EVOLUTION, ECOLOGY, CONSERVATION, AND MANAGEMENT OF HAWAIIAN BIRDS: A VANISHING AVIFAUNA

FRONTISPIECE: Hawai'i 'Ō'ō (*Moho nobilis*), largest of the 'Ō'ō's and best-known by the indigenous inhabitants of Hawai'i. Formerly widespread and common on the island of Hawai'i, it disappeared early in the 20th century, with the last known specimen from Ka'ū Crater on 13 May 1902 (Kepler et al. in press). Painting by H. Douglas Pratt, Jr.

EVOLUTION, ECOLOGY, CONSERVATION, AND MANAGEMENT OF HAWAIIAN BIRDS: A VANISHING AVIFAUNA

J. Michael Scott, Sheila Conant, and Charles van Riper, III, Editors

Studies in Avian Biology No. 22
A PUBLICATION OF THE COOPER ORNITHOLOGICAL SOCIETY

Cover photograph of 'Anianiau (*Hemignathus parvus*) foraging on kanawao (*Broussaisia arguta*) by Jack Jeffrey.

STUDIES IN AVIAN BIOLOGY

Edited by

John T. Rotenberry
Department of Biology
University of California
Riverside, CA 92521

Studies in Avian Biology is a series of works too long for *The Condor,* published at irregular intervals by the Cooper Ornithological Society. Manuscripts for consideration should be submitted to the editor. Style and format should follow those of previous issues.

Price $29.00 for softcover and $48.50 for hardcover including postage and handling. All orders cash in advance; make checks payable to Cooper Ornithological Society. Send orders to Cooper Ornithological Society, ℅ Western Foundation of Vertebrate Zoology, 439 Calle San Pablo, Camarillo, CA 93012.

ISBN: 1-891276-25-5 (cloth)   ISBN: 1-891276-18-2 (paper)

Library of Congress Control Number: 2001 131292
Printed at Allen Press, Inc., Lawrence, Kansas 66044
Issued: 16 March 2001
Revised: 8 March 2002

CONTENTS

RECOVERY AND MANAGEMENT

DEDICATION

This STUDIES IN AVIAN BIOLOGY volume is dedicated to Dean Amadon, Paul H. Baldwin, and David Woodside, colleagues and friends who laid the foundation for the recent renaissance of studies of the endemic birds of Hawai'i and a link with ornithologists of the late 19th century. It is because many of the researchers in Hawai'i, and those in particular who have contributed to this book, have anchored their scientific premises and hypotheses on the contributions of these three men, that we dedicate this STUDIES IN AVIAN BIOLOGY to them.

Dean Amadon was stationed with the U.S. Army in Hawai'i in 1944 and 1945, spending most of his time on the island of O'ahu, and two months on the Big Island as well. His interest in Hawaiian honeycreepers had been aroused earlier while he was at the American Museum of Natural History working with the ornithological collections of Lord Walter Rothschild. In Hawai'i, Amadon worked with Bishop Museum collections and got into the field to observe birds whenever he was free from his military duties. After the war he returned to academia to earn his doctorate at Cornell University. His dissertation, eventually published as *The Hawaiian Honeycreepers* (Amadon 1950), became a classic work on the systematics of the honeycreepers. It was the first thorough revision of the group based on Mayr's "modern synthesis" of evolutionary theory. While working on the Big Island, Amadon had been assisted by Paul Baldwin, whose research focused on life history and ecology of the honeycreepers.

Paul H. Baldwin was one of the true pioneers of Hawaiian ornithology. During the 1930s while Paul was working on his master's of science (on ocean crabs) at the University of Hawai'i, he was selected biologist for the Civilian Conservation Corps, stationed at Hawai'i Volcanoes National Park. It was at this position that Paul began collecting the first quantitative behavioral information on the Hawaiian avifauna. Following World War II, he enrolled at the University of California at Berkeley to complete his PhD. Coupling information that he had collected at Volcanoes National Park during the 1930s with intensive fieldwork in 1948–1949, Paul completed the first intensive behavioral work on banded Hawaiian honeycreepers. His study quantified for the first time physiological cycles, population movement patterns, avian diets, and evolutionary patterns in Hawaiian birds. He correlated these data with environmental factors (particularly climate), forest structure, and resource availability. Paul Baldwin's 1953 paper, *Annual cycle, environment and evolution in the Hawaiian honeycreepers (Aves: Drepaniidae)*, still stands as a milestone in Hawaiian ornithology. Paul's contributions to Hawai'i extend far beyond his 1953 work, with seminal papers on the Nēnē, a number on introduced birds (e.g., the Red-billed Leiothrix), economic impacts of the introduced mongoose, and impacts of cattle grazing on the native forests.

David Woodside was 15 years old when he began assisting George C. Munro in the field. Munro later published *Birds of Hawaii* (1944), which included the first comprehensive survey of the distribution of Hawaiian forest birds since the turn of the century. Woodside has worked with virtually every well-known ornithologist and agency that has engaged in research on Hawaiian birds, and has probably seen more Hawaiian birds and visited more haunts of Hawaiian birds than any living person. He was employed as a wildlife biologist for the Territory and later the State of Hawai'i for many years. After retiring from the state wildlife agency, he began working for the refuge branch of the U.S. Fish and Wildlife Service in 1980, where he continues to work today. Dave joined the Hawaii Audubon Society as a charter member when he was 15, and has contributed his time and expertise to studies and conservation of Hawaiian birds for a lifetime. Although he has witnessed the extinction of many Hawaiian birds, he is among the fortunate few living souls who have seen such birds as the O'ahu 'Alauahio, 'Ō'ū, Kāma'o, and Kaua'i 'Ō'ō.

LIST OF AUTHORS

DAVID G. AINLEY
H. T. Harvey and Associates
3150 Almaden Expressway, Suite 145
San Jose, CA 95118

CARTER T. ATKINSON
U.S. Geological Survey
Pacific Island Ecosystems Research Center
P.O. Box 218
Hawaii National Park, HI 96718

PAUL E. BAKER
U.S. Geological Survey
Pacific Island Ecosystems Science Center
P.O. Box 44
Hawaii National Park, HI 96718
(Present address: 8 Raglan Court, Silloth Cumbria,
    CA5 4BW, UK)

PAUL C. BANKO
U.S. Geological Survey
Pacific Island Ecosystems Research Center
Kilauea Field Station, P.O. Box 44
Hawaii National Park, HI 96718

WINSTON E. BANKO
U.S. Geological Survey
Pacific Island Ecosystems Research Center
Kilauea Field Station
Hawaii National Park, HI 96718
(Present address: 332 Redwood Place,
College Place, WA 99324)

KIM E. BERLIN
U.S. Geological Survey
Pacific Island Ecosystems Research Center
P.O. Box 44
Hawaii National Park, HI 96718

JEFFREY M. BLACK
Department of Wildlife
Humboldt State University
Arcata, CA 95521-8299

GREGORY J. BRENNER
U.S. Geological Survey
Pacific Island Ecosystems Research Center
P.O. Box 44
Hawaii National Park, HI 96718

REBECCA L. CANN
Department of Genetics & Molecular Biology
John A. Burns School of Medicine
University of Hawaii at Manoa
Honolulu, HI 96822

JOHN H. CAROTHERS
Museum of Vertebrate Zoology and Department of
    Zoology
University of California
Berkeley, CA 94720

EMILY B. COHEN
U.S. Geological Survey
Pacific Island Ecosystems Research Center
P.O. Box 44, Building 344
Hawaii National Park, HI 96718

MARK S. COLLINS
U.S. Geological Survey
Pacific Island Ecosystems Research Center
P.O. Box 44, Building 344
Hawaii National Park, HI 96718

SHEILA CONANT
Department of Zoology
University of Hawaii at Manoa
2538 McCarthy Mall
Honolulu, HI 96822

JOHN CURNUTT
Department of Ecology and Evolutionary Biology
University of Tennessee
Knoxville, TN 37919

REGINALD E. DAVID
Rana Productions
P.O. Box 1371
Kailua-Kona, HI 96745

LEAH DEFOREST
P.O. Box 6122
Hilo, HI 96720

DIANE DRIGOT
Environmental Department
Marine Corps Base Hawaii
MCBH Kaneohe Bay, HI 96863-3002

ANDREW ENGILIS, JR.
Ducks Unlimited, Inc.
3074 Gold Canal Drive
Rancho Cordova, CA 95670
(Present address: Department of
Wildlife, Fish, and Conservation Biology
University of California
Davis, CA 95616)

STEVEN G. FANCY
U.S. Geological Survey
Pacific Island Ecosystems Research Center
P.O. Box 44, Building 344
Hawaii National Park, HI 96718

ROBERT C. FLEISCHER
Molecular Genetics Laboratory
National Zoological Park
Smithsonian Institution
Washington, DC 20008

LEONARD A. FREED
Department of Zoology
University of Hawaii at Manoa
Honolulu, HI 96822

JON G. GIFFIN
Hawaii Dept. Land and Natural Resources
Division of Forestry and Wildlife
P.O. Box 4849
Hilo, HI 96720

CATHERINE GLIDDEN
Hawaii Volcanoes National Park
P.O. Box 52
Hawaii National Park, HI 96718-0052

PETER HARRITY
The Peregrine Fund
Keauhou Bird Conservation Center
P.O. Box 39
Volcano, HI 96785

PATRICK J. HART
Department of Zoology
University of Hawaii at Manoa
Honolulu, HI 96822

JEFF S. HATFIELD
U.S. Geological Survey
Patuxent Wildlife Research Center
Laurel, MD 20708-4017

STEVEN C. HESS
U.S. Geological Survey
Pacific Island Ecosystems Research Center
P.O. Box 44
Hawaii National Park, HI 96718

CATHLEEN S. NATIVIDAD HODGES
Haleakala National Park
Resources Management Division
P.O. Box 369
Makawao, Maui, HI 96768

FRANCIS G. HOWARTH
Department of Natural Sciences
Bernice P. Bishop Museum
P.O. Box 19000-A
Honolulu, HI 96819

DARCY HU
Hawaii Volcanoes National Park
P.O. Box 52
Hawaii National Park, HI 96718-0052

JAMES D. JACOBI
U.S. Geological Survey
Pacific Island Ecosystems Research Center
P.O. Box 44
Hawaii National Park, HI 96718

HELEN F. JAMES
Department of Vertebrate Zoology
National Museum of Natural History
Smithsonian Institution
Washington, DC 20560

SUSAN I. JARVI
Molecular Genetics Laboratory
National Zoological Park
Smithsonian Institution
3001 Connecticut Ave. NW
Washington, DC 20008
(Present address: Department of Biology
University of Hawaii-Hilo
200 W. Kawili St.
Hilo, HI 96720)

JAMES R. KOWALSKY
U.S. Geological Survey
Pacific Island Ecosystems Research Center
P.O. Box 44
Hawaii National Park, HI 96718

FRED KRAUS
Department of Land and Natural Resources
Division of Forestry and Wildlife
1151 Punchbowl Street
Honolulu, HI 96813

PAUL D. KRUSHELNYCKY
U.S. Geological Survey
Haleakala National Park Field Station
Box 39
Makawao, HI 96768

CYNDI KUEHLER
The Peregrine Fund
Keauhou Bird Conservation Center
P.O. Box 39
Volcano, HI 96785

JOPE KUHN
The Peregrine Fund
Keauhou Bird Conservation Center
P.O. Box 39
Volcano, HI 96785

MARLA KUHN
The Peregrine Fund
Keauhou Bird Conservation Center
P.O. Box 39
Volcano, HI 96785

LEONA P. LANIAWE
U.S. Geological Survey
Pacific Island Ecosystems Research Center
P.O. Box 44
Hawaii National Park, HI 96718

ALAN LIEBERMAN
The Peregrine Fund
Keauhou Bird Conservation Center
P.O. Box 39
Volcano, HI 96785

JILL S. LIPPERT
Hawaii Volcanoes National Park
P.O. Box 52
Hawaii National Park, HI 96718-0052

LLOYD L. LOOPE
U.S. Geological Survey
Pacific Island Ecosystems Center
Haleakala Field Station
P.O. Box 369
Makawao, Maui, HI 96768

JAMES S. MACIVOR
1207 Tedford Way
Oklahoma City, OK 73116

BARBARA MCILRAITH
The Peregrine Fund
Keauhou Bird Conservation Center
P.O. Box 39
Volcano, HI 96785

CARL E. MCINTOSH
Molecular Genetics Laboratory
National Zoological Park
Smithsonian Institution
Washington, DC 20008

ARTHUR C. MEDEIROS
U.S. Geological Survey
Haleakala National Park Field Station
Box 39
Makawao, HI 96768

JULIAN MEISLER
P.O. Box 851
Burlington, VT 05402

KARL E. MILLER
Department of Wildlife Ecology & Conservation
P.O. Box 110430
University of Florida
Gainesville, FL 32611-0430

MICHAEL P. MOORE
U.S. Geological Survey
Pacific Island Ecosystems Research Center
P.O. Box 44, Building 344
Hawaii National Park, HI 96718

MARIE MORIN
Department of Zoology
University of Hawaii at Manoa
2538 McCarthy Mall
Honolulu, HI 96822

MICHAEL P. MOULTON
Department of Wildlife Ecology & Conservation
P.O. Box 110430
University of Florida
Gainesville, FL 32611-0430

BERTRAM G. MURRAY, JR.
Graduate Program in Ecology and Evolution
80 Nichol Avenue
Rutgers University
New Brunswick, NJ 08901-2882

RONALD J. NAGATA, SR.
Haleakala National Park
Resources Management Division
P.O. Box 369
Makawao, Maui, HI 96768

JAY T. NELSON
U.S. Geological Survey
Pacific Island Ecosystems Research Center
P.O. Box 44, Building 344
Hawaii National Park, HI 96718

NADAV NUR
Point Reyes Bird Observatory
Stinson Beach, CA 94970

STUART PIMM
Department of Ecology and Evolutionary Biology
University of Tennessee
Knoxville, TN 37919

RICHARD PODOLSKY
Avian Systems
Fort Lee, NJ 07024

H. DOUGLAS PRATT
Museum of Natural Science
Louisiana State University
Baton Rouge, LA 70893

THANE K. PRATT
U.S. Geological Survey
Pacific Island Ecosystems Research Center
P.O. Box 44
Hawaii National Park, HI 96718

MICHELLE H. REYNOLDS
U.S. Geological Survey
Pacific Island Ecosystems Research Center
P.O. Box 44
Hawaii National Park, HI 96718

JUDITH M. RHYMER
Department of Wildlife Ecology
University of Maine
Orono, ME 04469

LENA SCHNELL
US Army, CDR, USAG-HI-PTA
Attn: Evironmental Office
APO AP 96556-5703

J. MICHAEL SCOTT
U.S. Geological Survey
IDCFWRU
College of Natural Resources
University of Idaho
Moscow, ID 83844-1141

CHERIE SHEHATA
Department of Genetics and Molecular Biology
John A. Burns School of Medicine
University of Hawaii at Manoa
Honolulu, HI 96822

JOHN C. SIMON
U.S. Geological Survey
Pacific Island Ecosystems Research Center
P.O. Box 44
Hawaii National Park, HI 96718

BETH SLIKAS
Molecular Genetics Laboratory
National Zoological Park
Smithsonian Institution
Washington, DC 20008

THOMAS B. SMITH
Department of Biology
San Francisco State University
1600 Holloway Ave.
San Francisco, CA 94132
(Present address: Center for Population Biology
University of California
Davis, CA 95616)

THOMAS J. SNETSINGER
U.S. Geological Survey
Pacific Island Ecosystems Research Center
P.O. Box 1319, Kaua'i Forest Bird Project
Kekaha, HI 96752

GREGORY SPENCER
P.O. Box 6122
Hilo, HI 96720

WILLIAM W. M. STEINER
U.S. Geological Survey
Pacific Island Ecosystems Research Center
3190 Maile Way
Honolulu, HI 96822

CHERYL L. TARR
Department of Biology and Institute of Molecular
  Evolutionary Genetics
208 Erwin W. Mueller Laboratory
Pennsylvania State University
University Park, PA 16802

ERIC A. TILLMAN
Department of Wildlife Ecology & Conservation
P.O. Box 110430
University of Florida
Gainesville, FL 32611-0430

JOHN TURNER
The Peregrine Fund
Keauhou Bird Conservation Center
P.O. Box 39
Volcano, HI 96785

ERIK J. TWEED
U.S. Geological Survey
Pacific Island Ecosystems Research Center
P.O. Box 44, Building 344
Hawaii National Park, HI 96718

MIKLOS D.F. UDVARDY (DECEASED)
California State University, Sacramento

ERIC A. VANDERWERF
University of Hawaii at Manoa
Department of Zoology
Edmonson Hall, 2538 The Mall
Honolulu, HI 96822

ELLEN M. VANGELDER
U.S. Geological Survey
Haleakala National Park
Box 369
Makawao, HI 96768

CHARLES VAN RIPER III
U.S. Geological Survey
Forest and Rangeland Ecosystem Science Center
Colorado Plateau Field Station
P.O. Box 5614
Northern Arizona University
Flagstaff, AZ 86011

BETHANY L. WOODWORTH
U.S. Geological Survey
Pacific Island Ecosystems Research Center
P.O. Box 44, Building 344
Hawaii National Park, HI 96718

FRIEDERIKE WOOG
Libanonstr. 66
70184 Stuttgart
Germany

Studies in Avian Biology No. 22:1–12, 2001.

INTRODUCTION

J. Michael Scott, Sheila Conant, and Charles van Riper, III

Hawai'i, a string of high and low islands stretching 1,900 km across the Central Pacific, has long captured the imagination of ornithologists. The Hawaiian Islands are the most isolated archipelago in the world, and as a result, were one of the last places on the planet to be populated (Fig. 1). The islands range from 25 million year-old Kure, at the extreme northwest end of the archipelago, to Hawai'i, the largest, southernmost, and the youngest island at less than 1 million years old (Fig. 2; Stearns 1966, Carson and Clague 1995). The climate varies dramatically from arid, tropical seashores receiving less than 26 cm (10 in) of precipitation on the leeward slopes of the main islands, to the windward peaks of the Alaka'i Swamp on Kaua'i, where it is not uncommon for torrential rains to drop 52 cm (20 in) in a day, or to record 1,152 cm (450 in) in a single year. The tropical lowland areas contrast dramatically with the high altitude, alpine ecosystems, and stone deserts, where it freezes every night. The landscape is as varied as it is dynamic. The tropical environments at sea level contrast dramatically with the snow capped peaks of Mauna Loa and Mauna Kea, which reach more than 4,000 m in height above sea level and more than 9,000 m from their base in the ocean from which they were born (Stearns 1966, Carson and Clague 1995). The Hawaiian archipelago is extremely dynamic, with Loihi Seamount, an incipient island, presently going through the birthing process at a depth of 950 meters 30 km off the southern coast of Hawai'i (Carson and Clague 1995).

Polynesians first reached the Hawaiian archipelago about 500 AD, and Europeans not until Captain James Cook's third voyage of discovery in 1778. With a little imagination and use of early voyagers' and naturalists' notes, one can create in the mind's eye a pre-Polynesian Hawai'i (Rothschild 1893–1900, Henshaw 1902a; Kirch 1982a, 1985). In these presettlement islands, millions of seabirds nested not only on offshore islets, isolated cliff faces, and barren subalpine areas where they are found today, but on the beaches and in adjacent forests, bringing tons of nitrates and phosphates from the sea. The transport of nutrients from marine environments by birds has significant impact on terrestrial environments, resulting in increased plant growth and increases in those species that depend on plants for habitat and food (Polis and Hurd 1996, Ryan and Watkins 1989; Anderson and

Polis 1998, 1999). As one moved inland, numerous species of geese, including ten that we know were flightless, grazed in the open grasslands. The forests must have been alive with various species of Hawaiian honeyeaters, honeycreepers, owls, and hawks, flightless species (such as rail and ibis), and a variety of largebilled finches. The dawn song chorus of this ghost avifauna will never again be heard, but one can dream.

Captain Cook's third voyage of discovery did not contribute greatly to our ornithological knowledge of the islands. Only 11 species and subspecies were described based on specimens collected during Cook's voyage, all from Kaua'i and Hawai'i (Medway 1981). The first comprehensive characterizations of Hawaiian birds were the almost simultaneous publications by Rothschild (1893–1900) and Wilson and Evans (1890–1899). These detailed descriptions of Hawaiian birds were augmented by the careful documentation of the natural history and ecology of these birds by Henshaw (1902a,b) and Perkins (1893, 1901, 1903). These works established a foundation from which all current Hawaiian ornithology is measured. In this monograph, we hope to provide another milestone of information on the avifauna of the Hawaiian Islands and the surrounding Pacific area, from which during the next century ornithologists might measure future changes in this avifauna. And most certainly there will be changes.

Historical changes to the Hawaiian avifauna started early, and only 100 years after Cook's exploration of the islands there were reports of species that had apparently gone extinct (Perkins 1903). At the turn of the century, R. C. L. Perkins (as cited in Munro 1944:69) wrote:

"When I first arrived in Kona, the Great Ohia trees, at an elevation of 2,500 feet, were a mass of bloom and each of them was literally alive with hordes of Crimson 'Apapane and Scarlet 'I'iwi; while continually crossing from the top of one great tree to another, the 'Ō'ō could be seen on the wing sometimes six or eight at a time .... The 'Amakihi was numerous in the same trees but less conspicuous and occasionally one of the long billed *Hemignathus*. Feeding on the fruit of the Ieie could be seen the Hawaiian Crow commonly and the 'Ō'ū in great abundance. The picture of this noisy, active, and often quarrelsome assembly

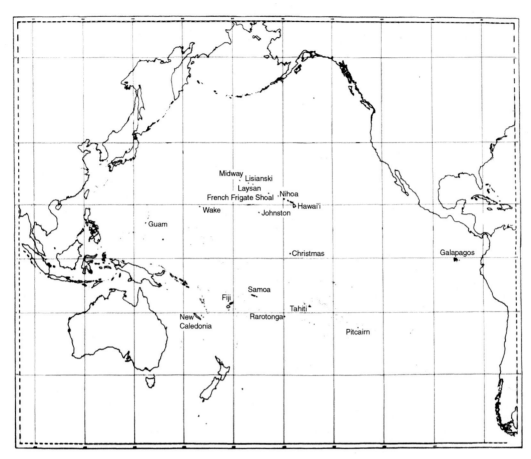

FIGURE 1. The Hawaiian archipelago and other major islands in the Pacific Ocean.

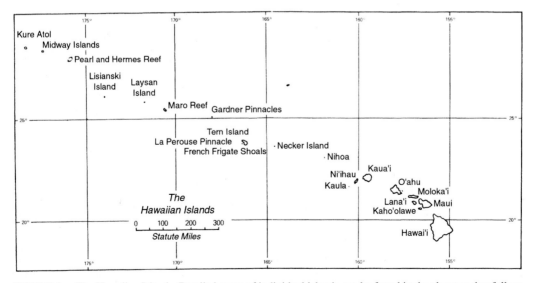

FIGURE 2. The Hawaiian Islands. Detailed maps of individual islands can be found in the chapters that follow.

of birds, many of them brilliant colors, was one never to be forgotten. After the flowering of the Ohia was over, the great gathering naturally dispersed, but even then the bird population was very great."

By 1930 however, things had changed greatly when Munro (1944:68) stated:

"Since civilization came to the Hawaiian Islands, the experience of the native perching birds has been tragic. My conclusions after the survey (1936–1937) were that 25 species have a fair chance of survival, while 30 species were gone or likely to become extinct."

Today native birds are almost absent from the remaining lowland forests of Kona. In their place is an eclectic group of alien species, the result of a large number of planned and unplanned releases (see Moulton et al. *this volume*). Today, only the 'Elepaio (*Chasiempis sandwichensis*), Hawai'i 'Amakihi (*Hemignathus virens*), 'I'iwi (*Vestiaria coccinea*), and 'Apapane (*Himatione sanguinea*) can be seen reliably, and these not in all areas. The large-billed finches, honeyeaters (species once ubiquitous), 'Ō'ū (*Psittirostra psittacea*), and 'Ōma'o (*Myadestes obscurus*) are gone, while the 'Ākepa (*Loxops coccineus*), 'Akiapōlā'au (*Hemignathus munroi*), and Hawai'i Creeper (*Oreomystis bairdi*) occur in vanishingly small numbers in fewer than five isolated pockets of native forest. At this writing, the number of free-flying 'Alalā (*Corvus hawaiiensis*) can be counted on one hand.

The true magnitude of these losses would, however, not be known until the pioneering research of the husband-and-wife team of Storrs Olson and Helen James (James and Olson 1991, Olson and James 1991). They documented the extinction of at least 50% of the Hawaiian avifauna prior to the first use of the Linnean System to describe a Hawaiian species. One hundred nine endemic species are known to have occurred in the Hawaiian Islands, 35 of which (32%) are still extant. Nineteen additional taxa were extant in the 18th century, and 55 (50%) are known only from the fossil and subfossil record (Table 1).

Reasons for losses of many Hawaiian bird species have been well documented, including the destruction of habitat (Cuddihy and Stone 1990) and taking of birds (van Riper and van Riper 1982, Banko et al. *this volume,* Hu et al. *this volume,* van Riper and Scott *this volume*), predatory mammals (Tomich 1969, Kramer 1971, Atkinson 1977), introduced birds (Schwartz and Schwartz 1949, Lewin 1971, Lewin and Lewin 1984, Mountainspring and

TABLE 1. BIRDS KNOWN FROM FOSSIL RECORDS OR KNOWN TO BREED IN THE HAWAIIAN ISLANDS

Group	Species known		Species extant	Endangered species	Populations	
	Fossil	Historic			≤50	51–500
Seabirds	1	22	22	2	2	1
Herons	0	1	0	0	0	0
Ibises	2	0	0	0	0	0
Waterfowl	10–11	3	3	3	0	0
Hawks	2	1	1	1	0	0
Rails	10	4	2	2	0	0
Stilts	0	1	1	1	0	0
Owls	4	1	1	0	0	0
Crows	3	1	1	1	1	0
Honeyeaters	0	6	1	1	1	0
Oldworld Flycatchers	0	1	1	0	0	0
Oldworld Warblers	0	1	1	1	0	0
Hawaiian Thrushes	0	6	2	1	0	1
Honeycreepers	13	31	20	9	4	3

Notes: Information on fossil birds includes only those records assigned species status (James and Olson 1991, Olson and James 1991). Additional species are being described. Historical status is based on several sources (Scott et al. 1989, Stone 1989, and Pyle 1997). In the last 11 years three species have become extinct: Kaua'i 'Ō'ō (*Moho braccatus*), Kāma'o (*Myadestes myadestinus*), and Oloma'o (*Myadestes lanaiensis*) based on the standard of extinct until proven extant (Diamond 1987). The 'I'iwi (*Vestiaria coccinea*) is declining in numbers and is disappearing from areas formerly occupied. The numbers of two other species have decreased to less than 50 individuals. Species with less than 50 and 500 censused individuals are provided as indicators of jeopardy. The effective population size for these species is unknown but likely to be one-half to one-quarter censused population size (Primack 1993). For the 29 species listed by the U.S. Fish and Wildlife Service as endangered, 8 continue to decline, 6 are of unknown status, and 15 are stable in numbers (USFWS 1996a).

Scott 1985), and diseases (Warner 1968, van Riper et al. 1986, Atkinson et al. 1993a,b,c, 1995; Jarvi et al. *this volume,* Shehata et al. *this volume*). The combined effect of these losses has been summarized in papers by Scott et al. (1986), van Riper and van Riper (1985), Ralph and van Riper (1985), Freed et al. (1993), and van Riper and Scott (*this volume*).

While many species have succumbed to extinction (Table 1), major steps have been taken recently to save Hawai'i's endangered species. The U.S. Fish and Wildlife Service has established two national wildlife refuges (Hakalau Forest and Kona Forest National Wildlife Refuges) on the island of Hawai'i with a primary objective of protecting endangered forest birds. Combined, these preserves total nearly 16,194 ha (40,000 acres). The National Park Service has eliminated goats (*Capra hircus*) and sheep (*Ovis aries*) from Hawai'i Volcanoes and Haleakalā National Parks. In addition, large acreages are now pig- (*Sus scrofa*) free in that park. Similar-

TABLE 2.　CHECKLIST OF THE BIRDS OF HAWAII

Symbols for status

R = Resident native species; normal does not leave islands: Re = Resident, endemic species, not extinct; Rx = Resident, endemic species, presumed extinct; Res = Resident; indigenous species, subspecies is endemic; Hawaiian; Ri = Resident; indigenous species, Hawaiian form is not endemic.
A = Alien introduced species; resident; normally does not leave the islands: Al = Alien; long established and breeding since before 1940; An = Alien, new introduced since 1950; apparently established; Ax = Alien; formerly long established and breeding for more than 25 years, but now no longer present in Hawaii.
E (or T) immediately preceding the genus name designates a species or subspecies currently listed as Endangered (or Threatened) on the Federal List of Endangered species.
B = Breeding species in Hawaii, native, most individuals leave Hawaii when not breeding: Bo = Breeder, species breeds only in Hawaii; Bes = Breeder, species also breeds elsewhere; Hawaiian subspecies breeds only in Hawaii; Bi = Breeder, Hawaiian form also breeds elsewhere.
V = Visitor species, breeds elsewhere, occurs in Hawaii when not breeding: Vc = Visitor, common migrant to Hawaii; Vr = Visitor, regular migrant to Hawaii in small numbers; Vo = Visitor, occasional to frequent migrant to Hawaii; Vs = Visitor, accidental straggler to Hawaii; Vd = Visitor, accidental straggler to Hawaii, recorded in Hawaii only as dead remains.

Common name	Scientific name	Status
GREBES	***PODICIPEDIDAE***	
Pied-billed Grebe	*Podilymbus podiceps*	Ri
Horned Grebe	*Podiceps auritus*	Vs
Red-necked Grebe	*Podiceps grisegena*	Vs
Eared Grebe	*Podiceps nigricollis*	Vs
ALBATROSSES	***DIOMEDEIDAE***	
Laysan Albatross	*Phoebastria immutabilis*	Bi
Black-footed Albatross	*Phoebastria nigripes*	Bi
Short-tailed Albatross	*E-Phoebastria albatrus*	Vo
PETRELS, SHEARWATERS	***PROCELLARIIDAE***	
Northern Fulmar	*Fulmarus glacialis*	Vo
Kermadec Petrel	*Pterodroma neglecta*	Vs
Herald Petrel	*Pterodroma arminjoniana*	Vs
Murphy's Petrel	*Pterodroma ultima*	Vs
Mottled Petrel	*Pterodroma inexpectata*	Vo
Juan Fernandez Petrel	*Pterodroma externa*	Vo
(Hawaiian Petrel)—Dark-rumped Petrel	*E-Pterodroma phaeopygia sandwichensis*	Res
White-necked Petrel	*Pterodroma cervicalis*	Vo
Bonin Petrel	*Pterodroma hypoleuca*	Bi
Black-winged Petrel	*Pterodroma nigripennis*	Vo
Cook's Petrel	*Pterodroma cookii*	Vs
Stejneger's Petrel	*Pterodroma longirostris*	Vd
Bulwer's Petrel	*Bulweria bulwerii*	Bi
Jouanin's Petrel	*Bulweria fallax*	Vs
Streaked Shearwater	*Calonectris leucomelas*	Vs
Flesh-footed Shearwater	*Puffinus carneipes*	Vo
Wedge-tailed Shearwater	*Puffinus pacificus chlororhynchus*	Bi
(New Zealand Shearwater)—Buller's Shearwater	*Puffinus bulleri*	Vs
Sooty Shearwater	*Puffinus griseus*	Vr
Short-tailed Shearwater	*Puffinus tenuirostris*	Vo
Christmas Shearwater	*Puffinus nativitatis*	Bi
(Newell's Shearwater)—Townsend's Shearwater	*T-Puffinus auricularis newelli*	Be
Little Shearwater	*Puffinus assimilis*	Vs
STORM-PETRELS	***HYDROBATIDAE***	
Wilson's Storm-Petrel	*Oceanites oceanicus*	Vs
Fork-tailed Storm-Petrel	*Oceanodroma furcata*	Vs
Leach's Storm-Petrel	*Oceanodroma leucorhoa*	Vr
(Hawaiian or Harcourt's Storm-Petrel)—Band-rumped Storm-Petrel	*Oceanodroma castro*	Bi
(Sooty Storm-Petrel)—Tristram's Storm-Petrel	*Oceanodroma tristrami*	Bi
TROPICBIRDS	***PHAETHONTIDAE***	
White-tailed Tropicbird	*Phaethon lepturus*	Ri
Red-billed Tropicbird	*Phaethon aethereus*	Vs
Red-tailed Tropicbird	*Phaethon rubricauda rothschildi*	Bi

TABLE 2. CONTINUED

Common name	Scientific name	Status
BOOBIES	***SULIDAE***	
(Blue-faced Booby)—Masked Booby	*Sula dactylatra personata*	Ri
Brown Booby	*Sula leucogaster plotus*	Ri
Red-footed Booby	*Sula sula rubripes*	Ri
CORMORANTS	***PHALACROCORACIDAE***	
Pelagic Cormorant	*Phalacrocorax pelagicus*	Vs
FRIGATEBIRDS	***FREGATIDAE***	
Great Frigatebird	*Fregata minor palmerstoni*	Ri
Lesser Frigatebird	*Frigata ariel*	Vs
HERONS, EGRETS	***ARDEIDAE***	
Great Blue Heron	*Ardea herodias*	Vs
Great Egret	*Ardea alba*	Vs
Snowy Egret	*Egretta thula*	Vs
Little Blue Heron	*Egretta caerulea*	Vo
Cattle Egret	*Bubulcus ibis*	An
(Green-backed Heron)—Green Heron	*Butorides virescens*	Vs
Black-crowned Night-Heron	*Nycticorax nycticorax hoactli*	Ri
IBISES	***THRESKIORNITHIDAE***	
White-faced Ibis	*Plegadis chihi*	Vs
GEESE, DUCKS	***ANATIDAE***	
Fulvous Whistling-Duck	*Dendrocygna bicolor*	Ri
(White-fronted Goose)—Greater White-fronted Goose	*Anser albifrons*	Vs
Emperor Goose	*Chen canagica*	Vo
Snow Goose	*Chen caerulescens*	Vs
Canada Goose	*Branta canadensis*	Vo
(Nēnē)—Hawaiian Goose	*E-Branta sandvicensis*	Re
Brant	*Branta bernicla*	Vo
(Whistling Swan)—Tundra Swan	*Cygnus columbianus*	Vs
Gadwall	*Anas strepera*	Vs
(European Wigeon)—Eurasian Wigeon	*Anas penelope*	Vs
American Wigeon	*Anas americana*	Vr
Mallard	*Anas platyrhynchos*	Al, Vo
(Koloa)—Hawaiian Duck	*E-Anas wyvilliana*	Re
Laysan Duck	*E-Anas laysanensis*	Re
Blue-winged Teal	*Anas discors*	Vo
Cinnamon Teal	*Anas cyanoptera*	Vs
Northern Shoveler	*Anas clypeata*	Vc
Northern Pintail	*Anas acuta*	Vc
Garganey	*Anas querquedula*	Vo
Green-winged Teal	*Anas crecca*	Vr
Canvasback	*Aythya valisineria*	Vs
Redhead	*Aythya americana*	Vs
Common Pochard	*Aythya ferina*	Vs
Ring-necked Duck	*Aythya collaris*	Vo
Tufted Duck	*Aythya fuligula*	Vs
Greater Scaup	*Aythya marila*	Vo
Lesser Scaup	*Aythya affinis*	Vr
Harlequin Duck	*Histrionicus histrionicus*	Vs
Surf Scoter	*Melanitta perspicillata*	Vs
Black Scoter	*Melanitta nigra*	Vs
Long-tailed Duck	*Clangula hyemalis*	Vs
Bufflehead	*Bucephala albeola*	Vo
Common Goldeneye	*Bucephala clangula*	Vs
Hooded Merganser	*Lophodytes cucullatus*	Vs
Common Merganser	*Mergus merganser*	Vs
Red-breasted Merganser	*Mergus serrator*	Vs
Ruddy Duck	*Oxyura jamaicensis*	Vs
HAWKS, EAGLES	***ACCIPITRIDAE***	
Osprey	*Pandion haliaetus*	Vo
Black Kite	*Milvus migrans*	Vs
Steller's Sea-Eagle	*Haliaeetus pelagicus*	Vs

TABLE 2. CONTINUED

Common name	Scientific name	Status
Northern Harrier	*Circus cyaneus*	Vs
Gray Frog-Hawk	*Accipiter soloensis*	Vs
('Io)—Hawaiian Hawk	*E-Buteo solitarius*	Re
Rough-legged Hawk	*Buteo lagopus*	Vs
Golden Eagle	*Aquila chrysaetos*	Vs
FALCONS	***FALCONIDAE***	
Merlin	*Falco columbarius*	Vs
Peregrine Falcon	*E-Falco peregrinus*	Vo
FRANCOLINS, OLD WORLD QUAIL, TURKEY	***PHASIANIDAE***	
Chukar	*Alectoris chukar*	Al
Gray Francolin	*Francolinus pondicerianus*	An
Black Francolin	*Francolinus francolinus*	An
Erckel's Francolin	*Francolinus erckelii*	An
Japanese Quail	*Coturnix japonica*	Al
Red Junglefowl	*Gallus gallus*	Al
Kalij Pheasant (Green Pheasant, Common Pheasant)—	*Lophura leucomelanos*	An
Ring-necked Pheasant	*Phasianus colchicus*	Al
Common Peafowl	*Pavo cristatus*	Al
Wild Turkey	*Meleagris gallopavo*	Al
NEW WORLD QUAIL	***ODONTOPHORIDAE***	
California Quail	*Callipepla californica*	Al
Gambel's Quail	*Callipepla gambelii*	Al
RAILS, GALLINULES, COOTS	***RALLIDAE***	
Laysan Rail	*Porzana palmeri*	Rx
Hawaiian Rail	*Porzana sandwichensis*	Rx
(Hawaiian Gallinule)—Common Moorhen	*E-Gallinula chloropus sandvicensis*	Res
(American Coot)—Hawaiian Coot	*E-Fulica alai*	Res
American Coot	*Fulica americana*	Vs
CRANES	***GRUIDAE***	
Sandhill Crane	*Grus canadensis*	Vs
PLOVERS	***CHARADRIIDAE***	
(Gray Plover)—Black-bellied Plover	*Pluvialis squatarola*	Vr
(Lesser or American Golden-Plover)— Pacific Golden-Plover	*Pluvialis fulva*	Vc
Mongolian Plover	*Charadrius mongolus*	Vs
Common Ringed Plover	*Charadrius hiaticula*	Vs
Semipalmated Plover	*Charadrius semipalmatus*	Vo
Killdeer	*Charadrius vociferus*	Vs
Eurasian Dotterel	*Charadrius morinellus*	Vs
STILTS	***RECURVIROSTRIDAE***	
(Hawaiian Stilt)—Black-necked Stilt	*E-Himantopus mexicanus knudseni*	Res
SANDPIPERS, WADERS	***SCOLOPACIDAE***	
Greater Yellowlegs	*Tringa melanoleuca*	Vs
Lesser Yellowlegs	*Tringa flavipes*	Vr
Wood Sandpiper	*Tringa glareola*	Vs
Solitary Sandpiper	*Tringa solitaria*	Vs
Willet	*Catoptrophorus semipalmatus*	Vs
Wandering Tattler	*Heteroscelus incanus*	Vc
(Siberian Tattler, Polynesian Tattler)— Gray-tailed Tattler	*Heteroscelus brevipes*	Vs
Spotted Sandpiper	*Actitis macularia*	Vs
Whimbrel	*Numenius phaeopus*	Vs
Bristle-thighed Curlew	*Numenius tahitiensis*	Vr
Far Eastern Curlew	*Numenius madagascariensis*	Vs
Hudsonian Godwit	*Limosa haemastica*	Vs
Bar-tailed Godwit	*Limosa lapponica*	Vo
Marbled Godwit	*Limosa fedoa*	Vs
Ruddy Turnstone	*Arenaria interpres*	Vc
Red Knot	*Calidris canutus*	Vs
Sanderling	*Calidris alba*	Vo

TABLE 2. CONTINUED

Common name	Scientific name	Status
Semipalmated Sandpiper	*Calidris pusilla*	Vs
Western Sandpiper	*Calidris mauri*	Vo
Red-necked Stint	*Calidris ruficollis*	Vs
Little Stint	*Calidris minuta*	Vs
Long-toed Stint	*Calidris subminuta*	Vs
Least Sandpiper	*Calidris minutilla*	Vo
Baird's Sandpiper	*Calidris bairdii*	Vs
Pectoral Sandpiper	*Calidris melanotos*	Vr
Sharp-tailed Sandpiper	*Calidris acuminata*	Vr
Dunlin	*Calidris alpina*	Vr
Curlew Sandpiper	*Calidris ferruginea*	Vs
Buff-breasted Sandpiper	*Tryngites subruficollis*	Vs
Ruff	*Philomachus pugnax*	Vo
Short-billed Dowitcher	*Limnodromus griseus*	Vo
Long-billed Dowitcher	*Limnodromus scolopaceus*	Vr
Common Snipe	*Gallinago gallinago*	Vo
Pin-tailed Snipe	*Gallinago stenura*	Vs
Wilson's Phalarope	*Phalaropus tricolor*	Vo
Red-necked Phalarope	*Phalaropus lobatus*	Vs
Red Phalarope	*Phalaropus fulicaria*	Vs
JAEGERS, GULLS, TERNS, NODDIES	*LARIDAE*	
South Polar Skua	*Stercorarius maccormicki*	Vs
Pomarine Jaeger	*Stercorarius pomarinus*	Vr
Parasitic Jaeger	*Stercorarius parasiticus*	Vs
Long-tailed Jaeger	*Stercorarius longicaudus*	Vs
Laughing Gull	*Larus atricilla*	Vo
Franklin's Gull	*Larus pipixcan*	Vs
Black-headed Gull	*Larus ridibundus*	Vs
Bonaparte's Gull	*Larus philadelphia*	Vo
Mew Gull	*Larus canus*	Vs
Ring-billed Gull	*Larus delawarensis*	Vo
California Gull	*Larus californicus*	Vs
Herring Gull	*Larus argentatus*	Vo
Slaty-backed Gull	*Larus schistisagus*	Vs
Western Gull	*Larus occidentalis*	Vs
Glaucous-winged Gull	*Larus glaucescens*	Vo
Glaucous Gull	*Larus hyperboreus*	Vs
Black-legged Kittiwake	*Rissa tridactyla*	Vs
Gull-billed Tern	*Sterna nilotica*	Vs
Caspian Tern	*Sterna caspia*	Vs
Great Crested Tern	*Sterna bergii*	Vs
Sandwich Tern	*Sterna sandvicensis*	Vs
Common Tern	*Sterna hirundo*	Vs
Arctic Tern	*Sterna paradisaea*	Vo
Little Tern	*Sterna albifrons*	Vs
Least Tern	*Sterna antillarum*	Vo
Gray-backed Tern	*Sterna lunata*	Bi
Sooty Tern	*Sterna fuscata oahuensis*	Bi
Whiskered Tern	*Chlidonias hybridus*	Vs
Black Tern	*Chlidonias niger*	Vs
(Common Noddy)—Brown Noddy	*Anous stolidus pileatus*	Ri
(Hawaiian Noddy, White-capped Noddy)— Black Noddy	*Anous minutus melanogenys*	Res
Blue-gray Noddy	*Procelsterna cerulea saxarilis*	Ri
(Common Fairy-Tern, Fairy Tern)— White Tern	*Gygis alba rothschildi*	Ri
AUKLETS, PUFFINS	*ALCIDAE*	
Cassin's Auklet	*Ptychoramphus aleuticus*	Vs
Parakeet Auklet	*Aethia psittacula*	Vd
Horned Puffin	*Fratercula corniculata*	Vs
Tufted Puffin	*Fratercula cirrhata*	Vd

TABLE 2. CONTINUED

Common name	Scientific name	Status
SANDGROUSE	*PTEROCLIDIDAE*	
Chestnut-bellied Sandgrouse	*Pterocles exustus*	An
DOVES	*COLUMBIDAE*	
Rock Dove	*Columba livia*	Al
(Chinese Dove, Lace-necked Dove)— Spotted Dove	*Streptopelia chinensis*	Al
(Barred Dove)—Zebra Dove	*Geopelia striata*	Al
Mourning Dove	*Zenaida macroura*	An
PARAKEETS	*PSITTACIDAE*	
Rose-ringed Parakeet	*Psittacula krameri*	An
CUCKOOS	*CUCULIDAE*	
Common Cuckoo	*Cuculus canorus*	Vs
Yellow-billed Cuckoo	*Coccyzus americanus*	Vs
BARN OWLS	*TYTONIDAE*	
Barn Owl	*Tyto alba*	An
TYPICAL OWLS	*STRIGIDAE*	
(Hawaiian Owl)—Short-earned Owl	*Asio flammeus sandwichensis*	Res
NIGHTHAWKS	*CAPRIMULGIDAE*	
Common Nighthawk	*Chordeiles minor*	Vs
SWIFTLETS	*APODIDAE*	
(Uniform, Island or Gray Swiftlet)—Guam Switflet	*Aerodramus bartschi*	An
KINGFISHERS	*ALCEDINIDAE*	
Belted Kingfisher	*Ceryle alcyon*	Vs
HONEYEATERS	*MELIPHAGIDAE*	
'Ō'ō'ā'ā—Kaua'i 'Ō 'ō	E-*Moho braccatus*	Re
O'ahu 'Ō'ō	*Moho apicalis*	Rx
(Moloka'i 'Ō'ō)—Bishop's 'Ō'ō	*Moho bishopi*	Rx
Hawai'i 'Ō'ō	*Moho nobilis*	Rx
Kioea	*Chaetoptila angustipluma*	Rx
CROWS	*CORVIDAE*	
('Alalā)—Hawaiian Crow	E-*Corvus hawaiiensis*	Re
MONARCH FLYCATCHERS	*MONARCHIDAE*	
'Elepaio	*Chasiempis sandwichensis*	
{Kaua'i 'Elepaio}—	*C. s. sclateri*	Re
{O'ahu 'Elepaio}—	*C. s. ibidis*	Re
{Hawai'i 'Elepaio}—	*C. s. sandwichensis, ridgwayi, bryani*	Re
LARKS	*ALAUDIDAE*	
(Eurasian Skylark)—Sky Lark	*Alauda arvensis*	Al, Vs
SWALLOWS	*HIRUNDINIDAE*	
Barn Swallow	*Hirundo rustica*	Vs
TITS	*PARIDAE*	
(Japanese Tit, Yamagara)—Varied Tit	*Parus varius*	Ax
BULBULS	*PYCNONOTIDAE*	
Red-vented Bulbul	*Pycnonotus cafer*	An
Red-whiskered Bulbul	*Pycnonotus jocosus*	An
OLD WORLD WARBLERS	*SYLVIIDAE*	
(Uguisu)—Japanese Bush-Warbler	*Cettia diphone*	Al
Millerbird	*Acrocephalus familiaris*	
{Laysan Millerbird}—	*A. f. familiaris*	Rx
{Nihoa Millerbird}—	E-*A. f. kingi*	Re
THRUSHES, SOLITAIRES	*TURDIDAE*	
(Shama Thrush)—White-rumped Shama	*Copsychus malabaricus*	Al
(Large Kaua'i Thrush)—Kāma'o	E-*Myadestes myadestinus*	Re
(O'ahu Thrush)—'Āmaui	*Myadestes woahensis*	Rx
Oloma'o	*Myadestes lanaiensis*	
{(Moloka'i Thrush)—Moloka'i Oloma'o}—	E-*M.l. rutha*	Re

TABLE 2. CONTINUED

Common name	Scientific name	Status
{(Lāna'i Thrush)—Lāna'i Oloma'o}—	*M. l. lanaiensis*	Rx
(Hawai'i Thrush)—'Ōma'o	*Myadestes obscurus*	Re
(Small Kaua'i Thrush)—Puaiohi	*E-Myadestes palmeri*	Re
BABBLERS	*TIMALIIDAE*	
Greater Necklaced Laughing-thrush	*Garrulax pectoralis*	Al
Gray-sided Laughing-thrush	*Garrulax caerulatus*	Al
(Melodious Laughing-thrush, Chinese Thrush)—Hwamei	*Garrulax canorus*	Al
(Pekin Nightingale, Japanese Hill-robin)—Red-billed Leiothrix	*Leiothrix lutea*	Al
WHITE-EYES	*ZOSTEROPIDAE*	
(Mejiro)—Japanese White-eye	*Zosterops japonicus*	Al
MOCKINGBIRDS	*MIMIDAE*	
Northern Mockingbird	*Mimus polyglottos*	Al
STARLINGS, MYNAS	*STURNIDAE*	
European Starling	*Sturnus vulgaris*	Vs
Common Myna	*Acridotheres tristis*	Al
PIPITS	*MOTACILLIDAE*	
Olive-backed Pipit	*Anthus hodgsoni*	Vs
Red-throated Pipit	*Anthus cervinus*	Vs
American Pipit	*Anthus rubescens*	Vs
EMBERIZIDS	*EMBERIZIDAE*	
Yellow-faced Grassquit	*Tiaris olivacea*	An
Saffron Finch	*Sicalis flaveola*	An
(Brazilian Cardinal)—Red-crested Cardinal	*Paroaria coronata*	Al
Yellow-billed Cardinal	*Paroaria capitata*	Al
Savannah Sparrow	*Passerculus sandwichensis*	Vs
Snow Bunting	*Plectrophenax nivalis*	Vs
CARDINALS	*CARDINALIDAE*	
(American or Kentucky Cardinal)—Northern Cardinal	*Cardinalis cardinalis*	Al
MEADOWLARKS, GRACKLES	*ICTERIDAE*	
Western Meadowlark	*Sturnella neglecta*	Al
Great-tailed Grackle	*Quiscalus mexicanus*	Vs
FINCHES	**FRINGILLIDAE**	
CARDUELINE FINCHES	**CARDUELINAE (subfamily)**	
(Linnet)—House Finch	*Carpodacus mexicanus*	Al
Common Redpoll	*Carduelis flammea*	Vs
(Green Singing-Finch)—Yellow-fronted Canary	*Serinus mozambicus*	An
(Canary)—Common Canary	*Serinus canaria*	Al
HAWAIIAN HONEYCREEPERS	**DREPANIDINAE (subfamily)**	
FINCH-BILLED HONEYCREEPERS	*PSITTIROSTRINI (tribe)*	
Laysan Finch	*E-Telespiza cantans*	Re
Nihoa Finch	*E-Telespiza ultima*	Re
'Ō'ū	*E-Psittirostra psittacea*	Re
Lāna'i Hookbill	*Dysmorodrepanis munroi*	Rx
Palila	*E-Loxioides bailleui*	Re
Lesser Koa-Finch	*Rhodacanthis flaviceps*	Rx
Greater Koa-Finch	*Rhodacanthis palmeri*	Rx
(Grosbeak Finch)—Kona Grosbeak	*Chloridops kona*	Rx
Maui Parrotbill	*E-Pseudonestor xanthophrys*	Re
SLENDERBILLED HONEYCREEPERS	*HEMIGNATHINI (tribe)*	
Hawai'i 'Amakihi	*Hemignathus virens*	
{Hawai'i 'Amakihi}—	*H. v. virens*	Re
{Maui 'Amakihi}—	*H. v. wilsoni*	Re
O'ahu 'Amakihi	*Hemignathus flavus*	Re
Kaua'i 'Amakihi	*Hemignathus kauaiensis*	Re

TABLE 2. CONTINUED

Common name	Scientific name	Status
(Lesser 'Amakihi)—'Anianiau	*Hemignathus parvus*	Re
(Green Solitaire)—Greater 'Amakihi	*Hemignathus sagittirostris*	Rx
Lesser 'Akialoa	*Hemignathus obscurus*	Rx
Greater 'Akialoa	*Hemignathus ellisianus*	
{Kaua'i 'Akialoa}—	*H. e. procerus*	Rx
{O'ahu 'Akialoa}—	*H. e. ellisianus*	Rx
{Lana'i 'Akialoa}—	*H. e. lanaiensis*	Rx
Nukupu'u	*Hemignathus lucidus*	
{Kaua'i Nukupu'u}—	*E- H. l. hanapepe*	Re
{O'ahu Nukupu'u}—	*H. l. lucidus*	Rx
{Maui Nukupu'u}—	*E-H. l. affinis*	Re
'Akiapōlā'au	*E-Hemignathus munroi*	Re
(Kaua'i Creeper)—'Akikiki	*Oreomystis bairdi*	Re
(Olive Green Creeper)—Hawai'i Creeper	*E-Oreomystis mana*	Re
(O'ahu Creeper)—O'ahu 'Alauahio	*E-Paroreomyza maculata*	Re
(Moloka'i Creeper)—Kākāwahie	*Paroreomyza flammea*	Rx
(Maui Creeper)—Maui 'Alauahio	*Paroreomyza montana*	
{Maui 'Alauahio}—	*P. m. newtoni*	Re
{Lana'i 'Alauahio}—	*P. m. montana*	Rx
(Kaua'i Ākepa)—'Akeke'e	*Loxops caeruleirostris*	Re
'Ākepa	*Loxops coccineus*	
{O'ahu 'Ākepa}—	*L. c. wolstenholmei*	Rx
{Maui 'Ākepa}—	*E-L. c. ochraceus*	Re
{Hawai'i 'Ākepa}—	*E-L. c. coccineus*	Re
RED AND BLACK HONEYCREEPERS	***DREPANIDINI (tribe)***	
Ula-'ai-hawane	*Ciridops anna*	Rx
'I'iwi	*Vestiaria coccinea*	Re
Hawai'i Mamo	*Drepanis pacifica*	Rx
(Perkins Mamo)—Black Mamo	*Drepanis funerea*	Rx
(Crested Honeycreeper)—'Ākohekohe	*E-Palmeria dolei*	Re
'Apapane	*Himatione sanguinea*	
{Laysan Honeycreeper}—	*H. s. freethii*	Rx
{'Apapane}—	*H. s. sanguinea*	Re
Po'ouli	*E-Melamprosops phaeosoma*	Re
OLD WORLD SPARROWS	***PASSERIDAE***	
(English Sparrow)—House Sparrow	*Passer domesticus*	Al
WAXBILLS, MANNIKINS	***ESTRILDIDAE***	
Red-cheeked Cordonbleu	*Uraeginthus bengalus*	An
Lavender Waxbill	*Estrilda caerulescens*	An
Orange-cheeked Waxbill	*Estrilda melpoda*	An
(Red-eared Waxbill)—Black-rumped Waxbill	*Estrilda troglodytes*	An
Common Waxbill	*Estrilda astrild*	An
(Strawberry Finch, Red Munia)—Red Avadavat	*Amandava amandava*	Al
African Silverbill	*Lonchura cantans*	An
(Ricebird, Spotted Munia)—Nutmeg Mannikin	*Lonchura punctulata*	Al
Tricolored Munia	*Lonchura malacca*	Al
Chestnut Munia	*Lonchura atricapilla*	An
Java Sparrow	*Padda oryzivora*	An

Notes: This table is modified from Robert Pyle's 1997 checklist of the birds of Hawaii. In all cases we have deferred to the American Ornithologist Union's 1998 Checklist of North American birds and the 42nd Supplement to the Checklist (AOU 2000) for common and scientific names and sequence of families and species. We have added macrons, diacritical marks, and glottal stops to all common names as indicated by Pyle (1997). Subspecies of resident species known to occur in the islands are indicated in brackets. Common names in parentheses are those commonly used in Hawai'i but not accepted by the AOU Check-list.

ly, The Nature Conservancy has pursued an aggressive control program for alien species that threaten the viability of native species populations and the ecological integrity of native Hawaiian ecosystems and established several large biological reserves. While the Sierra Club, Native Plant Society, Hawaii Audubon Society, and a number of state and federal agencies have all taken actions on behalf of Hawai'i's native flora and fauna, despite their efforts and extensive research efforts in the last 25 years (Banko et al. *this volume,* Steiner *this volume*), populations and species of native birds continue to be lost. Nonnative birds species comprise a large part of the current avifauna (Table 2).

If there is to be any hope of retaining even a majority of the currently endangered and threatened native Hawaiian species, more aggressive efforts are needed to seriously reduce agents known to be detrimental to native species (Smith 1985, 1989; Cuddihy and Stone 1990, Stone 1989, Banko et al. *this volume,* Scott and van Riper *this volume*). Despite widespread documentation of the impact of feral cats (*Felis catus*) on birds (Eberhard 1954, van Aarde 1978, Jehl and Parkes 1982, Tomkins 1985, Churcher and Lawton 1987, van Reusenburg and Bester 1988, Bloomer and Besler 1992, Seto and Conant 1996, Athens 1997, Radunzel et al. 1997), there are currently no cat control programs in place for passerine species and only limited efforts on behalf of seabirds (Hodges and Nagata *this volume*). Likewise, while the impact of rats (*Rattus* spp.) on Hawai'i's avifauna has yet to be fully documented, Atkinson's (1977) correlational study was suggestive, as was the extinction of five populations of native birds on Big South Cape Island in New Zealand shortly after the arrival of the roof rat (*Rattus rattus*; Atkinson 1985). Studies in New Zealand (Atkinson and Bell 1973) and elsewhere have shown the strong positive response of native species when nonnative rats are eliminated (Radunzel et al. 1997). In spite of this evidence, predator control programs are rare and are not being implemented over areas large enough to elicit a population response by native species. The elimination of rats from Midway Island is an exception (R. Shallenberger, pers. comm.).

In the absence of management activities to control or eliminate known causes of mortality to Hawaiian avifauna over areas comparable to the size of the distributional area of the threats, individuals will die, populations will be lost, and species will continue to go extinct. For some threats (e.g., predators, ungulates), known control techniques (e.g., Taylor and Katahira 1988, Katahira et al. 1993) only need be applied at a scale that is meaningful (the distributional area of a population or species). For others, such as avian malaria and avian pox, new techniques such as genetic engineering of disease resistant birds and introduction of sterile male mosquitoes must be developed and applied.

A first step to buy time and simultaneously to restore populations of other endemic Hawaiian species (plants and invertebrates) would be to restore the composition and structure of higher elevation xeric and mesic forest habitats on Maui and Hawai'i by eliminating alien animals and plants (e.g., rats, cats, ungulates, and fountain grass) from these areas. These recovered and restored habitats would act as refugia from avian diseases so prevalent at lower elevations.

The idea for this book came during informal discussions at the 67th annual meeting of the Cooper Ornithological Society in Hilo, Hawai'i, in April 1997. During that meeting there were 47 presentations on natural history, ecology and taxonomy of Hawaiian birds. We invited selected authors of those presentations to submit manuscripts for consideration in a peer reviewed book on the birds of Hawai'i. To fill gaps in topics covered we solicited eight additional manuscripts. There was a high degree of redundancy in references cited among authors. Because of this we chose to create a combined literature cited.

Common and scientific names of birds follow the 7th edition of the American Ornithologists Union Check-list (AOU 1998). Quentin Tomich's *Mammals in Hawaii* (Tomich 1986) was our reference for mammal names. For flowering plants we relied on *Manual of the Flowering Plants of Hawai'i* (Wagner et al. 1990 a,b). "Pronunciation of Hawaiian names is aided by the use of a reversed apostrophe ('), to indicate the glottal stop, a stopping of sound, as between the vowell sounds in oh-oh in English; and by macrons over vowels—ā, ē, ī, ō, ū—which denote long stress. An asterisk preceding a place name indicates that pronunciation is uncertain" (Armstrong 1983:231). The orthography follows the revised and enlarged *Hawaiian Dictionary* (Pukui and Elbert 1986). For place names we followed the revised and enlarged *Place Names of Hawaii* (Pukui et al. 1976). When names could not be located there the spelling in the *Atlas of Hawaii* (Armstrong 1983) was followed.

This monograph includes 35 papers, most of which were presented at the 67th meeting of the Cooper Ornithological Society in Hilo, Hawai'i, in April 1997. Each paper has been peer reviewed by the editors and at least one outside reviewer. We have grouped the 35 chapters in this book into six sections, each introduced with a historical review. Taken together, they report on the state of our knowledge concerning the Hawaiian avifauna at the end of the 20th century.

Hopefully, this synthesis volume will assist in some small way to help preserve the unique avifauna of Hawai'i and the Pacific islands so that future generations will be able to observe and hear some of the incredible sights and sounds that we have been privileged to experience during our short 'tour of duty' researching one of the most unique avifaunas on this planet.

ACKNOWLEDGMENTS

We thank Robert Pyle for permission to use a modified version of his Check-List of Hawaiian Birds and for his comments on drafts of Table 2. Sue McMurray tracked manuscripts and correspondence to author's queries. Sue McMurray and Andrea Reese completed the onerous task of combining references from individual papers into a single combined Literature Cited. Steve Mosher found a second home in the library as he checked references against the original publications. Lenny Freed was instrumental in launching the idea for publishing manuscripts from the Hilo meeting of the Cooper Ornithological Society as an integrated monograph in STUDIES IN AVIAN BIOLOGY and provided valuable comments on manuscripts. Melissa Madsen read all manuscripts for grammar and adherence to STUDIES IN AVIAN BIOLOGY format, consistency with place names of Hawa'i, and correct usage of glottal stops, macrons, and diacritical marks in the spelling of Hawaiian words. Kathy Merk's unfailing commitment to completing this book was a huge morale booster; she tracked manuscripts, corresponded with authors, and made edits on manuscripts as needed. John Rotenberry was the epitome of what a professional editor should be; his insightful comments, rigorous attention to detail, and manner of conveying need for change made him a pleasure to work with. H. Douglas Pratt graciously provided a painting of the Hawai'i 'Ō'ō for the frontespiece of this book, as well as the line drawings that precede each section. We thank Patrick Ching for the numerous drawings of native Hawaiian birds scattered throughout the text. Jack Jeffrey kindly provided the photograph of an 'Anianiau feeding on a kanawao that graces the cover. Funds for publication of this book and administrative support were provided by the U.S. Geological Survey, Idaho Cooperative Fish and Wildlife Research Unit, and the Department of Fish and Wildlife, University of Idaho, Moscow, Idaho. To all these individuals a special *mahalo nui loa* (deep thanks) for all that you have done.

Historical Perspectives

Studies in Avian Biology No. 22:14, 2001.

HISTORICAL PERSPECTIVES—INTRODUCTION

CHARLES VAN RIPER, III, SHEILA CONANT, AND J. MICHAEL SCOTT

The record of Hawai'i's avifauna is one of change; a change that is reflected in steadily diminishing numbers of species and abundance (Pratt 1994). Our historical perspectives provide insights into how many species there were and some documentation of their distribution, but only minor insights into their abundance, with size, shape, and bill forms allowing vague inferences concerning niches occupied and resources exploited. Nothing is known of clutch sizes, population characteristics, or ecological interactions of extinct species. For these reasons, more than 50% of Hawai'i's bird species will always be a ghost avifauna.

The history of ornithological exploration in Hawai'i is a legacy of missed opportunities, with the first extensive surveys of the avifauna coming 100 years after the discovery of the islands by Europeans in 1778 (Olson and James 1994a). Historically, recorded species are but a small fraction of what occurred in the islands prior to European colonization. Some species were simply overlooked; the Po'ouli (*Melamprosops phaeosoma*) was not discovered until 1972 (Casey and Jacobi 1974). Olson and James (1991, James and Olson 1991) nearly doubled the known number of endemic species based on their descriptions of new species from fossil and subfossil remains. New discoveries of fossil species continue today.

In the first chapter of this volume, Curnutt and Pimm estimate that the Pacific avifauna was composed of nearly 1,500 species, of which approximately 240 survive. For example, they estimate that there were 12 species of rails endemic to the Hawaiian Islands, versus the 7 currently described (Olson and James 1991; Table 2). In the second chapter, Michael Moulton and his co-authors document the introduction of 140 species in 14 different orders and ask, "Why do some introduced species succeed and others fail?"

Studies in Avian Biology No. 22:15–30, 2001.

HOW MANY BIRD SPECIES IN HAWAI'I AND THE CENTRAL PACIFIC BEFORE FIRST CONTACT?

JOHN CURNUTT AND STUART PIMM

Abstract. Since European settlement, extinctions of Pacific island birds have been widespread and well documented. Subfossil evidence indicates that the Polynesians caused extinctions of an even greater magnitude. Estimating the prehuman Pacific avifauna is difficult because the existing fossil record is inevitably incomplete. We use the theoretical framework of island biogeography to make estimates of the numbers of endemic rails, parrots, pigeons and doves that existed in the Pacific before human contact. We formulate two sets of estimates for each taxon by assuming that: (1) endemism is defined as a distribution limited to a single island, and (2) endemism is a distribution limited to a single-island group. These two assumptions lead to different results (884 compared with 242 endemic species). We refine our predictions by applying topographical and disturbance parameters. Our best estimate is that 332 endemic species of the three taxa once existed in the Pacific, of which 210 are not accounted for in the paleontological and historical data. Applying this ratio of known to missing species for all landbirds, we estimate the original Pacific avifauna to be composed of less than 1,500 species, of which approximately 230 survive. Our estimate of the original Pacific avifauna falls between two earlier conflicting predictions (800 and much greater than 2,000). Our predictions of the number of species missing on each type of island are testable. Our results can be used to focus research efforts on islands that are more likely to have held species of interest. Furthermore, our results can be interpreted to predict the risk of future extinctions that may result from habitat loss or rising sea levels.

Key Words: biogeography; doves; extinctions; Pacific Islands; parrots; pigeons; rails; sea level; tsunamis.

The Hawaiian Islands form one of the largest and most diverse archipelagoes in the Pacific. As a group, they lead the world in numbers of historically extinct and currently endangered species of birds (King 1985). This dismal legacy, however, did not befall the Hawaiian Islands alone. Untold bird extinctions doubtlessly occurred across the Pacific over the four millennia since humans first set sail there. What was the magnitude of the loss of bird species in the Pacific?

"The Pacific" denies an easy definition. Defined in the context of human settlement over the last 4,000 years, we will consider 41 island groups (Fig. 1). They span the Hawaiian Islands in the northeast, west to the Marianas and Palau, southwest through Vanuatu, south to New Zealand and east to Easter Island. Pratt et al.'s (1987) field guide covers all but Vanuata (for which see Bregulla 1992), New Zealand (see Falla et al. 1983), and Easter (which has no extant landbirds).

There are roughly 240 extant native species of landbirds in this region (Falla et al. 1983, Pratt et al. 1987, Bregulla 1992). The largest families are Pachycephalidae (whistlers; 40 spp.), Columbidae (pigeons and doves; 34 spp.), Muscicapidae (Old World flycatchers; 28 spp.), Rallidae (rails; 21 spp.), Psittacidae (parrots; 19 spp.), and Fringillidae (Hawaiian honeycreepers; 19 spp.).

To the above number of species we must add those that we know once existed but are now known only through historical records and fossils. Among the islands of the Pacific, the many vertebrate extinctions that occurred since the sixteenth century subsequent to the arrival of European explorers are well documented. For example, Diamond (1984) reported that, since 1600, Micronesia and Polynesia suffered roughly 100 bird species extinctions. The forces responsible for the loss of these species were the same as those that operate today, primarily habitat loss and the introduction of exotic species (Steadman 1997a,b). A much greater extinction event preceded the arrival of Europeans and was concurrent with the first human contact (Steadman 1997a,b). Beginning about 4,000 years ago with Melanesia and Micronesia and ending about 1,500 years ago with Hawai'i, Easter Island, and New Zealand, humanity brought the last habitable places on Earth under its domain (Rouse 1986).

European explorers found well-developed, agricultural-based societies on all of the larger Pacific islands. It is not known how many of the smaller, less suitable islands were visited only temporarily by the wandering islanders (Oliver 1961). Habitat loss and exotic species (including dogs and pigs) doubtlessly caused the extinction of many species of endemic birds on the permanently settled islands. Even on smaller uninhabited islands endemic species, many of them flightless rails that had evolved in the absence

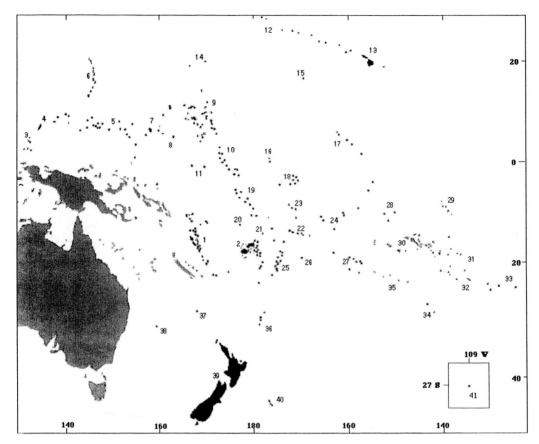

FIGURE 1.   The islands of the Pacific. Numbers refer to island groups referred to in the text and listed in Table 1.

of terrestrial predators, could have been harvested to extinction by temporary human occupants.

We have evidence of these unrecorded extinction events in the fossil record (Olson and James 1982a, 1991; Milberg and Tyrberg 1993). Archeological efforts in Hawai'i by Olson and James (1982a, 1991; James and Olson 1991) and throughout the rest of the Pacific (Balouet and Olson 1987; Steadman 1991, 1992, 1993, 1997a,b; Kirch et al. 1995), have uncovered a large number of avian fossils that were deposited concurrently with early human occupation of the islands. Not all islands have been searched, and even if they were, it is unlikely that all extinct species would be found. Thus, the total number of extant and extinct species identified to date is an underestimate of the diversity of the prehuman Pacific avifauna.

An exact count of the number of landbird species known only as fossils is difficult to tally because they are not clearly enumerated in some published accounts. The Hawaiian Islands held 62 fossil species (James and Olson 1991, Olson

and James 1991) and New Zealand held 44 species (Steadman 1995). The other islands of the Pacific that have been searched held something less than 100 additional species (Steadman 1995). Thus, roughly 200 species of Pacific landbirds are known only from the fossil record.

Summing the number of extant, historically extinct, and prehistorically extinct (fossil) species, there are 540 known species of landbirds in the Pacific. This number is too low because the fossil record is incomplete. An accurate estimate of the prehuman Pacific avifauna depends on an accurate estimate of the "missing" fossil species.

Pimm et al. (1994) estimated the prehuman number of Pacific island landbirds by applying sampling analyses to fossil data. Briefly, given the number of species known only by fossils, those known by modern observations (i.e., those that still survive and those extinct since European colonization), and those known by both fossils and modern observations one can deduce the number of "missing" species from an island. Applying this method to data on the landbirds of the tropical Pacific (including New Caledonia), Pimm et al. (1994) deduced that the number of known fossil species (ca. 200) is only half of the actual number of species that disappeared before European colonization. Pimm et al. (1994) estimated the original avifauna to include nearly 800 species of landbirds. Excluding data from New Caledonia and including data from New Zealand, to fit the boundaries to the current study, does not appreciably change these estimates.

A much higher estimate of the original Pacific avifauna was proposed by Steadman (1995, 1997). On finding fossil evidence of up to three or four now extinct species of flightless rails on islands he investigated, Steadman (1995, 1997a,b) suggested that the 800 major islands of the Pacific held more than 2,000 species of this taxon and lower numbers of other taxa—all driven to extinction as a result of first human contact. Steadman's (1995) approach set the question of original avifauna in the context of island biogeography.

In this paper we apply a robust theoretical framework, island biogeography theory (MacArthur and Wilson 1967a), to the Pacific islands to determine the number of islands that could have held endemic species of rails (Rallidae), pigeons and doves (Columbiformes), and parrots (Psittaciformes). We chose these taxa because they are well represented in the fossil record. Thus, we do not estimate the entire prehuman landbird fauna; instead our results can indicate the magnitude of the loss of bird diversity that has occurred since first human contact. We include in our analyses all named islands of New Zealand, Micronesia, central and eastern Melanesia, and Polynesia that experienced first human contact no earlier than 4,000 years before present (Rouse 1986). Unlike Steadman (1995, 1997), we incorporate data on habitat diversity, changing sea levels during the Holocene, and tsunamis. Each of these factors influences the effective size of islands for landbirds. Put simply, MacArthur and Wilson's (1967a) theory of island biogeography predicts more species on larger islands and those close to a source of immigrants, and fewer species on small or isolated islands. We perform two distance analyses: distance-from-source, as proposed by MacArthur and Wilson (1967a); and, distance between islands—isolated islands are more likely to produce species endemic to one island than those that have very near neighbors (Mayr 1963). By applying reasonable assumptions to this question, we hope to develop a more accurate estimate of the prehuman Pacific avifauna than has been produced to date.

We first identify those islands of the Pacific that have the potential to maintain populations of landbirds. We then extrapolate the numbers of endemic rails, pigeons, and parrots that could have existed on all of these islands by applying the known maximum of each taxon recorded on different island sizes and types. In fact, we calculate two estimates of the number of endemic species by using two definitions of endemism. We then refine our estimates by considering ecological and environmental characteristics.

IDENTIFYING THE BIRD ISLANDS

We do not expect all islands of the Pacific to hold birds. Some islands are too small to support viable populations of landbirds. Some islands may also fall outside of the known range of the taxa we are investigating. These limitations to bird distribution are diagrammed in Figure 2 Our first task, then, is to estimate how many islands there are in the Pacific, and which of these could support a population of landbirds.

How Many Islands

No one knows how many islands there are in the Pacific Ocean. Estimates range from 30,000 to less than half of that number (Bryan 1963). The distribution of island sizes is fractal—that is, as one looks at the Pacific at finer scales, one finds more islands in a characteristic way. Thus, most islands are very small. We limited our data to named islands. We obtained gazetteer data (latitude, longitude, name) from the U.S. Defense Mapping Agency's (DMA) database available on the Internet. This search yielded 3,463 islands.

We assigned each island to an island group according to an arbitrary grouping scheme. Obvious archipelagos were identified as groups (e.g., the Gilbert Islands), as were single islands not obviously associated with an archipelago (e.g., Rapa). The result was 41 island groups (Table 1; Fig. 1). As described below, we first grouped islands that are very close to each other. Our primary reason for this was to add small islets to the larger islands that they surround and to unite many "islands" that occur as parts of individual atolls. Second, we determined which islands are too far from a source of immigrants for each taxon. Finally, we determined the size and topography of each island.

Islands and Islets

If two islands were near enough to each other to allow a species to move between them, then neither would produce an endemic species (Ricklefs and Schluter 1993). But how close is close enough? No data exist on this subject for birds in the Pacific. We know that the limiting distances between islands are surely taxon spe-

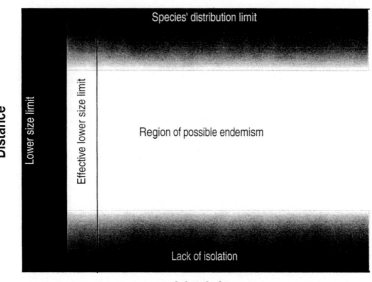

FIGURE 2.   Theoretical framework for endemism of Pacific island birds. Islands that are too small to maintain persistent populations will not produce endemic species (lower size limit), nor will larger islands subject to inhibitory disturbance regimes (effective lower size limit). Some islands are close enough to allow genetic exchange between populations and will not produce endemic species (lack of isolation), while others lay outside of the distribution of some taxa (species' distribution limit).

cific and this, in turn, is affected by the mode and propensity of movement exhibited by each taxon. For the three taxa we consider in this paper, rails have a higher wing load (ratio of weight to wing area) than pigeons or parrots (Rayner 1988). Thus, it would take relatively more energy for a rail to fly a fixed distance than it would a pigeon. Left free to speculate, we chose a minimum distance equivalent to 0.1° of latitude or longitude ($\approx$11 km at the equator) as sufficient for allowing isolation of breeding populations. We chose this distance primarily for ease of calculation, but also we feel that such a distance would provide an adequate barrier to movement for rails—the most stationary taxon because of its propensity to quickly evolve toward flightlessness (Trewick 1997).

We summed the sizes of all islands that were closer than 0.1° of latitude or longitude to each other. This grouping scheme reduced our data to 788 island sets. Hereafter, we refer to island sets as "islands."

WHICH ISLANDS ARE TOO FAR

Landbirds are not distributed evenly across islands. Just as islands that are too close will prohibit divergence; islands that are too distant from a source population may not be colonized at a rate sufficient to allow persistence (Ricklefs and Schluter 1993).

We tested for the effect of distance-from-source on the distribution of each of our three taxa with multiple regressions. All of the taxa we consider in this paper have their origins in the Old World (rails: Ripley 1977; pigeons: Goodwin 1983; parrots: Forshaw 1977). We used Map© (Apple Computers, Inc.) software to determine distances between geographic centers of island groups and the following (geologically) continental source areas: Australia (Brisbane), Papau New Guinea (New Britain), Philippines (Manila), and Taiwan (Taipei). Since island size is the most effective predictor of species diversity (MacArthur and Wilson 1967a), we performed stepwise multiple linear regression of the number of species on total area of each island group, then added distance. We repeated this process for each of the distances generated from the four sources listed above.

At best, these multiple regressions only weakly explained the variation in species numbers with distance ($R < 0.2$) and were only significant for parrots and pigeons ($P < 0.05$). For this analysis, it is better for the data to speak for themselves. Figure 3 shows the distribution of rails, parrots and pigeons among the 41 island groups of the Pacific. Rails are found throughout the region, reaching the most remote groups including Hawai'i and Easter Island. Paradoxically, rails, for which even the largest ocean is not

TABLE 1.   ISLAND GROUPS OF THE PACIFIC OCEAN IN-
CLUDED IN OUR ANALYSES

Group	Group number	No. of island sets	Area (km²)	Topography
Melanesia				
Vanuatu	1	38	11,400	H
Fiji Islands	2	74	1,860	H
Micronesia				
Palau	3	8	447	H
Yap	4	2	175	H
Chuuk	5	21	230	L
Mariana Islands	6	13	910	H
Pohnpei	7	2	360	H
Kosrae	8	1	100	H
Marshall Islands	9	28	255	L
Gilbert Islands	10	18	290	L
Nauru	11	2	36	L
Polynesia				
NW Hawai'i	12	2	8	L
Hawai'i	13	9	16,700	H
Wake	14	1	230	L
Johnson Atoll	15	1	2	L
Howland	16	1	10	L
North Line Islands	17	7	745	L
Phoenix	18	5	37	L
Tuvalu	19	6	27	L
Rotuma	20	1	49	H
Wallis and Futuna	21	2	275	H
Samoa	22	8	3,500	H
Tokelau Islands	23	3	13	L
North Cook Islands	24	5	10	L
Tonga Islands	25	18	563	H
Niue	26	1	258	L
South Cook Islands	27	9	234	H
South Line Islands	28	2	8	L
Marquesas Islands	29	11	1,062	H
Society Islands	30	10	1,710	H
Tuamotu Arch.	31	11	248	L
Gambier	32	6	21	L
Pitcairn Islands	33	2	8.5	H
Rapa	34	1	40	H
Tabuai Islands	35	4	120	H
Easter Island	41	1	170	H
Kermadec Islands	36	2	34	H
Norfolk	37	1	37	H
Lord Howe	38	1	10	L
New Zealand	39	33	267,800	H
Chatham Islands	40	4	1,085	H

"Group Number" refers to numbers shown on Figure 1. Island sets are named Islands that are within 0.1° latitude and longitude of each other. We include only those sets with combined areas of >150 HA. Topography is either high-relief (H) or low-relief (L).

large enough to prohibit colonization, can quick-ly evolve to flightlessness (Diamond 1991). The distribution of pigeons has apparently been lim-ited by the vast expanses of ocean that isolate Hawai'i and Easter Island, for neither has ap-parently held this taxon. For Easter Island, the nearest island to have ever held a pigeon is Pit-cairn (1,600 km), and for Hawai'i, it is the North Cook Islands (3,500 km). Parrots have been

found on Easter but not the Hawaiian Islands (nearest island with parrots–Marquesas, 3,800 km distant).

For our analyses, therefore, we consider all islands of suitable size as potential sites for rail colonization; all but the Hawaiian and North-west Hawaiian Islands for parrots; and, all but the Hawaiian groups and Easter Island for pi-geons.

SIZES OF ISLANDS

The final parameters we consider in determin-ing which island sets could maintain populations of landbirds are size and topography. We ob-tained data on the sizes of islands from various sources in the literature and from direct mea-surements from maps (ranging in scale from 1: 10,000 to 1:300,000). Some islands listed in the DMA database were not found on maps (or re-ferred to in any literature we searched), thus, we have no data on their sizes. However, we are confident that we have size estimates for all of the major islands (i.e., > 2 km²) and for many lesser islands, and those with missing data are from the smallest size classes. Our confidence lies in the fact that island sizes fall within a class of negative exponential distributions known as Zipf-Mandelbrot (Fairthorne 1969). For the is-lands for which we have data, we plotted the size distributions on log-log axes. The Zipf-Mandelbrot distribution predicts a straight line for this graph (Fig. 4), and we can interpret de-viations from the linear fit as "missing" islands. By extending the linear fit below 1 km² to our smallest recorded island size (10 ha), we predict that about 800 islands are missing from our is-land size data set.

While landbirds do occur on very small is-lands in the Pacific, these are members of sat-ellite populations of larger nearby islands. For example, the Antipodes Island Parakeet (*Cy-anoramphus unicolor*) is found in low numbers on Archway Island (6 ha)—the smallest of the Antipodes Islands (Taylor 1985). The species is also found on the 54-ha Bollons Island, which is much less than 1 km from Archway Island. The greatest part of this species' population, however, is on the 20 km² Antipodes Island—about 1 km from Bollons. The loss of the An-tipodes Island population would probably lead to the eventual extinction of this species. It would not make ecological sense to identify Archway Island as one suitable for sustaining a population of parrots. Similarly, we can safely ignore the existence of the 800 "missing" is-lands in our data because they are too small to hold endemic species of landbirds.

The smallest Pacific island known to hold an endemic rail is Wake Island, 6.5 km² and home

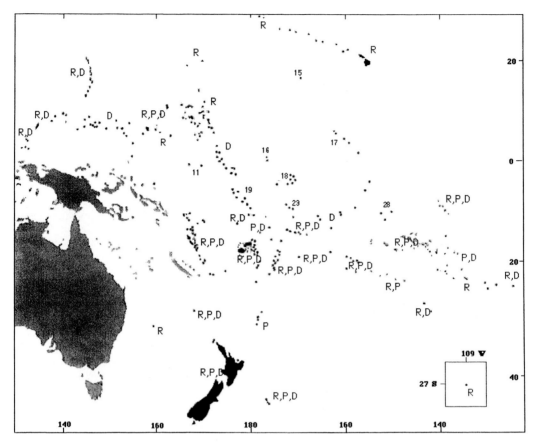

FIGURE 3.   The distribution of rails (R), parrots (P), and pigeons and doves (D) among the Pacific islands. Numbers correspond to group names in Table 1 and indicate island groups that hold none of the three taxa mentioned above.

to *Rallus wakensis*. The smallest island to hold an endemic pigeon is 28 km² Maketea (Tuamotu Archipelago), home to *Ptilinopus chalcurus*; and the smallest island to hold an endemic parrot is Norfolk Island (33.7 km²) where remains of *Nestor produetus* have been recovered.

These minima may not be actual; all islands have not been sampled. We performed a Monte Carlo simulation (Efron and Tibshirani 1993) to predict the minimum size of an island that should support an endemic species from the observed distribution of island sizes with endemic species. Using data on island sizes, we randomly selected a number of islands equivalent to the number that we knew held endemic species of each taxon. For example, 23 islands held at least one endemic species of rail. We randomly selected 23 islands from the entire set of 834 and recorded the minimum size of this subset. We then calculated the mean minimum value of 100 repetitions. By repeating this process with increasing cutoff values applied to the entire data

set, we determined the lower 95% confidence limit within which our known minimum island size fell (Fig. 5).

Some islands have held more than one endemic species of a taxon. For parrots and pigeons there were one and two islands, respectively. For these taxa we could not perform the above described simulation to determine the minimum island sizes for two or more species—the sample size is too small. For rails, however, of which 10 islands held more than one endemic species, we could estimate the minimum island size for two species by applying the simulation (with a sample size of 10). To determine which islands could have held more than two species of rail (or more than one species of parrot or pigeon), we assumed that the smallest island for which we had data was the actual minimum.

TYPES OF ISLANDS

Our measure of habitat diversity was very coarse. We described islands as "high-relief" or

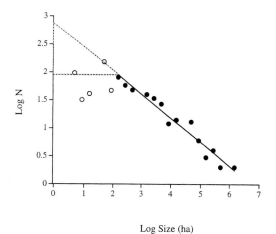

FIGURE 4. The relationship between island sizes and their frequency. The linear fit was calculated after excluding the two smallest size classes (open circles) and the three largest size classes (not shown). The area within the triangle represents islands with size data missing from our data set, assuming island sizes exhibit a Zipf-Mandelbrot distribution.

"low-relief." High-relief islands were those described in the literature as volcanic, hilly, or mountainous or whose representation on maps included hachures. Low-relief islands were all of those described as atolls or were lacking hachures on maps that normally include such data. High-relief islands are rich in habitat diversity compared to low-relief islands (Adler 1992). We apply the same topography to entire groups by summing the areas of all islands within groups and defining them as high relief if > 50% of the total area is attributed to high-relief islands.

EXTRAPOLATING ENDEMICS

To estimate the potential number of endemic species that each taxon held, we determined the known maximum number of endemics (living and fossil) on islands of different sizes and topographies throughout the Pacific. After estimating the size of the smallest islands which we would expect to find endemics on, we used these numbers to predict the maximum numbers of endemic species with reference to the distribution of island sizes and topographies within each island group (Fig. 6). We tallied the number of known endemics and the number of predicted endemics across taxa for each island group then

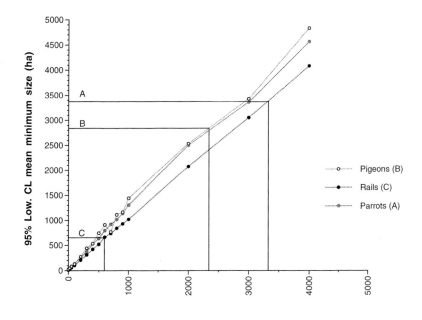

FIGURE 5. Results of a simulation whereby we randomly selected a number of islands equivalent to the number occupied by endemic species of each taxon. The x-axis represents the lowest value in the data set for each simulation, the y-axis is the 95% lower confidence limit of the mean of 100 repetitions. A, B, and C represent the actual minimum sizes for parrots, pigeons, and rails, respectively. The vertical lines intercept the x-axis at the smallest island size we would expect to find endemics of the respective species.

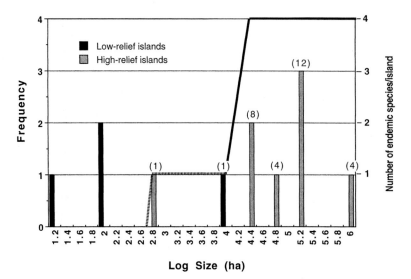

FIGURE 6. The size distribution of islands of the Hawai'i group classified as high relief and low relief. The solid line indicates the maximum number of endemic rails found on all high-relief islands in the Pacific while the dashed line indicates maxima for low-relief islands. We multiplied the maxima for each size class by the number of islands in each size class to predict the number of endemic rails that could have existed in each island group. Numbers in parentheses indicate the number of rails expected for each island size X the number of islands.

calculated the proportion of missing endemic species.

Our use of maxima reflects the potential lack of fossil data on some islands. For example, well-searched Mangaia of the South Cook Islands group held four endemic rails. Tofua of the Tonga Islands, with a similar size and topography, revealed none. For our estimates we assume that Tofua held four endemic rails. This may be incorrect; to paraphrase Montaigne, speciation is not so often the result of great design as of chance. There may never have been endemic rails on Tofua simply because no rails have survived there long enough to speciate.

Since the true number of prehistoric endemics cannot be known, we must be content with estimating this number by setting realistic limits based on the available data. Of the four factors we consider as affecting endemism, we have data on absolute lower island size and distance from source. Data do not exist for two other factors—effective lower island size (disturbance effects) and the minimum distance between islands needed to produce endemism (dispersal effects). Thus, we are left with the familiar quandary of decreasing our certainty as we increase the number of parameters. We address the problem of prehistoric disturbance on a group by group basis later. Our approach to effective distance between islands is as follows.

As noted earlier, we grouped all islands 11 km or closer to each other into sets. While an 11

km expanse of ocean may prohibit the movement of a flightless rail, it may have less effect on a strong-flying pigeon. We could further group our islands by different distances for each taxon, but this would be a series of educated guesses at best. Instead, we approach this problem by determining the maximum number of endemics that we know to occur in each island group. For example, the Red-bellied Fruit Dove (*Ptilinopus greyii*) is found on 28 islands of the Vanuatu group (total area of 11,000 km²). Thus, it does not fit our definition of a single-island endemic. It is, however, found only in the Vanuatu group, so it does exhibit a form of endemism. In Vanuatu, this species is found on both low- and high-relief islands. We conclude then that any island group that is dominated by high-relief islands and has a combined area the size of the Vanuatu group would hold an endemic pigeon.

We, therefore, produce two estimates for each taxon—the number of endemics at single islands and the number of endemics at island groups. The true number of endemic rails, pigeons, and parrots that have existed in the Pacific probably falls somewhere between these two values.

THE BIRDS

We chose rails, parrots, and pigeons for our analyses because they are well represented in the fossil record. We reviewed all available literature on the distribution of extant, historically ex-

TABLE 2. AN ESTIMATE OF THE NUMBER OF RAIL SPECIES IN THE PACIFIC BEFORE HUMAN COLONIZATION

Island size and topography	Number of islands	Number species/island	Predicted total number of species
<600 ha, high and low relief	578	0	0
600–1000 ha, high and low relief	44	1	44
<1000 ha, low relief	61	1	61
1000–6400 ha, high relief	86	2	172
<6400 ha, high relief	65	4	260
Total	834		537

Maximum numbers of species are gleaned from the data for each size/topography of island. The predicted number of species is the product of maxima and the number of islands.

tinct, and subfossil species of these taxa in the Pacific. We assigned each species to all islands on which it was known to occur.

RAILS

Single-island endemics

We catalogued 55 species of rails known to have occurred in the Pacific. Of these, only five (all extant) are not restricted to either single-island sets or single-island groups. Two-thirds of the species are known only from fossil data and 65% are endemic to one island. Endemic rails are found on only 13 of the 41 island groups

The results of our simulation show that the smallest island with an endemic rail (6.5 km^2) falls within a distribution that has a lower 95% confidence limit of 6 km^2. Both high- and low-relief islands have held single endemic species of rails, thus, we expect that all 256 islands that are larger than 6 km^2 held at least one species. Ten islands, all high relief, held more than one endemic species. The smallest of these was Lord Howe Island (10 km^2), which held two species, followed by Mangaia (64 km^2), which held four. Since four species of endemic rails is the maximum we encountered, we apply this value to all larger islands. Table 2 and Figure 6 illustrate our method of prediction of the number of rail species for the entire Pacific and specifically for the Hawaiian Island group.

We performed the same analysis on each island group and estimated that approximately 537 endemic rail species existed in the Pacific, of which 482 are not accounted for by a living or fossil species. Over one-third (36%) of the missing endemics are attributed to only two groups—Vanuatu (94) and Fiji (86). Whereas 13 groups hold no endemics nor are expected to, 14 others hold none but should. Of the remaining 13 groups, 11 hold fewer endemics than expected, and two (Wake Island and Lord Howe Island) hold the number of endemics we predict (one and two, respectively).

Island-group endemics

Eleven of the 55 species of rails in the Pacific are endemic to groups of islands. The occurrence of the Wake Island Rail (*Rallus wakensis*) on Wake Island, an island group in itself, insures the expectation of at least one endemic rail on all low-relief groups except Johnston Atoll, which is too small. For groups with high-relief islands, the maximum number of endemics ranges from two for groups as small as 10 km^2 (Lord Howe) to 12 for groups larger than 16,700 km^2 (Hawai'i). Summing over all groups, we expect 143 endemic rails in the Pacific based on our island group analysis.

PARROTS

Single-island endemics

Of the 24 species of parrots we catalogued, 9 are endemic to single islands. The majority of these (5) are found in the southwest Pacific. No low-relief islands hold endemic parrots. Norfolk Island (33.7 km^2) represents the smallest island to hold an endemic parrot (*Nestor produetus*). We estimated that the lower size limit of islands that would support endemic parrots is 28.5 km^2. Excluding the Hawaiian islands and Easter Island, there are 110 high-relief islands of 28.5 km^2 or greater. The only island with more than one species of endemic parrot is the largest in our data set—South Island, New Zealand (149,000 km^2). Thus, we attribute three species to this island only, for a total of 94 species ([91 islands * 1 species] + [1 island * 3 species]).

Island-group endemics

In contrast to the rails, a large proportion of parrot species (30%) in the Pacific show endemism to single groups of islands. The smallest group to hold an endemic is Norfolk (34 km^2), home to *Nestor produetus*. We apply this value of one endemic to 18 of the 22 island groups that contain high-relief islands. We predicted two endemic parrot species to Vanuatu and Fiji. New Zealand held four endemics. The total number of endemic parrots we expect from our analyses of island groups is a mere 29 species.

PIGEONS AND DOVES

Single-island endemics

We catalogued 43 species of pigeons and doves in the Pacific. Only nine of these are endemic to single islands. Of these, five are known only from fossil remains and are identified only to genus. Huahine of the Society Islands held the highest number of endemics with three of the unknown species (*Ducula* sp., *Gallicolumba* sp., and *Ptilinopus* sp.). Henderson Island of the Pitcairn group held two endemics—the extant Henderson Island Fruit Dove (*Ptilinopus insularis*) and a fossil *Gallicolumba* sp. The remaining four endemics were found on Rapa (Rapa Fruit Dove, *Ptilinopus huttoni*), Mangaia of the South Cook Islands (*Gallicolumba* sp.), Makatea of the Tuamotu Archipelago (Makatea Fruit Dove, *Ptilinopus chalcurus*), and Espiritu Santo of the Vanuatu group (Santa Cruz Ground Dove, *Gallicolumba sanctaecrucis*).

The smallest island to hold an endemic was Makatea of the Tuamotu Archipelago. Makatea is 28 km² and low relief. We estimate that the smallest island likely to hold an endemic pigeon or dove would be 20.7 km². Islands with more than one endemic are Henderson (36 km²) with two species and Huahine (75.5 km²) with three—both of these islands are high relief. Again, excluding Easter Island and the Hawaiian groups, our estimate of the total number of endemics is thus: (53 islands * 1 species) + (25 islands * 2 species) + (50 islands * 3 species) = 253 species.

Island-group endemics

Just as we saw that a greater proportion of parrots showed endemism to groups of islands than the less mobile rails, a full 51% of the pigeons and doves are restricted to single-island groups compared to 30% for parrots. Thus, there appears to be a positive relationship between flight ability and area over which endemism extends.

Vanuatu held the most species (6) of pigeons and doves that were restricted to an island group, and the Marianas held the next highest number (5). These, and the other large groups of islands (Chuuk, Fiji, New Zealand, the Society Islands, and Tonga) account for 39 of the total 64 species of island-group endemic pigeons and doves. Unlike parrots, endemic pigeons and doves are also found on large low-relief groups. Two species are restricted to the Tuamotu Archipelago, a fact that leads us to predict the same number of species on the Marshall Islands.

THE ESTIMATED NUMBER OF ENDEMICS

Our exercise produced two sets of estimates of the number of endemic species in each of three taxa. For estimates based on single-island endemism, we predict 537 species of rails, 94 species of parrots, and 253 species of pigeons and doves for a total of 884. We can account for only 57 single-island endemic species of the three taxa as either fossil, extinct or extant. Estimates based on island-group endemism yield 145 species of rails, 29 species of parrots, and 64 species of pigeons and doves (Fig. 7). We

can account for 40 of these as fossil, extinct, or extant. Thus, we predict that the total number of endemic species of these taxa that once occurred in the Pacific falls between 242 and 884.

TESTING THE MODELS: KNOWN VERSUS ESTIMATED ENDEMISM

We may now investigate factors that would refine our predictions. Which estimates better reflect the known distribution of endemic rails, parrots, and pigeons and doves in the Pacific—those derived from single-island endemics or those from island-group endemics? To answer this question, we compare our predicted values with the known distribution of endemic birds.

We calculated two indices of the proportion of total missing endemics (all taxa combined) per island group, one for each of our definitions of endemism. We added 1 to all values of the total number of endemics known to exist and to the totals predicted from our two definitions of endemism. We did this so that we could calculate proportions (number of known endemics/ number of predicted endemics) without having zero values in either the numerator or denominator. We arcsine transformed the proportions to make the distribution normal and ranked the results. We then compared the ranks by performing a linear regression of single-island endemic ranks on island-group endemic ranks (Fig. 8).

Not surprisingly, the linear fit was significant (F = 18.37, P < 0.01). The slope was less than unity (b = 0.56) suggesting that when the predicted number of endemics corresponds with the actual number of island-group endemics, the single-island prediction is low and vice versa. We tested for the influence of the number of islands in each group on both of our predictions. Neither set of predictions correlates with this parameter (r < 0.2 for both). Identifying each group as high relief (50% of total area is high relief) or low relief reveals the pattern responsible for the disparity between the two sets of ranks (Fig. 9). Predictions correspond best with known endemism for low-relief groups when endemism is defined as a single-island distribution. Conversely, for high-relief groups, predictions based on group endemism correspond best with the number of known endemics. We believe there are ecological reasons for this.

Groups of low-relief islands tend to have smaller islands than high-relief groups (ANOVA: F = 4.21, P = 0.04). For low-relief groups, an individual island approach to endemism would successfully identify those few large islands in the group that could support a large population of birds. In contrast, predictions based on group endemism would lead to overestimates because the area across each group is

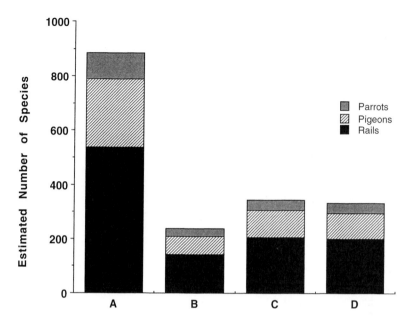

FIGURE 7. Total predicted numbers of endemic rails, parrots, and pigeons in the prehistoric Pacific under four sets of assumptions: (A) endemic species are those that occur on only one island; (B) endemic species are those that occur within single-island groups; (C) low-relief island groups produce endemic species at single islands and high-relief island groups produce endemics at island groups; and, (D) the same as (C) with modifications driven by patterns of disturbance (sea-level change and tsunamis).

summed. Conversely, the assumption of single-island endemism for the larger islands of high-relief groups ignores factors that potentially limit the size of bird communities. In his analysis of the assembly of the fruit-pigeon guild in New

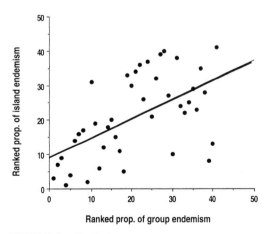

FIGURE 8. Ranked proportions of predicted numbers of endemic birds (rails, parrots, and pigeons combined) over known numbers of endemics. Values on the y-axis were generated using the assumption of single-island endemism while those on the x-axis were generated with the assumption of island-group endemism.

Guinea, Diamond (1975) showed that the entire species pool is never found in one locality. Some species never occurred together and some sets of species excluded particular species. This effect is primarily due to competition between species with closely related niches. Another ecological factor that over inflates the estimates for high-relief islands stems from our grouping across taxa. Some high-relief islands may provide habitat for each of the three taxa we discuss, but it may be unreasonable to assume that all of them do.

We can now refine our original estimates of endemism by calculating the totals for each taxon separately for low- and high-relief island groups using the appropriate assumptions of endemism (low-relief and single-island endemism; high-relief and island-group endemism). This yields 206 species of rails, 38 species of parrots, and 101 species of pigeons and doves (Fig. 7). These sum to 345 species across taxa.

WHERE THE ENDEMICS ARE AND WHERE THEY ARE NOT

Five island groups (Johnson Atoll, Howland, South Line, Gambier, and North Cook) are all low relief. They have no endemic species, nor are expected to under the assumption of single-island endemism. Our interpretation of the re-

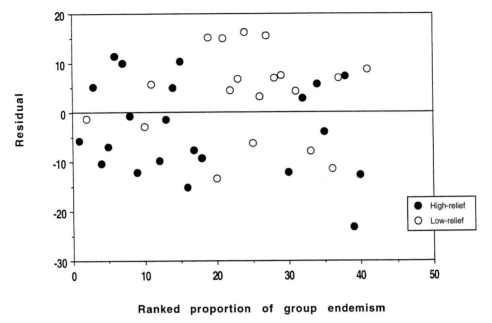

FIGURE 9.   Residuals of the linear relationship of predicted endemic species under single-island endemism versus island-group endemism (Fig. 8) with each island group defined as either high or low relief.

sults for the remaining 36 island groups depends on two assumptions. First, the maximum number of endemics recorded represents the actual maximum of each taxon that could occur on each type of island and, second, the recorded maxima on each island size/topography are applicable to all islands in each class. There is a chance that the first assumption is incorrect. Continued excavation of subfossil remains may well produce more species of birds, even on islands that are already well represented with endemics. The second assumption ignores differences in the history of islands across the Pacific. While there is little we can do to refine our predictions in light of the uncertainty of the first assumption, we can investigate the history of the Pacific islands to uncover patterns of species numbers on island groups.

The name "Pacific" belies this ocean's violent history. Natural disturbance of the Pacific islands can be a potentially limiting factor in speciation among birds. Stoddard and Walsh (1992) list five environmental factors that influence island ecosystems: vulcanicity and earthquakes, sea-level change, tsunamis, rainfall patterns, and hurricanes. We investigate two of these: sea-level change and tsunamis. We chose these factors because they operate at regional scales, their effects are unambiguous, and they occur across a temporal scale that is consistent with evolutionary time.

SEA-LEVEL CHANGE

A number of studies concerning sea-level change in the Pacific over the last 10,000 years have been reported in the literature (Ota et al. 1988, Pirazzoli and Montaggioni 1988, Yonekura et al. 1988, Pirazzoli 1991). Throughout the Pacific, sea level was much lower 10,000 years before present (BP) than any time since. At that time, global sea levels were rising rapidly with the melting of the glacial ice sheets. Indeed, the massive infusion of water into the oceans led to regions of hydroisostasy (depression of the ocean floor by water loading) and consequent elevated sea levels (Pirazzoli 1991). Thus, from 6,000 BP to as late as 1,200 BP some island groups had sea levels significantly higher than at present.

During the last glacial maximum (18,000 BP), when sea levels were nearly 150 m lower than today, all islands of the Pacific were larger. For example, the Fiji group currently has a combined area of 18,600 km^2, whereas at 18,000 BP its area was over 35,000 km^2 (Gibbons and Clunie 1986). With rising sea level there would have been a loss of area and habitat. Thus, many island groups probably held more endemic species in the distant past than they did even in prehistoric times. Isostatic effects have been recorded for French Polynesia, the South and North Cook Islands, and the Marquesas Islands

(Pirazzoli and Montaggioni 1988, Yonekura et al. 1988, Stoddard and Walsh 1992; Table 2). As late as 1,200 BP, these groups exhibited less surface area than today—with groups such as the Tuamotu Archipelago disappearing almost completely (Gibbons and Clunie 1986).

This scenario raises two important considerations for our estimates of the prehuman avifauna. First, the decrease in area of many large islands that began at 18,000 BP would have caused a decrease in the number of bird species. This decrease may not have been contemporary with the decrease in area. Diamond (1972) showed that the reduction of one large island, the D'Entrecasteaux Shelf, into a number of small fragments should have led to a reduction of the number of bird species to a new equilibrium. However, he suggests that the time to reach the new equilibrium is dependent on the size of the new island. Thus, there could be a lag time (of several thousands of years in the above case) before the actual species numbers reflect the restraints of the size of the new island. We are not aware of any studies similar to Diamond's (1972) that address the islands included in our analyses. We will assume that the avifauna of the islands was at equilibrium at 4,000 BP. In doing so, we risk underestimating the number of species on all islands but those affected by the above mentioned isostatic effect; for these islands, our estimates would be high.

The second consideration regarding sea level and endemism is the effect of elevated sea levels on low-relief islands. The low-relief island groups of Gambier, North Cook, and the Tuamotu Archipelago were affected by isostatic sea levels (Table 3). Of these, only Tuamotu is expected to have single-island endemics. We predict six species of rails and six species of pigeons—one pigeon exists (*Ptilinopus chalcurus*). Of this group's 60 islands, only five are greater than 30 km². Apparently, this species was able to survive the elevated sea level of 6,000–1,200 BP among these islands. The Fiji group is dominated by large high-relief islands but also holds a large number of surrounding low-relief islands. This group experienced sea levels nearly 2 m higher than present as late as 2,500 BP (Gibbons and Clunie 1986). Endemism would have been improbable in these islands up to that time because of the lower extent of the area. We predict that eight species of pigeons and 16 species of rails could have inhabited these low islands—none are known to have existed there. We removed the low-relief islands from the total area and calculated the number of endemic species we would expect on Fiji based on group endemism. This had no effect on our predictions. The size of Fiji's high-relief islands

TABLE 3. ISLAND GROUPS FOR WHICH PUBLISHED DATA EXIST ON MEAN SEA LEVELS (RELATIVE TO PRESENT; IN METERS) AT THREE PERIODS OF THE HOLOCENE (FROM PIRAZZOLI 1991); MAXIMUM SEA LEVEL AND TIME OF OCCURRENCE (OTA ET AL. 1988, PIRAZZOLI AND MONTAGGIONI 1988, YONEKURA ET AL. 1988, PIRAZZOLI 1991); AND MAXIMUM TSUNAMI RUN-UP HEIGHT (NATIONAL GEOLOGIC DATA CENTER)

| | Mean relative sea level | | | | |
| | Years before present × 10^3 | | | Maximum sea level | Maximum run-up |
Group	10	5	2.5		
Melanesia					
Vanuatu					0
Fiji		+1	0	2 (2500)	5.9
Micronesia					
Palau					0
Yap					1.9
Chuuk	−40	−2	−1		
Marianas		+4.5	+2.4		1.9
Pohnpei	−40	−5	−2		
Marshalls			+2.4		0
Gilbert		−3	+2.4		
Polynesia					
Hawai'i	>−15	0	0		16.8
North Line					0
Tuvalu			+0.6		
Samoa		−5	−2		1.9
North Cook				1 (1500)	0
Tonga					0
South Cook	−17	−1	+1	1.7 (3400)	0
Marquesas				1 (1500)	9
Society	>−20	+0.5	+1	1 (1500)	3.4
Tuamotu	>−20	+0.9	+0.9	1 (1200)	2.3
Gambier				1 (1500)	
Pitcairn					0
Rapa				1 (1500)	1.8
Tabuai				1 (1500)	
Kermadec				0	12
Norfolk				0	
New Zealand				0	5.9
Chatham				0	0

are near the maximum for the Pacific, and the removal of the low-relief islands did not lead to a change of the maximum number of species expected.

Johnson et al. (1996), investigating the evolution of cichlid fish, reported the most rapid vertebrate speciation known—on the order of 3,000 years. Thus, high sea levels up to 1,200 BP must have reduced bird speciation on some Pacific islands. The effect of our sea-level analyses on our predictions results in the removal of five species of pigeons and six species of rails from our total.

TSUNAMIS

Tsunamis are a series of high-energy waves propagated by a major displacement of earth un-

FIGURE 10.   Areas affected by tsunamis (shaded) and the direction of tsunamis (arrows) in the Pacific from 1900 to 1983 as reported in the Worldwide Tsunami Database (Lockridge and Smith 1984).

der the sea. They can have devastating effects on islands. For example, in the early morning hours of 1 April 1946 an earthquake in the Aleutian Islands, Alaska, caused a tsunami. Within minutes a manned lighthouse on Unimak Island had been obliterated with all hands lost. Four and a half hours later and over 3,000 km away the same tsunami hit the Hawaiian Islands. Reaching a maximum run-up height of nearly 17 m, it smashed into the Island of Hawai'i taking another 241 lives. This same series of waves caused casualties and property damage in California and as far south as central Chile (Lockridge and Smith 1984, Myles 1985).

Tsunamis of this magnitude are frequent with 14 occurrences in the Pacific Basin from 1900 to 1983 (Lockridge and Smith 1984). As with sea-level change, the effect of tsunamis on islands is variable. Islands without surrounding submarine shelves are more susceptible to remotely generated tsunamis because there is little to absorb the energy of the waves before they make contact. Topography and elevation above

sea level are also obvious factors in determining the effect of tsunamis on islands.

We accessed the Worldwide Tsunami Database, compiled by the National Geologic Data Center (http://julius.ngdc.noaa.gov/seg/hazard/tsudb.html), for recorded occurrences of tsunamis within our study site. Uninhabited islands are not well represented in the data set. For each occurrence we noted the location of the tsunami, its maximum run-up height, and its point of origin. We then classified our island groups as either susceptible to tsunamis or unaffected (Table 3).

The earliest recorded tsunami in our study area occurred in 1843. Since then over 130 tsunamis have been recorded. The Hawaiian Islands have seen the most tsunamis, a result of their central location relative to areas of seismic activity around the Pacific Rim and the lack of any energy-absorbing shelves around the group. Figure 10 shows regions affected by tsunamis and, when known, the direction traveled by tsunamis from their point sources.

We have data on tsunamis for 21 of our 41 island groups. Ten of these, however, have maximum recorded run-up heights of zero. That is, tsunami events do not noticeably affect these groups. Many of these fortunate island groups are low relief, including the extensive Marshall Islands. Ten of the remaining eleven groups are high relief and have experienced run-up heights from less than 2.0 to 16.8 m. The sole low-relief group affected by tsunamis is the Tuamotu Archipelago with a maximum run-up of 2.3 m.

The disturbance caused by tsunamis on high-relief islands is primarily limited to coastal areas, below the altitudinal distribution of most of the species we are concerned with. The effect of tsunamis on the fauna of the Tuamotu Archipelago, however, could be devastating. Most of the islands of this group are only a few meters in elevation, and the combined effect of higher sea level during the mid- and late-Holocene with tsunamis helps explain why this group has fewer endemics than we predict based on its size and topography. Finally, the Tonga group experienced a maximum run-up height of 4.0 to 6.0 m. This group is dominated by high-relief islands; however, 193 km² of its total 563 km² consists of low-relief islands. Assuming tsunamis were frequent and devastating enough to prevent endemism on these low islands, we can calculate a refined estimate of the number of endemics for this group by excluding all low-relief islands. This exercise results in the loss of one species of rail and one species of pigeon, leaving 35 rails, 12 pigeons, and 4 parrots attributed to the Tonga group.

Combining the effects of sea-level change and tsunamis, we can refine our previous estimate of predicted endemic species in the Pacific as follows: 199 endemic rails, 38 endemic parrots, and 95 endemic pigeons and doves (Fig. 7).

PROBLEM GROUPS

Even after incorporating the above adjustments to our predicted numbers of species, actual species account for less than half of the predicted numbers for 13 of the 23 high-relief groups. Six groups (Rotuma, Tabuai, Wallis and Futuna, Yap, Tonga, and Kermadec) have no actual island-group endemics although we predict from two to five species for these groups. For low-relief groups, 10 (Nauru, Northwest Hawai'i, Tokelau, Tuvalu, Gilbert, Niue, Phoenix, Chuuk, Marshall Islands, North Line Islands) have no actual single-island endemics although we predict from 1 to 20 species for these groups. In all, we predicted 210 species of rails, pigeons, and parrots that are not accounted for as either fossil, extinct, or extant.

DISCUSSION

We estimate that there were approximately 330 species of rails, pigeons, and parrots on the islands of the Pacific before human colonization began 4,000 years ago. Approximately one-third of these species are accounted for as either extant, historically extinct, or as fossils. Pimm et al. (1994), who looked for all landbirds, predicted that the fossil record was only half complete and that the original avifauna was about 800 species. In reviewing the fossil, historical, and current data, we could account for only one-third of the estimated number of species in the taxa we looked at. We should therefore apply a three-fold correction to the total number of known landbirds (540) and conclude that the entire Pacific landbird fauna was comprised of 1,620 or so species before human colonization. This simple multiplication, however, ignores differences in extinction rates between taxa. Steadman (1997a,b) suggested that flightless rails suffered a greater proportion of extinctions than any other taxon of birds. If so, an estimate of 1,500 species would be too high.

In comparing our results to Steadman's (1995) estimates, we must limit our consideration to rails—the only taxon that Steadman makes a quantitative estimate of. We estimate that the prehuman Pacific held about 200 species of rails, of which 21 are extant. Steadman's (1995) estimate (2,000+ species of rails) is an order of magnitude greater than ours. Like Steadman, we based our analyses on the roughly 800 larger islands of the Pacific. However, where Steadman simply multiplied a maximum number of rails per island by the number of islands, we incorporated into our analyses statistical probabilities and geographical, topographical and environmental data. Thus, we believe that Steadman's (1995) estimate of the prehuman avifauna is too high.

More fieldwork will inevitably bring new data to light. The discovery of more fossil species will potentially alter our estimates because of the multiplicative nature of our analyses. The discovery of one new fossil rail on a small island could conceivably add 800 to our current estimate of 200. This would still be half as much as the highest proposed number of rails (Steadman 1995). Currently, we suggest that the prehuman avifauna consisted of more than 800 and less than 1,500 species of landbirds. Further research (as outlined below) is needed to refine our estimates and to conserve the remaining species of the Pacific islands.

CONSERVATION CONCERNS

The loss to extinction of even our lowest predicted number of endemic species is disturbing.

Much more disturbing is the potential effect of this prehistoric loss on the biodiversity of the future. Habitat loss and the introduction of exotic species have had profound negative effects on endemic Pacific landbirds (Atkinson 1985, Pimm 1987). For rails, some of the progenitors of the clan of now extinct endemics may have themselves become extinct and anthropogenic disturbance on many islands may make recolonization by extant rails impossible. Thus, even for a rapidly speciating taxon like flightless rails, the potential for diversity has been greatly diminished.

Another conservation concern for Pacific landbirds is the rise of global sea levels. Although predictions of the rate of sea-level rise are rife with uncertainty, it is clear that global warming and subsequent rises in sea level will occur for centuries into the future (Hutter et al. 1990). Even with a moderate estimate of 4 to 6 cm per decade (Hutter et al. 1990, Wigley and Raper 1993) many low-relief islands will be inundated within the next few centuries.

FUTURE RESEARCH OPPORTUNITIES

Our predictions of the prehistoric Pacific island avifauna are testable. Using our results, researchers can focus excavation efforts on those islands that we predict will hold fossils of the greatest number of extinct species. Thus, we provide our analyses and results as a guide for continued work in this area of biodiversity. We conclude with the following suggestions for further study:

Where to look for subfossil birds

We predict that the greatest number of extinct landbirds existed on high-relief islands of at least 1 km^2 in size. The greatest part of the "missing" rails are from Fiji and Vanuatu. These areas should be surveyed intensely for subfossil remains. Searches should, perhaps, also include island shelves that are currently submerged. Gibbons and Clunie (1986) make a strong argument for extending archeological excavations to these areas because they were exposed and possibly colonized during the human expansion into the Pacific.

Analyze the loss of potential species richness

A thorough understanding of the phylogenetic relationship between the landbird species of the Pacific would serve to identify the mechanisms of speciation and the ancestral species that most contribute to the potential diversity of each taxon. A molecular genetic analysis and mapping of the relationship of these species may also uncover phylogenetic differences in speciation rates, dispersal, and habitat utilization.

Predict the effects of rising sea level on current bird diversity

We have described the effect of area and topography on bird species diversity. Currently, models are available that predict changes in sea level both globally and regionally (Wigley and Raper 1993). The application of sea-level change projections to Pacific islands would result in predicted size distributions of islands, to which our approach can be applied. This will allow us to predict the expected loss of bird species in the Pacific in the coming century. These analyses, coupled with more traditional efforts (e.g., Franklin and Steadman 1991) could also be used to map a survival strategy for Pacific biodiversity in light of the threat of future sea-level rise.

ACKNOWLEDGMENTS

We thank M. Moulton, D. Steadman, K. Reese, R. Walker, S. Conant, and one anonymous reviewer for their comments. SLP thanks the Pew Fellowship in Conservation and the Environment for support.

Studies in Avian Biology No. 22:31–46, 2001.

PATTERNS OF SUCCESS AMONG INTRODUCED BIRDS IN THE HAWAIIAN ISLANDS

MICHAEL P. MOULTON, KARL E. MILLER, AND ERIC A. TILLMAN

Abstract. At least 140 species of 14 different orders of birds have been introduced to the six main Hawaiian Islands. The introduced species came from six continents and the introductions were carried out by a variety of agents including state and local governments, private citizens, and the acclimatization society known as the Hui Manu. The introductions mostly occurred during the early to mid-twentieth century. Most (79%) of the intentional introductions were of species from three orders: Galliformes, Columbiformes, and Passeriformes.

Introduction success rates were significantly greater for passeriforms than for either columbiforms or galliforms, although the reasons for this are unknown. In predicting the fate of future introductions, only the columbiforms showed an "all-or-none" pattern of introduction history. Successful species had larger native geographic ranges than did unsuccessful species, which supports the hypothesis that range size is correlated with the ability to adapt to a new environment. Finally, in a partial test of the introduction effort hypothesis we found that galliforms successfully introduced to the island of Hawai'i were introduced in significantly larger numbers than unsuccessful species.

Key Words: doves; game birds; introduced species; introduction effort; introduction success; native range size; perching birds; pigeons.

Numerous species of birds from six continents have been introduced to the Hawaiian Islands (Caum 1933, Berger 1981, Long 1981, Pratt et al. 1987). These species were introduced by a variety of groups for a variety of reasons. As noted by Berger (1981), the first avian introduction came with early Polynesians who brought the Red Junglefowl (*Gallus gallus*) for food. Since that time, a number of private citizens have brought species to Hawai'i (e.g., Caum 1933). Some of these introductions were made inadvertently as individual birds escaped captivity (e.g., Melodious Laughingthrush or Hwamei, *Garrulax canorus,* on O'ahu), whereas others were intentionally released for aesthetic reasons or even as an attempt at biological control (Caum 1933). There also have been intensive efforts both by private citizens (e.g., Lewin 1971) as well as state and county agencies (Schwartz and Schwartz 1949; Walker 1966, 1967) to establish populations of various game birds for recreational hunting. In the early to mid-twentieth century, the acclimatization society known as the Hui Manu actively introduced several species to various islands (Caum 1933, Berger 1981).

Regardless of their source, a central question in any study of introduced birds is "Why do some species succeed and others fail?" In several papers we and our colleagues have argued that competition has played an influential role in determining the outcomes of passerine species' introductions in Hawai'i (Moulton and Pimm 1983, 1986a, 1987; Moulton 1985, 1993; Mountainspring and Scott 1985; Moulton et al. 1990; Moulton and Lockwood 1992). These arguments are based on three main findings. First, introductions tend to be less successful when more species of introduced birds are already present

(Moulton 1993; Moulton and Pimm 1983, 1986a). Second, there is a pattern of limiting similarity among congeneric pairs of introduced birds: differences in bill length are significantly greater in pairs that coexist than in pairs of species that were not able to coexist (Moulton 1985). And third, successful introduced passerines show a pattern of morphological overdispersion (Moulton and Pimm 1987, Moulton and Lockwood 1992); i.e., successful species are morphologically more different from each other than expected by chance.

Although these three patterns are consistent with predictions from competition theory, other explanations for patterns in introduction outcomes have been advanced. These include introduction history of a species (Simberloff and Boecklen 1991) and introduction effort (e.g., Pimm 1991, Veltman et al. 1996).

The idea that introduction history can predict future introduction outcomes is appealing in its simplicity. The concept comes from Simberloff and Boecklen (1991) who argued that whenever and wherever a given species is introduced, it tends to either always succeed or always fail. This leads to an "all-or-none" pattern in the distribution of birds introduced onto a series of islands: some species being successful on "all" the islands in the series and others being successful on "none" of the islands. If introduced birds actually follow this pattern, then predicting the outcome of future introductions would be greatly simplified. Moulton (1993) and Moulton and Sanderson (1997), however, argued that the all-or-none pattern reported by Simberloff and Boecklen (1991) for passerine birds was primarily an artifact of sample size.

Another factor that might influence the outcome of introductions is the effort invested in the introduction process. Griffith et al. (1989) found that introduction effort along with habitat quality were associated with introduction outcome. Similarly, Pimm (1991) studied introductions of seven game bird species (all of which had been successfully introduced somewhere in the world) in the western United States and found that there was a very high (360/424 = 85%) failure rate. Pimm's analysis indicated that the failure rate was particularly high when fewer than 75 individuals were released. More recently, studies of introduced birds in New Zealand (Veltman et al. 1996, Duncan 1997, Green 1997) have concluded that introduction effort is the most influential variable in determining which species succeed. In each of the three studies, the authors reported that successful species were introduced in larger numbers and more frequently than were unsuccessful species.

Several authors have reported a positive relationship between the size of the native geographic range of a species and its average abundance (e.g., Bock and Ricklefs 1983, Brown 1984). If widespread species tend to be ecologically more generalized than species with narrow distributions, we would predict that successful introduced species would tend to be those that have larger native ranges.

Many analyses of avian introduction success in Hawai'i have focused on passerine birds (e.g., Moulton and Pimm 1983, 1986a,b, 1987; Williams 1987, Moulton and Lockwood 1992), yet passerines represent fewer than half the total number of birds that have been introduced to the Hawaiian Islands (Berger 1981, Long 1981). Our objectives in this paper were to examine patterns of success for introduced species in Hawai'i across three taxonomic orders of birds: Galliformes, Columbiformes, and Passeriformes. Specifically, are the success rates of nonpasserine birds different from those of the passerines? Second, is an all-or-none pattern evident in the nonpasserine orders? Third, is native range size greater for successful introduced species than for unsuccessful introduced species in passerines and nonpasserines? And, fourth, does introduction effort play a role in determining the success of introduced birds in Hawai'i?

METHODS AND MATERIALS

We used Caum (1933), Schwartz and Schwartz (1949), Munro (1960), Walker (1966, 1967), Lewin (1971), Berger (1981), Long (1981), Lever (1987), and Pratt et al. (1987) to compile lists of nonindigenous birds introduced to the Hawaiian Islands. In compiling our lists we attempted to ascertain not only the current status of each species but also the date of first introduction. In our analyses we considered species to be successful if they were present on an island in 1990. We considered species to be unsuccessful if there were no recorded observations after 1990. Scientific names of 140 species introduced in the Hawaiian Islands are provided in Appendix 1. Scientific names of introduced species not included in our statistical analyses are provided in Appendix 2.

In order to determine success rates for the species in the different orders, we considered a species to be successful if it succeeded on any island, and unsuccessful only if it failed on every island on which it was released. By this approach, even if a species fails on all but one island, we believe that environmental conditions in the archipelago overall were potentially suitable for establishment and that perhaps differences in the mechanics of the release or interactions with other species might have occurred on islands where the species failed. We compared introduction success rates across orders with a chi-square test of equal proportions.

We used range maps in Long (1981) to estimate native range size for all introduced species, except *Garrulax caerulatus* and *Callipepla douglasii,* which were not included by Long. We used a grid method similar to the methods of Moulton and Pimm (1986b). We placed a small acetate grid over the native range map in Long (1981) and counted the number of squares that were intersected. Each square represented approximately 259,000 km^2. In earlier analyses of native range size of introduced passerines in Hawai'i (Moulton and Pimm 1986b), *Uraeginthus angolensis* and *U. cyanocephala* were omitted because of concern about the potential confusion with young *U. bengalus* in the field. However, we included all three *Uraeginthus* species in this analysis because Berger (1981) reported each was seen and identified in the wild.

We used Mann-Whitney tests for all our range size comparisons because data were not normally distributed. We compared native geographic range sizes of successful versus failed introductions, both within and across orders.

RESULTS

At least 140 species of nonindigenous birds from 14 orders have been released in the Hawaiian Islands (Table 1). Our results differ from earlier totals of 162 species (Long 1981) and 170 species (Berger 1981) for two reasons. First, those authors followed a somewhat different taxonomy. For example, Berger (1981) listed the Green Pheasant (*Phasianus versicolor*) as being a distinct species, whereas we followed Sibley and Monroe (1990) and treated it as being conspecific with the Ring-necked Pheasant (*Phasianus colchicus*). Second, at least among the passerines, we have excluded several species included by Long and Berger on grounds that simply too few individuals (i.e., < 5) were released. Simberloff and Boecklen (1991) list 14 of these species in their Appendix B, although based on Berger (1981) we included the two *Uraeginthus* species (*U. angolensis* and *U. cyanocephala*).

Although a great diversity of species has been released into the Hawaiian Islands, for the most

TABLE 1. SMALL SPECIES OF BIRDS INTRODUCED TO THE HA-
WAIIAN ISLANDS (CAUM 1933, BERGER 1981, LONG
1981)

Order	Number of species
Tinamiformes	1
Pelecaniformes	1
Ciconiiformes	3
Falconiformes	1
Galliformes	40
Turniformes	1
Gruiformes	1
Charadriiformes	2
Anseriformes	4
Columbiformes	18
Psittaciformes	14
Strigiformes	1
Apodiformes	1
Passeriformes	52

part three orders accounted for the bulk of the
introductions. These are the game birds (Galliformes), pigeons and doves (Columbiformes),
and perching birds (Passeriformes). These species represent 110 introductions (Appendices 3–
5). Berger (1981) lists 14 species of a fourth
order, Psittaciformes. However, according to
Berger (1981), 13 of these species were accidental introductions. Moreover, Pratt et al.
(1987) considered only one species of this order
(*Psittacula krameri*) to be successful in Hawai‘i.
Thus, we restricted our tests to the three orders
for which there was evidence for intentional in-

troductions: Galliformes, Columbiformes, and
Passeriformes.

HISTORICAL PERSPECTIVE

In order to develop a historical perspective on
the phenomenon of introductions for the galliforms, columbiforms, and passeriforms, we categorized introductions by time period (Fig. 1).
Historical peaks in the number of introductions
were evident for each order.

For galliforms, the number of species' introductions increased steadily from 1901 until the
early 1960s and then declined to zero. There has
not been an introduction of a new species of
galliform into the Hawaiian Islands since 1965
(*Francolinus adspersus*). For columbiforms, the
peak occurred in the 1920s. Indeed, there have
been only two introductions (*Zenaida asiatica* in
1961 and *Zenaida macroura* in 1962) of species
from this order since 1960. The passeriforms
also appear to show a decline in the number of
introductions after the 1960s (Fig. 1). Closer inspection reveals an even sharper decline in the
frequency of introductions, with only one new
passerine species introduced since 1980 (*Estrilda astrild* in 1981). The remaining nine species
were all present on other islands in the archipelago prior to 1975 and possibly arrived onto
new islands via interisland colonization.

SUCCESS RATES

Success rates differed significantly among orders ($\chi^2 = 14.59$, df = 2, P < 0.005). Among

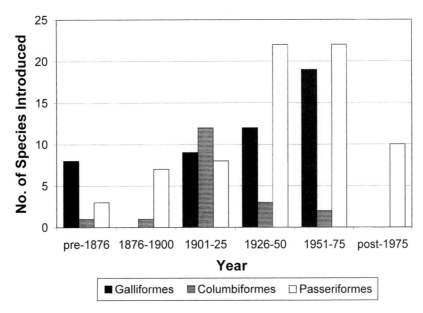

FIGURE 1. Chronology of species introductions to the Hawaiian Islands.

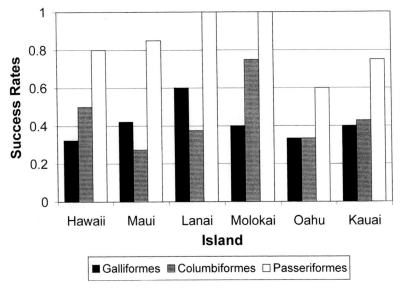

FIGURE 2. Success rates (number of successful introductions/total number of introductions) per order across the six main Hawaiian Islands.

passerines, 33 of 52 (64%) species have been successful on at least one island (Appendix 3). The success rates for galliform and columbiform species were not nearly so high. Only 12 of 40 (30%) introduced galliform species (Appendix 4) and 4 of 18 (22%) introduced columbiform species (Appendix 5) have been successful on at least one island.

Within islands the success rates also were variable (Fig. 2). For passerines, Moloka'i and Lāna'i shared the highest rates of success at 1.00 (13/13 for Moloka'i and 11/11 for Lāna'i). Lāna'i also had the highest success rate for galliforms (9/15, 0.60), whereas Moloka'i had the highest rate for columbiforms (3/4, 0.75; Fig. 2; Table 2). Although it is tempting to compare rates among islands across the different orders, results of any tests would be misleading because of the high potential for nonindependence. For example, with respect to passerines, only seven species were introduced to islands other than

O'ahu (five to Kaua'i and two to Hawai'i). For galliforms, only O'ahu and Hawai'i have any unique species.

ALL-OR-NONE PATTERNS

The hallmark of an all-or-none distributional pattern of introduced birds on islands would be presence of few, if any, mixed species. Mixed species are those that are successful on some islands and unsuccessul on others (Simberloff and Boecklen 1991). In principle, species released onto one island could show a mixed outcome if they spread to another island and then fail on one of the two islands. In practice this is very difficult to detect, because those species with the ability to spread to other islands could do so repeatedly giving the impression that they were established on the second island even if they were actually not able to survive there. This would be an example of what Brown and Kodric-Brown (1977) have termed a "rescue effect." With this in mind we believe that analyses for all-or-none patterns should be limited to those species that were physically introduced to more than one island.

In their analysis of introduced Hawaiian birds, Simberloff and Boecklen (1991) reported that among 19 introduced columbiform species, only one (*Pterocles exustus*) showed a mixed outcome, having succeeded on Hawai'i, and failed on Moloka'i and Kaua'i. However, Sibley and Monroe (1990) placed this species in the order Ciconiiformes. If this species is excluded, 18 columbiform species remain, 11 of which were

TABLE 2. SUCCESS RATES (NUMBER OF SUCCESSFUL INTRODUCTIONS/TOTAL NUMBER OF INTRODUCTIONS) PER ORDER ACROSS THE SIX MAIN HAWAIIAN ISLANDS

Island	Galliformes	Columbiformes	Passeriformes
Hawai'i	0.32	0.56	0.80
Maui	0.45	0.27	0.84
Lāna'i	0.53	0.43	1.00
Moloka'i	0.53	0.60	1.00
O'ahu	0.26	0.33	0.60
Kaua'i	0.40	0.375	0.75

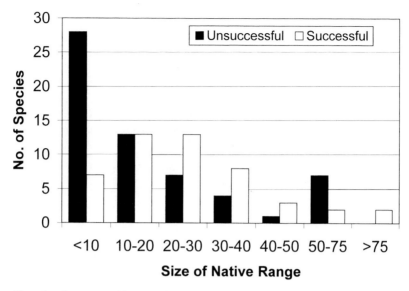

FIGURE 3. Size of native geographic range for unsuccessful versus successful introduced species. Range size measured in number of 259,000 km^2 map blocks (see Methods and Materials).

introduced onto more than one island. The observation of no mixed species out of eleven possible is evidence for an all-or-none pattern.

Among the Galliformes, 23 species were released onto two or more islands. At least seven of 23 (30%) have had mixed outcomes: *Callipepla californica, C. gambelii, Alectoris chukar, Coturnix japonica, Gallus gallus, Pavo cristatus, Meleagris gallopavo* (Appendix 4). Thus, there is not an all-or-none pattern among the introduced game birds.

Moulton and Sanderson (1997) and Moulton (1993) argued that mixed species tended to be those introduced onto more islands. With this in mind we compared the median numbers of islands of introduction for always unsuccessful, always successful, and mixed species. Medians differed significantly (H = 8.95, P = 0.012), with the highest median recorded for mixed species (6.0), and medians of 3.0 for always unsuccessful species and 6.0 for always successful species. As a further test we combined species that were always successful with those that were always unsuccessful and compared the combined median with that of the mixed species. These medians also differed significantly (H = 5.23, P = 0.022).

RANGE SIZE

We estimated native range size for 108 introduced species. Range size was significantly larger in successful species than in unsuccessful species (approximate χ^2 = 10.95, df = 1, P < 0.001; Fig. 3; Table 3). Within orders, range size differences were significant for passerines (P = 0.015) and marginally significant in game birds (P = 0.099). However median range size did not differ significantly between successful and unsuccessful columbiforms (P = 0.123). In all three orders, the successful species had larger median native range sizes than did unsuccessful species.

INTRODUCTION EFFORT

Data are available for only a partial test of the influence of introduction effort on introduction success. Lewin (1971) provided numbers of individuals released for 26 Galliformes on the island of Hawai'i (Table 4). Most of the data were derived from private releases by the owners of the Pu'u Wa'awa'a Ranch, but in some instances data from releases made by state agencies were included. We excluded *Coturnix japonica* because it already was successful, apparently having colonized the island from Maui and/or Lāna'i (Schwartz and Schwartz 1949), and there were no further releases by the state or the owners of the ranch. The median number of individuals introduced was 179 for successful galliform species (N = 9) and 14 for unsuccessful galliform species (N = 17). Medians

TABLE 3. RESULTS OF NATIVE RANGE SIZE COMPARISONS BETWEEN SUCCESSFUL (S) AND UNSUCCESSFUL (F) INTRODUCED SPECIES (MEAN NUMBER OF 259,000 KM^2 GRID SQUARES)

Order	S	F	P
Galliformes	22.2	16.6	0.099
Columbiformes	36.1	23.3	0.123
Passeriformes	33.0	17.5	0.015

TABLE 4. NUMBER OF INDIVIDUALS OF SPECIES OF GAME BIRDS, PIGEONS, AND DOVES RELEASED ON HAWAI'I (LEWIN 1971)

Species	Number released	Status
Colinus virginianus[a]	108	F
Oreortyx pictus	88	F
Callipepla squamata	14	F
Callipepla californica	412	S
Callipepla gambelii	546	F
Callipepla douglasii	113	F
Ammoperdix griseogularis	20	F
Cyrtonyx montezumae	8	F
Alectoris chukar	110	S
Alectoris barbara	104	F
Francolinus francolinus	226	S
Francolinus pintadeanus	10	F
Francolinus pondicerianus	214	S
Francolinus adspersus	4	F
Francolinus icterorhynchus	9	F
Francolinus clappertoni	10	F
Francolinus erckelii	179	S
Francolinus leucoscepus	27	F
Coturnix chinensis	8	F
Bambusicola thoracica	12	F
Lophura leucomelanos	67	S
Gallus sonneratii	14	F
Phasianus colchicus	244	S
Syrmaticus reevesii	180	F
Pavo cristatus	2	S
Meleagris gallopavo	115	S
Zenaida macroura	168	S
Zenaida asiatica	40	F
Streptopelia risoria (= decaocto?)	11	F
Streptopelia chinensis	8	S
Geopelia striata	18	S

[a] See Appendix 1 for common names.

were significantly different in a Kruskal-Wallis test (H = 5.25, P = 0.02).

Data for the columbiforms appear to be equally compelling, although we have not tested this group since there were just seven species introduced and two of these already were established on Hawai'i at the time of the introductions by the Pu'u Wa'awa'a Ranch (Lewin 1971).

DISCUSSION

The introduction process in the Hawaiian Islands has been highly nonrandom with respect to phylogeny. Thus 10 of the 14 orders are represented by five or fewer species. The three orders that are represented by more species are those that have been the focus of intentional introductions. Thus, most galliforms were likely introduced to enhance prospects for recreational hunting, and most columbiforms were introduced for recreational hunting or for aesthetic reasons. Passerines were introduced for a variety of reasons, including biological control and aesthetic reasons, as well as accidental releases of cage birds.

The phenomenon of avian introductions, at least for the three orders we have focused on here, appears to be historical, with most introduction efforts having come to a close. There have been no columbiform or galliform introductions to the Hawaiian Islands in more than 30 years. Moreover, no new passerine species have been introduced to the islands since 1981. This is not to say that there will not be future introductions from these, or other, taxa. Indeed, there have been recent sightings of various parrot species since 1990. For example, Pyle (1994) reported that 10 to 15 Nanday Parakeets (Nandayus nenday) were seen on the island of Hawai'i.

In terms of success rates, we found that passerine species had a significantly higher overall success rate than either of the nonpasserine orders. The reasons for this are unclear, but the pattern is highly significant. It is possible to explain some of this result via the propagule size hypothesis. We found a significant relationship between propagule size (i.e., introduction effort) and the success rates of galliforms introduced to the island of Hawai'i. Caum (1933) also noted that several columbiform species apparently were introduced in very small numbers. However, it remains to be shown that passerines were systematically released in larger numbers.

The simplest potential predictor of the outcome of species' introductions is introduction history (Simberloff and Boecklen 1991). If introduction history alone were an adequate predictor of introduction outcomes we should have detected clear all-or-none patterns within the orders we analyzed. Moulton (1993) and Moulton and Sanderson (1997) argued that the all-or-none patterns reported for passerines introduced to the Hawaiian Islands and elsewhere may be due to sampling artifact. When we extended the analysis here to include the columbiforms and galliforms, only the columbiforms show any evidence for such a pattern. Thus, we found little evidence to support the notion that introduction history is an adequate predictor of future introduction outcomes.

Our analyses suggested that one consistent predictor of introduction success was size of native geographic range. In all three orders we observed that successfully introduced species had larger native ranges than unsuccessful species. These results are consistent with the hypothesis that species with larger ranges are ecologically more generalized (Brown 1984) and hence better able to adapt to a new environment.

In a partial test of the introduction effort hypothesis, we found that galliforms introduced successfully to Hawai'i were introduced in larger numbers than were unsuccessful species. However, it should be noted that some species were successful with initial releases of as few as two individuals; e.g., a single pair of Peafowl (Pavo cristatus) released on the Pu'u Wa'awa'a Ranch in 1909 led to the successful establishment of the species on Hawai'i (Lewin 1971). Also, for 6 of the 15 unsuccessful species, >85 individuals were released (*Colinus virginianus, Callipepla douglasii, Callipepla gambelii, Syrmaticus reevesii, Oreotyx pictus, Alectoris barbara*; Table 4). We do not know if successful game birds on islands other than Hawai'i were introduced in higher numbers than were unsuccessful species. Because data are lacking for passeriform and columbiform species, a thorough test of the introduction effort hypothesis was not possible.

ACKNOWLEDGMENTS

We thank J. M. Scott, S. Conant, R. Walker, B. Dennis, and an anonymous reviewer for their comments on earlier versions of the manuscript. Florida Agricultural Experiment Station JS #R-07766. A. van Doorn assisted with review of the literature of psittaciform introductions. MPM wishes to thank C. J. Ralph, C. P. Ralph, and A. C. Ziegler for their kindness and hospitality during fieldwork in Hawai'i.

APPENDIX 1.   SCIENTIFIC AND COMMON NAMES OF 142 SPECIES INTRODUCED TO THE HAWAIIAN ISLANDS (NOMENCLATURE FOLLOWS SIBLEY AND MONROE 1990)

Scientific name	Common name
Acridotheres tristis	Common Myna
Agapornis roseicapillis	Rosy-faced Lovebird
Alauda arvensis	Skylark
Alectoris barbara	Barbary Partridge
Alectoris chukar	Chukar
Amandava amandava	Red Avadavat
Amazona ochrocephala	Yellow-crowned Parrot
Amazona viridigenalis	Red-crowned Parrot
Ammoperdix griseogularis	See-see Partridge
Anas discors	Blue-winged Teal
Anas platyrhynchos	Mallard
Ara macao	Scarlet Macaw
Bambusicola thoracica	Chinese Bamboo-Partridge
Brotegeris jugularis	Orange-chinned Parakeet
Bubulcus ibis	Cattle Egret
Cacatua galerita	Sulphur-crested Cockatoo
Cacatua moluccensis	Salmon-crested Cockatoo
Callipepla californica	California Quail
Callipepla douglasii	Elegant Quail
Callipepla gambelii	Gambel's Quail
Callipepla squamata	Scaled Quail
Caloenas nicobarica	Nicobar Pigeon
Cardinalis cardinalis	Northern Cardinal
Carpodacus mexicanus	House Finch
Cettia diphone	Japanese Bush-Warbler
Chalcophaps indica	Emerald Dove
Chrysolophus amherstiae	Lady Amherst Pheasant
Chrysolophus pictus	Golden Pheasant
Colinus virginianus	Northern Bobwhite
Collocalia vanikorensis	Uniform Swiftlet
Columba livia	Rock Pigeon
Copsychus malabaricus	White-rumped Shama
Copsychus saularis	Oriental Magpie-Robin
Coturnix chinensis	Blue-breasted Quail
Coturnix japonica	Japanese Quail
Coturnix pectoralis	Stubble Quail
Crax rubra	Great Currasow
Cyanoptila cyanomelana	Blue-and-White Flycatcher
Cygnus olor	Mute Swan
Cyrtonyx montezumae	Montezuma Quail
Eclectus roratus	Eclectus Parrot
Eolophus roseicapilla	Galah
Erithacus akahige	Japanese Robin
Erithacus komadori	Ryukyu Robin
Estrilda astrild	Common Waxbill
Estrilda caerulescens	Lavendar Waxbill
Estrilda melpoda	Orange-cheeked Waxbill

APPENDIX 1. CONTINUED.

Scientific name	Common name
Estrilda troglodytes	Black-rumped Waxbill
Falco (rusticolus ?)	Gyrfalcon?
Francolinus adsperus	Red-billed Francolin
Francolinus clappertoni	Clapperton's Francolin
Francolinus erckelii	Erckel's Francolin
Francolinus francolinus	Black Francolin
Francolinus icterorhynchus	Heuglin's Francolin
Francolinus leucosepus	Yellow-necked Spurfowl
Francolinus pintadeanus	Chinese Francolin
Francolinus pondicerianus	Grey Francolin
Gallicolumba luzonica	Luzon Bleeding-Heart
Gallus gallus	Red Junglefowl
Gallus sonneratii	Grey Junglefowl
Garrulax albogularis	White-throated Laughingthrush
Garrulax caerulatus	Grey-sided Laughingthrush
Garrulax canorus	Hwamei
Garrulax chinensis	Black-throated Laughingthrush
Garrulax pectoralis	Greater Necklaced Laughingthrush
Geopelia cuneata	Diamond Dove
Geopelia humeralis	Bar-shouldered Dove
Geopelia striata	Zebra Dove
Geophaps lophotes	Crested Pigeon
Geophaps plumifera	Spinifex Pigeon
Geophaps smithii	Partridge Pigeon
Geotrygon montana	Ruddy Quail-Dove
Gracula religiosa	Hill Myna
Grallina cyanoleuca	Magpie-Lark
Lagonosticta senegala	Red-billed Firefinch
Larus novaehollandiae	Silver Gull
Larus occidentalis	Western Gull
Leiothrix lutea	Red-billed Leiothrix
Leptotila verreauxi	White-tipped Dove
Leucosarcia melanoleuca	Wonga Pigeon
Lonchura cantans	African Silverbill
Lonchura malacca	Black-headed Munia
Lonchura oryzivora	Java Sparrow
Lonchura punctulata	Scaly-breasted Munia
Lophura leucomelanos	Kalij Pheasant
Lophura nycthemera	Silver Pheasant
Melanocorypha mongolica	Mongolian Lark
Meleagris gallopavo	Wild Turkey
Melopsittacus undulatus	Budgerigar
Mimus polyglottos	Northern Mockingbird
Myiopsitta monachus	Monk Parakeet
Nandayus nenday	Nanday Parakeet
Neochen jubata	Orinoco Goose
Nothoprocta perdicaria	Chilean Tinamou
Numida meleagris	Helmeted Guineafowl
Oreortyx pictus	Mountain Quail
Ortalis cinereiceps	Grey-headed Chachalaca
Paroaria capitata	Yellow-billed Cardinal
Paroaria coronata	Red-crested Cardinal
Paroaria dominicana	Red-cowled Cardinal
Parus varius	Varied Tit
Passer domesticus	House Sparrow
Passerina ciris	Painted Bunting
Passerina cyanea	Indigo Bunting
Passerina leclancherii	Orange-breasted Bunting
Pavo cristatus	Common Peafowl
Penelope purpurascens	Crested Guan
Perdix perdix	Grey Partridge
Phalacrocorax carbo	Great Cormorant
Phaps chalcoptera	Common Bronzewing
Phasianus colchicus	Ring-necked Pheasant
Phoenicopterus ruber	Greater Flamingo

APPENDIX 1. CONTINUED.

Scientific name	Common name
Platycercus adscitus	Pale-headed Rosella
Porphyrio porphyrio	Purple Swamphen
Psittacula krameri	Rose-ringed Parakeet
Pterocles exustus	Chestnut-bellied Sandgrouse
Pycnonotus cafer	Red-vented Bulbul
Pycnonotus jocosus	Red-whiskered Bulbul
Rhipidura leucophrys	Willie-Wagtail
Rollulus rouloul	Crested Partridge
Serinus leucopygius	White-rumped Seedeater
Serinus mozambicus	Yellow-fronted Canary
Sicalis flaveola	Saffron Finch
Streptopelia chinensis	Spotted Dove
Streptopelia decaocto	Eurasian Collared-Dove
Sturnella loyca	Long-tailed Meadowlark
Sturnella neglecta	Western Meadowlark
Syrmaticus reevesii	Reeve's Pheasant
Syrmaticus soemmerringii	Copper Pheasant
Tiaris olivacea	Yellow-faced Grassquit
Turnix varia	Painted Buttonquail
Tympanuchis cupido	Greater Prairie Chicken
Tympanuchus phasianellus	Sharp-tailed Grouse
Tyto alba	Barn Owl
Uraeginthus angolensis	Blue-breasted Cordonbleu
Uraeginthus bengalus	Red-cheeked Cordonbleu
Uraeginthus cyanocephala	Blue-capped Cordonbleu
Urocissa erythrorhyncha	Red-billed Blue Magpie
Vidua macroura	Pin-tailed Wydah
Zenaida asiatica	White-winged Dove
Zenaida macroura	Mourning Dove
Zosterops japonicus	Japanese White-Eye

APPENDIX 2. LIST OF 31 SPECIES FROM 11 ORDERS NOT INCLUDED IN STATISTICAL ANALYSES. WITHIN EACH CELL, THE FIRST LINE INDICATES DATE OF FIRST INTRODUCTION (OR FIRST REFERENCE TO INTRODUCTION) AND STATUS (S = SUCCESSFUL; F = FAILED); THE SECOND LINE INDICATES MODE OF INTRODUCTION (1 = PRIVATE; 2 = STATE OR COUNTY AGENCY; 3 = UNKNOWN, INCLUDES ESCAPE FROM CAPTIVITY; 4 = POLYNESIANS; 5 = HUI MANU); AND THE THIRD LINE INDICATES REFERENCE

Species	Oʻahu	Kauaʻi	Maui	Hawaiʻi	Molokaʻi	Lānaʻi
Nothoprocta perdicaria				1966 F 2 1		
Phalacrocorax carbo						1890s F 1 1
Phoenicopterus ruber		1929 F 1 1				
Bubulcus ibis	1959 S 1 7	1959 S 1 7	1959 S 1 7	1959 S 1 7	1959 S 1 7	1959 S 1 7
Pterocles exustus		1961 F 2 5,11		1961 S 2 5,11	1961 F 2 5,11	
Falco (rusticolus?)[a]				1929 F 1 1		

APPENDIX 2. CONTINUED.

Species	Oʻahu	Kauaʻi	Maui	Hawaiʻi	Molokaʻi	Lānaʻi
Turnix varia			1922 F		1922 F	
			2		2	
			1		1	
Poyphyrio porphyrio	1933 F			1928 F		
	3			2		
	1			1		
Larus novaehollandiae	1924 F					
	3					
	1					
Larus occidentalis	1933 F		1933 F			
	3		3			
	1		1			
Cygnus olor				1920 F		
				1		
				1		
Neochen jubata	1922 F					
	2					
	1					
Anas platyrhynchos[b]				1955 S		
				1		
				6		
Anas discors[c]	1932 F					
	2					
	1					
Tyto alba	1959 S	1959 S	1959 S	1958 S	1959 S	
	2	2	2	2	2	
	7	7	7	7	7,11	
Collocalia vanikorensis	1962 S					
	2					
	7					
Brotegeris jugularis	1933 F					
	3					
	1					
Cacatua galerita	1933 F					
	3					
	1					
Cacatua roseicapilla	1933 F					
	3					
	1					
Cacatua moluccensis	1981 F					
	3					
	7					
Ara macao	1933 F					
	3					
	1					
Melopsittachus undulatus	1933 F					
	3					
	1					
Psittacula krameri	1933 S	1981 S		1981 S		
	3	3		3		
	1,7	7,10		7,10		
Nandayus nenday	1981 F			1981 U		
	3			3		
	7			13		
Myiopsitta monachus	1970 F					
	3					
	7					
Amazona viridigenalis	1971 U					
	3					
	7					

APPENDIX 2. CONTINUED.

Species	O'ahu	Kaua'i	Maui	Hawai'i	Moloka'i	Lāna'i
Amazona ochrocephala	1969 F 3 7					
Eclectus roratus	1981 F 3 7					
Agapornis roseicapillis	1973 F 3 7					
Platycercus adscitus			1877 F 1 1			
Urocissa erythrorhyncha	1966 F 1 7					

References: 1 = Caum 1933; 2 = Schwartz and Schwartz 1949; 3 = Munro 1960; 4 = Walker 1966; 5 = Walker 1967; 6 = Lewin 1971; 7 = Berger 1981; 8 = Moulton and Pimm 1983; 9 = Scott et al. 1986; 10 = Pratt et al. 1987; 11 = Simberloff and Boecklen 1991; 12 = Moulton 1993; 13 = Pyle 1994; 14 = Wunz 1992.

[a] Caum (1933) listed *F. rusticolus* only as a tentative identification.

[b] May have interbred with natural migrants, as well as feral individuals.

[c] Species identity uncertain. Caum (1933) stated the species is *Querquedula discors* (Blue-winged Teal, *Anas discors*); however, he also reported that the individuals came from Australia where the Blue-winged Teal does not occur.

APPENDIX 3. INTRODUCED PASSERINES ON SIX MAIN HAWAIIAN ISLANDS (SEE APPENDIX 2 FOR EXPLANATION OF TERMS)

Species	O'ahu	Kaua'i	Maui	Hawai'i	Moloka'i	Lāna'i
Acridotheres tristis	1872 S 1 12	1883 S 3 8	1883 S 3 8	1883 S 3 8	1883 S 3 8	1883 S 3 8
Alauda arvensis	1867 S 3 12	1870 F 1 1,8	1886 S 3 8	1902 S 3 8	1917 S 3 8	1917 S 3 8
Amandava amandava	1900 S 3 12		1987 S 3 11	1987 S 3 11		
Cardinalis cardinalis	1929 S 3,5 1,8	1929 S 1 1,8	1949 S 3 8	1929 S 2 1	1951 S 3 8	1957 S 3 8
Carpodacus mexicanus	1870 S 3 12	1886 S 3 8	1886 S 3 8	1886 S 3 8	1886 S 3 8	1886 S 3 8
Cettia diphone	1929 S 1,2 1	1988 S 3 11	1980 S 3 11		1979 S 3 11	1980 S 3 11
Copsychus malabaricus	1939 S 5 11	1931 S 1 1				
Copsychus saularis	1932 F 5 1	1922 S 1 1,12				
Cyanoptila cyanomelana	1929 F 2,5 1,8			1937 F 5 8		
Erithacus akahige	1929 F 2 1					
Erithacus komadori	1931 F 3 8					
Estrilda astrild	1981 S 3 12					

APPENDIX 3. CONTINUED.

Species	O'ahu	Kaua'i	Maui	Hawai'i	Moloka'i	Lāna'i
Estrilda caerulescens	1965 S 3 12			1978 S 3 11		
Estrilda melpoda	1965 S 3 12		1989 S 3 MPM			
Estrilda troglodytes	1965 F 3 12			1975 S 3 11		
Garrulax albogularis		1919 F 1 1				
Garrulax caerulatus	1947 S 3 8					
Garrulax canorus	1900 S 3 1,8	1918 S 1 1,8	1902 S 1 1,8	1909 S 1 1,8	1909 S 1 1,8	
Garrulax chinensis		1931 F 1 1				
Garrulax pectoralis		1962 S 3 11				
Gracula religiosa	1960 S 3 11					
Grallina cyanoleuca	1922 F 2 1			1922 F 2 1		
Lagonosticta senegala	1965 F 3 11					
Leiothrix lutea	1928 S 2 1	1918 S 1 1	1928 S 2 1	1928 S 2 1	1928 S 2 1	
Lonchura cantans	1984 S 3 11	1984 S 3 11	1978 S 3 11	1972 S 3 11	1981 S 3 11	1979 S 3 11
Lonchura malacca	1936 S 3 8	1976 S 3 11				
Lonchura oryzivora	1964 S 3 12	1983 S 3 11	1986 S 3 11	1981 S 3 11		
Lonchura punctulata	1883 S 3 8,12	1883 S 3 8	1883 S 3 8	1883 S 3 8	1883 S 3 8	1883 S 3 8
Melanocorypha mongolica		1914 F 1 8				
Mimus polyglottos	1931 S 5 1,8	1946 S 3 8	1933 S 5 1,8	1959 S 3 8	1951 S 3 8	1970 S 3 11
Paroaria capitata				1973 S 3 11		
Paroaria coronata	1928 S 1,5 1,11	1928 S 3 8,11	1960 S 3 11	1976 S 3 11	1963 S 3 11	1976 S 3 11

APPENDIX 3. CONTINUED.

Species	O'ahu	Kaua'i	Maui	Hawai'i	Moloka'i	Lāna'i
Paroaria dominicana	1931 F 5 1					
Parus varius	1928 F 2 1,8	1890 F 1 1,8	1928 F 2 1,8	1928 F 2 1,8		
Passer domesticus	1871 S 3 1,8	1917 S 3 8	1917 S 3 8	1917 S 3 8	1917 S 3 8	1917 S 3 8
Passerina ciris				1937 F 5 8		
Passerina cyanea	1934 F 3 8			1937 F 5 8		
Passerina leclancherii	1941 F 5 8		1941 F 5 8,11			
Pycnonotus cafer	1966 S 3 11					
Pycnonotus jocosus	1965 S 3 11					
Rhipidura leucophrys	1926 F 2 1,8					
Serinus leucopygius	1965 F 3 11					
Serinus mozambicus	1964 S 3 11			1977 S 1 11		
Sicalis flaveola	1965 S 3 11			1966 S 3 11		
Sturnella loyca		1931 F 1 1				
Sturnella neglecta	1931 F 2 8	1931 S 1 1,11	1934 F 3 3			
Tiaris olivacea	1974 S 3 11					
Uraeginthus angolensis	1965 F 3 7					
Uraeginthus bengalus	1965 F 3 11			1973 S 3 11		
Uraeginthus cyanocephala	1969 F 3 12					
Vidua macroura	1962 F 3 12					
Zosterops japonicus	1929 S 2,5 1,11	1929 S 5 1,11	1938 S 3 8	1937 S 5 8	1938 S 3 8	1938 S 3 8

APPENDIX 4. INTRODUCED GAME BIRDS ON THE SIX MAIN HAWAIIAN ISLANDS (SEE APPENDIX 2 FOR EXPLAINATION OF TERMS)

Species	Oʻahu	Kauaʻi	Maui	Hawaiʻi	Molokaʻi	Lānaʻi
Crax rubra				1928 F 2 1		
Penelope purpurascens				1928 F 2 1		
Ortalis cinereiceps				1928 F 2 1		
Numida meleagris	1928 F 1 1,10	1874 F 1 1,10	1928 F 1 1,10	1928 F 1 1,10	1908 F 1 1,10	1914 F 1 1,10
Colinus virginianus	1906 F 2 1,4	1906 F 2 1,4	1906 F 2 1,4	1906 F 1 4	1906 F 2 1,4	1906 F 2 1,4
Oreortyx pictus		1929 F 2 1		1929 F 2 1		
Callipepla squamata				1961 F 2 6		
Callipepla californica	1855 F 3 1,10	1855 S 3 1,10	1855 S 3 1,10	1855 S 3 1,10	1855 S 3 1,10	1855 S 3 1,10
Callipepla gambelii	1958 F 2 4,10	1958 F 2 4,10	1958 F 2 4,10	1958 S 1,2 6,10		1958 S 2 4,10
Callipepla douglasii				1959 F 1 6		
Tympanuchus cupido	1895[a] F 1 1	1933[a,b] F 1 1				
Tympanuchus phasianellus				1932 F 2 1		
Cyrtonyx montezumae				1961 F 1 6		
Ammoperdix griseogularis				1959 F 1 6		
Alectoris chukar	1923 F 2 1,10	1957 S 2 4,10	1957 S 2 4,10	1949 S 2 5,10	1923 S 3 4,10	1923 S 3 4,10
Alectoris barbara			1961 F 2 4,10	1959 F 1,2 4,6	1961 F 2 4,10	1959 F 2 4,10
Francolinus francolinus		1959 S 2 9	1959 S 2 9	1959 S 1,2 6	1959 S 2 9	
Francolinus pintadeanus				1962 F 1 6		
Francolinus pondicerianus	1958 S 2 4,5,10	1958 S 2 4,5,10	1958 S 2 4,5,10	1959 S 1 6	1958 S 2 4,5,10	1958 S 2 5
Francolinus adsperus				1965 F 1 6		
Francolinus icterorhyn- chus				1961 F 1 6		

APPENDIX 4. CONTINUED.

Species	Oʻahu	Kauaʻi	Maui	Hawaiʻi	Molokaʻi	Lānaʻi
Francolinus clappertoni				1961 F 1 6		
Francolinus erckelii	1957 S 2 5,10	1957 S 2 5,10	1957 S 2 5,10	1958 S 1,2 6	1957 S 2 5,10	1957 S 2 5,10
Francolinus leucosepus				1959 F 2 6		
Perdix perdix		1910 F 1 1	1926 F 1 1	1929 F 2 1		
Coturnix chinensis	1922 F 2 1	1910 F 1 1	1922 F 2 1	1922 F 2 1	1922 F 2 1	
Coturnix pectoralis			1922 F 2 3			1922 F 2 3
Coturnix japonica	1921 F 3 2,10	1921 S 3 2,10	1921 S 2 1,10	1921 S 3 2,10	1921 S 3 2,10	1921 S 2 1,10
Rollulus rouloul	1924 F 2 1					
Bambusicola thoracica			1959 F 2 4,5,10	1961 F 1 6		
Lophura leucomelanos				1962 S 1 6,10		
Lophura nycthemera	1932 F 2 1	1870 F 1 1				
Gallus gallus	PH[c] S 4 2,10	PH S 4 2,10	PH F 4 2,10	PH F 4 2,10	PH F 4 2,10	PH F 4 2,10
Gallus sonnerati				1962 F 1 6		
Phasianus colchicus	1865 S 1 1,10	1865 S 1 1,10	1865 S 1 1,10	1865 S 1 1,10	1865 S 1 1,10	1865 S 1 1,10
Syrmaticus reevesii	1960 F 2 4,10	1960 F 2 4,10	1960 F 2 4,10	1959 F 1 6	1960 F 2 4,10	1960 F 2 4,10
Syrmaticus soemmerringii	1907 F 2 1	1907 F 2 1	1907 F 2 1			
Chrysolophus pictus	1932 F 2 1	1870 F 1 1				
Chrysolophus amherstiae	1932 F 2 1					
Pavo cristatus	1860 S 1 1,10	1860 F 1 1,10	1860 S 1 1,10	1928 S 1 1,10	1860 F 1 1,10	1860 F 1 1,10
Meleagris gallopavo	1815 F 1 1,10	1815 F 1 1,10	1815 S 1 1,10	1815 S 1 1,10	1815 S 1 1,14	1815 S 1 1,10

[a] May have been *Tympanuchus phasianellus* (Caum 1933).
[b] Based on "indefinite reports" (Caum 1933).
[c] Prehistoric introduction.

APPENDIX 5. INTRODUCED COLUMBIDS ON SIX MAIN HAWAIIAN ISLANDS (SEE APPENDIX 2 FOR EXPLANATION OF TERMS)

Species	Oʻahu	Kauaʻi	Molokaʻi	Hawaiʻi	Molokaʻi	Lānaʻi
Caloenas nicobarica		1928 F 2 1	1922 F 2 1			
Chalcophaps indica	1924 F 2 1					
Columba livia	1796 S 3 1	1796 S 3 1	1796 S 3 1	1796 S 3 1	1796 S 3 1	1796 S 3 1
Gallicolumba luzonica		1929 F 1 1				
Geopelia cuneata	1928 F 2 1		1929 F 2 1			
Geopelia humeralis	1992 F 2 1	1922 F 1 1	1928 F 2 1			
Geopelia striata	1922 S 2 1	1922 S 2 1	1922 S 2 1	1922 S 2 1	1922 S 2 1	1922 S 2 1
Geophaps lophotes	1922 F 2 1			1922 F 2 1	1922 F 2 1	1922 F 2 1
Geophaps plumifera			1922 F 2 1			1922 F 2 1
Geophaps smithii			1992 F 2 1			1922 F 2 1
Geotrygon montana			1933 F 3 3			
Leptotila verreauxi			1933 F 3 3			
Leucosarcia melanoleuca			1922 F 2 1			1922 F 2 1
Phaps chalcoptera	1922 F 2 1					
Streptopelia chinensis	1879 S 3 1	1890 S 3 8	1890 S 3 8	1890 S 3 8	1890 S 3 8	1890 S 3 8
Streptopelia decaocto	1928 F 1 1	1920 F 1 1		1928 F 2 1		
Zenaida asiatica				1961 F 2 6		
Zenaida macroura				1962 S 1 9		

Systematics

Studies in Avian Biology No. 22:48–50, 2001.

SYSTEMATICS—INTRODUCTION

HELEN F. JAMES

Unreachable to amphibians, reptiles, and most land mammals, the Hawaiian Archipelago has been colonized naturally only by the most vagile of vertebrates. The native terrestrial vertebrates of the islands consist entirely of birds and a couple of species of bats. Indeed, the islands are so remote from other complex terrestrial ecosystems that even birds have difficulty establishing themselves. The native birds that dwell as year-round residents in Hawai'i's terrestrial and wetland habitats can be traced to as few as 20 colonizing species (James 1991).

These successful colonists speciated and evolved in the islands to give rise to an avifauna with over 100 resident species. Sadly, many extraordinary species are extinct and known only through fossil remains. The fossil species include large flightless waterfowl, flightless woodland ibises, many flightless rails, a variety of raptors, three or four large crows, and diverse species of Hawaiian honeycreepers or drepanidines (Olson and James 1991, James and Olson 1991). Despite these losses, a host of remarkable endemic species survived in the islands long enough to be studied and appreciated by ornithologists. Most of the survivors are passerine forest birds, including many species in the adaptive radiation of drepanidines. Besides passerines, the only birds that escaped early extinction are a hawk, an owl that is probably a recent colonist, the Hawaiian Goose (*Branta sandvicensis*), and a variety of smaller waterbirds (including some that had moved into terrestrial habitats).

The Hawaiian Islands are one of the world's hottest of hot spots for the extinction of birds. Twenty-four endemic species of birds have become extinct there since 1778, and another eight are either recently extinct or imminently threatened (these figures vary slightly according to the taxonomy followed; Pratt 1994). In addition, the thirty-five fossil species that have been described and approximately twenty that are currently waiting to be described are thought to have disappeared mainly in the prehistoric period of human settlement (Olson and James 1991, James and Olson 1991). The causes of the decline and extinction of so many birds include habitat degradation and loss, introduced pathogens such as avian malaria and poxvirus, and introduced predators such as the small Indian mongoose (*Herpestes auropunctatus*).

Hawai'i's avifauna has garnered considerable attention from ecologists and evolutionary biologists. The extreme geographic isolation of the resident birds, the clear-cut barriers to dispersal within the archipelago (water gaps between islands), and the roughly linear progression of island ages (the islands to the northwest being older than those to the southeast), provide a relatively simple setting where the processes that underlie modern biogeographic patterns may be relatively accessible to inference. Classic papers on Hawaiian birds have addressed such topics as the allopatric model of speciation (Amadon 1950), character displacement (Bock 1970), dynamic equilibrium theory in island biogeography (Juvik and Austring 1979), and the processes underlying macroevolutionary change (Amadon 1950, Bock 1970, 1979). The basic information relied upon in these studies is the systematics and distribution of Hawai'i's endemic birds.

Formal study of the systematics and distribution of Hawai'i's birds began in the late eighteenth century, when the specimens collected on Captain James Cook's third voyage (in 1778–1779) reached England. The century that followed saw the steady addition of new species from Hawai'i, as subsequent voyages returned to western ports with specimens, and later, various foreigners took up residence in the islands and made their own collections (Olson and James 1991, 1994a). The lure of discovery finally inspired a period of intense exploration of the islands aimed specifically at collecting and describing the native birds and other endemic organisms. Between 1887 and 1902, the islands' birds were thoroughly sampled by Scott Wilson, R. C. L. Perkins, and especially by Lord Walter Rothschild's collectors Henry Palmer, G. C. Munro, and E. Wolstenholme, followed shortly by H. W. Henshaw (Olson and James 1994a). These efforts lead to three comprehensive publications (Rothschild 1893–1900, Wilson and Evans 1890–1899, Henshaw 1902a, and Perkins 1903).

Decades after this age of exploration and discovery, papers on the systematics and evolution of Hawaiian birds began to appear with regularity again. Miller (1937) studied anatomical adaptations for terrestriality in the Hawaiian Goose, while most other authors focused on the adaptive radiation of drepanidines (e.g., Amadon (1950) on eclectic systematics and speciation, Richards and Bock (1973) on functional anatomy, Raikow (1977) on myology, Sibley and

Ahlquist (1982) on DNA-DNA hybridization, Johnson et al. (1989) on protein electrophoresis, Tarr and Fleischer (1993, 1995) on mitochondrial DNA). Also, beginning in the 1970s, fossil birds were being found in Hawai'i with surprising frequency (e.g., Olson and Wetmore 1976, Olson and James 1982b, 1984, James et al. 1987, Olson and James 1991, James and Olson 1991).

As the papers in this volume attest, more effort is now focused on the systematics of Hawaiian birds than at any time since the 1890s. This coincides with a renaissance in phylogenetic research, spurred by advances in methods of analysis and by the technological revolution in molecular genetics. Hawaiian birds attract extra attention because of the urgency of studying species threatened with extinction, and the need to place the new fossil species in an evolutionary context.

The most active program in molecular genetics of Hawaiian birds is that of Robert C. Fleischer and his collaborators. A long-term goal of this program is to study the evolutionary genetics of each endemic lineage of Hawaiian birds. Fortunately, even the extinct fossil lineages can be studied, through amplification and sequencing of DNA fragments from fossil bones (Cooper et al. 1996, Paxinos 1998, Sorenson et al. 1999). By including appropriate outgroups and assuming a molecular clock based in part on earlier Hawaiian drepanidine research (Fleischer et al. 1998), Fleischer and McIntosh (*this volume*) are able to estimate the length of time that each lineage has been present in the islands. Their paper offers a glimpse of the types of questions we can answer with molecular genetics that we could only speculate about before, and also hints at the large number of molecular genetic studies of Hawaiian birds that are currently in progress.

The value of genetics and systematics to conservation of endangered species is exemplified by Judith Rhymer's contribution on the endangered Hawaiian Duck (*Anas wyvilliana*) and Laysan Duck (*Anas laysanesis*). Using a battery of molecular genetic techniques, Rhymer addresses several pressing questions that will affect the management plans for these two species. First, she shows that the Hawaiian and Laysan Ducks have separate evolutionary histories and certainly merit species rather than subspecies status. She also cites anecdotal evidence that Laysan Ducks rarely hybridize in captivity. Combined with her previous collaborative research showing that the former range of the Laysan Duck included the main Hawaiian islands (Cooper et al. 1996), this lays the groundwork for possible reintroduction of the Laysan Duck

in the main islands. Rhymer also develops molecular markers that can be used to monitor the extent of hybridization between Hawaiian Ducks and introduced Mallards. Such hybridization threatens the survival of Hawaiian Ducks on O'ahu but, so far, not on Kaua'i. The information and genetic tools provided by Rhymer will be indispensable in formulating management plans for these rare species.

Phylogenetic analysis can also contribute to conservation planning by providing a way to assess the phylogenetic "distinctiveness" of threatened species. The number of threatened species is disproportionate to the funding that is available to help them, forcing managers to make hard decisions about which species to focus upon. One objective of such decisions is to preserve evolutionary diversity. It is consequently useful to know to what degree a particular threatened species differs from its surviving relatives. The study by Fleischer et al. in this volume assesses the evolutionary relationships and phylogenetic distinctiveness of an endangered drepanidine, the Po'ouli (*Melamprosops phaeosoma*), using genetic and osteological data. Both datasets place the Po'ouli within the clade of drepanidines. However, an index of distinctiveness applied to both datasets also indicates that the Po'ouli is very different from other living drepanidines, both genetically and morphologically. Fleischer et al. conclude that saving the Po'ouli from imminent extinction would be well worth the effort from this perspective.

Douglas Pratt, who contributes a cladistic analysis of the drepanidine radiation based on eclectic phenotypic characters, recommends that no changes be made to his taxonomy in the light of molecular genetic data, which he regards as preliminary, inconsistent, and in the case of mitochondrial DNA sequences, perhaps giving a false signal due to hybridization (although there are no confirmed hybrids among the drepanidines). Where his results conflict with my dissertation research on drepanidine osteology (James 1998), he describes my work as perhaps based on superficial resemblances and illustrative of the weaknesses of "single character or single-complex analyses." My results are remarkably congruent with Raikow's (1977) early cladistic analysis of myology and external anatomy, but Pratt also considers Raikow's character analysis to be vague where it conflicts with his own results. I can only urge readers to consult the original sources and form their own opinions.

Two corrections should be made here, however. Pratt (p. 88, this volume) implies that my tree topologies bring together unrelated species with similar bill shapes in the red-and-black plumaged group and the green plumaged group.

Actually, my analysis (James 1998) recognized the red-and-black birds as a clade, including the full range of bill morphologies from "finch-like" to long and sickled. None of the green birds with parallel bill morphologies joined this clade. Also, whereas Pratt states that James and Olson (1991) previously suggested lumping *Loxioides* and *Chloridops,* we actually wrote that future research may justify merging *Loxioides* with *Telespiza.*

The contribution on species concepts by Pratt and Pratt is very much in the tradition of Pratt's dissertation (Pratt 1979), an eclectic assessment of alpha taxonomy with emphasis on vocalizations, plumages, and behavior as potential isolating mechanisms. Many allopatric populations of island birds were long ago demoted to subspecies by Ernst Mayr and others who embraced his biological species concept. For example, in his dissertation, which was supervised by Mayr, Amadon (1950) applied the biological species concept to the drepanidines and came up with many fewer species than were recognized by the late 19th century authorities (see Pratt 1979). However, Pratt and Pratt argue that Amadon and Mayr often erred in applying their own species concept, or simply lacked information that would have kept them from lumping. Properly applied, they feel that the biological species concept would elevate most of Amadon's allopatric subspecies to full species status. Although they stress potential isolating mechanisms in their evaluations, their way of applying the biological and phylogenetic species concepts result in very similar taxonomic lists. While the debate over species concepts continues, non-taxonomists can take comfort in knowing that, with the growth of knowledge about Hawaiian birds, the choice of species concept now appears to have little effect on the species-level taxa that are recognized.

This is an exciting time for evolutionary and biogeographic studies of Hawai'i's avifauna. The abundance of fossils enables us to study morphological change through time, calculate rates of species turnover and extinction using data with real time depth, and gain insight into the former ranges and habitat preferences of endangered species. With ancient DNA we can identify fossil species, place them on phylogenetic trees, and even study their population genetics over long stretches of time. Because the genetic divergences between isolated island populations cannot be older than the islands themselves, multiple local calibrations of the minimum rates of DNA sequence change are possible in Hawai'i. Putting aside differences of opinion on whether genetic or phenotypic data are best for phylogenetic analysis (see Pratt, *this volume,* and Fleischer and McIntosh, *this volume*), phylogenetic hypotheses can be strengthened and insights into character evolution can be gained through comparison of data and results from these two types of studies. The confluence of knowledge from these various sources is leading to a much improved picture of change in Hawai'i's avifauna through time. The growth of information from genetics, phylogenetics, and paleontology is contributing not only to basic knowledge, but in important ways to conservation management as well.

Studies in Avian Biology No. 22:51–60, 2001.

MOLECULAR SYSTEMATICS AND BIOGEOGRAPHY OF THE HAWAIIAN AVIFAUNA

ROBERT C. FLEISCHER AND CARL E. MCINTOSH

Abstract. The Hawaiian avifauna is exceptional for its high proportion of endemic taxa, its spectacular adaptive radiations, and its level of human induced extinction. Little has been known about the phylogenetic relationships, geographical origins, and timing of colonization of individual avian lineages until recently. Here we review the results of molecular studies that address these topics. Molecular data (mostly mitochondrial DNA sequences) are available for 14 of the 21 or more lineages of Hawaiian birds. We briefly review results of phylogenetic analyses of these data for lineages that have experienced major and minor radiations, and for single differentiated species and probable recent colonists. When possible, we determine the mainland species that are genetically most closely related. We find evidence that roughly half of the >21 lineages colonized from North America; not even a quarter appear to have come from South Pacific Islands. Our data also provide little evidence that Hawaiian bird lineages predate the formation of the current set of main islands (i.e., >5 Ma), as has been found for Hawaiian *Drosophila* and lobeliads.

Key Words: adaptive radiation; biogeography; Hawaiian avifauna; mitochondrial DNA; molecular systematics.

In 1943 Ernst Mayr published a short paper in *The Condor* summarizing his hypotheses about the geographic origins and closest living relatives of each known lineage in the Hawaiian avifauna. Mayr (1943) concluded that half of 14 hypothesized colonizations were of American origin and only two lineages arose from Polynesia. Therefore, although Hawai'i is considered part of the "Polynesian Region" because most of its biota and its human inhabitants had Polynesian ancestors, in terms of its birds Hawai'i is in the Nearctic Region. Since Mayr's paper, other authors have posited similar systematic hypotheses and biogeographic scenarios based on morphological, ecological, and distributional data (e.g., Amadon 1950, Pratt 1979, Berger 1981). Paleontology has offered only minor resolution of the relationships of ancestral lineages or the timing of speciation events; although there is an excellent Holocene fossil record in Hawai'i (Olson and James 1982a, 1991; James and Olson 1991), the pre-Holocene record is extremely limited (though one excellent fauna dates to >0.12 Ma ago; James 1987).

In recent years, molecular methods have proven extremely useful for inferring evolutionary relationships among taxa and the relative time frames during which taxa evolved (Avise 1994, Hillis et al. 1996). Inference from molecular data may be the best available way to reconstruct phylogenetic relationships and determine geographical origins and evolutionary time frames for Hawaiian taxa. In part this is because morphological or behavioral changes are often adaptive responses subject to natural or sexual selection (i.e., as part of the process of adaptive radiation), and they do not usually show constancy in their rates of change. Thus they can poten-

tially mislead on issues of common ancestry via homoplasy. DNA sequences, on the other hand, while obviously not evolving in a perfect clock-like fashion (see below), do change over time, and evolve more continuously than morphology. Also, with the exception of a relatively few non-synonymous changes within protein sequences, they generally evolve via mutation and drift (Nei 1987, Avise 1994), and are not as subject to homoplasy via convergence or stasis as are morphological or other characters. Thus major adaptive shifts in, for example, the bills of Hawaiian honeycreepers, may occur within some lineages (e.g., to thin and decurved in the nectarivorous 'I'iwi, *Vestiaria coccinea*), while not in others (e.g., conical and finchlike in the Laysan Finch, *Telespiza cantans*), in spite of an identical amount of time since evolving from their putatively "finch-billed" common ancestor. There are methods for detecting symplesiomorphic versus synapomorphic characters in phylogenetic analysis, but the higher variance in rates of change of morphological characters remains a problem for phylogenetic reconstruction (Hillis et al. 1996).

While there have been significant molecular investigations of particular Hawaiian plant and invertebrate taxa (especially *Drosophila*; e.g., Hunt and Carson 1983, DeSalle and Hunt 1987, DeSalle 1992), few molecular studies detailing evolutionary histories of the Hawaiian avifauna have been made until recently (e.g., Tarr and Fleischer 1993, 1995; Feldman 1994, Cooper et al. 1996; Fleischer et al. 1998, 2000, *this volume*; Paxinos 1998, Sorenson et al. 1999, Fleischer et al. in press, Rhymer *this volume*; C. Tarr, E. Paxinos, B. Slikas, H. James, S. Olson, A. Cooper, and R. Fleischer, unpubl. data).

TABLE 1. THE ELEMENTS OF THE HAWAIIAN AVIFAUNA

Taxon	Family	No. of species[a]	Geographic origin[b]	Comments[c]
Non-passeriformes:				
Ibises	Plataleidae	≥2	N.A.	minor radiation, flightless, *Apteribis*†
Night Heron	Ardeidae	1	N.A.	recent colonist, *Nycticorax nycticorax*
Moa-nalos	Anatidae	≥4	W. Hemisphere	minor radiation?, 3 flightless duck genera†
True Geese	Anatidae	≥3	N.A.	minor radiation, *Branta*,†**e**
Modern Ducks	Anatidae	2	N.A. and Asia	1 ± differentiated, 1 recent colonist, *Anas* **e**
Porzana Rails	Rallidae	≥12	Pacific/unknown	major radiation?, ≥2 colonizations†
Large rallids	Rallidae	2	N.A.?	recent colonists?, coot and moorhen
Black-necked Stilt	Recurvirostridae	1	N.A.	recent colonist, *Himantopus knudseni* **e**
Eagle	Acciptridae	1	Asia	recent colonist, *Haliaeetus leucophrys*†
Buteo	Acciptridae	1	N.A.	differentiated, *Buteo solitarius* **e**
Harrier	Acciptridae	1	Unknown	differentiated, *Circus dossenus*†
Long-legged Owls	Strigidae	4	Unknown	minor radiation, *Grallistrix* spp. 4†
Short-eared Owl	Strigidae	1	Unknown	recent colonist, *Asio flammeus sandwichensis*
Passeriformes:				
Crows	Corvidae	≥4	Unknown	minor radiation?, *Corvus* spp., 3†, 1 **e**
Millerbird	Sylviidae	1	South Pacific	differentiated, *Acrocephalus familiaris* **e**
'Elepaio	Myiagridae	≥1	Australasia	differentiated, *Chasiempis sandwichensis*
Thrushes	Muscicapidae	5	W. Hemisphere	minor radiation, *Myadestes* spp., 3†, 1 **e**
Honeyeaters	Meliphagidae	≥6	South Pacific	minor radiation, *Moho* spp., *Chaetoptila*, all†
Honeycreepers	Fringillidae	≥50	Asia or N.A.?	major radiation, drepanidines, most† or **e**
>21 lineages	*13 families*	*≥102 species*		

[a] Number of species within each lineage/family, based on James and Olson (1991), Olson and James (1991), and H. James (pers. comm.).
[b] N.A. = North America; W = West.
[c] † denotes at least some members extinct; **e** denotes at least some members endangered.

Components of the Hawaiian avifauna vary greatly in the degrees to which they have speciated and become modified morphologically and ecologically (Table 1). For example, the Hawaiian drepanidines (Hawaiian finches or honeycreepers) have evolved incredible morphological, ecological, and behavioral diversity across more than 50 species and are one of the most often cited cases of adaptive radiation (Rothschild 1893–1900, Perkins 1903, Amadon 1950, Raikow 1977, Freed et al. 1987a, James and Olson 1991, Tarr and Fleischer 1995, Fleischer et al. 1998). Several species of extinct, large,

flightless waterfowl (moa-nalos) show extreme morphological modification in their apparent shift into a ratite/grazing mammal/tortoise niche (Olson and James 1991; Sorenson et al. 1999). Other avian lineages have not speciated and have changed morphologically little or not at all from putative mainland relatives (e.g., Black-crowned Night Heron, *Nycticorax nycticorax hoactli*; Short-eared Owl or Pueo, *Asio flammeus sandwichensis*). Is this variance in levels of speciation and phenotypic differentiation related merely to the lengths of time that lineages have been evolving in the islands (Simon 1987, Car-

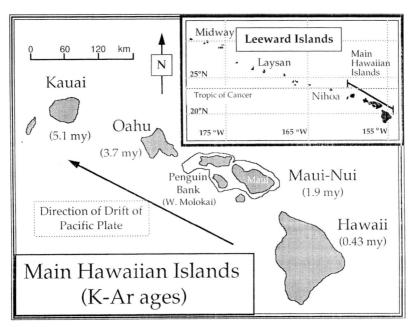

FIGURE 1. Map of the main Hawaiian Islands (plus inset map of main and leeward Hawaiian Islands). Ages of the oldest rocks from the main islands based on K-Ar dating are noted. Maui-Nui is composed of the islands of Maui, Lāna‘i, Kaho‘olawe, and Moloka‘i, all of which were connected until about 0.3–0.4 Ma ago and again during more recent periods of low sea level.

son and Clague 1995)? Or are there other factors that have promoted stasis in some lineages and change in others, regardless of length of time in the islands? As noted above, the fossil record provides little resolution of this question. Thus, estimates of the age of separation from ancestors outside of the Hawaiian Archipelago, or the age of a radiation within the islands, can only be inferred from molecular data.

The Hawaiian Islands and its avifauna are extremely isolated from continental and other Pacific island avifaunas. This is likely the primary reason for the relatively low number of independent taxonomic avian lineages that occur in the islands (Mayr 1943, Pratt 1979). While the total number of such lineages has been increased (and continues to increase) from recent fossil findings (Olson and James 1982a, 1991; James and Olson 1991), the islands still appear to have far fewer independent avian lineages than one might expect for a tropical archipelago of this size and topographic diversity, and there may be additional factors involved that limit the primary diversity of the avifauna.

Here we summarize molecular and other data relevant to systematics and biogeography of the Hawaiian aviafauna. We first provide a brief overview of the geological history of the Hawaiian Archipelago and its utility for calibrating rates of molecular evolution (Tarr and Fleischer

1993, Fleischer et al. 1998). We then consider the origins and phylogenetic histories of each lineage within the avifauna, addressing extensive and minor radiations, well-differentiated single species, and undifferentiated (and likely recent) colonists. We also apply a molecular clock approach to obtain rough estimates of the maximum period of time that a lineage could have existed in the Hawaiian Islands.

GEOLOGICAL HISTORY AND THE CALIBRATION OF MOLECULAR EVOLUTIONARY RATES

The Hawaiian Islands have an unusual geological history (Clague and Dalrymple 1987, Walker 1990, Carson and Clague 1995; Fig. 1). They form as the Pacific Plate drifts northwest over a "hot spot" where magma extrudes from the earth's mantle through the crust to build huge shield volcanos (often to >4 km above sea level). The extreme weight of a new island, combined with the cooling of the crust as it moves away from the hot spot, causes a relatively rapid subsidence in island elevation and area. Subsidence continues slowly beyond this point, as does erosion, and islands shrink to become small coral and sand atolls and ultimately undersea mounts (Fig. 1).

The Hawaiian Islands are ordered by age in a linear pattern, with the oldest main island in the northwest (Kaua'i at 5.1 Ma) and the youngest in the southeast (Hawai'i at 0.43 Ma; Fig. 1). This volcanic conveyor belt provides an exceptional system for evolutionary studies, as it sets up a temporal framework that can be used to estimate the timing of evolutionary events and rates of evolution. The age of an island is the maximum age for a population inhabiting the island. These ages can be used to calibrate rates of molecular change if phylogenies reveal that the pattern of cladogenesis parallels the timing of island formation, and if populations colonize near to the time of island emergence (Bishop and Hunt 1988, Tarr and Fleischer 1993, Givnish et al. 1995, Fleischer et al. 1998).

We used this rationale to calibrate part of the mitochondrial cytochrome *b* (cyt *b*) gene in Hawaiian drepanidines (Fleischer et al. 1998). The overall rate of cyt *b* divergence, corrected for minor saturation, transition bias, rate variation among sites, and potential lineage sorting is 1.6% sequence divergence/Ma. This value is similar to a rate we estimated for overall restriction site divergence in mitochondrial DNA (mtDNA) in drepanidines (~2%/Ma; Tarr and Fleischer 1993). Note that rates calibrated using this approach are based on a time period of divergence up to only about 4 Ma. Recently, Moore et al. (in press) showed through simulation modeling that cyt *b* sequence divergence is accurate as a predictor of time of divergence only to about 5 Ma (i.e., about 10% overall sequence divergence). Predictions of dates older than 5 Ma are generally underestimated. Nonlinearity of sequence divergence due to saturation and rate variation among sites appears to become problematic above about 10% overall sequence divergence for birds (Krajewski and King 1996, Randi 1996, Moore and DeFilippis 1997). Thus the drepanidine or other cyt *b* rates are not likely to be applicable to events that happened appreciably earlier than 5 Ma, and caution must be exercised when making predictions or calibrations from cyt *b* sequence divergences over 10%.

Our drepanidine rates (Tarr and Fleischer 1993, Fleischer et al. 1998) are within the range of estimates for avian and mammalian taxa based on calibrations derived from relatively recent fossil evidence of cladogenesis. This is true for both restriction fragment length polymorphisms (RFLPs) in total mtDNA and sequence divergence in the cyt *b* gene. Examples of avian rates include RFLP variation in geese at ~2%/Ma (Shields and Wilson 1987); cyt *b* sequences in partridges versus *Gallus* at 2.0%/Ma (Randi 1996; however, Arbogast and Slowinski [1998], corrected the divergences using an HKY [Hasegawa et al. 1985] model with a Γ-correction to

obtain a rate of about 5.0%/Ma); RFLP variation in New World quail at 2.0%/Ma (reported in Klicka and Zink 1997); woodpecker cyt *b* at 2.0%/Ma (Moore et al. in press); cyt *b* in cranes at 0.7%/Ma for Balearicines versus Gruines (old split) and up to 1.7%/Ma for comparisons within the Gruines (Krajewski and King 1996); and cyt *b* in albatross at 0.65%/Ma (Nunn et al. 1996, recalculated for total sequence change in Klicka and Zink 1997). In the crane and albatross studies the slower rates could be caused by the longer generation times in these species, or perhaps by reduced metabolic rates in these larger-bodied taxa (Martin and Palumbi 1993, Rand 1994, Bromham et al. 1996, Nunn and Stanley 1998). Alternatively, the difference may relate to the fossil dates used for calibration: for both studies these dates are older than 10 Ma, whereas for all but the partridge/*Gallus* comparison (Randi 1996) the dates are before 5 Ma. Both studies attempt to correct for saturation (Krajewski and King 1996, Nunn et al. 1996), but may severely underestimate divergence (Arbogast and Slowinski 1998). This could be considered an inverse prediction of the findings of Moore et al. (in press): using dates older than 5 Ma to calibrate may result in an underestimate of the rate. Supporting this is a negative correlation between divergence times and divergence rates (Spearman rho = −0.51, P = 0.042) from Table 2 of Martin and Palumbi (1993). Avian rates are similar to most mtDNA/cyt *b* rates calculated for mammal taxa (e.g., ~2%/Ma; Brown et al. 1979, Irwin et al. 1991, Stanley et al. 1994, Janacek et al. 1996).

In general, then, calibrated rates of mtDNA protein coding sequence divergence in birds and mammals do not appear to vary greatly from about 2%/Ma. Most rate variation appears to be correlated with variation in body size and its correlates (i.e., metabolic rate, generation time; Martin and Palumbi 1993, Rand 1994), although some of the variation may be due to differing selective constraints on proteins in different lineages or to fluctuations in population size (Ohta 1976). In summary, with the exception of the very rapidly evolving control region (which in some sections may be evolving an order of magnitude faster than the average for mtDNA; e.g., Quinn 1992), most avian and mammalian rate calibrations based on corrected mtDNA divergence and dates before 5 Ma ago reveal rates at about, or above, 2% divergence/Ma. Based on the rather detailed rationale described above we feel that mtDNA (RFLP or cyt *b*) sequence divergence between a Hawaiian taxon and its closest non-Hawaiian relatives that is below about 10% would indicate an origin near the time of or after the formation of the island of Kaua'i.

ORIGINS AND EVOLUTION OF THE HAWAIIAN AVIFAUNA

There were more than 102 species of native breeding land- or waterbirds (i.e., non-seabirds) in the Hawaiian Islands (Table 1; constructed from James and Olson 1991, Olson and James 1991; and H. James, pers. comm.). These 102 species sort into six songbird families (Passeriformes) and seven non-songbird families (Table 1). Some families have a relatively large number of species (i.e., >4) and, in some cases, it is fairly clear that each group of species in a family represents an in situ radiation from a single colonization (e.g., drepanidines, thrushes). It is clear that in some families (e.g., anatids, rallids) there has been more than a single colonization event, while for others (e.g., corvids, meliphagids) it is difficult to determine how many independent colonization events have occurred.

Avian biologists working in the islands have been fortunate to have an excellent Holocene fossil record (Olson and James 1982a, 1991; James and Olson 1991). Without this record, we would be missing a tremendous amount of information about distributions, phylogeny, biogeography, and ecology of these birds. Even so, additional fossil taxa continue to be discovered and, thus, our knowledge remains incomplete. The advent of genetic studies employing the polymerase chain reaction (PCR) has opened a new and exciting avenue for study of these fossils. Our laboratory has had considerable success amplifying mtDNA sequences from these subfossil remains. Here we summarize what has been learned about the evolution of Hawaiian birds from phylogenetic analyses of mtDNA sequences from a number of extinct and extant taxa.

EXTENSIVE RADIATIONS

The drepanidines (Hawaiian finches or honeycreepers) are by far the most speciose group in Hawai'i, with 33 species known from historical collections and more than 17 known from subfossil remains (totaling over 50 species; James and Olson 1991; H. James, pers. comm.). The drepanidine radiation is remarkable for its extreme morphological, ecological, and behavioral diversity (Rothschild 1893–1900, Perkins 1903, Amadon 1950, Baldwin 1953, Raikow 1977, Pratt 1979, Freed et al. 1987a, James and Olson 1991). However, major adaptive shifts appear to have modified many characters traditionally used for phylogenetic reconstruction, while others less subject to selection have been conserved and provide little or no phylogenetic information. The somewhat chimeric associations of morphological traits in the group have even

led to the suggestion that the drepanidines are not monophyletic (Pratt 1992a,b). Molecular data may prove especially useful for assessing evolutionary relationships in this group, and they do support a cardueline ancestry and, thus, far, monophyly of the drepanidines (Fleischer et al. 1998; Fig. 2c).

Molecular data may also be effective in estimating a time frame for the drepanidine radiation. The radiation of the drepanidines would seem quite deep based on their relative degree of phenotypic diversity. Molecular evolutionary rate estimates based on DNA-DNA hybridization data (Sibley and Ahlquist 1982) are in support of this prediction with an estimated split of drepanidines from a cardueline outgroup of about 15–20 Ma. Molecular rate estimates from both allozyme (Johnson et al. 1989, Fleischer et al. 1998) and mtDNA data (Tarr and Fleischer 1993, 1995; Fleischer et al. 1998), however, strongly contradict the results of Sibley and Ahlquist (1982) and suggest a basal split that began about 4 Ma ago and a separation from a mainland cardueline ancestor (not necessarily the closest outgroup; Fig. 2c) of <5–6 Ma ago. These mtDNA results are based on several internal rate calibrations estimated as outlined above for cyt *b*. Sibley and Ahlquist's (1982) results may be biased by their use of continental biogeographic points in their calibration (Quinn et al. 1991) or by use of too distant outgroups for comparison.

No other avian radiation in Hawai'i is so diverse in morphology or number of lineages as the drepanidines. Extinct flightless rails, classified as *Porzana* (Olson and James 1991), included perhaps more than 12 species, with as many as three species on each major island. Until recently it has not been clear whether these species comprise a single highly radiated clade, or represent a number of independent colonizations from mainland or other Pacific island sources. Molecular phylogenetic analyses (B. Slikas, S. Olson, R. Fleischer, unpubl. data) indicate that each of the two historically collected *Porzana* species resulted from independent colonizations. For *Porzana palmeri* the Kimura 2-parameter corrected distance (Kimura 1980; distance and SE calculated in MEGA, Kumar et al. 1993) for 197 base pairs (bp) of ATPase8 was 2.1 ± 1.1% distant from its closest non-Hawaiian *Porzana* relative. For *P. sandwichensis* the ATPase8 Kimura 2-parameter corrected distance was 5.9 ± 1.8% to its closest non-Hawaiian *Porzana* relative. Molecular analyses of *Porzana* taxa known only from subfossil remains are underway.

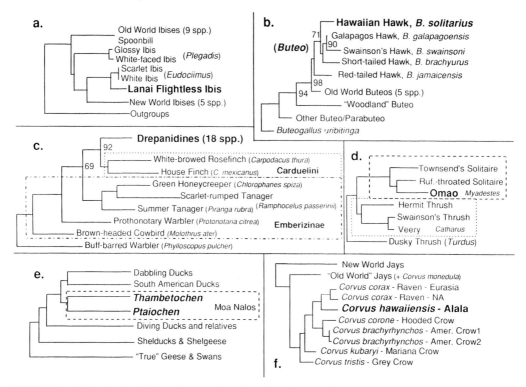

FIGURE 2.   Abbreviated phylogenetic reconstructions for six Hawaiian taxa. a. Summarized maximum parsimony tree based on 407 nucleotide sites of 12s ribosomal RNA (A. Cooper, S. Olson, H. James, R. Fleischer, unpubl. data). b. Summarized parsimony phylogram based on preliminary analysis of over 1500 bp of mtDNA sequence (ATPase8, ND2, cyt *b,* and COI) in *Buteo* and related taxa (R. Fleischer, P. Cordero, C. McIntosh, I. Jones, and A. Helbig, unpublished). c. Summary of relationships of outgroups and drepanidines based on parsimony analysis of 675 bp of cyt *b* sequence. d. Parsimony phylogram constructed from 700 bp of cyt *b* sequence from two *Myadestes* and three *Catharus* taxa with 'Ōma'o and *Turdus* outgroup. e. Parsimony tree of two moa-nalo genera and a wide sampling of other waterfowl taxa showing two moa-nalo genera to be sister taxa and related to dabbling ducks. Tree is summarized from Sorenson et al. (1999), and based on over 1200 bp of mtDNA sequence. f. Parsimony phylogram showing summary of jay relationships to *Corvus* and a sampling of *Corvus* taxa based on 1008 bp of cyt *b.* The 'Alalā is most closely related to the Common Raven.

MINOR RADIATIONS

Seven other Hawaiian avian groups have undergone what appear to be minor radiations, each with fewer than six species (Table 1). These include thrushes (genus *Myadestes*), honeyeaters (genera *Moho* and *Chaetoptila*), a lineage of owls (genus *Grallistrix*), several crows (genus *Corvus*), flightless ibises (genus *Apteribis*), and two waterfowl (Anatidae) lineages: true geese (genus *Branta*) and the highly modified dabbling duck relatives called "moa-nalos" (genera *Chelychelynechen*, *Ptaiochen*, and *Thambetochen*).

The five species of thrushes were placed originally in their own genus, *Phaeornis,* but were considered aligned with solitaires (*Myadestes*; Stejneger 1887, Amadon 1950), robins (*Turdus*) or nightingale-thrushes (*Catharus*; Ripley 1962).

Most of the morphological and other evidence (e.g., Kepler and Kepler 1983) clearly favors placement of thrushes in *Myadestes* (Pratt 1982). We analyzed variation in about 700 bp of the cyt *b* gene of mtDNA (C. McIntosh and R. Fleischer, unpubl. data), for the Hawai'i Thrush (or 'Ōma'o, *M. obscurus*), three *Catharus,* two American *Myadestes* and a *Turdus* species, along with outgroup taxa. The resulting trees clearly place the 'Ōma'o within the *Myadestes* clade, regardless of the tree building algorithm (i.e., maximum parsimony, Fig. 2d; maximum likelihood or minimum evolution). We could not resolve with certainty using this data set whether the 'Ōma'o is more closely related to *M. genibarbis,* a Caribbean solitaire, or *M. townsendi* of western North America. The Kimura 2-parameter corrected distance between the 'Ōma'o and the solitaires is 6.7% for the 700 bp.

The meliphagid genera *Chaetoptila* (Kioea; 2 spp.) and *Moho* (the 'Ō'ōs; 4 spp.) may represent independent colonizations from south Pacific meliphagids (Perkins 1903), although Mayr (1943) considers both genera derived from a single colonist. One species of *Moho* occurs on each of Kaua'i, O'ahu, Maui Nui (Maui, Lāna'i, Moloka'i, and Kaho'olawe), and Hawai'i, and this well-differentiated lineage (Pratt 1979) may provide an opportunity to estimate a rate calibration. The closest sister groups for the Hawaiian meliphagids are unknown, with some authors suggesting *Gymnomyza* of Fiji and Samoa (e.g., Mayr 1943) and others favoring *Foulehaio* of Samoa or the New Zealand tui's (*Prosthemadera*; e.g., Munro 1944, Pratt 1979). Molecular studies are underway to address the origin and monophyly of the Hawaiian forms and the possibility of a rate calibration from the four *Moho* species. A calibration could be used to estimate the date of separation from the most recent common ancestor. This date is important because we estimate from our drepanidine calibrations that nectarivorous drepanidines evolved only 2–3 Ma ago, while Givnish et al. (1995) used a calibration of chloroplast DNA restriction fragment variation to estimate that bird-pollinated flowering lobeliads (genus *Cyanea*) evolved 8–17 Ma ago. Thus it is highly unlikely that drepanidines "coevolved" with these plants in the islands (as was suggested by Givnish et al. 1995). The meliphagids are the only other known native, obligate nectarivores in the islands and, if they are older, could be the coevolved taxon.

At least four crows (*Corvus*) occurred in the islands (James and Olson 1991; H. James, pers. comm.). Three of these are known only from subfossils; two of which have been described and the fourth is the highly endangered Hawaiian Crow (*Corvus hawaiiensis*), hereafter referred to as 'Alalā. It is unclear at present whether these represent a single colonization and subsequent radiation, or multiple colonizations by the same or different ancestral taxa (James and Olson 1991). Preliminary phylogenetic analyses of the 'Alalā and seven other *Corvus* taxa indicate that it is more closely related to the Common Raven (*Corvus corax*) than to more typical crows, including two South Pacific island crows (R. Fleischer and C. McIntosh, unpubl. data; Fig. 2f). The Kimura 2-parameter corrected sequence divergence for 1,008 bp of cyt *b* between 'Alalā and North American Common Raven is about 8.4 ± 1.0%.

Subfossil bones and owl pellets are all that remain of four species of long-legged owls (*Grallistrix*) that apparently were morphologically adapted to feeding on birds. While no DNA analyses have yet been made on this group, it appears likely that they represent the results of a single colonization and subsequent minor radiation.

At least four lineages of waterfowl have colonized the Hawaiian Islands. Of these, only two, the moa-nalos (Olson and James 1991, Sorenson et al. 1999) and the modern geese (*Branta*; Olson and James 1991, Paxinos 1998; E. Paxinos et al. unpubl. data), have speciated beyond a single endemic species. All of the moa-nalos evolved to very large size, flightlessness, and highly modified cranial morphology. They have become convergent in morphology to ratites in terms of postcranial morphology, and one species in particular has converged to tortoise-like cranial morphology. Like the moas of New Zealand (Darwin 1859), the moa-nalos occupied a grazing mammal or tortoise niche (Olson and James 1991). One genus and species (*Chelychelynechen quassus,* the Turtlejawed Goose) is restricted to Kaua'i and one (*Ptaiochen*) to Maui, but *Thambetochen* is found on both Maui Nui and O'ahu, suggesting the genus may have originated on O'ahu and later walked across the Penguin Bank land bridge (Fig. 1) to Moloka'i. No moa-nalo is known from the young island of Hawai'i (but see below).

Olson and James (1991) suggested that the moa-nalos were related to either dabbling ducks or shelducks (tadornines) on the basis of skeletal characters, primarily the presence and shape of their syringeal bullae. Livezey (1996) tentatively concluded from a cladistic analysis of morphology that the moa-nalos were sister to a "true" geese and swan clade, and not to anatids. Mitochrondrial DNA analyses for two of the three genera (*Thambetochen* and *Ptaiochen*; Sorenson et al. 1999) have provided a phylogenetic hypothesis and estimates of minimum genetic divergence from anatid outgroups. The two genera form a well-supported clade that is itself sister to the "dabbling" ducks, although perhaps somewhat more similar to several South American *Anas* or *Anas* relatives than to North American dabblers (Fig. 2e). Molecular data do not support a close relationship with either tadornines or true geese. The distance between the moa-nalos and their closest anatid outgroup, based on 1,009 mtDNA sites, is 6.9 ± 0.5%.

The Nēnē or Hawaiian Goose (*B. sandvicensis*) is the only extant representative of what appears to be a minor radiation of *Branta* in the islands (Olson and James 1991, Paxinos 1998; E. Paxinos et al., unpubl data.). Nēnē are clearly derived from Canada Geese (*B. canadensis*; Quinn et al. 1991), and distances based on mtDNA restriction fragment and cyt *b* sequence data suggest that the two taxa shared a common ancestor sometime within the past 1 Ma (Quinn et al. 1991). At least two, and probably more than three additional *Branta* species existed in the islands (Olson and James 1991, Paxinos 1998; E. Paxinos et al., unpubl. data). One of these, the "very large Hawai'i goose" is the largest land vertebrate known from Hawai'i and is restricted in distribution to the island of Hawai'i (Giffin 1993). The species is highly modified morphologically with a massive body, short, stout wings (it was flightless, but may have used its wings for fighting; S. Olson, pers. comm.); and cranially quite similar to the moa-nalos. In fact, it appears to be a superb example of convergent evolution to the moa-nalos. Mitochondrial DNA sequence analyses (Paxinos 1998) strongly support placement of the very large Hawaiian goose *Branta* and also indicate a sister taxon relationship with the Nēnē and its close, larger relative, *B. hylobadistes*.

Two species of ibis (*Apteribis*) have been described from subfossil material (Olson and Wetmore 1976, Olson and James 1991). *Apteribis* had stouter legs and shorter wings than other ibises and were flightless. The two or more species were limited to Maui Nui, and the disconnection of Maui, Lāna'i, and Moloka'i 0.3–0.4 Ma ago may have initiated the speciation event(s). Analyses of mitochondrial 12S ribosomal DNA sequences of *Apteribis* and 21 other ibis species (Fig. 2a; A. Cooper, S. Olson, H. James and R. Fleischer, unpubl. data) indicate that the closest sister taxon to *Apteribis* is the New World White Ibis (*Eudocimus albus*). The Kimura 2-parameter pairwise distance between the two taxa for 407 bp of 12S rRNA sequence is $3.2 \pm 1.0\%$.

SINGLE DIFFERENTIATED SPECIES

Two raptors, a duck, and two songbirds represent single differentiated species. These taxa apparently colonized the islands and differentiated considerably from their ancestors but did not undergo subsequent speciation. The two raptors are the endangered Hawaiian Hawk or 'Io (*Buteo solitarius*) and an extinct accipiter-like harrier (*Circus dossenus*). The 'Io is currently restricted to the island of Hawai'i but has been found in fossil form on other islands (Olson and James 1991; S. Olson, pers. comm.). Like many other species of *Buteo*, the 'Io exhibits a light and a dark color morph. Preliminary phylogenetic analyses of more than 1,500 bp of mtDNA sequence in 18 species of *Buteo* (R. Fleischer, P. Cordero, C. McIntosh, I. Jones, and A. Helbig, unpubl. data) provides weak support for a clade containing the 'Io, the North American Short-tailed Hawk (*Buteo brachyurus*; to which it is least divergent; Fig. 2b), the North American

Swainson's Hawk (*Buteo swainsoni*; as suggested by Mayr 1943), and the endemic Galápagos Hawk (*Buteo galapagoensis*). The 'Io does not have a close relationship with any Old World *Buteo* we assessed. The Kimura 2-parameter (Kimura 1980) corrected sequence divergence from *Buteo brachyurus* is only $1.4 \pm 0.8\%$ for part of cyt *b*. We have no molecular data for the extinct and highly modified *Circus*.

The Laysan Duck (*Anas laysanensis*) is a relatively differentiated, small duck whose very small and vulnerable wild population inhabits only the tiny leeward island of Laysan. It has been consistently classified as either a subspecies of the Hawaiian Duck (*Anas wyvilliana*), hereafter referred to as Koloa, or of the Mallard (*Anas platyrhynchos*) on the basis of morphology and allozyme data (see Amadon 1950, Livezey 1991, Browne et al. 1993). Recent DNA analyses (Cooper et al. 1996; J. Rhymer, unpubl. data), however, have strongly countered the above scenarios, indicating instead that the Laysan Duck is differentiated from the Koloa and Mallard and may be more closely aligned with the South Pacific Black Duck (*Anas superciliosa*) clade. The Koloa, on the other hand, does cluster closely with the North American Mallard or Mottled Duck (*Anas fulvigula*) clades. Analyses of mitochondrial control region sequences of subfossil bones (Cooper et al. 1996) have also revealed that the Laysan Duck occurred in the main Hawaiian Islands well into the period of Polynesian settlement, and in forested habitats and higher elevations (>1,500 m) not considered typical for a dabbling duck. The level of mitochondrial control region sequence divergence between the Laysan Duck and its closest outgroup taxon is about 10%; overall mtDNA divergence is lower than this (J. Rhymer, unpubl. data).

The fourth "nonradiating" species, the 'Elepaio (*Chasiempis sandwichensis*), is polytypic at the subspecies level and occurs on the islands of Kaua'i, O'ahu, and Hawai'i (enigmatically, no fossils have been found of this species on Maui Nui; James and Olson 1991). The 'Elepaio is likely related to Polynesian flycatchers in the genus *Monarcha* (Mayr 1943, Amadon 1950) and is one of the few species for which differentiated subspecies have been identified on a single small island (Hawai'i; Pratt 1980). Molecular analyses of each island subspecies may, however, reveal differentiation sufficient to elevate them to species level.

PROBABLE RECENT COLONIZATIONS

Several taxa show little phenotypic divergence from mainland outgroups, suggestive of a very recent colonization (Table 1). These include the Black-necked Stilt (*Himantopus mexicanus knudseni*), Hawaiian Coot (*Fulica alai*), Common Moorhen (*Gallinula chloropus sandvicensis*), Koloa, Black-crowned Night Heron (*Nycticorax nycticorax hoactli*), an eagle (*Haliaeetus*), and the Short-eared Owl. Of these, only the Black-crowned Night Heron is not currently considered to be distinct from mainland forms at the subspecies or species levels, but the Short-eared Owl, in spite of its subspecific designation, is thought to be a post-Polynesian colonist (Olson and James 1991).

The Common Moorhen, Hawaiian Coot, Black-crowned Night Heron, and Short-eared Owl are extremely similar morphologically to outgroup relatives (Amadon 1950), but no DNA data currently exist with which to assess the age of their splits. As noted above, the Koloa is a very close relative of the Mottled Duck and Mallard (<3% mitochondrial control region divergence; Cooper et al. 1996). The endemic subspecies of the Black-necked Stilt differs from North American Black-necked Stilts (*H. m. mexicanus*) by only about 1.5 + 0.6% sequence divergence in 447 bp of mtDNA control region (R. Fleischer et al., unpubl. data). The North American Black-necked Stilts are considered to be the closest mainland relatives on the basis of morphology. Cyt *b* and 12S rRNA sequences from a subfossil bone of the extinct eagle (*Haliaeetus* sp.; Fleischer et al. 2000) are not different from the Old World White-tailed Eagle (*H. albicilla*), and the two species differ by 1.5% for the ATPase8 gene. Skeletal characteristics could not differentiate the Hawaiian eagle bones from either White-tailed Eagle or Bald Eagle (*H. leucocephalus*; Olson and James 1991). Thus, for at least three of these seven taxa the supposition of a recent split from a mainland ancestor and recent arrival in the islands is supported by the molecular data.

SUMMARY: GEOGRAPHIC ORIGINS AND TEMPORAL FRAMEWORK

Above we summarize recent molecular systematic studies of the Hawaiian avifauna. We use these data to infer, if possible, the closest living relatives and the geographic origins of the Hawaiian taxa we sampled. Our biogeographic analyses indicate (Table 1) that at least 9 or 10 of the ≥ 21 independent lineages appear to be of North American or at least Western Hemisphere origin, 4 appear to be of South Pacific or Australasian origin, 2 or 3 are of Asian origin, and 5 are of currently unknown geographic origin. Thus Mayr's (1943) conclusion that about half the Hawaiian avifauna is of American origin is still supported by our molecular data.

We found a relatively low level of molecular divergence between the Hawaiian taxa and their closest non-Hawaiian (mostly mainland) relatives (i.e., from zero to 10.3% sequence divergence for 14 lineages). Based on these results, none of these Hawaiian lineages split from mainland ancestors earlier than about 6.4 Ma. In fact, most of our estimates, although rough and lacking meaningful standard errors, fall well within the period of formation of the current set of main islands (i.e., Kaua'i at 5.1 Ma and later, Fig. 1). Only the drepanidines (10.3%), the corvids (8.4%), and perhaps the moa-nalos (6.9%) and the thrushes (6.7%) have Kimura 2-parameter sequence divergences from mainland relatives that suggest colonization prior to even the formation of O'ahu (3.7 Ma), and in each of these cases we may not have obtained sequence for the closest mainland outgroup (which we may not have sampled or it might be extinct). The overall picture suggests that while native Hawaiian *Drosophila* (Beverley and Wilson 1985, Thomas and Hunt 1991, DeSalle 1992, Russo et al. 1995) and lobeliads (Givnish et al. 1995) may have colonized the archipelago well before the formation of Kaua'i, thus far we have little evidence that any bird lineages have done so.

These findings lead us to consider factors beyond simple isolation by distance and the anthropogenically induced Holocene extinction that may help to explain Hawai'i's low primary avian diversity. First, the unique geology of the islands (Carson and Clague 1995) results in a situation in which individual islands have a limited "lifespan" (~5–7 Ma) as a high island. Lineages that have colonized older islands, but for some reason cannot succeed onto younger islands, will be ultimately lost as their island disappears into the sea (this may be especially true for forms that have evolved to be flightless). There may be reduced chance for taxonomic diversity to build up over long evolutionary periods relative to archipelagos with longer surviving islands. Secondarily, what secondary enrichment of avifaunal lineages by speciation that does occur in the islands may allow "niches" to be filled (perhaps by now locally adapted taxa) such that they are no longer available for occupation by new (and not locally adapted) colonists from elsewhere. Thus, primary diversity could be reduced by competitive exclusion. Continued paleontological research in the islands combined with studies of DNA sequence variation should help us to address these hypotheses. We hope these new fossils and sequences will continue to shed light on the systematics, biogeography, and timescale of avian evolution on the Hawaiian conveyor belt.

ACKNOWLEDGMENTS

We thank C. Tarr, S. Olson, H. James, E. Paxinos, A. Cooper, B. Slikas, J. Rhymer, B. Arbogast, S. Conant, M. Sorenson, T. Quinn, A. Helbig, I. Jones, A. Driskell, and T. Pratt for information concerning and discussion of many of the topics covered in this paper, and C. Tarr, B. Slikas, J. M. Scott, reviewer #1, and especially H. James for comments on an earlier draft of the manuscript. Samples for many of our analyses were provided by museum or field collections of tissues and we gratefully acknowledge the cooperation of C. Kishinami and A. Allison (B. P. Bishop Museum), S. Conant (University of Hawai'i), F. Sheldon (Louisiana State University), M. Robbins and B. Slikas (Academy of Natural Sciences-Philadelphia), P. Bruner (Brigham Young University-Hawai'i), E. Bermingham (Smithsonian Tropical Research Institute), S. Olson, P. Angle, and M. Braun (U.S. National Museum), R. Cann (University of Hawai'i), S. Rowher and S. Edwards (Burke Museum), and C. Cicero (Museum of Vertebrate Zoology-Berkeley). We greatly appreciate permission from Dave Swofford to use PAUP* (a gem of a program). Funding for many of the results presented above was provided by the Smithsonian Institution Scholarly Studies Program, Friends of the National Zoo, U.S. National Science Foundation, U.S. Fish and Wildlife Service, the National Geographic Society, and the Biological Resources Division of the U.S. Geological Survey.

Studies in Avian Biology No. 22:61–67, 2001.

EVOLUTIONARY RELATIONSHIPS AND CONSERVATION OF THE HAWAIIAN ANATIDS

JUDITH M. RHYMER

Abstract. The Hawaiian Duck or Koloa Maoli (*Anas wyvilliana*), hereafter referred to as Koloa, and Laysan Duck (*A. laysanensis*) are two endangered species of waterfowl in the mallard complex that are endemic to the Hawaiian Islands. These nonmigratory, nondimorphic species were thought to be derived from stray migratory, sexually dimorphic common Mallards (*A. platyrhynchos*), that subsequently lost the dimorphic plumage character. Laysan Ducks currently occur only on the tiny island of Laysan, while Koloa are found on Oʻahu, Hawaiʻi, and, primarily, Kauaʻi. Recent ancient DNA analysis shows that subfossil bones in deposits on the Big Island, Hawaiʻi, belong to the extant Laysan Duck. Similar fossils have been found on many of the major Hawaiian Islands, indicating that the species was formerly more widespread. Because of extensive hybridization between introduced Mallards and Koloa and the superficial morphological similarity between the Hawaiian taxa, their taxonomic status and phylogenetic relationships have been controversial. The perception that they may be subspecies of the Mallard, or even conspecific, has influenced their recovery programs. Molecular analyses indicate that Koloa and Mallard are distinct but very closely related species, whereas the Laysan Duck is very distinct from either. Some of the nondimorphic species in the mallard complex, such as the Laysan Duck, may have evolved from a nondimorphic ancestor rather than the common Mallard. Repeated bottlenecks, inbreeding, and small population size have likely contributed to a loss of genetic variation in the Laysan Duck, but it is now possible to plan a captive breeding program to preserve remaining variation for possible reintroduction of the species to other previously occupied Hawaiian Islands. Hybridization with Mallards is one of the factors contributing to the decline of Koloa on Oʻahu and Hawaiʻi. The Kauaʻi population represents a stronghold for the species, but thorough census data and basic information on the ecology of Koloa on Kauaʻi, essential for developing a specific conservation plan, are not available.

Key Words: *Anas laysanensis*; *Anas platyrhynchos*; *Anas wyvilliana*; ancient DNA; hybridization; molecular phylogeny; reduced genetic variation; species limits.

The Laysan Duck (*Anas laysanensis*) and Hawaiian Duck or Koloa Maoli (*A. wyvilliana*), hereafter referred to as Koloa, are endangered species of waterbirds endemic to the Hawaiian Islands. Laysan Ducks are restricted to the tiny 370 ha island of Laysan in the northwestern Hawaiian chain. They survived a severe bottleneck in the early part of the century, as their population was estimated to have plummeted to fewer than 10 individuals by 1911 (Moulton and Weller 1984). This precipitous population decline was caused by overhunting and by habitat destruction by introduced rabbits. A ban on hunting plus extermination of the rabbits allowed numbers of Laysan Duck to rebound to about 500 birds over the next few decades, but a severe drought in 1993 reduced the population to fewer than 150 individuals (Cooper et al. 1996), an indication of the extreme vulnerability of this species. Harsh environmental conditions on Laysan Island likely represent less than optimal habitat for the Laysan Duck.

Recent analysis of DNA isolated from late Holocene subfossils, found in lava tubes in forested habitats at elevations as high as 1,800 m on Hawaiʻi, indicates that they are Laysan Duck (Fig. 1), an indication that the species was once found elsewhere in the Hawaiian Islands (Cooper et al. 1996). Similar subfossil anatid speci-

mens found on Oʻahu, Kauaʻi, and Molokaʻi suggest that the range of Laysan Ducks was once more widespread. This situation is not unique: remains of over 30 other, now extinct, passerine and nonpasserine avian species of late Holocene age have also been found on Kauaʻi, Oʻahu, Molokaʻi, Maui, and Hawaiʻi (James and Olson 1991, Olson and James 1991). These prehistoric avian extinctions are attributed primarily to predation by Polynesians and introduced predators and to habitat destruction (Olson and James 1991). It may be possible to reintroduce Laysan Ducks to other islands, provided predators such as rats, mongoose, feral cats, and dogs are controlled and wetland and upland nesting habitats are protected.

Koloa once occurred on all the major islands in the lower Hawaiian chain except Lānaʻi and Kahoʻolawe (Griffin et al. 1989). The only substantial population is now found on the island of Kauaʻi, in montane areas and on the Hanalei National Wildlife Refuge. There are a few birds on Oʻahu, but hybridization with introduced common Mallards (*A. platyrhynchos*) is a serious problem there (Browne et al. 1993). The total population of Koloa has been roughly estimated at 2,500 birds, (2,000 on Kauaʻi-Niʻihau, 300 on Oʻahu, 25 on Maui and 200 on Hawaiʻi; Engilis and Pratt 1993), but in reality, there are few

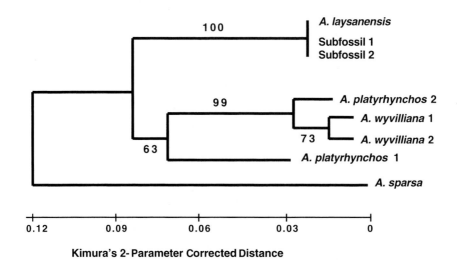

FIGURE 1. Neighbor-joining tree obtained with MEGA, based on Kimura's 2-parameter corrected distances using mtDNA control region sequences (after Cooper et al. 1996). Bootstrap values are shown. Sequences from Holocene subfossils are compared to those of extant Hawaiian anatids.

good data from which to estimate their current population size. Surveys do not cover montane streams and wetlands where most birds reside. In fact, little is known about their breeding ecology, reproductive success, movements, and annual habitat requirements. Specific conservation action has been limited, except for sporadic releases of captive-reared birds on O'ahu, Maui, and Hawai'i, which have had marginal success. Current recovery plans call for wetland protection and management and removal of the threat of hybridization (USFWS 1985). Management will include water level control, predator control, minimizing disturbance, improved census techniques, and monitoring of contaminants and avian disease.

The Laysan Duck and Koloa are thought by some to be derived from perhaps two waves of stray migratory Mallards that became isolated on the Hawaiian Islands and subsequently lost the Mallard's sexually dimorphic plumage (Weller 1980). They represent 2 of 14 closely related, nonmigratory, sexually nondimorphic species and subspecies in the worldwide mallard complex of waterfowl. The taxonomic status of many species in this complex has been controversial (e.g., Johnsgard 1961, Palmer 1976, Young and Rhymer 1998), and the specific status of Laysan Ducks and Koloa are no exception (Weller 1980). Detailed morphological analysis of the genus *Anas* by Livezey (1991) placed *wyvilliana* and *laysanensis* as sister species within a northern hemisphere mallard clade, not suprising given their close geographic distribution and small body size; they are about one-half to two-

thirds the size of common Mallards. Livezey (1991) considered them to be full species, as did Berger (1972) and the American Ornithologists' Union (AOU 1983). In other studies, their status has variously been described as (1) both Laysan Duck and Koloa as subspecies of the Mallard (Delacour and Mayr 1945, Johnsgard 1978, Weller 1980); (2) Koloa as a subspecies of Mallard, but Laysan Duck as a full species (Ripley 1960); (3) Koloa as a full species with Laysan Duck as a subspecies of Koloa (Brock 1951b, Griffin et al. 1989); and (4) Laysan Duck as a full species that evolved from Koloa (Warner 1963).

Three issues have been raised that have important implications for conservation of the Laysan Duck and Koloa: (1) recognition of species limits—are the Laysan Duck and Koloa distinct species from one another and from the common Mallard and, therefore, more worthy of protection? (2) hybridization with introduced species—what is the extent of hybridization with introduced Mallards and is it a possible threat to the species' integrity of Koloa? (3) loss of genetic variation—have small population size and population bottlenecks led to a loss of genetic variation in Koloa and Laysan Duck? These issues are addressed using molecular genetic analyses of mitochondrial and nuclear DNA.

METHODS

MOLECULAR ANALYSIS

As part of a larger study of phylogenetic relationships in the mallard complex of species, blood and/or muscle or heart tissue samples were collected from common Mallard (North America, N = 28; Europe, N

= 20); Koloa (Kaua'i, N = 19), Laysan Duck (founders of captive flock, Smithsonian Conservation Research Center, N = 15), African Black Duck (*A. sparsa*), the nondimorphic sister species to the mallard complex (Cooper et al. 1996, Johnson and Sorenson 1998, J. Rhymer, unpubl. data; captive flock, Wildlife Preservation Trust, N = 1); and Green-winged Teal (*A. crecca*; N = 2) as an outgroup (Johnson and Sorenson 1998). DNA was isolated from each sample using standard procedures (Rhymer et al. 1994).

Mitochondrial DNA (mtDNA)

The two most variable domains of the mitochondrial control region (631 base pairs, bp, from the 5′ and 3′ regions) were amplified using primers developed for waterfowl (Cooper et al. 1996). DNA sequencing was done on an ABI automated sequencer (model 373A) and sequences were aligned using Geneworks® (IntelliGenetics, Inc.) and by eye.

Single-copy nuclear DNA (scnDNA)

Five μg of DNA from each individual were digested with 10 enzymes that recognize six-base sequences. Fragments in digested samples were separated on 0.7%-1.2% agarose gels and transfered to nylon membranes (MSI Magnagraph) via Southern (1975) blotting. One avian oncogene, v-*myc* (Alitalo et al. 1983) and five anonymous single-copy nuclear DNA (scnDNA) clones were used as probes, for a total of 30 probe/enzyme combinations. Anonymous scnDNA clones were obtained using standard procedures (Quinn and White 1987a, Parsons et al. 1993). Two hundred ng of probe were labeled with ^{32}P for each hybridization, and membranes were then exposed to Kodak XAR film for 24−72 hours.

Amplified fragment length polymorphisms (AFLP)

The amplified fragment length polymorphisms (AFLP) technique is based on the detection of genomic restriction fragments by polymerase chain reaction (PCR) amplification, which produces fingerprints without prior sequence knowledge (Vos et al. 1995). Protocols provided with the AFLP™ Analysis System I and AFLP Starter Primer Kit (GibcoBRL) were followed. Briefly, this includes an initial restriction digestion of 150 ng genomic DNA with *Eco*R I and *Mse* I, followed by ligation of *Eco*R I and *Mse* I adapters, amplification of the restriction fragments, labeling of an *Eco*R I primer with [γ^{33}P]ATP, reamplification with the labeled *Eco*R I primer and an *Mse* I primer, and separation of labeled, amplified fragments on a 6.0% denaturing polyacrylamide sequencing gel. Primers used were *Eco*R I (AAG) with *Mse* I (CAG), and *Eco*R I (AA) with *Mse* I (CAA).

DNA fingerprinting with minisatellites.

Five μg DNA were digested with *Hae* III, fragments were separated on agarose gels, and were then transferred to nylon membranes via Southern blotting using standard procedures (Loew and Fleischer 1996). Membranes were hybridized with ^{32}P labeled Jeffrey's 33.15 minisatellite probe and exposed to Kodak XRP-1 x-ray film for 24 hours.

STATISTICAL ANALYSES

Phylogenetic relationships using mitochondrial DNA control region sequences were estimated using maximum parsimony (PAUP 3.1.1; Swofford 1993) and the neighbor-joining algorithm (Saitou and Nei 1987) with Kimura's 2-parameter model (MEGA 1.01; Kumar et al. 1993). One thousand bootstrap replications were performed to estimate robustness of tree topologies and decay indices (the number of additional steps in the shortest tree(s) without a given node) were also calculated (Bremer 1988). For AFLPs, alleles at polymorphic loci were scored as 1 (present) or 0 (absent), and the resulting data matrix was also analyzed using maximum parsimony. A strict consensus of most parsimonious trees was calculated.

For scnDNA data, genetic distances were estimated for each pair of species according to Nei's (1987) method for unmapped fragment data, using the analysis package RESTSITE (v1.1; Nei and Miller 1990), which allows for the inclusion of multiple individuals of each taxon analyzed with several probe/enzyme combinations. Relationships among species were estimated using the neighbor-joining method. Data were not available for an outgroup for either AFLP or scnDNA analyses.

Two methods were used to estimate genetic diversity within species. First, band-sharing coefficients were calculated from Jeffrey's 33.15 minisatellite DNA data, comparing unrelated individuals of Mallards (N = 5), Koloa (N = 5), and Laysan Ducks (N = 5) on the same gel. Second, proportion of polymorphic loci (P) were calculated for each species using AFLPs, as the number of loci at which the most common allele had a frequency of less than 0.95 divided by the total number of individuals in the sample.

RESULTS

RECOGNITION OF SPECIES LIMITS

Phylogenetic analysis of mtDNA control region sequences indicate that there are two divergent lineages of common Mallards in the world (Figs. 1 and 2), one that has a Holarctic distribution (Mallard 1) and one that is apparently found only in North America (Mallard 2; Young and Rhymer 1998). The Koloa is very closely related to the Mallard, particularly lineage 2 (as are the other North American nondimorphic mallard species, the Mottled Duck, *A. fulvigula,* and American Black Duck, *A. rubripes*; J. Rhymer, unpubl. data). Divergence of Laysan Duck from the Koloa/Mallard clade is well supported (Fig. 2).

The occurrence of two divergent mtDNA Mallard lineages suggests either retention of an ancestral polymorphism or hybridization among taxa in North America. One of the problems that can arise from analysis of maternally inherited mtDNA is the possibility that the gene tree is not congruent with the species phylogeny (Avise et al. 1990). This possibility prompted analysis of biparentally inherited nuclear DNA molecular markers (scnDNA and AFLPs) to determine if

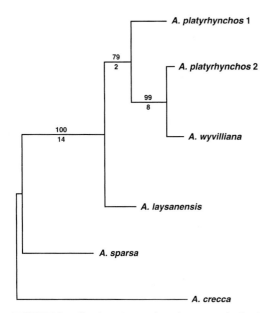

FIGURE 2.　Single most parsimonious tree obtained with PAUP 3.1.1, relating mitochondrial control region sequences for *A. platyrhynchos, A. wyvilliana, A. laysanensis* and *A. sparsa* (length = 127, CI excluding uninformative characters = 0.73, RI = 0.70). Tree rooted with *A. crecca* as an outgroup. Branch lengths are proportional to the number of inferred changes along each branch. Decay indices are shown below each node; bootstrap values are shown above

relationships among species suggested by the mtDNA results would be upheld. Only one lineage of Mallards was found at the nuclear level and both nuclear DNA datasets support the very close relationship between the common Mallard and the Koloa (Figs. 3 and 4). The divergence between Laysan Duck and Koloa was also highly repeatable, regardless of the nuclear DNA method employed.

HYBRIDIZATION WITH INTRODUCED SPECIES

Based on morphology, many of the Koloa-like birds on O'ahu appear to be hybrids. However, hybrid individuals are increasingly difficult to identify morphologically after more than one or two generations of backcrossing to one of the parental species (e.g., Rhymer et al. 1994). Molecular methods provide an unambiguous assessment of the extent of hybridization and introgression between species. One putative Koloa/Mallard hybrid has been analyzed with mtDNA and nuclear markers so far. This individual was phenotypically similar to Koloa but possessed a Mallard 2 mitochondrial haplotype. Analysis of nuclear DNA using AFLPs indicates that the hybrid is indistinguishable from Koloa (Fig. 4). These data suggest that the hybrid individual was not an F1 but a backcross into the Koloa. Further, because mtDNA is inherited only from the female parent, whereas AFLP loci are biparentally inherited, these data also indicate that the initial cross involved a female Mallard hybridizing with a male Koloa.

LOSS OF GENETIC VARIATION

There is considerably less mtDNA haplotype diversity in both Hawaiian and Laysan Ducks than in the Mallard. Five to ten haplotypes (with minor changes) have been found in each of the two Mallard lineages (Avise et al. 1990; J. Rhymer, unpubl. data), whereas only two haplotypes are found in the Koloa and one in Laysan Duck (Fig. 1). Analyses of minisatellite DNA and AFLPs also indicate an apparent loss of variation in Laysan Ducks (Table 1). Average numbers of scorable bands for the Jeffrey's 33.15 probe were similar for Mallards and Koloa but much reduced in Laysan Ducks. Similarly, band-sharing coefficients for Mallards and Koloa are within the range (0.2–0.5) for unrelated individuals in outbred avian populations (Haig and Avise 1996), while those for unrelated Laysan

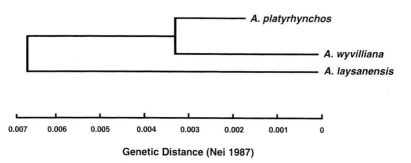

Genetic Distance (Nei 1987)

FIGURE 3.　Neighbor-joining tree obtained with RESTSITE 1.1, based on scnDNA data using Nei's (1987) distances for unmapped restriction sites for *A. platyrhynchos, A. wyvilliana,* and *A. laysanensis*

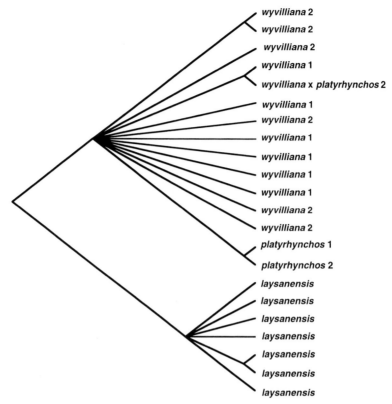

wyvilliana 2
wyvilliana 2
wyvilliana 2
wyvilliana 1
wyvilliana x platyrhynchos 2
wyvilliana 1
wyvilliana 2
wyvilliana 1
wyvilliana 1
wyvilliana 1
wyvilliana 1
wyvilliana 2
wyvilliana 2
platyrhynchos 1
platyrhynchos 2
laysanensis
laysanensis
laysanensis
laysanensis
laysanensis
laysanensis
laysanensis

FIGURE 4.   Strict consensus of 53 most parsimonious trees relating variation in AFLP loci of the two Mallard mtDNA lineages (*platyrhyncos* 1 and 2), Koloa (*wyvilliana* 1 and 2 refer to mtDNA haplotypes), and Laysan Duck (*laysanensis*). Several individuals are included to illustrate variation within and among taxa. One putative Koloa x Mallard hybrid with a Mallard 2 mtDNA haplotype clusters with Koloa, suggesting a backcross individual

Ducks were extremely high (> 0.8; Table 1). On two AFLP gels, the proportion of polymorphic loci (P; corrected for sample size) in Laysan Ducks was only about one-tenth that of Mallards with Koloa intermediate to the other two species (Table 1).

TABLE 1.   COMPARISON AMONG SPECIES OF NUMBER OF SCORABLE BANDS ($\pm$ SE) AND BAND-SHARING COEFFI-CIENTS (S), BASED ON JEFFREY'S 33.15 MINISATELLITE PROBE AND PROPORTION OF POLYMORPHIC LOCI (P), BASED ON AFLP DATA

| | Minisatellite DNA | | | AFLP[a] | |
| | # scorable bands | | | | |
	N	($\pm$ SE)	s	N	P
Mallard	5	42.8 $\pm$ 0.60	0.22–0.40	4	0.097
Koloa	5	43.4 $\pm$ 0.62	0.30–0.51	16	0.049
Laysan Duck	5	34.6 $\pm$ 0.26	0.82–0.90	10	0.014

[a] 104 of 401 scorable AFLP bands were variable.

DISCUSSION

Genetic analyses of both Laysan and Koloa provide insights into problems with systematics, hybridization, and loss of genetic variation of these endangered species that have important consequences for their conservation. Small body size of the two Hawaiian species places them together in recent systematic treatments based on detailed morphological analyses (Livezey 1991, 1993), but some plumage characters of the Koloa are more similar to Mallard than to Laysan Duck. Adding to the taxonomic confusion, however, are results of a recent allozyme study that showed a deep split between Mallard and Koloa (an order of magnitude greater than all anatid and most other avian congeneric genetic distances previously observed; Avise and Aquadro 1982), but virtually no differences between Laysan Duck and Koloa (Browne et al. 1993). In contrast, the analyses of mtDNA and nuclear DNA in this study show that the divergence of Laysan Duck from a Koloa/Mallard clade is robust, whereas the Koloa and Mallard are very closely related (with only a few species-specific diagnostic markers). It is possible that the anomalous protein results stem from the analyses of different tissue types in different samples, which could artificially inflate estimates of divergence among taxa.

Using a clock calibration of about 8% sequence evolution per million years (calculated for the more variable 5′ end of the mitochondrial control region by Sorenson and Fleischer 1996), it is estimated that the Koloa may have diverged from the North American lineage of Mallards (Mallard 2) as recently as 130,000 years ago, but from the Holarctic lineage (Mallard 1) as long ago as 0.8 million years ago (Ma). Divergence of the Laysan Duck from both common Mallard lineages, as well as from the Koloa, also appears to be on the order of 0.8 Ma. The evolution of these species from *A. sparsa* (about 1.7 Ma) is well supported even when all 14 species and subspecies in the mallard complex are included in the analysis (J. Rhymer, unpubl. data). In addition, some species in the mallard complex, such as the Laysan Duck, may well have evolved from the nondimorphic ancestor rather than the common Mallard (Fig. 2; see also Johnson and Sorenson 1998, Young and Rhymer 1998).

Confusion over the taxonomy and evolutionary history of these species has been compounded by the propensity of introduced Mallards to hybridize whenever possible with some of the nondimorphic species in the mallard complex, e.g., Grey Duck (*A. superciliosa*) in New Zealand (Rhymer et al. 1994), Black Duck and Mottled Duck in North America (Johnsgard 1967, Mazourek and Gray 1994), and the former Mexican Duck (*A. diazi*; Hubbard 1977). Extensive hybridization with introduced species can lead to a kind of genetic extinction of rare native flora and fauna (Rhymer and Simberloff 1996). As a result, the specific status of the taxa involved can be called into question, with important consequences for the protection of some endangered species (Meffe and Carroll 1994, Avise and Hamrick 1996). Nevertheless, current thinking does not consider the retained ability to interbreed as sufficient evidence to preclude specific status and protection (O'Brien and Mayr 1991, Rhymer and Simberloff 1996).

Hybridization between Koloa and introduced Mallards on Oʻahu has been so extensive that this population is no longer considered to have pure Koloa. Removal of the threat of hybridization is an essential component for the species recovery (USFWS 1985). As an aside, the contention that hybridization between Mallards and closely related nondimorphic species occurs primarily because females of the nondimorphic species are more attracted to the colorful Mallard male was not upheld in a detailed study of New Zealand Grey Ducks and introduced Mallards (Rhymer et al. 1994), and the same appears true for Koloa. Only one known Koloa x Mallard hybrid has been analyzed so far and this individual resulted from a Mallard female x Koloa cross. More importantly, there is a population of Koloa on Kauaʻi that is largely unaffected by hybridization, so far. Knowledge of the potential threat and the availability of diagnostic molecular markers can now help to monitor incursion of hybridization on this island. Apart from guarding against hybridization, detailed studies of Koloa ecology are of the utmost importance in understanding its population dynamics. It is the Kauaʻi population that will provide a stronghold for the Koloa, so it is suprising that little is known about the ecology of this endangered species. Captive breeding programs and/or translocations are a final resort. It is better to understand the species' ecology in planning the prevention of further declines.

The Laysan Duck is in an even more precarious situation with fewer than 150 individuals surviving the drought of 1993 (Cooper et al. 1996). In this case, a captive breeding program seems warranted. Results of mitochondrial and nuclear DNA analyses indicate that repeated bottlenecks, inbreeding, and/or low population numbers have probably contributed to a loss of genetic variation in this species. Only one mitochondrial haplotype remains and the number of minisatellite DNA bands and polymorphic loci (using AFLPs) is reduced compared to that found for either the Koloa or the Mallard. High levels of band sharing among apparently unrelated individuals suggest a history of inbreeding, similar to those observed in another species of endangered Hawaiian waterfowl, the Nēnē (*Branta sandvicensis*; Rave et al. 1994). Although few empirical data are available showing a direct link between loss of genetic variation (as indicated by molecular markers) and fitness (Lynch 1996), it is generally understood that adaptive evolutionary change is the primary means of responding to selective challenges (i.e., genetic variation is important for isolated species to adapt to environmental perturbations). All indications are that the beleaguered Laysan Duck does not adapt well to the harsh environmental conditions on Laysan Island. A captive program should be undertaken to reintroduce the Laysan Duck to other islands, provided predators are controlled and the habitat protected. It is now possible to plan a captive breeding program to maximize maintenance of the remaining genetic variation in this species (e.g., Haig et al. 1990).

We now know what the conservation issues are for the endangered Koloa and Laysan Duck and genetic considerations provide one starting point for developing comprehensive strategies to ensure their protection.

ACKNOWLEDGMENTS

I want to thank R. Fleischer for his encouragement over the years to work on the Hawaiian anatids. DNA fingerprints, using Jeffrey's 33.15 probe, were done in his lab at the National Zoological Park, while I was supported on a Smithsonian Institution Visiting Scientist Fellowship through the Migratory Bird Program. Thanks to A.J. Jeffrey for the use of his 33.15 mini-satellite probe. Also thanks to H. James and S. Olson for thought provoking discussions of evolution in Hawaiian waterfowl. Special thanks to D. Heckel for his encouragement, for allowing me the use of his lab at Clemson University for mtDNA sequencing and AFLP analysis, and for support through an NSF EPSCoR grant to University of South Carolina. I also want to thank L. Gahan for her expert advice on AFLP technology and E. Beedle for running sequences. The scnDNA RFLP analysis was done as part of a larger project on the North American mallard species complex at the Smithsonian Institution's Laboratory of Molecular Systematics under the direction of M. Braun, while I was supported on a Smithsonian Institution Molecular Evolution Postdoctoral Fellowship. I owe a deep debt of gratitude to the late Trish Sawaya for her many hours of enthusiastic and patient tutelage in lab techniques during that time.

Studies in Avian Biology No. 22:68–80, 2001.

THE INTERPLAY OF SPECIES CONCEPTS, TAXONOMY, AND CONSERVATION: LESSONS FROM THE HAWAIIAN AVIFAUNA

H. Douglas Pratt and Thane K. Pratt

Abstract. The Hawaiian Islands, with their unique geological history and geographic position, provide an excellent natural laboratory in which to evaluate currently competing biological (BSC) and phylogenetic (PSC) concepts of the species. Although the BSC as historically applied in archipelagic situations is shown to be flawed in producing overlumped polytypic species, it nevertheless remains the preferable concept for most practical purposes. A review of the taxonomic history and species limits in Hawaiian birds under both concepts reveals that, when properly applied, the BSC yields a species total remarkably close to that produced under the PSC, contrary to what many proponents of the latter have supposed. We propose that the widespread adoption of the PSC for conservation purposes is potentially harmful. The PSC trivializes the species taxon and introduces new problems of deciding when a population becomes diagnosable, the possibility that species could appear and disappear in a reticulate fashion, and the likelihood that genetically diagnosable but phenotypically identical, and therefore not field identifiable, populations could be ranked as species. All of these problems negatively impact such things as constructing credible and politically defensible lists of endangered species, the prioritization of limited conservation resources, and the gathering of field data. We contend the BSC is arguably a more rational concept that better supports the activities of both scientific and nonprofessional observers. Biological species limits in oceanic archipelagoes worldwide need to be reevaluated using modern concepts and technologies before rational conservation decisions can be made.

Key Words: avian conservation; biological species; endangered species; Hawaiian Islands; phylogenetic species; polytypic species; species limits.

Avian systematists have recently joined in a great debate over the definition of species. The long-accepted biological species concept (BSC) of Mayr (1942a) has been challenged by a new one from the field of phylogenetic systematics, usually called the phylogenetic species concept (PSC). As defined by Cracraft (1983), a phylogenetic species is a population or cluster of individuals "diagnosably different from other such clusters, and within which there is a parental pattern of ancestry and descent." Because diagnosability can be established by "any feature or set of features, ranging from single fixed nucleotide substitutions to major phenotypic (but genetically based) features" (Zink and McKitrick 1995), the PSC would elevate virtually all isolated subspecies to species and add many more based on small populations with one or more distinctive traits. Zink and McKitrick (1995) and Zink (1997) summarized the debate and argue in favor of the PSC, whereas Mayr (1992), with recent support from Snow (1997) and Collar (1997), defended the BSC. For popular overviews of the controversy, see Myers (1988) and Sibley (1997).

Many might regard this debate as purely academic. Recently, however, some conservationists have suggested that the PSC would better serve their purposes than the BSC, showing that such esoteric pursuits do, indeed, have relevance in the "real world." Hazevoet (1996) has even charged that the BSC "promotes the extinction of endangered birds," by classifying many distinctive island forms as subspecies. Because conservation efforts often focus only on "full" species (Collar et al. 1994), there is some validity to Hazevoet's claim. In this review, we use the avifauna of the Hawaiian Islands to demonstrate: (1) that proper application of the BSC in archipelagic situations can produce a species list much closer to one based on the PSC than has been previously appreciated; (2) that the BSC itself is sound and that the many problems with it cited by some conservationists and systematists arise from misapplication of the concept rather than weaknesses of it; and (3) that the PSC suffers from its own problems in practice such that a shift to it could be worse for conservation than maintaining the BSC (Collar 1997).

Because Hawai'i is the most isolated oceanic archipelago, with numerous large and ecologically varied islands, it has long been regarded as a superb natural laboratory for the study of evolution and biogeography. With the possible exception of Galápagos's birds, Hawai'i's is the best studied of any insular avifauna, and represents a much later stage of evolution than that of Darwin's younger islands, with a much higher level of endemism. Unfortunately, the Hawaiian Islands have also suffered considerably more ecological degradation (for a review, see Pratt 1994; Van Riper and Scott *this volume*) than the Galápagos and have more extinct and endangered birds than any comparable region. They also have the largest component of introduced species of any modern avifauna (Long 1981), but we will show that even alien birds can teach evolutionary lessons on islands. Thus Hawai'i's birds provide all the necessary ingredients for evaluating the relationship of the competing species concepts to each other and to conservation. They further provide an important counterpoint to Hazevoet's (1995) use of the Cape Verde Islands avifauna as evidence of the need to abandon the BSC.

AVIAN TAXONOMY IN HAWAI'I

Most recognizable forms of Hawaiian birds were first described as separate species under the Linnean typological or morphological species concept. Even some forms no longer regarded as subspecies were so described (e.g., the three populations of *Hemignathus virens wilsoni*; Wilson and Evans 1890–1899). All authors of the "classical period" of Hawaiian bird research (Wilson and Evans 1890–1899, Rothschild 1893–1900, Bryan 1901, Henshaw 1902a, Perkins 1903) used a morphological species concept, although all were evolutionists. Perkins's (1903) "family tree" of the Hawaiian honeycreepers, an endemic taxon variously ranked as the Drepanididae, Drepanidinae, or Drepanidini, was the first phylogenetic treatment of any Hawaiian birds. After the flurry of ornithological research in the islands around the turn of the twentieth century, a period of neglect ensued, with only a few scattered notes and papers on Hawaiian birds appearing over the next four decades, and avian taxonomy remained static.

Elsewhere during this quiescent period, systematists, with ornithologists prominent among them, were formulating the "modern synthesis" that culminated in Mayr's (1942a) classical definition of the biological species that has been memorized by generations of biologists. The BSC is operational, rather than morphological, and is based on the ability or inability of populations to interbreed freely. It introduced the concept of polytypic species (comprising several subspecies) for clusters of morphological "species" that could or would interbreed in nature. It thereby created the vexing problem of how to classify distinctive isolated (allopatric) forms whose ability or willingness to interbreed cannot be objectively demonstrated. Mayr (1942a) suggested the use of "potential isolating mechanisms" to gain inferences as to what might happen during a hypothetical future period of contact. He also suggested that systematists look to the degree of difference between related sympatric species as a guideline to evaluate allopatric forms in a given group. We will show that

properly applied, these precepts lead to species lists that can be corroborated by other procedures, such as phylogenetic analyses and genetic studies. However, early practitioners of the BSC too often ignored their own fundamental guidelines and engaged in hasty lumping of vaguely similar forms. One wag has dubbed the period "Lumparama." In many cases, no reasons other than general similarity and geographic separation were ever stated for lumping closely related forms previously considered separate species (see numerous examples in Mayr and Short 1970). It was taxonomy by decree.

Virtually all mid-century authors treated geographically replacing island populations the same as such populations on continents, even when differences were striking and consistent. However, subsequent genetic studies (e.g., Boag 1988) showed that island colonization is a unique phenomenon that differs fundamentally from the kind of isolation that results from habitat fragmentation, glacial cycles, and other continental phenomena. Diamond (1977) showed that speciation differed on islands as compared to continents, but his study suffered from the state of knowledge of the time in that several assumptions he made about Hawai'i in particular (e.g., that intraisland subspeciation has not occurred on islands smaller than New Zealand, but see Pratt 1980; that the Hawaiian Crow, *Corvus hawaiiensis*, represents a single colonization with no subsequent intra-archipelagal dispersal, but see Olson and James 1982b) have been shown to be false. The failure to appreciate the different character of insular allopatry was a basic misunderstanding that contributed to overlumping many island taxa.

The problem was exacerbated by Mayr's (1942a, 1969) clearly stated belief that allopatric populations of uncertain status should be considered subspecies. The "when in doubt, lump" precept may be appropriate for closely related isolates on continents (Snow 1997), but we will show that for traditional studies of archipelagic speciation, exactly the opposite bias ("when in doubt, split") is more likely to result in a species list that will stand up to independent corroboration. Indeed, every recent study of strikingly marked insular "subspecies" of which we are aware has revealed potential behavioral or ecological isolating mechanisms to support recognition of the forms as separate biological species. Although Mayr (1942a) introduced the concept of the superspecies for strongly differentiated allopatric species (allospecies), he stated that (p. 170): "It would be an abuse of this concept if an author were to call every polytypic species, composed of insular and thus well-marked subspecies, a superspecies." Again, it now appears that the real abuse of the superspecies concept is its under use in insular situations. Subsequently, Sibley and Monroe (1990) modified the Mayrian definitions for the BSC and recognized many well-marked island "subspecies" as allospecies. Even Mayr himself (E. Mayr and J. Diamond, unpubl. data) has elevated many of his earlier (Mayr 1945) subspecies to allospecies.

The first review of the Hawaiian avifauna to apply the "modern synthesis" was that of Bryan and Greenway (1944), who combined many geographically replacing morphological species. Amadon (1950) carried the process further, lumping many strikingly differentiated island forms into large polytypic species (his work dealt mainly with the honeycreepers, but he reviewed the other land and freshwater species in an appendix). His classification exemplifies mid-century evolutionary thinking. For example, Amadon (1950) considered plumage color relatively unimportant as an isolating mechanism, despite the fact that birds are highly visual organisms. The de-emphasis of coloration as a guideline to species limits was undoubtedly influenced by numerous hybridization studies during the period that lumped such different-looking continental forms as the three North American flickers (*Colaptes* spp.; Short 1965), the various "dark-eyed" juncos (*Junco* spp.; Mayr 1942b), "Black-crested" and Tufted titmice (*Baeolophus* spp.; Dixon 1955), Australian magpies (*Gymnorhina* spp.), silvereyes (*Zosterops* spp.), and many others (reviewed by Ford 1987), the "Northern" orioles (*Icterus* spp.; Sibley and Short 1964), Black-headed and Rose-breasted grosbeaks (*Pheucticus* spp.; West 1962), Eastern and Spotted towhees (*Pipilo* spp.; Sibley and West 1959), and numerous others. Some of these studies have withstood subsequent scrutiny, but many have not. The trend of the era led to lumping of such other taxa as Glossy and White-faced ibises (*Plegadis* spp.; Palmer 1962), Palearctic and Nearctic Green-winged Teal (*Anas* spp.; Delacour and Mayr 1945), "Black-shouldered" kites (*Elanus* spp.; Parkes 1958), the three "yellow-bellied" sapsuckers (*Sphyrapicus* spp.; Howell 1952), and Holarctic rosy-finches (*Leucosticte* spp.; Mayr 1927, French 1959), based solely on inference rather than actual studies. Most of the latter lumpings have subsequently been shown to be erroneous or ill-advised. We will show that, among Hawaiian birds, behavioral and genetic studies virtually always support the premise that those that *look* different, *are* different. Interestingly, although Amadon (1950) was applying the BSC, his work largely ignored the relatively little biological data available at the time and was based almost entirely on museum skins. But his study was state-of-the-art, and we should not be surprised that some of his polytypic "species" have subsequently been shown to be amalgams of several biological species (see section on 'Alauahios below). Amadon's (1950) classification of Hawaiian birds remained the standard for three decades.

The 1970s saw a renaissance in ornithological field studies in Hawai'i. Many observers, including the authors, confronted by overwhelming potential isolating mechanisms among many very strikingly marked "subspecies," began to question Amadon's (1950) taxonomy. H. Douglas Pratt conducted a complete review of available data from a variety of lines of inquiry and combined it with new information on vocalizations (Pratt 1996b), foraging behavior, nesting habits, and ecology to produce the first complete taxonomic revision of the endemic avifauna (Pratt 1979) since Amadon (1950). First appearing in a dissertation, his classification was the basis of that published by Berger (1981), who did not accept all of Pratt's splits at the species level. Berger's (and hence most of Pratt's) taxonomy was then adopted by the American Ornithologists' Union (AOU) Check-list (AOU 1983), which has been followed by most subsequent authors. Pratt et al. (1987) adopted all of Pratt's (1979) species limits, and in a series of papers expanding on his dissertation, Pratt (1982, 1987, 1989, 1992b) defended them, and all were eventually adopted by the AOU (1985, 1991, 1993, 1995).

Shortly after H. Douglas Pratt's work became widely known, another new classification appeared in the form of a review of recently discovered subfossil Hawaiian bird remains (Olson and James 1982b). As further discoveries came to light, these authors revised their classification and presented an updated version in tabular form (Olson and James 1991). Their arrangement of genera differs irreconcilably (Conant et al. 1998, Pratt *this volume*) with that of Pratt (1979) and the AOU Check-list (AOU 1998) as revised, but at the species level the two classifications differ only slightly and could eventually agree totally. In a footnote, Olson and James (1991) expressed the view that "distinctive, allopatric, insular forms" are best regarded as species. Their species-level taxonomy is thus the closest yet to application of the PSC to the Hawaiian avifauna.

During the 1970s, the first systematic studies of Hawaiian birds using the new technique of cladistics appeared. Raikow's (1977, 1986) anatomical studies produced the first cladistic phylogeny of Hawaiian honeycreepers (Pratt [1979] was influenced by this technique, but his first classification was not strictly cladistic). Since then, virtually all analyses of Hawaiian bird evolution have been cladistic. Until recently, cladistic methods did not affect decisions at the species level, but the PSC is itself an outgrowth of cladistic thinking (Cracraft 1983, Zink 1997). The recent split of the Oʻahu ʻAmakihi (*Hemignathus flavus*; see below) was based solely on a reconstruction of phylogenetic history through the study of mitochondrial DNA and shows that some decisions by proponents of the BSC come surprisingly close to PSC reasoning. Among Hawaiian birds, genetic studies at the molecular level have usually supported species limits determined by more traditional methods and are an important independent corroboration of them (Johnson et al. 1989; Tarr and Fleischer 1993, 1995; Fleischer et al. 1998). Indeed, many recent splits were not accepted until biochemical data supported them, but such data are not, in the operational sense of the BSC, biological (Greenwood 1997). Rather, biochemical systematists may base their decisions on the Mayrian technique of comparing degrees of difference, in this case genetic, between allopatric forms and those between related sympatric ones, or on measurements of the length of time allopatric populations have been evolving independently. Thus they implicitly subscribe to the BSC but deal with data that are outside the realm of traditional isolating mechanisms.

THE SPECIES OF HAWAIIAN BIRDS

The following is a review of all historically known Hawaiian land and freshwater birds and one nesting seabird whose species limits have been controversial. It shows that a near consensus on species limits has developed during the past decade. All lines of inquiry have contributed to it, and the result is a species list, based on the BSC, that differs little from one based on the PSC. It also suggests that in practice, application of the PSC is not as simple as it first appears.

Hawaiian Petrel

The Hawaiian petrel breeds in barren alpine zones of the Hawaiian Islands, with the main colony near the summit of Haleakalā on Maui. The birds' range at sea is poorly documented, but they are believed to remain in the central Pacific near Hawaiʻi year-round (Pratt et al. 1987). From the earliest days of its discovery, the similarity of the Hawaiian Petrel to the Dark-rumped Petrel (*Pterodroma phaeopygia*) of the Galápagos was obvious, and virtually all taxonomists regarded it as an allopatric subspecies *P. p. sandwichensis*. With the advent of technology that allowed detailed vocal comparisons of the two populations, differences in voice became apparent. Tomkins and Milne (1991) suggested that these differences were sufficient to be regarded as isolating mechanisms between species, and Sibley and Monroe (1993) recognized the Hawaiian Petrel (*P. sandwichensis*) as distinct. This case demonstrates a longstanding and increasing appreciation among BSC proponents of vocalizations as isolating mechanisms. Recently, strong genetic divergence of the two petrels was demonstrated using allozyme electrophoresis (Browne et al. 1997) and as yet unpublished mtDNA studies (G. Nunn fide R. Fleischer, pers. comm) had similar results. Because of their genetic diagnosability and geographic separation, the two forms would clearly qualify as phylogenetic species.

Endemic Ducks

The Hawaiian Islands have two endemic ducks that are apparent derivatives of the Mallard (*Anas platyrhynchos*). The form *wyvilliana* (Hawaiian Duck, hereafter referred to as Koloa) is known historically from the main islands, whereas *laysanensis* was historically restricted to Laysan. Both endemics were originally described as separate species, but Bryan and Greenway (1944), Munro (1944), and Amadon (1950) considered them conspecific but distinct from the Mallard. Delacour and Mayr (1945) lumped them all. For the next two decades most authors (e.g., Brock 1951a, Bailey 1956, Warner 1963) followed the former taxonomy, but Ripley (1960) advocated species status for the Laysan Duck while keeping the Koloa a subspecies of Mallard. Alternatively, Berger (1972) considered both endemics full species, whereas Weller (1980) again lumped both with the Mallard. Virtually all of these varied treatments resulted from subjective treatment of morphological characters with little consideration given to some rather obvious potential isolating mechanisms. For example, Mallards and their relatives are notorious hybridizers, especially in captivity. Yet Ripley (1960) indicated that captive Laysan Ducks failed to hybridize with Koloa when they had the opportunity. In a recent survey of waterfowl collections worldwide, only three of 46 collections holding Laysan Ducks reported that *laysanensis* hybridized with another duck species (M. Reynolds, pers. comm.). Ripley (1960) further described numerous ecological peculiarities of the Laysan Duck, but based his taxonomic reasoning solely on morphological characters such as distinctive downy plumage. For the Koloa, Pratt (1979) pointed out that migratory ducks form pair bonds on the wintering grounds, a fact overlooked by previous treatments of this complex. Koloa breed year-round (Swedberg 1967) and form pairs within sight of occasional wild Mallards. Swedberg (1967) further states that even on small ponds the local ducks tend to avoid wintering migrants, another obvious behavioral isolating mechanism. The near total genetic swamping of Koloa by domestic Mallards on O'ahu (Browne et al. 1993) does not negate the inference gained from earlier, more natural situations. Species status for the two endemic ducks is now also supported by both laboratory and paleontological studies. Browne et al. (1993), using allozyme electrophoresis, proposed that *A. wyvilliana* and *A. laysanensis* are sister taxa, separate from *A. platyrhynchos*. Discovery of subfossil remains of what appeared to be *laysanensis* on the main Hawaiian Islands (Olson and Ziegler 1995) suggested prehistoric sympatry with *wyvilliana*. Sequencing of mtDNA from the subfossil bones (Cooper et al. 1996, Cooper 1997, Rhymer *this volume*) indicated that they were close to the Laysan Duck but not the Koloa, strongly suggesting former sympatry. Rhymer's (*this volume*) results differ from those of Browne et al. (1993) in showing a close Mallard/Koloa relationship, with the Laysan Duck very distinct genetically. Whatever their phylogeny, these three forms appear to be good species under virtually any species concept.

HAWAIIAN COOT

All authors after Bryan and Greenway (1944) considered the Hawaiian Coot a subspecies of the American Coot (*Fulica americana*) until Pratt (1987) showed that its differences were of the same degree as those of other allospecies of the worldwide coot superspecies, and involved characters important in species recognition. He suggested it be classified as *F. alai* as originally described, and was followed by Sibley and Monroe (1990), Olson and James (1991), and the AOU (1993). Because it has consistent diagnostic characters that distinguish it from other coots, the Hawaiian Coot is also a phylogenetic species.

HAWAIIAN STILT

Like the coot, the endemic stilt of the Hawaiian Islands has been regarded by most authors as a subspecies of its North American counterpart, the Black-necked Stilt (*Himantopus mexicanus*). It is behaviorally quite similar but has many distinctive plumage features (Pratt et al. 1987) as well as adaptations to the unique Hawaiian environment. Mayr and Short (1970) recognized eight species of stilt in the superspecies *H. himantopus,* including the Hawaiian *H. knudseni,* rather than engage in "partial dubious lumping with insufficient knowledge." They stated that some forms "will undoubtedly prove

conspecific," and virtually no one followed their split. Olson and James (1991), without comment, ranked the Hawaiian Stilt as a full species. In light of what we now know about discrete plumage differences as indicators of relationship among island birds, that decision was probably sound. Under the PSC, the Hawaiian Stilt would unquestionably be a separate species because of its diagnostic plumage differences, and now molecular data (Fleischer and McIntosh *this volume*) show large genetic divergence as well. It likely is a valid biological species.

HAWAIIAN SOLITAIRES

The relationship of the Hawaiian thrushes (Turdinae) to the American solitaires (*Myadestes*) was hypothesized by the earliest researchers (Stejneger 1887, 1889) but was not generally accepted until Pratt (1982) reviewed and amplified the evidence supporting it. This classification has subsequently been corroborated by new osteological comparisons (Olson 1996) and genetic studies (Fleischer and McIntosh *this volume*). The various forms exhibit only slight variation in plumage, but differ strongly in bill morphology and vocalizations. They might all have been considered conspecific except for the fact that two of them are sympatric on Kaua'i. The smaller of those, the Puaiohi (*M. palmeri*), has always been considered a separate species, but mid-century workers regarded all the others as conspecific. Pratt (1982) documented the vocal differences mentioned by early researchers and showed by playback experiments that these were effective isolating mechanisms, at least between the Kāma'o (*M. myadestinus*) of Kaua'i and the 'Ōma'o (*M. obscurus*) of Hawai'i. The status of the then rare (and probably now extinct) form of Moloka'i (see Reynolds and Snetsinger *this volume*) and the extinct forms of O'ahu and Lāna'i had to be assessed by inference. Pratt (1982) recognized the Oloma'o (*M. lanaiensis*) as a species on the basis of its reportedly distinctive song. He found that the named subspecies on Lāna'i (nominate) and Moloka'i (*M. lanaiensis rutha*) could not be differentiated on the basis of plumage, but maintained the subspecies because of a reported difference in vocal behavior. Munro (1944) reported that the Moloka'i bird sang and the Lāna'i one did not. This difference disappeared, however, when Oloma'o on Moloka'i fell silent as they became rare and thinly distributed (pers. obs. based on reports of various field workers). Although the bird has been observed, its song has not been heard for decades. Because the O'ahu specimens had been lost, Pratt (1982) only tentatively recognized the 'Āmaui (*M. woahensis*) as an additional species. Following rediscovery of the two known specimens of the latter, Olson (1996) re-evaluated the O'ahu form and considered it a subspecies of *M. lanaiensis* pending comparison with subfossil remains from Maui (which lost its solitaire before the arrival of ornithologists). He emended the name to *M. lanaiensis woahensis*. If this arrangement stands up to further scrutiny, it will represent a pattern of speciation unique in the Hawaiian Islands. Whether the three populations of Oloma'o are phylogenetic species is difficult to say, given our limited knowledge of them, but the O'ahu form has a stronger claim to status under the PSC than the other two because of its slightly different coloration and longer period of isolation (Moloka'i and Lāna'i were joined with Maui to form Maui Nui during the last glaciation).

'ELEPAIOS

Hawai'i's monarchine flycatchers comprise the endemic genus *Chasiempis* and are distributed on Kaua'i (*sclateri*), O'ahu (*ibidis*; formerly *gayi* but see Olson 1989), and Hawai'i (*sandwichensis*), but are enigmatically absent from the Maui Nui cluster. The three island forms are strikingly different in coloration, but their voices, ecology, and general behavior are rather similar. Also, *sandwichensis* exhibits considerable intraisland variation and has three named forms (nominate, *ridgwayi,* and *bryani*) with zones of intergradation (Pratt 1980). The three major forms were first lumped by Bryan and Greenway (1944), and until very recently no one had challenged that classification. Pratt (1980) regarded them as megasubspecies (Amadon and Short 1976) to emphasize the two different levels of differentiation. Reflecting their previously stated beliefs about distinctive island forms, Olson and James (1991) recognized three species without elaboration, and Olson (1996) maintained that classification. Conant et al. (1998) were the first to document behavioral and ecological differences among 'elepaios. They showed that the obvious and diagnostic plumage differences are reinforced by other, more subtle potential isolating mechanisms. Conant et al. (1998) recommended biological species status for the Kaua'i 'Elepaio (*C. sclateri*), O'ahu 'Elepaio (*C. ibidis*), and Hawai'i 'Elepaio (*C. sandwichensis*), and we endorse their conclusion.

Whether the three subspecies of the Hawai'i 'Elepaio would be considered phylogenetic species is problematical because some of their observed intergradation may be primary and clinal rather than secondary (Pratt 1980). The three forms were presumably in constant genetic contact in the recent past, but because of habitat destruction the very distinctive Mauna Kea population (*C. sandwichensis bryani*) is now an isolate (Scott et al. 1986) with distinctive ecology as well as plumage. Preliminary studies of one zone of intergradation between *C. sandwichensis bryani* and *C. sandwichensis ridgwayi* on the southeastern flank of the mountain have found evidence of secondary contact with possibly some assortative mating (E. VanderWerf, pers. comm.). Thus *C. sandwichensis bryani* may be in the very earliest stage of speciation by the BSC. In a PSC view, none of the three intraisland variants would be recognized taxonomically while they remained in genetic contact, but presumably "*C. bryani*" is now a phylogenetic species.

MILLERBIRDS

The only Old World warblers (Sylviinae) native to the Hawaiian Islands are restricted to the Northwestern Hawaiian Islands. The extinct Laysan Millerbird (*Acrocephalus familiaris*) and the endangered Nihoa Millerbird (*A. kingi*) have long been considered conspecific, but Olson and Ziegler (1995) split them without elaboration. Biological support for such a split is presented by Morin et al. (1997), although they maintained the single species. Certainly the differences between them are of the same degree as those existing between other Pacific island *Acrocephalus* (Pratt et al. 1987), and separate species status is probably warranted. They clearly are phylogenetic species. The question has more than academic significance because of recent proposals to introduce Nihoa Millerbirds to Laysan (M. P. Morin and S. L. Conant, pers. comms.). If they are a different species from the original Laysan bird, the proposal should perhaps be reconsidered.

DREPANIDINE FINCHES

The finches of Laysan and Nihoa present an instructive example of differing appearance as an indicator of biological isolating mechanisms. They differ strikingly in overall size as well as relative size of bill. Plumages are similar but diagnostically different with females more divergent than males. Amadon (1950) and other midcentury authors regarded them as conspecific, but Banks and Laybourne (1977) split them after reporting very different molt and maturational sequences. Other authors (e.g., Ely and Clapp 1973, Clapp et al. 1977) reported differences in nesting behavior, and Pratt (1979, 1996a) described vocal differences. Because of the many potential isolating mechanisms, all recent authors have recognized both Laysan Finch (*Telespiza cantans*) and Nihoa Finch (*T. ultima*) as both biological and phylogenetic species. Recently, proof of biological species status was reported by James and Olson (1991), who found fossil remains of both species together on Moloka'i. Genetically, the two differ to the degree expected between pairs of closely related but biologically distinct species (Fleischer et al. 1998). These finches are one of many examples in which plumage differences that were dismissed by mid-century workers accurately predicted biological species status.

'AMAKIHIS

This is a group of small, black-lored olive green birds with down curved, short bills. The extinct Greater 'Amakihi (*Hemignathus sagittirostris*) of the island of Hawai'i had a longer, straighter bill and was probably a close relative, although some authors place it in the monotypic genus *Viridonia*. The 'Anianiau (*H. parvus*), a Kaua'i endemic, has a shorter, straighter bill and rather different coloration and, despite its occasional designation as "Lesser 'Amakihi," is probably not very closely related. Conant et al. (1998) reevaluated the morphological data and placed the 'Anianiau in the monotypic genus *Magumma,* and Fleischer et al. (1998) found genetic evidence to support their treatment. Both of these birds appear to have influenced the evolution of "typical" 'amakihis by character displacement: the Hawai'i form *H. virens virens* has the shortest bill in the complex, whereas the Kaua'i 'Amakihi (*H. kauaiensis*) has the longest (Pratt 1979). Mid-century authors regarded all typical 'amakihis as conspecific but almost always noted the much larger bill of the Kaua'i bird. The bill is both longer and heavier with virtually no overlap in measurements with any other form (Conant et al. 1998). The larger bill results in different feeding behavior and general ecology. Vocalizations of the Kaua'i 'Amakihi are also distinctive (Pratt et al. 1987, Pratt 1996b). Nevertheless, Berger (1981), and the AOU (1983), failed to follow Pratt's (1979) split. After biochemical data (Johnson et al. 1989, Tarr and Fleischer 1993) corroborated Pratt's findings, the split was accepted (AOU 1995), although the Check-list Committee cited no "traditional" data in support of the change. Conant et al. (1998) summarized the numerous potential isolating mechanisms of the Kaua'i 'Amakihi.

Surprisingly, Tarr and Fleischer's (1993) analysis of restriction-site variation in mtDNA showed that the O'ahu 'Amakihi (*H. chloris*), which had never been considered a biological species in modern times, was genetically distant from the morphologically, ecologically, and vocally similar 'amakihis of Maui Nui and Hawai'i. Furthermore, their evidence indicated that the O'ahu birds were the sister taxon to *H. kauaiensis* and therefore could not be conspe-

cific those of Maui Nui and Hawai'i. On this basis, the AOU (1995) accorded the O'ahu 'Amakihi species status. Then Fleischer et al. (1998) altered their earlier branching-sequence hypothesis as the result of a new analysis involving sequencing of mtDNA. They now believe the O'ahu taxon is, after all, sister taxon to the Maui/Hawai'i forms. Still, the genetic distance between the O'ahu 'Amakihi and its sister taxa is of the same order of magnitude as that between the Kaua'i and Maui/Hawai'i forms, so the species status of the O'ahu 'Amakihi is valid. This example shows why caution is dictated in making taxonomic innovations based solely on a single genetic study. The AOU (1995) decision, though now upheld for different reasons, could easily have proven incorrect and may have been premature.

Interestingly, the only clue that the O'ahu bird might be a separate species prior to the DNA studies was its distinctive plumage. Again, the character considered least important by mid-century workers was, in fact, the most telling. Male O'ahu 'Amakihi are more yellow below and more strikingly two-toned than other 'amakihis, with the typical pale eyebrow reduced to a small supraloral spot. Females are even more distinctive in being much less yellow or olive than others and especially in retaining as adults the pale wingbars seen in juveniles of all forms. O'ahu 'Amakihi can be distinguished from those of other islands with virtually 100% accuracy on plumage characters alone. Vocal differences, such as a higher pitched song (Pratt 1996b), may also exist but have not been adequately investigated.

The same cannot be said of the remaining two forms. Separate names were originally proposed for the populations on Moloka'i, Lāna'i, and Maui, but both Amadon (1950) and Pratt (1979) found them inseparable. As a group they differ on average from Hawai'i birds in coloration and bill length (longer), but overlap is so broad that only extreme individuals could be diagnosed on characters alone (Pratt 1979). Thus they form a biological subspecies *H. virens wilsoni*. Whether practitioners of the PSC would consider this form a species is unclear because despite their obviously divergent histories, they are not completely diagnosable on phenotypic characters.

'AKIALOAS

'Akialoas look like giant 'amakihis with extremely long bills. All forms are extinct, making biological assessment difficult. Forms are known historically from Kaua'i, O'ahu, Lāna'i, and Hawai'i, but those from the central islands are known only from a handful of specimens. Their classification has produced a nomenclatural tangle (Olson and James 1995), and their systematics is as yet unsettled. Most authors (e.g., Berger 1981, AOU 1983, Pratt et al. 1987, Sibley and Monroe 1990) follow Pratt (1979) in placing 'akialoas in a large genus *Hemignathus* defined on the basis of a suite of synapomorphies (Conant et al. 1998) in coloration, plumage sequence, and degree of sexual dimorphism, bill shape, and vocalizations, but Olson and James (1995) segregate them in their own genus *Akialoa.* (For a defense of "greater" *Hemignathus,* see Conant et al. 1998). At the species level, the situation is historically complicated. Bryan and Greenway (1944) lumped all forms, but Amadon (1950) recognized two species on the basis of the strikingly different relative bill lengths of the Kaua'i and Hawai'i forms. Having seen only two immature specimens of the Lāna'i form and none of the O'ahu one, he included both with the shorter-billed Hawai'i birds as *Hemignathus obscurus* and separated the Kaua'i 'Akialoa (*H. procerus* emended to *H. stejnegeri* by Olson and James 1995). Pratt (1979) and Olson and James (1982b) showed that the Lāna'i and O'ahu 'akialoas were actually closer to the Kaua'i 'Akialoa in bill length, and lumped all forms again. The AOU (1983), however, maintained Amadon's (1950) split. Pratt et al. (1987: 302) reviewed the situation and pointed out that if two species are recognized, the line of separation had to go between Lāna'i and Hawai'i with resultant nomenclatural changes. They suggested the names Lesser 'Akialoa (*H. obscurus*) for the Hawai'i bird and Greater 'Akialoa (*H. ellisianus*) for the other three forms; the AOU (1997) eventually adopted this two-species classification.

But the situation is complicated by recent paleontological data. James and Olson (1991) described a second species of 'akialoa, *H. upupirostris,* from Kaua'i and O'ahu that was sympatric with the historically known forms. Additionally Olson and James (1995) reported two sympatric prehistoric 'akialoas from Maui and a larger species sympatric with the Lesser 'Akialoa on Hawai'i, all as yet undescribed. Because the relationships of these forms are unresolved, Olson and James (1991, 1995) recommend recognition of all described forms as species: Hawai'i 'Akialoa (*Akialoa* = *Hemignathus obscura*), Maui Nui 'Akialoa (*A. lanaiensis*), O'ahu 'Akialoa (*A. ellisiana*), Kaua'i 'Akialoa (*A. stejnegeri*), and Hoopoe-billed 'Akialoa (*A. upupirostris*). Interestingly, plumage variation among the historically known forms is of the same degree as that in several other groups or pairs of species (e.g., 'amakihis, Hawaiian solitaires, O'ahu and Maui 'alauahios) and is nonclinal (for illustrations of all forms, see Pratt in

press). This case, perhaps more than any other, shows the folly of the old "if in doubt, lump" dictum. Obviously, 'akialoas cannot all be conspecific no matter what their interrelationships turn out to be. Presumably, the five species delimited by Olson and James (1995) can be considered phylogenetic as well as biological.

NUKUPU'US

The three island forms of Nukupu'u and the 'Akiapōlā'au comprise another group of honeycreepers with long, hooked bills. Each was described in the 1800s as a separate species: *Hemignathus lucidus* from O'ahu, *H. hanapepe* from Kaua'i, *H. affinis* from Maui, and *H. wilsoni* from Hawai'i. Bryan and Greenway (1944) combined all four, but Amadon (1950) separated the 'Akiapōlā'au because of its unique straight, rather than decurved, lower mandible. This taxonomy was supported by Olson and James' (1994) morphological studies and discovery of a specimen of Nukupu'u supposedly from Hawai'i (Olson and James 1994), indicating possible sympatry. Thus the Nukupu'u and 'Akiapōlā'au cannot even constitute a superspecies. Since Amadon's (1950) work, systematists have ignored the nukupu'u complex, and the AOU (1983) considered the Kaua'i and Maui forms as subspecies of *H. lucidus.* With all three taxa extinct or nearly so, their classification must depend on careful study of the fewer than 100 specimens scattered among a dozen museums from Honolulu to Berlin. Ongoing studies by T. K. Pratt and J. K. Lepson (pers. comm.) reveal that measurements and coloration consistently, and in some cases strikingly, distinguish the three nukupu'us from each other. The PSC would certainly consider them three species, but it is likely that by the criteria of the BSC the same outcome would be reached. Fleischer et al. (1998) identified the nukupu'us as a good test case for seeking a match between genetic divergence and sequence of colonizing new islands as they emerge down the Hawaiian chain.

'ALAUAHIOS

These small warblerlike birds of the genus *Paroreomyza* are confined to the central islands of O'ahu and the Maui Nui complex. Despite extreme interisland color variation that ranged from brilliant scarlet to dull gray, Amadon (1950) considered the four named forms of *Paroreomyza* conspecific with the two species of *Oreomystis* from Kaua'i and Hawai'i. Certainly, the inclusion of the brilliant scarlet Kākāwahie (*P. flammea*) of Moloka'i, with yellow and green birds from O'ahu, Maui, and Lāna'i, should have been a red flag indicating the existence of more than one species. But Amadon

(1950:166) stated that "variation from yellow to red is obviously accomplished readily and need not be considered as necessarily indicating specific difference." Lumping the Moloka'i, Lāna'i, and Maui forms meant that their striking differences had to have evolved since the breakup of Maui Nui, a period we now know to have been as little as 10,000 years. In fairness, we should point out that such geological information was unavailable in the period in which Amadon (1950) worked. Pratt (1979) hypothesized that the fact that the Kākāwahie was the largest *Paroreomyza* and had the heaviest bill, and the Maui/Lāna'i form was the smallest with the smallest bill suggested character displacement during a period of sympatry on Maui Nui. Olson and James (1982b) found paleontological evidence of such sympatry and agreed that *Paroreomyza* had to comprise more than one species. The other two Maui Nui forms, known historically from Lāna'i (*montana*) and Maui (*newtoni*), are very similar, differing only in that the Lāna'i birds are slightly brighter dorsally. No one since Bryan and Greenway (1944) has ever suggested that they are other than a single biological species, the Maui 'Alauahio (*P. montana*), but whether they qualify as phylogenetic species is problematical. The slight but consistent color differences they exhibit, rather than evolving in 10,000 years, may represent fragments of a former interisland cline, such as that shown by 'elepaios on Hawai'i (Pratt 1980), in which paler birds inhabited the lower and drier parts of Maui Nui and darker ones the rain forests of Haleakalā. The relatively few specimens from west Maui do appear somewhat intermediate in dorsal coloration. Questions such as at what point the fragments of a former cline become phylogenetic species show that the PSC is not free of subjective judgments (Collar 1997, Snow 1997). The O'ahu 'Alauahio (*P. maculata*), now possibly extinct, was considered conspecific with the Maui/Lāna'i bird by Olson and James (1982b), but later (James and Olson 1991) they joined other authors in separating it. Its bill is intermediate between those of *P. flammea* and *P. montana* but the coloration of both males and females is clearly different and diagnostic (Pratt et al. 1987).

'ĀKEPA

Representatives of the drepanidine "crossbills" (*Loxops*) were known from Kaua'i, O'ahu, Maui, and Hawai'i, with a distinct taxon on each island. Most forms are small birds with yellow or gray bills, the males red or orange-yellow, the females gray-green, and neither sex with any bold black patterning or other markings. The Kaua'i form is so distinctive that it was at first placed in its own genus *Chrysomitridops* (Wilson 1890). It is larger, with a proportionally larger blue bill. Both sexes are patterned in yellow and green with a prominent dark mask and pale forehead, although males are brighter than females. Bryan and Greenway (1944) recognized two species of *Loxops*: *L. caeruleirostris* ('Akeke'e) for the Kaua'i form, and *L. coccineus* ('Ākepa) for the O'ahu, Maui, and Hawai'i forms. Despite the striking plumage differences, which he did not consider great, Amadon (1950) believed it "by no means improbable that they all would interbreed freely were their ranges to overlap" and considered them all conspecific. Pratt (1979) showed that the plumage and bill differences were paralleled by others in vocalizations, but his recommendation of a return to Bryan and Greenway's classification was not adopted by Berger (1981). Thus the AOU (1983) maintained Amadon's single species of 'Ākepa. Further research by Pratt (1989) and others (summarized by Lepson and Freed 1997, Lepson and Pratt 1997) revealed fundamental differences in nest construction and ecology. As a result, the AOU (1991) finally recognized the 'Akeke'e as a separate species. This is yet another case in which plumage differences predicted potential isolating mechanisms in other aspects of the birds' biology.

The status of the three named forms of 'Ākepa is less clear because the O'ahu form (*wolstenholmei*) is extinct and known from only a few specimens, and the Maui one (*ochracea*) is very rare if not extinct and was never common in historical times. Males of each form can be distinguished with near 100% accuracy on coloration alone, but females are more difficult to identify visually. Whether the color differences are sufficient isolating mechanisms, in the absence of other data, for recognition of O'ahu and Maui 'ākepas as biological species is moot (Pratt 1989), and their status as phylogenetic species is likewise unclear. Perhaps biochemical data, as yet unavailable, will reveal clearer differences.

'APAPANES

The 'Apapane (*Himatione sanguinea*) is found in montane forests throughout the main Hawaiian Islands with no geographic variation. A now extinct related form on low, unforested Laysan was long regarded as a subspecies, but Olson and James (1982b, 1991) regarded it as a species (*H. freethi*) without comment. Schlanger and Gillett (1976) had considered the Laysan Honeycreeper a relict of the days when Laysan was a high island, but Olson and Ziegler (1995) believed it to be a colonizer from the main islands that has speciated on Laysan. With distinctive coloration (orangish rather than bright crimson body feathering, dingy pale brown rather than white undertail coverts), a shorter bill, and distinctive cranial osteology, it is unquestionably a species under the PSC. Olson and Ziegler (1995) split it on the basis of unspecified osteological differences. Overlooked in most discussions are several obvious potential isolating mechanisms of the Laysan Honeycreeper: distinctive song and song phenology (Rothschild 1893–1900); different feeding behavior (including often walking on the ground to forage among flowers; Fisher 1903); different nest placement and structure (Schauinsland 1899, Bailey 1956); and, most obviously, totally different habitat. A previously unreported anatomical difference, noticed by H. Douglas Pratt in preparing illustrations (Pratt in press) is that the Laysan bird has differently shaped tips to its primaries, lacking or possessing in very reduced form the truncation that produces the 'Apapane's wing noise. It now appears highly unlikely that these birds, adapted to two different worlds, could successfully interbreed, much less do so freely. Although Fancy and Ralph (1997) considered it a subspecies, future authors, including Pratt (in press), will likely split it, bringing the BSC and PSC into agreement on 'apapanes.

SUMMARY

A wealth of new morphological, behavioral, ecological, and genetic data have dramatically changed the systematics and taxonomy of Hawaiian birds. For example, a comparison of Amadon's (1950) classification of Hawaiian honeycreepers with the one we outline above shows that for 40 named taxa, the number of biological species (if all that have been proposed are accepted) swells from 23 to between 34 and 38, the final figure depending upon the classification of 'ākepas and nukupu'us. Correspondingly, the number of taxa designated as subspecies has dwindled from 17 to 6 or as few as 2! These two poorly differentiated taxa (Maui Nui 'amakihi and Lāna'i 'alauahio) amount to small pickings indeed over which to debate the BSC versus PSC. The status of the 25 undifferentiated, and therefore unnamed, island populations ('Ō'ū [*Psittirostra psittacea*], 'Apapane, and 'I'iwi on six islands, the three Maui Nui 'amakihis, and 'Ākohekohe [*Palmeria dolei*] on Moloka'i and Maui) does not change. Likewise, the 19 named populations of songbirds that are not honeycreepers have increased from 10 to 15 species, with one subspecies sunk, one in dispute, and one subspecies of Hawai'i 'Elepaio intergrading clinally with the nominate race, and another isolated but with limited and, as yet, little understood secondary contact.

Why is interisland endemism at the species level so striking in Hawai'i? The answer lies partly in the geographical setting: the Hawaiian Archipelago comprises moderately large islands with relatively few offshore islets and atolls inhabitable by landbirds. Distances between main island groups average 58 km, a formidable crossing for most sedentary songbirds. Birds newly colonizing one island from another could become quickly isolated genetically by weight of numbers. Because the pool of potential immigrants on neighboring islands is much smaller than would be the case if the source area were a continent or much larger island, conspecifics would arrive infrequently, and in low numbers they would enter a resident population numbering in the hundreds of thousands at least. Thus, adaptation to local conditions would proceed almost immediately without significant genetic input from ancestral populations, and evolution of endemic forms could proceed rapidly (Freed et al. 1987a).

Grant (1994) found that Hawaiian native finches exhibit less variability in bill measurements than Galápagos finches and attributed the difference to greater specialization in feeding habits, greater genetic distance among species, and near absence of hybridization. All of these comparisons relate to the very different geologic history of Hawai'i (Fleischer et al. 1998) as compared to the Galápagos, a tighter cluster of islands of relatively much younger age (Grant 1986). Species saturation was achieved in both archipelagos primarily by adaptive radiation of descendants of very few successful transoceanic colonizations (Diamond 1977, Juvik and Austring 1979), but levels of differentiation fit each unique situation. Because Hawaiian bird populations become genetically isolated virtually from the start, they can quickly evolve differences in plumage and voice, both of which are effective isolating mechanisms. Thus they soon become both biological and phylogenetic species, with only a brief period of intermediacy. The most straightforward case of this has been proposed by Fleischer et al. (1998), who provide genetic data indicating that the four 'amakihis originated from interisland colonizations that followed shortly after emergence of new islands in a conveyor-belt fashion as the archipelago moved across a mid-ocean "hot spot."

Nevertheless, interisland colonizations in Hawai'i obviously proceeded in both directions to produce the species-rich faunas of each island as well as the several examples of intra-archipelagic double invasions (*Myadestes* on Kaua'i, *Paroreomyza* on Maui Nui, 'akialoas on several islands, etc.). Also, some Hawaiian birds are widespread in the islands with no detectable interisland variation. The three Maui Nui 'amakihis and the two populations of 'Ākohekohe are fragments that were panmictic during recent periods of lower sea level, but other undifferentiated populations belong to species that disperse widely with relatively frequent intra- and interisland movements. Despite huge historical populations and the widest geographic range possible, two of those, the 'Apapane and 'I'iwi, are among the least genetically diverse of honeycreepers (Tarr and Fleischer 1995, Jarvi et al. *this volume*). Both may have suffered recent severe genetic bottlenecks then expanded their populations and ranges, and the recently extinct 'Ō'ū, which has not been investigated genetically, probably exhibited the same pattern. Absence of interisland variability in five species of Hawaiian waterfowl reflects large scale interisland movements and reproductively cohesive populations, as confirmed by banding studies (Engilis and Pratt 1993). The fact that far-ranging species move in both directions shows that not all speciation in Hawai'i has resulted from Fleischer et al.'s (1998) conveyor belt. Virtually all oceanic island avifaunas, though always depauperate in number of species as compared to continental areas, have very high levels of endemism (Stattersfield et al. 1998). Isolated, geologically old archipelagos with large interisland distances, such as the Marianas, Carolines, Tuamotus, Marquesas, and many others, can be expected to exhibit species-level endemism comparable to that of Hawai'i as their avifaunas are re-examined for the presence of potential isolating mechanisms.

Reflecting upon the history of avian systematics and taxonomy in Hawai'i, we repeatedly see that coloration, long regarded as relatively insignificant in determining species limits, may be the first and most reliable indicator. Consistent, unique vocalizations or discretely different bill size or shape also virtually always correspond to interspecific boundaries. In every case in which species limits determined on these bases have been tested by biochemical or paleontological data, decisions based on an enlightened use of traditional phenotypic investigations have been upheld. Far from being single characters that identify species, appearance and vocalizations predict where other more subtle isolating mechanisms exist. Because the Hawaiian Islands could well be regarded as the quintessential oceanic archipelago, the lesson is clear: island birds that look or sound different are very unlikely to be conspecific. Allopatric populations that have only average rather than diagnostic differences are little diverged genetically and can be recognized as subspecies. The old prejudice that similar allopatric populations should be classed as subspecies until proven otherwise has not

withstood the test of actual practice on oceanic islands, and the underlying assumptions that produced it must now be questioned or discarded, at least for insular taxa. Properly applied to island endemics, the BSC produces species limits comparable to those of the PSC, and further allows for the recognition of subspecies, a category the PSC would essentially eliminate (Snow 1997, Zink 1997). Because the taxonomy of island birds elsewhere in the tropical Pacific is still based largely on studies done in the first half of the century, we can anticipate a major increase in the number of biological species recognized in the region when the data are re-evaluated with the insights gained from the Hawaiian experience. However, we caution future workers not to follow their predecessors in making taxonomic changes based solely on inference.

SPECIES CONCEPTS AND CONSERVATION

Our paper began with, and was largely prompted by, the conflict between the BSC and PSC as debated by Hazevoet (1996) and Collar (1996). Because of the Hawaiian Islands' extremes of location and geologic history, their birds define the issue better than any other isolated insular avifauna. However, the outcome is unexpected: most diagnosable, allopatric taxa can be argued to be biological species on the criteria that they either (1) are not sibling species, or (2) were formerly reproductively isolated in sympatry but now live apart in contracted, relictual ranges, or (3) are genetically and morphologically distinct to a degree similar to related biological species living in sympatry. A few recognizable taxa do not qualify by these criteria, but we question whether these are either truly diagnosable (e.g., Maui 'Amakihi) or evolutionary units (three subspecies of Hawai'i 'Elepaio).

Changing views of biological species limits in Hawai'i has had surprisingly little impact on the course of conservation efforts because the U.S. Endangered Species Act of 1973 does not focus on, nor limit endangered status to, full species only. No named Hawaiian taxon deserving increased protection was omitted from the list because of its designation as a subspecies. Although undiagnosable and unnamed populations were not considered federally, a few were included in an otherwise parallel list of populations protected by the state of Hawai'i. Actual recovery efforts have been less encompassing, however, and reflect the need to engage in triage. Faced with a depressing list of 32 endangered birds, 13 of them on the brink of extinction, state and federal agencies focused their limited personnel and funding on managing tractable species such as Nēnē (*Branta sandvicensis*), Koloa, Laysan Duck, Newell's Shearwater (*Puffinus auricularis newelli*), and Hawaiian Crow, or 'Alalā. Beginning in the 1980s, recovery efforts began to focus on restoration and protection of habitat, to the benefit of entire bird communities. In the mid-1990s, special programs were initiated for two more endangered birds, the Puaiohi and Poʻouli (*Melamprosops phaeosoma*). The fact that these projects were funded, and not one to restore the Hawaiʻi 'Amakihi on Molokaʻi, shows that even with a program that focuses on populations, conservationists' attentions in Hawaiʻi as well as worldwide (Collar 1997) are inevitably closely tied to the species concept.

On what few phenotypic or genetic characters should one describe a phylogenetic species? Recent introductions of the endangered Laysan Finch, with subsequent rapid evolution in bill size (Conant 1988a), present proponents of the PSC with some yet-to-be resolved issues. For example, do diagnosable populations that evolved through founder effects and local adaptation in only two decades qualify as phylogenetic species? If not, at what point would they? Further, if introductions result in the creation of populations that are diagnosably distinct (Conant 1988b), and therefore are "new" phylogenetic species, how can this technique contribute to the conservation of the parent population? A related situation is that some introduced birds in Hawaiʻi, such as House Sparrows (*Passer domesticus,* Johnston and Selander 1964), may already be phenotypically diagnosable. Conservationists are unlikely to regard such introduced populations as endemic phylogenetic species. As Fleischer (1998) has proposed, artificially fragmented populations of endangered species in Hawaiʻi could become diagnosable at the molecular level through genetic drift and presumably therefore qualify as phylogenetic species. Recovery actions cannot save endangered species when new "species" are created from recently fragmented or introduced populations.

A second problem with the PSC is the possibility that species can appear and then disappear in a reticulate fashion (Zink 1997) because their delimitation does not require genetic isolation. Consider again the example of the 'Elepaio on Mauna Kea. Because its range is almost exactly congruent with that of the endangered Palila (*Loxioides bailleui*), it will be strongly affected by efforts to restore habitat for that species. If plans to connect the upper forests of Mauna Kea (the range of *Chasiempis sandwichensis bryani*) with the rain forests of Hakalau Forest National Wildlife Refuge (where *C. s.*

ridgwayi occurs) succeed, broad contact between two now isolated forms of 'Elepaio, each a potential phylogenic species, could be re-established, resulting in extensive interbreeding. As our Hawaiian examples show, automatic splitting of all populations with diagnosable differences (Cracraft 1997) under the PSC is not as simple in practice as it sounds (Collar 1997) and could undermine the use of such time-honored and successful management techniques as reintroduction and habitat restoration. We agree with Collar (1997) that the PSC would trivialize the species concept and severely stretch limited resources without providing any rational basis for formulating conservation priorities.

Even when, as in the United States, conservation authorities are enlightened about the sometimes arbitrary way that species limits are applied and protect endangered populations of whatever status, alpha taxonomy is still far more than just an academic exercise. Much more is involved in the conservation of island birds than just the decision as to which ones are officially listed as endangered. Often, the only information available on birds of remote islands comes from recreational birders, who seek out endemic species and generally ignore those that are "just subspecies" (see for example Pratt 1990, Wauer 1990a,b). One can argue the rationality of that mindset, but no one can deny that in the eyes of recreational birders, conservationists, and the general public, species status has almost magical properties. It is quite possible that many island species worldwide could become endangered or extinct without anyone noticing because birders ignored forms ornithologists called subspecies. Witness the case of the Island Scrub-jay (*Aphelocoma insularis*) endemic to Santa Cruz Island off California. Few birders were even aware of its existence before it was recognized as a species, but almost immediately afterwards, a small industry developed for the sole purpose of enabling people to see the bird (Atwood and Collins 1997). Had this been an endangered species, we believe the increased population monitoring would have contributed data valuable to the bird's recovery. An example of the latter phenomenon is the case of Bicknell's Thrush (*Catharus bicknelli*). No one voiced concern about its conservation status until it was elevated to species status (Thurston 1998).

Attention from birders may be important even before a bird is listed as endangered. For example, the Oʻahu 'Elepaio was rarely sought out except on Christmas Bird Counts because, as a subspecies, it did not score differently with birders. Thus, its sudden population crash in the past two decades (Pratt 1994) went largely unnoticed. Now that it is a candidate for species status

(Conant et al. 1998) as well as for listing as an endangered species (Conant 1995), birders have become more interested (Pratt 1993), and research on the species has resumed (VanderWerf et al. 1997, VanderWerf 1998a). Now, young visitors to Honolulu's Hawai'i Nature Center have their own species of 'Elepaio and 'amakihi on which to focus their local pride and interest. The fact that ecotourists would visit a locality for the sole reason of observing an endemic bird, or that school children take pride in and learn about their local avian specialty, increases public awareness and interest, especially in small countries with limited resources (Wille 1991) in whose hands the fate of many species ultimately lies.

Collar (1997) cited the numerous valuable contributions of recreational birders to taxonomy through their worldwide travel, tape recording, photography, and note taking on breeding biology and general natural history and behavior. Janzen et al. (1993) even refer to birders as "parataxonomists" in recognition of their contributions. We support Collar's (1997) observation that birders are today the ornithologist's most important ally in clarifying species limits and conservation status of birds, and managers of parks and reserves should encourage and facilitate birding rather than discourage it as has all too often been the case in some Hawaiian reserves (Pratt 1993, pers. obs.).

Conservationists and the general public need a rational and observable basis for species recognition. By increasing the number of trivial look-alike "species" to a bewildering and overwhelming degree, adoption of the PSC could destroy scientific credibility with governmental officials and the general public who have little interest in or knowledge of the subtleties of taxonomic philosophy. The BSC makes intuitive sense through its use of observable isolating mechanisms and the subspecies category for intermediate stages, and provides a credible basis for conservation strategies. Although Hazevoet (1996) may be correct that "taxonomic neglect" promotes extinction of island birds, his proposed solution of switching to the PSC will actually increase such neglect by augmenting the taxonomic workload, providing a confused taxonomy for conservation practices (Collar 1997), and recognizing "species" that defy common sense. Besides, his main goal (increasing the number of recognized species on islands) can be accomplished within the BSC without all of the disadvantages of the PSC. Proper application of the BSC, including a long overdue review of the taxonomic status of island taxa worldwide, will do far more for avian conservation than adoption of the phylogenetic species concept.

ACKNOWLEDGMENTS

We thank J. M. Scott for the initial inspiration for this paper, and R. C. Fleischer for thought provoking comments and insights from his unpublished data. S. Conant, M. Morin, and M. Reynolds kept us apprised of current conservation efforts in the Northwestern Hawaiian Islands. J. K. Lepson and E. VanderWerf shared their unpublished museum and field observations with us. Colleagues J. V. Remsen and F. Sheldon contributed thoughts to our formulation of the species concept debate and commented on the manuscript.

Studies in Avian Biology No. 22:81–97, 2001.

WHY THE HAWAI'I CREEPER IS AN *OREOMYSTIS*: WHAT PHENOTYPIC CHARACTERS REVEAL ABOUT THE PHYLOGENY OF HAWAIIAN HONEYCREEPERS

H. DOUGLAS PRATT

Abstract. A Phylogenetic Analysis Using Parsimony (PAUP) of 39 phenotypic characters of myology, osteology, tongue morphology, bill morphology, plumage and coloration, behavior, and ecology produced a tree that strongly supports, with a few exceptions, current American Ornithologists' Union classification of Hawaiian honeycreepers (Drepanidinae). These results are compared with those from three different biochemical and genetics laboratories and those of a cranial osteology study. The honeycreepers, including the aberrant genera *Melamprosops* and *Paroreomyza,* are shown to be monophyletic and a subgroup of the Fringillidae. The Maui Parrotbill *Pseudonestor xanthophrys* is related to thin-billed taxa rather than to the drepanidine finches. The genus *Hemignathus,* the present limits of which have been widely challenged, is shown to be strongly supported by a large suite of characters, except that the parrotbill may belong in it and the 'Anianiau (*H. parvus*) should be removed from it and placed in its own genus *Magumma. Hemignathus* can be divided into four or five subgenera. The generic pairs *Chloridops/Loxioides, Himatione/Palmeria,* and *Vestiaria/Drepanis* can justifiably be lumped as *Loxioides, Himatione,* and *Drepanis* respectively. The genera *Paroreomyza* and *Oreomystis* are not closely related, and the latter includes the Hawai'i Creeper (*O. mana*). Synapomorphies of the two species of *Oreomystis* include: lack of adult sexual dimorphism; lack of wing-bars; distinctive juvenal plumages; bill shape and coloration; foraging behavior; flocking behavior; juvenal begging calls; and a simple, narrow, nontubular tongue unique among honeycreepers. Hypothesized relationships of the Hawai'i Creeper with 'ākepas (*Loxops*) based on mtDNA studies, or to 'amakihis (*H. virens* and relatives) based on osteology, are incompatible with hypotheses based on a wide range of other characters.

Key Words: Drepanidinae; Hawai'i Creeper; Hawaiian honeycreepers; *Hemignathus*; *Magumma*; *Oreomystis*; *Pseudonestor*.

The classification of the Hawaiian honeycreepers (Drepanidinae) has been controversial since the American Ornithologists' Union (AOU) 1983) abandoned the longstanding classification of Amadon (1950) in favor of a new one based on Berger's (1981) use of my revision (Pratt 1979). This classification has been followed in most general references since, including Scott et al. (1986), Pratt et al. (1987), Sibley and Monroe (1990), and the AOU (1983, 1991, 1998), but its use has not been without criticism. Amadon (1986) felt that "the genera of the Hawaiian honeycreepers have been bandied about in rather cavalier fashion," and Olson and James (1995) bemoaned the wide acceptance of my classification "among non-taxonomists without any consideration having been given to its merits." Olson and James (1982) introduced a different classification, based largely on osteological studies, that has evolved in subsequent works (James and Olson 1991; Olson and James 1991, 1988, 1995), but has not as yet been widely adopted. The two schools have come to agreement on several points, and the remaining differences involve primarily the limits of the genera *Loxops* and *Hemignathus* and the placement of the Hawai'i Creeper (*Oreomystis mana* of AOU 1998 or *Loxops mana* of James and Olson 1991) and 'Akikiki or Kaua'i Creeper (*O. bairdi*). James

(1998) conducted a phylogenetic analysis of cranial osteology, the first study to include all taxa, both historical and subfossil. Her phylogeny (for historically known taxa only) is presented by Fleischer et al. (*this volume*). Recently, various allozyme (Johnson et al. 1989, Fleischer et al. 1998) and mtDNA studies (Tarr and Fleischer 1993, 1995; Feldman 1997; Fleischer et al. 1998; Fleischer et al. *this volume*) have suggested patterns of relationship that challenge both AOU (1998) and James and Olson's (1991) taxonomy. Because genetic technologies are still advancing, hypotheses of relationships based on them must be considered tentative. Each succeeding study seems to change the picture, the various methods show little concordance in their results, and the various laboratories do not agree even when performing essentially the same analyses. To their credit, the authors of these studies have been very conservative in recommending taxonomic changes. Molecular studies virtually never mention phenotypic characters, the traditional tools of systematists, because they consider such "adaptive" characters too subject to the vagaries of natural selection to be evolutionarily informative (R. Fleischer, pers. comm.). Also, no genetic study of Hawaiian honeycreepers has addressed the possibility that past hybridization could have a profound effect on perceived patterns of divergence, although hybridization has been shown to have played a major role in the adaptive radiation of the similar-aged Darwin's finches (Grant 1994). Although DNA studies may ultimately answer all phylogenetic questions, I agree with Raikow (1986) that concordance testing with more traditional methods is still the only reasonable way to evaluate their hypotheses. In this volume, Fleischer et al. do exactly that by using data from mtDNA along with phenotypic osteological characters to assess the phylogenetic placement of the Poʻouli (*Melamprosops phaeosoma*). In the two decades since my first effort (Pratt 1979), many new possible phenotypic synapomorphies have been discovered and others re-evaluated. Clearly now is the time to provide a cladistic analysis of this eclectic mix of traditional phenotypic characters, so that meaningful comparisons with genetic studies can be made.

METHODS

Scientific names used herein are those of the AOU (1998) unless otherwise noted. I conducted phylogenetic analyses of 39 characters (Table 1) derived from studies of myology, osteology, tongue morphology, bill morphology, plumage and coloration, behavior, and ecology using PAUP* (Swofford 1999) and MacClade 3.01 (Maddison and Maddison 1992). Table 2 shows the data matrix. The first 3 characters were segregated to simplify some manipulations done with them. The 26 taxa include the chaffinches (Fringillinae) and cardueline finches (Carduelinae) as outgroups. Groups are coded as possessing a character if any included species does so. Question marks indicate gaps in the data. I have liberally used vernacular names for three reasons: 1) to be as taxonomically noncommittal as possible in entering the data; 2) to make my trees directly comparable to others presented in this volume that also use Hawaiian names; and, most importantly, 3) because these are the only available names that have remained unambiguous for two centuries.

Phenotypic data are admittedly subject to some manipulation by the investigator because characters can be described in various ways. Thus the coding of several characters requires explanation. In Character 21, for example, long sickle-shaped bills are found among ʻakialoas (*Hemignathus* spp.) and in the ʻIʻiwi (*Vestiaria coccinea*) and mamos (*Drepanis* spp.), but they differ between the two groups in the nature of the bony support (Baldwin 1953). By combining two features, Character 21 codes this character without introducing known homoplasy. Tongue shape (Character 15) and bill shapes (Characters 19–22) could have been approached several different ways, but I found that qualitative descriptions worked better than quantitative ones. I also did not order these characters because whether they represent transformational series is uncertain. Character 26 (ʻamakihi coloration) represents a suite of possibly synapomorphic characters that appear to have evolved in tandem. ʻAmakihi coloration includes: 1) plumage olive green dorsally; 2) under-

parts yellow to olive green, paler than dorsum; 3) lores narrowly dark gray or black; 4) bill dark gray to black, usually with bluish base to mandible; 5) females and juvenals like males but less yellow; and 6) juvenals with at least faint wingbars. These characters must be grouped because they are not independent of one another.

I applied similar techniques and the same data set (plus other characters) in a different analysis that will be explained under the discussion of the Hawaiʻi Creeper below.

RESULTS

With all characters at the same weight, I conducted a heuristic search that yielded a total of 390 equally parsimonious trees. From those, a 50% majority rule consensus tree (Fig. 1a) was computed that had a length (L) of 130 steps, a consistency index (CI) of 0.546, and a retention index (RI) of 0.720. The numbers on the lines indicate the percentage of trees that possess the branch shown. The result produced some apparent anomalies. Although the two ʻalauahios (*Paroreomyza montana* and *P. maculata*) and the Kākāwahie (*P. flammea*) stand apart as I predicted (Pratt 1992b), the Poʻouli remains imbedded in the largest clade even though it also lacks the "defining characters" (Pratt 1992a), Characters 1–3 in Table 1, that presumably cause *Paroreomyza* to segregate in the tree. The difference for the Poʻouli is that it possesses an interorbital septum (Characters 11–12) like those of other Hawaiian honeycreepers (Zusi 1978; James and Olson 1991; Fleischer et al., *this volume*). Such a topology requires that the "defining" characters be secondarily lost in *Melamprosops*. This hypothesis lacks credibility because: 1) only these three among the 46 characters are virtually exclusive to Hawaiian honeycreepers as compared with all other passerines; 2) they probably represent gene complexes rather than single loci; and 3) they were favored by natural selection in the Hawaiian environment and retained in most of the drepanidine taxa, so it is difficult to discern how a reversal would be advantageous. If, as hypothesized by Pratt (1992a), drepanidine odor is a defense against predation, then for a lineage to lose it and have to compensate for the loss by the redevelopment of energy-taxing predator mobbing behavior (which dreps with the odor also lack), is certainly counterintuitive if not unparsimonious. Similarly, the loss of lingual wings (or conversely the development of a squared-off base to the tongue) seems unlikely to have occurred more than once among the honeycreepers because it has happened only one other time (among sunbirds) in the entire passerine order. A strict consensus tree of the same data set (Fig. 1b; L = 125, CI = 0.576, RI = 0.715) collapsed many of the nodes and revealed a lack of resolution among most taxa (but note that the *Hemignathus/Pseudonestor* clade, discussed below, survives, as do pairings of mamos and 'I'iwi, Palila and Kona Grosbeak, and the two creepers).

Consequently, I conducted a second analysis giving Characters 1–3 a weight of 2, with all others remaining weighted at 1. This run produced 150 equally parsimonious trees. The majority-rule consensus tree (Fig. 1c; L = 136, CI = 0.551, RI = 0.723) has a much more intuitively satisfying topology and is also more consistent with the findings of Fleischer et al. (*this* volume) and Pratt (1992a) with regard to *Melamprosops*. Furthermore, its topology is so robust that most of it survives in a strict consensus tree (Fig. 1d; L = 125, CI = 0.576, RI = 0.715).

These consensus trees support a number of hypotheses, some of which have taxonomic implications: 1) the Hawaiian honeycreepers, including *Melamprosops* and *Paroreomyza,* are monophyletic; 2) *Melamprosops* and *Paroreomyza* independently diverged from the "main line" of drepanidine evolution very early, before the "defining characters" of Pratt (1992a, b) evolved; 3) the drepanidine finches form a clade that does not include the 'Ō'ū (*Psittirostra psittacea*), Lāna'i Hookbill (*Dysmorodrepanis munroi*), or the Maui Parrotbill; 4) the genera *Chloridops* and *Loxioides* are sister taxa, as suggested by James and Olson (1991); 5) the 'amakihis, 'akialoas, and "heterobills" form a clade that corresponds to the currently recognized genus *Hemignathus* (AOU 1998) except that 6) the 'Anianiau (*H. parvus*) is not included in it, as suggested by Conant et al. (1998); 7) *Pseudonestor* may be a *Hemignathus*; it is more closely related to the thin-billed taxa than to the drepanidine finches as suggested very early by Perkins (1903) and later by Bock (1970) and Pratt (1979) but not accepted by the AOU (1983); 8) the remaining honeycreepers may divide into two clades along the traditional "red" vs. "green" lines; 9) several of the "red" genera are closely related and possibly warrant merger; 10) *Paroreomyza* is not closely related to *Oreomystis*; which 11) includes the Hawai'i Creeper. Several of these require further comment.

DISCUSSION

DREPANIDINE FINCHES

Amadon (1950) placed all the drepanidine finches (except the hookbill, which he regarded as an aberrant specimen) in the genus *Psittirostra* rather than recognizing the five genera previously named, most of which at the time would have been monotypic. This arrangement also re-flected his hypothesis that these birds' finchlike characters were secondarily derived from a thin-billed ancestor. Greenway (1968) split the genus into *Psittirostra* for the 'Ō'ū and *Loxioides* for the rest, and Banks and Laybourne (1977) advocated re-establishment of the original five genera, primarily on the basis that Amadon's *Psittirostra* was morphologically too broad, and breaking it up reflected degrees of phenotypic divergence comparable to those among various mainland finch genera. With a cardueline ancestry fairly well established, Amadon's large *Psittirostra* also appeared to represent a paraphyletic assemblage based on plesiomorphies (Pratt 1979). Olson and James (1982b) maintained Amadon's *Psittirostra* but recognized five subgenera. Later (James and Olson 1991), they recognized all five genera, several of which by then had gained new members described from prehistoric remains, and added several new finchlike genera. Although my phylogeny would support Greenway's (1968) classification, I would caution against making any sweeping taxonomic changes at this time. This study included relatively few characters that could differentiate the finch genera, so the apparent monophyly of the group could easily be an artifact. Any changes, with the possible exception of the merger of *Chloridops* and *Loxioides* suggested by both this study and James and Olson (1991), should await publication of James's (1998) dissertation, new fossil discoveries, and ongoing studies based on ancient DNA extracted and amplified from prehistoric remains (R. L. Fleischer, pers. comm.).

MAUI PARROTBILL

Not only does the parrotbill cluster with the thin-billed taxa *contra* previous classifications (Raikow 1977, AOU 1983), but it may belong in the genus *Hemignathus*. Once the conflation of its huge but fundamentally different bill with the large bill of the 'Ō'ū (Raikow 1977) is eliminated, the similarities of the parrotbill to the hemignathines, especially the 'Akiapōlā'au (*H. munroi*), are overwhelming. Synapomorphies are as varied as a modified jaw muscle (Zusi 1989) and juvenile call notes (pers. obs.). Interestingly, the mtDNA phylogeny of Fleischer et al. (1998, *this volume*) also supports a close 'Akiapōlā'au/parrotbill relationship, although not necessarily the current composition of *Hemignathus* (see below). The parrotbill's tongue (Character 16) is unique among the honeycreepers, elongated with lateral and terminal projections. It looks very much like a drepanidine tubular tongue that has simply been unrolled, and can easily be seen as derived from a tubular ancestor. However, osteological studies (James 1998, Fleischer et al. *this volume*) group the par-

TABLE 1.   CHARACTER STATES FOR PAUP* ANALYSES OF HAWAIIAN HONEYCREEPERS

Characters used in Figure 1

Defining characters of Hawaiian honeycreepers (Pratt 1992a):
    1. Drepanidine odor
        0. Absent
        1. Present
    2. Proximal end of tongue
        0. With prominent "lingual wings."
        1. Squared off, with no large backward projections.
    3. Mobbing behavior
        0. Present
        1. Absent
Anatomy:
    4. Pattern of insertion of the 3 branches of *M. flexor digitorum longus* (Raikow 1978)
        0. ABB
        1. ABA
    5. Condition of *M. peroneus brevis* tibial head (from Raikow 1978)
        0. Absent
        1. Present
    6. Condition of *M. pterygoideus retractor* (Zusi 1989)
        0. Not enlarged
        1. Highly enlarged
    7. Tibial head of the shank muscle *M. peroneus brevis* (Raikow 1977, 1978)
        0. Absent
        1. Present
    8. Coracoidal head of the upper forelimb muscle *M. deltoideus minor* (Raikow 1977)
        0. Absent
        1. Present
   *9. Condition of *M. plantaris* (Raikow 1977)
        0. Present
        1. Absent
        2. Variable within taxon.
   10. Solid bony palate (Sushkin 1929, Amadon 1950)
        0. Absent
        1. Present
   11. Interorbital septum thickness (Zusi 1978)
        0. Thin, single-walled
        1. Thick, double-walled
        2. Thick, double-walled but with thin area in center
   12. Fenestration of interorbital septum (Richards & Bock 1973, Zusi 1978)
        0. Large fenestrae
        1. Solid
        2. Small fenestrae or none (variable)
   13. Floor of cranial fenestra in profile (Zusi 1978)
        0. With hump or upward protrusion
        1. Flat
   14. Palatine process of the premaxilla (Bock 1960, Richards & Bock 1973)
        0. Present
        1. Absent (= fused) with lateral flange at anterior end
        2. Absent (= fused) with reduced lateral flange
Tongue adaptations:
   *15. Overall shape
        0. "Nontubular, fleshy above, corneous below and caudolaterally" with "a rounded
            tip edged with small papillae" (James et al. 1989).
        1. As above but "far less fleshy, more slender" (Gadow 1899).
        2. Straight and shallowly troughlike (Richards and Bock 1973).
        3. Thin, tubular for half or more of length.
        4. Fleshy but narrow, with spoonlike tip (Bock 1978).

TABLE 1. CONTINUED

Characters used in Figure 1

*16. Tongue margins
  0. Smooth, not raised dorsad (Gadow 1899, Gardner 1925, Clark 1912, Amadon
      1950, Raikow 1977, James et al. 1989).
  1. Slightly raised, with short lateral and terminal laciniae at distal end
      (Gadow 1899, Richards and Bock 1973).
  2. Slightly raised, with long lateral and terminal laciniae
      (Rothschild 1893–1900).
  3. Strongly raised and curved inwards progressively toward tip,
      lateral laciniae interlaced distally (Gadow 1899, Raikow 1977).
*17. Seed-cup modifications
  0. Mixed within taxon.
  1. No specialization for seeds
  2. Seed-cup tip (Gadow 1899, Amadon 1950)
Bill morphology (mostly pers. obs.):
  18. Nasal Operculum (Raikow 1977, James et al. 1989)
  0. Not expanded downward
  1. Partially developed
  2. Expanded downward to nearly cover nostril
  19. Finchlike bill shape
  0. Finchlike
  1. Finchlike but elongated (i.e. tanager-like)
  2. Not finchlike
*20. Unique morphologies
  0. Bill shape represented elsewhere among passerines
  1. Heavy, hooked maxilla
  2. Heavy, parrotlike bill
  3. Slightly crossed bill tips
  4. "Heterobill" morphology
*21. Sickle-shaped bills
  0. Not sickle-shaped
  1. Sickle-shaped, thin
  2. Sickle-shaped, thick
  22. Inflation of bill
  0. Bill not inflated
  1. Bill highly inflated, subglobose
*23. Profile of gonys
  0. Strongly convex
  1. Slightly convex
  2. Straight to slightly concave
  3. Strongly concave
Plumage and Coloration (pers. obs.)
  24. Sparrow-like streaking
  0. Present at least in juveniles
  1. Never present
*25. Juvenal plumage
  0. No age-related plumage variation
  1. Juvenile distinct but patterned like adult female
  2. Juvenile patterned differently from either adult
  26. Presence of "amakihi coloration" (see text for details):
  0. Not present
  1. Present
  2. Present with secondary modifications
  3. Present with loss of distinctive female and juvenile plumages
  27. Purring or cooing wing note in flight
  0. No
  1. Yes

TABLE 1.   CONTINUED

Characters used in Figure 1

28. Primaries with truncate tips
    0. No
    1. Yes
29. Plumage texture
    0. Soft, non-shiny
    1. Shiny or hardened
*30. Predominant plumage colors
    0. Yellow-green, yellow, or red
    1. Black, red, and/or yellow
    2. Brown and black
    3. Dull green or gray
    4. Variable in group

Behavior and ecology
*31. Song quality
    0. Canarylike (Perkins 1903, Pratt 1996a)
    1. Dissonant whistles, bell-like and mechanical sounds
        (Perkins 1903, Bryan 1908, Pratt 1996a)
    2. Lively, quiet chittering (Engilis 1990, Kepler et al. 1996)
    3. Lively whistles interspersed with call-like notes
        (Pratt 1992b, Pratt 1996a)
    4. Song of simple trills or warbles (Perkins 1903, Henshaw
        1902, Pratt 1996a)
*32. Song complexity (Newton 1973; Pratt 1979, 1996)
    0. Complex
    1. Mixed complex and simple
    2. Simple
*33. Distinct juvenal call beyond fledging
    0. Absent or unrecognized
    1. Rapid juvenal begging calls in flocks (Scott et al. 1979; Fig. 2)
    2. Evenly spaced "sound beacon" from solitary chick
        (BNA; pers. obs.)
34. Whisper songs (Pratt 1979, 1996a, b)
    0. No whisper song
    1. Whisper songs similar to primary songs.
    2. Whisper songs distinct from primary songs.
35. Nest sanitation
    0. Absent at some point in nesting cycle (Newton 1973; van Riper
        1980a; Pletschet and Kelly 1990; Morin 1992a, b; BNA)
    1. Throughout nesting cycle.
*36. Primary adult diet (Perkins 1903, Berger 1981, BNA)
    0. Seeds
    1. Soft fruits
    2. Nectar
    3. Mixed
    4. Invertebrates
37. Nest construction roles (Newton 1976, Morin 1992b, BNA)
    0. Construction by female only.
    1. Construction mainly by female with limited help from male.
    2. Construction by both sexes.
38. Size of territory (Newton 1976, BNA)
    0. Large territories.
    1. Small territories in immediate area of nest.
*39. Display flights over breeding area (Newton 1976, Morin 1992a, BNA)
    0. Absent
    1. Present

TABLE 1. CONTINUED

Characters used in Figure 1

*40. Presence of red in plumage
    0. Yes
    1. No
*41. Bill color
    0. Pale throughout (may have darker tip)
    1. Pale with dark culmen
    2. Brown or gray with pale base
    3. Black with bluish base to mandible
    4. All black
*42. Attenuation of bill
    0. None
    1. Slight
    2. Moderate
    3. Pronounced
    4. Extreme
*43. Presence of yellow in plumage (adult male)
    0. Yellow head only
    1. No yellow (or very little)
    2. Yellow underlying entire plumage, nowhere bright
    3. Yellow throughout plumage, with bright areas
    4. Nearly all yellow.
*44. Black or gray feathering in face
    0. None
    1. Broad, not confined to lores
    2. Confined to lores
*45. Presence of wing bars
    0. Never present
    1. Faint in juveniles, absent in adults
    2. Present in juveniles only
    3. Present in some adults
*46. Color pattern of crown and supraloral area
    0. Uniformly colored
    1. Indistinct pale eyebrow
    2. Bold, distinct eye stripe
    3. Contrasting crown and forehead
    4. Pale supraloral fleck

Notes: All characters ordered except those with asterisks. Citations for every data point not given. Summaries are cited where useful. The abbreviation BNA refers to the Birds of North America series of the American Ornithologists' Union (Baird 1994; Fancy and Ralph 1997, 1998; Lepson 1997, Lepson and Freed 1997, Lepson and Pratt 1997, Pratt et al. 1997, Simon et al. 1997, Lindsey et al. 1998; Olson 1998a,b,c; Snetsinger 1998; Baker and Baker 2000a,b; Sykes et al. in press).

rotbill with two other taxa that have strongly hooked bills ('Ō'ū and hookbill), but different tongues. This grouping could easily be viewed as the result of homoplasy or just superficial resemblances. It is reminiscent of Raikow's (1977: 113) clustering of the parrotbill with the 'Ō'ū on the basis of their vaguely similar bill shape and the fact that such placement was "not refuted by other characteristics." That placement is now refuted by many other characters, and the parrotbill, despite its large bill, clearly belongs among the thin-billed taxa. However, I do not suggest merger of *Pseudonestor* and *Hemignathus* until the relationships are better understood, even though my findings seem to show that, with

Pseudonestor excluded, *Hemignathus* is paraphyletic.

HEMIGNATHUS AND LOXOPS

Except for the *Pseudonestor* problem, the above results clearly support current AOU (1998) taxonomy that restricts *Loxops* to the 'ākepas and groups the 'amakihis, 'akialoas, and heterobills in *Hemignathus*. However, the current inclusion of the 'Anianiau in the latter genus is not justified. For a detailed discussion of the reasoning behind these conclusions, see Conant et al. (1998). DNA studies also support recognition of a monotypic *Magumma* for the 'Anianiau. Tarr and Fleischer's (1995) restriction-

TABLE 2.   DATA MATRIX FOR PAUP* ANALYSIS OF HAWAIIAN HONEYCREEPERS USING CHARACTER STATES FROM TABLE 1

Taxon	Character state															
	1	2	3	4	5	6	7	8	9	10	11	12	13	14	15	16
Chaffinches	0	0	0	1	0	0	0	0	0	0	0	0	0	0	0	0
Cardueline finches	0	0	0	0	1	0	0	1	0	1	1	1	1	1	0	0
Telespiza finches	1	1	1	1	?	0	0	1	0	1	1	1	1	1	0	0
Palila	1	1	1	?	?	?	?	?	?	?	1	1	1	?	0	0
koa finches	1	1	?	?	?	?	?	?	?	?	1	1	1	?	0	0
Kona Grosbeak	1	1	?	?	?	?	?	?	?	?	1	1	1	?	0	0
'Ō'ū	1	1	1	0	1	0	0	1	0	?	1	1	1	?	0	0
Lāna'i Hookbill	?	?	?	?	?	?	?	?	?	?	1	1	1	1	0	0
Po'ouli	0	0	0	?	?	?	?	?	?	?	2	2	1	?	4	0
Kākāwahie/'alauahios	0	0	0	?	?	?	?	?	?	0	0	0	1	2	2	1
Maui Parrotbill	1	1	1	?	?	1	?	?	?	?	2	2	1	?	1	2
Hawai'i Creeper	1	1	?	?	?	?	?	?	1	?	2	2	1	1	2	1
'Akikiki	1	1	1	0	1	?	0	1	0	?	2	2	1	?	2	1
'ākepas/'Akeke'e	1	1	1	?	?	?	?	?	?	1	2	2	1	1	3	3
'Anianiau	1	1	1	?	?	?	?	?	?	?	2	2	1	?	3	3
Greater 'Amakihi	1	1	?	?	?	?	?	?	?	?	2	2	1	?	3	3
'amakihis	1	1	1	0	1	0	1	1	1	?	2	2	1	2	3	3
'akialoas	1	1	?	0	1	0	1	1	0	1	2	2	1	1	3	3
nukupu'us	1	1	?	0	1	?	?	?	?	?	2	2	1	?	3	3
'Akiapōlā'au	1	1	1	0	1	1	0	1	0	?	2	2	1	?	3	3
'Ula-'ai-hawane	1	1	?	?	?	?	?	?	?	?	2	2	1	?	3	3
'Apapane	1	1	1	0	1	0	1	1	1	1	2	2	1	1	3	3
'Ākohekohe	1	1	1	1	1	0	1	1	1	?	2	2	1	?	3	3
'I'iwi	1	1	1	0	1	0	0	1	1	1	2	2	1	2	3	3
Black Mamo	1	1	?	?	?	?	?	?	?	?	?	?	1	?	3	3
Hawai'i Mamo	1	1	?	?	?	?	?	?	?	?	?	?	1	?	3	3

fragment mtDNA study of a limited number of taxa found the 'Anianiau widely separated from the 'amakihis in a clade of its own. Fleischer et al.'s (1998, *this volume*) mtDNA sequencing study included additional taxa and grouped the 'Anianiau with the heterobilled 'Akiapōlā'au (*H. munroi*) and the parrotbill. James's (in Fleischer et al., *this volume*) osteological phylogeny, however, maintains the grouping of the 'Anianiau with the 'amakihis, which may reflect the superficial resemblance that led to the former name "Lesser 'Amakihi" and my own (Pratt 1979) uncritical placement of this species in *Hemignathus* before closer scrutiny (Conant et al. 1998).

James and Olson (1991: Table 14) restricted *Hemignathus* to 'akialoas and the heterobills, and later (Olson and James 1995) subdivided it and placed the former in a new genus *Akialoa*. They grouped the 'amakihis with the 'ākepas, 'Anianiau, and Hawai'i Creeper in *Loxops*. Thus constituted, *Loxops* would be close to Amadon's (1950) characterization (Pratt 1979, Conant et al. 1998). James's (1998) newly analyzed osteological data (Fleischer et al., *this volume*) provide no support for such an arrangement. In fact, her phylogeny not only supports restriction of *Loxops* to 'ākepas, but can be interpreted as sup-

porting a large *Hemignathus* as currently recognized. The 'amakihis, heterobills, and akialoas are members of a single clade even on osteological grounds, but the picture is complicated by the inclusion of the "red" honeycreepers in the same clade. This result reveals one of the weaknesses of single-character or single-complex analyses. With only one suite of characters, the computer program has no way of distinguishing homoplasy or parallelism from synapomorphy. The bill morphologies among the "red" birds (i. e., short down-curved bills, long sickle-bills, etc.) parallel those found in *Hemignathus,* but other characters (i. e., behavior, plumage type, sequence of plumages, and vocalizations) show that these resemblances are not synapomorphic with similar morphologies among the "green" birds (Perkins 1903, Amadon 1950). I suspect that a combination of the osteological data with my own would resolve this discrepancy and bring James's (1998) phylogeny and mine into substantial agreement. With the red birds removed, James's uppermost clade fairly closely approximates *Hemignathus* as currently delimited (AOU 1998).

Fleischer et al.'s (1998) mtDNA sequence phylogeny supports neither an enlarged *Hemignathus* nor an enlarged *Loxops*. In it, the heter-

TABLE 2. EXTENDED.

												Character state										
17	18	19	20	21	22	23	24	25	26	27	28	29	30	31	32	33	34	35	36	37	38	39
0	0	0	0	0	0	1	0	1	0	0	0	0	4	?	2	0	0	1	0	0	0	0
0	0	0	0	0	0	1	0	1	0	0	0	0	4	0	0	0	1	0	0	0	1	1
1	0	0	0	0	0	0	0	1	0	0	0	0	0	0	0	0	0	0	0	0	1	0
2	0	0	0	0	1	0	1	1	0	0	0	0	0	0	0	0	1	0	0	1	1	1
2	0	0	0	0	0	1	1	1	0	0	0	0	0	?	?	?	?	?	0	?	?	?
2	0	0	0	0	1	0	1	0	0	0	0	0	0	0	0	?	1	?	0	?	?	1
1	1	1	1	0	0	0	1	1	0	0	0	0	0	0	0	0	0	?	1	?	?	1
1	1	2	1	0	0	0	1	?	0	0	0	0	0	?	?	?	?	?	?	?	?	?
1	?	1	0	0	0	0	1	1	0	0	0	0	2	2	0	0	0	1	4	2	?	0
1	1	2	0	0	0	1	1	1	0	0	0	0	0	3	1	0	2	1	3	?	1	1
1	0	2	2	0	0	0	1	1	2	0	0	0	0	4	2	2	2	0	4	1	0	0
1	1	2	0	0	0	2	1	2	0	0	0	0	3	4	2	1	0	1	4	1	1	0
1	1	2	0	0	0	2	1	2	0	0	0	0	3	4	2	1	2	1	4	?	?	?
1	2	2	3	0	0	2	1	1	0	0	0	0	0	4	2	0	2	0	4	0	1	1
1	2	2	0	0	0	2	1	1	0	0	0	0	0	4	2	0	2	1	3	1	1	0
1	2	2	0	0	0	2	1	0	3	0	0	0	0	4	2	?	?	?	4	?	?	?
1	2	2	0	1	0	3	1	1	1	0	0	0	0	4	2	0	2	0	3	1	0	1
1	2	2	0	1	0	3	1	1	1	0	0	0	0	4	2	?	?	?	3	?	?	?
1	2	2	4	1	0	3	1	1	1	0	0	0	0	4	2	?	?	?	4	?	?	?
1	2	2	4	1	0	1	1	1	1	0	0	0	0	4	2	2	2	1	4	0	?	0
1	2	1	0	0	0	1	1	2	0	?	0	1	1	?	?	?	?	?	?	?	?	?
1	2	2	0	0	0	2	1	2	0	1	1	1	1	1	0	0	0	1	2	2	1	1
1	2	2	0	0	0	2	1	2	0	1	0	1	1	1	0	0	2	1	2	0	1	1
1	2	2	0	2	0	3	1	2	0	1	1	1	1	1	0	0	0	1	2	1	1	0
1	2	2	0	2	0	3	1	0	0	1	0	0	1	1	?	?	?	?	2	?	?	?
1	2	2	0	2	0	3	1	0	0	1	0	1	1	1	?	?	?	?	2	?	?	?

obills group with the parrotbill and 'Anianiau, the 'amakihis are sister-group to the red birds, and the Hawaii Creeper is sister-group to the 'ākepas. The analysis does not include the Greater 'Amakihi or the 'akialoas. According to R. Fleischer (pers. comm.) the branching sequence among the thin-billed honeycreepers is not well defined by the techniques used in their study, so I believe we should await further developments before tinkering with a taxonomy so well supported by phenotypic characters.

Although the phenotypic data support a large *Hemignathus,* they also support the recognition of four (or five if *Pseudonestor* is included) subgenera within it: *Hemignathus* for the heterobills; *Akialoa* for the 'akialoas; *Chlorodrepanis* for the "typical" 'amakihis; and *Viridonia* for the Greater 'Amakihi. The latter two cannot be combined as has been done in the past (Greenway 1968) because such a construct would be paraphyletic. In fact, future studies should consider the possibility that the Greater 'Amakihi, like the 'Anianiau, warrants a genus of its own.

THE "RED-AND-BLACK" GENERA

Every study reviewed herein shows that the members of this subgroup, recognized from the time of Perkins (1903), do indeed form a well-defined clade. R. C. Fleischer (pers. comm.), on the basis of the small degree of genetic difference between them, believes all of the "red" genera could justifiably be merged. On phenotypic grounds, the genera *Vestiaria* and *Drepanis* differ solely on a relatively minor red-to-yellow color shift, hardly a generic-level distinction by modern standards, but my earlier suggestion (Pratt 1979) that they should be merged was not accepted by Berger (1981). Also, the 'Apapane and 'Ākohekohe (*Palmeria dolei*) are close structurally and behaviorally, although the latter's unique plumage features make it look superficially rather different. The lumping of *Himatione* and *Palmeria* is not as strongly supported by my phylogeny as the *Vestiaria/Drepanis* merger.

HAWAI'I CREEPER

So now we come to the one species whose taxonomic position is the subject of the widest disagreement among competing evolutionary hypotheses and hence the namesake of this paper. The Hawai'i Creeper is a small, drab Hawaiian honeycreeper endemic to the island of Hawai'i (Scott et al. 1979). Its dull gray-green

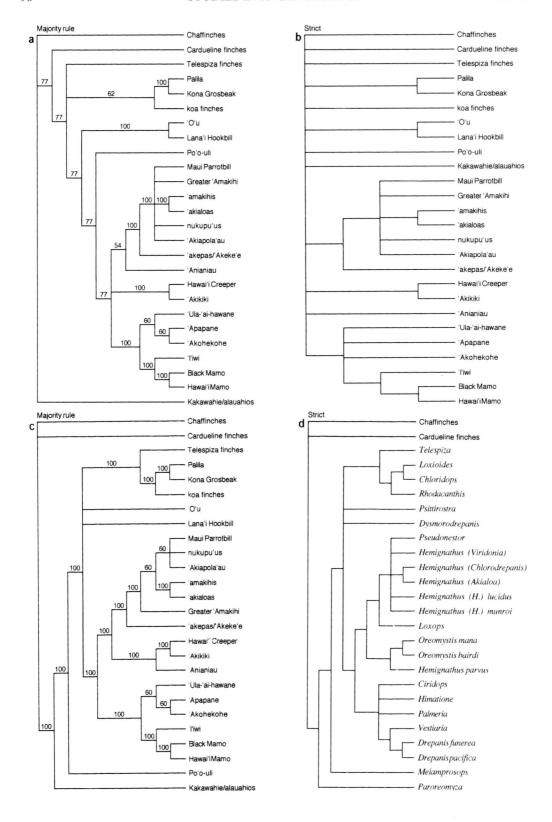

coloration and generally inconspicuous behavior may have contributed to the fact that the Hawaiians did not distinguish it from the Hawai'i 'Amakihi (*Hemignathus virens*; Perkins 1903). It was first described (Wilson 1891) as *Himatione mana,* but Amadon (1950) included it in his large genus *Loxops* as one of the subspecies of the "Creeper," a "species" subsequently shown to be a grouping of five species in either 2 (Pratt 1979, 1992b) or 3 (Olson and James 1982b, James and Olson 1991) genera. The O'ahu, Moloka'i, and Maui/Lāna'i components of Amadon's "Creeper" are now placed in the enigmatic genus *Paroreomyza,* which now appears to represent a very early divergence in the evolution of the honeycreepers (Tarr and Fleischer 1995, Fleischer et al. 1998, this study). The genus *Oreomystis* comprises the remaining two species, the 'Akikiki or Kaua'i Creeper, *O. bairdi,* and the Hawai'i Creeper, *O. mana.* Johnson et al. (1989), Feldman (1997; phylogeny reproduced in Freed 1999) and Fleischer et al. (1998, *this volume*) present strong allozyme, mtDNA, and osteological evidence that *O. bairdi* is the sister-group of *Paroreomyza,* although the placement of that clade varies among the studies. For this relationship to hold, the honeycreepers' squared-off tongue base (Character 2) would have to have evolved twice independently, an unlikely prospect as discussed earlier. This study achieved very different results (Fig. 1) in which *Paroreomyza* and *Oreomystis bairdi* are as far apart as any other two drepanidine genera. Tarr and Fleischer's (1995) restriction-site study supports this finding, but is out of step with their later mtDNA sequence analyses.

On osteological grounds, Olson and James (1982) and James and Olson (1991) place the Hawai'i Creeper in their large *Loxops* and considered it closely related to the 'amakihis (Olson and James 1995). However, James's (1998) phylogeny (see Fleischer et al., *this volume*) shows it only as a sister group to most of the other thin-billed honeycreepers, a position rather close to where it appears in my study (except that the 'Akikiki is paired with it). Thus the osteological phylogeny and mine actually differ more strikingly on the placement of *O. bairdi* than on that of the Hawai'i Creeper. The osteological phylogeny, if correct, would require either the creation of a new monotypic genus for the creeper or the recognition of a huge genus *Drepanis* that would include everything from the creeper to heterobills to mamos. If the red birds were removed from this assemblage as suggested above, the creeper could be in *Hemignathus.* Interestingly, Feldman's (1994) independent mtDNA study showed the Hawai'i Creeper as sister group to the red honeycreepers which clade in turn formed an unresolved trichotomy with the 'amakihis and 'ākepas. Although distinctive, this hypothesis is closer to those derived from osteology and this study than to the other mtDNA results. Fleischer et al. (1998, *this volume*) hypothesize on the basis of mtDNA sequencing that the Hawai'i Creeper forms a clade with the 'ākepas which in turn is sister to an odd assemblage that includes the heterobills, parrotbill, and 'Anianiau. So is this enigmatic little bird an odd offshoot of its own, sister to the 'Apapane (*Himatione sanguinea*) and 'I'iwi, a non-crossbilled 'ākepa, or an *Oreomystis*?

The question of whether *Oreomystis* is related to *Paroreomyza* is independent of whether the Hawai'i Creeper and the 'Akikiki are congeners. So numerous are the phenotypic similarities of the Hawai'i Creeper to the 'Akikiki that manuscript reviewers of Pratt (1992b) questioned even considering them separate species, let alone members of different genera. The Hawai'i Creeper is vaguely similar in overall coloration to female and juvenile 'amakihis, female 'Ākepa (*Loxops coccineus*), and both sexes of 'Akeke'e (*L. caeruleirostris*; Scott et al. 1979, Pratt et al. 1987), but differs in important details. Unlike 'amakihis and 'ākepas, adults are not sexually dichromatic. They have a broad gray mask, shaped more like the black mask of *L. caeruleirostris* than the narrow black lores of 'amakihis. Unlike 'amakihis but resembling 'ākepas, neither adults nor juveniles ever have wing-bars. And unlike both 'amakihis and 'ākepas, juveniles have a distinctive plumage with pale feathering in the lores and over the eye. In plumage features, the Hawai'i Creeper closely resembles *Oreomystis bairdi,* which also lacks sexual dichromatism as an adult, has a distinctive pale-faced juvenile plumage, and lacks wing-bars.

The creeper's bill is nearly straight with a concave gonys (Pratt 1992b), pale except for a dusky tinge, variable in extent, along the culmen. In overall shape it is somewhat intermediate between that of an 'amakihi and that of an 'ākepa (without crossed tips) and resembles that

←

FIGURE 1. Phylogenetic trees of Hawaiian honeycreepers: a) unweighted tree, 50% majority-rule consensus; b) unweighted strict consensus tree; c) majority rule tree with Characters 1–3 weighted 2; d) strict consensus of weighted trees, with AOU (1998) scientific name equivalents and *Hemignathus* divided into four subgenera. See Tables 1 and 2 for data and coding. See text for analysis details.

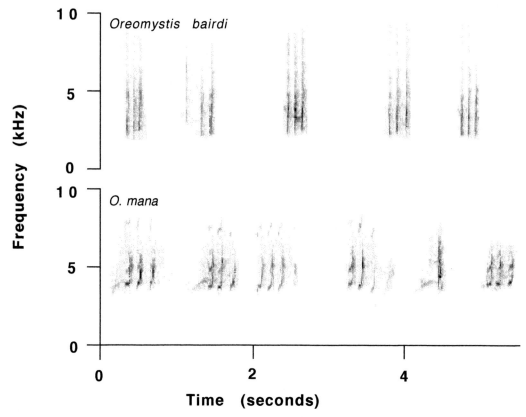

FIGURE 2.   Juvenile begging calls of the 2 species of *Oreomystis*. *O. bairdi* recorded 6 August 1997 by David Kuhn near the Mohihi Trail above Koaʻie Stream, Alakaʻi Wilderness Preserve, Kauaʻi (not archived). *O. mana* recorded by the author 4 May 1977 at Keauhou Ranch, Kaʻu District, Hawaiʻi (Cornell Laboratory of Ornithology, Library of Natural Sounds No. 05274). Audiospectrograms prepared on a Macintosh computer using Canary© software program.

of *Oreomystis bairdi* in nearly every detail except that it is somewhat thinner, light gray rather than pale pink, and has somewhat more dark pigment above (Pratt et al. 1987). Because their bills are nearly identical in shape, the most parsimonious hypothesis would seem to be that the two creepers share a common ancestry, but bill shape does not argue strongly against an ʻākepa relationship for them both.

The nuthatch-like foraging of the Hawaiʻi Creeper differs from that of *Oreomystis bairdi* only in that the chosen substrates average larger for the latter (Pratt 1992b). Of all the ʻamakihi species, the Kauai ʻAmakihi (*H. kauaiensis*) is the most frequent bark-picker, but it would never be characterized as nuthatch-like (Conant et al. 1998). Nor does the Hawaiʻi Creeper forage in any way resembling the feeding of either species of *Loxops* (Lepson and Pratt 1997, Lepson and Freed 1997). Following fledging, tightly structured family groups of both Hawaiʻi Creeper (Scott et al. 1979, Pratt et al. 1987) and ʻAkikiki

(Pratt 1992b, Conant et al. 1998) forage together with frequent begging notes from the juveniles. Both may later join larger mixed-species flocks with ʻamakihis, ʻākepas, and other species (Pratt et al. 1976, Lepson and Freed 1997, pers. obs.). Similar tightly structured family foraging groups with distinctive calls have not been reported in ʻamakihis or ʻākepas (Lepson and Pratt 1997, Lepson and Freed 1997), although they both join looser flocks. Because the hypothesized ancestor of the drepanidines was a seed-eating cardueline finch, the nuthatch-like foraging of the two creepers can be viewed as a synapomorphy.

The song of the Hawaiʻi Creeper is a short trill similar to that of *O. bairdi,* but many other drepanidine species also sing short trills, so adult songs reveal little about relationships (Scott et al. 1979, Pratt et al. 1987, Pratt 1992b, Pratt 1996). One noteworthy difference is that songs of both *Oreomystis* are highly stereotyped, whereas those of such potential relatives as 'amakihis and 'ākepas are highly variable even when uttered by the same individual (Pratt 1979,1996; Pratt et al. 1987). The begging notes of Hawai'i Creeper juveniles flocking with their parents after fledging are very similar to those of juvenile 'Akikiki (Fig. 2) in similar context, which were first recorded in 1997 and are thus not included in recently published tapes (Pratt 1996). The individual notes of 'Akikiki juveniles are slightly shorter and cover a somewhat wider frequency range than those of the Hawai'i Creeper, but they have a similar syncopated rhythm, with notes grouped in short bursts (Fig. 2). Although a few other Hawaiian honeycreepers (e. g. *Pseudonestor xanthophrys, Hemignathus munroi*) have distinctive juvenile begging notes that persist long after fledging, none have the same sound or rhythmic pattern of the two creepers. No long-persisting juvenile begging notes have been reported among either 'amakihis or 'ākepas, nor among carduelime finches, and thus the juvenile calls appear to be another synapomorphy linking the two *Oreomystis*.

But it is the tongues that present the most enigmatic observations. The Hawai'i Creeper's tongue is narrow and nontubular, with a notched, slightly frayed tip (Richards and Bock 1973) and resembles the tongue of *O. bairdi* in virtually every detail (Pratt 1992a). Such a tongue tip differs strikingly from that of the hypothetical ancestral Hawaiian honeycreeper (Raikow 1977), is found only in the Hawai'i Creeper and the 'Akikiki, and, unlike that of the parrotbill, is difficult to envision as a derivative of the highly derived drepanidine tubular type. The most likely explanation for two taxa sharing in detail such a complex derived morphology is that they both inherited it from a common ancestor. The simple, notched tongue certainly appears to be a defining synapomorphy in *Oreomystis*.

If Raikow (1977, 1985, 1986) is correct that the tubular drepanidine tongue defines a major clade of the Drepanidinae that includes both the "green" and "red" groups, *Oreomystis* cannot belong to it unless its distal tongue morphology is secondarily derived from the tubular form. Of course, such derivation is clearly possible. Both the DNA and osteology trees of Fleischer et al. (*this volume*) require this secondary derivation for the Hawai'i Creeper but not the 'Akikiki. My unweighted tree (Fig. 1a) shows the two-member *Oreomystis* as one branch of an unresolved trichotomy with the "red" clade on the one hand and the "green" clade on the other, but my weighted tree (Fig. 1c) places it, like both of those of Fleischer et al. (*this volume*), in a position that requires secondary derivation of the *Oreomystis* tongue from a tubular ancestor.

This result prompted me to conduct an additional analysis that focused on the "green" birds, including all species-level taxa and additional characters (40–46 in Table 1) that, for reasons mentioned earlier, could not be used with the broader sample of taxa. I included the three *Paroreomyza* species and the monotypic *Psittirostra* for comparative purposes and so that the relationships of *Pseudonestor* would also be reexamined. All characters were unweighted in this analysis, and Character 35 (nest sanitation) was ordered rather than unordered as previously. Table 3 is the data matrix for this analysis. A heuristic search of the 46 characters produced 180 trees, from which majority-rule and strict consensus trees (Fig. 3; L = 109, CI = 0.661, RI = 0.732) were derived. This time, the two *Oreomystis* sorted out as the sister group to the entire clade defined by the tubular tongue (but including *Pseudonestor*), which I believe is a reasonable placement for it. Note that the earlier pairing of *Oreomystis* with 'Anianiau did not hold up in this more detailed analysis, and I regard it as an artifact.

Problems of possible homoplasy complicate analysis of another anatomical feature that has figured prominently in the taxonomic history of the creepers. Raikow (1976) found that some Hawaiian honeycreepers, like many other passerines, have lost the plantaris, a minor muscle of the shank. Of the taxa he studied, only the 'amakihis and the "red" genera *Himatione, Palmeria,* and *Himatione* lacked the plantaris. Unfortunately, he included neither an 'ākepa nor any of the "creepers" (which were all then considered conspecific) other than *Oreomystis bairdi*. Nevertheless, Raikow (1977) separated "the Creeper" generically from the 'amakihis based on the loss of the plantaris in the latter. If the loss of the plantaris is a uniquely derived character state within the honeycreeper taxon, then the logical conclusion is that the taxa that share this condition form a clade ('amakihis plus the red-and-black birds), a grouping that appears in Fleischer et al.'s (1998) mtDNA tree. Subsequent dissections (S. L. Olson, pers. comm.) revealed that the Hawai'i Creeper lacks the plantaris, a result that might also seem to support a relationship to 'amakihis. How useful is loss of the plantaris as a key to phylogeny? Clearly, it cannot be considered a synapomorphy in any broad sense, because it has occurred several times among passerines generally, and at least twice among the Carduelinae (Raikow 1976, 1977, 1978). Furthermore, avian muscles have been shown to be subject to evolutionary reversals (i. e., to become re-established in a lineage after loss; Raikow et al. 1979) as well as sufficiently variable individually to present problems for phylogenetic studies based on few specimens

TABLE 3. DATA MATRIX FOR PAUP* ANALYSIS OF "HEMIGNATHINE" SPECIES OF HAWAIIAN HONEYCREEPERS USING CHARACTER STATES FROM TABLE 1

Taxon	1	2	3	4	5	6	7	8	9	10	11	12	13	14	15	16	17	18	19	20	21
Psittirostra	1	1	1	1	1	0	0	1	0	?	1	1	1	?	0	0	1	1	1	1	0
Paroreomyza maculata	0	0	0	?	?	?	?	?	?	0	0	0	1	2	2	1	1	1	2	0	0
Paroreomyza montana	0	0	0	?	?	?	?	?	?	0	0	0	1	2	2	1	1	1	2	0	0
Paroreomyza flammea	0	0	0	?	?	?	?	?	?	0	0	0	1	2	2	1	1	1	2	0	0
Pseudonestor	1	1	1	?	?	1	?	?	?	?	2	2	1	?	1	2	1	0	2	2	0
Oreomystis mana	1	1	1	?	?	?	?	?	1	?	2	2	1	1	2	1	1	1	2	0	0
Oreomystis bairdi	1	1	1	0	1	?	0	1	0	?	2	2	1	?	2	1	1	1	2	0	0
Loxops coccineus	1	1	1	?	?	?	?	?	?	1	2	2	1	1	3	3	1	2	2	3	0
Loxops caeruleirostris	1	1	1	?	?	?	?	?	?	?	2	2	1	?	3	3	1	2	2	3	0
Hemignathus sagittirostris	1	1	?	?	?	?	?	?	?	?	2	2	1	?	3	3	1	2	2	0	0
Hemignathus virens	1	1	1	0	1	0	1	1	1	?	2	2	1	2	3	3	1	2	2	0	1
Hemignathus flava	1	1	1	0	1	0	?	1	1	?	2	2	1	2	3	3	1	2	2	0	1
Hemignathus kauaiensis	1	1	1	0	1	0	?	1	1	?	2	2	1	2	3	3	1	2	2	0	1
Hemignathus parvus	1	1	1	?	?	?	?	?	?	?	2	2	1	?	3	3	1	2	2	0	0
Hemignathus ellisianus	1	1	?	0	1	0	1	1	0	1	2	2	1	1	3	3	1	2	2	0	1
Hemignathus obscurus	1	1	?	?	?	?	?	1	0	1	2	2	1	1	3	3	1	2	2	0	1
Hemignathus lucidus hanapepe	1	1	?	?	?	?	?	?	?	?	2	2	1	?	3	3	1	2	2	4	1
Hemignathus lucidus lucidus	1	1	?	?	?	?	?	?	?	?	2	2	1	?	3	3	1	2	2	4	1
Hemignathus lucidus affinis	1	1	?	?	?	?	?	?	?	?	2	2	1	?	3	3	1	2	2	4	1
Hemignathus munroi	1	1	1	0	1	1	1	1	0	?	2	2	1	?	3	3	1	2	2	4	1

(Raikow et al. 1990). Further complicating matters is the lack of information on the plantaris condition of 'ākepas, the Greater 'Amakihi, and the 'Anianiau. Thus the hypothesis that the plantaris has been lost more than once in drepanidine evolution is by no means far-fetched, and the usefulness of this character in reconstructing phylogeny is severely compromised. Nevertheless I included it (Character 9) in my analyses as an unordered character.

The case for inclusion of the Hawai'i Creeper in *Oreomystis* based on "traditional" taxonomic data is straightforward, unequivocal, and supported by every tree topology in this study, although the placement of that genus among the others remains controversial. The phenotypic evidence in this case, which includes certain and probable synapomorphies of plumage sequence, coloration, bill and tongue morphology, vocalizations, social behavior, and ecology are too numerous and varied to be dismissed out of hand, as has been done in recent molecular studies, none of which have even mentioned this striking conflict of genetic and phenotypic data. Nor in my opinion can so many similarities be credibly attributed to convergence or homoplasy.

R. L. Fleischer (pers. comm.) has suggested that a past hybridization event could produce the re-

TABLE 3. EXTENDED.

												Character state												
22	23	24	25	26	27	28	29	30	31	32	33	34	35	36	37	38	39	40	41	42	43	44	45	46
0	0	1	1	0	0	0	0	0	0	0	0	0	?	1	?	1	?	1	0	1	0	0	1	0
0	1	1	1	0	0	0	0	0	3	1	0	2	1	3	?	?	?	1	1	0	3	1	3	2
0	1	1	1	0	0	0	0	0	3	1	0	2	1	3	?	1	1	1	1	0	3	2	1	0
0	1	1	1	0	0	0	0	0	3	1	0	2	1	3	?	?	?	0	1	0	1	0	0	0
0	0	1	1	2	0	0	0	0	4	2	2	2	0	4	1	0	0	1	1	2	3	2	1	2
0	2	1	2	0	0	0	0	3	4	2	1	0	1	4	1	0	0	1	1	0	2	1	0	0
0	2	1	2	0	0	0	0	3	4	2	1	2	1	4	?	?	?	1	1	0	1	0	0	0
0	2	1	1	0	0	0	0	0	4	2	0	2	0	4	0	1	1	0	0	0	1	0	0	0
0	2	1	1	0	0	0	0	0	4	2	0	2	1	4	2	?	0	1	0	0	3	1	0	3
0	2	1	0	2	0	0	0	0	4	2	?	?	?	4	?	?	?	1	3	3	2	2	0	1
0	3	1	1	1	0	0	0	0	4	2	0	2	0	3	0	1	1	1	3	2	3	2	2	1
0	3	1	1	1	0	0	0	0	4	2	0	2	?	3	1	?	?	1	3	2	3	2	3	4
0	3	1	1	1	0	0	0	0	4	2	0	2	1	3	1	0	0	1	2	3	3	2	2	1
0	2	1	1	0	0	0	0	0	4	2	0	2	1	3	1	1	0	1	1	1	4	0	0	0
0	3	1	1	1	0	0	0	0	4	2	?	?	?	3	?	?	?	1	2	4	3	2	1	1
0	3	1	1	1	0	0	0	0	4	2	?	?	?	3	?	?	?	1	2	4	2	2	2	1
0	3	1	1	1	0	0	0	0	4	2	?	?	?	4	?	?	?	1	4	4	3	2	1	0
0	3	1	1	1	0	0	0	0	4	2	?	?	?	4	?	?	?	1	3	4	3	2	1	0
0	3	1	1	1	0	0	0	0	4	2	?	?	?	4	?	?	?	1	4	4	3	2	1	2
0	1	1	1	1	0	0	0	0	4	2	2	2	1	4	1	?	0	1	4	4	3	2	1	0

sults seen here, but considers convergence more likely. The name *Oreomyza* (= *Oreomystis*) *perkinsi* was based on a possible hybrid specimen of which one parent was a Hawai'i Creeper (Amadon 1950:176–177), so hybridization is neither unprecedented nor unreasonable. Furthermore, if Tarr and Fleischer (1995) and Fleischer et al. (1998) are correct that the drepanidine radiation resulted from a recent rapid burst of speciation, then hybridization need not indicate "next-of-kin" relationship, especially because intergeneric hybrids are fairly frequent in birds (Bledsoe 1988a). In the similarly rapidly evolving Darwin's finches, hybridization has clearly played a role (Grant 1986, 1994), and as Freeland and Boag (1999:584) pointed out, "it is extremely difficult with existing data to differentiate between the effects of lineage sorting and hybridization." Recently, P. R. Grant (pers. comm. *fide* Thane Pratt) reported a pattern of hybridization and subsequent backcrossing among the Geospizinae that, if it occurred among Hawaiian honeycreepers, could explain the apparent conflict of phenotypic and genotypic data for the Hawaii Creeper. In such a scenario, hybrids would involve primarily, or only, male *Oreomystis* mating with female 'ākepas or 'amakihis. Given the song vari-

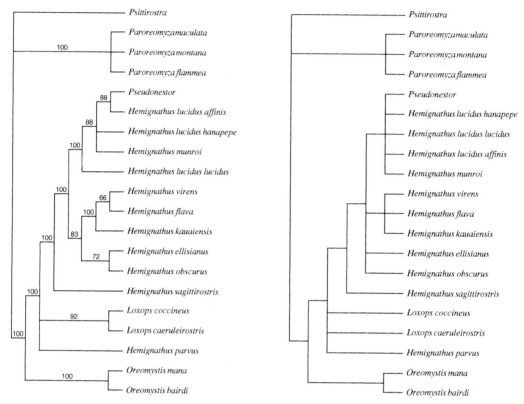

FIGURE 3.   Species-level phylogeny of "hemignathine" Hawaiian honeycreepers plus *Paroreomyza* and *Psittirostra*. Left, 50% majority-rule consensus tree; right, strict consensus tree. Taxonomy follows AOU (1998).

ation of the latter two groups and the relative uniformity of *Oreomystis* songs, non-*Oreomystis* females might be more likely to mate with a male *Oreomystis* than *Oreomystis* females to mate with a non-*Oreomystis* male. Offspring of such matings would then mate preferentially with *Oreomystis* or hybrids because males would sing the songs of their fathers and females would respond to songs of their fathers. If the birds with mixed ancestry became the ancestors of the Hawai'i Creeper, then they could retain all of the phenotypic synapomorphies of *Oreomystis* but possess mtDNA, which represents solely the female line of descent, "stolen" from another species. Ongoing studies of nuclear DNA (R. Fleischer, pers. comm.) may help to solve this problem. Of course, the past hybridization event might not have involved the Hawai'i Creeper at all; it could instead be the reason why the 'Akikiki turns up in the "wrong" place in some phylogenies. Indeed, the molecular and osteological phylogenies reviewed here are more similar in their placement of the Hawai'i Creeper than the 'Akikiki.

Removal of the Hawai'i Creeper from the genus *Oreomystis* at this stage would clearly be prema-

ture, especially because we would have no unequivocal alternative. At present, the DNA laboratories offer us three different hypotheses. This analysis of phenotypic characters shows very strong support for the current taxonomy, which is somewhat weakly corroborated by osteological studies and one mtDNA analysis. Furthermore, plausible hypotheses can be offered to explain the observed lack of genetic and phenotypic congruence. Until nuclear DNA studies are completed and possible hybridization is addressed, the prudent course is to avoid taxonomic changes based solely on molecular data. If future studies prove that the evolution of the Hawai'i Creeper was entirely independent of *Oreomystis bairdi*, then the large number and varied character of apparent synapomorphies of these two species will represent one of the most remarkable and noteworthy examples of convergence ever demonstrated. That finding would be exciting, but the burden of proof clearly lies with those who would remove the Hawai'i Creeper from *Oreomystis*. Why is the Hawai'i Creeper an *Oreomystis*? Because that is what the most consistent available evidence shows it to be.

SUMMARY

This study shows that the alpha taxonomy of the Hawaiian honeycreepers currently in use (AOU 1998) has a solid foundation in phenotypic characters. None of the taxa, with the possible exception of *Hemignathus,* are paraphyletic, and generic limits, with a few minor exceptions, are reasonable. Hypothesized relationships at variance with current usage and based on genetic studies must be considered preliminary and tentative until consistent results are achieved. Taxonomic and sequence changes suggested by these results include: 1) the merger of *Chloridops* and *Loxioides,* or at least adjacent placement in the taxonomic order; 2) removal of the 'Anianiau from *Hemignathus* and classification as *Magumma parva*; 3) recognition of four subgenera of *Hemignathus* (*Hemignathus, Akialoa, Chlorodrepanis,* and *Viridonia*); 4) the placement of *Pseudonestor* adjacent to *Hemignathus* in taxonomic sequence, or even merger of the two genera; 5) lumping of *Vestiaria* into *Drepanis* and probably also *Palmeria* into *Himatione*; and 6) movement of *Melamprosops* and *Paroreomyza* to the beginning of the sequence, preceding *Telespiza.*

ACKNOWLEDGMENTS

I thank D. Kuhn for recording the 'Akikiki juveniles for this study. Students and staff of the Louisiana State University Museum of Natural Science helped in numerous ways: D. Lane and M. Cohn-Haft assisted in preparation of the audiospectrograms, F. Burbrink taught me how to use PAUP and MacClade, and J. V. Remsen and F. H. Sheldon made numerous suggestions that improved the manuscript. Colleagues R. L. Fleischer, H. James, S. Olson, L. Freed, T. Pratt, J. Lepson, B. Slikas, C. McIntosh, and R. Raikow made valuable input by their challenging comments and sharing of unpublished information. J. M. Scott, S. Conant, and J. Rotenberry made helpful comments on earlier versions of the manuscript.

Studies in Avian Biology No. 22:98–103, 2001.

PHYLOGENETIC PLACEMENT OF THE PO'OULI, *MELAMPROSOPS PHAEOSOMA*, BASED ON MITOCHONDRIAL DNA SEQUENCE AND OSTEOLOGICAL CHARACTERS

Robert C. Fleischer, Cheryl L. Tarr, Helen F. James, Beth Slikas, and Carl E. McIntosh

Abstract. The Po'ouli (*Melamprosops phaeosoma*) is a small oscine songbird first discovered on Maui in the early 1970s and originally described as a member of the Drepanidini (Hawaiian honeycreepers). A recent study suggested that the Po'ouli may not be a drepanidine because it lacks most of a small set of drepanidine synapomorphies (e.g., specialized tongue morphology and distinctive odor). We conducted phylogenetic analyses of the Po'ouli and a number of drepanidine and potentially related songbird taxa. Our character sets included mitochondrial DNA sequences (obtained for *Melamprosops* via PCR of DNA isolated from museum specimens) and osteological characters. Analyses support the placement of the Po'ouli within the drepanidine clade, although the position of the Po'ouli within the clade is not strongly supported by either data set. Our results indicate that the Po'ouli is relatively distinct phylogenetically among drepanidines. If a goal of biodiversity conservation is to retain as much genetic diversity as possible then the Po'ouli should be considered a species of very high priority for conservation efforts.

Key Words: ancient DNA; Drepanidini; *Melamprosops phaeosoma*; mitochondrial DNA; osteology; phylogeny; Po'ouli.

In 1973 a new genus and species of Hawaiian bird was discovered by a group of student researchers in a small area of rainforest on the north slope of Haleakalā Volcano on Maui. It was described from two collected specimens as the first new, living species of Hawaiian honeycreeper (Drepanidini) to be found in over 50 years (Casey and Jacobi 1974). Later, however, doubts arose concerning whether this small, brown, snail-eating bird is a drepanidine or some other type of songbird (Pratt 1992a). It was given the scientific name *Melamprosops phaeosoma,* and the common Hawaiian name Po'ouli (which means "black-faced" in reference to its prominent black mask). The Po'ouli is now on the verge of extinction. Recent and intensive efforts to locate the species has resulted in detection (and marking) of only three individuals (S. Reilly and M. Collins, pers. comm.; Reynolds et al. *this volume*). It is possible that this number represents the entire living population for the species.

Although the Po'ouli differs in morphology, behavior and ecology from other living Hawaiian birds (Pratt et al. 1997b), its phylogenetic uniqueness and closest relatives remain uncertain (Bock 1978, Pratt 1992a). According to Pratt (1992a), *Melamprosops* completely lacks the few synapomorphies that define the Drepanidini, most notably the unique musty odor and specialized tongue characteristics. It also differs from all known drepanidines in plumage color and pattern, bill morphology, vocalizations, diet (i.e., specialization on snails), and other aspects of behavior (Pratt 1992a). Knowledge about the

relationships and phylogenetic uniqueness of the Po'ouli will help in deciding how much effort should be expended to recover the species (Faith 1992, Krajewski 1994). Here we present cladistic analyses of mitochondrial DNA sequences and skeletal morphology that indicate that this troubling (and troubled) little bird is a Hawaiian honeycreeper, albeit an extremely distinctive one.

METHODS

SAMPLED TAXA

We compared DNA and skeletal characters of *Melamprosops* to a sampling of taxa from within the Drepanidini, Carduelini, Fringillini, Emberizinae, and other outgroups. Common and scientific names of North American and Hawaiian taxa follow the AOU Checklist (1998). Common and scientific names of other taxa, and subfamily classifications, are from Monroe and Sibley (1993).

Drepanidini analyzed for mtDNA sequence or osteology (see Figs. 1 and 2) include Nihoa Finch, *Telespiza ultima*; Laysan Finch, *T. cantans*; Palila, *Loxioides bailleui*; 'Ō'ū, *Psittirostra psittacea*; Lāna'i Hookbill, *Dysmorodrepanis munroi*; Maui Parrotbill, *Pseudonestor xanthophrys*; Kaua'i Creeper, *Oreomystis bairdi*; Hawai'i Creeper, *O. mana*; Maui 'Alauahio, *Paroreomyza montana*; 'Akeke'e, *Loxops caeruleirostris*; 'Ākepa, *L. coccineus*; 'Akiapōlā'au, *Hemignathus munroi*; Lesser 'Akialoa, *H. obscurus*; 'Anianiau, *H. parvus*; Kaua'i 'Amakihi, *H. kauaiensis*; O'ahu 'Amakihi, *H. flavus*; Maui 'Amakihi, *H. virens wilsoni*; Hawai'i 'Amakihi, *H. v. virens*; 'I'iwi, *Vestiaria coccinea*; Hawai'i Mamo, *Drepanis pacifica*; 'Apapane, *Himatione sanguinea*; and 'Ākohekohe, *Palmeria dolei.*

Carduelini analyzed include the White-browed Rosefinch (*Carpodacus thura,* Genbank number

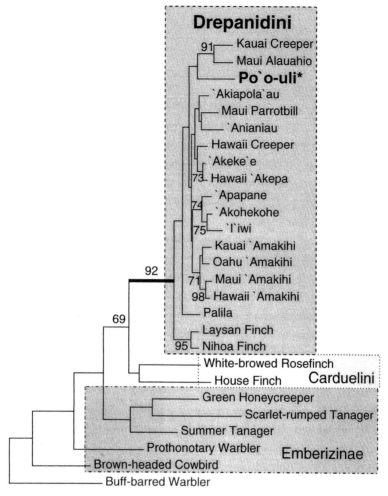

FIGURE 1. Phylogenetic tree constructed using a maximum parsimony criterion from mitochondrial DNA cytochrome *b* sequences. The phylogram is one of two maximum parsimony trees of (weighted) length 1255 and CI of 0.53. The numbers at particular nodes are the percentage of trees containing the node following a 500 repetition bootstrap. Nodes with percentages below 50% are not noted. These nodes are assumed to be unresolved and their branches collapse to a polytomy. See Methods for scientific names of taxa exhibited here.

AF015765), House Finch (*C. mexicanus*; Fleischer et al. 1998), Common Rosefinch (*C. erythrinus*), Purple Finch (*C. purpureus*), Spot-winged Grosbeak (*Mycerobas melanozanthos*), Evening Grosbeak (*Hesperiphona vespertina*), Desert Finch (*Rhodopechys obsoleta*), Golden-winged Grosbeak (*Rhynchostruthus socotranus*), European Greenfinch (*Carduelis chloris*), Pine Siskin (*C. pinus*) Red Crossbill (*Loxia curvirostra*), Yellow-fronted Canary (*Serinus mozambicus*), Grey-headed Bullfinch (*Pyrrhula erythraca*), Pine Grosbeak (*Pinicola enucleator*), and Asian Rosy Finch (*Leucosticte arctoa*). The Common Chaffinch (*Fringilla coelebs*) is a fringilline outgroup.

Emberizines include the Green Honeycreeper (*Chlorophanes spiza*; Fleischer et al. 1998), Scarlet-rumped Tanager (*Ramphocelus passerinii*; U15717), Summer Tanager (*Piranga rubra*; U15725), Prothonotary War-

bler (*Protonotaria citrea*; this study), Brown-headed Cowbird (*Molothrus ater*; this study), Northern Cardinal (*Cardinalis cardinalis*), Black-and-white Warbler (*Mniotilta varia*), Vesper Sparrow (*Pooecetes gramineus*), White-lined Tanager (*Tachyphonus rufus*), Redwinged Blackbird (*Agelaius phoeniceus*), and Saffron Finch (*Sicalis flaveola*). Outgroups are the House Sparrow (*Passer domesticus*) and the Buff-barred Warbler (*Phylloscopus pulcher*; Y10732).

MITOCHONDRIAL DNA

DNA was isolated from samples taken from the only two *Melamprosops* museum specimens that exist. The tip of one small secondary feather was removed from the B. P. Bishop Museum specimen (holotype: BBM-X147112; under the care of C. Kishinami and A. Allison), and a small piece of skin from the ventral open-

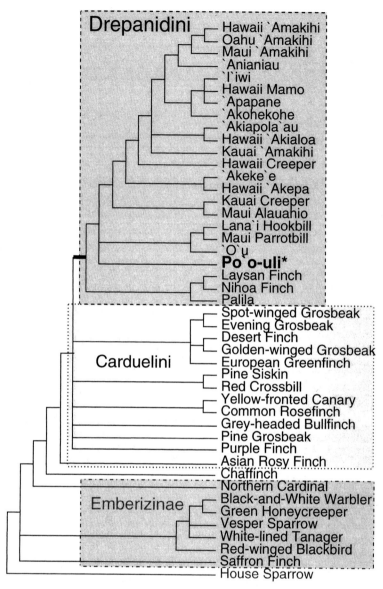

FIGURE 2.   Phylogenetic tree constructed using a maximum parsimony criterion from a matrix of osteological characters. A strict consensus of 128 optimal trees found by repeated random searches of these data (500 replicates, closest addition sequence with ten trees held at each step, initial tree improved upon with TBR branch swapping; optimal tree length 286 steps). See Methods for scientific names of species included in the tree.

ing was taken from the American Museum of Natural History specimen (paratype: AMNH-810456; under the care of G. Barrowclough). Museum specimen DNA was isolated in a small laboratory dedicated to ancient DNA analyses using "ancient DNA" procedures (e.g., Cooper et al. 1996, Paxinos et al. 1997). Modern DNA analyses were conducted in a laboratory separated by >500 m from our ancient laboratory. Briefly, DNA was isolated by digesting skin or feather pulp overnight at 55° C in a DTT-SDS-EDTA buffer with proteinase K, followed by phenol and chloroform

extractions and centrifugal dialysis to remove buffer and other solutes (as in Paxinos et al. 1997).

We amplified and sequenced two regions of mtDNA from the museum and modern specimens (Fig. 1) using the polymerase chain reaction and specific primers: (1) 675 bp of the Cytochrome b (Cyt b) gene in two overlapping pieces (see Fleischer et al. 1998); and (2) 224 bases of the 5' end of the mitochondrial control region (CR; Tarr 1995). Cyt b and CR sequences were also obtained for some non-drepanidine songbird species from Genbank (see Fig. 1). The Cyt b sequence was amplified only from the AMNH specimen, and analyzed with 18 other drepanidine taxa as reported in Fleischer et al. (1998). The CR segment was amplified from the BPBM specimen only, and from an additional 6 drepanidine species. PCR controls were negative (i.e., no apparent product produced) for the study skin amplifications for both Cyt *b* and CR. Sequences were produced either manually as in Fleischer et al (1998) or on an ABI-373 automated DNA sequencer as in Greenberg et al. (1998), and were aligned with Sequencher 3.0. Phylogenetic reconstructions and other analyses utilized PAUP*4.0d64 (D. Swofford, pers. comm.) and MacClade 3.01 (Maddison and Maddison 1992), and are described in the results section below.

OSTEOLOGY

A subset of data from a separate study of cranial osteology and phylogeny in the drepanidines (James 1998) was used to determine if the Poʻouli is supported as part of the drepanidine clade. The original study involved 72 characters and 55 species of drepanidines, including 17 fossil species that became extinct following human settlement of the archipelago less than two thousand years ago (James and Olson 1991). For the present study, the fossil taxa were excluded in order to specifically examine the phylogenetic placement of *Melamprosops* relative to extant or historically extinct drepanidines. Twenty-one other species of nine-primaried oscines were included so that other potential relationships might be revealed. *Passer domesticus* was included as an outgroup. The resulting matrix had 45 terminal taxa and 57 informative characters.

The osteological matrix was analyzed using a parsimony criterion. All characters were run as ordered characters except for seven multistate characters that were run as unordered because the states were not judged to be sequential. Ten characters had an essentially binary distribution of states except that a few taxa showed intermediate conditions. In these instances, the intermediate condition was scored as a third state, but the character was assigned a weight of 0.5 for the parsimony analyses, to prevent intermediate conditions from exerting an undue influence on tree length. All other characters were unweighted.

RESULTS

MITOCHONDRIAL DNA

Cladistic parsimony analyses of the Cyt *b* sequences consistently place the Poʻouli within the Drepanidini (Fig. 1). We initially ran a heuristic search in PAUP* with replicated, random addition and no character weighting, and obtained seven equally most parsimonious trees for drepanidines and carduelines. A maximum likelihood (ML) estimate of the transition-to-transversion ratio was then made using the tree with the lowest ML score (ts:tv ~ 4.0:1). This ratio was used to weight transversional changes, and a heuristic search generated two maximum parsimony trees of length 1255 (unweighted for the same topology is 685 steps) and a consistency index of 0.53 (Fig. 1). Placement of Melamprosops within the Drepanidini, however, occurs re-

gardless of whether transversions are weighted 4.0:1, 10.0:1, or unweighted relative to transitions (although weighting and additional outgroup taxa does affect the topology of drepanidine relationships). Forcing the Poʻouli from the Drepanidini to the Carduelini (in MacClade; Maddison and Maddison 1992) increases the length of the tree (unweighted) in Figure 1 by 12 additional steps. This constrained tree is significantly longer than that of Figure 1 based on both parsimony (Kishino-Hawegawa test, t = 2.69, P = 0.0072; Kishino and Hasegawa 1989) and maximum likelihood (G = 52.71, P < 0.001; Felsenstein 1988) tests. Making Melamprosops the sister to each emberizine clade also significantly increases tree length (by 20–27 additional steps; Kishino-Hasegawa test, t = 3.56, P < 0.001).

Distance analyses further support a drepanidine relationship for *Melamprosops*. Kimura 2-parameter and gamma-corrected distances were lower for comparisons of the Poʻouli and drepanidines (0.086 ± 0.002, range 0.062–0.102) than for comparisons of the Poʻouli and carduelines (0.147 ± 0.005, range 0.142–0.152) or emberizines (0.196 ± 0.010, range 0.170–0.218).

The CR sequence analyses also place the Poʻouli within the Drepanidini. First, three single-base deletions found in the Fringillini and Carduelini CR sequences do not occur in drepanidines nor in Melamprosops CR sequence (Table 1). Second, 1000 replication bootstraps of maximum parsimony trees (with gaps and transversions weighted 10:1 or 5:1 over transitions; heuristic search) reveal 88% and 90% support, respectively, for monophyly of the drepanidines, including the Poʻouli. Last, forcing the Poʻouli from the Drepanidini into the Carduelini (i.e., sister to *Carduelis chloris*) or Emberizinae (i.e., as a sister to *Melospiza georgiana*) increases unweighted tree length by 4 and 10 steps, respectively. The constrained trees are significantly longer (Kishino-Hasegawa test, t = 2.15, P = 0.032 when sister to *Carduelis*; t = 2.32, P = 0.021 when sister to *Melospiza*).

OSTEOLOGY

Parsimony analysis produced 128 equally most parsimonious trees from which we derive a strict consensus tree (Fig. 2). The Poʻouli is nested within the drepanidine clade in all of the 128 trees. Moving the Poʻouli outside the drepanidine clade to a position as sister to either cardueline terminal taxa or cardueline resolved clades adds 9 to 23 additional steps to the total tree length. Making the Poʻouli a sister taxon to *Fringilla* or any emberizine outgroup adds 13 to 20.5 steps.

TABLE 1. LISTED ARE 67 VARIABLE NUCLEOTIDE SITES (OF 224 TOTAL) FROM THE 5'-END OR LEFT DOMAIN OF THE MITOCHONDRIAL CONTROL REGION ASSESSED FOR ONE EMBERIZINAE (*MELOSPIZA GEORGIANA*; GREENBERG ET AL. 1998) AND TEN FRINGILLINAE, INCLUDING THREE FRINGILLINI (*FRINGILLA*; MARSHALL AND BAKER 1997), ONE CARDUELINI (*CARDUELIS*; MARSHALL AND BAKER 1997), AND SIX EXTANT MEMBERS OF THE DREPANIDINI (TARR 1995)

```
                        1         2         3         4         5         6
                 1234567890123456789012345678901234567890123456789012345678901234567
                 |||||||||||||||||||||||||||||||||||||||||||||||||||||||||||||||||||||

Melospiza georgiana      TAGCCACGACACCTTATTATGAA-CCACTAGTGA-A-AACACTCCCGTAGGTATATTCAATAGATAG

Fringilla teydea         ....TGTA.-.T.....A.C..TA..T....A..-.-.G.TA..T...T....-.GCTTC.TA.C..

Fringilla montifringilla ....T.TAG-..AC..........-..T.CC.GA.-.-.G.TA......T.....-.GCTTC.TA.C..

Fringilla coelebs        C....G...T..........A..-A.T....A..-.-.G.TA......T.....-.GCTTC.TAGC.A

Carduelis chloris        .CAAT.A....GT.......A.TAA.CT...GA.-G-.GA.A..T....ACAT-GCCTGCCTAGC..

Paroreomyza montana      .CA...A...GATC.....C.CTA.AC.AG.GAGG.TGG.......ACT.......C..C.T..C..

Loxioides balleui        .CA.T.A....G....C..C.CCAA.T.AC.C..G.G.G........GT......C...C.T.....

Telespiza cantans        .CA...A...GGT.C.C...ACCA.AC.A.....G.G.G.....NNNNN......C...C.TT.C..

Hemignathus parvus       .CA...A...GA......G.ATCAAAC.A..A..G.NNG.......AGT....G....TC.T..C..

Hemignathus kauaiensis   .CA.T.A...GA........ACCCAAC.A..A..A.A.G...C...CAC....AG.C.TC.T..CC.

Himatione sanguinea      .C..TTA...G.......C.CTAAAC.ATCAC.G.NNG....A.T..T...CG..C.TC.T..C..

Melamprosops phaeosoma   .CA.T.A........C.....TTC.AT.A..A..G.NNG...NNNNNNN......GCTTC.T..C..
```

Note: *Melamprosops phaeosoma* sequence is from this study. A "." indicates identity of the nucleotide to the topmost base and an "N" indicates a base that could not be called. A "-" indicates a gap or deletion in the sequence. Note the three insertions found in all drepanidines relative to fringillines (at sites 35, 37, and 54). In addition, there are three drepanidine transversional synapomorphies (22, 26, and 29). See Fig. 1 for common names of drepanidine taxa.

DISCUSSION

In spite of Pratt's (1992a) assessment that the Po'ouli might not be a drepanidine, we find consistent evidence to the contrary. Pratt (1992a) notes that the Po'ouli should be considered a "nine-primaried oscine of uncertain affinities," and that it "does not look, smell, act, or sound like a Hawaiian honeycreeper." Our DNA evidence places *Melamprosops* within the drepanidines, and osteological characteristics indeed make the Po'ouli "look" like a honeycreeper. How does one reconcile the apparent morphological, ecological, and behavioral distinctiveness of the Po'ouli (Pratt 1992a; Pratt et al. 1997b, *this volume*) with our results? Two explanations may account for this: (1) some of the phenotypic traits that Pratt emphasizes (i.e., those associated with foraging mode and feeding) may be affected by adaptive radiation and thus we might expect to see wide diversity in their character states; and (2) some of the 17 extinct drepanidine species known only from fossils may have shared these traits with the Po'ouli, thus making it different only in the context of living or historically extinct taxa. We do not know what factors effected the evolution of the brownish coloration and the black facial mask, nor why *Melamprosops* (and apparently *Paroreomyza*; Pratt 1992b) lack the distinctive drepanidine odor.

While our results indicate that the Po'ouli is a Hawaiian honeycreeper, the relationships of the Po'ouli within the drepanidines are not well resolved by the mtDNA data (Fig. 1). Majority rule bootstrap analysis results in collapse of supporting branches such that *Melamprosops* becomes a basal drepanidine lineage. On the strict consensus for the morphological trees, the Po'ouli joins at a node proximal to the finch-like species but distal to most other living drepanidines. It is not depicted as the sister group of any living drepanidine species. Thus, in both mtDNA and osteological trees the Po'ouli appears to represent a unique drepanidine lineage. Its lineage may have diverged from other drepanidine lineages prior to evolution of the synapomorphic characters defined by Pratt (1992a).

How phylogenetically distinct is the Po'ouli among living drepanidines? To answer this we estimated the contribution of each taxon to the total minimum evolution score for the Cyt *b* tree in Figure 1. In PAUP*, we constrained the tree topology, pruned a taxon from the tree, then recalculated the ME score. The process was repeated for each drepanidine taxon; each ME score was subtracted from the total ME score to provide a phylogenetic "distinctiveness" score (U) for the taxon (essentially that of Faith 1992). The Po'ouli had the highest U (0.044) among the 19 drepanidines (mean and SE of U for the other 18 taxa was 0.015 ± 0.002). To evaluate the Po'ouli's distinctiveness in the osteology-based tree we constrained the tree in Figure 2 in MacClade 3.01. A drepanidine taxon was removed and the length of the reduced tree was subtracted from the length of the total tree. The procedure was repeated for each of the 23 drepanidines, and revealed that the Po'ouli was the fourth most distinctive taxon based on osteology (after Maui and Kauai creepers and the 'Akiapōlā'au). Thus we consider the Po'ouli to be phylogenetically unique among the drepanidines, and the taxon that individually contributes most to extant drepanidine phylogenetic diversity.

The closest corrected genetic distance between the Po'ouli and other drepanidines is 0.062. Applying a corrected internal rate calibration for Cyt *b* in honeycreepers of about 0.016 ± 0.005/MY (from Fleischer et al. 1998) suggests that the Po'ouli split from its nearest living drepanidine relative about 3.8 ± 0.9 MY

ago (fairly early in the drepanidine radiation; Tarr and Fleischer 1995, Fleischer et al. 1998). Of course extinct fossil drepanidines (James and Olson 1991) not included here, such as *Xestospiza,* may turn out to be more closely related genetically. Nonetheless, in comparison to other extant drepanidines, the Po'ouli has had a long, independent evolutionary history. This long period of independent evolution can perhaps explain some of *Melamprosops'* unique phenotypic characteristics. Such phylogenetic distinctiveness also increases the Po'ouli's conservation value, in that the species represents a significant fraction of the genetic diversity of the drepanidines (Faith 1992, Krajewski 1994). Along with its singular ecological, behavioral, and morphological characteristics, the Po'ouli's unique evolutionary history convinces us that serious efforts should be undertaken to avoid its impending extinction.

ACKNOWLEDGMENTS

We gratefully acknowledge C. Kishinami and A. Allison of the B. P. Bishop Museum, and G. Barrowclough of the American Museum of Natural History, for allowing us to sample from the precious Po'ouli specimens under their care. The Smithsonian Institution's Walcott and Wetmore Funds, the National Geographic Society, and the Friends of the National Zoo provided funding for our Hawaiian honeycreeper research. We thank T. Pratt and S. Reilly for providing information and discussion, and D. Pratt, C. van Riper and S. Conant for reading and evaluating the results in the manuscript.

Status and Trends

Studies in Avian Biology No. 22:106–107, 2001.

STATUS AND TRENDS—INTRODUCTION

J. Michael Scott and Charles van Riper, III

The first postcontact attempts to assess the status of Hawai'i's birds were the collection of birds by naturalists of Cook's third voyage of exploration (Medway 1981). Additional 18th and 19th century attempts to document the occurrence of birds in Hawai'i were sporadic and incompletely reported, and are documented in detail elsewhere (Olson and James 1994a). In the last decade of the 19th century and in the first years of the 20th century, there was renewed interest in the birds of Hawai'i. Henry Palmer collected for Walter Rothschild, and S. B. Wilson obtained specimens that resulted in publication of his and Evans's monumental works on the avifauna of Hawai'i (Wilson and Evans 1890–1899, Rothschild 1893–1900). The Nihoa Finch (*Telespiza ultima*) was described in 1917 (Bryan 1917) and the Nihoa Millerbird (*Acrocephalus familiaris*) in 1924 (Wetmore 1924), but the Po'ouli (*Melamprosops phaeosoma*) would not be described until 1973 (Casey and Jacobi 1974). During this same period, Henshaw (1902a) and Perkins (1903) added much to our knowledge of the turn of the century status and distribution of birds in Hawai'i. It was not until George C. Munro's efforts to survey the avifauna of the islands from 1935 to 1937 that anyone would attempt to systematically ascertain the 20th century status of Hawai'i's native avifauna (Munro 1944).

The husband and wife team of Charles and Elizabeth Schwartz conducted an 18-mo survey of the game birds of the territory of Hawai'i (Schwartz and Schwartz 1949). The objectives of this survey were "to ascertain the game birds present on the Hawaiian Islands, their distribution and abundance and factors upon which their welfare depends." Several surveys of the Leeward Islands followed (Bailey 1956, Amerson 1971, Amerson et al. 1974, Clapp et al. 1977, Woodward 1972). Richardson and Bowles (1964) conducted an exhaustive survey of Kaua'i, one that resulted in the last documented field observations of the 'Akialoa (*Hemignathus ellisianus*). Their observation that all of the species known to have occurred on Kaua'i could still be found there resulted in the state of Hawai'i setting aside the Alaka'i Swamp as a reserve.

John Sincock and Gene Kridler, both of the U.S. Fish and Wildlife Service, set up a statistically defensible set of transects allowing an estimate of the population size of Laysan Finch (*Telespiza cantans*) and the Nihoa Millerbird in the Leeward Islands (Conant et al 1981, Conant and Morin *this volume*). These transects have since been monitored continuously and constitute the first estimate of the numbers of Hawaiian birds that included variances. Sincock followed his efforts in the Leeward Islands by establishing a set of transects in the Alaka'i Swamp that were used to establish the population size of the endangered forest birds of Kaua'i (reported in Scott et al. 1986). Interagency efforts were initiated in the 1950s to monitor the numbers of waterbirds (Engilis and Pratt 1993) and to assess the number and distribution of the Nēnē (Hawaiian Goose, *Branta sandvicensis*; Black and Banko 1994). In 1976, nearly 100 years after its discovery (Wilson and Evans 1890–1899), the first ever attempt to estimate the population size of the Palila (*Loxiodes bailleui*) was conducted (van Riper et al. 1978). That effort established that the Palila was more abundant than previously thought, thus documenting the value of statistically based surveys of the entire range of a species. Winston Banko provided an exhaustive review of the literature on Hawaiian birds and documented all known records (Banko 1979, 1980a,b,c,d; 1981a,b; 1984a,b; 1986)

The second range-wide survey of the Palila occurred in 1980 (Scott et al. 1984) and used the variable circular count. This census method has been used in all subsequent attempts to estimate population size of the Palila (Jacobi et al. 1996). It was in part the success of the Palila surveys that prompted the Hawaiian Forest Bird Survey (HFBS) 1976–1981 (Scott et al. 1986), an effort to survey all the forest bird habitat in Hawai'i. The HFBS was initiated in the forests of Ka'ū on Hawai'i in 1976 and ended deep in the heart of the Alaka'i Swamp on Kaua'i in 1981. The objectives of this survey were to determine the numbers, distribution, habitat associations, and possible limiting factors of the endangered forest birds of the high islands of Hawai'i. The only islands not surveyed were O'ahu (Shallenberger and Vaughn 1978) and the privately owned Ni'ihau. Since completion of this HFBS, segments of HFBS transects have been surveyed irregularly (Reynolds et al. *this volume*). The challenges of estimating the number of birds in Hawai'i were the motivation for an international symposium on estimating the number of terrestrial birds (Ralph and Scott 1981).

Authors in this section report on more recent efforts to assess the numbers of Hawai'i's avifauna. David Ainley and his coauthors use a combination of field observations and modeling to assess the status of the Hawaiian subspecies of Townsend's Shearwater (*Puffinus auricularis newelli*), hereafter referred to as Newell's Shearwater, whereas the late Miklos Udvardy and Andrew Engilis report on 50 years of data on the migratory Northern Pintail (*Anas acuta*). Mich-

elle Reynolds and Thomas Snetsinger describe their efforts to monitor the status of the rarest birds in Hawai'i, reporting on thousands of person-days of field effort. Paul Baker describes the status and distribution of the rarest of Hawai'i's terrestrial birds, the Po'ouli (*Melamprosops phaeosoma*) and finds three birds remaining. The dilemma of what management actions are dictated by such a rare species has challenged the talents of scientists and managers alike.

Studies in Avian Biology No. 22:108–123, 2001.

THE STATUS AND POPULATION TRENDS OF THE NEWELL'S SHEARWATER ON KAUA'I: INSIGHTS FROM MODELING

David G. Ainley, Richard Podolsky, Leah Deforest, Gregory Spencer, and Nadav Nur

Abstract. We assessed the status of the endemic subspecies of Townsend's Shearwater, hereafter referred to as Newell's Shearwater (*Puffinus auricularis newelli*), on Kaua'i, Hawaiian Islands, where the only sizable population of this species remains. First, to index recent population trends, we analyzed data gathered on the 1,000–2,000 fledglings attracted to lights and picked up annually by the "Save Our Shearwaters" (SOS) Program over a 17-year period, 1978–1994. Second, to calibrate and to provide a demographic context to these data, we quantified breeding productivity and mortality in a mountain colony and mortality due to anthropogenic factors in the urban corridor that encircles the breeding areas during seven years: 1980–1985 (summary of previous study), 1993, and 1994. Finally, we entered rates of productivity and mortality into a Leslie model to integrate these data, to evaluate the demographic importance of different sources of mortality, and to assess the utility of SOS in mitigating mortality from anthropogenic factors.

During 17 years of data collection, an average 1,432 fledglings that were attracted to lights were picked up by SOS each year; 90% were banded and released alive. Considering all of Kaua'i during the study period, more fledglings were picked up, if breeding effort and success were higher, and the full moon occurred in early October well before the mid-month peak of fledging. Overall, the annual totals of fledglings (1) gradually decreased on the southern shore, where the level of urbanization (and lighting) has grown to double that of the entire remainder of the island; (2) remained approximately stable on the eastern shore (moderate urbanization); but (3) increased markedly on the northern shore, where urbanization is low but grew dramatically during the study period. The relationships to urbanization were corroborated by natural experiments when lighting was curtailed. Research in the breeding colony revealed (1) a high incidence of nonbreeding (46% of burrow occupants) even among experienced adults, typical of many petrel species; (2) predation (2.5% of individuals) on subadults and adults in the colonies by introduced house cats (*Felis catus*) and Barn Owls (*Tyto alba*); and (3) breeding success (0.66 chicks/pair) comparable to other shearwaters with stable populations. Research in the urban corridor revealed, conservatively, that (1) about 15% of an estimated 9,600 fledglings produced each year are picked up by SOS, (2) annual mortality of fledglings following light attraction during autumn is about 10%, and (3) annual mortality to adults and subadults from collisions with power lines during spring and summer (without light attraction) is 0.6–2.1%/yr. Only 15 of the 23,000 fledglings (<0.1%) initially banded by SOS have been recovered in subsequent years, but recoveries show that first breeding occurs at about 6 yrs of age and that 1-yr-olds do not visit Kaua'i.

A Leslie model, using parameters determined for the Newell's Shearwater, supplemented by those from the very closely related Manx Shearwater (*P. p. puffinus*), indicated a balanced/stable population when extrinsic mortality of anthropogenic origin was excluded. Factoring in predation on adults and subadults in the colonies and mortality of fledglings and adults/subadults due to collisions with human-made structures produced decadal declines of 30–60% in the population, with variation depending on the parameter values used. The model also showed that the SOS program is critical to reducing the rate of population decline. Predation from introduced animals proved to be the most important cause of decline, but collisions with structures by adults and mortality of fledglings following light attraction were also significant.

Key Words: bird impacts; cat predation; Hawai'i; Kaua'i; light attraction; Newell's Shearwater; oceanic island; population model; *Puffinus auricularis*; transmission line; urbanization.

Many populations of tropical seabirds that nest on oceanic islands with large human populations have been decimated by introductions of mammalian predators, habitat destruction, and urbanization, though the details are known only generally. Several large tropical petrels are now endangered or recently extinct, for example, the Bermuda Petrel (*Pterodroma cahow*), Jamaican Petrel (*Pt. hasitata*), Madeiran Petrel (*Pt. mollis madeira*), Fiji Petrel (*Pt. macgillivrayi*), and Magenta Petrel (*Pt. magentae,* of New Zealand; Croxall et al. 1984, Warham 1990, Ehrlich et al. 1992, Nettleship et al. 1994). Included in this group are those petrels nesting among the main Hawaiian Islands, the endemic subspecies of Townsend's Shearwater (*Puffinus auricularis newelli*), hereafter referred to as Newell's Shearwater, and Dark-rumped Petrel (*Pt. phaeopygia sandwichensis*), both of which are listed by the U.S. Endangered Species Act (USFWS 1982a). Newell's Shearwater and Dark-rumped Petrel have been extirpated from most of their former nesting islands, but on Kaua'i they are still relatively abundant (Telfer et al. 1987, Harrison 1990).

The Newell's Shearwater, or 'A'o, was considered extinct as of 1908, but on Kaua'i in 1947 it was rediscovered and, in 1967, confirmed to be breeding (King and Gould 1967, Sincock and Swedberg 1969). A small breeding population has been confirmed recently on the island of Hawai'i (Reynolds et al. 1997a, Reynolds and Ritchotte 1997), and the species may also nest in very low numbers on Moloka'i and O'ahu (Harrison 1990). Rediscovery of Newell's Shearwater coincided with rapid growth in urban development on Kaua'i, when hundreds of fledglings were found, having been attracted to and, typical of all petrels (Reed et al. 1985), apparently blinded by man-made lighting as the birds made their way from nest to ocean on their nocturnal fledgling flight (King and Gould 1967). This annual "fallout" became a major source of mortality, because fledglings die after being run over by cars or colliding with lights, utility poles and wires, and buildings (Byrd et al. 1984, Telfer et al. 1987). Shielding lights reduced attraction by as much as 40% in experimental areas (Reed et al. 1985); for example, a reduction in the intensity of yard lights at the Hanalei Plantation Hotel in 1965 reduced the fallout there significantly (King and Gould 1967). New building codes established in the late 1980s request measures to shield lights (State of Hawaii 1987); however, compliance has been inconsistent (D. Ainley and R. Podolsky, pers. obs.).

Attempting to decrease the mortality associated with fallout, the U.S. Fish and Wildlife Service (USFWS) and the State of Hawaii, Department of Land and Natural Resources (DLNR), organized the "Save Our Shearwaters" (SOS) Program in 1978 (Telfer et al. 1987, Rauzon 1991). Residents who found fallen shearwaters were encouraged, by advertisements in the news media, to place them in bird boxes at "Shearwater Aid Stations." The captured birds were then picked up each morning and taken for release from a coastal cliff. In the 17 years through 1994, about 23,000 shearwaters have been retrieved, banded, and released (T. Telfer, unpubl. data).

The current relatively high abundance and easy access of the Newell's Shearwater on Kaua'i provided the opportunity to understand the species' ecology in the context of interactions with human activity, and to test the utility of SOS before the species' status becomes desperate and conservation attempts costly. What is learned may help to protect this and similar seabirds as development and tourism spread to more and more tropical islands (e.g., Croxall et al. 1984, Croxall 1991). We report here our findings during a study that included both fieldwork

and analysis of existing unpublished data gathered by SOS and by government researchers since the late 1970s. The assembled information provided inputs into a demographic model of population growth under various scenarios of mortality. The model was used to evaluate the impact of three important factors indicated in the field studies: predation of adults from introduced animals, mortality of fledglings after fallout, and mortality of adults from collisions with power lines. In addition, we use the population dynamic model to project long-term stability of the Newell's Shearwater population on Kaua'i.

METHODS

FIELDWORK

We conducted fieldwork in a mountain colony above Kalāheo (Fig.1), where the species breeding biology was studied in the early 1980s as part of an effort to determine whether Newell's Shearwaters could be cross-fostered by the much more abundant Wedge-tailed Shearwater (*P. pacificus*; Byrd et al. 1984). Access to the colony was difficult but nevertheless was easier by far than to any other colony known for Newell's Shearwater. Elevation of the Kalāheo colony is about 600 m. We searched for burrows among the vegetation on the >65 degree slopes between May and November 1993. Burrows were marked and a line of small sticks was erected across entrances to indicate burrow use when brushed aside by entering or departing birds; we also noted the presence or absence of excrement and feathers. We used a miniature infrared TV camera (Furhman Diversified, Inc.) on a stiff coaxial cable "snaked" down each burrow to determine the presence of eggs or chicks. Once an egg or chick was found, we rechecked the nest's status monthly. We attempted to set up a second study colony at a site called Kaluahonu, on the southern part of the island, but found that few birds still nested there compared with the early 1980s. In 1994, due to a shortfall in funding and a request from the committee overseeing the project (see Acknowledgments), we diminished work in the Kalāheo colony and allocated our efforts elsewhere. Therefore, we checked contents of burrows found the previous year on four occasions between late August and mid-November. We compared our findings on breeding productivity with the results of Telfer (1986), who participated in the cross-fostering studies from 1981 to 1985. Results over the seven seasons were combined in the demographic model described below.

To guard against intrusions of feral cats (*Felis catus*) and rats into our study colony, we placed a network of live-capture traps at the entrance to our ridge-top trails. Traps were baited every three days. In addition, we carried no food of our own into the colony for fear of attracting mammals.

To assess survival from the proportion of colony occupants that may have been banded by SOS (when birds were fledglings), we captured adult shearwaters by blocking the burrow entrance just before dark and waiting nearby. Upon arrival, the birds sat by the entrance and could be picked up easily. We checked

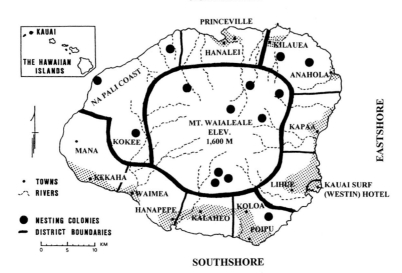

FIGURE 1.   Map of Kauaʻi, Hawaiian Islands, showing breeding colonies of Newell's Shearwaters (from Ainley et al. 1995) and the 10 districts used by SOS to summarize data (modified from Telfer et al. 1987). Bold boundaries indicate the Southshore, Eastshore, and Northshore areas on Kauaʻi into which we combined SOS districts in our analysis. Shading indicates the current extent of urban and suburban areas.

these birds for bands and banded them if none was present. We quantified mortality due to collisions with power lines during summer and to fallout during autumn; results are reported elsewhere (Ainley et al. 1995, Podolsky et al. 1998).

ANALYSIS OF SOS DATA

To assess temporal and regional trends in the number of birds retrieved, we analyzed data contained in annual reports of the SOS program from 1980 to 1993 (project W-18-R, Hawaii DLNR), as well as raw data computerized by SOS from 1987 to 1993. We did not use data from 1978 or 1979 in most analyses because effort by the citizenry was reduced in the first two years of the program relative to subsequent years (citizens learned of the program each fall through advertisements in newspapers and radio).

A ledger on which persons could record the place where each bird was found was provided by SOS at each shearwater station. In 10–15% of cases the specific pickup locality was not recorded, and in some of these (e.g., when a citizen was commuting to/from work) it was likely that birds were turned in at stations some distance from the pickup locality. Beginning in 1982, to determine geographic variation in the relative strength of fallout, SOS divided Kauaʻi into ten districts (Fig. 1) and apportioned the birds of unknown locality to the various districts according to the SOS station at which these birds were turned in (Telfer et al. 1987). We combined the districts into broader regions, a procedure that further diluted the effect of any incorrect apportionment. The regions, and the districts/drop-off stations comprising them, were (see Fig. 1): (1) Northshore—Hanalei-Princeville; (2) Eastshore—Kīlauea-Anahola, Kapaʻa, Līhuʻe, Westin Lagoons (Kauaʻi Surf) Hotel; and (3) Southshore—Kō-

loa-Poʻipū, Kalāheo, Hanapēpē-Waimeae, Mānā-Kekaha (including Barking Sands Naval Air Station). Nāpali-Kōkeʻe is included in the Northshore, but being mostly wild land, it contributed little to SOS data.

In analyses where year was an important consideration, we did not use data from autumn 1992 or from 1993, because Kauaʻi was much different in ways critical to our study. Hurricane Iniki devastated human structures on the island in September 1992, just before the shearwaters had begun to fledge and SOS would have swung into action. The hurricane obliterated all bright lights; all hotels were closed due to damage and fewer than 10% of street lights or power lines were left standing. Life on Kauaʻi did not return to normal until summer 1994. Hurricane Iwa, in 1982, did not pass over Kauaʻi until November, after shearwater fallout had been completed, so the fallout data were not affected and were included in analyses.

To maintain robust sample sizes in the data, we made some reasonable assumptions to categorize certain data rather than discarding them from analysis. First, dead adults were distinguished from dead fledglings in the 1987–1993 SOS data, but this was not the case in the 1980–1986 data. With no organized search effort in 1987–1990, the average number of dead adults/subadults found was 17/yr (see Results). So, to estimate the number of dead fledglings reported by SOS each autumn, 1980–1986, we assumed that the age ratio and search effort were the same as in 1987–1990 and, therefore, subtracted 17 "adults" from the total number of dead shearwaters reported in each of those years.

Second, dead adults reported during spring and summer were logged by SOS beginning in 1987. It was not until 1991–1992, however, that a concerted search effort for adults/subadults was made, in effect, equal to the effort for fledglings in autumn. In 1991, some especially interested and knowledgeable citizens (C. Berg, C. Orr, and K. Viernes) undertook this task and it was continued by us in 1993 and 1994. We assumed that patterns revealed in 1991–1994 were similar to those in the older SOS data. Next, we assumed that "adults" reported as dead in the SOS data after 15 September of each year included many individuals incorrectly aged for two reasons. First, in SOS records, peaks in number of dead birds recorded as "adults" (many of which are flattened and thus hard to assess) corresponded exactly to peaks of fledglings (Ainley et al. 1995). Second, few adults visit the colonies and no banded adults/subadults have been found after this date (see Results). Adult shearwaters desert their young a week or two before the fledgling departs (see Warham 1990); therefore, we considered all birds found after 15 September (the beginning of the fledging and fallout period) to be fledglings. To be sure, a few adults are found after that date (T. Telfer, pers. comm.).

Finally, it was not until 1982 that stainless steel bands were used by SOS on all fledglings. Prior to then, most were banded with monel bands. Therefore, our analyses based on return rates of banded birds do not include the data for the 1978–1981 cohorts, assuming that the monel bands were lost rapidly as a result of immersion in sea water (Boekelheide and Ainley 1989).

To assess trends in SOS totals in the context of urbanization, we indexed the urbanization of Kaua'i in two ways. Ultimately, we were interested in the number and dispersion of shearwaters, the number and dispersion of lights to attract them, and the number of people available to report birds or carcasses to SOS. Not having direct data on urbanization (e.g., the rate at which building permits were issued), we chose two surrogates. First, we used growth in numbers of year-round human residents (data from the U.S. Census Bureau, 1930–1990), and compared these among the three regions to which the SOS data had been partitioned (Fig. 1). From this population are the persons who participate in SOS, with participation depending only on the acts of encountering a shearwater, picking it up, and delivering it to an SOS station. In the small, close community of residents (currently 48,000 persons), more and more persons would know about SOS as the years passed and the proportion of interested persons would not decrease. Efforts to advertise SOS remained constant throughout the period. Next, to index trends in growth of the infrastructure developed for the tourist industry (i.e., coastal hotels, condominiums, lighted tennis courts and driving ranges, etc.), which would not necessarily track the requirements of permanent residents, we obtained data from the state of Hawai'i on the number of passengers using the Līhu'e Airport each year from 1960 to 1993. This infrastructure (and attendant lights) would be the source of fallout. Tourists would not know about SOS.

The following assumptions were used to relate trends in the SOS data to urbanization. First assumption: the number of fledglings retrieved by SOS in any year is proportional to breeding population size and reproductive success. Reproductive output, or at least SOS totals, appears to have exhibited no continuous trend through time, except for the occasional outlying year (see Results). Second assumption: the number of fledglings reported to SOS is strongly affected by the number and distribution of lights to attract them. This effect of lights, proposed also by Telfer et al. (1987), was verified experimentally when lighting was severely reduced at the Hanalei Plantation Hotel in the 1960s (King and Gould 1967), at the Kaua'i Surf/Westin Lagoons Hotel after 1983, and throughout Kaua'i as a result of Hurricane Iniki during 1992–1993 (see Results). Third assumption: the number of citizens present on Kaua'i also directly affects the number of birds reported. The latter two factors (i.e., number and distribution of lights plus number of persons available to encounter birds) would determine the proportion of fledglings produced that were attracted to lights, went aground, and were picked up. Final assumption: because the shearwater population incurs a cost through mortality from fallout (i.e., some birds die regardless of SOS), the cost, if high enough, can lead to population decline (i.e., too many fledglings die due to effects of urbanization). It is possible that the proportion of fledglings attracted and picked up could become saturated (i.e., an asymptote is reached whereby additional lights and people do not lead to more birds retrieved). This would argue also, however, for fallout cost to reach a maximum early in the growth of urban development (an important consideration; see below).

MODELING

We developed a population-dynamic model for the Newell's Shearwater, using assumptions similar to those used by others in analogous contexts (e.g., Simons 1984, Beissinger 1995, Shannon and Crawford 1999), to project population trajectory with and without mortality due to anthropogenic factors and to quantify the relative impact of those threats. We used a Leslie model (Leslie 1945), which combines age-specific fecundity and survival to estimate population growth rates. Due to lack of information about year-to-year variation in demographic parameters, which is the case for the vast majority of demographic studies of wild, long-lived vertebrates, we assumed average (constant) values for the parameters. Owing to lack of data regarding age-related variation in demographic parameters among shearwaters and other procellariiforms (e.g., Bradley et al. 1989, Wooller et al. 1989), and consistent with the efforts of other researchers, we also made the simplifying assumption of age-constant survival and reproductive success for individuals that have reached adulthood.

Our approach, first, was to determine the combination of parameter values that produced a stable population. Against this, current population parameters could be compared to show that, in the absence of recent anthropogenic activity, Newell's Shearwaters can maintain their numbers. Second, we used conservative, best estimates for each parameter and compared population projections that did and did not include various factors affecting population growth. The factors considered were: (1) mortality of fledglings attracted to lights and subsequently grounded during autumn (fallout), (2) mortality of adults and subadults that collide with utility structures during spring and summer, (3) predation of adults and subadults in the breeding

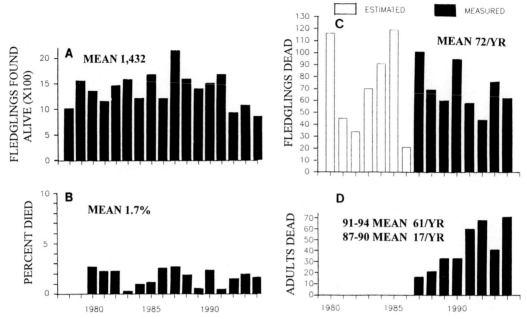

FIGURE 2.   Summary of SOS data for Newell's Shearwaters on Kaua'i, Hawaiian Islands: (A) total fledglings retrieved annually, 1980–1994; (B) percentage of fledglings that died in captivity during those years; (C) the number of fledglings, and (D) number of adults, respectively, as reported dead on the road (not retrieved). The number of dead fledglings was estimated for years prior to 1987 (see Methods).

colonies, and (4) reduction of mortality to fledglings as a result of the SOS program in autumn.

For all analyses, we used the computer package STATA (Computer Resource Center 1993). Averages are reported with ± 1 SE.

RESULTS

BREEDING EFFORT AND SUCCESS

Telfer (1986) monitored 36–47 burrows in the Kalāheo colony during 1981–1985, and we monitored 58–65 burrows, including many in Telfer's sample, in 1993–1994. Among the burrows checked in 1981–1985, the proportion in which breeding adults occurred (i.e., eggs or chicks found) averaged 46.5% ± 6.4% (range 30% to 62%). In 1993, the proportion was 26%, although this is a minimum as some eggs probably were lost before we finished our search for burrows (which took two months). In 1994, our effort was insufficient to derive an estimate of reproductive effort (see Methods). In 1993, 58 burrows were visited by shearwaters (88%); thus, a high level of nonbreeding (no eggs laid) was apparent. Not determined in 1981–1985 was the proportion of burrows that actually were active (i.e., used regularly regardless of whether an egg was laid).

Among nests in which eggs were laid, an average 66.0% ± 6.4% (range 49–75%) succeeded each year, from 1981 to 1985; in 1993 only 27%

succeeded and in 1994 81% succeeded. Like Telfer in 1981–1985, we could not ascertain the cause of mortality of most chicks. Only three of the 1994 chicks were from burrows in which eggs were laid in 1993; conversely, among the sites that produced chicks in 1994, 11 were active but none of these produced eggs or chicks in 1993. In total, the Newell's Shearwater produced 0.66 chicks/breeding pair/yr during the 1981–1985 period.

On average, 1,432 fledglings were reported to SOS each year, ranging from 950 (1992) to 2,200 (1987; Fig. 2A). Some of the variation was explained by differences in the timing of moon phases from one year to the next. It appears that when the full moon occurs in mid-October, the peak of fledging (Telfer et al. 1987, Ainley et al. 1997b), as in 1981, the total number of individuals found during all of the fledgling period (mid-September to early November) is much lower than if the full moon occurs at the periphery of peak fledging, i.e., in early or late October (Fig. 3). Breeding effort and success probably also affect the number of fledglings picked up; for instance, 1987 was a year when ocean productivity in the shearwaters' feeding grounds was unusually high (see Discussion) and the number of fledglings picked up was higher than expected. Nineteen eighty-seven

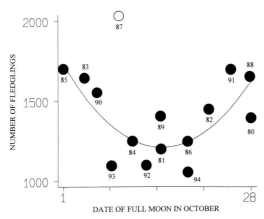

FIGURE 3. The total number of fledgling Newell's Shearwaters on Kaua'i, Hawaiian Islands, retrieved by SOS each autumn (Sept–Nov), 1980–1994, as a function of how closely the full moon coincided with the peak of fledging (mid-October). The point for 1987 was not used to generate the regression line (r^2 = 0.572, $F_{2, 11}$ = 7.36, P = 0.009; see text). Number by black and white circles indicates year.

was also a year when the full moon did not occur during the middle of fledging and, thus, the two factors (high ocean productivity, timing of full moon) combined to produce high fallout numbers. Finally, curtailment of lighting, as Hurricane Iniki accomplished in 1992–1993 (and even into 1994 somewhat), brought fewer fledglings to ground (Fig. 2A). The same pattern can be seen locally at the Kaua'i Surf/Westin Lagoons Hotel when lighting was adjusted during renovations in 1983 (Fig. 4B) as subsequent fallout was much lower.

MORTALITY

Breeding colony

We found one fresh adult carcass and six skeletons of adults or subadults in the colony during 1993. In 1994, we found 23 dead shearwaters. All were skeletons of adults that had been killed in the early spring during courtship two months before our first visit, and each had marks on the sternum to suggest eating by a cat. Almost all dead birds were found in the lower two-thirds of the study area indicating that the cat entered the colony from the sugarcane fields below the colony rather than using our access above the colony. Telfer (1986) found cat predation to be significant especially during the second year of his five year study.

We caught one cat and eight rats during 1993, but caught neither rats nor cats in 1994. Each year, we found rat droppings deposited throughout the colony before our arrival. During our work at night in 1993, we often saw or heard

introduced Barn Owls (*Tyto alba*). Barn Owls prey on Newell's Shearwaters (Byrd and Telfer 1980), and it was clear that they homed in on the Newell's Shearwater vocalizations that we occasionally played from a tape recorder (Ainley et al. 1995). During the day or evening only, we infrequently saw Short-eared Owls (*Asio flammeus*), but whether they prey on shearwaters is not known.

Urban corridor

The number of fledglings that died each year during SOS processing averaged 1.7% of the total turned in (Fig. 2B). The number of fledglings logged by SOS as dead on the road, but not deposited at SOS stations, averaged an additional 6% of the total each year (Fig. 2C). Almost all of these birds were checked for bands.

During 1991–1994, when a concerted search for dead adults was conducted, 42–72 were found in spring and summer each year (mean = 61 ± 7/yr; Fig. 2D; see also Ainley et al. 1995, Podolsky et al. 1998). Before the directed search, an average 17 ± 2 dead adults were reported per year by SOS (1987–1990). In 1993–1994, among 30 adults that could be sexed (not overly smashed), the male:female ratio was 8:9, and 7 (23%) were breeders. The average mass of dead adults was 381 ± 8 g (N = 35), a value important to our estimate of adult survival (see below).

RATES OF BAND RECOVERIES

Recoveries and band-return rates of fledgling and adult shearwaters were unexpectedly low. None of 15 fledglings banded in 1993–1994 and none of 52 banded in the study colony during 1980–1985 were picked up subsequently by SOS.

In 1993, we captured nine adults in the colony, but none had been banded previously. Only 1 of 30 adults/subadults found dead in 1993–1994 was banded. That one individual had been banded as a fledgling by SOS during fallout on the Southshore. Thus, we found 1 (2.6%) banded birds among 39 adults/subadults examined in the colony in 1993–1994. Similarly low band returns are evident in a sample of 14 adults banded in 1983 (T. Telfer, unpubl. data). These birds were attracted one night to a camp light in the Kōke'e forest (Fig. 1). One of these birds (7.1%) was subsequently recovered upon hitting a power line.

An equally low recovery rate is evident among adults found dead along power lines and roadways. Thus far, only 15 of the 23,000 fledglings banded and released by SOS have been recovered as adults or subadults during subsequent years (Table 1). Excluding data from the

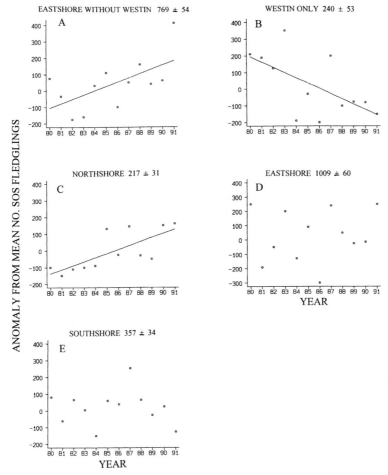

FIGURE 4.   Deviations from the mean number of Newell's Shearwater fledglings on Kaua'i, Hawaiian Islands, retrieved by SOS each year, 1980–1994, on the: (A) Eastshore with data from the Kaua'i Surf/Westin Hotel (district) removed [$Y = -2201 + 26.2X$; $r^2 = 0.365$, SE = 10.9, P = 0.038]; (B) Kaua'i Surf /Westin Lagoons Hotel only [$Y = 2723–31.6X$; $r^2 = 0.381$, SE = 12.7, P = 0.032]; and totals for (C) Northshore [$Y = -2062 + 24.1X$; $r^2 = 0.543$, SE = 6.9, P = 0.006], (D) Eastshore [P = 0.7], and (E) Southshore [P = 0.8].

first few years, when weak monel bands were used, the recovery rate was only 0.1% (12 of 12,443 birds banded in 1982–1990 and recovered in 1989–1994). Looked at in another way, among 351 adults reported to SOS, from 1987 to 1994 (when search effort was quantified), 12 (3.4%) had been banded. Three-fourths of the recoveries occurred during the past four years, when search effort was much greater than it had been (Ainley et al. 1995). No birds <2 yrs of age have been recovered.

POPULATION TRENDS

For all of Kaua'i, numbers of fledglings picked up each year were about the same during the period 1980–1990 (Fig. 2A). Thereafter, even after 1987 numbers declined each year (in-

cluding years beyond those of this study, through 1997; SOS unpubl. data, T. Telfer, pers. comm.). Results separated by region of retrieval showed a steeply growing number of fledglings for the Northshore (Fig. 4C, D, and E). No sloping trend was evident for the Eastshore (Fig. 4D), unless data for the Kaua'i Surf/Westin Lagoons Hotel were analyzed separately (Fig. 4B). Then, positive growth in the number of fledglings was evident (Fig. 4A). Similarly, no sloping trend was evident for the Southshore overall, although a decline not evident in the other regions is apparent after 1988 (Fig. 4E).

The growing number of SOS-processed birds on the East- and especially the Northshore occurred in concert with the doubling and quadrupling, respectively, of urban development (size

TABLE 1. THE TIME OF YEAR THAT BANDED NEWELL'S SHEARWATERS OF KNOWN AGE WERE RECOVERED ON KAUA'I FROM 1980 TO 1994[a]

Age (Yr)	May			June					July				August				
	<18	18	25	1	8	15	22	29	6	13	20	27	3	10	17	24	31
2–3				1	1	1	1	2	1		1						
4–5	1				2						1						1
≥6	1													1			

[a] Dates represent the first day of one-week periods.

of the human population) since 1970 (Fig. 5A). On the Southshore, where the human population has always exceeded that elsewhere on Kaua'i, it also increased during 1970–1990, but in this case it was returning to a level reached previously in the 1940s. The infrastructure to support tourists (lights included), indexed by the number of persons passing through the Līhu'e Airport, increased more than 12-fold in recent decades

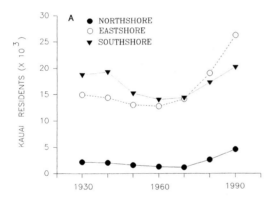

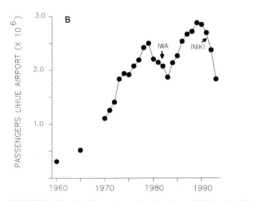

FIGURE 5. Indices to urbanization of Kaua'i, Hawaiian Islands: (A) Number of permanent residents on North-, East-, and Southshores, 1930–1990 (cf. Fig. 1); (B) Number of passengers at Līhu'e Airport (mostly tourists who need to reside at hotels, condominiums, etc.), 1960–1993 (data from State Airports Commission). Another commercial but private airport opened in Princeville ca. 1980 (but no data on passengers are available).

(Fig. 5B). We hypothesize that this growth, too, with its accompanying lights, probably affected the ability of urban areas to attract fledglings. Many coastal hotels, restaurants, sporting facilities, etc., have been built to accommodate these tourists and the resident population to service them. To summarize, then, on portions of Kaua'i where urbanization has been increasing recently, more and more fledglings have been recovered by SOS; where urbanization has been even denser and more widely spread for a long time, no trend in SOS retrievals has occurred. We hypothesize that either the proportion of fledglings attracted to lights and the retrieval capabilities of SOS have become saturated in those areas, or an increasingly greater proportion of fledglings are being attracted and the shearwater population has suffered greater mortality due to fallout and, in effect, has declined (see Discussion). In other words, the decline is masked because an increasing proportion of fledglings are being attracted to lights.

POPULATION MODELING

To put our results into perspective, we developed a Leslie model (Leslie 1945), that incorporates the various parameters of productivity and mortality. Before doing this, and in order to estimate mortality rates, we had to estimate the total number of fledglings produced on Kaua'i. The average 9,636 fledglings/yr was derived by multiplying three values: (1) 84,000, the estimated total population of Hawaiian Newell's Shearwaters (excluding fledglings; Spear et al. 1995); (2) 0.637, the proportion of total population of breeding age, i.e., 6 yrs or older, derived from the stable age distribution (see below); and (3) 0.547, the proportion of adults that bred in any given year (see below). The result was 14,600 breeding pairs, which produced 0.66 fledglings per pair. Our estimate of fledgling numbers does not correct for the few that would occur on Hawai'i (where radar studies indicate far fewer Newell's Shearwaters than on Kaua'i; Ainley et al. 1997b, Reynolds et al. 1997a).

PARAMETERS USED IN THE POPULATION MODEL

Five demographic parameters were required in the Leslie model: survival of adults (i.e., those

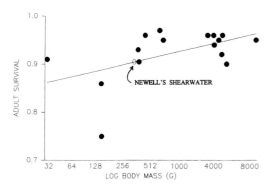

FIGURE 6.   Relationship between body mass and annual adult survival among procellariiforms; data extracted from Gaillard et al. (1989) and Dunning (1992). A significant relationship (P = 0.045) exists between log (adult survival) and log (body mass).

birds physiologically mature); survival of juveniles and subadults (i.e., birds between fledging and 12 months of age and those after the first year of life but before adulthood, respectively); age of first breeding; reproductive success; and breeding probability (i.e., the probability that an adult will breed in a specific year). Before discussing model results, we present values for these parameters here, incorporating empirical results and those from the literature.

Annual survivorship

Annual survivorship, as in most seabirds, has not been studied in Newell's Shearwater. We estimated annual adult survival to be 0.905, a value reported for a population of the very closely related Manx Shearwater (*P. p. puffinus*; taxonomy summarized in Ainley et al. 1997a), whose numbers have been stable and which has been exhaustively studied since the 1950s (Brooke 1990). This value is consistent with those reported for procellariiforms of similar mass (Croxall and Gaston 1988) and with an allometric relationship to body mass (381 g; see above) among procellariiforms (Fig. 6). From this regression, the predicted value for adult survival of a Newell's Shearwater was 0.904 ± 0.017, with an approximate 95% prediction interval of 0.870–0.934.

Juvenile and subadult survival

Juvenile and subadult survival also have not been studied in Newell's Shearwater and are poorly known in procellariiforms and most wild birds. The well-studied Manx Shearwater, again, can provide some insight. After adjusting for dispersal, Brooke (1990) estimated that 33.3% of Manx Shearwater fledglings survived from fledging to breeding age (age 6 yrs or older). We

incorporated this value into the simulations for Newell's Shearwaters, after considering the following patterns in the few other seabird species for which empirical data are available. Annual survival of juvenile and subadult alcids (e.g., Common and Thick-billed murres [*Uria aalge* and *U. Lomvia*], the size of which is similar to Newell's Shearwater) at ages 1, 2, and 3 yrs, respectively, is 60%, 82–83%, and 95–96% of the adult value; from the fourth year on, subadults have attained 100% of the adult value (Nur 1993, De Santo and Nelson 1995; S. Beissinger and N. Nur, unpubl. data). A similar pattern has been observed among male Western Gulls (*Larus occidentalis*; Spear et al. 1987), South Polar Skuas (*Catharacta maccormicki*; Ainley et al. 1990), also similarly sized to Newell's Shearwater, as well as among the heavier-bodied Adélie Penguin (*Pygoscelis adeliae*; Ainley and DeMaster 1980) and African Penguin (*Spheniscus dermersus*; Shannon and Crawford 1999). This pattern of age-specific survival was maintained by us for the Newell's Shearwater while scaling survival upward to achieve a total survival of 0.333 between fledging and age 6 yrs. The result was annual survival estimates of 0.654, 0.78, 0.89, and 0.905 in the first four years of life, and 0.905 for each year of life thereafter (within 1 SE of 0.904, the value obtained from the allometric regression, above).

These survival values, consistent with those for other seabird species, if anything, may be a bit high rather than too low. For example, survival from fledging to age 6 yrs in a growing population of Cory's Shearwater (*Calonectris diomedea*; Mougin et al. 1987) was estimated to be in the interval 0.230–0.334; Simons (1984) assumed survival from fledging to breeding age of 0.268 for a stable population of Dark-rumped Petrels; and for five alcid species, survival to average breeding age ranged 0.244–0.345 (Hudson 1985). As pointed out below, given an adult survival of 0.905, survival from fledging to breeding age would need to be at least 0.333 to produce a stable population; therefore, we retained this estimate.

Age of first breeding

On the basis of an average age of first breeding in the Manx Shearwater of six to seven years (Brooke 1990) and data presented in Table 1, we assumed that no Newell's Shearwater breeds before age 6 yrs, and from age 6 yrs onward, all individuals breed with probability, *p* (see below). Among 15 banded, known-age Newell's Shearwaters recovered by SOS during the past several years (Table 1), essentially all <5 yr of age were found from the period of late-egg laying onward, suggesting that they did not breed.

Of the two birds 6–7 yrs old, one was found in the prelaying period, consistent with a bird arriving early enough to breed. We further estimated that $1-p$ fraction of 6-yr-old Newell's Shearwaters would not breed in a given year. The result of this assumption is that the actual mean age of first breeding is between 6 and 7 yrs in all of our simulations, which is consistent with values not just for Manx Shearwater but also for the other shearwater species for which empirical data are available: 7 yrs in the Short-tailed Shearwater (Bradley et al. 1989) and 9 yrs in Cory's Shearwater (Mougin et al. 1987).

Longevity

We assumed a maximum age of 36 yrs for Newell's Shearwater. This corresponds to the maximal age observed among other shearwaters (e.g., Bradley et al. 1989).

Productivity

We used a breeding success value of 0.66 fledglings/breeding pair, a value determined in our study, to simulate the current trajectory of the Kaua'i population. In the Manx Shearwater, reproductive success was 0.70 (Brooke 1990), a value consistent with that reported for Short-tailed Shearwater (Wooller et al. 1989). We used 0.70 to simulate a balanced Newell's Shearwater population.

The low numbers of fledglings picked up by SOS during 1992 and 1993 may be due to several factors: (1) strong El Niño conditions that negatively affected food availability and, thus, shearwater breeding success (see below); (2) the possibility that Hurricane Iniki killed many birds, forcing a need for much new pairing and construction of burrows, two factors that result in lower breeding success in other seabirds (but this is unlikely; see above); (3) an absence of bright lights (which attract fledglings) on Kaua'i for many months after the storm (see above); and (4), at least for 1992, the effect of the full moon during fledging (Fig. 3). None of these explanations are likely to explain the pattern entirely, however, because the numbers of fledglings found by SOS continues to decline even through 1998 (SOS, unpubl. data; T. Telfer, pers. comm.). We hypothesize that recently we have begun to see the effects of the costs of fallout and adult mortality on the stability of the shearwater population (see below).

The low number of birds turned in during fall 1978 was certainly a result of the start-up nature of the SOS program. The large number found in 1987 was unusual, but is consistent with that year being at the start of one of the strongest La Niñas of recent decades. At that time, unusually productive waters existed in the eastern tropical Pacific, where Newell's Shearwaters feed (cf. Ribic et al. 1992, Spear et al. 1995). Thus, in 1987, breeding success may have been unusually high, and, in that year, the timing of the full moon would not have decreased the numbers of fledglings found.

It is not known whether the fewer fledglings found in some years, as a function of moon phase, is due to their greater ability to see structures in the moonlight (hence, fewer crashes), or whether fledglings are attracted away from civilization by the very bright moon (as suggested by Reed et al. 1985). The moon is clearly the brightest light source around and is low on the horizon just after sunset; our surveys indicated that most fallout occurs during the three hours after sunset (Ainley et al. 1995). Also hypothesized as a possibility by Reed et al. (1985), but determined to be false by us, is that moon phase affects the fledging rate, i.e., young may not fledge during the bright full moon (Ainley et al. 1995).

Breeding probability

The breeding probability parameter refers to the proportion of adults occupying a burrow in which no egg is laid. In Newell's Shearwater, 46% of occupied burrows produced an egg during the 1981–1985 period. Some of these burrows were surely occupied by prebreeding individuals. Assuming that (1) all 4- and 5-yr-old Newell's Shearwaters occupied burrows but did not breed (see above), (2) all individuals >5 yr of age occupied burrows and bred with probability p (see above), and (3) 4- and 5-yr-olds composed 15.9% of all individuals 4 yr or older (as determined from simulations described below), we can solve for the fraction of breeding-aged individuals that bred. Dividing 46% by 84.1% (proportion of burrow-holding population that has the potential to breed) yields an annual breeding probability of 0.547. In the Manx Shearwater, 20% of adults that had bred previously do not breed in a given year (Brooke 1990); in Short-tailed Shearwater, 12% of adults do not attend the colony and 19% maintain burrows but do not lay an egg (i.e., breeding probability is 0.69; Wooller et al. 1989).

There are two sources of uncertainty concerning our estimate of breeding probability. First, sampling error is associated with the estimate of 46% of pairs breeding among those occupying burrows (SE = 0.035; 95% CI = 0.39–0.53). Second, uncertain is our assumption that 15.9% of burrows are occupied by prebreeding individuals (i.e., that all 4- and 5-yr-olds occupy burrows but do not breed and that 2- and 3-yr-olds do not occupy burrows). If 3-, 4- and 5-yr-olds occupy burrows, this implies that 22% of bur-

TABLE 2. PARAMETER ESTIMATES USED IN LESLIE MODELS UNDER DIFFERENT SCENARIOS

	Balanced: Manx Shearwater	Best estimate: Newell's Shearwater		
		W/O Power line mortality, predation, or fallout	W/Power line mortality, predation, and fallout	W/Power line mortality, and fallout, but W/O predation
Survival: adult	0.909	0.905	0.896	0.904
Survival: fledgling to adulthood	0.333	0.333	0.239	0.327
Age first breeding	6–7	6–7	6–7	6-7
Breeding success	0.70	0.66	0.634[a]	0.634[a]
Breeding probability	0.80	0.547	0.547	0.547
λ	1.000	0.968	0.939	0.963

[a] 0.66 chicks fledge per breeding pair but 4% of fledged chicks die in fallout (not rescued by SOS); therefore, 0.66 × 0.96 = 0.634.

rows are occupied by prebreeders; alternatively, if only 5-yr-olds occupy burrows, this implies that 11% of burrows are occupied by prebreeders. In turn, this implies that breeding probability may vary between 0.60 (if only 5-yr-olds hold burrows) and 0.50 (if 3-, 4- and 5-yr-olds all hold burrows). We used 80% breeding probability for simulating a balanced population (Manx Shearwater), but 54.7% for simulating the contemporary Newell's Shearwater population.

The factors that affect breeding probability in Newell's Shearwater are not known for certain. Why reproductive effort was so low especially in 1993 is difficult to ascertain. As in 1983, the year that Telfer (1986) found the fewest burrows with eggs, 1993 was a year of major El Niño. Characteristic of such years, seabirds forgo reproduction because of a lack of food reserves (Schreiber and Schreiber 1984, Ainley and Boekelheide 1990). The 1993 breeding season also closely followed the devastation of Hurricane Iniki (September 1992). We saw some evidence of terrain slumping and a few uprooted trees at Kalāheo. Thus, the high level of nonbreeding could have been related to storm damage, but we saw little evidence of major burrow excavation, and many burrows used in 1993–1994 was not unusual for this population. It is not clear why breeding probability is low in the Newell's Shearwater (54%), but it may result from a high level of mate loss (itself a result of excessive mortality, see below) because, among seabirds, breeders who have lost their mates usually cannot obtain a new one quickly (e.g., Ainley and DeMaster 1980, Boekelheide and Ainley 1989). It could be, too, that our estimates are biased.

SIMULATION OF A BALANCED POPULATION

Incorporating values from the Manx populations (Table 2), our model produced a population that was nearly balanced but still declined slowly at 0.65% per year (λ, the finite population

growth rate = 0.994). Thus, after 10 years, the population will have declined by 6.3%. Increasing adult survival from 0.905 to 0.909, however, produced a stable population: λ = 1.000. An adult survival rate of 0.909, within 1 SE of Brooke's (1990) estimate of 0.905, is statistically reasonable.

Substituting a breeding probability of 0.547 and a reproductive success of 0.66 in the model, i.e., Newell's Shearwater values, produced a population that declined at 3.2%/yr (λ = 0.968). This is our best estimate of the current population trajectory of the Newell's Shearwater in the absence of additional mortality due to fallout, collisions with power lines, or from introduced predators (see below). In other words it is an idealistic scenario. The main factor affecting the declining growth rate was the fact that breeding probability was 0.547, rather than 0.8. Substituting 0.547 into the model was by itself sufficient to reduce population growth rate from 1.000 to 0.978. A breeding success of 0.66 (versus 0.70) and adult survival of 0.905 (versus 0.909) were of minor influence in lowering population growth rate, accounting for an additional drop from 0.978 to 0.968.

POPULATION STABILITY WITH MORTALITY OF FLEDGLINGS DURING FALLOUT

We next added mortality to fledglings during fallout to the simulation, i.e., attraction to lights and subsequent death owing to a complex of factors (see Introduction). This mortality occurs in spite of the efforts of SOS.

On the basis of the SOS data gathered by an opportunistic effort, the percent of fledglings that died annually, among those encountered by SOS, was 7.7% (see above; Fig. 2). However, on our night surveys in which search effort was quantified, 43% of fledglings were found dead (Ainley et al. 1995, Podolsky et al. 1998). The discrepancy with SOS must be due partly to different areas being surveyed, our sampling of areas that were less frequented by citizens (e.g.,

TABLE 3. FLEDGLING MORTALITY AS A FUNCTION OF MORBIDITY AND DISCOVERY RATES[a] OF NEWELL'S SHEARWATERS ON KAUA'I, HAWAIIAN ISLANDS

Morbidi-ty rate	Discovery rate			
	100%	80%	67%	50%
7.7%	0.011	0.014	0.017	0.023
15%	0.022	0.028	0.033	0.044
25%	0.037	0.046	0.056	0.074
43%	0.064	0.080	0.096	0.127

[a] Morbidity = percentage dead among downed fledglings; discovery = percentage of downed fledglings found by SOS.

TABLE 4. POPULATION GROWTH RATES (λ) IN RELATION TO FLEDGLING MORTALITY, ADULT, AND SUBADULT MORTALITY AND PREDATION OF NEWELL'S SHEARWATER ON KAUA'I, HAWAIIAN ISLANDS

Fledgling mortality	Adult/subadult power line-caused mortality			
	None	Low	Medium	High
Without predation from introduced animals:				
0.02	0.966	0.965	0.963	0.962
0.04	0.965	0.963	0.962	0.960
0.06	0.964	0.962	0.960	0.959
0.08	0.963	0.961	0.959	0.958
0.10	0.961	0.960	0.958	0.957
With predation from introduced animals:				
0.02		0.941	0.939	
0.04		0.939	0.938	
0.06		0.938	0.937	
0.08		0.937	0.936	
0.10		0.936	0.934	

sugarcane fields, secondary roads), and the reluctance of the public to salvage dead birds for SOS. The true mortality could be approximated better if we knew the number of birds that citizens rescued from our circuits each night before we passed through. Our regular checks of SOS shearwater drop-off stations in the vicinity of our circuits, however, revealed a few (1–5) but not disproportionately large numbers of additional live birds. Clearly, a greater proportion of each year's fledgling cohort dies than is revealed by SOS data. This hypothesis is supported by the fact that SOS reported none of 44 dead birds tagged and left in place by us during autumn 1993 and 1994 (Ainley et al. 1995, Podolsky et al. 1998). Thus, the true morbidity, i.e., probability that a downed fledgling dies, is likely between 7.7% and 43% of all fledglings. In our simulations, we considered these extremes as well as intermediate values of 15% and 25%.

Finally, we estimated the proportion of all downed fledglings encountered by the public and (if alive) brought to SOS stations, i.e., discovered. An extreme assumption would be that citizens discovered (and recorded) all downed fledglings. This scenario is unlikely, because some fledglings fall in inaccessible areas, such as sugarcane fields (which occupy a huge proportion of Kaua'i's coastal plain and are crossed by many kilometers of power lines), as well as other factors that could prevent discovery (e.g., birds moved by predators, birds hiding in the bushes). On the other hand, without recording them, some citizens find birds and release them into the ocean at the beach (probably jeopardizing the shearwaters, which are not anatomically prepared to deal with surf). The proportion of individuals that escape on their own are not our concern here. Therefore, we have considered four scenarios: 100%, 80%, 66.7%, and 50% of all downed fledglings are discovered by SOS.

Combining four levels of morbidity and four levels of discovery yields 16 combinations of total fledgling mortality (Table 3). We recognize that the two dimensions, morbidity and discov-

ery, are likely related: the more fledglings that come down in areas not covered efficiently by citizens, the higher the level of morbidity, since many fledglings will not be able to recover (e.g., it would take days, if ever, for a shearwater to extricate itself from the tall, dense foliage of a sugarcane field). However, our intention is merely to indicate the range of fledgling mortality likely to be sustained by this population. Total fledgling mortality due to fallout for the 16 different combinations of morbidity and discovery ranged 1.1% to 12.7%. Thus, in the most optimistic scenario, 1,432 out of 9,636 fledglings are downed and 7.7% of the 1,432 die (110/9,636 = 0.011). In the most pessimistic scenario, 2,864 fledglings are downed and 43.1% of these die (1,232/9,636 = 0.128).

We simulated the effects of fledgling mortality due to fallout, allowing the fraction of fledglings dying to vary from as low as 0.02 to as high as 0.10, where all other parameter values corresponded to our best estimate model (Table 2). High fledgling mortality (0.10) lowered λ by 0.5%, compared to low fledgling mortality (0.02; Tables 4, 5; Fig. 7A).

POPULATION STABILITY WITH SUBADULT AND ADULT MORTALITY DUE TO POWER LINE COLLISIONS

As indicated above, about 61 subadults and adults have been found dead as a result of power line collisions each year. This by no means includes all such individuals, as an adequate search of inland power lines, of which there are about 40 km across sugarcane fields, was beyond our resources (Ainley et al. 1995, Podolsky et al. 1998). We assumed true island-wide mortality to be either 122 birds (i.e., twice the measured level: "low power line mortality"), 244

TABLE 5. COMPARISON OF POPULATION GROWTH RATES (λ) AT DIFFERENT LEVELS OF SPONTANEOUS ESCAPEMENT BY DOWNED NEWELL'S SHEARWATER FLEDGLINGS ON KAUAʻI, HAWAIIAN ISLANDS, WITH AND WITHOUT PREDATION FROM INTRODUCED ANIMALS AND WITHOUT THE SOS PROGRAM

Fledgling mortality	25% of downed fledglings escape		0% of downed fledglings escape	
	Population	Difference[a]	Population	Difference[a]
	Growth rate		Growth rate	
Low-level power line mortality for adults/subadults, without predation:				
0.02	0.958	0.0071	0.955	0.0096
0.06	0.955	0.0073	0.952	0.0099
0.10	0.952	0.0075	0.949	0.0102
Low-level power line mortality for adults/subadults, with predation:				
0.02	0.934	0.0062	0.932	0.0085
0.06	0.932	0.0063	0.930	0.0087
0.10	0.929	0.0066	0.926	0.0091

[a] Absolute difference in λ, comparing population growth rate for a population with (see Table 4) and without SOS program (in which 25% or 0%, respectively, of the 1,432 fledglings turned in each year would escape on their own).

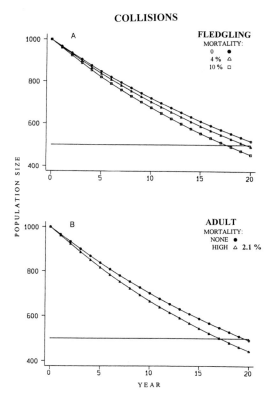

FIGURE 7. Results of simulations showing effects on population growth in the Newell's Shearwater caused by: (A) fledgling mortality of 0, 4, and 10% due to fallout; and (B) no versus high adult/subadult mortality due to collisions with power lines. The horizontal line indicates 50% population level.

birds (i.e., 4 × 61, "medium power line mortality"), or 350 dead birds ("high power line mortality"; see Ainley et al. 1995, Podolsky et al. 1998, for derivation). In addition, such mortality is apparently age specific: subadults appear more vulnerable than breeding adults. First, as noted above, 20% of the birds found and necropsied by us were active breeders, yet an estimated 35% of such birds exist in the population (on the basis of the model, 0.637 × 0.547). Second, an additional sample of 15 known-aged (banded) subadult and adult individuals killed by power lines (Table 1) indicated that only two (13%) were 6 yrs of age or older (i.e., of breeding age); the remainder were 2–5 yrs of age (subadults). Thus, the two samples yielded similar adult:subadult ratios.

On the basis of these data, we assumed either 24, 48, or 70 dead breeders per year (122, 244, or 350 × 0.2). Dividing 24, 48, and 70 by the total number of adults at the colony yielded mortality rates of 0.046%, 0.092%, and 0.131%, respectively, for the three levels of power line mortality. For subadults ages 2–5 yrs (Table 1), depending on the level of power line mortality, we derived mortality rates of 0.60%, 1.20%, and 1.72%, respectively.

We simulated population growth rate incorporating these levels of subadult and adult mortality, together with a range of fledgling (fallout) mortality values (Table 4). The effect of high subadult and adult power line mortality compared to no such mortality was to lower population growth rate by 0.5% for a given level of

fledgling mortality. Low and intermediate subadult and adult power line mortality generated intermediate levels compared to high and no power line mortality. It appears that the magnitude of the effect of power line mortality on population growth rate is roughly comparable to the estimated effect of fledgling mortality (i.e., depressing the population growth rate by as much as 0.5%). We considered the high level of power line mortality to be the best estimate of such (Ainley et al. 1995, Podolsky et al. 1998). Nevertheless, for analyzing effects of predation and efficacy of the SOS program, to err on the side of caution given the uncertainties involved, we used our most conservative estimates of power line mortality.

POPULATION STABILITY WITH PREDATION OF BURROW OCCUPANTS

Mortality due to predation from introduced animals should be considered additional to mortality already discussed, since most studies of shearwaters have been conducted at sites where predation of subadults and adults is low. Some Manx Shearwaters are taken by Great Skuas (*Catharacta skua*) and large gulls (*Larus* spp.), but numbers of these avian predators are extremely low because of control programs (Furness 1987). Predation by humans had a marked effect on the Cory's Shearwater population (Mougin et al. 1987).

We found 30 dead subadults and adults among the estimated 600 individuals in the Kalāheo colony (about 150 burrows × 2 yrs × 2 individuals/burrow/yr; Ainley et al. 1995). This yielded a crude estimate of 5% mortality among burrow holders. We modeled this as an extra 2.5% morality averaged over all adults and subadults (excluding 1-yr-olds). We chose to use 2.5% mortality (rather than 5%) to reflect the fact that some individuals killed might have been transients and not burrow holders, and some nonbreeders of breeding age might not have been present at the burrows at all, as in the Short-tailed Shearwater (Wooller et al. 1989; see above). As shown below, even 2.5% mortality of subadults and adults has a dramatic effect on population growth rate. We have not considered mortality of adults or chicks due to predation by rats, for we have no data on rat predation, a most difficult factor to quantify (Thompson 1987, Seto 1995, Seto and Conant 1996).

We also considered that predation, especially from owls, is age specific. Active breeders are inconspicuous, so we assumed that they incurred a very low predation rate, whereas 4- and 5-yr-olds, who attempt to gain both a burrow and a mate, are most conspicuous of all and suffered the highest predation rate. We assumed that inactive breeders (individuals that bred in a previous year, but not the current year) and 2-and 3-yr-olds incur intermediate levels of predation. Taking into account our subjective assessment of predation risk, 2- and 3-yr-olds were assigned a mortality rate due to predation of 5%; 4- and 5-yr-olds a rate of 10%; and breeding age individuals (whether active or inactive) a predation rate of 1%. Averaged over all individuals 2 yrs of age or older, mortality due to predation was 2.5%.

The effect of predation on population growth was dramatic (Tables 4, 5). Simulations indicated a decline of 0.023–0.024 in the finite population growth rate, depending on the level of mortality assumed for fledglings, subadults, and adults. Thus, the two most important factors in determining population growth (and in this case, decline) were the low breeding probability compared with that of stable shearwater populations (0.547 versus 0.80) and the apparently high mortality rate due to introduced predators. The two may well be related; loss of mates (due to pre-

dation, hurricanes, or power line collision, see above) may lead to a reduced breeding probability for the current or subsequent breeding season.

POPULATION STABILITY WITH SOS REDUCTION OF FLEDGLING MORTALITY

There is little information regarding the number of fledglings that come to ground but then, in the absence of SOS, spontaneously escape to the sea. Here, to assess the impact of SOS, we consider two possibilities: 0% and 25% of downed fledglings escape on their own. Telfer et al. (1987) proposed that few fledglings that fallout would be capable of survival on their own. In fact, we observed two fledglings who took off after being grounded (it was windy and they were in a large, unobstructed expanse— empty parking lots; Ainley et al. 1995).

In the simulations (Table 5), 2.0–10.0% of all fledglings were assumed to have died as a result of hitting power lines, etc., just as was implemented in the simulations shown in Table 4, and then an additional 1,432 (due to not being rescued by SOS participants, assuming 0% spontaneous escape) or 1,074 (assuming 25% spontaneous escape) fledglings die. The decline in population growth rate in the absence of SOS was 0.62–0.75% if 25% of downed fledglings escaped on their own, and ranged 0.85–1.02% in the absence of spontaneous escape. Therefore, the SOS program has had a significant effect on population growth of the Kaua'i population: fledgling mortality, in the presence of SOS, lowered the population growth rate by 0.12–0.62% but, in the absence of SOS, lowered it by an additional 0.62–1.02%.

MODELED POPULATION TRAJECTORIES

Finally, we modeled the population trajectory for the Kaua'i population of Newell's Shearwaters under four scenarios, assuming an arbitrary starting population size of 1,000 individuals (of all ages >1 yr; Fig. 8A). All scenarios assumed a "low" level of subadult and adult mortality due to power lines and 4% mortality of fledglings due to fallout (see above). Scenarios 1 and 3 assumed the continued operation of the SOS program, but scenarios 2 and 4 assumed no such program, and further assumed that 25% of downed fledglings spontaneously escape (see above). Scenarios 1 and 2 included no provision for mortality due to introduced predators; scenarios 3 and 4 included such mortality.

We also considered results for these scenarios with values of breeding probability and reproductive success from the Manx Shearwater (Table 2, Fig. 8B; Brooke 1990). After all, Newell's Shearwater eggs raised in the absence of pred-

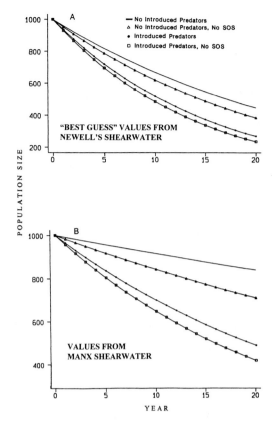

FIGURE 8. Results of simulations showing effects on population growth of shearwaters in the face of low-level mortality to fledglings due to fallout (SOS in operation), low levels of mortality to adults/subadults due to collisions, and low levels of predation on adults/subadults in the breeding colonies, assuming: (A) demographic parameters estimated currently for the Newell's Shearwater, and (B) demographic parameters estimated for the Manx Shearwater.

ators (by Wedge-tailed Shearwaters) attained a success equal to that of the Manx Shearwater (Byrd et al. 1984). Moreover, Manx values, when combined with other parameter values, produced a population declining slightly, whereas Newell's values produced a population declining steeply (see above). If one concludes that the Newell's population is declining slightly rather than steeply, one should adopt Manx values. Whatever values one uses, however, qualitatively similar results are produced: the cessation of the SOS program would accelerate the decline of the Newell's Shearwater population by two fold (in the absence of predation).

DISCUSSION

Comparing the spatial and temporal patterns in the SOS data with those evident in urbaniza-

tion, as well as modeling results, we interpret the trends seen in fallout as follows. The shearwater population on the Southshore is decreasing. The increased urbanization there, which is compensated somewhat by the slightly increased use of shielded lights (since 1987), should lead to more shearwaters being found, all else being equal. The opposite pattern observed, however (no increase in fallout), is consistent with an added cost (mortality that is not uncompensated) and a declining population. The severe reduction in the size of the Southshore colony at Kaluahonu (few occupied burrows present in 1992–1993 compared to the early 1980s; Ainley et al. 1995) is consistent with this trend. In fact, because our inputs to the demographic model were gathered on the Southshore (Kalāheo colony, routes to quantify mortality), our model results duplicate well what we propose is happening to the Southshore Newell's shearwater population on the basis of SOS results.

In contrast to the Southshore, shearwater colonies on the Eastshore and Northshore are facing increased urbanization (well beyond historical levels; Fig. 5A) and, as predicted with more lights, more birds are being reported to SOS (Fig. 4A, C). The very recent growth in urbanization is so dramatic that the increased use of shielded lights (although still minimal) must be having little compensatory effect on shearwater fallout. Due to mortality and ensuing population decline, the fallout pattern for the North- and Eastshore eventually should duplicate the trend seen on the Southshore: level or decreasing fallout. Indeed, following our study, the number of fledglings found in 1995, 1996, 1997, and 1998 (T. Telfer, pers. comm.) continued the "unexplained" gradual lowering of SOS totals that began in 1992 (or even 1987).

In the absence of fallout, power line-caused mortality, and introduced predators, the model showed that the Kaua'i population of Newell's Shearwaters should be able to maintain its numbers, i.e., no other important factors affect population instability. The SOS program goes far to reduce one of these mortality factors, death of fledglings due to fallout. Even with SOS, however, there is significant mortality of fledglings; >2% and as much as 10% or more of fledged shearwaters likely die as a result of fallout. Mortality of subadults and adults due to power line collisions also depresses population growth, but depending on the actual rates obtained, it may or may not be as important. Firm quantification of the significance of power line-caused mortality among subadults and adults awaits further study. In the absence of the SOS program, however, fallout-caused mortality of fledglings would likely be more important than power line-caused mortality of subadults and adults.

Evidence points clearly to two factors that importantly affect population growth of the Newell's Shearwater: low breeding probability and high rates of predation on adults and subadults. The cause of the low breeding probability are not readily apparent, but rates would be exacerbated by mortality of breeders and prebreeders due to predation, disturbance by predators, and collisions with power lines. Otherwise, even if the Newell's Shearwater breeding population is not currently declining (i.e., the model is wrong and the SOS results are not a valid index of population size), our results indicate the vulnerability of the Newell's Shearwater population. A reduction in the production and survival of fledglings will only be felt many years later, at the time when such fledglings would have begun breeding. Remember, the longevity of this species is about 30 yrs, and not even one generation has passed since urbanization began to expand rapidly. We ask, Are the low SOS totals continuing past 1987 and the unusually low banded-bird recovery rates finally indicating decreased survival? Seen in this context, mortality of adults and subadults due to collisions is still of great concern for recovery of Newell's Shearwater (see USFWS 1982a).

Alternative hypotheses exist, of course, to explain some of the trends revealed by our research and simulations. The regional difference in trends could be a result of an increasing population of shearwaters on the Northshore due either to immigration from colonies on the Southshore (in turn to help explain the decrease there) or much better breeding success on the Northshore than on the Southshore. A shift from the Southshore to the Northshore is problematic given the high degree of philopatry characteristic of procellariiforms (Warham 1990). The very low recovery rate of shearwaters initially banded as fledglings by SOS could be a result of a lower-than-natural survival rate of these birds (deemed to have been "rescued" by SOS only because they were able to fly away). Another possibility is that the large majority of fledglings picked up by SOS were produced on the Northshore—and eventually recruited to Northshore

colonies as adults—but having reached the sea were attracted back to land by coastal lights on the more brightly lighted South- and Eastshores. Until 1995, the Northshore had lacked the power lines that effectively "sample" adults and subadults in the population, although following completion of our study high, deep arrays of lines have been installed. Thus, sampling efficiency may have increased and we can see whether or not the number of banded birds found also increases. Additional research in the colonies on the Northshore also could easily determine whether many banded shearwaters nest there.

In conclusion, then, the population of Newell's Shearwaters on Kaua'i appears to be declining. On the basis of demographic modeling, the prospects appear to be poor for the continued existence of a robust population of this species on this island. A reversal of the indicated population trends will be possible only with more strict controls of lighting (such as on the Big Island, where the astronomical observatories require minimal upward light radiation), fencing and predator control in several important shearwater breeding areas, and, possibly, the burying of power lines in a few especially critical areas (Ainley et al. 1997a, Podolsky et al. 1998).

ACKNOWLEDGMENTS

T. C. Telfer (Hawaii DLNR) introduced us to shearwaters and petrels on Kaua'i, contributed much insight, lent equipment to us, and provided access to past data from the SOS program. He chose not to accept authorship of this paper. Assistance, too, was provided by R. Voss and K. Viernes (USFWS), Kilauea Point National Wildlife Refuge. C. Berg was very helpful and supplied much information early on that improved our knowledge of Kaua'i. We also thank Kaua'i Electric Company and the Electric Power Research Institute (EPRI) for funding, and the coordination provided by J. Huckabee and M. Fraser (EPRI). The counsel received from the EPRI Scientific Advisory Panel was also of great value: D. Boersma (University of Washington), G. Breece (Georgia Power and Southern Company Services), S. Conant (University of Hawai'i), E. Colson (Pacific Gas and Electric, and Colson and Associates), E. Flint (Pacific Islands Office, USFWS), L. Ginzburg (Applied BioMathematics), and S. Kress (National Audubon Society). Finally, B. A. Cooper, R. H. Day, M. Fraser, T. C. Telfer, L. B. Spear, S. Conant, and several anonymous reviewers provided many good comments on the manuscript.

Studies in Avian Biology No. 22:124–132, 2001.

MIGRATION OF NORTHERN PINTAIL ACROSS THE PACIFIC WITH REFERENCE TO THE HAWAIIAN ISLANDS

Miklos D. F. Udvardy and Andrew Engilis, Jr.

Abstract. Northern Pintails (*Anas acuta*) regularly occur as winter visitors on most Pacific islands with suitable habitat. Their breeding distribution includes both sides of the Pacific Rim. While large populations breed in Siberia and winter in California, numerous North American breeders also winter in areas near the Sea of Japan, Hawaiian Islands, and other Pacific island groups. Though pintail flights across the Pacific have not been well documented, scrutiny of banding returns shows that an exclusive California-Hawai'i flyway does not exist, as was earlier proposed. Data support a more complex movement of birds from numerous breeding locations in the Holarctic. We summarize movements of Holarctic nesting pintails to wintering grounds in the Hawaiian Islands that include birds originating from northeastern Siberia, Alaska, and the interior prairie provinces and states of North America. We also summarize pintail movements to other Pacific archipelagoes. Finally, to close the circle around the North Pacific, we summarize movements of birds between Canadian and Alaskan breeding grounds to wintering sites in Japan. We also discuss other panmictic, Holarctic migrants and their colonization attempts in Hawai'i.

Key Words: *Anas acuta*; banding return; Holarctic; migration; Northern Pintail; Oceania; panmixis.

The primary interest of a faunist is in establishing the list of species that regularly occur in the area under scrutiny. Data of a species' regular occurrence increase knowledge of their total distribution, which is the aim of the zoogeographer. Regularly occurring species are recognized as influential members of local ecosystems; thus, they play a prominent role in ecogeographical studies. Often less attention is paid to scarce, rare, or irregularly occurring species, for chance seems to determine their detection, and their role in community ecology appears negligible.

Regarding these "lesser" elements of local fauna, interest increases when a chance visitor comes from afar. Lately, the study of rarities became important on two accounts. First, it is realized that bird species are to an extent dynamic; the "stray" individuals caught outside of their regular distributional range are all potential colonists. The trends in their occurrence outside the "normal" range and throughout a longer time period may reveal the nature and extent of the pioneering tendency of the species. Second, it is also realized that species composition of faunas fluctuates; thus rare visitors may reveal trends in faunal changes.

Holarctic waterfowl are among the most successful colonizers owing to their exceptional powers of flight between breeding and nonbreeding areas. Their ability to move long distances and tendency for dispersal have resulted in establishment of waterfowl on many remote land masses where food and freshwater resources are available (Weller 1980).

As with all remote oceanic islands, the Hawaiian Archipelago received its endemic avifauna through over-water dispersal and subsequent local speciation. The Hawaiian avifauna consists of year-round residents (the landbirds) and seasonal but regular visitors (seabirds that come to breed, and Anseriformes and Charadriiformes that winter in Hawai'i). Thirty-three species of migratory waterfowl have been recorded in the Hawaiian Islands (Pyle 1997). Ten species are annual visitors with Northern Pintail (*Anas acuta*), Northern Shoveler (*Anas clypeata*), Lesser Scaup (*Aythya affinis*), American (*Anas americana*) and Eurasian (*A. penelope*) wigeons, and Green-winged Teal (*Anas crecca*) accounting for 95% of those birds wintering in the islands (Engilis 1988).

Our focus in this paper, the pintail, is a regularly occurring winter visitor in Hawai'i and is a scarce or irregular visitor to other Pacific island groups. Reliable but general historical accounts claim that pintail came in large numbers to Hawai'i (Munro 1944). Earlier evidence is suggested by the fact that the Hawaiians recognized two species by name: pintail (Koloa Māpu) and shoveler (Koloa Mohā), indicating that they were an obvious component to the Hawaiian avifauna before Captain Cook discovered the islands in the 1770s. Surveys have documented migratory ducks exceeding 10,000 birds in the mid-1950s (Medeiros 1958). We examined the data from biannual waterbird surveys conducted on most lowland wetlands since the 1940s (Table 1). We omit data collected from 1960 through 1977 (Ni'ihau, Hawai'i, and Moloka'i not regularly surveyed during those periods). These data, summarized in Engilis (1988), confirm that the population size of wintering pintails in Hawai'i have declined tenfold. This decline has led to added interest by conservationists to address habitat needs in the Hawaiian Islands benefiting migratory waterfowl and

TABLE 1.   CENSUS OF PINTAILS IN HAWAI'I

Year	Total Pintails
1950	1,593
1951	1,875
1952	7,094
1953	8,226
1954	1,950
1955	2,653
1956	3,045
1957	1,619
1958	1,126
1959	1,249
1978	897
1979	490
1980	923
1981	377
1982	150
1983	60
1984	235
1985	150
1986	501
1987	203

Notes: Data from 1950 to 1959 from Meideros (1950–1959). Counts were taken on Maui, Hawai'i, O'ahu, and Kaua'i. Data from 1978 to 1987 from Engilis (1988). During 1960–1977 not all islands were surveyed and records are sketchy. The period of 1978–1987 represents the best modern data set as all eight main islands including Ni'ihau were surveyed.

shorebirds. Understanding pintail movements to Hawai'i will assist in these efforts.

Medeiros (1958) documented the movement of pintails between the Hawaiian Islands and North America, speculating a California-Hawai'i flyway. Although this connection is correct, the true migration patterns are more complex. We analyzed banding data from the U.S. Migratory Bird Management Office (MBMO), Yamashina Institute for Ornithology, Japan, and the Russia Bird Ringing Center. Included in our data collection was a summary of available literature, examination of specimens from the American Museum of Natural History (AMNH), National Museum of Natural History (USNM), and Bernice P. Bishop Museum (BPBM), examination of bird observation records from the Hawaii Rare Bird Database (HRBD), and fieldwork conducted by us (Udvardy 1958–1960 and Engilis 1984–1997). These sources enabled us to gather considerable amounts of data indicating that pintails from at least half of the species circumpolar distribution are potential winter visitors to Hawai'i and that their movements across the Pacific are complex. In the following discussion we try to document these assumptions.

NORTHERN PINTAIL MIGRATION TO THE HAWAIIAN ISLANDS

Of the 2,811 pintails banded in Hawai'i, 107 have been recovered on the North American mainland and 16 have been retrapped on the islands. Additionally, a pintail banded on Maui in October 1952 was reported taken a month later from Pukapuka (Danger) Atoll in the Tuamotu Archipelago. Significantly, the Tuamotus are almost due south from the Hawaiian chain, as are the Line Islands, where two pintails were recovered two to three months after same-year autumnal banding in North America (MBMO data). Medeiros' analysis of these returns lead him to the conclusion that the islands' wintering pintail population is not blown off course but are deliberately flying from central California to, and return there from, their wintering areas in Hawai'i. Of the above mentioned 107 Hawai'i-banded pintails, 45 were recovered in the San Francisco Estuary, California (Fig. 1). These returns also confirmed that pintails return to the islands one or several years after the initial banding there. Thus, pintails repeatedly and deliberately visit Hawai'i to spend the winter, with some flying further southward after having used the islands in transit (Medeiros 1958). Medeiros speculated that the autumnal flight probably used the northerly trade winds that originate outside central California, while for the return flight in the spring the ducks probably are helped by the westerlies.

According to the MBMO banding/recovery data, 165 pintails have been banded in Hawai'i and recovered (including 16 in Hawai'i) between 1953 and 1960 (Fig. 1). The data reveal that the high number of California returns in the total of Hawai'i-banded ducks matches the distribution pattern, at banding, of 14 pintails banded from 1951 to 1954 in North America and later recovered in the Pacific (Fig. 2). In addition, the proportion of California's share in the total of 165 records is 77.6% against all other localities; if we compare California only with the coastal entities of Alaska, British Columbia, Washington, and Oregon, the proportions are 128 against 24, or 84.2%.

In order to assess the relation of mainland populations of pintail to the population visiting the Hawaiian Islands, according to the banding and recovery results, we have compared the figures of banding effort, recoveries, and hunting pressure on the Pacific coastal areas of North America for the years of Medeiros's project (Tables 2, 3). We excluded Alaska from these tables because there were no data available for hunting pressure or banding efforts in Alaska for the 1950s.

Comparing the data in Tables 3 and 4, we concluded that during the 1950s, California pintails were indeed providers of over 90% of the birds annually harvested by hunters in the temperate Pacific Coast of North America and also

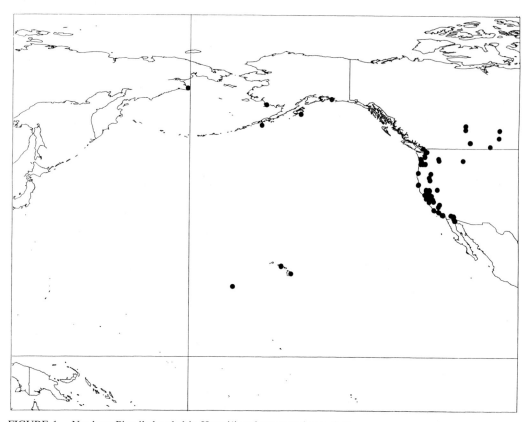

FIGURE 1.   Northern Pintails banded in Hawai'i and recovered anywhere.

of pintails annually banded there. The recoveries in California are predominately from the fall when hunting pressure is at its highest. Also, pintails arrive in California earlier than most species of migratory waterfowl, boosting the California figures (Miller 1985). These facts, overlooked by Medeiros, contributed to the predominance of California in the Hawaiian banding and recovery data. However, California remains a critical area for pintail, supporting over 50% of those wintering in the United States (Heitmeyer et. al. 1989); thus it probably serves as a principle staging area for Hawaiian-bound pintails. This still needs to be confirmed through modern marking and tracking studies. We note that banding recoveries support the notion that pintails could equally originate from other Pacific Coast localities such as Mexico, Oregon, or Washington (Figs. 1, 2).

A second pattern of movement can be seen from birds banded in Hawai'i and recovered in the Arctic. Five birds banded in Hawai'i in the 1950s were recovered in the Arctic: one in the Aleutian Islands; another in the Yukon-Kuskokwin Delta, an important breeding ground in western Alaska; and two on Alaska's South Coast (Fig. 1). One bird was recovered in the Anadyr Region of eastern Russia (lat. 62° 5′ N, long. 179° 1′ E). The later bird was a hatching-year male banded on Maui, Hawai'i, 22 February 1954. It was shot on the breeding grounds 29 May 1960. These multiple recoveries straddling the Bering Sea provide another migration link from the Holarctic to the Hawaiian Islands. We speculate that Arctic nesting pintail probably make the transoceanic flight direct from southern Alaska/Siberia to the Hawaiian Islands, intercepting the leeward islands (e.g., Midway and Laysan), resting, and then moving to the main islands. Just as plausible, however, is a movement of Alaskan birds south along the Pacific Coast of North America, into California, and then across the Pacific. This movement may be indirectly supported by banding evidence of Alaskan birds as nearly 80% of those recovered have been taken in California (Austin and Miller 1995). The early arrival of pintails to California—males arrive in numbers by late August (Miller 1985)—could allow time for birds to refuel and make the flight to the Hawaiian Islands. Again, this high return rate of Alaskan-banded

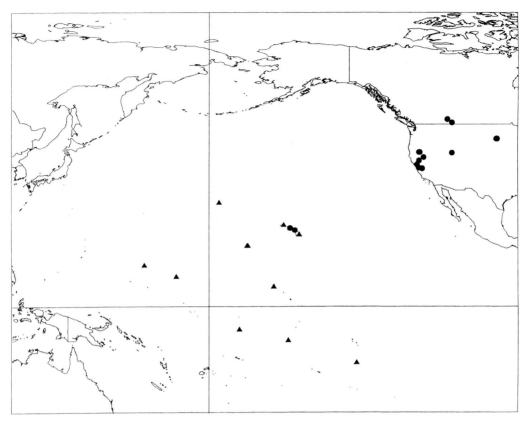

FIGURE 2. Northern Pintails banded anywhere and recovered in the Pacific Ocean (triangles = recovery location, dots = banding location).

pintails can be biased by the high number of birds shot in California.

POPULATION DEMOGRAPHY OF PINTAIL WINTERING IN THE HAWAIIAN ISLANDS

From Medeiros's banding data we note that Hawai'i had a sex ratio skewed towards females (Table 4). This is atypical for what has been reported for pintails (and other ducks) of North America, where males tend to outnumber females in most studies on the wintering and breeding grounds (Bellrose et al. 1961, Miller 1985, Rienecker 1987, Austin and Miller 1995, Migoya and Baldassarre 1995). The higher number of males recorded in waterfowl populations has been speculated to be the result of a high mortality rate (increased predation due to habitat fragmentation) of adult females during the

TABLE 2. HUNTING PRESSURE[a] ON PINTAIL 1950–1956 AT PACIFIC COASTAL AREAS

Year	British Columbia	Washington	Oregon	California
1950	69,600	109,500 (est.)	—	1,945,300
1951	94,830	114,900	—	2,966,000
1952	72,620	111,250	—	4,659,000
1953	94,940	97,800	—	4,599,500
1954	93,940	112,600	—	3,461,600
1955	70,490	128,200	—	3,312,700
1956	71,940	117,700	—	3,526,000
Totals	568,360	791,950	913,620 (est.)	24,470,100
Yearly Mean	81,194	113,136	130,517	3,495,729

[a] Figures represent reported birds taken by hunters during the legal hunting season of each year. Source: state and provincial hunting records obtained in writing by M.D.F. Udvardy.

TABLE 3. BANDING OF PINTAIL 1950–1956 AT PA-
CIFIC COASTAL AREAS

Year	British Columbia	Washington	Oregon	California
1950	28	110	234	9,334
1951	26	774	544	19,360
1952	31	656	102	17,570
1953	0	433	574	16,737
1954	5	143	1,000	16,514
1955	5	625	2,931	21,475
1956	0	988	1,651	15,759
Total	95	3,729	7,036	116,749

Source: U.S. Migratory Bird Management office records.

breeding season (Johnson and Sargeant 1977).
The disproportionate numbers of females seen in
Hawai'i may therefore be the result of female
pintail's tendency to exhibit philopatry to their
winter quarters (Rienecker 1987, Anderson et al.
1992), coupled with the effort required to reach
the Hawaiian Islands. In addition, pintails undergo a sex-segregated migration as males move
to molting grounds earlier than females, in some
cases arriving months earlier (Fuller 1953, Oring
1964, Salomonsen 1968, Bellrose 1976). Both
sexes appear prone to wander, particularly young
birds, as is revealed in the specimen record. Of
the 42 pintail specimens examined from Pacific
islands, 25 were hatching-year birds and 17 were
adults. Medeiros's trapping and banding data
also revealed a decline in pintail age ratio
throughout his study (Table 5). This decline was
also reflected in the Pacific flyway pintail population and was the result of a severe drought in
the prairie provinces of Canada depressing continental waterfowl populations (Ducks Unlimited 1990).

The timing of pintail migration to Hawai'i has
apparently changed in the past five decades. The
decline of pintails in North America has been
well documented, and we have seen a similar
decline in Hawai'i (Engilis 1988, Ducks Unlimited 1990, Austin and Miller 1995). Not only has
there been a decline in numbers, but the period
of arrival has decreased as well. In the 1950s,
Medeiros documented birds arriving, in numbers, as early as mid-September. His banding records revealed that the early arrival was marked
by small flocks of males, followed by females
and hatching-year birds that arrived in October.
Pintail numbers peaked in November. This sex-
segregated migration pattern has been documented for other waterfowl in North America,
particularly in California where male pintail
comprised over 90% of the total birds arriving
in August but only 53% of the total wintering
population once females arrived (Miller 1985).

By the mid-1980s to present, pintail arrival

TABLE 4. SEX RATIOS OF BIRDS BANDED IN THE HA-
WAIIAN ISLANDS (MEDEIROS 1950–1959)

Year	N	Sex ratio (Males to Females)
1951	417	0.63
1952	856	0.84
1953	644	0.65
1954	446	0.94
1955	478	0.50

patterns changed in Hawai'i. A more abbreviated migration occurs with the main bulk of pintail arriving in the islands, marked by hatching-
year birds (based on the timing of their body
molt; A. Engilis, unpubl. data) by late October,
peaking in November, and stabilizing at a few
hundred birds through the winter. We speculate
that the early arrival of male pintails to Hawai'i
was lost during the years of continental decline
(mortality?) from 1975 to 1985 leading to the
observed, abbreviated migration and decline in
Hawai'i. In the late 1990s, a few early flocks
have again been observed in late September;
most are comprised of male birds (A. Engilis
and A. J. McCafferty, pers. obs.). During the
same period, pintail numbers have increased on
the continent (USFWS 1996b).

MOVEMENT OF NORTHERN PINTAIL ACROSS THE PACIFIC

To complete the assessment of pintails migrating across the Pacific, we assembled data for
pintail banded in North American and recovered
in Eurasia. One movement of birds between the
continents has been documented, with part of the
population breeding in eastern Siberia and wintering in the western United States (Dement'ev
and Gladkov 1952, Henny 1973). Again the
banding recoveries (N = 423) yield a more complex pattern of movement across the North Pacific than first thought. To make sense of these
data, we combined the patterns of movement
into three groups.

TABLE 5. RATIOS OF WINTERING NORTHERN PINTAIL
ADULTS TO JUVENILES IN THE PACIFIC FLYWAY AND THE
HAWAIIAN ISLANDS BASED ON BANDING RECORDS (MED-
EIROS 1950–1959)

Year	Hawai'i	Pacific Flyway[a]
1951	1.19	3.50
1952	2.07	3.70
1953	0.51	0.50
1954	0.72	0.50

[a] Extrapolated from Bellrose et al. 1961.

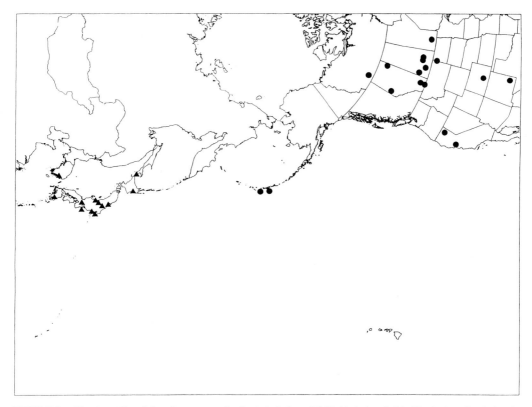

FIGURE 3.   Northern Pintail banding recoveries in Asia below 50° N; birds banded in North America (triangles = recovery location, dots = banding location).

GROUP 1

Three birds were recovered in Europe and one in western Siberia. The first bird, a drake, was banded in northern California and shot eight years later in western Siberia. Another drake, also from California, and was recovered two years later from the Arctic coast of Russia's Kara Sea. A third, an immature drake from the Canadian maritime province of Nova Scotia, was found in Chechia two and a half years later. These records provide an example of the mechanism whereby these circumpolar, wetland species mix their genotype so that no specialization could occur, supporting the notion that the Holarctic pintail population remains panmictic and opportunistic, thus adapted to varying climate conditions (Udvardy 1969:180–181). The last of these cases defies all speculations; an adult female from northern California that was found six years later in the Ukraine (Rienecker 1987, 1988).

The remaining 420 pintails mentioned above were divide into two groups: those recovered in Asia below 50° N (group 2) and those above it (group 3).

GROUP 2

Below the 50° N parallel, 21 North American-banded pintails have been recovered in Japan, 1 in Korea, and 2 in Sakhalin Island, Russia. Of these 24 birds, all were winter visitors: 5 were banded on the Aleutian Islands; a scattering came from the tundra or northern parklands of Canada; 11 were in a cluster from the southern Canadian and northern U.S. prairies; and another scattering originates in California and other western states (Fig. 3). These data corroborate Henny's data (1973) and, in addition, show that there is an unknown, but sizable number of North American pintails that regularly winter in the region of the Sea of Japan, the area which is also a wintering ground for some portion of the East Asian breeding population (Dement'ev and Gladkov 1952, Ornithological Society Japan 1974, Meyer de Schauensee 1984). Further, four female pintails, all banded within 5 days of one another on the Aleutian Islands, were recovered in Japan: three of them 40, 52, and 64 days after their banding date, respectively. The fourth was recovered, also in Japan, a year later. These four females, banded in "immature" plumage, ex-

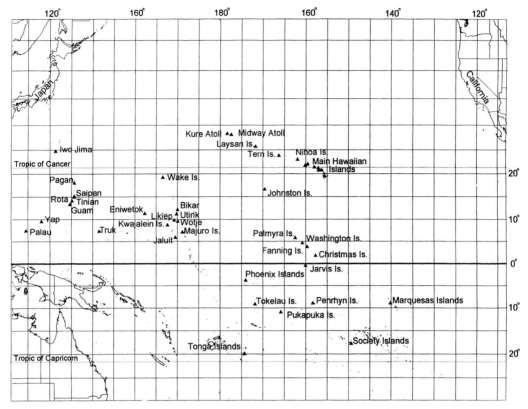

FIGURE 4. Localities where Northern Pintails have been recorded in the Pacific Ocean (banding, sight and specimen records). Sources: Reichenow (1899, 1901), Schnee (1901), Baker (1946), Gallagher (1958–1959), Yocum (1964), Fosberg (1966), Amerson (1969), Ely and Clapp (1973), Palmer (1976), Pratt et al. (1987), Engilis (1988), Stinson et al. (1997), specimens from American Museum of Natural History, National Museum of Natural History, Bernice P. Bishop Museum, and sight observation records Hawaii Rare Bird Database).

emplify the regularity of visiting and returning to winter grounds (cf. philopatry of Rohwer and Anderson 1988), reminding us of similar data from Medeiros's banding returns in the Hawaiian Islands. It is tempting to suggest a Canada-Japan flyway on a great circle route from the North American prairies through the Aleutian Chain, Kamchatka, and the Kuril Islands.

GROUP 3

The remaining 396 banded birds recovered in Asia were there predominantly as spring-summer arrivals because 338 of them were found from April to July, 55 in the fall months, and only 3 in the winter. Beside Henny (1973), a number of publications deal with drought displacement of pintails to Alaska and beyond (Derksen and Eldridge 1980; Hestbeck 1995, 1996). Thus, there is a sizable movement between breeding grounds in eastern Siberia and wintering areas in North America. It is not known whether these birds fly over the ocean or

in a great circle route or follow a coastal route along the Pacific Rim.

To close the circle around the pintails of the Hawaiian Islands, we looked at the rest of Oceania (Fig. 4). Our scrutiny of the pertinent literature, banding records, and museum specimens shows that every island group of central Oceania has received pintail visitors, often in numbers. We mention here two special cases as extremes. During the period when the Marshall Islands were German colonies, Anton Reichenow reported in 1899 about an autumnal duck migration viewed at Jaluit Atoll by reliable public officers and documented by specimens sent to the Berlin Museum as pintails, Green-winged Teals, and Canvasbacks (*Aythya valisineria*). "*In ununterbrochener Folge ungeheure keilformige Schwärme*" (large numbers in uninterrupted sequence of enormous v-shaped flocks) moved over the atolls of Bikar, Utirik, Ailuk, Jemo, Likiep, and Wotje from north to south in the fall, and back again in May (Reichenow

1899, 1901). Another observed migration toward north and north-east in the vicinity of Kwajalein Atoll was documented in May 1900 (Schnee 1901).

The pintail is also an uncommon, but regular winter visitor to the Mariana Islands, occurring regularly on the main islands of Guam (numerous sites), Saipan (Lake Susupe), and Tinian (Hagoi Marsh; Stinson et al. 1997). Kuroda (1961) linked the pintail that reach Micronesia to the "Nearctic Hawaiian Flyway" (cf. Baker 1953), referring to the now unrecognized North American race (*A. acuta tzitzihoa*). However, with the prevailing storms across Japan moving east and southeast, it is conceivable that the North American connection to the Marianas are actually birds originating from the "Canada-Japan" corridor.

SUMMARY OF COLONIZATION EVENTS BY HOLARCTIC MIGRANTS IN HAWAI'I

The winter range of Northern Pintail is perhaps the most widespread distribution area of all species of waterfowl (Palmer 1976, Austin and Miller 1995). Pintail are prone to disperse and wander as is evident by the banding, observation, and specimen information synthesized here. The species has been recorded on all continents except Antarctica and shares ancestry with the endemic island form in the Southern Hemisphere, Eaton's Pintail (*Anas eatoni*). Holarctic species prone to wandering have given rise to the majority of known endemic waterbirds and most landbirds of North Pacific islands (Fleischer and McIntosh *this volume*). The majority of the species that have colonized are those whose resources naturally fluctuate, both on a regional and seasonal pattern. Many of these are representative of highly volatile species such as fringillid finches, frugivorous thrushes, waterbirds (rallids, shorebirds, and ducks), and raptors, the latter whose populations erupt relative to fluctuating small mammal numbers. Colonization events have been rarely documented on island groups, and although pintail have yet to be recorded nesting in Hawai'i, other Holarctic migrants have. We summarize three cases where colonization has led to, or is suspected to have lead to, a Hawaiian breeding population of a Holarctic migrant.

FULVOUS WHISTLING-DUCK

The Fulvous Whistling Duck (*Dendrocygna bicolor*) apparently reached Hawai'i under its own power in 1982 when a flock of six birds suddenly appeared on O'ahu (Leishman 1986). They began nesting on O'ahu's North Shore, expanding to nearly 30 birds in under five years. Dispersal records of individual birds were doc-

umented on Moloka'i, Maui, and Kaua'i during the late 1980s. After the decline of wetlands and aquaculture on O'ahu's North Shore in 1992, the population of Fulvous Whistling Ducks crashed dramatically, so that by 1998 only one bird remained on the James Campbell National Wildlife Refuge (A. Engilis, Jr., pers. obs.). It is of interest to note that the whistling duck has high populations on the Pacific Coast of North America only in western Mexico. Thus it is conceivable that these birds originated from there, as could migratory pintail as stated earlier. A Mexico-Hawai'i tie is also suggested by other vagrants that have occurred in Hawai'i: e.g., Little Blue Heron (*Egretta caerulea*), Laughing Gull (*Larus atricilla*), and Great-tailed Grackle (*Quiscalus mexicanus*; Pyle 1997).

PIED-BILLED GREBE

The Pied-billed Grebe (*Podilymbus podiceps*) has bred in Hawai'i since the mid-1980s. A single bird arrived to overwinter in 1984 on 'Aimakapā Pond, located on the Kona Coast of Hawai'i. It left in the spring of 1985. Two birds returned the following fall, remained, and gave rise to a population on the pond that remained stable at a dozen birds throughout the late 1990s (R. David, unpubl. data). These two birds remained and have given rise to a population on the pond that remains stable at about a dozen birds. Dispersal records on Kaua'i, Maui, and on other wetlands of the island of Hawai'i are becoming more frequent in recent years, probably representing young birds that may have originated from 'Aimakapā Pond (HRBD, unpubl. data).

GREAT BLUE HERON AND WHITE-FACED IBIS

Although they have not yet been recorded breeding, two Holarctic ciconids are now regular residents in small numbers, the Great Blue Heron (*Ardea herodias*) and White-faced Ibis (*Plegadis chihi*). Great Blue Herons continue to wander through the chain and at times form small groups, often roosting among nesting colonies of Cattle Egrets (*Bubulcus ibis*) and Black-crowned Night Herons (*Nycticorax nycticorax*).

What drives these birds to disperse to the Pacific islands remains unclear, as do the mechanisms of how they navigate to the islands year after year (wintering shorebirds and waterfowl). Mayr (1953) discussed the migration of birds across the Pacific speculating that historically the islands of the Pacific were more massive, thus providing better opportunity for colonization. He also suggested two patterns affecting Holarctic birds, that of route abbreviation and route prolongation. The Northern Pintail might more readily fall into the latter group of migrants, a species whose migration patterns have been elongated as a result of global climate changes and expanding breeding range northward, away from traditional wintering grounds. Baker (1953) further alluded to the fact that oceanic islands provide excellent wintering grounds due to the absence of mammal and reptilian predators. Both authors discussed their findings with an emphasis on northern nesting shorebirds, including those species where the majority of the known population winters in the Pacific: Bristle-thighed Curlew (*Numenius tahitiensis*), Pacific Golden Plover (*Pluvialis fulva*), Wandering (*Heteroscelus incanus*) and Gray-tailed (*H. brevipes*) Tattlers, and Bar-tailed Godwit (*Limosa lapponica*; Baker 1951, Mayr 1953).

Finally, migration out over the Pacific Ocean has rarely been observed, owing to paucity of observers and opportunities. A great "corridor" of migrating Alaska pintails was observed in the fall in southern British Columbia, and another one moving from Alaska southwest across the Pacific has been postulated (Bellrose 1976, Campbell 1990) and backed by observations (Martin and Myres 1969). We uncovered one specimen of American Wigeon (AMNH 131716) collected by C. H. Townsend in 1891 from the USS Albatross, "500 miles NW of Oʻahu", documenting yet another species' movement across the Pacific. Perhaps new technologies for tracking large birds (satellite telemetry and Doppler radar) may help shed light on these movements. The evidence bears out a complex setting for migratory waterfowl in the Pacific, fortunately observers of the past had the foresight to band pintails to help us elucidate these movements herein. What has become clear is that pintail remain a regularly occurring component of the Pacific island avifauna, representing a link to the mechanics of island colonization from the Holarctic faunal region.

ACKNOWLEDGMENTS

In assembling the data for this paper we received enthusiastic help and data from many fellow wildlife researchers such as C. Kessler, B. H. Powell, J. M. Sheppard, K. Smith, and G. J. Wiles, all of the U.S. Geological Survey. The following provided banding data for our studies: B. Trost of the U.S. Fish and Wildlife Service for information on pintail banded in North America; M. Yoshii of the Yamashina Institute for Ornithology for information on pintail in Japan; in the 1960s, A. Vinckurov of the Russia Ringing Center, Moscow, for data on pintails in Russia. The original hunter and banding data from the 1950s has been courteously provided by the departments of wildlife of Hawaiʻi, Alaska, British Columbia, California, Oregon, Washington, and the U.S. Fish and Wildlife Service. B. O'Hara and A. Morton of Ducks Unlimited created all figures and M. Doyle helped with many of the technical details while working on the data. We would also like to thank M. LeCroy (AMNH), P. Angle (USNM), and C. Kishinami and R. L. Pyle (BPBM) for access to specimens and assistance while working with collections. K. Evans and J. M. Scott provided helpful comments on the manuscript. The junior author thanks M. Udvardy and family for their support of the manuscript after M. D. F.'s untimely passing.

Studies in Avian Biology No. 22:133–143, 2001.

THE HAWAI'I RARE BIRD SEARCH 1994–1996

MICHELLE H. REYNOLDS AND THOMAS J. SNETSINGER

Abstract. We compiled the recent history of sightings and searched for 13 rare and missing Hawaiian forest birds to update status and distribution information. We made 23 expeditions between August 1994 and April 1996 on the islands of Hawai'i, Maui, Moloka'i, and Kaua'i totaling 1,685 search hours, 146 field days, and 553 person days. During our surveys we found four critically endangered birds: the Po'ouli (*Melamprosops phaeosoma,* five to six individuals), Maui Nukupu'u (*Hemignathus lucidus affinis,* one individual), 'I'iwi (*Vestiaria coccinea*) on Moloka'i (one individual), and the Puaiohi (*Myadestes palmeri,* 55–70 individuals). Detection rates for each species were 0.013, 0.002, 0.012, and 0.318 detections/hr, respectively. Although not visually confirmed during our surveys, auditory detections, unconfirmed sightings, and other reports suggest the possible existence of 'Ō'ū (*Psittirostra psittacea*) on Hawai'i, Kaua'i Nukupu'u (*Hemignathus lucidus hanapepe*), and Maui 'Ākepa (*Loxops coccineus ochraceus*) in perilously low numbers. Six undetected forest bird populations, Kāma'o (*Myadestes myadestinus*), Kaua'i 'Ō'ō (*Moho braccatus*), Bishop's 'Ō'ō (*Moho bishopi*), 'Ō'ū on Kaua'i, Greater 'Akialoa (*Hemignathus ellisianus*), and Kākāwahie (*Paroreomyza flammea*) have high probabilities of being extinct. Oloma'o (*Myadestes lanaiensis*) from Moloka'i are probably extirpated from the areas searched on that island but may persist on the unsurveyed Oloku'i Plateau.

Key Words: bird survey; critically endangered; extinct; Hawai'i; 'I'iwi; Nukupu'u; Po'ouli; Puaiohi.

Descending from a small number of original colonizers, Hawai'i's native plants and animals are an evolutionary panoply. Species underwent explosive adaptive radiation and specialization in the world's most isolated island chain (Carlquist 1974, Scott et al. 1986, Freed et al. 1987a, Howarth et al. 1988, James and Olson 1991, Olson and James 1991, Wagner and Funk 1995, Pratt and Pratt *this volume*). Striking examples of speciation occurred among the lobelioids, fruit flies, land snails, and Hawaiian honeycreepers (Fringillidae: Drepanidinae), with more than 50 known species having evolved from one cardueline finch colonizer (Johnson et al. 1989, Tarr and Fleischer 1995).

The isolation that allowed such unique adaptations also predisposed the ecosystem to vulnerability due to human caused and stochastic natural disturbances. Multiple pressures have resulted in catastrophic species extinctions; habitat destruction and nonnative species introductions, including ungulates, mammalian predators, pathogens, and disease vectors, have had the most extensive and detrimental effects on Hawai'i's island ecosystem (Atkinson 1977, Ralph and van Riper 1985, Scott et al. 1986, Loope et al. 1988, Atkinson et al. 1995). Recent fossil evidence indicates at least 50% of the original avifauna went extinct after the arrival of the Polynesians about 400 AD, and today 75% of the historically known native birds are either extinct or endangered (James and Olson 1991, Olson and James 1991, Ehrlich et al. 1992).

Coincident with increased human development and the spread of the *Culex* mosquito since the 1900s, Hawai'i's remaining native avifauna has experienced a steady decline with low-ele-

vation and specialized species suffering particularly heavy losses (Baldwin 1953, Warner 1968, Scott and Kepler 1985, van Riper et al. 1986, Pratt 1994). Many species that were abundant or common into the early 1900s had low population densities during the extensive U.S. Fish and Wildlife Service (USFWS) Hawaiian Forest Bird Surveys (HFBS) of the 1970s and 1980s (e.g., 'Ō'ū [*Psittirostra psittacea*], Maui 'Ākepa [*Loxops coccineus ochraceus*], 'Ō'ō [*Moho* spp.], Hawaiian Crow [*Corvus hawaiiensis*] or 'Alalā, Moloka'i's Oloma'o [*Myadestes lanaiensis rutha*], and Kāma'o [*Myadestes myadestinus*]; Bryan and Seale 1901, Henshaw 1902a, Perkins 1903, Bryan 1908; Banko 1980a, 1980b, 1981a, 1984a, 1986; Scott et al. 1986). Today the existence of more than half Hawai'i's critically endangered (Mace and Lande 1991) birds is seriously in question (Pratt 1994, USFWS 1996a).

The Convention on International Trade in Endangered Species and the World Conservation Union (WCU 1982) have set 50 years of no sightings as the arbitrary limit to declare species extinction. This may be a useful definition in some cases, but it is hardly appropriate when periodic intensive search effort or surveys by qualified personnel make it possible to evaluate the likelihood of extinction objectively. While most of Hawai'i's endangered endemics are rare, often cryptic species that inhabit remote, rainy, and treacherous terrain where search effort is irregular (further complicated by difficulties in gaining access to rare bird habitat on both public and private lands), the periodic survey and intensive search methodology initiated in Hawai'i in the 1960s (Richardson and Bowles 1964, Sincock et al. 1984) allows for a quicker, more objective assessment of a species' status than the WCU criterion. This regular monitoring approach is essential in island ecosystems, where ecological collapse and extinction can be swift (e.g., Guam's forest bird community crashed within 35 years of the introduction of the brown tree snake [*Boiga irregularis*]; Savidge 1987a).

Species accounts written over the last century provide a sobering historical review of their disappearance (Perkins 1903, Munro 1944; Banko 1980a, 1980b, 1981a, 1981b, 1984a, 1984b, 1986; Berger 1981, Scott et al. 1986; Pratt et al. 1987, 1997b; Fancy and Ralph 1998, Lepson and Freed 1997, Snetsinger et al. 1998), but fundamental questions remain unanswered: Which species persist? What is their distribution? How many remain? Are these populations viable? Through our surveys we sought to clarify the status of extremely rare Hawaiian endemics from four families: corvids (one species), turdids (three species), fringillids (eight populations, representing seven unique taxa), and melephagids (two species; Ellis et al. 1992a).

New conservation tools from New Zealand using alien predator removal and translocation of vulnerable species will improve our ability to preserve native biodiversity (Merton 1975, Butler and Merton 1992, Saunders 1994, Serna 1995). With more than 450,000 ha in Hawai'i now designated as reserve, the development of captive propagation and release tools for Hawai'i's passerines (Kuehler et al. 1994, 1995, 1996; Fancy et al. 1997), and improved understanding of the pathology of avian pox and malaria (Warner 1968, Ralph and van Riper 1985, Atkinson et al. 1995), conservation and management opportunities are expanding enormously. To apply these methods effectively and to make more defensible management decisions, basic knowledge about which species remain, their population and distribution, is essential.

STUDY SITES AND METHODS

EVALUATION OF RECENT REPORTS

We reviewed published and unpublished reports of all critically endangered bird detections during the last 20 years in *'Elepaio*; *Hawaii's Forests and Wildlife*; the B. P. Bishop Museum *Sightings* database; and USFWS, Biological Resources Division of the U.S. Geological Survey (U.S. Geological Survey), and Hawaii Department of Land and Natural Resource (DLNR) files. For those species not reported, we reviewed Scott et al. (1986) and Banko (1980a, 1980b, 1981a, 1981b, 1984a, 1984b, 1986) for descriptions of the most recent sightings.

STUDY AREA

We conducted 28 rare bird search expeditions from August 1994 to April 1996, selecting search areas with

suitable habitat above 1,000 m or above the avian malaria belt (van Riper et al. 1986, Atkinson et al. 1995; Table 1). Native vegetation dominated survey sites, and we took care to reduce the accidental introduction of weeds into pristine areas by using new gear on each island, inspecting and cleaning clothing and equipment, and not cutting trails. Most search areas had historical sightings or had received little attention from ornithologists due to their remoteness and rough terrain. We reached remote sites by helicopter and hiked established trails to less isolated areas.

Rainfall averages up to 10 m/yr, and rainy periods often last for weeks (Scott et al. 1986, van Riper et al. 1986). The mountainous terrain is often precipitous, with flooding drainages, sheer cliffs, and gorges. Thick vegetation obscures treacherous volcanic earth cracks and lava tubes. Besides the hazardous and difficult field conditions, we found that access to many promising areas was restricted. Thus, we could not search several promising tracts.

We surveyed remote state and federal lands on the islands of Hawai'i: Ka'ū Forest Reserve (Ka'ū; 19°22' N, 155°48' W), Upper Waiākea Forest Reserve (Upper Waiākea; 19°40'49" N, 155°16'64" W), South Kona (19°11' N, 156°30' W), and Pu'u Maka'ala Natural Area Reserve (Pu'u Maka'ala; 19°12'30" N, 155° W); Maui: Hanawī Natural Area Reserve (Hanawī; 20°45' N, 156°06' W), Kīpahulu Valley (20°44'30" N, 156°' W), Kuiki (20°43'30" N, 156°10'30" W), and Waikamoi Preserve (Waikamoi; 20°43' N, 156°10'30" W); Moloka'i: Kamakou Preserve and Pelekunu Valley (Kamakou-Pelekunu; 21°08'15" N, 156°54'30" W); and Kaua'i: Alaka'i Swamp Wilderness Preserve: Koai'e (22°07' N, 159°34'30" W), Mōhihi-Waiakōali-Kōali (22°08' N, 159°31' W), Halehaha-Halepa'akai (22°06' N, 159°31' W), North Kawaikōī (22°09'30" N, 159°34' W).

OBSERVER TRAINING

Skilled field ornithologists knowledgeable in the identification of Hawaiian forest birds learned island-specific vocalizations and improved species identification skills through rigorous training: supplemental surveys in endangered forest bird habitat (25 field days not included in search effort; Table 1), practice with Hawaiian bird recordings (Cornell Laboratory of Ornithology 1995) on Bird Song Master 2.2 (Microwizard 1995) and *Voices of Hawaii's Birds* (Pratt 1996a), examination of museum skins, and study of field guides and historical references (Perkins 1903, Munro 1944, Berger 1981, Pratt et al. 1987).

SURVEY METHODOLOGY

For our surveys we used continuous observation during timed searches, a modified form of the "area search method," which uses 20–30 min timed searches (Ralph et al. 1993). Two-person survey teams conducted searches from base camps at helicopter drop sites or from satellite camps reached by backpacking. We used binoculars and listened for vocalizations to search for rare species. We incorporated the use of periodic playbacks (Johnson et al. 1981) for rare species with available recordings (Cornell Laboratory of Ornithology 1995): Kāma'o, 'Ō'ō 'ā'ā (*Moho braccatus*) or Kaua'i 'Ō'ō, 'Ō'ō, Po'ouli (*Melamprosops phaeo-*

TABLE 1. RARE BIRD SURVEY RESULTS AND SUMMARY OF SEARCH EFFORT AUGUST 1994–APRIL 1996

Island	Search area	Dates	Search effort (hr)[a]	Overall weather[b]	Number of critically endangered birds (unique individuals by expedition)	Observation time (hr:min:sec)[c]	Detection rate (detections/hr)
Maui	Waikamoi	20–21 Aug 1994	8.0	Poor	—	—	—
Maui	Hanawī	22 Aug–8 Sept 1994	154.0	Poor	Po'ouli (3)	0:05:20	0.02
Maui	Hanawī	19–27 Oct 1994	210.0	Fair	'Ākepa (1-auditory)	0:00:10	—
					Nukupu'u (1)	0:00:30	< 0.01
					Po'ouli (2)	0:00:55	0.01
Hawai'i	Upper Waiākea	7–8 Feb 1995	6.0	Fair	—	—	—
Maui	Hanawī	17–24 Feb 1995	94.0	Good	Po'ouli (2)	0:05:30	0.02
Maui	Hanawī	28 Feb–2 Mar 1995	64.0	Good	—	—	—
Moloka'i	Kamakou-Pelekunu	17–23 May 1995	85.0	Good	'I'iwi (1)	0:00:30	0.01
Hawai'i	South Kona	15, 22, 31 May–3 Jun 1995	88.0	Good	—	—	—
Maui	Hanawī	13–17 Sept 1995	60.0	Good	Nukupu'u (1)	0:01:15	0.02
Hawai'i	Ka'ū	26–27 Oct 1995	7.0	Good	—	—	—
Hawai'i	Hakalau (Training)	31 Oct–3 Nov 1995	105.0	Fair	—	—	—
Hawai'i	Hanawī (Training)	10–14 Nov 1995	21.8	Good	—	—	—
Hawai'i	Hanawī (Training)	28 Nov–1 Dec 1995	24.0	Fair	—	—	—
Maui	Kīpahulu Valley	27 Nov–1 Dec 1995	36.0	Poor	'Ākepa (1-auditory)	0:00:30	—
Maui	Kīpahulu Valley	27 Nov–3 Dec 1995	80.8	Poor	—	—	—
Maui	Kuiki	5–12 Dec 1995	126.0	Good	—	—	—
Hawai'i	Ka'ū	9–13 Jan 1996	59.5	Fair	—	—	—
Hawai'i	Kīlauea-Keauhou (Training)	16–19 Jan 1996	36.0	Good	—	—	—
Hawai'i	Upper Waiākea	22–26 Jan 1996	38.8	Poor	—	—	—
Hawai'i	Pu'u Maka'ala	12, 14 Feb 1996	6.3	Good	—	—	—
Kaua'i	Koai'e (Training)	8–13 Feb 1996	30.0	Fair	—	—	—
Kaua'i	Mōhihi	10–12 Feb 1996	17.3	Poor	Puaiohi (2)	0:21:00	0.23
Kaua'i	Southeast Interior-Upper Halepa'akai	20 Feb–1 Mar 1996	49.3	Poor	—	—	—
Kaua'i	North Kawaikōī	7–14 Mar 1996	77.4	Good	—	—	—
Kaua'i	Halehaha-Halepa'akai	14–21 Mar 1996	122.8	Good	Puaiohi (7)	0:28:08	0.06
Kaua'i	Mōhihi-Waiakōali	28 Mar–12 Apr 1996	132.8	Good	Puaiohi (27–34)	3:35:25	0.70
Kaua'i	Mōhihi-Kōali-Kawaikōī	17, 21–26 Apr 1996	95.4	Good	Puaiohi (28–31; 11 new)	2:10:00	0.60
Kaua'i	Halehaha-Halepa'akai	21–27 Apr 1996	66.8	Good	Puaiohi (12–14; 6 new)	0:27:39	0.30

[a] Search effort = cumulative party hours (e.g., two teams searching in different areas for 8 hr each = 16 hr of search effort).
[b] Weather: Good = ≥ 75% of search effort without precipitation (ppt) and wind < 11 kmph; Fair = ≥ 50% of search effort without ppt and wind < 20 kmph; Poor = > 50% of search effort with ppt and/or wind ≥ 20 kmph or with canceled surveys due to wind and rain (i.e., search effort = 0 hr).
[c] Total time observed = total time a critically endangered species was observed or heard.

TABLE 2. STATUS AND RECENT DETECTIONS OF HAWAI'I'S CRITICALLY ENDANGERED FOREST BIRD SPECIES

Species	Distribution	Status and sightings (*Unconfirmed)	References
'Alalā	South Kona, Hawai'i	1) 1 bird 1991 on Hualālai, plus S. Kona population; 2) 4 birds 1999	1) J. Giffin, DLNR, pers. comm.; 2) D. Ball, USFWS, pers. comm.
Kāma'o	Alaka'i Swamp, Kaua'i	1) 2 birds 1985; 2) *2 birds 1989; *2 1993[a]; 3) *1 bird 1995[b]	1) in Pyle 1985b; 2) in Pyle 1989, 1993; 3) D. Holmes and C. Hayward, U.S. Geological Survey, pers. comm.
Oloma'o	Kamakou and Oloku'i Plateau, Moloka'i	1) 2–3 seen 1975; 2) 3 plus *3 sightings 1980; 3) *1 bird 1988	1) Scott et al. 1977; 2) in Scott et al. 1986; 3) DLNR unpubl. data
Puaiohi	Alaka'i Swamp, Kaua'i	1) 18 birds in 1994; 2) 145 ± 19 in 1996	1) DLNR/USFWS unpubl. data; 2) Reynolds et al. 1997b
'Ō'ō'ā'ā	Alaka'i Swamp, Kaua'i	1) 1 pair 1981; 2) 1 bird 1985; 3) 1 heard 1987	1) Scott et al. 1986; 2) in Pyle 1985b; 3) in Pyle 1988
Bishop's 'Ō'ō	Northeast slope Haleakalā, Maui	1) *2 auditory 1973[c]; 2) *seen 1980[d]; 3) *seen 1981; 4) *seen 1983[3]	1) J. Jacobi in Sabo 1982, W. Banko and P. Banko in Banko 1981a; 2) Scott et al. 1986; 3) Sabo 1982; 4) D. Boynton, pers. comm., field notes
'Ō'ū	Alaka'i Swamp, Kaua'i Windward districts, Hawai'i Island	1) 2 birds in 1989 on Kaua'i; 2) 1 in 1987 from 'Ōla'a Forest, Volcano	1) in Pyle 1989; 2) USFWS, unpubl. data in Pyle 1989.
Greater 'Akialoa	Alaka'i Swamp, Kaua'i	1) 1 bird 1965; 2) *1 bird 1969	1) Huber 1966; 2) P. Bruner in Ellis et al. 1992a
Kaua'i Nukupu'u	Alaka'i Swamp, Kaua'i	1) Several seen 1985; 2) 1 bird 1987; 3) 2 birds 1995	1) In Pyle 1985a, 1985b; 2) by T. Telfer, USFWS/DLNR, unpubl. data; 3) T. Casey and J. Jeffery, pers. comm.
Maui Nukupu'u	Northeast slope Haleakalā, Maui	1) 1 bird 1986; 2) 2 birds 1989; 3) 1 bird 1994; 4) resighted 1995, 1996	1) Engilis 1990; 2) R. Fleischer, pers. comm.; 3) J. Jeffery and M. Reynolds, pers. comm.; 4) M. Reynolds, K. Berlin, pers. comm.
Kākāwahie	East slopes, Moloka'i	1) 2 seen 1961, 3 seen 1962, 3 seen 1963	1) Pekelo 1963
O'ahu 'Alauahio	Ko'olau Mountains, O'ahu	1) *41 reports 1941-1975 few with details; 2) 3 seen 1977-1978; 3) 2 juveniles seen 1985[e]; 4) *3 possible sightings 1984-1993[f]	1) Shallenberger and Pratt 1978; 2) Shallenberger and Vaughn 1978; 3) A. Engilis et al. in B. P. Bishop Museum Sightings database; 4) B. Eilerts et al., D. Woodside and R. Saito, and E. VanderWerf in Sightings database

TABLE 2. CONTINUED.

Species	Distribution	Status and sightings (*Unconfirmed)	References
Maui 'Ākepa	Northeast slope Haleakalā, Maui	1) 2 birds seen 1988; 2) *1 audio 1994; 3) *1 audio 1995	1) Engilis 1990; 2) T. Snetsinger; 3) T. Casey, pers. comm.
'I'iwi on Moloka'i	East slopes, Moloka'i	1) 1 bird 1995	1) J. Jeffery, USFWS, and T. Casey, KSBE, pers. comm. (DLNR, unpubl. data)
Po'ouli	Northeast slope Haleakalā, Maui	1) 1 bird 1993; 2) 5 birds sighted 1994-1995; 3) 6 in 1996	1) B. Gange and T. Pratt, pers. comm.; 2) Reynolds and Snetsinger 1994; 3) T. Pratt, U.S. Geological Survey, pers. comm.

[a] Brief sightings reported as possible Kāma'o or Puaiohi.
[b] Field notes described a dull brown thrush quivering its wings. Observed for 1 min with binoculars in good light from 20 m away. Reported from Kukui Trail well below 1,000 m elevation in dry, scrubby forest, in an area unlikely to support Kāma'o.
[c] Auditory detections of Bishop's 'Ō'ō calls tracked down were mimicry by 'Ākohekohe (*Palmeria dolei*), but observers appear to indicate that there was a detectable difference in mimic calls and actual *Moho* sp. calls.
[d] Described by observers as a large unidentified black bird, not 'Ākohekohe.
[e] Poamoho Trail, 21 December 1985, detailed notes and sketch.
[f] June 1984 Wai'alae Iki Ridge (identification termed "uncertain" by observers); 30 June 1989 N. Hālawa near HW-3 tunnels; 15 January 1993 Mānana Stream detailed notes (identification termed "uncertain" by EV).

soma), and Puaiohi (*Myadestes palmeri*). We recorded survey effort in hours (search hours) as the difference between start and end times for each two-person survey team. We recorded weather data (wind speed and precipitation) at the start of surveys and recorded any changes throughout the search period. We classified survey weather conditions as good (wind speed < 11 kmph and no precipitation), fair (wind speed > 11 kmph or light precipitation), or poor (wind and/or rain contributing to 20%–50% loss in visual or auditory detections; Ralph et al. 1995b). Survey effort during high wind (> 32 kmph), heavy rain, or other circumstances that severely hampered the ability of the observers to identify species, was excluded in the calculation of search hours.

We defined a "confirmed" sighting as one sighting of a bird by two observers or at least two separate sightings in the same vicinity by different experienced observers. We calculated the number of "confirmed" rare bird detections per search hour. These detection rates (detections/hr) served as an index of species rarity. When possible, we identified individual birds based on plumage, age, distance from previous detections, repeated sightings, and territorial behavior such as response to playback recording.

Subtle differences between species' call notes and some song types complicated by mimicry and an incomplete collection of Hawaiian forest bird vocalizations made auditory detection of critically endangered species as much art as science. Auditory records were not considered "confirmed" detections by the authors unless birds were sighted. We reported auditory records here only if two knowledgeable observers heard the vocalization and agreed on its identity. However, we did not consider these records as confirmation of the species' persistence and did not include auditory detections in the calculation of detection rates.

DATA ANALYSIS

We calculated detection probabilities for species undetected during our surveys to evaluate the likelihood of extinction. Scott et al. (1986) calculated the probability (p) of detecting one bird from a randomly distributed population of n individuals as:

$$p = 1 - \left(1 - \frac{a}{A}\right)^n \quad (1)$$

We approximated a, the effective search area, on either side of the search transects using the effective detection distance (EDD) for each species. We used the EDD for each species calculated from HFBS data (Table 6 in Scott et al. 1986). We measured survey distances using a planimeter (Numonics model 1250) on topographic maps. A is the last known range of the species (Tables 10 and 11 in Scott et al. 1986). We note that many rare species have experienced range contraction since the HFBS, making our detection probabilities more conservative. We used Scott et al.'s (1986) detection probabilities, p, from the HFBS for Kona and Ka'ū because we used the same transects, but we recalculated new p for all other areas. We used 10 birds as the hypothetical population size, n.

Reed (1996) modified Guynn et al.'s (1985) statistical methods to infer species extinctions:

TABLE 3. DETECTION PROBABILITIES (DP) FOR ONE BIRD FROM A POPULATION OF 10 BIRDS RANDOMLY DISTRIBUTED ACROSS THE KNOWN RANGE

Island	Species	Range[a] (km²)	EDD[b] (m)	Independent visits[c] (N)	Effective search area[d] (km²)	DP during surveys	N_{min} = Visits[c] Needed (L = 3 km)[e] for DP = 95%, 99%	Probability of zero detection in N visits, (L = 3 km)[e]
Hawai'i	'Ō'ū	145	66	17	16.28	0.70	110, 169	0.628
	'Alalā	253	282	16	54.45	0.91	45, 69	0.342
Maui	Bishop's 'Ō 'ō	23[a]	75	67	10.04	>0.99	16, 24	<0.0001
	'Ākepa	23	34	67	4.55	0.89	34, 52	0.0026
Moloka'i	Oloma'o	16, 8[f]	23	9	1.75	0.69, 0.92[f]	35, 54	0.459
	Kākāwahie	16[a], 8[f]	28	9	2.13	0.76, 0.95[f]	29, 44	0.387
	Kāma'o	25	60	54 (+208)[g]	9.13	0.99	21, 32	0.0004
Kaua'i	'Ō'ō'ā'ā	25	150	54 (+208)[g]	16.07	>0.99	9, 13	<0.0001
	'Ō'ū	25	66	54 (+208)[g]	9.83	>0.99	19, 29	0.0002
	'Akialoa	25[a]	39	54 (+208)[g]	6.65	0.96	32, 49	0.0062
	Nukupu'u	25	39	54 (+208)[g]	6.65	0.96	32, 49	0.0062

[a] Range given by Scott et al. (1986). Range used for Bishop's 'Ō'ō was the same as Maui 'Ākepa, Kākāwahie was same as Oloma'o, Greater 'Akialoa was the same as other endangered Kaua'i forest birds.
[b] Effective detective distances (EDD) are given by Scott et al. (1986).
[c] Visits are defined as 10 hr search effort in good weather; 20 hr search effort in fair to poor weather.
[d] Effective Search Area = 2*EDD*Survey Length (L). Repeated searches of the same area were added into L only once.
[e] L = 3 km is a conservative value. This was the minimum survey length during our searches.
[f] Range excluding Oloku'i Plateau (i.e., assuming a population of 10 birds distributed in the Kamakou and Pelekunu Valley area).
[g] Additional fieldwork in the Koai'e-Mōhihi drainages by Puaiohi Recovery Project field crew not included in calculation of p(0).

$$\text{Prob}(k) = \binom{N}{k} p^k (1 - p)^{N-k}$$

N is the number of independent visits made to search for the missing species, k is the number of sightings ($k = 0$ for an undetected species), and p is the probability of detection. We defined N conservatively and weighted it by weather conditions, assuming species will be more difficult to detect with decreasing visibility or deteriorating auditory conditions. We defined one "visit" as 10 hr of search effort in good survey weather or 20 hr under fair to poor weather conditions. We calculated the minimum number of visits,

$$N_{min} = \frac{\ln \alpha}{\ln(1 - p)}$$

N_{min}, needed for 95% ($\alpha = 0.05$) and 99% ($\alpha = 0.01$) probability of detection: We calculated p from Equation 1 with our minimum survey length = 3 km in 10 hr of good weather. Lastly, we calculated the probability of detecting zero birds during N visits using a conservative 3-km survey length.

DATA COMPARISON

Most forest bird censuses during the last 20 years have used the variable circular plot (VCP) method (Reynolds et al. 1980, Ramsey and Scott 1981) designed to determine multispecies bird densities in structurally complex habitat (Johnson 1995). Rare species require a much larger number of sampling points than common species, and the results of VCP censuses for rare species have yielded large confidence intervals. A sampling technique specific to the target species is most effective for censusing rare species. Differences in methodology preclude direct comparison of densities with results from previous surveys (Ralph et al. 1995b), but a review of the recent history of detec-

tions of each of these species is instructive in evaluating their status and distribution.

RESULTS

Since the comprehensive HFBS (Scott et al. 1986) and Avian History Reports (Banko 1979, 1980a, 1980b, 1981a, 1981b, 1984a, 1984b, 1986), little information on the distribution of Hawai'i's rare birds' has been published. Through our search of published and unpublished reports of critically endangered bird detections we found that many descriptions lack supporting documentation or fall into the status of unconfirmed detection according to our criteria. Table 2 summarizes status and recent detection information with sources for all of Hawai'i's critically endangered forest birds.

Search effort totaled 1,685.2 hr. We spent 146 field days and 553 person days in the field for surveys on the islands of Hawai'i (205.6 hr), Maui (832.8 hr), Moloka'i (85.0 hr), and Kaua'i (561.8 hr). Table 1 provides a summary of search effort, weather conditions, and species detections.

We failed to detect seven species during our surveys, but coverage was insufficient to infer extinction (P ≥ 0.95) for one species, and our results for two species on Moloka'i were inconclusive (Table 3). Due to restricted access, we were unable to search the Oloku'i Plateau on Moloka'i, one of the last areas on that island to harbor that island's endemics. Unconfirmed detections of two species (Maui 'Ākepa and Kaua'i Nukupu'u [Hemignathus lucidus hana-

pepe]) by skilled observers provide some hope of their continued survival (Table 2). Below we summarize, by island, survey efforts during the last two decades. Within that context we provide species accounts that include results from our surveys, additional details on historical status, and recent records from published and unpublished sources.

HAWAI'I

Survey effort

Variable circular plot surveys conducted after HFBS (1976–1978) on Hawai'i (Scott et al. 1986) include: Hakalau National Wildlife Refuge Surveys (USFWS, unpubl. data 1987–1997); Hāmākua and Ka'ū Forest Bird Survey (DLNR, unpubl. data 1993–1994); Geothermal East Rift Forest Bird Surveys (Jacobi et al. 1994); Kapāpala Forest Bird Surveys (U.S. Geological Survey, unpubl. data 1993–1994); Kīlauea-Keauhou Forest Bird Surveys (Kamehameha Schools Bishop Estate [KSBE], unpubl. data 1993–1996); Kūlani Prison Forest Bird Surveys (U.S. Geological Survey, unpubl. data 1990–1998); Hawai'i Volcanoes National Park Bird Surveys (U.S. Geological Survey, unpubl. data 1991–1994); Ka'ū-Kona 'Alalā Surveys (J. Klavitter et al., unpubl. rep.; Pacific Islands Ecoregion Office, USFWS, unpubl. data), and our rare bird search expeditions 1994–1996 (Table 2).

Species accounts

The Hawaiian Crow (*Corvus hawaiiensis*), hereafter called the 'Alalā, is a raven-sized, primarily frugivorous corvid. It is now found in a single tiny population in South Kona, Hawai'i (National Research Council 1992). Intensive surveys by the USFWS in 1995 using playback recordings in areas of recent reports and over broad areas of Ka'ū and Kona failed to confirm 'Alalā outside known territories in South Kona (USFWS, unpubl. data). We searched an additional 66.0 hr in Ka'ū without detections. While efforts to locate 'Alalā in Ka'ū and Kona were insufficient to be confident of their extirpation from these areas (for $P \geq 0.95$), other surveys have also failed to find this species and it is unlikely to be present (USFWS, DLNR, unpubl. data). As of 1999, in addition to the wild population of 4 'Alalā (Table 1), more than 21 are held in captive breeding facilities (C. Kuehler, The Peregrine Fund [TPF], pers. comm.).

'Alalā once ranged over much of Hawai'i Island but suffered rapid range contraction and population decline from the early 1900s through the 1940s (Banko 1980a). By the 1950s continued habitat degradation, avian diseases, predation, and persecution fragmented the population,

resulting in more rapid population declines. The last confirmed sighting outside the current distribution was in 1991 (Table 2).

The 'Ō'ū is a heavy-set, frugivorous Hawaiian honeycreeper with a thick pink bill, and was once common and wide-ranging on all the main Hawaiian Islands (Snetsinger et al. 1998). We failed to find 'Ō'ū during surveys for rare birds on Hawai'i Island in 1994–1996. We are confident that 'Ō'ū are extirpated from South Kona ($P \geq 0.95$). However, search effort was insufficient in Ka'ū, Upper Waiākea, and Pu'u Maka'ala to be confident (for $P \geq 0.95$) of their absence (Table 3). While observers had auditory detections consistent with 'Ō'ū in Ka'ū some of these detections were mimicry by 'Apapane (*Himatione sanguinea*) in response to 'Ō'ū playbacks. During a 1994 survey J. Jeffrey (USFWS, pers. comm.) reported 'Ō'ū whistles without the use of playbacks, but the vocalizing bird could not be found.

The most recent population estimate on Hawai'i Island (1976–1978) was 400 ± 300 individuals (95% CI) with a high density pocket (101–200 birds/km^2) in Upper Waiākea (Scott et al. 1986). Lava flows from Mauna Loa destroyed much of this high density 'Ō'ū habitat in 1984, and no subsequent concentrations of 'Ō'ū have been found since. The last confirmed sighting on the island of Hawai'i was in 1987 (Table 2).

Insufficient visits to promising habitat and poor weather conditions during Upper Waiākea searches make additional effort necessary to determine the status of 'Ō'ū on Hawai'i. The historical concentrations of 'Ō'ū in Upper Waiākea, superior coverage of potential habitat in other areas, and periodic tantalizing reports of 'Ō'ū from this vicinity make it the most likely forest to harbor remnant individuals.

MAUI

Survey effort

Specific searches to locate Maui's rarest forest birds were undertaken in 1967 and 1981 Kīpahulu Valley expeditions (Banko 1968, Conant 1981, Conant and Kjargaard 1984). In 1980 (Scott et al. 1986), 1992, and 1996, VCP censuses were conducted along HFBS transects (U.S. Geological Survey, USFWS, DLNR, unpubl. data). Additional surveys were conducted in 1981 (Conant 1981), 1983 (Conant and Kjargaard 1984), 1994–1995 (rare bird surveys; Table 2), and 1994–1996 (Maui Forest Bird Project surveys; U.S. Geological Survey, unpubl. data). After our findings, the Po'ouli Recovery Project 1995–1998 continued surveys in the area (U.S. Geological Survey, unpubl. data). Our 1995 rare bird surveys in Kīpahulu Valley were limited to the upper shelf and plagued with poor weather. Maui ʻĀkepa, Maui Nukupuʻu (*Hemignathus lucidus affinis*), and Poʻouli distribution may occur in these undersampled areas.

Species accounts

Bishop's ʻŌʻō (*Moho bishopi*) is a honeyeater reportedly preferring lobelioid nectar (Perkins 1903, Sykes et al. in press). Despite excellent coverage of its presumed range, we did not detect this species during our searches, and it is probably extinct (P > 0.95). Search effort was sufficient to be confident of detecting Bishop's ʻŌʻō from combined search areas (Table 3).

Although Bishop's ʻŌʻō is historically known only from Molokaʻi, Sabo (1982) described an ʻŌʻō thought to belong to this species seen on Maui in 1981. It is known from two sightings and several putative auditory detections (Table 2). Fossil remains identified as *Moho* sp. (Olson and James 1991) support the historic presence of an ʻŌʻō on Maui as do other reports summarized by Banko (1981a).

Maui Nukupuʻu are honeycreepers with long decurved maxillas used for boring out invertebrate prey and nectivory (Amadon 1950). We confirmed the existence of Maui Nukupuʻu (one individual; Table 1). Our detection rate was 0.002 detections/hr. Total observation time was 105 sec. All recent sightings (1994–1996) were of an adult male with bright yellow plumage from Hanawī at 1,890 m (Table 2).

The Maui Nukupuʻu has been rare historically with infrequent sightings (Banko 1984b; Table 2). The HFBS in 1980 detected one Nukupuʻu and they estimated the population size at 28 ± 56 individuals (95% CI). Last indication of breeding was a pair exhibiting courtship behavior in 1989 (R. Fleischer, Smithson. Inst., pers. comm.).

Maui ʻĀkepa, a subspecies of the Hawaiʻi ʻĀkepa (*Loxops coccineus*), were locally common in the 1890s (Perkins 1903) but have been rare since the early 1900s. Songs identified as ʻĀkepa's were heard on 25 October 1994 in Hanawī at 1,882 m (T. Snetsinger, F. Warshauer, pers. comm.) and 28 November 1995 from Kīpahulu Valley at 1,872 m (T. Casey, S. Hess, pers. comm.), but were not confirmed visually (Table 2). Auditory detections of Maui ʻĀkepa require visual confirmation because of possible confusion or mimicry with similar songs of Maui Parrotbill (*Pseudonestor xanthophrys*).

Observers of the HFBS of 1980 detected eight ʻĀkepa in East Maui from Waikamoi, Hanawī, and Kīpahulu. Scott et al. (1986) described the population as relictual with a patchy distribution, estimated at 230 ± 290 individuals (95% CI).

The last well-documented visual detections occurred in 1988 (Table 1).

The Poʻouli is a bark and an epiphyte forager discovered in 1973 (Casey and Jacobi 1974). We confirmed the continued existence and successful breeding of the Poʻouli (five to six individuals; Table 2) in 1994 after nearly two years without a sighting (Pratt et al. 1993). The detection rate for Poʻouli was 0.013 detections/hr. Total observation time was 11.75 min (Table 1). Sightings were from Kūhiwa drainage of Hanawī and included discovery of a family group (two adults and one fledgling) on 1 September 1994 at 1,890 m elevation (Table 2). We observed the fledgling Poʻouli begging and being fed. We found additional birds at 1,890 m and 1,500 m elevations and had an auditory detection at 1,902 m elevation east of the main Kūhiwa drainage (Table 2). Typical Poʻouli vocalizations are simple chips that readily blend with the call notes of several of Maui's other honeycreepers. During our searches we observed Maui ʻAlauahio (*Paroreomyza montana*) and Maui Parrotbill respond to Poʻouli playbacks. Thus, auditory detections for this species should be confirmed visually.

Our results prompted the initiation of a project to collect more life history information, manage introduced mammalian predators, and evaluate other management strategies required to recover this very rare honeycreeper (Reynolds and Snetsinger 1994).

The Poʻouli's population has plummeted since it was first described (Banko 1984a, Kepler et al. 1996, Baker *this volume*). The 1980 HFBS recorded three birds, and Scott et al. (1986) estimated total population size as 140 ± 280 individuals (95% CI). Only a few observations have been documented since that time (Table 2).

MOLOKAʻI

Survey effort

Molokaʻi birds were surveyed in 1979, 1980 (Scott et al. 1986), 1988, and 1995 (DLNR, unpubl. data). An active presence of visitors and staff at The Nature Conservancy (TNC) Kamakou Preserve has not detected any rare species in the area, except an ʻIʻiwi (*Vestiaria coccinea*) in 1995 (Ed Misaki, TNC, pers. comm.). Ornithologists have not surveyed the Olokuʻi Plateau, ungulate-free and one of the most pristine locations in the Hawaiian Islands, since 1988; Olokuʻi may still harbor critically endangered birds.

Species accounts

Olomaʻo, or Molokaʻi Thrush, was abundant into the early 1900s (Perkins 1903) but was rare and declining before 1930 (Munro 1944). Detection probabilities suggest the Oloma'o has been extirpated from Kamakou-Pelekunu (assuming a population of 10 outside of the Oloku'i Plateau), but additional searches are required to improve confidence levels (Table 3). The extremely high density of the vociferous, dull gray-brown, Japanese Bush Warbler (*Cettia diphone*) throughout the native forest of Moloka'i further reduced the chance of detecting Oloma'o (DLNR, USFWS, unpubl. data). We did not search the remote Oloku'i Plateau, and it may still harbor the small population of Oloma'o present during the 1980 HFBS. The last well-documented sightings of Oloma'o were from 1963 (Pekelo 1963), 1975, (Scott et al. 1977) and 1980 (Scott et al. 1986), with additional unconfirmed detections since that time (Table 2).

Kākāwahie (*Paroreomyza flammea*), also called Moloka'i Creeper, was common in 1907 (Bryan 1908) but extremely rare by 1930 (Munro 1944). The likelihood of the Kākāwahie being extirpated from Kamakou-Pelekunu was also high based on detection probability (P ≥ 0.95; Table 3). Searches have been unsuccessful in finding Kākāwahie since the last sighting in 1963, including surveys on the Oloku'i Plateau in 1980 and 1988 (Table 2). Considering our results and the failure of previous surveys to find this species since 1963, we believe the Kākāwahie to be extinct.

The 'I'iwi is a largely nectivorous honeycreeper, abundant in the high elevation forests of Hawai'i, Maui, and Kaua'i. It is rare on O'ahu, Moloka'i, and West Maui, but the state of Hawai'i lists it as endangered only on O'ahu. VanderWerf and Rohrer (1996) recently discovered a small resident population on O'ahu. Observers found one 'I'iwi on Moloka'i during the 1995 Moloka'i Forest Bird Survey and Rare Bird Search (Table 2; DLNR, unpubl. data) at 1,220 m above Kamalō Gulch on 23 May 1995 (Table 1). The detection rate was 0.012 detections/hr, and total observation time was 30 sec. The HFBS (Scott et al. 1986) found 12 'I'iwi from Kamakou Preserve and Oloku'i Plateau and estimated the population at 80 ± 65 individuals (95% CI).

The 'I'iwi is extremely susceptible to mortality from avian malaria (Atkinson et al. 1995). The remains of a juvenile 'I'iwi from forests of Lāna'i (T. Pratt, U.S. Geological Survey, and R. Pyle, B. P. Bishop Museum, pers. comm.) and the 'I'iwi's high-flying habits lead us to speculate that 'I'iwi found on Moloka'i may have been from a source population on Maui.

KAUA'I

Survey effort

Portions of the Alaka'i Swamp Wilderness Area, along HFBS transects, have received sig-nificant forest bird monitoring effort while other areas on Kaua'i remain unexplored by knowledgeable ornithologists. All of Kaua'i's historical avifauna was present into the 1960s (Richardson and Bowles 1964). Extensive surveys by John Sincock from 1968 to 1973 (Sincock et al. 1984), an eight-day expedition in 1975 by Conant et al. (1998), and the HFBS surveys in 1981 turned up all but the Greater 'Akialoa (*Hemignathus ellisianus*; Scott et al. 1986). In the last two decades, Hurricanes Iwa (1982) and Iniki (1992) raged through the forests, home to at least five of Kaua'i's most critically endangered birds. Engilis and Pratt (1989) and Pyle (1983) reported devastating effects of Hurricane Iwa on several species. USFWS and DLNR have conducted extensive VCP surveys (1985, 1989, 1993, 1994) along the 1981 survey transects. We conducted rare bird surveys from 1995 to 1996 (Table 1). The Puaiohi Recovery Project, based at a field camp along Koai'e and Kawaikōī streams (August 1995–1999), averages 600 person hr/mo of field effort. While most of Kaua'i's rain forest is remote and difficult to get to, easy access to intact native forest makes the Kōke'e area one of the most extensively bird-watched areas in the Hawaiian Islands.

Species accounts

The Kāma'o was sighted regularly until 1985 (T. Telfer, DLNR, pers. comm.). Our coverage of the search area was extensive, and we had a high probability of detecting Kāma'o present in the combined search areas (Tables 1 and 3). We detected none, and the Kāma'o is probably extinct (P ≥ 0.95; Reynolds et al. 1997b). Periodic reports of this species since 1995 are unconfirmed (Table 1).

We found Puaiohi, or the Small Kaua'i Thrush, in greater numbers than expected (55–70 individuals). They were widely distributed across the Alaka'i Plateau from 1,060 to 1,280 m elevation, occupying five main drainages (South Kawaikōī-Kōali, Mōhihi, Waiakōali, Halehahā-Halepa'akai, and Koai'e streams). The detection rate was 0.318 detections/hr and the total observation time was 7.04 hr (Reynolds et al. 1997b). We observed a fledgling on 26 April 1996. One nest and six birds were discovered in the Koai'e study site in 1995 (T. Casey, KSBE, pers. comm.) and 50 nests and 75 birds were monitored in 1996 (U.S. Geological Survey, unpubl. data). Our data in combination with unpublished research on the Mōhihi-Koai'e population indicate the Puaiohi population may exceed 200 birds (Reynolds et al. 1997b; T. Snetsinger and C. Herrmann, unpubl. data). In 1996, 4 Puaiohi were hatched in captivity at Keauhou Bird Conservation Center from eggs collected at the Koai'e study site, 10 were added to the flock in 1997, and 16 were hatched from eggs produced in captivity 1998 (C. Kuehler, TPF, pers. comm.).

The sedentary behavior and infrequent vocalizations of the Puaiohi make this species difficult to census. Some Puaiohi responded readily to playbacks of calls and songs. The most recent Puaiohi population estimate was 20–34 individuals (95% CI; Scott et al. 1986). Scott et al. (1986) noted the sampling design may have been biased against Puaiohi, which is associated with streams.

The 'Ō'ō'ā'ā, a black, large-bodied nectarivore, is vocally conspicuous and responds well to playbacks (Conant et al. 1998; T. Telfer, DLNR, pers. comm.). We did not detect the 'Ō'ō'ā'ā during our surveys. Detection probability was very high for 'Ō'ō'ā'ā in combined search areas, and our failure to find the species suggests it is extinct (P ≥ 0.95; Table 3). The population estimate for 'Ō'ō'ā'ā from surveys 1968–1973 was 36 ± 29 individuals (95% CI; Sincock et al. 1984). Observers regularly sighted two or three 'Ō'ō'ā'ā from 1975 to 1981, but these birds had vanished by the 1989 DLNR survey (Table 2). We found that White-rumped Shama (*Copsychus malabaricus*) answered 'Ō'ō'ā'ā recordings and heard 'I'iwi mimic parts of 'Ō'ō'ā'ā song.

The last published 'Ō'ū sighting from Kaua'i was in 1989 in the southeastern Alaka'i (Engilis and Pratt 1989, Pyle 1989). From our detection probabilities, we believe the 'Ō'ū is extinct on Kaua'i (P ≥ 0.95; Table 3). Auditory detections in 1995 to 1997 (U.S. Geological Survey, unpubl. data) along Koai'e Stream were unconfirmed. Estimated population size in 1968 to 1973 was 62 ± 82 individuals (95% CI; Sincock et al. 1984) and 3 ± 6 individuals (95% CI) in 1981 (Scott et al. 1986).

Greater 'Akialoa on Kaua'i, common in the 1890s (Perkins 1903), was last well documented in 1964 (Huber 1966). The likelihood of Greater 'Akialoa being extinct was high based on detection probability (P ≥ 0.95; Table 3). An unconfirmed 1969 report may have been the last sighting (Table 2). Vocalizations of this species were never recorded. Greater 'Akialoa's extraordinary bill length of 6 cm (S. Johnson, unpubl. data) would make visual identification unquestionable.

Kaua'i Nukupu'u, historically an uncommon species, was extremely rare by 1960 (Perkins 1903, Richardson and Bowles 1964). We did not record Kaua'i Nukupu'u during our surveys nor did observers with the HFBS observe it (Scott et al. 1986). However, skilled observers reported three (unconfirmed) sightings of at least one male and one female) in 1995 near the Koai'e Gauging Station (Table 2; T. Casey and J. Jeffrey in Conant et al. 1998). Our lack of detections combined with our analysis of detection probability (P ≥ 0.95) suggest the population is less than 10 birds.

Despite extensive fieldwork, J. Sincock observed Kaua'i Nukupu'u only twice from 1968 to 1973 (Sincock et al. 1984). Conant et al. (1998) report a 1975 sighting, and several observers provide convincing reports from the 1980s and 1990s (Table 2). Other Nukupu'u reports require additional confirmation due to the possible confusion with Kaua'i 'Amakihi (*Hemignathus kauaiensis*).

DISCUSSION

Six of the 13 missing Hawaiian birds are likely to be extinct (Kāma'o, 'Ō'ō'ā'ā, Bishop's 'Ō'ō, 'Ō'ū on Kaua'i, Greater 'Akialoa, and Kākāwahie), three of which disappeared in the last decade. Moloka'i's endemic Oloma'o could probably be added to this list, but to be confident of its extinction a thorough search of the restricted Oloku'i Plateau is warranted. Five of Hawai'i's rarest forest birds still exist ('Alalā, Puaiohi, Po'ouli, 'I'iwi on Moloka'i, and Maui Nukupu'u), and the results of our surveys and investigation were inconclusive for three additional populations (Kaua'i Nukupu'u, Maui 'Ākepa, 'Ō'ū on Hawai'i). Reports of Kaua'i Nukupu'u in the Alaka'i Swamp (1994, 1995), and 'Ō'ū from the Ka'ū (1993, 1995) and Pu'u Maka'ala (1991, 1992, 1996) reported to U.S. Geological Survey or the Bishop Museum (R. Pyle, pers. comm.) suggest that a few individuals of these species may still exist. Auditory detections of Maui 'Ākepa (1995, 1996) in combination with sightings within the last decade (Engilis 1990; T. Casey, pers. comm.) and insufficient coverage of the potential range make its status unknown.

Rare Hawaiian birds have been rediscovered after they were presumed extinct or have been found in larger populations than expected (Richards and Baldwin 1953, Richardson and Bowles 1964, Banko 1968, Shallenberger and Vaughn 1978, Sabo 1982, VanderWerf and Rohrer 1996, Reynolds et al. 1997b, VanderWerf et al. 1997). We hope this will also be the case for some of Hawai'i's rare species that we failed to find. While we searched habitat with historical records and/or high native-species diversity to increase our chances for rare bird detections, similar habitat with recent sightings of critically endangered species outside our search area exists.

Long-term declines in Hawaiian native bird populations signal the need for additional action against known threats such as feral ungulates, alien weeds, introduced predators, and avian disease vectors (Richardson and Bowles 1964, Atkinson 1977, Sincock et al. 1984, Jacobi and Scott 1985, Vitousek et al. 1987, Atkinson et al. 1995). Active ecosystem management is the best way to conserve endangered species before they become rare and a species-by-species approach is impractical. Fortunately, endemic and endangered species occur in many areas held by federal and state agencies or private landowners with strong interests in conservation. Aggressive management and long-term population monitoring are essential to protect these areas and the endangered species they harbor.

We believe those birds not sighted in the last 20 years with high probabilities of being extinct should be taken off the Federal Endangered Species List to update the list, heighten awareness of Hawai'i's extinction crisis, and focus recovery on ecosystems and the species that we can assist. We encourage field observers to take detailed notes and report or publish their sightings so that monitoring the status of Hawai'i's rare birds will be easier.

ACKNOWLEDGMENTS

We thank the participants and the staff of rare bird search expeditions (except where noted, personnel were U.S. Geological Survey staff or volunteers): R. Allen, S. Anderson (National Park Service [NPS]), G. Balauss, A. Carter, T. Casey (KSBE), R. Chesser, K. Fluetsch, B. Haus (NPS), S. Hess, C. Hodges (NPS), G. Homel, J. Jeffery (USFWS), K. Karwacky, D. Kuhn, C. Lott, D. Pratt, J. Simon, B. Smith, E. VanGelder, R. Warshauer. We received logistical assistance from a host of people and agencies: B. Evanson (DLNR), R. Nagata (NPS), and J. Simon (U.S. Geological Survey) on Maui; T. Telfer (DLNR) Alaka'i Wilderness Preserve on Kaua'i; P. Conry (DLNR) and J. Yoshioka (TNC) during DLNR Moloka'i Forest Bird Survey (1995); and J. Giffin (DLNR) and J. Klavitter (USFWS) during the 'Alalā Surveys of Ka'ū and South Kona. We thank T. Pratt for support on Maui and providing Kaua'i and Moloka'i survey data. J. Jacobi, H. Love and L. Young provided invaluable administrative support. We also thank C. Kishinami and R. Pyle (B. P. Bishop Museum) for providing access to specimens of our target rare bird species and sharing information on recent sightings. A National Biological Service competitive grant provided funding for most of these surveys. We thank T. Casey, S. Hess, G. Lindsey, B. Ostertag, and T. Pratt for reviewing earlier versions of this manuscript. Lastly, we thank G. Brenner and J. Hatfield for statistical advice.

Studies in Avian Biology No. 22:144–150, 2001.

STATUS AND DISTRIBUTION OF THE PO'OULI IN THE HANAWĪ NATURAL AREA RESERVE BETWEEN DECEMBER 1995 AND JUNE 1997.

PAUL E. BAKER

Abstract: The Po'ouli (*Melamprosops phaeosoma*), a critically endangered Hawaiian honeycreeper first discovered in 1973 on east Maui, Hawai'i, is on the brink of extinction. The population was estimated at 140 ± 280 (95% CI) in 1980, but has since declined rapidly. No birds were seen between 1989–1993, but sightings in 1993–1994 prompted the development of this study. Aims were to locate all remaining Po'ouli and other critically endangered forest birds, to identify causes of decline, and to develop and implement management to help the recovery of the species. Intensive searching and revisiting (752 person-days) of 700 ha including most of the historical distribution, between December 1995 and June 1997, resulted in 81 sightings and one audible contact of Po'ouli involving five birds: three males, one female, and one immature (possibly female) in three home ranges. One other male was heard singing in a fourth home range but was never seen. Playbacks were used to assist detection of critically endangered birds on 171 occasions. In the first six months of 1997, only three Po'ouli could be found (two males, one possible female), one bird in each of the three home ranges. These birds are believed to be the last of their species. No individuals of two other critically endangered forest bird species, the Maui 'Ākepa (*Loxops coccineus ochraceus*) and Maui Nukupu'u (*Hemignathus lucidus affinis*), were found in the study area.

Key Words: distribution; endangered; Hawaiian honeycreeper; *Melamprosops phaeosoma*; Po'ouli.

One of the most secretive and elusive of the Hawaiian honeycreepers (Fringillidae: Drepanidinae), the Po'ouli (*Melamprosops phaeosoma*) was discovered in the remote, montane cloud forest of northeastern Maui in 1973 (Fig. 1; Casey and Jacobi 1974, Mountainspring et al. 1990). At that time, several pairs were found between the east and west Hanawī streams (Unit 1; Fig. 2) and two were collected so the species could be described (Casey and Jacobi 1974). The Hawaiian name Po'ouli literally translates as "black-headed," but it has been interpreted as meaning black-faced (Casey and Jacobi 1974).

The first Hawai'i Forest Bird Survey in 1980 estimated the population at 140 ± 280 (95% CI), calculated from three sightings of Po'ouli along one transect (Scott et al. 1986). Intermittent field work documented the decline of the Po'ouli over the next 15 years. Mountainspring et al. (1990) estimated the population density in Hanawī to be 76 birds/km² in 1975, but by 1985 they noted a decline to only 8 birds/km². These authors offered circumstantial evidence suggesting that the decline of the Po'ouli was related to the increase in feral pig (*Sus scrofa*) activity in the area (431% during 1975–1985), resulting in extensive damage to the understory and ground layer.

Only two Po'ouli nests were ever found and monitored; both were constructed in 1986 by the same pair of birds just east of the east Hanawī stream at 1,800 m (Kepler et al. 1996). Po'ouli were next seen in 1988, when five were encountered between the east Hanawī stream and the eastern boundary of the Hanawī Natural Area Reserve (Hanawī NAR; Engilis 1990). The last sightings near the Hanawī streams were in September 1993; one at the former nest site, the other just 400 m to the west across the east Hanawī stream (U.S. Geological Survey, USGS, unpubl. data). No Po'ouli were found during four years of intensive field work (1994–1997) between the Hanawī streams (USGS, unpubl. data).

In 1994–1995, the Biological Resources Division of the U.S. Geological Survey (then known as the National Biological Service) led searches for critically endangered birds on Maui. The known distribution of the Po'ouli (U.S. Geological Survey, unpubl. data) was included and the searches resulted in sightings of five Po'ouli between the upper watersheds of the Kūhiwa and Helele'ike'ōhā streams, involving two adults and a dependent juvenile, and single adults in two other locations. Thus, prior to our field work the Po'ouli had disappeared from its type locality, but a small number remained 1–2.5 km to the east. All well-documented sightings of Po'ouli have been between 1,400–2,100 m elevation in approximately 13 km² on northeastern Maui (Scott et al. 1986, Mountainspring et al. 1990).

As a result of this recent survey, Hawaiian conservation agencies in November 1994 produced a three-point plan to investigate the decline of this species and assist any recovery (U.S. Fish and Wildlife Service, USFWS, unpubl. data). Two other critically endangered species, the Maui 'Ākepa (*Loxops coccineus ochra-*

FIGURE 1.   Adult male Po'ouli in the Hanawī Natural Area Reserve in 1997. Photo by Paul E. Baker.

ceus) and Maui Nukupu'u (*Hemignathus lucidus affinis*) were to be included in the project if encountered. Objectives of the plan were to (1) locate (by surveys) and continuously monitor all remaining individuals through banding and observation of known birds; (2) investigate the population ecology of the bird, abundance and diversity of invertebrate food resources, and effects of avian diseases on the population; and (3) control small, nonnative mammalian predators in Po'ouli home ranges by means of approved techniques. Consequently, U.S. Geological Survey was contracted for two years (1995–1997) to conduct the work. This paper reports the results of the primary goal of the project, namely the intensive search of the historical distribution of the Po'ouli and nearby areas to determine the current distribution and number of birds.

METHODS

STUDY SITE

Most of the historical distribution of the Po'ouli lies within the Hanawī NAR, which is managed by the State of Hawai'i Department of Land and Natural Resources, Division of Forestry and Wildlife (DOFAW). The reserve was established in 1986 to protect a diversity of native ecosystems, and rare and endangered plant and bird populations. The reserve also preserves

Maui's most important watershed. The Hanawī NAR is 3,036 ha of mesic to wet cloud forest between 610–2,286 m elevation on northeastern Maui in the Hana district (described in Mountainspring 1987, Wagner et al. 1990a,b). Haleakalā National Park (HNP) lies to the south and southeast (Kīpahulu Valley) of the Hanawī NAR, while the Hanā and Ko'olau Forest reserves lie to the east and west (Fig. 2).

Extensive habitat degradation by feral pigs in the Hanawī NAR prompted a large-scale fencing and pig removal program by DOFAW to restore habitat and exclude pigs in the most pristine upper reaches of the reserve. Fencing and pig removal was completed in three stages important to the partitioning of the study area: Unit 1 (198 ha) by 1991; Unit 2 (172 ha) in 1993; and Unit 3 (405 ha) in 1996 (Fig. 2). The resulting ungulate-free zone of 775 ha between 1,584–2,286 m included almost all of the historical distribution of the Po'ouli. Adjacent forest to the south in HNP was fenced in 1989 and was almost pig free during our study (part of Unit 5). The remainder of Unit 5 to the east of the Hanawī NAR and the forest below the NAR fence to the north (Unit 4) both had pigs and were managed by DOFAW.

To locate Po'ouli, 'Ākepa, and Nukupu'u, all suitable habitat within the historical distribution of the Po'ouli and some adjacent areas were systematically searched (Fig. 2), except as noted below. The eastern two-thirds of Unit 2, all of Unit 3, as well as forest bordering the fences in Units 4 and 5 were searched. Also, approximately 100 ha to the south in HNP's por-

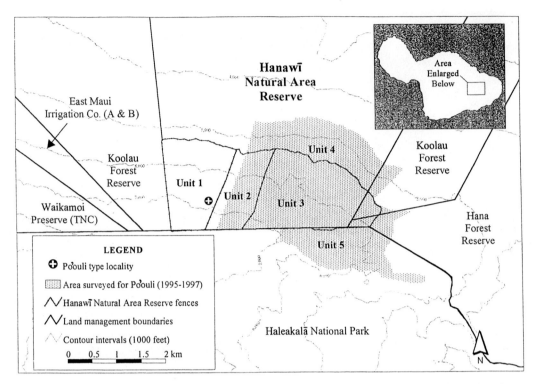

FIGURE 2.   The Hanawī Natural Area Reserve showing Po‘ouli type locality, study area units, and total area searched.

tion of Unit 5 were searched, which included mostly land that had never been searched for the focal species before. Despite the former presence of Po‘ouli down to 1,400 m elevation, the searches only went to 1,432 m, because below that point the severely degraded habitat was infested with nonnative weeds that I did not want to spread. The area between the Hanawī streams (including Unit 1) was not searched because the 1994–1995 survey failed to find the three focal species at that location, and because the above-mentioned research project of 1994–1997 was concurrently conducting intensive surveys there with the same result (U.S. Geological Survey, unpubl. data).

TRAINING

All survey participants were trained to recognize the appearance, calls, and songs of all Hawaiian honeycreepers and nonnative passerines inhabiting the study area. Training involved playing and identifying recorded vocalizations and field identification sessions until everyone was competent at identification. Vocalizations of Maui ‘Ākepa and Maui Nukupu‘u have never been recorded, so recordings of the most closely related taxa (Hawai‘i ‘Ākepa, *L. c. coccineus*; ‘Akiapōlā‘au, *Hemignathus munroi*; and Maui Parrotbill, *Pseudonestor xanthophrys*) were used. Perkins (1903) commented that the calls and song of Maui Parrotbill were virtually identical to those of the Maui Nukupu‘u.

SEARCHES

The subdivision of the Hanawī NAR into fenced units greatly facilitated searches, reducing the study area into manageable sections. Main trails were marked with flagging in each unit. The terrain was very rugged and the study area remote, so for safety reasons survey participants worked in pairs. All teams carried first aid kits, compasses, radios, and emergency locating transmitters (ELT/EPIRB). Teams used main trails to access areas quickly, then slowly searched through dense vegetation off the trail or used minor trails while looking for birds. Several teams worked in the same unit simultaneously to facilitate communication and detection of birds. Trail maps, fences, and use of compasses ensured complete coverage of each unit.

Searches began in Unit 2, then moved eastward into Units 3, 4, and 5. Each unit was searched twice for the presence of Po‘ouli, Maui Nukupu‘u, and Maui ‘Ākepa. Additional searches were done at a different time of year, in case these species were less detectable during certain months. All vocalizations sounding similar to Maui Parrotbill were investigated, as were all "chip" calls and any unknown or unusual vocalizations. ‘I‘iwi (*Vestiaria coccinea*) and ‘Apapane (*Himatione sanguinea*) were generally ignored, as they are not known to associate with the critically endangered species. All other native birds were observed for any associating focal species by using 10 x 42 binoculars.

TABLE 1.   PERSON-DAYS SPENT SEARCHING FOR PO'OULI IN EACH UNIT ON MAUI, NUMBER OF BIRDS FOUND, AND NUMBER OF BIRDS RELOCATED DURING SUBSEQUENT VISITS TO EACH LOCALITY

	Unit 2	Unit 3	Unit 4	Unit 5	Total
Person-days searching	46	200	40	32	318
No. times Po'ouli found while searching	1[a]	10[a]	1[a,b]	1[a]	13
Person-days resighting	90	336	8	0	434
No. times Po'ouli resighted	3[a,c]	66[a]	0	0	69
Actual no. of individual Po'ouli located	1[d]	5[d]	1[b]	1[e]	5(+1[b])

[a] Sightings were: 21 in home range 1, 1 near home range 1, 46 in home range 2, 13 in home range 3, plus 1 audible contact in home range 4.
[b] Bird heard singing and was not seen.
[c] All sightings occurred in home range 3.
[d] Home range 3 straddled Units 2 and 3, so the bird in Unit 2 is also one of the Unit 3 birds.
[e] Unit 5 bird is probably one of the birds from home range 1 in Unit 3 to the north, because of the proximity to this home range.

Whenever Po'ouli were found, observers took detailed descriptions of the appearance and behavior of the bird and I later compared these with published descriptions of birds to determine the age and sex of each bird (Casey and Jacobi 1974, Engilis et al. 1996). Following initial detections, the surrounding forest (up to 70 ha) was searched repeatedly to relocate the bird. These visits were made each day, beginning when possible with the day after discovery and continuing for a week. If no bird was seen, at least 18 follow-up visits would be made over a period of a month. If a bird was found again, further visits were made each month to study it. During 19 months of surveying and monitoring, we spent 729 person-days searching and revisiting areas. A person-day was defined as 8–11 hours of searching by each person in a pair (i.e., two person-days per pair on one day), because each person often searched independently while in the same area. Searches were discontinued during periods of poor weather that reduced detectability of birds.

PLAYBACKS

Playbacks of recorded calls and songs of Hawai'i 'Ākepa, Maui Parrotbill, 'Akiapōlā'au, Po'ouli, and Maui 'Alauahio (*Paroreomyza montana newtoni*) were used on a total of 171 occasions during searches to help locate critically endangered forest birds. Recordings were obtained from various U.S. Geological Survey personnel in Hawai'i, or made by participants using a Sony PBR-330 parabolic reflector and Sony Walkman recorder. Calls and songs recorded on 3-min endless loop cassette tapes were broadcast from 5-watt speakers. Playbacks were used most frequently between December to May during the breeding season of the honeycreepers on Maui when their response to playback was greatest (P. Baker and H. Baker, pers. obs.). During favorable weather conditions of good visibility and no wind or rain, teams would stop when "chewee" calls were heard and would play either Maui Parrotbill or 'Akiapōlā'au calls and song to attract the bird for identification. This call is given by Maui Parrotbill, Po'ouli, and Maui Nukupu'u. Hawai'i 'Ākepa calls and song were played in areas where audible contact with Maui 'Ākepa had been reported by biologists previously working in the reserve (U.S. Geological Survey, unpubl. data). Calls and songs of Maui Parrotbill, 'Akiapōlā'au, and Hawai'i 'Ākepa were also played where Po'ouli had been seen to determine which individual birds and species would respond. Po'ouli calls were played only in areas where Po'ouli had been seen, as were Maui 'Alauahio "chip" calls. Both Maui 'Alauahio and Maui Parrotbill make a "chip" call similar to that of the Po'ouli.

MAPPING SIGHTINGS OF PO'OULI

A Rockwell PLGR 96 Federal Global Positioning System unit (GPS unit), accurate to < 10 m, was used to obtain coordinates for Po'ouli locations. These locations were mapped with Arcview software. The area within a cluster of sightings, which probably represented the home range of a Po'ouli, was determined by the minimum convex polygon method.

RESULTS

SEARCHES

Between September 1995 and October 1996, 700 ha were searched for Po'ouli during 318 person-days (Fig. 2). Six Po'ouli were found on 13 occasions in four areas during searches. In addition, between December 1995 and June 1997, Po'ouli were found on another 69 occasions during 434 person-days that were spent revisiting three areas to study five of the six birds found (Table 1). No Maui 'Ākepa or Maui Nukupu'u were found during these searches.

An adult male and an immature of unknown sex, possibly female by the small size of the facial mask, were found at 1,908 m elevation in the Hanawī NAR. These birds were found within 100 m of the Hanawī NAR/HNP boundary fence in March and April 1996, respectively. This area was designated home range 1 (Fig. 3). The immature's plumage was not typical of either adult or juvenile as described by Engilis et al. (1996) and did not resemble any adult Po'ouli I had personally observed. I determined that this bird (pers. obs.) was definitely an immature by comparison with the holotype specimen and the photographs of the paratype (Casey and Jacobi 1974). This suggests that the bird was hatched in 1995, indicating successful breeding by one pair in that year. No adult female was seen with either the male or the immature. One or both birds were seen 18 times in

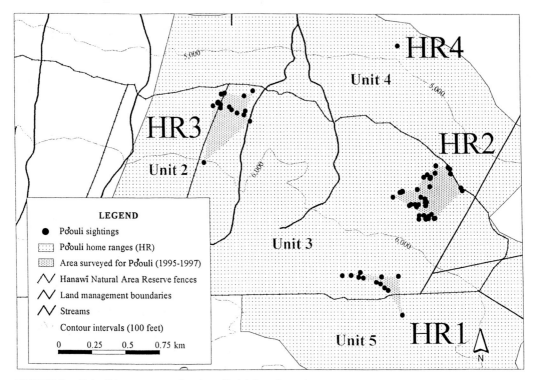

FIGURE 3.   Po'ouli home ranges showing all sightings in each area.

home range 1 until July 1996, but they were never seen together. There were no more sightings in this area until February 1997, when one bird, possibly an adult female, was seen. An adult bird was then seen once each month in April and May 1997 in this same area, but the sex was not determined.

A pair of Po'ouli was found in an area between 1,768 and 1,584 m within Unit 3, north of home range 1, in an area designated as home range 2 (Fig. 3). The adult male was found in March 1996 and seen 10 times during March and April, but the female was only seen twice, in June–July 1996, and both times with or near the male. The male was seen 24 times during 1996. It was captured and banded in January 1997 (Baker 1998), and was then seen 22 times between January and the end of May 1997; no other Po'ouli were seen in this area.

A single bird, probably male based on plumage, was located in December 1995 at 1,866 m and then at 1,816 m in the vicinity of the boundary fence between Units 2 and 3. I designated this area home range 3 (Fig. 3). Revisiting this area on 90 person-days between December 1995 and May 1997 (with thorough searching) produced only 11 more sightings. An adult, possibly male, was relocated in this area twice on one day in February 1997 at 1,860 m (T. Snetsinger,

pers. comm.). There were also two sightings of a single male in March 1997 at 1,880 m (west of the fence) and 1,860 m (east of the fence). A single adult bird (male) was seen several times in this same area in late May and early June 1997, giving a total of 13 sightings in home range 3. (This bird was seen flying away at a distance on two occasions, enabling further estimation of home range size, hence Figure 3 has 15 points rather than 13.) No pair was ever confirmed visually.

Po'ouli song was heard once at 1,493 m on transect # 9 in Unit 4 during March 1996. This locality was designated home range 4 (Fig. 3). Re-searching this area produced no more contacts.

There were no definite sightings of Po'ouli in Unit 5, but a bird that may have been a Po'ouli was glimpsed near transect # 10 on HNP land, and it may have been from home range 1.

PLAYBACKS

No Po'ouli were attracted to either recorded Po'ouli "song" or calls. I discovered that the recording previously thought to be song (H. D. Pratt, pers. obs.) was actually the alarm call of the Po'ouli, and I observed two different individuals give these calls when distressed. Recorded Po'ouli "chip" calls were played (on

TABLE 2. NUMBERS OF HAWAIIAN HONEYCREEPERS LURED BY PLAYBACK OF THEIR OWN AND OTHER SPECIES' CALLS AND SONGS

	Playback tape used (song and calls)				
Species lured	Po'ouli	Maui Parrotbill	'Akiap-ōlā'au	Hawai'i 'Ākepa	Maui 'Alau-ahio
Po'ouli	0	1	1	1	0
Maui Parrotbill	0	30	13	6	0
Maui Nukupu'u	0	0	0	0	0
Maui 'Ākepa	0	0	0	0	0
Number of times playback tried	6	78	38	41	8

three occasions) to an adult male Po'ouli that was very responsive to calls of other species (see below) and elicited no interest or response at all. I also tried the same calls in home range 1, and did not attract any Po'ouli either. Playbacks of Po'ouli calls were not used again.

The male Po'ouli in home range 2 was very attracted to playback of Maui Parrotbill "chewee" calls and song. He was also attracted to playback of 'Akiapōlā'au song and Hawai'i 'Ākepa calls and song. Playback of Maui Parrotbill was used unsuccessfully to try to attract Po'ouli in the other areas where we had found them, and elsewhere (Table 2).

Maui Parrotbill, 'Akiapōlā'au, and Hawai'i 'Ākepa playback attracted most species of honeycreeper at least briefly but were a strong attractant for Maui Parrotbill. Maui Parrotbill were attracted to Hawai'i 'Ākepa song and calls in both areas where possible Maui 'Ākepa were reported, as well as in four other areas. Playback would be a useful census tool to locate Maui Parrotbill. Prior to using playback, we had mapped all Maui Parrotbill located during our searches. Playback did not attract pairs in any areas, other than where we had known them to be based on our mapping. From these findings, the current known population of Po'ouli in 1997 is three individuals in 7 km². Despite intensive searching no other Po'ouli were found, or are known from elsewhere on Maui, so we presume the Po'ouli to be on the brink of extinction.

MAPPING PO'OULI HOME RANGES

All sightings of Po'ouli during this study between December 1995 and June 1997 are illustrated in Figure 3. Using Arcview to determine distances between sightings of Po'ouli within each home range, we were able to determine minimum home range sizes of 3.2 ha for home range 1, 11.2 ha for home range 2, and 10.2 ha for home range 3. Unfortunately, there was only a single audible (song) contact in home range 4,

so no estimation of home range size could be made (Fig. 3).

The longest linear distance (determined using Arcview) between two sightings in each home range was 548 m in home range 1, 537 m in home range 2, and 672 m in home range 3. Linear distances between home ranges were: 469 m between home ranges 1 and 2, 1,382 m between home ranges 1 and 3, 1,817 m between home ranges 1 and 4, 1,247 m between home ranges 2 and 3, 961 m between home ranges 2 and 4, and 1,170 m between home ranges 3 and 4.

DISCUSSION

NUMBER AND DISTRIBUTION OF PO'OULI

In 1996, there were six Po'ouli in the Hanawī NAR, which were confined to four distinct home ranges 0.45–1.81 km apart. The banded bird was only seen in home range 2 despite intensive searching by my crew beyond its home range area, suggesting Po'ouli are sedentary. Although Po'ouli may have home ranges of > 10 ha, they do not use the area equally. Po'ouli seem to use intensively particular areas, perhaps as small as 4 ha, then, after some time, they may move and use another area within the home range and occasionally visit the previous area (pers. obs.). This observation is supported by this survey, in which Po'ouli were located in each of the three general areas, but not at the same places where the 1994–1995 survey had found them. The apparently small size of home range 1 is probably due to such behavior. Initially, birds were found in the eastern portion of home range 1, but all recent sightings have been on the western "edge" bordering an area that is inaccessible to survey crews due to steep terrain and deep gulches. This inaccessible area is only about 200 m east of where a Po'ouli family had been seen prior to this study, but the birds were never found there despite many days of searching during this project, suggesting periodic changes in the use or position of a home range. From observations of Po'ouli behavior, it is unlikely that Po'ouli are sensitive to disturbance on the ground by humans and, in fact, they often approach closely showing curiosity.

Given a fairly sedentary nature and the long distances between home ranges, it is unlikely that the remaining Po'ouli in the Hanawī NAR may wander into each other's home ranges. Distances moved by birds within and between home ranges calculated with Arcview do not take into account the rugged terrain but only the linear distance between points or areas. The extremely rugged terrain may also reduce the distances moved by Po'ouli because they may prefer the habitat found in gulches or low lying areas rather than that on ridges.

Many other Hawaiian honeycreeper species are easy to locate as pairs during the breeding season. In the 1980s, Po'ouli were frequently found in pairs (Scott et al. 1986; B. Gagne, pers. comm.). Only one pair of Po'ouli were observed during this study, on two occasions in 19 months of intensive field work. Adult female Po'ouli were seen only three times. There has also been no evidence of successful reproduction based on nest building or dependent fledglings since 1995. I believe that all remaining Po'ouli and their home ranges within the known historical distribution of the species have now been located, and it is highly unlikely that any were overlooked; so no viable pairs currently exist in this study area. Therefore, a great problem is that the remaining birds cannot find each other and attempt to breed.

Although it is unlikely that Po'ouli are to be found elsewhere on Maui, it is remotely possible that there are birds outside the study area. Parts of Kīpahulu Valley have been searched, but large areas remain to be thoroughly searched. Habitat that may be suitable for Po'ouli also lies all along the northern flank of east Maui from Hanawī, as far west as the Waikamoi Preserve near Makawao, where there was one record of Po'ouli in 1983 (Mountainspring et al. 1990). There have been no other records despite several surveys on established transects throughout the area by biologists from the Hawai'i Forest Bird Survey and the Nature Conservancy of Hawai'i. Much of this habitat where Po'ouli may occur has been damaged by pigs (Scott et al. 1986). Even so, this does not account for the current critically low number of Po'ouli, or their distribution, because much relatively undamaged habitat remains within the Hanawī NAR and elsewhere that should be suitable for Po'ouli.

OTHER CRITICALLY ENDANGERED MAUI FOREST BIRD SPECIES

No Maui Nukupu'u were seen during this study, despite over 90 person-days of searching the area where a bird was reported in 1995 (U.S. Geological Survey, unpubl. data), as well as all the other searching through the Hanawī NAR. Playback of both Maui Parrotbill and 'Akiapōlā'au was utilized, especially during the breeding season. The tapes attracted Maui 'Amakihi (*Hemignathus virens wilsoni*), Maui 'Alauahio, 'I'iwi, and Maui Parrotbill (nine Maui Parrotbill

were captured in mist nets in the immediate area where the Maui Nukupu'u was reported to have been because they responded to the playback).

Possible audible contacts of Maui 'Ākepa have been reported several times in the Hanawī NAR since 1994 (T. Snetsinger and T. Casey, pers. comm.), but my crew was unable to confirm their presence. Three of my crew experienced with Hawai'i 'Ākepa all reported hearing and seeing Maui Parrotbill producing song and "chewee" calls that they believed could be mistaken for that of the Hawai'i 'Ākepa. Maui Parrotbill are resident in each area where Maui 'Ākepa contacts were reported. These were the only 'Ākepa-like vocalizations heard by the crew. I have noticed a lot of individual variation in pitch and intonation for different Maui Parrotbill, from the usual sounding birds to those that make high-pitched, squeaky vocalizations rather like Hawai'i 'Ākepa. The USGS crew in Unit 1 of the Hanawī NAR has not reported any definite sightings of either Maui Nukupu'u or Maui 'Ākepa from 1994–1997. No viable populations of Maui Nukupu'u and Maui 'Ākepa now exist within the 700 ha study area in the Hanawī NAR.

ACKNOWLEDGMENTS

I thank my patient wife Helen, who reviewed this manuscript and "allowed my absence" for half of every month over the last two years. Thanks to T. Pratt, J. Bruch, and V. Stein, who also reviewed this manuscript or earlier drafts. Words cannot express the gratitude to all staff and volunteers who had the arduous task of searching the 7 km² area during the project, thank you all: staff J. Isaacs, Y. Chan, S. Sandin, J. Bruch, J. Kowalsky, V. Stein, and P. Dunlevy; and interns M. Walther, A. Spauldin, A. Illes, D. Mather, R. Chester, Z. Machado, L. Pechjar, S. Prosser, T. Pearson, C. Suppa, T. Savre, J.Moran, J. Beadell, M. Layes, and J. Turner. Thanks also to T. Pratt and office staff of USGS for their handling of logistics, finances, advice, and support; W. Evanson of DOFAW for information, use of camps, and especially for access to the Hanawī NAR; Resources Management staff of Haleakalā National Park for use of their facilities, camps, land, and for their assistance with helicopter safety, training, and flight management; Windward Aviation Inc. for their sterling service and flight expertise; and special thanks also to S. Jo and the Hawai'i Ecosystems at Risk project for their support and production of all maps. This research was supported by the Pacific Islands Ecosystems Research Center of U.S. Geological Survey, USFWS, DOFAW, The Nature Conservancy of Hawai'i, and HNP.

Ecology

Studies in Avian Biology No. 22:152–153, 2001.

ECOLOGY—INTRODUCTION

SHEILA CONANT

Subsequent to the publication of several major, descriptive works (e.g., Wilson and Evans 1890–1899, Rothschild 1893–1900, Henshaw 1902a, Perkins 1903) at the turn of the last century, research on Hawai'i's birds nearly came to a standstill. George Munro, who assisted in some of the fieldwork leading to the above-mentioned publications, continued doing fieldwork, eventually publishing his own book, *Birds of Hawaii,* in 1944. Charles and Elizabeth Schwartz came to Hawai'i specifically to work on the ecology, life history, and distribution of its introduced game birds (Schwartz and Schwartz 1949), and Harvey Fisher and Paul Baldwin (birds of Midway, breeding cycles of seabirds; Fisher and Baldwin 1946a,b) carried out general life history and ecology studies of seabirds (Fisher 1948a,b, 1949, 1951, 1965, 1967, 1968, 1969). From 1944–1969, Paul Baldwin reported on the natural history of the endemic birds of Hawai'i (Baldwin 1945, 1969a,b). His monograph on the annual cycle, environment, and evolution in Hawaiian honeycreepers (Baldwin 1953) was the first systematic use of banded birds in the study of Hawaiian honeycreepers, and his paper on the life history of the Laysan Rail (*Porzana palmeri*) was the first and last detailed description of that extinct species (Fisher and Baldwin 1945, 1946a; Baldwin 1947b). Richardson and Bowles' (1964) survey of the birds of Kaua'i made the last collections of the Greater 'Akialoa (*Hemignathus ellisianus*) and 'Ō'ō'ā'ā or Kaua'i 'Ō'ō (*Moho braccatus*) while simultaneously decrying their declines. The 1960s saw a revival of interest in the ecology of Hawaiian birds, beginning with the work of Andrew Berger, who initiated studies on the ecology and natural history of native and introduced species (Berger 1966, 1967, 1969a,b,c, 1970a,b, 1974, 1975a,b,c,d,e,f, 1977a,b,c,d,e) and published a widely read book (Berger 1972, 1981). His students studied life history and ecology of both native (Eddinger 1970, Conant 1977; van Riper 1978, 1980a,b, 1984) and introduced birds (Guest 1973, Hirai 1975). Richards and Bock (1973) published an extensive study of the feeding apparatus of Hawai'i 'Amakihi (*Hemignathus virens*), 'Ākepa (*Loxops coccineus*), 'Anianiau (*Hemignathus parvus*), O'ahu 'Alauahio (*Paroreomyza maculata*), and 'Akikiki (*Oreomystis bairdi*), all of which were then in the genus *Loxops*. Studies by U.S. Fish and Wildlife Service biologists

John Sincock, Eugene Kridler, and Winston Banko included surveys and general ecological observations of both forest birds and seabirds. They were often joined in their fieldwork by Department of Land and Natural Resources biologists David Woodside, Ernie Kosaka, Gerry Swedberg, and Ron Walker. Rediscovery of several endangered species (Newell's Shearwater [*Puffinus auricularis newelli*], Sincock and Swedberg 1969; Maui Parrotbill [*Pseudonestor xanthophrys*] and Maui Nukupu'u [*Hemignathus lucidus affinus*], Warner 1967, Banko 1968) inspired ornithologists to get out into remote field areas. The results of additional fieldwork included the discovery of the Po'ouli (*Melamprosops phaeosoma*; Casey and Jacobi 1974, see also Baker *this volume*), a species that has gone from discovery to near extinction in 25 years (Reynolds and Snetsinger *this volume*). Richard Warner's landmark paper on avian diseases (1968) brought the first critical attention to the problem of disease as a limiting factor for the distribution of Hawai'i's forest birds. Carpenter's and MacMillen's studies on foraging ecology and territory in the 'I'iwi (*Vestiaria coccinea*) and 'Apapane (*Himatione sanguinea*; Carpenter 1976a,b; Carpenter and MacMillen 1976, 1980; MacMillen and Carpenter 1980) were part of a larger set of ecological studies conducted under the auspices of the International Biological Program (Mueller-Dombois et al. 1981a,b). Moulton and Pimm's (1983) and Mountainspring and Scott's (1985) studies on competition were the first efforts to quantify the role of competition among native and nonnative species of birds. The U.S. Forest Service initiated an intensive study of the ecology and life history characteristics of endemic species (Ralph and Fancy 1994a,b,c, 1995, 1996) to complement the extensive surveys of distribution, abundance, and habitat associations conducted by the U.S. Fish and Wildlife Service and Hawaii Department of Land and Natural Resources (Scott et al. 1977, 1984, 1986; van Riper et al. 1978, Mountainspring and Scott 1985, Mountainspring et al. 1990, and references cited therein). Building on those large area surveys researchers have framed hypotheses regarding distributional anomalies (e.g., Hart *this volume*). Others conducted detailed ecological studies of the Palila (*Loxioides bailleui*) and other endemic species.

In this group of papers, Steve Hess and coauthors document the temporal response of 'I'iwi,

'Apapane, and Palila to different habitat types and the occurrence of seed pods and nectar-producing flowers. Bethany Woodworth and coauthors report on the demography of the endangered Hawai'i Creeper (*Oreomystis mana*), implicating nest failure as a major limiting factor for this species. Lenny Freed's study of the significance of old growth forests to the Hawai'i 'Ākepa (*Loxops coccineus coccineus*) is the first of its kind in Hawai'i and has major implications for the conservation of this species. Patrick Hart's comparisons of demographic traits of high and low density of 'Ākepa populations is pioneering and has major implications for con-

servation of Hawai'i's endangered bird species. Three papers shed light on the ecology of one of Hawai'i's rarest birds, the 'Ākohekohe (*Palmeri dolei*). Ellen VanGelder and Thomas Smith characterize the breeding ecology of this species, while Kim Berlin and colleagues demonstrate a positive correlation with the timing of breeding in the 'Ākohekohe and abundance of the 'ōhi'a-lehua (*Metrosideros polymorpha*) bloom. John Carothers' study documents that age-related differences in diet for 'Apapane and 'Ākohekohe are affected by differential growth demands of immatures and adults and complements the work of Hess et al., VanGelder and Smith, and Kim Berlin et al., all in this volume.

Studies in Avian Biology No. 22:154–163, 2001.

DREPANIDINE MOVEMENTS IN RELATION TO FOOD AVAILABILITY IN SUBALPINE WOODLAND ON MAUNA KEA, HAWAI'I

Steven C. Hess, Paul C. Banko, Michelle H. Reynolds, Gregory J. Brenner, Leona P. Laniawe, and James D. Jacobi

Abstract. Flowers of the māmane tree (*Sophora chrysophylla*) are the primary nectar source for Hawaiian honeycreepers in subalpine woodland on Mauna Kea Volcano on the island of Hawai'i. Māmane seeds are the primary food resource of the endangered Palila (*Loxioides bailleui*), which is now restricted to subalpine woodland on Mauna Kea. The objectives of this study were to determine the patterns and relative scales of movements of the drepanidine community in relationship to food availability and tree density on leeward Mauna Kea. 'I'iwi (*Vestiaria coccinea*) and 'Apapane (*Himatione sanguinea*) densities were related to māmane flower abundance. Palila densities were related to māmane pod abundance. These species also had higher densities in māmane woodland than in naio-māmane woodland, unlike the more insectivorous Hawai'i 'Amakihi (*Hemignathus virens*) whose densities did not differ between woodland types. Palila and Hawai'i 'Amakihi do not make movements on the same scale as 'I'iwi and 'Apapane, whose densities changed by more than an order of magnitude. Ungulate eradication, grass reduction, fire management, and restored corridors of māmane woodland would benefit all drepanidines on Mauna Kea, particularly the Palila.

Key Words: 'Apapane; food resources; Hawai'i 'Amakihi; *Himatione sanguinea*; *Hemignathus virens*; 'I'iwi; *Loxioides bailleui*; Palila; subalpine woodland; *Vestiaria coccinea*.

Drepanidines (Hawaiian honeycreepers—Fringillidae: Drepanidinae) in dry subalpine woodland of Mauna Kea Volcano, on the island of Hawai'i (Fig. 1), may make movements in response to nectar and pod availability of the leguminous māmane tree (*Sophora chrysophylla* [Salisb.] Seem.). These movements may be limited by site tenacity (Fancy et al. 1993b), habitat fragmentation, or the use of alternate food resources. Movements of drepanidines have been described in Hawaiian wet forests (Baldwin 1953, MacMillen and Carpenter 1980; Ralph and Fancy 1994a, 1995), but there have been few comprehensive studies of drepanidine movements within subalpine woodland (van Riper 1978, 1980a,b, 1987; van Riper et al. 1978, Fancy et al. 1993b, Ralph and Fancy 1995).

'Apapane (*Himatione sanguinea*) and 'I'iwi (*Vestiaria coccinea*) are primarily nectarivorous and breed mostly in wet forests of the Hawaiian Islands, but they make seasonal and daily movements from wet forest to subalpine woodland and leeward dry woodlands, following availability of nectar (Ralph and Fancy 1995). Hawai'i 'Amakihi (*Hemignathus virens*) have a larger component of arthropods in their diet than other nectarivores (van Riper 1978) and may not need to make large-scale movements in response to availability of food resources (Baldwin 1953). Palila (*Loxioides bailleui*), an endangered drepanidine finch, is primarily a māmane seed and flower predator living exclusively in subalpine woodlands of Mauna Kea. Palila are highly de-

pendent on māmane woodlands for food and nesting sites (van Riper 1980a). Drepanidines may also take advantage of other superabundant and relatively aseasonal plant resources, such as the flowers or fruits of the naio tree (*Myoporum sandwicense* A. Gray) when māmane seeds and flowers are scarce.

Subalpine woodland habitat has been reduced and degraded by herbivorous feral mammals since the arrival of Europeans in Hawai'i (Warner 1960, Scowcroft and Giffin 1983). Māmane regeneration has recently improved after feral mammals were reduced beginning in 1981 (Hess et al. 1999). However, Palila have not recovered in much of their former range, despite improvement in habitat conditions around Mauna Kea. The 1980–1995 mean population of 3,390 Palila has been inhabiting a 139 km^2 area that is <5% of their historical distribution (Scott et al. 1984, 1986; Jacobi et al. 1996). This entire area is now susceptible to destruction by fire due to invasion by nonnative grasses, making Palila highly vulnerable to catastrophic habitat loss.

The objectives of this study were to determine the patterns and relative scales of movements of the drepanidine community in relationship to food resource availability and tree density on leeward Mauna Kea. The quality and extent of māmane habitat on Mauna Kea may be important for drepanidines as seasonal foraging grounds during periods of nectar scarcity in wet forests. Palila are probably more affected than other drepanidines by subtle changes in subalpine woodland habitat because of their special-

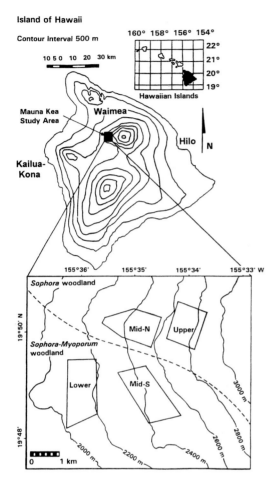

FIGURE 1.   Map of Hawaiian Islands (upper inset), island of Hawai'i, study area (lower inset), and four study sites (Upper; Mid-N, mid-elevation-North; Mid-S, mid-elevation-South; Lower) with elevation contours on the west slope of Mauna Kea Volcano, Hawai'i.

ized diet and restricted range. If Palila do not exploit temporal-spatial patterns of food resource availability, then translocation may be necessary to reestablish populations or to expand their current range (Fancy et al. 1997). However, if Palila do make movements that correspond to gradients in food resources, then connecting isolated fragments of suitable habitat by improving corridors of marginal subalpine woodland may be more affective in expanding Palila range and population (Scott et al. 1984).

METHODS

STUDY AREA

Four study sites, each with five transects, were located on a gradient from 1,978 to 2,816 m in leeward, dry subalpine woodland in the Mauna Kea Forest Re-

serve, on the island of Hawai'i (19°50 'N, 155°35 'W; Fig. 1). The sites were designated, in order of descending elevation: upper, mid-elevation north, mid-elevation south, and lower. The upper- and mid-elevation north sites above 2,317 m were dominated by māmane with 5–30% canopy cover, whereas the mid-elevation south and lower sites below 2,437 m contained a high proportion of codominant naio with as much as 60% overall canopy cover. Overall canopy cover averaged 30% and canopy height was generally short (3–8 m). Vegetation structure and plant phenology were described by van Riper (1980b) and Hess et al. (1999). Climate was investigated by Juvik and Nullet (1993) and Juvik et al. (1993).

TREE DENSITY

We sampled five transects from each of the four sites (Fig. 1) using the point-centered quarter method for estimating mature tree density (Mueller-Dombois and Ellenberg 1974). Transect length varied from 900 to 1,200 m. In each study area, we randomly selected 20 point-centers along two transects and ten point-centers along three transects. We selected the nearest mature tree within each quarter that had a crown size >2 m high and wide. We measured the distance from the center of the selected tree's crown to the sample point ± 0.5 m. All conspecific stems emerging from the ground within 1 m radius of the selected tree were considered to be from the same selected tree. We also measured elevation at each point-center.

PHENOLOGY

We counted the number of expanded green pods (face of the seeds >3 mm) and the number of open flowers on the nearest māmane tree >2 m tall located at 150 m intervals along the same transects where we estimated mature tree density. We multiplied the mean number of pods and flowers for each transect by the estimate of tree density at each transect to estimate availability of flowers and pods per ha. We log transformed both independent variables and analyzed them with the General Linear Model (GLM) procedure (SAS Institute 1985) to test for differences among study sites and assessment periods. Although Palila eat the fruit of naio, availability of this resource was not included in the analysis because it constituted <10% of food items consumed, and it was superabundant during the entire study in the two study sites where naio was codominant (S. Hess and P. Banko, unpubl. data). Nectarivorous drepanidines also used naio flowers but to a lesser extent than māmane flowers.

POINT COUNTS

We used variable circular-plot (VCP) counts (Reynolds et al. 1980) to estimate the densities of drepanidines on the four study sites. VCP counts were conducted six times at irregular intervals from July 1994 until August 1996 concurrently with phenological measurements. Observers received 2–3 months training in identification of local bird vocalizations and distance estimation (Kepler and Scott 1981). During 6-minute count periods between 05:45 A.M. and 11:00 A.M., we recorded the distance to every bird seen or heard (Scott et al. 1984). Counts were not conducted when wind speed exceeded 30 km/hr or during rain.

Cloud cover was recorded in 10% increments and wind speed was recorded on the Beaufort scale.

ANALYSIS

We calculated tree densities with Pollard's (1971) formula for an unbiased population density estimate. We log transformed mature māmane tree densities and analyzed these data by transect with the GLM procedure (SAS Institute 1985). We used Tukey's studentized multiple range test to determine which sites differed in māmane density and ANOVA contrasts to determine the significance of orthogonal comparisons. We averaged drepanidine densities by transect across the six bird counts, log transformed the data, and related them to the estimate of māmane density by transect with ANOVA (α = 0.05).

We analyzed VCP counts by adjusting detection distances by the significant effects of different observers, weather variables, and time of day with respect to a reference condition (Ramsey et al. 1987, Fancy 1997). The reference condition was: an experienced observer (P. Banko) common to all counts at 9:00 A.M. hours with no clouds or wind. We pooled observers having <26 detections of a species with the reference observer. Detection distances at each station were adjusted by only the significant regression coefficients of the model under the actual conditions when the station was sampled. We analyzed adjusted distances with the program DISTANCE (Laake et al. 1994) to calculate the effective area surveyed under reference conditions and bird density by transect. We calculated variation in the effective area surveyed with 5,000 bootstrap samples from a random normal distribution centered on the mean effective area using the computer program VCPADJ (Fancy 1997).

We used analysis of covariance (ANCOVA) to relate the log transformed densities of the four drepanidine species to māmane flowers/ha (each by transect), and the class covariates of assessment period and study site, in that order, with the GLM procedure (SAS Institute 1985). We also related Palila density to māmane pods/ha with the same design. We used ANCOVA because the bird counts were not conducted at standard intervals and because we had a combination of numerical and class variables to examine simultaneously. The model assumed equal slopes over the levels of the class variables. We used conservative alpha levels (α = 0.01) to control type I error due to autocorrelation from repeated sample points (Hatfield et al. 1996). We used ANOVA contrasts to determine the significance of orthogonal comparisons.

Additionally, we present māmane phenological data from both the upper and mid-elevation north study sites for April 1990–April 1994. During this period, we conducted monthly counts of pods and flowers using the same methodology described above. We multiplied the mean number of pods and flowers per transect by the 1996 estimate of tree density, and then averaged the five transects to obtain a monthly estimate of resource availability for each year. Data from the month of October 1993 are not represented. We also present mist net capture data standardized by effort for the four species of drepanidines from years 1989 to 1993. Four fixed mist net stations were operated in the vicinity of each of the four study sites. Ten

12 × 2 m nets were operated between 07:30 A.M. and 05:30 P.M. hours at each station. Effort was variable among years. Sampling was conducted each month in at least three different years, except for January for which there are only two years of data.

RESULTS

TREE DENSITY

Mature māmane tree densities differed significantly among study sites (ANOVA, df = 3, P < 0.005). The upper study site had a higher density of mature trees than the other three sites (df = 1, P < 0.001; Fig. 2). The māmane dominated upper and mid-elevation north sites had higher densities of māmane (df = 1, P < 0.001) than mixed naio-māmane woodland in the lower and mid-elevation south study sites. Differences in naio densities between māmane and mixed naio-māmane woodland sites (df = 1, P < 0.001) resulted from the rarity of naio in the upper and mid-elevation north sites and abundance of naio in the lower and mid-elevation south sites (Fig. 2).

PHENOLOGY

Mean monthly māmane flower and pod availability varied throughout the year (Fig. 3). The lowest period of annual flower availability was July in both the upper and mid-elevation north study sites. Flower availability peaked in September–December in the upper site and October–December in the mid-elevation north site. A second, more variable period of flowering occurred in January–March at both sites. Pod availability was lowest in November in the upper site and September in the mid-elevation north site.

During the concurrent phenology and point count study period, māmane flower availability differed among study sites (ANCOVA, df = 3, P < 0.001; Fig. 4). The upper study site had higher flower availability than the other sites (df = 1, P < 0.001) and the two māmane woodland study sites had higher flower availability than the naio-māmane woodland sites (df = 1, P < 0.001). Flower availability also differed significantly among assessment periods (df = 5, P < 0.001; Fig. 5). Flower availability in September 1995 was higher (df = 1, P < 0.001), and in July 1994, it was lower (df = 1, P < 0.001) than other assessment periods. Overall flower availability was not related to pod availability (df = 1, P > 0.37).

Pod availability also differed among study sites (df = 3, P < 0.001; Fig. 4), being highest in the upper study site (df = 1, P < 0.003). The two māmane woodland study sites had higher pod availability than the naio-māmane study sites (df = 1, P < 0.001). Pod availability also

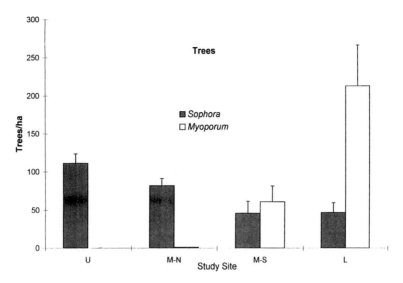

FIGURE 2. Density of *Sophora chrysophylla* and *Myoporum sandwicense* >2 m tall (trees ha^{-1} ± SE) at 4 study sites (U = Upper, M-N = Mid-elevation-North, M-S = Mid-elevation-South, L = Lower) on the west slope of Mauna Kea Volcano, Hawai'i.

differed among assessment periods (df = 5, P < 0.001; Fig. 5). Pod availability in July 1994 was higher (df = 1, P < 0.001), and in September 1995, was lower (df = 1, P < 0.001) than other assessment periods. Overall pod availability was not related to flower availability (df = 1, P > 0.36).

VCP COUNTS

In addition to observers, time of day affected VCP detection distances for both Palila and Hawai'i Amakihi (df = 1, P < 0.001). Detection distances decreased with time of day. Weather variables did not significantly affect detection distances of Palila, I'iwi, or 'Apapane (df = 1, P > 0.05); however, detection distances increased with cloud cover for Hawai'i Amakihi (df = 1, P < 0.001). We adjusted detection distances for only the significant effects of the models (Fancy 1997).

DREPANIDINE ABUNDANCE IN RELATION TO FOOD AND HABITAT

The majority of known-age 'Apapane (84%) and 'I'iwi (74%) were captured in the postbreeding months of September–November (Fig. 6), corresponding to peak flowering in the upper elevation study site (Fig. 3). In contrast, resident Palila and Hawai'i 'Amakihi were captured in all months of the year, with annual low capture rates during the postbreeding months of July–August for Hawai'i 'Amakihi and July–September for Palila.

Palila density, determined by point counts,

was not as strongly related to flower availability (ANCOVA, df = 1, P > 0.06) as it was related to pod availability (df = 1, P < 0.001), assessment period (df = 5, P < 0.003; Fig. 5), and study site (df = 3, P < 0.001; Fig. 4). Although Palila density was not related to māmane density (df = 1, P > 0.80), it was higher in the two māmane dominated sites than the naio-māmane sites (df = 1, P < 0.001).

'Apapane density was related to flower availability (df = 1, P < 0.001; Fig. 5), assessment period (df = 5, P < 0.001), study site (df = 3, P < 0.001; Fig. 4), and māmane density (df = 1, P < 0.04). 'Apapane in the māmane dominated sites approached significantly higher densities than in the naio-māmane sites (df = 1, P < 0.013).

'I'iwi density was related to flower availability (df = 1, P < 0.009), assessment period (df = 5, P < 0.003; Fig. 5), and study site (df = 3, P < 0.001; Fig. 4), but it was not related to māmane density (df = 1, P > 0.67). However, 'I'iwi density was higher in the māmane dominated sites than the naio-māmane sites (df = 1, P < 0.001). 'I'iwi were not detected in the lower elevation study site.

Hawai'i 'Amakihi density was not related to flower availability (df = 1, P > 0.19), but it was related to assessment period (df = 5, P < 0.002; Fig. 5) and study site (df = 3, P < 0.001). Hawai'i 'Amakihi density was not related to māmane density (df = 1, P > 0.089) nor was it different between the two māmane dominated

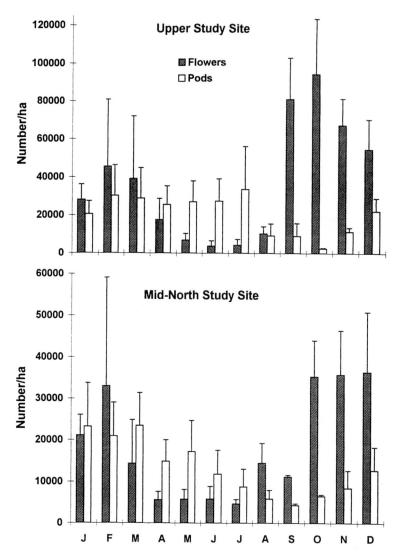

FIGURE 3.   Mean monthly *Sophora chrysophylla* flower and pod availability and annual variation (number ha^{-1} ± SE) at two study sites on the west slope of Mauna Kea Volcano, Hawai'i from April 1990 to April 1994.

sites and the naio-māmane sites (df = 1, P > 0.26).

Hawai'i 'Amakihi exhibited the least variable change in density of the four drepanidine species over time (Figs. 4, 5), with only 34% coefficient of variation. Palila exhibited only slightly greater change in density than Hawai'i Amakihi, with CV = 89%. 'Apapane exhibited the largest change in density, CV = 198%. 'I'iwi also had high relative change in density, CV = 188%.

DISCUSSION

Lower densities of mature māmane in mixed naio-māmane woodland sites relative to māmane woodland sites are probably a result of browsing

by introduced feral ungulates (Warner 1960, Scowcroft 1983, Scowcroft and Giffin 1983, Scowcroft and Sakai 1983, Juvik and Juvik 1984, Mountainspring et al. 1987), because māmane sapling density was at least as high in mixed naio-māmane woodland as in māmane woodland (Hess et al. 1999). Feral sheep and mouflon sheep prefer māmane foliage over other plant species (Giffin 1976, 1982). Therefore, browsing may have selectively reduced māmane in the mixed-species woodland sites, resulting in a shift towards naio dominance (van Riper 1980b, Hess et al. 1999). Other comparable subalpine woodland sites with high ungulate browsing pressure, such as Kīpuka 'Alalā on Mauna

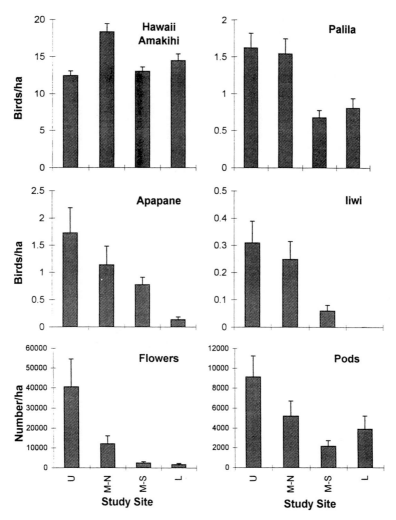

FIGURE 4.   Mean densities of four species of drepanidines and availability of *Sophora chrysophylla* flowers and pods (number ha^{-1} ± SE) at four study sites (U = Upper, M-N = Mid-elevation-North, M-S = Mid-elevation-South, L = Lower) on the west slope of Mauna Kea Volcano, Hawai'i.

Loa, also exhibit extremely high naio regeneration concurrent with extremely low māmane regeneration (P. Banko, unpubl. data). If ungulate browsing is controlled, the plant community will probably shift towards increased māmane density in the future.

Tree density was a strong determinant of food resource availability. The highest māmane flower and pod availability occurred in the upper elevation site, where māmane density was highest. Annual development of flowers and pods occurs first at higher elevations (van Riper 1980b; P. Banko, unpubl. data). Rainfall, another primary determinant of flower and pod production, was approximately 25% greater in 1994 and 50% less in 1995 than the long-term average (J. Ju-

vik, unpubl. data). Pod availability in 1994 and 1995 was relatively low, but flower availability was normal (P. Banko, unpubl. data). In 1994, rainfall was normal during the flowering period but declined sharply afterwards, which may have resulted in limited pod development. Pod availability in 1995 was less than the other years due to below normal rainfall for the entire year. The year of highest pod availability was 1996, which also coincided with the greatest number of nest attempts by Palila (P. Banko, unpubl. data).

Palila densities were greater at sites dominated by māmane and peaked during the breeding season when pod availability was greatest. The importance of pods in relation to movement and

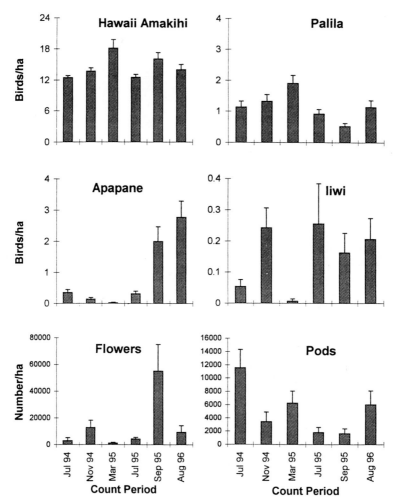

FIGURE 5. Mean densities of four species of drepanidines, and availability of *Sophora chrysophylla* flowers and pods (number ha^{-1} ± SE) during six count periods (July 1994, Nov. 1994, March 1995, July 1995, Sept. 1995, and August 1996) on the west slope of Mauna Kea Volcano, Hawai'i.

breeding of Palila has been well documented (van Riper et al. 1978, van Riper 1980a, Scott et al. 1984, Fancy et al. 1993b, Lindsey et al. 1995a). Palila probably dispersed from higher elevation sites after the breeding season because of declining pod availability. During January–March 1995, a period of extremely low pod availability in the lower elevation site, Palila were present and were observed eating naio fruit, indicating that they had switched to alternate food resources (S. Hess, unpubl. data). Palila densities fluctuated least in the mixed naio-mämane woodland, although Palila densities in these areas were never as great as in mämane dominated sites.

van Riper (1987) found that Hawai'i 'Amakihi nested in higher density in predominantly mämane habitat; however, we did not find Ha-

wai'i 'Amakihi in greater density in mämane woodland than in mixed naio-mämane woodland, unlike the other drepanidines. This pattern may be related to the higher proportion of naio flowers and arthropods in the diet of Hawai'i 'Amakihi (Baldwin 1953, van Riper 1978), and, for the other species, preference for mämane food resources, as well as reduced predator densities in mämane woodland (Amarasekare 1993, 1994). At the lower elevation study site, only one 'I'iwi was captured during four years of mist netting operations and none were detected during the three years of point counts. Although 'I'iwi are very susceptible to introduced avian malaria, it is unlikely that mosquito-vectored disease is responsible for the rarity of this species (van Riper et al. 1986, Atkinson et al. 1995). There is no larval mosquito habitat pres-

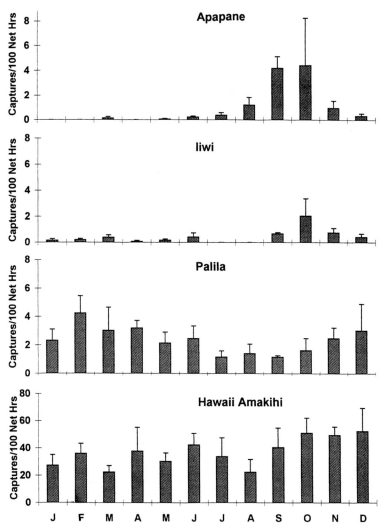

FIGURE 6.   Mean monthly capture rates and annual variation (captures/100 net hours ± SE) of four species of drepanidines on the west slope of Mauna Kea Volcano, Hawai'i from 1989 to 1993.

ent at this site and thermal constraints would inhibit parasite development within vectors dispersing from lower elevations (D. LaPointe, unpubl. data). The rarity of 'I'iwi was most likely due to other habitat features such as food resources or predators. If māmane density continues to increase in the mixed naio-māmane woodland, drepanidine densities may also increase, although predators may ultimately limit bird densities (Amarasekare 1993, 1994).

Banding data and point count data show similar patterns and scales of movement for each of the four drepanidine species. Hawai'i 'Amakihi exhibited the least change in overall mean densities during the study. Palila exhibited only slightly greater change in densities than Hawai'i

'Amakihi, indicating small-scale movements, and generally high site tenacity (Fancy et al. 1993b), or scarcity of māmane pods in accessible adjacent areas during the study. 'Apapane exhibited the largest proportional change in mean density of any drepanidine, consistent with their movements between windward to leeward slopes. 'Apapane are known to have the greatest change in densities among drepanidines (Baldwin 1953, Scott et al. 1986, van Riper 1987; Ralph and Fancy 1994a, 1995). A small population of breeding 'I'iwi (T. Pratt, unpubl. data) resides in the study areas, but there was also high change in 'I'iwi densities, which was second to 'Apapane, thus indicating large-scale movements.

Baldwin (1953:354) observed that Hawai'i 'Amakihi, 'Apapane, and 'I'iwi near the summit of Kilauea Volcano and slopes of Mauna Loa Volcano, "...occur quite consistently throughout the year where they occur at all." Contrasting with Baldwin's findings, in subalpine woodlands of Mauna Kea, 'Apapane are not resident but make annual movements to and from other areas. We found a small number of 'I'iwi are resident in subalpine woodland throughout the year, while a greater number make annual movements to and from other areas. Hawai'i 'Amakihi have a large resident population with the least fluctuation in annual densities. Baldwin (1953) also stated that postbreeding dispersal results in widely and thinly distributed drepanidine populations in late summer months. This period corresponds to the highest annual densities of 'Apapane and 'I'iwi in subalpine woodland. Palila, with a protracted breeding season (van Riper 1980a, Pletschet and Kelly 1990), may also have a postbreeding dispersal that extends later into winter months than other drepanidines. Family groups of Palila with radio transmitters moved from upper and mid-elevation nesting areas to lower elevation areas after young had fledged in 1995 (L. Miller, unpubl. data); however, this did not occur in 1994 when family groups stayed close to their nesting territories. The 1995 postbreeding dispersal corresponded simultaneously with the lowest measured Palila densities and pod availability during this study. Although decreased vocalization rates could also be consistent with the calculated low density, Palila were also much more difficult to capture during this period, indicating that they had dispersed from the study area (L. Miller, unpubl. data).

Palila, as seed and flower predators, reduce their most important food resource and the most important food resources of other nectarivorous drepanidines when they eat flowers and flower buds. Although Palila eat more flowers and flower buds than seeds, they spend a greater proportion of time eating seeds and presumably consume more seed mass and receive more nutrition from seeds than from flowers (van Riper 1980a; S. Hess, unpubl. data). Other drepanidines, such as Hawai'i Amakihi, 'Apapane, and 'I'iwi, may provide an essential service through pollination of flowers that ultimately develop into pods. The loss of pollinating birds in subalpine woodland could result in reduced pod crops and may be detrimental to both Palila and māmane woodland. Continuous, high-quality subalpine woodland habitat must be available near Mauna Kea for wetland forest drepanidines in search of seasonal nectar sources.

Palila make short-range movements within the west slope of Mauna Kea to follow māmane pod availability, but they do not exhibit the dramatic change in densities that 'Apapane or 'I'iwi do. 'Apapane and 'I'iwi may make movements of many kilometers to follow nectar resource availability among different forest types. Peak annual abundance of 'Apapane and 'I'iwi appears to be related to the peak availability of māmane flowers in subalpine woodland and the period of lowest annual *Metrosideros* flower availability in wet forests (Ralph and Fancy 1995). Subalpine woodland is an important foraging ground for a high proportion of young birds that may move from wet forests during periods of nectar scarcity. Fifty-one percent of 'Apapane and 53% of 'I'iwi captured on the west slope of Mauna Kea were hatching-year (HY) birds (G. Lindsey, unpubl. data), whereas the proportion of HY Palila ranged only from 3.1% to 22.6% (Lindsey et al. 1995a). High-elevation subalpine woodland may also serve as an important refuge for Hawaiian birds susceptible to avian poxvirus or avian malaria (*Plasmodium relictum*) epizootics that may occur in late summer months (see Jarvi et al. *this volume*). Birds that make movements to higher elevation risk less chance of becoming infected by these pathogens than those that move to lower elevations. Subalpine woodland may serve to maintain higher population levels of these species during periods of nectar scarcity in wetland forests by conferring higher survivorship through seasonally abundant food resources and reduced disease transmission. However, seasonally migrating birds may also bring avian pox to subalpine woodlands.

If corridors of quality māmane habitat eventually connect relatively distant isolated tracts of larger māmane woodland, such as the north and south slopes of Mauna Kea, Palila and other drepanidines may be able to disperse longer distances, make seasonal use of other areas, and breed where there are sufficient food resources. Nearby habitat accessible to Palila should be protected from ungulates, replanted with māmane, and allowed to recover sufficiently for Palila to exploit shifts in pod availability (Scott et al. 1984, 1986; Fancy et al. 1993b, Fancy 1997). Palila are at high risk of extinction as long as they continue to breed in the single largest habitable tract of māmane woodland on Mauna Kea, where the probability of habitat destruction by fire is extreme. Ungulate eradication, predator reduction, grass reduction, fire management, and restoration of māmane woodland would benefit all drepanidines on Mauna Kea (Scott et al. 1986, USFWS 1986). These efforts may also be less expensive, more effective, and longer lasting than intensive single-species recovery efforts, such as translocation of Palila (Fancy et al. 1997).

ACKNOWLEDGMENTS

We gratefully acknowledge the many volunteers and staff of the U.S. Geological Survey, Biological Resources Division, who helped in this study: S. Barker, C. Crooker, D. Bogardus, K. Ellison, S. Howlin, L. Johnson, L. Miller, L. Niebaur, S. Legare, T. Male, J. Meyer, T. Overbey, D. Payne, R. Rounds, B. Smith, C. Smith, S. Sepulveda, T. Snetsinger, M. Stapleton, H. Townsend, and M. Wiley. Thanks to S. Fancy for the dBase program used to calculate elevation on the upper sites. Thanks to the State of Hawai'i Division of Forestry and Wildlife for allowing us to work in the Mauna Kea Forest Reserve. Thanks to J. Hatfield for detailed statistical guidance and to S. Conant, S. Fancy, J. Hatfield, T. Pratt, J. Rotenberry, and J. M. Scott for reviewing early drafts of this manuscript.

Studies in Avian Biology No. 22:164–172, 2001.

BREEDING PRODUCTIVITY AND SURVIVAL OF THE ENDANGERED HAWAI'I CREEPER IN A WET FOREST REFUGE ON MAUNA KEA, HAWAI'I

BETHANY L. WOODWORTH, JAY T. NELSON, ERIK J. TWEED, STEVEN G. FANCY, MICHAEL P. MOORE, EMILY B. COHEN, AND MARK S. COLLINS

Abstract. We studied the demography of the endangered Hawai'i Creeper (*Oreomystis mana*) from 1994–1999 at three sites in Hakalau Forest National Wildlife Refuge (NWR). Hawai'i Creepers bred from January to June, with peak breeding in February through May (about 120–180 days), and molted from May to August. A small proportion (4.9%) of individuals overlapped breeding and molting activities. We located and monitored the fates of 60 nests. Mean clutch size was 2.1 eggs, nest building required 19 days, incubation was 16 to 17 days, and nestling period lasted 18 days. Of all nest attempts, 25% were abandoned before egg laying, 6.7% were removed for captive propagation, 13.3% had undetermined fates, 38.3% failed during incubation or nestling periods, and 16.7% were successful. Thus, of 33 nests that were active through egg laying and outcome was confirmed, only 30% were successful. The daily survival rate of active nests was 0.960 ± 0.009 SE. An average of 1.7 chicks fledged from successful nests. Thirty-two percent of hatch-year birds were alive and in the study area at least one year later. Annual adult survival was high (0.88 ± 0.03). The primary factors limiting productivity of Hawai'i Creeper in Hakalau Forest NWR appear to be low reproductive potential in combination with high rates of nesting failure. Further research into the causes of nest failure, the length of the breeding season, and renesting behavior of females is needed, and protection of the forest from the degrading impacts of introduced mammals is paramount.

Key Words: endangered species; Hawai'i Creeper; nesting success; *Oreomystis mana*; productivity; survival.

The high elevation, wet forests on the island of Hawai'i are important habitat for many native Hawaiian honeycreepers, several of which are endangered (Scott et al. 1986). These high-elevation forests act as refugia for Hawaiian honeycreepers from the devastating effects of habitat loss and disease, which have led to the extirpation of most lower-elevation populations (Warner 1968, van Riper et al. 1986). However, most of these wet forest habitats are not pristine; forest composition and associated ecological processes have been degraded by the activities of feral ungulates. The forest is also home to high densities of introduced mammals and birds. Introduced mammals may act as nest predators (Atkinson 1977) and damage or destroy native plants and create areas of disturbance, and introduced birds may compete for food or nest sites with native species (Banko and Banko 1976, Mountainspring and Scott 1985). These factors may threaten the persistence of native bird species by affecting their nesting success, recruitment, and survival.

The Hakalau Forest National Wildlife Refuge (Hakalau), located at 1,600 m elevation on the windward slope of Hawai'i, contains some of the best remaining habitat for native forest birds on the island. The forest harbors important populations of several endangered forest birds, including the 'Akiapōlā'au (*Hemignathus munroi*), 'Ākepa (*Loxops coccineus coccineus*), and

Hawai'i Creeper (*Oreomystis mana*). In this paper, we report on the demography and ecology of the Hawai'i Creeper, a small, 15-g insectivorous bird that forages by creeping along the trunks and major branches of large trees, gleaning insects from the bark (Scott et al. 1979, Mueller-Dombois et al. 1981b). Hawai'i Creepers defend a small (10–20 m radius) area immediately surrounding the nest, and forage over a 4–7 ha home range during the breeding season (Ralph and Fancy 1994a, VanderWerf 1998b). Females do all or most of the nest building and incubate, brood, and feed the chicks; males assist by feeding the female both on and off the nest and by feeding the young (Sakai and Johanos 1983, VanderWerf 1998b; J. Nelson, unpubl. data). During the nonbreeding season, pairs range over a wider area (about 11 ha) and join other forest birds in mixed-species flocks (VanderWerf 1998b). At Kīlauea Forest and Keauhou Ranch study sites on Hawai'i, creepers breed from about January to June (Sakai and Johanos 1983, Ralph and Fancy 1994b) and have relatively high adult survival (Ralph and Fancy 1994a). However, only 17 nests of this species have been documented (Sakai and Ralph 1980a, Scott et al. 1980, Sakai and Johanos 1983, VanderWerf 1998b), and little is known about their nest success, ability to renest, or seasonal fecundity.

The Hawai'i Creeper was once widely distrib-

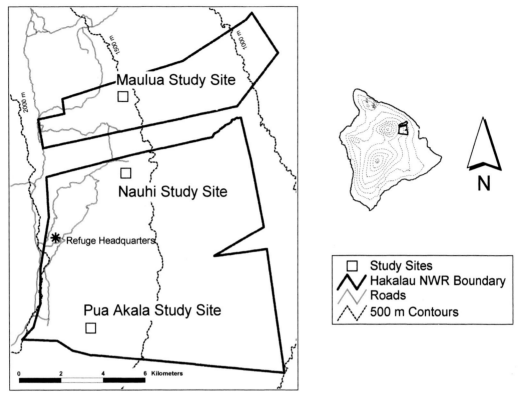

FIGURE 1.   Map of Hakalau Forest National Wildlife Refuge on the windward slope of Mauna Kea, Hawai'i, showing the location of the three study areas: Maulua, Nauhi, and Pua 'Ākala.

uted in dry and wet habitats on the island of Hawai'i as low as 600 m in elevation (Scott et al. 1986). As of 1979, the creeper was confined to four disjunct populations in wet and mesic forests, primarily above 1,500 m (Scott et al. 1986). Two populations near Kona totaled only about 300 birds, and a third, near Ka'ū, consisted of about 2,100 birds. Hakalau, where 10,000 ± 1,200 birds reside, is the location of the largest remaining population of Hawai'i creepers (Scott et al. 1986). Our ability to assess and monitor the health and persistence of this core population depends on reliable estimates of the birds' recruitment and survival. Here we present data on population density, nesting success, productivity, juvenile and adult survival, and natal dispersal in order to understand further the population dynamics and conservation status of the creeper in Hakalau, and to assess potential management and restoration actions.

METHODS

STUDY AREA

We studied the wet forest bird community in Hakalau (19°51'N, 155°18'W), a tropical montane rain forest at 1,600 m elevation on the windward slope of Mauna Kea, Hawai'i (Fig. 1). Data were collected during 1994–1999 as part of an ongoing study of the wet forest bird community at three study sites within the refuge (Pua 'Ākala, Nāuhi, and Maulua), ranging in elevation from 1,500–1,640 m (Fig. 1). The forest canopies of all three study areas are dominated by 'ōhi'a (*Metrosideros polymorpha*) and koa (*Acacia koa*), but sites differ in their disturbance history and the composition of the understory. Common shrubs and subcanopy trees are 'ōlapa (*Cheirodendron trigynum*), ōhelo (*Vaccinium dentatum*), pūkiawe (*Styphelia tameiameiae*), and hāpu'u tree ferns (*Cibotium* sp.). Permanent markers were placed at 50 m or 75 m intervals in a 56–110 ha grid on each study area, where resighting, nest searching, and censusing were conducted, and at 25 m intervals on a smaller "intensive" grid within the larger grid at two of the study areas (350 × 450 m at Nauhi, 500 × 500 m at Pua 'Ākala), where banding was also done.

MIST NETTING AND BANDING

We captured birds in nylon mist nets (12 m × 2.6 m, 36 mm mesh) placed at a height of 6 m on two-tiered poles or suspended at 10–15 m height from branches in the canopy. Nets were operated from approximately 0700 to 1600 hours, except during inclement weather. From February 1994 to April 1996, we operated about 20 nets for 3–12 days at least quarterly at each of the three study areas. From January 1997 to June 1998, we netted only at the Nauhi study area, and operated from 18 to 48 nets approximately 14 days/mo. We moved each net approximately once each month to ensure complete coverage of the intensive grid each year. Banding effort through 1998 totaled 74,097 mist-net hours (13,214 net-hours at Pua 'Ākala, 56,953 net-hours at Nāuhi, and 3,930 net-hours at Maulua). From 1994–1998, we captured and banded 84 adult and 49 hatch-year Hawai'i Creepers.

POPULATION DENSITY

Densities of Hawai'i Creeper on the study areas were estimated using the variable circular-plot method (Reynolds et al. 1980) and the analysis techniques described in Fancy (1997). Counts were located 150 m apart at 36–48 stations on each study area and were conducted quarterly from February 1994 (Pua 'Ākala, Nāuhi) or August 1994 (Maulua) to August 1997. Observers were field biologists with extensive experience with the birds in Hakalau and were trained or recalibrated in distance estimation before each count. Observers counted all birds heard or seen during 8-minute counts, and estimated the horizontal distance to each bird. All counts were conducted between dawn and 1100 hours, and were discontinued in periods of heavy wind or rain.

We combined data for 37 surveys, which included a total of 685 detections of Hawai'i Creeper. We examined the effects of wind, rain, cloud cover, and time of day on detection distance using multiple linear regression following methods described in Ramsey et al. (1987); the effect of each of these variables was nonsignificant ($P > 0.50$). Variation between observers in hearing acuity and distance estimation skills can lead to differences in their effective detection distances (Ralph and Scott 1981 and papers therein, Scott et al. 1986). Buckland et al. (1993) recommended 60–80 detections for each observer as a practical minimum for estimating a detection function. Because of the rarity of the Hawai'i Creeper, the sample size of detections for most observers was inadequate for inclusion in the regression model, and so we were unable to correct for the effect of observers on detection distance.

We used the program DISTANCE (Laake et al. 1994) to calculate effective area from detection distances for Hawai'i Creeper. We truncated the distribution of detection distances by 4% to remove the elongated tail of the distribution (96 percentile distance = 96 m). Based on between-model goodness-of-fit tests, we grouped data into seven intervals of 13.5 m width, which resulted in an estimated effective detection distance (m) of 37.03 ± 1.06 SE (uniform key, χ^2 = 4.6, df = 3, P = 0.21). Density was estimated at each station by dividing the number of creepers detected at that station by the effective area surveyed.

BREEDING SEASON AND MOLT

We banded birds with a U.S. Fish and Wildlife Service (USFWS) aluminum band and a unique combination of three colored leg bands. Birds were weighed using an electronic platform scale or 100-g Pesola spring scale, and measured for exposed culmen length and bent wing chord. Male and female Hawai'i Creepers cannot be reliably sexed using plumage characteristics, so sex was determined when possible by the presence of an active brood patch or swollen cloacal protuberance (Pyle et al. 1987). Brood patches were recorded as smooth (breast feathers molted but breast not yet vascularized), vascularized (fully developed, fluid-filled), or receding (wrinkled and/or pin feathers coming in around edges). Cloacal protuberances were classified as absent, small, medium, or large. Because birds with a smooth brood patch or small cloacal protuberance might be confused with nonbreeding birds in the field, we excluded such birds from analysis of breeding season and molt-breeding overlap. Juvenile (hatch-year) birds were identified by their plumage, primarily by the presence of a yellowish-white superciliary stripe and paler undersides (Scott et al. 1979). Birds were also examined for presence of flight or body molt, fat, and active pox lesions or missing digits (which may be indicative of past pox infection).

NESTING BIOLOGY AND SUCCESS

We systematically searched the study areas for color-marked birds for an average of 34 hr/mo (total = 1,235 hr) from 1994 through 1997, resulting in 236 observations of color-banded birds. Overall, about 40% of the Hawai'i Creepers on our study area were banded, as indicated by both our mist-netting and resighting data. We recorded data on social interactions, foraging behavior, and breeding activity of all color-marked creepers encountered. We located nests by following nest building or incubating birds to the nest. In general, we monitored nests every 2–8 days. Most nests were inaccessible and were monitored from concealed locations from a distance of about 25 m. We determined nesting stage by behavioral clues of the parents (incubation, egg turning, brooding, nest sanitation, or feeding). Monitoring visits typically lasted 30–60 minutes, and longer nest watches were conducted at some nests. We returned to nests at 5–7 day intervals three or more times after the nest became inactive and searched an approximately 100 m radius area for signs of renesting attempts.

We calculated daily nest survival rate and its associated variance using the Mayfield method (Mayfield 1975, Johnson 1979). We estimated transition dates between nest stages by forward dating or back dating from known events in the nesting cycle, assuming (1) a nest-building period of 16 days, (2) incubation period of 16 days, and (3) nestling period of 18 days (Sakai and Johanos 1983, VanderWerf 1998b; this paper). Where no other data were available, we assumed the event to have occurred on the date midway between intervals of checking the nest (Mayfield 1975). Abandonment was inferred if the nest was inactive for at least one hour on at least three consecutive visits. Hawai'i Creeper nest-building activity slows considerably in the few days before egg laying (U.S. Geological Survey, unpubl. data). Based on this, if a nest was abandoned <5 days after active building ceased, we assumed that eggs were never laid, although we recognize that we may have missed cases of egg predation very early in the nesting cycle. Nests that received eggs but fledged no young were classified as failed. Finally, a nest was successful if it fledged at least one chick; in all cases success was confirmed by observation of the fledglings on the nest rim or out of the nest. In calculating the Mayfield estimate, we included exposure days for six nests with partial histories (four nests where eggs were removed for captive propagation, and two nests where fieldwork ceased before nest outcome was known).

Beginning in 1996, alien mammals were experimentally removed from one-half (48 ha) of the Nāuhi grid in conjunction with a concurrent study of the influence of introduced predators on nesting success and productivity of forest birds. Although this manipulation of predator numbers may have influenced nest success rates in this study, due to small sample size, statistical power to detect a difference in Hawai'i Creeper nest success between predator control and reference grids was low. There was no statistically significant effect of the treatment on creeper nest success rates (B. Woodworth, unpubl. data), and so we present the data for predator control and reference grids combined. Details of the predator control and its implications for other wet forest birds will be presented elsewhere.

Nest and nest-site characteristics were recorded for 52 nests in 1997–1999. Nests were classified as one of three types: (1) open cup; (2) pseudo-cavity, nest situated behind a bark slab or limb scar with more than two routes of ingress and <90% hidden; and (3) cavity, nest situated behind a bark slab or limb scar with one route of ingress and >90% hidden. Nest height was measured from the base of the nest tree using a clinometer and tape measure.

Adult and Juvenile Survival Rates and Dispersal

We estimated survival from 58 captures of 43 color-marked adult birds captured or resighted on the Nāuhi study area between 1994–1997. We used the program JOLLY (Pollock et al. 1990) to produce estimates of survival rate under five different capture-recapture models that vary in their assumptions about capture and survival probabilities. The reliability of Jolly-Seber estimates requires that data meet several assumptions (treated in detail in Pollock et al. 1990). First, all birds present in the population at the time of a given sample must have the same probability of being captured in that sample (homogeneity of capture probabilities). We excluded data from the Pua 'Ākala and Maulua study areas because mist netting ended there in April 1996. Second, all birds present in the population immediately after a given sampling period must have the same probability of surviving until the next sampling period (homogeneity of survival probabilities). Because juvenile survival rate is likely to be less than that of adults, we handled juveniles separately (see below). Although survival rates may vary between male and female honeycreepers (e.g., Lepson and Freed 1995), sample size was too low to account for differences in survival rates between sexes in this study. The third assumption is that bands are not lost or overlooked. Fourth, the sampling period must be short relative to the survival period. To approximate this assumption, we limited analysis to data collected from February to April each year (the months with the most complete data). JOLLY provides goodness-of-fit tests to assess the fit of a model to a given data set. Where several models fit the data, likelihood ratio tests were used to test between models. The simplest adequate model was preferred because fewer parameters were estimated, and it therefore resulted in a more precise estimate. Survival rates are presented as mean ± SE. For comparison of survival rates, we used the program CONTRAST (Hines and Sauer 1989), which uses the chi-square statistic proposed by Sauer and Williams (1989).

Juvenile survival was estimated by enumeration, because sample size was insufficient to use model-based estimators. Juvenile survival rate was calculated as the proportion of birds originally banded as hatch-year birds that were recaptured or resighted in a subsequent year. Only hatch-year birds banded at the Nāuhi study area were included because other study areas had inconsistent coverage in later years. Mortality of juvenile birds is highest during the first few weeks after fledging (reviewed in Ricklefs 1973, Anders et al. 1997), but because recent fledglings are less mobile than older hatch-year birds, they are less likely to be captured in our mist nets. This will tend to increase our estimate of juvenile survival.

Natal dispersal is usually measured as the distance between the natal nest and the first breeding nest (Greenwood and Harvey 1982); because these data were not known in this study, we approximated natal dispersal by measuring the distance between a bird's first capture as a juvenile and its first capture as an adult. We recognize that birds dispersing long distances are less likely to be detected, and so the observed dispersal distance will be an underestimate of true dispersal distance, a limitation in all studies of dispersal that cover finite areas.

RESULTS

Population Size and Density

Our quarterly variable circular-plot counts indicate that Hawai'i Creepers are more common at the Pua 'Ākala study area (2.18 ± 0.50 birds/ha) than at Nauhi (1.09 ± 0.29 birds/ha) or Maulua (0.57 ± 0.23 birds/ha), indicating a decreasing south-north gradient in density (GLM, df = 2, P < 0.001; Fig. 2a). Estimated density of creepers declined each November, probably reflecting a seasonal decrease in singing frequency (and therefore detectability) in the fall (Ralph and Fancy 1994b). In contrast, capture rates of Hawai'i Creepers, summed over all years, are similar among the three sites (Fig 2b; 0.348 birds/100 net-hours in Pua 'Ākala, 0.360 birds/100 net-hours at Nāuhi, and 0.229 birds/100 net-hours at Maulua; Kruskal-Wallis χ^2 = 1.3, df = 2, P = 0.53), perhaps because Hawai'i Creepers forage fairly high in the canopy above the reach of most of our nets. Overall capture rate for the three study areas was 0.351/100 net-hours. For comparison, overall capture rates of the more common species at our study sites were 3.76/100 net-hours for 'I'iwi (*Vestiaria coccinea*) and 2.28/100 net-hours for Hawai'i 'Amakihi (*Hemignathus virens*).

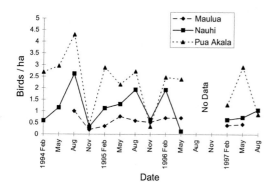

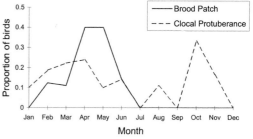

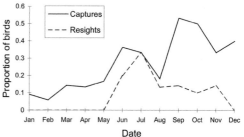

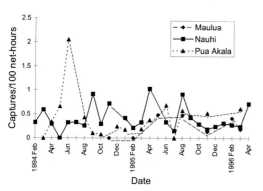

FIGURE 2. (a) Seasonal population density (birds/ha) of Hawai'i Creepers in Hakalau Forest National Wildlife Refuge on Pua 'Ākala, Nāuhi, and Maulua study areas, 1994–1997. (b) Capture rates of Hawai'i Creeper by month in Hakalau Forest National Wildlife Refuge on Pua 'Ākala, Nāuhi, and Maulua study areas, 1994–1996.

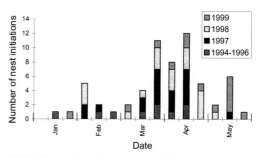

FIGURE 3. Breeding season of Hawai'i Creeper in Hakalau Forest National Wildlife Refuge. (a) Frequency of birds caught with an active brood patch or enlarged cloacal protuberance by month, 1994–1997. (b) Frequency of mist net captures and sightings of hatch-year birds by month, 1994–1997. (c) Dates of nest initiation (beginning of nest building) by 10-day intervals, 1994–1999.

BREEDING SEASON AND MOLT

We used four different indicators of breeding season in Hawai'i Creepers. First, mist-netting data from 131 recaptures of 61 adult Hawai'i Creepers over four years (1994–1997) showed that females were in breeding condition from February to June, with a peak in May and June. In contrast, males with enlarged cloacal protuberances were captured over a protracted period from February to November (Fig. 3a). Second, hatch-year birds began to appear in the population in large numbers in June and peaked in September and October, based on mist-netting data (Fig. 3b). Similarly, hatch-year birds in our resight sample also increased in June, but then decreased, possibly because it was more difficult to identify late season hatch-year birds in the field than in the hand. Third, nest initiations peaked from February through May (Fig. 3c). Finally, one banded female began building her first (known) nest on about 12 February, and her last known nest failed on 11 May 1997. Thus,

the breeding season of this female lasted at least 3 months (none of her three nests were successful).

In 1998, when an El Niño event caused a severe drought from December to March, many Hawai'i Creepers delayed breeding in our study area until late March and April. Despite this late start to the breeding season, no new nests were initiated after the end of May.

Breeding was followed closely by feather molt (Fig. 4). Molting of flight feathers and body feathers peaked during June–August and overlapped breeding by about 2 months. However, only 3 of 61 adult birds (4.9%) were in breeding condition (i.e., had an active brood patch or an enlarged cloacal protuberance) while simultaneously molting body or flight feathers. This is

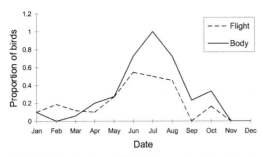

FIGURE 4. Timing of flight (wing and tail) and body molt of Hawai'i Creeper in Hakalau Forest National Wildlife Refuge, 1994–1997.

TABLE 1. FATE OF 60 HAWAI'I CREEPER NESTS, HAKALAU FOREST NATIONAL WILDLIFE REFUGE, HAWAI'I, 1994–1998

Fate of Nests	Number of nests[a] (percent)
Abandoned prelaying	15 (25.0)
Eggs pulled during incubation for captive propagation	4 (6.7)
Failed	23 (38.3)
Successful	10 (16.7)
Fate undetermined	8 (13.3)

[a] Data are from all study areas and years combined.

consistent with the frequency of molt-breeding overlap found in other studies of tropical birds (e.g., 3.1–8.5% of individuals; Payne 1969, Foster 1975, Ralph and Fancy 1994b).

NESTING BIOLOGY AND SUCCESS

We found a total of 60 nests, the majority (>90%) during nest-building activity and incubation. At least one member of the pair was color-banded at 29 of these nests. Nests were built in a variety of locations, from major forks in branches to clusters of small twigs and cavities, with a mean nest height (m) of 13.9 ± 5.0 SD (range 2.8–24.1, N = 52). Most (50/58) were open-cup nests, three were built in cavities, and five in pseudo-cavities (no data for other three nests). Nests were most often built in 'ōhi'a trees (88.5%, N = 60), and the remainder in large koa. This is not different from the percentage of 'ōhi'a trees available on the study area ('ōhi'a trees comprise 88.6% of the trees >30 cm dbh on the study area; B. Woodworth, unpubl. data). An analysis of creeper nest-site selection in relation to habitat availability will be presented elsewhere.

It is unknown whether Hawai'i Creepers routinely breed in their first year, but one banded female in this study was confirmed nesting in her first year. Nest building occupied 19 days at one nest, and mean clutch size in eleven nests was 2.1 eggs. Based on 4 eggs that were artificially incubated, incubation lasted 16–17 days, and captive-reared chicks fledged at 18 days of age (C. Keuhler, pers. comm; compare incubation period of 13–14 days and nestling period of 18–21 days in Sakai and Johanos 1983, VanderWerf 1998b). Pairs renested after failure, as indicated by ten renesting attempts by eight different pairs (two pairs nested three times within a season). The interval between failure of one nest (removed from the wild for captive propagation) and initiation of the replacement clutch was 22 days. Young remained dependent

on the parents for at least 23 days at one nest. Two pairs attempted to raise a second brood after a successful nesting attempt.

An estimated 25% of all nests that we found were abandoned before egg laying was begun (N = 60, Table 1). Fate of eight nests was undetermined because we left the study area or because we were unable to determine nest outcome. Eggs from four nests were collected and taken to a captive propagation facility to develop methods for rearing Hawaiian honeycreepers. Of the remaining nests (N = 33), nest failure occurred during egg laying, incubation, or nestling stages in 70% of nests (Table 1). Four of these failures coincided with severe wind or rainstorms (in one case the nest tree was toppled, destroying the nest). Seven successful nests fledged an average of 1.7 chicks each (range 1–2; number of chicks in three other successful nests could not be determined). We observed kleptoparasitism of nest material at six nests by I'iwi, 'Apapane (*Himatione sanguinea*), and Hawai'i 'Amakihi.

The daily survival rate of active nests was 0.960 (95% C.I. 0.942–0.977, N = 34 nests, 470.5 exposure-days). Based on this estimate, overall survival for the 34-day nesting cycle (from egg laying to fledging) would be about 25%.

ADULT AND JUVENILE SURVIVAL RATES AND DISPERSAL

Jolly-Seber Model D, which assumes constant survival and capture probability, was selected as the simplest adequate model to explain the data. Based on this model, annual adult survival rate from 1994–1997 on the Nāuhi study area was 0.88 ± 0.03, and capture probability over the four years was 0.37 ± 0.02.

Nine of 28 (32%) hatch-year birds captured in our mist nets were caught or resighted as adults. These hatch-year birds dispersed between 36–700 m from their first capture site to their first relocation as adults (median dispersal distance = 240 m; median time to relocation = 1.25 yr).

DISCUSSION

PRODUCTIVITY

Nesting success

Hawai'i Creepers built a large number of nests that never received eggs (25%). VanderWerf (1998b) also documented a high rate of abandonment (33%, N = 6 nests with known outcomes). Although human disturbance may cause abandonment (reviewed in Götmark 1992), most nests in this study were inaccessible and were observed from a distance, so nest disturbance was minimal. Disturbance from predators, an approaching end to the breeding season, disagreement between mates regarding a nest site, interference from other nesting birds, death of a mate, or the habit of building "dummy" nests for courtship or roosting may all result in building of inactive nests (Nolan 1978). In Hakalau, kleptoparasitism of nest material by other birds appears to be a frequent occurrence, having been noted at six nests in this study and in two nests by VanderWerf (1998b). Other passerines have been reported to build a high proportion of nests that did not receive eggs, e.g., four species of Hawaiian honeycreepers, 16–32% (Eddinger 1970); Prairie Warbler (*Dendroica discolor*), 23% (Nolan 1978); Laysan Finch (*Telespiza cantans*), 20% (Morin 1992b); and Puerto Rican Vireos (*Vireo latimeri*), 28% (Woodworth 1997).

In this study, 70% of active nests failed during incubation or nestling stages. Because nest contents could not be monitored in most nests, we could not confirm the cause of nest failure; disease, predation, starvation, exposure, and addling (failure to hatch) are all potential causes. Avian pox (*Poxvirus avium* sp.) and malaria (*Plasmodium relictum*) may infect and kill nestling birds (C. Atkinson, pers. comm.) and may decrease breeding activity of adults (E. VanderWerf, pers. comm.). However, the primary mosquito vector, *Culex quinquefasciatus*, is rare above 1,200 m elevation. Only about 3% of all birds of any species showed signs of pox infection during our study, and of 137 captures and 116 recaptures of Hawai'i Creeper over five years, we observed only one Creeper with an active pox lesion and one with a missing digit. The bird with pox lesions survived the infection and was recaptured and resighted several times over the following 15 months. Malaria antibodies were detected in only 6.6% of all birds captured and sampled at Nāuhi in 1998 (N = 242), and none of nine Hawai'i Creepers sampled showed evidence of past or active infection (J.

Lease, pers. comm.). Furthermore, mosquitoes are not known to breed in Hakalau; three surveys of mosquito breeding sites (Nov 1994, Feb 1995, Oct 1997) that sampled a total of 1,024 water sources at the three study areas (1,500–1,700 m elevation) failed to discover any larvae. The presence of disease at higher elevations may be the result of irregular or seasonal "disease events," whereby mosquitoes are carried by winds from lower elevations, or when mobile birds such as 'I'iwi or 'Apanane return from lower elevations with infection. Although we have no data on other potential diseases (e.g., *Mycoplasma*), we have no reason to suspect disease as a frequent cause of nest failures in Hakalau. Wind storms and heavy rains may cause nest failure; four of the nest failures during this study coincided with severe wind or rain, including one nest which was destroyed when the nest tree was toppled by heavy winds.

Nest predation is the most frequent cause of nest failures in small landbirds (Nice 1957, Martin 1992a), and predation is likely to be an important cause of nest failures in Hawaiian wet forests. Hakalau is home to six species of introduced mammals, most of which are potential predators on bird nests: feral cats (*Felis catus*), mongoose (*Herpestes auropunctatus*), roof rats (*Rattus rattus*), Polynesian rats (*R. exulans*), Norway rats (*R. norvegicus*), and house mice (*Mus musculus*). Of these, the roof rat is the most common and arboreal, and is potentially a major cause of nesting mortality in Hakalau (Lindsey et al. 1999; B. Woodworth, unpubl. data). Two avian predators are also found on the study area: the 'Io (*Buteo solitarius*) is common and has been observed preying upon nestling 'Amakihis on our study area, and the Barn Owl (*Tyto alba*) is present in low numbers.

Combining abandonments before egg laying and failure of active nests, about 79% of all Hawai'i Creeper nest starts failed to produce young (excluding 8 nests where outcome was unknown and 4 nests pulled for captive propagation). Similarly, in Kīlauea Forest and Keauhou Ranch, 89% (N = 9) of nests found were unsuccessful (reviewed in Sakai and Johanos 1983); and at a site upslope from our Pua 'Ākala study area, 50% of six known-outcome nests failed (VanderWerf 1998b). In contrast, nest mortality rate averaged 51% in 24 studies reviewed by Nice (1957) and 56% in 36 studies reviewed by Martin (1992a). The high rate of nest failure observed in this study is alarming, and further study is needed to elucidate the causes of these failures. If introduced mammals are responsible for a large proportion of failures, then controlling exotic predators in these habitats should have a large positive effect on forest bird productivity, and may be an important management tool in Hawaiian native forests.

Breeding season and renesting

Additional important components of annual productivity are the probability that a female will renest after nest failure and successful nesting, and the length of time available for birds to breed. Data from marked pairs suggest that Hawai'i Creepers readily renest after failure, but we have no data on how often they raise a second brood. The closely related 'Alauahio (*Paroreomyza montana*) is not known to renest after fledging young (Baker and Baker in press). Parent Hawai'i Creepers feed fledglings for at least three weeks post-fledging, but within one month of leaving the nest young are foraging independently for food (although still following parents; VanderWerf 1998b; U.S. Geological Survey, unpubl. data). If a complete nesting cycle requires about 50 days plus postfledging care, and breeding seasons typically last at least 120 days, then there appears to be ample time for pairs to start a second brood. However, a daily nest failure rate of 5% might effectively prevent this from occurring very often. For example, one female that nested three times over the 1997 breeding season suffered two failures and one abandonment, and to our knowledge did not succeed in fledging young that season. Using a model of seasonal fecundity (Pease and Grzybowski 1995), based on the nesting data presented herein, we estimated that the average female probably fledges only about 1.85 young (0.93 females) per season.

Although nests of the Hawai'i Creeper have been located from January to August (Sakai and Ralph 1980a, Scott et al. 1980, Sakai and Johanos 1983, VanderWerf 1998b; this study), and despite our presence on the study area year-round 1994–1997, only four of our nests were found outside of the period February to May. Consistent with this, our data indicated a breeding season of about four months from February to May, based on breeding condition of females, the appearance of juvenile birds in the population, the timing of nest initiations, and the timing of molt. Ralph and Fancy (1994b) found a similar pattern based on mist netting and resight data at Keauhou Ranch and Kīlauea Forest. The 'Alauahio also breeds from late March to late July, peaking in April and May (Baker and Baker 2000a).

The breeding season of Hawai'i Creepers is long compared to that of many neotropical migrants (50–90 days; Ricklefs 1969, Nolan 1978), and compared to the nectivorous 'I'iwi and 'Apapane in the same habitat (Ralph and Fancy 1994b). However, it is more restricted than those of birds in wet lowland tropical areas, which may extend for up to 10 months (Ricklefs 1973). The ultimate factors controlling the length of the breeding season are unknown. At high-elevation montane sites, breeding seasons might be constrained by weather or food availability. Food (or food quality) may be too limited later in the season for parents to successfully feed nestlings; birds may need to accomplish postbreeding molt before the "lean season"; or if survival rates of late-fledging chicks are poor, selection may act to limit late-season reproduction. In Hawai'i 'Amakihi, the major breeding effort coincides with the time of year of maximum resource availability (when māmane, *Sophora chrysophylla,* bear the maximum number of flowers; van Riper 1987). Similarly, 'Apapane and 'I'iwi breed during the peak in 'ōhi'a flowering (Ralph and Fancy 1994b). Reproduction in tropical House Wrens (*Troglodytes aedon*) is generally timed so that postbreeding activities such as molt and dispersal of young coincides with the peak in arthropod abundance (Young 1994). However, Ralph and Fancy (1994b) found no predictable seasonal pattern in the biomass of insects available on 'ōhi'a foliage or 'ōhi'a terminal buds at a nearby site of similar elevation. As they point out, it is possible that insects found on bark substrates where creepers forage show a more marked pattern of seasonal abundance than do foliage insects.

What, then, are the factors controlling the onset and end of breeding in Hawai'i Creepers at Hakalau? This problem has important significance for conservation of the creeper and other Hawaiian wet forest birds: through the combined effects of disease and habitat loss, the species may now be confined to high elevation breeding habitats where their breeding season is too short to allow annual productivity to balance survival. The problem is exacerbated by the presence of mammalian predators which were historically absent from Hawai'i.

SURVIVAL AND DISPERSAL

Survival rate of adult birds in our sample (0.88 ± 0.03) was similar to that documented by Ralph and Fancy (1994a) of 0.73 ± 0.12 ($\chi^2 = 1.54$, df = 1, P = 0.21). Baker and Baker (2000a) report a similarly high adult survival rate for the 'Alauahio (87% by enumeration methods). Both estimates are remarkably high, especially considering the small size and insectivorous habit of these species. Karr et al. (1990) found that the annual survival rates of 35 tropical and temperate species averaged 56%; Martin (1995) found an average survival of 53% for 34 temperate species; and Johnston et al. (1997) found an average survival of 65.3% for 17 Trinidadian species. Other Hawaiian passerines have similarly high survival rates, for example the Hawai'i 'Ākepa, 0.70 ± 0.12 SE (Ralph and Fancy 1994a) and 0.82 ± 0.04 SE (Lepson and Freed 1995); and 'Apapane, 0.72 ± 0.12 SE (Ralph and Fancy 1995).

The high survival rate of Hawai'i Creepers in Hakalau in part may reflect the rarity of disease in this high-elevation refugia, above the level of mosquito populations. However, a preliminary population model indicated that the population growth rate of Hawai'i Creepers is strongly influenced by adult survival (B. Woodworth, unpubl. data). Thus, the invasion of disease into these areas could have severe consequences for the population. Controlling the spread of mosquitoes into upper elevations (including control of feral pigs, which create mosquito breeding sites through their foraging activities) should be a high priority for management.

In general, reproductive potential of the creeper appears to be low due to its small clutch size, relatively long developmental period, and limited breeding season. This low reproductive potential is exacerbated by the high rate of nesting failures documented in this study, possibly due to the introduction of mammalian nest predators to Hawai'i. High adult and juvenile survival rates may compensate to some extent for low annual productivity, but if disease were to reach the upper elevation rain forests it could have devastating effects. More detailed demographic data are needed to assess the implications for population persistence of Hawai'i Creeper in this high-elevation refuge. Finally, maintenance of the native wet forest bird communities on Hawai'i will require preserving the integrity of the habitat and its essential quality for the breeding birds—in particular, mosquito control, feral ungulate control, and rodent control will be important tools for management.

ACKNOWLEDGMENTS

This research would not have been possible without the contributions of C. Driehaus, A. Grover, S. Langridge, J. Townsend, K. Wakelee, and dozens of volunteer field assistants over the years. Special thanks are due to D. Wass, J. Jeffrey, and other staff of Hakalau Forest National Wildlife Refuge, who gave permission to work on the refuge, provided logistical support, and donated their time and expertise throughout the project. Financial support was provided by the Pacific Island Ecosystems Research Center, Biological Resources Division of the U.S. Geological Survey (formerly USFWS and National Biological Survey), and the U.S. Fish and Wildlife Service, Ecological Services Division. K. Berlin, S. Conant, L. Freed, and T. Pratt reviewed and improved earlier drafts of this manuscript.

Studies in Avian Biology No. 22:173–184, 2001.

SIGNIFICANCE OF OLD-GROWTH FOREST TO THE HAWAI'I 'ĀKEPA

Leonard A. Freed

Abstract. The Hawai'i 'Ākepa (*Loxops coccineus coccineus*) is an endangered Hawaiian honeycreeper that nests obligately in tree cavities of 'ōhi'a-lehua (*Metrosideros polymorpha*) and koa (*Acacia koa*). Comparative evidence from cavity-nesting birds elsewhere suggests that the distribution and abundance of the Hawai'i 'Ākepa may depend on large trees. During a seven-year study of the bird at Hakalau Forest National Wildlife Refuge, 54 trees were used by the birds. I documented size and growth form of these trees and compared them to trees randomly selected and to large trees that were inventoried. The trees used by the birds are the largest 'ōhi'as, which are in the rarest size classes, and large koas. The 'ōhi'a and koa trees fit many criteria of old-growth forest. Particularly striking is the association of cavities with large trees. Growth form is also important since cavities occur almost exclusively in monopodial (single-trunked) 'ōhi'as, and the birds use cavities in monopodial koa trees over those in sympodial (multiple-trunked) trees. Regeneration of old-growth forest involves both the transition of large trees into cavity trees and the growth of seedlings into a monopodial form. Disturbance to the forest over the last 100 years has generated problems at both scales of regeneration. Trees with cavities are likely falling at a faster rate than cavities develop in smaller trees, and increased light levels in the understory and at edges of the forest appear to promote sympodial growth in seedlings.

Key Words: Acacia koa; distribution and abundance; Hawai'i 'Ākepa; koa; *Loxops coccineus coccineus*; *Metrosideros polymorpha*; 'ōhi'a; old-growth forest; regeneration; tree cavities.

Old-growth forests have specific relevance to both evolutionary and conservation biology. Free from human or natural disturbance for a much longer time than second-growth forests, old-growth forests appear to be unique environments in which some resident species evolved their life histories and behaviors (Wesołowski 1983, Piotrowska and Wesołowski 1989). These forest types are often associated with conservation hot spots where some species have their highest densities. Spotted Owls (*Strix occidentalis caurina*), Red-cockaded Woodpeckers (*Picoides borealis*), and Marbled Murrelets (*Brachyramphus marmoratus*) are prominent avian examples for old-growth coniferous forests (Forsman et al. 1984, James 1991, Ralph et al. 1995a). The macroecological approach to the study of correlation between distribution and abundance suggests a hot spot exists because the niche requirements of the species in it are best met (Brown 1984, Brown et al. 1995, Terborgh 1995). This is best illustrated by temporal changes in a population of Acorn Woodpeckers (*Melanerpes formicivorous*) in New Mexico associated with a decline in old, partly dead cottonwood trees (*Populus angustifolia*) used as stable granaries for storing acorns (Ligon and Stacey 1996).

The most extensive forest type on the main Hawaiian islands consists of 'ōhi'a-lehua (*Metrosideros polymorpha*, hereafter referred to as 'ōhi'a), frequently in association with koa (*Acacia koa*) as a co-emergent (Scott et al. 1986, Wagner et al. 1990a,b). However, the concept of old-growth forest has not yet been applied to this or any other forest type in Hawai'i. There may be several reasons for this including (1) inability to age 'ōhi'a and koa trees based on growth rings (Sastrapradja 1965, Burgan 1970, Wick 1970); (2) elimination of large trees by repeated hurricanes (Shaw 1981, Schroeder 1993) and by humans as forests were destroyed (Kirch 1982a); (3) steep topography, which would limit tree size for biomechanical reasons of soil support (Garwood et al. 1979, Sidle et al. 1985, Mattheck 1991) and exposure to wind (Telewski 1995), or for physiological reasons of water stress caused by exposure to wind and excessive drainage (Kozlowski and Pallardy 1997a); and (4) growth in soils on older islands with fewer nutrients (Crews et al. 1995, Vitousek et al. 1995). In addition, on the volcanically active island of Hawai'i, elimination of forests by lava flows (Carson et al. 1990) and youth of regenerating forests on lava do not provide the pattern for recognizing old-growth forests. The phenomenon of "'ōhi'a dieback," where cohorts of mature trees but not saplings die synchronously (Mueller-Dombois 1987), also does not promote the concept of old-growth forest with large live specimens standing and large dead specimens on the ground (Franklin et al. 1981, 1986).

The Hawai'i Forest Bird Survey (Scott et al. 1986) was the first comprehensive attempt to analyze the distribution and abundance of native forest birds in relation to features of habitat. However, there was no formal incorporation of variables that could identify old-growth forest.

Scott et al. (1986) indicate that tree diameter was measured at selected stations, but these data were not incorporated as variables in the habitat response analysis designed to identify aspects of habitat that were associated with high and low densities of birds. Rather, forest development was indexed as tree biomass, calculated as crown cover (in percent) times canopy height (m). For many aspects of the survey this was appropriate, as in other studies attempting to estimate canopy volume for comparative purposes (Sturman 1968, Karr and Roth 1971, Sabo 1980, Rice et al. 1983). However, dense stands of tall, thin trees could have the same value of tree biomass as thinner stands of large (in diameter) trees of similar height but with wider canopies. Such stands could even have higher estimated tree biomass than areas with more widely separated trees that are large in diameter and of the same height. Without formally incorporating variables of tree diameter, there would be no way in which old-growth forest, based on the presence of large trees, could be identified.

Some anomalies in the habitat response analysis might be attributed to the absence of a variable that could represent old-growth forest. The Hawai'i 'Ākepa *(Loxops coccineus coccineus)* is a Hawaiian honeycreeper (Drepanidinae) that exists exclusively in 'ōhi'a or 'ōhi'a-koa forests on the island of Hawai'i (Scott et al. 1986). The bird forages mainly in the terminal foliage of 'ōhi'a (Perkins 1903) and is unique among forest birds in being able to extract caterpillars from the inside of 'ōhi'a leaf buds (Richards and Bock 1973, Freed et al. 1987a). The main 'Ākepa populations, in the Hāmākua study area on Mauna Kea and in the Ka'ū study area on Mauna Loa (Fig. 1), varied in their response to habitat variables (Scott et al. 1986). The 'Ākepa in the Ka'ū site showed no relationship between density and tree biomass, whereas the 'Ākepa in the Hāmākua site showed a negative relationship between density and tree biomass. A negative response could occur if the birds were more likely to be detected, or were more abundant, in highly disturbed forest with large trees than in second growth forest with smaller trees. It is possible that large 'ōhi'a trees in a pasture may be more important to the niche of the Hawai'i 'Ākepa than dense stands of smaller 'ōhi'a trees with native understory. A second variation in response was that birds in the Ka'ū site were negatively associated with koa, whereas birds in the Hāmākua site were positively associated with koa. This pattern could occur if large koa trees were associated with large 'ōhi'a trees in the Hāmākua but not the Ka'ū study site. In fact, the southeastern portion of the Ka'ū site with the most 'Ākepa has large 'ōhi'a but no koa, where-

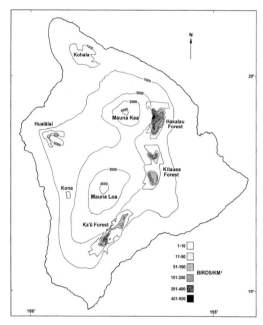

FIGURE 1.   Distribution and abundance of Hawai'i 'Ākepa on the island of Hawai'i based on Hawai'i Forest Bird Survey (Scott et al. 1986). Contour lines at 1,000 m. Birds were found at Hakalau Forest, Ka'ū Forest, Kona. and Hualālai; distribution is represented by irregular enclosures. Hakalau Forest and Kīlauea Forest were within the Hāmākua study area of the survey. Ka'ū Forest was within the Ka'ū study area. Pua 'Ākala study site in current study is located at the highest Hawai'i 'Ākepa density (solid black) in Hakalau Forest. Hart (*this volume*) compared 'Ākepa at Pua 'Ākala with those in a site of reduced density north of Pua 'Ākala.

as the northwestern portion with koa has few 'Ākepa (Jacobi 1978, Scott et al. 1986).

The location of nests of the Hawai'i 'Ākepa may be the link between the density of birds and the presence of large trees in old-growth forests. The 'Ākepa appears to be the only honeycreeper that nests obligately in cavities in trees (Scott et al. 1980, Freed et al. 1987b, Lepson and Freed 1995), and all reported nests were located in large trees (Sincock and Scott 1980, Collins 1984, Lepson and Freed 1997). A variety of cavities were used, including holes in trunks or branches, snags, and even open areas where the bark and wood had separated (Sincock and Scott 1980, Collins 1984, Freed et al. 1987b). There are no primary cavity-nesting (excavating) birds such as woodpeckers in Hawai'i. Therefore, cavities must form naturally in trees, and large trees might be much more likely than small trees to form cavities, as has been found with *Eucalyptus* in Australia (Lindenmayer et al. 1991a, 1993; Bennett et al. 1994). Studies of secondary cavity-nesting birds, which use existing cavities, indicate that nests are located in cavities in large trees (Saunders et al. 1982, van Balen et al. 1982, Wesołowski 1989). No study of relationship between cavities and tree size has occurred in Hawai'i.

As part of a long-term study of the breeding biology and mating system of the Hawai'i 'Ākepa, I documented 'ōhi'a and koa trees used by the birds as nest sites and compared the trees used as nest sites with other trees available in the same study area. This provided a basis for establishing the nonrandom use of trees in the forest. In addition, I investigated the relationship between cavities and tree size. This relationship is the basis for identifying old-growth forest in Hawai'i and the critical role that exceptionally large trees have in the nesting niche of the Hawai'i 'Ākepa.

METHODS

The relations among tree size, tree form, presence of cavities, and use of cavities for nesting by Hawai'i 'Ākepa were studied in the Pua 'Ākala Tract of Hakalau Forest National Wildlife Refuge. This section of the refuge has the highest density of 'Ākepa on the windward slope of Mauna Kea (Fig. 1). The study site within the tract was a 500 × 600 m area at an elevation of 1,900 m. The land had been partially cleared and extensively grazed by cattle for over 100 years (Tomonari-Tuggle 1996). As a result, the site has a parkland-like structure of large 'ōhi'a and koa trees, with introduced grasses as the primary understory species in cleared areas. Within this structure are sections of less altered forest with an understory of native ferns and *Rubus hawaiensis,* and a midstory of native woody trees and shrubs, mainly *Cheirodendron trigynum, Myrsine lessertiana, Coprosma ochracea, Vaccinium calcynum, Ilex anomala,* and *Styphelia tameiameiae.*

'Ākepa nesting had been studied within the site for 7 years (Lepson and Freed 1995, 1997). I measured the diameter at breast height (dbh) in cm using a dbh tape of the 54 'ōhi'a and koa trees that had been used by the birds. The diameter of the part of the tree that contained the cavity was estimated as a percentage of dbh based on comparing units of a ruler subtended by the part and by the trunk at dbh height viewed from a similar distance. I also identified the growth form as the height of first forking in relation to the measurement of standard dbh (height of 1.3 m). Trees that forked above this height were considered single-trunked (monopodial). Trees that forked below this height were considered sympodial, with co-dominant trunks (forks). Size of sympodial trees was measured below the fork. In addition, the diameter of each fork was measured. These trees are the basis of comparison with other trees sampled in this study.

The size of trees available to the birds was determined by sampling trees in the same study area. Sampling stations were located 50 m apart along transects 50 m apart, based on a randomly selected initial starting point near the corner of the study area. At each of the 133 stations where a tree was within 20 m of the

TABLE 1. TYPES OF CAVITIES USED AT 71 NEST SITES BY HAWAI'I, 'ĀKEPA

Cavity entrance	Proportion
Smooth hole	0.34
Rough crack	0.24
Rough hole	0.20
Smooth crack	0.11
Niche	0.04
Long crack	0.01
Unknown	0.06

station, the dbh and trunk type was determined for the closest tree with dbh above 5 cm. At 16 of these stations, the closest tree in each of four quadrants was measured. This resulted in a sample of 162 'ōhi'a and 10 koa trees. *Ilex, Coprosma,* and *Cheirodendron* together resulted in four trees. Sizes of 'ōhi'a and koa available and used were compared to illustrate the significance of large and old trees to the breeding niche of the bird.

The relationship among tree size, growth form, and presence of cavity was determined by inventorying large trees within a 200 × 500 m subarea. Sections of the subarea were investigated in relation to prominent landmarks to ensure complete coverage. All trees >60 cm dbh, the smallest tree size known among the 54 trees used by nesting 'Ākepa, were measured in the inventory. In addition, some specimens were included that were measured and found to be <60 cm dbh. Diameter at breast height, growth form, presence of cavity, and use of cavity by 'Ākepa were documented for each tree in the inventory. Trees used by the birds in previous years were already marked. The inventory included 229 trees (172 'ōhi'a, 57 koa).

Unless indicated otherwise, all statistical analyses of metric variables were done using a two-sided t-test, and tests of proportions involved a binomial test.

RESULTS

CHARACTERISTICS OF CAVITIES AND TREES

The birds used cavities with several types of entrances (Table 1, Fig. 2). The sample size of 71 cavities in 54 trees reflects the fact that about one-third of the trees had more than one cavity present and used, but never during the same breeding season. The holes and cracks were cavities formed by openings within the wood. The niche cavity was an opening formed by the separation of the bark away from the wood, as was reported for an 'Ākepa nest in the Ka'ū Forest Reserve on Mauna Loa (Freed et al. 1987b). Both rough and smooth openings were used equivalently (0.44 and 0.45, respectively), indicating that the type of opening does not appear to be important. The heights above ground of cavities used ranged from 1.5 to 19.5 m (mean 10.2 m). This wide range suggests that the presence of a cavity may be more relevant than its height above the ground. The range includes the

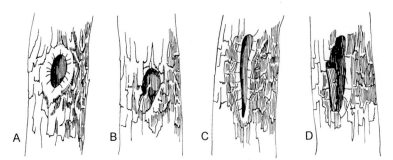

FIGURE 2. Four major types of openings of cavities used for nesting by Hawai'i 'Ākepa. A = smooth hole, B = rough hole, C = smooth crack, D = rough crack. Ontogenetic differences are discussed in text.

highest nest known for 'Ākepa (Collins 1984, Freed et al. 1987b); however, height of the first 'Ākepa nest discovered in the Ka'ū Forest Reserve by Sincock and Scott (1980) was the lowest at 1 m.

The birds used only large trees for nest sites. For 'ōhi'a, the trees used are on average more than twice the size of trees available based on the random sample (P < 0.001; Fig. 3); for koa, there was no significant difference (P = 0.42; Fig. 4). However, the random sample of koa contained only one tree <75 cm dbh (10%), unlike the random sample for 'ōhi'a, in which 77% of trees were <75 cm dbh. The rarity of smaller koa trees appears to be the result of cattle ranching for the last 100 years and faster growth and possibly shorter life of koa (Cooray and Mueller-Dombois 1981, Spatz and Mueller-Dombois 1981). I have observed cows seek young koas as food with the result that koa regeneration has probably been suppressed over the past century (Baldwin and Fagerlund 1943). Nevertheless, all nests were located in enormous 'ōhi'a and koa trees, averaging 1 m dbh with a minimum of 60 cm dbh. Trees of this size would be expected in an old-growth forest, thus revealing the essential role of such a forest in the niche of the 'Ākepa.

ASSOCIATION BETWEEN CAVITIES AND TREES

The presence of cavities in 'ōhi'a in the inventory area and the use of trees with cavities by 'Ākepa was related to the size of tree. Only monopodial trees are considered for the analysis of 'ōhi'a. Within the set of large 'ōhi'a trees that were inventoried, cavity trees are an average of 20 cm greater in dbh than 'ōhi'a trees without cavities (P < 0.001), and cavity trees used by the birds for nesting are about 14 cm greater in dbh than unused cavity trees (P = 0.04; Fig. 5). It appears that the birds are tracking the largest 'ōhi'a trees in the forest, a finding further supporting the hypothesis of old-growth forest niche for the 'Ākepa.

There is a similar relationship between tree size and presence of cavity for koa. Within the set of large koa trees sampled, trees with cavities were an average of 35 cm larger in dbh than non-cavity koa trees (P < 0.001; Fig. 6). However, unlike 'ōhi'a, there was no significant difference in the size of koa trees with cavities that were used and those with cavities that were unused (P = 0.80; Fig. 6). The birds do not appear to be tracking the largest koa trees in the forest.

The difference between 'ōhi'a and koa may be compared directly. Within the inventory area, there were 48 'ōhi'a and 33 koa trees with cavities. Although the proportions of use of these trees by the birds are not significantly different (P = 0.72), within the limited sample of 15 trees used, the direction favors 'ōhi'as (0.21) rather than koas (0.15). This, plus the tracking of large 'ōhi'a trees, is consistent with the dependence of the bird on 'ōhi'a rather than koa in its distribution.

Both 'ōhi'a and koa trees varied in the height of forking below and above the 1.3 m height of dbh. A mixture of monopodial and sympodial large trees is a characteristic of the forest. Approximately 50% of the large 'ōhi'a trees in each of the size classes in the inventory area are monopodial (overall 52%; Fig. 7). More koa are monopodial (79%; P < 0.001), suggesting that large 'ōhi'a trees have a more variable growth form than large koas, presumably reflecting differences in apical dominance between the species. In my random sample of 164 'ōhi'as, 80% of the trees were monopodial. However, of the 28 trees in this sample with dbh >60 cm, 64% were monopodial, statistically indistinguishable from the area sample (P = 0.17). An interesting finding is that within the random sample of 'ōhi'a, trees <60 cm dbh were more likely to be monopodial than trees >60 cm dbh (84% versus 64%; P = 0.034). As will be discussed below, this may reflect differences in early growth conditions for the trees of different ages.

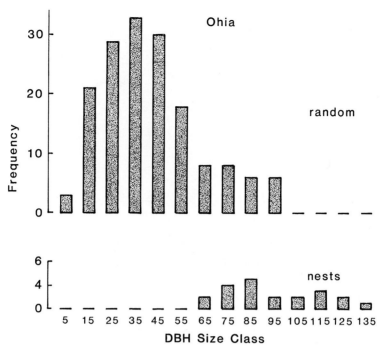

FIGURE 3.   Diameter at breast height (DBH size class in cm, midpoint shown) of 'ōhi'a trees sampled through-out the study area (upper) and those used as nests in the same area (lower).

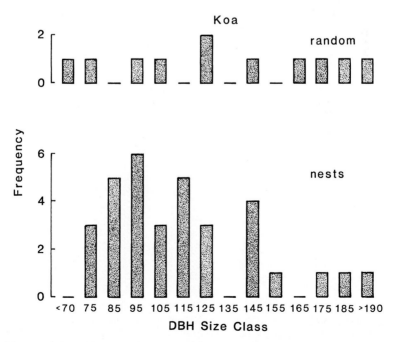

FIGURE 4.   Diameter at breast height (DBH size class in cm, midpoint shown) of koa trees sampled throughout the study area (upper) and those used as nests in the same area (lower).

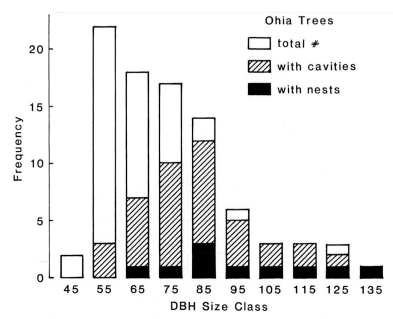

FIGURE 5.   Diameter at breast height (DBH size class in cm, midpoint shown) of large 'ōhi'a trees within inventory area. Height of the bar represents the total number of trees. Diagonal hatching is overlaid on that bar to show the trees with cavities, and the solid fill is further overlaid to show the trees with cavities that were used by Hawai'i 'Ākepa.

Sympodial 'ōhi'a trees, whose diameter was measured below the bifurcation, were not significantly smaller than monopodial 'ōhi'a trees within the inventory area (P = 0.51; Figs. 3, 5). However, only 2 of the 83 sympodial trees had cavities visible to researchers, in contrast to the 46 of 89 monopodial trees in the same area

(Fisher exact test, P < 0.001). Among the 21 'ōhi'a trees used by 'Ākepa in the entire study area, only one was sympodial, which was consistent with the rarity of cavities in trees of this form.

The situation with koa is more complex. Sympodial koa trees in the inventory area were an

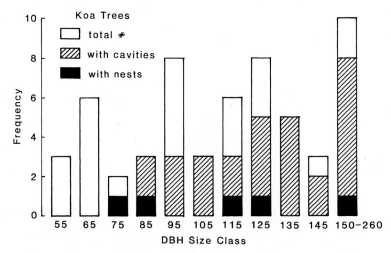

FIGURE 6.   Diameter at breast height (DBH size class in cm, midpoint shown) of large koa trees within inventory area. Height of the bar represents the total number of trees. Diagonal hatching is overlaid on that bar to show the trees with cavities, and the solid fill is further overlaid to show the trees with cavities that were used by Hawai'i 'Ākepa.

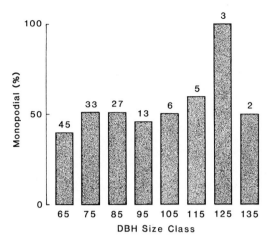

FIGURE 7. Proportions of 'ōhi'a trees of different size (midpoint shown) that were monopodial within the inventory area. (DBH is diameter at breast height.)

average of 33.1 cm greater in diameter than monopodial trees (P = 0.015). In addition, 10 of 12 (0.83) sympodial koa trees had cavities in contrast to 23 of 45 (0.51) monopodial trees (Fisher exact test, P = 0.055). Among the 33 koa trees used by 'Ākepa in the entire study

area, only 2 were sympodial. A higher proportion of sympodial koa trees than sympodial 'ōhi'a trees had cavities (10 of 12 koa versus 2 of 83 'ōhi'a with cavities in the inventory area; Fisher exact test, P < 0.001), indicating that sympodial koa trees with cavities were underutilized by the birds (Fisher exact test, P < 0.001).

'Ōhi'a and koa trees differ in the pattern of growth form, size of tree, and presence of cavity. The relationship among these variables seems to be based on the size of the forks in the sympodial trees. Only rarely, even in the largest sympodial 'ōhi'a trees, are forks of diameter >63 cm (Fig. 8), the diameter of the smallest monopodial trees with cavities used by 'Ākepa. It appears then that the growth form of the tree, determined as height of first forking, influences the likelihood that a cavity will develop. Sympodial 'ōhi'a trees appear to be larger than they really are with respect to cavity formation, since the forks available for cavity formation are smaller than the measured diameter on the short main trunk. In contrast, as documented above, sympodial koas are larger than monopodial koas, and all sympodial koas had at least one fork that fell within the size range of monopodial koas with cavities ≥ 70 cm in diameter.

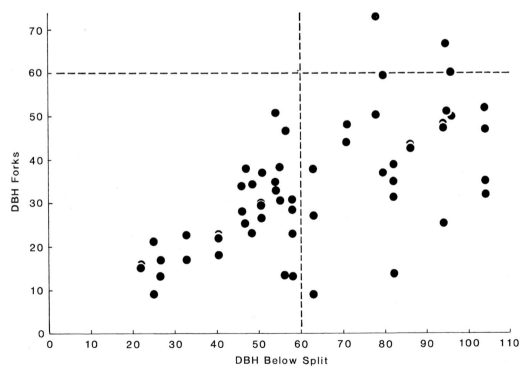

FIGURE 8. Diameter of forks (cm) in relation to size of trunk below the first fork (cm) in sympodial 'ōhi'a trees. (DBH is diameter at breast height.)

TABLE 2. PORTIONS OF TREE OF 71 CAVITIES USED AS NEST-SITES

Location of cavity	Proportion
Branch	0.48
Trunk	0.24
Fork	0.15
Snag	0.10
Unknown	0.03

Cavities in trees used by the Hawai'i 'Ākepa were found in a variety of locations (Table 2). Almost one-half of cavities used were in branches and approximately one-quarter were in primary trunks, reflecting the rarity of cavities in forks and the rarity of snags. Parts of trees with cavities used must generally be >20 cm in diameter, based on median and first quartile displayed in Figure 9.

Particularly relevant is the size of branches with cavities. There is a significant relationship between the size of the branch (or snag) with cavities and the size of the primary trunk of the tree for 39 trees (linear regression, $P = 0.015$; Fig. 10). While larger trees have larger branches, absolute branch or snag size appears to be important since over two-thirds of the cavities used were in parts with a diameter >20 cm ($P = 0.005$).

DISCUSSION

Large 'ōhi'a and koa trees are clearly part of the ecological niche of the Hawai'i 'Ākepa. The large trees that have cavities are rare and for 'ōhi'a are almost exclusively monopodial in growth form. Here I will relate these findings to more general issues associated with the distribution and abundance of the Hawai'i 'Ākepa, attempt to identify characteristics of forests with large 'ōhi'a and koa trees that could be considered old-growth, and identify problems in regeneration of old-growth 'ōhi'a-koa forest based on variation in growth form of 'ōhi'a.

DISTRIBUTION AND ABUNDANCE OF THE HAWAI'I 'ĀKEPA

The dependence of the Hawai'i 'Ākepa on large trees with cavities can be considered the Big Tree Hypothesis concerning the distribution and abundance of the bird. The hypothesis has the potential to explain otherwise puzzling aspects of these phenomena both historically and recently. Early naturalists reported that the bird had a spotty distribution on the island, but that it was locally common in certain areas (Wilson and Evans 1890–1899, Rothschild 1893–1900, Henshaw 1902a, Perkins 1903). According to the Big Tree Hypothesis, the areas in which the bird was locally common were forests with large trees with cavities. On active volcanoes such as Mauna Loa, Kīlauea, and Hualālai (Fig. 1), big trees would most likely be present in areas that had escaped lava for extensive periods of time, and also escaped fire and high winds. Kohala and Mauna Kea (Fig. 1), as inactive volcanoes, would have consistently older substrates free from lava. However, geographical heterogeneity of tree size could still be generated by tree fall

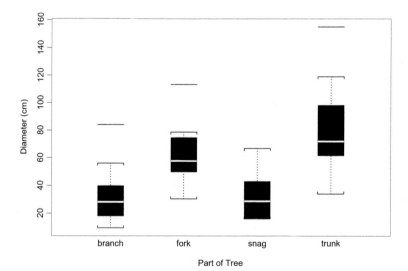

FIGURE 9. Diameter of part of tree with cavity that was used by Hawai'i 'Ākepa. Horizontal white line is the median, top and bottom of shaded box represent first and third quartiles. Brackets show range. Isolated black lines represent outliers.

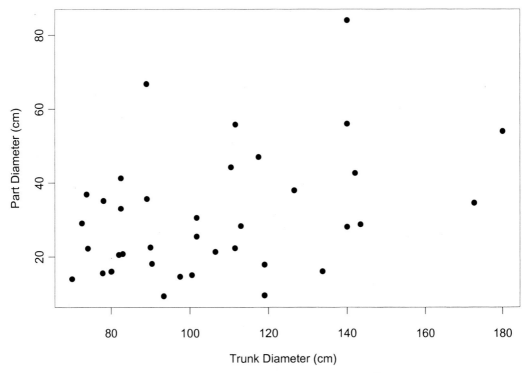

FIGURE 10. Diameter of branches and snags with cavities used by Hawai'i 'Ākepa in relation to size of trunk (diameter at breast height).

associated with high wind, torrential rains, and perhaps fire.

An attempt to document historical forest structure is difficult at best with species with growth rings from which ages of standing trees can be estimated (Harper 1977). The lack of distinct annual growth rings in 'ōhi'a and koa, as in many other tropical trees (Kozlowski and Pallardy 1997b), makes it even more difficult. However, both large 'ōhi'a and koa trees become nursery logs when they fall over and begin to decompose (Scowcroft 1992). In principle, it would be possible to document the presence of large trees in an area in the past by including dead nursery logs as well as live specimens, and including large trees that show evidence of past nursery logs through their stilt-like roots arranged around an opening. An interesting project in historical biogeography would be to determine if the distribution of large trees (standing and as logs) was as spotty as the distribution of the bird.

The Big Tree Hypothesis can also account for current patterns of distribution and abundance. For example, Scott et al. (1986) identified a series of distributional anomalies for the Hawai'i 'Ākepa. These were defined as unexpectedly low abundance in areas with presumably the ap-

propriate tree biomass. Such anomalies were identified as elevational and lateral. Elevational anomalies, where the birds were rare in suitable habitat at lower elevations, could be generated by less visible factors such as *Culex* mosquitoes as vectors and pathogens such as malaria (*Plasmodium*) and poxvirus (*Poxvirus avium*) (Scott et al. 1986). An increasing body of evidence supports this interpretation of elevational anomalies since both the mosquito and *Plasmodium* fare better at lower and warmer elevations (van Riper et al. 1986, Atkinson et al. 1995, Jarvi et al. *this volume*). However, disease is much less likely as an explanation for the lateral anomalies within an elevation. A specific prediction of the Big Tree Hypothesis is that large trees will be rarer where the Hawai'i 'Ākepa is rarer, consistent with other studies of hole-nesting birds (von Haartman 1971).

The Kīlauea Forest Reserve is the only other site on the island of Hawai'i where both bird densities and tree sizes have been measured. Consistent with the Big Tree Hypothesis, 'Ākepa densities there were lower than at Pua 'Ākala during the Hawai'i Forest Bird Survey (Scott et al. 1986), and sizes of 'ōhi'a and koa reported in Cooray and Mueller-Dombois (1981) do not achieve those documented here. The possibility exists that the lower 'Ākepa densities at the Hakalau tract of Hakalau Forest National Wildlife Refuge, documented by Hart (*this volume*), may be associated with lower densities of large trees.

OLD-GROWTH FOREST AND CAVITIES

Habitat quality and critical resources are fundamental aspects of management. Given the attention that old-growth forests have received in the journal *Conservation Biology* during the last 10 years, it is pertinent to consider the forest at Pua 'Ākala as potentially indicative of old-growth in Hawai'i. While the focus on old-growth will be with respect to the Hawai'i 'Ākepa, it is also relevant to note a general correlation in distribution and abundance between the 'Ākepa and other endangered birds of 'ōhi'a-koa forest (Scott et al. 1986). This suggests that old-growth forests may be important to endangered forest birds such as Hawai'i Creeper (*Oreomystis mana*) and 'Akiapōlā'au (*Hemignathus munroi*). While the Hawai'i 'Ākepa depends on large trees for nest sites, it is possible that the bark of large trees may support more arthropods for the Hawai'i Creeper and the wood more insects for the 'Akiapōlā'au than that of smaller trees. At minimum, large trees provide larger patches of foraging substrate that could reduce travel costs of foraging birds.

There are two approaches to defining old-growth forest. The process approach is based on stand development (Oliver and Larson 1996). Events since the last major disturbance are the key in distinguishing transitional old-growth and true old-growth. There may be relic large trees that germinated before the last major disturbance. Stands that still contain such trees, with younger trees growing upward, could be considered transitional old-growth. In contrast, with sufficient time, the relic large trees may have germinated after the last major disturbance and the entire stand would consist entirely of trees that grew upward from beneath. This is considered true old-growth. While much work has been done on stand development of 'ōhi'a and koa on younger substrates (Mueller-Dombois 1987), it is impossible to know the conditions under which the large 'ōhi'a trees at Pua 'Ākala germinated relative to a major disturbance. However, charcoal from underneath lava flows in the region has been dated at approximately 5,000 years (Wolfe et al. 1997). Volcanic rocks closer to the summit have been aged between 65,000 to 4,000 years ago (Wolfe et al. 1997). At least with respect to geological events, there has been sufficient time for true old-growth conditions to occur.

The second approach to defining old-growth forest is based on structure (Oliver and Larson 1996). Criteria include many large, old trees, often at a wide spacing; standing dead trees as snags; large logs on the ground; and long time free from human disturbance (Franklin and Waring 1979; Franklin et al. 1981, 1986). Pua 'Ākala has all of these characteristics but with human disturbance. Logging, or clearing and burning for cattle ranching, has occurred more outside of the forest than inside. Disturbance inside the forest is due primarily to the direct effects of cattle. As herbivores, cattle have a major impact on the understory and regeneration but little impact on established trees. The time scale of disturbance by cattle, 100 years, has not been long enough to modify the structure of the emergent canopy. Studies of 'ōhi'a (Porter 1973) and koa (Spatz and Mueller-Dombois 1981) growth indicate that the large emergent canopy trees are much older than 100 years. Also, cattle would have no effect on the presence of large fallen logs, which are included in the criteria of old-growth.

Although not formally recognized by Oliver and Larson (1996), the presence of cavities can also be used as a criterion of old-growth. The association of cavities with very large trees at Pua 'Ākala is consistent with studies in old-growth forests in Australia (Lindenmayer et al. 1993), similar to Hawai'i in lacking an avian excavator. A similar association of cavities with large trees was detected in an unmanaged stand in Europe for cavities that were not formed by woodpeckers (Wesołowski 1989). Cavities have the potential to be a simple way to identify old-growth forests. The definition of old-growth forest in Hawai'i, in relation to cavities, has the advantage that the growth form of 'ōhi'a is implicit as a variable since large sympodial trees have few cavities. This is important because a forest of primarily sympodial 'ōhi'a trees does not provide the specialized niche requirement of the Hawai'i 'Ākepa.

While the age of the Pua 'Ākala forest is not known, several lines of evidence suggest that 'ōhi'a trees with diameters of >1 m are extremely old. Porter (1973), based on size specific growth studies of 'ōhi'a on younger substrates and primarily lower elevations, estimated that 'ōhi'a trees that were 65 cm in diameter were 300 years old. Trees that are 1 m and larger would be considerably older given the sigmoidal growth curves of trees with increasingly slower growth after the inflection point (Evans 1972). The disproportional use of the largest 'ōhi'a trees by Hawai'i 'Ākepa may involve trees that are surprisingly old. For example, some trees in mountain ash (*Eucalyptus regnans*) forests in Australia may not develop cavities large enough for vertebrates until they are over 400 years old (Lindenmayer et al. 1991b). Slow growing 'ōhi'a may require a much longer time.

Why do cavities form primarily in larger and older trees? Cavities form as a tree isolates a wound through compartmentalization of wood decayed by microorganisms (Shigo 1984, 1991; Mackowski 1984). Although some microorganisms can gain entry through injuries to sapwood (Adaskaveg and Ogawa 1990), most access is through wounds exposing the heartwood (Carey and Sanderson 1981). Branches large enough to form heartwood may themselves be damaged and decay may then proceed into the heartwood of the trunk. This may be the key reason why older and larger trees are more likely to have cavities. Such trees may be the only ones with branches sufficiently large to have heartwood. An element of chance is also involved because a sufficiently large branch must break to form a cavity. The increasing association of cavities with age or size of trees can represent the greater exposure to rare events of older trees. The rough holes associated with cavities may represent cases where the smaller unit was ripped off the larger unit, along with part or all of the trunk collar (Shigo 1991; Fig. 2). The smooth holes may represent cases where the smaller unit was broken and subsequently rotted off the larger unit, leaving the trunk collar largely intact. The ontogenetic difference between smooth and rough cracks, involving wounded wood on the borders (Shigo 1991; Fig. 2), is less clear.

Under this model, the rarity of cavities among the sympodial trees is based on the relatively small size of the forks. The short main trunk of sympodial trees might have sufficient heartwood for formation of cavities, but each fork may only have the heartwood of a smaller monopodial tree in which cavities are rare or nonexistent. In addition, the short main trunk does not have branches that could break to initiate formation of cavities. A detailed comparison of forks and their branches versus a monopodial tree of the same diameter and its branches might reveal constraints on growth of sympodial trees relevant to cavity formation.

REGENERATION OF OLD-GROWTH 'ŌHI'A-KOA FOREST

The large 'ōhi'a trees used for nesting by 'Ākepa at Pua 'Ākala are old specimens. Their replacement involves regeneration at two different scales of time and size. The first involves the growth of smaller trees, of monopodial growth form, into the size classes in which cavities are likely to develop. The second involves regeneration of monopodial specimens at the seedling stage. There are problems at each scale that may

be involved with human disturbance of the forest.

The large 'ōhi'a (and koa) trees used by the birds for nesting appear to be falling at a faster rate than they are being replaced. The Pua 'Ākala Tract experiences high winds that can exceed 145 km/hr during winter storms. Some trees fall during this time, perhaps more than in pristine forest because exposed trees may now be more vulnerable to wind. Of the 54 nest-site trees, 9 (16.7%) are no longer standing. This mortality has occurred during a 7-year period. At the rate of 0.3 cm growth in diameter per year, the maximum identified by Porter (1973) for trees growing on loamy soil at 1,200 m elevation, a tree would grow about 2 cm during that time (perhaps less at the 1,900 m elevation at Pua 'Ākala and if the growth rate decreases with size). If cavities take a long time to develop after a suitable accident that forms a wound, it is unlikely that there were 9 monopodial trees that had no cavities at the beginning of the study but developed cavities within the seven years to replace the fallen trees. While more effort is required to identify the balance between cavities gained and cavities lost over a given time period, it is clear that a cavity can be lost more quickly due to disturbance than can be gained through growth of trees.

A related concern is that existing cavities become unsuitable even though the tree is still standing. This has happened at least three times where we could observe deterioration of the cavity over time. Thus the balance between cavities gained and cavities lost must include loss of cavities within trees still standing as well as fallen trees.

Replacement of large old trees with cavities ultimately requires regeneration of trees of appropriate growth form. 'Ōhi'a has pseudodichotomous branching (Porter 1973), meaning that forking occurs when the apical meristem aborts or is injured, thereby releasing dominance over the lateral buds which then develop into shoots that represent the two forks (Bell 1991). The height of first forking probably reflects the actual height of the event since no trees, among thousands inspected, have been found with an intermediate form of one fork lost and one present below the first intact forking. The form would be evident by the remaining fork forming an angle to the trunk below it. Growth form appears to be set early in the growth of a seedling. Thus the different proportions of monopodial and sympodial trees in larger and smaller size classes found in this study suggest that environmental conditions for growth were different for the trees when they were seedlings.

Direct and indirect effects of cattle ranching

have consequences for regeneration of trees. The effect most recognized is mortality of seedlings through herbivory (Stone 1985). However, there are two consequences related to growth form that do not involve mortality. One of these is herbivory that involves removing the apical bud of seedlings. This action releases dominance over the lateral buds, thereby promoting sympodial growth form. There are large numbers of 'ōhi'a seedlings on nursery logs within or at the margins of pastures with a dbh of 0.5 to 2 cm and repeated forking beginning at a height of 10 cm or less. While these seedlings are now the most conspicuous indicator of regeneration, the results of my study indicate that these are unlikely to develop cavities when they reach large size.

The second consequence of cattle ranching, without seedling mortality, is that seedlings are regenerating now in the presence of more light. A significant role of gap dynamics for regeneration within an otherwise intact forest has been identified (Cooray and Mueller-Dombois 1981, Burton and Mueller-Dombois 1984). However, the size of gaps associated with human clearing of forest for cattle ranching, and the destruction of the understory by herbivory, have jointly resulted in seedlings exposed to more light than expected in natural gaps caused by tree falls. Even though cattle have been eliminated at Pua 'Ākala for 10 years, there is a continuing edge effect between pasture and forest and lesser midstory within forests. Light is considered one of the important variables that influences apical dominance over lateral buds at the same level (Brown et al. 1967; Kozlowski and Pallardy

1997a,b). My observations of young 'ōhi'a seedlings indicate that over 90% have forked by the time they reach a height of 0.25 m. It is difficult to identify among existing seedlings those that may become the monopodial giants whose height of first forking can occur as high as 20 m.

Based on this study, regeneration of old-growth 'ōhi'a-koa forests involves growth form as well as presence and size of trees. One of the great challenges to managing restoration and regeneration in disturbed areas is how to mimic the conditions that have produced the monopodial giants in the past. The future of the endangered Hawai'i 'Ākepa depends on implementation of appropriate management of regeneration over wide areas at upper elevations. Provision of artificial cavities may be an appropriate stop-gap management technique. At least five different pairs of birds have used such cavities at Pua 'Ākala and nested successfully. Artificial cavities may be essential if the birds are to persist at high density despite loss of cavity trees and slow regeneration of new ones.

ACKNOWLEDGMENTS

I dedicate this paper to Doug Ackerman, architect of Hakalau Forest Biological Field Station of the University of Hawai'i, with whom I have worked closely for several years. Our mutual interests in wood extend from strength and beauty for construction and finish work to conservation of forests and the animals that depend on trees. I thank J. Lepson for finding most of the 'Ākepa nests, and for helping me document the characteristics of trees used by the birds. P. Hart, S. Fretz, J. Rohrer, M. Burt, and J. Bennett helped gather data in both the inventory and sampling areas. Thanks also to S. Monden for most of the artwork, and to J. Lepson, S. Conant, and J. M. Scott for helpful comments.

Studies in Avian Biology No. 22:185–193, 2001.

DEMOGRAPHIC COMPARISONS BETWEEN HIGH AND LOW DENSITY POPULATIONS OF HAWAI'I 'ĀKEPA

Patrick J. Hart

Abstract. A comparison of demographic traits between large and small populations is a promising tool for revealing proximate causes of rarity in the smaller population. In the Hakalau Forest National Wildlife Refuge on the island of Hawai'i, a "distributional anomaly" for the endangered Hawai'i 'Ākepa, *Loxops coccineus coccineus,* has persisted for at least 15 years in which population densities decrease by over an order of magnitude within 5 km of similar forest at similar elevations. I compared demographic and individual fitness characteristics of 'Ākepa within high and low density populations in relation to hypotheses of regulation. No important differences were detected in annual adult survival, reproductive success, age structure, mean fat level, mean weight, external indicators of disease, or sex ratios. This is evidence that, for the period of this study, populations were being regulated in a similar way. Most importantly, predation and disease do not appear to be affecting the low density site disproportionately, nor have stochastic effects played a role in misshaping population structure at that site. Since both populations have been relatively stable over the past 15 years, these results indicate that differences in environmental carrying capacity, possibly through nest-site availability, maintain current patterns of density.

Key Words: 'Ākepa; demographic comparison; distributional anomaly; *Loxops coccineus coccineus*; small population.

To conserve and manage many threatened populations in a natural setting, it is necessary to understand the factors that determine a population's average abundance and changes in numbers (Smith et al. 1991). As a general rule, population regulation is considered density dependent when birth rate decreases and/or mortality increases with increasing population size (Nicholson 1933, Murray 1994b). For birds, this type of population regulation is often associated with carrying capacity of the environment. Food limitation (Lack 1954, 1966; Klomp 1980, van Balen 1980, Dunning and Brown 1982, Martin 1987, Newton 1991) and nest-site limitation (Cavé 1968, van Balen et al. 1982, Bock et al. 1992, Dobkin et al. 1995) are the most important aspects of carrying capacity. Density dependent mechanisms of population regulation not closely related to carrying capacity include predation (Perrins and Geer 1980, Marcström et al. 1988, Potts and Aebischer 1991) and disease (Anderson and May 1978, Anderson 1979, Hudson 1986). In contrast, population regulation is considered density independent when frequent severe weather or other environmental disturbance is most important in limiting population size (Andrewartha and Birch 1954). For birds, severe weather has often been shown to periodically reduce population densities in otherwise density dependent populations (Kikkawa 1977, Valle and Coulter 1987, Smith et al. 1991).

The Hawai'i 'Ākepa, (*Loxops coccineus coccineus*) is a specialized, long-lived, honeycreeper that was once widespread in 'ōhi'a (*Metrosideros polymorpha*) and 'ōhi'a-koa (*Acacia koa*) forests throughout the island of Hawai'i (Perkins 1903). The bird now exists mainly in four widely separated populations (Scott et al. 1986). Habitat destruction, primarily from cattle ranching, and mosquito (*Culex quinquefasciatus* and *Aedes albopictus*) transmitted disease appear to be the two major factors responsible for the decline of this bird over much of its former range (van Riper et al. 1986, Lepson and Freed 1997). However, huge tracts of apparently suitable 'ōhi'a-koa forest exist at elevations above the upper range of disease carrying mosquitoes in which these birds are rare or absent. This scarcity of birds in what appears to be suitable habitat was first identified as a "distributional anomaly" by the 1986 Hawai'i Forest Bird Survey and has since been corroborated by annual surveys. In the 13,247 ha Hakalau Forest National Wildlife Refuge on the eastern slope of Mauna Kea, the Hawai'i 'Ākepa exists in populations that vary linearly in density by over three orders of magnitude in what qualitatively appears to be the same habitat (Scott et al. 1986). This distribution provides a natural experiment for comparing population structure and dynamics, and aspects of carrying capacity, between sites that appear to vary mainly in density of birds.

The aim of this study was to use a demographic comparison between high and low density populations (1) to examine the relative importance of various nonmutually exclusive hypotheses for regulation or limitation at each site, and (2) to determine if the mechanisms of regulation or limitation are different between sites. An examination of the way demographic characteristics such as survival rate, reproductive

TABLE 1. PREDICTIONS OF FOUR HYPOTHESES FOR MAINTENANCE OF DIFFERENT POPULATION DENSITIES BETWEEN PUA ʻĀKALA AND PEDRO

Hypotheses	Predictions[a]						
	Adult survival rate	Reproductive success	Age-structure	Fat	Weight	Disease	Sex ratio
Food limitation	S	S	S	S	S	S*	S*
Nest-site limitation	S*	S	S*	S*	S*	S*	S*
Predation	L	L	D	S*	S*	S*	D
Disease	L	L	D	L	L	H	S*

[a] (L) lower at Pedro; (H) higher at Pedro; (D) different; (S) similar; (S*) no particular difference is logically specified by hypothesis.

success, age structure, fat levels, weight, disease, and sex ratios are similar or different between sites should point to the cause of rarity of the smaller population. The nonterritorial nature of the ʻĀkepa makes it an appropriate species for this comparison because the demographic effects of resource limitation (environmental carrying capacity) can be distinguished from the mediating effects of territorial behavior. Approximately 10 years of demographic information from the high density site indicate that the ʻĀkepa is a species whose life-history characteristics have been shaped by carrying capacity of the environment. These birds are extremely long lived (>11 yr), have high annual adult survival (0.81) for a 10–12 g passerine, have small clutch sizes (mean = 2), and are highly specialized cavity nesters (Lepson and Freed 1995). In addition, population size in this area has not undergone large fluctuations in density during the past 10–15 years (J. Jeffrey, pers. comm.).

An assumption of this study is that the high density site (Pua ʻĀkala) represents a healthy and relatively stable ʻĀkepa population. Under the food limitation and nest-site limitation hypotheses, birds at the low density site (Pedro) are being regulated in a similar way to those at the high density area, but carrying capacity is lower. A prediction of these hypotheses is that demographic and fitness characters will be similar between sites (Table 1). Since similar limiting factors should affect population structure in similar ways, this would be evidence that the smaller population is a merely a "scaled down" version of the larger and not under a disproportionate external threat. For example, predation and outbreaks of disease have been shown to decrease annual adult survival (Perrins and Geer 1980). Similar annual adult survival between sites would indicate that predation or levels of lethal disease are not greater at Pedro. Alternately, under the predation and disease hypotheses, carrying capacity is similar at each site, but birds at the low density site are being regulated below carrying capacity by predation or disease

(Table 1). For example, lower annual adult survival at Pedro would point to greater levels of predation or disease there. Of course, differences in one demographic parameter must be examined in relation to differences in others. For example, food limitation could also be responsible for lower annual adult survival at one site but not if fat levels and mean weights are similar.

METHODS

This study was conducted from January 1994 through December 1996 at two sites separated by approximately 5 km of contiguous old growth (>200 yr) forest within Hakalau Forest National Wildlife Refuge (Fig. 1). The elevation of the high density site (Pua ʻĀkala) ranges from 1,850 to 1,900 m and the low density site (Pedro) ranges from 1,750 to 1,800 m. Mean annual rainfall was 225 cm during the study period. The canopy at both sites is from 15 to 30 m in height and is comprised almost exclusively of ʻōhiʻa and koa. Over a century of use as a cattle ranch has resulted in a degraded understory dominated by introduced grasses, but native ferns, shrubs, and small trees (primarily *Cheirodendron trigynum* and *Myrsine lessertiana*) are patchily abundant at both sites.

Beginning in January 1994, a system of canopy-level mist nets was established to capture ʻĀkepa. At Pua ʻĀkala, I added 6 mist nets to 15 erected by earlier researchers. At Pedro, I established 20 new nets at similar heights and orientation to foliage as those at Pua ʻĀkala. All individuals captured were extensively measured, examined for external disease, molt, and breeding condition, and given a unique combination of one aluminum U.S. Fish and Wildlife Service band and three plastic color-bands for individual identification in the field. Adult males and females of this sexually dichromatic bird were identified by plumage and presence of a cloacal protuberance or brood patch during the breeding season. Fledgling and hatch-year birds (<9 mo) were identified by plumage and behavior. Second-and third-year males were distinguished by intermediate plumage characteristics following criteria reported by Lepson and Freed (1995). Age class of females could not be accurately determined in the field.

Relative ʻĀkepa density at each site was estimated using mist-net capture rates (number of individuals captured per net hour) and yearly fixed-plot censuses. These censuses were conducted each January–March

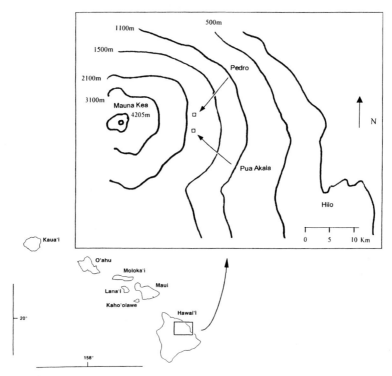

FIGURE 1.   Map of the main Hawaiian Islands with inset showing location of study areas.

within 25-m radius stations set at 100-m intervals along established transects. All adult 'Ākepa seen or heard within 5 min at each station were recorded.

Annual adult survival rate is an important demographic parameter with respect to the food limitation, predation, and disease hypotheses (Table 1). Annual adult survival at both sites was estimated by weighted enumeration (total number of individuals captured or resighted relative to the total number available for detection). 'Ākepa are year-round residents at the study site and have relatively small home ranges (female mean = 3.07 ha, male mean = 4.49 ha; Ralph and Fancy 1994a). Because recapture and resighting probabilities are high for this bird, enumeration estimates of survival are similar to those for the SURVIV (White and Garott 1990) and JOLLY (Brownie et al. 1986) programs (Lepson and Freed 1995).

Annual reproductive success has importance to all four hypotheses being examined here (Table 1). It was estimated as the proportion of hatch-year birds to adults within mixed-species, postbreeding flocks. These flocks usually form soon after 'Ākepa fledge each June and are joined by most individuals, regardless of breeding success (P. Hart, pers. obs.). Flocks were followed from the ground and color-banded individuals were identified with Leica 10 × 42 binoculars. All hatch-year birds within a given area were easily counted because of their conspicuous and highly vocal begging behavior that lasts approximately two months. My estimate of reproductive success therefore is for individuals within two months of fledging. Most subadult and adult 'Ākepa (mean = 8.6, SE = 1.1) in

an average flock (mean = 35, SE = 2.1) were identified within the first one and one-half hours of observation. In contrast, nest-site observation did not yield sufficient information about reproductive success at the population level. Because this technique is so time-consuming, I was never able to adequately monitor more than 12 nests per season.

Age structure is important with respect to the food limitation, predation, and disease hypotheses (Table 1). Age structure may reveal information about present limiting factors or past disturbance within the population. For example, significantly more sub-adult males at Pedro could indicate higher adult mortality there within the past one to three years. Age-structure estimates for males were based on mist-net capture data at both sites and were calculated simply as the proportion of captured subadult and adult males.

For this study, fat level and weight are considered comparative measures of individual fitness. An analysis of the way fat and weight vary between sites may be important with respect to the food limitation and disease hypotheses (Table 1). These measurements were also obtained from mist-net captured birds. Subcutaneous fat deposits within the furcula were categorized from zero to three with zero as no fat visible. Bird weight was measured to the nearest 0.1 g using a 30-g Avinet scale.

External indications (sores, lesions, or missing appendages) of past or active avian pox (*Poxvirus avium*) were noted through thorough examination of feet, legs, and mandibular regions of all captured birds. Blood samples (mean volume = 50 μl) were taken from the

TABLE 2. 'ĀKEPA POPULATION DENSITY ESTIMATES

Method	Pua 'Ākala	Pedro	Ratio P.A./Pedro
Fixed-plot census[a]	1.46/station	0.45/station	3.24
Mist-net[b]	0.0386 captures/net hour	0.0133 captures/net hour	2.9

[a] Fixed plot censuses were conducted at 70 stations per study site.
[b] Mist-netting was conducted for a total of 854 net hours at Pua 'Ākala (P.A.) and 2554 net hours at Pedro.

brachial vein of each captured bird to detect the presence of avian malaria (*Plasmodium relictum*).

Sex ratio estimates were based on capture data at both sites and were calculated as the proportion of males and females captured during the three-year study period.

RESULTS

POPULATION DENSITY ESTIMATES

Both censusing and mist-netting demonstrated that there were approximately three times more 'Ākepa at Pua 'Ākala than at Pedro in the years 1995 and 1996 (Table 2). A similar difference in population size between these two areas was reported by Scott et al. (1986), based on surveys conducted from 1976 to 1983. At that time, 'Ākepa density ranged from 400 to 800 birds/km[2] at Pua 'Ākala and from 100 to 200 birds/km[2] at Pedro. My fixed-plot census information extrapolates to 743 birds/km[2] at Pua 'Ākala and 229 birds/km[2] at Pedro. These data indicate that the general difference in population size between sites has persisted for at least 15 years.

DEMOGRAPHIC CHARACTERISTICS

Annual adult survival was slightly higher at Pedro than at Pua 'Ākala between 1995 and 1996. Forty-three individually marked adults were known to exist in 1995 at Pua 'Ākala and 26 (60%) were resighted the following year in 326 search hours. At Pedro, 21 birds were known in 1995 and 17 (81%) were resighted in 1996 in 299 search hours. This estimate for an-

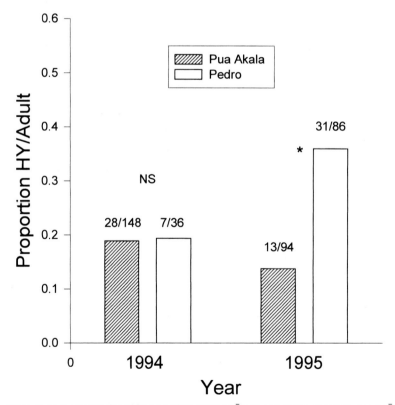

FIGURE 2. Reproductive success for 1994 and 1995 of Pua 'Ākala and Pedro populations of 'Ākepa. Sample sizes are shown above and an asterisk indicates significant difference at P < 0.05.

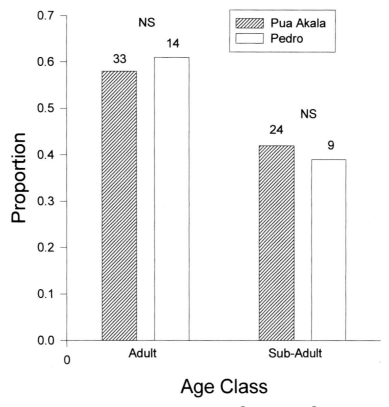

FIGURE 3.   Proportional representation by age class of male 'Ākepa at Pua 'Ākala and Pedro from 1994 to 1996. Sample sizes are shown above. NS indicates no significant difference (P > 0.05).

nual adult survival at Pedro is identical to estimates provided by Lepson and Freed (1995) based on five years of data at Pua 'Ākala using similar techniques. Subsequent searches (320 hours) at Pua 'Ākala in winter and summer of 1997 detected only two additional 'Ākepa known in 1995 and not seen in 1996. My estimate for adult survival at Pua 'Ākala is low compared to past years and appears to reflect an unusually bad year for adults there. No additional 'Ākepa were detected at Pedro in 1997 (150 search hours).

There was no difference in reproductive success between sites in 1994 (χ^2 = 0.005, P = 0.94), but reproductive success was higher at Pedro in 1995 (χ^2 = 12.00, P = 0.001; Fig. 2). For 1996, reproductive success at Pua 'Ākala increased to 0.64 fledglings per adult, the highest value for either site during the study, but there was insufficient information collected from Pedro to make an appropriate comparison. There was no difference in age structure between sites for males for 1994 through 1996 (χ^2 = 0.06, P = 0.80; Fig. 3), suggesting that the balance between adult mortality and recruitment of young males was similar.

The condition of birds was similar between sites. There was little difference in mean fat level for 1995 (two-sample t = −1.68, P = 0.10), but Pedro birds were significantly fatter in 1996 at the low fat levels characteristic of all honeycreepers captured during this study (t = 3.32, P = 0.002; Fig. 4). In addition, there was no difference in mean weight between sites for the years 1995 (t = −1.49, P = 0.14) and 1996 (t = 1.35, P = 0.19; Fig. 5). There was also little external evidence of disease for the years 1994–1996 at either site. At Pua 'Ākala (N = 112), an otherwise healthy adult male was missing a toe, a likely sign of past poxvirus. At Pedro (N = 42) there was no external evidence of present or past disease. A laboratory analysis of blood samples for presence of malaria during this study period has not yet been completed, but prior laboratory tests (N = 47) revealed no instances of infection at Pua 'Ākala (Feldman et al. 1995).

For 1994–1996, there was no difference in

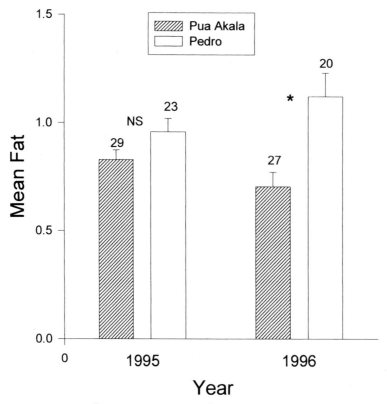

FIGURE 4.   Mean fat level of 'Ākepa sampled at Pua 'Ākala and Pedro during 1995 and 1996. Error bars indicate SE, sample sizes are shown above, and an asterisk indicates a significant difference at P < 0.05.

sex ratio of Hawai'i 'Ākepa between sites (χ^2 = 0.027, P = 0.87; Fig. 6). The 1.13 male to 1 female sex ratio I found for Hawai'i 'Ākepa at Pua 'Ākala agrees well with the 1.14 male to 1 female ratio reported by Lepson and Freed (1995) for Hawai'i 'Ākepa at Pua 'Ākala between the years 1988 and 1993.

DISCUSSION

This study has shown that Hawai'i 'Ākepa populations persist in two locations that differ in density by a ratio of 3:1. In addition, most demographic parameters of the two populations are similar. Elsewhere I will present a demographic model reflecting the stability of the two populations at different densities. Here, I will discuss these findings in relation to four hypotheses that have been proposed to account for regulation or limitation of bird populations. The relatively close proximity and similar elevations of the two sites logically rules out the idea of disproportionately severe weather.

PREDATION AND DISEASE

Given sufficient resources and favorable conditions, 'Ākepa populations theoretically have

the capacity to double each year, or at least to recover relatively quickly after bad years. The mean clutch size for 'Ākepa at Pua 'Ākala (N = 5) is two and second-year birds of both sexes are physiologically capable of reproduction (Lepson and Freed 1995). The sympatric 'Elepaio (*Chasiempis sandwicensis*) also has a mean clutch size of two, and E. VanderWerf (pers. comm.) found population densities of this bird to increase 58% within one year following a year of disease-related high mortality. In addition, most replacement was by known second-year birds from within the population. The fact that the densities of 'Ākepa have not significantly increased in 15 years at Pedro constitutes initial evidence that either the carrying capacity is different there or that cycles of disease or predation act with more frequency there.

Introduced predators, especially rats (*Rattus rattus, R. norvegicus,* and *R. exulans*) are thought to be responsible for the reduction and possible extinction of numerous native Hawaiian birds (Atkinson 1977, Berger 1981). Introduced avian disease, especially malaria and poxvirus, have played perhaps the largest role in shaping

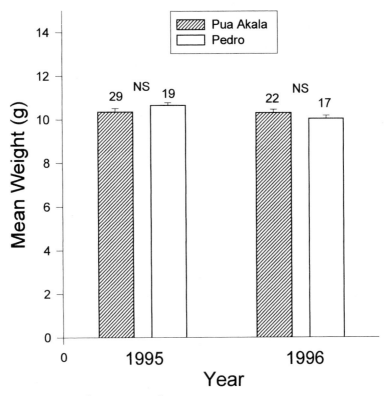

FIGURE 5.   Mean weight of 'Ākepa at Pua 'Ākala and Pedro during 1995 and 1996. Error bars indicate SE, sample sizes are shown above. NS indicates no significant difference (P > 0.05).

the present distributions of native Hawaiian forest birds (Warner 1968, van Riper et al. 1986, Jarvi et al. *this volume*). It is not unreasonable to assume then that predation and/or disease are largely responsible for the anomalous distribution of 'Ākepa within Hakalau Forest NWR. Indeed, data from the Biological Resources Division of the U.S. Geological Survey show the refuge to contain some of the highest rat densities ever reported for a natural area (S. Fancy, pers. comm.). While rats have been shown to be efficient nest predators, the extent to which they prey on adult forest passerines in Hawaii is still unclear. Under the predation hypothesis, higher levels of rat predation at Pedro are responsible for lower 'Ākepa density there. This would be reflected through lower annual adult survival, reproductive success, and possibly a different population age structure. If levels of disease were greater at Pedro, annual adult survival, reproductive success, age structure, fat levels, and weight might all be lower. With a few exceptions, the demographic data presented here show great similarity between the high and low density populations and thus fail to support the predation or disease hypotheses.

Annual adult survival and reproductive success at Pedro were similar to or higher than at Pua 'Ākala. The 81% adult survival rate I found for Pedro is identical to mean annual survival at Pua 'Ākala (Lepson and Freed 1995). Reproductive success was similar in 1994 and greater at Pedro in 1995, but not outside of the known range for Pua 'Ākala (1996 reproductive success at Pua 'Ākala = 0.64). The high adult survival rate and similarities in reproductive success and age structure at Pedro reduce the importance of rat predation to the maintenance of different population densities. The similarities in adult survival, reproductive success, age structure, fat, weight, and the near complete absence of external indications of disease indicate that within the past three years, disease has not affected the low density site disproportionately.

FOOD AND NEST-SITE LIMITATION

The apparently persistent difference in population size coupled with the similarity in demographic characteristics supports the hypothesis that the two populations are being regulated in a similar, density dependent way. The most likely way to have relatively long-term stability in

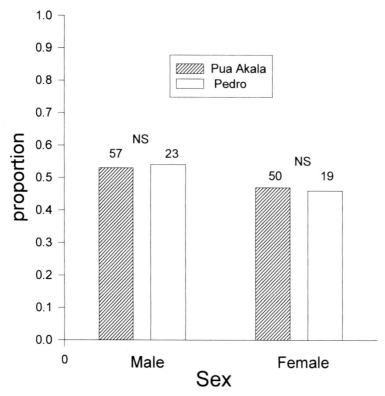

FIGURE 6.   Proportion of male and female ʻĀkepa captures at Pua ʻĀkala and Pedro from 1994 to 1996. Sample sizes are shown above. NS indicates no significant difference (P > 0.05).

population size and similar demographic characteristics between years is if the carrying capacity, in terms of food or nest-site availability, is different between sites. Based on available information, it appears that the Pedro population is a "scaled down" version of the one at Pua ʻĀkala. This idea seems counterintuitive because there is little apparent qualitative difference in habitat between sites.

It is possible that the sites vary in subtle but ecologically important ways. For example, differences in tree age, architecture, or canopy cover might affect abundance of arthropods, the primary source of food for ʻĀkepa. However, the food hypothesis was not supported by weight or fat levels. Nest-site availability may also differ between sites. ʻĀkepa are the only Hawaiian honeycreeper known to nest in natural cavities obligately (Freed et al. 1987b). Numerous studies have shown that nest sites are often in short supply for hole-nesting birds (Von Haartman 1956, Perrins 1979, Gustafsson 1988). All known ʻĀkepa nests (N = 98) have been located in cavities or holes in large, old growth ʻōhiʻa or koa trees (minimum 60 cm dbh; Lepson and Freed 1995). Furthermore, growth form (single

versus multiple trunks) is an important determinant of nest-site availability in ʻōhiʻa trees; appropriate cavities almost exclusively form in single-trunk trees (Freed this volume). Since soil type, soil age, or degree of previous human disturbance may vary between sites, it is possible that the abundance of large koa, and large single-trunk ʻōhiʻa varies also. Under the nest-site limitation hypothesis, ʻĀkepa density at each site is determined by the availability of nest cavities. A prediction of this hypothesis is that density of ʻĀkepa varies in direct proportion to availability of large trees with cavities. Preliminary data support this prediction. Based on intensive habitat sampling in more than 60 15-m radius quadrats at each site, there are three times more large ʻōhia trees (>60 cm dbh) at Pua ʻĀkala than at Pedro (P. Hart and L. Freed, unpubl. data). A relevant way to evaluate nest-site limitation would be to determine the proportion of "floaters" at each site or the response to artificial cavities. The nonterritorial nature of the ʻĀkepa makes it difficult to identify floaters. There has been limited response at each site to artificial cavities. This is inconsistent with other cavity nesting birds studied elsewhere. Von

Haartman (1971) and Copeyon et al. (1991) found that experimental increases in nest cavities may dramatically increase population size of temperate, hole-nesting species. However, artificial cavities set up for passerines in neotropical forests have also been sparingly used (J. Terborgh, pers. comm.).

How viable is the Pedro population? Theoretical predictions (MacArthur and Wilson 1967b) and empirical evidence (Terborgh and Winter 1980, Belovsky 1987, Pimm et al. 1988) show that the dynamics of small populations are often different from those of larger populations, mainly because smaller populations are more vulnerable to stochastic environmental and demographic perturbations (Shaffer 1981, Gilpin and Soulé 1986). If population level characteristics such as sex ratios are greatly different between sites, this could indicate that the population has fallen to the critical level at which stochastic events have begun to misshape population structure. Small population size itself would be implicated in the maintenance of low densities, even if the original factor responsible for the decline (e.g., disease) is no longer operating. That there is no difference in sex ratios between sites indicates that the Pedro population is not so small that stochastic processes have begun to misshape population structure. It would be of interest to examine how sex ratios and other demographic characteristics might vary in an even smaller, more isolated population of 'Ākepa.

ACKNOWLEDGMENTS

I thank L. A. Freed for advice through all stages of this project and J. Lepson for his pioneering work on the Pua 'Ākala population. I also thank the U.S. Fish and Wildlife Service and the staff of Hakalau Forest National Wildlife Refuge, in particular R. Wass and J. Jeffrey for their support of research at the refuge. For assistance in the field I thank E. VanderWerf, J. Bennett, J. Rohrer, S. Fretz, M. Burt, M. Ono, and S. DeLima. Financial support was provided by a grant from the John D. and Catherine T. MacArthur Foundation (to L. Freed, R. Cann, and S. Conant), the EECB program at the University of Hawai'i, and a Maybelle Roth Scholarship from the ARCS foundation at the University of Hawai'i.

Studies in Avian Biology No. 22:194–201, 2001.

BREEDING CHARACTERISTICS OF THE 'ĀKOHEKOHE ON EAST MAUI

ELLEN M. VANGELDER AND THOMAS B. SMITH

Abstract. The breeding biology of the endangered 'Ākohekohe (*Palmeria dolei*) was studied from 1992 to 1993 in the Waikamoi Reserve on east Maui. Nesting success was examined in relationship to habitat characteristics, inter- and intraspecific interactions, and other biotic and abiotic factors. Twenty-four nests were examined and all were constructed in 'ōhi'a (*Metrosideros polymorpha*) trees between 1,655 and 1,836 m elevation. Nesting occurred during months of high rainfall, January through late June. Nesting success was higher in 1992, when weather was drier and 'ōhi'a flowering was believed to be more profuse. The number of fledglings produced per successful nest was similar between years. The majority of nest failures occurred during the nestling stage. Chases directed at non-conspecifics were observed more frequently at nests that failed than at successful nests during 1993. 'Apapane (*Himatione sanguinea*) were the target of 46% of chases, while chasing of intraspecifics was rare and no chases involving nonnative species were observed. Whereas predation, especially by Short-eared Owl (*Asio flammeus sandwichensis*), and weather were implicated in some nest failures, further research will be required to determine their importance. Although 'ōhi'a nectar was found to be the single most important food source, the variety of plants on which 'Ākohekohe were found to forage stresses the importance of maintaining undisturbed forest understories and subcanopies. To reduce the extinction risk of 'Ākohekohe populations, restoration of existing habitats is critical.

Key Words: 'Ākohekohe; breeding biology; endangered birds; Hawai'i; Hawaiian honeycreeper; *Palmeria dolei.*

The Hawaiian honeycreepers (subfamily Drepanidinae), endemic to the Hawaiian Islands, represent perhaps the most celebrated example of an avian adaptive radiation in the world (Freed et al. 1987a, Tarr and Fleischer 1995). They also comprise a large proportion of one of the world's most critically endangered avifaunas. At least 14 species, known only from subfossils, went extinct after Polynesian settlement (circa 400 A.D.) but before European contact in 1778 (Olson and James 1982b, James and Olson 1991). Less than 75% of the historically known species remain today (Scott et al. 1986). Of these, the 'Ākohekohe or Crested Honeycreeper (*Palmeria dolei*) is one of 13 drepanids listed as endangered (Scott et al. 1986, Pyle 1990). Once endemic to the islands of Maui and Moloka'i, the 'Ākohekohe is now found only in the eastern, high-elevation rain forests on Maui. Like most honeycreepers, numerous factors threaten the remaining population (Smith and Fancy 1998), including habitat loss and alteration by humans and alien species (Scott et al. 1986), competition with alien species (Mountainspring and Scott 1985), and disease (Warner 1968, van Riper et al. 1986, Atkinson et al. 1995).

Maintaining viable 'Ākohekohe populations will depend on sound knowledge of their life-history characteristics and ecology. Much of the available information is anecdotal, consisting of observations made by naturalists over the last century (Perkins 1903). While recent research has provided information on population size, distribution (Scott et al. 1986), and competition

(Mountainspring and Scott 1985, Carothers 1986a), information on the breeding biology is lacking.

Here we report observations of the first recorded nests of the 'Ākohekohe. We describe and document its breeding biology, particularly those aspects that potentially will be useful in managing the remaining populations. These include: nest and nest-site selection, nesting success and timing of nesting in relation to biotic and abiotic factors, and other aspects of breeding that may be important in their conservation.

METHODS

STUDY AREA

Fieldwork was conducted for 10 months (10 March–27 June 1992, and 3 February–20 July 1993), in The Nature Conservancy's Waikamoi Reserve. This 2,100 ha reserve is located on the north slope of Haleakalā Volcano between 1,400 and 2,600 m elevation. The 25 ha study site is located between 1,640 and 1,880 m elevation in the western portion of the reserve and includes 3 km of foot trails (VanGelder 1996). Vegetation of the study area consists primarily of wet forest (Kitayama and Mueller-Dombois 1992) and 'ōhi'a (*Metrosideros polymorpha*) comprises >25% of the canopy cover (Scott et al. 1986).

Precipitation on Haleakalā's north slope is largely determined by prevailing trade winds and temperature inversions (Lyons 1979). The temperature inversion occurs between approximately 1,900 and 2,000 m elevation (Kitayama and Mueller-Dombois 1992) and limits the up-slope movement of clouds. Below the inversion adiabatic cooling produces up to 7,000 mm of annual rainfall (Giambelluca et al. 1986), making the windward slopes of Haleakalā one of the wettest places on earth. The greatest rainfall generally occurs from October to April, when trade winds are less frequent and storm related rainfall is more common (Giambelluca et al. 1986); however, seasonality in wet areas is less pronounced than in dry areas. The annual rainfall regime of wet windward areas usually consists of three seasonal peaks. At west Honomanū (elevation 915 m) on Haleakalā's windward slope, peaks in rainfall occur during December, March–April, and August (400 to 650 mm), with lows during June, October, and January (300 to 400 mm; Giambelluca et al. 1986). Rainfall during both years was considerably below the annual average and coincided with an El Niño period. Annual rainfall during 1992 and 1993 was 892 mm and 1,094 mm, (34% and 25% below average), respectively (U.S. Department of Commerce 1993).

NEST CHARACTERISTICS

Nest searches were conducted throughout the study and, while not quantified in 1992, exceeded 380 person-hours in 1993 (VanGelder 1996). To identify factors important in nesting success, seven nest-placement variables were recorded, including species of nest tree, nest and nest tree height, direction of the nest from the trunk, percentage of foliage cover above the nest, nest location in the canopy, and orientation of twigs supporting the nest (see VanGelder 1996). In addition, broad habitat characteristics at nest sites were estimated by sampling a 16-m radius circular plot centered on the nest tree. The percentage canopy and subcanopy cover were estimated at 1, 8, and 16 meters in each cardinal direction by holding a 0.5 m diameter metal ring overhead at arm's length. Trees >12 m were considered canopy, 4.5–12 m subcanopy, and <4.5 m understory. Estimates for each plot were averaged to obtain mean percentage of cover for the canopy and subcanopy. Percentage of cover of seven native understory plants on which 'Ākohekohe are known to forage (e.g., *Myrsine* sp., *Melicope* sp., *Vaccinium reticulatum*, *Rubus hawaiiensis*, *Styphelia tameiameiae*, *Broussaisia arguta*, *Cheirodendron trigynum*) were estimated within 1-m radius subplots located at 8 m and 16 m in each of the four cardinal directions from the trunk of the nest tree. In addition, the number of canopy trees (not including the nest tree) within the nest plot, their condition (live or dead) and the diameter at breast height (dbh) of each tree in the plot were measured to obtain a mean plot dbh. Nest tree dbh and distance from the trunk of the nest tree to the nearest canopy tree within the plot were also measured. Elevation of the nest tree was recorded at the trunk using an altimeter, and slope was measured from the trunk of the nest tree to a point at least 16 m downslope using a clinometer.

To identify important factors in nest-site selection, we compared variables from known nest trees with those from 18 randomly chosen trees (VanGelder 1996). Sites were generated such that an equal number of random sites were located at low (<1,730 m), middle (1,731–1,790 m) and high (1,790–1,850 m) elevations to control for elevational differences.

BEHAVIOR, ABUNDANCE, AND 'ŌHI'A FLOWERING

'Ākohekohe nests were observed daily or every other day, for one to four hours between 0530 and 1900.

Observations were conducted using binoculars or a 10 × spotting scope from a concealed location at least 20 m from the nest. Because nests were located in the crowns of trees and observers could not see into the nest, various nest stages were approximated from the behavior of adults (VanGelder 1996). These behaviors included building (carrying nesting material), incubation (sitting on nest for extended periods), brooding (actively feeding, removing fecal sacs, etc.), and fledging (see VanGelder 1996 for details). The period that a nest was active was determined by backdating from the day of fledging or, if the nest did not fledge young, from the estimated hatch date. 'Ākohekohe chase behavior was recorded two to three times a week at selected nests for a total of 19 and 104 hours during 1992 and 1993, respectively. For each chase we recorded number, species, and age of individuals chased. A chase was defined as an adult rapidly flying toward an individual(s) of any species in an aggressive manner and occurring within 30 m of the nest. Foraging behavior was quantified during 1993 by recording all foraging observed and included recording plant species, substrate (e.g., leaf or flower), and location (e.g., canopy, subcanopy, understory). Only foraging observations at least three minutes apart were used in analysis to minimize autocorrelation of behavior on the same bird.

Relative number of adults and juveniles were estimated from surveys in 1993. Approximately 3 km of trails were walked biweekly from 11 March to 20 July by one of two trained observers at a rate of approximately 0.54 km/hr. When an 'Ākohekohe was sighted, it was observed for 5 min and its behavior was recorded, as well as the time, age (juvenile or adult), location, and weather (VanGelder 1996). After 5 min an observer would then walk approximately 90 m before searching for another individual.

'Ōhi'a flower abundance was estimated twice during February and once a month thereafter during 1993. Estimates of flower abundance were made at 80 fixed locations, 30 m apart. The canopy in flower was visually estimated from a randomly chosen quarter of a 30-m diameter circular plot centered on a fixed location on the trail. After the subplot was selected, it was used for all subsequent sampling. Flowering was categorized visually as 1 = trace (<1%), 2 = low (1–5%), 3 = medium (6–25%), and 4 = high (26–50%).

RESULTS

NESTING SUCCESS

Nesting occurred during months of high rainfall, from January through late June, with peak nesting earlier in 1993 (March) than in 1992 (May; Fig. 1). Twenty-four nests were found during the study, 11 in 1992 and 13 in 1993 (Table 1). From these nests a total of 20 chicks successfully fledged. Nesting success was twice as high in 1992 when weather was drier and 'ōhi'a flowering was believed to be more profuse (VanGelder 1996) than in 1993 (Table 1). The number of fledglings produced per successful nest, however, was similar between years.

Of the nine nest failures, the majority oc-

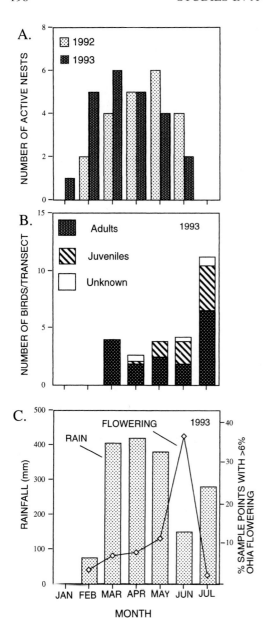

TABLE 1. SUMMARY OF 'ĀKOHEKOHE NEST PRODUC-
TIVITY IN WAIKAMOI RESERVE, MAUI, FOR 1992 AND
1993 (NUMBERS IN PARENTHESES ARE PERCENTAGES)

	Year		
	1992	1993	Total
Nests	11	13	24
Successful nests[a]	8 (73)	4 (31)	12 (50)
Failed nests[a]	2 (18)	7 (54)	9 (38)
Abandoned	1	1	1
Unknown	1	1	2
Nesting success[b]	0.80	0.36	0.57
Fledging success[c]	1.30	0.64	0.95
Fledglings/successful nest	1.63	1.75	1.67

[a] Number of successful versus failed nests approached significance between years (Fisher's Exact test, P = 0.056).
[b] Proportion of nests that produced young out of total number of nests
of known outcome.
[c] Number of fledglings produced out of the total number of nests of
known outcome.

meus sandwichensis) were seen in the nest vicinity either on the day of failure, or within 48
hours prior, and owls were observed flying within 10 m of the nest at two of these nests. Owls
were observed on the study area on 32 (21%) of
151 days during 1993, often flying low over the
canopy. Although we never found remains of
nestlings, we did find remains of an adult 'Ākohekohe on the ground near a stump where an
owl had been sighted.

Three failures (two during the nestling stage,
one during incubation) were associated with periods of high winds and rain. In one case we
observed a nest slowly disintegrating over several days until only a small corner remained.
One of two chicks disappeared during this period, while the other remained perched on a remnant piece of nest and eventually fledged. One
nest failed after 16–18 days of incubation. The
protracted incubation period suggests that this
failure could have resulted from embryo death
or infertility.

Renesting occurred on two occasions, each at
different localities. In 1992, a pair fledged two
young from one nest, and within 48 hours after
the last chick fledged, a second nest was discovered in a tree approximately 8 m away from the
first nest tree. The fledglings from the first nest
were observed begging from the adults as the
adults built the second nest. In 1993, a single
pair apparently nested three times and could
have been responsible for half of all fledged
young produced for the year. For this pair, the
first nest failed after at least 16 days of incubation, and within two days adults built a second
nest in a tree approximately 17 m from the first
nest tree. Twelve days after two young fledged
from the second nest, adults built a third nest

FIGURE 1. Seasonal trends in: (A) monthly nesting
activity of 'Ākohekohe during 1992 and 1993. Active
nests are those in incubation or nestling stage. (B) Relative abundance of 'Ākohekohe as determined by transects, and (C) rainfall and 'ōhi'a flowering. No rainfall
data were collected during January, and no abundance
data were collected for January or February (see
VanGelder 1996).

curred during the nestling stage. Three occurred
when chicks were 5 to 8 days old, three at 12
to 14 days old, and one at 18 days old. At three
of the failed nests, Short-eared Owl (*Asio flam-*

TABLE 2. 'ĀKOHEKOHE NEST PLACEMENT CHARACTERISTICS IN WAIKAMOI PRESERVE, MAUI (DATA FROM 1992 AND 1993 ARE COMBINED)

Characteristic		N	χ^2	P
Location in forest	Canopy	23		
	Subcanopy	1	20.17	0.001
Location within canopy	Top 20%	14		
(of nest tree)	Mid 40%	8		
	Bottom 40%	1	11.14	0.004
Estimated	0–33%	0		
foliage cover over nest cup	34–66%	1		
	67–99%	21	38.45	0.001
Orientation of twigs	Vertical	13		
supporting nest	Horizontal	10	0.39	0.532
Canopy quadrant in	NE	9		
which nest is located	NW	8		
	SE	6		
	SW	0	8.55	0.036

within 6 m and in the same tree as the first nest. Fledglings were seen begging from an adult during building and could be observed near the nest tree through fledging of the third nest. Adults often chased these juveniles from the nest tree and adjacent areas. Other evidence of renesting is more circumstantial but suggests that renesting was widespread. Evidence includes the discovery of new nests in the immediate area of recently fledged or failed nests (N = 2), observations of recently fledged or juvenile birds approaching active nests (N = 2), and repeated observations of pairs of juvenile birds observed in the immediate area of an active nest (N = 3).

Chases directed at non-conspecifics were observed more frequently at nests that failed than at successful nests during 1993. For the 11 nests monitored, 0.96 chases/hr were recorded at failed nests, whereas the chase rate at successful nests was only 0.06 chases/hr (χ^2 = 25.62, P < 0.001). This suggests that chases may have been a factor leading to nest failure; however, determining the relative importance of chases on nesting is complicated by the fact that in 1992 when nesting success was higher, we observed a much greater rate of chasing (3.0 chases/hr). All nests monitored for chases in 1992 were successful, so comparisons with failed nests for this year were not possible.

'Ākohekohe chases for both years (N = 123) were directed at four native species, 'Apapane (*Himatione sanguinea*), 'I'iwi (*Vestiaria coccinea*), Hawai'i 'Amakihi (*Hemignathus virens*), and Maui Creeper (*Paroreomyza montana*), although the species could not be determined in 49% of the chases. 'Apapane was the target of 46% of chases, the highest proportion, while chasing of intraspecifics was recorded rarely. We observed no chases involving nonnative species.

NEST-SITE SELECTION

All nests were constructed in 'ōhi'a trees between 1,655–1,836 m elevation. The distance to the nearest nest ranged from zero (in the case of renesting) to 263 m. However, the majority of nests (83%) were constructed within 80 m of the nearest nest, producing a clustered distribution. All but one nest were located in the canopies of large 'ōhi'a trees in the top 20% of the canopy and had dense foliage above the nest (Table 2). The one exception was located in a small 'ōhi'a on the edge of a dieback area where few trees were taller than 12 m. Mean nest height was 15.33 m (N = 13, SE = 0.55).

Random sites and nest sites were significantly different for 4 of the 15 habitat variables (Table 3). Canopy cover, percentage of *Myrsine* sp., percentage of living trees, and tree density were all significantly higher at nest sites than at random sites. The relative importance of any single variable is difficult to determine because all variables except percentage of *Myrsine* sp., were positively correlated (r_s < 0.6, P < 0.001), and sample size was insufficient for multivariate analyses. Nevertheless, results suggest that 'Ākohekohe selected nest trees with greater canopy cover in denser stands of live trees where the percentage of ground cover of *Myrsine* sp. was high.

Subcanopy cover, slope, and elevation were significantly lower at successful nests than failed nests (Table 4). This suggests that birds that chose to nest in areas with sparser subcanopies, on sites with less slope, and at slightly lower elevations were more successful. However, as was the case for nest-site selection, all variables are significantly correlated (r_s < 0.5, P < 0.01). No differences were found between successful

TABLE 3. SIGNIFICANT HABITAT VARIABLES (MEAN ± SE) COMPARING RANDOM SITES (N = 10) WITH NEST SITES (N = 16) OF 'ĀKOHEKOHE

Variable	Nest Site	Random Site	U[a]	P
Percentage canopy cover	28.16 ± 2.01	21.21 ± 2.24	117	0.051
Percentage *Myrsine* sp. cover	2.64 ± 0.49	0.73 ± 0.38	133	0.005
Percentage living trees	9.50 ± 1.04	5.80 ± 1.01	124	0.021
Number canopy trees	10.56 ± 0.97	6.00 ± 1.01	133	0.005

[a] U = Mann-Whitney U statistic.

and unsuccessful nests with respect to their location within the canopy of the nest tree (Fischer's exact test, N = 20, P > 0.10), or orientation of twigs supporting the nest (Fisher's exact test, N = 20, P > 0.1).

NESTING PERIODS

Nest building

Building activity was recorded at seven nests. Although birds were not individually marked, it appeared that one adult of each pair did the majority of the building, and the second adult was often present and commonly called near the nest. Material was collected from up to 50 m from the nest (VanGelder 1996). Nests were cup shaped and constructed of twigs, lichens, and mosses. Two nests collected after fledging in 1992 measured 104 mm and 65 mm in depth, and 153 and 180 mm in diameter, respectively. The deeper nest consisted of two distinct layers, suggesting a second nest had been built on top of an existing nest. Both nests were deposited in the Bernice P. Bishop Museum (Catalogue No. BPBM 1992.223).

Laying and incubation

Date for egg laying and incubation could only be estimated from behavior patterns exhibited by birds at nests. Irregular nest visits occurred one to two days prior to onset of incubation. This period of irregular visitation was assumed to be the laying period. The incubation period was recorded at seven nests and varied from 14–16 days, but the period could only be estimated because of the difficulty in determining when egg

laying had ceased and incubation had begun. Incubation bouts typically lasted 20 to 30 minutes, separated by absences of 1–10 minutes. It appeared as though one bird, possibly the female, did almost all of the incubating. During this period, what was presumed to be the male fed the female both on and off the nest.

Nestling period

The complete nestling period was observed at six nests and lasted 20 to 27 days (Fig. 1). Young were first visible at approximately 6–8 days of age. At this time they were partially covered with white or gray down. One 14-day-old nestling collected off the ground in 1993 had feathers half emerged from their shafts (VanGelder 1996). Plumage at fledging was slate gray with brown nape feathers. During the first week after hatching, adults were occasionally observed removing what appeared to be fecal sacs from the nest. By 6–8 days of age, chicks ejected feces over the side of the nest. Both adults fed chicks by regurgitation. During the last week of the nestling stage, chicks sometimes exhibited behavior characteristic of foraging and were seen probing 'ōhi'a flowers and foliage near the nest with their bills.

Fledging and postfledging

The earliest and latest fledging dates recorded over the two years were 3 March 1993 and 27 June 1992. Fledging was a gradual process. Chicks initially ventured a few centimeters from the nest, then gradually increased the time and distance. A nestling was described as fledged

TABLE 4. SIGNIFICANT HABITAT VARIABLES (MEAN ± SE) COMPARING SUCCESSFUL NESTS (N = 9) WITH UNSUCCESSFUL NESTS (N = 9) OF 'ĀKOHEKOHE

Variable	Successful	Unsuccessful	U[a]	P
Percent subcanopy cover	14.41 ± 1.15	20.48 ± 2.09	14	0.034
Slope	11.94 ± 1.54	17.20 ± 1.28	14	0.019
Elevation	1710.44 ± 9.19	1748.65 ± 14.29	15	0.024

[a] U = Mann-Whitney U statistic.

when it moved more than 3 m from the nest. Postfledging activity was noted at three nests. During the first few days, fledglings perched or explored via climbing or fluttering in the canopy, remaining within approximately 40 m of the nest, and often perching under dense leaf clusters usually within a few meters, and sometimes a few centimeters, from a sibling. During this period, fledglings were fed regularly by the parents. Five to six days after fledging, young were observed aggressively pursuing adults and begging (VanGelder 1996). By 14 days after fledging, young foraged on their own but still uttered persistent begging calls while pursuing and begging from adults. Throughout this period, the adults occasionally fed the young birds but also frequently chased them for short distances. The oldest fledgling observed being fed by an adult was at least 33 days old. Two young were observed in the nest area for up to 32 days, and one young up to 41 days after it fledged.

IMPORTANCE OF 'ŌHI'A

Percent 'ōhi'a flowering varied significantly through the 1993 season (χ^2 = 87.937, df = 12, P < 0.001), showing a steady increase between February and May, a high peak in June, and marked decrease in July (Fig. 1). The abundance of juveniles and adults peaked in July, which was after nesting had ceased and one month after peak 'ōhi'a flowering (Fig. 1). Juvenile and adult abundance in July was, respectively, two and three times higher than in June.

Although 'Ākohekohe were observed foraging on 13 plant species (VanGelder 1996), the majority (75%) of the 1,222 observations were on 'ōhi'a, either taking nectar from flowers or feeding on invertebrates from leaves in the canopy. Across all species 63% of foraging events were on nectar from flowers and 46% foraged on invertebrates on leaves. Among all food sources, 'ōhi'a was the most important for both adults and juveniles in all months (χ^2 = 52.170, df = 5, P < 0.001 and χ^2 = 21.755, df = 2, P < 0.001, respectively). In addition to 'ōhi'a, other foods were seasonally important for adults. For example, during February, 78% of feeding observations were on kōlea (*Myrsine* sp.), and in March 91% were on either kōlea or 'alani (*Pelea* sp.). In addition, 'ākala (*Rubus* sp.) flowers appear to be important sources of nectar in June (VanGelder 1996). Thus, these plants, in addition to 'ōhi'a, represent important foods or substrates for foraging during the breeding season.

DISCUSSION

In many respects the breeding characteristics we recorded for 'Ākohekohe are similar to those described for other Hawaiian honeycreepers (Baldwin 1953, Eddinger 1970, van Riper 1980a, Pletschet and Kelly 1990, Morin 1992a, Ralph and Fancy 1994b, Lepson and Freed 1995). There is a protracted breeding season in which the fledging period broadly overlaps with peak 'ōhi'a flowering, a pattern similar to that reported for the 'I'iwi and 'Apapane (Baldwin 1953, Eddinger 1970, Ralph and Fancy 1994b). Although we can not directly compare nesting success with other studies of honeycreepers because we could not determine clutch size or hatching success, the level of nesting success we estimated is within the range of that for other drepanids (Eddinger 1970, van Riper et al. 1982, van Riper 1987, Pletschet and Kelly 1990, Morin 1992a).

Use of nonnectar food sources during the nesting cycle, especially between February and May, likely reflected the need for protein during egg production and nestling growth (Ricklefs 1974, Walsberg 1983). Our results support historical observations by Perkins (1903), who pointed out the importance of species other than 'ōhi'a for foraging during certain times of year. Although we found 'ōhi'a to be the single most important food source, the variety of plants on which 'Ākohekohe forage stresses the importance of maintaining undisturbed forest understories and subcanopies.

A number of authors have suggested that honeycreepers move in search of flowering 'ōhi'a trees and track 'ōhi'a flowering over the season (Baldwin 1953, MacMillen and Carpenter 1980). Carpenter (1976b) found a two week lag between the onset of high 'ōhi'a flowering and the influx of 'Apapane, but found no such lag for 'I'iwis. Our data for 1993 strongly suggest such a lag between peak flowering and 'Ākohekohe abundance. Since this period also coincides with fledging and the end of nesting, it is unclear whether the dramatic increase in 'Ākohekohe numbers could have been due in part to greater visibility of resident adults and recently fledged offspring. It seems somewhat doubtful, however, that these factors could completely explain the threefold increase in adults from June to July. Other evidence for the movement of 'Ākohekohe into the study area is supported by the occurrence in July of individuals with vocalizations typical of the populations in Hanawī, on the far side of Haleakalā crater (VanGelder 1996). These data are also consistent with assertions by others suggesting 'Ākohekohe may show seasonal movements (Conant 1981).

Despite small sample sizes, breeding success of 'Ākohekohe approached being significantly different between years. Although we have no quantitative information on 'ōhi'a flowering in

1992, flowering was apparently greater in 1992 (E. VanGelder, pers. obs.) and might explain the higher breeding success that year. Nectar availability has been shown to be a limiting factor influencing honeycreeper breeding success (van Riper 1984, 1987) and has been shown to be a limiting resource for larger nectarivores (Carpenter and MacMillen 1980, Pimm and Pimm 1982). Assessing the importance of 'ōhi'a flowering is difficult, however, because flowering is patchy and nectar quality and quantity are unpredictable (Carpenter 1976b). Further research over multiple years of differing resource levels will be needed to fully evaluate the relationship between 'ōhi'a flowering and reproductive success in the 'Ākohekohe.

In addition, weather, especially rain and associated high winds, may influence nesting success in given years. For the Hawaiian nectarivores, resources and weather are closely coupled (Carpenter 1976b, Carpenter and MacMillen 1976). First, storms have been implicated in breeding failures (Baldwin 1953, Eddinger 1970, Morin 1992a). Rain imposes thermal stress on adults and nestlings, and wind dislodges nests from trees and young from nests, as we found in 1993. Second, the typically cold, wet environment of Hawaiian high-altitude forests results in high energy requirements, and rain causes low nectar production rates and dilutes nectar in 'ōhi'a (Carpenter 1976b). Thus, rainy periods place higher energetic and foraging demands on individuals, especially adults feeding nestlings. It is interesting that although rainfall was greater in 1993 than in 1992, it was still 25% below normal. This begs the question of what breeding success is like in a year receiving average rainfall. Other research on the breeding biology of the 'Ākohekohe by the Biological Resources Division of the U.S. Geological Survey may shed light on this important question.

While we found no evidence of interference competition between 'Ākohekohe and nonnative species, we did find such evidence with the 'Apapane. 'Ākohekohe chased 'Apapane at significantly higher rates at nests that subsequently failed than they did at successful nests, suggesting possible negative fitness consequences associated with chasing. Our observations are consistent with those of other researchers who recorded interference competition between 'Ākohekohe and 'Apapane (Perkins 1903, Carothers 1986a). However, determining whether 'Apapane populations have negative effects on overall breeding success of 'Ākohekohe will require further work. Nests observed in 1992 were successful, although chase rates were three times those of failed nests in 1993. However, the nests we chose to observe for chasing behavior in

1992 were all successful, not allowing a comparison of chase rates at failed and successful nests for the year. It is possible that the variability in chase behavior and its consequences depend on resource availability (Carpenter and MacMillen 1976), and future work will be required to determine this. Nevertheless, it is intriguing that the 'Apapane, the native species that is most resistant to avian malaria, is responsible for the highest levels of interference competition (C. Atkinson, pers. comm.). This raises the question of whether 'Apapane populations are greater than they were historically, and, if so, whether they are having negative impacts on other native species.

Many variables such as proximity to food resources, concealment from predators, protection from weather, and predator and competitor detection may play important roles in nest-site selection and nesting success (Calder 1973, van Riper 1984; Martin 1987, 1988; van Riper et al. 1993, With 1994). Our results show nonrandom nest placement with respect to several habitat variables. Pairs nest in denser stands of living trees where the canopy cover is higher. This preference could provide either greater shelter for nests, concealment from predators, or both. Successful nests had more open subcanopies, were on less extreme slopes, and occurred at slightly lower elevations than unsuccessful nests. However, what other factors may correlate with these variables is unclear. It could be that these variables are simply correlated with important microhabitat variables we did not measure. van Riper et al. (1993) found that 'Amakihi on the southwest slope of Mauna Kea nested predominantly on the southwest side of tree canopies. They reasoned that this was due to microhabitat influences on ambient temperature and associated advantages in thermoregulation. In contrast, we found 'Ākohekohe nested predominantly in the northern sector of tree canopies (never in the southwest quarter) on the north facing slope of Haleakalā and, thus, directly exposed to the northeast trade winds and accompanying precipitation.

We found only circumstantial evidence that predation may affect breeding success. While predation is the primary cause of nest failure for many bird species (Skutch 1985, Martin 1993), the possible impact of predation is difficult to assess in this study. We found circumstantial evidence that Short-eared Owls may have taken some nestlings, but the overall affect of this predation on breeding success is unclear. Although we found no evidence that alien mammals were preying upon 'Ākohekohe nests, the probability of detecting such predation in this study was very low.

CONSERVATION PRIORITIES

To reduce the extinction risk of 'Ākohekohe populations, restoration of existing habitats is critical. In particular, our results suggest that maintaining undisturbed understory and subcanopies in addition to healthy stands of 'ōhi'a is important, since they represent important foraging areas for 'Ākohekohe. Although disease is a concern for many regions (Scott et al. 1986, Atkinson et al. 1995, Jarvi et al. *this volume,* Shehata et al. *this volume*), translocations of 'Ākohekohe to other previously occupied regions, once they are restored, should also be considered.

Additional research also needs to be carried out to evaluate the impact of predation on 'Ākohekohe populations and the importance of resource tracking. It should not be assumed that changes in abundance will be gradual. Rapid declines frequently occur in populations subject to stochastic events (Temple 1985, 1986). The year to year variation in breeding success found in this study and reported in other honeycreepers (Eddinger 1970, van Riper 1987, Morin 1992a) suggests yearly monitoring of populations may be essential.

ACKNOWLEDGMENTS

We thank S. Ashe, R. Aburomia, C. Barber, and B. Keitt for their assistance in the field, and F. Duvall, C. Chimera, P. Conry, K. Rosa, M. White, and the employees of the Olinda Endangered Species Propagation Facility, Haleakalā National Park, Hawai'i's Department of Land and Natural Resources, and the Maui office of The Nature Conservancy of Hawai'i for their support. We thank The Nature Conservancy of Hawai'i for allowing us access to Waikamoi Reserve; and T. Pratt, J. Simon, K. Berlin, B. Larison, J. Carothers, S. Conant, P. Sykes, C. van Riper III, M. Defley, H. Freifeld, D. Goley, A. Medeiros, H. Baker, and M. Scott for discussion and comments. We thank the U.S. Fish and Wildlife Service Pacific Island Office, Hawai'i's Department of Forestry and Wildlife, The Nature Conservancy, Haleakalā National Park, San Francisco State University, and B. Tribbensee for financial assistance.

Studies in Avian Biology No. 22:202–212, 2001.

'ĀKOHEKOHE RESPONSE TO FLOWER AVAILABILITY: SEASONAL ABUNDANCE, FORAGING, BREEDING, AND MOLT

KIM E. BERLIN, JOHN C. SIMON, THANE K. PRATT, JAMES R. KOWALSKY, AND JEFF S. HATFIELD

Abstract. We studied the relationship of flower availability to the seasonality of life history events of the 'Ākohekohe (*Palmeria dolei*), a primarily nectarivorous and endangered Hawaiian honeycreeper from montane rain forests on Maui, Hawai'i. For comparison, we also investigated temporal bird density and foraging behavior of three other competing Hawaiian honeycreepers: 'Apapane (*Himatione sanguinea*), 'I'iwi (*Vestiaria coccinea*), and Hawai'i 'Amakihi (*Hemignathus virens*). All species except 'amakihi fed primarily on nectar of 'ōhi'a-lehua (*Metrosideros polymorpha*), which produced flowers year-round but had an annual flowering peak in January. Flowers of several subcanopy shrubs and trees were important components of the diet for all nectarivores, and these were available seasonally depending upon the species. 'Ākohekohe densities did not change temporally, suggesting a relatively stable population residing above 1,700 m. Monthly densities of 'Apapane, 'I'iwi, and Hawai'i 'Amakihi were positively correlated with monthly 'ōhi'a-lehua flower abundance, and 50–80% of these populations departed temporarily from our high-elevation site in July. There was a positive correlation with the timing of 'Ākohekohe breeding and high abundance of 'ōhi'a-lehua bloom. Molt followed breeding. From a conservation perspective, these results show that 'Ākohekohe maintain a relatively stable population above the mid-elevation zone of disease transmission, particularly during the fall when 'ōhi'a-lehua bloom decreases and mosquitoes increase. 'Ākohekohe remain on their territories partly by switching their foraging to subcanopy trees and shrubs, most of which require protection from feral pigs (*Sus scrofa*).

Key Words: 'Ākohekohe; breeding; foraging; Hawaiian honeycreeper; *Metrosideros*; *Palmeria dolei*; phenology.

The seasonal rhythms of breeding, molt, and population movements in birds are often correlated with the temporal availability of primary food resources (Skutch 1950; Stiles 1975, 1980, 1985; Clutton-Brock 1991). Breeding is often timed to peak availability of food resources such that the young are adequately nourished and adults can satisfy the energetic demands for breeding (Stiles 1985, Ralph and Fancy 1994b). Birds breed and molt throughout the year in the tropics, but some are restricted to breeding and molting during certain times of the year based on a species' foraging niche (Skutch 1950; Stiles 1980, 1988; Poulin et al. 1992; Ralph and Fancy 1994b). Altitudinal bird migrations are also found to be in response to fluctuating food supplies and occur predominantly among nectarivores and frugivores (Wolf et al. 1976; Stiles 1985, 1988; Loiselle and Blake 1991). In general, these birds have limited food choices and must be highly mobile to locate new sources of flowers or fruits.

Nectarivorous Hawaiian honeycreepers (Fringillidae: Drepanidinae) respond to seasonal fluctuations of flower abundance (Baldwin 1953, van Riper 1984, Carothers 1986a; Ralph and Fancy 1994b, 1995). For example, at one site on the island of Hawai'i, breeding and molting periods of 'Apapane (*Himatione sanguinea*), 'I'iwi (*Vestiaria coccinea*), and Hawai'i 'Amakihi (*Hemignathus virens*) were associated with nec-tar availability, but insectivorous species, which had a more constant food supply, had longer, less defined breeding and molting periods (Ralph and Fancy 1994b). 'Apapane and 'I'iwi practice altitudinal movements on the island of Hawai'i, dictated by the timing of bloom of certain nectar producing plants (Baldwin 1953, Ralph and Fancy 1995). The larger 'Ākohekohe (*Palmeria dolei*), the focus of our study, also feeds primarily on nectar. The 'Ākohekohe has undergone extirpation on the island of Moloka'i, is currently endangered (USFWS 1998), and survives only in montane rain forest on the windward slope of east Maui. 'Ākohekohe are closely associated with 'ōhi'a-lehua (hereafter 'ōhi'a, *Metrosideros polymorpha*), the dominant tree of Hawaiian rain forests. 'Ākohekohe feed primarily on 'ōhi'a nectar and nest exclusively in 'ōhi'a canopies (Carothers 1986a,b; Van-Gelder 1996, VanGelder and Smith *this volume*).

Flowering 'ōhi'a trees can be found at all times of the year in different areas of forest as flowering progresses from high elevations in winter to lower elevations in spring and summer (Baldwin 1953, Bridges et al. 1981). However, at most sites honeycreepers do not permanently inhabit the lowest elevations, where higher incidence of contact with introduced avian diseases has apparently depleted the birds' populations (Scott et al. 1986, Ralph and Fancy 1995). Mosquitoes (*Culex quinquefasciatus*) can

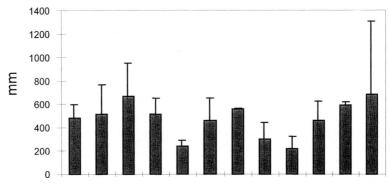

FIGURE 1. Mean monthly rainfall at 2,100 m elevation in the Hanawī Natural Area Reserve, Maui, Hawai'i, for the period January 1995 through May 1997.

spread avian malaria (*Plasmodium relictum*) and poxvirus (*Poxvirus* spp.) and are most abundant at elevations below 1,500 m (van Riper et al. 1986). The prevalence of these diseases appears to restrict most native bird populations to high-elevation forests where mosquitoes are less abundant or absent (Warner 1968, Scott et al. 1986, van Riper et al. 1986, Atkinson et al. 1995). Seasonal migrations to lower elevations, where mosquitoes exist in greater abundance, would compromise native birds that have little or no tolerance to these alien diseases. Conservation of native habitats and bird species must therefore consider how seasonal availability of dominant food sources such as 'ōhi'a affect bird behavior and the timing of life history events.

In this paper we examine the relationship between availability of flowers, particularly 'ōhi'a, with seasonality in bird abundance, foraging ecology, breeding, and molt in the 'Ākohekohe. We compare seasonality in abundance and foraging of 'Ākohekohe with the three other nectarivorous honeycreepers ('Apapane, 'I'iwi, and Hawai'i 'Amakihi) on our study site. We also present data on seasonality of mosquito presence and discuss the possible influence of habitat quality and flower availability on bird movements and mortality from avian disease.

METHODS

STUDY AREA

Our study was conducted continuously from April 1994 to December 1997 between the east and west forks of Hanawī Stream at 1,550–2,125 m elevation on the windward slope of Haleakalā Volcano, east Maui, Hawai'i (20° 44' N, 156° 8' W). The topography is rugged, steep, and dissected by many small ravines and wide valleys. The forest canopy, dominated by 'ōhi'a trees, is dense and continuous throughout most of the study site. The subcanopy is also dense with trees and shrubs including 'ōlapa (*Cheirodendron tri-*

gynum), pilo (*Coprosma ochracea*), na'ena'e (*Dubautia plantaginea, D. reticulata*), kāwa'u (*Ilex anomala*), 'alani (*Melicope clusiifolia* mainly, also *M.* spp.), kōlea (*Myrsine lessertiana*), pūkiawe (*Styphelia tameiameiae*), and 'ōhelo (*Vaccinium calycinum*), with kanawao (*Broussasia arguta*), 'ākala (*Rubus hawaiensis*), ferns, grasses, sedges, and mosses dominating the understory, and epiphytes cloaking the branches (Jacobi 1989, Kitayama and Mueller-Dombois 1992; this study). Rare plants producing flowers sought by birds included lobelias (*Clermontia,* 4 spp.; *Cyanea,* 3 spp., and *Lobelia* spp.) and mint (*Stenogyne kamehamehae*).

The climate is dictated by the northeasterly trade winds; fog and mist occur almost daily, and rainfall is among the highest in the state. We set two standard 26-inch (66.3 cm) National Weather Service rain gauges at 1,700 m and 2,125 m elevation. Annual rainfall at these sites averaged 5,154 mm ± 1,192 SE and 5,114 mm ± 1,359 SE, respectively, for the period January 1995 through May 1997. Precipitation was not seasonal, although monthly and year-to-year fluctuations were high (Fig. 1). Average monthly temperatures ranged from 9 to 13° C, with slightly cooler temperatures and sharply decreased solar radiation in winter months for the same period (T. Giambelluca, unpubl. data, as further described in Berlin et al. 2000).

FLOWERING PHENOLOGY AND BIRD DENSITY

Data on flowering phenology of ten native plant species and bird counts were taken during the first or second week of every month from January 1995 through December 1997. We established four transects running downslope from 2,150 to 1,550 m elevation; each transect had ten stations at approximately 150-m intervals. Transects ran along parallel, nonadjacent ridges roughly 100 m apart. We used ridge trails due to the difficult terrain encountered off the ridges, but the geography was such that we could hear birds in adjacent valleys and on facing ridges.

At each station, we recorded flowering activity of the following native plants: 'ākala, 'alani, kanawao, kāwa'u, kōlea, 'ōhelo, 'ōhi'a, 'ōlapa, pilo, and pūkiawe. The species selected were represented on the four transects across elevations and constituted the majority of the woody flora at this site. We tagged individual plants (N = 275) that (1) were of minimum size to be expected to flower, (2) were the closest to the station without being on the trail to minimize bias in selecting plants, and (3) could be viewed clearly. With the aid of binoculars, we counted the number of flowers ('ākala) or inflorescences (hereafter referred to as "flowers" for kanawao, 'ōhi'a, and 'ōlapa), or estimated the percentage of live stems with flowers (all others). For the purposes of this paper, we report mean number of 'ōhi'a flowers per month during the three year study (i.e., the total number of flowers for all trees in a given month divided by the number of trees). For nine tree and shrub species other than 'ōhi'a, we calculated the monthly percentage of species with flowering peaks (i.e., the number of species for which flowering peaked in a given month divided by the total number of species). Detailed statistical analyses of phenology of all species is reported in Berlin et al. (2000).

Bird counts were conducted beginning one-half hour after sunrise and continuing usually no later than 12:00, weather permitting. Two nonadjacent transects were chosen per day to avoid recording the same birds from two observers. We believe this was achieved, as effective detection distances range from 32 m for Hawai'i 'Amakihi to 46 m for 'Ākohekohe (Scott et al. 1986), a small fraction of the distance between our transects. All counts were conducted at designated stations and began from the highest elevation and continued downhill. In models testing variables influencing counts, we found no significant effect for time of day that might confound effects of elevation (unpubl. data). We estimated bird density following the variable circular-plot method (Reynolds et al. 1980, Fancy 1997). The estimated distance of a bird either seen or heard from each station was recorded during eight-minute counts. Weather conditions were recorded using the Beaufort scale for wind speed, and cloud cover was recorded to the nearest 10%. Rain was recorded on a scale of 0 to 4, with 0 = no rain, 1 = mist or fog, 2 = light drizzle, 3 = light rain, and 4 = heavy rain. Counts were postponed if sustained wind speeds exceeded 13 mph or rain was greater than 3.

Analyses of densities for each Hawaiian honeycreeper were performed using four-way nested analysis of variance (ANOVA; SAS Institute 1987) to investigate temporal and spatial variability in densities. Elevation was divided into three categories based on habitat changes within the site that appear to influence 'Ākohekohe distribution. Between 2,040 m and 2,130 m (N = 8 stations, mean elevation = 2,092 m), the habitat is a transition between shrubland found on the upper slopes beyond our study area and 'ōhi'a forest, which, in this zone, is shorter in stature than the forest at lower elevations. Within the mid-section of our site, from 1,750 m to 2,039 m (N = 20 stations, mean elevation = 1,897 m), the canopy of 'ōhi'a trees is taller and more continuous. At the lowest elevations of our study area, from 1,567 m to 1,749 m (N = 12 stations, mean elevation = 1,659 m), the 'ōhi'a canopy becomes more sparse. Thus, our four-way ANOVA model included the main effect variables of month, year, elevation category, and station, with stations nested within elevation categories, along with the various

two-way and three-way interaction terms of month, year, and elevation category.

To compare bird densities with 'ōhi'a flowers, we calculated the mean number of 'ōhi'a flowers at each station for each month and year and included this variable as a continuous covariate in the four-way model above. This five-way analysis of covariance (ANCOVA) was then used to test for the significance of 'ōhi'a flower abundance on bird densities, at the scale of the station level.

We ran some simpler analyses at a much broader scale, the scale of the entire study area, rather than at the scale of each station. We calculated the mean densities for each species and for 'ōhi'a flowers for each month, averaged over the entire time period, and calculated the Pearson's correlation coefficient (N = 12 per species) between mean densities and mean 'ōhi'a flowers for each species. We also ran some simple ANCOVAs in which we calculated the means by both month and elevation category (N = 36 per species), and tested for association of bird densities and mean 'ōhi'a flowers along with elevation categories and the interaction of elevation and 'ōhi'a flowers. This is similar to the correlation coefficients, except that it tests for whether elevation category is important in the association between mean bird densities and mean 'ōhi'a flower abundance. Finally, one last ANCOVA (N = 108 per species) added year along with all the interactions to learn whether year effects were important in the associations among mean bird density, mean flower abundance, and elevation for each species.

FORAGING

Foraging behavior was recorded for the four nectarivorous honeycreepers between December 1994 and June 1997. All observations were taken between 07:00 and 18:30 during various weather conditions. Foraging observations were not taken sequentially and were treated as independent events. Upon detecting a bird, the observer waited ten seconds, then recorded the first foraging maneuver by the bird. For each observation, we recorded the bird's age class, foraging maneuver (e.g., probing, plucking), plant species, substrate type (e.g., flower, twig, leaf), food type, estimated foraging height, and estimated canopy height. Age of the bird was classified as immature or adult and was determined at the time of observation based on plumage characteristics (Simon et al. 1998). Sex was determined for 37 adult and 25 immature 'Ākohekohe based on other behavioral data or morphometric analyses of color-banded individuals (Simon et al. 1998). We used a two-way ANOVA to analyze sex and age categories of 'Ākohekohe in comparing monthly foraging heights, and chi-square contingency tables to compare monthly categorical data on plant species used, stratum occupied (canopy, subcanopy, understory), and food type.

SEASONALITY OF BREEDING AND MOLT

We examined breeding biology and molt of 'Ākohekohe between December 1994 and June 1997. Throughout the study, we searched the study area for nests, repeatedly covering all trails over a 3–4 day period. We located nests between November and May by observing nest building, nest defense, or courtship, by following adults going to and from the nest, and by occasional chance discovery. Most nests were observed with a spotting scope at 2–3 day intervals from a blind to determine nesting status. Mean incubation and mean nestling periods were calculated for nests for which laying, hatching, and fledging could be closely approximated; these means were used to back-date the start of incubation and the presence of hatched chicks for nests found later in their cycle. The proportion of juveniles in the sample of birds observed foraging was also used as an index of breeding activity.

Feather molt was recorded from birds captured in multilevel mist nets primarily from May to October (Simon et al. 1998). Birds were netted either near banding stations or selectively as they visited blooming shrubs. The presence of either flight or body molt was calculated for second-year and older adults combined. We used Pearson's correlation to analyze the timing of breeding and molting with 'ōhi'a flowering.

DISEASE

Culex quinquefasciatus, the only mosquito found routinely at elevations above 1,200 m (Goff and van Riper 1980), serves as the main vector for avian malaria and avian pox (van Riper et al. 1986) and is easily attracted to artificial breeding sites (Reiter 1987). The presence of mosquitoes along the elevational gradient was determined monthly at 24 oviposition pans set along the same transects used for plant phenology and bird counts. We placed one plastic pan in a flat area on the forest floor at every other station and one at the lower most station on each transect. Rabbit food and soil were put into each pan and combined with rainwater to create an organic mixture suitable for mosquito larvae. Any evidence of mosquito eggs, larvae, pupae, or adults in the pans was recorded. The liquid contents of the pans were drained after inspection to remove mosquitoes. Rainfall refilled the pans each month, except in a few monthly checks (<5%) during dry periods. Food and soil were replenished periodically as needed.

Evidence for avian pox was also checked upon examination of all birds captured in mist nets. We recorded the presence or absence of poxlike lesions, such as missing toes and open or closed sores.

RESULTS

FLOWERING PHENOLOGY AND BIRD DENSITY

'Ōhi'a flowers were present year-round with an annual peak evident in January; flowering increased gradually such that flowers were relatively abundant for 4–5 months (Fig. 2a). In summer months, 'ōhi'a flowering had virtually ceased at high elevations but continued at elevations below 1,750 m. Understory trees and shrubs flowered at various times of the year; peaks occurred predominantly from April to June (Fig. 2b). Of the species most visited by nectarivorous birds, 'ākala and 'ōhelo flowered in spring months, and kanawao flowered between August and October.

'Ākohekohe densities averaged 2.89 birds/ha ± 0.07 SE throughout the study site for all years.

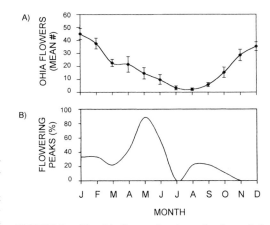

FIGURE 2. Monthly flower abundance for the period January 1995 through December 1997. A. Monthly mean number of 'ōhi'a flowers per marked tree over three years with standard error bars (N = 92 trees). B. Monthly percentage of understory plant species with flowering peaks (N = 183 plants of 9 species).

Significant differences were found among months ($F_{11,1295}$ = 4.38, P < 0.001), years ($F_{2,1295}$ = 16.74, P < 0.001), and elevation categories ($F_{2,37}$ = 64.98, P < 0.001), and also many of the higher-order interactions of these variables (P < 0.05). No strong pattern existed among consecutive months (Fig. 3a), but the highest densities occurred in 1996 (mean = 3.34 birds/ha) while 1995 and 1997 were very similar (mean = 2.72 and 2.61 birds/ha respectively). Elevation was such a significant factor because nearly the entire population (93%) resided above 1,700 m elevation. The highest average density occurred in the mid-elevation category, with a mean of 4.08 birds/ha (Fig. 3b). The high-elevation area had a mean of 2.69 birds/ha, and the low-elevation area had the lowest average at 1.04 birds/ha (Fig. 3b). When the ANCOVA was performed by adding the 'ōhi'a flower variable to the four-way ANOVA, there was no significant effect of 'ōhi'a flowers on 'Ākohekohe densities ($F_{1,1292}$ = 0.17, P = 0.678), at least at the scale of stations over which we measured these variables.

Among the other nectarivorous species, 'Apapane densities were the highest, with an average of 14.42 birds/ha ± 0.29 SE (Fig. 3a). 'I'iwi densities were 3.59 birds/ha ± 0.09 SE over the study area and lowest of the nonendangered species, while Hawai'i 'Amakihi had a mean of 11.82 birds/ha ± 0.23 SE. As for the 'Ākohekohe, months and years were very significant (P < 0.001) for 'Apapane, 'I'iwi, and Hawai'i 'Amakihi in the four-way ANOVA. Concerning months, highest mean densities occurred in January for 'Apapane and Hawai'i 'Amakihi, and in October for 'I'iwi, although January had the

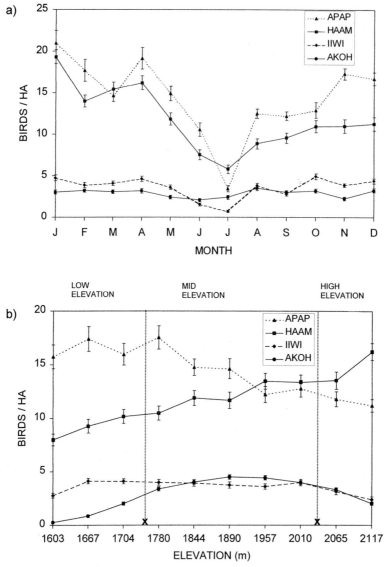

FIGURE 3.   Mean bird density (birds/ha) and standard error bars for four nectarivorous Hawaiian honeycreepers (A) by month, and (B) by mean elevation.

second highest mean for that species. Lowest densities occurred in July for all three species (Fig. 3a). The highest densities occurred in 1997 for 'Apapane and in 1996 for Hawai'i 'Amakihi and 'I'iwi. Elevation category was also very significant in explaining variability in densities for all three species ('Apapane, $F_{2,37} = 10.25$, P < 0.001; 'I'iwi, $F_{2,37} = 6.61$, P = 0.004; Hawai'i 'Amakihi, $F_{2,37} = 25.83$, P < 0.001). Like the 'Ākohekohe, the 'I'iwi had the highest mean density in the mid-elevation area, while the highest mean density occurred in the low-elevation area for the 'Apapane and in the high-

elevation area for the Hawai'i 'Amakihi (Fig. 3b). However, as in the 'Ākohekohe analysis, the 'ōhi'a flower variable was not significant in explaining any of the variability in bird densities for these species in these ANCOVAs ('Apapane, $F_{1,1292} = 0.01$, P = 0.935; 'I'iwi, $F_{1,1292} = 0.03$, P = 0.854; Hawai'i 'Amakihi, $F_{1,1292} = 1.44$, P = 0.230), at least at the scale of the station level.

However, using the 12 monthly averages over the entire time period for the number of 'ōhi'a flowers and densities of each species, and performing Pearson's correlation, the correlation coefficients were positive and significant for

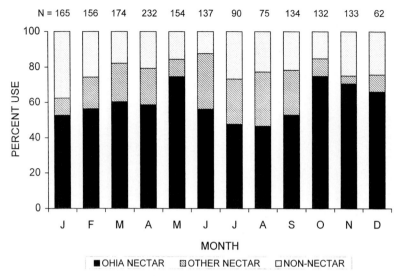

FIGURE 4. Percentage of monthly observations for 'Ākohekohe foraging, by food type: 'ōhi'a flowers, other flowers (subcanopy trees and shrubs listed in Methods), and substrates other than flowers. Sample sizes appear above graph.

three of the four species ('Ākohekohe, r = 0.22, P = 0.484; 'Apapane, r = 0.81, P = 0.001; 'I'iwi, r = 0.58, P = 0.047; Hawai'i 'Amakihi, r = 0.86, P < 0.001; N = 12 for each species). This implies that, at the scale of the entire study area, these species tended to move into the area when 'ōhi'a flowers were most abundant (in the winter), but this relationship does not hold up at the scale of individual stations (at least the way we measured 'ōhi'a flowers at each station by counting the same 2–3 trees per visit). When we ran the ANCOVA on these means, adding in elevation category, year, and the interactions, year effects were significant in three of the four species (P < 0.005 for all but 'I'iwi, for which P > 0.05, N = 108 per species), but the conclusions for mean bird densities versus mean 'ōhi'a flower abundance and elevation categories were similar, so we prefer to present the simpler models without year effects (see below).

These simpler ANCOVA models tested for an association between mean bird densities, mean 'ōhi'a flower abundance, elevation, and the interaction of elevation and 'ōhi'a flowers. For 'Apapane and 'I'iwi densities, 'ōhi'a flowers were significant ('Apapane, $F_{1,30}$ = 28.05, P < 0.001; 'I'iwi, $F_{1,30}$ = 12.09, P = 0.002; N = 36 per species), but elevation category and the interaction were not significant (P > 0.05), implying that over the scale of the entire study area, these birds are moving into the different elevation bands at the time when the 'ōhi'a flowers are most abundant there. (Recall that elevation was very significant in the five-way ANCOVA

for these species.) Hawai'i 'Amakihi densities also had a significant association with mean 'ōhi'a flowers ($F_{1,30}$ = 25.16, P < 0.001), but there was a significant elevation effect, too ($F_{2,30}$ = 5.92, P = 0.007), implying that something more complicated was happening. For the 'Ākohekohe, however, we found no association between mean densities and 'ōhi'a flower abundance even at the scale of the entire study area ($F_{1,30}$ = 1.54, P = 0.225), but as in the four-way and five-way analyses, there was a very significant elevation effect ($F_{2,30}$ = 35.01, P < 0.001). This suggests that, despite small fluctuations among months and years, 'Ākohekohe density was not associated with 'ōhi'a flower abundance as it was for the other three species. However, statistical power may be a problem, considering that the 'Ākohekohe had the lowest densities of the four species.

FORAGING

Foraging maneuvers of 'Ākohekohe (N = 1,544) were classified as probing (63%) into a flower or the base of a leaf cluster, gleaning (23%) primarily for invertebrates from the surface of leaves or bark, and biting (12%). Other maneuvers such as drilling, tapping, or hawking were less common and collectively composed <1% of all foraging observations.

'Ōhi'a nectar was the primary food for 'Ākohekohe and constituted 50–75% of the monthly foraging observations throughout the year (Fig. 4). Nectar of many subcanopy trees and shrubs, particularly 'ākala, kanawao, and 'ōhelo, was

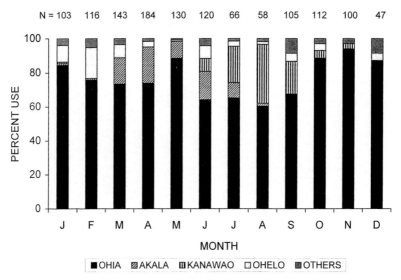

FIGURE 5. Percentage of monthly observations for 'Ākohekohe foraging on flowers. Sample sizes appear above graph.

also important in the diet (Fig. 5). Use of 'ākala and kanawao was seasonal and constituted up to 20–35% of 'Ākohekohe monthly foraging observations when 'ōhi'a bloom declined. 'Ākala was utilized most between March and July, and kanawao mainly between July and September. 'Ōhelo flowers were most numerous in winter and spring, but were used by 'Ākohekohe year-round. Other nectar sources included 'alani, kō-lea, 'ōlapa, and pūkiawe, but these composed <10% of the monthly foraging observations (Fig. 5). 'Ākohekohe foraged in the canopy during 64% of all observations (N = 1,956) at a mean height of 9.5 m ± 0.90 SE. There were no significant differences between adults and juveniles or between males and females in monthly

comparisons of foraging height, location in the forest strata, food type, or plant species used.

'Ākohekohe use of nonnectar foods (entirely invertebrates) did not change among months (Fig. 4). 'Ākohekohe foraged for invertebrates primarily on 'ōhi'a (35–75% of observations per month) and secondarily on 'ōhelo and 'alani (Table 1). 'Ākala and kanawao, which were important sources of nectar for 'Ākohekohe, were infrequent sources of nonnectar foods.

'Apapane and 'I'iwi had foraging preferences for nectar similar to 'Ākohekohe, but Hawai'i 'Amakihi foraged more generally upon five species: 'ōhi'a, 'ākala, kanawao, 'ōhelo, and pūkiawe (Table 2). Visits to 'ōhi'a flowers composed only 26% of the total observations for Hawai'i

TABLE 1. PERCENT OF OBSERVATIONS OF 'ĀKOHEKOHE FORAGING ON SUBSTRATES OTHER THAN FLOWERS[a]

Plant species	Month											
	J	F	M	A	M	J	J	A	S	O	N	D
'Ōhi'a (Metrosideros polymor-pha)	42	35	39	69	75	59	63	71	48	65	48	73
'Ōhelo (Vaccinium calycinum)	27	38	35	13	4	6	21	0	10	5	3	7
'Alani (Melicope spp.)	8	13	10	0	4	6	4	29	17	5	15	13
Kōlea (Myrsine lessertiana)	5	5	10	10	4	12	0	0	10	0	0	0
'Ōlapa (Cheirodendron trigyn-um)	8	8	3	4	0	0	0	0	7	10	15	0
Pūkiawe (Styphelia tameiameiae)	0	3	0	0	0	12	4	0	3	5	0	0
'Ākala (Rubus hawaiensis)	0	0	0	0	8	6	8	0	0	0	0	0
Kanawao (Broussaisia arguta)	3	0	0	2	0	0	0	0	0	5	9	0
Kāwa'u (Ilex anomala)	3	0	0	0	0	0	0	0	3	0	6	7
Pilo (Coprosma ochracea)	3	0	0	2	4	0	0	0	0	5	3	0
Na'ena'e (Dubautia spp.)	0	0	3	0	0	0	0	0	0	0	0	0

[a] By plant species and month from December 1994 through June 1997 (N = 360 observations).

TABLE 2.   PERCENT OF OBSERVATIONS OF FOUR HA-
WAIIAN HONEYCREEPERS FORAGING ON FLOWERS

Plant species	'Ākohekohe	'I'wi	'Apapane	Hawai'i 'Amakihi
'Ōhi'a	77	57	69	26
'Ākala	8	22	9	25
Kanawao	6	4	12	15
'Ōhelo	6	9	4	16
Pūkiawe	<0.5	0	4	11
'Alani	2	0	1	5
'Ōlapa	<0.5	2	1	0
Pilo	0	1	0	2
Lobelia	<0.5	3	0	0
Stenogyne	<0.5	2	0	0
Kōlea	<0.5	0	0	1
Kāwa'u	<0.5	1	0	0
Sample size	1284	116	94	132

TABLE 3.   PERCENT OF OBSERVATIONS OF FOUR HA-
WAIIAN HONEYCREEPERS FORAGING ON SUBSTRATES OTH-
ER THAN FLOWERS, MAINLY FOR INVERTEBRATES

Plant species	'Ākohekohe	'I'wi	'Apapane	Hawai'i 'Amakihi
'Ōhi'a	54	33	64	25
'Ōhelo	17	40	16	19
Pilo	2	7	4	17
'Ōlapa	6	13	0	6
Kōlea	5	7	8	2
'Alani	9	0	8	4
'Ākala	1	0	0	11
Pūkiawe	2	0	0	10
Kanawao	2	0	0	5
Kāwa'u	2	0	0	1
Na'ena'e	<0.5	0	0	0
Sample size	360	15	25	100

'Amakihi but 57–77% for the other three honeycreepers. 'Ākala, kanawao, and 'ōhelo were a
substantial portion of all honeycreeper nectar diets. For nonnectar foraging, a wide variety of
understory and canopy species were utilized, but
'ōhi'a and 'ōhelo were visited the most by all
honeycreepers (Table 3).

SEASONALITY OF BREEDING AND MOLT

'Ākohekohe bred during the coldest, wettest
time of the year, with the shortest day length,
and when 'ōhi'a flowers were most abundant
(Fig. 6). The breeding season lasted seven
months with peak nesting between January and
April. The number of nests active per month was

positively correlated with mean monthly abundance of 'ōhi'a flowers (Pearson's r = 0.66, P
= 0.01). The first nests were initiated in November, while 'ōhi'a bloom was increasing. Nesting
peaked in March, two months after peak 'ōhi'a
bloom in January, and continued through May.
The percentage of active nests declined with declining 'ōhi'a bloom.

Juvenile 'Ākohekohe were observed mainly
between March and October (Fig. 7). The highest proportion of observations of juveniles occurred in May, two months after peak nesting
when many understory plants were in flower.
Observations on juveniles declined temporarily
in July, coincident with the lowest densities of

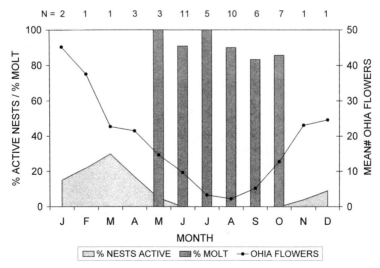

FIGURE 6.   Timing by month of 'ōhi'a bloom, 'Ākohekohe breeding, and 'Ākohekohe molt. Line graph: mean
number of 'ōhi'a flowers (N = 92 trees and 3,312 observations). Area graph: breeding activity measured by
percentage of nests active/mo (N = 49 nests). Bar graph: molting period measured by percentage of birds ≥
second year in either flight or body molt (N = 38). Monthly sample sizes for molt appear above graph.

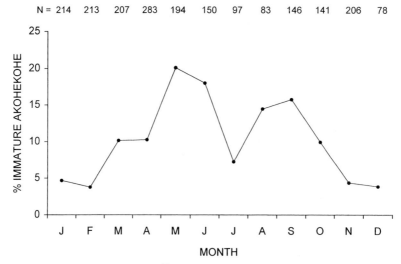

FIGURE 7. Monthly proportion of juvenile 'Ākohekohe seen during foraging observations. Sample sizes appear above graph.

'Apapane, 'I'iwi, and Hawai'i 'Amakihi, as well as the lowest flower availability (see Figs. 2, 3a).

'Ākohekohe molt began abruptly in May as nesting activity declined and was recorded at high frequencies through October (Fig. 6). In no case did individual birds exhibit breeding and molting conditions simultaneously, but there was slight breeding-molt overlap in May and June for the population overall. The percentage of birds in molt per month with years pooled was negatively correlated with mean monthly 'ōhi'a flowering (Pearson's r = −0.82, P < 0.001).

DISEASE

Mosquitoes were collected from oviposition pans only in the months of September, October, and November. During these three months, 16.5% of the pans (N = 24/mo) had mosquitoes. Larvae were found only below 1,650 m, with the exception of one pan at 2,100 m elevation in November 1997.

The prevalence of birds captured with physical signs of avian pox was low: 'Apapane 3.4% (N = 147), 'I'iwi 3.2% (N = 62), Maui Creeper (*Paroreomyza montana*) 1.0% (N = 96), and Hawai'i 'Amakihi 5.6% (N = 268) were caught with open or closed lesions on the legs, or missing toes. The most severe case was an 'Apapane that was missing its upper mandible in addition to having other lesions. Because bacterial infections from other causes can create similar lesions, we cannot be sure of the real prevalence of avian pox in this sample. No endangered or introduced bird species were found with poxlike lesions.

DISCUSSION

TEMPORAL AND SPATIAL ABUNDANCE OF 'ŌHI'A BLOOM AND HAWAIIAN HONEYCREEPERS

'Ākohekohe densities did not vary greatly by month nor correlate with abundance of 'ōhi'a flowers, suggesting that this species is relatively sedentary and that recruitment and loss rates are roughly equivalent. 'Ākohekohe are heavily dependent upon 'ōhi'a as a nectar source, but our data indicate that this species is able to maintain its population at high elevation during periods of depleted 'ōhi'a flowering. 'Ākohekohe are highly aggressive and displace 'Apapane, 'I'iwi, and Hawai'i 'Amakihi from foraging sites (Mountainspring and Scott 1985; Carothers 1986a,b; VanGelder 1996, VanGelder and Smith *this volume*). This dominance may enable 'Ākohekohe, especially adults, to remain at high elevation, whereas most juvenile 'Ākohekohe and individuals of other species are forced to depart. For example, during periods of depleted 'ōhi'a flowers, 'Ākohekohe actively defended patches of blooming 'ākala and kanawao (K. Berlin et al., pers. obs.). In contrast, monthly densities of 'Apapane, 'I'iwi, and Hawai'i 'Amakihi were temporally associated with 'ōhi'a bloom. Densities of all three species were lowest in July concurrent with the lowest availability of 'ōhi'a and understory flowers (see Figs. 2, 3a). These data suggest that a substantial proportion of nectar-feeding birds depart from high elevations and are consistent with the hypothesis that the birds follow 'ōhi'a flowering as it progresses downhill below the study area. The presence of juvenile 'Ākohekohe also declined temporarily in July, and may indicate that juveniles, subordinate to adults (Carothers 1986a,b), must also disperse (Scott et al. 1986). On the island of Hawai'i, 'Apapane and 'I'iwi make daily long-distance foraging and roosting flights and seasonal altitudinal movements in response to fluctuating 'ōhi'a flowering (Baldwin 1953, MacMillen and Carpenter 1980, Ralph and Fancy 1995). Daily foraging and roosting flights do not occur on Maui to the extent found on Hawai'i (Mountainspring and Scott 1985; Pacific Island Ecosystems Research Center, PIERC, unpubl. data), but the positive correlation of 'ōhi'a flowering with densities of all nonendangered nectarivorous birds supports the hypothesis of seasonal altitudinal movements on Maui.

FORAGING

'Ōhi'a nectar was the food source most frequently exploited by 'Ākohekohe (Fig. 4). Even in summer months when 'ōhi'a flowers were scarce, use of 'ōhi'a decreased only slightly. 'Ākala and kanawao flowered most heavily during spring and summer, respectively, coincident with the period of declining or low 'ōhi'a bloom. Alternate food sources such as 'ākala and kanawao were used frequently in summer months, although their use remained secondary to 'ōhi'a. In two other studies, 'alani and kōlea were the main alternate sources of nectar for 'Ākohekohe during spring and fall months (VanGelder 1996, VanGelder and Smith *this volume*; H. Baker and P. Baker, unpubl. data). Native lobelias (Campanulacae) have also been noted as a nectar source for many Hawaiian birds (Spieth 1966, Lammers and Freeman 1986). Lobelias in our study area bloomed from summer through fall (PIERC, unpubl. data), producing nectar for honeycreepers when the high-elevation 'ōhi'a bloom declined. Because a variety of flowering understory plants supplement the diets of 'Ākohekohe and other honeycreepers, habitats must therefore contain a diversity of these plants to maintain populations of nectarivorous birds.

Our study did not show any age- or sex-related differences in 'Ākohekohe foraging preferences. However, J. Carothers (*this volume*) recorded that immature 'Ākohekohe fed less frequently on 'ōhi'a nectar than did adult 'Ākohekohe, and more often on arthropods. He attributed this difference to the nutritional need of immatures for a high-protein diet during the early postfledging stage of development. We cannot say whether the difference between our results and Carothers' can be explained by differences in methodology or the habitats studied.

'Apapane and 'I'iwi had similar foraging preferences to 'Ākohekohe, confirming prior observations of interspecific competition among these species (Mountainspring and Scott 1985; Carothers 1986a,b). 'Ākohekohe dominate 'Apapane, 'I'iwi, and Hawai'i 'Amakihi and often defend food sources from these species (Carothers 1986a,b). Hawai'i 'Amakihi foraged more generally and did not show a strong preference for any particular plant species or food type. Baldwin (1953) also found that Hawai'i 'Amakihi forage more generally, and Carothers (1986a) noted that Hawai'i 'Amakihi did not forage extensively in 'ōhi'a canopies and were not involved in as many interspecific interactions as were 'Ākohekohe, 'Apapane, or 'I'iwi. Hawai'i 'Amakihi are at the bottom of the nectarivorous hierarchy, and 'Ākohekohe, 'Apapane, and 'I'iwi probably prevent them from utilizing higher-quality nectar sources (Pimm and Pimm 1982; Carothers 1986a,b).

SEASONALITY OF BREEDING AND MOLT

'Ākohekohe initiated nesting during the coolest, wettest time of the year when the photoperiod was decreasing and 'ōhi'a bloom was increasing. Decreasing daylight and heavy rainfall are considered to be an unfavorable time for plants to flower and for birds to breed, and in most humid tropical forests these events occur during the dry period (Foster 1974, Frankie et al. 1974, Stiles 1978). However, hummingbirds in Costa Rica breed during the coolest, wettest time of the year when the greatest numbers of ornithophilous flowers are in bloom at high elevations (Wolf et al. 1976, Stiles 1985).

'Ākohekohe nesting was positively correlated with 'ōhi'a bloom, although peak nesting lagged two months behind peak bloom. 'Ōhi'a flowering has been associated with the timing of breeding of nectarivorous birds on the island of Hawai'i, but the timing and sequence of these peaks is variable (Baldwin 1953, Ralph and Fancy 1994b). Along the western periphery of native forest on eastern Maui and at a slightly lower elevation, 'ōhi'a bloom peaked two months after peak 'Ākohekohe nesting (VanGelder 1996, VanGelder and Smith *this volume*). We question whether peak bloom at this site corresponded instead with the flowering of glabrous 'ōhi'a, which are more common at mid-elevations than the pubescent varieties predominating at our site (Berlin et al. 2000). On the island of Hawai'i, breeding of 'Apapane and 'I'iwi coincided with 'ōhi'a bloom (Ralph and Fancy 1994b).

As with most Hawaiian honeycreepers (Ralph and Fancy 1994b), molt in 'Ākohekohe followed breeding (Simon et al. 1998). Molt did not coincide with flowering 'ōhi'a, but instead was initiated while many understory plants were flowering. Flowering of these understory species in spring and summer months may provide adequate resources during the energetically costly molting period and allow populations to maintain an extended breeding season as 'ōhi'a sources diminish.

IMPLICATIONS FOR CONSERVATION

'Ōhi'a is the single most important element in the habitat of the 'Ākohekohe and other nectarivorous Hawaiian honeycreepers at Hanawī. It is the main structural component of the forest community (Jacobi 1989) and provides the principal source of food (Carothers 1986a, VanGelder and Smith *this volume*) and nest sites (VanGelder and Smith *this volume*; PIERC, unpubl. data; this paper) for these birds. In this paper, we have also demonstrated that for the 'Ākohekohe, 'ōhi'a bloom probably influences timing of breeding and molt. The health and extent of 'ōhi'a populations is therefore of concern for the survival of Hawaiian honeycreepers. The phenomenon of 'ōhi'a dieback—when a stand of 'ōhi'a dies simultaneously and is replaced by a new cohort of 'ōhi'a—has been much studied (Mueller-Dombois 1980, Jacobi et al. 1988) and dictates the need for large reserves to sustain extensive forests of 'ōhi'a in a landscape of patchy dieback and cyclical succession. Reserve design must also take into account the variation with elevation in phenology of 'ōhi'a bloom (Berlin et al. 2000). An elevational gradient within a reserve increases the seasonal availability of 'ōhi'a flowers, particularly for 'Apapane and 'I'iwi which travel greater distances between patches of bloom.

When 'ōhi'a bloom declines in the summer, nectarivorous birds switch to other sources of nectar and many emigrate, perhaps because they are denied access to limited resources by 'Ākohekohe or are even driven out by 'Ākohekohe. The switch to foraging on understory plants underscores their importance in two respects, first as an alternate source of food, and second as a means of lessening emigration. Prior to the introduction of avian malaria, avian pox, and disease-transmitting mosquitoes, birds could emigrate from higher elevations with few risks and follow the summer 'ōhi'a bloom downslope (as proposed in van Riper et al. 1982). At present, such movements pose great risks of exposure to avian diseases so prevalent below 1,500 m. Indeed on the island of Hawai'i, epizootics happen during fall (van Riper et al. 1986; C. Atkinson, pers. comm.). On Hawai'i and at our Maui site, this problem is exacerbated by the upslope movement of mosquitoes during the fall (van

Riper et al. 1986; D. LaPointe, pers. comm.). A further consideration is that some populations of 'Apapane and Hawai'i 'Amakihi have greater resistance to avian malaria (Jarvi et al. *this volume*), and the movement of infected individuals to higher elevations may facilitate the transmission of diseases. We never captured any 'Ākohekohe with physical signs of disease. However, Feldman et al. (1995) detected avian malaria through blood sampling of one bird above 2,000 m elevation. The low prevalence of disease detected in 'Ākohekohe coupled with the species' confinement to elevations above 1,300 m (Scott et al. 1986) may indicate high susceptibility and mortality of infected 'Ākohekohe.

The best action to increase 'Ākohekohe populations at elevations above the lethal mosquito zone is to restore the vegetation of the birds' habitat to its former complexity and diversity. Forest understory across the east Maui watershed has been damaged to varying degrees by feral pigs (*Sus scrofa*), which in places have removed the understory and caused severe erosion. Enclosures where pigs have been removed have substantially recovered an understory of tree seedlings, 'ākala, kanawao, lobelias, and ferns. Eight rare lobelia species found at Hanawī presently grow epiphytically or clinging to cliff faces where they survived beyond the reach of pigs. In protected habitats, some of these lobelias are now growing on the forest floor, a positive sign for habitat recovery. Recovery of understory plants increases the year-round nectar supply for 'Ākohekohe and other honeycreepers. We emphasize that removal of pigs and restoration of the forest understory will provide food for birds that otherwise, during the summer and fall, may be forced to emigrate, never to return.

ACKNOWLEDGMENTS

This project was made possible through funding from the U.S. Fish and Wildlife Service, the Pacific Island Ecosystems Research Center of the U.S. Geological Survey-Biological Resources Division, the Hawai'i Department of Land and Natural Resources, and The Nature Conservancy of Hawai'i. We thank the Natural Area Reserves System, Hawaii Department of Land and Natural Resources for access to the Hanawī Natural Area Reserve, the many volunteers and biologists that assisted this project, Haleakalā National Park for their cooperation and assistance with helicopter operations, Windward Aviation for providing safe transportation to our study site, and T. Giambelluca and members of the HaleNet Project for supplying weather data from the Hanawī Natural Area Reserve. The following individuals provided unpublished information: C. Atkinson, H. Baker, P. Baker, and J. Carothers. S. Fancy provided statistical advice. Drafts of this paper were critically reviewed by C. Atkinson, P. Banko, E. VanGelder, and B. Woodworth.

Studies in Avian Biology No. 22:213–217, 2001.

AGE-RELATED DIET DIFFERENCES IN TWO NECTAR-FEEDING DREPANIDINES: THE 'ĀKOHEKOHE AND THE 'APAPANE

JOHN H. CAROTHERS

Abstract. Nectar-feeding birds face special dietary demands because the amino acid content of nectar is very low. I studied foraging ecology of two Hawaiian drepanidines, the 'Apapane (*Himatione sanguinea*) and the 'Ākohekohe (*Palmeria dolei*), to see how differential growth demands of immatures and adults might be reflected in diet choice. Interference interactions affect foraging, but when this effect was factored out immatures still appeared to favor arthropod prey more than adults did. Diet differences were significant for three-month-old immatures but were indistinguishable for those nine months of age, as they are probably at adult mass. This difference in diet could be explained by the lower mass of immatures and their growth needs for attaining adult mass. These observations suggest that growing juveniles may have higher protein/calorie requirements than adults, causing differences in their foraging ecology. Differential diet demands on breeding adults were controlled, but breeding and other factors besides growth are also expected to influence diet choice.

Key Words: age and diet; 'Ākohekohe; 'Apapane; Drepanidinae; *Himatione sanguinea*; insectivory; nectar feeder; *Palmeria dolei*.

Foraging differences between adult and immature birds have been observed for a variety of species and may result from three different age-related factors: inexperience at foraging, behavioral interference by adults, or differences in dietary requirements. Inexperience is particularly relevant when prey items require skilled detection and active pursuit and capture of prey (Amadon 1964, Recher and Recher 1969, Buckley and Buckley 1974, Searcy 1978, Porter and Sealy 1982), whereas interference interactions are important for socially interacting species which feed at a common food source (reviews in Murray 1971, 1981; Collins et al. 1990). Dietary preferences would differ among individuals facing differing metabolic demands (e.g., Sedinger 1997).

In this study, I examine which factors cause differences in the foraging behavior of adults and immatures in two nectar-feeding Hawaiian drepanidine species. These birds primarily feed upon the nectar of a single tree species (Berlin et al. *this volume*), although they also forage upon arthropods. Because of their manner of foraging and the nature of the food they consume, inexperience is unlikely to play an important role in the types of food they consume and hence unlikely to cause any differences observed. As with other nectar-feeding species (Wolf 1978, Murray 1981, Collins et al. 1990), interference interactions within and among these species are high and have an important affect upon their foraging behavior (Carothers 1986a,b; Mountainspring and Scott 1985; Scott et al. 1986). Immature Hawaiian drepanidines are subordinate to adults in the dominance hierarchy, and thus they are often excluded from nectar by defending adults (Carothers 1986a,b).

Amino acid and protein levels are low in nectar (Baker and Baker 1973, 1975), but they are significant diet components and they play major roles in foraging decisions (Pulliam 1975, Gass and Montgomerie 1981). Nectar feeders certainly need protein (e.g., Brice and Gray 1991, Brice 1992). Various authors have suggested that ontogenetic diet shifts occur in birds because of differing physiological needs of immatures undergoing growth to adulthood; immatures progressing toward the attainment of adult body mass have higher protein requirements than adults (Ricklefs 1968, Fisher 1972, Morton 1973, Foster 1978, Pyke 1980, O'Connor 1984). Although it is a general observation that nestlings are fed arthropods by their parents (O'Connor 1984), there are almost no studies comparing diets of immature (postfledgling) and adult nectar-feeding birds. This paper investigates if ontogenetic diet differences occur in two species of Hawaiian drepanidines, and whether such differences can be more likely attributed to interference behavior or to differing dietary demands.

METHODS

STUDY AREA

Birds were observed in the Ko'olau Forest Reserve, on the north slopes of Haleakalā volcano on the island of Maui, Hawai'i, for three periods: 15 May to 25 July 1980 (Summer 1), 10 July to 10 August (Summer 2), and 10 to 27 December 1981 (Winter 1). This rain forest habitat is mainly composed of one tree species, the 'ōhi'a (*Metrosideros polymorpha*), which has a flowering canopy and is a main food source for the nectar-feeding Hawaiian honeycreepers at all times of the year (Baldwin 1953, Carpenter 1978; Carothers 1986a,b; Berlin et al. *this volume*). The forest contains a diversity of smaller trees and shrubs that provide other locations for foraging for arthropods and as minor nectar sources.

THE BIRDS

The two species I studied are the 'Apapane (*Himatione sanguinea*) and the 'Ākohekohe (*Palmeria dolei*). Although both are sexually monochromatic, adults have brightly colored plumages whereas immatures are cryptically colored, allowing one to readily distinguish the two age classes (Carothers 1986a, Fancy et al. 1993a). Weight data on tags of museum specimens in University of California, Berkeley's Museum of Vertebrate Zoology collected by Baldwin (1953) on the island of Hawai'i provide evidence that adult male 'Apapanes ($\bar{x}$ = 16.35 g, S_E = 0.17, n = 34) are heavier than immatures (14.85 g, S_E = 0.32, n = 10; t-test, P < 0.01). 'Ākohekohe specimens were not available, but the trend occurs in the closely-related 'I'iwi (*Vestiaria coccinea*) as well: adult males ($\bar{x}$ = 20.96 g, S_E = 0.18, n = 13) had a higher average mass than immature males ($\bar{x}$ = 16.62 g, S_E = 0.64, n = 6; t-test, P < 0.01). Because drepanidines are sexually dimorphic in size (Amadon 1950) we used data from males only.

'Ākohekohes are territorial, with a single adult or mated pair and perhaps one or more immature individuals (presumably offspring) foraging in a given tree (Carothers 1986a). In contrast, 'Apapanes are nomadic, flying about and often foraging in small flocks (Carpenter 1978, Carothers 1986a). 'Ākohekohes of either age class dominate 'Apapanes, and within each species adults dominate immatures (Carothers 1986a). Another nectar-feeding drepanidine that occurs in the Maui rain forests, the 'I'iwi, also dominates 'Apapanes, but too few data on the diets of immature 'I'iwi were available to include this species in the comparative analyses.

OBSERVATIONS

Observations were conducted both from the ground and by climbing trees to observe birds at relatively close range (usually 15–20 m) in nearby trees. The following data were recorded for each individual observation: date, time, species, age of individual (by plumage), plant species occupied, stratum occupied, foraging site, and presence and identity of co-occurring birds. The presence or absence of others was recorded in order to determine the effects of dominants upon the foraging behavior of subordinates.

FORAGING COMPARISONS

There were yearly and seasonal variations in both resource availability and relative abundances of the two age classes of both bird species, necessitating the subdivision of all comparisons. Because sufficient sample sizes for immatures were not available for all three field seasons, data for each species were only analyzed for two seasons. Two types of analyses were performed. In the first, the general foraging behaviors of immature and adult conspecifics were compared to see if the two age classes differed. These analyses compared plant species foraged upon and food items selected to establish if basic differences in foraging ecology occurred between age classes.

The second set of analyses focused specifically on foraging behavior in 'ōhi'a trees (their main foraging site). Here I compared stratum occupied, foraging site, and food item of adult and immature conspecifics. To investigate differences in dietary preference on foraging behavior in 'ōhi'a trees, I needed to eliminate the effect of interference interactions by dominant individuals. Dominants defend nectar resources, inhibiting immatures from use of nectar; this should bias subordinates towards insectivory (Carothers 1986a). To control for the effect of interference interactions upon feeding preference, comparisons were made with a data set in which observations with a dominant present in the same tree were excluded. (Experimental removal of dominants, the "ideal" way of testing this hypothesis, is not feasible, as 'Ākohekohes are on the U.S. Endangered Species List). Because adult 'Ākohekohes dominate all others, no observations of their foraging behaviors needed to be excluded. For immature 'Ākohekohes, observations were excluded if adults were present. Foraging observations of 'Apapane adults were excluded if 'Ākohekohes or 'I'iwis were present; for immature 'Apapanes, observations with any co-occurring 'Ākohekohes, 'I'iwis, or adult 'Apapanes were excluded. As noted above, comparisons were made within a given season. Contingency table analyses with G-tests were used to compare frequencies of use of plant species, strata occupied, foraging sites, and food items taken. Raw frequency data (not percentage of use) were used in all tests. When a single cell size was < 5, Yate's correction was employed. Where both cell sizes were < 5, the cells were excluded from the analysis.

RESULTS

Adults and immatures of both species differ in their use of plant species (Table 1). Except for comparisons of 'Ākohekohes during the winter season, immatures fed less frequently from the nectar producing 'ōhi'a trees than adults did. This demonstrates a lesser reliance upon 'ōhi'a nectar by immatures, as reflected in the generally lower levels of nectar foraging (Table 1).

Comparisons of foraging characteristics in 'ōhi'a trees in the absence of dominants show significant differences between age classes in stratum of tree occupied, foraging site, and food items taken (Table 2). In these comparisons, immatures fed less often in the flower-filled canopy. Sites occupied by arthropods (leaf buds and axils, branches and twigs) were favored foraging sites, with the result that arthropods were taken more often than was nectar. These results held for all but the winter 'Ākohekohe adult and immature comparisons, which showed no differences.

Insects occupy flower clusters and could be taken while birds are visiting flowers for nectar. However, my observations indicate that such a behavior is not prominent: when foraging on flowers, birds displayed little evidence of doing anything other than feeding on nectar. In either case, such behavior does not change the fact that

TABLE 1. PERCENTAGES OF USE OF PLANT SPECIES AND OF ARTHROPODS AND NECTAR BY IMMATURE AND ADULT 'APAPANE AND 'ĀKOHEKOHE (SAMPLE SIZES IN PARENTHESES)

	'APAPANE				'ĀKOHEKOHE			
	Summer 1		Summer 2		Summer 2		Winter 1	
	Immature (71)	Adult (246)	Immature (2284)	Adult (1884)	Immature (1613)	Adult (458)	Immature (42)	Adult (458)
PLANT SPECIES								
Acacia koa	0	0	0.26	0	0	0	0	0.44
Broussaisia arguta[a]	1.41	4.47	0	0	0.06	0	0	0
Cheirodendron trigynum	8.45	2.08	0.79	0	0.31	0	0	3.72
Coprosma sp.	0	0	0.18	0	0.12	0	0	0
Gouldia sp.	0	0	0	0	0.06	0	0	0
Ilex anomola	0	0	0	0	0.06	0.22	0	0
Metrosideros polymorpha[a]	78.87	90.24	95.53	99.29	93.49	98.03	100	37.55
Myrsine lessertiana	0	0	0	0	1.80	1.09	0	0.44
Rubus hawaiiensis[a]	1.41	1.22	0	0	0	0	0	0
Pelea clusiaefolia	1.41	0	0.61	0.11	3.35	0.66	0	1.75
Stenogyne sp.[a]	0	0	0	0	0.37	0	0	1.75
Styphelia sp.	4.23	1.22	0.61	0	0.06	0	0	0.44
Vaccinium calycinum	4.23	0.81	0.88	0	0.31	0	0	53.93
G[b]	7.47**		63.57**		14.77*		65.65**	
FOOD ITEM								
Arthropods	57.8	24.2	10.4	2.1	21.9	12.3	29.5	23.3
Nectar	42.3	75.8	89.6	97.9	78.1	87.7	70.5	77.0
G[b]	27.15**		131.22**		22.95**		0.91	

[a] Mainly a nectar source.
[b] G-test compairing distribution of observations between immature and adults.
* denotes P < 0.05
** denotes P < 0.01

juveniles preferentially foraged on strata bearing insects.

DISCUSSION

Differences in body mass between immature and adult drepanidines are consistent with the expectation that immatures are still growing and have not yet attained adult body mass. Thus, any age-related differences in use of forage plant species and use of arthropods or nectar as a food source can be attributed at least in part to the metabolic demands of immatures for continued growth. While such considerations do not mean that this is necessarily an actual cause of diet differences, they are important for considering this hypothesis.

The few data available on other passerines (e.g., Ricklefs 1975, Austin and Ricklefs 1977) are evidence that the greatest increase in body mass of birds occurs before fledging, with more modest increases continuing into adulthood. During this postfledging period body lipid mass appears to stay constant or decrease, while protein containing components of body tissue (measured by lean dry weight) continue to increase. Thus protein/calorie considerations, while not as influential as during the prefledging period, may well be important in diet selection of immatures after fledging.

Foraging characteristics of adults and immatures reveal that they differ significantly in diet, with immatures foraging less often on flowers of 'ōhi'a trees (the main nectar source) than adults. These results also demonstrate that immatures feed on arthropods more often than adults. Interference competition by dominants keeping out subordinates from 'ōhi'a flowers is an expected cause of at least part of this bias (Carothers 1986a,b). However, the data on comparative foraging in 'ōhi'a trees presented here suggests the importance of dietary requirements in the foraging of immatures. In these comparisons, which statistically controlled for effects of interference interactions, immatures foraged in places where they are more likely to encounter arthropod prey items; this decreased the proportion of nectar in their diet. These results indicate that immatures indeed preferentially feed on arthropods compared to adults, despite the effect that interference interactions has in determining the foraging behavior of immatures, primarily immature 'Apapanes.

For 'Ākohekohe immatures, the presence of adults likely does not have an important influence on food selection. A difference between immatures of the two species is expected, given the comparatively higher levels of interference interactions directed against immature 'Apapa-

TABLE 2. PERCENTAGES OF USE AMONG DIFFERENT FORAGING CATEGORIES IN 'ŌHI'A TREES BY IMMATURE AND ADULT 'APAPANE AND 'ĀKOHEKOHE (SAMPLE SIZES IN PARENTHESES)

	'APAPANE				'ĀKOHEKOHE			
	Summer 1		Summer 2		Summer 2		Winter 1	
	Immature (36)	Adult (36)	Immature (849)	Adult (1233)	Immature (447)	Adult (1355)	Immature (172)	Adult (42)
STRATUM								
Canopy	58.3	86.3	94.1	98.6	94.4	91.0	95.2	94.1
Subcanopy	41.7	13.7	4.4	1.2	4.4	8.3	4.8	5.9
Branches	0	0	1.5	0.2	1.2	0.7	0	0
G[a]		13.1**		32.2**		9.7**		0.05
FORAGING SITE								
Flower	54.3	80.6	83.8	98.4	83.9	90.2	73.8	71.5
Leaf Bud	8.6	5.3	6.6	0.5	5.2	0	21.4	11.6
Leaf Axil	0	0	5.7	0.6	7.5	1.3	4.8	11.1
Twig	0	0	1.5	0.2	0.7	6.5	0	0
Branch	37.1	14.1	2.5	0.6	2.6	2.0	0	5.8
G[a]		10.8**		160.4**		107.8**		5.0
FOOD ITEM								
Arthropod	47.2	79.7	16.3	1.6	16.1	9.8	26.2	28.5
Nectar	52.8	20.3	83.7	98.4	83.9	90.2	73.8	71.5
G[a]		10.4**		160.3**		11.1**		0.09

[a] G-test comparing distribution of observations between immatures and adults.
** denotes P < 0.01.

nes, which are at the bottom of the dominance hierarchy (Carothers 1986a). Immature 'Ākohekohes are dominated only by conspecific adults, and because the adults with which they co-occur in trees are probably their parents, the levels of interference interactions are quite low (Carothers 1986a). Thus, interference interactions are unlikely to influence foraging choices of immature 'Ākohekohes. Hence, the observed dietary preferences probably resulting from differing physiological requirements are the main factor responsible for the observed age-related foraging differences. For 'Apapanes, both diet preference and interference interactions play roles in the foraging ecology difference between adults and immatures.

One group of data did not fit the predictions of differing diet, those for immature and adult 'Ākohekohes during the winter. Here no significant differences existed between the age classes; yet what at first seems to contradict the predictions actually supports them. With all other comparisons being of newly fledged summer immatures (approximately three months old), the immature 'Ākohekohes observed in the winter were a full six months. Thus, they were very likely at adult body mass despite the lack of attainment of adult plumage. Accordingly, with their body growth phase completed, their metabolic demands for protein, and resulting dietary preferences and ecology, should have been and was similar to those of adults. (Data for corroboration were unavailable on 'Apapanes during this same period). In another study of nectar-

feeding birds, Thomas (1980) found that for two meliphagid species that emphasized nectar, immatures also ate more arthropods but shifted to more nectar as the season progressed. Some studies (Young 1971, Hainsworth 1977, Thomas 1980) have partly attributed seasonal differences in diet to differences in nectar availability. However, because adult-immature comparisons in this study are made within seasons, any differences between the age classes cannot be attributed to differing availabilities.

A factor not addressed in this paper that may seasonally obscure diet differences based upon differing physiological requirements is the effect of reproduction. It is expected that adult females during the breeding season would eat more arthropods while they are forming eggs (Ricklefs 1974, Montgomerie and Redsell 1980, O'Connor 1984). Both adult male and female nectar feeders may increase the proportions of arthropods they capture when they are feeding young in the nest (for trochilids see Wagner 1946, Hainsworth 1977, Carpenter 1976a, Gass and Montgomerie 1981, Stiles 1995; for meliphagids see Halse 1978, Thomas 1980). These breeding effects would confound the detection of differing diet preferences of adults and immatures. However, the birds in this study were observed both before and after, but not during, the spring breeding season. In this way, diet differences that may have resulted from these breeding affects were eliminated. Future studies on the possible influence of reproduction (and molting) on diet choice in these and other nectar-feeding birds should prove rewarding, and more work on the diets of adult and immatures in other species of nectar-feeding or fruit-eating (Morton 1973, Foster 1978) birds, which also have lower than average protein contents in their diets is needed.

ACKNOWLEDGMENTS

I thank K. Brown, R. Etemad, D. Good, R. Hansen, S. Harvey, S. Mountainspring, M. Weiss, and M. Williams for field assistance, and the Hawaiian Audubon Society, the American Museum of Natural History (Chapman Fund), Sigma Xi (Grant-in-Aid of Research), and the Department of Zoology and the Museum of Vertebrate Zoology (Carl B. Koford Fund) at University of California, Berkeley, for grant support. The personnel of Haleakala National Park and the U.S. Fish and Wildlife Service (especially C. Crivellone, R. Fox, C. and K. Kepler, A. Medeiros, S. Mountainspring, K. Murless, and J. M. Scott) provided help in many ways. Bausch and Lomb kindly provided binoculars, and C. J. Ralph assisted greatly in data entry. R. Ricklefs and several anonymous reviewers offered constructive comments. The Nature Conservancy, Hawai'i, allowed me access to preserve land. Mahalo nui to the above for support.

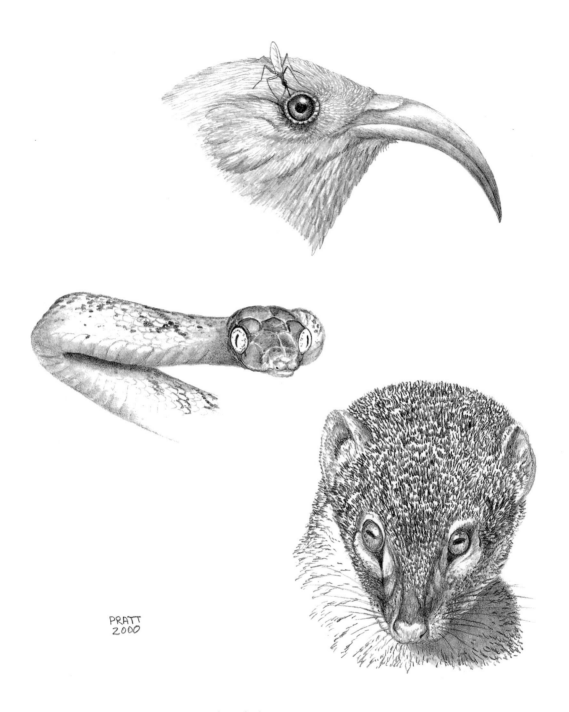

PRATT
2000

Limiting Factors

Studies in Avian Biology No. 22:220, 2001.

LIMITING FACTORS—INTRODUCTION

J. MICHAEL SCOTT AND CHARLES VAN RIPER, III

Speculation for reasons for the decline in numbers and extinction of Hawaii's endemic birds date back to at least the end of the 19th century. Scott Wilson and A. H. Evans in their classic *Aves Hawaiienses: The Birds of the Sandwich Islands* (1890–1899:ix), stated:

"The regrettable extinction of certain of the rarer woodland birds is due to the absence of the trees which supply a large part of their diet: for other causes have undoubtedly contributed to their loss, and it has been well remarked that, for all we know to the contrary, the destruction of some particular insect might result in the simultaneous disappearance of one or more of members of the avifauna."

Repeated observations of continuing loss of endemic species and mounting threats have been made by generations of observers of Hawaiian bird life (see Loope et al. *this volume* and van Riper and Scott *this volume* for details). In the papers that follow, the role that limiting factors play in the ongoing loss of species and their habitats is well documented.

In the introductory chapter to this section, "Limiting Factors Affecting Native Birds of Hawai'i," Charles van Riper, III, and J. Michael Scott provide a comprehensive overview of six limiting factors: (1) habitat changes, (2) human predation, (3) nonhuman predation, (4) avian competition, (5) avian parasites and diseases, and (6) abiotic factors. The influence of each of these is discussed along a time line of cultural influences, i.e., prehuman contact prior to 500 BC, post-Polynesian contact from 500 to 1778 AD, and post-European contact from 1778 to 1998 AD. Their chapter provides the background for the other eight papers in this section.

Darcy Hu and her colleagues characterize Dark-rumped Petrel (*Pterodroma phaeopygia sandwichensis*) nest sites in southeast Mauna Loa at two spatial scales and use population viability assessment to suggest that, with current demographic characteristics, the population may not persist.

Paul Krushelnycky, Cathleen Hodges, Arthur Medeiros, and Lloyd Loope's study of interactions between the Dark-rumped Petrel and the Argentine ant (*Linepithema hunile*) indicate that the alien ant species is not significantly influencing the nesting success rate of Dark-rumped Petrels under current ecological conditions.

Eric VanderWerf's correlation of avian pox-like lesions with demography of 'Elepaio (*Chasiempis sandwichensis*) populations on Mauna Kea is one of the first to relate the demographics of an endemic Hawaiian bird to avian diseases.

Susan Jarvi, Carter Atkinson, and Robert Fleischer provide an excellent overview of the role of avian malaria in the decline of Hawai'i's endemic avifauna. Cherie Shehata, Leonard Freed, and Becky Cann's study of changes in native and introduced bird populations on O'ahu suggest that genetic resistance and/or tolerance factors to avian malaria are evolving on O'ahu. This paper has major implications for the siting of new nature reserves. Similar studies on the low elevation populations of Hawai'i 'Amakihi (*Hemignathus virens virens*) found on Moloka'i and Hawai'i (Scott et al. 1986) might be instructive regarding putative disease resistant populations found there.

Steven Fancy and Thomas Snetsinger's speculation on what caused the population decline of the Bridled-white Eye (*Zosterops conspicillatus rotensis*) on Rota, in the Mariana Islands, has implications for future management of Hawaiian birds. Bertram Murray discusses in detail the evolution of passerine life histories on ocean islands and implications for the dynamics of population decline and recovery in bird populations in Hawai'i and other islands.

The chapter on newly emergent and future threats of alien species to Pacific birds and ecosystems (Loope et al. *this volume*) is a comprehensive survey of potential threats to Hawaiian endemic flora and fauna. However, their findings have implications for endemic flora and faunas worldwide.

Studies in Avian Biology No. 22:221–233, 2001.

LIMITING FACTORS AFFECTING HAWAIIAN NATIVE BIRDS

CHARLES VAN RIPER, III AND J. MICHAEL SCOTT

Abstract. Hawai'i has lost more than half of its endemic avifauna. Causes have varied, but habitat loss, hunting, predation by introduced predators, and disease are those for which we have the best evidence. With the exception of actions taken on behalf of birds in the Leeward Islands, the scale of management actions has not matched the scale of the threats. Species like the 'Akiapōlā'au (*Hemignathus munroi*), 'Ākepa (*Loxops coccineus*), Palila (*Loxioides bailleui*), and Po'ouli (*Melamprosops phaeosoma*) are threatened over their entire range. Despite this, management actions are typically limited to areas less than 1% of species ranges. In the absence of any near future means to eliminate avian diseases, the survival of Hawai'i's endemic avifauna depends on elimination of habitat modifiers such as feral cattle (*Bos taurus*), pigs (*Sus scrofa*), goats (*Capra hircus*), feral sheep (*Ovis aries*), and mouflon (*Ovis musimon*). Introduced predators such as cats (*Felis catus*), rats (*Rattus* spp.), feral dogs (*Canis familiaris*), and small Indian mongoose (*Herpestes auropunctatus*) must be eliminated or significantly reduced in numbers over all, or a significant part of, the ranges of the threatened and endangered species of the islands. Failure to do so will result in all but two or three of the commonest species becoming extinct.

Key Words: disease; Hawai'i; honeycreeper; endangered species; management; predation.

Limiting factors responsible for the declines and extinctions of so many native Hawaiian birds have long interested biologists. Virtually every imaginable factor has been set forward at one time or another for the demise of this avifauna, but too often with little supporting evidence. Many have claimed one factor or another as "the" cause of extinction, but with endangered species, there is virtually never a single limiting factor. Instead, a spectrum of intertwining causes all contribute toward what exists today (Ehrlich et al. 1992).

We will critically examine six limiting factors that have been operative on the native Hawaiian avifauna: habitat changes, human predation, nonhuman predation, avian competition, avian parasites/diseases, and abiotic factors. Each factor will be discussed along a time line, starting with pre-human contact (prior to 500 BC), followed by post-Polynesian contact (400–1700 AD), and ending with post-European contact (1778–1998 AD). We will then try to understand the historical and current factors impacting native birds of the Hawaiian Islands. Hopefully, this will provide a foundation from which future research and management can be soundly based. Without some appreciation of these factors, we will have little hope of taking positive steps toward preventing further losses of this unique avifauna.

LIMITING FACTOR I: HABITAT CHANGES

PRE-HUMAN CONTACT

To properly examine anthropogenic habitat change in the Hawaiian Islands, it is necessary to recreate the condition of habitat and birds prior to arrival of the first humans. This is of course largely speculative, because the early humans in Hawai'i kept no written accounts of the habitat conditions that they encountered. Therefore, we must use archaeological records, observations of the first European explorers, paleontological records, pollen profiles from bogs, and general knowledge of the reactions of biota to various types of impacts.

In pre-human Hawai'i, major habitat changes were restricted primarily to plant community succession and abiotic factors. However, arrival of new species and subsequent adaptive radiation resulted in a constantly changing composition, structure, and function of native ecosystems. One significant influence to vegetation communities was undoubtedly the frequent volcanic eruptions that occurred in the islands, both directly through the impact of lava and volcanic dust and indirectly through fire, as it still does today. The creation of kīpuka's (habitat islands) by lava served to isolate the less mobile species, especially the flightless ones, and must have greatly contributed to the high degree of insular avian adaptive radiation in Hawai'i. Vegetation changes were also wrought by climate shifts caused by El Niño and the ice ages (Allen 1997). Changes in sea level modified low-lying coastal habitats (Nunn 1990). Another factor influencing habitat, and thus the pre-Polynesian birds, would have been infrequent tropical hurricanes. These storms can have a devastating effect on forests and species inhabiting them (Pérez-Rivera 1991, Wauer and Wunderle 1992, Wunderle et al. 1992, Herbert et al. 1999), and any avian species restricted to small forest patches would be subject to local extinctions. Raffaele (1977) attributed the extinction of a Bullfinch (*Loxigilla portoricensis grandis*) from St. Kitts Island to two hurricanes.

Carlquist (1970:173) claimed that before human occupation, no significant herbivory occurred on the islands because there were no grazing land mammals. These ancient forests had, in fact, a considerable array of large herbivorous birds that were probably quite common. One such grazer, a goose, was described from fossil remains more than 50 years ago (Wetmore 1943). Since then, Olson and James (1982b:33–34) have found an array of geese and other potential grazing birds, up to 3 or 4 species from each island, including 10 extinct species, as well as the still extant Hawaiian Goose (*Branta sandvicensis*), hereafter referred to as Nēnē. Some of these extinct birds were quite large, flightless, and even possessed toothlike projections on their beak, apparently an adaptation for grazing on plant parts. In addition, there was a plethora of finch-billed Hawaiian honeycreepers, some of which fed on leaves of plants, as a few still do today. This large grazing avian component undoubtedly influenced habitat changes in pre-human Hawai'i, as did plant feeding insects.

POST-POLYNESIAN CONTACT

The early Hawaiians kept no written records of what habitat changes they wrought to the islands (Kirch 1974). So again, we are forced to rely on inferential reasoning as to what occurred to Hawaiian habitats following Polynesian arrival. We argue that habitat, between the post-Polynesian period of 440 and 1700 AD, would have experienced dramatic changes. The lowlands up to about 1,500 m would have been burned and converted to agricultural lands, thus eliminating a large portion of the very distinct avifauna of these habitats (Cuddihy and Stone 1990). Many of the native plant species, found today only in remnant lowland patches, undoubtedly flourished (Rock 1913). Evidence from Kirch's (1982b) studies of land snails and Olson and James's (1982b) studies of pre-Polynesian fossil birds leaves little doubt that the diversity of the fauna and flora in the lowlands was astounding. Analysis of soil cores dating to 3660 BP in a limited number of sites found that Pritchardia palms and other tree species throughout the lowland forests on O'ahu steadily declined following arrival of Polynesians (Allen 1997, Athens 1997). Additionally, soon after the arrival of humans in the islands, signs of cultivation and erosion were evident. Cultivation of hillsides accelerated erosion, and sediment began to fill coastal lagoons inhabited by species such as the Common Moorhen (*Gallinula chloropus sandvicensis*) and Hawaiian Duck (*Anas wyvilliana*), hereafter referred to as Koloa.

The Polynesian pig's (*Sus scrofa*) impact on forested regions away from human habitation is unknown. There is some evidence that it was not widespread in remote mountainous areas (reviewed by Cuddihy and Stone 1990), although the evidence varies (Ellis 1917, Tomich 1986). They almost certainly foraged widely in lowland areas where they would have significantly modified the vegetation in a manner similar to their activities today. The Polynesian rat (*Rattus exulans*) consumes many of the fruits, seeds, and drupes of native plants.

Much of the reasoning surrounding the thought that Polynesians greatly altered avian habitat in the islands comes from estimates of the human populations, which range from 200,000 to twice that many (Schmitt 1971). Whatever the true population, it was of a size that has not yet been reached even today on six of the eight main islands. This was a population largely dependent upon resources of the land. The warm and relatively deep waters surrounding Hawai'i are not the most productive for fish or invertebrates, although these resources were used extensively and supported large numbers of seabirds.

A massive agricultural system was necessary to support this human population. The excellent work of archaeologists in Hawai'i has provided extensive evidence of intense cultivation, pointing to widespread agriculture ranging from the coast up to 900 m and in some areas to 1,500 m elevation (Yen et al. 1972, Smith and Schilt 1973, Kirch and Kelly 1975; Kirch 1982a,b). The early Hawaiians diverted streams and had massive irrigation projects that enabled them to grow crops in many areas that did not have adequate rainfall and were thus marginal for agriculture.

Fire was used extensively by Polynesians to clear land for cultivation (Kirch 1982a,b; Cuddihy and Stone 1990), and the resultant loss of habitat was a major factor in the massive extinction of birds in the lowlands, and also an important factor in the upland areas. This use of fire in the clearing of large areas of native forest was a regular practice. As we can see today in other Pacific Islands, fire results in a steady encroachment of "cultivated" land, as each burn enters a bit farther into the normally wet, fire-resistant mesic forest (Allen 1997, Spriggs 1997).

The pervasiveness of this land clearing is apparent from pollen records that suggest a lowland vegetation much different from that experienced by early European explorers, who described lowlands on all islands as largely devoid of trees and shrubs and very similar among all the islands. For example, Cook (1785) and Vancouver (1798) describe a scene of dry lowlands devoid of trees and covered with grass on all the main islands. Some of the smaller islands, such as Kahoʻolawe, Lānaʻi, and Niʻihau, were also reported to be completely barren of trees by members of Cook's crew. All this argues that by the time Europeans arrived, much of the damage to lowland birds and their habitats had been done.

The extensive modifications of pre-Polynesian landscapes by the first human inhabitants of the islands is counter to the popular notion that the Polynesians were somehow special in the annals of humans, living harmoniously with their environment and taking only the surplus production of the land and the sea. The evidence that we have today suggests that what forests and avian habitat that were left at European contact remained only because the limited Polynesian technology prevented them from more fully exploiting their environment.

POST-EUROPEAN CONTACT

With the arrival of the Europeans, alteration of upland habitats, which in part had escaped the massive destruction by Polynesians, began in earnest. The first commercial use of Hawaiian forests was the harvesting of sandalwood (*Santalum* sp.), a tree prized for its fragrant wood, in the late 1700s and early 1800s and subsequent exportation to China (Rock 1974). This over-exploitation caused the demise of what once was a fairly common species whose flowers and fruits provided nectar and food for many native birds.

Today sandalwood is quite rare. Since the sandalwood trade died out, there has been relatively inconsistent use of the native forests. There have been numerous attempts at using extant forests for commercial ends, but almost all have been financially unsuccessful. Among these was the cutting of ʻōhiʻa (*Metrosideros polymorpha*) trunks for a variety of products, including railroad ties in the western United States (Rock 1974:333). Koa (*Acacia koa*), the largest native tree, has had the longest history of commercial use in Hawaiʻi. Koa is highly prized among woodworkers because of its unique and interesting grain, being used today for specialty products, hardwood paneling, and flooring. The steady use of the larger trees has been a fairly continuous process, leaving now only remnant stands. Koa harvesting is usually coupled with the introduction of feral herbivores, especially cattle (*Bos taurus*). This tree, a legume, when young is exceedingly palatable to herbivores. Consequently, it is largely unable to regenerate under grazing pressure (Baldwin and Fagerlund 1943).

The conversion of native forests to pasture is probably the most comprehensive change to have taken place in the post-European period in upland native bird habitat. The usual scenario is the initial felling of the forest, resulting in clearing and piling up windrows of logs. The cattle then have access to a variety of native plants, many of which are very palatable. The resulting grazing pressure of cattle prevents regeneration of any native plants except those that are growing on sides of steep gullies or as epiphytes (Cuddihy and Stone 1990).

The introduced animal that probably has had the greatest impact on altering native vegetation is the cow. Vancouver brought the first cattle to Hawaiʻi in 1793, placing seven ashore at two locations on Hawaiʻi Island. In the following year, he landed five more on that island (Vancouver 1798). Cattle were brought to Hawaiʻi in hopes of establishing a permanent food source for both the Polynesians and visiting ships' crews. To this end, Vancouver persuaded King Kamehameha I to place a kapu, or prohibition, for 10 years on the killing of any cattle.

The cattle soon multiplied and dispersed, and by 1801 were being used extensively for beef on Hawaiʻi (Tomich 1986). By 1813, 20 years after being introduced, cattle had so multiplied that they became a nuisance, and Brennan (1974) indicates that they were "devouring and trampling the natives' crops of potatoes, ravishing their taro patches, and, in short, raising havoc with whatever was planted." By 1846 there were an estimated 25,000 wild and 10,000 domestic cattle on the islands of Hawaiʻi. They not only ravished cultivated lands, but also devastated large tracts of native forest. There was little action taken to control them until the early 1900s. Judd (1936) presented a summary of actions taken, including fencing, shooting, trapping, and stock removal. Tomich (1986) credited cattle with totally denuding the Waimea Plain and much of the Hāmākua forests on Hawaiʻi. In fact, vegetation was damaged extensively on each of the islands that had cattle. Today, feral cattle exist in any numbers only on Hawaiʻi (van Riper and van Riper 1982).

Goat (*Capra hircus*) were first released in 1778 on Niʻihau (Cook 1785), and Tomich (1986) felt that they were fairly well distributed throughout Hawaiʻi by 1793. Since the species originated in arid Mediterranean regions, it is well suited to the dry, rugged lava terrain in Hawaiʻi. The vegetation degradation that cattle started was compounded by the many feral goats that had proliferated in the late 1800s. Goats are much more agile than cattle, and they could, therefore, obtain forage in many areas where cattle had been excluded. Goats are prolific, and they move in small herds or family groups (van Riper and van Riper 1982). The product of this was extensive browsing pressure in localized areas. Many of the fragile dry areas in Hawai'i were almost totally denuded of overstory vegetation because of high goat densities. Goats became a significant factor in forest and range deterioration and in the extinction of some specialized plant forms in the islands (Tomich 1986). At one time feral goats inhabited all the main islands, but today they are absent from Ni'ihau and Lāna'i. Indicative of the possibilities for eliminating goats from native ecosystems is the history of goat eradication in Hawai'i Volcanoes National Park. After years of mixed management, including sustained yield hunting, as late as 1970 park personnel fenced the park into quadrants from which goats could be removed using a variety of methods (Yocum 1964, 1967; Tomich 1986). Today the goat only occurs as an occasional straggler in the park. However, elsewhere in the islands it continues its negative impact on native ecosystems.

The effects of feral sheep (*Ovis aries*) on Hawaiian vegetation has been more localized than that of either cattle or goats, being restricted to the islands of Hawai'i and Kaho'olawe. Sheep were first introduced to Hawai'i by Captain James Colnett in 1791 (Wyllie 1850). Vancouver added more in 1793 and 1794. Like other introduced herbivores, feral sheep multiplied rapidly. By the mid-1800s, there were more than 3,000 on Hawai'i, and by the 1930s, there were over 40,000 just on Mauna Kea (van Riper and van Riper 1982). Domestic sheep were also raised on Ni'ihau and Lāna'i, and due to heavy overstocking, there was much damage to the vegetation (Tomich 1986). However, after the closing of the Humu'ula sheep ranch on Hawai'i Island in 1963 (Brennan 1974), the sheep industry all but disappeared in the islands.

Feral sheep and goats were cited as major factors in the decline of the māmane (*Sophora chrysophylla*) forest on Mauna Kea (Warner 1960). In a precedent-breaking decision, the United States Ninth Circuit Court stated that the presence of sheep, goats, and mouflon (*Ovis musimon*) in the māmane forest inhabited by the endangered Palila (*Loxioides bailleui*) was a violation of Section 9 of the Endangered Species Act by causing "harm" to the Palila. In 1979 the state of Hawai'i was directed to remove the feral ungulates from Palila habitat (Bean and Rowland 1997). Twenty years later there are still hundreds of feral sheep, mouflon, and hybrids on the mountain. The example provided by the National Park Service in Hawai'i Volcanoes National Park indicated it is possible to remove ungulates from areas the size of Mauna Kea. Why this population has been allowed to persist is a mystery, as the damage caused to native plants

and the response when ungulates are removed is well documented (Scowcroft 1983, 1992; Scowcroft and Giffin 1983, Scowcroft and Sakai 1984, Scowcroft and Hobdy 1987).

Damage to the vegetation of Hawai'i by feral pigs has been extensive (Giffin 1978, Cooray and Mueller-Dombois 1981, Ralph and Maxwell 1984, Tomich 1986). Pigs of English stock were brought to Hawai'i by Cook (1785) on his first voyage, and a number of subsequent introductions have occurred (Tomich 1986). When new strains were introduced, the Polynesian pig interbred readily with the European varieties. Feral pigs are now distributed throughout the upland pastures and forests of the six largest islands that they inhabit (Tomich 1986). Hawai'i Island has the largest and densest pig population in the archipelago, and pig populations may reach densities of 0.4 animals per ha in pasture areas and 1.2 per ha in rain forest habitat (Giffin 1978). At these high densities, damage to the environment can be extensive. In some remote forested areas, such as Kohala Mountain, pigs have totally removed the understory vegetation, and all that remains are tree-fern skeletons and a quagmire of mud. This removal of understory vegetation and suppression of regeneration of canopy species has undoubtedly had a negative impact on native birds. For example, Rock (1974) noted that the Kohala Mountain area was one of the richest for lobelioids, a favorite nectar source of many native birds. Today, lobelioids are rare on Kohala Mountain and elsewhere as well, and the forest has also lost many of its native birds (van Riper 1982).

Recently introduced plants have resulted in marked vegetation changes in the islands (Cuddihy and Stone 1990). More than 1,000 species of nonnative plants were outplanted in forest reserves between 1910 and 1960 (Skolman 1979). This was in part the result of early statements that native plants were doomed (Lyon 1918). In the 1930s a number of the higher forests were cleared and replanted to eucalyptus (*Eucalyptus* sp.) plantations (Judd 1936). Other mid-to-upper native forests have been converted to nonnative conifers. However, the affected area has been relatively small as compared to conversion to pasture. Other species such as lantana (*Lantana camara*), firetree (*Myrica faya*), and banana poka (*Passiflora mollissima*), as they spread throughout the islands have had negative effects on the composition, structure, and function of native ecosystems. This is perhaps best documented in the national parks (Loope et al. 1992) where firetree has had a major impact (Vitousek 1992, Whiteaker and Gardner 1992). Recent studies have shown changes not only in the species composition of Hawaiian ecosystems but also in their structure and ecological processes (Vitousek 1992). Those forests where nonnative species have become pervasive have usually been perturbed severely by other factors, apparently enabling the entry and spread of introduced species. Not all the impacts have been negative; in fact, the prolific flowers of the banana poka are a favored food source by some native birds (e.g., Berger 1981:155). The introduction of predaceous insects has resulted in the decline of many native insects, many of which serve as prey for native birds or as pollinators of flowering plants on which the nectivorous species feed (Banko and Banko 1976, Howarth and Mull 1992).

Post-European habitat changes were also greatly influenced by new types of agriculture. With the influx of Europeans in the early 1800s, the types of crops grown in the lowland areas changed (e.g., sugar cane and pineapple), and there was some increase in area farmed by the Polynesians, but this increase has not been well documented. Many areas, especially along streams, that were once used by the Polynesians for banana and wetland taro have now reverted back to second-growth habitat. However, they have not usually reverted to native forest but to introduced species of trees and shrubs. Many of the former lowland taro fields were converted to rice cultivation, and this shift probably had a temporary positive effect upon water birds. Early accounts describe the large numbers of ducks frequenting ponds (Berger 1981). Fossils of Laysan Ducks (*Anas laysanensis*) in lava taken on Pu'u Wa'awa'a and other upland locations suggests they may have been more wide-ranging than previously thought. However, more recently, drainage for housing developments and the decrease in farming has resulted in a reduction of wetland habitat. Thus, the advent of western farming continued to have a negative impact on native birds, albeit much reduced from that of the Polynesians.

Even the leeward island habitats were greatly altered, illustrated by the destruction of native vegetation by the European rabbit (*Oryctolagus cuniculus*) introduced to Laysan Island by guano miners in 1903. By the time of the Tanager Expedition in 1923, four of the five endemic landbirds were heading to extinction (Wetmore 1925). The last Laysan Honeyeater (*Himatione sanguinea freethii*) was observed just prior to a three-day windstorm on Laysan Island in 1923 (Wetmore 1925, Bailey 1956).

We are thus left today, on all the Hawaiian Islands, with only remnants of habitat suitable for native bird occupancy and a fraction of the original avifauna.

LIMITING FACTOR II: HUMAN PREDATION

PRE-HUMAN CONTACT

What would have impressed people the most, if they could have viewed pre-human Hawai'i, would have been the spectacular assemblage of seabirds. The large land area and relative absence of predators probably made the Hawaiian Islands home to many millions of terns, shearwaters, petrels, boobies, albatrosses, and other seabirds, the remnants of which today throng only on the leeward and some offshore islands. Due to the remoteness of the islands, insular adaptive radiation flourished and there was a suite of flightless birds, including geese, moa nolas ibises, and rails on each island (James and Olson 1991, Olson and James 1991, Curnutt and Pimm *this volume*). Thus the stage was set for human exploitation of the native avifauna through indiscriminate hunting, as has been demonstrated on other isolated oceanic islands (Steadman 1997a,b).

POST-POLYNESIAN CONTACT

The large number of flightless Hawaiian birds must have been a welcome sight to the early Polynesians. Such a food source, probably fairly abundant, soon succumbed to human predation. Flightless Hawaiian birds followed the same path to extinction as the moas (e.g. *Dinornis torosus, Eurapteryx gravis*) in New Zealand (Anderson 1984, 1989) and other oceanic island birds (e.g., Anderson 1984, Diamond and Veitch 1981; Steadman 1997a,b). Another group that was particularly hard hit by Polynesian hunting was seabirds. Especially vulnerable were the burrow nesting species, such as the Dark-rumped Petrel (*Pterodroma phaeopygia sandwichensis*), whose young were collected by skewering them with a barbed stick just prior to fledging (Munro 1944). Adult petrels and other nocturnal seabirds were also netted as they flew into their nesting grounds after dark (Simons 1985). By 1778, nesting seabirds were all but gone except for the most isolated or inaccessible areas. Their absence was a direct result of continued egg, chick, and adult predation by humans. For example, after protection, Sooty Terns (*Sterna fuscata oahuensis*) increased from few or no birds on Mānana Island off O'ahu to about 100,000 breeding pairs in 1972 (Brown 1976). The large numbers of seabirds transported large masses of nutrients from the sea to the land. This has been demonstrated to be a major factor in the growth of plants and other species elsewhere (Ryan and Watkins 1989, Polis and Hurd 1996, Polis et al. 1997; Anderson and Polis 1998, 1999; Stapp et al. 1999).

After the flightless and unwary birds had been disposed of, the Polynesians resorted to a great variety of bird-catching techniques including birdlime and nooses for the other species (Perkins 1903). Most of these methods were indiscriminate. Polynesians hunted a number of native Hawaiian birds for their feathers, but the prized species included the 'Ō'ō (*Moho* spp.), Hawai'i Mamo (*Drepanis pacifica*), 'Ō'ū (*Psittirostra psittacea*), 'Apapane (*Himatione sanguinea*), and 'I'iwi (*Vestaria coccinea*; Brigham 1899). Not only were feathers collected, but also, in all likelihood, the birds were themselves eaten (Wilson and Evans 1890–1899, Berger 1981), especially considering the relative scarcity of protein in this agricultural society. Although it took an estimated 80,000 birds to construct a small feather cape (Rose et al. 1983), harvesting by prehistoric Hawaiians probably did not have a major detrimental effect on native birds that could fly.

POST-EUROPEAN CONTACT

With the introduction of firearms to the islands, coupled with an active trade of feathered artifacts, hunting probably contributed significantly to the final demise of several highly prized species, particularly the Hawai'i Mamo and 'Ō'ō. Perkins (1903) reports on over 1,000 'Ō'ō (*Moho nobilis*) shot over several weeks above Hilo, Hawai'i. The mid-elevation species were probably hardest hit by hunting for the feather trade, as were the leeward island birds (Berger 1981).

Historic hunting for food and sport during the post-European period had its greatest impact on the extant larger native birds. Swedberg (1967) was convinced that the demise of the Koloa could be attributed directly to hunting pressure. The Nēnē was also subjected to intensive hunting, and there is little doubt that its precipitous decline was directly related to this factor (Baldwin 1945, Kear and Berger 1980). The goose was hunted during its breeding season (September through February) in the early 1900s, thus magnifying the impact.

Today, hunting seasons are closed for all native birds in Hawai'i. However, occasional shooting still occurs. In 1970 we found the plucked remains of two Nēnē on the summit of Hualālai. During the private release of introduced birds in the early 1970s at Pu'u Wa'awa'a, the Hawaiian Hawk (*Buteo solitarius*) was eliminated from this area (pers. obs.). Through the 1980s, the Hawaiian Crow (*Corvus hawaiiensis*), hereafter referred to as 'Alalā, was shot for sport (J. Giffin, pers. comm.). Munro (1944) believed that shooting was one of the chief reasons for the 'Alalā's decline at the turn of the century.

LIMITING FACTOR III: NON-HUMAN PREDATION

PRE-HUMAN CONTACT

Undoubtedly, many of the seabirds that nested on cliffs along the coasts of the main Hawaiian Islands lost young to predatory fish, who would concentrate off shore to prey on young that had just fledged into the ocean. The majority of terrestrial predation on the native avifauna, prior to the arrival of humans, was limited primarily to other avian species. Many of the Hawaiian paleontological specimens have been retrieved from fossilized owl pellets of extinct bird-eating owls in sinkholes (Olson and James 1982b, Olson and James 1991, Giffin 1993). Researchers have also found a number of extinct predatory birds such as Long-legged Owls (*Grallistrix* spp.), an eagle (*Haliaeetus* sp.) and a harrier (*Circus dossenus*) (Olson and James 1991). We know that the Hawaiian Hawk, although a buteo, takes a number of avian prey species (Griffin et al. 1998), as does the Hawaiian subspecies of the Short-eared Owl (*Asio flammeus sandwichensis*) or Pueo. The 'Alalā diet includes a large number of other passerine species (Sakai et al. 1986, Sakai and Carpenter 1990).

POST-POLYNESIAN CONTACT

The Polynesians brought the pig (Kirch 1985, Tomich 1986), Polynesian rat, and dog (*Canis familiaris*), and these early introductions must have greatly affected birds that had never encountered mammalian predators. Native Hawaiian birds evolved in the absence of mammalian predators and were thus extremely vulnerable to these introduced mammals. What portion of the prehistoric avian extinctions can be attributed directly to mammalian predation cannot be determined. However, the view that these introductions by the Polynesians were essentially without impact seems to us without merit. The Polynesian rat, widespread and abundant, is a known predator on 15 species of seabirds (Atkinson 1985) and consumes many of the fruits, seeds, and drupes of native plants. The Polynesian rat is carnivorous and will readily take birds and their eggs (e.g., Kepler 1967, Woodward 1972). Introduced rats have been implicated in the complete breeding failure of several seabird species on Kure Atoll (Moors and Atkinson 1984). Feral pigs are well-known predators of ground-nesting seabirds (Challies 1975). The feral dog is a known predator on seabirds and their eggs (Moors and Atkinson 1984, Atkinson 1985, Johnstone 1985) and has been implicated in the extinction or extirpation of a number of seabird species and populations. Feral dogs almost certainly preyed on eggs and young of both ground-nesting and burrowing colonial nesting seabirds in the lowlands (Johnstone 1985). They are known predators on Nēnē (reviewed in Tomich 1986) and colonial nesting seabirds such as the Wedge-tailed Shearwater (*Puffinus pacificus chlorohynchus*; Byrd and Boynton 1979, Stone et al. 1983).

The Polynesian pig and rat most likely confined initially to the areas around settlements, but within a very few years undoubtedly experienced explosive population increases and dispersed into the forests. (See previous discussion on this topic.) An introduction of an animal into a novel environment often results in such a population explosion, overrunning an area, and only in later years drops to a more restrained population level. Ground-nesting and -feeding birds were probably most affected, and many did not survive long after these mammalian predators were introduced (Olson and James 1982a, 1991; James and Olson 1991). The declines and extinctions caused by these introduced predators is a pattern that was repeated throughout the world (King 1985, Steadman 1995, 1997a,b).

POST-EUROPEAN CONTACT

A number of additional potential predators of birds were introduced into Hawai'i following European discovery, including the cat (*Felis catus*), small Indian mongoose (*Herpestes auropunctatus*), two species of rat (roof rat, *R. rattus*, and Norway rat, *R. norvegicus*), and the Barn-Owl (*Tyto alba*). Of these, the one with probably the most impact on birds was the roof rat. Atkinson (1977) provides convincing evidence implicating this rat as one of the major causes of the declines of native birds in the early 1900s. He observed that the chief effect of the roof rat on passerine birds was through predation on eggs, nestlings, and sometimes adults. It is fairly certain that this rat caused the extinction of the Laysan Finch (*Telespiza cantans*) and Laysan Rail (*Porzana palmeri*) from Midway Island (Munro 1944; Baldwin 1945, 1947b). More recently, Seto and Conant (1996) showed that 46 of 58 known nest failures of Bonin Petrels (*Pterodroma hypoleuca*) on Midway Island were due to loss of eggs thorough rat predation. Eddinger (1970) found that roof rats destroyed a number of 'Anianiau (*H. parvus*) and 'I'iwi nests that he had studied on Kaua'i. On Hawai'i, van Riper (1978) reported predation of roof rats at two Hawai'i 'Amakihi (*H. virens*) nests found on Mauna Kea. Roof rats have been implicated in the loss of five species of birds from South Cape Island in New Zealand (Bell 1978). The Norway rat is a known predator on more than 100 bird

species (Atkinson 1985), has caused significant declines in many, and has been implicated in the extinction of the Lord Howe Island Starling (*Aplonis fuscus carunculatus*) and South Island Saddleback (*A. f. hullionus*; Hindwood 1940, Atkinson and Bell 1973). King (1985) stated that rats have been implicated in the greatest number of extinctions due to any predator (54%).

The cat was introduced to Hawai'i with the first Europeans, quickly became feral, and is now established in the wild on all eight main islands (Tomich 1986). It lives in all habitats throughout Hawai'i, but is more abundant in drier areas. Cats worldwide are known to prey on birds (e.g., Johnstone 1985, Veitch 1985), and Hawai'i is no exception. Twenty-six percent of bird extinctions on islands by nonnative predators are attributed to cats (King 1985). Perkins (1903) reported that he found the bodies of no less than 22 native birds that were eaten by cats on a single trail over a two-day period on Lāna'i. Richardson and Woodside (1954) reported that cats preyed on the endangered Dark-rumped Petrel on both Hawai'i and Maui. Tomich (1969) found feral cats on Mauna Kea with remains of the introduced Skylark (*Alauda arvensis*) in their stomachs. On this same mountain, van Riper (1978) reported that 55% of trapped cats had bird remains in their stomachs. Native birds were the Hawai'i 'Amakihi and 'Elepaio (*Chasiempis sandwichensis*). He also found one nest of the endangered Palila from which the female had been taken by a cat. In the Kīlauea forest on Mauna Loa, Hawai'i, Tomich (1981b) found 'Ōma'o (*Myadestes obscurus*) in a cat stomach. There is no doubt that the cat has had and continues to have a negative effect on the native birds of Hawai'i.

The small Indian mongoose was released in Hawai'i in 1883 along the Hāmākua coast of Hawai'i (Bryan 1938). Subsequent releases were made on all of the main islands except Lāna'i and Kaua'i (Baldwin et al. 1952). Mongooses are principally predators on ground-nesting birds (King 1985). They have been identified as a primary factor in the extinction of the ground-nesting Jamaican Least Pauraque (*Siphonorhis americanus americanus*) and at least one other Jamaican species also known as predators on seabirds (King 1985). Their impact would, therefore, be felt more heavily on native seabirds, ducks, geese, and those passerines that frequent the ground.

La Rivers (1948), Baldwin et al. (1952), Kami (1964), and Tomich (1986) have treated at length the question of whether the mongoose is a negative factor in relation to landbirds. They reported that the small Indian mongoose now preys principally on game birds, and occasionally some of the introduced passerine species. King and Gould (1967) felt that this predator was responsible for the disappearance of the endemic subspecies of Townsend's Shearwater (*Puffinus auricularis newelli*), hereafter referred to as Newell's Shearwater, from most of the main Hawaiian Islands. The mongoose is probably now having the greatest impact on the Nēnē (Baldwin 1945, Elder 1958, Walker 1966, Baker and Russell 1979). Banko (1992, Banko et al. 1999) believes that the poor reproductive success of the goose in recent years is a direct result, in part, of mongoose predation on eggs, goslings, and adults. Without proper control of this predator, it is doubtful if the Nēnē will ever be able to maintain its numbers in the wild. However, inadequate food resources appear to be a significant factor in failure to restore the Nēnē to nonendangered status citation.

In studies conducted on the feeding habits of the Barn Owl (*Tyto alba*), native landbirds constituted only a small portion of their diet (Tomich 1971, 1981b, Byrd and Telfer 1980, Snetsinger et al. 1994; C. van Riper, pers. comm.). However, owls near seabird colonies have some effect (Byrd and Telfer 1980), and feral dogs and pigs have been known to prey on the Nēnē and Koloa (Swedberg 1967, Tomich 1969, Giffin 1982).

Perkins (1903:394) felt that the Common Myna (*Acridotheres tristis*) was a major predator on eggs and young of other avian species. He said that it "probably exceeds in numbers the whole of the native land-birds put together," and felt it had "greatly extended its range through the forest." In the 1890s the species was in an expansion phase of a population increase, and may well have had marked negative effects on native birds. Today, it is much rarer in native forests, and its impact on other birds probably not nearly so severe.

LIMITING FACTOR IV: AVIAN COMPETITION

PRE-HUMAN CONTACT

Interspecific avian competition was undoubtedly a significant force driving evolution of the pre-human avifauna on the Hawaiian Islands. The disharmonic fauna and equitable environment rapidly selected for different forms, each sped along their evolutionary pathways through avoidance of competition from their avian counterparts.

POST-POLYNESIAN CONTACT

The only additional component of potential interspecific competition added to the Hawaiian avifauna during the Polynesian era was the Red Junglefowl (domestic chicken—*Gallus gallus*).

It is not clearly understood how this species interacted with the terrestrial native birds, how it competed for resources, and what diseases might have been introduced with it, but the introduction of this bird by the Polynesians as a domestic animal probably had some impact. At present the Red Junglefowl is found in numbers only on Kaua'i, which lacks the mongoose, but it was formerly established in the wild on all the main islands. Its reproductive potential is high, and it is omnivorous. It seems very likely to us that this species in large numbers could have been a potent competitor to some species of ground-foraging native birds, such as the smaller rails, only one of which survived into historical times.

POST-EUROPEAN CONTACT

Competition with native birds by introduced avian species is one of the favorite themes of biologists who have compiled armchair lists of potential causes of the demise of the Hawaiian avifauna. In addition, much of yesterday's ecological literature emphasizes the role of competition in shaping communities (e.g., MacArthur 1972). There have been, however, no unequivocal studies establishing competition as a cause of extinctions in Hawai'i, and none is likely to be soon forthcoming. The study of competition in birds is one of correlation and comparison because of the difficulty in designing a crucial experiment with field populations. The Japanese White-eye (*Zosterops japonicus*) is considered a prime candidate as a harmful competitor. Although introduced about 1929, after most native bird extinctions had already occurred, it is widely known as an abundant generalist, spending a good deal of time gleaning for insects but also venturing with facility into frugivory and nectarivory (van Riper 2000).

There have been few published studies that actually examined data that may have some relevance to introduced versus native bird competition in Hawai'i (Moulton and Pimm 1983, 1986a; Mountainspring and Scott 1985). Mountainspring and Scott (1985) examined the correlations between densities of different birds in different areas to determine if any negative relationships emerged. That is, if one bird became less common while another became more common, it could indicate a competitive interaction. Of 170 partial correlations, just 6% were significantly negative, only slightly more than the 5% expected by chance alone. However, the authors felt that two relationships were especially important: (1) the Japanese White-eye and the 'Elepaio, and (2) the Japanese White-eye and 'I'iwi. Even if competition is involved in these two cases, clearly by this measure at least, it is not a pervasive and continuous force. However, when they examined the entire set of set of correlations, Mountainspring and Scott (1985) found that there was a more pervasive pattern. The native/introduced species pairs had a significantly greater proportion of negative partial correlations (37%) than either native/native (8%) pairs, or introduced/introduced (0%) pairs. The authors suggest that many of the native/introduced species pairs experience at least small population depressions due to competition.

It seems unlikely to us that introduced granivores and frugivores could be competitors with native birds, since critical seed and fruit resources are used by relatively few historic native birds and because they are superabundant (Wagner et al. 1990a,b). Some native birds that use fruit resources (largely the thrushes) are themselves still generally common (van Riper and Scott 1979, Wakelee 1996). Similarly, the presumed granivores that became extinct, such as the large-billed finches, used food resources that are still common, and there were essentially no introduced species that could have completed with them for this food resource (however, see Moulton et al. *this volume*).

LIMITING FACTOR V: AVIAN PARASITES/ DISEASES

PRE-HUMAN CONTACT

Because of Hawai'i's isolation, many avian diseases and their vectors were not able to reach the islands prior to the arrival of humans. The first avian parasites to reach the islands undoubtedly arrived with early immigrating birds, and they subsequently evolved with their avian hosts. Endemic coccidia and nematodes have been reported from Hawai'i (Levine 1980, Cid del Prado Vera et al. 1985) and many ectoparasites also appear endemic (Garrett and Haramoto 1967, Goff 1980). It is unknown what impact these diseases had on prehistoric bird populations.

POST-POLYNESIAN CONTACT

It is not known what avian parasites/diseases arrived in Hawai'i from 400 to 1700 AD. Alicata (1947) lists a number of diseases in gallinaceous birds, and it is possible that some of these were introduced to Hawai'i with the Polynesian chicken. Additional avian parasites could have been introduced to the islands during this period by migrating birds, but because of distances to mainland source areas (e.g., 5,000 km to North America), certainly birds with heavy parasite levels would have been less likely to survive the long flight. The impact of infectious diseases introduced by Polynesians and their commensals is unknown but may have been significant (Daszak et al. 2000).

POST-EUROPEAN CONTACT

The parasites and diseases that have accumulated in Hawaiian birds subsequent to European contact are varied. Protozoa, various helminths, ectoparasites, viruses, bacteria, and fungi are all represented (van Riper and van Riper 1985). Although most diseases appear to be of little importance in regulating avian populations in Hawai'i, avian poxvirus and malaria have had an important influence. These two diseases have such an influence on the native birds that of all the limiting factors presently operative in Hawai'i, disease is now recognized as the single factor having the greatest impact on the continued survival and potential recovery of native birds.

The negative impact of diseases on native Hawaiian birds was probably felt most strongly when avian poxvirus, one of the first new diseases, was introduced to the islands following colonization by Europeans. Perkins (1893) recorded a number of native species from O'ahu and Hawai'i, including the 'Apapane, Lesser 'Akialoa (*H. obscurus*), 'Elepaio, Palila, and Kona Grosbeak (*Chloridops kona*) with extensive swellings on their legs and feet. Rothschild (1893–1900) and Wilson and Evans (1890–1899) also mention numerous birds that they encountered with lesions on their legs, feet, and heads. Avian pox was first confirmed in an 'Ākepa on Hawai'i by Henshaw (1902a). Munro (1944) associated the increasing numbers of domestic poultry with the spread of avian pox throughout the islands. In any event, by the late 1800s, it is clear that avian pox was widespread in the islands. It is, therefore, probable that it played a role in the massive extinctions of the native birds at the turn of the century. Today, this disease is still impacting native forest birds (Jenkins et al. 1989, VanderWerf *this volume*, van Riper et al. in press).

Malaria, a parasitic disease caused by blood protozoan infections (*Plasmodium* spp.), was the second important disease introduction, probably brought in with caged passerine birds in the early 1920s (Laird and van Riper 1981, van Riper and van Riper 1985). The mosquito vector for malaria, *Culex quinquefasciatus*, was present on all the main islands at that time, and then spread the parasite to previously unexposed native avian species. This mosquito is present up to 1650 m elevation, the highest reaches of the extant wet forests on Hawai'i Islands, but its abundance is quite low at the upper elevations (Goff and van Riper 1980). Despite this, infected birds are found at all elevations, and malaria transmission in Hawai'i does occur quite successfully at relatively low vector densities. The key observation of van Riper et al. (1986) is that the altitudinal distribution of the parasite is not a direct reflection of vector densities. At lower elevations, *C. quinquefasciatus* is numerous, and the avian malarial parasite level low. At the mid-elevation ranges (about 800–1,300 m), malarial parasite levels increase disproportionately to the number of vectors. These are also the lowest elevations at which native birds are normally present. It thus appears that a directional selection pressure, exerted by the pathogenicity of the malarial parasite, is presently forcing the native avifauna into higher forest areas. It affects young birds, as in Hawai'i where first-year birds have up to six times greater parasitemia levels than do adults, particularly in native species. Laysan Finches from mosquito-free Laysan Island have been shown to be very susceptible to *Plasmodium* infections (Warner 1968), with 100% mortality in test birds (van Riper and van Riper 1985). In other Hawaiian birds, there are varying degrees of susceptibility to malaria (Atkinson et al. 1995, 2000; Jarvi et al. *this volume,* Shehata et al. *this volume,* Yorinks and Atkinson 2000), and these differences are observed even between populations of the same species, depending upon their length of historical exposure to mosquitoes (van Riper et al. 1986).

Because the endemic avifauna apparently evolved in the absence of many disease factors, it is probable that the native birds have lost some immunogenetic mechanisms. So, when confronted with newly encountered diseases, naive native birds are more susceptible than their introduced counterparts with a long history of exposure and natural selection. This situation has been documented in North America birds, for example, where introduced birds succumb more readily to native eastern equine encephalitis (Karstad 1971b). In Hawai'i, avian pox and malaria, the two introduced diseases which have probably had the greatest negative impact on native birds, appear to have an attenuated pathology when compared to continental strains (C. van Riper, pers. obs.). In addition, populations of some species (e.g., Hawai'i 'Amakihi) seem to have developed some resistance to the present *Plasmodium* parasite. Recently, there have been some preliminary indications that genetic resistance to some introduced diseases may be evolving (Shehata et al. *this volume,* Atkinson et al. 2000, S. Jarvi pers. comm.,).

The pattern of historical decline in native Hawaiian birds is bimodal. The initial reduction of native birds was in the mid- and late 1800s and was unlikely due to disease. However, the second phase of extinctions in the early 1900s was the most likely result of a number of factors, including introduced predators and habitat loss,

but avian pox and malaria were likely the primary causes. Other than avian pox and malaria, the majority of avian diseases present in Hawai'i are relatively non-pathogenic. Harm to infected individuals varies with the parasite, and some parasites typically produce more negative effects on their hosts than others. *Ascaridia* larvae, for example, migrate through and damage various organs in route to their final destination, whereas for other parasites (e.g., acanthocephalans and cestodes), only the localized sites of parasite attachment may become inflamed. Many parasites, such as *Dispharynx* and *Capillaria,* feed only on intestinal contents, rarely disrupting their host's condition. The greatest threat of most maladies is the lowering of the host's resistance so that other stresses can cause death. For example, *Histomonas meleagridis* inflections become more severe when certain types of intestinal bacteria are present (Kemp and Springer 1978), and the severity of *Ascaridia galli* infections is influenced by levels of coccidia and some viruses (Levine 1980).

Many parasites require intermediate hosts, while others facultatively rely upon them for increased success of transmission. The gapeworm (*Syngamus trachea*) does not require an intermediate host, but birds that feed on earthworms are more severely infected (Levine 1980). The eyeworm (*Oxyspirura mansoni*) is the most widespread helminth infecting avian hosts in Hawai'i. This parasite is probably found in all birds that regularly eat the intermediate host, the burrowing cockroach (*Pycnoscelus surinamensis*). There are a number of other examples where intermediate hosts limit the types of birds infected in Hawai'i. Because of their influence on parasite and disease transmission, intermediate hosts could be important targets in a parasite control program. Alicata (1947) reported success in controlling the poultry eyeworm by the introduction of toads to poultry yards in Hawai'i. Mosquito eradication is well documented as a successful means of malaria control.

Other disease pathogens might have a similar influence in the future; it is vital that no new diseases and parasites or their vectors be introduced to the islands (Loope et al. *this volume*). Arboviruses, Newcastle disease, and possibly avian influenza, are absent, based on preliminary surveys by Quisenberry and Wallace (1959), Wallace et al. (1964), and Okamoto (1975). The obvious solution is careful control in the importation of birds, including the monitoring and clearing of all parasites in these birds.

Species being reintroduced into the wild from captive populations, such as the Nēnē, in particular, should be monitored for diseases and parasites (Griffith et al. 1989, Snyder et al. 1996).

Care should be taken to insure that released birds do not carry diseases or parasites that are absent in wild populations. For instance, *Cyathostoma,* a gapeworm infecting geese, has never been reported in Hawai'i, but Avery (1966) reported it from captive Nēnē at a rearing facility in Slimbridge, England. Life cycles of this parasite are similar to *Syngamus trachea,* and disease symptoms can be quite severe (Levine 1980). Avery (1966) also reported tuberculosis and two species of tapeworms, *Menatoparataiena southwelli* and *Fimbiaria fasiolaris,* from captive Nēnē in England. It is not known if these parasites have reached Hawai'i in captive birds that have been released in the past from Slimbridge, but great care should be taken to prevent their introduction.

In summary, there is compelling evidence today that a few diseases are presently playing a major role in influencing the numbers and distribution of native birds (Daszak et al. 2000). In order to preserve and properly protect these birds, it is imperative that the importance of diseases and parasites be recognized as limiting factors for endemic birds and that efforts be made to reduce breeding sites for known vectors and to conduct research on development of disease-resistant populations for repopulating historical range (Fancy and Ralph 1997, Cann and Douglas 1999, Jarvi et al. *this volume,* Shehata et al. *this volume*).

LIMITING FACTOR VI: ABIOTIC FACTORS

PRE-HUMAN CONTACT

Hurricanes, fires, floods, volcanic eruptions, and other short-duration high-energy abiotic events cause infrequent environmental perturbations that often greatly impact species and ecosystems. These phenomena can be so large as to influence all or a significant portion of an endangered species range, as seen in other areas of North America. For example, Hurricane Hugo in 1989 resulted in the loss of half of the population of the endangered Puerto Rican Parrot (*Amazona vittata*). Hugo had similar devastating effects on Red-cockaded Woodpecker (*Picoides borealis*) when it destroyed 95% of the suitable nesting trees at the Francis Marion National Forest in South Carolina, home to 20% of the known Red-cockaded Woodpecker population (USFWS 1989). The Short-tailed Albatross (*Phoebastria albatrus*) was thought to be extinct, the result of volcanic eruptions on its nesting grounds (Hasegawa 1984). However, birds that were apparently at sea during the eruptions later recolonized the former nesting colonies, and the species is making a slow recovery. Abiotic influences were most likely the major lim-

iting factor to Hawaiian birds prior to human arrival. Not only did the extensive lava flows destroy habitat, but they also created partial dispersal barriers to birds, especially flightless species. Extreme weather events such as hurricanes, floods, and El Niño oscillations all influenced avian survival in pre-human Hawai'i as did massive landslides, subsidence, changes in sea level, and tsunamis (Strearns 1966, Carson and Clague 1995).

POST-POLYNESIAN CONTACT

As the lowland native vegetation was eliminated by Polynesians, habitat patch size concomitantly decreased. These smaller patches were much more susceptible to abiotic perturbations. Strong winds would have felled solitary trees, while hurricanes could have potentially destroyed many of the smaller lowland habitat patches. Assuming that the upland forests were still somewhat intact, hurricanes would not have had as great an impact, in fact probably providing openings for forest regeneration.

Volcanic eruptions and subsequent lava flows would have had a greater impact on the post-Polynesian contact native birds because habitat patch in the lower forests was continually being reduced. As the lowland patches became further apart, any destruction of remaining patches by lava flows would have increased barriers to dispersal and ultimately resulted in less habitat for birds.

El Niño oscillations would have continued to influence avian resources, but with smaller habitat patches spaced further apart, ultimately the variable weather conditions would have had a greater negative impact on food resources and ultimately upon avian populations.

POST-EUROPEAN CONTACT

As Europeans further reduced available avian habitat through agricultural and residential clearing, and the activities of their introduced ungulates, abiotic factors would have escalated their impact on the native birds. In Hawai'i the current ranges of many of the endangered species are extremely small, frequently less than 10,000 ha (Scott et al. 1986). Small distributional areas make endangered Hawaiian species extremely vulnerable to stochastic abiotic perturbations of their environment. For example, Scott et al. (1986) estimated the 'Ō'ū population on the island of Hawai'i to number 300 individuals and have a distributional of less than 5,000 ha. In 1984 a flank eruption of Mauna Loa resulted in lava flows and subsequent fires that eliminated all habitat where the greatest number of 'Ō'ū had been observed (Reynolds and Snetsinger *this volume*). This habitat loss, due to an abiotic event, undoubtedly hastened the decline of this species in that it has not been reliably reported from Hawai'i since 1987 (Pyle 1992, Reynolds and Snetsinger *this volume*). The impact on lowland populations of the 'Ōma'o, Hawai'i 'Amakihi, and 'Elepaio went undocumented.

Probably the most significant example of recent abiotic impacts on native birds occurred on the island of Kaua'i, and is summarized by Pratt (1994). The historic avifauna, although confined to the Alaka'i Plateau with some populations very reduced, still retained all species through 1960 (Richardson and Bowles 1964). Montane forest birds on Kaua'i and other islands formerly moved to lower elevations in great numbers during storms (Henshaw 1902a). Beginning in 1980s, a series of hurricanes destroyed a large portion of the remaining Alaka'i Plateau habitat, and many individuals were driven to lower elevations, thus exposing them to introduced diseases; thus followed the extinction of many native species. Following Hurricane Iwa, the 'Ō'ō'ā'ā (*Moho braccatus*) population was reduced to a single male, and no individuals have been reported since 1987 (Pyle 1989). The 'Ō'ū, common to the 1980s (Scott et al. 1986), was reduced to a few birds by the 1990s (Pratt 1994). The Kāma'o (*M. myadestinus*), once one of Kaua'i's most abundant native birds, declined to several hundred individuals by 1973 (Sincock et al. 1984), to several dozen in 1981 (Scott et al. 1986), and to only several individuals by 1989 (Pyle 1989). In 1992 Hurricane Iniki caused even more devastation to the small remnant of existing native bird habitat on the Alaka'i Plateau. Pratt (1994) questions if the Kāma'o, Puaiohi (*Myadestes palmeri*), 'Ō'ū, and Nukupu'u (*H. lucidus hanapepe*) will survive the ravages of Iniki. To make matters even worse, Atkinson et al. (1995) have now found avian malaria in the Alaka'i birds, where prior to recent hurricanes, they demonstrated that this parasite was absent from these forests.

The last individuals of the Laysan Honeyeater were seen just prior to a severe three-day windstorm in 1923 (Wetmore 1925, Baily 1956). The Palila, known only from 13,900 ha of māmane forest on the island of Hawai'i, is at great risk from loss of habitat due to fire. Two hundred ha were lost to fire in 1979. A similar size fire in the māmane forest with highest densities of Palila could remove habitat for 800 birds, 12% to 40% of population estimates for the species (Scott et al. 1984).

Clearly, abiotic disturbances can have a major impact on species with small populations and restricted distributions. However, it is important to note that in all the cases we have cited, the abiotic events were able to impact significant portions of species' ranges only because they had been decreased by other factors. In the case of the Short-tailed Albatross, the birds had been eliminated from all but one of their nesting islands by individuals killing birds for their feathers, and to habitat loss as the result of grazing by cattle. In the case of the Laysan Honeycreeper, its habitat had been destroyed by rabbits that had been introduced to provide meat to guano workers. Loss of vegetation may have also contributed to the severity of the windstorm. The 'Ō'ū occurred in less than 5% of its historical range as the result of introduced predators and disease (Scott et. al. 1988).

Restoring species to all or a significant portion of their historic range is the surest way to guard against loss of species to abiotic threats. In Hawai'i, this will require that recovery actions be put in place over much larger areas than in the past. Current populations of several of Hawai'i's endangered species (e.g., three Po'ouli [*Melamprosops phaeosoma*]) are so small that lack of genetic diversity may be contributing to their decline. However, this remains one of many unstudied questions.

CONCLUSIONS

The composition of the flora and fauna of Hawai'i has been shaped by a number of biotic and abiotic factors. Prior to the arrival of Polynesians about 400–500 AD, all these factors were natural; new diseases, parasites, and new competitors arrived on their own and all evolved in the absence of the hand of humans. The arrival of the first Polynesians' voyages changed all that, for with them came the dog, Polynesian rat, and pig, all known predators on a very vulnerable avifauna. The nature of introduced diseases on plants and animals remains unknown. But the record of species lost directly at the hand of humans—directly, through hunting and habitat modification, or indirectly, as the result of predation and habitat modification of our commensals—while incomplete, is well documented. At least 50% of the known species were lost. The arrival of Europeans and later other ethnic groups brought new and more powerful tools for habitat modification and hunting as well as large ungulate browsers and grazers that were capable of inflicting unprecedented habitat change on the Hawaiian landscape. With the Polynesians, conversion of landscapes to anthropogenic cover types was largely restricted to elevation below about 1,600 m. After 1778 there were no elevational limits, and loss of habitat extended to the tree line at 3,000 m on Mauna Kea. With this increase in loss and modifications of habitat, and the introduction and continuing introduction of a host of alien species and diseases, the Hawaiian avifauna experienced its second extinction spasm, one that continues to this day. Efforts to save species have largely failed, in large part because of the failure of recovery actions to match the scale of the threat. Recovery actions, with the exception of those on the smaller islands in the leeward chain, have not been conducted over all or a significant part of threatened and endangered species' ranges. As a result, species responses have been at the level of increases in survival or reproduction for individual animals, not at the population, subspecies, or species level required for recovery. Perhaps the best example is the Nēnē. Efforts to save this species date back to at least 1950 (Kear and Berger 1980); captive breeding efforts resulted in release of thousands of birds on Hawai'i and Maui. Efforts to control predators focused on small predator-free exclosures or in the immediate vicinity of nesting pairs. However, these efforts have been over but a very small fraction of the Nēnē's range.

Contrast these recovery efforts with those on behalf of the congeneric Aleutian Canada Goose (*Branta canadensis leucopareia*). The factors associated with the decline of these species are similar: hunting and introduced predators. While hunting of both species was largely eliminated, the story with respect to introduced predators is quite different. The introduced Arctic Fox (*Alopex lagopus*) was eliminated from entire islands on which the Aleutian Canada Goose bred. The population has increased from 790 in 1975 to more than 24,000 in 1998 (V. Byrd, pers. comm.). The number of Nēnē continues to decline (USFWS 1996a, c). This demonstrates clearly that the management response has to match the scale of the threat to a species.

The islands of Hawai'i are so large that elimination of known predators on native birds will be extremely difficult. Cats have been eliminated from areas as large as 2,180 ha (Veitch 1985). Norway rats have been eliminated from islands only as large as 100 ha, while it has been suggested that 100 ha are the largest area from which elimination of rats is possible. The recent elimination of rats over 1,000 ha on Midway Island (R. Shallenberger, pers. comm.) gives hope for effective removal of rats over areas at least that large on the major islands. The māmane forest on Mauna Kea and 'Akiapōlā'au (*H. munroi*) habitat in Hakalau Forest National Wildlife Refuge would make excellent areas to demonstrate that rats could be removed from biologically significantly sized areas in structurally complex habitats. Removal of feral ungulates, as demonstrated by the successful removal of pigs and goats from Hawai'i Volcanoes National Park, appears to be limited only by our desire to do so.

If we fail to eliminate or control nonnative predators and ungulates from all or a significant part of the range of Hawai'i's endangered bird species, we will continue to catalog the demise of an avifauna. Since the completion of the Hawai'i Forest Bird Survey (Scott et al. 1986), the 'Ō'ū, 'Ō'ō'ā'ā, Kāma'o, and Moloka'i Oloma'o (*Myadestes lanaiensis rutha*) are presumably extinct, and the Po'ouli (*Melamprosops phaeosoma*), with only three individuals known, is functionally extinct. Despite this record of loss, current efforts to save the species are conducted at scales (individual animals) inappropriate to the challenge (species ranges). Unless we act now to eliminate introduced mammals from all or a significant part of the ranges of these species, all is lost.

While additional biological reserves are needed, the current "system" of biological reserves (national parks, national wildlife refuges, Nature Conservancy reserves, and Hawai'i Department of Natural Resources wildlife management areas) provides a framework to initiate an aggressive habitat restoration initiative (Holt and Fox 1985). Much of what has to be done was documented fifteen years ago in a detailed summary of threats, their impacts, and actions till then (Stone 1985). Not much has changed. More areas have been dedicated to long-term conservation of native species. The Hakalau Forest National Wildlife Refuge, Kona Forest National Wildlife Refuge, and The Nature Conservancy's Waikamoi Preserve on Moloka'i are but three examples (see Holt and Fox 1985 for a listing of extant reserves in 1985). Nonetheless, with few exceptions (Katahira et al. 1993) we have consistently failed to act on available information and use existing methods to eliminate sheep, goats, mouflon, rats, and cats over biological significant areas. A similar conclusion was made 11 years ago (Stone and Stone 1989).

A lot has been accomplished. Much more could be accomplished by working cooperatively and using currently available methods. Economies of scale in cost and efficiency will be gained as new techniques become available. The biological impact on birds, their habitats, and other endemic plants and animals is well documented (see citations in this article; Stone 1985, Stone and Stone 1989). We will be judged poorly by future generations of conservationists if we fail to act aggressively on that information.

Studies in Avian Biology No. 22:234–242, 2001.

HABITAT USE AND LIMITING FACTORS IN A POPULATION OF HAWAIIAN DARK-RUMPED PETRELS ON MAUNA LOA, HAWAI'I

DARCY HU, CATHERINE GLIDDEN, JILL S. LIPPERT, LENA SCHNELL, JAMES S. MACIVOR, AND JULIAN MEISLER

Abstract. Through field surveys and geographic information system analysis, Dark-rumped Petrel (*Pterodroma phaeopygia sandwichensis*) nest sites on southeast Mauna Loa were characterized at two scales. Regionally, nests occurred in weathered pāhoehoe flows, most over 2,000 years old. At the scale of the individual burrow, nearly half the active nests occurred in human-modified pits; the rest were placed in various naturally occurring openings. In 1995, when feral cat (*Felis catus*) predation was limited, the nest success rate was independent of burrow type. However, in 1996, when predation was heavier, burrows placed in human-altered pits suffered higher losses. Population viability analysis suggests that at current rates of predation, the southeast Mauna Loa population of Dark-rumped petrels may not persist.

Key Words: bird catching; Dark-rumped Petrel; excavated pits; feral cats; nest success; population viability analysis; predation; *Pterodroma phaeopygia sandwichensis*; 'Ua'u.

The Hawaiian Dark-rumped Petrel (*Pterodroma phaeopygia sandwichensis*) was one of five procellariid seabirds found in the main Hawaiian Islands prior to human contact, three of which remain today (Olson and James 1982b). Breeding only in Hawai'i, these petrels enter and exit underground burrows nocturnally during the late February to November nesting season (Simons 1985). The subspecies is federally listed as endangered (USFWS 1983b). Recent electrophoretic comparisons have bolstered earlier suggestions, based on morphology and behavior, to reclassify the Hawaiian and Galápagos subspecies as full species (Browne et al. 1997).

Historical, ethnographic, archeological, and paleontological evidence suggest that prior to human arrival, the Dark-rumped Petrel occurred on all the main Hawaiian Islands from sea level to at least mid-elevations. At low elevations, it was found both offshore (e.g., Makuko'oniki [probably a variant or misspelling of Mokuho'oniki] Islet off Moloka'i, Banko 1980d; Mānana Island off O'ahu, Handy and Handy 1972) and on the main islands themselves (e.g., 'Ewa Plains sinkholes on O'ahu, Olson and James 1982b; near South Point on Hawai'i, Moniz 1997). Munro (1960) states that the Dark-rumped Petrel nested up to 1,524 m, and large quantities of petrel bones have been found at archeological sites at approximately 1,830 m, possible evidence of nesting in the vicinity (J. Moniz, pers. comm.).

The Dark-rumped Petrel was abundant across a range of elevations as well. It was the "most abundantly represented bird in the [sea level] O'ahu deposits" examined by Olson and James (1982b:43) and was the most common species found in a paleontologically rich lava tube on Hualālai that runs from 1,310 to 1,890 m elevation (Giffin 1993).

Presently, Dark-rumped Petrels breed on Haleakalā on Maui (Hodges and Nagata *this volume*), on Mauna Loa on the island of Hawai'i, and on Kaua'i (Simons 1983, Hodges 1994, Ainley et al. 1997a). Colonies may still occur on Lāna'i, Moloka'i, and elsewhere on Hawai'i (Hirai 1978, Banko 1980d, Berger 1981, Conant 1980, Pyle 1987, Bartle et al. 1993). Estimates of the statewide population range from the thousands to perhaps low tens of thousands (Simons and Hodges 1998).

The Haleakalā colony is the subspecies' largest known population. The primary threat to its 500 or more breeding pairs is predation from introduced mammals: roof rats (*Rattus rattus*), small Indian mongooses (*Herpestes auropunctatus*), feral cats (*Felis catus*), and dogs (*Canis familiaris*; Simons 1983, Hodges 1994, Hodges and Nagata *this volume*). An ongoing and aggressive predator control program has halted most losses, and this important colony appears secure.

When found fortuitously in 1990, the southeast Mauna Loa population of the Dark-rumped Petrel was already under attack by feral cats. After the initial discovery, consisting of 11 depredated carcasses (P. Banko, unpubl. report), several subsequent surveys yielded a handful of active nests, most in the vicinity of the original site (C. Hodges, unpubl. report). Little additional work was conducted prior to the start of our fieldwork. Our goals were to locate as many nests as possible to allow us to (1) characterize habitat use at both regional and local scales, (2) estimate nest success, and (3) assess the seriousness of the predation threat.

METHODS

We report here on work conducted between July 1993 and April 1997 within Hawai'i Volcanoes Na-

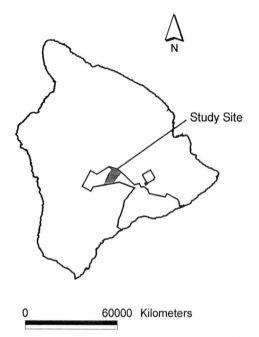

FIGURE 1. Dark-rumped Petrel study area within Hawai'i Volcanoes National Park on the island of Hawai'i. The study area lies between approximately 8,000 and 9,500 ft elevation.

TABLE 1. NEST SUCCESS DEFINITIONS USED FOR ACTIVE DARK-RUMPED PETREL BURROWS MONITORED ON MAUNA LOA, HAWAI'I[a]

Outcome	Criteria
Fledged monitored >1 time	droppings or footprints seen up to mid-Sept., and down at burrow entrance after mid-Sept.; or droppings or footprints seen up to mid-Sept. and activity after mid-Sept., although down (due to large entrance, recent rain, or a late check) not detected.
Fledged monitored once in Sept. or later	down at entrance; or evidence of recent entry or occupation (droppings or footprints), but down not detected (entrance large, recent rain, or late check).
Failed	carcass in or near burrow entrance, or quantities of feathers inside; or egg fragments at burrow entrance and no down present late in season; or activity (droppings, footprints) prior to mid-Sept., but no sign of later entry or exit, and no down at burrow entrance.
Unknown	checked only once late in season and older droppings present (indicating probable activity earlier in season), but down not detected (due to large entrance, rain, or lateness of season); or activity noted on midseason check(s), but not monitored between mid-Sept. and mid-Nov.

[a] Modified from Hodges (1994).

tional Park (HVNP) between approximately 2,440 and 2,900 m elevation on the southeast flank of Mauna Loa (Fig. 1). Because Mauna Loa is an active volcano, last erupting in 1984, its slopes are a patchwork of lava flows of different ages and textures. On older flows, vegetation at these elevations consists of sparse subalpine scrub, with native shrubs predominating. Newer flows are unvegetated. Due to limited funding, we confined our surveys to pāhoehoe lava flows, which were previously identified as the most likely substrate for use by nesting Dark-rumped Petrels (C. Hodges, unpubl. report). Pāhoehoe lava is relatively fluid when molten; once hardened, it has a smooth, sometimes ropey surface (Hazlett 1993).

Surveys consisted of searches on foot to look for active nests, indicated by droppings splashed around the burrow entrance, or past use as evidenced by petrel remains. In most areas, we also listened for calling birds at night as an indication of active nests in the vicinity.

Whenever possible, burrow locations were recorded using a global positioning system with a typical accuracy of approximately 8 m. Locations of a few nests found early in the study were recorded with an instrument accurate only to within 25 m. Nest locations were then mapped on a geographic information system-generated flow map. Beginning in 1996, we also noted the type of geologic or archeological feature used for nesting. Some burrows found early in our work and not revisited lack this information. Since few nests had accessible or visible nest chambers, we used a variety of indirect cues to assess burrow activity and success.

These included posting toothpick 'fences' across burrow entrances and then returning to look for signs of entry or exit, as well as the presence of footprints, feathers, tufts of down, splashes of excrement, and the musty smell characteristic of petrels. Nests then were categorized as inactive or active, and active nests were assigned a fate of fledged, failed, or unknown (Table 1). From these data we calculated nest success, the proportion of active nests that fledged a chick (Hodges 1994). All tests of independence were calculated using the G statistic and Williams' correction (Sokal and Rohlf 1981).

To assess the effect of observed predation on HVNP's Dark-rumped Petrel population, we conducted a population viability analysis (PVA) using Version 7 of the program VORTEX (Lacy et al. 1995). VORTEX models population growth deterministically, but can also include stochastic, demographic, genetic, and environmental processes, including catastrophes, that imperil small populations. All simulations were iterated

TABLE 2. INPUT PARAMETERS FOR FIVE SIMULATIONS OF THE DARK-RUMPED PETREL POPULATION IN HAWAI'I VOL-
CANOES NATIONAL PARK USING THE POPULATION VIABILITY ANALYSIS PROGRAM VORTEX

Model parameter	Stable population	Mauna Loa predation		Stochastic predation	
		1995	1996	A	B
Inbreeding depression	recessive lethal	recessive lethal	recessive lethal	recessive lethal	recessive lethal
Age at 1st reproduction	6	6	6	6	6
Age at last reproduction	35	35	35	35	35
Adult males in breeding pool	89%	89%	89%	89%	89%
Density dependence	yes	yes	yes	yes	yes
First year mortality ± SD[a]	34.0 ± 10%	38.5 ± 15%	41.7 ± 15%	34.0 ± 10%	34.0 ± 10%
2nd–5th year mortality ± SD[a]	19.7 ± 10%	19.7 ± 10%	19.7 ± 10%	19.7 ± 10%	19.7 ± 10%
Adult mortality ± SD[a]	7.0 ± 10%	8.3 ± 10%	17.4 ± 10%	7.0 ± 10%	7.0 ± 10%
Starting population	1000	1000	1000	1000	1000
Carrying capacity ± SD[a]	2500 ± 10%	2500 ± 10%	2500 ± 10%	2500 ± 10%	2500 ± 10%

Model parameter	Stable population	Mauna Loa predation		Stochastic predation	
		1995	1996	A	B
El Niño catastrophe					
Probability of occurrence	3%/y	3%/y	3%/y	3%/y	3%/y
Effect on reproduction	−43%	−43%	−43%	−43%	−43%
Effect on survival	−0%	−0%	−0%	−0%	−0%
Eruption catastrophe					
Probability of occurrence	0.49%/y	0.49%/y	0.49%/y	0.49%/y	0.49%/y
Effect on reproduction	−33.3%	−33.3%	−33.3%	−33.3%	−33.3%
Effect on survival	−16.7%	−16.7%	−16.7%	−16.7%	−16.7%
Predation catastrophe					
Probability of occurrence	not included	not included	not included	33.3%/y	20%/y
Effect on reproduction				−7.7%	−7.7%
Effect on survival				−10.4%	−10.4%

[a] Standard deviations reflect environmental variation.

1,000 times and modeled population growth over a 200-year time span. Initially, we modeled a stable population based largely on Simons' (1984) population model of the Haleakalā colony. Two additional runs substituted mortality data collected from HVNP in 1995 and 1996. Because cats in the subalpine habitats appeared to range widely, were absent from some nest groups in both years, and may not necessarily encounter petrel breeding areas at a time when birds are most vulnerable (i.e., when adults are calling or when fledglings emerge prior to departure), the final two runs modeled cat predation as a catastrophe with different probabilities of occurrence (Table 2). The effects of catastrophic predation on reproduction and survival were based on the predation-related mortality documented in 1996.

RESULTS

To date, we have surveyed approximately two-thirds of the appropriate habitat. Because of time and funding constraints, the northeast portion of the study area was surveyed more thoroughly than the less accessible southwest end. In total, we found 50 nests ranging in elevation from 2,440 to 2,800 m.

At a regional scale, most nests were clustered into four distinct groups, with all or most nests within each group placed on the same lava flow.

Utilized flows ranged in age from 2,000 to 8,999 years old (Fig. 2). A few additional nests found outside the main groups were on flows 1,000–2,999 years old. Despite the extensive age range, the surfaces of all nesting flows were oxidized and broken.

At the scale of the individual nest, 21 (52.5%) of the 40 burrows we classified were located in various naturally occurring features including lava tubes (12 nests), cracks in tumuli (fractured hills on the surface of pāhoehoe flows; Hazlett 1993; three nests), spaces created by the uplift of pāhoehoe slabs (three nests), and miscellaneous natural features (three nests). The remaining 19 burrows were located in pāhoehoe pits that showed evidence of human modification. Modification consisted of excavation of chunks of pāhoehoe, as evidenced by more recently exposed (less weathered) surfaces both on excavated material and pit edges. It is unclear if excavations were performed to enlarge existing holes or to create new ones. Regardless, the resultant pits provide access to the space between the surface and the underlying flow (Fig. 3) where petrels currently nest. Based on our examinations to date, it appears excavations were

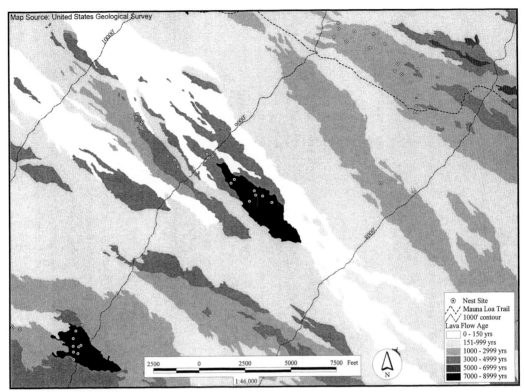

FIGURE 2.   Distribution of Dark-rumped Petrel nests found during this study in relation to age of surface lava flows on southeast Mauna Loa, Hawaiʻi. Geologic map courtesy of F. Trusdell and J. Lockwood (unpubl. data), U.S. Geological Survey, Hawaiian Volcano Observatory.

performed either prehistorically (pre-1778) or in early historical times.

In 1995, monitored burrows in the easternmost group of nests suffered limited cat predation. A single cat was trapped in late summer, probably preventing more extensive losses. We noted no predation following the capture, and success for all nests that year was 61.5%. In 1996 we conducted no trapping. Nest success dropped to 41.7%, mainly due to cat predation in one of the central nest groups (Table 3). Nest success was associated with year (G_{adj} = 6.43, P = 0.040, df = 2, N = 63). In 1995, the year of limited predation, success was independent of burrow type (G_{adj} = 1.70, P = 0.42, df = 2, N = 35). In 1996, the year of heavy predation, success was associated with burrow type (G_{adj} = 7.54, P = 0.023, df = 2, N = 24): nests placed in anthropogenic pits failed more frequently than those placed in natural features.

All runs of the PVA began with a population of 1,000 individuals. Because Mauna Loa surveys are incomplete, this starting population size was based on our crude approximation that the 50 known nests represent one-fourth of the breeding population and the estimate that some 40% of the population is nonbreeding (Spear et al. 1995). Applying mortality figures given by Simons (1984) for his hypothetical, stable Dark-rumped Petrel population resulted in an exponential growth rate, r, of near zero and persistence of the population in 97.5% of the iterations (Table 4). Substituting success and mortality figures from our 1995 work resulted in 28% of the iterations going extinct in an average of 158 years and the remaining populations slowly declining. Use of 1996 data resulted in the extinction of all 1,000 iterations in an average of 65 years. Compared to runs which modeled predation deterministically, the two runs in which predation was modeled as a stochastic variable yielded intermediate results for number of iterations going extinct, mean time to extinction, and mean growth rate of those iterations persisting. However, even the most optimistic scenario, in which severe predation of the magnitude observed in 1996 occurred only approximately every five years, resulted in the extinction of over half the iterations and a declining growth rate for those persisting 200 years.

FIGURE 3. A human-modified pit on Mauna Loa, Hawai'i. Rocks in the foreground were broken to make or enlarge the opening visible in the background. Photo by C. Glidden.

TABLE 3. OUTCOMES OF ACTIVE DARK-RUMPED PETREL NESTS ON MAUNA LOA, HAWAI'I IN 1995 AND 1996

Nest outcome	1995	1996
Fledged	24	10
Failed	5	10
Unknown	10	4
Total	39	24

DISCUSSION

Throughout the Hawaiian Archipelago, Dark-rumped Petrels still display considerable diversity in nesting habitat. On Maui, most petrel burrows are excavated in cinder substrate (Hodges 1994). Kaua'i lacks subalpine habitat, as do the other main islands where the species may persist; birds on these islands may nest on cliff faces or thickly vegetated ridges. This diversity in nesting habitat suggests that should factors now limiting the species ever be adequately controlled, Dark-rumped Petrels would not be behaviorally or physiologically limited to currently occupied nesting areas, some of which may have marginal temperature and humidity ranges for eggs and chicks.

In Mauna Loa's subalpine zone, Dark-rumped Petrels appear fairly narrowly circumscribed in their nesting by the presence of appropriate flows. However, the wide age range of utilized flows (1,000–8,000 yrs old) suggests age is an imperfect indicator of suitable substrate, and perhaps only correlated with other factors, such as the presence of shallow, accessible lava tubes. In many pāhoehoe flows, lava tube networks arise and are briefly active as part of the flow emplacement process. Freeze-thaw regimes and other forms of weathering subsequently create breaks in the surface, providing access to these tubes. The pace of weathering is not strictly a linear function of age but is also influenced by elevation, aspect, slope, and localized weather (B. Camara, pers. comm.). On Mauna Loa, lava tubes are favored for nesting both in their natural form and when access is provided via anthropogenic pits.

Archaeologically, the presence of human-modified pits at elevations ranging from 2,400 to 2,800 m is puzzling. The archaeological literature about Hawai'i proposes several functions for these types of features, none of which seem reasonable at this location. Possible functions include use as quarries for the extraction of building material or abrader blanks (Bevacqua 1972, Kirch 1979) or for growing crops (Barrera 1971; L. Carter, unpubl. report; J. Pantaleo et al., unpubl. report). Use of Mauna Loa pits for extracting building material is unlikely, as the project area lacks habitation sites. Nor does it seem like-

TABLE 4. RESULTS [MEAN (SE)] OF FIVE POPULATION VIABILITY ANALYSIS SCENARIOS FOR DARK-RUMPED PETRELS ON MAUNA LOA, HAWAI'I

	Stable population	Mauna Loa predation 1995	Mauna Loa predation 1996	Stochastic predation A	Stochastic predation B
Probability of extinction	0.0250 (0.0049)	0.276 (0.014)	1.00 (0.0)	0.958 (0.0063)	0.580 (0.016)
Years to extinction	161 (6.3)	158 (1.81)	65 (0.45)	123 (1.02)	146 (1.36)
Final size of surviving populations	921 (22.8)	280 (16.5)		19.0 (3.24)	98.4 (10.4)
Population growth rate (r)[a]	−0.0001 (0.0003)	−0.0174 (0.0003)	−0.0960 (0.0008)	−0.0481 (0.0005)	−0.0293 (0.0004)

[a] Growth rate is calculated from all simulated populations and prior to carrying capacity truncation.

ly that pits were used to extract abrader blanks, since the pāhoehoe in the area is large and blocky and unsuitable for manufacturing abraders.

The last proposed function, using the pits for growing crops, also is unlikely. Hawaiian varieties of sweet potato, the most likely crop, cannot tolerate the combination of cold, aridity, and lack of soil evident at this altitude on Mauna Loa (Yen 1974). At similar altitudes (approximately 2,750 m) in New Guinea, latitude 6° S, sweet potato growth is necessarily seasonal due to cold winter temperatures. Crops cultivated at high altitudes in New Guinea take from 7 to 12 months to mature, compared to 5 to 6 months in the lowlands (Bourke 1982). As in the drier regions elsewhere on the island, sweet potatoes would have been grown directly in the Mauna Loa pits with the addition of mulching material. Mulch would have been essential for crop growth, but the lack of vegetation in the vicinity of the pits would have made the collection of mulching material a time consuming and difficult practice. Finally, the lack of soil within this environment severely restricts the growth potential of all plants.

We speculate that pits in the subalpine lava flows on Mauna Loa instead may have been modified for catching seabirds, including Dark-rumped Petrels. These birds would have been an attractive food source for a number of reasons: they nest synchronously and colonially, their breeding chronology (including fledging) is predictable, they have high nest-site fidelity, and many species are somewhat awkward on land (Moniz 1997). Consistent with the hypothesis that these pits were modified for catching petrels, one explanation for the difference in failure rates we observed under heavy predation is that nests placed in modified pits are more accessible to predators.

Prehistorically, Dark-rumped Petrels were a favored source of food for Hawaiians. Strongly flavored adults were salted (Munro 1960, Wichman 1985), while nestlings were more highly prized and reserved for ruling chiefs (Henshaw 1902a, Munro 1960). On the island of Hawai'i, H. C. Shipman recounted stories from his childhood in which he heard of "native Hawaiians claiming different caves or nesting areas, presumably in the mountains, for capturing young for food" (Banko 1980d:3). Methods of capture included placing nets over burrow entrances (Wichman 1985) and insertion of long sticks into burrows to pluck the nestlings out while twisting the pole into the soft down (Henshaw 1902a). Midden remains of Dark-rumped Petrels found in many locations on Hawai'i substantiate the use of this species for food (Banko 1980d).

Ethnographic information indicates that Hawaiians may have attempted to harvest Dark-rumped Petrels in a sustained manner: "The bird catchers did not take all the birds from a hole but took only from one to three and no more, so as to keep the birds in that hole, nor were the parents taken lest there be no birds there. . ." (Kahiolo 1863:1016). Although there is no location information attached to this account, the description further indicates that birds were nesting in close proximity, perhaps several pairs to a hole, as may have been the case in the modified pits found on Mauna Loa.

Most of the Dark-rumped Petrel nests we found on Mauna Loa had nest chambers that could not be viewed directly, necessitating indirect monitoring techniques that sometimes resulted in ambiguous reproductive outcomes. This was especially true for burrows with large openings, where fledgling down was both less likely to be snagged and more difficult to detect if present. In such instances, if there was no other sign of either success or failure and previous checks had indicated activity, we categorized those nests as successful. The rationale for this decision was that failure, especially predation, usually was quite obvious—either carcasses or large quantities of feathers at or near the burrow entrance. Thus, the risk here is of inflated estimates of nest success. When the year's initial surveys were conducted well into or even at the end of the breeding season, as widely occurred in 1996, early failing nests were more likely to have been wrongly classified as inactive for the season, again inflating nest success estimates. While these methodological shortcomings dictate that our estimates of nest success should not be considered highly precise, they are within the 35–72% range found by Simons (1984) and similar to the 42% and 57% figures (for areas without and with predator control) reported by Hodges (1994).

We also attempted to err conservatively on the following additional model parameters for which we lacked substantial information: density dependence, environmental variation in age-specific mortality, and inbreeding depression. While we feel these parameters did not substantially impact the results of the PVA, we discuss them here in the interest of completeness and repeatability of results.

Density dependence probably operates for this species, with the most important effects manifested at low population levels. Because the Dark-rumped Petrel previously existed at much higher numbers, it seems unlikely that even large increases in existing populations would strain at sea-food resources (Simons 1985) or create shortages in nest sites (D. Hu, pers. obs.).

However, prospecting petrels may use the calls of other birds to select nesting colonies; attraction of Galápagos Dark-rumped Petrels (*P. p. phaeopygia*) was strongest to the sounds of a busy, thriving colony (Podolsky and Kress 1992). Thus, an Allee effect is possible at low numbers. The magnitude of such an effect may be somewhat ameliorated by the ability of petrels to prospect over large areas relatively quickly and easily in search of other calling birds.

VORTEX can include the following density dependence equation. We chose to include it in all runs:

$$P(N) = (P(0) - [(P(0) - P(K))(N/K)^B])$$

$$\times [N/(N + A)]$$

where

P(N) = percent females breeding at population size N;

P(0) = percent females breeding at population size near zero;

P(K) = percent females breeding at K;

B = relationship between percentage breeding and population size at large values of N;

A = the magnitude of the Allee effect.

For all runs, we set P(0) = 90% and P(K) = 80%. This was based in part on Simons' (1984) determination that 89% of adult Dark-rumped Petrels at Haleakalā bred annually, presumably reflecting the level of activity in a substantially reduced population. We followed the general recommendation for mammals and specified B = 2, prescribing a quadratic relationship for the density dependence curve (Fowler 1981). The Allee effect term equaled one in all runs, describing a mild decline in breeding activity at very low population levels.

We had little data on the amount of variation in mortality rates due to environmental variability. Choosing to include some variation, we arbitrarily set the SD in mortality at 10% for all age classes in the stable population simulation and in the two runs which modeled predation stochastically. Based on our two years of nest success data, we increased the SD in first year mortality to 15% for the two runs in which predation was modeled deterministically.

The final problematic input parameter was inbreeding depression. Here again, for the sake of realism we chose to incorporate the effect. However, we used the simpler, faster, but less realistic of the two models of inbreeding depression offered in VORTEX. In the recessive lethal model, the population contains a single recessive lethal allele. Each founder individual is heterozygous for the lethal allele, and progeny that inherit two lethal alleles are eliminated. Thus, the allele is slowly purged from the population. While Lacy et al. (1995) caution that this model underestimates the impact of inbreeding, we used it because the alternative heterosis model ran prohibitively slowly.

We included two catastrophes in all VORTEX runs: Occurrences of a severe El Niño-Southern Oscillation (ENSO) event and volcanic eruptions in which lava covers nesting habitat. The frequency of severe ENSOs was based on data from 1800 to the present (Glynn 1988). Their effect on petrel reproduction was determined by comparing fledging success from Haleakalā for 1982 to a multiple-year mean (C. Hodges, unpubl. data). We assumed no affect on adult survival. The frequency of Mauna Loa eruptions was taken from Kauahikaua et al. (1995). Effects on survival and reproduction were estimated by assuming that an eruption on Mauna Loa would impact only one of the known nest groups (western, central, or eastern), that only one adult would be in the burrow at any time, and that nests were roughly evenly distributed among the three general areas.

The lack of data for these parameters and other more basic life history components highlights the need for long-term monitoring of the species. For this population, we now face the dilemma of drawing erroneous conclusions because of our short-term view of the situation, or waiting to accumulate more data, perhaps only to document the local demise of the species.

Certainly, more data should be collected if possible. However, within the limits of current information, we believe our PVA results are robust. Modeling predation deterministically within VORTEX yielded qualitatively similar results to Simons's (1984) Leslie matrix model; even limited predation caused population decline, and more severe predation resulted in relatively quick population extirpation. When severe predation was modeled stochastically in VORTEX, the population responded similarly. Clearly, even without more data on the frequency and severity of predation on Mauna Loa petrels, control of feral cats should be the highest priority recovery action.

To conserve this population, cat control must occur regularly (Hodges and Nagata *this volume*) and in perpetuity, a commitment that requires considerable institutional support. However, any control efforts will benefit other members of Mauna Loa's avian subalpine community. Methodological improvements and related research also may aid the considerable number of bird species elsewhere in Hawai'i that are impacted by feline predation.

ACKNOWLEDGMENTS

Thanks to the following for invaluable assistance in the field: J. Chase, H. Hoshide, D. Kuwahara, B. Pelke, K. Sherry, and the Resources Management staff at HVNP. B. Lacy, Jr., and D. Okita provided helicopter transport, frequently under adverse conditions. C. N. Hodges loaned equipment and provided guidance in the development of field techniques. H. Leong lent predator control expertise, and J. Moniz provided references and unpublished data. R. Loh and S. Margriter helped solve GPS mysteries. F. Trusdell provided advance copies of Mauna Loa flow maps, and P. Graves produced Figure 1. B. Camara taught us geology and gleaned references, and with L. Schuster, helped us formulate ideas on archaeology. S. Conant and J. M. Scott made helpful suggestions on an earlier draft. Our work was partially funded by Hawai'i Volcanoes National Park, the U.S. Fish and Wildlife Service, and the University of California at Davis.

Studies in Avian Biology No. 22:243–246, 2001.

INTERACTION BETWEEN THE HAWAIIAN DARK-RUMPED PETREL AND THE ARGENTINE ANT IN HALEAKALĀ NATIONAL PARK, MAUI, HAWAI'I

PAUL D. KRUSHELNYCKY, CATHLEEN S. N. HODGES, ARTHUR C. MEDEIROS, AND LLOYD L. LOOPE

Abstract. The invasive immigrant Argentine ant (*Linepithema humile* Mayr) has spread to occupy roughly 120 ha, or 15%, of the nesting habitat of the endangered Hawaiian Dark-rumped Petrel (*Pterodroma phaeopygia sandwichensis*) in Haleakalā National Park on the island of Maui, Hawai'i. The colony at Haleakalā is responsible for most of the known reproduction of the endemic seabird, and concern arose that the Argentine ant may reduce petrel breeding success at this important site. Investigations in ant-infested areas of the petrel colony, however, showed that the nesting success rate (53.7%) was not significantly different from the nesting success rate in adjacent ant-free areas (50.0%). While the ant occurred more frequently at the entrances of burrows with recent petrel activity, high numbers of ants or foraging trails within the petrel burrows were seen only rarely. Cold soil surface temperatures may inhibit ant foraging into the deeper parts of the burrows, where incubation and chick development occur. At current levels, the Argentine ant is not believed to significantly influence the nesting success rate of the Hawaiian Dark-rumped Petrel.

Key Words: Argentine ant; Hawaiian Dark-rumped Petrel; *Linepithema humile*; *Pterodroma phaeopygia sandwichensis*.

The Argentine ant (*Linepithema humile* Mayr) was first recorded in Haleakalā National Park in 1967 (Huddleston and Fluker 1968) and has since proved to be highly invasive and destructive to native biota (Fellers and Fellers 1982, Cole et al. 1992). As an aggressive predator and scavenger, *L. humile* reduces populations of native arthropods in high-elevation subalpine shrublands (Cole et al. 1992). The entire endemic biota of the Hawaiian Islands is believed to have evolved in the absence of ant predation; endemic arthropod species, for example, are highly vulnerable to the effects of immigrant ants (Gillespie and Reimer 1993). Recently, concerns were raised that this immigrant ant may also reduce the breeding success of a native seabird, the endangered Hawaiian Dark-rumped Petrel (*Pterodroma phaeopygia sandwichensis*).

The disturbance of nesting behavior and direct depredation of hatchlings by ants has been documented in a number of species of birds, including seabirds. While most of these cases involve the red imported fire ant (*Solenopsis invicta* Buren; Ridlehuber 1982, Sikes and Arnold 1986, Drees 1994, Dickinson 1995, Lockley 1995), several other species of ants have also been implicated, including *Monomorium pharaonis* (Linnaeus) (Parker 1977), *S. xyloni* (McCook) (Hooper 1995), and *S. geminata* (Fabricius) (Stoddard 1931, Kroll et al. 1973). The Argentine ant could have a similar effect. Its polygynous unicolonies form high densities of co-operating nests that dominate habitat and have the ability to recruit large numbers of workers to attractive food sources. In fact, *L. humile* has

been observed to recruit quickly and heavily to the pipped eggs of the endangered ground-nesting Hawaiian Goose (Nēnē; *Branta sandvicensis*) on the island of Hawai'i, requiring human intervention to prevent depredation on the emerging goslings (F. Duvall, pers. comm.).

The Hawaiian subspecies of the Dark-rumped Petrel has been listed as endangered since 1967 (USFWS 1983b). Once apparently abundant throughout the islands at lower elevations, the Hawaiian Dark-rumped Petrel's numbers have declined precipitously with the advent of hunting by Polynesians, loss of breeding habitat, and depredation by introduced mammals (Banko 1980c, Olson and James 1982a, Simons 1985, Hodges 1994). Today, the high-elevation cliffs (2,400–3,055 m) near the summit of Haleakalā Volcano on Maui serve as one of the last, and largest, remaining parcels of breeding habitat for the imperiled bird. Although significant numbers of adult Hawaiian Dark-rumped Petrels have been sighted on other Hawaiian Islands, Haleakalā National Park protects approximately 95% of the estimated 450–650 known breeding pairs in the islands (Simons and Hodges 1998).

Currently, the greatest threat to the petrel's survival is introduced mammalian predators such as rats, mongoose, and feral cats and dogs (Hodges 1994). Because the petrel has a conservative reproductive strategy typical of Procellariiformes, with monogamous pairs producing a maximum of only one chick per year, depredation of adults and chicks is particularly damaging to the health of the colony (Simons 1984). Consequently, predator removal is an important part of the park's management plan for the petrel.

Beginning in the late 1980s, park employees noticed Argentine ants over large areas of the petrel colony. In the early 1990s the ant distribution was mapped and discovered to occupy an entire section of cliff face from crater rim to crater floor. Today this area comprises approximately 120 ha, or 15% of the known petrel nesting habitat in the park (Hodges 1994). Despite the cold temperatures and extreme weather that can limit ant foraging at this elevation, the Argentine ant is expanding its range. Concerns were raised by biologists and managers that this ant could become another major threat to the survival of this endangered seabird. Possible effects included direct depredation of newly hatched or emerging chicks; disruption of courtship and mating behavior, incubation of eggs, and the brooding and feeding of chicks; and abandonment of nesting burrows in ant-infested areas. The purpose of this study was to determine if Hawaiian Dark-rumped Petrel nesting success was being affected by the Argentine ant.

METHODS

The Dark-rumped Petrel nesting season at Haleakalā begins in late February and ends in mid-November (Simons 1985). In July 1994, 110 potential petrel burrows were located within the area infested by the Argentine ant at 2,440 to 2,740 m. In December 1994, 71 of these burrows were determined to be active. Of the 71 active burrows, 55 were randomly selected for monitoring during the entire 1995 nesting season.

This study followed the protocol utilized by the Resources Management Division of Haleakalā National Park for long-term monitoring of the park's petrel colony (Hodges 1994). Because the petrels excavate winding burrows from 1 to 10 m deep in the volcanic cinder substrates (Simons 1985), opportunities for seeing the nest chamber are rare. Accordingly, monitoring is largely based on external signs of burrow activity. Records were taken on whether or not each burrow had been entered, as well as on the presence of various signs of petrel activity such as fresh droppings, feathers, and down; egg shell fragments; and petrel tracks at the burrow entrance. Data were collected during monthly surveys of all 55 study burrows from March to October and subsequently during biweekly surveys until the end of November, resulting in a total of 11 monitoring surveys.

A row of toothpicks placed across the burrow entrance at an interval of 3 cm served as a trip entry indicator (as in Simons 1983, Hodges 1994). Disruption of this row was used to determine whether a burrow had been entered. By using toothpick monitoring paired with other evidence of petrel activity such as droppings, tracks, feathers and egg shells, active burrows were easily recognized over the course of the season.

Burrows that remained active into late October and November and that had characteristic gray chick down

at the entrance were believed to have fledged a chick (Hodges 1994). Nesting success, defined here as the percentage of active burrows (active with breeders and nonbreeders) that fledged a chick, was compared among the ant-infested study area and the adjacent ant-free areas of the petrel colony monitored by National Park Service personnel during the 1995 season.

At all study burrows, ant presence or absence inside and outside the burrow entrance was recorded. This was defined as inside or outside the row of toothpicks spanning the entrance, which delineated the border between the perpetually shaded, relatively constant microhabitat of the burrow interior and the highly variable microhabitat outside the burrow (variable in vegetation, exposure to sun, other weather conditions, food sources). The presence of ten or more ants inside a burrow and the presence of foraging trails leading directly into a petrel burrow were also noted.

In 1997, soil surface temperatures were measured inside and outside 14 burrows during two days of warm weather in August, the warmest month of the year. Temperatures inside burrows were measured using a LI-COR soil heat probe resting on the shaded ground, recorded every 0.5 m from the burrow entrance until the nest chamber or a distance of 2.0 m was reached. Soil surface temperatures outside the burrow entrances were measured with an Everest Interscience infrared surface thermometer. These temperatures were recorded in exposed direct sunlight, exposed overcast sunlight, and shaded soil directly outside the burrow entrances. All temperatures were measured during the time period of 12:00 to 17:00, the warmest part of the day for ground temperatures.

RESULTS

Fifty-four of the 55 study burrows (98.2%) were active during the 1995 nesting season. Of the 54 active burrows, 29 (53.7%) fledged a chick. In the adjacent ant-free areas monitored by the National Park Service in 1995, 36 of 72 active burrows (50.0%) fledged a chick. There was no significant difference between these nesting success rates in ant-infested and ant-free areas of the petrel colony ($\chi^2_1 = 0.055$, P $>$ 0.05).

Each of the 54 active burrows was checked on 11 occasions for a total of 593 burrow checks. These burrows were entered by petrels 419 times and not entered 174 times. Of the checks in which active burrows had been entered, at least one Argentine ant was found inside the burrow on 230 occasions, or 55.9% of the time. Of the checks in which active burrows had not been entered, ants were found inside the burrow on 62 occasions, or 35.6% of the time. There was a significant difference between the rates of incidence of ants inside entered and not entered active burrows ($\chi^2_1 = 17.52$, P $<$ 0.01). The single inactive study burrow had ants within its entrance in only 1 of the 11 monitoring checks in 1995.

Twenty-one of the 54 active burrows were found to have ten or more ants inside their en-

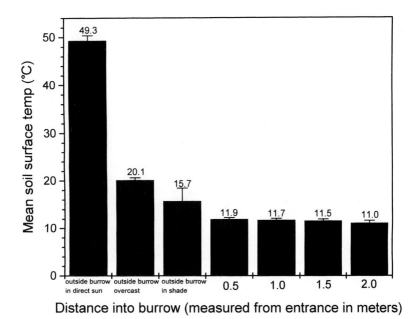

FIGURE 1. Mean soil surface temperatures inside and outside Dark-rumped Petrel burrows during August in Haleakalā National Park, Maui, Hawai'i. Bars indicate one SE (N = 14).

trances on at least one occasion. Fifteen of these burrows (71.4%) fledged a chick. Five of the 21 burrows were found to have a visible foraging trail of ants leading directly into the burrow on at least one occasion, and four of these (80.0%) fledged a chick. The fifth burrow contained large pieces of egg shell approximately 1 m inside the entrance, which appeared to be the destination of the foraging trail.

Means of the soil surface temperatures measured inside and outside 14 burrows in August 1997 are shown in Figure 1. Temperatures drop sharply from the exposed sun-heated cinders just outside burrow entrances to the shaded soil as near as 0.5 m inside burrow entrances. Soil surface temperatures steadily decrease with increasing distance into the burrow.

DISCUSSION

Observations determining whether the Argentine ant directly encounters petrels or petrel chicks in the nest chamber were not obtainable in this study. All data collected, however, indicate that such interactions are unlikely. There was no significant difference between the nesting success rates in ant-infested and ant-free areas of the petrel colony. In addition, 98.2% of the study burrows active in the 1994 season were active again in 1995. Because adult Hawaiian Dark-rumped Petrels use the same burrow year after year (Simons 1985), this high return rate may indicate that the ant's presence is

not discouraging the adult petrels from returning to their burrows.

While the ant presence data show that the ant seems to be attracted to active petrel burrows, with ants occurring significantly more frequently inside the entrances of recently active burrows, this is likely related to the attraction of the Argentine ant to the guano, feathers, fish oil, broken eggs, and invertebrates characteristic of active petrel burrows. Because these data only indicate the presence of a single ant inside the burrow entrance, they do not provide evidence for the mass recruitment that would be necessary for serious disturbance of petrel nesting activity. Furthermore, increased ant presence did not appear to detract from breeding success. Among the 21 burrows that were found to have ten or more ants inside their entrances on at least one occasion, 71.4% fledged a chick. While this nesting success rate represents a small sample size and should therefore be viewed with caution, it is nevertheless considerably higher than that of the study area as a whole. Similarly, of the five burrows found to have a visible trail of foraging ants leading directly into them on at least one occasion, four fledged a chick.

In all instances where ant trails were found, it was impossible to determine the distance to which the ants were foraging inside the burrows. Even with flashlights, it was difficult to see much past 1 m into the burrow. Burrow temperature data, however, suggest that the Argentine ant does not forage far into petrel burrows. As can be seen in Figure 1, there is a large difference in soil surface temperature between the exposed sun-heated cinders outside burrow entrances and the shaded soils inside burrow entrances. Additionally, soil surface temperatures steadily decrease with increasing distance into the burrow. These burrow temperatures fluctuate relatively little throughout the day (Simons 1985), as the burrows are always shaded and air currents into and out of the burrows are probably minimal.

The mean temperatures of approximately 11 to 12° C (Fig. 1) thus encountered by a foraging ant inside a petrel burrow are near the minimum temperature required for Argentine ant foraging and above ground activity (Newell 1908, Markin 1970; P. Krushelnycky, unpubl. data). These temperatures correspond fairly closely to the average temperature of 9.59° C measured at petrel burrow nest chambers during the month of October by Simons (1985). It should be pointed out that while fluctuations of soil surface temperatures over time within individual and averaged burrows are small, the range of soil surface temperatures encountered in different burrows is considerably larger. This is dependent on the shape and depth of each burrow. Deep, narrow burrows can have soil surface temperatures of 8 to 9° C, whereas wide, shallow burrows may have soil surface temperatures of up to 13.5° C.

So while temperature data indicate that some burrows may be more thermally accessible to ants (and therefore more vulnerable) than others, both the nesting success data and the ant presence data suggest that these differences are not important. Perhaps this is because even the warmest burrows are still cold enough to discourage extensive foraging by ants. Indeed, we suspect that cold burrow temperatures are the major reason why high numbers of ants occurred inside burrow entrances so infrequently: foraging trails were seen inside burrows only eight times throughout the study period.

The foraging trails observed on these several occasions were most likely destined for food sources relatively close to the burrow entrances. While ants were seen opportunistically feeding on the carcass of one petrel chick found at its burrow entrance, we presently have no evidence that the Argentine ant is responsible for petrel chick mortality or disruption of breeding behavior. It would nevertheless be wise to periodically monitor the ant-infested section of the colony to ensure that nesting success remains at a level comparable to that of adjacent ant-free areas. Continued research into the ecological interactions of the Hawaiian Dark-rumped Petrel should remain an important aspect of the conservation of this endangered species.

ACKNOWLEDGMENTS

We would like to thank C. Chimera, P. O'Connor, S. Joe, J. Lienau, C. Barr, and R. Ho for their assistance with fieldwork. We also thank T. Simons and T. Giambelluca who provided important consultation on temperature measurements, and P. Thomas who assisted in database design and data processing.

Studies in Avian Biology No. 22:247–253, 2001.

DISTRIBUTION AND POTENTIAL IMPACTS OF AVIAN POXLIKE LESIONS IN 'ELEPAIO AT HAKALAU FOREST NATIONAL WILDLIFE REFUGE

ERIC A. VANDERWERF

Abstract. I studied distribution of avian poxlike lesions and demography of 'Elepaio (*Chasiempis sandwichensis*) at three sites in Hakalau Forest National Wildlife Refuge on Hawai'i from 1994 to 1997. Birds were mist-netted, banded, visually inspected for lesions, and monitored for survival and reproductive success. Prevalence of avian poxlike lesions in 'Elepaio was much higher at Maulua (40%) at 1,550 m elevation, than at two Pua 'Ākala sites (2%) at 1,800–1,900 m. All infected 'Elepaio had old, healed lesions, not active ones, indicating a past epizootic that had ended. Ages of infected birds revealed that an epizootic occurred at Maulua in 1992; 70% of birds hatched in 1992 or before had healed lesions, but all birds hatched in 1993 or after showed no sign of infection. Birds with healed lesions did not differ from healthy birds in annual survival (0.87 versus 0.86, respectively) or reproductive success (0.71 versus 0.62, respectively), demonstrating that birds surviving the initial infection were no longer affected. 'Elepaio population density at Maulua was 49% lower than at Pua 'Ākala in 1994 (0.66 versus 1.29 birds/ha), but recovered rapidly after the epizootic ended and increased 65% to 1.09 birds/ha by 1996, while density at Pua 'Ākala did not change. As population density increased, more subadults were excluded from the breeding population. Poxlike lesions appeared to reduce numbers of 'Elepaio in certain breeding cohorts at Maulua. The frequency of poxlike epizootics is unknown, but would have important implications for persistence of bird populations in Hawai'i.

Key Words: *Chasiempis sandwichensis*; disease; 'Elepaio; Hawai'i; population reduction; poxlike lesions; reproductive success; survival.

The 'Elepaio (*Chasiempis sandwichensis*) is a small monarch flycatcher that comprises a genus endemic to the Hawaiian Islands of Hawai'i, O'ahu, and Kaua'i. Forms on each island currently are regarded as subspecies (Pratt 1980, Berger 1981, Pyle 1997) but formerly they were treated as separate species (Henshaw 1902b, MacCaughey 1919). 'Elepaio are fairly common and widely distributed at higher elevations on Hawai'i and Kaua'i (Richardson and Bowles 1964, Sincock et al. 1984, Scott et al. 1986), but on O'ahu they have seriously declined in the last few decades and they have a fragmented distribution (Williams 1987, VanderWerf et al. 1997, VanderWerf 1998a). Factors causing the decline of 'Elepaio on O'ahu and limiting their distribution on other islands are not completely understood, but introduced mosquito-borne diseases are one of the primary threats, particularly avian malaria (*Plasmodium relictum*) and avian poxvirus (*Poxvirus avium*; Warner 1968, van Riper et al. 1986, Atkinson et al. 1995, Cann et al. 1996, VanderWerf et al. 1997). The high susceptibility of Hawaiian honeycreepers (Drepanidinae) to avian malaria and avian pox has been well documented by laboratory challenge experiments, and the range of many native Hawaiian birds appears to be limited by these diseases (Warner 1968, Scott et al. 1986, van Riper et al. 1986, Atkinson et al. 1995). However, information is lacking about the effects of disease on the demography of wild populations of Hawaiian birds, and the prevalence and distribution of avian pox are not well-known.

Most species of birds are susceptible to at least some of the 13 described species of avian pox (Kirmse 1967, Tripathy 1993). Some species of avian pox are very host specific, especially in wild birds, and pathogenicity can vary considerably among hosts (Tripathy 1993). Poxvirus isolated from one host species can produce severe infection or no reaction at all in other groups of birds, and inoculation with one type of poxvirus may not provide protection against other species of poxvirus (Tripathy 1993). Avian pox symptoms were first observed in Hawaiian birds over a century ago (Henshaw 1902a, Perkins 1903) and now have been found in many species, including 'Elepaio and most other endemic forest birds, several species of seabirds, and several introduced game birds and passerines (van Riper and van Riper 1985). The year when avian pox was introduced to Hawai'i and its place of origin are not clear, and it is possible that more than one species has reached Hawai'i (Warner 1968).

Poxvirus infects a bird through a break in unfeathered skin or in the oral or respiratory mucous membranes, and can be transmitted by either an arthropod bite or by direct contact with a contaminated surface, such as another bird, a perch, or a nest (USFWS 1987, Tripathy 1993). At least 11 species of Diptera have been reported as vectors of avian pox (Akey et al. 1981), but the principal vector in Hawai'i is the introduced mosquito *Culex quinquefasciatus* (Warner 1968, van Riper et al. 1986, Atkinson et al. 1995). Avian pox infection occurs in two forms. The cutaneous form is characterized by wartlike nodules and tumorous lesions on unfeathered body areas, including the feet, legs, face, and around the bill and eyes. Symptoms of the less common diphtheritic form, or wet pox, include soft yellowish cankers and lesions on membranes of the upper respiratory and digestive tracts and in the mouth (USFWS 1987, Tripathy 1993). Local swellings and lesions first develop at the site where the virus entered; these may increase in size and erupt into granular nodules and tumors, and may be followed by viremia, secondary lesions, and spread to various internal organs (Tripathy 1993). In more severe and advanced cases, lesions may become necrotic and often are accompanied by hemorrhaging and secondary bacterial infections (Warner 1968, van Riper and van Riper 1985, Tripathy 1993). Severity and duration of infection vary considerably among individuals; some birds develop only small lesions and recover rapidly, but others develop very large and debilitating lesions (Warner 1968). Cutaneous lesions on the feet, wings, bill, and eyes can cause difficulty in perching, flight, feeding, and vision, and may inhibit foraging and lead to emaciation and starvation (Docherty et al. 1991, Pearson et al. 1975, Orós et al. 1997). Munro (1960:117) described a Kaua'i 'Akialoa (*Hemignathus e. procerus*) as being "so disabled with lumps on legs and bill that it could scarcely fly." Diphtheritic lesions on the larynx and trachea can cause respiratory difficulty, gasping, and eventually suffocation, while lesions on the tongue, palate, or esophagus can interfere with eating and drinking (Tripathy 1993). Birds that recover from avian pox often have scars and deformities, such as misshapen or missing claws or digits (Greenwood and Blakemore 1973, Tripathy 1993). The mortality rate may depend on the susceptibility of the host population, the virulence of the avian pox, concurrent physical or environmental stress, and other infections (Tripathy 1993). Avian pox can persist in lesions for up to 13 months (Kirmse 1967), may occur as a latent infection that becomes active again during times of stress (Olsen and Dolphin 1978), and can survive for years in dried scabs (Tripathy 1993).

As part of a long-term study of demography and plumage variation in 'Elepaio, I investigated disease prevalence and monitored survival and reproductive success of 'Elepaio at Hakalau Forest National Wildlife Refuge on Hawai'i Island. Hakalau protects part of one of the largest tracts of native forest left in the state, and it supports the largest populations of several species of native passerine birds, including 'Elepaio. My objectives were to determine the spatial and temporal distribution of poxlike lesions in 'Elepaio, measure survival and reproduction of 'Elepaio, and understand how poxlike lesions are related to changes in 'Elepaio populations. In particular, previous surveys showed that 'Elepaio and several species of endangered insectivorous honeycreepers were less abundant at Maulua, near the northern end of the refuge, than at Pua 'Ākala, at the southern end of the refuge (Scott et al. 1986), but whether disease is a factor in causing this pattern is not known. The 'Elepaio is an especially suitable species in which to study the effects of disease because it is nonmigratory and territorial year-round (VanderWerf 1998a), making it a good indicator of local disease prevalence and easy to find and monitor.

METHODS

STUDY SITE

I conducted this study from 1994 to 1997 at Hakalau Forest National Wildlife Refuge (Hakalau) on the east slope of Mauna Kea on the island of Hawai'i (Fig. 1). Habitat in this region originally was montane rain forest, but some areas were used historically for cattle ranching and logging, resulting in a mosaic of relatively dense, closed-canopy forest and highly disturbed open-canopy woodland. I studied 'Elepaio at three sites on the refuge; a closed-canopy site at middle Pua 'Ākala (MPA) at 1,800 m elevation, an open-canopy site at upper Pua 'Ākala (UPA) at 1,900 m elevation, and another open-canopy site at Maulua at 1,550 m elevation. The two Pua 'Ākala sites were contiguous, but the Maulua site was about 10 km to the north (Fig. 1). At all three sites, 'ōhi'a (*Metrosideros polymorpha*) and koa (*Acacia koa*) were the dominant tree species, and other fairly common trees included 'ōlapa (*Cheirodendron trigynum*), kōlea (*Myrsine lessertiana*), kāwa'u (*Ilex anomala*), and pilo (*Coprosma montana*). Common shrubs included 'ōhelo (*Vaccinium calycinum*), 'ākala (*Rubus hawaiensis*), and pūkiawe (*Styphelia tameiameiae*). Ground cover consisted of native forbs and ferns, and introduced grasses.

STUDY SPECIES

'Elepaio are insectivorous, socially monogamous, nonmigratory, and territorial year-round (Conant 1977, van Riper 1995, VanderWerf 1998a). The foraging behavior of 'Elepaio is extremely varied and plastic (VanderWerf 1994), they are generalized in habitat selection (VanderWerf 1993), and are one of the most successful Hawaiian forest birds in adapting to disturbed habitats and introduced plant species (Conant 1977, VanderWerf et al. 1997). 'Elepaio populations have persisted at low elevations in some areas where most other native birds have disappeared, suggesting 'Elepaio may have greater immunity to introduced diseases than many Hawaiian birds (VanderWerf 1998a). 'Elepaio are sexually mature and sometimes breed when one year old, but have a two-year delay in plumage maturation in both sexes, resulting in distinct first

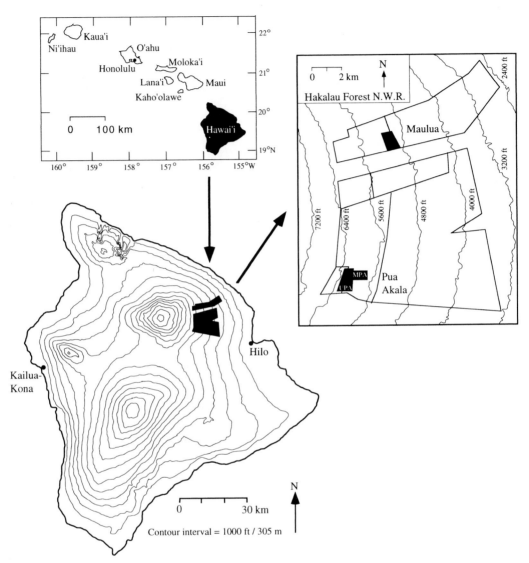

FIGURE 1. Location of three study sites (shown in black) at Hakalau Forest National Wildlife Refuge on Hawai'i Island. MPA = middle Pua 'Ākala at 1,800 m elevation, UPA = upper Pau 'Ākala at 1,900 m elevation, and Maulua at 1,550 m elevation.

basic, second basic, and definitive basic (adult) plumages (VanderWerf 1998a). Adults are generally dominant over subadults, and subadults act as floaters until they acquire a territory. 'Elepaio occur in all three study sites at Hakalau, but, at the start of this study in 1994, population density was 49% lower at Maulua than in similar habitat at Pua 'Ākala (E. VanderWerf, unpubl. data).

POXLIKE LESIONS

To measure prevalence of poxlike lesions at each site, I captured birds in mist nets and visually examined them for symptoms. I also collected a small blood sample from the ulnar vein of each bird to test for malaria. "A presumptive diagnosis of avian pox can be made from the gross appearance of growths on body surfaces" (USFWS 1987:141). However, I did not clinically confirm the field diagnoses of avian pox in 'Elepaio because biopsy was judged to be too invasive and I did not want to exacerbate any lesions or deformities. I believe that avian pox is the most likely cause of the cutaneous lesions found in 'Elepaio at Hakalau. Other diseases, such as laryngotracheitis and trichomoniasis, can cause symptoms similar to those of the diphtheritic form of avian pox (van Riper and van Riper 1985, Tripathy 1993), and mites can cause lesions and warty growths typical of the cutaneous form of avian pox. I therefore assumed birds with cu-

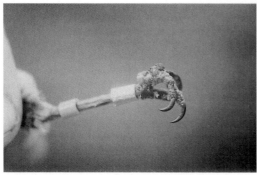

FIGURE 2.   'Elepaio feet with avian poxlike symptoms: left, active lesions; right, missing and deformed toes typical of healed lesions.

taneous lesions, wartlike growths, or soft swellings had active avian pox; those with missing or deformed toes had healed pox; and those with no external symptoms were healthy (Fig. 2). The timing of epizootics was determined by the cohorts of 'Elepaio having poxlike lesions, with ages of birds based on plumage. For example, birds that had first basic plumage in 1994 must have hatched in 1993, those with second basic plumage in 1994 must have hatched in 1992, and those with definitive adult plumage in 1994 must have hatched in 1991 or earlier.

DEMOGRAPHY

I monitored survival and reproductive behavior of banded birds on regular visits to each territory throughout the year. If a bird was not found in its traditional territory and another bird was found in its place, I assumed the original bird was dead. I believe this assumption is valid because 'Elepaio remain on their territory year-round and have extremely high territory fidelity in both sexes, approximately 97% (E. VanderWerf, unpubl. data). I made extensive searches of surrounding areas in all directions, but only twice relocated a bird that had disappeared from its territory. Because emigration was rare and the probability of resighting a bird that was alive and on the study area was reliably high (0.993; E. VanderWerf, unpubl. data), I calculated annual survival by enumeration

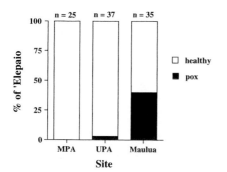

FIGURE 3.   Incidence of avian poxlike lesions in 'Elepaio at three study sites in Hakalau Forest National Wildlife Refuge, Hawai'i Island.

(Lepson and Freed 1995). I calculated reproductive success as the proportion of pairs fledging at least one chick. Only pairs I observed feeding fledglings were counted as successful. Fledglings are fed by their parents for at least a month, are easy to locate by their begging calls, and remain on their natal territory until chased away by the parents at the onset of the subsequent breeding season. I estimated population density at each site by converting the average territory size to numbers of birds/ha. This method thus estimates the breeding population because it includes territory holders and excludes nonbreeding floaters and juveniles. I mapped territories through observations of boundary disputes, and in some cases by playbacks (Falls 1981), and calculated territory size by the minimum convex polygon method using WILDTRAK (Todd 1992).

RESULTS

POXLIKE LESIONS IN 'ELEPAIO

Prevalence of poxlike lesions in 'Elepaio differed dramatically among sites at Hakalau (χ^2 = 25.3, df = 2, P < 0.001). At both Pua 'Ākala sites combined, only one of 62 'Elepaio (1.6%) had poxlike lesions, but at Maulua 40% of 35 'Elepaio had poxlike lesions (Fig. 3). No 'Elepaio were captured with active lesions; all infected birds had deformed or missing toes. The deformities and healed lesions generally were not severe and did not appear debilitating. Most birds had from one to three deformed toes or claws, and a few had a slightly deformed foot. The most severe case observed was a bird that was missing most of two toes and had two other toes and claws deformed. No 'Elepaio were captured with large deformities on the feet, legs, or head. It is possible, however, that birds with more severe infections did not survive and died before this study began.

Prevalence of poxlike lesions in 'Elepaio at Maulua varied over time (χ^2 = 15.8, df = 1, P < 0.001), which was revealed by the cohorts that contained infected birds. Seventy percent of birds that hatched in 1992 or earlier had healed

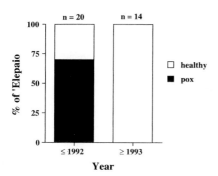

FIGURE 4. Incidence of avian poxlike lesions in 'Elepaio at Maulua over time.

lesions, but all birds hatched in 1993 or later showed no signs of lesions (Fig. 4). The population density of 'Elepaio at Maulua increased 65% during the study, from 0.66 birds/ha in 1994, to 1.03 in 1995, and 1.09 in 1996. Age structure of the breeding population at Maulua also changed over the same period, from 50% subadults in 1994, to 42% in 1995, and 8% in 1996. All new territory holders at Maulua were only one or two years old. Two 'Elepaio that were banded as juveniles in 1994 each obtained a territory and a mate in 1995 close to their natal territories. In contrast, at upper Pua 'Ākala, where habitat was similar to that at Maulua but where few birds had lesions, population density remained relatively constant from 1994 to 1996 (1.25–1.27 birds/ha), and the proportion of the breeding population consisting of subadults was consistently small (4–20%). By 1996, Maulua and upper Pua 'Ākala were similar in population density (1.09 versus 1.26 birds/ha, respectively) and in age structure (8% versus 4% subadults, respectively).

No birds with active lesions were caught, but survival of 'Elepaio with healed lesions (0.89, N = 45 bird-years) was very similar to that of 'Elepaio without lesions (0.87, N = 47 bird-years). Survival was independent of whether a bird was healthy or had healed lesions (χ^2 = 0.06, df = 1, P = 0.81). Reproductive success at Maulua of pairs in which at least one bird had healed lesions (0.71, N = 38 pair-years) was similar to that in pairs with two healthy birds (0.62, N = 29 pair-years), and did not differ between these two groups (χ^2 = 0.60, df = 1, P = 0.44). Whether or not a bird was infected was independent of whether its mate was infected (χ^2 = 1.63, df = 1, P = 0.20).

DISCUSSION

Poxlike lesions were much more prevalent at Maulua than at either Pua 'Ākala study site, which probably at least partly explains the lower population density of 'Elepaio found at Maulua in previous surveys (Scott et al. 1986) and at the start of this study. The cohorts of 'Elepaio with poxlike lesions indicated higher infection rates at Maulua in 1992 that decreased by spring 1993. Prevalence of deformed birds at Maulua was very high with 70% of birds missing digits. Population density apparently was greatly reduced in 1992, but increased rapidly and by 1996 had returned to a level similar to that at upper Pua 'Ākala, where there was no evidence of lesions. When population density was low at Maulua, many young birds were able to acquire territories and breed, but as the population recovered and density increased, most subadults were excluded from the breeding population and acted as floaters, as seen each year at Pua 'Ākala. The differences in demography and population dynamics between Maulua and Pua 'Ākala and the recovery of the Maulua population provide strong circumstantial evidence that avian pox caused the low density of 'Elepaio at Maulua. Additional factors currently being investigated that also may be partly responsible for the lower population density at Maulua include habitat structure and arthropod abundance.

Higher disease prevalence at Maulua may also be responsible for the low densities of other bird species, such as Hawai'i 'Ākepa (*Loxops c. coccineus*), Hawai'i Creeper (*Oreomystis mana*), and 'Akiapōlā'au (*Hemignathus munroi*; Scott et al. 1986). These endangered honeycreepers may be more susceptible than 'Elepaio to introduced diseases like malaria and avian pox, making them more vulnerable to local extinction. Below I discuss the implications of these findings for the importance of poxlike lesions in reducing Hawaiian forest bird populations in general and at Maulua in particular.

Poxlike lesions were probably more prevalent at the Maulua study site because the site is at a lower elevation than the Pua 'Ākala study sites (1,550 versus 1,800–1,900 m). In other areas of the island of Hawai'i, van Riper et al. (1986) demonstrated that the proportion of birds with malaria was lower at high elevations, with almost no infected birds above 1,600 m. Goff and van Riper (1980) found that the upper-elevational limit of *Culex* mosquitoes was 1,500 m in most months, but occasionally up to 1,650 m. In this study, poxlike lesions were common at 1,550 m elevation at Maulua in some years, but very rare at 1,800–1,900 m at Pua 'Ākala, demonstrating a consistent upper limit to the distribution of disease in different areas of the island. The similar upper-elevational limits of poxlike lesions and mosquitoes suggest that mosquitoes may be the primary vector of avian pox among Hawaiian forest birds. Incidence of poxlike lesions also was independent between mates, which would not be expected if transmission occurred primarily by contact with an infected bird, perch, or nest.

Elevations from 1,500–1,600 m may be especially important and demographically interesting due to the dynamic nature of disease prevalence and transmission (Atkinson et al. 1995). Contact between native birds and disease vectors is most frequent at these elevations, but abundance of vectors and thus of disease transmission may vary among seasons (van Riper et al. 1986) and among years (this study), resulting in periodic epizootics of disease separated by varying lengths of time. Recovery of the 'Elepaio population at Maulua was rapid in this case and required only four years, but the frequency of epizootics is unknown and could have important effects on persistence and variation in size of bird populations. If epizootics are infrequent, populations of most bird species may fully recover between disease episodes, and populations may be large most of the time. If epizootics are frequent, population sizes may be smaller and below carrying capacity much of the time, and species that are highly susceptible may have insufficient time to recover between disease episodes, resulting in ever-dwindling populations and eventual extinction. Species that are somewhat more resistant, perhaps such as 'Elepaio, may be able to maintain larger populations during epizootics, and their population remnants would recover more quickly. Whether a particular species can persist in an area thus may depend on the interaction between frequency of epizootics and susceptibility to disease of that species. Recovery also may be more rapid in areas with less habitat disturbance because population remnants are larger or closer together.

'Elepaio may be more dispersive and better able to recolonize vacant habitat than the endangered Hawai'i 'Ākepa and Hawai'i Creeper because of their life histories. Both 'Elepaio and these honeycreepers have high site fidelity as adults (VanderWerf 1998a, Woodworth et al. *this volume*), but young 'Elepaio may be forced to disperse more often than young honeycreepers because the highly territorial nature of adult 'Elepaio forces young birds to search for vacant space (VanderWerf 1998a). The honeycreepers are less territorial, and young birds may have more opportunity, and may prefer, to return to their natal area to breed (Lepson and Freed 1995, VanderWerf 1998b, Woodworth et al. *this volume*).

If an 'Elepaio can survive initial infection, its future survival and ability to reproduce are not affected. Such birds probably also develop a greater degree of immunity to subsequent infec-

tions by the same pathogen (Karstad 1971a,b; Tripathy 1993). Mortality rate among birds with active infections could not be measured in this study, but on O'ahu preliminary evidence indicates annual mortality of 'Elepaio with active poxlike lesions is quite high, approximately 40% (VanderWerf et al. 1997; E. VanderWerf, unpubl. data). Birds with mild infections, in which only the toes are affected, frequently recover, and loss or deformation of a few toes does not appear to be debilitating. More severe infections of the feet, legs, and head often may lead to mortality. No 'Elepaio with large healed lesions on the feet, legs, or head were captured in this study. If certain populations or individuals are discovered to have greater immunity to avian pox, these should be selected for use in any captive breeding efforts. In particular, captive breeding and reintroduction have been proposed as conservation measures for the O'ahu 'Elepaio (Ellis et al. 1992a). Use of disease-resistant birds could greatly increase the success of reintroductions and thus the value of captive breeding, and this issue should be investigated before any captive breeding is begun.

Vaccines against some forms of avian pox have been developed, primarily for use in the poultry industry, but vaccination of wild bird populations against poxvirus probably is not a practical long-term conservation strategy. Birds must be captured in order to be vaccinated cutaneously, which is the most effective method (Nagy et al. 1990). Mass inoculation of wild birds through vaccines in food supplements or drinking water cannot ensure that birds obtain an adequate immunogenetic dose and is potentially dangerous because it may select for resistant forms of the virus. Immunogenicity of vaccines also varies considerably among viral species (reviewed in Tripathy 1993) and it is not known which or how many species of avian pox occur in Hawai'i. Furthermore, immunity acquired through vaccination may provide some short-term protection for very young offspring via maternal antibodies, but it will not be heritable and will not provide long-lasting protection. The effort and cost required to continually capture and vaccinate generation after generation of wild birds is likely to be prohibitive. A more practical approach may be to limit transmission of avian pox by controlling the primary vector, mosquitoes, or to identify naturally resistant populations or individuals.

Ideally, it would be best to control vectors year-round to maximally reduce disease transmission. In reality, funding for vector control is likely to be limited, and managers will have to choose when and where to apply vector control so that it is most effective, and this decision should be based on several factors. There is accumulating evidence in birds that nutritional limitation causes a trade-off between reproductive effort and ability to resist parasitic infection (Gustafsson et al. 1994), resulting in greater susceptibility to disease during times of stress, such as egg production (Allander and Bennett 1995, Oppliger et al. 1996) and feeding of nestlings (Norris et al. 1994, Richner et al. 1995). On the other hand, rate of disease transmission is likely to be influenced by vector abundance, resulting in higher disease prevalence when vectors are more common (van Riper et al. 1986). In areas of Hawai'i where mosquitoes are common year-round, such as low elevations forests on O'ahu, vector control might be most effective at reducing the effects of disease during the spring breeding season when birds are stressed by producing eggs, incubating, and feeding offspring. At higher elevations, perhaps such as Hakalau, or in drier areas where mosquito populations vary seasonally with temperature and rainfall, vector control might be most effective in fall and winter when mosquito abundance peaks (Goff and van Riper 1980).

In addition to Hakalau, poxlike lesions have been found in 'Elepaio at Hawai'i Volcanoes National Park, Manukā Natural Area Reserve, and Pōhakuloa Training Area on Hawai'i Island, on the Alaka'i Plateau on Kaua'i, and in many areas of O'ahu (Herrmann and Snetsinger 1997, VanderWerf et al. 1997; C. Atkinson, pers. comm.; E. VanderWerf, unpubl. data). Poxlike lesions are widespread and very common in some areas, and avian pox may be reducing many 'Elepaio populations, making it one of the most important threats to this species.

The results of this study further illustrate the importance to native Hawaiian birds of high-elevation forests as refuges from mosquito-borne diseases. Populations of 'Elepaio at Pua 'Ākala from 1,800–1,900 m elevation were dense, stable, and relatively unaffected by disease during this study. However, prevalence and distribution of vectors and disease vary from year to year (van Riper et al. 1986), and bird populations at

elevations above the usual "mosquito zone" may occasionally be at risk. Maulua had no disease and presumably few mosquitoes in most years, but periodic epizootics may be sufficient to make populations of sensitive bird species fluctuate dangerously at Maulua. Upper Pua 'Ākala at 1,900 meters likely is subject to disease very infrequently, but a few 'Elepaio were infected even there, indicating small numbers of mosquitoes occasionally reach even that high elevation. Much as civil engineers must deal with "100-year floods," avian conservation biologists in Hawai'i should consider the eventuality of a "100-year epizootic" that would affect populations of forest birds at elevations traditionally considered safe from disease. Such an event could be catastrophic and would be difficult to contend with, but development of safe, practical methods of mosquito control would be extremely valuable in reducing the severity of any epizootic. Additional management techniques such as removal of feral pigs to reduce mosquito breeding habitat, removal of introduced predators like roof rats (*Rattus rattus*) and cats (*Felis catus*) to increase nest success, and habitat restoration to increase food supply, population size, and range may help by relieving other potential threats so recovery can be as rapid and complete as possible following the epizootic.

ACKNOWLEDGMENTS

This research was supported by grants and awards to E. VanderWerf from the Ecology, Evolution, and Conservation Biology Program of the University of Hawai'i, the ARCS Foundation, Sigma Xi, the Hawaii Audubon Society, and by a grant from the MacArthur Foundation to L. Freed, R. Cann, and S. Conant. I thank the staff of Hakalau Forest National Wildlife Refuge, especially refuge manager R. Wass and refuge biologist J. Jeffrey, for permission to work and logistical help. Valuable field assistance was provided by J. Bennett, M. Burt, M. Ono, and J. Rohrer. T. Yoshikawa and K. Asoh helped with histological preparations. The manuscript was improved by comments from S. Conant, L. Freed, A. Taylor, and C. van Riper. I greatly benefited from discussions about disease in Hawaiian birds with C. Atkinson, R. Cann, L. Freed, S. Jarvi, D. LaPointe, B. Nielsen, and C. van Riper.

Studies in Avian Biology No. 22:254–263, 2001.

IMMUNOGENETICS AND RESISTANCE TO AVIAN MALARIA IN HAWAIIAN HONEYCREEPERS (DREPANIDINAE)

SUSAN I. JARVI, CARTER T. ATKINSON, AND ROBERT C. FLEISCHER

Abstract. Although a number of factors have contributed to the decline and extinction of Hawai'i's endemic terrestrial avifauna, introduced avian malaria (*Plasmodium relictum*) is probably the single most important factor preventing recovery of these birds in low-elevation habitats. Continued decline in numbers, fragmentation of populations, and extinction of species that are still relatively common will likely continue without new, aggressive approaches to managing avian disease. Methods of intervention in the disease cycle such as chemotherapy and vaccine development are not feasible because of efficient immune-evasion strategies evolved by the parasite, technical difficulties associated with treating wild avian populations, and increased risk of selection for more virulent strains of the parasite. We are investigating the natural evolution of disease resistance in some low-elevation native bird populations, particularly Hawai'i 'Amakihi (*Hemignathus virens*), to perfect genetic methods for identifying individuals with a greater immunological capacity to survive malarial infection. We are focusing on genetic analyses of the major histocompatibility complex, due to its critical role in both humoral and cell-mediated immune responses. In the parasite, we are evaluating conserved ribosomal genes as well as variable genes encoding cell-surface molecules as a first step in developing a better understanding of the complex interactions between malarial parasites and the avian immune system. A goal is to provide population managers with new criteria for maintaining long-term population stability for threatened species through the development of methods for evaluating and maintaining genetic diversity in small populations at loci important in immunological responsiveness to pathogens.

Key Words: avian malaria; Drepanidinae; genetics; Hawai'i honeycreeper; *Mhc*; *Plasmodium relictum*.

The Hawaiian honeycreepers (Drepanidinae) are a morphologically and ecologically diverse subfamily of cardueline finches that probably evolved from a single finch species that colonized the Hawaiian Islands an estimated 4–4.5 million years ago (Tarr and Fleischer 1993, 1995; Fleischer et al. 1998). The honeycreepers radiated very rapidly to fill a variety of ecological niches. While the progenitor of the subfamily was presumably a finch-billed, granivorous form, the more than 50 species and subspecies of honeycreepers derived from this ancestor had great diversity of morphological types ranging from nectivores with long, decurved sickle bills to seedeaters with massive, powerful beaks (Perkins 1903, Amadon 1950, Raikow 1977, Freed et al. 1987a, James and Olson 1991).

While the Drepanidines have long been considered an exceptional example of adaptive radiation, they, along with many other Hawaiian birds, are also an unfortunate paradigm of extinction and endangerment (Scott et al. 1986, 1988; James and Olson 1991). Of a total of 54 described species, 14 became extinct after Polynesian colonization and are known only from subfossil remains. Another 14 became extinct following Western contact and are present in museum collections from the 1800s. Of the remaining 26 species, 18 are currently listed as endangered by the U.S. Fish and Wildlife Service and many of these are perched on the brink of extinction, and some may be extinct (Jacobi

and Atkinson 1995, Reynolds and Snetsinger *this volume*). Although a large number of factors contributed to the extinction of Hawaiian honeycreepers (Ralph and van Riper 1985, Scott et al. 1988, James and Olson 1991), introduced disease and disease vectors are likely the greatest threat facing them today, particularly at elevations lower than 1,500 m (Warner 1968, van Riper et al. 1986, Atkinson et al. 1995).

PARASITES IN PARADISE

There are no native mosquitoes in Hawai'i, but a bird-biting species (*Culex quinquefasciatus*) was accidentally introduced to Maui in 1826 (Hardy 1960). The spread of this mosquito throughout low- and mid-elevation habitats and introduction and release of domestic fowl, game birds, and cage birds allowed two introduced diseases to escape into native populations, avian malaria (*Plasmodium relictum*), and avian pox (*Poxvirus avium*). Although there is little direct evidence that diseases caused by these organisms were responsible for the major declines and extinctions of honeycreepers during the past 100 years, considerable indirect evidence has accumulated in recent years that supports this hypothesis. Anecdotal reports by early naturalists of sick and dead birds with large pox-like tumors suggests that avian poxvirus was having major impacts on forest bird populations as early as the 1890s (Perkins 1903). It is less clear when malaria was first introduced to Hawai'i since the

TABLE 1. MORTALITY IN NONNATIVE FOREST BIRDS IN HAWAI'I EXPERIMENTALLY INFECTED WITH HAWAI'I ISOLATES OF *P. relictum*

Species	Sample-size	Route of inoculation	% Mortality
Red-Billed Leiothrix[a] (*Leothrix lutea*)	5	Blood inoculation	0 (0/5)
Japanese White Eye[a] (*Zosterops japonicus*)	5	Blood inoculation	0 (0/5)
Nutmeg Mannikin[b] (*Lonchura punctulata*)	7	Mosquito bite	0 (0/7)

[a] van Riper et al. (1986).
[b] Atkinson et al. (1995).

TABLE 2. MORTALITY IN HONEYCREEPERS EXPERIMENTALLY INFECTED WITH HAWAI'I ISOLATES OF *P. relictum*. (SCIENTIFIC NAMES FOR ALL BIRD SPECIES LISTED BELOW CAN BE FOUND IN TABLE 2 FOLLOWING THE INTRODUCTION OF THIS VOLUME.)

Species	Sample size	Route of inoculation	% Mortality
Laysan Finch[a]	5	Blood inoculation	100 (5/5)
'I'iwi[a]	5	Blood inoculation	60 (3/5)
'I'iwi[b]	10	Mosquito bite	90 (9/10)
Maui 'Alauahio[c]	4	Mosquito bite	75 (3/4)
'Apapane[a]	5	Blood inoculation	40 (2/5)
'Apapane[e]	8	Mosquito bite	63 (5/8)
Hawai'i 'Amakihi[a] (high elevation)	6	Blood inoculation	66 (4/6)
Hawai'i 'Amakihi[a] (low elevation)	5	Blood inoculation	20 (1/5)
Hawai'i 'Amakihi[d] (high elevation)	20	Mosquito bite	65 (13/20)

Note: Mosquito bite method of inoculation duplicates natural conditions more closely and provides a more accurate estimate of expected mortality in the wild.
[a] van Riper et al. (1986).
[b] Atkinson et al. (1995).
[c] C. T. Atkinson (unpubl. data).
[d] Atkinson et al. (2000).
[e] Yorinks and Atkinson (2000).

earliest blood smears from native birds date only to the 1940s, and it is unlikely that early naturalists would have recognized signs and lesions of the disease. van Riper et al. (1986) has hypothesized that the introduction occurred in the 1920s, since this corresponds to a time when large numbers of exotic cage birds were imported from throughout the world and released into the wild. Limited collections of blood smears prepared from native species prior to 1950 also show little evidence of infection in native species, suggesting that spread of this disease in forest bird populations may be responsible for the major wave of extinctions in mid-elevation habitats that occurred in the second half of the 20th century (van Riper et al. 1986, van Riper 1991).

From historical collections and observations, as well as subfossil distributions, many honeycreeper taxa were known to have occurred at lower elevations prior to the introduction and spread of mosquitoes, pox, and malaria (Warner 1968, van Riper et al. 1986, James and Olson 1991). With the exception of several relatively common species, most honeycreeper taxa now occur only at elevations above 1,200 m. With few exceptions, they show little or no overlap with the current range of *C. quinquefasciatus*, even though otherwise suitable habitat is available at lower elevations (Goff and van Riper 1980, Scott et al. 1986). While nonnative passerines show little morbidity or mortality following infection with Hawaiian isolates of *P. relictum* (Table 1), most honeycreeper taxa tested thus far are severely debilitated and usually killed by acute anemia associated with fulminating erythrocytic infections (Warner 1968, van Riper et al. 1986; Atkinson et al. 1995, 2000; Yorinks and Atkinson 2000; Table 2).

Experimental studies (van Riper et al. 1986, Atkinson et al. 1995, Yorinks and Atkinson 2000) have provided evidence that elevational

and geographical anomalies in honeycreeper distribution may largely be due to relative resistance or susceptibility to avian malaria (Fig. 1). Morbidity and mortality in 'I'iwi (*Vestiaria coccinea*), Hawai'i 'Amakihi (*Hemignathus virens*), 'Apapane (*Himatione sanguinea*), and Maui 'Alauahio (*Paroreomyza montana*) were extraordinarily high after a minimal dose of a single mosquito bite (Table 2). Both Maui 'Alauahio and 'I'iwi, two species that rarely occur below 1,500 m, are most susceptible with fatality rates of 75% and 90%, respectively. The range of both species appears to be contracting, particularly in mid-elevation habitats where mosquito populations have increased in recent years as a consequence of feral pig activity and human development (Goff and van Riper 1980). Mortality was lower for 'Apapane and 'Amakihi, although those individuals who recovered underwent a severe, acute illness that caused significant declines in food consumption, weight, and activity levels (Atkinson et al. 2000, Yorinks and Atkinson 2000). Laysan Finches (*Telespiza cantans*) are also highly susceptible to and suffer high mortality from malarial infection, based on experimental infection and exposure of caged captive birds to infected mosquitoes in lowland habitats (Warner 1968, van Riper et al. 1986). Much less is known about other threatened and

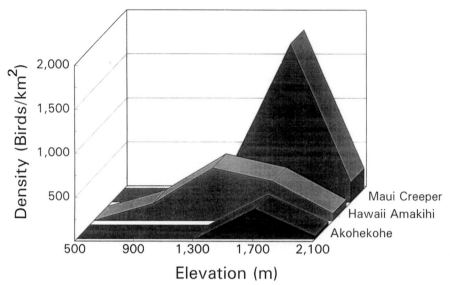

FIGURE 1. Differences in density of three species of honeycreepers on the northeastern slope of Haleakalā Volcano, island of Maui. Data are extracted from density maps published in Scott et al. (1986) to illustrate the lower elevational limits of species that are likely to be highly susceptible to avian malaria (i.e., Maui ʻAlauahio and ʻĀkohekohe, *Palmeria dolei*) and those more resistant to this disease (i.e., Hawaiʻi ʻAmakihi).

endangered species, but it is likely that they share a similar high susceptibility to infection.

Interestingly, several of the more abundant honeycreeper species, i.e. Hawaiʻi ʻAmakihi, Oʻahu ʻAmakihi (*Hemignathus flavus*), and ʻApapane, appear to have fragmented but apparently stable populations in low- and mid-elevation habitats where pox and malaria transmission occurs. Based on differential mortality between mid- and high-elevation Hawaiʻi ʻAmakihi that were infected experimentally with *P. relictum* (Table 2), van Riper et al. (1986) hypothesized that these low-elevation populations were evolving "immunogenetic" resistance to malaria from continual exposure to the parasite. van Riper (1991) also found some evidence that Hawaiian isolates of *P. relictum* are less virulent than those found on mainland North America, suggesting that both native hosts and introduced malaria are exerting strong selective pressures on each other and actively coevolving (Atkinson et al. 1995). There is some evidence that selection for less virulent strains of pox may also be occurring, since the massive, debilitating lesions that were described by workers in the early 1900s are found rarely today in naturally infected honeycreepers (C. T. Atkinson, unpubl. data). Evidence for this is still limited but consistent with current evolutionary theory that predicts selection for intermediate levels of virulence and host susceptibility after a pathogen is introduced into a highly susceptible host population (Anderson and May 1982, Ewald 1994).

This putative genetic basis for resistance to malaria in low-elevation honeycreeper populations could involve only a single gene of the immune system, such as a locus of the major histocompatibility complex. Or, like genetically based resistance to malaria in humans, there could be many loci and genetic systems involved to varying degrees, with epistasis also a possible factor (Nagel and Roth 1989, McGuire et al. 1994, Hill 1996, Riley 1996, Weatherall 1996, Hill and Weatherall 1998). If there is a genetic basis to resistance to malaria, then individuals who are resident at higher elevations represent a population that has not been tested significantly or subjected to natural selection by malarial infection. These individuals act as a control for the experimental or selected population that has lived with malaria at low elevations for many generations. Thus by comparing allele frequencies or heterozygosities of different genetic markers between these two populations, we may find evidence for the previous (and likely continuing) action of natural selection. This linkage disequilibrium caused by selection (Ghosh and Collins 1996) might also allow us ultimately to identify the specific target(s) of selection.

To understand why and how some species and individuals within species appear to be able to survive disease epidemics, while others succumb, requires knowledge of the complex interactions between malarial parasites and the avian immune system and how these interactions may place selective pressures on both parasite and host. We have initiated research on genes of the immune system in Hawaiian honeycreepers and ribosomal genes and selected cell-surface molecules of Hawaiian isolates of *P. relictum* as a first step toward developing a better understanding of these complex relationships.

AVIAN IMMUNE SYSTEMS AND THE MHC

Many of the genes and molecules involved in immune system processes that are described in mammals are also known in birds and many were, in fact, initially discovered in birds. The domestic chicken (*Gallus domesticus*) has long served as the "laboratory mouse" of avian research, largely because of its agricultural importance and domestication. Thus, much of the current knowledge of avian immune systems comes from studies completed in chickens. Avian immune system cells appear to function in a way similar to those in mammals, but obvious distinctions in structure and distribution of lymphoid tissue exist in birds. Birds lack the lymph nodes that are so common in mammals, but they have unique avian lymphatic tissues such as the oculo-nasal Harderian gland and the bursa of Fabricious (Eerola et al. 1987). Early studies illuminating the role of the bursa of Fabricious in antibody production established the foundation for the T-cell, B-cell concept (Glick et al. 1956). The B-cell system involves production of specific antibody (humoral immunity) and the T-cell system involves cell-mediated immunity. This duality of the immune system is now known to be universal among all vertebrates. In mammals and birds, both humoral and cell-mediated responses are involved in the immune response against malaria. Among the many cells and molecules with important roles in immunity (e.g., antibodies, macrophages, neutrophils, natural killer cells, and a variety of cell communication molecules, such as interleukins and cytokines), molecules encoded by genes within the major histocompatibility complex (*Mhc*) are of special significance due to their critical role in both humoral and cell-mediated immunological responses.

Mhc class I and class II genes have been found in all well-characterized vertebrates and date as far back as cartilaginous fish. The *Mhc* was first identified as the genetic locus responsible for allograft (tissue) rejection, but it is now known to be responsible for determining what is viewed as "self" versus "non-self" by the immune system. Class I molecules are present on essentially all nucleated cells in the body (including erythrocytes in birds), whereas class II molecules are present on only certain cells of the immune system. *Mhc* molecules function to distinguish foreign invaders by presenting a peptide fragment of the invader (i.e., a parasite of any kind, or peptides from a foreign graft) in the antigen-binding region (ABR) of the molecule to T-cell receptors. This initiates a cascade of events that leads to production of lymphocytes, cytokines, and antibodies, and eventual elimination of the parasite.

The *Mhc* is polymorphic (multiallelic) and multigenic in most species investigated to date. The human *Mhc* is known to contain over 200 genes, many of which are directly involved in the adaptive immune response. The chicken *Mhc* (*B* system; Briles et al. 1948) is the smallest known *Mhc*, containing only 19 known genes coupled to a large family of B-G genes (Kaufman et al. 1999). Studies of the avian *Mhc* have recently been extended to galliformes other than chickens and include pheasants (Jarvi and Briles 1992, Jarvi et al. 1996; Wittzell et al. 1994, 1995), turkeys (Emara et al. 1993), and quail (Shiina et al. 1995) as well as passeriformes (Edwards et al. 1995, Vincek et al. 1995; S. I. Jarvi et al., unpubl. data) and cranes (Jarvi et al. 1995, 1999). B-G molecules are expressed on a variety of tissues in chickens (Miller et al. 1990, Salomonsen et al. 1991), but their function is still unknown. B-G genes have been shown to exist in pheasants (Jarvi and Briles 1992, Jarvi et al. 1996) and cranes (Jarvi et al. 1995, 1999). Recently a second cluster of at least two *Mhc* class I and two class II genes (called *Rfp-Y*) has been identified in chickens (Briles et al. 1993; Miller et al. 1994a,b) and pheasants (Wittzell et al. 1995, Jarvi et al. 1996). The function and expression of these genes is currently under investigation. The simplicity of *Mhc* structure and function in birds as compared to mammals has been thought to account for the more obvious associations of *Mhc* genotype and susceptibility to infectious disease (for review see Kaufman and Wallney 1996).

One of the earliest reported *Mhc* associations with infectious disease was in chickens with Marek's disease (Hansen et al. 1967, Briles and Oleson 1971). Marek's disease is a naturally occurring, herpes-virus induced lymphoma of chickens. The virus initially infects B-cells and macrophages, and eventually T-cells, which result in lethal lymphomas. Birds possessing the B21 *Mhc* haplotype show strong resistance (as much as 95% survival; Pazderka et al. 1975, Longenecker et al. 1976; Briles et al. 1977, 1980, 1983; Bacon and Whitter 1980). The B21 haplotype occurs frequently in many apparently unrelated populations of chickens, including Red Jungle Fowl (*Gallus gallus*; the hypothesized species progenitor), indicating that it may have special survival value for the species (Longe-necker and Mossman 1981).

Rous Sarcoma virus (RSV) is a retrovirus which causes fatal tumors in some chickens but not others. When studied in congenic strains of chickens, *Mhc* haplotype B12 is involved with tumor regression (more resistant to RSV) where-as B4 is a progressor (more susceptible to RSV; reviewed in Plachy et al. 1992). Further studies show the existence of 17 virally derived peptides that are capable of binding the major B12 class I molecule, whereas only two virally derived peptides were identified with the motif of the major B4 class I molecule (Kaufman and Wall-ney 1996). This may partially explain the resis-tance (or enhanced immune response) that oc-curs in B12 chickens. Other strong disease as-sociations with different *Mhc* alleles in chickens include coccidiosis (Clare et al. 1989) and fowl cholera (Lamont et al. 1987). Association be-tween specific *Mhc* alleles and resistance to dis-ease in humans exists, but it is not as apparent. Substantial evidence exists for protective alleles against severe malaria in some human popula-tions but not in others (Hill et al. 1991, 1994; Riley 1996, Hill and Weatherall 1998, Gilbert et al. 1998), and that particular class II haplotypes affect the probability that a hepatitis B infection will become persistent (Thursz et al. 1995).

It has been shown that *Mhc* heterozygotes have higher hatchability and viability than ho-mozygotes (Schultz and Briles 1953), and that individual *Mhc* haplotypes are associated with level of hatchability and viability in chickens (Briles and Allen 1961). Evidence for overdom-inance of *Mhc* alleles (heterozygous advantage) was demonstrated very early in chickens for traits such as viability, hatchability, body weight, and survivor egg production (Briles 1954, Briles et al. 1957, Abplanalp et al. 1992, Sato et al. 1992) and in humans for susceptibil-ity to hepatitis B infection (Thursz et al. 1997) and survivorship to HIV-1 infections (Carring-ton et al. 1999). Retention of polymorphism (multiple alleles) as well as heterozygosity for genes in the *Mhc* is likely important for long-term population stability. The *Mhc,* therefore, appears to be an excellent candidate gene region in which to search for disease relationships in Hawaiian honeycreepers.

GENETIC ANALYSES OF HOSTS

We know that susceptibility to malaria differs among and within honeycreeper species and that relative susceptibility or resistance can explain their current elevational distribution to this dis-ease. To investigate the natural evolution of dis-ease resistance in honeycreepers, we have initi-ated studies of the *Mhc* in Hawai'i 'Amakihi, a species with some evidence of natural resistance to malaria, and also the 'I'iwi, a highly suscep-tible species with declining numbers that is cur-rently limited to high-elevation habitats. Be-cause of the extreme variability and putative dis-ease and fitness associations of the *Mhc,* a num-ber of authors have suggested that selection for increased *Mhc* diversity occurs via interactions of the molecule with diverse antigen types, but the type of selection has been open to debate (e.g., Hughes and Nei 1988, Hedrick et al. 1991). Selection may be directional in situations where a particular *Mhc* variant provides immu-nity to a particular disease (Hedrick et al. 1991). If a number of different diseases infect a popu-lation over time, selection could balance the fre-quencies, resulting in a high level of variability (i.e., frequency dependent selection; Hedrick et al. 1991). If a population, such as low-elevation 'Amakihi, experiences a devastating epidemic of a single disease, we may see the "signature" of the selection as a greatly increased or modified frequency of a particular haplotype in the pop-ulation of survivors. Alternatively, selection may favor heterozygous individuals (heterozy-gote advantage), because the *Mhc* products of two alleles can recognize more, different anti-gens (i.e., polypeptide products) of a particular disease than one allele.

What sample sizes are needed to have suffi-cient power to detect this selection? We are cur-rently comparing samples from low- and high-elevation Hawai'i 'Amakihi. Most of the low-elevation populations have been in contact with mosquitoes and malaria for 50–100 yrs. Given mortality rates of 50–70% in malaria-challenged high-elevation birds, there is potential for very strong selection with coefficients of 0.5 or high-er. Using equations from Hartl and Clark (1989), we have modeled the potential impacts of direc-tional selection by malaria on single-locus allele frequencies and on the power to detect signifi-cant differences (Cohen 1988) given sample sizes of 50 low- and 200 high-elevation birds (Fig. 2). Whether we use 50 or 100 generations of selection, or have an initial allele frequency of the positively selected allele as 5% (based on a "typical" *Mhc* haplotype frequency in chick-ens), or 30% (based on the survival rate in high-elevation challenges), we generally have suffi-cient power (>80%) to detect selection coeffi-cients as low as 0.02 with our sample. Satta et al. (1995) recently estimated overdominant se-lection coefficients on mammalian *Mhc* loci to range from about 0.002 to 0.05; thus, this type of comparison should be able to detect at least the higher range of their values.

Our model does not include the ameliorating effects of migration. However, the 'Amakihi is

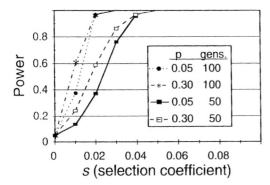

FIGURE 2. Power (Cohen 1988) to detect frequency differences between low- and high-elevation populations after 50 or 100 generations of malaria selection (Hartl and Clark 1989) in low-elevation populations.

TABLE 3. POWER TO DETECT FREQUENCY DIFFERENCES BETWEEN SURVIVORS AND NONSURVIVORS AFTER DIRECTIONAL MALARIA SELECTION AT THE GIVEN SELECTION COEFFICIENT (S) WITH THE GIVEN SAMPLE SIZE (N)

N	Selection coefficient			
	0.05	0.10	0.25	0.50
25	0.061	0.077	0.153	0.440
100	0.077	0.120	0.354	0.915
250	0.097	0.184	0.655	0.999

known to have high breeding and natal philopatry (van Riper 1984; U.S. Geological Survey, unpubl. data), and it is our view that migration is not sufficient to counter the expected selection intensities. We also assessed the power to detect significant differences in allele frequencies between malaria challenge survivors, fatalities, and controls (Table 3). In this case, selection must be very strong (>0.25) in order for us to detect a significant difference given sample sizes from recent challenge experiments (Atkinson et al. 1995).

Our goals are to perfect genetic methods for evaluating *Mhc* diversity among and within species to look for elevation-dependent allele frequency distributions. Birds involved in experimental malaria challenges are also included in this ongoing study with the hopes of developing methods for identifying individuals with a greater ability to survive malarial infection. General methodology includes the use of the polymerase chain reaction (PCR) to amplify the *Mhc* antigen-binding region (ABR) of class II (beta) genes from the genomic DNA from several individuals (S. I. Jarvi et al., unpubl. data). This targets the gene region in which much of the variability of *Mhc* molecules is concentrated. Products from PCR were cloned using methods that allow specific cloning of homoduplex PCR products by either PCR+1 (Borriello and Krauter 1991) or single-stranded conformational polymorphism (SSCP) isolation (Oto et al. 1993), PCR reamplification, and direct cloning. Both strands of the cloned products were sequenced using a 373 ABI automated sequencing system, and sequences verified as originating from the class II ABR by comparison with numerous known class II sequences available through Genbank.™ Restriction fragment-length polymorphism (RFLP) analyses of 'Amakihi and

'I'iwi class II genes were carried out (Figs. 3a and 3b, respectively). All blots were produced by digestion of approximately 15 μg of genomic DNA with either *PvuII, PstI,* or *HindIII.* Blots were then hybridized with a mixture of cloned, sequenced, ^{32}P-labeled *Mhc* class II antigen-binding region from Hawai'i 'Amakihi and 'I'iwi at 50°C in a rotating hybridization oven. Blots were washed in 1 × SSC for at least one hour and autoradiograms were produced. Band sharing coefficients (s) were calculated (using methods described in Lynch 1988) from banding patterns derived from individuals on four 'Amakihi blots and four 'I'iwi blots. Data are presented as composite histograms in Figures 3a and 3b. The *Mhc* class II banding patterns of 'Amakihi and 'I'iwi are markedly distinct, as is reflected by a mean band sharing coefficient of 0.617 over four 'Amakihi blots (Figure 3a) and 0.883 over four 'I'iwi blots (Figure 3b). The actual number of bands varies depending on restriction enzyme used (either *HindIII, PvuII,* or *PstI*). Digestion of genomic 'Amakihi DNA results in a range of four to nine bands/lane whereas 'I'iwi generally have from one to four bands/lane. One would expect these two species to possess a similar number of class II genes since they are thought to be monophyletic, and also since some 'I'iwi were found with six or more bands/lane. Therefore, the observed decrease in bands/lane among 'I'iwi as compared to 'Amakihi (particularly a decrease in polymorphic bands, i.e., an increase in band-sharing coefficients) likely represents a decrease in class II *Mhc* diversity. The limited *Mhc* diversity found in 'I'iwi could play a role in the high mortality observed in this species. That is, if *Mhc* class I and class II antigen-binding variability is low, it is less likely that malarial-encoded peptides will be presented to or be recognized by the host's immune system. Insufficient stimulus to the immune system could explain the prolonged parasitemias that are common in honeycreepers with acute infections, where the parasite reproduces unchecked in the bloodstream. This is in stark contrast to nonnative species where parasitemias peak sharply and immediately decline

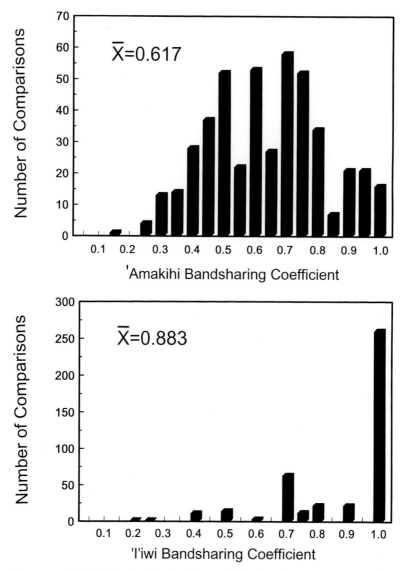

FIGURE 3.   Summary of RFLP (Southern blot) analyses of Hawaiian honeycreeper *Mhc* class II genes. Data are compiled as the percentage of shared bands between individuals (i.e., the bandsharing coefficient, computed according to methods of Lynch 1988) versus the number of individual comparisons. A. Four Hawai'i 'Amakihi Southern blots include a total of 58 different individuals originating from several elevations on the island of Hawai'i. B. Four 'I'iwi blots include a total of 41 different individuals originating from high elevations on the island of Hawai'i.

(van Riper et al. 1986; C. T. Atkinson, unpubl. data).

Comparisons of mitochondrial DNA gene sequences derived from 'I'iwi and 'Amakihi reveal predictable levels of nucleotide diversity among 'Amakihi, but all sequences derived from 'I'iwi are invariant (Feldman 1994; C. Tarr, pers. comm.). Further studies are needed to clarify any potential selective role of the parasite.

In addition to systematically analyzing varia-tion at the *Mhc* for its possible relationship to disease resistance, other genetic markers can be used to identify different genetic systems that may also confer resistance. These markers can include putatively random ones (such as micro-satellites, minisatellites, Randomly Amplified Polymorphic DNA (RAPDs), or Amplified Frag-ment Length Polymorphisms (AFLPs)), or gene systems known to play a role in malaria resis-tance in humans (e.g., G6PDH, TNF-a, etc.;

Riley 1996, Weatherall 1996). Microsatellites have been developed for drepanidines (Tarr 1995, Tarr et al. 1998), and panels of chicken cDNA probes are available (Bumstead et al. 1995) for screening immune system and other genes. These markers may prove useful for three primary purposes: (1) An alternative measure of variability will be available for comparisons among elevations and susceptibility classes in 'Amakihi, and among different honeycreeper species. This tests whether a correlation between *Mhc* gene diversity (heterozygosity) and resistance is due to the variation within the *Mhc* itself (and/or its linked genes) or to genomic variability in general. (2) Markers can be assayed to determine if particular allelic variants or heterozygotes show strong associations with malaria resistance (i.e., differ between low and high elevation or challenge survivors and fatalities). This approach is standard in medical genetics and is outlined by Ghosh and Collins (1996) as the "linkage disequilibrium" approach, as it requires that the actual disease resistance mutations be in linkage disequilibrium with particular alleles. (3) Microsatellite and AFLP markers are excellent for the construction of linkage maps. Such a map would be important for locating the relative position of the *Mhc* and other immune system genes, or any other markers that show a relationship with disease resistance.

While mapping disease resistance to the *Mhc* is strong evidence favoring that *Mhc* itself is responsible, it does not rule out other genes linked within the region. In fact a number of other genes coding for immune system molecules have been localized to the *Mhc* region in mammals and birds (Bumstead et al. 1995), including tumor necrosis factors (Hedrick et al. 1991), complement proteins (Hedrick et al. 1991), proteasomes for antigen degradation (Fehling et al. 1994), and transporter-associated antigen processing proteins (de la Salle et al. 1994, Suh et al. 1994, Bumstead et al. 1995). Some of these may be involved in disease resistance and serve as the targets of selection.

GENETIC ANALYSIS OF PARASITES

A second key to understanding disease resistance in Hawaiian honeycreepers concerns genetic diversity of malarial parasites themselves and how they may exert selective pressure on the host. The malarial parasites of vertebrates (*Plasmodium* spp.) are a closely related group of Apicomplexan parasites that share common morphological and developmental characteristics in all of the reptilian, avian, and mammalian hosts in which they occur (Garnham 1966). Species of *Plasmodium* are thought to have diverged from other members of the Apicomplexa ap-

proximately 129 million years ago (Escalante and Ayala 1994), possibly explaining why more species are found in reptiles and birds (110+) than in mammals (40+; Levine 1988). Most of what we know about the life cycles, pathogenicity, and immunology of the avian parasites was established during the first half of the 20th century when several species that readily infect domestic birds (e.g., *P. gallinaceum* and *P. lophurae*) were used as primary laboratory models for studies of human malaria. With the development of rodent, primate, and in vitro models, research shifted away from avian parasites in the 1950s and we consequently know relatively little about how unique avian immune system molecules and processes might influence parasite interactions with the avian host.

Having successfully persisted in a variety of vertebrate species over such a long period of time, *Plasmodium* spp. have necessarily evolved effective mechanisms for survival. Immune-evasion strategies and the processes involved in natural immunity to malaria are complex and poorly understood, even in mammalian hosts where most research has focused in recent years. Much of this complexity is due to multiple stages of the parasite life cycle that alternate between the vertebrate host and the mosquito vector. In mammals, transmission occurs to a new host when an infected anopheline mosquito inoculates sporozoites into the bloodstream during a blood meal. These invade hepatocytes, undergo one generation of asexual reproduction, and release merozoites into the bloodstream, which invade circulating erythrocytes. Multiple cycles of asexual reproduction occur in the circulating blood cells, during which some merozoites are produced that invade erythrocytes and develop into gametocytes. These circulating gametocytes complete the vertebrate phase of the life cycle and are capable of infecting new mosquito hosts. The complex interactions that occur between developing parasites, host cells, and the host immune system in mammals results in production of antibodies, activation of a variety of different effector cells, production of lymphokines, and a cascade of events that control parasite numbers without completely eliminating the infection. Production of nonsterilizing immunity is characteristic of *Plasmodium* in its various vertebrate hosts, including birds, and has been termed concomitant immunity.

A number of key differences exist between the life cycles of avian and mammalian malarial parasites that may be important in how parasites interact with the immune system. The pre-erythrocytic stages of avian parasites (i.e., those that develop from sporozoites) invade and develop in blood forming cell types, such as hemocytoblasts, and cells of the lymphoid-macrophage system rather than hepatocytes (Huff 1969). These cell types include macrophages, stem cells, and endothelial cells that line blood capillaries. Avian parasites undergo several cycles of reproduction in these cell types before invading erythrocytes and, unlike most mammalian parasites that have a self-limiting cycle in the host liver, persist in cells of the lymphoid-macrophage system for the duration of the infection and most likely for the life of the host. These persistent tissue stages provide a source of parasites for relapsing erythrocytic infections and, more importantly, stimulate concomitant immunity in the host, providing protection from reinfection with homologous strains of the parasite.

We have initiated genetic studies of Hawaiian isolates of *P. relictum* to determine if multiple strains that differ in pathogenicity are present in Hawai'i and whether they are responsible for periodic epidemic outbreaks that occur in mid-elevation habitats (C. T. Atkinson, unpubl. data). We are also interested in developing reliable PCR-based methods for diagnostic purposes. To accomplish this, we are evaluating diversity of regions of several genes including the more conserved 18S ribosomal genes (Waters and McCutchan 1989, Feldman et al. 1995), and several variable genes encoding cell-surface proteins including thrombospondin-related analogous protein (TRAP), circumsporozoite protein (CSP), and merozoite surface antigen 2 (MSA-2). The genes encoding cell-surface proteins were initially characterized in *P. falciparum,* and we are currently developing PCR primers specific for the homologous gene regions in *P. relictum* (Felger et al. 1993, 1994; McCutchan et al. 1996, Templeton and Kaslow 1997). The 18S ribosomal genes have a low mutation rate of approximately 2% per 110 million years (Ochman and Wilson 1987, Wilson et al. 1987) and are especially useful for phylogenetic analyses (e.g., Escalante and Ayala 1994). Sporozoite and merozoite cell-surface proteins are all quite variable and are thought to be under positive Darwinian selection by the host immune system, i.e., amino acid variability is higher, especially within certain gene regions of the molecules, than would be expected under circumstances of neutrality (Hughes and Hughes 1995). Balanced host-parasite interactions may likely involve selective pressure by the parasite on molecules of the immune system (e.g., *Mhc* molecules) as well as selection on variable parasite molecules (e.g., TRAP, CSP, MSA-2) by the host's immune system. These highly variable parasite molecules are important in fundamental primary mechanisms of immune evasion, antigenic diversity and antigenic variation. Antigenic diversity refers to the expression of different alleles of a gene in different populations, whereas antigenic variation is the process by which a clonal parasite population can switch its antigenic phenotype (reviewed in Reeder and Brown 1996). In fact, polymorphic regions of the CSP have been shown to serve as T-cell epitopes (Good et al. 1988).

We are using a variety of molecular techniques to evaluate these genes or portions of these genes in *P. relictum* as a means of identifying variation sufficient to warrant strain divergence. We are also using these techniques to develop a PCR-based diagnostic test for *P. relictum* that will supplement both the PCR test described by Feldman et al. (1995) and serological tests for antibodies to the parasite that we are currently using (Atkinson et al. 2001).

We began analyses of the 18S ribosomal genes using highly conserved PCR primers specific for an approximately 580 base pairs (bp) segment of 18S ribosomal genes (Feldman et al. 1995, Shehata et al. *this volume*). We selected individuals that had been previously screened for the presence or absence of *Plasmodium* by blood smear and immunoblot methods (C. T. Atkinson, unpubl. data) to provide a basis for comparison. PCR-based techniques for studies of human *Plasmodium* spp. are generally used in combination with serological or other immunological methods due to the high percentage of false negatives (0.05) and false positives (0.16) in PCR-based diagnostic tests (reviewed in Weiss 1995). These ribosomal primers are also highly conserved. This means that they would likely anneal to ribosomal regions of DNA of any number of organisms under the appropriate conditions, as has been demonstrated in other species (Perkins and Martin 1999). In our hands we have found that these primers amplify multiple fragments from individuals which makes it difficult to distinguish the (theoretically) *Plasmodium*-specific 580 bp band from other similar-sized bands that may also be amplified from whole blood. Upon cloning and sequencing amplified DNA from 20 individuals, we have found that the length of this region varies, ranging from approximately 570 to 600 bp in length. From initial nucleic acid comparisons (MEGA and PC Gene), no distinct groupings were seen based on geographic origin of the samples.

The actual number of ribosomal genes in *P. relictum* is unknown but ranges from 4–10 rDNA units in other *Plasmodium* species (McCutchan 1986). For understanding more completely the diversity levels in this gene region, we are using an SSCP-based approach. The patterns produced by SSCP reveal the presence of as many as 10 bands, suggesting that *P.*

relictum, if haploid, contains multiple rDNA gene units with a minimum copy number of five. We have cloned and sequenced a nearly full length TRAP gene from *P. relictum* in order to obtain DNA sequence for designing strain-specific primers (S. I. Jarvi, unpubl. data); these are for use in diagnostic tests to supplement the currently available PCR test that is based on ribosomal genes (Feldman et al. 1995, Shehata et al. *this volume*), as well as for use in evaluating diversity at a variable and likely selected gene.

Because the bionomics of the mosquito vectors of avian malaria can affect evolution of the bird-parasite interactions, research on dispersal, host preferences, behavior, susceptibility, and genetics of *C. quinquefasciatus* is needed to help interpret findings from research being conducted on both honeycreepers and malarial parasites. It is beyond the scope of this paper to report in detail on projects in progress, but field and laboratory studies currently underway are using mitochondrial DNA and a number of microsatellite markers as well as other techniques for examining geographic diversity, patterns of introduction, dispersal rates, and vectorial capacity of *Culex* populations in Hawai'i (Fonseca et al. 1998; D. A. Fonseca, D. A. LaPointe, C. T. Atkinson, and R. C. Fleischer, unpubl. data).

CONCLUSIONS

Genetic studies that help to clarify the complex interactions between host and parasite can provide information critical for the survival and management of native forest birds. Immunogenetic studies of honeycreepers will provide natural resource managers new criteria for maintaining and increasing genetic diversity in fragmented populations of threatened or endangered species. Because of dynamic coevolutionary interactions among hosts, parasites, and vectors, the best overall strategy may be to aggressively use translocations and captive propagation to maximize heterozygosity to prevent loss of rare alleles, especially at loci important in immunological responsiveness to pathogens. At the same time, detailed information about genetic diversity in parasite populations can have important applications in monitoring epidemics and developing quarantine protocols for preventing introductions of new strains of the parasite. Recent data indicates that the dispersal and flight range of *Culex quinquefasciatus* in densely forested habitats may be much greater than initially anticipated, making it less likely that vector-control techniques based on elimination of breeding sites or application of environmentally compatible larvicides will be effective unless applied over large geographic areas (D. A. LaPointe, C. T. Atkinson, unpubl. data). Other approaches for breaking the disease cycle, such as chemotherapy or vaccine development, are even less feasible because of efficient immune-evasion strategies evolved by the parasite, technical difficulties associated with treating wild avian populations, and the increased risk of selecting for more virulent strains of the parasite. Until we know more about genetic diversity and its relationship to disease susceptibility in remaining threatened and endangered forest bird populations, protection of high-elevation habitats, prevention of new introductions of pathogens, and intensive management of adjacent mid-elevation forests to reduce oviposition sites for *Culex* mosquitoes may be the best short-term approach for preventing further extinctions.

ACKNOWLEDGMENTS

We thank J. Ballou, S. Bonner, D. LaPointe, J. Lease, C. McIntosh, J. Schultz, C. Tarr, and J. Wilcox for technical assistance and helpful discussions. The *Mhc* studies of honeycreepers were supported by a Smithson grant (to RCF), a Smithsonian Molecular Evolution Postdoctoral Fellowship (to SIJ), and a Smithsonian Institution Scholarly Studies grant to (RCF, SIJ, and J. Ballou). This work was also supported by the U.S. Geological Survey-Biological Resources Division, Pacific Island Ecosystems Research Center (parasite and pathogenicity studies).

Studies in Avian Biology No. 22:264–273, 2001.

CHANGES IN NATIVE AND INTRODUCED BIRD POPULATIONS ON O'AHU: INFECTIOUS DISEASES AND SPECIES REPLACEMENT

CHERIE SHEHATA, LEONARD FREED, AND REBECCA L. CANN

Abstract. Bird species with their blood parasites have been introduced to the Hawaiian Islands in the last 150 years and alien bird species now outnumber native species in most lowland habitats. We conducted a survey of malarial prevalence in birds at one low-elevation site in urban Honolulu over a three-year period. In screening 311 birds (15 taxa) with a sensitive and accurate DNA-based diagnostic, we discovered that the average prevalence of avian malaria was about 10%, but that significant differences in prevalence existed among species at this site. Not a single case of malarial infection was detected in the 43 native birds, primarily O'ahu 'Amakihi (*Hemignathus flavus*), that were tested by polymerase chain reaction (PCR). It is well established that 'Amakihi (e.g., *Hemignathus virens*) on other islands are suitable hosts for *Plasmodium* strains present in Hawai'i, and that they survive at lower rates than introduced species when given malaria experimentally. Five introduced species have prevalence rates in excess of 20% and appear to be some of the primary reservoirs for maintenance of the disease among passerines on O'ahu. Five other introduced species showed no evidence of active malarial infections. Recaptures allowed us to discover that some alien species effectively cleared their parasites in 3 to 8 months after initially testing positive for *Plasmodium.* The survival of relict populations of native birds on O'ahu suggests that genetic resistance and/or tolerance factors to avian malaria are evolving; this is consistent with observations that 'Amakihi on other islands vary in their survival when experimentally challenged with malarial pathogens. In habitats where prevalence of malaria may be seasonal and at low levels, testing for avian malaria using blood smears is likely to underestimate the true impact of the disease. Successful management of honeycreeper relatives may now depend on identifying the genetic loci responsible for disease resistance, using the 'Amakihi model.

Key Words: Birds; disease; endangered species; Hawai'i; malaria.

The introductions of more than 125 alien bird species to the Hawaiian Islands since 1865 (Pimm 1991) and an appropriate mosquito vector in the early 1800s (van Riper et al. 1986) have had devastating consequences for native Hawaiian birds. As a group, native Hawaiian birds are now at about half the level of species diversity that existed 200 years ago, and half of these species are currently endangered (Freed et al. 1987a, Stone and Stone 1989). The extinction process of native species has accelerated with the rediscovery of the Hawaiian Islands by western explorers, such that the pattern of historical decline has been called bimodal (Ralph and van Riper 1985). This historical pattern parallels the near extinction of Native Hawaiian peoples to infectious diseases after the rediscovery of Hawai'i in 1778 (Stannard 1989), where models for virgin soil epidemics consider evolution in geographic isolation and modes of transmission to be important features for predicting changes in pathogen virulence (Ewald 1994).

The Hawaiian Islands have more alien bird species than any other place on earth, and most of these species have been introduced since 1893 (Pratt 1994). The islands were once geographically remote, extremely isolated habitats, even for birds (Olson and James 1982a). That status changed with the arrival of Polynesian and European explorers, who brought with them a host of predators, pathogens, and avian competitors (van Riper et al. 1986). The association of the current decline in native bird populations with the continued introduction of alien species is attributable to at least two hypotheses: (1) direct competition between natives and aliens for food, nesting, or other resources (Moulton and Pimm 1983); and (2) greater susceptibility (morbidity, mortality) of natives to infectious diseases and novel strains of pathogens that arrive with each introduction (Warner 1968, van Riper et al. 1986, Atkinson et al. 1995, Cann et al. 1996).

There is little direct evidence to support the first hypothesis because habitats with ecological variables that appear suitable for native birds are sometimes completely devoid of them (Scott et al. 1986, Freed and Cann 1989). Steep distributional gradients now mark the ranges of many endangered species on the high-elevation islands as if there were some invisible but deadly force restricting species recovery though their habitats are now protected.

The continued decline during the last 30 years of native birds in low-elevation forests on the island of O'ahu (Williams 1987, Pratt 1994) also is especially problematic. These are the habitats of native species most accessible to educators and their students, naturalists, ecotourists, and policy makers. Yet these forests have few native birds. Remnant populations of less than 1,000 individuals spread over 32 km may not represent truly viable groups. One thinks immediately of the case of the O'ahu 'Elepaio (*Chasiempis sandwichensis ibidis*), a territorial species with disjunct populations isolated on two separate mountain ranges (VanderWerf et al. 1997).

Declines in the absence of habitat degradation or obvious competitors and predators are consistent with the disease hypothesis. All Hawaiian forests have alien bird species, and the distribution of native birds is generally limited to elevations where the introduced *Culex* mosquito is rare (van Riper et al. 1986). Alien birds are linked to habitat loss, predation, competition, and introduced diseases, all of the major factors thought to account for the wave of extinctions between 1893 and 1910 (Ralph and van Riper 1985). It is also possible that the alien birds introduced since 1910 pose an even greater disease threat to native birds than previously thought. Newly introduced organisms can bring with them novel pathogens and may also acquire the parasite faunas of resident species, altering disease transmission patterns. Alien vertebrates can even reduce their parasite load upon translocation to new habitats (Lewin and Holmes 1971), especially if intermediate hosts are lacking in the new environment or dietary changes accompany the shift in range.

In the midst of all these difficulties, isolated pockets of native birds exist in low-elevation forest habitats on at least two Hawaiian Islands, where mosquitoes are present year-round in high densities and researchers suspect there are very high rates of *Plasmodium* infection (Scott et al. 1986). We have identified such a population of honeycreepers in the O'ahu 'Amakihi (*Hemignathus flavus*) at Lyon Arboretum, a protected, second-growth forest habitat that is affiliated with the University of Hawai'i on the island of O'ahu. We have a special interest in this study site, because it is also the focus of native plant restoration attempts and, as such, is an important resource in the battle to conserve tropical biodiversity (Turner and Corlett 1996).

Only two species of native honeycreepers, the O'ahu 'Amakihi and the 'Apapane (*Himatione sanguinea*), are present at Lyon Arboretum. The 'Amakihi is a year-round resident, while the much rarer 'Apapane is usually found only when floral resources are abundant in the arboretum and low to absent elsewhere. In contrast, at least 30 alien species of birds are normally sighted at the location, some of them escaped exotics from an adjacent tropical garden. These alien species

are known to host a variety of parasites (van Riper and van Riper 1985).

Birds living in the arboretum, which has been reforested with a mixture of exotic tree species since the 1920s, are also potentially coexisting with a variety of disease vectors. Any native bird surviving in this habitat has experienced more than 70 generations of breeding in association with multiple vectors, parasites, and reservoirs. Native birds in this habitat are therefore prime candidates for evolving genotypes tolerant or resistant to malaria. The exotic bird species included in this study and the estimated date of their introduction to Hawai'i are shown in Table 1.

We previously devised a PCR-based test that was capable of detecting malarial infection in many species of passerine birds. The test used a 50 µl blood sample taken during the mist-netting and banding of birds (Feldman et al. 1995). Data from this test documented the presence of malaria in high-elevation zones previously thought to be safe habitats for native birds, but the assumption of safety was based on only limited knowledge of the dynamics of the disease in low-elevation habitats containing large numbers of introduced birds and mosquitoes (Cann et al. 1996). An extensive survey of malarial prevalence at the Lyon Arboretum site was therefore initiated to more accurately estimate the true importance of this disease for bird populations living in relict, lowland Hawaiian forests and to help address the continued decline of native birds on O'ahu.

METHODS

Birds were caught in pole-based and aerial mist nets using standard ornithological methods and following all animal safety regulations. Blood samples were taken from birds by puncturing the wing vein with a sterile 26-gauge needle. A total of 311 individual birds were bled and examined visually for signs of ectoparasites and poxlike lesions. Each bird was tagged with a unique color band and/or a standard aluminum identification band and was measured, photographed, and released.

Approximately 50 µl of blood was withdrawn as per Feldman et al. (1995), and total genomic DNA was prepared using the low-volume modification method of Quinn and White (1987b). Amplification of a fragment of the 18s rRNA gene from either the disease agent or the bird was performed and scored as in Feldman et al. (1995). All birds were tested in at least two separate amplification reactions, with appropriate extraction and with positive and negative controls. Only unambiguous birds were scored in this test, with the 18s rRNA gene fragment of the host bird's cell serving as an internal control for successful amplification.

Infectious state (positive or negative) was analyzed using a logistic regression with status (native or introduced) as a class variable and species within status as a nested variable. Chi-square tests were derived from

TABLE 1. MALARIA FOUND IN BIRDS SAMPLED AT LYON ARBORETUM, HONOLULU, HAWAI'I, FROM 1994 TO 1996

Species	Place of origin	Time introduced	Number Positive	Total	Percentage
Native Honeycreepers					
O'ahu 'Amakihi			0	42	0
'Apapane			0	1	0
Total			0	43	0
Introduced species					
Common Myna	India	1879	0	2	0
Common Waxbill	Africa	early 1900s	1	36	2.8
House Finch	North America	1800s	0	3	0
Java Sparrow	South-east Asia	before 1965	0	10	0
Japanese White-eye	East Asia	1929	4	87	4.6
Northern Cardinal	North America	1929	0	6	0
Nutmeg Mannikin	India	1865	6	27	22.2
Red-billed Leiothrix	South Asia	1918	1	19	5.2
Red-vented Bulbul	India	1965	1	2	50
Red-whiskered Bulbul	India	1966	11	40	27.5
Spotted Dove	South-east Asia	1800s	1	5	20
White-rumped Shama	South-east Asia	1940	6	26	23.1
Zebra Dove	Australia	1922	0	5	0
Total			31	268	11.6
Sample Total			31	311	10

the generalized linear model functions of S-Plus (Venables and Ripley 1994).

RESULTS

Native birds had significantly lower prevalence of malarial infection than did introduced birds (P = 0.002; Table 1). In fact, none of the native birds tested positive despite being sampled at the same time and place during which introduced birds tested positive. The species screened and numbers of malaria positive individuals identified during the three-year period (1994–1996) are listed in Table 1. Eight of the 15 species tested were found to be infected with the pathogen.

There were also significant differences in prevalence rates (P = 0.002) among the species of introduced birds (Table 1). The highest rates of malaria (>20%) were found in White-rumped Shama (*Copsychus malabaricus*), Red-whiskered Bulbul (*Pycnonotus jocosus*), Red-vented Bulbul (*Pycnonotus cafer*), Nutmeg Mannikin (*Lonchura punctulata*), and Spotted Dove (*Streptopelia chinensis*). Five species of introduced birds that were free of malaria at the time of testing were Common Myna (*Acridotheres tristis*), House Finch (*Carpodacus mexicanus*), Java Sparrow (*Padda oryzivora*), Northern Cardinal (*Cardinalis cardinalis*), and Zebra Dove (*Geopelia striata*). Low, but non-zero, rates of infection were observed in Common Waxbill (*Estrilda astrild*), Japanese White-eye (*Zosterops japonicus*), and Red-billed Leiothrix (*Leiothrix lutea*). Malaria affected 12% of the birds that were screened in 1994, 9% in 1995,

and less than 9% in 1996 (Fig. 1). Overall prevalence of malaria at the study site for the three-year period was 10%.

DISCUSSION

WHAT ABOUT THE SICK BIRDS THAT CAN'T FLY?

It is possible that we failed to find native and alien birds on O'ahu infected with malaria because sick birds do not normally fly into mist nets. We never encountered dead or moribund birds in the forest during our hours of mist-netting, but the overall probability of such discovery is low. A single 'Apapane has been discovered near death by arboretum staff at this site in the last six years of our working there. We simply cannot say that our sample of mist-netted individuals represents an adequate survey of all birds present in the habitat. Perhaps all native birds contract malaria, and the only ones well enough to fly are those with immune systems capable of clearing the parasites to tolerable levels that are below our ability to detect them with current techniques.

We can, however, evaluate the likelihood that our total sample was insufficient to discover infected birds across the board by reference to standard epidemiological modeling. A sample size of 246 individuals is sufficient to estimate within 5 percentage points the true value of disease incidence, with 95% confidence, if the value of the true rate is unlikely to exceed 20% (Lwanga and Lemeshow 1991:25). Our sample of 311 birds therefore appears to have been sufficiently large to have uncovered infected birds,

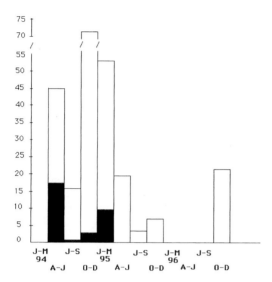

Prevalence in 8 introduced species showing

some positive individuals over 1994-1996

FIGURE 1. Capture history of diseased birds over the 1994–1996 study interval. Data for the eight species showing malaria are grouped in 3-month intervals, with total number of birds captured in any interval shown on the y axis and the number of diseased birds in that sample indicated by shading. J–M = January, February, and March; A–J = April, May, and June; J–S = July, August, and September, and O–D = October, November, and December. The number under the first quarter indicates the year of the sample for the following intervals. O'ahu 'Amakihi were captured in each.

if they truly existed, over the study period. If there is a general prevalence of malarial infection of 10%, and 14% of the total sample were native birds, it is somewhat unusual that not a single native bird was scored positive, given our knowledge of their susceptibility to this pathogen when experimentally challenged.

Additionally, the possibility that native birds were differentially affected at the nestling and fledgling stages, where their decreased mobility or immature immune systems might render them even more susceptible to parasitic infection (Ricklefs 1992), can be addressed. Of the 42 'Amakihi sampled, 4 were hatch-year birds, 6 were second-year birds, and 32 were after hatch-year birds. We therefore expect that some fraction of the 10 youngest 'Amakihi in this sample might still have circulating evidence of a past malarial infection, because other studies have tested how long after a deliberate inoculation with *Plasmodium* that a PCR signal can detected. C. Atkinson and C. van Riper (pers. comm) have followed experimentally challenged birds

and estimate that the PCR detectable sequence is present for a year post-infection.

Challenge experiments with adult native 'Amakihi after a single bite from an infected mosquito show that an acute stage of parasitemia develops within 10 days, killing approximately 60% of the birds within 3 weeks of infection (Atkinson et al. 2000, Jarvi et al. *this volume*). Birds surviving this challenge show PCR-positive results for up to a year after infection, though some of these experimentally infected Amakihi are PCR negative (C. Atkinson, pers. comm.). Thus, it is likely that if 'Amakihi on O'ahu are easily infected, our sample of juvenile and young individuals should have contained a few birds still harboring enough parasites to render them PCR positive. All 42 'Amakihi that were tested appeared free of infection, consistent with their local evolution of genetic characteristics rendering them tolerant or resistant to malaria. Affected individuals of eight alien species were present in the same habitat (Fig. 1) during the same time that 'Amakihi were tested, showing that the vector is prevalent, and the 'Amakiki are known to be year-round residents of the area.

THE RELEVANCE OF THE 'AMAKIHI MODEL

We infer that the O'ahu 'Amakihi population sampled in this study has evolved some mechanism(s) of genetic resistance that now allows it to survive in lowland forests where malaria is prevalent. This hypothesis is consistent with the observation that 'Amakihi populations from the island of Hawai'i contain individuals capable of surviving experimental challenge with malaria (van Riper et al. 1986, Atkinson et al. 2000). The 'Amakihi populations of O'ahu may be similar to the case reported for the New Zealand Bellbird (*Anthornis melanura*), where recovery is apparently unrelated to a decline in predators or a decline in habitat destruction (Steadman et al. 1990). If the adaptive radiation of Hawaiian honeycreepers truly began less than 10 million years ago (Johnson et al. 1989, Tarr and Fleischer 1995), the 'Amakihi population sampled here represents the Rosetta Stone for potentially manipulating the genomes of many endangered honeycreepers, with whom they share most of their evolutionary history.

'Amakihi are small nectivores/insectivores that exhibit some aspects of territorial behavior during breeding. Their nesting and foraging behaviors are well documented (van Riper 1987), and they have become important surrogates for research into captive propagation of endangered Hawaiian honeycreepers (Kuehler et al. 1996). 'Amakihi are generalists that exist in large numbers on the islands of Kaua'i, Maui, and Hawai'i, and are considered one of the most adaptable of the remaining honeycreeper species (Scott et al. 1986). Populations on the older islands of O'ahu and Kaua'i are accorded separate species designations, whereas Maui and Hawai'i populations are considered separate subspecies (Pratt et al. 1987).

We investigated the genealogical relationships between 'Amakihi using mitochondrial DNA (mtDNA) sequences from the cytochome *b* gene to explore whether there were deep phylogenetic subdivisions that might restrict the utility of classic genetic mapping for disease loci in this genus. Sequences were amplified from total genomic DNA using conserved primer sequences as in Kocher et al. (1989), and we used additional sequences as in Feldman (1994). Based on an alignment of approximately 220 nucleotides of cyt *b* for 68 birds, we confirmed that O'ahu lineages form a separate island group of maternal genealogies in the genus, and we have identified at least five separate maternal lineage groups that currently exist in 'Amakihi using distance, parsimony, and likelihood clustering methods (Cann and Douglas 1999). We estimated from this study that the coalescence of the mitochondrial genome for the O'ahu sample was approximately 300,000 years ago, based on an assumption of a crude rate of substitution at 2% per million years for the cyt *b* gene as a whole (Irwin et al. 1991).

All O'ahu birds tested negative for *Plasmodium,* so presumably the mutations conferring tolerance or resistance arose in a common ancestral lineage, but this might be shared with the Kaua'i population. Maui and Hawai'i 'Amakihi lineages belong to a different set of maternal genetic lineages; therefore, we suspect that the ability to tolerate or resist malarial pathogens has arisen independently in these birds since the introduction of the mosquito as an appropriate vector.

THE DYNAMICS OF DISEASE TRANSMISSION

In Hawai'i, the disease relationships between native and introduced bird species are by no means clear. Native birds are known to show a higher degree of susceptibility to malaria when exposed experimentally, and they have more severe infections than introduced species (Warner 1968, van Riper et al. 1986, Atkinson 1995). This pattern fits the virgin soil model, where initial exposure can result in the loss of up to 95% of the host population in as few as two generations. Stochastic factors (Lande 1988) might then finish off the remaining population, as fragmented groups suffer from highly skewed sex ratios and loss of behaviorally experienced individuals. Twenty years of monitoring infectious

disease in Hawaiian birds has convinced most conservationists that malaria is a major factor limiting the recovery of native forest bird populations below 1,800 m (van Riper et al. 1986).

Researchers now generally considered that only a single species, *Plasmodium relictum capistranoae,* is currently infecting bird populations (Laird and van Riper 1981), and that a single species of *Culex* mosquito is primarily responsible for the transmission of this pathogen. Unfortunately, *Culex quinquefasciatus,* is abundant year-round on O'ahu in habitats below 1,600 m. The mosquito is also capable of transmitting avian poxvirus, a disease that can cause blindness by secondary bacterial infections and can inhibit the ability of perching birds to forage efficiently due to the loss of digits (see also VanderWerf *this volume*). As predicted by the disease model, the distribution of native birds on most islands is inversely related to the density of mosquitoes (Scott et al. 1986).

Various authors commenting on avian extinctions have speculated about a potential role introduced bird community may play in serving as a disease reservoir (van Riper et al. 1986, Steadman et al. 1990, Pimm 1991, Feldman et al. 1995), especially given the continued decline of native birds on O'ahu following analysis of the Audubon Society's Christmas Bird Count (Williams 1987). At least 22 new species of birds were recorded on O'ahu during the 1960s (Moulton and Pimm 1983), and at least some of these introductions resulted in the establishment of new breeding populations.

The Red-whiskered Bulbul, introduced to O'ahu in 1966, shows a prevalence of 27.5% malarial infection over the period of this study, consistent with its potential to act as a potent source of pathogens in the resident bird community. Of the species with prevalence rates in excess of 20%, however, Nutmeg Mannikins (22.2%) and Spotted Doves (20%) represent older introductions to Hawai'i from India and Southeast Asia in the 1800s, and five introduced species (including some recently introduced taxa) were completely free of infection. New studies should now focus on strain identification of the pathogens and their associations with particular species, in order to address the question of recently introduced species and more virulent pathogen genotypes.

The hypothesis of alien species-as-disease reservoir was also deemed less likely by the discovery that native birds on the island of Hawai'i are commonly infected with malaria in low-elevation forests (Atkinson et al. 1995). This finding showed that the native populations are capable of maintaining their own disease reservoir and has led some researchers to discount the impact introduced species have had on the continuing disappearance of native forest birds. Our results documenting a higher level of malaria in alien birds on Oʻahu suggest that the ecology of disease transmission may be different on the two islands, perhaps because the communities of native and introduced species differ in their exact makeup (Pratt et al. 1987).

INFECTION VERSUS DISEASE AND MECHANISMS OF DISEASE RESISTANCE

Genetic loci implicated in resistance to malaria are often members of the major histocompatibility complex (*Mhc*), a supergene family containing sequences important in presenting fragments of degraded molecules to cells of the immune system (see, e.g., Jarvi et al. *this volume*). The family also contains complement, collagen, proteasome-like, transporter, cytokine, and heat shock genes (Klein 1986, Trowsdale et al. 1991, Hughes and Nei 1992, Klein and OʻhUigin 1994). The bird model for the *Mhc*, the domestic chicken, has duplicated the *Mhc* regions (B@ and RFP-Y@) on two ends of microchromosome 16 (Fillon et al. 1996). So far, no association has been made between particular *Mhc* loci and resistance to malaria in birds (Stevens 1996).

Resistance to or tolerance of malaria, however, cannot be understood simply from the perspective of the *Mhc*. Owing to the fact that malarial infections involve a parasite that cycles between sexual and asexual life phases, uses several hosts, and undergoes rapid change in surface antigens presented to the host, it is possible to control its proliferation at many points. Natural resistance to malaria in humans has also been linked to Duffy blood group antigens, glucose 6-phosphate dehydrogenase variants, sickle-cell hemoglobins, alpha and beta thalassemias, and various transport proteins, as well as the *Mhc* class 1 and 2 genes (Weiss 1993).

Much of the epidemiological evidence associating a particular *Mhc* haplotype or variant with disease resistance to malaria is actually indirect (Mascie-Taylor 1993), and of a questionable experimental nature owing to systematic underestimates of the prevalence of malaria in well-studied populations (Bottius et al. 1996). In mice, natural immunity to malaria appears to be linked to a non-*Mhc* major gene (Malo and Skamene 1994) with contributions from other loci. Thus, resistance to malaria should be treated as a quantitative genetic trait, and it may be misleading to search only among the ʻAmakihis *Mhc* for variants conferring natural immunity to *Plasmodium* parasites.

Birds that can tolerate a certain number or strain of parasites, because of genetic factors, may be capable of harboring a *Plasmodium* infection but never show clinical symptoms of malaria. We are therefore incapable of stating at this time that birds scored as infected using the PCR test have now or have had in the past full-blown malaria. Atkinson's followup of our PCR negative samples by serological tests indeed identified an Oʻahu ʻAmakihi with immunological evidence of past infection (C. Atkinson, pers. comm.). Studies like the one performed by Hulier et al. (1996), which follow the development of parasites in infected organs of the host animal, will be necessary to differentiate between these two states. Animals that survive infection, however, might serve to illustrate the first stage of adaptation and be used as models for illustrating different levels of genetic resistance.

Dobson and May (1986) have shown that the major factor in the time it takes for a native host population to evolve a significant degree of genetic resistance to an introduced pathogen is the cohort generation time of the host species, and that initial frequency of the resistance gene, gene dominance, or strength of selection for resistance (and therefore fitness of both heterozygotes and homozygotes) affect resistance time only in a logarithmic fashion. Resistance typically arises in 5 to 50 generations. ʻAmakihi are capable of breeding within six months of hatching (van Riper 1987), so it appears that an appropriate length of time has elapsed for natural selection to have resulted in the evolution of resistant genotypes to certain infectious diseases in Hawaiʻi, assuming native birds are breeding *at minimum* on an annual cycle. Epizootic malarial transmission in Hawaiʻi probably began sometime between the 1826 introduction of a suitable vector (Warner 1968) and the decade beginning 1870 when Skylarks (*Alauda arvensis*), Spotted Doves, Common Mynas, and House Sparrows (*Passer domesticus*) appeared on Oʻahu. Thus, a minimum of 170–125 generations has elapsed for natural selection to result in the evolution of resistant genotypes.

Our finding that at least three species of introduced birds were capable of clearing malarial infections in 3–8 months, based on recapture data, is also consistent with the hypothesis that introduced birds coevolved in their native ranges with the *Plasmodium* pathogens for a longer period of time, and that they now contain greater numbers of individuals in their populations with malarial-tolerant genotypes. Immunity to malaria is generally strain specific, may be stage specific as well, and can also entail a number of cellular mechanisms that help limit the life cycle of the pathogen (Wakelin 1996). A host may have the ability to restrict or modify the movement of *Plasmodium* parasites during invasion of cells, or can prime the synthesis of additional cytokines, helper T cells, or other mediators. In addition, the host may be able to prevent binding of the parasite to vessel endothelia, or to neutralize the toxins produced when schizonts rupture host cells. A host may also have the ability to control the reproductive stage of the parasite.

Any genetic mutation in the host genotype affecting the growth of one strain or species of *Plasmodium* during infection does not necessarily confer immunity to another strain. Resistance/susceptibility may be due to primarily *Mhc*-T cell interactions for one strain and B cell factors for another. Molecular studies can eventually map all the loci contributing to resistance in each species of bird, but these features underscore the need to search beyond *Mhc* loci for genetic resistance/susceptibility to malaria.

IMPLICATIONS FOR MANAGEMENT AND RECOVERY

van Riper and van Riper (1985) drew attention to the continuing threat of disease to bird populations of Hawai'i, and the role that management must play in monitoring and vector control. Nothing has changed since that report cataloged the known avian disease pathogens of Hawai'i and their hosts. Captive and domesticated birds continue to be imported, as well as captive-bred native species, like the Hawaiian Goose (*Branta sandvicensis*), or Nēnē. Stepped-up efforts at captive rearing of the goose and the Hawaiian Crow (*Corvus hawaiiensis*), or 'Alalā, have resulted in more stringent quarantine protocols at rearing facilities, but game birds, natives, and exotics from around the world continue to mix in our forests and in mosquito-laden zoo environments. It appears that arboviruses, Newcastle disease, and avian influenza have still not made it to Hawai'i, and extreme care is necessary to maintain this condition, especially now that animal quarantine regulations have been relaxed. If anything, the threats and problems caused by infection and disease (Scott et al. 1988) have increased in magnitude, with the rediscovery of tiny populations of some endangered species.

Prior to our analysis, the only comprehensive study of disease pathogens in the introduced bird populations on O'ahu examined 121 individuals from 21 species (Smith and Guest 1974). That study documented protozoan infections (*Coccidia* and *Trichomonas*) in 20 birds and found evidence of helminths infecting 40, but it did not identify malaria as a significant component of the parasite load in these species. The site of study in this instance was the western slope of Diamond Head, a significantly drier habitat than the arboretum in the Manoa Valley where we

worked. It is possible the malaria was not a significant disease at that time, but it is more probable that limited resources did not allow a full exploration of potential disease pathogens, and that the level of parasitemia may have been too low for detection by classical blood-smear methods.

The full impact of malaria on bird populations can only be evaluated with an efficient diagnostic that can detect very low levels of the parasite. The reported absence of protozoan parasites in the Cook Islands (Steadman et al. 1990), attributed to a very low level of prevalence in native and colonizing species, may actually be due to inadequate methods of detection using diagnosis by blood smears. We suggest that no population be considered *Plasmodium*-free unless PCR-based diagnostics are employed. If disease prevalence is not measured accurately, continued discussion about characteristics of successful invasions (e.g., Pimm 1991) in Hawai'i and elsewhere is likely to omit crucial pieces of data. Most ecologists sample their systems in coastal forests below 610 m in elevation. In Hawai'i, such low-elevation sites are highly degraded and are usually characterized by a mixture of predominantly introduced species. Our suggestion that the disease hypothesis more fully accounts for the continued decline of native birds, rather than the effects of competition between introduced and native species, is based on our findings that malarial infections have been systematically underreported in all species tested prior to PCR-based assays. (A more complete discussion of these issues can be found in the appendix to this paper). What remains to be examined is the direct role of malaria in limiting survival and recruitment, using populations of banded birds and continual monitoring over several annual cycles of reproduction.

Captive rearing efforts using Hawai'i 'Amakihi (*H. virens*) as a surrogate species for studies of rearing, release, and restoration of endangered birds have been unsuccessful to date, because all birds reared succumbed to massive *Plasmodium* infections after their release (Kuehler et al. 1996). Eggs were taken from nests for hand-rearing from an area where the population was known to be highly susceptible to malaria (van Riper et al. 1986). If eggs are chosen with more attention to disease characteristics, it is likely that post-hacking survival will increase.

One can anticipate pressure to exhibit captive-reared native honeycreepers to the public, in order to justify the extraordinary expenditure of resources aimed at preserving a few endangered species. However, this action needs to be weighed against the relative risks of introducing novel pathogens to the remaining native bird community, which is the predicted result of aviculture of many species in a common rearing environment. New molecular methods to designate birds disease-free should be supported by specialists in captive rearing and employed to screen potential candidates for either exhibition in nonmosquito proof cages or release into the wild.

Translocation studies of native birds into and between forests within the mosquito zone should consider the probability of enhanced long-term survival by the judicious choice of individual birds, especially if variation in natural immunity to mosquito-borne diseases exists among target species. If important factors (sex, age, appropriate genetic markers, vocal patterns, nest-building behaviors, plumage variation) are otherwise balanced, it seems wise to begin these translocations with birds that have a better possibility of tolerating malaria. Reuse of nest sites can also increase the probability of disease transmission (Loye and Carroll 1995), so some obligate cavity nesters may be more vulnerable to these dangers upon translocation.

Emergence of more virulent pathogens is one potential outcome of enhancing the frequency of resistant hosts by both natural and artificial selection (Ewald 1994). Management decisions that result in incomplete removal of parasites, through baited pharmaceuticals, may fail due to the inability to control drug dosages in natural populations of free-flying birds and will likely be counterproductive. We therefore cannot advocate treating malarial infections in endangered bird populations by offering them food items laced with antimalarials. Until effective vaccination is possible, vector control efforts offer the only sure route of breaking epidemic disease cycles.

Removal of certain alien bird species known to harbor malaria in critical habitats of highly endangered birds is a last resort. Such management action is likely to be a stopgap at best, but for alien species known to have sedentary or territorial behaviors placing them in direct competition with resident natives it may work as a short-term strategy, especially if vector numbers are low or fluctuate seasonally. To be effective, this action would depend on baseline knowledge of seasonal disease prevalence in the bird populations, some degree of geographic isolation between habitats, and effective year-round monitoring for infection.

CONCLUSIONS

This study documents a new, hopeful outlook on malaria as a factor limiting the recovery of native Hawaiian bird populations in urban, lowland habitats. Native birds coexisting with malarial pathogens represent individuals with genotypes that have effectively solved one infectious disease problem. Molecular markers offer us the opportunity to identify the genetic loci responsible for natural immunity, and to boost the numbers of individuals carrying these loci in natural populations. O'ahu 'Amakihi populations should be examined for DNA markers of disease resistance and used as the sires and dams in captive-rearing experiments. Long-term maintenance of genes for disease resistance or tolerance may require a metapopulation to be operating that geographically structures resistance genes and allows cycles of local population extinction with recolonization (Thompson 1996). This can be enhanced by judicious translocation and captive rearing.

ACKNOWLEDGMENTS

This study was funded by a grant from the John D. and Catherine T. MacArthur Foundation, World Environment and Resources Program. Support for this research was also provided by a grant from the Howard Hughes Medical Institute (HHMI) through the Undergraduate Biological Sciences Education Program. C. Shehata was an HHMI Undergraduate Research Fellow at the time of this study. We thank C. Atkinson, G. Massey, C. van Riper, III, B. Nakamura, L. Goff, D. La Pointe, M. Burt, J. Rohrer, E. VanderWerf, D. Haderman, M. Ono, K. Fernandez, D. Tupper, L. Douglas, and J. Maag for their samples, help, and discussion. An anonymous reviewer greatly improved this paper.

APPENDIX.

EFFECTIVENESS OF THIS SCREEN FOR DETECTION OF INFECTED BIRDS

A. Is the PCR test reliable?

Colleagues have asked us to address the question of reliability for the diagnostic employed here, compared to traditional smear-based methods involving light microscopy that they are more familiar with. They fear we have an unknown rate of false positives, as well as false negatives, associated with our PCR-based test, and that the high rate of infection seen for some alien species is an experimental PCR artifact. We can report on our own experience with this type of comparison, as well as relay data that exist in the literature for screening of subpatent malarial infections in humans, lizards, and rodents. There is general agreement among specialists in the field that PCR-based tests are preferred to smear diagnostics when parasitemia levels are low, when mixed infections are present, and when new dipstick-style tests are to be evaluated (Humar et al. 1997).

Information was already presented by Feldman et al. (1995) showing that, in two blind samples of Hawaiian birds, the PCR test using appropriate 18s rRNA primers correctly identified all birds judged infected by smear diagnostics. What we did not report in that publication was the finding that the PCR positive birds we identified, but which were not found initially by smear tests to contain *Plasmodium* infected cells, were later reexamined with additional effort and found to be indeed infected (C. Atkinson, pers. comm.). We felt this was evidence that the assay was indeed more sensitive than we could measure adequately at the time, because DNA extracted from avian blood contains primarily the host DNA from nucleated erythrocytes, which could have reduced the efficiency of PCR amplification to target the parasite gene.

This comparison allows us to have greater confidence in the assertion that low-levels of infection sufficient to give a positive PCR result are often missed on blood smears for reasons that can range from time and effort of the slide reader to the physiological sequestering of parasites during certain stages of infection. It is estimated that roughly 200 times more blood cells are assayed in the PCR test than would be counted in microscopic fields (Snounou et al. 1993), and a study specifically designed to examine subpatent infections in humans estimates that in total sensitivity, PCR is 100 to 1,000 times more sensitive than microscopy (Bottius et al. 1996). A comparison of PCR with nested primers versus smear efficiency in western fence lizards (*Scleroperous occidentalis*) infected with the parasite *Plasmodium mesicanum* found that the more sensitive nested PCR easily detected very low-level infections, those scored as <1 parasite per 10,000 erythrocytes (Perkins et al. 1998), and this is also the conclusion of a second comparison (Khoo et al. 1996) with *Plasmodium falciparum* in humans.

Following the publication of an early PCR-based test using ribosomal primers for human *falciparum* malaria (Barker et al. 1992) different from the ones employed here and based on different cycling parameters, it was suggested that false positive rates of 16% and false negative rates of 5% were associated with the PCR method (Weiss 1995). False positives result from nonspecific priming of ribosomal gene families and their pseudogenes, and this can be controlled by better choice of primer sequences as well as nested primers in a two-step test. False positives can also be the result of sample contamination, which can be managed by good laboratory practices and is easily detected with appropriate positive and negative controls. False negatives are based on the failure of signal to amplify, either because some reagent is faulty, cycling parameters are not optimum, or due to stochastic effects with low parasite target numbers during early amplification stages. All these problems can be addressed by appropriate controls and multiple PCR runs on the same samples.

On the surface, a rate of 16% for false positives appears alarmingly high. However, this must be compared to an even higher but as yet largely uncalibrated rate of false negatives associated with classical smear tests. For human malarial diagnostics where correct drug treatment places high demands on testing accuracy, values in the literature range from 9% to 67%, reflecting a variety of field and laboratory conditions encountered by biologists (Kain et al. 1993, Ntoumi et al. 1995, Bottius et al. 1996, Khoo et al. 1996).

Snounou et al. (1993) demonstrated that correctly performed PCR can achieve an absolute, i.e. all or none detection accuracy, when titrated against controls (infected, cultured cells). Additionally, one quantitative study of malaria parasite development in mice has suggested that PCR methods previously criticized as inaccurate correctly predict infections when as few as 500 injected sporozoites are followed by a variety of quantitative biochemical measures, with implications for vaccine development (Hulier et al. 1996). In the lizard study cited previously (Perkins et al. 1998), it was found that false negatives (those samples scored as not infected after the blood smear, but found infected via PCR) were approximately 5%, but that a greater proportion of infections was detected only by PCR at a site deliberately chosen to study low prevalence transmission dynamics, where malarial infections were averaging about 6% of the total population (50% versus 9%). This was also the conclusion of the study of transmission dynamics with human malaria in Malaysia (Khoo et al. 1996). Under conditions where 50% of the infections in a population are characterized by low parasite counts, rare transmission appears to select parasite genotypes that sustain low parasitemia, as predicted by Ewald (1994). Decreasing parasite loads also result in a generally more complex genotypic array of parasites sequestered in the hosts body (Ntoumi et al. 1995). Given this information, it is clear that PCR technology brings many advantages, increasing our understanding of malarial epizootics in Hawaiian birds.

We should sensibly adopt the general position that sensitivity of both PCR and smear methods to correctly detect infection decreases as the number of parasites decreases. Evaluation of various diagnostic techniques under low levels of infection now posits that microscopy has an 83–86% sensitivity rate compared to PCR (Humar et al. 1997, Pieroni et al. 1998). Even with high sensitivity, birds with *Plasmodium* may be infected but may not suffer from malaria, emphasizing the importance of long-term studies on banded populations of birds where recaptures can be evaluated for disease status. As a rule, all birds should be screened at least twice by a PCR-based test in order to be considered free of *Plasmodium*. In addition, immunological tests that assay for the presence of past infection through western blot technology (Sambrook et al. 1989) have revealed that at least one of our 'Amakihi samples that was scored as negative by PCR showed evidence of antibodies to erythrocytic stages of *P. relictum* (C. Atkinson, pers. comm.). This clearly reveals that a PCR negative bird may have a negligible parasite status at the moment, but it may be impossible to say that a bird was never truly infected by a parasite, only that it is capable of mounting an immune response that limits infection.

B. Under what conditions might extra (>2) amplification products be produced?

Aside from known problems associated with failure to optimize PCR reactions involving low annealing temperatures, unbalanced deoxynucleotide ratios, extra cycling steps forcing carryover products, contamination by human cells, and magnesium concentrations, there are other factors that may lead to the occasional appearance of more than the two fragments expected in the Feldman test. An obvious one is that organisms undergo mutational change, and divergence in genetic sequences can be due to both length changes as well as substitution changes. If two pathogens coexisting in the same host were to undergo sexual recombination, their genetic sequences might represent a new combination of information not previously seen in either parental strain. The new pathogen might have a gene fragment longer or shorter than the one expected on the basis of sequences currently found in Genbank.

Humans are commonly infected with multiple genetic strains and species of malarial pathogens, and the genetic characteristics of these strains change over the course of an infection (Ntoumi et al. 1995). *Plasmodium falciparum* is known to harbor six sets of rRNA genes per haploid genome (Rogers et al. 1995) that are expressed in stage specific manner (McCutchan et al. 1995). Judging from this example, birds in the wild probably contain an unknown number of different strains and/or species of pathogens, and to date no systematic molecular analysis of pathogen species diversity has been undertaken for Hawaiian birds. Additionally, *Plasmodium* contains an obligate plastid-like organelle (Kohler et al. 1997) with its own 35 kilobase circular genome containing multiple ribosomal sequences. There remain important questions to explore involving the use of ribosomal genes to identify species, but ribosomal genes are usually the genes of choice for molecular taxonomy of parasites.

In theory, a variety of nuclear, mitochondrial, and plastid ribosomal sequences are potential amplification targets. These accessory targets reduce the efficiency of amplification of parasite nuclear ribosomal fragments using the Feldman primers. Under certain conditions, one might mistake amplification products of the host's ribosomal sequences for that of an intracellular parasite, giving rise to false positives. In our case, however, we would have to account for 100% of the 'Amakihi sample giving false negatives. We find this suggestion unlikely. Finally, if we subtract out a false positive rate as high (19%) as that suggested to plague certain early PCR tests in humans, we still have significantly higher infection levels (50–19 = 31%) than the previously reported 4% for alien species in Hawaiian lowland forests (van Riper et al. 1982) using the smear method.

Nested primer design, correct magnesium titration for different instruments with different cycling parameters, and high annealing temperatures help to ensure that PCR amplification is accurate and specific. We suggest that it may be necessary to sequence amplification products in each new species tested to verify their source, and that direct sequencing of amplification products is the only accurate way to study the individual selection of parasite genomes within different species of bird host cells over the course of an infection. This precaution should be taken with both the 18s rRNA amplification products produced by the reactions we use and the additional TRAP gene test under development (Jarvi et al. *this volume*).

Studies in Avian Biology No. 22:274–280, 2001.

WHAT CAUSED THE POPULATION DECLINE OF THE BRIDLED WHITE-EYE ON ROTA, MARIANA ISLANDS?

Steven G. Fancy and Thomas J. Snetsinger

Abstract. The Bridled White-eye (*Zosterops conspicillatus rotensis*) was once thought to be common and widespread on Rota, Commonwealth of the Northern Mariana Islands, but is now restricted to several patches of native limestone forest in and adjacent to the Sabana region. Surveys conducted in 1990 indicated that the population had declined by 87% between 1982 and 1990 for unknown reasons. The low density and restricted habitat association of the Bridled White-eye on Rota contrasts with the situation on Saipan, Tinian, Agiguan, and formerly on Guam, where the Bridled White-eye is the most common forest bird and occurs at all elevations and in all habitat types. We surveyed the entire range of the Rota Bridled White-eye in 1996 to estimate its current numbers and distribution. We also reviewed existing information on the white-eye and evaluated potential causes of its decline, including predation by Black Drongos (*Dicrurus macrocercus*), rats (*Rattus* spp.), and the brown tree snake (*Boiga irregularis*); pesticides; avian disease; and habitat loss and alteration. We found that 94% of the extant population of 1,165 white-eyes on Rota was restricted to four patches of old-growth, native limestone forest covering only 259 ha. We believe that the population decline and current localized distribution is primarily a result of habitat changes due to agricultural development and typhoons, but the absence of white-eyes from several stands of native forest above 200 m remains unexplained. The Rota white-eye may be a different species from white-eyes found on Saipan, Tinian, Agiguan, and Guam, with different habitat preferences.

Key Words: Black Drongo; Bridled White-eye; brown tree snake; conservation; *Dicrurus macrocercus*; Mariana Islands; Rota; *Zosterops conspicillatus*.

Mosquito-borne avian diseases have had major effects on the distribution and population dynamics of Hawaiian forest birds, and yet the absence of certain native and nonnative species from apparently suitable habitat suggest that factors other than avian disease may be responsible for large-scale changes in bird distribution and numbers. Studies of declining bird populations on islands elsewhere in the Pacific where avian disease is not a confounding factor may help to explain some of the declines documented for Hawaiian species. The Bridled White-eye (*Zosterops conspicillatus*) is a small, flocking passerine species known only from Guam and the Commonwealth of the Northern Mariana Islands (CNMI) in Micronesia. Three subspecies are currently recognized: *Z. c. conspicillatus,* formerly on Guam but extinct since 1983; *Z. c. saypani* on Saipan, Tinian, and Agiguan; and *Z. c. rotensis* on Rota. On Saipan, Tinian, and Agiguan, the Bridled White-eye is by far the most abundant forest bird, with densities reaching 3,000 birds/km² on Tinian and 2,000 birds /km² on Saipan and Agiguan (Engbring et al. 1986). On Saipan, Craig (1996) found Bridled White-eyes at all elevations and in all habitats including limestone forest, secondary forest, beach strand, and disturbed habitats. On Guam, the white-eye was once found in coastal strand, grasslands, foothills, and mature forests (Jenkins 1983). Craig (1989, 1990; J. Craig, pers. comm.) found similar foraging behavior between the Rota subspecies and white-eyes on Saipan.

The status of the Bridled White-eye on Rota differs greatly from populations on Saipan, Tinian, and Agiguan, and the Rota subspecies is being considered for listing as endangered by the U.S. Fish and Wildlife Service. White-eyes were once found at lower elevations on Rota (Baker 1951, Craig and Taisacan 1994) but are currently found only above 170 m elevation in fragmented patches of forest on the upper plateau of the Sabana region and at the base of cliffs surrounding the Sabana (Fig. 1). All reports on the status and population trends of the Rota Bridled White-eye during the past 15 years agree that the population has been declining, but the reason for the decline has not been determined. Engbring et al. (1986) estimated the Rota Bridled White-eye population at 10,763 birds in 1982, with 93% of the birds in the Sabana. Surveys in 1990 using a combination of variable circular-plot (VCP; Reynolds et al. 1980) counts and area searches resulted in population estimates of < 300 birds by Greg Witteman and 1,500 birds by Stan Taisacan of the Division of Fish and Wildlife of the CNMI (CNMI-DFW), suggesting an 87% decrease in eight years (Craig and Taisacan 1994). Craig and Taisacan (1994) reported a linear decline based on monthly surveys in 1989–1990 and predicted that the white-eye population might be extinct by January 1997 if no action was taken. F. Ramsey and A. Harrod (unpubl. data) analyzed data from VCP surveys in 1994 that focused on the Bridled White-eye and reported a 53% decrease in densities between 1982 and 1994.

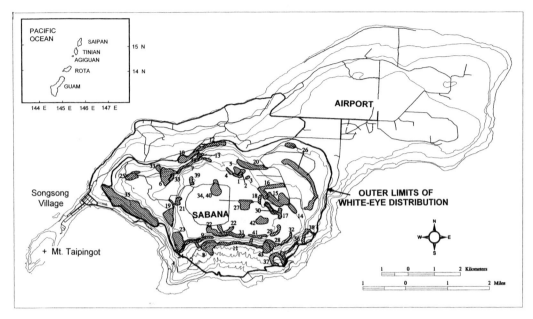

FIGURE 1.   Areas searched (hatching) and distributional limits of the Rota Bridled White-eye.

At the request of the U.S. Fish and Wildlife Service, an interagency team of biologists surveyed Rota in September 1996 to determine the current status and trends of the Bridled White-eye population. We reviewed all published and unpublished reports on the white-eye and possible reasons for its decline, and we evaluated data from previous surveys after taking into account differences in survey coverage, weather conditions, and observer differences that might affect population estimates. Our primary objectives were to provide data for a habitat conservation plan being developed for Rota, and to recommend specific research and management actions to assist the recovery of the Rota Bridled White-eye.

METHODS

Based on previous surveys on Rota, we expected Bridled White-eyes to be patchily distributed in dense vegetation where detection distances are usually <50 m. Because of low numbers of white-eyes detected during past plot counts along transects, we stratified the species' distribution on Rota based on previous survey data and vegetation maps (Falanruw et al. 1989), and optimally allocated search effort to each stratum based on expected densities (Fig. 1). This approach allowed us to search a greater proportion of the known range and to follow flocks to get additional information on flock size and composition. Two-person teams of biologists from the U.S. Geological Survey, U.S. Fish and Wildlife Service, CNMI-DFW, and Guam Division of Aquatic and Wildlife Resources conducted area searches between daybreak and late afternoon during 4–19 September 1996. Teams delin-

eated the areas they searched on 1:10,000 scale aerial photos and 1:25,000 topographic maps that were later digitized. We calculated the density of white-eyes in each search area from the number of white-eyes detected (midpoint if a range was given); the total area searched; and the percentage of the area that the team was able to effectively search, taking into account the effects of vegetation and terrain on detection distances.

To extrapolate density estimates for each search area to the larger area they represented, we adjusted the original stratum boundaries based on numbers of white-eyes found in various areas, descriptions of the forest provided by participants, vegetation boundaries delineated by Falanruw et al. (1989), and our own photointerpretation of 1994 aerial photos and comparisons with 1987 photos. This approach resulted in 17 polygons that were assigned a density class of high, low, very low, or zero white-eyes (Fig. 2). Map boundaries were digitized and areas within each polygon were calculated with a geographic information system. Densities of all search areas within the four high-density and single low-density polygons were averaged, and the overall mean density and 95% confidence limits were calculated using equations 2.15–2.16 of Manly (1992: 29).

RESULTS

In all, 247–296 individual white-eyes were detected. Some flocks were heard but not seen, and ranges provided by some teams represented uncertainty about the number of birds in a flock or whether the team had already detected a particular bird. Based on location and timing of detections, 26–29 white-eyes may have been counted by more than one team. We estimate

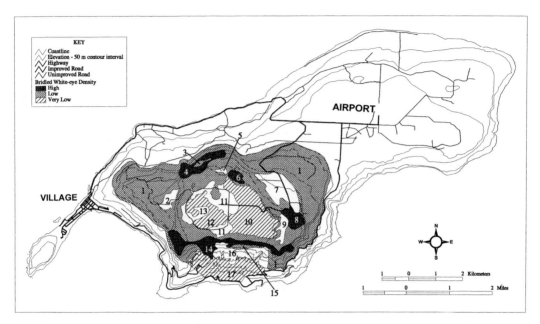

FIGURE 2.   Polygons delineating areas of high, low, very low, and zero density of Bridled White-eyes on Rota.

that 221–267 different white-eyes were detected during these surveys.

Ninety-four percent of the resulting population estimate of 1,165 ± 390 (95% CI) Rota Bridled White-eyes occurred in four polygons totaling 259 ha (Table 1). We found the highest density of 6.51 birds/ha in Polygon 8 (Fig. 2) in relatively pristine limestone forest dominated by *Elaeocarpus*. Polygon 6, with a density of 5.47 birds/ha, also had several stands of relatively pristine forest dominated by *Elaeocarpus* and *Hernandia* with numerous epiphytes, although portions of this polygon were dominated by *Pandanus* with only scattered trees. Polygon 4, on the northern slopes of the Sabana, had a density of 4.94 birds/ha. Forests along the top and at the base of the southern cliffs of the Sabana (Polygon 14 of Fig. 2) had an estimated 398 white-eyes, including one flock that was observed foraging in an introduced stand of bam-

boo at 200 m elevation. The low-density Polygon 1 in Figure 2 included 747.7 ha, and we estimate that 71 white-eyes occurred there based on a mean density of 0.094 birds/ha (N = 25 search areas). Our total population estimate of 1,165 ± 390 (95% CI) white-eyes represents an 89% decline from the 1982 estimate of 10,763 white-eyes.

DISCUSSION

Several hypotheses for the population decline and range contraction of the Rota Bridled White-eye have been stated in the published and unpublished literature or in interviews with biologists familiar with Rota. The hypotheses evaluated here include declines caused by (1) Black Drongo (*Dicrurus macrocercus*) predation; (2) brown tree snake (*Boiga irregularis*) predation; (3) rat (*Rattus* spp.) predation; (4) pesticides; (5) avian disease; and (6) habitat

TABLE 1.   NUMBER OF BRIDLED WHITE-EYES IN HIGH AND LOW DENSITY POLYGONS OF FIGURE 2

Polygon	Areas sampled	Total area (ha)	Density		Population size	
			Mean	SE	Mean	±95% CI
1–Low	25	747.72	0.0944	0.0313	70.6	46.7
4–High	3	65.21	4.9367	2.2191	321.9	289.4
6–High	5	19.31	5.4700	1.0086	105.6	39.0
8–High	1	41.15	6.5100	—	267.9	—
14–High	9	133.07	2.9944	0.9578	398.5	254.9
Total	43	1006.46	1.1570	0.1940	1164.5	390.4

change, including losses and modification of habitat because of agriculture, development, and damage from typhoons. We evaluated information supporting and refuting each hypothesis, and provide the following summary of our investigation.

BLACK DRONGO PREDATION HYPOTHESIS

Craig and Taisacan (1994) suggested that the Black Drongo, a medium-sized, flycatcher-like bird introduced from southeast Asia, was responsible for the distributional change and population decline of the Rota Bridled White-eye and several other native bird populations. Most biologists and Rota residents support this view. Craig and Taisacan (1994) noted that the Black Drongo became abundant on Rota in the 1960s, at the time when the decline in the Bridled White-eye population was first noted. Drongos are most abundant at lower elevations and in open habitats, whereas white-eyes are absent or rare in these places. Craig and Taisacan argued that white-eyes are particularly susceptible to predation by drongos because they are small and feed on the exposed upper branches of the forest canopy where they can be preyed upon by drongos. They also observed that bird species too large for drongo predation were abundant and widespread on Rota.

Occasional predation on small birds by Black Drongos is well documented (Vernon 1959, Beaty 1966, Ali and Futehally 1970, Drahos 1977, Maben 1982; G. Perez, unpubl. data), and drongos are known for their "belligerence in territorial defense" (Maben 1982:3) and their frequent chases of Rufous Fantails (*Ripidura rufifrons*), white-eyes, Eurasian Tree Sparrows (*Passer montanus*), and larger birds. However, it is very unlikely that the Black Drongo, which is primarily insectivorous (Thyagaraju 1934, Ali and Futehally 1970, Drahos 1977, Maben 1982) could have caused an island-wide range contraction and major population decline of the Bridled White-eye. On Guam, Drahos (1977) found only trace samples of bird bones in 82 drongo stomachs, and Maben (1982) found bird bones in only one of 113 drongo stomachs. Maben (1982:73) wrote that "despite this well-documented ability to eat small birds, I did not observe drongos regularly attempting to capture and eat small birds even when seemingly available," and she concluded that predatory interactions between drongos and other birds were not a significant factor in the decline of Guam's forest bird populations.

The drongo hypothesis does not explain why white-eyes are absent from several blocks of seemingly pristine limestone forest at higher elevations where drongos do not occur, nor why

populations of Micronesian Honeyeaters (*Myzomela rubratra*) and Rufous Fantails have not experienced similar population declines. However, considering the current low number of white-eyes on Rota and the greater amount of edges around remaining patches of intact limestone forest, the apparently low rate of predation by drongos on white-eyes and frequent harassment could have a measurable affect on the white-eye population if no action is taken.

BROWN TREE SNAKE PREDATION HYPOTHESIS

The accidental introduction of the brown tree snake to Guam in the late 1940s has led to the nearly complete extirpation of native bird species there (Savidge 1987a), as well as considerable economic losses because of frequent power outages and interference with cargo shipments (Fritts et al. 1987, 1990; Rodda et al. 1992, 1997). Rota receives much of its cargo from Guam, and two dead brown tree snakes were found in 1991 in construction equipment from Guam. The Bridled White-eye was the first forest bird species to go extinct on Guam as the brown tree snake expanded its distribution and population size (Savidge 1987a). It is possible that a small, undetected population of brown tree snakes occurs on Rota, but if the snake were widespread and numerous enough to have caused an island-wide range contraction and major population decline of the Bridled White-eye during the past 25 years, at least one live snake should have been detected on Rota by now. Rota has a high prey base of rats, geckos, small birds, and other prey, and we would expect brown tree snakes to multiply rapidly as they did on Guam. Heightened public awareness of the snake and extensive land clearing for housing developments and agriculture on Rota in recent years would increase the probability of detecting a snake if they occurred on Rota. Efforts to prevent the spread of the brown tree snake to Rota and other islands in Micronesia remain a top priority for conservation of Micronesian avifauna.

RAT PREDATION HYPOTHESIS

In Hawai'i, New Zealand, and other Pacific Islands, rats have been found to be important predators of native birds to the point where they cause population declines or the extinction of native birds (e.g., Atkinson 1977, 1985; Robertson et al. 1994, Innes et al. 1995, van Riper and Scott *this volume*). No detailed work on rats has been conducted on Rota, but opportunistic trapping (G. Beauprez, pers. comm.; S. Derrickson, pers. comm.) and the many observations of rats active during the daytime suggest that Rota has a very high density of rats. It has been assumed in the past that most rats trapped and seen on

Rota are either the roof rat *Rattus rattus* or the Polynesian rat *R. exulans,* because these species are found on most islands throughout the Pacific. However, Flannery (1995) indicates that *R. rattus* has never occurred in Micronesia because it is excluded by the Asian house rat, *R. tanezumi.* The two species are distinguishable only by chromosomal characteristics or by "morphological and biochemical traits" that have never been clearly outlined (Wilson and Reeder 1993:658, Flannery 1995).

The role of rats in the decline of forest birds on Rota is unknown. If rat densities are higher at low elevations on Rota, this could help explain changes in the white-eye distribution there. However, there is no evidence for a range contraction and major population decline of other species on Rota such as the Rufous Fantail and Micronesian Honeyeater, which would be expected if rats caused the population decline and range contraction of the Bridled White-eye. Nevertheless, rat predation may be an important mortality factor for the white-eye and other forest birds on Rota, and additional information is needed on rat populations and predation on Rota.

PESTICIDES HYPOTHESIS

Concern over pesticide use arose after Baker's (1946) report and other documents indicating that the U.S. military had liberally sprayed, dusted, and fogged DDT on Guam, Rota, and other islands in the Marianas during and after World War II (Jenkins 1983:52, Grue 1985). Grue (1985) found that DDT and DDE concentrations in bird carcasses and guano were not high enough to cause mortality in birds and concluded that there was no evidence for pesticides being responsible for bird declines on Guam. Organophosphates or carbamates have been used on Rota and other islands in recent years for agricultural and public health reasons (Engbring 1989, USDA 1989; CNMI-DFW, unpubl. data), but these pesticides break down rapidly and do not persist in the environment.

Small passerine populations are able to double or triple in size within a few years if adequate habitat is available and limiting factors are removed, and heavy use of pesticides would need to continue on an annual or biannual basis to keep bird populations depressed if pesticides were the primary cause of declines. Pesticide spraying also occurred on Saipan and Tinian, but the Bridled White-eye on those islands has not declined as it has on Rota. Even if pesticides caused mortality and distributional changes on Rota in the past, the pesticides hypothesis does not explain current patterns and trends seen on Rota with various forest bird species. We conclude that pesticide use cannot explain distributional changes and population declines in the Rota Bridled White-eye.

AVIAN DISEASE HYPOTHESIS

In Hawai'i, native forest birds are rare or absent from lower-elevation forests because of the presence of *Culex quinquefasciatus,* a cold-intolerant vector for avian malaria and avian pox that has a feeding preference for birds (Warner 1968, van Riper et al. 1986, Atkinson et al. 1995, Jarvi et al. *this volume,* Shehata et al. *this volume*). Avian malaria and avian pox have been documented for Mariana birds (Savidge 1986, Savidge et al. 1992), and several species of mosquitoes that might transmit avian diseases, including *C. quinquefasciatus,* also occur there (Savage et al. 1993).

We cannot rule out the possibility that avian disease restricts Bridled White-eyes to higher elevations, but we think that this is unlikely for several reasons. First, the elevational range on Rota is probably not great enough to restrict a disease vector to lower elevations. We found white-eyes as low as 170 m elevation, and most of the population occurs at elevations between 300 m and 496 m, the highest elevation on Rota. *Culex quinquefasciatus* in Hawai'i is common to elevations well above 1,500 m (Atkinson et al. 1995), and with even warmer temperatures in the Marianas we would expect it to be found at all elevations there. Second, if avian disease were an important factor, we would expect other species of native forest birds to be more abundant at higher elevations, but they are not. Third, if a disease vector restricts the white-eye to higher elevations on Rota, why is it found only in undisturbed native forest there and not in disturbed areas and second-growth forest as it is on Saipan and Tinian? Avian disease cannot be ruled out as a mortality factor on Rota without field sampling for vectors and parasites, but the avian disease hypothesis cannot adequately explain the population decline and range contraction of the Bridled White-eye.

HABITAT CHANGE HYPOTHESIS

We believe that historical changes in the distribution and population size of the Rota Bridled White-eye are primarily a result of habitat loss and modification, coupled with differences in habitat selection between the Rota white-eye and the white-eyes found on other islands in the Marianas. We found flocks of white-eyes in all areas where they have been recorded since the 1970s where the native limestone forest is relatively intact. We failed to find them in agricultural areas and most second-growth forests. Many of the areas mapped as tall limestone forest by Falanruw et al. (1989) based on 1987 ae-rial photos were damaged by super typhoon Roy in 1988 and are now poor habitat for white-eyes. White-eyes now have a patchy distribution among remnant stands of relatively pristine na-tive forest separated by areas cleared for agri-culture or supporting only scattered trees and *Pandanus* (Fig. 2).

Based on 1987 aerial photos, 58% of Rota was covered by native limestone forest (Falan-ruw et al. 1989), but much of this was second-growth or disturbed forest that may lack some attribute of old-growth forest important to the Rota Bridled White-eye. Between 1932 and 1935, more than a third of the island was cleared for sugar plantings (Bowers 1950), and addition-al clearing by the Japanese administration oc-curred until World War II. Areas that currently support relatively undisturbed tracts of native limestone forest were spared because the soil was too thin for agriculture or the terrain was too steep, as along the base of cliffs surrounding the Sabana (Fosberg 1960). Rota was one of the most heavily bombed islands in the Pacific, and by the end of World War II, few stands of un-disturbed limestone forest remained.

Aerial photographs from 1946 and historical maps indicate that more than half of the Song-song Peninsula on and around Mt. Taipingot (el-evation 143 m; Fig. 1) was forested just after the war, and many areas just above the village that have been cleared for small farms had more in-tact forest. The fact that white-eyes have not been seen in Songsong Village since the 1950s or in other lower-elevation areas as remembered by Rota elders may be a case of habitat degra-dation and fragmentation. As the village ex-panded and more of the forest around Mt. Taip-ingot and above the village was modified, the connectivity among habitat fragments for the white-eye was lost and flocks of white-eyes oc-cupying those areas disappeared. It is possible that white-eyes observed at lower elevations were transients or dispersers from preferred hab-itats at higher elevation where white-eye density was much greater, and that as the population de-clined from habitat loss and modification during and following the war, white-eyes were no lon-ger seen at low elevation. It is interesting that all of the reports of white-eyes at low elevation are for areas surrounding the Sabana, and no white-eyes have ever been reported for the east-ern third of the island.

The habitat hypothesis assumes that Rota Bri-dled White-eyes require native limestone forest and does not explain why the species is absent from several areas currently supporting good stands of native forest at lower elevation. Also, Bridled White-eyes on Saipan and Tinian, and formerly on Guam, are found at all elevations and in all vegetation types, including nonnative and highly disturbed native forests. We believe that these discrepancies occur because the Bri-dled White-eye on Rota is a different species, with different habitat preferences, than the white-eyes on other islands in the Marianas. Pre-liminary findings from DNA analyses support this belief (R. Fleischer, pers. comm.). Every taxonomist that has studied the Bridled White-eye has commented on the differences between the birds on Rota and those on other islands (Oustalet 1895, Pratt et al. 1987). Pratt et al. (1987) stated that differences in plumage and song among subspecies of Bridled White-eye in the Marianas are as great as among many sym-patric species of *Zosterops* elsewhere (e.g., *Z. lateralis* and *Z. explorator* in Fiji). They wrote that the Rota form resembles Caroline Islands birds (*Z. semperi*) in plumage but behaviorally is more like other Mariana Islands white-eyes. Pratt et al. (1987:283) suggest that "*Z. conspi-cillatus*" in Micronesia may have originated from two directions (a Melanesian ancestor and continental forms to the north) and may be more than one species.

Two puzzling aspects of our argument are that most white-eyes in Micronesia are habitat and foraging generalists, and that we found no white-eyes in several stands of seemingly high-quality native forest above 170 m elevation where we would have expected them. Forests in the Marianas have been referred to as "typhoon forests" because disturbance is a characteristic feature of them. Most Micronesian forest birds are versatile in their use of foraging sites, as would be expected on islands that are periodi-cally defoliated by typhoons (R. Craig, pers. comm.). White-eyes on other islands in the Ma-rianas occur at high density and forage in all habitat types, and only on Rota do they appear to be habitat specialists. The Rota Bridled White-eye does occasionally forage in intro-duced stands of bamboo and in second-growth forest (R. Craig, pers. comm.; this study), but the great majority of observations are in old-growth limestone forest. Two additional excep-tions to the rule that white-eyes in Micronesia are generalists are the Samoan White-eye, *Z. sa-moensis*, that is restricted to mountaintops above 900 m on Savaii in Western Samoa, and the Great Truk White-eye, *Rukia ruki*, that is com-mon only at the summit of Tol Island (Pratt et al. 1987).

Several stands of forest that we searched for white-eyes appeared to be suitable old-growth limestone forest and were at elevations above 170 m (the lowest elevation where we found white-eyes), and yet no white-eyes were found there. All of these areas, such as the hillside below Polygon 4 or below the easternmost portion of Polygon 14 (Fig. 2), are immediately adjacent to areas where white-eyes occur at high density, although white-eyes have never been documented there. This distributional pattern is inconsistent with the notion of habitat limitation, and yet predation and avian disease cannot easily explain this result either. In addition to the need for further work on the taxonomic status of the Rota Bridled White-eye, research on microhabitat selection and nesting ecology, and removal experiments involving Black Drongos and rats, are needed to understand distributional anomalies and determine appropriate management actions for conservation of this species.

IMPLICATIONS FOR CONSERVATION OF HAWAIIAN FOREST BIRDS

In Hawai'i, it is now widely accepted that mosquito-borne avian diseases, primarily avian malaria, are responsible for the absence of native forest birds from forests at lower elevations where the mosquito *C. quinquefasciatus* is common throughout the year. This has resulted in a conservation strategy in Hawai'i of protecting and restoring native forests at higher elevations where disease transmission is reduced, and has recently prompted research to develop tools for identifying disease-resistant individuals that might be used as founders for starting new populations at lower elevations (e.g., Shehata et al. *this volume*). In both Hawai'i and Rota, however, we still cannot explain why certain bird species are absent from areas of seemingly suitable habitat. On Rota, for example, the Bridled White-eye has never been found in several patches of forest that seem to have the same forest structure and plant composition as nearby stands where the white-eye occurs. In Hawai'i, several introduced species that are presumably resistant to avian malaria, such as the Japanese White-eye (*Zosterops japonicus*) and the Red-billed Leiothrix (*Leiothrix lutea*), are missing from some lower-elevation forests, and there are "distributional anomalies" for native species as well (e.g., Scott et al. 1986, Ralph et al. 1998). The Red-billed Leiothrix may now be extinct on Kaua'i (Male and Snetsinger 1998) and its numbers have declined in lower-elevation forests on the island of Hawai'i in the past 40 years for unknown reasons (Ralph et al. 1998). These findings from Rota and the Hawaiian Islands suggest that factors other than avian disease may be responsible for large-scale changes in bird distribution and numbers, and they highlight the need for additional work in both high- and low-elevation forests to identify or rule out factors so that appropriate management actions can be taken.

ACKNOWLEDGMENTS

This study would not have been possible without the cooperation and contribution of numerous biologists and agencies in the CNMI, Guam, and Hawai'i. We thank F. Toves, S. Taisacan, B. Sablan, and C. Kessler of the CNMI-DLNR; T. Aguon, R. Beck, G. Beauprez, and G. Wiles of the Guam Division of Aquatic and Wildlife Resources; D. Grout, M. Lusk and A. Marshall of the U.S. Fish and Wildlife Service; and M. Reynolds and S. Mosher of the U.S. Geological Survey, Biological Resources Division. We also thank the many biologists who have previously worked on Rota who provided input into this study: J. Engbring, R. Craig, J. Reichel, S. Derrickson, G. Olsen, J. Savidge, G. Rodda, T. Fritts, E. Campbell, and T. Pratt. Funding for the study was provided by the U.S. Fish and Wildlife Service. S. Conant and J. M. Scott provided helpful comments on the manuscript.

Studies in Avian Biology No. 22:281–290, 2001.

THE EVOLUTION OF PASSERINE LIFE HISTORIES ON OCEANIC ISLANDS, AND ITS IMPLICATIONS FOR THE DYNAMICS OF POPULATION DECLINE AND RECOVERY

Bertram G. Murray, Jr.

Abstract. The Seychelles Archipelago in the Indian Ocean lies a few degrees south of the equator, about 1,600 km east of Kenya. The Galápagos Archipelago in the Pacific Ocean lies on the equator about 1,000 km west of Ecuador. The Hawaiian Islands straddle the Tropic of Cancer and are about 3,500 km southwest of California. The Seychelles Warbler (*Acrocephalus sechellensis*) has a long life, usually begins breeding at age four, lays a one-egg clutch, and is single brooded (a combination that is extraordinary for a small passerine). In contrast, the Large Cactus Finch (*Geospiza conirostris*) of the Galápagos has a short life (some cohorts live no more than seven years), usually begins breeding at age one (but some may begin at age two or three), lays a large clutch (about four eggs), and successfully rears as many as six broods per year (occasionally, it rears none). The life history of Hawaiian passerines appears to be intermediate between these extremes. These differences are attributable to environmental differences affecting the length of the breeding season, survivorship, and reproductive success.

Many island populations are threatened with extinction because of introduced disease, such as avian malaria, and predators, such as rats, cats, and humans, as well as destruction of their habitats by introduced animals, such as goats, and by humans. Island populations are at greater risk of serious population decline than mainland populations because of the limited amount of habitat and because they have evolved a small biotic potential (r_{max}). The small biotic potential results from the evolution of long life expectancy and small clutch size in environments that were virtually predator- and disease-free prior to their discovery by the human species. Conservation of endemic island populations will require, at least, the preservation of suitable habitat and control of predator and disease organisms.

Key Words: age of first breeding; biotic potential, breeding season; clutch size; demography; Galápagos; Hawai'i; life history; population dynamics; r_{max}; Seychelles; survival.

Clutch-size variations in birds are well-known, the most prominent of which is the increase in clutch size with increasing latitude (Lack 1947, 1948; Cody 1966, 1971; Klomp 1970). Clutch size also tends to be smaller on oceanic islands than on the nearest mainland in the temperate zone, but not in the tropics, where clutch size is about the same on islands and on the adjacent mainland (Lack 1968, Cody 1971). On oceanic islands within the tropics, however, clutch size in passerines varies from one egg in the long-lived, single-brooded Seychelles Warbler (*Acrocephalus sechellensis*) to four eggs in the short-lived, multibrooded Large Cactus Finch (*Geospiza conirostris*). In this paper I explore the evolution of life-history variations of passerines on tropical oceanic archipelagos.

The theory on the evolution of clutch size, proposed to explain this variation in life histories among passerines on oceanic archipelagos, will be used to explore the evolution of a species' biotic potential (i.e., r_{max}), that is, its maximum rate of increase in natural habitat in uncrowded conditions. A species' biotic potential is a measure of the rate of recovery of a population when the environment is managed for that population.

THE BIRDS

The Seychelles Warbler is endemic to Cousin Island in the Seychelles Archipelago in the western Indian Ocean. In 1959 the global population of Seychelles Warbler numbered 26 individuals, and in 1968 the International Council for Bird Preservation undertook management of the island for the preservation of the species. Because the coconut palms (*Cocos nucifera*) were prevented from regenerating and the indigenous vegetation was allowed to flourish, the warbler population grew to over 300 birds by 1982 (Komdeur 1994a). In 1988, 29 birds were transferred to Aride Island, and in 1990 another 29 were transferred to Cousine Island. Both introductions have been successful (Komdeur 1994a).

On Cousin Island, the Seychelles Warbler is long-lived with an annual adult survival rate of 0.82 (Table 1). One bird survived to its 28th year (S. Dykstra, pers. comm.). Females begin breeding at age four and rarely lay more than one one-egg clutch per year (Komdeur et al. 1995, 1997). On Aride and Cousine islands, where the populations are still growing, females begin breeding at age one, lay a larger clutch, and often rear more than one brood per year (Komdeur 1994a, 1996).

The life history of the Large Cactus Finch on Isla Genovesa in the Galápagos Archipelago (Grant and Grant 1989) is strikingly different from that of the Seychelles Warbler (Table 1).

TABLE 1. LIFE-HISTORY CHARACTERISTICS OF FIVE PASSERINE SPECIES FROM THREE OCEANIC ARCHIPELAGOS

	Seychelles Warbler[a]	Palila[b]	Hawai'i 'Ākepa[c]	'Ōma'o[d]	'Elepaio[e]	Large Cactus Finch[f]
Age of first breeding	4	3 (males) 1–2 (females)	2 (males) 1 (females)	—	1	1–3
Mean clutch size	1	1.9	2–3	1–2	2	3.5
Maximum broods per year	1	3	1	—	2	0–6
Breeding season length (mo)	12	6–7	4	12 (peak May–July)	3	0–6
Survival of fledglings	0.44	0.36	0.43	0.40	—	0.10
Adult survival	0.81	0.65 (males) 0.62 (females)	0.83 (males) 0.80 (females)	0.66	0.88 (males) 0.80 (females)	0.62[g]

[a] Komdeur (1992, 1994a), Komdeur et al. (1997).
[b] van Riper (1980a), Lindsey et al. (1995), T. K. Pratt (pers. comm.).
[c] Lepson and Freed 1995, L. A. Freed (pers. comm.).
[d] Berger (1981), Ralph and Fancy (1994c).
[e] van Riper (1995), Vander Werf (unpubl. abstract).
[f] Grant and Grant (1989).
[g] See text.

Females usually begin breeding at age one or two, but some females do not breed until age three, and lay a modal clutch size of four eggs. Annual variation in number of clutches laid varies greatly, from zero in severe drought years to as many as seven in wet years (see Fig. 4.6 in Grant and Grant 1989). Consistent with high reproduction is the short life of Large Cactus Finches, four of five reported cohorts of females surviving no more than seven years (males tend to survive longer, one cohort of males surviving beyond ten years). About 10% of fledglings survive their first year (see Tables 3.1 and 3.2 in Grant and Grant 1989). Although Grant and Grant (1989, Table 3.2) use subsamples to give estimates of annual adult survival for males of 0.81 and for females of 0.78, the largest sample (1,244 banded birds known to have fledged in the years 1978 to 1983) gives an annual adult survival of 0.50. This is probably an underestimate (with annual adult survival of 0.50, we should expect to see 1 in 1,000 reach age eight). Annual adult female survival may be closer to 0.62 (Table 3.2 in Grant and Grant 1989). With this survival rate, we should expect 1 in 1,000 females to reach age ten). This may also be an underestimate (P. R. Grant, pers. comm.). Annual adult female survival of 0.78, however, is too great (1 in 1,000 expected to reach age 19).

The life histories of the Medium Ground Finch (Geospiza fortis) and Common Cactus Finch (Geospiza scandens) on Isla Daphne Major are similar to that of the Large Cactus Finch (Grant and Grant 1992). Most females begin breeding between ages one and three. One of four cohorts (1975, sexes combined) of each species survived to age 15 (G. fortis) and 16 (G. scandens), and the 1978 cohorts had three (G. scandens) and five (G. fortis) survivors at age

13. However, there was no cohort of G. fortis produced in 1977, and the 1976 cohort had only one bird survive two years. One cohort (1977) of G. scandens did not survive three months, and another (1976) had one bird survive two years. Although adult survivorship appears to be high (about 80%) in some cohorts, the mean life expectancy of the average bird from the time of its being laid as an egg is short. Females of both species lay a modal clutch of four eggs (Grant and Grant 1989).

The Seychelles Warbler and the Geospiza finches seem to represent extremes in the evolution of life histories on tropical oceanic islands. The Seychelles Warbler has a long life and low reproductive rate, whereas the Geospiza finches have short life expectancies and high reproductive rates.

Intermediate are the indigenous Hawaiian passerines (Table 1). For example, the Palila (Loxioides bailleui) has a clutch size of 1.9 (van Riper 1980a). Females begin breeding at age one or two and rear at most three broods in a season (T. K. Pratt, pers. comm.). Survivorship of fledglings is 0.36, and annual adult survivorship is 0.63 (Lindsey et al. 1995a). T. K. Pratt et al. (unpubl. data) found a small difference in survivorship between males and females, 0.65 and 0.62, respectively.

In other Hawaiian passerines, clutch size varies between two in the Po'ouli (Melamprosops phaeosoma; Pratt et al. 1997b) and 'Elepaio (Chasiempis sandwichensis; van Riper 1995, VanderWerf 1998a) and 3.2 in the Laysan Finch (Telespiza cantans; Morin 1992a). Adult survivorship varies between 0.55 in the 'I'iwi (Vestiaria coccinea; Ralph and Fancy 1995), 0.80 for female and 0.83 for male Hawai'i 'Ākepa (Loxops coccineus; Lepson and Freed 1995), and

0.78 for female and 0.87 for male 'Elepaio (VanderWerf 1998a). Most females produce at most a single brood a year. Unfortunately, survivorship from the laying of the egg through the first year is poorly known in all these species.

THE ENVIRONMENTS

The granitic central islands of the Seychelles Archipelago are the remains of the breakup of Gondwanaland. The climate is relatively benign (Court 1992). The drier southeast monsoon occurs from May through October, and the wetter northwest monsoon occurs between December and March. The mean annual precipitation of 1,500 to 2,200 mm is distributed throughout the year, varying from 61 and 64 mm in June and July to 296 and 387 mm in December and January (at Point La Rue international airport; Court 1992). Temperature varies slightly, from a mean low of 23.9° C in December to a mean high of 31.3° C in April (Court 1992).

Although the availability of food and the probability of success in rearing young from a breeding attempt varied considerably, some breeding activity (nest building, incubation, and feeding of young) on Cousin and Cousine islands occurred throughout the year (Komdeur 1994a, 1996; Komdeur et al. 1995). On Aride Island, where the Seychelles Warbler has recently been introduced, some breeding activity occurred in almost 100% of territories in every month of the year.

In contrast, the climate of the volcanic Galápagos Archipelago is more variable, severe, and unpredictable, especially with regard to rainfall (Grant and Boag 1980, Grant 1986, Grant and Grant 1989). Normally, a warm wet period from about January to May is followed by a cool dry period from about June to December, in response to the annual north-south movements of the southern, cooler Humboldt Current and the warmer, tropical current flowing from the Gulf of Panama. Temperature varies between a mean high of about 30° C in March to a mean low of about 19° C in September at the Charles Darwin Research Station. According to Grant (1986:25), "The most striking feature of the Galápagos climate is the extraordinary year-to-year variation in rainfall." During the wet season, rainfall varies from completely absent (in 1985) to quite heavy (116 mm in February 1980, compared with a mean precipitation of about 18 mm per month from January to May in years without El Niño rainfall; Grant and Grant 1989). Superimposed on these variations are El Niño-Southern Oscillation (ENSO) events, which occur every 2 to 11 years (averaging 7 years). At these times precipitation can be very heavy, even during the "dry" season (e.g., 505 mm on Isla Genovesa

in July 1983; Grant and Grant 1989). Nevertheless, the average monthly rainfall during the wet season in the Galápagos (55 mm from 1978 through 1988; Grant and Grant 1989) is considerably less than the mean monthly low during the five drier months of the southeast monsoon at the Seychelles (91 mm from May through September; Court 1992).

The food supply for the finches varies with the amount of rainfall (Grant and Grant 1989), and thus breeding activity of the birds is extraordinarily variable. During drought years, breeding may not occur at all, and during wet years breeding may continue for seven to eight months, during which females may lay as many as seven clutches and rear as many as six broods (Grant and Grant 1989).

Lying about 20° north of the equator, the "Hawaiian Islands are justly famous for mild, uniform, subtropical weather . . . " (Carlquist 1970: 63). The northeast trade winds blow throughout most of the year (averaging about 300 days), and the difference between the mean summer (May to October) and mean winter (November to April) temperature is only 4° C. During the winter the wind sometimes shifts to the south (Kona winds), bringing hotter, stickier weather. Rain falls throughout the year but varies considerably between leeward and windward sides and with elevation. Hilo, on the island of Hawai'i, is the wettest city in the United States (3,300 mm per year), whereas on the leeward side of the islands rainfall may be as little as 250 mm.

Despite the year around near uniformity of the climate, the length of the breeding season of the endemic passerines varies from as short as two months (Po'ouli; Pratt et al. 1997b) to year-round ('Ōma'o [*Myadestes obscurus*]; Ralph and Fancy 1994c).

DISCUSSION

THE EVOLUTION OF CLUTCH SIZE

The clutch size of birds on oceanic islands tends to be smaller than on the nearest mainland in the temperate zone and about the same size in the tropics (Cody 1966, Lack 1968). The clutch sizes of Galápagos finches are exceptional in being larger than those of passerine species on the Santa Elena Peninsula of Ecuador (Marchant 1960), which in turn are larger than typical for tropical species (Marchant 1960, Cody 1966, Lack 1968, Skutch 1985). The clutch size of the Seychelles Warbler is exceptional in being the smallest for a passerine species.

If we are to understand the evolution of life-history variations, we must keep three facts in mind. First, the relationship between clutch size and other demographic parameters is given by the clutch-size equation (Murray and Nolan 1989),

$$C = \frac{a + 1}{\sum_{\alpha}^{\omega} \lambda_x \sum_{1}^{n} P_i},$$ (1)

where a is the primary sex ratio (assumed to be one in birds), λ_x is the probability of surviving from birth (in birds, from the laying of the egg) to age class x of those individuals from successful clutches or litters, α is the mean age class of first breeding, ω is the age class of last breeding, and $\sum_{1}^{n} P_i$ is the mean number of broods successfully reared during a breeding season. $\sum_{1}^{n} P_i = P_1 + P_2 + \ldots + P_n$, where P_1, P_2, and P_n are the probabilities of the females of a genotype successfully rearing at least one, two, and n broods during a breeding season. Furthermore, $P_1 + P_2 + \ldots + P_n = c_1 s_1 + c_2 s_2 + \ldots + c_n s_n$, where c_1, c_2, and c_n are the mean number of clutches laid in producing a first, second, and nth brood, and s_1, s_2, and s_n are the probabilities that first, second, and nth brood clutches produce at least one young to independence (Murray 1991a,b). Equation 1 must hold, regardless of one's explanation for the evolution of clutch size (Wootton et al. 1991, Murray 1992a).

With high quality data (large samples for almost 20 years), such as are available for the Florida Scrub-Jay (*Aphelocoma coerulescens*; Woolfenden and Fitzpatrick 1984), the equation works exceptionally well (Murray et al. 1989). The equation has been applied to data on only two other species, each producing a very good estimate of clutch size (Prairie Warbler [*Dendroica discolor*], Murray and Nolan 1989; House Wren [*Troglodytes aedon*], Kennedy 1991).

Second, if the probability of nest contents (eggs or nestlings) surviving from one day to the next is less than one, then smaller clutches always have a higher probability of having young leave the nest (s_i) than larger clutch sizes (Murray 1999). For example, a two-egg clutch always has a greater s_i than a three-egg clutch, and a four-egg clutch always has a higher s_i than a five-egg clutch because, in each case, the larger clutch always requires at least one more day to rear young to nest-leaving. The difference is small, but inasmuch as small differences may have big evolutionary effects (Fisher 1930), we should probably ask whether this small difference in survival of clutches of different size has evolutionary significance.

By "always" I am referring to a particular clutch laid by a particular female. I am not referring to a comparison between a five-egg clutch laid in May with a four-egg clutch laid in July, or a five-egg clutch laid by a female of one species with a four-egg clutch laid by a female of another species. If we are observing a female that has just laid a fourth egg in a clutch, we may ask, would she increase her probability of rearing any young from that clutch by laying an additional egg? The answer is, no. The only apparent exception: a female that lays two eggs and begins incubation with the first egg can do better than if she had laid one egg (Murray 1994a). If she began incubation with the second egg, however, s_i would be less than if she had laid one egg.

Third, it is important to understand that we cannot compare one or two components of a life history within, between, or among species and draw a conclusion about fitness (Murray 1992b, 1997a), much less make a prediction of what we should find in nature. We must consider the combination of factors explicit in Equation 1. For example, if annual adult survival is greater in one species than in another, we should not expect that it should necessarily have the smaller clutch. If juvenile survival of the first species were poorer than in the second, each species could have the same clutch size, or the first could have a larger clutch size. If age of first breeding were later in the first species than in the second, then each species could have the same clutch size, or the first could have a larger clutch size. In comparing species, we must be careful to control for or at least consider the possibility of multiple demographic differences between them.

With these constraints in mind, I have proposed that selection favors those females that lay as few eggs or bear as few young as are consistent with replacement because they have the highest probability of surviving to breed again, their young have the highest probability of surviving to breed, or both (Murray 1979, 1991a, 1999). What this means is that the genotype that has a clutch size that can replace itself has the greatest Malthusian parameter, the best measure of fitness (Murray 1992b, 1997a). Genotypes with clutch sizes smaller than replacement have negative Malthusian parameters because they are not producing enough young to replace themselves. Genotypes with larger clutch sizes have smaller Malthusian parameters than the replacement genotype because of the reduced reproductive success or survivorship imposed by the extra egg(s). This is a hypothesis that should be tested against empirical fact. So far, this hypothesis has led to several predictions that seem confirmed by the empirical evidence (Murray 1979, 1985, 1991a, 1999).

According to this hypothesis, selection favors the mean clutch size that just balances the im-

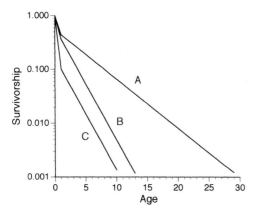

FIGURE 1. Survivorship curves for three species of passerines (data in Table 1). A = Seychelles Warbler, B = Palila, C = Large Cactus Finch.

pact of environmental factors affecting longevity (i.e., $\Sigma \lambda_x$) and the age of first breeding (i.e., α), both of which affect $\Sigma_\alpha^\omega \lambda_x$, and the probability of rearing young successfully from brood i (i.e., s_i, which affects $\Sigma_1^n P_i$). Such factors include the intensity of predation, disease, competition, and inclement weather, and the length of the breeding season. The latter especially affects $\Sigma_1^n P_i$. A long breeding season increases the number of opportunities (c_1) to rear a successful first brood (i.e., increasing P_1) and increases the probability of rearing several broods during a breeding season, increasing $\Sigma_1^n P_i$.

Unfortunately, the reported demographic data on the Seychelles Warbler, the Hawaiian passerines, and the Galápagos finches are not suitable for a rigorous comparative analysis. Data on one or more important parameters are usually lacking, based on small samples, or incorrectly calculated. Nevertheless, there are enough data (Table 1; Fig. 1) to support a preliminary analysis that may spur further investigation. Further investigation may change the numbers, but it probably would not change the interpretation.

Environmental conditions on the Seychelles certainly allow for a long life in the Seychelles Warbler. According to this hypothesis, selection should favor a small clutch size and few breeding attempts. Although the climate is suitable for breeding year-round on Cousin Island, where the population is limited by suitable breeding habitat, females normally lay only one egg per year. Furthermore, Seychelles Warblers live so long that initial breeding can be postponed, which in turn allows for the evolution of helpers at the nest (Komdeur 1992). On Aride and Cousine islands, however, where the species has recently been introduced, breeding often begins at age one, females often lay more than one egg per

year, and, initially, young disperse to breeding territories rather than postpone breeding and act as helpers (Komdeur et al. 1995, Komdeur 1996).

In contrast, climatic variation on the Galápagos is so severe that life expectancy of the Large Cactus Finch at hatching is short (only about 10% survive the first year, whereas 10% of Palila survive to beyond age three and 10% of Seychelles Warbler to age eight [Fig. 1]), some females are forced to postpone breeding until suitable conditions occur, and in some years no breeding occurs at all. Under such conditions, the Galápagos finches must evolve a large clutch size and rear multiple broods when conditions favor breeding or become extinct.

The climate of the Hawaiian Islands is benign. Breeding may be year-round in some species (e.g., ʻŌmaʻo; Ralph and Fancy 1994c) but short in others, three to seven months in the ʻElepaio (van Riper 1995) and only two months in the Poʻouli (Pratt et al. 1997b). Nevertheless, breeding occurs each year, during which as many as two or three broods may be reared. Juvenile survivorship (0.36 in Palila and 0.40 in ʻŌmaʻo [Table 1]) is greater than in the Large Cactus Finch, but adult survivorship may be more typical of temperate zone birds (e.g., 0.62 in Palila and 0.66 in ʻŌmaʻo) or as great as in the Seychelles Warbler (e.g., 0.8 in female ʻElepaio and Hawaiʻi ʻAmakihi). An intermediate clutch size between those of the Seychelles Warbler and Large Cactus Finch is not surprising in these species.

The life histories of the passerines in the Seychelles, Galápagos, and Hawaiian islands seem consistent with the notion that the clutch size is adjusted to the population's life expectancy, age of first breeding, and probability of rearing one or more broods during a breeding season, which are constrained by environmental variables such as the intensity of predation, disease, competition, and inclement weather, and by the length of the breeding season.

Alternative hypotheses on the evolution of clutch size, such as Lack's hypothesis that the clutch size reflects the amount of food available for laying eggs and rearing young (Lack 1947, 1948, 1954, 1968) or the nest-predation hypothesis of Skutch (1949) and Martin (1992b), imply that the rest of a population's demographic characteristics are adjustments to the evolved clutch size. Thus, according to these hypotheses, populations with small clutch sizes, which have evolved in response to a limited food supply or to a high incidence of predation on nest contents, have evolved longer life (i.e., greater adult survivorship) or longer breeding seasons and multibroodedness. It is difficult to imagine how a population could evolve a longer life when lacking sufficient food for rearing a larger family or how a longer breeding season and multi-broodedness could evolve in response to heavy predation on nest contents.

On the other hand, if reduced predation, disease, competition, and other sources of mortality result in increased longevity, and if s_i (the probability of rearing any young from a clutch) is greater for smaller clutches, then longer life should easily lead to the evolution of smaller clutches. If a population lives in a region that provides suitable conditions for breeding for much of the year (say, the tropics), it could evolve small clutches because s_i is greater for smaller clutches and females could lay more replacement clutches after failure (increasing c_i) and produce second, third, or more broods (increasing $\Sigma_1^n P_i$), whereas a population in a region with short breeding seasons (say, at higher latitudes), where few replacement clutches could be laid and no more than a single brood could be reared, should have a large clutch size.

It seems more likely that humans, whales, albatrosses, and the Seychelles Warbler have small litter and clutch sizes because they have evolved a long life, rather than because they have limited amounts of food available for rearing young or suffer high predation rates. It seems more likely that pigs, mice, phasianids, and the Large Cactus Finch have large litter and clutch sizes because they have a short life expectancy, rather than because they have access to a more abundant food supply or have fewer predators than longer lived species.

Equation 1 provides another clue. The only life history parameter that can be predicted from knowledge of the others is a population's mean clutch size. The other parameters of Equation 1, $\Sigma_\alpha^\omega \lambda_x$ and $\Sigma_1^n P_i$, are composites of two or more life history parameters, age-specific survivorship and age of first breeding in the former, and probability of rearing young from a clutch and number of clutches laid in rearing a brood in the latter. All kinds of life history combinations (of juvenile survival, adult survival, age of first breeding, single- or multibroodedness) may have the same clutch size. Philosophically, it seems more likely that the clutch size is a consequence of the evolution of the other life-history traits.

This study points out the need for high quality demographic data in evaluating evolutionary hypotheses. In order to predict clutch size from other demographic parameters, we need to know the number of clutches laid per female in rearing a first, second, or later brood (i.e., c_1, c_2, ... , c_n); the probability of rearing a first, second, or later brood from a clutch (i.e., s_1, s_2, ... , s_n); the mean age of first breeding (i.e., α); and annual survival rates (from which we calculate λ_x). In order to understand the evolution of clutch size, we will need to know further the influence of the factors affecting these parameters, such as the intensity of predation, disease, and competition, and the length of the breeding season (i.e., egg-laying season).

IMPLICATIONS FOR THE DYNAMICS OF POPULATION DECLINE AND RECOVERY

This analysis of clutch-size variations of island passerines is based on a conception of population dynamics different from that prevailing during the fifty years since Lack (1947, 1948, 1954, 1966) proposed that the clutch size reflected the maximum number of young the parents could rear on average and that the excess production was eliminated by density-dependent mortality, especially prior to the age of first breeding. This view was consistent with the older view of a population's "biotic potential" being kept in check by "environmental resistance" (Chapman 1928). Modifications to Lack's clutch-size hypothesis do not change the dynamics. Cody (1966) suggested that the clutch size was a function of the amount of energy available to the parents for reproduction, and Williams (1966) and Charnov and Krebs (1974) suggested that the clutch size was an "optimum," balancing the benefit of current reproduction against the costs of decreased future reproduction. The implication of these hypotheses seems to be that natural selection favors maximizing reproduction to the extent allowable by environmental conditions.

In contrast, I proposed that natural selection for longer life (by reducing age-specific mortality) is the driving force in the evolution of life histories, with clutch size being minimized to the extent allowable by mortality, and that population size was limited, not regulated, by the availability of resources, predation, disease, or other sources of mortality or reduced reproductive success (Murray 1979, 1982, 1986, 1991a).

These fundamentally different perspectives of population dynamics may have implications for conservation biology, especially with regard to our understanding of the rates of decline and recovery. Consider a simple model of population growth (Murray 1979). In Figure 2 the birth and death rates in pristine natural conditions (i.e., before human interventions) are shown by the solid lines. Between the lower critical density (LCD) and the upper critical density (UCD) resources are sufficiently abundant that individuals have equal access to the resources that permit the expression of the maximum birth rate (given their evolved fecundity) and minimum death rate. Above the UCD the birth rate decreases

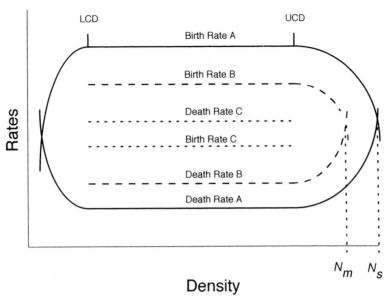

FIGURE 2. Relationship between a population's birth (*b*), death (*d*), and growth (*r*) rates, $r = \ln(1 + b—d)$, and its density. Birth and death rates A are natural rates unaffected by human intrusion. Birth and death rates B are those resulting from a moderate amount of anthropogenic increases in mortality. Birth and death rates C are those resulting from further anthropogenic increases in mortality, leading to eventual extinction. LCD = lower critical density, UCD = upper critical density, N_s = mean steady state size of population in natural conditions, and N_m = mean steady state size of population subjected to anthropogenic mortality rate B.

and death rate increases because of decreasing per capita availability of resources (e.g., food, space) or increasing levels of predation, disease, or other source of mortality. The population normally fluctuates in size around the mean steady-state size, N_s. Below the LCD the birth rate may decrease and the death rate may increase because the population is so small that individuals have difficulty in finding one another or in defending themselves from predators or other sources of mortality (e.g., Allee effects).

Second, consider that the exponential rate of change in numbers of a population (*r*) is a function of the difference between the birth (*b*) and death (*d*) rates (Murray 1997b),

$$e^r = \lambda = 1 + b - d, \qquad r = \ln(1 + b - d),$$

where *e* is the base of the natural logarithms and λ is the finite rate of change in population size. Between the LCD and UCD in Figure 2, $r_{max} = \ln(1 + b_{max} - d_{min})$, which corresponds to the population's natural biotic potential.

In Figure 2 the long dashed lines show the effects on birth and death rates of a moderate increase in mortality (the birth rate decreases with increasing mortality because of a changing age structure; Murray 1979). With moderate mortality, the mean steady-state population size, N_m, is smaller than N_s. With greater anthropo-

genic mortality, the death rate increases and the birth rate decreases further. If the death rate exceeds the birth rate (*r* < 0), as shown by the short dashed lines in Figure 2, the population declines toward extinction (i.e., size and density decrease).

The rate at which a population recovers from decline (that is, increases in numbers, *r*) is a function of how well humans have managed to clean up the environment and to reduce predation, disease, and other sources of anthropogenic mortality. The maximum rate of increase is r_{max}, that is the population's theoretical biotic potential, unless management has also reduced the natural causes of mortality.

Indeed, anthropogenic activity may affect all species, reducing predator populations as well as prey. A decline in predators could result in increasing r_{max} of the prey and greater N_s, but the latter only if predation limited population size. I suspect that populations of most passerine species, if not most species of birds, are limited by territorial behavior (Murray 1979, 1982). The elimination of predators in territorial species could result in a greater r_{max} but not in a greater population size, N_s. The beauty of the model in Figure 2 is that one can plot the consequences of multiple causes of mortality, as shown in greater detail in Murray (1986).

TABLE 2. LIFE HISTORY PARAMETERS OF GROWING (r_{max} = 0.05) LONG-LIVED (A) AND SHORT-LIVED (B) POPULATIONS

Parameter	Population	
	A	B
Survival during first year ($s_{x = 1}$)[a]	0.40	0.15
Survival after first year ($s_{x > 1}$)[a]	0.80	0.50
Age class[a] of first breeding (α)	4	2
Maximum age class[a] (ω)	27	10
Mean fecundity of breeders (m_x)[a]	1.1420	3.8685
Generation time (T)	7.8861	2.9824
Birth rate (b)	0.4058	0.8266
Death rate (d)	0.3545	0.7754
r_{max}	0.05	0.05

[a] x = age class = age + 1 (Murray 1997b).

We can examine the dynamics of population change further by comparing, quantitatively, the effects on a population's growth rate (r) of increasing amounts of pollution, predation, or disease in populations with different life histories. For illustration (Table 2), I have created for comparison a long-lived, low-fecundity population, A, and a short-lived, high-fecundity population, B. I have assumed for each an r_{max} of 0.05 in pristine environments. With increasing intensity of mortality, the death rate increases, the birth rate decreases, and, thus, r decreases (Fig. 3). What is striking in this example is the much greater risk of extinction of the short-lived, high-

fecundity population exposed to the same intensity of anthropogenic mortality as the long-lived, low-fecundity population. This result seems counterintuitive.

Indeed, Freed (1999) has pointed out that species of endangered Hawaiian honeycreepers (Kaua'i Creeper [*Oreomystis bairdi*] and Kaua'i 'Ākepa [*Loxops caeruleirostris*]) have small clutch sizes and tend to be single brooded, compared with the more abundant species (Kaua'i 'Amakihi [*Hemignathus kauaiensis*], 'Apapane [*Himatione sanguinea*], and I'iwi'i) living in 'ōhi'a-koa forest on Kaua'i. These data and the result shown in Figure 3 indicate to me that, for some reason, low-fecundity species must have a smaller r_{max} than high-fecundity species. Low-fecundity species are at greater risk because of a naturally low r_{max} rather than a low fecundity per se. We should consider how differences in r_{max} could evolve.

First, if age-specific survival and longevity (i.e., s_x and l_x, respectively) reflect density-dependent responses to the evolution of clutch size and, therefore, fecundity (i.e., m_x = (mean clutch size × mean number of clutches)/2), as implied by Lack (1947, 1948, 1954, 1966) and Cody (1966), or if clutch size, survival, and longevity are optimized, as suggested by Williams (1966) and Charnov and Krebs (1974), the situation described in Table 2 and Figure 3 is possible. We should expect to find some long-lived, low-fecundity species with an r_{max} that is equal to or

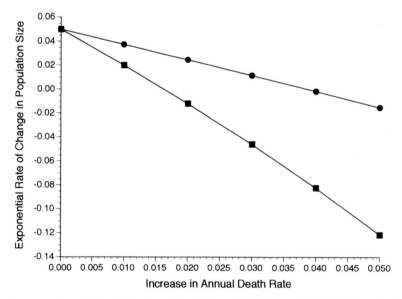

FIGURE 3. A comparison of the effect of r_{max} (i.e., between the LCD and UCD in Figure 2) of increases in the death rate from increasing anthropogenic causes of mortality in a long-lived, low-fecundity population A (circles) and short-lived, high-fecundity population B (squares). The data for each population when r_{max} = 0.05 are given in Table 2.

TABLE 3. LIFE HISTORY PARAMETERS OF LONG-LIVED (C) AND SHORT-LIVED (D) STEADY-STATE ($r = 0$) POPULATIONS

Parameter	Population	
	C	D
Survival during first year $(s_{x\,=\,1})^a$	0.310	0.126
Survival after first year $(s_{x\,>\,1})^a$	0.710	0.476
Age class[a] of first breeding (α)	4	2
Maximum age class[a] (ω)	27	10
Mean fecundity of breeders $(m_x)^a$	1.4621	4.164
Generation time (T)	6.4418	2.8971
Birth rate (b)	0.4834	0.8063
Death rate (d)	0.4834	0.8063
r_{max}	0.0000	0.0000

[a] x = age class = age + 1 (Murray 1997b).

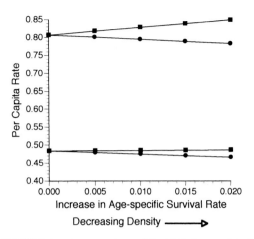

FIGURE 4. A comparison of the birth (squares) and death (circles) rates of long-lived population C (lower) and short-lived population D (upper) when their age-specific survival is increased above what is at N_s. Data for populations at N_s are in Table 3.

even greater than the r_{max} of some short-lived, high-fecundity species. In the long-lived population in our example, the mean annual m_x is 1.1420 of breeders (some females should be laying three or more eggs [i.e., mean = 2 × 1.1420] per year) and is sufficient to maintain r_{max} at 0.05 with its survivorship schedule. In the short-lived population, the mean annual m_x is 3.8695 of breeders (some females should be laying eight or more [i.e., mean = 2 × 3.8695] eggs per year) and is sufficient to maintain r_{max} at 0.05 with its survivorship schedule.

According to the theories of Lack, Cody, Williams, and Charnov and Krebs, there is no apparent reason for r_{max} to be smaller in a low-fecundity, long-lived population. For example, suppose a mutation occurs that allows the long-lived females in population A (Table 1) to lay on average an additional egg per year (m_x = (2.284 + 1)/2 = 1.642). Suppose further that the larger fecundity reduces survival during the first year from 0.40 to 0.35 and survival of females of breeding age from 0.80 to 0.75. Under these conditions, r_{max} = 0.0576. Thus, the benefit of an increase in fecundity exceeds the cost of decreasing survival, resulting in an increase in r_{max}. If the new, larger fecundity should evolve because it is "optimal," we should expect to find at least some low-fecundity species with a high r_{max} and, therefore, with a lower risk of extinction than some high-fecundity species.

On the other hand, according to my theory, selection acts on clutch size when the population is fluctuating around the population's mean size, N_s, that is, when $r = 0$ over evolutionary time (Murray 1999). If natural selection favors the genotype whose females lay as few eggs as are consistent with replacement because they have the highest probability of surviving to breed again, their young have the highest probability of surviving to breed, or both, as I have pro-

posed (Murray 1979, 1991a, 1999), then we should expect r_{max} to be smaller in long-lived species than in short-lived species, according to the following argument.

We can examine the demography of populations of different life histories by creating two new populations, a long-lived (C) and a short-lived (D) steady-state population (Table 3). According to the population dynamics model (Fig. 2), we should expect that the birth rate would be greater and the death rate smaller at population sizes less than N_s, compared with the birth and death rates at N_s. Assuming that age-specific fecundity within each population is the same at all densities, we can calculate the birth, death, and growth rates when age-specific survival is increased, simulating the effect of densities below N_s. For the same change in age-specific survival, the relative and absolute changes in birth and death rates are greater in the high-fecundity population than in the low-fecundity population, resulting in greater r (i.e., $\ln(1 + b - d)$) in the high-fecundity population (Fig. 4).

As far as I am aware, the notion that the clutch size reflects the fewest eggs that a female can lay, consistent with replacement, is the only explanation for the evolution of a smaller r_{max} in long-lived populations than in short-lived populations. Long-lived populations are not at greater risk of extinction than short-lived populations because of their lower fecundity per se but because of their smaller r_{max}. However intuitive it is that low-fecundity species should be at greater risk for extinction and have slower rates of recovery than high-fecundity species, current life-history theory does not explain it. On the other hand, the comparison of the demography of species at risk and not at risk comprises a small sample. Further comparisons would be desirable.

If selection results in a mean clutch size that just balances average mortality, as my theory asserts (Murray 1979, 1991a, 1999), then we should expect that island species, which usually have evolved in environments with little predation, disease, and other causes of mortality, should have greater mean life expectancy and lower fecundity than species exposed to greater natural mortality. Populations on islands, which have been assaulted by the introduction of disease (e.g., avian malaria), brood parasites (e.g., Glossy Cowbird [*Molothrus bonariensis*]), predators (e.g., rats, cats, and humans), as well as loss of habitat (e.g., to goats and humans), suffer disproportionately. Mainland populations, natu-

rally subjected to higher mortality than island populations, have evolved larger clutch sizes and, thus, greater r_{max}. The mortality effects of a newly introduced predator should probably not be additive because the new predator would be expected to be competing with the already present predators, reducing the old predators' populations and their effect on the prey.

The conservation of endemic island populations will require preservation or restoration of suitable habitat and protection from predation and disease.

ACKNOWLEDGMENTS

I thank J. Burger, L. A. Freed, M. Gochfeld, P. R. Grant, J. R. Jehl, Jr., and J. M. Scott for reading and commenting on the manuscript. I thank L. A. Freed, T. K. Pratt, and C. J. Ralph for drawing my attention to papers on the Hawaiian avifauna.

Studies in Avian Biology No. 22:291–304, 2001.

NEWLY EMERGENT AND FUTURE THREATS OF ALIEN SPECIES TO PACIFIC BIRDS AND ECOSYSTEMS

LLOYD L. LOOPE, FRANCIS G. HOWARTH, FREDERICK KRAUS, AND THANE K. PRATT

Abstract. Although the devastating effects of established alien species to Pacific birds and ecosystems are generally well recognized by the avian conservation community, we raise the under appreciated issue of effects of incipient and future invasions. Although special attention to Pacific bird species "on the brink" is to a certain extent appropriate and necessary, a comparable focus on stopping new invasions appears desperately needed. All indications suggest that introductions will escalate with the trend toward ever increasing commerce and unrestricted trade unless stronger preventative measures are implemented very soon. The threat to Pacific island avifaunas from the brown tree snake (*Boiga irregularis*) is well-known, but as many as several hundred of the world's snake species, some of which are repeatedly smuggled illegally as pets, might have similar impacts on native birds if transported to Pacific islands. We touch upon a sampling of obviously severe potential future threats, with the hope of raising awareness and resolve to fix the current woefully inadequate system for prevention of and rapid response to new invasions.

Key Words: biological invasions; invasion and biological diversity; invasive amphibians; invasive invertebrates; invasive plants; invasive reptiles; invasive vertebrates; newly emergent alien species; quarantine; snake invasions of islands.

The biotas of oceanic islands in general, and the Hawaiian Islands and other Pacific islands in particular, are highly susceptible to damage caused by alien plants, animals, and microorganisms transported by humans. The high susceptibility is related to the evolutionary history of island organisms that generally evolved with reduced exposure to certain physical (e.g., fire) and biotic (e.g., ungulates, snakes, ants) forces (Loope and Mueller-Dombois 1989). Although habitat destruction by humans was a very important factor in the decimation of Hawaiian landbirds in the past, the greatest current threats are from alien species. The most important threats include avian diseases transported by mosquitoes; predation by rats, cats, dogs, and mongooses; competition for food and other resources by alien species, especially arthropods and birds; and habitat degradation by feral ungulates, especially pigs, which also facilitate spread of alien plants (Cuddihy and Stone 1990, Jacobi and Atkinson 1995). Alien species also prevent the recovery of native ecosystems after disturbances, thus seriously exacerbating the effects of habitat destruction. We concur that the current focus of conservation agencies on mitigating these threats, with special attention to "species on the brink," is appropriate and necessary. However, we aim in this paper to call attention to the intuitively obvious but seldom mentioned reality that although existing invasions pose formidable threats, the situation promises to get much worse as additional invasive species are introduced and established. We ask the conservation community and public agencies to recognize and address the problem of continued alien species introduction.

Located near the middle of the Pacific Ocean, Hawai'i is increasingly important as an international transportation hub. Honolulu International Airport is the seventeenth busiest airport in the world in terms of total passenger traffic; military air traffic is also substantial. The state is a social melting pot, with much movement of cultural trappings such as ethnic fruits and vegetables as well as the ever increasing repertoire of the international horticulture and pet trades. Tourism is the primary industry, and visitors arrive from all over the world. Agriculture is also an important industry, which routinely moves living material into and out of Hawai'i. All these activities result in the frequent arrival of new alien species (Holt 1996). Furthermore, the increasing globalization of the world economy and the increasing scope of free trade agreements promise to expedite the flow of species (Jenkins 1996).

Our focus on this topic was heightened by recent experience on a technical panel convened by the U.S. Federal Aviation Administration, the Hawaii Department of Transportation, and the U.S. Fish and Wildlife Service to examine likely impacts on endangered species of an expanded airport at Kahului, Maui. We were asked to predict what new species might arrive, particularly on new direct flights from Asia and eastern United States, and how their arrival might challenge the currently minimal quarantine system.

The analysis below makes no attempt to be comprehensive, but only to highlight a range of taxonomic groups and pathways posing obvious threats, with emphasis on potential vertebrate invaders, especially snakes. Our aim is to present a range of examples in sufficient detail to illustrate the scope of the problem and to highlight the urgency of finding solutions. Although most examples are for Hawai'i, since that is the island group with which we are most familiar, conclusions largely apply to other Pacific islands. The analysis includes suspected modes of entry, potential threats, and examples of high-risk species not yet known to be established.

VERTEBRATES

Nearly all alien vertebrate species in Hawai'i are pests in some situations, although some also have economic benefits (Stone 1985). The mammals are the best known and provide the best examples of the dilemma created by alien species introductions; this is especially clear with the ungulates. Ungulates have been the most destructive group for native ecosystems but are among the most important groups economically (Cuddihy and Stone 1990). Other herbivorous and frugivorous vertebrates are often important threats to native species and are pests of agriculture as well. The insectivorous and carnivorous species are potentially extremely detrimental to native birds and other animals.

Vertebrates as a group are particularly destructive because of their relatively large size (which gives them more food and water reserves and consequently wider environmental tolerances than smaller animals). They are also often generalist feeders, more mobile, and thus more effective competitors than most invertebrates. On the other hand, an observational bias makes it easier for humans to recognize impacts from vertebrates, especially for the larger species. A few terrestrial vertebrates (especially the smaller ground and den-inhabiting species) can disperse as stowaways in cargo and aircraft, and aquatic species may arrive in ballast. However, by far the most important avenue of dispersal of vertebrates into Hawai'i has been purposeful introductions for economic, recreational, or cultural purposes, often by persons or groups unfamiliar with the potential negative consequences of such introductions.

SNAKES

Hawai'i and virtually all other oceanic Pacific islands lack native terrestrial snakes (Loveridge 1945, Allison 1996). Consequently, the native birds lack adaptive behaviors to deal with these predators. The apparently inadvertent introduction after World War II of the brown tree snake (*Boiga irregularis*) into Guam well illustrates the effects alien snakes may have on native island ecosystems. Within 40 years of introduction, the brown tree snake had attained peak densities of 100/ha, had exterminated nine of Guam's 12 native forest birds and approximately

half the native lizard fauna, and had left the three surviving forest bird species and remaining fruit bat highly endangered (Savidge 1987a; Wiles 1987a, 1987b; Rodda and Fritts 1992, Rodda et al. 1998). Huge reductions have also been observed in the populations of introduced birds, mammals, and lizards on Guam (Savidge 1987a, Rodda et al. 1998). The loss of the avifauna has had unknown affects on the native forest ecosystem, but loss of pollinators and fruit dispersers are likely to have important repercussions over several decades (Savidge 1987b). For example, there has been a dramatic bloom in spider populations coincident with the loss of the insectivorous avifauna (Rodda et al. 1998).

It is sometimes claimed or implied that the brown tree snake is somehow unique in its ability to wreak ecological devastation on island communities and that other snake species would not present similar problems (e.g., McKeown 1996:144–145). But this argument derives from ignorance of snake ecology and the fact that the brown tree snake invasion of Guam is the only snake invasion to be well studied to date. In fact, several snake species have invaded other islands (or, in the case of peninsular Florida, areas ecologically similar to islands), and damage to native biotas has been documented or inferred in some instances. Additional snake invasions include the wolf snake *Lycodon aulicus* on Reunion and Mauritius in the 1800s (Cheke 1987), on Christmas Island in the 1980s (Fritts 1993), and perhaps throughout the Philippines and western Indonesia in the past few centuries (Leviton 1965); *Elaphe guttata* (corn snake) on Grand Cayman Island (Schwartz and Henderson 1991); *E. taeniura* (striped racer), *Protobothrops elegans,* and cobras (of an unspecified species) on Okinawa (Rodda et al. 1997, Ota 1998); *Natrix maura* (viperine watersnake) on Mallorca (Corbett 1989); *Boa constrictor* in Florida and Cozumel (Dalrymple 1994, Butterfield et al. 1997; T. Fritts, pers. comm.); and possibly *Acrochordus* in southern Florida (P. Moler, pers. comm.). Especially successful has been the spread of the parthenogenic (lacking a requirement for fertilization) blind snake *Ramphotyphlops braminus* throughout the tropics over the past century, primarily as a stowaway in potting soil associated with horticultural shipments. The invasion of *Lycodon* on Reunion is thought to have resulted in the near extinction of a native lizard (Cheke 1987). An endemic frog, *Alytes muletensis,* is endangered on Mallorca, apparently because of the introduction there of *Natrix maura* (Corbett 1989). The recent introduction of *B. constrictor* to Cozumel is expected to pose a serious threat to the survival of nesting seabirds and several endemic birds and mammals

(T. Fritts, pers. comm.). But most snake invasions remain poorly studied, and their ecological consequences remain largely undocumented.

There is every reason, however, to be concerned with snake invasions more generally; the brown tree snake may be only the vanguard of a potentially great ecological problem. There is nothing especially remarkable about the ecology of the brown tree snake. Its clutch size of 4–12 (mean = 8) eggs (Shine 1991, Rodda et al. 1998) is unexceptional and lower than that of many snakes (Fitch 1985, Seigel and Ford 1987, Shine and Seigel 1996). The brown tree snake apparently produces at most a single clutch per year in its native range (Shine 1991) but may produce two per year in Guam (Rodda et al. 1998); hence, its intrinsic rate of increase is probably fairly low. It is not adapted to extremes of either temperature or humidity, judging from its natural geographic, elevational, and ecological range (McCoy 1980, Cogger 1992, O'Shea 1996, Rodda et al. 1998). The most noteworthy features of the ecology of the species are its catholic diet of vertebrates (Savidge 1988, Greene 1989, Campbell 1996); its arboreal proclivities, which allow it greater access to forest birds than most snakes would have; and its nocturnal habits. But these features are by no means unique to brown tree snakes: many snakes are general vertebrate predators, many are arboreal, and many are nocturnal, especially in the tropics and subtropics. Many arboreal snakes specialize on birds or feed on them opportunistically and could be expected to devastate Pacific avifaunas if they were to become established. Lastly, any snakes to become established on oceanic islands would be in environments largely free of predators and disease organisms, as is the brown tree snake in Guam (the widely touted, terrestrial and diurnal mongoose would have no affect on nocturnal or arboreal snakes, nor on pit vipers, whose strike is faster than the mongoose). Hence, introduced snakes on most oceanic islands could be expected to lack significant predators or other sources of premature mortality. A reasonable estimate is that several hundred of the world's approximately 3,000 snake species could prove damaging to island avifaunas previously unexposed to snakes, although the major effects of many of these would be primarily on ground-dwelling birds. Several potentially invasive snake species are dangerously venomous and could be expected to have negative consequences for humans too.

Snakes are likely to be introduced to islands in two ways. The first is by hitchhiking in cargo or on vessels used for transportation. This is how the brown tree snake is thought to have arrived on Guam (and other islands) and how

Lycodon and *Ramphotyphlops* have moved around the Indo-Pacific region. The second is by deliberate introduction as pets followed by escape or intentional release. Most of the free-roaming snakes captured in Hawai'i each year are clearly in the latter category (based on examination of Hawaii Department of Agriculture records), as are the foreign snakes established or commonly seen in Florida (Dalrymple 1994; P. Moler, pers. comm.).

The number of snake species that would prove adept at hitchhiking is unknown but probably fairly small. Secretive and nocturnal species having high densities and with facultative (Schuett et al. 1997) or obligate (McDowell 1974, Nussbaum 1980) parthenogenesis are likely to make the most successful hitchhikers. While the group of snakes meeting these specifications is relatively small, it has nevertheless furnished the most accomplished invasive snake agents of ecological destruction so far.

In Hawai'i, the past three decades have seen a dramatic increase in the rate of pet reptile introduction, release, and establishment. Given the burgeoning number of species bred and available within the mainland pet trade, Hawai'i and other Pacific islands remain highly vulnerable to further introductions. Many snake species introduced for the purpose of furnishing pets may well prove just as great a threat to native avifaunas as has the brown tree snake, judging from their ecological attributes. Among the commonly kept species, boas, pythons, rat snakes (*Elaphe*), bullsnakes (*Pituophis*), and most pit vipers (Crotalinae) specialize on endothermic prey, and many of the rat snakes and pit vipers have an ontogenetic switch from ectothermic to endothermic prey. King snakes (*Lampropeltis*) are vertebrate generalists. Many boas, pythons, pit vipers, and rat snakes are arboreal and feed primarily, or to a large extent, on avian prey. All these taxa have clutch sizes of the same magnitude as brown tree snakes or, in the case of the commonly kept *Boa, Eunectes* (anaconda), and *Python* species, are much larger (30–>100; Fitch 1985, Stafford 1986, Seigel and Ford 1987). Several of these species can potentially produce two or more clutches per year when food is freely available (Tryon and Murphy 1982, Tryon 1984), as it is in Hawai'i, where the environment is artificially enriched with an abundance of alien rodents, lizards, and birds. Furthermore, some species are suspected to be facultatively parthenogenic (Schuett et al. 1997), an attribute whose significance for colonizing oceanic islands should be obvious. Most of these species are nocturnal. The only ecological parameter for which some of these common pet species cannot match brown tree snakes is elevational range. In its native New Guinea, brown tree snakes can live at elevations from sea level to 1,400 m (O'Shea 1996). Most commonly kept pythons and boas probably cannot live at such high altitudes, although many *Elaphe, Lampropeltis, Pituophis,* and pit vipers would have no trouble doing so, judging from their native latitudinal and elevational ranges. The significance of these considerations for Hawai'i, and perhaps other islands, is that most of the snakes captured and identified in Hawai'i are in the genera *Boa, Python, Elaphe,* and *Pituophis.* That these snakes have not elicited the same level of concern in Hawai'i that brown tree snakes have is remarkable and probably attributable to the general ignorance about snakes and their biology that prevails at any location in which they are naturally absent.

OTHER REPTILES

A host of other alien reptile species could also be expected to have negative consequences for native Pacific avifaunas, though they perhaps may not be as damaging as snakes. A handful of large aquatic turtles are noteworthy for their predation upon waterbird chicks (Ernst et al. 1994). Included in this group are several soft-shelled turtles (Trionychidae), of which two species have been introduced to Hawai'i (McKeown 1996), and other turtles such as the snapping turtle (*Chelydra serpentina*) that have been established elsewhere (McCoid 1995). Several monitor lizards (*Varanus*) grow to large sizes, feed to some extent on birds, and are adept at climbing trees (Daniel 1983, Green and King 1993). These could be expected to have negative consequences for at least some native birds. Reports of wild monitor lizards occur occasionally in Hawai'i and frequently in Florida (Dalrymple 1994).

Of potentially significant impact is the introduction of arboreal insectivorous lizards because these species can often reach high population densities and may seriously impact the food resources of native insectivorous birds. Especially problematic in this regard is Jackson's chameleon (*Chamaeleo jacksoni*), which provides an illustrative case history of illegal alien vertebrate establishment in Hawai'i and ineffectual management response to the threat. The Jackson's chameleon became popular in the international pet trade in the 1970s. Some reached O'ahu legally in 1972 under a pet store import permit. These were illegally released in the importer's Kāne'ohe backyard (McKeown 1996), subsequently became free-ranging, and served as the source for a rapidly expanding distribution and trade. The species spread throughout O'ahu during the 1970s and 1980s, reached Maui by the

early 1980s, and is now found on most or all of the main islands. In an effort to curb the spread of the species, Hawaii Department of Agriculture prohibited the keeping of Jackson's chameleons in the state until 1994, when the regulation was rescinded because of its ineffectiveness. However, during this same time, sale and export were allowed, providing an economic incentive for people to move the lizards around surreptitiously to begin new populations that could serve as a source of saleable animals. Consequently, the spread of the species to other islands and to new localities within islands was rapid, despite its illegality.

Jackson's chameleon is native to cloud forest (1,800–2,400 m) in Kenya, where temperatures range from 25° C during the day to 10° C at night (McKeown 1996). It forms dense populations at lower elevations (400–1,100 m) in Hawai'i and can be expected to invade forested upland habitats, perhaps as high as the upper tree line. There was an unconfirmed sighting of an individual at Hosmer Grove (elev. 1,830 m) of Haleakalā National Park, Maui, in June 1994. In 1996, Haleakalā Chief Ranger K. Ardoin found one crossing the road at 1,800 m elevation in ranchland just below the park boundary.

In addition to being a voracious and efficient predator of arthropods, Jackson's chameleon attains sufficiently large size that there is concern about its potential ability to take native forest bird nestlings as prey items, although this concern has yet to be scientifically investigated. Other chameleons attain a larger size, are known to eat nestling birds (Schmidt and Inger 1957; C. Raxworthy, pers. comm.), and are available in the pet trade.

Another concern is that any introduced lizard species could serve as an additional food source for many species of introduced snakes, thereby serving to keep introduced snake populations at an artificially high level and thus maintaining a high predation pressure on native birds. This is one means by which brown tree snakes have maintained phenomenally high population densities on Guam, even after the extirpation of most native birds (Campbell 1996, Rodda et al. 1997). The high densities of alien geckos and skinks in Hawai'i suggest a similar scenario could obtain there should snakes become established.

AMPHIBIANS

Frogs represent another under appreciated potential threat to native Pacific avifaunas. Bullfrogs (*Rana catesbeiana*), already introduced to Hawai'i, attain a large size and will consume anything they can cram into their mouths, including all classes of vertebrates (Bury and

Whelan 1984). In the western United States, where this species has also been introduced, it has been observed to eat adult passerines, snakes, frogs, fish, and bats, and is partly responsible for the endangered status of one snake and several frogs (Rosen and Schwalbe 1995). It is reasonable to expect bullfrogs to exert some predation pressure on waterbird chicks where they co-occur.

A more insidious threat may be posed by a variety of arboreal tropical frogs, loosely termed "treefrogs" but representing a diverse array of taxonomically unrelated species. It is reported that the Cuban hylid *Osteopilus septentrionalis* is established on O'ahu (McKeown 1996). In 1997, two species of leptodactylids were reported for the first time in the Hawaiian Islands: *Eleutherodactylus coqui* and *E. planirostris* (Kraus et al. 1999). The first is arboreal and has a loud, piercing call; the latter is terrestrial with a quieter chirp. Both species originated in the Caribbean and are associated in Hawai'i, as elsewhere (Conant and Collins 1991, Kaiser 1992, Dalrymple 1994), with greenhouses and nurseries. Both species are currently spreading from nurseries to surrounding areas and are also being transported and established by landscaping of resorts and residential areas with plants from infected nurseries. These species are easily spread in plants and associated soil because eggs are hidden in these areas and directly develop into small froglets, bypassing a tadpole stage and, hence, any need for standing water. *E. coqui* occurs to elevations of 1,200 m in its native ranges (Schwartz and Henderson 1991), has already established at higher elevations in Hawai'i, and, hence, has potential to invade upland rain forest in Hawai'i.

Both species of established Hawaiian *Eleutherodactylus* and many other species of hylid, leptodactylid, and rhacophorid "treefrogs" form high-standing biomass and can be expected to exert a significant impact on native insect faunas and, indirectly, on the insectivorous birds dependent upon them (Kraus et al. 1999). Because they will have few or no predators in the Pacific, such species may serve as energy sinks, producing large quantities of biomass that do not get transferred to higher trophic levels and, consequently, may exert ecosystem-level changes as well (Dalrymple 1994).

Again it needs to be emphasized that unsupported claims that only a single species of treefrog "has the capacity to do great harm to island ecosystems" (McKeown 1996:20) and that other alien species would be beneficial if introduced to Hawai'i are simply statements of faith combined with a studious disregard for general ecological principles. It is usually impossible to comprehend fully the potential ecological impacts of a species before it is introduced. However, an invasion is unlikely to benefit most native species because all species engage in a web of interactions with a large host of other species. The nonlinear nature of many of these interactions makes complete prediction of a species' effects inherently difficult, but breaking established webs or creating energy sinks (e.g., amphibians discussed above) will inevitably be detrimental to some native species. Consequently, blanket claims that particular aliens are "kama'āina" (native-born) species or "harmless" or "helpful" (e.g., throughout McKeown 1996) can clearly be seen to be unscientific statements deriving from a different agenda than the impartial description of reality. Dissemination of such complacent ignorance of and unconcern for the native biota is perhaps the greatest long-term threat to the Pacific avifauna.

BIRDS

Alien birds threaten native birds directly through competition and transmission of diseases and parasites, and indirectly through aiding habitat conversion and ecosystem alteration by dispersal of seeds of alien plants (Stone and Loope 1987). Over 150 species of alien birds have been introduced to the Hawaiian Islands (Hawaii Audubon Society 1989), but only 54 have successfully established breeding populations (Pyle 1997).

In contrast to Florida (James 1997), opportunities for alien bird stowaways and "natural" colonizations of Pacific islands are highly limited. In Hawai'i, all successfully established alien bird species were deliberately brought to the islands for some purpose. Therefore, limiting introductions has mainly relied on regulating trade in live birds. If this trend continues, future introductions of alien birds are likely to be derived from four main groups: waterfowl, galliforms (chickenlike birds), psittacids (parrotlike birds), and passerines (perching birds), especially finches. Birds are also increasingly smuggled as eggs, which means that almost any species might be introduced in the future.

Escaped Mallards (*Anas platyrhynchos*) threaten the endangered Hawaiian Duck or Koloa (*A. wyvilliana*) ecologically and genetically through hybridization (USFWS 1985, Rhymer *this volume*). Apart from Mallards and Cattle Egrets (*Bubulcus ibis*), all populations of alien waterfowl have been ephemeral (Berger 1981). New wild populations derived from collections belonging to resorts or private individuals are likely, but their long-term establishment is less likely, because Hawai'i has relatively few wetlands and the largest of these are managed for native wildlife by government agencies.

All wild populations of galliforms in Hawai'i (12 species) have been authorized releases. Such releases still take place, but now for the purpose of providing birds to shoot rather than to establish new populations. This unmonitored practice appears to involve mainly the Ring-necked Pheasant (*Phasianus colchicus*) and Wild Turkey (*Meleagris gallopavo*), but the practice has the potential for escalating. The small trade in "ornamental" galliforms (tropical pheasants, etc.) could be a latent source of new introductions.

Over the history of releases in Hawai'i, there has occurred an important shift in the taxa released. Besides establishing the Mallard and many galliforms, early acclimatization projects and escapes successfully introduced the Cattle Egret, Chestnut-bellied Sandgrouse (*Pterocles exustus*), Barn Owl (*Tyto alba*), Guam Swiftlet (*Aerodramus bartschi*), 13 species of insectivorous and frugivorous passerines, and 19 species of finches (Pyle 1997). The egret, owl, and swiftlet were government releases for biological control.

Since 1970, all new introductions have been unauthorized and have included parrots and finches. This shift has resulted from a tightening of restrictions imposed on importers by the state of Hawai'i and by changes in federal laws regarding importation and quarantine of birds into the country, particularly by the Wild Bird Conservation Act of 1992. Importers prefer seed-eating birds that can survive the long wait through quarantine rather than the more delicate insectivores and frugivores with their difficult diets; however, other passerines continue to appear occasionally in Honolulu pet stores.

Hundreds of species of parrots and other psittacids are available through the pet trade, and their availability is increasing as new populations are established in captivity. Fortunately, members of the most potentially damaging group, the lories and lorikeets, are prohibited from legal importation into Hawai'i, yet in the past small colonies have been illegally held by private breeders. Many species of these aggressive nectar feeders would thrive in high-elevation rain forests and compete for food with endangered Hawaiian honeycreepers.

Unfortunately, there is little or no accountability for releases of parrots. Three species have established breeding populations, and others are trying. The world's most successfully invasive parrot, the Rose-ring Parakeet (*Psittacula krameri*) now inhabits Kaua'i, O'ahu, Maui, and Hawai'i, though no population estimates exist (Hawaii Audubon Society 1993). From three

birds, an O'ahu population of Red-crowned Amazons (*Amazona viridigenalis*) grew to more than 30 individuals by the late 1980s (T. K. Pratt, pers. obs.). While there are no recent estimates for this parrot, a flock of 40 was seen in 1998 (E. VanderWerf, pers. comm.), suggesting a slow rate of increase. Rapidly growing colonies of Mitred Conure (*Aratinga mitrata* and, possibly, related species) appeared on O'ahu, Maui, and Hawai'i in the 1990s (T. K. Pratt and L. L. Loope, pers. obs.). The Maui, and perhaps the Hawai'i, population of conures stem from deliberate releases. The population in the Huelo area of Maui is expanding, and now numbers at least 80 (F. Duvall, pers. comm.). This species may well become numerous, being adapted in its original range to open and disturbed habitats. We expect escapes and releases of parrots to increase as the number of parrots bred in captivity exceeds the demand for these long-lived birds as pets.

Parrot invasions would seem to pose a threat of additional diseases to Pacific birds. Certainly, agricultural and ecological problems caused by parrots are well-known. Viewed by farmers as little more than winged rodents, parrots damage seed and fruit crops. In Hawai'i, parrots have depredated crops of corn, mangos, and lichee; permits have been issued for their control (T. K. Pratt, pers. obs.). A very serious concern is the potential ecological role of parrots as seed predators and herbivores of native trees. Sulfur-crested Cockatoos (*Cacatua galerita*) introduced to Palau depredate native palms. Cockatoos "fed heavily on the heart of two species of endemic palms, and large stands of these trees have been destroyed" (Engbring 1992:32). The native Hawaiian flora includes many trees and shrubs with large seeds potentially vulnerable to predation by parrots. The role of parrots in the spread of alien plants is unclear. Research is needed to determine which seeds are digested and which are viable after passage. Seeds that pass undigested will be transported long distances by parrots.

Nineteen species of finches (Fringillidae and Passeridae) now swarm the gardens and grasslands of Hawai'i (Pyle 1997). Yet only the House Finch (*Carpodacus mexicanus*), Northern Cardinal (*Cardinalis cardinalis*), Yellow-faced Grassquit (*Tiaris olivacea*), Nutmeg Mannikin (*Lonchura punctulata*), and Common Waxbill (*Estrilda astrild*) reside in edges or gaps in native forests (Scott et al. 1986; T. K. Pratt, pers. obs.). Apart from the House Finch, which serves as a reservoir of avian poxvirus (Warner 1968, Docherty and Long 1986), introduced finches play an undetermined role in transmission of diseases.

Another important component of alien bird

species issues arises from past, successful introductions currently restricted to only one or a few islands but with potential for spread to other islands. Species raising concern include the insectivorous and frugivorous species, which have a potentially great effect on native birds through their ability to colonize native ecosystems and compete with endemic species.

The Red-vented Bulbul (*Pycnonotus cafer*) and Red-whiskered Bulbul (*P. jocosus*), among the worst of all possible avian alien seed dispersers, have been established on Oʻahu since the 1960s (Long 1981) and threaten to spread to other islands. Red-vented Bulbuls discovered on both Maui (F. Duvall, pers. comm.) and Hawaiʻi (R. Bachman, pers. comm.) have been eliminated. The Red-vented Bulbul is a major disperser of the notoriously invasive tree *Miconia calvescens* in Tahiti (Meyer 1996). Continued exclusion of bulbuls from Hawaiian Islands besides Oʻahu must continue to be a very high priority.

The Kalij Pheasant (*Lophura leucomelanos*), a forest pheasant native to Nepal and adjacent countries in central Asia (Long 1981) was legally introduced to Puʻu Waʻawaʻa Ranch on the island of Hawaiʻi in 1962 (Lewin and Lewin 1984). It dispersed rapidly and by the late 1980s had reached the forests of Hawaiʻi Volcanoes National Park on the opposite side of the island, but it has not as yet spread to other islands. Every effort should be made to keep this disperser of alien plants (Lewin and Lewin 1984) off other islands.

Currently, the main source of new alien bird species is the pet trade. The list of birds permitted into the state should be reassessed to eliminate species with high risk of invasion. But even more important is the commitment to eliminate incipient wild populations and to hold owners of released or escaped birds responsible for the effort and cost of recovering free-flying birds.

MAMMALS

Mammals, especially ungulates, rats, and mongooses, have been and continue to be the single group of alien organisms in Hawaiʻi most damaging to native ecosystems. For jeopardizing survival of native birds, impact of mammals is challenged for primacy only by diseases and parasites. As with birds, most established mammals in Hawaiʻi have been intentionally introduced (Tomich 1986). The highly significant exceptions to date are the rats (*Rattus rattus, R. exulans, R. norvegicus*) and mice (*Mus domesticus*), which have successfully established as stowaways on most Pacific islands.

The greatest newly emergent mammalian threat for Hawaiʻi may be the European rabbit (*Oryctolagus cuniculus*). Rabbits have been liberated on at least 700 islands throughout the world. Devastation resulting from their establishment has been well documented in several areas, most notably Laysan, in the Northwest Hawaiian Chain, and Round Island, near Mauritius in the Indian Ocean (Atkinson 1989). The threat of rabbits to Hawaiʻi has been raised by the case of their incipient establishment and eradication (100 removed) in Haleakalā National Park on Maui in 1989–1991 (Loope et al. 1992). Hawaiʻi state statutes permit importation and possession of rabbits, but they specify that they must be kept in cages off the ground (to prevent tunneling). In practice, rabbits commonly escape, and no agency has been given the responsibility for preventing their establishment. Rabbits released in areas without free-ranging dogs (usually, but not necessarily, at high elevations) are likely to multiply and result in geometrically increasing, uncontrollable populations within one to two years; the Haleakalā population was detected after nine months and prompt action taken.

Aside from the usual array of domestic mammals, few other species are commonly kept in captivity in Hawaiʻi. Importation of mammals is tightly regulated, first by authorizing few species for import and second by a lengthy quarantine for rabies in state run facilities, at least for the carnivorous species. We see the rate of new mammalian introductions as much lower than that for other groups of vertebrates. Nineteen species of mammals are established in the wild in Hawaiʻi (Miller and Eldredge 1996). Most invading mammal species still occur on only a few islands, and none have reached their full potential distributional range within Hawaiʻi. Preventing their further spread and mitigating their damage would be worth the effort, as their effects on vulnerable native ecosystems and avifauna can be predicted from evidence of damage where they occur. Hawaiʻi and other Pacific islands should not relax vigilance, since new rodents and insectivores, such as the musk shrew (*Suncus murinus,* nonindigenous in the Mariana Islands), can arrive with increased shipping activity. Undetermined North American shrews have been found alive in shipments of Christmas trees to the islands. The Asian rat, *R. tanezumi,* which is virtually indistinguishable externally from *R. rattus,* is found in the Marianas (Musser and Carleton 1993) and on many other Pacific islands but has not yet been discovered in Hawaiʻi.

For deliberately imported mammals, we view monkeys as the most serious threat to Pacific ecosystems. *Macaca fascicularis,* transported to Mauritius in the seventeenth century, is among the most destructive of alien mammals there, severely damaging native trees and epiphytes and dispersing alien plants (Strahm 1996). We note with alarm that three species of monkeys have become established in Florida (Layne 1997), including the squirrel monkey (*Saimiri sciureus*). A fenced colony of squirrel monkeys maintained by Pana'ewa Zoo in Hilo could potentially be freed by the next hurricane to strike the island of Hawai'i. Ferrets and other small wild carnivores, which are commonly kept as exotic pets (although illegally in Hawai'i; Tomich 1986), also represent serious threats to native birds if any become established.

INVERTEBRATES

Nearly 4,000 species of alien invertebrates have been recorded from Hawai'i (Miller and Eldredge 1996), but many species remain undiscovered, especially the smaller, cryptic ones. More than three-quarters of the established alien invertebrates in Hawai'i are arthropods, which are represented by over 2,500 insect species and over 500 other arthropods (Nishida 1994). Between 15 and 20 alien species of arthropods are added to the list each year (Beardsley 1979), and one or more become pestiferous. Most alien invertebrates arrived inadvertently through commerce, or associated with their purposely introduced hosts. Over one-fifth of the insects and a few other invertebrates were purposefully introduced for biological pest control.

For most of the recorded alien species of invertebrates little is known of their biology and even less of their impacts on native species. What is known indicates that some species can affect native ecosystems in profound ways (Howarth 1985a, Howarth and Ramsay 1991). Alien invertebrates have invaded virtually all ecosystems from the seacoast to the summits of the highest mountains, and probably few native species escape at least some feeding damage. Some change ecosystem processes; for example, earthworms change nutrient cycling in soils thus favoring invasion by alien species (Vitousek and Walker 1989). Over two-thirds of the 750 native land snails are extinct or endangered, and alien predators (particularly the purposefully introduced predatory snail *Euglandina rosea*) are believed to be the major culprits in their decline (Cowie et al. 1995). *Euglandina* has not yet reached its full potential range, and as it expands, it threatens additional populations.

Four phyla contain species that can potentially invade and directly affect the survival of landbirds in Hawai'i. Three of these (Platyhelminthes, Acanthocephala, and Nematoda) include parasitic worms capable of causing disease in birds. A few alien bird-infecting species are known from Hawai'i (references in Miller and Eldredge 1996), but many additional harmful species could be introduced with alien hosts brought in through the pet trade (Nilsson 1981).

The major groups of arthropods affecting native birds are the parasitic and blood-feeding species (including several mites, fleas, and flies) and the insectivorous species (especially wasps) that compete for avian food (Howarth 1985a; G.J. Brenner, pers. comm.). The parasitic and blood-feeding species affect birds not only by causing disease and worrying their hosts, but also by serving as vectors for avian diseases (van Riper 1991). Mosquitoes, especially *Culex quinquefasciatus*, are considered among the most severe current threats to Hawaiian landbirds because they are the vector for malaria, bird pox, and other diseases among wild bird populations (van Riper and van Riper 1985, Jarvi et al. *this volume*, Shehata et al. *this volume*). Only five blood-sucking mosquitoes are established in Hawai'i, but several hundred more could potentially invade if given the chance. Many of these are associated with leaf axils and could be imported with bromeliads, which are currently popular in horticulture. The Central American mosquito, *Wyeomyia mitchellii*, is believed to have arrived in this way in the 1980s.

Unlike many introduced vertebrates, most invertebrates are narrowly specialized to exploit particular environments; thus, to succeed, invading invertebrates generally must find a new environment that closely matches their requirements. Hawai'i, with its benign, perpetual spring-like climate and great range of elevation, temperature, and moisture regimes, could host a large percentage of the world's tropical, subtropical, and warm temperate invertebrates since they could find a suitable environment if given the opportunity. With increasing travel and world commerce, the pool of potential invaders is immense, and a thorough analysis of their potential threats daunting. Thus, we describe examples from just two arthropod groups to illustrate the scope of the problem in hopes of divining long-range solutions.

ANTS (HYMENOPTERA: FORMICIDAE)

Ants are notorious invaders and recognized as a cause of native species extinctions, both in Hawai'i and elsewhere (Cole et al. 1992, Gillespie and Reimer 1993, Hölldobler and Wilson 1994, Reimer 1994, Wilson 1996). Ironically, many of the same invasive ant species are also regarded as beneficial for their role as biocontrol agents (Way and Khoo 1992), and some species have been purposely introduced to new areas for biocontrol (Greenslade 1965, Way and Khoo 1992, Zenner de Polania and Wilches 1992). For example, in the 1980s, a group of businessmen introduced the ant, *Paratrechina fulva,* into Colombia, South America, in an effort to control snakes at lumber mills. Subsequently, Zenner de Polania and Wilches (1992) reported that species richness decreased over 90% in areas invaded by the ant. Native ant species were especially affected, but other arthropods and some vertebrates also declined or completely disappeared from invaded areas.

There are no native ants known in Hawai'i. About 40 species of alien ants are established (Nishida 1994), and of those the 16 species with large, aggressive colonies are the most troublesome (Howarth 1985a, Reimer 1994). There are numerous other ant species that could invade new habitats or attack different prey if they became established in Hawai'i. Two examples are described: the fire ants, which are currently serious invaders of southern North America, and the weaver ants, which are dominant forest canopy predators in the Old World tropics and subtropics.

Fire ants

Two species of fire ants were inadvertently introduced from South America into southeastern United States: *Solenopsis richteri,* which arrived about 1918, and *S. invicta,* which arrived about 1940, and both have become problem invasive species (U.S. Congress 1993, Callcott and Collins 1996). *S. invicta,* especially, has been implicated in the extirpation of native species in areas where it has invaded. *Solenopsis* nests in the ground, usually in open habitats and open woodlands. If these warm temperate species established in Hawai'i, they probably would invade at least low- and mid-elevation dry forests and open country. Their upper elevation limit is unknown, but their subterranean nests are protected from most frosts.

Two species of fire ants already occur in Hawai'i and are widespread on all the main islands. The native North American fire ant, *S. geminata,* prefers to nest in loose soil and sandy areas, and in Hawai'i it remains confined to sandy coastal habitats and in dry leeward areas up to 300 m altitude, mostly in disturbed sites (Huddleston and Fluker 1968, Reimer 1994). *S. papuana* prefers wetter habitats and forests, nesting under rocks or wood on the ground in wet to mesic forests between 300 and 1,100 m. Its large polygyne (multiple-queen) colonies may contain over 1,000 workers (Reimer 1994).

Fire ants are voracious predators of small animals, feeding the protein to their larvae. Few native invertebrates would escape their depredations. Naive ground-nesting birds would be especially vulnerable, if the ants can survive near the bird colonies. Adult ants also feed on sweets such as nectar and honeydew. Thus, they could disrupt reproduction and survival of native plants and favor invasions of certain alien plants and honeydew-producing insects. Many plant and animal extinctions would be expected to occur in invaded habitats.

A colony of *S. invicta* was intercepted in Honolulu in a package from Texas in 1991 (CGAPS 1996). As the species expands its range in North America, it will have greater opportunity to be transported to Hawai'i. *S. invicta* reproduces in two ways: individual fertile queens establishing new colonies, and polygyne colonies dividing and part of the colony walking to a new nest site (Shoemaker and Ross 1996). Polygyne colonies pose a greater invasive threat and are more likely to establish if transported, but they are also far less likely to disperse long distances, although they might be transported to Hawai'i in a containerized shipment or in soil on earth-moving or construction equipment. Fertile females, on the other hand, could become stowaways in planes, cargo, and containers.

Weaver ants

The Asian arboreal weaver ant (*Oecophylla smaragdina* [Fab.]) is widely distributed from Asia to Australia, where it occupies a wide range of forest habitats from savanna and monsoon dry forests to more mesic habitats and rain forests (Hölldobler and Wilson 1994). A closely related species lives in Africa. Weaver ants use their larvae as spindles to weave nests in the canopy, and their ability to select an optimal environment within the canopy for their nests gives the group a wide tolerance for different forest types. Given the Asian weaver ant's known distribution and preferred environments, it would be able to invade all forested habitats in Hawai'i except perhaps the wettest and coldest rain forests.

The ant is a voracious arboreal predator, which can exclude all sensitive animals from its nest tree as well as closely neighboring trees. Colonies can contain 500,000 or more workers and can control a territory of a dozen or more large trees (Hölldobler and Wilson 1994). They control the entire tree surface from the ground up and kill virtually all animals found within their territory (Hölldobler and Wilson 1994). Native forest birds would be naive to such a competitor and probably would be unable to nest or forage near an active ant nest. Both native invertebrates and several native forest bird species, as well as the endangered tree-roosting native bat, would be severely affected, and the extinction of many currently listed species as well as many currently nonendangered species would be expected if this species established in Hawai'i.

The Asian weaver ant is often considered beneficial by farmers, who have lionized the ants and introduced them to their orchards for pest control for centuries (Way and Khoo 1992). The species has been introduced to south Pacific islands for biocontrol of palm pests (Greenslade 1965). However, its effects on either the intended target or potential nontargets have not been recorded. It could be introduced into Hawai'i illegally by well-intentioned gardeners returning from Asia. Less likely is the possibility that fertile queens could arrive as stowaways in aircraft or in shipments of cut flowers or other plant material.

The weaver ant's exceptionally complex behavior makes them popular research animals. The related African species is established in entomological laboratories in the continental United States (Hölldobler and Wilson 1994) and could be moved to Hawai'i. Hölldobler and Wilson (1994) describe a method to transport small colonies within hand luggage on aircraft.

BITING MIDGES (DIPTERA: CERATOPOGONIDAE: *CULICOIDES*)

Biting midges in the genus *Culicoides* are important veterinary and public health pests in most areas of the world (Linley and Davies 1971). There are over 1,000 valid species, and many more still to be discovered and described (Borkent and Wirth 1997). Over 175 species are known from Japan and Southeast Asia (Arnaud 1956, Wirth and Hubert 1989), and about 135 from North America (Wirth 1965). The biology of most species remain unknown. The larvae are scavengers or predators on tiny invertebrates in semi-aquatic and aquatic habitats; larval substrates include damp rotting plant material, animal dung, mud, and soil in tree holes, leaf axils compost heaps, rotting vegetation, margins of water bodies, and a variety of aquatic habitats (Jamnback 1965, Howarth 1985b). Each species prefers particular larval habitats, and in concert most potential larval substrates are exploited.

Adult females of many species are specialized to suck vertebrate blood: some generalists, some attacking birds, others small or large mammals, reptiles, amphibians, or even larger arthropods (Jamnback 1965, Wirth and Hubert 1989). They are important transmitters of diseases, including blood protozoans (especially the primitive bird malarias), filarial worms, viruses, and other parasites among birds (Kettle 1965, Wirth and Hubert 1989). In addition, they also would increase the spread of mechanically transmitted diseases of birds (e.g., avian pox). Adult females of most species are readily dispersed by wind (Linley

and Davies 1971) and attracted to lights at night (Howarth 1985b); thus they could become stowaways on aircraft departing infested areas at night. Leaf axil breeding species could be introduced in bromeliads and other plant material. *Culicoides* are very small; most adults are less than 2 mm long. Unless the species bit humans (which many do) or otherwise became conspicuous, their impact on endangered birds would go unnoticed until too late. To illustrate the potential impacts of these alien species in Hawai'i, the potential threats posed by two species will be described: *C. arakawae* and *C. obsoletus*.

Culicoides arakawae

C. arakawae is widespread in Asia from Japan south to the Indonesian islands and west to India (Arnaud 1956, Wirth and Hubert 1989). The species does well in both tropical and temperate climates, but whether its range results from different strains is unknown. Arnaud (1956) reported it to be the most abundant and widely distributed *Culicoides* in Japan. It breeds in mud and soil at water margins, especially where polluted, such as animal wallows, ditches, flumes, streams, and pools (Kitaoka and Morii 1963, Howarth 1985b). Near Tokyo (35°–36° N), the species has two to three generations per year with a minimum life cycle of 30 days (Kitaoka and Morii 1963). The species probably can breed continuously in the tropics; adults were collected in most months of the year in Laos (Howarth 1985b).

The adults readily attack birds and sometimes mammals (Arnaud 1956), and the species is considered to be the most important vector of the bird protozoan parasite *Leucocytozoon caulleryi*, a serious disease of poultry in east Asia (Kitaoka 1978), and fowl poxvirus (Fukuda et al. 1979). Fowl pox is already recognized as a severe disease among Hawaiian endangered birds (van Riper and van Riper 1985); thus the establishment of an efficient new vector would pose a significant new risk. Adult *C. arakawae* are readily attracted to lights (Arnaud 1956) and are easily transported on the wind; they are, therefore, potential stowaways on aircraft departing from infested areas at night.

Female *C. arakawae* disembarking in Hawai'i would find abundant ideal breeding habitats in the immediate area surrounding most island airports. For example at Kahului, Maui, Kanahā Pond and the irrigation ditches and pools in and near neighboring cane fields would be ideal. From these lowland habitats the species could easily disperse on the wind to rain forest habitats on both east and west Maui. The endangered waterfowl at Kanahā Pond and other wetlands could be severely impacted both from exsanguination and from exposure to new diseases. Breeding habitats may be more limited in the upland rain forests, except for pig wallows and some natural pool margins; however, the species might adapt over time to breed in the constantly moist soil in the wet forests of Hawai'i. If it did become abundant, it could cause the declines of several native forest birds.

Culicoides obsoletus

C. obsoletus is one of the most widespread species of biting midges, occurring in North Africa, Eurasia, and North America (Jamnback 1965). It is recorded from both South Korea and Japan, where it is widespread on Honshu and Hokkaidō (Arnaud 1956). In North America *C. obsoletus* is found from southern Canada to North Carolina and Tennessee in the east and from British Columbia and Alberta to northern California in the west (Jamnback 1965). It is a serious pest of humans and animals on Hokkaidō (Arnaud 1956) and in North America (Jamnback 1965). There are two generations a year (Kitaoka and Morii 1963).

The wide range of larval breeding habitats indicates that the species could become invasive in Hawai'i. Suitable breeding habitats include stream and pond margins and irrigation ditches in the lowlands, as well as moist forest floor in rain forests. If overwintering larvae diapause, they would not be successful in lowland habitats, except as continual re-invaders from upland sites, but this species would probably survive very well in cool upland forests where the major populations of endangered forest birds survive. Emerging females do not require a blood meal to develop their first clutch of eggs, making establishment of colonizers more likely but perhaps decreasing their role in disease transmission. In suitable habitats, they can become incredibly abundant, severely worrying their hosts. Like *C. arakawae,* adult *C. obsoletus* are readily attracted to lights and are potential stowaways on aircraft. Additionally, immatures of this and other problematic species could be inadvertently imported on sphagnum or other moist materials used to pack shipments of living organisms and cut flowers.

In summary, the prospect is grim for future invertebrate introductions unless we can learn how to prevent them and are given the political support (including adequate funding for quarantine) to apply what we have learned. The examples above give only the merest glimpse of the thousands or tens of thousands of potentially damaging species with potential to reach Pacific islands.

PLANTS

Invasions by alien plants can alter the population dynamics and community structure of native species and change the large-scale functioning of native ecosystems (Vitousek 1992). The prevention of recruitment of native plant species by invasive alien plant species is often the mechanism of long-term conversion of ecosystem structure and function (Macdonald et al. 1989). Alien plant invasion in Hawai'i frequently alters ecosystems, jeopardizing and eventually eliminating habitat for most native birds (e.g., Scott et al. 1986, Cuddihy and Stone 1990, Stone et al. 1992). For example, invasion of the vine banana poka (*Passiflora mollissima*) reaches elevations as high as 1,500 m and smothers koa and 'ōhi'a forest, killing mature trees and preventing recruitment, and degrading habitat for native birds (Warshauer et al. 1983, Jacobi and Scott 1985). Shrubs and trees such as clidemia (*Clidemia hirta*), strawberry guava (*Psidium cattleianum*), kāhili ginger (*Hedychium gardnerianum*), firetree (*Myrica faya*), Australian tree fern (*Cyathea cooperi*), and miconia (*Miconia calvescens*) can potentially reach similarly high elevations, alter ecosystems, and degrade bird habitat. At Kanahā and Keālia ponds on Maui, dense thickets of fleabane (*Pluchea indica*) convert extensive areas of habitat for Hawaiian Stilts (Ae'o; *Himantopus mexicanus knudseni*) and Hawaiian Coots ('Alae ke'oke'o; *Fulica alai*) to nonhabitat. In Tahiti, 40–50 species of the 107 plant species endemic to the island are believed to be on the verge of extinction primarily because of invasion of miconia (Meyer and Florence 1997). Effects on bird habitat in Tahiti remain unanalyzed.

Alien plant invasions of Hawai'i and Pacific islands already pose an acute problem in preservation of ecosystems and bird habitat. Much effort is expended in Hawai'i and elsewhere on weed control. Managers of natural areas and agencies are struggling to address immediate problems through manual, chemical, and biological control of invasive alien plants. However, most weed control programs get underway only after an alien species is an obvious problem. Managers and agencies normally have their resources directed at dealing with the major weed problems that are already highly conspicuous.

There is a concurrent urgent need for dealing with incipient and future plant invasions which is only beginning to be addressed. Whereas approximately 100 plant species are currently recognized as serious invaders of native ecosystems in Hawai'i (Smith 1985, Stone et al. 1992), over 8,000 plant species had been introduced to Hawai'i by the late 1980s (Yee and Gagne 1992),

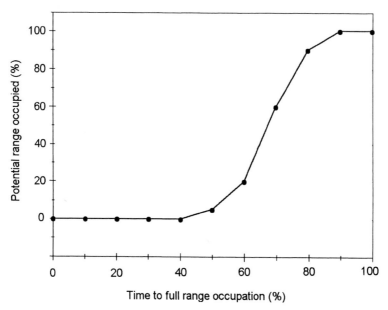

FIGURE 1.   Stylized representation of the spread of an invasive plant species over time (Hobbs and Humphries 1995).

and at least 861 had been recognized as exhibiting reproduction in the wild (Wagner et al. 1990a,b). An ongoing up-to-date analysis of plant introductions in Hawai'i places the number at over 13,000 (G. Staples, Bishop Museum, pers. comm.), or roughly 3–4% of the world's known vascular plant species. A substantial number of the world's most invasive plant species are already present in Hawai'i but not yet widely perceived to exhibit alarming invasiveness. Examples include *Arundo donax* (giant reed), *Cinchona pubescens* (quinine), *Cryptostegia grandiflora* (rubber vine), *Hiptage benghalensis, Ligustrum* spp. (privet), *Lonicera japonica* (Japanese honeysuckle), *Pittosporum undulatum,* and *Thunbergia grandiflora.* Some of these were not included in the 861 species regarded as naturalized by Wagner et al. (1990a,b), and others were included as "sparingly naturalized." Most of them are probably in a so-called "lag phase" (see below).

Furthermore, whereas there is currently government scrutiny of proposed legal introductions of animal species in Hawai'i and many other Pacific islands, there is still almost no government-sponsored effort to prevent the potentially invasive plant species which have not yet reached the shores from being introduced. The phasing out of sugar cane and pineapple in Hawai'i is contributing to a quest for agricultural diversification and experimentation. And with increasing travel combined with botanical curiosity and industry, the number of possible future

experiments in invasive potential becomes enormous. One proponent of enriching Hawai'i's flora with more introductions recently wrote (Bezona 1996), "After visiting Ecuador, I realize we have barely tapped the potential for new plant materials, including bamboo in Hawai'i." A recent effort in Hawai'i at developing defoliator-resistant, nitrogen-fixing trees which can aggressively invade degraded lands of the tropics has hybridized 22 species in the genus *Leucaena* on O'ahu (Brewbaker and Sorensson 1994), creating a source for a new wave of invasion in the Pacific by that genus.

A large amount of literature on alien plant biology, impacts, and management exists in Hawai'i (e.g., Smith 1985, Stone et al. 1992) and worldwide (e.g., Cronk and Fuller 1995, Hobbs and Humphries 1995). Experience in Hawai'i and elsewhere suggests that plant species which have proved invasive when introduced to one part of the world are highly likely to be invasive when introduced to similar habitats elsewhere (Cronk and Fuller 1995, Loope and Stone 1996, Reichard and Hamilton 1997). However, there is often a "lag phase," in which a newly introduced potentially invasive species is slow in spreading and therefore easily controllable (Figs. 1, 2).

Recognizing (1) the desirability of early detection and local eradication of such species (as advocated by Hobbs and Humphries 1995, Westbrooks and Eplee 1996, Loope and Stone 1996), and (2) the increasing danger of arrival of ad-

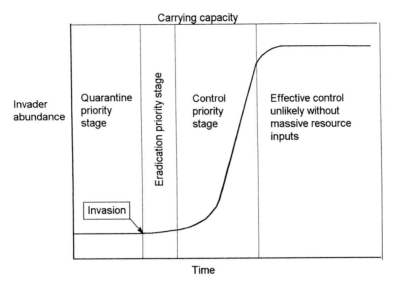

FIGURE 2.   Phases of weed invasion and priorities for action at each phase. Ease of treatment of an invasion problem declines from left to right (Hobbs and Humphries 1995).

ditional potentially invasive species because of accelerating international trade (Jenkins 1996), prompt action to deal with newly emergent and future plant threats is obviously urgently needed. Two examples of the consequences of being "slow on the draw" follow.

Firetree, a small tree from the Azores, Madeira, and the Canary Islands, provides a representative example of the potential for rapid alteration of natural areas. One of the worst invaders in Hawai'i Volcanoes National Park, firetree often forms dense stands that shade out native competitors. It fixes nitrogen in root nodules and alters early successional ecosystems through nutrient enrichment (Vitousek and Walker 1989). Brought to Hawai'i in the 1920s for reforestation, firetree was an incipient invader in Hawai'i Volcanoes National Park in the 1960s, at which time an intense debate arose over whether aggressive control or allowing natural succession to take its course was the proper response (D. Reeser, National Park Service, pers. comm.). In an eight-year period between 1978 and 1986, firetree expanded its range twentyfold within the park (Whiteaker and Gardner 1992). It currently occupies 14,800 ha within Hawai'i Volcanoes National Park in spite of concerted control efforts (Satchell 1997).

The most dramatic current example of an incipient invasive plant threat in the Pacific involves the invasive tree *Miconia calvescens* (Melastomataceae), native to neotropical forests at 300–1,800 m elevation, and now known to be an unusually aggressive invader of moist island habitats. Introduced to Tahiti in 1937, dense thickets of miconia had by the 1980s replaced the native forest over most of the island, with dramatic reduction of biological diversity. After the late F. R. Fosberg saw this species in Tahiti in 1971, he reported that "it is the one plant that could really destroy the native Hawaiian forest." Yet because of its attractive purple and green foliage, it had already been brought to Hawai'i as an ornamental in the 1960s, and nobody did anything about it until it got well established. After its detection on Maui by conservation agencies in 1990, an alarm was raised; miconia seemed to be an especially severe threat to the high-elevation rain forest habitat of many forest birds. Now miconia has become something of a household word in Hawai'i and an aggressive campaign against it is being conducted, especially on the islands of Maui and Hawai'i (Conant et al. 1997, Medeiros et al. 1997), at costs that will soon approach $1,000,000. The government of French Polynesia is also aggressively involved in preventing miconia from taking over forests in islands neighboring Tahiti (e.g., Meyer and Malet 1997). *Miconia* needs to be stopped, and we need to watch out for future miconias.

Unless a proactive approach is taken by governments to prevent continued or even accelerated introduction of invasive weeds, we are very likely to have many more examples like firetree and miconia in the future.

PROSPECTS FOR IMPROVEMENT IN SLOWING INVASIONS

We have attempted to describe the nature of the threats that we believe loom ominously below the tip of the iceberg represented by the currently recognized threats to avian "species on the brink" and Pacific ecosystems in general. Hawai'i is the biological invasions capital of the United States (and consequently the endangered species capital of the United States) and in many ways is at the forefront in confronting the problem, if not yet in effectively dealing with it. Yet biological invasions constitute a national and global problem (Vitousek et al. 1997), and Hawai'i could well be regarded as a laboratory for addressing alien species issues.

Hawai'i is a microcosm—a small world in itself where boundaries are clear, allowing opportunity as well as challenge in dealing with alien species problems. Lessons learned in Hawai'i are highly relevant to other Pacific islands and to continental situations. The state of Hawai'i, dominated by urban politics (with 75% of the state's population on O'ahu, which has <10% of the state's land area), is clearly overwhelmed with the problem. Much more attention to the problem from the federal government as well as from the state government is clearly warranted and desperately needed.

The Honolulu-based interagency Coordinating Group on Alien Pest Species (CGAPS) is an alliance of biodiversity, agriculture, health, and business interests that has been working since 1995 to seriously address the alien pest crises in Hawai'i (Holt 1996). A major public relations campaign was launched in late 1996 to increase public awareness of alien species problems (CGAPS 1996). The intentions of CGAPS are extremely good, but their effectiveness remains to be demonstrated, largely because of an inadequate political (and thus bureaucratic) response to the challenge.

A better-funded, better-staffed, better-equipped, and better-legislated quarantine system for Hawai'i is desperately needed (yet the Hawai'i legislature and agencies involved are not pushing for it). Additionally, early detection and treatment of invaders before explosive spread occurs

can potentially prevent many future problems. As of late 1997, agencies and individuals on the island of Maui, which have been working together at a grassroots level for six years to deal with the weed tree miconia invasion, envision evolution toward an interagency working group with subcommittees dealing with major categories of invaders. The group sees itself as a grassroots component of CGAPS. An island-wide plan would establish categories (exclusion, eradication, containment, large-scale management), and set priorities and responsibilities for pest management. The greatest challenge appears to involve obtaining funding and personnel to do the control work in an era of shrinking government. Is success possible? All agree that public education is a crucial ingredient of the anti-alien species strategy, to gain broad political support. Direct public involvement in selected eradication efforts is an important tool. Achieving and publicizing success stories is an effective strategy. Given much more resources than are currently on the political horizon, Maui's successes and failures could guide efforts statewide.

Concurrent research is needed to (1) examine and explain the lag phase phenomenon for both plants and animals; (2) detect and predict what specific incipient invader populations need attention statewide; (3) determine the specific pathways by which these recent invaders arrived and are being spread in the state; (4) develop techniques for eradicating various groups of invaders once detected; and (5) develop the biological basis for needed legal tools to ameliorate current problems and prevent future problems.

ACKNOWLEDGMENTS

LLL thanks D. Reeser for inspiration, practical progress, and insight for how to realistically confront alien species issues in Hawai'i. FGH thanks N. L. Evenhuis, S. E. Miller, and R. H. Cowie of Bishop Museum for reviewing earlier drafts of the invertebrate section and for locating critical references. FK thanks E. Campbell, R. Crombie, G. Rodda, P. Rosen, and A. Wolf for assistance in locating relevant references.

PRATT
2000

Recovery and Management

Studies in Avian Biology No. 22:306–307, 2001.

RECOVERY AND MANAGEMENT—INTRODUCTION

J. MICHAEL SCOTT AND SHEILA CONANT

Hawai'i has 29 threatened and endangered bird species (see Table 2 following the Introduction to this volume). The most recent assessment of their status indicated that none of the populations are improving, 15 are stable, 8 are declining, and 6 are of uncertain status (USFWS 1996a,b). Despite large increases in personnel and funds for research and management of endangered birds in Hawaii, this disappointing record persists since the passage of the Endangered Species Act in 1973 (Steiner *this volume*). Reasons for this failure to restore species to healthy self-sustaining populations are indicative of the complexity of the problem and the pervasiveness of threats. There are examples where a limiting factor is clearly identified and its impact on the species is fully documented and we still failed to take action over areas large enough to be biologically meaningful.

Perhaps the best documented example is the loss of habitat for the Palila (*Loxioides baileui*) across its range by feral ungulates browsing on māmane (*Sophora chrysophylla*), an important plant to the Palila (Warner 1960, Scowcroft 1983, Scowcroft and Giffin 1983, Juvik and Juvik 1984, Scowcroft and Sakai 1984, Scott et al. 1984). In 1979, the Ninth Circuit Court ruled that feral sheep (*Ovis aries*) and goats (*Capra hircus*) maintained by the state of Hawai'i for hunting were threatening the survival of the Palila. The feral ungulates browsed on māmane trees that provide food, nesting sites, and cover for Palila. Damage to Palila habitat by these feral species was found to be a violation of Section 9 of the Endangered Species Act, in response to a suit filed by the Sierra Club "Palila vs. Hawaii Department of Natural Resources" ("Palila II") by the Ninth Circuit Court of Appeals (Bean and Rowland 1997). In 1985, this decision was affirmed and broadened to include mouflon (*Ovis musimon*). Methods to eliminate ungulates from such large areas are well documented and have been clearly demonstrated in Hawai'i at Hawai'i Volcanoes National Park and Haleakalā National Park (Taylor and Katahira 1988). Despite a clear legal mandate, 20 years later there are still hundreds of sheep and mouflon within critical habitat of the Palila on Mauna Kea (M. Sherwood, pers. comm.). Additionally, there is no systematic effort to eliminate rats (*Rattus* spp.) and cats (*Felis catus*), known avian predators, from this area. If there is an inability, or unwillingness of the responsible agency, in this case the Hawaii Department of Land and Natural Resources, to intervene on behalf of the last remaining individuals of an endangered endemic Hawaiian bird, can we hold out much hope for the endangered plants and invertebrates?

A number of very positive things have been done on behalf of Hawai'i's beleaguered endemics. The Nature Conservancy has established nature reserves on Maui, Moloka'i, and O'ahu. These areas are being managed for the long-term viability of native species. As previously stated, goats and pigs (*Sus scrofa*; Katahira et al. 1993) have been eliminated from Hawai'i Volcanoes National Park and Haleakalā National Park. Native vegetation is coming back in these areas and the endangered Hawaiian silversword (*Argyroxiphium sandwicense*) has increased dramatically in numbers. On privately owned Keauhou Ranch, scarification of soil and replanting of koa trees (*Acacia koa*) have resulted in dramatic increases in the numbers of endangered 'Akiapōlā'au (*Hemignathus munroi*; T. Pratt pers. comm.). The Ōla'a, Kilauea, partnership involving Hawai'i state prisons, Kamehameha Schools, and Hawai'i Volcanoes National Park is managing more than 10,000 hectares of mid-elevation native forests to benefit native species. Such public-private partnerships bode well for the future (Stone 1985).

Other actions taken on behalf of endangered birds are documented in the following articles. Cathleen Hodges and Ronald Nagata demonstrate the importance of predator control for cats and small Indian mongoose (*Herpestes auropunctatus*) in improving the reproductive success of the Dark-rumped Petrel (*Pterodroma phaeopygia sandwichensis*). However, despite this and other earlier demonstrations of the harm caused by nonnative predators and the effectiveness of predator control in improving nesting success of burrowing seabirds (Coulter et al. 1985, Johnstone 1985, Tomkins 1985, Veitch 1985), there are breeding colonies on Hawai'i and Kaua'i where no predator control actions are being taken. Such failure to act on behalf of this endangered species is extremely disappointing. Frederike Woog and Jeffery Black discuss the role of managed grasslands in providing quality food for the Nēnē (*Branta sandvicensis*). Diane Drigot documents the role of ecosystem management in enhancing waterbird habitat on military lands. Sheila Conant and Marie Morin ask why the Nihoa Millerbird (*Acrocephalus familiaris kingi*) is not extinct and discuss the management possibilities for the dangerously small population. Steven Fancy and co-authors document methods used in translocating small passerine species, whereas Cyndi Kuehler and co-authors document methods suitable for the captive rearing of endemic Hawaiian birds. Paul Banko and co-authors provide details regarding the effectiveness of ongoing recovery efforts, and William Steiner concludes with an assessment of costs.

Studies in Avian Biology No. 22:308–318, 2001.

EFFECTS OF PREDATOR CONTROL ON THE SURVIVAL AND BREEDING SUCCESS OF THE ENDANGERED HAWAIIAN DARK-RUMPED PETREL

CATHLEEN S. NATIVIDAD HODGES AND RONALD J. NAGATA, SR.

Abstract. Haleakalā, Maui, hosts the world's largest known nesting colony of endangered Hawaiian Dark-rumped Petrels (*Pterodroma phaeopygia sandwichensis*), or ʻUaʻu, with about 900 known nests. In 1979, introduced predators were identified as significant limiting factors for the Hawaiian Dark-rumped Petrel at Haleakalā National Park. Small Indian mongooses (*Herpestes auropunctatus*) were identified as major predators, with cats (*Felis catus*) being secondary. In 1981, the National Park Service implemented an extensive trapping program to protect the Hawaiian Dark-rumped Petrel colony and outlying areas from predators. Since then, about 300 live traps of various sizes have been monitored.

This paper expands on a 1993 National Park Service study comparing reproductive success before and after trapping, and in areas protected and unprotected from predators. Significant differences in nesting activity and nesting success varied from year to year. In all years except two, protected sites showed significantly higher nesting activity and success. This suggests that predator control has a positive effect on protecting the Hawaiian Dark-rumped Petrel nesting habitat.

Key Words: Dark-rumped Petrel; endangered species; Haleakalā birds; Hawaiian Petrel; predation; predator control; seabird breeding success; seabird management; ʻUaʻu.

There are two subspecies of Dark-rumped Petrels (*Pterodroma phaeopygia*): the Hawaiian Dark-rumped Petrel (*P. p. sandwichensis*), and the Galápagos Dark-rumped Petrel (*P. p. phaeopygia*). Both are endangered under the federal Endangered Species Act of 1973. The Hawaiian Dark-rumped Petrel, hereafter referred to by its Hawaiian name ʻUaʻu, was once numerous throughout the Hawaiian Islands. Munro (1955) refers to comments by people on the island of Molokaʻi of ʻUaʻu arriving at Pelekunu Valley in numbers large enough to darken the sky. Populations are now confined to higher elevations (Banko 1980d).

Habitat loss, predation, and hunting are major causes of endangerment of the world's island birds (King 1984). In Hawaiʻi, several species of introduced mammals contributed to the decline of native bird populations (Moors and Atkinson 1984, Stone 1989, Bailey and Kaiser 1993, Seto 1994, Seto and Conant 1996). Introduced herbivores, such as cattle and goats, browse on vegetation in seabird colonies and often trample nests. On island ecosystems such as Hawaiʻi, mammalian predators feast on seabirds that have, for the most part, evolved in predator-free environments. The effects of an individual predator, such as a small Indian mongoose (*Herpestes auropunctatus*), can be extremely destructive to a population of colony-nesting seabirds (Simons 1983, Bartle et al. 1993). Most seabirds are long-lived and have low adult mortality, delayed maturity, small clutch sizes, long nesting periods, and low annual productivity. Continuous predation of breeding adults by an individual predator can cause extinction of a seabird population. Seabird life-history patterns prevent rapid replacement of depredated adults (Moors and Atkinson 1984, Simons 1984).

Natural and unnatural events affect the reproductive success of seabirds. Natural events include climate changes such as El Niño events (Wilson 1991, Ribic et al. 1992, Duffy 1993), direct and indirect disturbance by native predators (Tomkins 1985, Furness and Monaghan 1987, Reichel and Glass 1989, Paine et al. 1990, Burness and Morris 1993), and competition with other seabird species (Furness and Monaghan 1987, Harrison 1990). Unnatural events, such as habitat degradation and loss, predation by introduced predators, and direct and indirect disturbance by humans, are extremely detrimental to seabird breeding success (Simons 1983, Feare 1984, Vermeer and Rankin 1984, Atkinson 1985, Litvinenko 1993, Bailey and Kaiser 1993, Seto 1994, Seto and Conant 1996).

Olson and James (1982a) found fossil evidence of breeding ʻUaʻu near sea level. It appears that Polynesian activities in lowland areas exterminated ʻUaʻu populations before European arrival to the Hawaiian Islands. Predation by dogs (*Canis familiaris*), pigs (*Sus scrofa*), and Polynesian rats (*Rattus exulans*) introduced by the Polynesians (see van Riper and Scott *this volume*) further decreased the numbers of ʻUaʻu. However, the primary cause of ʻUaʻu decline may have been the large-scale harvest of the chicks by the Polynesians, as evident by abundant fossils found in middens and lava tubes (Olson and James 1982a, Moniz 1997). The Polynesians considered 'Ua'u nestlings a delicacy for exclusive consumption by chiefs (Henshaw 1902a). Each season, the chiefs sent hunters to retrieve these delicacies. Hunters used dogs to locate 'Ua'u nests in the early 1900s (Kramer 1971). They inserted sticks into the burrows then twisted the stick to become entangled into the downy feathers of the chicks. The chicks were then easily pulled out of the nests and taken.

European arrival to the islands in the late 1700s brought the introduction of additional predators including roof rats (*Rattus rattus*), Norway rats (*R. norwegicus*), cats (*Felis catus*), and more dogs. Rats have been identified as predators of burrow-nesting seabirds. On Midway Atoll, Hawai'i, roof rats preyed upon Bonin Petrel (*Pterodroma hypoleuca*) eggs significantly decreasing Bonin Petrel reproductive success (Seto 1994, Seto and Conant 1996).

In 1883 sugar planters brought the small Indian mongoose to Hawai'i to control rats in the cane fields (Kramer 1971). Simons (1983) identified mongooses as the primary predator of the 'Ua'u. In 1979, he observed high rates of predation (34% of active burrows) and initiated a trapping scheme to remove this predator from the Haleakalā colony.

Europeans introduced, in the late 1700s to 1800s, several domesticated animals as gifts to the Hawaiian royalty (Kramer 1971). Cattle (*Bos taurus*), horses (*Equus caballos*), sheep (*Ovis aries*), and goats (*Capra hircus*) were released into the wild. The Hawaiian royalty protected these animals with a kapu (forbidding law), much to the detriment of the Hawaiian environment and the already shrinking seabird habitat. Newcomers also introduced game animals such as the European wild boar (*Sus scrofa*), axis deer (*Axis axis*), and mouflon sheep (*Ovis musimon*) to Hawai'i, compounding the habitat alteration.

There is no documentation that feral goats or pigs prey upon 'Ua'u. However, together with other introduced herbivores, these animals cause indirect negative affects on the 'Ua'u. These herbivores devastated Hawai'i's natural landscape by overgrazing and accelerated erosion by trampling over the landscape (Haleakalā National Park, unpubl. data). Simons (1983) noted negative effects of goats and pigs on 'Ua'u nesting areas. Goats chose bedding sites on or near 'Ua'u burrows and caused burrows to collapse. Furness (1988) found that sheep (*Ovis* sp.) and elk (*Cervus elaphus*) preyed upon tern and skua chicks living on Foula, Shetland. Pigs in the Galápagos destroyed petrel burrows by rooting and preyed upon both birds and eggs (Harris 1970).

The known surviving populations of 'Ua'u are probably nesting in suboptimal high-elevation habitat. Maui (Krushelnycky et al. *this vol-*

ume) and Hawai'i (Hu et al. *this volume*) are the only Hawaiian Islands with known active 'Ua'u nests. Currently, about 95% of the known breeding population occur in and around Haleakalā Crater of Haleakalā National Park on the island of Maui (Fig. 1). About 50 nests are on the island of Hawai'i at the higher elevations of Hawai'i Volcanoes National Park on Mauna Loa (Hu et al. *this volume*; D. Hu, pers. comm.). Although nests have not been found, a nesting population of 'Ua'u is thought to exist on Kaua'i (Ainley et. al 1997a; B. Cooper and R. Day, unpubl. report). 'Ua'u have been heard on the islands of Lāna'i and Moloka'i, but nests have not yet been found (Simons 1983).

On Maui, J. Larson (unpubl. report) conducted the initial studies in 1967 that identified and mapped the first 'Ua'u burrows near the summit of Haleakalā. From 1968 to 1980, J. Kunioki (unpubl. report) found and observed about 400 of the 900 known burrows that are now monitored. His work was limited to the summer months and did not include the fledgling season. Simons (1983) from 1979 to 1981 was the first to conduct comprehensive monitoring of 'Ua'u nests throughout the entire breeding season. Nest checks were continued by W. Han from 1982 through 1984 (unpubl. report).

Simons (1983) trapped extensively for predators in the 'Ua'u colony from 1979 through 1981. In 1981, the National Park Service expanded upon Simons' initial predator trapping program to include much of the western area outside the primary 'Ua'u colony. Since then, live traps of various sizes have been checked and baited on a weekly basis.

Haleakalā National Park began regular, thorough monitoring of 'Ua'u nests in 1988. Nests were checked at least once a month from mid-February through the end of October. Monitoring efforts were concentrated in the inner west rim of Haleakalā Crater. Other areas were visited as time and personnel allowed. Visits to these peripheral subcolonies were sometimes limited to once or twice during the entire breeding season.

Haleakalā National Park initiated construction of a boundary fence in 1976. The goal was to protect the park's ecosystems from feral animals, particularly pigs and goats. The fence is made of 1.2-m high hog wire, with two strands of barbed wire running parallel to the top of the hog wire. The maximum height of the fence is 1.5 m. Approximate mesh size is 15 cm^2. Since completion of the boundary fence around the Crater District of the park in 1988, goat and pig populations have been reduced to zero, with occasional ingress of animals. These vagrant ani-

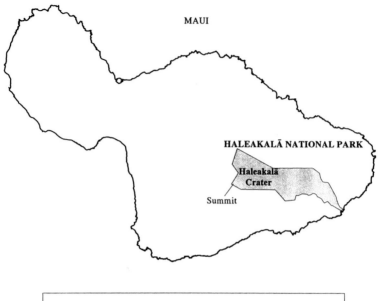

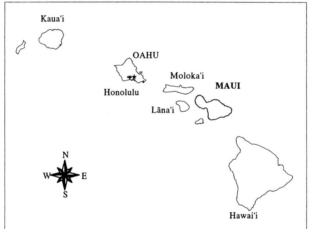

FIGURE 1. Major Hawaiian Islands and Haleakalā National Park on the island of Maui.

mals are immediately removed when found (Haleakalā National Park, unpubl. data).

In 1993, Hodges (1994) conducted a study to determine the effectiveness of predator control on the breeding success of the 'Ua'u. This study found that predator control has a positive effect on 'Ua'u breeding success and survival. The study also found that habitat protection through feral animal fencing and eradication may provide additional protection for the 'Ua'u nesting colony.

In this paper, we further examine the effects of predator control on 'Ua'u nesting activity and success. We also make inferences on the effects of feral ungulate control on 'U'au nesting. We utilize all available data collected from previous years.

METHODS

STUDY SITE

Mount Haleakalā is a dormant shield volcano that defines east Maui and is over half the land mass of the island of Maui. Haleakalā National Park extends from sea level to the 3,055 m summit of Mount Haleakalā (Fig. 1). Haleakalā Crater is a large erosional depression, about 1,000 m deep, and is about half the land area of Haleakalā National Park.

The highest concentration of 'Ua'u nests are along the inside west rim of Haleakalā Crater from about 2,400 to 3,055 m above sea level (Fig. 2). Other nests are in other locations of the crater and along the outer west slope. The nesting habitat consists of large boulders, rocky outcrops, and cinder fields (Simons 1983, Brandt et al. 1995). Vegetation is still sparse (probably resulting from almost 200 years of feral herbivore

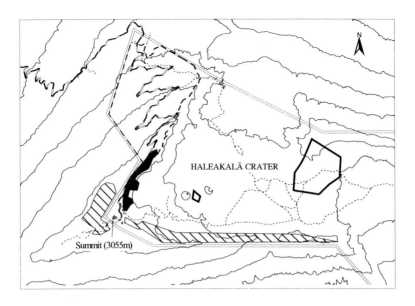

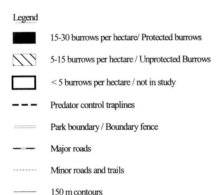

FIGURE 2.   Location of 'Ua'u burrows, predator control traps, and fences.

browsing) and consists of native shrubs and bunch grass. Shrubs are within 0.1 to 5 m of 'Ua'u burrows.

PREDATOR CONTROL

There are about 300 live traps protecting the 'Ua'u and the endangered Hawaiian Goose or Nēnē (*Branta sandvicensis*) populations of Haleakalā National Park (Fig. 2). Traps are along the park's boundary, road sides, ridge tops, hiking trails, pathways where predators have been sighted, and near buildings. Sixty-eight traps are directly within the 'Ua'u colony, while the remaining traps are at lower elevations outside the colony (Fig. 2). We use live traps as a precaution against accidental capture of the ground-nesting 'Ua'u and Nēnē. Both birds have been caught in these traps (Haleakalā National Park, unpubl. data).

Predator control has been continuous since 1981. Information on predator catch was used as a measure of predator activity inside and outside the 'Ua'u colony. We calculate catch per trap day from all trapping information collected from 1981 to 1996 to examine trends in predator catch.

NEST MONITORING

'Ua'u are at the Haleakalā colony from mid-February through late November (Simons 1983; Haleakalā National Park, unpubl. data). Nests were checked during these months.

Nests were monitored using direct and indirect methods. Direct methods involved viewing nests by looking through the burrow entrance or other opening to the nest chamber with a flashlight, or by use of a remote camera. Indirect methods involved placing toothpicks, about 2.5 cm apart, at the burrow entrance and recording any signs of 'Ua'u activity. Simons (1983) and Hodges (1994) found that the indirect method of using toothpicks was as valid at determining nesting activity and nesting success as were direct methods. Prior to the start of each season and after

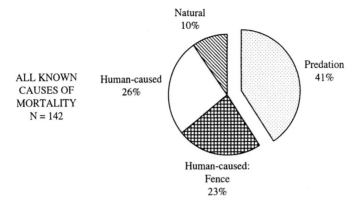

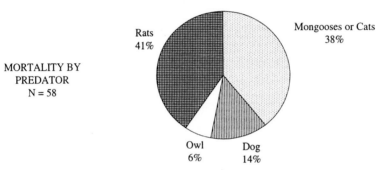

FIGURE 3.   Known causes of 'Ua'u mortality 1964–1996.

every burrow check, each burrow was cleared of all signs of 'Ua'u activity.

We classified each burrow as "entered" or "not entered" by 'Ua'u. Adult 'Ua'u weigh about 435 g, the body size of a small chicken, and have a wing span of about 98 cm (Simons 1983). 'Ua'u leave prominent foot prints and guano at the burrow entrances. Nests were considered "entered" by 'Ua'u if at least three consecutive toothpicks were displaced during subsequent checks and foot prints or guano were evident. "Not entered" were those burrows with all toothpicks intact, or displacement of single or alternate toothpicks (i.e., down, up, down). The distinction between intact and alternately displaced toothpicks were recorded as possible rat entries may occur. In addition, any signs of activity (evidence of burrow excavation, feathers, eggshells, etc.) in and near the burrow were noted.

We determined the final status of each nest at the end of each season. Burrows that were "entered" for three or more checks throughout the season were considered "active." Simons (1983) indicated that failed and nonbreeders depart by mid-September. 'Ua'u chicks exiting burrows prior to fledging leave large amounts of downy feathers in front of nests (Simons 1983, Hodges 1994). Burrows were documented as "fledged chick" if "active" after 15 September and downy feathers were present at the burrow entrance.

NESTING ACTIVITY AND SUCCESS

To determine the effectiveness of the predator control program, we compared nesting activity and nesting success between protected and unprotected sites (Fig. 2). Protected sites were near predator control traps. Unprotected sites were those not in protected areas. Although the southeastern colony lies within the park's boundary fence, we considered those nests unprotected since traps have never been placed in that area. The fence mesh is large enough for easy entry to the colony by mongooses, cats, and rats.

Numbers of burrows surveyed and frequency of checks varied from year to year. We used all available data from 1982, when traps were placed in the 'Ua'u colony, to 1996 to determine the effectiveness of predator control.

Data from 7- to 10-day checks indicated that monthly checks were as accurate as 7- to 10-day checks to determine nesting activity. Burrow checks occurring twice a month were as accurate as 7- to 10-day checks to determine nesting success. (See below for definitions of nesting activity and nesting success.) We therefore used data from burrows that were checked at least once month from February through September, and twice a month from September through November. We also used data from years where at least 30 bur-

TABLE 1.   Comparison of nesting activity and nesting success of 'Ua'u between protected and unprotected sites

Year	Nesting activity (%)			Nesting success (%)		
	Protected	Unprotected	Pa	Protected	Unprotected	Pa
1982	37.25	35.00	0.074	32.73	0	0.002
1990	78.13	80.00	0.082	49.18	10.00	0.0006
1991	69.70	53.09	0.003	48.64	25.58	0.003
1992	54.96	23.08	<0.001	16.97	15.15	0.79
1993	66.47	33.68	<0.001	38.19	32.81	0.414
1994	43.45	35.46	0.09	23.01	44.00	0.002
1995	75.00	64.71	0.11	50.00	31.82	0.03
1996	70.39	88.17	0.001	46.73	28.05	0.009

[a] P-value derived from chi-square and Fisher's exact tests comparing protected and unprotected nests.

rows per site were checked. Years with sufficient data on 'Ua'u nests surveyed for both the protected and unprotected sites were 1982 and 1990 through 1996.

Simons (1983) found that nesting activity is a good indicator of 'Ua'u population health. We defined nesting activity as the proportion of burrows surveyed that show signs of burrow activity. We defined nesting success as the proportion of active burrows that show signs of fledging chicks. Nesting activity and success were compared between protected and unprotected sites using chi-square test and the Fisher exact test for comparing two proportions (Zar 1984).

MORTALITIES

Information on 'Ua'u mortalities is available from 1964 to 1996. All carcasses or abandoned eggs were examined and cause of mortality was identified when possible. From 1992 to 1996, prior to the return of 'Ua'u to the crater each year, all areas were cleared of 'Ua'u carcasses and abandoned eggs. Causes of mortality were placed into one of four categories: (1) natural causes; (2) human-caused; (3) human-caused by fence; and (4) predation. Mortality by natural causes included death due to old age, eggs pushed out of nests that were not disturbed by predators, 'Ua'u flying into rocky outcrops, etc. Human-caused mortality included road kills, caved-in burrows, collision into human-built structures, etc. We defined the boundary fence as a separate category (human-caused by fence) of human-caused mortality to identify the impact of the boundary fence, and to modify the fence to decrease 'Ua'u mortality. Mortality from predation and all other causes were compared.

PREDATION IDENTIFICATION

Characteristics of predation by each type of predator have been identified (Simons 1983, Tomkins 1985, Hodges 1994). We used these characteristics to identify predation by mongoose, dog, cat, rat, or owl on the 'Ua'u. Mongooses punctured a small hole on the side of the egg, licked out the contents of the egg, punctured the back of the bird's neck, and possibly decapitated adults. Dogs scattered limbs and feathers over a wide area and mutilated carcasses. Cats crunched the back of the 'Ua'u skull and left both wings attached to a slightly chewed carcass stripped of most flesh (often called a "bridle carcass"). Rats left remnants of unevenly chewed pieces of eggshell,

moved eggs out of burrows, drank or ate the contents, and abandoned the almost empty shell. Rats also dragged chick carcasses from the burrows to sheltered areas (called 'ratteries') where food debris including petrel bones, accumulated. Rats left fresh droppings at burrows of missing chicks, and the vegetation platforms used as 'Ua'u nests were scattered. Owls neatly plucked the 'Ua'u body and usually only ate viscera and pectoral muscles.

RESULTS

NESTING ACTIVITY

Five of eight years showed significant differences in nesting activity between protected and unprotected sites (Table 1). Years with significant differences (P < 0.10) were 1991, 1992, 1993, 1994, and 1996. In all years except 1996, nesting activity was significantly higher in protected sites.

NESTING SUCCESS

Six of eight years showed significant differences in nesting success between protected and unprotected sites (Table 1). Years with significant differences (P < 0.10) were 1982, 1990, 1991, 1994, 1995, and 1996. In all years except 1994, nesting success was significantly higher in protected sites.

MORTALITIES

Data from 1964 through 1996 indicate 230 documented mortalities of birds and eggs with 142 having known causes. Predation accounted for 41% of all known mortalities (Fig. 3). Of these instances of predation, 41% were rats, 39% were cats or mongooses, 14% were dogs, and 6% were owls.

Human-caused mortalities accounted for 49% of all known mortalities (Fig. 3). These mortalities were due primarily to collision with human structures such as poles, buildings, vehicles, lights, and fences. The park's boundary fences accounted for 23% of all mortalities. Ten percent of all mortalities were from natural causes.

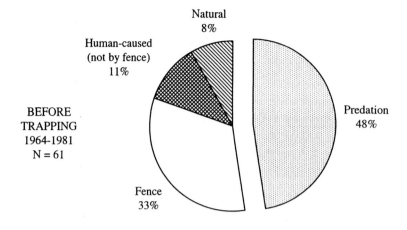

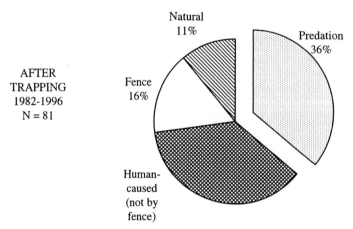

FIGURE 4.   Causes of 'Ua'u mortality before and after trapping.

Comparison of mortalities before (1964–1981) and after (1982–1996) trapping indicates that known instances of predation decreased from 48% of all known mortalities (Fig. 4; N = 61) to 36% (N = 81). However, there was no significant difference between predation and other causes of mortality before and after trapping (P = 0.159).

Since the inception of the predator control trapline, there have been only seven instances of cat and mongoose predation in 15 years. Instances of predation by other predators (rats, dogs, owls) remain minimal (25 in 15 years), but still persist. Dog predation was relatively high from 1990 to 1993 (4, 2, 2, and 1 instance per year, respectively) with all instances occurring outside the park's fence and in a colony that is adjacent to a state of Hawai'i public hunting

area. Gut content analysis of one dog caught in that area revealed 'Ua'u remains.

PREDATOR CATCH AND ACTIVITY

The majority of catches from the traps within the 'Ua'u colony were rats (Fig. 5). Data from traplines outside the 'Ua'u colony are useful for determining the source of predators to the 'Ua'u colony. Rat catches were higher outside the colony, but have been consistent for the past 15 years (Fig. 6). This suggests that rats persist within the colony and that trapping simply keeps rat populations from increasing.

Mongooses and cats were caught at very low numbers both in and outside the 'Ua'u colony, but they were caught at higher rates outside the colony (Fig. 6). Inside the colony, mongooses and cats were rarely caught, but outside the col-

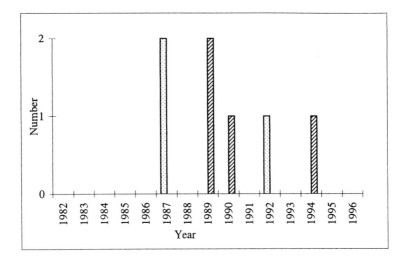

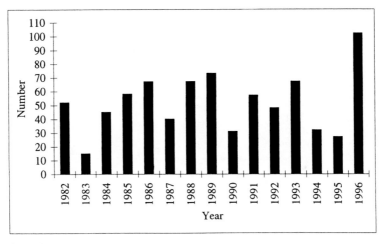

Legend

☐ MONGOOSES
▨ CATS
■ RATS

FIGURE 5. Numbers of predators caught within the 'Ua'u colony.

ony the catch increased. There has been no observed predation from cats or mongooses in the years when these predators were caught in the colony. This suggests that the few mongooses and cats that enter the 'Ua'u colony are trapped before they are able to cause harm to the 'Ua'u.

DISCUSSION

EFFECTS OF INTRODUCED PREDATORS

Significant differences in nesting activity and nesting success suggest that predator control trapping has positive effects on the 'Ua'u. Except for 1994 and 1996 in which the unprotected sites had a higher nesting activity and nesting success rates, respectively, all other years showed higher activity or success in protected sites (Table 1).

The fact that nesting activity and nesting success rates from within and outside areas subject to trapping did not differ significantly in some years is not surprising. Mongooses and cats in areas without traps (unprotected burrows) may

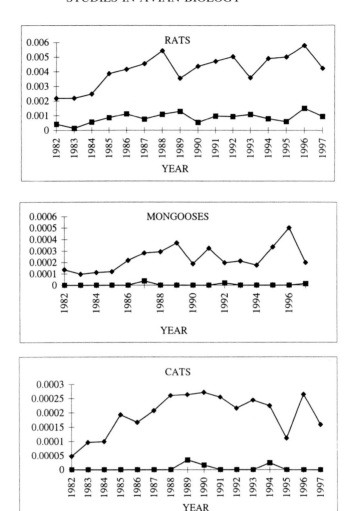

CATCH PER TRAP DAY

Legend

→ OUTSIDE

→ WITHIN

FIGURE 6. Yearly rat, mongoose, and cat catches from outside and within the 'Ua'u colony.

travel into areas with traps and may subsequently be captured. Also, numbers of predators near the 'Ua'u colony may be low since removal efforts have been continuous for 15 years. Existing traps may be capturing predators that would otherwise travel to untrapped areas.

The higher catch of mongooses and cats at lower elevations indicates that these predators will continue to pose a threat to the high-elevation 'Ua'u colonies (Hu et al. *this volume*). Simons (1983) found that one mongoose or one cat could prey upon large numbers 'Ua'u. It is possible for mongoose or cat predation to go undetected in the 'Ua'u colonies. Areas where egg-shell fragments are found should be thoroughly examined for mongoose or cat presence.

There is continuous catch of cats and mongooses and evidence of these predators breeding in lower elevations (Hodges 1994). These adjacent areas may be acting as a source habitat for predators and that our 'Ua'u colony may be a sink (Pulliam 1988, Howe et al. 1991). The source for predators from areas outside the park is high. Maui County Humane Society annual reports (unpubl. data) from 1992, 1993, and 1995 show that almost 6,000 cats and about 3,000 dogs were received each year. Of six possible location sources throughout Maui, 34% of the cats and 44% of the dogs came from the area adjacent to the park.

It is conceivable that cats, and possibly mongooses, travel far into the 'Ua'u nesting area. Rood (1986) cites the home range of mongooses in Fiji as 0.39 km² where population densities were 50 mongooses per km². Apps (1986) found that the home range of cats was 0.62 to 1.50 km² on Marion Island, South Africa, where population densities were 4 to 5 cats per km². Future research may be needed to determine the home range of cats and mongooses at Haleakalā.

Feral cats are frequently sighted throughout the park (Haleakalā National Park, unpubl. data). Cats are captured, but some appear evasive to current predator control techniques. Field personnel continuously report cat tracks and droppings in areas with traps. This indicates that cats persist within the park and continue to threaten the 'Ua'u population. Small-scale predation can be detrimental to endangered bird populations such as the 'Ua'u (Karl and Best 1982, van Reusenburg and Bester 1988, Rodriguez-Estrella et al. 1991). Cats from these studies severely decreased populations of nesting birds.

It is clear that trapping is only partially effective on rats since rat predation is still being detected. Rodent populations persist in the 'Ua'u colony and appear to have both direct and indirect negative effects on reproductive success. Rats appear to have preyed upon eggs and to have disturbed breeding adults. On Midway Atoll, rat predation on Bonin Petrel eggs caused a dramatic decline in the breeding population (Seto and Conant 1996). Arthropods and vegetation in the 'Ua'u colonies, many of which are endemic, are prominent diet items and allow rats to persist at higher elevations (F. Cole et al., unpubl. report). Healthy populations of house mice (*Mus domesticus*) exist at elevations equivalent to the 'Ua'u colony throughout the year. Together with the persistent rat population, these rodents serve as prey bases for mongoose and cat populations (Stone 1989). This allows for the potential existence of mongooses and cats in the 'Ua'u colony, even after the 'Ua'u have left from the Haleakalā colony for the season. Seto and Conant (1996) found that control of rats with a rodenticide significantly suppressed rat numbers on Midway Atoll. This decreased the instances of rat predation on eggs and increased Bonin Petrel breeding success. In January 1997, diphacinone (an anticoagulant) was placed in the 'Ua'u colony to lower rat populations. The effectiveness of this toxicant needs to be examined.

OTHER IMPACTS ON 'UA'U

The boundary fence protects Haleakalā's ecosystem from ingress of goats and pigs. Unprotected areas had higher nesting success in 1994, and nesting activity in 1996. This may be attributed to habitat regeneration. Revegetation and soil retention has improved within the park's boundary since removal of feral ungulates (Haleakalā National Park, unpubl. data). It is therefore conceivable that 'Ua'u benefit from overall habitat protection. Feral ungulates no longer pose a threat by collapsing nests. Soil retention may make for more suitable habitat for these burrowing birds. Additionally, the boundary fence prevents dogs from entering the colony and preying upon 'Ua'u.

The boundary fence has, unfortunately, caused 'Ua'u mortalities since 1976. The bulk of the mortalities occurred from 1986 to 1988. Fences are routinely inspected for breaks, thus making detection of fence-caused mortality very thorough. Most of the 'Ua'u caught were found impaled on the barbed wire portion of the fence. Beginning in 1987, Haleakalā National Park crews removed these two top strands of barbed wire in all the areas where 'Ua'u were snagged. This reduced the fenced-caused mortality of 'Ua'u to almost zero (Haleakalā National Park, unpubl. data). Although 'Ua'u mortalities occur because of the fence, new nests that produce young each year are constantly found. Additionally, the number of total nests have increased from 659 in 1990 to 986 in 1996. Goat herds as large as 50 have been sighted in the southwestern 'Ua'u colony outside the park as recently as January 2000. If fences are removed to prevent further mortality, goats and pigs would return to the park and reverse 10 years of ecosystem recovery in the crater. Larger predators such as lost hunting dogs might enter the park and through breaks in the fence devastate the main 'Ua'u colony.

Our data found that few 'Ua'u were killed by owls. Harris (1970) found owls to be prominent predators on the Galápagos Dark-rumped Petrel. The native Short-eared Owl (*Asio flammeus sandwichensis*), known by its Hawaiian name Pueo, are frequently sighted throughout the park and appear to be increasing. Sightings of the introduced Barn Owl (*Tyto alba*) in the park have increased (Haleakalā National Park, unpubl. data). Owl predation may have been minimal in the past because the owl population consisted only of the crepuscular Pueo. Predation upon the nocturnally active 'Ua'u by owls may increase as the nocturnally active Barn Owl population expands.

A recent threat to the Haleakalā ecosystem is

the increasing population of axis deer on Maui. Recent observations and high-end estimates put the axis deer population at up to 10,000 on East Maui (Maui Axis Deer Group, pers. comm.). The park's fences are too low to prevent the deer from jumping into the park. However, higher fences may result in a significant increase in 'Ua'u mortality as observed in the past. If this deer becomes established in the park, its destructive activities will be far worse than feral goats. Current axis deer management at Haleakalā includes monitoring of deer during fence inspections and trapline maintenance. Sightings inside the park's fence are followed up by ground or helicopter removal of the deer.

A dynamic system of factors influences the survival and breeding success of the endangered Hawaiian Dark-rumped Petrel. Without an active management program, 'Ua'u populations would be subjected to heavy impacts by predators such as cats, mongooses and dogs, and by habitat destruction by ungulates. The surviving Maui 'Ua'u populations probably exist because of the high-elevation nesting environment which may be too hostile for most of the introduced predators to endure.

Current management efforts to control predators, remove ungulates, and maintain the boundary fences have reduced predation and provided for habitat recovery. However, predation will persist and the habitat will always be threatened by ungulates.

A persistent population of rats serves as a prey base for cats and mongooses, and appears to have negative effects on 'Ua'u breeding success. Since traps have not eradicated rats in the 'Ua'u colony, increased use of rodenticides may be needed to remove this prey base in order to deprive mongooses and feral cats of their primary food source. Rodent removal may benefit not only the 'Ua'u, but other native birds, endemic arthropods, and native vegetation at Haleakalā.

Habitat destruction is the primary threat to all of Hawai'i's remaining native biota (Stone 1989). The State of Hawai'i's increasing human population and associated development, the constant influx of new alien species, and the spread of the most aggressive aliens have accelerated habitat loss for these endangered species.

MANAGEMENT RECOMMENDATIONS

The ultimate management objective for the 'Ua'u population at Haleakalā is to ensure survival of the species. Simons (1984) emphasized the importance of adult survival for population growth. Our findings show that continual management of 'Ua'u is necessary for species survival.

1. Predator control is necessary to keep predator populations low. The use of traps and approved toxicants such as diphacinone are means of predator control. To avoid a detrimental dietary shift from rats to 'Ua'u, it is extremely important to control cats and mongooses while controlling rats. A multispecies toxicant may be useful in decreasing the labor-intensive live-trapping program.
2. Continual monitoring of 'Ua'u nests is necessary to determine changes in nesting activity and success. Monthly monitoring using toothpicks is an inexpensive and valid means of determining nesting activity but is also labor-intensive.
3. Maintaining feral animal control fences is necessary to keep ungulates from reentering the recovering nesting habitat. Special modifications to select portions of the existing boundary fences may be required due to the newly emerging axis deer threat.
4. Searching other islands for productive nesting colonies of Hawaiian Dark-rumped Petrels is necessary for species survival.

ACKNOWLEDGMENTS

We thank all those who worked to protect the 'Ua'u colony; J. Tamayose and R. Takumi, are key field workers whose continual dedication contributes to the survival of the 'Ua'u and other species. J. Medeiros, and J. G. Massey, DVM, provide continual support of this project both outside and inside the park. We thank T. Simons for providing comments on the manuscript. E. Nishibayashi, V. Greive, W. Han, T. Simons, the late J. Kunioki, and many others provided monitoring efforts and support. We also thank the dedicated Resources Management staff, past and present, paid or volunteer, who have worked to protect and preserve Haleakalā's unique ecosystem by planning, building, and maintaining the fences; controlling alien plants; removing feral animals; and processing the paperwork that allowed the fieldwork to be performed. Finally, we thank the State Division of Forestry and Wildlife on Maui and the U.S. Fish and Wildlife Service Ecological Services Division in Honolulu for their continued support of this program.

Studies in Avian Biology No. 22:319–328, 2001.

FORAGING BEHAVIOR AND TEMPORAL USE OF GRASSLANDS BY NĒNĒ: IMPLICATIONS FOR MANAGEMENT

FRIEDERIKE WOOG AND JEFFREY M. BLACK

Abstract. We studied foraging behavior of Hawaiian Geese (*Branta sandvicensis*) hereafter referred to as Nēnē, visiting a variety of grasslands in Hawai‘i Volcanoes National Park. For the purpose of this study, two overgrown sites were mowed and subsequently compared with established sites that had previously been mowed or grazed by livestock. Relative grazing pressure varied among sites and at different times of the year. Sites differed in plant species composition and quality, seedhead production, grass height, and rainfall. Most of the plants were introduced species. Nēnē grazed more in areas with the sward-forming Kikuyu grass (*Pennisetum clandestinum*) than in areas with bunch grasses, selecting sites that had grass with a high water content. Water content in the grass was correlated with protein content. Grazing pressure decreased in grass taller than 11 cm and geese used grasslands less during dry periods. Plant quality in the newly mown sites was relatively low and did not attract birds. Nēnē remained in established sites and did not move to newly managed sites. Based on our results, we suggest that grasslands could be managed at a height below 11 cm, irrigated in drought periods, and fertilized to encourage feeding opportunities for this endangered species.

Key Words: *Branta sandvicensis*; endangered species; foraging; grassland management; habitat use; Hawaiian Goose; Nēnē.

In spite of major conservation efforts, the Hawaiian Goose, hereafter Nēnē, (*Branta sandvicensis*), is still one of the most endangered waterfowl species in the world. The Nēnē's breeding success in the wild remains low, and without releases of captive-bred birds, its numbers may rapidly decline (Black and Banko 1994). Predation by introduced mammalian predators and the poor availability of food are thought to be the main obstacles on the Nēnē's route to recovery (Baldwin 1947a, Stone et al. 1983, Banko 1992, Black 1995). The low incidence of nesting suggests that many females cannot accumulate sufficient body reserves for egg laying and incubation due to poor foraging conditions (Banko 1992). Recent studies on gosling mortality showed that lack of adequate nutrition is especially detrimental for young birds (P. Baker and H. Baker, pers. comm.).

We do not know what habitats Nēnē used in the times prior to Polynesian and European settlement. Today, birds nest and roost in open shrubland in lava deserts where they feed on berries and on grasslands created by humans, such as ranches, golf courses, and lawns near housing areas and campgrounds, where they fatten up prior to breeding and rear their goslings (Black et al. 1994). This pattern follows that of many Arctic geese that forage on agricultural fields and pastures during migration and at their wintering grounds (reviewed by Black et al. 1994). After removal of ungulates within Hawai‘i Volcanoes National Park, previously grazed pastures, mainly consisting of introduced grass species, have become overgrown (Cuddihy and Stone 1990) and thickets have formed, which are not used by the geese. We studied the foraging behavior of the Nēnē at several of the sites that had been mowed. We asked whether the vegetation composition and cover, seedhead abundance, grass height, protein and water content of grass, rainfall, temperature, and time of year contributed to the variation in grazing pressure.

We discuss the implications of our findings for grassland management and the role managed grasslands could potentially play in the recovery of Nēnē.

STUDY AREA AND METHODS

We collected data at Hawai‘i Volcanoes National Park and the adjacent Kapāpala Ranch (Fig. 1). Hawai‘i Volcanoes National Park comprises an area of 85,000 ha and holds a population of about 160 Nēnē. We studied grazing behavior in the breeding season from December 1994 to March 1995 and in the pre-breeding and breeding season from August 1995 to March 1996. The grasslands varied in size, boundary type, management regime, soil, and other environmental factors. We measured the size of the grasslands with the Global Positioning System 'Pathfinder.' The grasslands ranged in size from 0.1–4 ha and were mowed or livestock-grazed periodically. A boundary index was recorded ranging from open to very enclosed (1 = open, short grass; 2 = open, surrounded by tall grass and bushes; 3 = open, tall grass and bushes surrounding and within; 4 = closed, a few trees surrounding and within; 5 = closed, many trees surrounding and within; Table 1). Most soils were porous, not holding water.

Sites 2 and 6 were previously overgrown with mainly Kikuyu grass (*Pennisetum clandestinum*) until they were mowed in November 1994. Site 7 was initially mowed in 1992, whereas the other sites were mowed or grazed much earlier. Site 3 has been a recreational picnic area since the early 1940s, and later became a campground, and the grasslands at sites 5 and 8 were

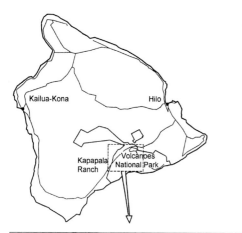

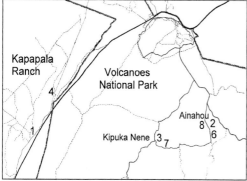

FIGURE 1: Location of Hawaiʻi Volcanoes National Park, Kapāpala Ranch, and study sites.

periodically mowed for geese by the National Park Service since 1992.

We made observations of the behavior of the geese at sites 2 and 8 during 13 days between November 1994 and March 1995 (149 hours), and during 11 days between August 1995 and March 1995–1996 (119 hours). Observations were spread throughout the season. The majority of birds observed were nonbreeders or failed breeders. The behavior of all geese present in an area was scan sampled from dawn to dusk (for a daily average of 11 hours, total of 268 hours). An au-

dio beeper gave a signal every 10 minutes and the behavior of all individually marked birds visible at that instant was recorded (Martin and Bateson 1986). Behaviors included vigilance, feeding, loafing, preening, walking, and social interactions (courtship, aggressive encounters; Inglis 1977).

We measured weekly grazing pressure by counting and removing droppings, which had accumulated in seven days prior to measurement, within a 1.12 m radius of randomly placed stakes (each plot covering an area of 4 m²; Owen 1971, Summers and Stansfield 1991). The number of plots ranged between 9 and 25, according to area size. We visually estimated percentage of vegetation cover to the species level in each dropping plot to the nearest 5%. Species covering <5% were estimated to the nearest percent. We subsequently classified vegetation types using TWIN-SPAN (two-way indicator species analysis; Hill 1979). This allowed us to distinguish two vegetation types at each site, which we refer to as patch types (Table 2). All scientific names and families (Wagner et al. 1990a,b) of the prevalent plant species are listed in the Appendix. Grass species growing in tufts are called bunch grasses as opposed to sward-forming species. All plants under study were introduced species.

Hawaiʻi Volcanoes National Park was dominated by the sward-forming Kikuyu grass and the Kapāpala Ranch was dominated by grass of the genus *Paspalum*. In Hawaiʻi Volcanoes National Park most of the Kipuka Nēnē area contained bunch grasses; the ʻĀinahou area had less bunch grasses and was dominated by Kikuyu grass and the sedge *Kyllinga brevifolia*. Plant species with high average cover were also widespread and abundant, but some of the species with a low average cover occurred regularly.

In the 1994–1995 Nēnē breeding season, we took 10 random measurements of grass height in each dropping plot every three weeks and calculated a mean for each plot. The grass height measurements were divided into three classes: short (1.6–5.5 cm), medium (5.6–11.5 cm), and tall (11.6–23.5 cm). We determined the production of seedheads in the 1995–1996 breeding season once a month, by counting them in a 50 cm × 50 cm area in each dropping plot. In the same time period we collected fresh Kikuyu grass monthly in each of the grasslands. Samples were sorted, weighed, and dried at 70°C overnight for subsequent analysis of crude protein (nitrogen × 6.25, Kjehldahl; Wagner 1970), and expressed as percentage dry weight (Owen

TABLE 1. AREA SIZE, BOUNDARY INDEX, AND MANAGEMENT REGIME OF THE STUDY SITES ON THE ISLAND OF HAWAIʻI

Site	Area size (m²)[a]	Boundary	Management	
1	ʻĀinapō Corral (Kapāpala Ranch)	29,110	1	overgrazed by cattle
4	Halfway House (Kapāpala Ranch)	40,000 (est.)	1	overgrazed by cattle
3	Kipuka Nēnē Campground	1,520	5	mowed/goose grazed[b]
7	Kipuka Nēnē mowed area	2,140	2	mowed
8	ʻĀinahou, Pen 11	5,200	3	mowed/goose grazed
5	ʻĀinahou, Pine area	1,160	4	mowed
2	ʻĀinahou, Big Pen	5,290	4	mowed/horse grazed[b]
6	ʻĀinahou, Lower mowed area	5,210	5	mowed

[a] Area sizes only account for managed grassland; islands of tall vegetation within the grasslands were excluded.
[b] Areas that were kept at least partially short by the geese were considered to be goose grazed.

TABLE 2.   PATCH TYPES AND TOTAL MEAN VEGETATION COVER FOR THE STUDY SITES DESCRIBED IN TABLE 1

Site	Patch	Prevalent plants	% Vegetation cover
1	1 (10)[a]	*Paspalum*, some *Lotus* and *Sporobulus*	102 ± 6
	2 (5)	*Eleusine*, some *Solivia* and *Portulaca*	101 ± 9
2	1 (11)	*Pennisetum, Kyllinga*	106 ± 3
	2 (6)	*Pennisetum, Kyllinga*, some *Digitaria*	114 ± 3
3	1 (7)	*Pennisetum*, some *Sporobulus*	119 ± 7
	2 (8)	*Sporobulus*, some *Chloris* and *Vulpia*	87 ± 11
4	1 (10)	*Paspalum, Desmodium* and *Kyllinga*	115 ± 1
	2 (10)	*Paspalum, Desmodium, Trifolium*, and *Kyllinga*	115 ± 2
5	1 (9)	*Paspalum, Kyllinga, Desmodium*, some *Trifolium*	120 ± 7
6	1 (19)	*Pennisetum, Kyllinga*	83 ± 2
7	1 (4)	*Pennisetum* and *Desmodium*, some *Melinis*	95 ± 9
	2 (9)	*Digitaria, Andropogon*	59 ± 10
8	1 (13)	*Pennisetum, Kyllinga*	116 ± 5
	2 (12)	*Pennisetum, Kyllinga*, some *Desmodium*	88 ± 6

[a] Numbers in parentheses indicate number of plots.

1971). The water content of the samples was obtained by subtracting dry weight from fresh weight. We focused on Kikuyu grass because it is readily eaten by the geese and is widespread, allowing a comparison among sites (Black et al. 1994).

To examine the effects of rainfall and temperature on grassland usage, we placed minimum-maximum thermometers and rain gauges in each area and checked them weekly. At Kipuka Nēnē and 'Āinahou we used weather data collected by the National Park Service.

STATISTICAL METHODS

All analyses were undertaken using general linear models, with either binomial or Poisson error structure. The resultant changes in deviance are equivalent to the chi-squared statistic and were tested accordingly (Crawley 1993, NAG 1993).

Diurnal patterns of grassland usage

We used the maximum count within each hour to reflect the number of birds present in the course of a day (Black et al. 1991). To compare the yearly, seasonal, and daily variation in the time the geese spent grazing, we used an analysis of variance with a binomial error distribution in GLIM (Crawley 1993, NAG 1993). The average number of birds feeding within an hour was the response variable, and the average number of birds within an hour was the binomial denominator. Factors were location, date, year, and hour (time of day). Small sample sizes (e.g., hours with only 1 scan and days with <25 scans) were excluded from the analysis. We tested differences among sites and categories of behavior with nonparametric chi-square tests.

Grazing pressure

We employed several analyses of variance and covariance models to determine which variables affected grazing pressure. Initial fits to the models indicated that the dropping count data were over dispersed, and consequently the constraints imposed by the declaration of Poisson error distribution were modified by adjustment of the scale parameter. This was achieved by

dividing the Pearson chi-square statistic of the final model by the residual degrees of freedom (Crawley 1993). Explanatory variables were location, date, season, protein and water content of the grass, grass height, vegetation type and cover, elevation, number of seedheads, rainfall, and temperature. Not all of these were fitted to the same model. Variables that caused a significant increase in deviance were retained in the model. Insignificant terms were removed. We also tested all biologically meaningful interaction terms.

To reduce effects of data dependency, only the number of droppings accumulated over certain time periods were used for analysis (monthly, per season, and over an entire year). Each season amounted to 23 weeks: the 1994–1995 breeding season (24 Oct 1994–29 Mar 1995), the 1995 summer (19 Apr 1995–18 Sept 1995) and the 1995–1996 breeding season (10 Oct 1995–13 Mar 1996). Sample sizes indicate the number of plots.

GLIM was also used to compare differences among classes. In multiple comparisons, significance levels were controlled by using sequential Bonferroni tests; otherwise, the significance level was set at $P < 0.05$. Percentage data were arcsine transformed prior to analysis.

RESULTS

DIURNAL PATTERNS OF GRASSLAND USAGE

Birds flew from their desert roosting places to the grasslands between 0615 and 0730 hours, and left the grassland between 1600 and 1745 hours. Numbers of geese varied throughout the day, ranging between 1 and 24. The mean maximum number of geese per hour (Fig. 2), reached a peak at 1400 hours, and then declined until the geese left the area. At site 8, goose numbers varied throughout the day (F = 7.2, df = 12, $P < 0.01$) and with date (F = 8.56, df = 20, $P < 0.01$). There was no difference between the two breeding seasons (1994–1995 and 1995–1996), or between arrival and departure times of the geese between the two years (Mann-Whitney U-tests for flying in: W = 135, N = 12 and 7,

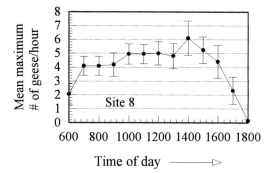

FIGURE 2. Mean maximum number of Nēnē per hour counted on 24 observation days at study site 8.

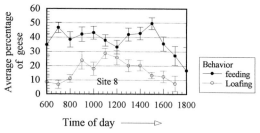

FIGURE 3. Average percentage of Nēnē scanned for behavior (feeding or loafing) throughout the day.

P < 0.022; and departing: W = 98, N = 10 and 8, P < 0.82. The percentage of birds feeding peaked at 800 and 1500 hours and was lowest at 1200 hours (Fig. 3). The percentage of geese feeding and loafing varied throughout the day. The hourly pattern of use was significant for loafing (χ^2 = 24.78, df = 12, P < 0.025).

The percentage of birds feeding varied between sites 2 and 8 (χ^2 = 5.63, df = 1, P < 0.025) and dates (χ^2 = 38.18, df = 21, P < 0.025), but there was no significant difference between the two breeding seasons. The geese spent more time feeding and less time loafing at the newly established site 2 (inside the enclosure; χ^2 = 6.14, df = 1, P < 0.025), compared to the more established site 8 (Fig. 4). The time spent feeding at site 2 decreased from 57% in 1994–1995 to 47% 1995–1996.

GRAZING PRESSURE

The yearly grazing pressure varied among sites (χ^2 = 228.7, df = 7, P < 0.001; Fig. 5). Grazing pressure was highest at sites 2, 3, and 8, intermediate at site 7, and low at sites 1 and

4 (Kapāpala Ranch); site 6 had the lowest grazing pressure. Some of the between-site variation in grazing pressure might be explained by differences in management and boundary type (Fig. 6). All management types were significantly different from each other (χ^2 = 6.94–80.96, df = 1, P < 0.01–0.001). There were significant differences in yearly grazing pressure among sites with different boundary types. Sites 2 and 3, 2 and 4, and 4 and 5 were significantly different (χ^2 = 4.–13.36, P < 0.001–0.03). The geese apparently selected the mowed and grazed grassland sites (Fig. 6a) and used open sites less than closed ones (Fig. 6b). Sites with an extensive tree canopy were used less than sites with only a few trees (χ^2 = 12.49, df = 1, P < 0.001). Area size did not affect grazing pressure. At some sites, goose-grazing pressure increased after mowing or horse-grazing.

The observed preferences for a certain vegetation type were persistent through all seasons (Table 3). Grazing pressure was higher in the Kikuyu grass patch compared to the bunch grass patch (χ^2 = 22.09, df = 1, P < 0.001; Fig. 7). When having the choice between a mixed patch type with Kikuyu and a legume (*Desmodium sandwicense*) and pure Kikuyu, the geese grazed

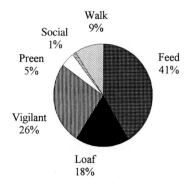

Site 8 (n=21 days)

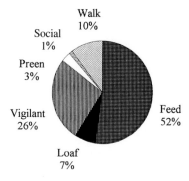

Site 2 (n=10 days)

FIGURE 4. Activity budgets of Nēnē at sites 2 and 8.

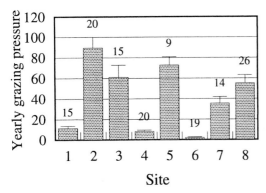

FIGURE 5. Variation in yearly Nēnē grazing pressure by sites. Values indicate the yearly accumulated number of droppings/4 m², sample sizes indicate the number of plots in each location, means are among plots.

more in the mixed type ($\chi^2 = 5.4$, df = 1, P < 0.025; Fig. 7).

Vegetation cover may also explain grazing pressure variation in some sites. In areas with short Kikuyu, the geese grazed more in dense grass cover ($\chi^2 = 14.87$, df = 1, P < 0.001; Fig. 8a), whereas in areas with taller grass, they grazed more in less dense grass cover (Fig. 8b). The association with a lower cover of *Kyllinga* (Fig. 8c) was detected at site 4 ($\chi^2 = 9.37$, df = 1, P < 0.005), and of *Sporobulus* (Fig. 8d) at site 8 ($\chi^2 = 5.48$, df = 1, P < 0.01).

At site 4, the grazing pressure was also influenced by the topography; it varied between vegetation patch types, but the elevation of the plots explained more of the variation. The higher-elevated plots were grazed more ($\chi^2 = 13.09$, df = 1, P < 0.001).

Seedheads of grasses were most abundant in winter months (October–January; Fig. 9), however, in general, a higher number of seedheads did not attract more geese. We tested this by fitting the number of droppings accumulated in

the four weeks prior to the seedhead count as a response variable, and the number of seedheads in each plot as an explanatory variable. Site 4 on Kapāpala Ranch was an exception to the general finding, but only in August ($\chi^2 = 4.23$, df = 1, P < 0.05, N = 18), when a high number of seedheads apparently attracted more geese.

The use of different grass heights varied among sites. In Hawai‘i Volcanoes National Park, grazing pressure was greatest in grass of medium heights (5.6–11.5 cm; $\chi^2 = 16.61$, df = 2, P < 0.001; Fig. 10). The tallest grass height class (11.6–23.5 cm) had by far the least goose usage. Shorter grass heights were used on the intensively cattle-grazed Kapāpala ranch (2.4–7.9 cm).

The correlation between protein and water content of grasses was significantly correlated at site 3 (r = 0.782, df = 6, P < 0.05), site 8 (r = 0.831, df = 6, P < 0.02), and site 2 (r = 0.742, df = 6, P < 0.05) and for all locations combined (Fig. 11). Kikuyu grass with low water content was also low in protein. Water content in the grass and monthly precipitation were not correlated.

Protein and water content in Kikuyu grass changed over the study period and differed among sites (Fig. 12). Paired t-tests showed that the grass at the newly managed site 6 had a significantly lower protein content than the established site 8 (t = 2.58, N = 8, P = 0.036) and also a significantly lower water content (t = 2.6, N = 8, P = 0.035). Nēnē rarely used site 6. The minimum temperature ranged between 6 and 8°C and did not influence grazing pressure.

To test for regular grazing cycles at the different sites, we plotted autocorrelation functions (ACFs) of the weekly grazing pressure using SYSTAT. There was no regular cyclical pattern to the observed fluctuations in grazing events.

Variation in grazing pressure might be explained by more factors than the quality of the grassland alone. Birds might be absent because

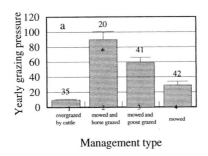

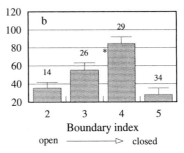

FIGURE 6. (A) Yearly grazing pressure by management types. (B) Yearly grazing pressure by types. Sample sizes indicate the number of plots, * indicates the periodic presence of captive birds; the yearly grazing pressure is expressed as the mean number of droppings/4 m² accumulated over a year, means are among plots.

TABLE 3. COMPARISON OF DROPPINGS ACCUMULATED OVER A PERIOD OF ONE YEAR (24 OCTOBER 1994 – 24 OCTOBER 1995) IN TWO DIFFERENT VEGETATION TYPES WITHIN A SITE, DF = 1

Site	χ^2	P<	Type with higher dropping density	Type with lower dropping density
2	9.31	0.05	*Pennisetum, Digitaria*	*Pennisetum, Kyllinga*
3	22.09	0.001	*Pennisetum*	*Sporobulus, Chloris, Vulpia*
4	6.27	0.025	*Paspalum, Desmodium, Trifolium*	*Paspalum, Desmodium, Kyllinga*
8	5.40	0.025	*Pennisetum, Desmodium*	*Pennisetum, Kyllinga*

they are nesting or molting, or because there are seasonally better resources in the neighbouring shrublands. In our final models we included these variations as an intrinsic date or season effect. At all sites, grazing pressure varied significantly among months. At many sites either year or rainfall caused a significant change in deviance, but year and rainfall were not significant in the same model (Fig. 13; Table 4). After controlling for location (χ^2 = 853.4, df = 7, P < 0.001), the grazing pressure was different between months (χ^2 = 76.26, df = 17, P < 0.001). At most locations grazing pressure varied also between season and/or years and/or with rainfall (see Table 4). There was an intrinsic seasonal pattern and a departure from that pattern caused by rainfall. It is, however, difficult to tease them apart, as rainfall itself followed a seasonal pattern.

DISCUSSION

Managers once believed that Nēnē would thrive in volcanic shrubland at high elevation, where the last remaining birds were found. However, birds reintroduced into these areas had poor survival rates compared with those in mid and low elevations where they had access to managed agricultural habitats (Black et al. 1997). Many healthy goose populations throughout the world are making use of man-made sites to meet their daily energetic requirements (reviewed by Black et al. 1994). Nēnē have adapted to man-made habitats and readily use introduced plant species for foraging.

Understanding variation in grazing pressure in

geese is not an easy task, as it cannot be explained by a single factor. In our study, Nēnē selected habitats with food plants of a high protein content. They favored vegetation patches with Kikuyu grass sward as opposed to patches with bunch grasses, and grazed more in mixed grass-legume than in pure grass sward. Kikuyu grass sward is higher in protein than bunch grasses, and legumes have even higher levels of protein than Kikuyu grass (Black et al. 1994). Research on many herbivores, including other geese, has confirmed the suitability of crude protein as an indicator of forage quality (Owen 1981, Sedinger and Raveling 1984, Festa-Bianchet 1988), and geese are able to select forage of high nutritional quality when available (Owen 1971, Sedinger and Raveling 1984, Prop and Deerenberg 1991). Our study indicates that Nēnē are no exception to these findings.

That the geese used most grasslands less during dry periods could have two explanations. Grass with a low water content is proportionally higher in fiber (Owen 1981) and, as shown in this study for Kikuyu grass, lower in protein, which increases the physical effort of grazing and digestion (Prop and Vulnik 1992). Especially in periodically dry areas, the amount of rainfall may explain plant quality and quantity, and the subsequent grazing behavior of geese. Further research is needed into the short-term effects of rainfall on the vegetation (daily measurements) and the effects of rainfall duration on grazing pressure.

Nēnē used newly managed sites less than other, longer established ones. The new sites may

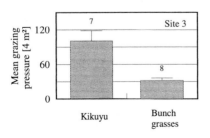
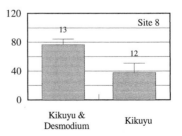

FIGURE 7. Variation of yearly grazing pressure with vegetation type (droppings accumulated between October 1994 and October 1995). Species names indicate plants with the highest cover, sample sizes indicate the number of plots.

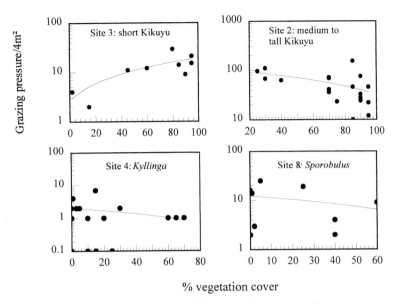

FIGURE 8.   Nēnē grazing pressure in Kikuyu grass, *Kyllinga* and *Sporobulus* with varying cover. The dropping density accumulated eight weeks before and after the vegetation cover assessment (between 18 Jan 1995 and 3 May 1995) was used to indicate relative grazing pressure.

have been unfamiliar to the birds; furthermore, the protein content in Kikuyu grass was lower. In other goose species, individuals using sites with a high forage quality spend less time feeding (Bédard and Gauthier 1989, Black et al. 1991). In our study, Nēnē spent less time feeding in the established site, suggesting the plant quality and abundance was better than at the newly managed site. From 1994 to 1995, we found a decrease in feeding time by 10% in the newly managed site. This might be explained by an increasing forage quality after repeated mowing of this previously unmanaged site. In many grass species, repeated mowing or grazing increases the protein content (Ydenberg and Prins

1981, Sedinger and Raveling 1986, Gadallah and Jefferies 1995). Thus, given good initial forage quality and sufficient rainfall, geese may themselves be able to improve the quality of the sward to a certain extent.

Colonization of new habitats is likely to occur with a change in selection pressure. Many Arctic geese shifted to new habitats after their populations had increased and some of their traditional habitats had deteriorated (Owen and Black 1991, Black et al. 1991). In contrast, the Nēnē population in our study is in danger of further decrease, and although more extensive measurements are needed, we provided data that new sites were nutritionally less attractive than estab-

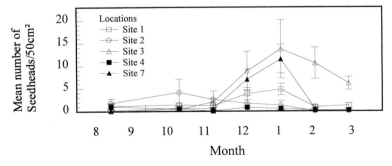

FIGURE 9.   The change of the mean number of seedheads over time (August 1995–March 1996). Predominant species at site 1 and 4: *Paspalum* and *Digitaria,* at site 3 and 7: *Sporobulus* and other mixed bunch grasses and at site 2: *Digitaria.* In February site 7 was mowed, hence the sudden absence of seedheads. Sample sizes are equal to the number of plots in each site.

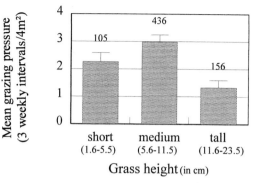

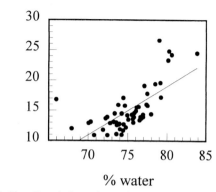

FIGURE 10.   Nēnē grazing pressure in different grass heights in Hawai'i Volcanoes National Park. Measurements were taken at 3-week intervals at five locations over a period of 21 weeks. The droppings accumulated in the three weeks prior to the grass height measurements indicated the relative grazing pressure. Sample sizes indicate the number of plots the grass height was measured in.

FIGURE 11.   Correlation of protein and water content in Kikuyu grass (all locations: r = 0.688, df = 52, P < 0.0001)

lished, traditional ones. To attract Nēnē to new sites, they must offer a higher-quality forage, and even then geese might not shift to them, especially if the established sites are not overcrowded. The size of the managed areas has to be adapted to the population size.

Nēnē are faced with a variable climate, and hence fluctuating forage quality. Droughts are a fairly common phenomenon in the normally wet winter months, but they are unpredictable. If the vegetation quality deteriorates during the critical time of incubation and brood rearing, birds might not be able to successfully rear their offspring. An adequate growth rate for goslings is only possible if accessible supplies of high quality forage are available (Gadallah and Jefferies 1995). Black et. al (1994) showed that the forage plants of Nēnē are depleted throughout the season and do not regenerate quickly, especially in unmanaged areas. Reduced supplies of forage due to earlier grazing are thought to cause reduced growth rates in Black Brant (*Branta bernicla*; Sedinger and Flint, 1991) as well as in Snow Geese (*Chen caerulescens*; Cooch et al. 1991). Adult Nēnē fly to better sites when food resources get low (Black et al. 1994); when leading goslings, however, they cannot travel far and must use what is available in the area. The nutritional inadequacy of the grasslands seems especially detrimental for goslings (P. Baker and H. Baker, pers. comm.) and may be the key factor in limiting population growth.

Today, most endangered species recovery plans emphasize the importance of an ecosystem approach (Martin 1994), but little attention is given to the management of disturbed habitats

which are used by endangered species. Species like the Nēnē utilize disturbed habitats and benefit from introduced plants as a food resource (Black et al. 1994). Although the restoration of disturbed habitats remains a long-term objective (Stone and Scott 1985a,b), the adaptability of the Nēnē can be turned into an advantage for the recovery of the species. Managing grasslands adjacent to nesting areas is a quick and comparatively inexpensive means of providing the birds with food. By managing grasslands that are overgrown by introduced grass species like Kikuyu, molasses grass (*Melinis minutiflora*), beard grass (*Schizachyrium condensatum*), and broomsedge (*Andropogon virginicus*) for the geese, some disturbed ecosystems may benefit. Corridors of short grass serve as effective firebreaks in areas with high fire risk. Most native plant species are not adapted to fire (Mueller-Dombois 1981), and fire also facilitates invasion by alien species (National Park Service 1989). From a conservation point of view, a reduction in the seed production of introduced grass species is favorable as it reduces the spread of these species into noninvaded areas.

Golf courses meet our criteria of grasslands as they have short, nutritious grass, and many Nēnē use them. However, various problems are

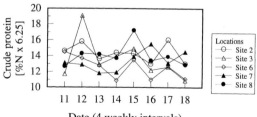

FIGURE 12.   The change of protein content in Kikuyu grass over time (July 1995–March 1996).

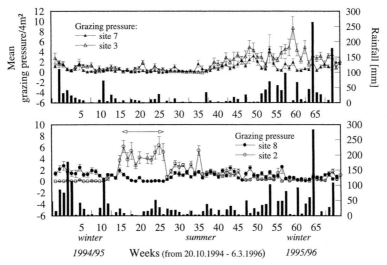

FIGURE 13.   The change of mean weekly grazing pressure (lines) by Nēnē and rainfall (bars) over time. Sample sizes correspond with the number of plots in each site (site 2: N = 20, site 3: N = 15, site 7: N = 14, site 8: N = 26). Weekly values are presented for detail, because of temporal autocorrelation between the weekly data, however, only monthly accumulated values were analyzed. The arrow indicates a periodic presence of semicaptive birds at site 2.

associated with this use. Geese get killed or crippled by golf balls, the adjacent nesting sites are usually cut off by roads, which causes roadkills, pesticides are used freely, and parent geese leading goslings are vulnerable to disturbance. A possible solution would be to create areas on golf courses that are set aside for geese and are nutritionally more attractive and concentrate geese away from human activity.

In 1997, the State of Hawai'i passed the Hawai'i Endangered Species Recovery Act, which allows incidental take of an endangered species on private land. The act opens new possibilities for the reintroduction of endangered species on private land. Some ranches, for example, pro-

vide excellent feeding opportunities for Nēnē. Prior to future reintroductions, however, the vegetation and seasonal local rainfall patterns should be assessed and only adequate grasslands with adjacent shrubland for nesting habitat should be considered. Dry habitats should be avoided. Adequate predator control in these areas remains vital to ensure breeding success of the geese.

The population of the Nēnē on Kaua'i is increasing steadily for two apparent reasons: (1) they use lush, cattle grazed and irrigated pasture vegetation in the lowlands, and (2) the number of introduced predators is low. Providing high quality pastures enables more birds to accumu-

TABLE 4.   The effect of month, year, rainfall, and patch type on grazing pressure (October 1994-March 1996) by Nēnē

Site	Month χ^2	(df = 12) P<	Year χ^2	(df = 1) P<	Rainfall χ^2	(df = 1) P<	Patch type[a] χ^2	(df = 1) P<
1	47.94	0.001	39.84	0.001	—	n.s.	5.51	0.025
1	48.16	0.001	—	n.s.	32.9	0.001	5.51	0.025
2	342.9	0.001	21.34	0.001	—	n.s.	25.06	0.001
2	303.6	0.001	—	n.s.	41.39	0.001	24.6	0.001
3	192.9	0.001	26.4	0.001	5.086	0.025	131.3	0.001
4	26.74	0.01	—	n.s.	—	n.s.	14.91[b]	0.001
5	310.8	0.001	—	n.s.	—	n.s.	only 1 type	
6	132.2	0.001	—	n.s.	—	n.s.	only 1 type	
7	78.01	0.001	14.23	0.001	—	n.s.	18.67	0.001
7	82.37	0.001	—	n.s.	15.27	0.001	18.79	0.001
8	105.9	0.001	13.39	0.001	—	n.s.	50.35	0.001

[a] Patch type was characterized by the vegetation type.
[b] At site 4 the elevation of the plot is used instead of the vegetation type.

late sufficient body reserves for breeding and results in higher fledgling success. Furthermore, strong and healthy birds may be more likely to escape predation.

Increased breeding success in the wild is the main goal for recovery. To achieve that goal, we emphasize the importance of large-scale sanctuaries in the wild, including both intensively managed grasslands and natural shrubland nesting habitats coupled with predator control. To determine the required size of sanctuaries, we recommend detailed studies on the carrying capacity of Nēnē habitat. Good management can result in doubling the carrying capacity of grasslands (Owen 1977). Furthermore, a study on different management regimes including mowing, livestock grazing, irrigation, fertilization, and burning treatments could reveal which treatments yield the highest carrying capacity and are most applicable financially.

IMMEDIATE MANAGEMENT IMPLICATIONS

Our immediate conclusions and implications for grassland management include the following:

1. Nēnē grazed most heavily on an intermediate grass height (approx. 5–11 cm). Mowing or grazing grass higher than 11 cm will optimize grasslands for the geese.
2. The geese used grasslands less during drought periods. Irrigation could be useful as a management tool, especially during the breeding season.
3. The geese grazed more in grass sward than in areas with bunch grasses. Although seedheads of bunch grasses are eaten by the geese, they are only seasonally plentiful, whereas short grass sward is scarce but with adequate management could be available year-round. Repeated mowing favors grass sward growth and reduces bunch grasses.
4. Geese grazed more in areas with grass high in protein. Fertilizer application is likely to improve grassland quality.
5. Management activities in grasslands should be carried out when bird numbers using the area are low (e.g., during molting), or after

1600 hours, when most birds leave the grasslands and fly to roosting sites.

ACKNOWLEDGMENTS

We are grateful to the Resources Management and the Research Division of Hawai'i Volcanoes National Park, the State Division of Forestry and Wildlife, the U.S. Geological Survey, The Wildfowl and Wetlands Trust, Slimbridge, The Peter Scott Trust for Education and Research in Conservation, and Sandy and Jill Friedman, Honolulu, for financial and logistical support. British Airways Assisting Conservation sponsored our flights between Europe and the United States. The German Academic Exchange Service (DAAD) kindly financed Friederike Woog in 1996. Many people helped in the field; M. Pfiz, M. Fujura, C. Walz, J. Edwards, A. Böhmler, and S. Straub were of invaluable assistance. L. Katahira, D. Hu, H. Hoshide, C. Terry, and P. C. Banko were very supportive throughout the study. The laboratory of the Agricultural Extension Service at University of Hawai'i at Manoa analyzed the protein content in the grass samples. Special thanks go to R. Pettifor, M. Rowcliffe, M. Kershaw, J. Bowler, A. Lang, and J. Hutchinson for statistical advice and to E. Zimmermann, M. Rowcliffe, and U. Zillich for commenting on earlier drafts.

APPENDIX. SCIENTIFIC AND COMMON NAMES OF PREVALENT PLANT SPECIES (WAGNER ET AL. 1990A,B)

Family	Latin name	Common name
Poaceae	*Pennisetum clandestinum*	Kikuyu grass
	Melinis minutiflora	Molasses grass
	Andropogon virginicus	Broomsedge
	Eleusine indica	Wiregrass
	Paspalum conjugatum	Hilo grass
	Sporobulus africanus	Rattail grass
	Digitaria violascens	Violet crabgrass
	Vulpia bromoides	Brome fescue
	Chloris virgata	Finger grass
Cyperaceae	*Kyllinga brevifolia*	Kaluhā
Fabaceae	*Lotus subbiflorus*	
	Desmodium sandwicense	Spanish clover
	Trifolium repens	White clover

Studies in Avian Biology No. 22:329–337, 2001.

AN ECOSYSTEM-BASED MANAGEMENT APPROACH TO ENHANCING ENDANGERED WATERBIRD HABITAT ON A MILITARY BASE

Diane Drigot

Abstract. Improving and sustaining endangered waterbird habitat has proven challenging but possible at Marine Corps Base Hawaii (MCBH), an active military installation on Hawai'i's most urbanized island of O'ahu. Such results have been possible through an ecosystem-based approach to resource management. This approach integrates stakeholder involvement into habitat enhancement schemes. Annual military maneuvers and frequent community volunteer assistance in invasive vegetation control have become an integral part of MCBH's waterbird habitat management routine for more than fifteen years. This approach has contributed to a doubling of Hawaiian Stilts (*Himantopus mexicanus knudseni*) counted, increased habitat availability for stilt nesting, and improved awareness among involved stakeholders of collaborative stewardship efforts needed to sustain these gains. This approach is applicable elsewhere.

Key Words: Black-necked Stilt; ecosystem health recovery; ecosystem management; endangered waterbird habitat; Hawaiian Stilt; military training; U.S. Marine Corps.

Improving and sustaining endangered waterbird habitat has proven challenging but possible at Marine Corps Base Hawaii (MCBH), an active military installation in the Hawaiian Islands. In 15 years, the Hawaiian Stilt, an endemic subspecies of the Black-necked Stilt (*Himantopus mexicanus knudseni*), population at the base's Nu'upia Ponds grew from about 60 to over 130 birds—10% of the state's entire population (Rauzon et al. 1997). MCBH resource managers are working to minimize stilt exposure to predators, alien plant habitat intrusions, competitors, disease vectors, and human disturbances. They have the added challenge of doing this in the context of military mission priorities and other resource use pressures.

This case study will show how an ecosystem-based management approach integrates the seemingly conflicting management priorities of combat readiness at a military installation and species preservation. Multiple objectives have been achieved, such as habitat enhancement through military training maneuvers and the development of a shared regional vision of restored ecosystem health through a sustained community volunteer weed removal program. The lasting success of MCBH projects such as alien pickleweed (*Batis maritima*) and red mangrove (*Rhizophora mangle*) control to recover endangered species habitat is the result of using this approach. Lessons learned are applicable elsewhere.

GEOGRAPHIC SETTING AND MANAGEMENT CONTEXT

The site of this case study is Mōkapu, a 1,194 ha peninsula on the northeast, windward side of O'ahu, separated from downtown Honolulu by the 35 km Ko'olau Range (Fig. 1).

Although relatively small in size, this peninsula supports a surprising diversity of wildlife and other natural and cultural resources, besides being a busy military community of over 17,000 residents. The base's Ulupa'u Crater supports a colony of over 3,000 Red-footed Boobies (*Sula sula rubripes*) within an active weapons firing range (Rauzon 1992). Within the cliffs below the crater, next to a grenade range, the oldest fossil bird deposit yet found in the Hawaiian Islands has attracted national scientific interest (James 1987, Olson and James 1991).

Along the 17.6 km shoreline of Mōkapu peninsula, over 50 different species of waterbirds, migratory shorebirds, and seabirds have been noted in 50 years of bird count records (Rauzon 1992). Legally protected sand dunes contain thousands of ancient Native Hawaiian burials and support a variety of native seastrand vegetation. Sixty-two cultural resources have been recorded, 50 of which are archaeological or historic World War II sites eligible for or already listed in the National Register of Historic Places (Schilz 1996). The peninsula has a storied landscape, rich in Hawaiian legends and considered sacred by some contemporary Hawaiians (Maly and Rosendahl 1995). Like many other military bases on the continental United States, MCBH has become a de facto refuge of diverse natural and cultural resources surrounded by an urbanized region (e.g., Advisory Council on Historic Preservation 1994, Steinitz 1996, Leslie et al. 1996).

The base contains a busy military airfield, whose aircraft flight paths, noise limitations, accident risks to nearby communities, and bird-

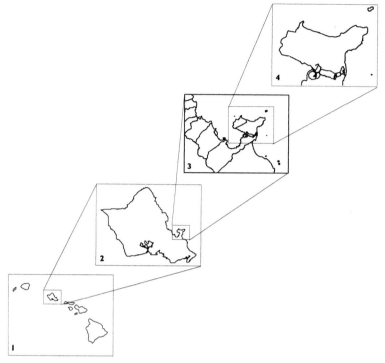

FIGURE 1. Map of (1) Hawaiian Islands; (2) island of Oʻahu; (3) Koʻolau Poko District; and (4) Mōkapu Peninsula (from Wilcox et al. 1998).

aircraft strike hazards must be carefully managed in a manner that considers the surrounding environment and community concerns. Marine training operations occur around the peninsula in water assigned the most stringent water quality standards in the state (Hawaiʻi State Administrative Rules Chapters 11–54). Marines share this water space with public boating, fishing, swimming, and protected species such as coral reefs, threatened green sea turtles (*Chelonia mydas*), endangered Hawaiian monk seals (*Monachus schauinslandi*), and humpback whales (*Megaptera novaeangliae*; Drigot et al. 1991).

In addition to these many and varied resources, uses, and demands, Mōkapu supports a major breeding population of Hawaiian Stilt. This bird is currently listed as endangered by the U.S. Fish and Wildlife Service (35 Federal Register 16047). The peninsula's primary stilt habitat is mudflat shoreline around the Nuʻupia Ponds, originally part of an ancient Hawaiian aquaculture complex and now an MCBH-designated Wildlife Management Area (WMA). This 195-ha area is comprised of an interconnected complex of eight shallow ponds, associated wetland areas, and a vegetative buffer zone, which links the peninsula to the rest of the island of Oʻahu (Fig. 2). In the past 15 years, biannual

censuses of Hawaiian Stilt at these ponds have shown growth from about 60 to over 130 birds. The pond stilt population now comprises nearly 10% of the state's total estimated population of 1,500–1,800 birds (Rauzon et al. 1997). Recent (1994–1996) intensive MCBH stilt monitoring surveys have confirmed this growth, with band returns showing some dispersal to other habitats off the base. Increases in number of nests made, eggs laid, and chicks hatched have been particularly noted in pond areas subject to deliberate vegetation manipulation (Rauzon and Tanino 1995, Rauzon et al. 1997).

This aspect of the increased breeding success of MCBH Hawaiian Stilt is the result of the application of ecosystem-based management principles. These principles emphasize that resource management decisions should be based not only on the "best science" but on the recognition that resource "management objectives are a matter of social choice," and that "ecosystems must be managed in a human context" (McDowell 1997).

BACKGROUND AND METHODS

Ecosystem management (EM) is an important priority for federal agencies (Grumbine 1997). The Department of Defense (DoD) is one of 14

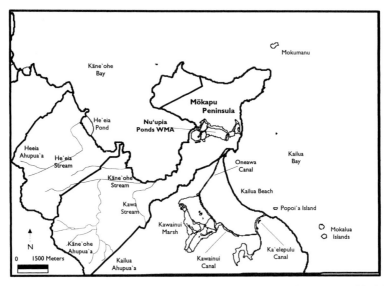

FIGURE 2.   Nu'upia Ponds Wildlife Management Area (WMA) in regional context modified from Wilcox et al. (1998).

federal land management agencies that on December 15, 1995, signed an interagency "Memorandum of Understanding to Foster the Ecosystem Approach" to resource management (Council on Environmental Quality et al. 1995). The goal of EM as stated in the Memorandum of Understanding (MOU) is:

> . . . to restore and sustain the health, productivity, and biological diversity of ecosystems and their overall quality of life through a natural resource management approach that is fully integrated with social and economic goals . . .

The MOU further defines an ecosystem approach as:

> . . . a method for sustaining or restoring ecological systems and their functions and values. It is goal driven, and it is based on a collaboratively developed vision of desired future conditions that integrates ecological, economic, and social factors. It is applied within a geographic framework defined primarily by ecological boundaries . . .

EM emphasizes humans as part of the ecosystem, basing resource management decisions not only on "best science" but on "associated cultural values," "improved communication with the general public," and "forming partnerships" with government, nongovernmental agencies, "and other stakeholders."

DoD Instruction 4715.3 of May 3, 1996, promulgates ten "Ecosystem Management Principles and Guidelines" to be followed by all U.S.-based military installations (DoD 1996). These ecosystem management principles (EMPs) are listed below and explained in Appendix 1.

1. Maintain and improve the sustainability and native biodiversity of ecosystems.
2. Administer with consideration of ecological units and time frames.
3. Support sustainable human activities.
4. Develop a vision of ecosystem health.
5. Develop priorities and reconcile conflicts.
6. Develop coordinated approaches to work toward ecosystem health.
7. Rely on the best science and data available.
8. Use benchmarks to monitor and evaluate outcomes.
9. Use adaptive management.
10. Implement through installation plans and programs.

In fiscal year 1997 alone, one-third of the DoD's $100 million conservation budget supported the development of Integrated Resource Management Plans (IRMPs). These IRMPs are seen as the primary vehicle for promulgating EMPs. DoD's ambitious goal is to complete baseline IRMPs for 425 major military installations spanning approximately 10 million ha of U.S. land by the year 2001 (Boice 1997). One of DoD's "Conservation Measures of Merit" to assess progress in implementing EMPs is the timely completion of these plans (L. P. Boice, pers. comm.). Congress's recent reauthorization and update of the Sikes Act addressing natural resources conservation on DoD installations now mandates development of these plans and periodic reports to Congress on plan implementation progress (Sikes Act Improvement Act of 1997—P.L. 105-95).

In the Results and Discussion section that follows, some of MCBH's endangered species habitat recovery activities over the past 15 years and elements of the base's recently completed Integrated Resource Management Plans (Wilcox et al. 1997, Wilcox 1998) will be reviewed in the context of the concomitant EMPs upon which they are based. To that end, there will be parenthetical references to one or more of the ten EMPs in the sections where they are most pertinent.

RESULTS AND DISCUSSION

Ecosystem-based Approach to Resource Management at MCBH (EMPs 1, 2, 3)

Although terms such as "ecosystem-based management" and the emphasis on humans as part of managed ecosystems are relatively new, MCBH resource management approaches have long reflected the notion that humans do not just generate "anthropogenic effects" *on* ecosystems but are an integral *part of* ecosystems being managed. Application of this broader, human-emphasized perspective is illustrated as follows. First, since MCBHs primary military mission is to maintain facilities and services that support the combat readiness of Marines, base resource managers must view the primary goods and services derived through the air, land, and water resource management zones in and around the peninsula as those which serve this central mission requirement. From this perspective, a primary function of the Nu'upia Ponds Wildlife Management Area is as a valuable security buffer and helicopter overflight corridor between the military installation and the surrounding civilian community (EMP 3).

Secondly, federal mandates also require that base resource managers identify and protect significant cultural and natural resources within their jurisdiction. From this perspective, the dual status of Nu'upia Ponds as an endangered species habitat and an ancient Hawaiian fishpond of national historical significance (Keeper of the National Register 1984) must be recognized. In fact, the valued "natural" waterbird habitat functions of the base's Nu'upia Ponds resulted from a human construct in the first place—a walled fishpond complex whose remnant fishpond features have archaeological and indigenous cultural values contributing to Nu'upia Ponds eligibility for inclusion in the National

Register of Historic Places (Drigot and Tuggle 1984). Although no longer actively managed for fish harvesting, the shoreline mudflats bordering the interconnected fishpond rock wall alignments are now used by the Hawaiian Stilt and other protected waterfowl. Historic preservation requirements associated with these features often influence how, when, and where wildlife habitat improvements are made in this area (EMPs 1, 2).

In summary, MCBH is required by federal laws to integrate historic Polynesian and present military functions of the pond landscape in their wildlife habitat recovery schemes. By recognizing that such mandated resource uses are an integral part of the ecosystem, rather than a constraint to overcome, unique opportunities to recover an endangered species as discussed below became apparent.

Resolving Management Conflicts into Opportunities (EMPs 1, 3, 5)

From the mid-1960s through the mid-1970s, Hawaiian Stilt counts at Nu'upia Ponds were at much lower levels than today. For example, the average number of stilts counted on 27 censuses between 1965 and 1975 was 54 birds (Rauzon et al. 1997). During this time, Amphibious Assault Vehicles (AAVs) used the northern shoreline of this wetland as their daily transit corridor to the nearest beach maneuver area.

When Hawaiian Stilts attempted to nest in tire tracks left in the mud by these 26-ton tracked vehicles, wildlife biologists were called in to move the birds. In the process of addressing this immediate problem, what was initially seen as a conflict between a military training exercise and an endangered species came to be viewed as a "swords into plowshares" opportunity. State and federal wildlife biologists worked with MCBH environmental and Marine personnel to capitalize on the fact that these birds were attracted to the open mudflat areas cleared of invasive alien vegetation by these vehicles. The immediate conflict was resolved by moving the AAVs' daily transit corridor upland to the north, out of the wetland mudflats. However, on a supervised, annual basis, just before the onset of the breeding season, MCBH began to deliberately deploy these AAVs in plowing-like maneuvers within this mudflat shoreline (Fig. 3). These actions are directed by resource managers in such manner as to avoid culturally sensitive features and break open thick mats of alien invasive plants (primarily pickleweed and some red mangrove) for expanded stilt nesting and feeding opportunities (EMP 5).

Coincident with the past 15 years of performing this annual back and forth AAV plowing ac-

FIGURE 3. Marine amphibious assault vehicles plowing mudflats of Nu'upia Ponds, crushing invasive weeds, and opening water channels to expand and improve Hawaiian Stilt nesting and feeding opportunities. (Photo by D. Drigot).

tion, biannual stilt counts have more than doubled. Direct observations and monitoring studies have confirmed the creation of improved nesting and feeding substrate as significant contributing factors in attracting these birds (Rauzon 1992, Rauzon and Tanino 1995, Rauzon et al. 1997). A predator trapping program and minimization of human disturbances have also played a role. The moat-and-island terrain created by the AAV plowing action reduces the risk of egg predation by mongooses and helps the young, newly hatched stilt gain more ready access to food, water, and shelter. This is important since they are precocial at hatching and must fend for themselves (EMP 1).

As for the immediate human benefit, this action goes beyond compliance with federal resource stewardship mandates by providing the Marines an unexpected opportunity to practice working their vehicles in uncustomary terrain in a normally restricted area (EMP 3).

Thus, what may be construed as inherently destructive military maneuvers have been turned into an environmentally benevolent action. The Marines have become an integral part of the dynamics of this managed ecosystem, both providing and receiving a valuable service. Through this deliberate controlled disturbance once a year, the habitat becomes more available to the birds. In exchange, Marines get a novel training opportunity recognized by favorable media coverage, publications (e.g., Drigot 1996), and national awards earned in interservice military competitions (e.g., 23 Secretary of the Navy Natural Resources and/or Secretary of Defense Environmental Security Awards over 25 years). A sense of pride about environmental stewardship has grown, consistent with the Marine Corps' ethic about doing what is right and being protectors.

The Marines have adopted their own name— "Annual Mud Ops"—for this annual plowing ritual (Compton 1997). In response to base community interest, the base elementary school has even changed its mascot from a stallion to a stilt. When a ritual is thus born, acquires a name, and is adopted by the community, these are signs that it is sustainable and will have lasting affect, despite the constant rotation off the base of the individual Marines involved (Kent and Preister 1997; J. Kent, pers. comm.).

In summary, a potential conflict was turned into an unexpected opportunity to synergistically support valued military and wildlife functions of the pond landscape by applying an EM approach to integrated resource management (EMPs 1, 2, 3, 5).

DEVELOPING A REGIONALLY SHARED, SUSTAINABLE VISION OF AND COORDINATED APPROACHES TOWARD ECOSYSTEM HEALTH (EMPs 4, 6)

Another aspect of how MCBH's early EM approach has improved stilt habitat in a sustainable fashion has been the collaborative manner by which alien invasive red mangrove has been removed from the ponds using volunteer labor, thus cultivating a shared vision of desirable future ecosystem conditions in the region.

Introduced to the islands in the early 1900s for erosion control, red mangrove has spread throughout much of Hawai'i's coastal wetlands (Wester 1981). This invasive species has become a major threat to Hawaiian wetland habitats and to cultural resources as well. At Nu'upia Ponds, if left unchecked, mangrove can overgrow and destroy remnant ancient fishpond walls and valuable mudflat bird nesting and feeding habitat. These plants also clog waterways, alter native aquatic and wetland habitat, and out compete native wetland plants.

Using volunteer labor, in the early 1980s, MCBH began to tackle removal of this invasive alien plant in areas of the ponds not readily accessible by amphibious vehicles or other mechanized equipment. The intention was, with limited labor and funds, to discourage further eastward expansion across the fishpond complex.

In the process of involving diverse groups of volunteers (e.g., Sierra Club, Scouts, Marines, and school and church organizations), modest view planes were cleared into the pond habitat. In so doing, a shared vision of what was possible began to develop as more people were literally drawn into the landscape and established direct connection with the resource (EMP 4). Numerous schools and community groups, both on- and off-base, were successfully encouraged to incorporate pond mangrove-pulling events into their institutions' regular service schedules (Burrows 1997; EMP 3).

Over the years, by publicizing the positive results and coordinating a number of regular, volunteer weed-clearing services, further mangrove encroachment has been curtailed, while a sustained regional commitment to promoting ecosystem health has been fostered (EMPs 2, 3, 6).

Early and regular involvement of these "stakeholders" laid the foundation for sustaining the later benefits of an early 1990s infusion of Congressional Legacy Program funds. These competitively awarded funds helped MCBH to clear 17 acres, or 95% of remaining mangrove vegetation from the ponds, by a combination of contractor-assisted hand and heavy equipment techniques. In a few years, a quantum leap in habitat recovery and cultural landscape restoration was made at MCBH. These gains are being sustained by the continued services of various volunteer groups that have become part of the maintenance routine over the years (EMP 3).

Cultivation of this shared vision and service routines also has been instrumental in creating community awareness of the beneficial effects of a cooperative approach to restoring regional ecosystem health (EMP 6). Thus, cooperation is beginning to expand among resource managers, volunteers, concerned citizens, and groups in multiple ecosystems of the Kāne'ohe Bay region also involved in mangrove control, fishpond restoration, bird habitat enhancement, environmental education, or other ecosystem recovery efforts.

One of these groups, the Kāne'ohe Bay Regional Council, serves a community of interest encompassing the entire Kāne'ohe Bay shoreline adjacent to Mōkapu peninsula. This council is particularly concerned about the adverse effects of mangrove encroachment on Kāne'ohe Bay's shorelines and property values. They are using MCBH's experience and study results to build support for more mangrove removal along the shoreline fronting the bay, outside U.S. Marine Corps jurisdiction but within the jurisdiction of other public and private stakeholders (Kaneohe Bay Task Force 1997, Tully 1997). As awareness thus spreads, it is expected that a more coordinated interagency approach to mangrove control will emerge that will disperse the regional resource stewardship burden more evenly among all eligible stakeholders.

ADAPTING MANAGEMENT PRACTICES (EMPs 7, 8, 9, 10)

Legacy funds for mangrove removal at Nu'upia Ponds also supported systematic evaluation of improved environmental quality and stilt habitat along restored shorelines and adjacent waters (EMPs 7, 8). Careful observations of stilt response showed immediate expansion of bird nesting in the mudflats of the mangrove-cleared areas (Rauzon et al. 1997). Localized improvements in water quality chemistry were documented in areas recently cleared of heavy mangrove infestation (Cox and Jokiel 1997). Cultural features of this historic fishpond complex were more clearly exposed, mapped, and recorded through archaeological monitoring studies (McIntosh and Carlson 1996).

Fish surveys in the ponds documented the presence of at least 16 native fish species (Brock 1994). Fish tagging experiments demonstrated the critical value of the ponds as a nursery area for growing fry of native fish populations who later migrate into surrounding bay or ocean waters where they are caught by sports and commercial fishermen (Cox and Jokiel 1997; EMPs 7, 8).

Parallel research on historical human settlement patterns and former hydrologic regimes of the pond area through archival studies, oral histories, and group discussions led to renewed connections with early century residents and their descendants. Many traditions of resource use and stewardship have been recorded through these indigenous sources (Maly and Rosendahl 1995, Maly et al. 1997; EMP 2).

As public awareness of pond ecosystem health recovery spreads, potential conflicts in future envisioned uses of the Nu'upia Ponds are anticipated. Some interest groups have already requested that the Marines restore former fishpond harvesting techniques for subsistence purposes. However, the large-scale fish harvesting techniques likely needed to realize this vision are not compatible with either military security or endangered waterbird requirements for minimum human disturbance in the area.

MCBH is addressing these and other use pressures within the context of its integrated resource management planning process (Wilcox et al. 1997, Wilcox 1998). Data and insights revealed during this ecosystem-based management planning process have revealed an alternative way of addressing fishpond use pressure through a revival of Native Hawaiian use of these ponds in a way that may be more compatible with the needs of the Marines, the birds, and the interested publics: restoring the easternmost pond to its original saltworks configuration (Wilcox et al. 1997; EMPs 5, 7, 9, 10).

Throughout most of the 1,000 years of the ponds' cultural history, this area of the complex was managed as a saltworks. There is a strong tradition of salt gathering in several locations of the peninsula (Maly and Rosendahl 1995, Maly et al. 1997). Hawaiian Stilt not only can tolerate hypersaline conditions, but restored saltpans will support food sources attractive to stilts (e.g., brine shrimp and flies; Guinther 1985, Rauzon et al. 1997). Restoration of the high salinity extreme in the eastern end of the mixed salinity regime of Nu'upia Ponds will likely improve the heterogeneity of feeding habitats for Hawaiian Stilt there (Guinther 1983, 1985; E. Guinther, pers. comm.).

Restoring the saltworks would involve closing a channel created in the 1920s by the Territorial Game Farm (Cordy 1984). This would solve a current problem of sand migrating into the pond through the channel from the sand dune shoreline of the adjacent beach, enhancing the possibility of exposing Native Hawaiian burials located in this protected archaeological site.

To further develop this emerging vision of a possible restored saltworks, MCBH is looking to local and indigenous sources of knowledge. Thus, for example, oral histories of former Mōkapu residents about early twentieth century salt harvesting traditions and the experiences of other respected Hawaiian elders ("kupuna"), are being reviewed, some of whom still manage saltworks elsewhere in Hawai'i today (Maly and Rosendahl 1995, Maly et al. 1997). MCBH resource managers are also becoming familiar with contemporary Hawaiian cultural resource restoration techniques, having already employed Native Hawaiian stonemasons on a wall replication elsewhere on the peninsula (Kakesako 1997).

Such limited, localized, controlled public use/ harvesting of the ponds' resources in an endangered species habitat and historic landscape on a military base may be more manageable and compatible than fish harvesting uses, and more consistent with cultural precedent and recommendations (Maly and Rosendahl 1997; EMPs 5, 9).

CONTINUED USE OF ADAPTIVE MANAGEMENT APPROACH TO INSTALLATION IRMPS (EMPs 9, 10)

Successful EM requires the recognition that ecosystems are open, changing, and complex. Management practices need to be flexible in accommodating dynamic changes in scientific understandings, management concerns, and public issues. As seen above, they must also often include taking local and indigenous knowledge and ideas into account in addressing resource management problems and opportunities. Effective EM must be a collaborative learning process (Daniels and Walker 1996).

MCBH is following an adaptive management approach to striking a balance among the valued natural and cultural resources services provided by Nu'upia Ponds. This involves a continuous process of identifying and balancing natural, sociocultural, institutional, and economic opportunities and constraints, and framing the process within a consciously defined ecosystem boundary in a regional context. To further ensure that management actions and priorities are continuously effective, the recently developed IRMPs and implementation strategies are subject to regular review and updating (EMPs 9, 10).

CONCLUSION

In the application of EM principles at MCBH, it was discovered that endangered species restoration is possible, even on a busy military installation, so long as it is linked with the community's lifeways and cultural values, both past and present. These findings are similar to those of a recent national survey of over 100 ecosystem management projects in the United States, both public and private (Yaffee et al. 1996). This survey revealed that many pioneering efforts now underway hold promise of restoring ecosystem health through a more holistic approach to resource management. However, these efforts often face resistance if focused on the biophysical aspects of such restoration, with insufficient attention to the viewpoints of many different stakeholders affected by a given restoration scheme. MCBH's experience indicates the potential for sustainable ecosystem recovery is greater using an ecosystem-based management approach focusing on the following elements:

1. Acknowledge and incorporate human influences—past, present, and future—into ecosystem management schemes.
2. Understand that people form cultural attachments over time to an area where ritual activities take place (Kent and Preister 1997). If ways can be found to incorporate people's daily routines or valued rituals (e.g., military training, community service) into ecological restoration projects, then the chances of sustained ecological recovery are increased (J. Kent, pers. comm.).
3. Seek to adapt and refine solutions to emergent resource management challenges in a collaborative manner by regularly reviewing and refining one's vision of possibilities in light of mission requirements, best science, and stakeholder involvement.
4. Realize that such an approach to ecosystem management draws out the natural stewardship values in people. With an unstable funding climate for ecological restoration projects, securing public allegiance and support in this manner is an effective way to sustain the gains made.

ACKNOWLEDGMENTS

Mahalo nui (Much thanks!) to B. Wilcox and J. Kent for their valuable reflections as this manuscript evolved; to S. Conant, M. Morin, M. Scott, and one anonymous reviewer for their suggestions and comments; to state and federal wildlife biologists R. Saito, R. Walker, R. Shallenberger, T. Coleman, T. Burr, V. Byrd, and consultants M. Rauzon and L. Tanino, all of whom played a crucial advisory role over the years on the synergistic interaction possibilities between Amphibious Assault Vehicles and Hawaiian Stilt; and to all the Marines of Amphibian Assault Detachment, Combat Support Company, 3rd Marines, who are the real heroes in this Hawaiian Stilt recovery story. However, the views expressed in this article are those of the author, and do not necessarily reflect the positions of the U.S. Government, the U.S. Department of Defense, and the U.S. Marine Corps.

APPENDIX

ECOSYSTEM MANAGEMENT PRINCIPLES AND GUIDELINES, REPRINTED FROM ENCLOSURE (6) OF DEPARTMENT OF DEFENSE INSTRUCTION 4715.3 OF MAY 3, 1996, ENVIRONMENTAL CONSERVATION PROGRAM, PREPARED BY THE OFFICE OF THE DEPUTY UNDER SECRETARY OF DEFENSE (ENVIRONMENTAL SECURITY), 3400 DEFENSE PENTAGON, WASHINGTON D.C. 20301-3400

A. GOAL OF ECOSYSTEM MANAGEMENT

To ensure that military lands support present and future training and testing requirements while preserving, improving, and enhancing ecosystem integrity. Over the long-term, that approach shall maintain and improve the sustainability and biological diversity of terrestrial and aquatic (including marine) ecosystems while supporting sustainable economies, human use, and the environment required for realistic military training operations.

B. PRINCIPLES AND GUIDELINES

1. *Maintain and Improve the Sustainability and Native Biodiversity of Ecosystems.* Ecosystem management involves conducting installation programs and activities in a manner that identifies, maintains, and restores the "composition, structure, and function of natural communities that comprise ecosystems," to ensure their sustainability and conservation of biodiversity at landscape and other relevant ecological scales to the maximum extent that mission needs allow.
2. *Administer with Consideration of Ecological Units and Time Frames.* Ecosystem management requires consideration of the effects of installation programs and actions at spatial and temporal ecological scales that are relevant to natural processes. A larger geographic view and more appropriate ecological time frames assist in the analysis of cumulative effects on ecosystems that may not be apparent with smaller and shorter scales. Regional ecosystem management efforts are generally more appropriate than either national or installation-specific efforts. Consideration of sustainability under long-term environmental threats, such as climate change, is also important.
3. *Support Sustainable Human Activities.* People and their social, economic, and national security needs are an integral part of ecological systems, and management of ecosystems depends on sensitivity to those issues. Consistent with mission requirements, actions should support multiple use (e.g., outdoor recreation, hunting, fishing, forest timber products, and agricultural outleasing) and sustainable development by meeting the needs of the present without

compromising the ability of future generations to meet their own needs.

4. *Develop a Vision of Ecosystem Health.* All interested parties (federal, state, tribal, and local governments, nongovernmental organizations, private organizations, and the public) should collaborate in developing a shared vision of what constitutes desirable future ecosystem conditions for the region of concern. Existing social and economic conditions should be factored into the vision as well as methods by which all parties may contribute to the achievement of desirable ecosystem goals.

5. *Develop Priorities and Reconcile Conflicts.* Successful approaches should include mechanisms for establishing priorities among the objectives and for conflict resolution during both the selection of the ecosystem management objectives and the methods for meeting those objectives. Identifying "local installation objectives" and "urban development trends" are especially important to determine compatibility with ecosystem objectives. Regional workshops should be convened periodically to ensure that efforts are focused and coordinated.

6. *Develop Coordinated Approaches to Work Toward Ecosystem Health.* Ecosystems rarely coincide with ownership and political boundaries so cooperation across ownerships is an important component of ecosystem management. To develop the collaborative approach necessary for successful ecosystem management installations should:

   a. Involve the military operational community early in the planning process. Work with military trainers and others to find ways to accomplish the military mission in a manner consistent with ecosystem management.

   b. Develop a detailed ecosystem management implementation strategy for installation lands and other programs based on the vision developed in subsection B.4., above, and those principles and guidelines.

   c. Meet regularly with regional stakeholders (e.g., state, tribal, and local governments; nongovernmental entities; private landowners; and the public) to discuss issues and work toward common goals.

   d. Incorporate ecosystem management goals into strategic, financial, and program planning and design budgets to meet the goals and objectives of the ecosystem management implementation strategy.

   e. Seek to prevent undesirable duplication of effort, minimize inconsistencies, and create efficiencies in programs affecting ecosystems.

7. *Rely on the Best Science and Data Available.* Ecosystem management is based on scientific understanding of ecosystem composition, structure, and function. It requires more and better research and data collection, as well as better coordination and use of existing data and technologies. Information should be accessible, consistent, and commensurable. Standards should be established for the collection, taxonomy, distribution, exchange, update, and format of ecological, socioeconomic, cartographic, and managerial data.

8. *Use Benchmarks to Monitor and Evaluate Outcomes.* Accountability measurements are vital to effective ecosystem management. Implementation strategies should include specific and measurable objectives and criteria with which to evaluate activities in the ecosystem. Efficiencies gained through cooperation and streamlining should be included in those objectives.

9. *Use Adaptive Management.* Ecosystems are recognized as open, changing, and complex systems. Management practices should be flexible to accommodate the evolution of scientific understanding of ecosystems. Based on periodic reviews of implementation, adjustments to the standards and guidelines applicable to management activities affecting the ecosystem should be made.

10. *Implement Through Installation Plans and Programs.* An ecosystem's desirable range of future conditions should be achieved through linkages with other stakeholders. "Specific DoD activities" should be identified, as appropriate, in INRMPs and ICRMPs and in other planning and budgeting documents.

Studies in Avian Biology No. 22:338–346, 2001.

WHY ISN'T THE NIHOA MILLERBIRD EXTINCT?

SHEILA CONANT AND MARIE MORIN

Abstract. We used the extinction model VORTEX to assess population viability for the Nihoa Millerbird (*Acrocephalus familiaris kingi*), an endangered reed-warbler, endemic to the small Hawaiian Island of Nihoa. VORTEX was used to simulate establishment (via translocation) of new populations. Some population and life history parameters are known and others were estimated based on available data for similar tropical passerine birds. In these simulations, occasional population supplementation was the key to success, probably because it maintained genetic diversity. When current estimates of carrying capacity and environmental variation were used, 1,000-year simulations of 100 iterations each generated very high probabilities of extinction, but 100-year simulations were more optimistic. Because conservative estimates of some parameters (e.g., carrying capacity) always resulted in extinction, we used the more liberal estimates of some values. The model may need to be adjusted for populations such as this one that have had a long history of small size, probable numerous bottlenecks, and may no longer suffer severe negative effects from inbreeding or low levels of heterozygosity. We recommend that conservation measures for this species include an assessment of genetic variation (past and present) and that planning for translocation be undertaken without delay.

Key Words: Acrocephalus; conservation; endangered species; extinction; Hawaiian birds; Millerbird; population viability analysis (PVA); translocation; VORTEX.

The Nihoa Millerbird (*Acrocephalus familiaris kingi*) is endemic to tiny (63 ha) Nihoa Island in the Hawaiian Islands National Wildlife Refuge (NWR). Nihoa Millerbird was listed as endangered because of its small population (recent estimates have ranged from 30 to 730 birds), limited natural range, and the fragility of its native ecosystem (USFWS 1984a, Morin et al. 1997). The Laysan Millerbird (*A. f. familiaris*), which was endemic to Laysan Island (1,060 km northwest of Nihoa and also in the NWR), became extinct between 1916 and 1923, during a period when feral rabbits were destroying the vegetation on Laysan Island (Ely and Clapp 1973). According to the Northwestern Hawaiian Islands Passerines Recovery Plan (USFWS 1984a), the major threats to the continued existence of the Nihoa Millerbird are accidental introduction of alien plant and animal pests and environmental catastrophes. Due to difficulty of access, Nihoa may be less susceptible to accidental introductions of alien species than other northwestern Hawaiian islands. Consequently, the U.S. Fish and Wildlife Service has not actively pursued extraordinary conservation measures such as establishment of alternative populations and captive propagation. However, major environmental perturbations, such as hurricanes or severe drought, may occur at any time.

The genus *Acrocephalus* (reed-warblers) is relatively widespread in Eurasia and Africa and among the Pacific islands, where it has colonized numerous islands, many of which are small and often remote (Pratt et al. 1987). Based on its patchy, apparently relictual distribution, Pratt et al. (1987) speculate that the genus has been in the Pacific for a long time and note that

the Pacific island forms have diverged substantially in morphology from continental relatives. In the Hawaiian Islands *Acrocephalus* is known to occur only on Laysan and Nihoa islands. Despite extensive paleontological exploration in a variety of sites in the main islands (James and Olson 1991), no fossils of this genus have been found.

Vertebrate populations with limited ranges and of small size (similar to that of the Nihoa Millerbird) are thought to be at risk of extinction due to demographic and environmental stochasticity and loss of genetic variation (Soulé 1987). In the early 1980s, basing their estimates primarily on genetic considerations, biologists (e.g., Franklin 1980, Soulé 1980, Shaffer 1981) suggested that an effective population size (N_e) of at least 50 was the minimum viable population size (MVP) for which we might expect a species to survive for up to 100 years. The idea of a specific number was quickly recognized to be an oversimplification of the issue. Lande and Barrowclough (1987) and Soulé (1987), among others, revised the notion of MVP, stating that 500 was a much safer MVP for vertebrates, if, indeed, it was wise to specify an MVP in the first place. Those same authors also provided an extensive discussion of the MVP concept, cautioning that numerous factors (e.g., genetic, demographic, environmental, populational) must be considered in any estimation of MVP for a particular species. Recently, Lande (1995) addressed the MVP issue in the context of genetic variation, concluding that most vertebrate populations should number at least 5,000 if they are to survive at least 100 more years. Unfortunately many, if not most, endangered vertebrate populations number fewer than 5,000. Many conservation biologists and managers generally agree that ecosystem protection is the best way to conserve viable populations (e.g., Tear et al. 1993); nevertheless, recovery plans for endangered species often specify a minimum census population size (often smaller than 5,000) as a means of judging whether a species has sufficiently recovered to be considered "secure."

The notion of MVP seems to have been developed largely in a context of concern for the conservation of vertebrate species (or populations) that have undergone relatively recent (in the last century or two) and dramatic declines in total population size and/or geographic range. The MVP concept has no doubt provided a good framework for conservation planning for endangered vertebrates. However, we wondered if the concepts and the models (in this case, VORTEX; Lacy 1993, Lacy et al. 1995) developed for population viability analysis (PVA) of rare vertebrates were appropriate for small populations that may have been "naturally" small for several thousands of years and whose geographic range has also been small for a similar length of time. In other words, do "naturally" small populations, such as those endemic to small, remote islands, have the same risk of extinction as populations that have become small due to recent, dramatic declines?

Frankham (1995) discussed the role inbreeding may play in extinction. He pointed out that the susceptibility of island populations to extinction has been attributed to nongenetic causes and cautioned that inbreeding is probably also an important cause of extinction on islands. But is this really true? And, if it is, how could we distinguish between extinctions due to genetic causes, including inbreeding depression and loss of heterozygosity, and those due to demographic and environmental stochasticity? Although we have not been able to answer that question with the work reported here, our results prompt us to reiterate that genetic, demographic, and environmental factors all need to be addressed when PVAs are used as a basis for planning management actions aimed at conserving rare species (Mills et al. 1996). Although VORTEX allows us to assess all these factors, we found that its estimates of extinction probabilities for the Nihoa Millerbird still seem unrealistic.

METHODS AND MATERIALS

VORTEX is a computer model that provides a stochastic simulation of the extinction process (Lacy et al. 1995). The model uses basic life history (e.g., age at first reproduction, age-specific reproductive success) and genetic parameters to estimate the probability of extinction within a particular time frame (usually 100

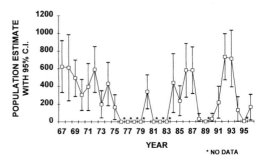

FIGURE 1. Nihoa Millerbird population estimates from 1967 to 1996.

to 1,000 years). Like any model, VORTEX makes a number of assumptions that can be violated for any particular analysis.

Although we have some data about the life history of the Nihoa Millerbird (Conant et al. 1981, Morin et al. 1997), we found it necessary to estimate a number of parameters. To do this we conducted a literature survey on life history of small tropical passerines, including those endemic to islands or archipelagoes and, especially, *Acrocephalus* species (Rowley and Russell 1991; Komdeur 1992, 1994a, 1997). We also examined unpublished data (made available to us by colleagues) on life history parameters of other endemic Hawaiian passerines. Presently we have no data on baseline genetic diversity in this subspecies or in the extinct Laysan Millerbird; however, blood samples from live Nihoa Millerbirds have been collected and tissue samples could be taken from museum specimens to resolve some of the genetic issues.

THE EXISTING KNOWLEDGE

Population size and carrying capacity

Between 1967 and 1996, the U.S. Fish and Wildlife Service (USFWS) censused the Nihoa Millerbird population 21 times. The estimates ranged from a low of 31 birds to a high of 731 birds, with a mean of 380, a median of 395, and an average 95% CI of $\pm$ 211.5 (N = 21, range 61–374; Fig. 1; see also Appendix 2 in Morin et al. 1997). Strip transects 3 m wide were used for all estimates (see Conant et al. 1981 for a detailed description of the method), and estimates are based on the assumption that all birds are detected within those transects. The 95% CI for these estimates are quite large, due, in large part, to effects caused by observers (Conant et al. 1981, and see Morin and Conant 1994 for a discussion of effects of observer variability on population estimates).

Using spot mapping and habitat evaluation, Conant et al. (1981) estimated that 40 ha of Nihoa Island's 63 ha of habitat are suitable for Nihoa Millerbird territories. Territory size ranges from 0.2 to 0.4 ha, so the number of territories on the island could be 100 to 200. There is insufficient data to assess what proportion of the population consists of pairs with territories and what proportion consists of floaters. According to the recovery plan for the endangered passerines of the Northwestern Hawaiian Islands (USFWS 1984a), the carrying capacity (K) is 600, and, although we used

TABLE 1. EXSTING KNOWLEDGE (MORIN ET AL.1997) OF NIHOA MILLERBIRD LIFE HISTORY PARAMETERS

40 ha of Nihoa Island's 63 ha useable for territories

Territories are 0.2 to 0.4 ha, permitting 100 to 200 territories

Pairs stay on territories year-round, are monogamous, and retain mate from year to year

Clutch size is 2 to 3 (mean = 2.2, N = 16)

Pairs can breed more than once per year

From 1967 to 1996, population averaged 380 birds (N = 21, range = 31–731).

Carrying capacity (K) for Nihoa Island ~ 600 (USFWS 1984a), SD of environmental variation estimated at 200

K for extinct Laysan Millerbird on Laysan Island estimated at 1,500, SD of environmental variaion at 500

this figure in our analyses, we think it may be an overestimate.

Life history parameters

Pairs remain on their territories year-round, are monogamous, and retain pair bonds from year to year (Morin et al. 1997). Clutch size is two or three eggs (mean = 2.2, N = 16), and pairs may breed more than once per year, though this has been documented for only one pair (Morin et al. 1997). Existing knowledge about the Nihoa Millerbird is summarized in Table 1. We needed to estimate a number of additional parameters in order to use VORTEX.

ESTIMATES OF PARAMETERS FOR A STANDARD RUN OF THE MODEL

Due to the dearth of information about this species, we estimated many of the parameters in order to run the model in VORTEX. In this section we provide a detailed discussion of and justification for those estimates.

Reproduction and mortality

We assumed a monogamous breeding system. The VORTEX model assumes random recombination of pairs each year (Lindenmayer et al. 1995), so that any advantage to reproductive success or survival conferred by mate fidelity is apparently not modeled. We were unable to assess the importance of this attribute of the VORTEX model. We know that banded pairs remained together on their territories, and both parents incubated eggs and cared for their young (Morin et al. 1997); this type of mating system would certainly limit, if not preclude, opportunities for extra-pair copulations. We assumed that the parents at the nest were the genetic parents of the young in that nest, although we do not have genetic information to confirm this assumption. Craig (1992) found that the Nightingale Reed-warbler (*Acrocephalus luscinia*), endemic to Saipan, was largely or entirely monogamous and that males defended relatively large territories on which most were sedentary for the two years of the study. In contrast, Brooke and Hartley (1995) found, in a single study season, that Henderson Reed-warblers (*A.*

vaughani taiti) bred cooperatively, as the Seychelles Warbler (*A. sechellensis*) will do under certain conditions (Komdeur 1994b). Age at first breeding is not known for the Henderson or Nightingale reed-warblers.

We assumed that females and males breed at one year of age. Although we do not have data for the Nihoa Millerbird, we do know that the Hawai'i 'Ākepa (*Loxops coccineus;* Lepson and Freed 1997), and the 'Elepaio (*Chasiempis sandwichensis*; VanderWerf 1998a) sometimes breed at one year of age, although quality of habitat and food probably influence the age at which birds breed. Seychelles Warblers may breed as early as eight to nine months of age, or reproduction may be considerably delayed (up to six years) if habitat quality is low (Komdeur 1992, 1994a,b). We assumed that the maximum, cumulative number of young per female per year is four, an assumption based on observations of a single banded pair of birds with two successful clutches in one breeding season (Morin et al. 1997). In the VORTEX equation for percentage of females that breed, we assumed that when the population is well below K, 95% of females breed, and when the population is at K, 65% of females breed. We assumed that all males would be in the breeding pool when the population was below K.

Environmental variation and reproduction

We assumed that environmental variation in reproduction and survival are correlated and that reproduction is density dependent. The population is limited to a small island that probably has a limited food supply, and the quality and amount of food and shelter are strongly affected by environmental factors, such as amount and distribution of rainfall, which, in turn, probably affect reproductive success. Komdeur and colleagues (Komdeur et al. 1991; Komdeur 1992, 1994a,b, 1997) have documented that reproduction in the Seychelles Warbler is strongly influenced by environmental variables, and that reproduction is density dependent. We assumed that the Allee effect would be zero because the island is so small that it is unlikely individuals would have difficulty finding mates if they were available. Territorial males advertise with a distinctive territorial song that "floater" females should be able to detect as they are moving about. VORTEX asks the investigator to choose one of several formulas that describes the shape of the curve (B) describing density dependence. We did not have information on the true shape of this curve for our species. We chose B = 8 because this curve best fit our expectation that, due to limited available habitat, a steep decrease in breeding would occur at high population densities as is the case for the Seychelles Warbler (Komdeur 1992, 1994b). We modeled three types of environmental catastrophes and based our estimates of their frequencies on available weather data and historical accounts of fire on the island. We assumed that there would be a severe drought every 50 years, a remarkable hurricane every 100 years, and a major fire every 200 years. Although hurricanes frequently occur near Hawai'i, between 1904 and 1967 only four came close enough to affect the islands (Mueller-Dombois et al. 1981a). According to Armstrong (1983) 14 hurricanes occurred near Hawai'i between 1950 and 1983, but none of

TABLE 2. STANDARD CONDITIONS FOR VORTEX SIMULATIONS FOR THE NIHOA MILLERBIRD

Simulations to run for 100 or 1,000 years, 100 iterations each
No inbreeding depression
Environmental variation in reproduction and survival are correlated
Three catastrophes in Nihoa Model:
- Droughts: 2/100 yrs, 0.5 effect on reproduction, 0.8 on survival
- Hurricanes: 1/100 yrs, 0.5 effect on reproduction, 0.75 on survival
- Fires: 1/200 yrs, 0.5 effect on reproduction, 0.5 on survival

Monogamous breeding system
Females and males breed at 1 year of age
Maximum age is 10 years
Sex ratio at birth is 1:1
Maximum cumulative young fledged per female per year is 4
Reproduction is density dependent
In equation for percentage of breeding females: $P(0)^a = 95\%$, $P(K)^b = 65\%$, $B^c = 8$, $A^d = 0$
For breeding females:
- 35% fledge 1/yr 45% fledge 2/yr
- 15% fledge 3/yr 5% fledge 4/yr
- SD = 5%

70% mortality from fledging to 1 yr (20% EV^e) both sexes
- 15% mortality 1 yr to 10 yrs (5% EV) females
- 10% mortality 1 yr to 10 yrs (3% EV) males

All males in breeding pool
Stable age population
Initial (1996) population = 200
K = 600
Standard deviation (EV) in K = 200
No harvest or supplementation

[a] P(0) = probability of extinction observed.
[b] P(K) = probability of carry capacity.
[c] B = curve describing density dependence.
[d] A = Allee effect (difficulty in finding a mate).
[e] EV = environmental variation.

these did any serious damage. Since then, only two storms, Hurricane Iwa in 1983 and Hurricane 'Iniki in 1992 have caused serious structural damage to natural habitats. Droughts are a regular feature of El Niño events, which occur roughly every 20 years, but remarkable droughts occur less frequently (Armstrong 1983). Smith and Tunison (1992) summarized what is know about the role of fire in Hawai'i's natural ecosystems, concluding that it played a minor role until the establishment of human populations and alien species, particularly grasses. Our estimate that one catastrophic fire would occur every 200 years takes into account a low natural rate of fire and a substantially higher fire risk associated with human visitation to Nihoa Island.

Initial population size, carrying capacity (K), length of runs, and inbreeding depression

We assumed the Nihoa Millerbird population would have a stable age distribution, that K was 600, as stated in the recovery plan, and that the standard deviation of K was 200. We used the 1996 population estimate of 200 birds as the initial population size. There could be no supplementation of this population because it is the only one in existence, and harvesting is not currently permitted. We ran both 100- and 1,000-year simulations of 100 iterations each. For our standard condition runs of the model, we assumed that there would be no inbreeding depression because the population has been small for a substantial, though unknown,

length of time. We included inbreeding depression in a few other runs to see what would happen, and those results are discussed below. Other PVAs (Bustamante 1996) have assumed no inbreeding depression as part of the standard conditions for their VORTEX runs.

Appropriateness of estimates

Although we based our estimates of most life history parameters on data for similar species, we do admit to a certain amount of bias generated by our early attempts at running the model. For example, we feel that the estimate of K = 600 from the recovery plan for this species is rather high. We note that the average population estimate is 380 birds, well below 600. If K is actually 600 and the standard deviation of K is actually 200, then the average of the population estimates and the confidence intervals for those estimates should more closely approach 600 and 200, respectively. However, we found that if we attempted to run the model with a K lower than 600, the probability of extinction [P(E)] was so high that, if the model is correct, the Nihoa Millerbird should have gone extinct long ago. We regard some of our estimates of other parameters (e.g., age-specific reproductive success for females) "optimistic" as well but found that lower estimates caused the model to "crash" consistently. These problems will be discussed later.

Standard conditions we used to run the model are shown in Table 2.

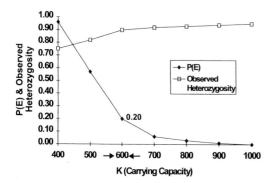

FIGURE 2. Probability of extinction [P(E)] and observed heterozygosity in Nihoa Millerbirds for 100-year VORTEX run of 100 iterations. Environmental variation (EV) = 200 for different carrying capacities K, "standard" condition being K = 600.

RESULTS

RESULTS OF 100- AND 1,000-YEAR SIMULATIONS

The results of the 100-year simulation of 100 iterations at the standard conditions specified above are illustrated in Figure 2. At a K of 600, the probability of extinction [P(E)] is 0.20. In this example (Fig. 2) the model is very sensitive to K; that is, P(E) increases dramatically as K decreases. Observed heterozygosity and the number of alleles increases with K, more rapidly up to K = 700 than at higher K. The results of a 1,000-year simulation (using identical input and also performed with 100 iterations) provide a much less optimistic outlook (Fig. 3). At K = 600, P(E) in the 1,000-year run is 0.96 and decreases to 0.42 at K = 700. Observed hetero-

zygosity and number of alleles are much lower in this simulation, an indication of the effects of heterozygosity on the P(E).

EFFECTS OF ENVIRONMENTAL VARIATION

To examine the effect of environmental variation (EV) in K, we varied the standard deviation (EV) of K, which, in the previously discussed simulations, was 200. When EV decreases from 200 to 150 in the 100-year simulation, observed heterozygosity rises from 0.90 to 0.93 and P(E) drops from 0.20 to 0.04 (Fig. 4). For the 1,000-year simulations P(E) remains high regardless of the magnitude of EV; however, it dropped to <0.40 when EV was only 150. We believe that EV may actually be much higher than 150. In the 1,000-year simulations, when EV was 250, all Nihoa Millerbirds in these iterations went extinct by year 400, and when EV was 300, they went extinct by year 200.

Under our "standard conditions" (Table 2), which included no inbreeding depression, the mean final population for successful cases of 100-year simulations was 278 Nihoa Millerbirds (SD = 168.5), and the mean final population for successful cases of 1,000-year simulations was 170 Nihoa Millerbirds (SD = 125.2). When we changed the inbreeding depression to the Recessive Lethal Model and kept all other conditions the same, the mean final population for successful 100-year simulations was 240 Nihoa Millerbirds (SD = 129.6), and the mean final population for successful 1,000-year simulations was 309 Nihoa Millerbirds (SD = 92.2)

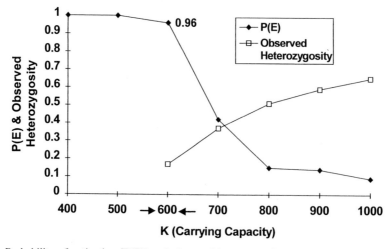

FIGURE 3. Probability of extinction [P(E)] and observed heterozygosity in Nihoa Millerbirds for 1,000-year VORTEX run of 100 iterations. Environmental variation (EV) = 200 for different carrying capacities K, "standard" condition being K = 600.

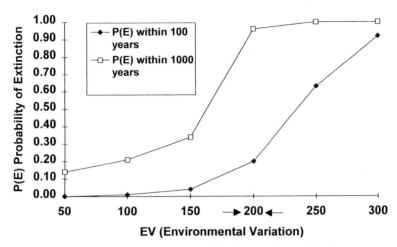

FIGURE 4.   Probability of extinction [P(E)] in Nihoa Millerbirds for K = 600 when environmental variation (EV) ranges from 50 to 300, for 100-year and 1,000-year VORTEX runs. All runs resulted in extinction by year 400 in the 1,000-year runs when CV = 250, and all runs resulted in extinction by year 200 when EV = 300.

EFFECTS OF VARIATION IN MORTALITY REGIMES

Because we lack data on mortality regimes for this species, we decided to examine how P(E) would vary with different mortality regimes. Figure 5 shows the results of both 100- and 1,000-year simulations in nine different mortality regimes. We ran a simulation with three different adult mortality regimes and three different first-year mortality regimes. Perhaps the most striking result shown in Figure 5 is the difference in P(E) for the 100- and 1,000-year simulations. Only in the most pessimistic mortality regime (shown in the first column of Fig. 5) does the P(E) for the 100-year simulation resemble that of the 1,000-year simulation. The P(E) for any single 1,000-year simulation was never less than 0.70; whereas all but one of the 100-year simulations had P(E) values of less than 0.25.

DISCUSSION

INFLUENCE OF CARRYING CAPACITY K ON PROBABILITY OF EXTINCTION P(E)

As we mentioned above, we believe that the estimation of K = 600 in the recovery plan

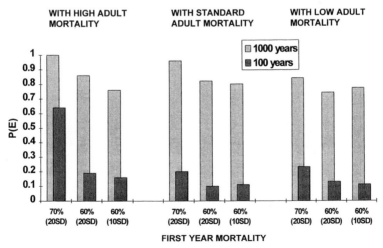

FIGURE 5.   Probability of extinction [P(E)] for Nihoa Millerbirds under three different first-year and adult mortality regimes. First year mortality was 70% (SD = 20) or 60% (SD = 10 and SD = 20). In addition there were three adult mortality regimes. High mortality: adult females 20% (SD = 10%), adult males 15% (SD = 5%); "standard" conditions: adult females 15% (SD = 5%) adults males 10% (SD = 3%); low mortality: adult females 10% (SD = 3%), adult males 10% (SD = 3%).

(USFWS 1984a) for this species is a substantial overestimate. We feel it would be more realistic to use the mean population estimate (380) derived from 21 censuses that were made during the last 30 years (Fig. 1). However, when we attempted to use K = 380, all simulations had very high P(E). Furthermore, we feel that 200 may be an unrealistically low estimate of EV, again because the censuses (Fig. 1) show such a great deal of variation from year to year. However, if we use an even higher estimate of EV than 200, all simulations result in extinction very quickly. This suggests to us that environmental variation could, in reality, be much smaller than we think. Furthermore, the possibility that K changes, perhaps considerably, from year to year seems very reasonable. The negative effects of the 1997–1998 El Niño phenomenon on environmentally mediated reproduction and survival of many Hawaiian birds appears to have been dramatic (P. Banko, H. D. Pratt, and A. Engilis, pers. comm.)

LIFE HISTORY PARAMETERS

In the model, the percentage of breeding females is a function of population size, but the percentage of breeding males is fixed for any single simulation. We speculate that the percentage of breeding males may also be a density dependent function. If we have underestimated reproductive potential, the population may be more resistant to extinction than our results suggest. For example, if Nihoa Millerbirds breed in response to vegetation flushes brought on by rainfall, then they may have much higher reproductive rates in some years, making the results of our simulations overly pessimistic. It could be that Nihoa Millerbirds, like the Seychelles Warbler (Komdeur 1994a, 1997), may often raise two broods a year. Another consideration here is that, because this model assumes random reassignment of mates each year, it may underestimate reproductive success associated with multiyear mate fidelity. Thus, the effects of multiyear mate fidelity on the probability of extinction remain unknown for the Nihoa Millerbird.

However, even if we have underestimated reproductive potential and overestimated mortality, these values are considerably less important than overestimates of K in the model. As mentioned above, because the simulations using lower values for K almost always went to extinction rapidly (much higher P(E) values), we were somewhat liberal in estimating some life history parameters.

We were surprised at how insensitive the model seemed to be to different mortality regimes (see Fig. 5). Lower mortality regimes did not always have higher probabilities of extinc-

tion. Perhaps the mortality regimes we used overlapped sufficiently to mask such differences.

THE ROLE OF GENETIC VARIATION IN THE MODEL

VORTEX allows the investigator to specify whether or not the population experiences inbreeding depression. The VORTEX simulations used to generate Figures 2–5 were run without inbreeding depression. However, using the rest of the standard conditions (Table 2), we added inbreeding depression for a 100-year and a 1,000-year simulation with both the Heterosis Model (using the default mammalian values of 3.14 lethal equivalents per genome; Ralls et al. 1988) and the Recessive Lethal Model. The P(E) for 100 and 1,000 years for the Heterosis Model were: 0.28 (28 of the 100 simulations went extinct in 100 years) and 1.0 (all simulations went extinct by the year 300), respectively. In contrast, the P(E) for the Recessive Lethal Model were actually the same or slightly more optimistic than those values VORTEX generated when no inbreeding depression was specified: P(E) = 0.18 for 100 years and P(E) = 0.93 for 1,000 years. The choice of "no inbreeding depression" (standard conditions in Table 2) generated a 100-year P(E) = 0.20 and a 1,000-year P(E) = 0.96 (Figs. 2, 3).

We decided to eliminate inbreeding depression from our simulations because our population was so small, and had been small for possibly thousands of years. Population estimates over the last 30 years show considerable fluctuation in population size, which is not surprising because of the harsh, variable habitat Nihoa provides. Thus, we expect the population has been subject to frequent and severe bottlenecks, allowing it to adapt a relatively high level of inbreeding. We note that our populations lost heterozygosity quickly in the simulations, and that this factor may have played an important role in the generation of high extinction probabilities. We speculate that our population may not be as severely affected by this factor as populations that have undergone recent, dramatic declines but are at a loss to do more than speculate on the role such a difference might play in scaling the model somewhat differently for our population. This issue could be addressed if we could make a comparison of genetic variation between Laysan and Nihoa Millerbird populations (via the use of museum specimens), as well as a comparison of Nihoa specimens collected in the 1920s and blood samples collected 70 years later in 1992 and 1993. The latter comparison would allow us to compare VORTEX estimates of genetic change in the population over time with actual data.

100-Year Simulations Versus 1000-Year Vortex Simulations

A number of PVAs reported in the literature or performed by or for management agencies report on the results of simulations that are much shorter than 1,000 years (e.g., Ellis et al. 1992a,b; Bustamante 1996, Mills et al. 1996). Our results indicate that 100-year simulations are not very useful for long-term conservation goals, since they give the illusion that populations may be secure, when this may only be true for the short-term (i.e., 100 years) and not the long-term. If management programs are based on results of short-term simulations, they may become locked into simplified or superficial short-term goals due to lack of in-depth understanding of how the population could behave. Populations judged to be "secure" in the short-term may become genetically depleted to the point that they may not recover from their endangered status if management goals are based on results of short-term PVAs.

Should The Nihoa Millerbird be Translocated to Other Islands?

VORTEX predicts that as K increases P(E) will decrease, all else being equal. This suggests that management efforts for this species should focus strongly on increasing K. Our simulations clearly showed that the higher the value of K, the more extinction resistant the population will be. Because Nihoa Island is limited in size, predator free, and relatively undisturbed, there is little likelihood that managing the habitat there could increase the carrying capacity. The most expedient method of increasing the carrying capacity of Nihoa Millerbird would be to establish one or more additional populations that are geographically separated from the Nihoa population, so that environmental, demographic, and genetic factors affecting extinction probabilities will vary independently for the different populations. Establishment of two alternative populations of the Seychelles Warbler by translocations has certainly brought the species back from the brink of extinction (Komdeur 1997). The potentially devastating effects of an accidental rat introduction (see Fisher and Baldwin 1946a for a description of the extinction of the Laysan Finch [*Telespiza cantans*] and Laysan Rail [*Porzana palmeri*] from Midway within two years of accidental rat introduction) suggest that establishing additional Nihoa Millerbird populations would probably be the single most effective conservation measure that could be undertaken at this time.

To explore translocation as a means of increasing Nihoa Millerbird K, we simulated an

TABLE 3. VORTEX SIMULATIONS OF NIHOA MILLERBIRD INTRODUCTION TO LAYSAN ISLAND, HAWAI'I

	P(E)[a]	Observed heterozygosity	Final number of alleles
100-year scenarios			
40 males and 40 females	0.24	0.92	30.1
No supplementation			
Suppl: 5yr-old males 5yr-old females 1 × per 10 yrs	0.0	0.96	74.1
1,000-year scenarios			
20 males and 20 females	0.0	0.77	29.5
Suppl: 5yr-old males 5yr-old females 1 × per 10 yrs			

[a] P(E) = Probability of extinction.

introduction to Laysan Island. Laysan is probably the best choice for establishing a second population because the Laysan Millerbird once occurred there, the island is predator-free, and there are a number of native and introduced arthropods for food sources. Based on the size of Laysan Island, in particular the size of its vegetated area (~190 ha), we estimated that K = 1,500 Nihoa Millerbirds. We estimated that on Laysan, EV = 500, then we simulated several scenarios for the introduction (Table 3). In these simulations, we incorporated hurricanes and droughts with the same frequencies and effects as those in the Nihoa simulations (see Table 2), but we did not include fire because we felt that fires on Laysan are far less likely to get started, as well as to move very far due to damp soil conditions and lack of significant dry fuel.

In the first pair of 100-year simulations, we introduced 40 males and 40 females each time. In one case, there was no supplementation, and, in the second case, the population was supplemented with five-year-old males and five-year-old females every ten years. Without supplementation, the first introduction had a 0.24 P(E) in 100 years. With supplementation the P(E) was zero. Although observed heterozygosities at the end of the 100 years were similar (0.92 for the unsupplemented introduction and 0.96 for the supplemented introduction), the final number of alleles in the supplemented was 74.1, compared to only 30.1 in the unsupplemented population. VORTEX predicts that even a very modest level of supplementation will give the population much higher odds for survival. Supplementation is the key to success for these translocation scenarios, because it allows a much higher level of heterozygosity to be maintained. To mimic an even more practical translocation, we ran a 1,000-year simulation that involved the introduction of 20 males and 20 females, and which was supplemented every 50 years with five-year-old males and five-year-old females. This simulated translocation had an extinction probability of zero as well, a most encouraging result.

We have not suggested the establishment of an alternative population in captivity because it seems likely that this alternative would be prohibitively expensive and may carry unacceptable risks. The passerines of Laysan and Nihoa islands have been isolated from avian diseases such as pox and malaria for a long, though unknown, period of time. Current knowledge of the serious impacts of these diseases on endemic Hawaiian passerines (e.g., van Riper and van Riper 1985, van Riper et al. 1986, Feldman et al. 1995, Jarvi et al. *this volume*, Shehata et al. *this volume*, van Riper and Scott *this volume*), as well as documentation of the Laysan Finch's susceptibility to avian malaria (Warner 1968, Throp 1970) suggest that the risks of moving birds from a captive propagation facility to one of these remote and isolated islands are likely to be quite serious. Furthermore, insectivorous birds are known to be highly sensitive to capture and captive conditions (Komdeur et al. 1994a), so that the remoteness of the population will make any kind of hands-on management involving transport of birds very risky.

The results of both our VORTEX Nihoa Millerbird PVA, as well as the translocation simulations, encouraged us to speculate that the Nihoa Millerbird's historical distribution may have included additional islands (e.g., Lisianski, French Frigate Shoals, Necker, Kaua'i), although this is not yet substantiated by paleontological findings (but note that Curnett et al., *this volume*, discuss how recent paleontological discoveries have reduced the number of single-island endemics throughout Pacific island groups). Alternatively, or perhaps additionally, there may have been a small, nevertheless significant, amount of gene flow between the Laysan and Nihoa populations of this species. Either of these possibilities might well provide the answer to the question posed by our title. More importantly, our results suggest that the species is in serious danger of going extinct during the next two or three decades if an alternative population is not established.

We should be able to refine our population viability analysis of this species if we have better data on several life history parameters: age-specific mortality, annual age-specific reproductive success, proportion of breeding adults of each sex in the population. In addition, we need a more realistic idea of what the carrying capacity really is on Nihoa Island and how much it varies. Finally, and perhaps this will be the easiest issue to assess, we need to know the nature of genetic variation in both the Laysan and Nihoa Millerbird populations.

In his paper, "Inbreeding and Extinction: a threshold effect," Frankham (1995) warns that, "there may be little warning of impending extinction due to inbreeding in wildlife, especially with species that are not intensively monitored." We concur and further add that monitoring should include assessing genetic variability as well as the usual parameters examined for rare populations, such as population size and annual reproductive success. Because samples are readily available, an assessment of genetic variation in the species should be undertaken immediately. This assessment should include a comparison of the Laysan and Nihoa Millerbird populations as well as an examination of genetic variation over time for the Nihoa population. Although the population is censused in most years, there is no monitoring aimed at assessing variation in reproductive success, which is unfortunate. Lack of access to the island and the disturbance such monitoring may cause to other wildlife and plants can be serious, however. If establishment of new populations by translocation to Laysan Island (or other islands, such as Midway Atoll or Lisianski Island) is a possibility, planning and data acquisition should begin immediately.

At this point in time we have the luxury of being able to ask, "Why isn't the Nihoa Millerbird extinct?" If action to conserve the species is not taken soon, we may be asking, "Why did the Nihoa Millerbird go extinct?"

ACKNOWLEDGMENTS

We thank the U.S. Fish and Wildlife Service and the National Marine Fisheries Service for financial and logistic support for fieldwork. M. S. Collins, M. J. Rauzon, D. P. McCauley, D. R. Hopper, and V. H. Gauger assisted with fieldwork, J. L. Simasko assisted with figures, and the U.S. Fish and Wildlife, J. K. Lepson, L. A. Freed, and E. VanderWerf made their unpublished data available to us. J. M. Scott and an anonymous reviewer made a number of helpful suggestions on the first draft of this paper.

Studies in Avian Biology No. 22:347–353, 2001.

REINTRODUCTION AND TRANSLOCATION OF 'ŌMA'O: A COMPARISON OF METHODS

STEVEN G. FANCY, JAY T. NELSON, PETER HARRITY, JOPE KUHN, MARLA KUHN, CYNDI KUEHLER, AND JON G. GIFFIN

Abstract. We reintroduced 25 captive-reared 'Ōma'o (*Myadestes obscurus*) and translocated 16 wild-caught 'Ōma'o to former range in the Pu'u Wa'awa'a Wildlife Sanctuary on the island of Hawai'i to develop and refine methods that might be used in the recovery of the closely related and critically endangered Puaiohi (*Myadestes palmeri*) on Kaua'i. Captive-reared 'Ōma'o were soft-released from two hacking towers at 66–57 days of age, whereas wild birds (all adults) were hard-released on the same day as capture or after a 1–9 day holding period. The fate of all birds was monitored daily for two months using radiotelemetry. Only 16 of 76 (21%) wild-caught 'Ōma'o were translocated because of problems with active avian poxlike lesions, an imbalanced sex ratio, or because birds would not eat during holding. Survival to 30 days postrelease was similar for birds released by the two methods: three captive-reared 'Ōma'o were killed by predators, and four wild 'Ōma'o died of handling/transport stress. 'Ōma'o populations are highly male biased, and a sex ratio of captive-hatched eggs of 18 males to 6 females suggests that the sex ratio may not be 1:1 at hatching. Translocation of hatching-year 'Ōma'o would not be practical because of very low capture success for juvenile 'Ōma'o and the skewed sex ratio. Fidelity to the release site was higher for captive-reared birds, and this approach is less expensive for 'Ōma'o and more likely to result in successful establishment of a new population in continuous habitat.

Key Words: captive propagation; Hawai'i; Hawaiian honeycreepers; *Myadestes obscurus*; 'Ōma'o; reintroduction; translocation.

Major management programs have been initiated in recent years by federal, state, and private agencies in Hawai'i to protect and restore portions of native ecosystems deemed critical for the survival of endangered Hawaiian forest birds. In several areas, there has been notable recovery of both the structure and composition of the native vegetation, but reintroductions of captive-reared birds or translocations of wild birds will be needed to speed the recovery of avian populations. The U.S. Fish and Wildlife Service (USFWS) has entered into a long-term agreement with The Peregrine Fund to propagate Hawaiian forest birds in captivity in efforts to restore several species of endangered birds, and captive propagation and release are included in recovery plans for many Hawaiian species. However, considering the relatively poor track record of bird reintroductions on the mainland (Griffith et al. 1989, Snyder et al. 1996, Wolf et al. 1996), the critically low population sizes of some Hawaiian species, and the unique situation where mosquito-borne diseases (Warner 1968, van Riper et al. 1986) and introduced mammalian predators (Atkinson 1977, Scott et al. 1986) have devastated the Hawaiian avifauna, further development and refinement of reintroduction and translocation methods are needed for Hawaiian species before these tools can be used effectively in recovery efforts.

The development of captive propagation and reintroduction methods is recommended in the recovery plan (USFWS 1983a) for two species

of critically endangered Hawaiian solitaires on Kaua'i, the Kāma'o (*Myadestes myadestinus*) and Puaiohi (*M. palmeri*). The Kāma'o was once the most common forest bird on Kaua'i but is now extremely rare or extinct (Scott et al. 1986, Reynolds et al. 1997b, *this volume*; Conant et al. 1998), whereas an estimated 300 Puaiohi survive in a 10 km² area in the Alaka'i Wilderness Area (T. Snetsinger, unpubl. data). The rear-and-release approach described in this paper has been proposed for establishing new populations of Puaiohi on Kaua'i beginning in 1999. In 1996 and 1997, 14 Puaiohi were hatched by The Peregrine Fund and transported to the Keauhou Bird Conservation Center (KBCC) for captive breeding and subsequent release of offspring to the wild.

The closest relative of these critically endangered solitaires is the 'Ōma'o (*M. obscurus*), a solitary, highly sedentary species (van Riper and Scott 1979, Ralph and Fancy 1994c) that is common in high-elevation, windward forests on the island of Hawai'i. 'Ōma'o now occupy only 30% of their former range on Hawai'i (van Riper and Scott 1979, Scott et al. 1986). The most plausible explanation for the peculiar present day distribution of 'Ōma'o (Fig. 1) is that a virulent strain of avian disease that has since attenuated or disappeared caused the extinction of 'Ōma'o and several other species in leeward Hawai'i and the Kohala Mountains in the late 1800s, followed by the development of resistance and subsequent dispersal by 'Ōma'o in

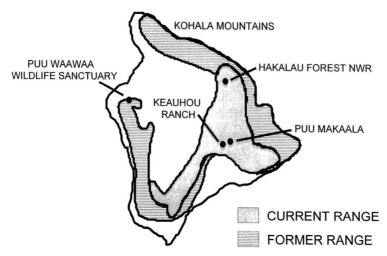

FIGURE 1.   Current and former range of ʻŌmaʻo on the island of Hawaiʻi.

windward forests (Scott et al. 1986, Atkinson et al. 1995). Mosquitoes are a vector for avian malaria (*Plasmodium relictum*) and avian pox (*Poxvirus avium*), which have dramatically affected the numbers and distribution of Hawaiian birds (Warner 1968, van Riper et al. 1986, Jarvi et al. *this volume*), and almost all of the ʻŌmaʻo's former range in the Kona and Kohala districts is within the zone of mosquito occurrence (Scott et al. 1986). Breeding populations of ʻŌmaʻo are now found below 1,200 m elevation where mosquitoes occur throughout the year, and the presence of malarial antibodies in ʻŌmaʻo and initial findings for captive ʻŌmaʻo challenged with *Plasmodium relictum* (C. Atkinson, unpubl. data) suggest that some ʻŌmaʻo are resistant to or tolerant of avian malaria.

The main objective of this study was to compare two approaches for reestablishing ʻŌmaʻo in former range based on their practicality and the initial fate of released birds. The reintroduction approach involved collecting eggs from nests in the wild, hatching and raising ʻŌmaʻo in captivity, and releasing them to the wild using soft-release procedures. Translocation involved capturing juvenile and adult ʻŌmaʻo in mist nets, transporting them to the release site after disease screening and a short holding period, and releasing them immediately or after a short holding period. Secondary objectives were to develop captive-rearing and release procedures for Puaiohi using ʻŌmaʻo as a surrogate. The ʻŌmaʻo was an ideal species for this study for several reasons: (1) information obtained from this study will be immediately applicable to recovery of the Puaiohi and possibly the Kāmaʻo, and it has important implications for the recovery of other endangered Hawaiian species; (2)

ʻŌmaʻo are locally abundant and nonendangered, thus it is possible to collect eggs and translocate a large number of wild birds without jeopardizing the population; (3) the species is highly sedentary, territorial, vocal, and large enough to carry a transmitter, making it highly tractable for monitoring the fate of individuals following release to the wild; (4) the species has been successfully held in captivity by several zoos, and procedures to hold and feed birds have already been developed; (5) the geographical distribution of ʻŌmaʻo is ideally suited to investigations of distributional anomalies through translocation studies, and careful monitoring of the fate of translocated birds may assist in identifying factors limiting populations of native birds; (6) a detailed study of the life history of the ʻŌmaʻo, including its breeding and foraging ecology, was completed in 1996 (Wakelee 1996); and (7) reintroduction of ʻŌmaʻo to former habitat is an important step, in terms of both research and applied management, in restoring native ecosystems in Hawaiʻi.

Our decision to release ʻŌmaʻo in an area where they had been extinct for almost a century was based on several factors involving avian disease and habitat recovery. ʻŌmaʻo are highly sedentary (van Riper and Scott 1979, Ralph and Fancy 1994c, Wakelee 1996), and much of their former range is separated from the current distribution by heavily grazed, disturbed, or unforested areas, such that natural recolonization would probably occur slowly. The occurrence of breeding populations of ʻŌmaʻo at elevations below 3,000 m in windward Hawaiʻi where mosquitoes and avian disease are common, the rapid recovery from malarial infections by ʻŌmaʻo challenged with *Plasmodium,* and the occurrence of breeding populations of several native forest bird species at the release site all suggested that avian disease would not preclude the reestablishment of 'Ōma'o in leeward Hawai'i. Also, recent studies of 'Ōma'o habitat requirements (Ralph and Fancy 1994c, Wakelee 1996) and initial surveys of the release site, which is recovering from past cattle grazing, suggested that adequate food, nesting sites, and other requirements were present at the release site.

METHODS

We collected 'Ōma'o eggs and mist-netted wild 'Ōma'o at three study sites in windward forests on the island of Hawai'i, and released all birds at the Pu'u Wa'awa'a Wildlife Sanctuary on the northern slope of Hualālai volcano in leeward Hawai'i (Fig. 1). Subfossil records indicate that 'Ōma'o formerly ranged between 200 and 1800 m elevation on Hualālai (J. Giffin, unpubl. data). The Pu'u Maka'ala study area where 'Ōma'o eggs and adult birds were collected was a closed-canopy forest characterized by 'ōhi'a (*Metrosideros polymorpha*), *Cibotium* tree ferns, 'ōlapa (*Cheirodendron trigynum*), and kōlea (*Myrsine lessertiana*). This study area was at an elevation of 1,000 to 1,150 m where mosquitoes occurred throughout the year, and included portions of the Pu'u Maka'ala Natural Area Reserve and the Upper Waiakea Forest Reserve along the Stainback Highway. The Keauhou Ranch study area, at 1,800 m elevation, had a discontinuous canopy dominated by 'ōhi'a and naio (*Myoporum sandwichense*). The Keauhou Ranch site has had a long history of grazing and koa (*Acacia koa*) logging. The Hakalau study area was located at 1,570 m elevation near Nāuhi Camp, in the Hakalau Forest National Wildlife Refuge, in a 'ōhi'a- and koa-dominated closed forest with a relatively intact native understory. Mosquitoes rarely occur at the Keauhou Ranch and Hakalau study areas because of cooler temperatures at those sites.

The 15.4 km² Pu'u Wa'awa'a Wildlife Sanctuary is located between 1,220 and 1,830 m elevation on the northern slope of Hualālai volcano (Fig. 1). The western half of the sanctuary where we released 'Ōma'o has a open- to closed-canopy forest of 'ōhi'a and koa, with an understory of pilo (*Coprosma* spp.), native ferns, and introduced Kikuyu grass (*Pennisetum clandestinum*). The understory has been disturbed by more than 100 years of livestock grazing, and banana poka (*Passiflora mollissima*), a climbing vine from South America, is common in the area (Warshauer et al. 1983).

Eight volunteers and one biologist searched for 'Ōma'o nests during April and May 1996 at the Pu'u Maka'ala, Keauhou Ranch, and Hakalau study areas. In addition, two eggs were collected from a single nest at the Hakalau site in August 1995. Nests were located using cues provided by vocalizations and parental behavior (Martin and Geupel 1993), and by carefully following birds to their nest. Eggs were collected by hand, lowered from the tree in a thermos filled with warm millet, and transported to the Keauhou Bird Conservation Center in a portable incubator. Methods for incubation and hatching 'Ōma'o eggs, hand-rearing

chicks, and releasing captive-reared birds will be published elsewhere (C. Kuehler, unpubl. data).

Wild 'Ōma'o were captured in 12-m mist nets placed on 6-m poles at the Pu'u Maka'ala and Keauhou Ranch study areas during September–November 1996. 'Ōma'o with an active brood patch or with active lesions characteristic of avian pox were released at the net. Wild 'Ōma'o were initially transported by vehicle to the Biological Resource Division's (BRD) field station in Hawai'i National Park where each bird was weighed and measured, banded with a numbered USFWS band and three colored plastic bands, screened for avian disease (G. Massey, unpubl. data), and fitted with a 1.5-g radio transmitter using an elastic figure-eight harness (Rappole and Tipton 1991, Wakelee 1996). Blood was drawn by jugular venipuncture for disease screening and for DNA analysis to determine sex (Zoogen, Inc.). 'Ōma'o are sexually monochromatic, and wing-chord measurements accurately sexed only 79% of museum specimens (Fancy et al. 1994).

One of the first two 'Ōma'o that was transported by vehicle to Pu'u Wa'awa'a and released the same day died < 24 hours after release, and it was obvious that the 6–8 hour holding time necessary for transport and disease screening before same-day release was too long. We therefore held the next four 'Ōma'o overnight at the BRD field station in 30 × 30 × 60 cm cages provided with perches, water, and native fruits before transporting them by vehicle to Pu'u Wa'awa'a the next morning on 21 September 1996. This approach was also abandoned, as three of the four 'Ōma'o died < 24 hours postrelease. The third strategy used with wild 'Ōma'o was to hold them for 2–5 days in a 4 × 5 × 5 m aviary near the KBCC, transport them to Pu'u Wa'awa'a, and then hold them individually for 1–2 days in 60 × 100 × 122 cm cages suspended 2 m above the forest floor. Six 'Ōma'o were successfully released by this method, but two mortalities occurred before birds were transported. The final strategy was to hold birds in 60 × 122 × 122 cm cages near the mist net where they were captured and to release any birds that would not eat native fruits or fruit cocktail within 4 hours of capture. Four birds were successfully translocated by this approach following a 2–5 day holding period at the capture site or KBCC aviary, and another four were released at the capture site because they would not eat or lost > 10% of their body weight while in captivity.

Captive-reared birds were held and released from two hacking towers at Pu'u Wa'awa'a located 1,200 m apart at 1,640 m elevation, as described by C. Kuehler et al. (unpubl. data). Following a test release of two 'Ōma'o in January 1996, we released four groups of five to seven 'Ōma'o during August–October 1996 after holding them for 6–9 days in the hacking boxes at Pu'u Wa'awa'a. All captive-reared birds were banded with colored leg bands and fitted with transmitters as described for wild 'Ōma'o. Artificial foods and native fruits were provided at the hacking boxes for 2–4 weeks following release (C. Kuehler et al., unpubl. data).

We attempted to locate all 'Ōma'o released at Pu'u Wa'awa'a at least daily using radiotelemetry, and to monitor behavior and social interactions by visual sightings. On 5 November 1996 we used an airplane

TABLE 1. Summary of reintroduction and translocation methods for 'Ōma'o at Pu'u Wa'awa'a Wildlife Sanctuary, Hawai'i, in 1996

Reintroduction Method	Translocation Method
31 eggs collected	76 'Ōma'o captured in mist nets
2 eggs dead/inviable	39 probable males released
29 viable eggs	13 with active poxlike lesions released
2 embryo deaths	5 wouldn't eat in captivity and released
27 eggs hatched	2 died during holding prior to translocation
2 chicks died during rearing	1 with active brood patch released
25 chicks fledged	16 'Ōma'o translocated to Pu'u Wa'awa'a
All fledged chicks survived holding/transport/release	4 died within 24 hr of release
25 'Ōma'o released at Pu'u Wa'awa'a	12 'Ōma'o alive 30 d postrelease
3 killed by predators	7 dispersed
22 'Ōma'o alive 30 d postrelease	5 translocated 'Ōma'o at Pu'u Wa'awa'a in mid-December 1996
2 dispersed	
20 reintroduced 'Ōma'o at Pu'u Wa'awa'a in mid-December 1996	

to search for several birds that could not be located from the ground. We found most of those birds 2–5 km south of the release site on Hualālai Ranch or in the Kaloko Mauka subdivision. We determined that a bird had dispersed if we located it by radiotelemetry outside of the Pu'u Wa'awa'a sanctuary, and if changes in the location and amplitude of its signal over one or more days clearly indicated that it was moving.

Prior to and during the release, we controlled rats (*Rattus* spp.) at Pu'u Wa'awa'a using diphacinone rat poison and Victor snap traps, and we trapped feral cats (*Felis catus*) and small Indian mongooses (*Herpestes auropunctatus*) using cage traps. Bait stations with Eaton's molasses and peanut butter-flavored bait blocks were placed at 75 m intervals along twelve 1,950 m long transects between 1,500 and 1,800 m elevation. Seventy-two snap traps baited with coconut were placed near hacking towers to determine rat species composition and relative abundance.

RESULTS

Locating 'Ōma'o nests proved to be difficult, particularly in lower-elevation forests where 'Ōma'o density was low and dense understory vegetation made it difficult to follow 'Ōma'o or observe them from a distance. Many nests were found in the nestling stage, but we did not take nestlings because of the extensive procedures required to prevent the introduction of disease to the captive-breeding facility. Furthermore, removal of eggs instead of chicks is a better conservation strategy for Puaiohi and 'Ōma'o, as it increases the chances of double clutching in wild pairs; for Puaiohi one chick in the typical two-chick clutch usually dies before fledging (T. Snetsinger, unpubl. data). We located 18 nests in the construction or incubation stage and collected 33 eggs after > 360 person-days of searching, for a yield of one egg per 11 person-days of search effort. Four eggs were infertile or dead when collected, and 25 chicks were fledged from

the 29 viable eggs and subsequently released at 66–157 days of age (Table 1). The sex ratio for 'Ōma'o hatched from eggs, based on wing-chord measurements and postrelease behavior of the first two 'Ōma'o, and DNA analysis of blood for the remaining birds, was 18 males, 6 females, and 1 unknown, different from the expected 1:1 ratio (Exact binomial test, $P = 0.008$).

Thirty 'Ōma'o were captured in mist nets (N = 4,108 net-hr) at the Pu'u Maka'ala study area during September and October 1996. Twelve (40%) of these were released at the net because they had open lesions characteristic of avian pox, one was released because it would not eat in captivity, and one was released because it had an active brood patch. Twelve of 14 'Ōma'o captured at Pu'u Maka'ala and sexed by DNA analysis (results were not available until after they were translocated) were males. Because of the highly male-biased ratio of 'Ōma'o at Pu'u Maka'ala and the low capture rate of 'Ōma'o at Pu'u Maka'ala, we began capturing 'Ōma'o at the Keauhou Ranch site where 'Ōma'o were more abundant and we only kept those with wing-chord lengths <95 mm that were probably females (Fancy et al. 1994). Forty-six 'Ōma'o were captured at Keauhou Ranch (N = 2,762 net-hr), but only three of these were translocated to Pu'u Wa'awa'a. We released 39 of the 46 'Ōma'o because they were probably males based on wing-chord length; four others were released because they would not eat within 4 hours of capture, and one bird was released because it had active poxlike lesions (Table 1).

The 25 captive-reared 'Ōma'o all survived the transport and holding period in hacking boxes and were released at Pu'u Wa'awa'a. Twenty-two of these 'Ōma'o survived more than 30 days

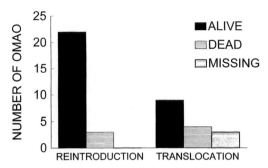

FIGURE 2. Comparison of survival > 30 days postrelease of reintroduced and translocated 'Ōma'o.

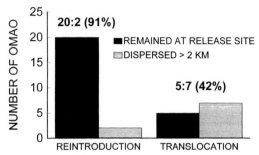

FIGURE 3. Comparison of fidelity to release site of reintroduced and translocated 'Ōma'o within 60 days postrelease.

postrelease (Fig. 2). The remaining three 'Ōma'o were killed by predators: one by an Hawaiian Hawk (*Buteo solitarius*), one by a pet cat after the 'Ōma'o dispersed to a housing subdivision 5 km west of the release site, and one by a rat. Two of the three depredated 'Ōma'o were females. Five captive-reared birds left the study area 1–2 days after release: two of these returned 30–40 days later after dispersing 1.5–2.5 km west of Pu'u Wa'awa'a, one was observed near the hacking tower in June 1997, one was depredated, and one had not returned by mid-December when its transmitter's batteries expired. In mid-December when intensive monitoring ended, 20 of the 22 surviving captive-reared 'Ōma'o remained at the Pu'u Wa'awa'a study area (Fig. 3).

Sixteen wild 'Ōma'o were translocated to Pu'u Wa'awa'a, but four of these died within 48 hours of release, probably because of the stresses of handling and transport. Including these four mortalities, survival to 30-days postrelease of wild 'Ōma'o (12/16) did not differ from that of captive-reared 'Ōma'o (22/25, $\chi^2 = 2.0$, 1 df, P = 0.20). Eight of the remaining 12 'Ōma'o dispersed 2–5 km west of Pu'u Wa'awa'a to Hualālai Ranch and the Kaloko Mauka subdivision within 3 days of release. Three wild 'Ōma'o that dispersed > 2 km from Pu'u Wa'awa'a returned after a 1–8 week absence, and by mid-December, five wild-caught 'Ōma'o remained at Pu'u Wa'awa'a. Fidelity of wild 'Ōma'o to the release site was lower than that for captive-reared 'Ōma'o ($\chi^2 = 9.67$, 1 df, P = 0.0037). It is interesting that three of four wild 'Ōma'o that were held in a hacking box at Pu'u Wa'awa'a for 7–9 days before release remained there (one dispersed but returned after 6–8 days), suggesting that holding translocated birds in hacking boxes may increase site fidelity.

In December 1996, we observed two of the captive-reared 'Ōma'o copulating, and another 'Ōma'o was observed carrying nesting material.

In June 1997, we searched an area of 150 ha surrounding the hacking towers and found nine 'Ōma'o, including one unbanded juvenile that was observed near the site where an 'Ōma'o was seen with nesting material 6 months earlier. Seven of the eight adult 'Ōma'o that were identified were captive-reared birds and one was a wild, translocated bird. We estimated, based on a variable circular-plot count, that 15 'Ōma'o remained within the 150 ha area, compared to 25 'Ōma'o in the same area in mid-December (Nelson and Fancy 1999). In May 1998, one person spent three days at Pu'u Wa'awa'a and sighted four 'Ōma'o, two of which appeared to be a breeding pair. The two individual 'Ōma'o that were identified by their colored leg bands were both captive-reared males. An additional search for 'Ōma'o at Pu'u Wa'awa'a will be made during summer 1998.

DISCUSSION

With one exception, all of the birds that dispersed from Pu'u Wa'awa'a flew to the west, to Hualālai Ranch and the Kaloko Mauka subdivision, along a gradient of increasing moisture. The Pu'u Wa'awa'a Wildlife Sanctuary is bordered on the north by heavily grazed and arid ranchlands, and to the south and east by shorter, dry 'ōhi'a forest and shrublands dominated by pūkiawe (*Styphelia tameiameiae*). 'Ōlapa, a preferred food of 'Ōma'o (van Riper and Scott 1979; C. J. Ralph, unpubl. data) that was abundant at the Pu'u Maka'ala and Keauhou Ranch study sites, is mostly absent from Pu'u Wa'awa'a because of livestock grazing, but it is common in the Kaloko Mauka subdivision. A fire burned the eastern third of Pu'u Wa'awa'a Wildlife Sanctuary in March 1995 and the more open, drier forest to the east may have limited the dispersal of 'Ōma'o in that direction.

Our initial results suggest that the rear-and-release approach, where birds are soft-released in the same year that eggs are collected, is more likely to result in establishment of a self-sustaining population at the release site, primarily because of greater site fidelity. Assuming that a captive propagation facility is already available, reintroduction was more practical and less costly than translocation, although both methods were labor-intensive and expensive. The reintroduction method required 11 person-days of search effort for each egg found, after which one or two persons were needed to hatch, raise, and release the birds. For the translocation method using a nine person field crew, our capture rate was 0.73 'Ōma'o/100 net-hours at the lower-elevation site and 1.67 'Ōma'o/100 net-hours at Keauhou Ranch where 'Ōma'o density is high (Ralph and Fancy 1994c). Furthermore, we had to release 60 of 76 (79%) 'Ōma'o because of problems with active poxlike lesions, the excess of males, or because some individuals would not eat in captivity. Only two hatch-year 'Ōma'o were kept, but both died during their first night in captivity before they could be translocated. In 1992, a group of biologists from several mainland zoos also found that the majority of wild-caught 'Ōma'o would not eat in captivity, and they released 8 of 11 (73%) adult 'Ōma'o (S. Derrickson, pers. comm.). At our higher rate of capture and retention, it would require > 2,500 net-hours of effort to obtain 20 adult 'Ōma'o for translocation, and > 22,600 net-hours (ca. 161 days using 20 nets for 7 hr/d) for 20 hatch-year 'Ōma'o, and even then there would be a shortage of females.

'Ōma'o are the most sedentary of any closely studied Hawaiian forest bird species (van Riper and Scott 1979, Ralph and Fancy 1994c), and yet most of the wild 'Ōma'o released at Pu'u Wa'awa'a quickly dispersed from the study area. Similar results were found during two translocations of second-year and adult Palila (Loxioides bailleui; Fancy et al. 1997; L. Johnson, unpubl. data), as more than half of the birds returned to the source population. Because of the difficulty and high cost involved in reintroduction and translocation efforts, high fidelity to the release site is critical to the successful establishment of a new population, and the reintroduction approach offers better chances for success.

Age is a confounding variable in our comparisons of survival and site fidelity between hatch-year, captive-reared 'Ōma'o and adult, wild-caught 'Ōma'o, but our objective was to develop a practical management tool, not to compare survival and fidelity between hatch-year and adult 'Ōma'o. For efficiency and cost purposes, the reintroduction approach requires that 'Ōma'o be released as juveniles, whereas translocation of juvenile 'Ōma'o is impractical because of the difficulty in capturing enough juveniles of each sex that will survive the translocation.

There was no indication that avian disease was involved in any of the mortalities that occurred by mid-December when intensive monitoring ended. For the 16 wild 'Ōma'o translocated to Pu'u Wa'awa'a, all of the deaths occurred within 48 hours of their release and seemed to be a direct result of capture stress and handling. Predators were responsible for the three deaths among 25 captive-reared 'Ōma'o (six from low-elevation populations where mosquitoes are present and 19 from high-elevation populations).

Mosquitoes were observed at Pu'u Wa'awa'a during the time that birds were being released, and avian malaria and avian pox have been documented there. G. Massey (unpubl. data) found that 4.9% of 209 Hawai'i 'Amakihi (Hemignathus virens) captured at Pu'u Wa'awa'a in 1994 had poxlike lesions and two Hawai'i 'Amakihi had active malarial infections. Additionally, H. Baker (unpubl. data) in 1995 found that 11.5% of Hawai'i 'Amakihi had poxlike lesions. Disease related mortalities of native birds are greatest in the warmer months of August–November because of increased abundance of cold-intolerant mosquitoes at higher elevations where native birds are more common (C. Atkinson, unpubl. data). Although avian disease has been documented at Pu'u Wa'awa'a, and our study was conducted during the warmer months when disease transmission would be expected to be highest, our data are too limited to determine whether avian disease prevents the recolonization of Pu'u Wa'awa'a by native birds such as 'Ōma'o and 'Akiapōlā'au (Hemignathus munroi). However, our results and findings from challenge experiments that 'Ōma'o quickly recover from avian malaria infections (C. Atkinson, unpubl. data) suggest that avian disease would not preclude the establishment of 'Ōma'o in lower-elevation forests such as Pu'u Wa'awa'a or the Kohala Mountains.

The highly male-biased sex ratio was a problem, and we were surprised that 18 of the 24 known-sex young from captive-hatched eggs were males. Additional validation of the DNA sexing method for Hawaiian solitaires is needed, but blood samples from three 'Ōma'o that died and were necropsied were all correctly sexed as males by Zoogen. Two field studies of banded 'Ōma'o populations found male-biased sex ratios (Wakelee 1996; C. J. Ralph, unpubl. data). It is usually assumed that a skewed adult sex ratio results from differential mortality between sexes (Breitwisch 1989, Lindsey et al. 1995a), but the excess of male 'Ōma'o in our sample of eggs is unexplained. It is interesting that Wakelee (1996) found a 2:1 male : female ratio among hatch-year and second-year 'Ōma'o, which could mean either that juvenile females have higher mortality than males, or that the sex ratio of 'Ōma'o is not 1:1 at hatching as our data suggest.

Most translocations and reintroductions require multiple releases of birds before a self-sustaining population is established (Griffith et al. 1989, Wolf et al. 1996). We observed breeding activity by captive-reared 'Ōma'o in December 1996 and found a juvenile 'Ōma'o at the release site in June 1997, but it is unlikely that a viable 'Ōma'o population will become established on Hualālai since the founding population contained only eight females by December 1996. Our results from the comparison of the two methods indicate that the reintroduction approach is more likely to result in successful establishment of Puaiohi and other endangered birds because reintroduced birds had greater fidelity to the release site. However, additional translocation experiments should be conducted to determine whether holding wild birds in hacking towers for > 7 days or translocating juvenile birds will increase fidelity to the release site. We support the recommendation, made more than 20 years ago by J. M. Scott and C. van Riper (pers. comm.), to reestablish 'Ōma'o in the Kohala Mountains and forests of leeward Hawai'i as part of the restoration of native Hawaiian ecosystems.

ACKNOWLEDGMENTS

We thank A. Lieberman, P. Oesterle, T. Powers, and the 16 volunteer nest searchers and mist netters for assistance with capturing, hatching, raising, releasing, and monitoring 'Ōma'o. We thank G. Massey for veterinary assistance, and C. Atkinson, J. Lease and N. Shema for assistance with holding and screening 'Ōma'o for avian disease. T. Work necropsied dead 'Ōma'o. We thank T. Casey and managers of Kamehameha Schools Bishop Estate lands for allowing us to collect 'Ōma'o from Keauhou Ranch. M. Kato of Pu'u Wa'awa'a Ranch also gave permission to access private lands. We thank C. Atkinson, S. Conant, L. Johnson, A. Lieberman, M. Morin, J. M. Scott, and T. Snetsinger for helpful comments on the manuscript. Funding for much of the field work was provided by the U.S. Fish and Wildlife Service.

Studies in Avian Biology No. 22:354–358, 2001.

RESTORATION TECHNIQUES FOR HAWAIIAN FOREST BIRDS: COLLECTION OF EGGS, ARTIFICIAL INCUBATION AND HAND-REARING OF CHICKS, AND RELEASE TO THE WILD

Cyndi Kuehler, Alan Lieberman, Peter Harrity, Marla Kuhn, Jope Kuhn, Barbara McIlraith, and John Turner

Abstract. In 1993, The Peregrine Fund (TPF), in cooperation with the U.S. Fish and Wildlife Service, the state of Hawai'i, and the 'Alalā Partnership, began a new restoration program for endangered Hawaiian birds. Through this program, eggs produced in the wild and in captivity are incubated and hatched, the chicks are hand-reared, and the juveniles are subsequently released to the wild. To date, 153 endemic passerine chicks have been artificially hatched, with the wild population of the endangered Hawaiian Crow (*Corvus hawaiiensis*), or 'Alalā, being the first species to benefit from these efforts. Beginning with four nonendangered species in 1995 and 1996—Hawai'i 'Amakihi (*Hemignathus v. virens*), 'Ōma'o (*Myadestes obscurus*), 'I'iwi (*Vestiaria coccinea*), and Hawai'i 'Elepaio (*Chasiempis s. sandwichensis*)—TPF's program has expanded to include construction of a captive propagation facility on the Big Island and the operation of a second facility on Maui. Cooperative projects are underway for the Puaiohi (*Myadestes palmeri*), Palila (*Loxioides bailleui*), Hawai'i Creeper (*Oreomystis mana*), 'Ākohekohe (*Palmeria dolei*), and Maui Parrotbill (*Pseudonestor xanthophrys*), in addition to continuing work with the 'Alalā. Conservation partnerships have been formed with private landowners, government agencies, Kamehameha Schools Bernice Pauahi Bishop Estate, and the Zoological Society of San Diego to implement these restoration activities.

Key Words: captive propagation; conservation; endangered birds; Hawai'i; restoration.

Human modification of the environment in the Hawaiian Islands is causing the steady extinction of endemic bird populations. Loss of secure habitat due to the encroachment of introduced plants, birds, insects, mammals, and disease is contributing to the decline. Long-term, holistic programs involving habitat management and conservation education are required to preserve the remaining natural areas and ensure the survival of Hawai'i's unique avifauna (Ralph and van Riper 1985, Scott et al. 1988, Atkinson et al. 1995).

For some bird species habitat enhancement and protection may not occur quickly enough to guarantee a safe haven for populations on the verge of extinction. In these cases manipulation of wild birds and hands-on intervention can be useful management tools. For example, captive breeding programs to produce birds for reintroduction have proven to be a valuable conservation strategy for endangered Peregrine Falcons (*Falco peregrinus*) and California Condors (*Gymnogyps californianus*; Cade et al. 1988, Kuehler and Witman 1988). However, long-term propagation of birds in captivity is labor-intensive, costly, and not an effective recovery tool for all species (Griffith et al. 1989, Snyder et al. 1996). For some island endemics, such as Ultramarine Lories (*Vini ultramarina*), translocation to secure habitat on another island is a preferable option, if the founder population is large enough to support collection of wild individuals (Kuehler et al. 1997, Lieberman et al. 1997). Cross-

fostering is also an intervention technique that has been successfully utilized for the management of Chatham Island Black Robins (*Petroica traversi*). The success of this strategy with robins was partly due to the availability and suitability of using Chatham Island Tits (*Petroica macrocephala chathamensis*) as foster parents (Butler and Merton 1992). However not all endangered birds are as tolerant of intensive nest manipulation as robins, or have accommodating nesting pairs from similar species available to act as foster parents.

An alternative to cross-fostering, translocation, or long-term captive breeding is a short-term intervention strategy termed "rear and release," which involves manipulating wild populations by collecting eggs, artificially hatching and rearing chicks in captivity, and immediately releasing juveniles back to the wild. This conservation management tool increases the reproductive rate through double clutching, and/or providing a protected artificial environment during the incubation and nestling period, normally a period of high mortality in the wild for many bird species. "Rear and release" also decreases the need for long-term maintenance of breeding birds in captivity. Except for the endangered San Clemente Island Loggerhead Shrike (*Lanius ludovicianus mearnsi*), passerine recovery programs have not incorporated "rear and release" techniques into recovery plans due to insufficient technical information relating to the transport and artificial incubation of passerine eggs, hand-rearing of chicks, and release of juveniles to the wild (Kuehler et al. 1993).

In 1992, legal actions relating to the recovery of the Hawaiian Crow (*Corvus hawaiiensis*), hereafter referred to as the 'Alalā, instigated the formation of a National Academy of Science Committee to evaluate recovery actions for this species (Duckworth et al. 1992). The "rear and release" strategy was recommended for implementation.

Beginning in the 1970s, propagation of endangered Hawaiian forest birds in captivity was supervised by the U.S. Fish and Wildlife Service (USFWS) and the state of Hawai'i's Division of Forestry and Wildlife (DOFAW) at the Olinda Endangered Species Propagation Facility, Pohakaloa Breeding Facility, and the Patuxent Wildlife Research Center. In 1993, the USFWS and DOFAW requested The Peregrine Fund (TPF) to begin a cooperative restoration program for the 'Alalā. Based on the initial success with this species, in 1995 TPF's Hawaiian Endangered Bird Conservation Program was expanded to include developing techniques for endangered native honeycreepers and thrushes, and construction of a captive propagation facility, the Keauhou Bird Conservation Center (KBCC), on the Big Island. Additionally, in 1996, DOFAW requested that TPF assume the operation of a second facility, the Maui Bird Conservation Facility (MBCC), on Maui (formerly the Olinda Endangered Species Propagation Facility). Cooperative projects are underway for five endangered species: the Puaiohi (*Myadestes palmeri*), Palila (*Loxioides bailleui*), Hawai'i Creeper (*Oreomystis mana*), 'Ākohekohe (*Palmeria dolei*), and Maui Parrotbill (*Pseudonestor xanthophrys*), in addition to continuing work with the 'Alalā.

METHODS

EGG COLLECTION

Nest searching and collection of Hawaiian forest bird eggs is accomplished by biologists from the USFWS, DOFAW and U.S. Geological Survey-Biological Resources Division (BRD), in collaboration with TPF. Eggs are collected and transported, and chicks are hatched at facilities on the island of origin to minimize transport time. Eggs are transported in portable incubators (Dean's Animal Supply, Orlando, FL) and helicopters are used if the terrain is rough or the driving distance long.

ARTIFICIAL INCUBATION OF EGGS AND HAND-REARING OF CHICKS

Eggs are incubated in forced-air incubators (Humidaire models 20 and 21; Humidaire Incubator Co., New Madison, OH) under parameters used to hatch similar passerine species: 37.5–38.1° C (dry bulb), 30.0–33.3° C (wet bulb). Mass (water loss) is monitored by weighing eggs throughout incubation and

eggs are transferred to hatchers when chicks pip the air cell (Kuehler and Good 1990; Kuehler et al. 1993, 1994, 1996).

Chicks are hand-reared using techniques previously developed for related passerines and subsequently tested on nonendangered surrogate Hawaiian forest birds. Chick mass, vitality, developmental changes and food intakes are recorded. Nutrient analysis of hand-rearing diets is accomplished using the N2 Animal Nutritionist software program which compiles and analyzes the nutrient content of individual food items (Kuehler et al. 1993, 1994, 1996).

BIRD RELEASES

Prior to reintroduction, birds are conditioned in enclosures to (1) develop flight and foraging capabilities, (2) enhance release site tenacity, and (3) provide natural exposure to avian malaria under field conditions where supplemental feeding is available ('Alalā). The length of the acclimation period is species-dependent. For example, 'Alalā spend several months learning to forage prior to release, while 'Ōma'o (*Myadestes obscurus*) require approximately two weeks. Supplemental foods are decreased gradually while the released birds are weaned, and in response to their ability to forage on native foods. The larger, heavier species (e.g., corvids and thrushes) are fitted with transmitters for monitoring, (the smaller size of some species of honeycreepers makes the use of radiotelemetry less practical). Predator control to increase habitat security is undertaken prior to release (Kuehler et al. 1995, 1996; Fancy et al. *this volume*).

RESULTS

Since 1993, 153 endemic passerine chicks have been artificially hatched and the techniques have been developed to hand-rear 11 species of native Hawaiian songbirds, including Hawai'i 'Amakihi (*Hemignathus v. virens*), 'Ōma'o, 'I'iwi (*Vestiaria coccinea*), Hawai'i 'Elepaio (*Chasiempis s. sandwichensis*), 'Apapane (*Himatione sanguinea*), Puaiohi, Palila, Hawai'i Creeper, 'Ākohekohe, Maui Parrotbill, and 'Alalā. Subsequently four species of native passerines have been released: 'Alalā, Hawai'i 'Amakihi, 'Ōma'o, and 'I'iwi. Overall hatchability of viable eggs = 87.4%, survivability of chicks for 30 days = 87.6% (Table 1).

'ALALĀ (1993–JUNE 1998)

Five, seven, four, and eight hand-reared 'Alalā were released into historical habitat in the South Kona District on the island of Hawai'i in 1993, 1994, 1996, and 1997, respectively. All 24 birds survived 180 days post-release and 12 birds survive to date (50% survivability to June 1998). First-year survivability of wild passerine populations (parent-rearing) has been reported to range between 2% and 63% (Sullivan and Roper 1996). Known mortality of reintroduced 'Alalā has largely been due to 'Io (*Buteo solitarius*) predation in areas of high 'Io population densi-

TABLE 1. SUMMARY OF HAWAIIAN FOREST BIRD EGGS ARTIFICIALLY INCUBATED AND CHICKS HAND-REARED BY THE PEREGRINE FUND 1993–JUNE 1998

Species	Viable eggs collected	Hatched (%)	Survive (%) (30 days)
Hawai'i 'Amakihi	26	21 (80.8)	19 (90.5)
'I'iwi	2	2 (100)	2 (100)
'Ōma'o	29	27 (93.1)	25 (92.6)
'Elepaio	2	1 (50.0)	1 (100)
Palila	22	21 (95.5)	11 (52.4)
Puaiohi	32	30 (93.8)	29 (96.7)
	6	6 (100)	5 (83.3)
'Ākohekohe	9	9 (100)	9 (100)
Hawai'i Creeper	1	1 (100)	1 (100)
Maui Parrotbill	2	2 (100)	2 (100)
'Apapane	44	33 (75.0)	30 (90.9)
'Alalā	175	153 (87.4)	134 (87.6)

ties (D. Ball, pers. comm.). In 1997 the USFWS began translocation and removal of predatory 'Io in 'Alalā release areas.

Eighteen 'Alalā currently reside in captivity in two facilities on Maui and the Big Island (MBCC and KBCC). Thirty-three 'Alalā have been hatched in TPF facilities from 1993 to June 1998.

HAWAI'I 'AMAKIHI (1995)

In 1995, 16 nonendangered Hawai'i 'Amakihi were artificially incubated and hatched, hand-reared, and experimentally released in low-elevation forest (1,212 m) containing predators and mosquito-transmitted avian disease. This surrogate project required the development of egg transport, artificial incubation, and hand-rearing procedures for honeycreepers and tested the efficacy of releasing birds in compromised habitat. Eleven of the released birds were known to have died due to avian malaria and pox. This experiment showed that, although it was possible to artificially incubate and hand-rear honeycreepers, the release techniques developed for juvenile 'Alalā, which are capable of surviving avian malaria and pox infection, would not be applicable to honeycreepers even under conditions of supplemental feeding. Restoration of endangered honeycreepers may be possible only in mosquito-free and predator controlled release sites in Hawai'i (Kuehler et al. 1996).

'ŌMA'O (1995–JUNE 1998)

In 1995 and 1996, the first restoration attempt of a small Hawaiian passerine to predator controlled habitat with a low incidence of disease was made with the release of captive-reared 'Ōma'o into Pu'u Wa'awa'a Forest Reserve (PWW); where this species has been absent for

nearly 100 years. In 1995, two birds were reintroduced as a preliminary test release, and in 1996, 23 birds were released in cohorts numbering from two to seven birds. Of the 25 released birds, the two birds released in 1995 were observed one year later, and 22 of the 1996-hatched birds were monitored and known to have survived for at least 30 days post-release (duration of transmitters). In December 1996 the two captive-reared 'Ōma'o released in 1995 were observed copulating and carrying nesting material. An unbanded juvenile was observed in the same area six months later.

Additionally, during fall 1996, an experimental translocation of 'Ōma'o was undertaken by BRD biologists in the same area to compare the fate of captive-reared release birds and translocated wild 'Ōma'o (Fancy et al. *this volume*). This evaluation of techniques for nonendangered 'Ōma'o provides information for the development of conservation strategies for the endangered Puaiohi. A follow-up survey was conducted during the week of May 18, 1997, by BRD and TPF biologists. Fifteen 'Ōma'o were estimated to remain within 2 km of the release aviaries. Eight birds were identified by bands (seven captive-reared and one translocated), although most birds had moved to higher elevation areas where fruit was more abundant. Additional 'Ōma'o are known to have dispersed elsewhere, and recent reports of sightings have been made by residents of a subdivision about 5 km away from the release site. The results of the 'Ōma'o study suggests that using founder release cohorts of captive-reared birds may enhance reestablishment of wild populations in secure/managed areas, due to their greater site fidelity after release. An additional 'Ōma'o survey will be conducted by BRD and TPF biologists in summer 1998 (Fancy et. al. *this volume*).

PUAIOHI (1996–JUNE 1998)

In 1995, BRD, DOFAW, USFWS, and TPF began a cooperative project to establish additional breeding populations of the critically endangered Puaiohi in the Alaka'i Wilderness Area on Kaua'i. The total wild population of this species is estimated to be approximately 300 individuals (T. Snetsinger, pers. comm.).

In 1996 and 1997, wild eggs were collected to provide breeding stock for propagation and release; 14 chicks were hatched. Four females hatched in 1996 subsequently laid a total of 15 infertile eggs in captivity during the 1997 breeding season (there were no males in the flock).

As of June 1998, 15 second generation Puaiohi chicks were produced via captive-breeding at the KBCC on the Big Island. These birds will comprise the first release cohort of Puaiohi scheduled for reintroduction in the Alaka'i Wilderness Area in February 1999.

'ĀKOHEKOHE (1997)

Historically, 'Ākohekohe populations were found in the wet forests of Moloka'i and in eastern and western Maui (Perkins 1903). Currently one population of approximately 3,500 birds remains on the windward side of Haleakalā (T. Pratt, pers. comm.).

In 1997, six 'Ākohekohe eggs were collected in cooperation with BRD and DOFAW in Maui; six chicks hatched, and five were hand-reared. 'Ākohekohe are being maintained in captivity to develop the breeding and release techniques for future re-introduction into managed habitat.

MAUI PARROTBILL (1997–JUNE 1998)

The estimated wild population of Maui Parrotbill is about 500 birds and is restricted to the remaining high-elevation rain forests of East Maui (T. Pratt, pers. comm.). This species has a low reproductive rate and lays a single egg clutch (Simon et al. 1997).

In cooperation with BRD, one nest of this species was located in 1997 and one chick was reared from the single egg collected. No wild nests were located by DOFAW biologists in 1998 to provide a mate for this single bird. If possible, in 1999, additional wild eggs will be collected to establish a captive breeding flock. Given the low reproductive rate and scarcity of nests, "rear and release" is not a practical strategy for this species.

HAWAI'I CREEPER (1997–JUNE 1998)

Hawai'i Creepers are found in several disjunct populations; approximately 12,500 birds existed in the wild in the late 1970s (Scott et al. 1986). In order to develop the restoration techniques for Hawai'i Creepers and to serve as a model for other rare insectivorous species, four eggs were collected from Hakalau Forest National Wildlife Refuge with BRD assistance in 1997 and five eggs were collected in 1998. Hawai'i Creepers will be bred in captivity to produce birds for future release into secure habitat.

PALILA (1996–PRESENT)

Historically Palila occurred on the slopes of Mauna Kea, Mauna Loa, and Hualālai. Today a few thousand birds are restricted to the montane māmane forests of Mauna Kea (Jacobi et al. 1996).

Eleven Palila were reared in 1996, with ten surviving for more than one year. Because of the identification of possible disease infection (*Mycoplasma* spp.) in the wild and captive flocks in 1996, these birds are being held for captive propagation and research. Offspring will be candidates for captive breeding and/or release in 1999 (B. Rideout, pers. comm.).

Currently, BRD researchers are translocating wild juvenile Palila to determine the feasibility of introducing young Palila to new habitat. This study will determine the advisability of using either translocation, or captive-breeding and reintroduction as a restoration strategy for Palila (P. Banko, pers. comm.).

DISCUSSION

Recovery techniques involving birds in captivity are costly strategies which have been the subject of considerable debate in the conservation arena. "Better dead than captive-bred" is a familiar refrain. Although hands-on manipulation of wild birds has helped endangered California Condors and Peregrine Falcons, lack of thoughtful planning has also resulted in inappropriate efforts for some species (Griffith et al. 1989, Hutchins and Conway 1995, Hutchins et al. 1995, Snyder et al. 1996). Captive propagation techniques, in concert with habitat management, can only be effective conservation tools when (1) thorough knowledge of species biology exists, (2) the causes of decline are understood and ongoing programs to reverse the trend are being implemented, (3) captive propagation technology and expertise is available, (4) release techniques exist which result in behaviorally competent birds, (5) adequate funding and facilities are available, (6) recovery objectives and goals are clear, and (7) acceptable, secure release sites are available in the wild.

Unique management techniques for artificially incubating eggs and subsequently rearing and releasing passerines are currently being developed as restoration tools for endangered Hawaiian birds. These strategies are being used as stop-gap measures to increase reproductive output in rare bird populations during this period of environmental crisis. Intervention techniques provide a means to preserve options until the habitat is secure and wild populations are stabilized. However, without commensurate action to protect and enhance the habitat, these hands-on restoration efforts cannot establish viable self-sustaining wild populations.

ACKNOWLEDGMENTS

There are many individuals and organizations who contribute to this program. Our cooperators, including the USFWS, U.S. Geological Survey-Biological Resources Division (BRD), the state of Hawai'i Division of Forestry and Wildlife (DOFAW), the Zoological Society of San Diego (ZSSD), and Kamehameha Schools Bernice Pauahi Bishop Estate (KSBE) and their many personnel have our sincere thanks. To name a few: USFWS—R. Smith, K. Rosa, S. Johnston, and D. Ball;

BRD—S. Fancy, J. Nelson, T. Snetsinger, C. Herrmann, P. Banko, L. Johnson, S. Dougill, C. Atkinson, T. Pratt, and J. Simon; DOFAW—M. Buck, P. Conry, C. Terry, J. Giffin, T. Telfer, E. Pettys, and G. Massey. We also acknowledge our ZSSD collaborators—B. Rideout, D. Janssen, P. Morris, N. Harvey, and M. Lam. Dr. S. Grune graciously donates veterinary clinical care. Our land-manager partners include: C. and R. Salley, K. Unger, B. McClure, N. Zablan, N. and J. Santimer, and T. Stack; and KSBE—O. Stender, T. Casey, J. Melrose, P. Simmons, and B. Lindsey. This program is funded by the USFWS (Pacific Islands Ecoregion Office) and DOFAW with significant contributions from The Cooke Foundation, Atherton Foundation, and Hawaii Electric Industries. Our volunteers were invaluable—M. Fancy, N. Janssen, L. DiSante, L. Neibaur, and M. Schwartz. Finally we acknowledge our colleagues at The Peregrine Fund—B. Burnham, P. Burnham, J. Cilek, J. Holly, L. Kiff, P. Oesterle, and T. Powers.

Studies in Avian Biology No. 22:359–376, 2001.

CONSERVATION STATUS AND RECOVERY STRATEGIES FOR ENDEMIC HAWAIIAN BIRDS

PAUL C. BANKO, REGINALD E. DAVID, JAMES D. JACOBI, AND WINSTON E. BANKO

Abstract. Populations of endemic Hawaiian birds declined catastrophically following the colonization of the islands by Polynesians and later cultures. Extinction is still occurring, and recovery programs are urgently needed to prevent the disappearance of many other species. Programs to recover the endemic avifauna incorporate a variety of conceptual and practical approaches that are constrained by biological, financial, social, and legal factors. Avian recovery is difficult to implement in Hawai'i because a variety of challenging biological factors limit bird populations. Hawaiian birds are threatened by alien predatory mammals, introduced mosquitoes that transmit diseases, alien invertebrate parasites and predators that reduce invertebrate food resources, and alien animals and plants that destroy and alter habitats. Life in the remote Hawaiian Archipelago has imposed other biological constraints to avian recovery, including limited geographical distributions and small population sizes. Recovery of the endemic avifauna is also challenging because resources are insufficient to mitigate the many complex, interacting factors that limit populations. Decisions must be made for allocating limited resources to species teetering on the brink of extinction and those in decline. If funds are spent primarily on saving the rarest species, more abundant species will decline and become more difficult to recover. However, critically rare species will disappear if efforts are directed mainly towards restoring species that are declining but not in immediate danger of becoming extinct. Determining priorities is difficult also because management is needed both to supplement bird populations and to restore habitats of many species. Rare species cannot respond quickly to management efforts intended only to improve habitat and reduce limiting factors. Recovery is slow, if it occurs at all, because years or decades are generally required for habitat rehabilitation and because small populations of birds initially increase slowly even when habitat conditions are favorable. Consequently, even as habitat conditions begin to improve, small populations may disappear unless they are supplemented directly. Hawaiian bird conservation is also affected by social and legal factors, including hunting alien game species, commercial land use practices, and lawsuits and policies concerning endangered species and critical habitat. Influenced by this mixture of conflicting and competing issues, Hawaiian bird recovery programs range from management of single species and some components of their habitats to limited forms of community or ecosystem management. Although the effectiveness of most programs is difficult to evaluate because of monitoring limitations, several programs exemplify species and community management. Programs primarily intended to recover single species include Hawaiian Goose or Nēnē (*Branta sandvicensis*), Hawaiian Crow or 'Alalā (*Corvus hawaiiensis*), and Palila (*Loxioides bailleui*). Programs attempting to manage entire communities of forest birds include Hakalau Forest National Wildlife Refuge and Hawai'i Volcanoes National Park on Hawai'i, and Waikamoi Preserve, Hanawī Natural Area Reserve, and Haleakalā National Park on Maui.

Key Words: conservation; extinction; habitat management; Hawaiian birds; recovery strategy; species management.

The Hawaiian avifauna is renowned for the spectacular radiation of specialized species evolving from relatively few founders, widespread extinctions of endemic forms following human colonization, and recent inundation by alien species. In the wake of sweeping changes to native ecosystems wrought by humans, biologists and resource managers must struggle just to protect remaining species from extinction and prevent further degradation to habitats. Restoring whole communities of birds and entire ecosystems seems only a distant hope. Only during the last several decades have conservationists begun to appreciate the complexity of factors limiting Hawaiian bird populations and threats to their habitats (see van Riper and Scott, *this volume*). Success in recovering the remaining avifauna depends on developing and implementing strategies that overcome problems inherent in managing small populations in fragmented, degraded ecosystems and that mitigate the effects of alien species.

THE HAWAIIAN AVIFAUNA AND ITS COLLISION WITH CIVILIZATION

Indigenous and alien bird species inhabit the entire length of the Hawaiian Archipelago from Kure Atoll to the still-growing island of Hawai'i (2,683 km); endemic species are distributed from Laysan to Hawai'i (1,925 km; Fig. 1). Nearly 150 native species occupied this remote island chain before humans arrived. Isolation from continents and other island groups led to a high degree of endemism of the nonmigratory, terrestrial avifauna prior to the introduction of many new bird species during the 1900s. In contrast, relatively few marine species nest exclusively in the Hawaiian Islands, and resident

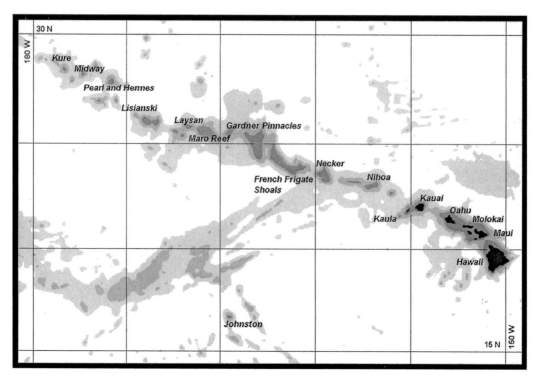

FIGURE 1. The Hawaiian Archipelago extends 2,683 km from Kure (the oldest island) to Hawai'i (the youngest island). Islands are formed and sustained sequentially as the Pacific lithospheric plate slides slowly over a "hot spot" (upwelling of magma) in the earth's mantle.

freshwater birds have differentiated only slightly from continental forms (Pratt et al. 1987, James and Olson 1991, Olson and James 1991, Pyle 1997). In addition, 51 species regularly or occasionally visit the islands and another 114 rarely occur but do not breed in the archipelago (Pyle 1997). More than 165 alien bird species have been introduced to the Hawaiian Islands, and at least 50 have established breeding populations persisting for 25 years or longer (Long 1981, Pyle 1997; R. E. David, unpubl. data).

The larger Hawaiian Islands, which extend 598 km from Kaua'i to Hawai'i, are home to most endemic terrestrial birds; however, marine species are more numerous in the smaller Northwestern Hawaiian Islands, which extend 1,837 km from Nihoa to Kure. Geological age of the archipelago increases with latitude, and island size and height decrease with age. The oldest major island, Kaua'i, is 5.1 million years old (K-Ar), whereas new land continues to be added to the youngest island, Hawai'i (Carson and Clague 1995). Two volcanic peaks rise over 4,100 m above sea level on Hawai'i, which is larger than all other remaining islands and atolls combined. Steep elevation and rainfall gradients, rugged topography, and a mosaic of substrate

types resulting from lava flows of different ages characterize the major islands. In this setting, Hawaiian birds have become adapted to a variety of habitat types, foraging substrates, and food resources, resulting in a spectacular radiation of forms (Freed et al. 1987a).

Endemic species declined markedly in numbers and distribution following human colonization in approximately 400 AD (James and Olson 1991, Olson and James 1991). Since then, about 95 (67%) of the 142 endemic bird species and subspecies known from collected specimens (71 taxa; Pyle 1997) or nonmineralized fossils (71 taxa; James and Olson 1991, Olson and James 1991, Giffin 1993; J. G. Giffin, pers. comm.) have become extinct. About 50% (71/142) of the endemic taxa were extirpated during Polynesian colonization and were unknown to nineteenth century naturalists, while an additional 17% (24/142) were extirpated after 1825. About 69% (31/45) of the remaining endemic taxa are listed as endangered or threatened, and others are being considered for listing by the U.S. Fish and Wildlife Service. In addition, at least 11 taxa listed as endangered are unrecoverable because they are very rare or extinct.

During Polynesian colonization, about 77%

TABLE 1. DECLINE OF ENDEMIC HAWAIIAN BIRD TAXA BY ORDER THROUGH TIME

Order	Prehistoric (<1778)	Historic (>1778)	Current (2000)
Procellariiformes (petrels, shearwaters)	3	2	2
Ciconiiformes (ibises)	3	0	0
Anseriformes (geese, ducks)	13	3	3
Falconiformes (eagles, hawks)	4	1	1
Gruiformes (rails, gallinules, coots)	18	4	2
Charadriiformes (stilts)	1	1	1
Laridae	1	1	1
Strigiformes (owls)	5	1	1
Passeriformes (perching birds)	94	58	36[a]
TOTAL	142	71 [50%]	47 [33%][b]

[a] Includes four taxa that have not been seen for 10–30 years and are undoubtedly extinct, although they are still listed as endangered, and seven other taxa that are so rare that recovery is unlikely and extinction is imminent or may have already occurred. For specific details on recent sightings see Reynolds and Snetsinger (*this volume*).

[b] Percentage of total ancient taxa surviving shown in brackets.

(37/48) of the endemic nonpasserine taxa, mostly ground nesters and raptors, vanished; the 11 surviving forms are primarily wetland and marine birds (Table 1; Olson and James 1991). In contrast, about 38% (36/94) of endemic passerine taxa were extirpated, primarily in dry lowland habitats (James and Olson 1991, Giffin 1993; J. G. Giffin, pers. comm.). After 1825, another 23% (22/94) of endemic passerines disappeared from low and mid elevations, which were inundated by disease vectors, mammalian predators, food competitors, ungulates that destroyed and modified habitats, and weeds (Scott et al. 1986). About 61% (22/36) of all remaining endemic passerine taxa are endangered, and only half have any chance for recovery.

Naturalists explored the Hawaiian avifauna and investigated taxonomy and life history during the nineteenth and early twentieth centuries (Peale 1848, Wilson and Evans 1890–1899; Rothschild 1892, 1893–1900; Henshaw 1902a, Perkins 1903, Munro 1944). Following decades of neglect, modern Hawaiian ornithology began with investigations of the status, distribution, and ecology of native and introduced birds throughout the archipelago (Baldwin 1945, 1947a,b, 1953, 1969a,b; Fisher 1948a,b, 1949, 1951, 1965, 1967, 1968, 1969; Fisher and Baldwin 1945, 1946b, 1947; Richardson 1949, 1954, 1957, 1963; Richardson and Woodside 1954, Richardson and Bowles 1964).

Significantly, Baldwin (1953) conducted his detailed study of three common honeycreepers in Hawai'i National Park, which was established in 1917 to make available to the world the wonders of Kīlauea, Mauna Loa, and Haleakalā volcanoes. The Pacific Remote (formerly Hawaiian) Islands National Wildlife Refuge Complex was established in the same year to protect seabirds, migratory birds, and endemic landbirds of the tiny atolls and islands of the northwestern portion of the archipelago. These were the first areas in Hawai'i intended for conservation, and they have since become critical nodes for bird recovery and ecosystem management in the Pacific.

Despite a degree of legal protection and the establishment of conservation areas, it was clear that Hawaiian birds were becoming increasingly imperiled, prompting concern for at least some of the more conspicuous species. The first recovery efforts were directed at breeding and releasing Nēnē (*Branta sandvicensis*) or Hawaiian Geese after it was shown that their numbers and range had decreased precipitously (Baldwin 1945, Smith 1952, Elder and Woodside 1958, Scott 1962, Kear and Berger 1980). Today, Nēnē have been saved from extinction, but the species serves as a reminder that avian recovery in Hawai'i requires great persistence, effort, and resources to accomplish even modest gains.

AVIAN CONSERVATION ALONG THE ARCHIPELAGO

The distribution of avian habitats and breeding species varies considerably along the length of the Hawaiian Archipelago. Seabirds and shorebirds occur from Kure to Hawai'i, native passerines and waterfowl are found from Laysan to Hawai'i, and wetland birds and raptors are found primarily in the main islands from Kaua'i to Hawai'i. The largest tracts of forests, woodlands, shrublands, and grasslands occur on Hawai'i, followed by those on Maui, Kaua'i, and O'ahu. Wetlands are most available on Kaua'i, O'ahu, and Maui. Seabirds nest primarily on the small islands and atolls of the Northwestern Hawaiian Islands, where alien mammalian predators are absent, and relict populations persist in areas on the main islands where predators are locally absent or scarce.

Bird species are protected by state and federal

TABLE 2. MANAGERIAL JURISDICTION OF AVIAN HABITATS IN HAWAI'I

Jurisdiction	Wet forest, shrubland & bog	Mesic forest & shrubland	Dry forest, shrubland & grassland	Coastal wetlands	Shoreline	Small islands & atolls
National Park Service	X	X	X	X	X	
U.S. Fish & Wildlife Service	X	X		X	X	X
Military[a]		X	X	X	X	
Natural Area Reserve	X	X	X			
Forest Reserve & Wilderness	X	X	X			
Game Management Area	X	X	X			
The Nature Conservancy	X	X			X	
Private	X	X	X			
Government & Private Partnership	X	X				

[a] Excludes areas used for active training and operations.

laws, but habitats are managed by a variety of jurisdictions and organizations, each with somewhat different objectives (Table 2). The Hawaii Department of Land and Natural Resources, the National Park Service, and the U.S. Fish and Wildlife Service manage most Hawaiian bird habitat, including forests and shrublands, wetlands, and small islands and atolls used by seabirds.

The most significant gaps in habitat protection occur in areas essential to endemic forest birds. Scott et al. (1986) delineated areas on Hawai'i, Maui, Moloka'i, and Kaua'i as being essential for long-term survival of native forest birds. These areas represented the core and surrounding habitat where native bird communities were most intact and where the rarest species were found during the Hawai'i Forest Bird Surveys. On Hawai'i, four such areas were identified: the māmane (*Sophora chrysophylla*) and naio (*Myoporum sandwicense*) forest on the southern and southwestern side of Mauna Kea, the windward rain forest, the Ka'ū forest, and the remaining mesic to wet forest in South Kona (Fig. 2). On Maui, essential habitat included the higher-elevation rain forest on the northeastern slope of Haleakalā and the upper reaches of Kīpahulu Valley (Fig. 3). On Moloka'i, the forest of Kamakou Preserve and Oloku'i plateau were considered essential (Fig. 3). On Kaua'i, essential habitat consisted of the core of the Alaka'i Swamp (Fig. 4).

Most essential forest bird habitats on Maui, Moloka'i, and Kaua'i fall within areas that are primarily intended for conservation management, but on Hawai'i there are extensive areas that lack even nominal protection, especially in leeward locations. Preserving and restoring native biodiversity in additional areas of essential habitat would greatly benefit bird conservation. Critical habitat has been designated only for the Palila (*Loxioides bailleui*). Unlike critical habitat, essential habitat has no legal definition or implications.

On Hawai'i, endemic passerine populations and efforts to recover them are mostly restricted to highland native forest, because lowland areas have less remaining native habitat and more problems associated with alien species and disease (Scott et al. 1986, van Riper et al. 1986). Therefore, opportunities for avian recovery have been limited to areas that for many species represent the upper range of their historical distribution. Some of these areas may be marginal due to cooler temperatures and lower richness of food resources.

Endemic birds have persisted with varying degrees of success on different islands (Table 3). The present number of endemic species and subspecies on each island ranges from 26% to 67% of what existed prehistorically. Although much of this range simply reflects differences in the completeness of fossil and historical records, it is clear that endemic birds have declined dramatically throughout the archipelago. Even on Kaua'i, where about 62% of the known prehistoric avifauna survives, bird species are disappearing.

HAWAI'I

The island of Hawai'i presently supports 20 endemic bird species, of which 13 are listed as endangered or threatened (USFWS 1996a). Of the 11 surviving endemic forest passerines, 6 are endangered. The 'Alalā (*Corvus hawaiiensis*), or Hawaiian Crow, is nearly extinct in the wild but may be saved by captive breeding and release. Prospects for recovering the 'Ō'ū (*Psittirostra psittacea*) are hopeless because wild populations on all islands are exceedingly rare or extinct, and there are there are no birds in captivity. The other four species, Palila, 'Akiapōlā'au (*Hemignathus munroi*), Hawai'i Creeper (*Oreomystis mana*), and Hawai'i 'Ākepa (*Loxops coccineus*),

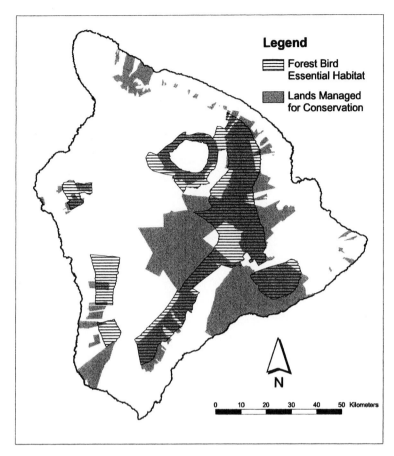

FIGURE 2.   Essential forest bird habitat on Hawai'i requires additional protection in many areas but especially on the western side of the island.

are likely to persist for decades longer, but their recovery cannot be taken for granted. Even among the five species not considered endangered, there are troubling downward trends. For example, the 'I'iwi (*Vestiaria coccinea*) has disappeared or is declining in many areas. Nonetheless, Hawai'i is the only island where there is a viable population of endemic thrush, the 'Ōma'o (*Myadestes obscurus*). Although today most passerines occupy wet and mesic native forests, many extinct species occurred in dry forest, formerly the most botanically rich habitat on the island (Rock 1974; Wagner et al. 1990a,b; James and Olson 1991, Olson and James 1991). Dry forests now exist mainly as highly altered remnants, but portions receive limited protection.

The 'Io (*Buteo solitarius*), or Hawaiian Hawk, the sole surviving falconiform species in the islands, is a widely distributed hawk in forests and woodlands. It is limited to Hawai'i, although fossil evidence indicates a wider range prehis-

torically, and it is listed as endangered. The endemic subspecies of the Short-eared Owl (*Asio flammeus sandwichensis*), or Pueo, is the only other surviving raptor of the nine known to have occurred prehistorically or historically (Olson and James 1991). The Short-eared Owl occurs in forests, woodlands, and shrub-grasslands on Hawai'i and all the other major islands.

The endangered Nēnē inhabits agricultural lands and managed grasslands in addition to native shrublands and grasslands. Three endangered waterbirds, the Koloa (Koloa maoli, *Anas wyvilliana*), or Hawaiian Duck; Hawaiian Coot ('Alae ke'oke'o, *Fulica alai*); and an endemic subspecies of the Black-necked Stilt, the Hawaiian Stilt (Ae'o, *Himantopus mexicanus knudseni*), survive primarily in the small wetlands along the western coast. In recent years, populations of Hawaiian Coot and Black-necked Stilt have increased significantly in the Kona area due to the construction of aquaculture ponds at

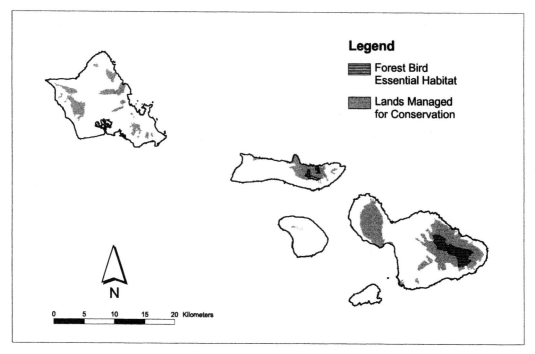

FIGURE 3.   Essential forest bird habitat on Maui and Molokaʻi are designated for conservation, but essential habitat was not identified on Oʻahu, Lānaʻi, or Kahoʻolawe.

the Natural Energy Laboratory at Keāhole and sewage treatment ponds.

The endangered Dark-rumped Petrel (ʻUaʻu, *Pterodroma phaeopygia sandwichensis*), or Hawaiian Petrel, once abundant on the island, now is limited to relic nesting colonies in remote lava fields at high elevation (Hu et al. *this volume*). The remoteness of these sites inhibits predation by introduced small mammals that long ago overran lowland breeding sites on the island (Simons and Hodges 1998). The threatened endemic subspecies of Townsend's Shearwater, here-

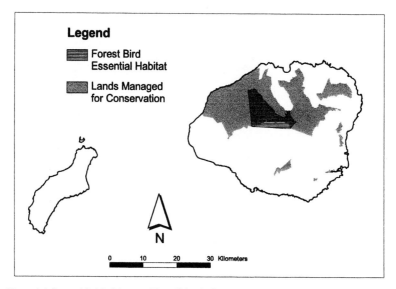

FIGURE 4.   Essential forest bird habitat on Kauaʻi is designated for conservation.

TABLE 3. DISTRIBUTION AND SURVIVAL OF ENDEMIC TAXA (INCLUDING SUBSPECIES) IN THE HAWAIIAN ARCHIPELAGO THROUGH TIME

Island	Prehistoric (<1778)	Historic (>1778)	Current (2000)
Northwestern Islands	9	9	6 [67%][a]
Kaua'i	34	22	22 [65%]
O'ahu	43	17	11 [26%]
Moloka'i	37	18	11 [30%]
Lāna'i	11	11	6 [55%]
Maui	48	19	16 [33%]
Hawai'i	46	31	20 [43%]

Notes: Data adapted from James and Olson (1991), Olson and James (1991), Giffin (1993, pers. Comm.), and Pyle (1997). Values for prehistoric and historic avifauna on different islands will increase as fossils continue to be identified, revealing new species and range extensions of already-described species.

[a] Percentage of surviving prehistoric taxa are shown in brackets.

after referred to as Newell's Shearwater ('A'o, *Puffinus auricularis newelli*), has been reduced to tiny, relic colonies nesting in pit craters in low- and mid-elevation forest on the southern and eastern portions of the island and along cliffs in the northern Kohala mountains (Ainley et al. 1997b, Reynolds and Ritchotte 1997, Ainley et al. *this volume*). The Hawaiian subspecies of the Black Noddy, or Hawaiian Noddy (Noio; *Anous minutus melanogenys*), nests along sea cliffs on the eastern and southern coasts.

MAUI

Maui, to the northwest of Hawai'i, is older and smaller, and this geochronological trend continues northwestward along the archipelago. Although once much larger, these older islands now support relatively reduced areas of forest, thereby limiting opportunities for avian recovery. Nevertheless, a moderately large proportion of high-quality native forest on Maui is protected and supports ten endemic bird taxa; of these, five are endangered. Three of these taxa, Maui Nukupu'u (*Hemignathus lucidus affinus*), Maui 'Ākepa (*Loxops coccineus ochraceus*), and Po'ouli (*Melamprosops phaeosoma*), are so rare that recovery seems highly improbable (Reynolds and Snetsinger *this volume*). Although Maui Parrotbill (*Pseudonestor xanthophrys*) and 'Ākohekohe (*Palmeria dolei*) populations and ranges are relatively small, their remaining habitat is at least minimally protected and managed. Populations of three endangered endemic wetland birds, Koloa, Hawaiian Coot, and Black-necked Stilt, occur in the wetlands on the isthmus between east and west Maui. The two largest wetlands, Kanahā and Keālia, are protected and managed. As on the island of Hawai'i, the Dark-rumped Petrel nests primarily in high-elevation habitats within Haleakalā National Park

(Simons and Hodges 1998, Hodges and Nagata *this volume,* Krushelnycky et al. *this volume*), and the Black Noddy nests along sea cliffs and offshore sea stacks.

LĀNA'I

Lāna'i, once connected to Maui and Moloka'i, now contains only a tiny area of forest. The 'Apapane (*Himatione sanguinea*), one of the most abundant forest birds on the major islands today and in the past, is the only endemic passerine surviving on Lāna'i. Even the once common Maui 'Amakihi (*Hemignathus virens wilsoni*) is no longer found on Lāna'i (Lindsey et al. 1998). However, the Short-eared Owl still occurs on the island (Scott et al. 1986). In addition, two endangered wetland birds, Hawaiian Coot and Black-necked Stilt, are observed rarely at sewage treatment ponds. The colony of Dark-rumped Petrels that once nested on Lāna'i (Simons and Hodges 1998) has recently disappeared. Black Noddies, however, continue to nest in small numbers on the island (Harrison 1990).

MOLOKA'I

The native forest on Moloka'i is much reduced, and no more than five endemic forest bird species remain. However, the Moloka'i Oloma'o or Moloka'i Thrush (*Myadestes lanaiensis rutha*) was last seen in 1979–1980 (Scott et al. 1986), and the Kākāwahie or Moloka'i Creeper (*Paroreomyza flammea*) was last seen in 1963 (Pekelo 1963). Both species are almost certainly extinct, although they continue to be listed as endangered (but see Reynolds and Snetsinger *this volume*). Only 'Apapane and Maui 'Amakihi are relatively common. 'I'iwi are very rare today, although they were once abundant on this and other major islands (Scott et al. 1986). Two endangered endemic wetland birds, Hawaiian Coot and Black-necked Stilt, still survive. The Short-eared Owl is the only survivor of the five raptorial taxa formerly known from Moloka'i. The Dark-rumped Petrel and Newell's Shearwater still nest in the valley walls deep in the interior of the island. The Black Noddy nests along the ocean cliffs.

O'AHU

Five endemic forest bird species remain on O'ahu; however, populations generally are in decline (VanderWerf and Rohrer 1996, VanderWerf et al. 1997). Although listed as endangered, the O'ahu 'Alauahio (*Paroreomyza maculata*), or O'ahu Creeper, is probably extinct. The O'ahu 'Elepaio (*Chasiempis sandwichensis ibidis*) is being considered for listing as an endangered species (Conant 1995), although subspecies on Hawai'i and Kaua'i are still relatively common. The O'ahu 'Amakihi (*Hemignathus flavus*) is still relatively common and is even reappearing in some lowland habitats after decades of absence (VanderWerf 1997). 'Apapane are now scarce, and 'I'iwi are very scarce. Four species of endangered endemic waterbirds still occur on O'ahu: Common Moorhen (Hawaiian Gallinule, 'Alae'ula; *Gallinula chloropus sandvicensis*), Hawaiian Coot, Black-necked Stilt, and Koloa, which was reintroduced from releases of captive stock. Mallards (*Anas platyrynchos*) have genetically swamped Koloa on O'ahu through extensive hybridization (Browne et al. 1993). The Short-eared Owl is the only endemic raptor and the Black Noddy is the only endemic seabird still nesting on O'ahu.

KAUA'I

The endemic avifauna on Kaua'i is somewhat more intact than on other islands, but many forest bird species are declining or have recently become extinct. Of the seven forest bird species not listed as endangered, the 'Akikiki (*Oreomystis bairdi*), or Kaua'i Creeper, has declined significantly and become uncommon. Of the six forest bird species listed as endangered, recovery may be possible only for the Puaiohi (Small Kaua'i Thrush, *Myadestes palmeri*). Kāma'o (Large Kaua'i Thrush, *Myadestes myadestinus*), 'Ō'ū, and Kaua'i Nukupu'u (*Hemignathus lucidus hanapepe*) are too rare to be recovered. The 'Ō'ō'ā'ā (*Moho braccatus*), or Kaua'i 'Ō'ō, was last observed in 1987 (Pyle 1987a, Conant et al. 1998) and the Kaua'i 'Akialoa (*Hemignathus ellisianus procerus*) was last seen in 1969 (P. Bruner in Pyle 2000); both are almost certainly extinct (Reynolds and Snetsinger *this volume*).

Endemic nonpasserines on Kaua'i include two seabirds that nest in forest habitats: the endangered Dark-rumped Petrel and the threatened Newell's Shearwater. The Black Noddy nests along sea cliffs. Four endangered wetland birds also reside on Kaua'i: Koloa, Common Moorhen, Hawaiian Coot, and Black-necked Stilt. The Short-eared Owl inhabits forests and shrubgrasslands. The Nēnē has been reintroduced to Kaua'i, and populations are growing rapidly in and around agricultural lands and golf courses (Banko et al. 1999).

SPECIES AND HABITAT APPROACHES TO AVIAN CONSERVATION

The Hawaiian avifauna has become so depleted and habitats have been destroyed and altered on such a large scale that designing and implementing recovery programs is daunting, especially given the limited resources available for conservation in Hawai'i. As a consequence,

recovery actions in Hawai'i are often opportunistic and seldom reflect a coherent, overall strategy (van Riper and Scott *this volume*). Avian conservation in Hawai'i, therefore, is attempted along a continuum of levels, including individuals, populations, species, communities, habitats, and ecosystems. Although recovery of species is mandated by the Endangered Species Act of 1973, avian recovery in Hawai'i requires habitat management. Degradation of native plant communities and introductions of alien predators, disease vectors, and food competitors have caused widespread and pervasive problems for Hawai'i's avifauna (Warner 1968, Atkinson 1977, Banko and Banko 1976, Ralph and van Riper 1985, Scott et al. 1986, van Riper et al. 1986, Pratt 1994, Atkinson et al. 1995, Jacobi and Atkinson 1995, van Riper and Scott *this volume*). Recovery plans have been developed for most species (USFWS 1982a,b,c,d, 1983a,b,c, 1984a,b,c, 1985, 1986), but specified recovery actions have not been fully implemented.

The "species approach" often involves monitoring populations, studying life history and limiting factors, protecting species from predators, providing artificial nest sites and supplemental food, manipulating habitat or enhancing nesting or feeding opportunities, translocating species, captive breeding and release, and rehabilitating injured individuals. Species management should start when populations begin to decline, not when they are listed as endangered. By this criterion, nearly all endemic species in Hawai'i birds require some level of management; however, there are too many species requiring management to devote resources to each one. Resource managers are quickly overwhelmed even if they concentrate their efforts on the most critically endangered birds, the ones at the very end of the "extinction conveyor belt." In addition, by trying first to save the most endangered birds, managers are unable to stop the decline of the many less-threatened species. This results in desperate, if not hopeless, attempts to restore primarily "species on the brink" while reducing opportunities for recovering species for which there is a greater chance of success. Focusing avian recovery at the species level also diverts resources and attention from improving the quality of habitats.

The "habitat approach" assumes that bird communities are sustainable in the long-term when suitable resources are adequately distributed along appropriate environmental gradients and in large areas. It also assumes that bird populations will respond positively to changes in their habitat and that there is sufficient habitat to sustain bird communities for the long-term. For example, we know that seabirds thrive when predators are removed, and removing rats (*Rattus* spp.) may benefit forest bird species. However, we do not yet know that birds respond to changes we observe in plant communities following pig (*Sus scrofa*) removal. Nevertheless, we believe pig removal will result in fewer disease-transmitting mosquitoes, and it may result indirectly in more food resources for birds. Therefore, we should manage habitats before birds become uncommon, because a long time may pass before populations respond. In addition, we should manage large areas of habitat for the long-term. The habitat approach often incorporates removing or controlling alien species, such as ungulates, predators, disease vectors, and food competitors, and it should involve monitoring bird abundance to evaluate progress.

EXAMPLES OF SPECIES CONSERVATION

How do we allocate research on the endemic taxa that remain? The greatest effort is spent on studying nesting, food habits, movements, territory, limiting factors, habitat use, and population monitoring. We still know little about the nine species that are very rare or functionally extinct. The most intensively studied species include: Dark-rumped Petrel (Hodges and Nagata *this volume,* Hu et al. *this volume,* Krushelnycky *this volume*), Nēnē, 'Alalā, O'ahu 'Elepaio (VanderWerf *this volume*), Palila, Laysan Finch (*Telespiza cantans*), and Hawai'i 'Ākepa (Freed *this volume,* Hart *this volume*). Considerable research has also been directed towards 'Io, Hawai'i 'Elepaio (*Chasiempis sandwichensis sandwichensis*), Puaiohi, Hawai'i 'Amakihi (*Hemignathus virens virens*), 'Ākohekohe (Berlin et al. *this volume,* Carothers *this volume,* VanGelder and Smith *this volume*), Maui Parrotbill, 'Ōma'o (Fancy *this volume*), 'Apapane (Carothers *this volume*), 'I'iwi, and Nihoa Millerbird (*Acrocephalus familiaris kingi*; Conant and Morin *this volume*).

How is management allocated among endemic species? Searches were recently conducted for very rare birds with the idea that management might be implemented if target species were located (Reynolds and Snetsinger *this volume*). However, this approach was abandoned because few rare species were found and the futility of restoring tiny, elusive populations was realized. When endangered species are managed, efforts are generally aimed at population monitoring, captive propagation and translocation, and controlling predators in limited areas; some efforts have also been made to attract cavity nesters to artificial nests. Most endangered species management is directed towards Dark-rumped Petrel, Nēnē, Palila, Maui Parrotbill, 'Akiapōlā'au, Hawai'i Creeper, Hawai'i 'Ākepa, 'Ākohekohe,

and three critically endangered species: 'Alalā, Puaiohi, and Po'ouli. The 'Ōma'o has been the only nonendangered species receiving management, and a major justification for doing so was to develop techniques for restoring endangered thrushes.

NĒNĒ

The first attempt to recover an endemic Hawaiian bird species began with the release to the wild of captive-reared Nēnē (Kear and Berger 1980). By 1950, the wild population had declined to 30–50 individuals and there was no prospect for natural recovery. The initial phase of the recovery program involved building captive populations in Hawai'i and England and developing techniques for captive propagation and release. After much effort and persistence, breeding and releasing Nēnē became routine and 2,450 captive-reared Nēnē were released on Hawai'i, Maui, and Kaua'i over 40 years (Banko et al. 1999); however, a program of habitat management to complement the release of the captive birds was not sufficiently developed and supported. Consequently, most wild populations are not self-sustaining due to predation by introduced species of small mammals and poor food availability (Banko 1992, Black and Banko 1994, Banko et al. 1999, Scott and Banko 2000). Although extinction was prevented, the program demonstrates that species cannot be recovered without effective habitat management. Small Indian mongooses (*Herpestes auropunctatus*), feral cats (*Felis catus*), and feral dogs (*Canus familiaris*) prey on eggs, goslings, and adults in many areas; these predators are difficult and expensive to control. On Kaua'i, where mongooses are absent, predation is less of a problem and the Nēnē population is growing rapidly (Telfer 1995, 1996; Banko et al. 1999).

In addition to the difficulty of controlling predator numbers, many birds were released into areas that were not historically important for nesting (Henshaw 1902a). Over 1,000 Nēnē were released in the highlands on Hawai'i where habitat conditions were marginal (Black et al. 1997, Banko et al. 1999). Most released birds died and the survivors produced few offspring during the drought period of 1976–1983. Drought had somewhat less affect on the Nēnē population that was reintroduced to high-elevation habitat on Maui, probably because birds were able to graze on pasture grasses. Similarly, the Nēnē population reintroduced into Hawai'i Volcanoes National Park is slowly growing where nesting females and goslings have access to areas of managed grass. On Kaua'i, released birds mainly inhabit lowland pastures or other areas of managed grass where foraging opportunities are greatest (Telfer 1995, 1996).

The availability of managed grass enhances Nēnē breeding and survival (Woog and Black *this volume*); however, pastures, golf courses, lawns, roadsides, and other unnatural settings should be considered as ancillary to natural habitats. Nonetheless, it is better to have Nēnē in pastures than only in zoos. In addition, populations that utilize highly altered habitats can serve as genetic reservoirs and as safeguards when populations in wild habitats decline or disappear due to drought and other perturbations. However, maintaining at least some populations in shrub-grassland habitats dominated by native species should be a major goal. Towards this end, native plants that are nutritious and palatable to Nēnē should be encouraged to flourish in areas where predators can be controlled (Banko et al. 1999).

Conservationists around the world acclaimed the rescue of the Nēnē from extinction. Unfortunately the program was not critically evaluated until many birds had been released into habitats that could not support nesting and rearing. Substantial effort and money would have been saved if more thorough monitoring and more complete studies of limiting factors had been initiated earlier. Nonetheless, the Nēnē restoration program played an important role in attracting public attention to conserving Hawai'i's natural heritage.

'ALALĀ

The 'Alalā recovery program parallels that of the Nēnē in several ways. Recovery began when the population, range, and recovery options had become greatly reduced. The initial phase of recovery has emphasized captive propagation and release of birds to supplement the wild population. As with early Nēnē propagation, building viable breeding flocks of 'Alalā and developing avicultural techniques has been difficult and slow. Starting with three wild fledglings salvaged in 1972, only now is captive propagation becoming a viable management tool. In addition to breeding 'Alalā in captivity, wild eggs have been harvested and hatched in captivity. Young from some wild eggs have been incorporated into the captive breeding populations on Hawai'i and Maui while others have been released to the wild along with offspring of captive pairs. Since 1993, 27 captive-reared fledglings have been released in or adjacent to the new South Kona Unit of Hakalau Forest National Wildlife Refuge. Although survival of these captive-reared birds is higher than of parent-reared wild juveniles during the past 30 years (Banko and Banko 1976, National Research Council 1992), all but 6 of the 27 have died or disappeared since their release. The six surviving birds were returned to captivity until better management can be applied and habitat conditions improve. Disease and predators are proving to be a major hindrance to recovery, and the availability of suitable food needs to be investigated. Although releasing animals into habitats where limiting factors have not been managed reduces the chances of successful recovery (Griffith et al. 1989, Wolf et al. 1996), releasing 'Alalā into the wild has helped to identify some major limiting factors.

The endangered 'Io and alien small mammals are important predators of 'Alalā. Captive-reared 'Alalā and the few remaining wild individuals have frequently been chased, struck, or otherwise harassed by 'Io. Older 'Alalā are killed about as frequently as younger birds, suggesting that experience does not provide a critical benefit in avoiding predation. 'Io outnumber 'Alalā in their range in South Kona, and they will likely limit their recovery until many more 'Alalā have been released or methods are developed for reducing the threat of 'Io predation and harassment. In response to the fatalities of released birds, the eight captive-reared birds remaining in the wild were captured in 1998 and held in captivity until a plan for reducing the impact of 'Io could be developed. Subsequently, five of the eight birds were released to the wild for a second time. After one disappeared and another died, the three remaining birds were again recaptured and incorporated into the captive flock, which included the three other birds that had previously been released to the wild.

Although 'Io have killed many captive-reared 'Alalā, disease organisms, such as the protozoan *Toxoplasma gondii,* the bacteria *Erysipelas rhusiopathae,* and an unidentified fungus, have been implicated in the deaths of some birds (Work et al. 1999, 2000; unpubl. data). Feral cats are the carriers of toxoplasmosis (Wallace 1973), and birds scavenging a cow carcass may have encountered *E. rhusiopathae.* Diseased 'Alalā may be more vulnerable to 'Io predation, thus complicating the identification of mortality factors. An unexpected result of the captive-release program has been the low incidence of illness and mortality due to avian malaria and pox, which has been proposed as the most important factors preventing population recovery (Jenkins et al. 1989). Prior to their release into the wild, captive-reared birds are maintained in large, netted aviaries where they develop flight and social skills. While in this protected environment, they are exposed to mosquitoes, vectors of malaria and pox. The prevalence of *Plasmodium relictum* is uncommonly high in the South Kona mosquito population, and the aviary birds inevitably are bitten (C. T. Atkinson, pers. comm.).

Because their diet in captivity is excellent and they are treated prophylactically for malaria, 'Alalā survive with only short-term, mild symptoms of the disease, if any. Exposure to malaria while in the aviaries seems to confer immunity to the birds after their release and switch to a natural diet in the wild. Since captive-reared birds have not yet nested in the wild, it is not known whether their offspring will suffer more from avian malaria and pox without access to the high-quality diet available inside the aviaries.

The suitability of the habitat for supporting wild nestlings is poorly known, and this may be the next important challenge to managers after they have reduced predation rates. As with Nēnē, therefore, predator control and habitat management are needed to recover the species.

PALILA

In contrast to recovering endangered species on the brink of extinction, a program has begun to begin recovery of the endangered Palila before it becomes critically rare or limited in distribution. The program is distinguished by the fact that years of habitat improvement and research into the Palila's life history and limiting factors have preceded the development of more intensive techniques, such as translocation and captive propagation. Palila are the last remaining finch-billed species in the main islands and rely on seeds, flowers, and caterpillars taken from māmane trees. The annual Palila population estimate fluctuates considerably, and long-term viability of the species is in doubt (Jacobi et al. 1996, Banko et al. 1998, Gray et al. 1999). Palila are not increasing in numbers or distribution despite years of increasing māmane stand density and crown size of individual trees following the reduction of ungulate populations (see van Riper and Scott *this volume*); therefore, it is time to manage the species more actively.

The Palila population is becoming increasingly concentrated on the western slope of Mauna Kea Volcano where the māmane forest is large and extends along a substantial gradient of elevation. The forest on the eastern slope is truncated along its lower margin by pastures (van Riper et al. 1978, Scott et al. 1984), and the Palila population is steadily declining (Jacobi et al. 1996, Banko et al. 1998). Management options are, therefore, limited. Similarly, opportunities to restore the diminished population on the southern slope of Mauna Kea are limited, although the forest is relatively extensive. Instead, ranching and military training inhibit population restoration. To mitigate the effects of realigning Saddle Road through Palila habitat on the southern slope, efforts are being made to reestablish Palila in recovering forest on the northern slope, where Palila have been absent for over 25 years (van Riper et al. 1978).

In 1993, 35 adult Palila were translocated to the eastern slope to determine whether recovery could be expedited in an area where predators were controlled (Fancy et al. 1997). Although several pairs nested, about half of translocated birds returned to their original habitat on the western slope after 2 to 6 weeks. In order to further develop translocation as a management tool, 53 juveniles (> 3 months) and adults were moved to the northern slope during three trials in 1997–1998; however, most birds returned to the western slope or were killed by predators (U.S. Geological Survey, unpubl. data). Concurrently, techniques for hatching wild eggs in captivity have been developed, and a small captive population has been established with the hope of releasing birds to the wild (Kuehler et al. *this volume*).

Palila exist today primarily because foresters rehabilitated māmane forests on Mauna Kea by removing tame and feral cattle (*Bos taurus*) and reducing populations of feral sheep (*Ovis aries*) from 1921 to 1946 (Bryan 1947). However, the sheep population, consisting of about 500 animals in 1949, was allowed to increase and was maintained in the low 1,000s when sustain-yield game hunting was popularized in the 1950s (Tomich 1986). In addition, mouflon (*O. musimon*), which hybridized with feral sheep, were introduced to Mauna Kea in 1962 to enhance game hunting (Tomich 1986). Sheep and mouflon browsed māmane seedlings and foliage, severely damaging the forest (Giffin 1976, 1982).

In 1979 and 1986, district federal court ruled that feral sheep and goats (*Capra hircus*) must be eradicated to allow Palila habitat to recover (Pratt et al. 1997a). Populations of sheep and mouflon have been reduced substantially and māmane recruitment is evident (Hess et al. 1999). However, fire risks have escalated as alien grasses have increased. Understanding fire ecology in montane and subalpine dry forests and developing appropriate management schemes will be critical to recovery efforts.

Other habitat factors are also important to Palila recovery. For example, the primary insect food of nestling Palila is native caterpillars, *Cydia* spp. (Tortricidae), which eat māmane seeds (U.S. Geological Survey, unpubl. data). *Cydia* are parasitized by at least three alien and one native wasp species, possibly limiting Palila productivity where parasitism is heavy. Introduced small mammals also prey on Palila eggs, chicks, and adults. Feral cats and roof rats (*Rattus rattus*) pose the greatest threats, and may limit natural population expansion and recovery in some areas (Pratt et al. 1997a). Investigations into predator impacts and control methods continue. Unlike most other forest birds in Hawai'i, Palila are distributed above the range of mosquitoes, and avian malaria and pox seldom affect them. However, other disease organisms may impact wild Palila (U.S. Geological Survey, unpubl. data). We presume that Palila living near tree line today may not be as productive as when populations ranged much lower in elevation (Perkins 1903). Reintroducing Palila to low-elevation habitats, however, must wait until biological and political obstacles are resolved.

EXAMPLES OF HABITAT CONSERVATION

The primary goal of some programs in Hawai'i is to restore habitats or ecosystems with the expectation that many species will benefit. The National Park Service and U.S. Fish and Wildlife Service attempt to manage relatively large areas, whereas the state Natural Area Reserve System and The Nature Conservancy of Hawai'i manage habitats on a somewhat smaller scale.

Hawai'i Volcanoes and Haleakalā national parks focus primarily on landscape-scale habitat conservation. Although both parks contain many listed endangered species, the priority is removing alien animals and plants that degrade native habitats. Since the early 1970s, feral pigs, goats, and other ungulates have been removed from large, fenced areas (Anderson and Stone 1993, 1994). Vegetation recovering in these ungulate-free management units may eventually support more native birds and other species.

Similarly, habitat recovery is beginning at Hakalau Forest National Wildlife Refuge because of recent alien pest and weed management. These wet and mesic forests are vitally important for many common and endangered forest birds. In addition to removing feral animals that degrade native forests, the refuge is planting native trees and shrubs in highland areas denuded by grazing, logging, and fire. Native birds are beginning to use these emergent habitats, and they will benefit more as forest structure and composition become increasingly complex and diverse.

In an encouraging trend, adjacent landowners jointly manage portions of their land for conservation. On the island of Hawai'i, for example, Kamehameha Schools Bishop Estate, Hawai'i Volcanoes National Park, Hawaii Department of Land and Natural Resources, and Hawaii Department of Public Safety cooperate with the U.S. Fish and Wildlife Service, U.S. Geological Survey, and the U.S. Forest Service to manage the 'Ōla'a-Kīlauea Management Area. This project, encompassing over 12,000 ha of land on the upper, windward slopes of Mauna Loa Volcano, includes extremely important native koa (*Acacia koa*) and 'ōhi'a (*Metrosideros polymorpha*) forest habitat, which supports significant populations of rare and common native birds. The landowners and cooperating agencies that form the East Maui Watershed Partnership have taken a similar approach to reduce the stress of invasive plant and animal species in wet forest habitats on Maui. These joint efforts can serve as models for protecting large, continuous tracts of forest bird habitat over landscapes that have multiple ownership.

CONSERVATION STRATEGIES AND OPTIONS

GOALS AND PRIORITIES FOR AVIAN CONSERVATION

Recovery plans have been written, and in a few cases revised, for all endangered Hawaiian bird species, yet there is no comprehensive strategy to conserve endemic birds generally. The goal of "no more bird extinctions in Hawai'i" is impractical, given the number of species that are critically endangered. Neither does it seem likely that many bird populations will recover naturally in response to limited habitat restoration, such as removing select alien species. Forests and other avian habitats have been so severely damaged by alien stressors that restoration of native vegetation structure and composition may take many decades. There have been few opportunities to evaluate the response of native invertebrate and bird communities to habitat changes following the removal of ungulates. In the best known example, Palila populations have been slow to respond to the increased regeneration of māmane trees resulting from the reduction of feral sheep and mouflon. Therefore, restoring many endemic birds will require species management in addition to removing or reducing factors that damage habitats.

Avian conservation in Hawai'i requires evaluating areas of essential habitat to determine which management actions will best promote the recovery of native bird communities. Lowland habitats should not be overlooked since virtually all bird species once occurred there. It also is necessary to take into account that lava flows, hurricanes, fires, cycles of forest senescence and rejuvenation, and other natural disruptions to avian habitats will occur. The scale of conservation activities must encompass large regions and cannot be limited to existing wildlife refuges, reserves, and parks. There presently is no basis for deciding what size habitats should be to sustain communities of Hawaiian birds.

Information and improved techniques also are

needed to accelerate the development of avian conservation strategies in Hawai'i. Major factors limiting endemic bird populations have been identified, although additional research is needed to guide managers' efforts to overcome negative effects of these factors. Research should include investigative and manipulative approaches to provide managers with information about the underlying nature of limiting factors and the consequences, both intended and unintended, of their mitigation.

It may be useful to investigate the factors limiting alien bird populations, particularly in lowland habitats, to help restore endemic forest birds. If alien birds are relatively resistant to avian malaria and pox (van Riper et al. 1986, Atkinson et al. 1995), what factors limit their populations and potentially inhibit native species recovery? The Red-bill Leiothrix (*Leiothrix lutea*), for example, seems to be disappearing from some habitats where it once was common and increasing in some areas where it was scarce, yet there is no research into the factors responsible for this.

Birds play important roles in ecosystem function by pollinating and dispersing native and alien plants. Management strategies must account for the potential harm done to native ecosystems by birds facilitating the spread of noxious weeds and the potential benefit to bird populations that forage heavily on fruit and nectar of alien plant species. We need to determine in more detail how bird and plant interactions may affect conservation goals. Birds may also affect native and alien insect populations, as they do elsewhere (Holmes 1990), but the nature or consequences of these relationships have not been investigated in Hawai'i. Similarly, birds may affect nutrient cycling and soil development. For example, seabirds once nested in much greater numbers over a far larger area (Olson and James 1982b, 1991); their guano and burrowing may have influenced mineral availability and the dynamics of plant communities (M. Friedland and P. Vitousek, unpubl. data). Determining the function of birds in native ecosystems in greater detail will help in designing conservation strategies.

Priorities

- Identify, characterize, and prioritize habitats essential to Hawaiian birds and develop management strategies for areas where restoration of native birds and their habitats is likely to be effective. Leeward areas of Hawai'i merit special consideration. Habitats to be managed for avian recovery include dry, mesic, and wet forests and woodlands; shrub-grasslands; wetlands, including rivers, streams, estuaries,

marshes, and bogs; coastlands, atolls, and islets; marine waters.
- Determine the geographical scale appropriate to recovering and maintaining viable populations of wide-ranging and sedentary species. Promote partnerships and public appreciation to manage large areas of habitat for avian and other conservation values.
- Determine additional management requirements of species that may not respond naturally or quickly to habitat management. Investigate factors that limit alien bird populations to evaluate endemic bird requirements.
- Investigate the functional role of endemic and alien birds in Hawaiian ecosystems.

HABITAT ALTERATION AND STRESSORS

Human activity and invasive alien plants and animals can affect the Hawaiian biota at population, community, and ecosystem levels. Gross changes in ecosystems and community structure and composition began with Polynesian colonization and continue today as native forests are converted to tree plantations and other agricultural or social uses. Few endemic Hawaiian birds have survived major, or even subtler, changes to their habitats. Passerine birds have suffered the most from habitat alteration. Remaining species generally inhabit only the uppermost extremes of their former distributions where they contend least with disease vectors, predators, and alien weeds and pests. Nevertheless, a few species actually thrive in highly altered habitats. For example, fossils of Short-eared Owl are not known from the period prior to human colonization, and populations may not have become established until humans modified habitats, introduced rodents, and perhaps reduced populations of other raptors (Olson and James 1991). The Nēnē is readily attracted to short, growing grasses found in pastures, golf courses, lawns, and roadsides (Black et al. 1994, Banko et al. 1999); however, they may have fared as well or better when the full array of native food plants were available. The 'Io, too, preys on introduced animals and occupies agricultural and other altered habitats in addition to native forest. All endemic wetland birds survive in habitats dominated by alien plants. We can only guess about their status in pristine habitats.

Terrestrial habitat management in Hawai'i is meaningless without eradicating or substantially reducing populations of feral ungulates. Forest bird recovery plans and management plans for federal, state, and private natural area reserves and parks acknowledge this fact. Ungulates are the greatest threats to forest habitats (Ralph and van Riper 1985, Scott et al. 1986, Cuddihy and Stone 1990, Pratt 1994), but there has been significant progress in controlling their populations in relatively few areas. Prime examples of successful control programs include Hawai'i Volcanoes National Park, Haleakalā National Park, Waikamoi Preserve, Hanawī Natural Area Reserve, and Kamakou Preserve. In addition, ungulate control is under way in Hakalau Forest Wildlife Refuge. Sheep, goats, and mouflon are being controlled in Mauna Kea Forest Reserve, but pigs are maintained for sustained-yield hunting. The added benefit of feral pig control in moist areas is the likely reduction of mosquito populations and lower transmission rates of malaria and pox (Scott et al. 1986, van Riper et al. 1986, Atkinson et al. 1995). Feral ungulates destroy and modify Hawaiian bird habitats by eating native plants, disrupting soil processes, and increasing erosion, facilitating the spread of alien plants, and creating breeding sites for disease vectors (van Riper and Scott *this volume*). Their removal should be the highest management priority in Hawaiian bird habitats. It is important, however, to be prepared for the possible increase of some alien plants following ungulate removal.

The dominance of alien weeds in many avian habitats affects avian conservation programs in a variety of ways. Most importantly, alien plants may fundamentally change habitat structure and composition, resulting in changes in the availability of suitable foraging and nesting substrates. Some alien species affect ecosystem function by altering the availability of resources (e.g., soil chemistry, light), changing trophic relationships (e.g., seed predation and dispersal, pollination), and intensifying or speeding disturbance (e.g., facilitating invasion by other invasive species; Vitousek and Walker 1989). Therefore, it is crucial to Hawaiian bird conservation to reduce many populations of alien weeds and pests that have already invaded native ecosystems and to prevent the introduction and spread of other invasive species (Loope et al. *this volume*). Some of the most insidious species invading Hawaiian forests include *Miconia calvescens, Passiflora mollissima, Psidium cattleianum, Shinus molle, Clidemia hirta, Rubus ellipticus, Myrica faya,* and *Hedychium gardnerianum*. These and many other invasive plants crowd out native species that are sources of fruits, seeds, or invertebrates to endemic birds. Furthermore, changes in plant community structure and composition due to alien plants generally negate foraging benefits to birds. Serious threats to shrub-grasslands and woodlands include alien grasses (*Pennisetum setaceum, P. clandestinum,* and *Schizachyrium condensatum*), *Ulex europaeus, Leucaena leucocephala, Lantana camara,* and a number of other species. The introduced mangrove, *Rhizophora mangle,* and *Pluchea in-*

dica threaten some wetland habitats (Allen 1998, Loope et al. *this volume*). Weeds are also a concern on the small islands of the northwestern chain. Habitat conditions for the Laysan Finch have improved now that *Cenchrus echinatus* has been nearly eradicated. Hawai'i Volcanoes and Haleakalā national parks have stopped the spread of some alien plants (e.g., Medeiros et al. 1997). They have shown that allocating sufficient resources and managing ungulates, fire, and other environmental stressors are important in controlling many weed species. Additional research is required to develop techniques, including biological control and chemical applications, for efficiently removing weeds. Monitoring the responses of native communities, including birds, should accompany the removal of alien species.

Forest health is critical to conserving Hawaiian forest birds, and many forests are dominated by only one or two native tree species. Pathogens or insects affecting dominant forest components would devastate native forest bird populations. Three species of endemic trees are essential to endemic passerines today: 'ōhi'a, koa, and māmane. Trees alone are not sufficient to sustain forest bird populations; understory diversity is also needed. Managers must know what agents and processes potentially threaten dominant tree species. The phenomenon of 'ōhi'a dieback is relatively well understood (Mueller-Dombois 1980, Jacobi 1993), but continued research and monitoring are warranted to avoid overlooking a pathogenic cause of tree mortality. Modeling spatial and temporal patterns of forest senescence should help guide research when large areas of forest begin to lose vigor. There is little research into the prevalence or pathogenicity of disease agents of endemic plants (but see Gardner 1997). Additional studies would help develop strategies for preventing the loss of large forest tracts to alien pathogens. Neither is there sufficient effort to prevent the establishment of insect pests that attack plants that provide important food resources to birds.

A pressing management concern in dry Hawaiian forests and woodlands is fire. Alien annual grasses greatly facilitate fire through the accumulation of dead leaves and stems, which burn rapidly. As previously discussed, fire seriously threatens the Palila population on the dry, western slope of Mauna Kea. Fire also disrupts shrubland and woodland communities in the lower elevations of Hawai'i Volcanoes National Park (Hughes et al. 1991), although Nēnē may opportunistically use areas that are recovering from burns (Banko et al. 1999). Hawai'i Volcanoes National Park actively manages fire threats, a policy that is needed at Pōhakuloa

Training Area, Mauna Kea Forest Reserve, and other areas where alien grass cover is high.

Hawaiian forest bird populations have declined in part because alien predators and parasites have depleted invertebrate food resources (Banko and Banko 1976; U.S. Geological Survey, unpubl. data). The loss of native invertebrates may hinder the recovery of some bird species. Techniques for controlling invertebrate pests, however, are largely undeveloped and managers have few tools and little expertise at their disposal. Efforts generally consist of reducing yellow jacket (*Vespula pensylvanica*) populations in a few localities. Controlling yellow jackets and other invertebrate predators and parasites over large areas may prove to be very difficult (Cole et al. 1992). Therefore, efforts should focus on preventing the introduction and spread of the most damaging alien species, while developing techniques for control at the landscape level (Loope et al. *this volume*).

Priorities

- Permanently remove feral ungulates from essential avian habitats.
- Control the spread of alien weeds and remove them from important avian habitats.
- Develop and implement plans for managing fire threats.
- Restore native plant communities following ungulate and weed removal.
- Determine the distribution of alien invertebrate pests that deplete avian food resources and develop and implement management techniques.
- Identify threats to habitats posed by plant pathogens and herbivorous invertebrates and develop strategies and techniques for their prevention or control.

POPULATION MONITORING

Monitoring bird species is important because managers need information on population trends to plan and develop recovery efforts. Surveys of species distributions, densities, and habitat associations were conducted throughout the state in forested areas during 1976–1983 (Scott et al. 1986). However, plans to survey each major island every five years since the baseline was established have not been carried out. Although there may be little practicality in learning that rare species are becoming rarer, trends of more common species are important to determine.

At Hakalau Forest National Wildlife Refuge, where there is a comprehensive monitoring program, counts are conducted annually, sometimes seasonally, and there is a relatively long history of monitoring. Trends suggest that there has not been sufficient management or time to determine changes in bird populations. The avian community is dominated by common nectarivorous or omnivorous species, although the refuge was established primarily for three endangered insectivorous species, 'Akiapōlā'au, Hawai'i 'Ākepa, and Hawai'i Creeper. Annual monitoring of forest bird populations has recently been implemented in 'Ōla'a-Kīlauea, Keauhou, and Haleakalā. Mauna Kea Forest Reserve has the longest record of continuous population monitoring (20 years in the year 2000) and is the largest tract of forest that is surveyed annually. Until recently, counts on Mauna Kea have focused mainly on endangered species.

Select species are monitored regularly in some areas; for example, Nēnē and Dark-rumped Petrels at Hawai'i Volcanoes National Park. In addition, forest birds in Kīpahulu Valley are now being monitored annually in Haleakalā National Park. Many seabird species are monitored annually on Laysan, Tern, and Midway in the Hawaiian/Pacific Islands National Wildlife Refuge Complex. The Laysan Duck (*Anas laysanesis*) and Laysan Finch are surveyed frequently, if not annually, whenever trained observers are available. All bird species are surveyed on Nihoa at about 2–3 year intervals. Annual counts of waterbirds are conducted throughout the state. The Bishop Museum maintains a database of unusual bird observations (R. L. Pyle, pers. comm.). There is no comprehensive, systematic, or long-term monitoring of migratory bird populations in Hawai'i, except perhaps for Kōlea (*Pluvialis fulva*; Johnson and Johnson 1993).

Priorities

- Monitor population trends of common and endangered birds to evaluate conservation priorities, strategies, and tactics.
- Monitor endangered passerines whose populations occur in the low 100s or 1,000s and that have some prospect for recovery, including Nihoa Millerbird, Puaiohi, Laysan Finch, Nihoa Finch (*Telespiza ultima*), Palila, Maui Parrotbill, 'Akiapōlā'au, Hawai'i Creeper, Kaua'i 'Ākepa or 'Akeke'e (*Loxops caeruleirostris*), Hawai'i 'Ākepa, and 'Ākohekohe.
- Evaluate responses of avian populations to changes in plant and invertebrate communities generated by the removal of alien species and other management.
- Determine the abundance and distribution of nesting Dark-rumped Petrels and Newell's Shearwaters and develop conservation strategies.

REINTRODUCTION, TRANSLOCATION, AND CAPTIVE PROPAGATION

Many endemic species must be reintroduced to portions of their historic or prehistoric range, because their reproductive potential and dispersal capabilities are limited. Recovering the Laysan Duck, for example, must include reintroducing populations to other islands and atolls in the northwestern chain; it may also involve reintroduction to some of the major islands where it once occurred (Olson and Ziegler 1995, Cooper et al. 1996, Moulton and Marshall 1996; J. G. Giffin, pers. comm.). Reintroduction and translocation may also be necessary to restore other species, such as 'Akiapōlā'au and Hawai'i Creeper, in habitats recovering from ungulate damage, for example in Hawai'i Volcanoes National Park and Mauna Kea Forest Reserve. Experimental reintroductions of Palila and 'Ōma'o, however, suggest that results may vary according to species and habitat (Fancy et al. *this volume*).

Where a species or subspecies has been extirpated, it may be possible to introduce a close relative. For example, it may be possible to introduce the Nihoa Millerbird to Laysan Island, where the Laysan Millerbird (*A. f. familiaris*) became extinct after introduced rabbits denuded the island. This may reduce the threat of extinction on one island while helping to restore the terrestrial community on the other (Morin et al. 1997).

In addition to expanding their distribution, reintroducing and translocating Nēnē to former range may help establish adaptive traditions of seasonal movement to more suitable habitats. For example, Nēnē families translocated from one island or habitat to another might return to their original breeding grounds after the goslings fledge. When mature, some females might return with their mates to nest in the new area, thereby promoting adaptive patterns of movement and possibly survival and productivity. When Nēnē are reintroduced to Moloka'i (C. Terry, pers. comm.), there will be opportunities to experiment with establishing interisland movement to Maui.

Releasing captive-reared birds to reintroduce or bolster populations is an alternative or supplement to translocating wild individuals and has been used with Nēnē, 'Alalā, 'Ōma'o, and Puaiohi. In addition, common species, such as the Hawai'i 'Amakihi, have been experimentally reared and released (Kuehler et al. 1996).

Nests of 'Alalā and Nēnē have been managed in the wild to enhance productivity, and other species may be similarly manipulated to facilitate their restoration. 'Alalā eggs were removed from the wild and hatched in captivity to provide new stock for release to the wild and for captive breeding (Kuehler et al. 1995). Manipulated pairs renested within 2 weeks of egg removal, but no chicks fledged. Palila eggs were removed from the wild for the same purpose, but all stock was retained for captive breeding. Manipulated pairs renested within 2 weeks and some fledged chicks (U.S. Geological Survey, unpubl. data). Wild Puaiohi also renested readily when their eggs were removed to establish a captive breeding flock (Snetsinger et al. 1999). Nēnē eggs have been salvaged from abandoned nests and the goslings were raised in captivity for later release, thereby increasing wild recruitment (Baker and Baker 1996).

In contrast to terrestrial bird reintroduction, reestablishing seabirds and waterbirds in former range may involve only controlling predators and attracting birds with calls and artificial nest sites. This technique might be especially effective for reestablishing breeding colonies of Dark-rumped Petrels and Newell's Shearwaters.

Priorities

- Develop strategies and priorities for reintroducing species into habitats that are recovering from ungulates and other stressors and for supplementing populations that have reached critically low levels.
- Develop techniques for hatching, rearing, and releasing species that may be difficult to recover by other methods.

PREDATOR CONTROL

Alien predators threaten Hawaiian birds in all habitats found on the major islands. Conserving endemic birds, therefore, requires reducing or eliminating predatory threats posed by introduced small mammals, particularly rats, feral cats, and mongooses. Preventing the establishment of ground predators on the islands and atolls of the Hawaiian/Pacific Islands National Wildlife Refuge Complex is crucial to conserving resident seabirds and endemic passerines.

Rats have been controlled in Hawai'i primarily in an experimental context to demonstrate their effects on bird survival and productivity. Although rats prey on birds, they may also compete for fruits, seeds, insects, snails and other food items and they may modify habitats by lowering plant productivity, recruitment, and survival. As in New Zealand, rat control may be on the verge of becoming a viable management tool in at least a few areas in Hawai'i. For example, rats have been eradicated from Kure Atoll (D. Smith, pers. comm.) and Midway Atoll (R. J. Shallenberger, pers. comm.). Rats and other predators are being reduced in portions of

Hanawī Natural Area Reserve (M. S. Collins, pers. comm.), Keauhou forest (T. L. C. Casey, pers. comm.), Hakalau Forest National Wildlife Refuge (J. T. Nelson, U.S. Geological Survey, unpubl. data), and Mauna Kea Forest Reserve (P. C. Banko, U.S. Geological Survey, unpubl. data).

The mongoose limits the abundance and distribution of many ground-nesting birds. On Kaua'i, where mongooses are absent, Newell's Shearwaters and Nēnē are relatively abundant. Although controlling mongooses is possible on a local scale, it requires great effort and expense over large areas (Stone et al. 1995). Controlling feral cats is also necessary to protect populations of ground-nesters, such as Dark-rumped Petrels (Hu et al. *this volume*). In addition, cat control is important to maintaining passerine populations, including Palila and 'Alalā. Because disposing of cats elicits strong emotional responses from some people, control programs must include public education. Controlling rats and mongooses, on the other hand, seems to create comparatively little concern among the public.

Priorities

- Prevent mongooses from becoming established on Kaua'i, Lāna'i, and Kaho'olawe.
- Test, register, and implement more economical and effective methods for distributing mongoose poisons.
- Convince legislators and the public of the necessity to eradicate feral cat populations and develop, register, and implement methods for their control.
- Accelerate research for developing efficient techniques for landscape-scale rodent control.

DISEASE

Avian malaria and pox are potent factors limiting populations of many Hawaiian birds (Warner 1968, Scott et al. 1986, van Riper et al. 1986, Jarvi et al. *this volume,* Shehata et al. *this volume,* van Riper et al. *this volume,* VanderWerf et al. *this volume*). Recent research has confirmed the pathogenicity of malaria in 'I'iwi, a once widespread, common species that is declining in most portions of its range (Atkinson et al. 1995). The ecology of the most important vector of avian diseases in Hawai'i, the mosquito (*Culex quinquefasciatus*), is being investigated to guide management (D. LaPointe, pers. comm.). Feral pigs create breeding sites for mosquitoes, but pig removal and mechanical reduction of breeding sites does not reduce mosquito populations in areas apparently smaller than the dispersal range of mosquitoes (C. T. Atkinson and D. LaPointe, pers. comm.). This reinforces the importance of conducting management over large areas of habitat to conserve birds.

Immunogenetics and resistance to avian malaria are being investigated in Hawaiian honeycreepers with a view towards developing methods for maintaining population stability through maintaining genetic diversity at loci important in immunological responsiveness to pathogens (Jarvi et al. *this volume*). Evidence that some species are co-evolving with malaria may be suggested by the persistence and reappearance of 'Ōma'o, O'ahu 'Amakihi, O'ahu 'Elepaio, and Hawai'i 'Amakihi in some low-elevation localities where mosquitoes are abundant. Research into the genetic, physiological, and ecological bases for the persistence of lowland endemic bird populations will help guide conservation strategies. Similar research is needed to understand the persistence of some endemic species in South Kona, Hawai'i, where the abundance of mosquitoes and prevalence of malaria are high. Investigating the role of diet in the survival of young birds infected by mosquitoes may partially explain malaria resistance, as observed in wild-released 'Alalā.

Hawaiian wetlands also require management to reduce avian disease. Avian botulism outbreaks have occurred at Aimakapā Pond, Hawai'i, as recently as 1996 and killed most Hawaiian Coots, some Black-necked Stilts, and many other waterbirds (Morin 1996).

Priorities

- Prevent the establishment of species or strains of mosquitoes adapted for high elevations (>1,500 m).
- Evaluate the effects of landscape-scale removal of feral pigs on mosquito populations and develop other methods for reducing mosquitoes.
- Remove breeding sites of mosquitoes on Midway Atoll to prevent avian pox outbreaks.
- Investigate immunogenetics and resistance to malaria of low-elevation bird populations and develop strategies for genetic management.
- Determine the possible synergistic relationship between nutrition and resistance to malaria and pox.
- Manage wetlands to prevent outbreaks of avian botulism.
- Determine the role of other infectious diseases in lowering the hatchability and survival of forest birds.

CONCLUSIONS

Large-scale habitat management is essential but not sufficient in itself to recover many endemic Hawaiian species. Preserving biodiversity over large areas is difficult, expensive, and often controversial where other human activities conflict. Strategies for avian conservation, therefore, must be effective, efficient, and justifiable to the public. Techniques for landscape-scale predator control are not yet available but are being developed. Ungulate control, on the other hand, is applicable over large areas and may reduce the incidence of avian disease vectors and reduce the spread of weeds. However, public attitudes towards killing vertebrate species, whether alien or not, often hamper control programs. Efforts to educate and counter negative perceptions must be launched on a broad scale. Alien weeds and invertebrates also negatively impact native ecosystems and are very difficult to control. More effective control efforts are needed and new invasive species must not become established.

Opportunities are limited for managing areas not already designated for conservation. Therefore, it is essential to manage areas adjacent to protected lands in partnership with other landowners, as seen in the 'Ōla'a-Kīlauea and East Maui Watershed partnerships.

Reintroduction, translocation, captive breeding, and other techniques are necessary tools for recovering and conserving uncommon species. There is now expertise, facilities, and stable funding to support such specialized management actions. However, at least 11 taxa on four islands are probably not recoverable because they are so rare. We regret the loss of these species but must act swiftly to combine habitat and species management approaches to save species for which there is more hope.

ACKNOWLEDGMENTS

We thank M. Scott, S. Conant, and L. Loope for reviewing earlier drafts and making helpful comments and suggestions. We salute the many dedicated biologists and conservationists, past and present, who have worked hard to preserve what remains of the extraordinary Hawaiian avifauna.

Studies in Avian Biology No. 22:377–383, 2001.

EVALUATING THE COST OF SAVING NATIVE HAWAIIAN BIRDS

WILLIAM W. M. STEINER

Abstract. Approximately $94 million has been spent on avian research and management in Hawai'i over the past decade. This figure represents a large investment in refuges and reserves as well as research across five state and federal agencies and The Nature Conservancy. This level of funding has made a substantial contribution to local economies, far outweighing even any contribution that local hunters make. Yet only one firm success story exists, the Nēnē (*Branta sandvicensis*), which has been brought back from the edge of extinction to more than 300 birds on two islands today. This paper examines the accomplishments gained by this level of funding, and the problems that still remain to be examined. Niche dimensions, territory sizes, impact of introduced birds, diet preferences, plant associations, invertebrate hosts, disease avoidance mechanisms, behavioral barriers all await study in rare species. Complex models of interaction must be built to better define the decline process. Avian genetics and the consequences of hybridization, important for future recovery efforts, are poorly studied and will likely become future focal points for research. It is recognized that a need exists to integrate future restoration efforts with tourism, the primary income generator for the Hawaiian Islands. One way to do this is through ecotourism and attraction of the birding community. Continued public support is necessary to maintain current and future funding levels or research and management of birds, and the need to develop outreach and education programs for the public is recognized as well. Hawai'i and the research community should seize the opportunity to integrate economic needs of the state and resource management needs that can then serve as a model for other states and countries.

Key Words: avian biology and research; economics; ecotourism; endangered species; Hawaiian Islands.

We are all familiar with the cost of saving endangered species. This cost is not strictly related to restoration. It includes, in any final analysis, costs of saving habitats, and conducting research into the biology, genetics, and other useful facts about the species of concern. Hawai'i, with its many endangered bird species, is a case in point. It turns out, as shown below, that currently about $9,451,664 is spent each year on providing, saving, and managing bird habitat. This includes research concerning all aspects of avian biology and ecology. But this figure may be important to providing other benefits as well, a fact which needs to be pointed out and discussed in open forum to identify and verify exactly what those benefits are. And it should not be overlooked that these species play important roles in the Hawaiian environment in terms of pollination, seed dispersal, and insect predation.

The rate of spending has not declined over the years; yet the Nēnē (*Branta sandvicensis*) program is the only telling success story concerning increase in a Hawaiian bird to date though not without its own setbacks and problems (Banko 1992, Black and Banko 1994, Black et al. 1997, Banko et al. *this volume*; see also Scott and Banko 2000). In fact, the increase of this species has not allowed its removal from the endangered species list, and is due as much to the length of the recovery program (40 years) as dollars spent. This belies the fact that investments in avian conservation often take long periods of time to yield returns since habitats often require considerable restoration (P. Banko, pers. comm.). Ban-

ko et al. (*this volume*) show that densities of many of the endangered species under study for the last half century have either remained steady or have declined. In a few cases, investigation of what was thought to be just a few remaining individuals of some rare species uncovered larger and/or additional populations than originally thought to exist (Scott et al. 1986), but this occurred only after intensive field studies. This type of success is due to improved field observation and technique and so it is not accurate to attribute these increases to restoration efforts. Finding additional individuals or populations of a species may serve to establish the extent of extant populations, population subdivision, and more accurate estimation of remaining numbers, thus allowing rank ordering of need for restoration under a regime of limited resource dollars.

In this paper I address the actual cost of research and management in Hawai'i over the past decade and raise two related questions: what have we accomplished with this expenditure? And where do we need to go from here? These questions are important if there is a need for directional change or a program refocus, or if particular points need to be reexamined. There may also be a need to determine if current funding allocations are adequate to get the job done.

The amount spent in Hawai'i with regard to saving the declining native avian resource can be broken into several categories. The first concerns what was spent directly on the resource for research and management, including studies of avian biology and conservation and purchase of lands for refuges and reserves. The second concerns what was spent that indirectly impacted birds and other related resource components. It includes, for example, dollars spent on avian disease characterization or for study of predator biology. A third category, that in which dollars spent on the avian resource indirectly benefited other endangered (e.g., plant) resources will not be considered here but is worthy of some future examination since it gives a measure of "fallout" effect from dollars spent to protect trust species in general. It is important to note that one very good reason an assessment is needed is to better focus limited restoration and recovery dollars on species that have a good chance of benefiting from the attention.

THE ACCUMULATED AND AVERAGE COSTS OF SAVING HAWAIIAN AVIFAUNA

For over a decade, the U.S. Department of Interior, the state of Hawai'i, and various other agencies have, sometimes under legislated mandate or under court order, invested considerable sums to save the endangered bird species of Hawai'i. A rough summation demonstrates this figure to lie somewhere around $37,765,530 for research and $56,751,110 for habitat acquisition and management over the past decade, totaling $94,516,640 (Table 1). These estimates are limited to the dollars spent during the past decade because this has been a critical period in determining the extent of the avian population decline in Hawai'i. Since 1994, this figure includes $5,804,000 of base funding which the Biological Resources Division of the U.S. Geological Survey (National Biological Service prior to 1996) has invested in understanding the biology and other factors influencing survival of Hawai'i's shrinking avian resource. The annual amount for the BRD figure previously would have been found in the U.S. Fish and Wildlife Service (USFWS) budget.

The figure of $94.5 million is astonishing. It has increased over the 1980s in part because of environmental action and lawsuits associated with the Endangered Species Act. These legal actions demonstrated that the Endangered Species Act would have to be taken seriously and put the onus on land management agencies to establish baseline data concerning avian species population densities. But a large portion of the increase is also due to USFWS land acquisition initiatives and increased funding for management costs associated with the Natural Area Reserve System and Natural Area Partnership funding by the state. The figure does not include some costs due to restoration efforts currently underway in Hawai'i and related to the Peregrine Fund's own effort to rear and release en-

TABLE 1. MINIMUM ESTIMATES OF AGENCY EXPENDITURES FOR AVIAN RESEARCH AND MANAGEMENT IN HAWAI'I, 1987–1997

Source	Estimated annual dollars	
	Research	Management
State of Hawai'i[a]	$ 764,560	$ 1,575,111
U.S. Fish and Wildlife Service[b]	$ 849,993	$ 500,000
U.S. National Park Service[c]	$ 12,000	$ 600,000
U.S. Geological Survey Biological Resources Division[d]	$ 1,451,000	-0-
U.S. Department of Defense (1996–1997 based on Palila)	$ 99,000	not known
The Nature Conservancy[e]	$ 600,000	$ 3,000,000
Average annual expenditure for avian research, 1987–1997	$ 3,776,553	$ 5,675,111
Total spent/year, last ten years	$ 9,451,664	

Note: This table does not include federally funded research to university scientists or visiting scientists whose work may comprise major sources of information prior to or during this period. In some cases figures may be only an approximation of annual expenditures.

[a] Information provided by Paul Conry, Hawaii Dept. of Land and Natural Resources. The estimate includes 50% of the cost of the Natural Areas Reserve program since the reserves provide habitat for endangered birds among other species. Section 6 dollars are included in the research component.

[b] Includes dollars spent on rearing facilities and management of refuges. Estimate for research is based on a seminar by Adam Asquith (USFWS) March 1996 and covers the period from 1992 to 1995. Based on contracts to the BRD-PIERC, this figure probably holds for post-1995 years as well. Management estimate includes dollars provided to The Peregrine Fund rate bird rearing facility by the USFWS for construction, rearing, and management.

[c] This estimate includes prorated dollars spent for rodent and special ecological area research through the NRPP program, and dollars spent for management of feral pigs, Nēnē, and Dark-rumped Petrel (*Pterodroma phaeopygia*). Information provided by Drs. Lloyd Loope and David Foote of BRD.

[d] Between 1991 and 1995, the U.S. Geological Survey Biological Resources Division did not exist and NBS was in formation. Spending on avian research during this period averaged $995,467 annually. This was 47.4% of the budget of the NBS center at its formation in October of 1994. By 1997 this had grown to 54.1% of the annual budget for the center and has been declining since.

[e] Estimates provided by Dan Orodenker and Alan Holt for The Nature Conservancy includes land acquisitions, which eventually formed the basis for many of the refuges that now exist in the Hawaiian Islands. The refuges harbor endemic avian species in protected habitats.

dangered birds, nor does it include the cost of Department of Defense efforts on military lands (this information was unavailable at the time of writing this paper; see Drigot *this volume* for an example of what is being done on military lands). Thus the estimate is likely low. The figure does, however, include efforts by the state of Hawai'i in the early 1990s to rear endangered species, such as the Hawaiian Crow, hereafter referred to as the 'Alalā (*Corvus hawaiiensis*), at the old rearing facility on Maui.

In a sense, the annual expenditure flowing into and/or within Hawai'i has become a force to be reckoned with at social, cultural, and economic levels, as well as biological. This expenditure is easily ten times the economic value, for example, of hunting in Hawai'i, assuming that about 900 hunters in the state spend an average of $1,000 each to exercise the privilege. The hunting expenditures are offset by earmarked dollars that come to Hawai'i via the Pittman-Robertson bill, which supports research and management of nongame species. Still, hunting expenditures are an important consideration because wild pigs, feral goats and cattle, mouflon sheep, and deer lie at the root of claims to any cultural right of hunting. All of these introduced mammals impact avian habitats and have contributed substantially to the observed and continuing decline in endemic avifauna as well as plants and invertebrates. It is a consideration that the average taxpayer should be seriously concerned with, for their dollars help finance the battle to save Hawai'i's birds.

ACCOMPLISHMENTS OF AVIAN RESEARCH AND MANAGEMENT IN HAWAI'I

Despite the understanding gained about endemic Hawaiian bird biology and establishing the beginnings of restoration for the Nēnē, it is difficult to assess how successfully research results have been applied to avian conservation in Hawai'i. In a sense, we are in the "investment phase" of conservation program building in Hawai'i (T. K. Pratt, pers. comm.), because many of the accomplishments deal with placing lands under protection; starting recovery projects for specific species of birds; and building and maintaining the infrastructure of captive propagation facilities, field stations, reserves, and refuges (including building of roads and fences). T. K. Pratt (pers. comm.) rightly points out that the present generation of conservation managers, workers, and scientists have inherited a very bad situation and has had to start from scratch to build conservation programs and do land acquisition and capital improvements. We need to invest in species and ecosystem management now or biological losses will be greater in the future. T. K. Pratt (pers. comm.) raises a very important question: is it realistic to expect turnaround in population trends in the short-term? And, if not, what time frame should we use? Expenditures must accompany whatever the length the time frame will be.

There is no question the past decade of research has dramatically increased our understanding of avian biology in Hawai'i, and that this increase of knowledge has been driven in part by the threat of losing so many endangered species. We now have better understanding of avian behavior, demography, and life cycles, and their population fluctuations, diet, and disease distribution and transmission; we have even begun research via observation into the effects of climate change on various bird species (Table 2). These important studies provide baseline information at a critical time.

But nonbird advantages have also accrued, giving a larger 'bang-for-the-buck" as it were. These accomplishments secured by funding avian research and management include:

- Established habitat protection for many listed species of plants.
- Established habitat protection and refuge for undescribed and unstudied arthropod species endemic to the Hawaiian Islands, including insects, snails, and "happy-face" spiders, many of which are dependent on endangered plants and so must in turn be endangered themselves.
- Saved the last remaining native rain forests on several islands from destruction and development.
- Created refuges for culturally important plants and animals for the remaining Polynesian society, thus ensuring continuation of cultural diversity.
- Contributed toward ecological and thus economic stability of the islands by saving the concept of "original paradise."
- Contributed toward saving coral reefs just offshore by stabilizing ecology on steep volcanic slopes such that erosion, as a marine polluting process, is reduced.
- Saved the original watersheds that provide abundant and wholesome water to the human populace of the islands by preventing increased run-off due to erosion.

For example, establishing bird habitats has also served to save or provide sanctuary for many of the endangered plant species and natural communities remaining in Hawai'i, in addition to an unknown number of rare arthropods, some of which may be crucial to avian diets. Refuges and reserves have saved some of the last pristine native semitropical rain forest left in Hawai'i from development. It is probably impossible to tease apart those funds which have actually served to stop bird declines from those which have effectively prevented decline of remaining

TABLE 2. SPECIFIC ACCOMPLISHMENTS RELATED TO AVIAN RESEARCH IN HAWAI'I

Accomplishment	Author(s)
Summarized the known biology, habitat associations, density, and distribution of endemic surviving bird species	Scott et al. 1986, Conant et al. 1998
Determined sex and age in native Hawaiian birds	Fancy et al. 1993a, 1994; Jeffrey et al. 1993; Pratt et al. 1994
Determined nesting behavior and reproductive biology in several native birds	Banko and Williams 1993, Fleischer et al. 1994; Ralph and Fancy 1994a,b,c; Kepler et al. 1996
Determined insectivorous behavior of forest birds on alien plants versus native plants	Waring et al. 1993
Demonstrated demography, change over time, movement, diet, life history, survival, and recognition of specific Hawaiian birds	Engilis and Pratt 1993; Fancy et al. 1993a,b; Ralph and Fancy 1994a,b,c; Snetsinger et al. 1994, Lindsey et al. 1995a, Ralph and Fancy 1995, Engilis et al. 1996, Jacobi et al. 1996, Ralph and Fancy 1996, Fancy et al. 1997
Led to understanding pathogenecity and avian disease and distribution in Hawai'i	Atkinson et al. 1993a,b; Atkinson et al. 1995, Herrmann and Snetsinger 1997
Proved that introduced mammals were predators of native birds	Snetsinger et al. 1994
Demonstrated a link between climate changes and native forest bird population change	Lindsey et al. 1997
Demonstrated the potential for translocation of existing bird populations to serve as a conservation tool to build population density and replenish a native species in the archipelago	Fancy et al. 1997

biological ecosystems and communities. And most crucial, and completely unstudied, is the value this may have for developing and promoting ecotourism, currently considered an economically important income "wave of the future" in Hawai'i.

Technical contributions also exist. A very useful statistical procedure, analyzing bird densities from variable circular-plot counts (Reynolds et al. 1980, Fancy 1997), has proven valuable for inventorying and monitoring island bird species. Hughes' celluloid leg bands in various color combinations have been used to identify individual birds carrying them. However, Lindsey et al. (1995b) found that under Hawaiian conditions the bands may undergo color changes, rendering them questionable for long-term use in the field. Additionally, taking blood samples from small birds is always difficult, so finding that Hawaiian honeycreepers were not affected by blood sampling was encouraging (Pratt et al. 1994).

Clearly, there are gaps in our knowledge of Hawaiian birds and how to conserve them. There is a need to develop genetic profiles *before* a species' decline becomes threatening, yet there is still no comprehensive gene data bank for native Hawaiian birds. Genetic profiling might prove extremely valuable as Hawaiian avian research moves into a restoration phase. Information on the nature of genetic differences between apparently the same species or even subspecies across islands would be useful in assessing probability for bird survival and determining management approaches. An example can be found in 'Elepaio (*Chasiempis sandwichensis*), which is now being considered for listing by the USFWS because of its declining status on O'ahu. Subpopulations of this species exist on Hawai'i and might serve as transplant donor populations if no reproductive barriers exist. The importance of this can be seen in two recent studies. Although Franklin and Frankham (1998) maintain that an effective population size of 500 to 1,000 individuals is enough to maintain genetic variation for evolutionary change under mutation and random genetic drift load, Lynch and Lande (1998) question this figure, saying that it should be revised upward by at least five-fold because selection plays a defining role in quantity and quality of genetic variation. At the very least, the 'Elepaio subpopulations could act to increase genetic variance via hybridization when and if the two populations are brought together. Knowledge about what portion of genetic variation is lost during a population decline could give clues to a species ability to adapt to new conditions. As we gain understanding of gene structure and function, this knowledge could also provide insight as to why declines are occurring.

There also appears to be no information on compatibility of crosses (hybridization) of subspecies from different islands. This information would prove valuable if decline of a species on one island forces drastic measures to be taken which demand forsaking genetic purity of the subspecies. Unanswered questions here concern survival of hybrids, fertility, genetic compatibility, disruption of behavior, etc., all of which can effect any transition period before a new species stability is reached. If success does result (e.g., an endangered subspecies is successfully propagated as a hybrid to save some portion of its gene pool), information on how the hybrid fits into the old ecosystem and survives threats posed by that ecosystem, especially the threats that led to the decline of the original subspecies, is desirable. This type of research might teach us new ways of looking at the interaction of a species with its environment. Needless to say, any approach using hybridization to save a portion of a gene pool must be carefully weighed against other approaches, such as whether to concentrate limited human and cash resources on saving ecosystems or saving avian species that have not yet reached some critical stage of decline.

Even more critical work is necessary to better understand the interactions of each of Hawai'i's avian species with macro and micro components of its ecosystem. Niche dimensions, territory sizes, impact of introduced birds, diet preferences, plant associations, invertebrate hosts, disease avoidance mechanisms, and behavioral barriers all await study in rare species. Complex models of interaction must be built to better define the decline process. We have learned a lot in the past decade, but we still do not know enough.

WHAT DOES THE FUTURE HOLD?

The meeting and research results summarized in this volume led to a roundtable discussion and a list of the following action items:

WHAT CAN WE DO TO STOP NATIVE BIRD DECLINES?

Funding

1. The percentage of the total budget devoted to conservation by the state of Hawai'i, about 1%, is inadequate; work to get the state to commit more funding and encourage the state to put more funding into supporting the Department of Forestry and Wildlife and hiring more biologists for management of its lands.
2. Coordinate efforts between federal agencies so that joint funding initiatives can be developed for congressional action taking advantage of the great rate of loss and listing of endangered and threatened species in Hawai'i.

Education

3. Encourage agencies to develop and conduct outreach and public education programs.

Children 9 to 14 years of age should be targeted in education programs. Outreach efforts need to reach into schools on a regular basis (don't wait for the invitation).
4. In support of outreach, encourage USFWS to reprioritize their funding programs to place education programs near the top.
5. Make an attempt (by survey?) to find out what is relevant to the public and encourage education programs that address this relevancy and use this as a wedge to make the public more environmentally aware. In this regard, develop programs that take advantage of modern marketing techniques to create the *need* for the public to know.
6. Get on a first-name basis with as many news reporters and writers as possible, and actively promote newsworthy projects and problems.
7. Work toward establishing some Hawaiian "flagship" successes in species recovery, habitat recovery, etc., to create a "positive" mood in the public and a "can do" attitude in the research and management agencies.
8. Accept the mixed (alien and native) biology we are stuck with and use established alien species to educate the public while working to conserve the natives that remain.

Ecotourism

9. Encourage the city, country, and state governments to support, expand, and promote Hawaiian zoos, aviaries, botanical gardens, and aquariums that feature Hawaiian organisms and tell their stories to the tourist trade.
10. Promote ecotourism that is nonharmful to the sensitive Hawaiian environment; to this end, encourage the state of Hawai'i to build roads, trails, boardwalks, etc., that can bring tour groups in more immediate touch with natural Hawai'i and its biota.
11. Encourage development of adequate marketing programs in ecotourism.
12. Encourage the cities and counties to include information brochures on endangered species at tourist information kiosks.
13. Work to include the Secretariat of Conservation as a member of the Hawaii Visitors Bureau.

HOW CAN WE BRIDGE THE GAP BETWEEN RESEARCHERS AND MANAGEMENT?

14. Work to coordinate research and management strategies better.
15. Examine the way we develop strategies to address conservation problems.
16. Publish research reports and technical reports in a more timely manner to make them available to the management agencies.

WHAT BENEFITS HAVE ACCRUED TO HAWAIIAN CONSERVATION EFFORTS BEYOND THOSE WHICH HAVE BEEN SPENT STUDYING AND MANAGING ENDANGERED BIRD SPECIES?

17. Conduct monitoring surveys to determine how endangered plant species are doing in critical bird habitat. Do the same for endangered invertebrates.
18. Link findings from the above surveys to outreach programs targeting groups in Native Hawaiian cultural programs (such as kumu hulu halaus who use native plants in their ceremonies) in order to demonstrate relevance of biodiversity and broader impact of specific management and research programs for cultural needs and practices.
19. Determine contribution at the landscape level to ecosystem sustainability.
20. Determine contribution to decision support systems to support management functions.

To some extent, the action items are responses to embedded questions, which remain unanswered today and require serious efforts to resolve in the future. For example, action item 1 under funding addresses the implicit question "is support of avian conservation adequate by the state of Hawai'i?" Discussion at the meeting implied that support is not adequate. Action items related to what can we do to stop native bird declines are most telling in terms of what we have not done or have not done well. Here, effort must be expanded in the areas of funding, education, and ecotourism. The state of Hawai'i has spent some $23,396,715 in the past decade, mostly on providing management of reserves for saving critical bird habitat. Yet the figure for state-sponsored research is declining; it is thought to represent less than ½ of one percent of the total state budget in the current (1998) economy. Part of this decline is due to a lack of understanding and appreciation of the problem by the public and state legislatures. Part of it is due to harsh economic times; tourism is the state's main income generator and declines in the Far East economy and the Japanese tourist base in 1998 has resulted in hotel occupancy rates that have fallen 15% or more in recent months.

For management purposes, funding is needed to control predators; prevent fires, especially in El Niño years; and provide protection from ungulates and introduced and feral grazing animals. Federal management funds for which the state could compete if it had matching dollars go begging or go elsewhere. Although the state has recently provided funding to hire more law enforcement officers for management and oversight of marine fisheries resources, similar efforts are needed to protect natural ecosystems and endangered terrestrial species. Instead, the Hawaii Department of Land and Natural Resources has undergone budget cuts. These cuts come at a critical time for mounting unified efforts to understand and halt avian declines.

There is a great need to educate the public about Hawai'i's conservation problems. Excellent programs now exist in some of the elementary schools in the state. These programs should be identified, singled out for reward, and used as examples for other schools. Although education starts with the children, it should not end there because it will take the children at least a decade to reach voting age, when they make a difference by going to the polls. The remaining Hawaiian avifauna might very well go extinct in the waiting period. For this reason, effective adult education programs, perhaps led by state community colleges, and enhancement of existing conservation biology programs in local universities should be considered. An example is seen in *Miconia calvescens,* a highly competitive, invasive, South American plant (with the ability to replace native rain forest) that occurs on Maui. An education program on this island has mobilized the public to help eradicate the plant. The success of this program demonstrates how effective public education can be.

Much could be gained by recognizing and establishing the economic value of having rare bird species within relatively easy accessibility. This is an economic component that resource managers are either unaware of or have no way to assess. More than $50 million dollars was poured into promoting tourism in the state of Hawai'i in 1998. Little, if any, was used to promote the beautiful avifauna, although some was used to promote whale-watching. The Maui "Whalefest" is an example. Held in March, this event not only promotes whale-watching to tourists, but sponsors the "Lahaina Whalefest Essay" competition in which local high school students win opportunities to attend advanced courses on whales at Costeau Catalina Island Camp in California. Where the humpbacked whale (*Megaptera novaeangliae*) is making a comeback, the endemic avifauna is not with the exception of the Nēnē. Yet the Nēnē can be most easily seen, even occurring on golf courses in the state! Reports suggesting that birders and their organizations contribute hundreds of millions of dollars to local community economies with their birding visits need to be brought to the attention of local resource managers, tourism boards, and the Hawai'i Visitors Bureau. Figures published by the USFWS and others suggest that over $29.2 billion was spent as an industry output for watching wildlife in 1996, and the ripple effect in America was over $85 billion. Already individual bird-watching guides take small parties into the mountains to see Hawai'i's rare avifauna and the state's Na Ala Hele Trail and Access program is planning on opening nearly 40 trails on four islands to limited commercial hiking tours. The Hawai'i Ecotourism Association is preparing a manual for use by ecotour hikers. The McCandless Ranch on the island of Hawai'i offers tours to see the rare 'Alalā and other native plants and birds, such as the Hawaiian 'Io (*Buteo solitarius*), the endemic subspecies of the Short-eared Owl (*Asio flammeus sandwichensis*), the 'I'iwi (*Vestiaria Coccinea*) and 'Elepaio. Studies need to be done to determine just how many tourists take time to bird in Hawai'i. Integration of economic need with the natural resource need could prove highly successful.

Effective management is not purely a textbook enterprise; it relies on and must integrate good science and the research that derives from it. Studies are needed on the population biology of alien birds and how they affect competition for food and nest sites, as well as disease transmission. We do not know if we need to control alien birds or not, yet these may have as large an impact as predatory rats, feral cats, and mongoose. If alien bird species undergo declines in frequency, it may be that these can serve as a harbinger of problems to come for native birds. Habitat protection on a larger geographical scale, assessment of current management practices, and population ecology of low-elevation populations deserve research attention.

The considerations mentioned herein suggest that an annual average research expenditure of $3.7–$3.8 million (Table 1) should continue if not increase. Given the educational component mentioned above, this figure needs to be expanded so that the role and nature of the educational component can be developed as well as studied. Unlike nongovernmental organizations like The Nature Conservancy, design of federal and state conservation programs, after recognizing an existing or potential problem, has rarely taken into consideration the need for public education. Yet the success of such programs are inherently related to the willingness of the public to support them and pay for them. P. Banko (pers. comm.) has pointed out that "... the amount spent ... might seem astonishingly high ... until the costs of other activities undertaken by society are considered. For example, $50 million was spent in one year to promote tourism in Hawai'i ..." This provides a benchmark against which to compare amounts spent on research and education.

I suggested that given the need for avian restoration and the need for research, Hawai'i, with its defined island boundaries, high number of endemic endangered bird species that occur across a wide variety of ecosystems and habitats, and upscale tourist industry, presents a unique opportunity to build an integrated model of conservation and economics. Without such a model, the current expenditures on research may eventually become as extinct as the birds they are intended to save, as the public fails to grasp the moral, ethical, and economic importance of why their dollars need to be spent on understanding avian biology and on restoration of native birds.

ACKNOWLEDGMENTS

I thank my colleagues in the Department of Land and Natural Resources, the U.S. Fish and Wildlife Service, the National Park Service, and The Nature Conservancy who helped me to compile the dollar figures in Table 1. J. M. Scott deserves a big mahalo for being understanding while I struggled to gather the information and write this paper around rigorous demands on my time, and for his encouragement to even make the attempt. This paper grew out of a discussion with Mike Scott about just what had been accomplished over the years. S. Conant, P. C. Banko, and T. K. Pratt provided insightful comment. However, all interpretations made in this paper are my own and I take full responsibility for them. This paper is not meant as an endorsement of any private or public technologies, comments, or concerns by the Biological Resources Division of the U.S. Geological Survey.

LITERATURE CITED

ABPLANALP, H., K. SATO, D. NAPOLITANO, AND J. REID. 1992. Reproductive performance of inbred congenic leghorns carrying different haplotypes for the major histocompatibility complex. Poultry Science 71:9–17.

ADASKAVEG, J. E., AND J. M. OGAWA. 1990. Wood decay pathology of fruit and nut trees in California. Plant Disease 74:341–352.

ADLER, G. H. 1992. Endemism in birds of tropical Pacific islands. Evolutionary Ecology 6:296–306.

ADVISORY COUNCIL ON HISTORIC PRESERVATION. 1994. Defense department compliance with the national historic preservation act. Prepared by Advisory Council on Historic Preservation, Washington, D.C.

AINLEY, D. G., AND R. J. BOEKELHEIDE (EDITORS). 1990. Seabirds of the Farallon Islands: ecology, structure and dynamics of an upwelling system community. Stanford University Press, Palo Alto, CA.

AINLEY, D. G., AND D. P. DEMASTER. 1980. Survival and mortality in a population of Adélie Penguins. Ecology 61:522–530.

AINLEY, D. G., R. PODOLSKY, L. DEFOREST, AND G. SPENCER. 1997a. New insights into the status of the Hawaiian Petrel on Kauai. Colonial Waterbirds 20:20–34.

AINLEY, D. G., R. PODOLSKY, L. DEFOREST, G. SPENCER, AND N. NUR. 1995. The ecology of Newell's Shearwater and Dark-rumped Petrel on Kauai, Hawaii. Tech. Rep. 3521–02 (EPRI TR-105847-V2), Kauai endangered seabird study. Vol. 2. Electric Power Research Institute, Palo Alto, CA.

AINLEY, D. G., C. A. RIBIC, AND R. C. WOOD. 1990. A demographic study of the South Polar Skua *Catharacta maccormicki* at Cape Crozier. Journal of Animal Ecology 59:1–20.

AINLEY, D. G., T. C. TELFER, AND M. H. REYNOLDS. 1997b. Townsend's and Newell's Shearwater (*Puffinus auricularis*). *In* A. Poole and F. Gill (editors). The Birds of North America, No. 297. The Academy of Natural Sciences, Philadelphia, PA, and American Ornithologists' Union, Washington, D.C.

AKEY, B. L., J. K. NAYAR, AND D. J. FORRESTER. 1981. Avian pox in Florida wild turkeys: *Culex nigripalpus* and *Wyeomyia vanduzeei* as experimental vectors. Journal of Wildlife Diseases 17:597–599.

ALI, S., AND L. FUTEHALLY. 1970. Common Indian birds. International Publication Service, Calcutta, India.

ALICATA, J. E. 1947. Parasites and parasitic diseases of domestic animals in the Hawaiian Islands. Pacific Science 1:69–84.

ALITALO, K., J. M. BISHOP, D. H. SMITH, E. Y. CHEN, W. W. COLBY, AND A. D. LEVINSON. 1983. Nucleotide sequence of the v-*myc* oncogene of avian retrovirus MC29. Proceedings of National Academy of Sciences (USA) 80:100–104.

ALLANDER, K., AND G. F. BENNETT. 1995. Retardation of breeding onset in Great Tits (*Parus major*) by blood parasites. Functional Ecology 9:677–682.

ALLEN, J. 1997. Pre-contact landscape transformation and cultural change in windward O'ahu. Pp. 230–247 *in* P. V. Kirch and T. L. Hunt (editors). Historical Ecology in the Pacific islands. Yale University Press, New Haven, CT.

ALLEN, J. A. 1998. Mangroves as alien species: the case of Hawaii. Global Ecology and Biogeography Letters 7:61–71.

ALLISON, A. 1996. Zoogeography of amphibians and reptiles of New Guinea and the Pacific region. Pp. 407–436 *in* A. Keast and S. E. Miller (editors). The origin and evolution of Pacific island biotas, New Guinea to Eastern Polynesia: patterns and processes. SPB Academic Publications, Amsterdam, the Netherlands.

AMADON, D. 1950. The Hawaiian honeycreepers (Aves, Drepaniidae). Bulletin of the American Museum of Natural History 95:151–262.

AMADON, D. 1964. The evolution of low reproductive rates in birds. Evolution 18:105–110.

AMADON, D. 1986. The Hawaiian honeycreepers revisted. 'Elepaio 46:83–84.

AMADON, D., AND L. L. SHORT. 1976. Treatment of subspecies approaching species status. Systematic Zoology 25:161–167.

AMARASEKARE, P. 1993. Potential impact of mammalian nest predators on endemic forest birds of western Mauna Kea, Hawaii. Conservation Biology 7:316–324.

AMARASEKARE, P. 1994. Ecology of introduced small mammals on western Mauna Kea, Hawaii. Journal of Mammalogy 75:24–38.

AMERICAN ORNITHOLOGISTS' UNION. 1983. Check-list of North American birds. 6th edition. Allen Press, Lawrence, KS.

AMERICAN ORNITHOLOGISTS' UNION. 1985. Thirty-fifth supplement to the American Ornithologists' Union check-list of North American birds. Auk 102:680–686.

AMERICAN ORNITHOLOGISTS' UNION. 1991. Thirty-eighth supplement to the American Ornithologists' Union check-list of North American birds. Auk 108:750–754.

AMERICAN ORNITHOLOGISTS' UNION. 1993. Thirty-ninth supplement to the American Ornithologists' Union check-list of North American birds. Auk 110:675–682.

AMERICAN ORNITHOLOGISTS' UNION. 1995. Fortieth supplement to the American Ornithologists' Union check-list of North American birds. Auk 112:819–830.

AMERICAN ORNITHOLOGISTS' UNION. 1997. Forty-first supplement to the American Ornithologists' Union check-list of North American birds. Auk 114:542–552.

AMERICAN ORNITHOLOGISTS' UNION. 1998. Checklist of North American Birds. 7th edition. American Ornithologists' Union, Washington, D.C.

AMERICAN ORNITHOLOGISTS' UNION. 2000. Forty-second supplement to the American Ornithologists' Union check-list of North American birds. Auk 117:847–858.

AMERSON, A. B. 1969. Ornithology of the Marshall and Gilbert Islands. Atoll Research Bulletin 127:1–348.

AMERSON, A. B., JR. 1971. The natural history of French frigate shoals, Northwestern Hawaiian Islands. Atoll Research Bulletin No. 150.

AMERSON, A. B., JR., R. B. CLAPP, AND W. O. WIRTZ,

II. 1974. The natural history of Pearl and Hermes Reef, Northwestern Hawaiian Islands. Atoll Research Bulletin No. 174.

ANDERS, A. D., D. C. DEARBORN, J. FAABORG, AND F. R. THOMPSON, III. 1997. Juvenile survival in a population of neotropical migrant birds. Conservation Biology 11:698–707.

ANDERSON, A. 1984. The extinction of moa in southern New Zealand. Pp. 728–740 in P. S. Martin and R. G. Klein (editors). Quaternary extinctions: a prehistoric revolution. University of Arizona Press, Tucson, AZ.

ANDERSON, A. J. 1989. Prodigious birds Moas and Moa hunting in prehistoric New Zealand. Cambridge University Press, Cambridge, MA.

ANDERSON, M. G., J. M. RHYMER, AND F. C. ROHWER. 1992. Philopatry, dispersal, and the genetic structure of waterfowl populations. Pp. 365–395 in B. D. J. Batt, A. D. Afton, M. G. Anderson, C. D. Ankney, D. H. Johnson, J. A. Kadlec, and G. L. Krapu (editors). Ecology and management of breeding waterfowl. University of Minnesota Press, Minneapolis, MN.

ANDERSON, R.M. 1979. Parasite pathogenicity and the depression of host population equilibria. Nature 279: 150–152.

ANDERSON, R. M., AND R. M. MAY. 1978. Regulation and stability of host-parasite population interactions: I. regulatory processes. Journal of Animal Ecology 47:219–247.

ANDERSON, R. M., AND R. M. MAY. 1982. Coevolution of hosts and parasites. Parasitology 85:411–426.

ANDERSON, S. J., AND C. P. STONE. 1993. Snaring to control feral pigs Sus scrofa in a remote Hawaiian rain forest. Biological Conservation 63:195–201.

ANDERSON, S. J., AND C. P. STONE. 1994. Indexing sizes of feral pig populations in a variety of Hawaiian natural areas. Transactions of the Western Section of the Wildlife Society 30:26–39.

ANDERSON, W. B., AND G. A. POLIS. 1998. Marine subsidies of island communities in the Gulf of California: evidence from stable carbon and nitrogen isotopes. Oikos 81:75–80.

ANDERSON, W. B., AND G. A. POLIS. 1999. Nutrient fluxes from water to land: seabirds affect plant nutrient status on Gulf of California islands. Oecologia 118:324–332.

ANDREWARTHA, H. G., AND L. C. BIRCH. 1954. The distribution and abundance of animals. University of Chicago Press, Chicago, IL.

APPS, P. J. 1986. Home ranges of feral cats on Dassen Island. Journal of Mammology 67:199–200.

ARBOGAST, B. S., AND J. B. SLOWINSKI. 1998. Pleistocene speciation and the mitochondrial DNA clock. Science 282:1955a.

ARMSTRONG, R. W. (EDITOR). 1983. Atlas of Hawaii. 2nd edition. University of Hawaii Press, Honolulu, HI.

ARNAUD, P. 1956. The heleid genus Culicoides in Japan, Korea and Ryukyu Islands (Insecta: Diptera). Microentomology 21:84–207.

ATHENS, J. S. 1997. Hawaiian native lowland vegetation in prehistory. Pp. 248–270 in P. V. Kirch and T. L. Hunt (editors). Historical ecology in the Pacific Islands. Yale University Press, New Haven, CT.

ATKINSON, C. T., R. J. DUSEK, AND W. M. IKO. 1993a. Avian malaria fatal to juvenile I'iwi. Hawaii's Forests and Wildlife 8:1, 11.

ATKINSON, C. T., R. J. DUSEK, AND W. M. IKO. 1993b. Epidemic pox and malaria in native forest birds. Hawaii's Forests and Wildlife 8:10.

ATKINSON, C. T., R. J. DUSEK, AND J. K. LEASE. 2001. Serological responses and immunity to superinfection with avian malaria in experimentally-infected Hawaiian Amakihi. Journal of Wildlife Diseases 37: 20–27.

ATKINSON, C. T., R. J. DUSEK, K. L. WOODS, AND W. M. IKO. 2000. Pathogenicity of avian malaria in experimentally-infected Hawaii Amakihi. Journal of Wildlife Diseases 36:197–204.

ATKINSON, C. T., W. HANSER, J. PRICE, L. SILEO, D. LAPOINTE, M. L. GOFF, C. LOCHER, AND L. TAM. 1993c. Role of disease in limiting the distribution and abundance of Hawaiian forest birds. Annual Report, work unit 932.11, period 24 April 1992–1 June 1993. Hawaii Volcanoes Field Station, National Wildlife Health Research Center, HI.

ATKINSON, C. T., K. L. WOODS, R. J. DUSEK, L. S. SILEO, and W. M. IKO. 1995. Wildlife disease and conservation in Hawaii: pathogenicity of avian malaria (Plasmodium relictum) in experimentally infected Iiwi (Vestiaria coccinea). Parasitology 111: S59-S69.

ATKINSON, I. A. E. 1977. A reassessment of factors, particularly Rattus rattus L., that influenced the decline of endemic forest birds in the Hawaiian Islands. Pacific Science 31:109–133.

ATKINSON, I. A. E. 1985. The spread of commensal species of Rattus to oceanic islands and their effects on island avifaunas. Pp. 35–81 in P. J. Moors (editor). Conservation of island birds. International Council for Bird Preservation Technical Publication No. 3. Cambridge, UK.

ATKINSON, I. A. E. 1989. Introduced animals and extinctions. Pp. 54–75 in D. Western and M. C. Pearl (editors). Conservation for the twenty-first century. Oxford University Press, New York, NY.

ATKINSON, I. A. E., AND B. D. BELL. 1973. Offshore and outlying islands. Pages 372–392 in G. B. Williams (editor). The Natural History of New Zealand. A. H. and A. W. Reed, Wellington, New Zealand.

ATWOOD, J. L., AND C. T. COLLINS. 1997. The Island Scrub-Jay: origins, behavior, and ecology. Birding 29:476–485.

AUSTIN, G. T., AND R. E. RICKLEFS. 1977. Growth and development of the Rufous-winged Sparrow (Aimophila carpalis). Condor 79:37–50.

AUSTIN, J. E., AND M. R. MILLER. 1995. Northern Pintail (Anas acuta). In A. Poole and F. Gill (editors). The Birds of North America, No. 163. The Academy of Natural Sciences, Philadelphia, PA, and American Ornithologists' Union, Washington, D.C.

AVERY, R. A. 1966. Helminth parasites of wildfowl from Slimbridge Gloucestershire. I. Parasites of captive Anatidae. Journal of Helminthology 40:269–280.

AVISE, J. C. 1994. Molecular markers, natural history and evolution. Chapman and Hall, New York, NY.

AVISE, J. C., C. D. ANKNEY, AND W. S. NELSON. 1990. Mitochondrial gene trees and the evolutionary relationship of Mallard and Black Ducks. Evolution 44: 1109–1119.

AVISE, J. C., AND C. F. AQUADRO. 1982. A comparative summary of genetic distances in the vertebrates: patterns and correlations. Pp. 151–185 in M. K. Hecht, B. Wallace, and G. T. Prance (editors). Evolutionary biology. Vol. 15. Plenum Press, New York, NY.

AVISE, J. C., AND J. L. HAMRICK. 1996. Conservation genetics: case histories from nature. Chapman and Hall, New York, NY.

BACON, L. D., AND R. L. WHITTER. 1980. B2 determines resistance of Marek's disease tumor in contrast to B5 in F5 chickens. Federation Proceedings 39:938.

BAILEY, A. M. 1956. Birds of Midway and Laysan islands. Denver Museum Pictorial No. 12. Denver, CO.

BAILEY, E. P., AND G. W. KAISER. 1993. Impacts of introduced predators on nesting seabirds in the northeast Pacific. Pp. 218–226 in K. Vermeer, K. T. Briggs, K. H. Morgan, and D. Siegel-Causey (editors). The status, ecology, and conservation of marine birds of the North Pacific. Canadian Wildlife Service, Ottawa, Ontario.

BAKER, H., AND P. E. BAKER. 2000a. Maui 'Alauahio (Paroreomyza montana). In A. Poole and F. Gill (editors). The Birds of North America, No. 504. The Academy of Natural Sciences, Philadelphia, PA, and American Ornithologists' Union, Washington, D.C.

BAKER, H. G., AND I. BAKER. 1973. Amino-acids in nectar and their evolutionary significance. Nature 241:543–545.

BAKER, H. G., AND I. BAKER. 1975. Studies of nectar constitution and plant-pollinator coevolution. Pp. 100–140 in L. E. Gilbert and P. H. Raven (editors). Coevolution in animals and plants. University of Texas Press, Austin, TX.

BAKER, J. K., AND C. A. RUSSELL. 1979. Mongoose predation on a nesting Nēnē. 'Elepaio 40:51–52.

BAKER, P. E. 1998. A description of the first live Poouli captured. Wilson Bulletin 110:307–310.

BAKER, P. E., AND H. BAKER. 1996. Nene report: egg and gosling mortality in Haleakala National Park, 1994–1995. Final report submitted to Hawaii Department of Land and Natural Resources, Division of Forestry and Wildlife, Honolulu, HI.

BAKER, P. E., AND H. BAKER. 2000b. Kākāwahie (Paroreomyza flammea) and O'ahu 'Alauahio (Paroreomyza maculata). In A. Poole and F. Gill (editors). The Birds of North America, No. 503. The Academy of Natural Sciences, Philadelphia, PA, and American Ornithologists' Union, Washington, D.C.

BAKER, R. H. 1946. Some effects of the war on the wildlife of Micronesia. Transactions of the North American Wildlife Conference 11:205–213.

BAKER, R. H. 1951. The avifauna of Micronesia, its origin, evolution, and distribution. University of Kansas Publications of the Museum of Natural History 3:1–359.

BAKER, R. H. 1953. Divisional discussion on problems of bird migration in the Pacific. Pp 383–387 in Proceedings of the Seventh Pacific Science Congress. Vol. 4. Whitcomb and Tombs, Auckland, New Zealand.

BALDWIN, P. H. 1945. The Hawaiian Goose, its distribution and reduction in numbers. Condor 47:27–37.

BALDWIN, P. H. 1947a. Foods of the Hawaiian Goose. Condor 49:108–120.

BALDWIN, P. H. 1947b. The life history of the Laysan Rail. Condor 49:14–21.

BALDWIN, P. H. 1953. Annual cycle, environment and evolution in the Hawaiian honeycreepers (Aves: Drepaniidae). University of California Publications in Zoology 52:285–398.

BALDWIN, P. H. 1969a. The Hawaiian Hawk from 1938 to 1949. Elepaio 29:95–98.

BALDWIN, P. H. 1969b. The 'Alalā (Corvus tropicus) of western Hawaii Island. Elepaio 30:41–45.

BALDWIN, P. H., AND G. O. FAGERLUND. 1943. The effect of cattle grazing on koa reproduction in Hawaii National Park. Ecology 24:118–122.

BALDWIN, P. H., C. W. SCHWARTZ, AND E. R. SCHWARTZ. 1952. Life history and economic status of the mongoose in Hawaii. Journal of Mammalogy 33:335–356.

BALOUET, J. C., AND S. L. OLSON. 1987. A new extinct species of giant pigeon (Columbidae: Ducula) from archeological deposits on Wallis (Uvea) Island, South Pacific. Proceedings of the Biological Societies of Washington 100:769–775.

BANKO, P. C. 1982. Productivity of wild and captive Nene populations. Pp. 12–32 in Proceedings of the Fourth Hawaii Volcanoes National Park National Science Conference. Cooperative National Park Studies Unit, University of Hawaii, Honolulu, HI.

BANKO, P. C. 1992. Constraints on productivity of wild Nene or Hawaiian Geese Branta sandvicensis. Wildfowl 43:99–106.

BANKO, P. C., J. M. BLACK, AND W. E. BANKO. 1999. Hawaiian Goose (Nene) (Branta sandvicensis). In A. Poole and F. Gill (editors). The Birds of North America, No. 434. The Academy of Natural Sciences, Philadelpia, PA, and American Ornithologists' Union, Washington, D.C.

BANKO, P. C., S. C. HESS, L. JOHNSON, AND S. J. DOUGILL. 1998. Palila population estimate for 1997. 'Elepaio 58:11,14–15.

BANKO, P. C., AND J. WILLIAMS. 1993. Eggs, nests, and nesting behavior of Akiapolaau (Drepanidinae). Wilson Bulletin 105:427–435.

BANKO, W. E. 1968. Rediscovery of Maui Nukupuu, Hemignathus lucidus affinis, and sighting of Maui Parrotbill, Pseudonestor xanthophrys, Kipahulu Valley, Maui, Hawaii. Condor 70:265–266.

BANKO, W. E. 1979. History of endemic Hawaiian birds specimens in museum collections. Avian History Report 2. Cooperative National Park Resources Studies Unit, University of Hawaii, Honolulu, HI.

BANKO, W. E. 1980a. History of endemic Hawaiian birds. Part 1. Population histories—species accounts, forest birds: Hawaiian Raven/Crow. Avian history report 6B. Cooperative National Park Resources Studies Unit, University of Hawaii, Honolulu, HI.

BANKO, W. E. 1980b. History of endemic Hawaiian birds. Part 1. Population histories—species accounts, forest birds: Hawaiian thrushes. Avian History Report 6C–6D. Cooperative National Park Resources Studies Unit, University of Hawaii, Honolulu, HI.

BANKO, W. E. 1980c. History of endemic Hawaiian

birds. CPSU/UH Avian History Report 026/10. Co-operative National Park Resources Studies Unit, University of Hawaii at Manoa, Honolulu, HI.

BANKO, W. E. 1980d. History of endemic Hawaiian birds. Part I. Population histories—species accounts, sea birds: Hawaiian Dark-rumped Petral (Uau). Avian History Report 5B. Cooperative National Park Resources Studies Unit, University of Hawaii at Manoa, Honolulu, HI.

BANKO, W. E. 1981a. History of endemic Hawaiian birds. Part 1. Population histories—species accounts, forest birds: 'Elepaio, Oo, Kioea. Avian History Report 7A–7B. Cooperative National Park Resources Studies Unit, University of Hawaii, Honolulu, HI.

BANKO, W. E. 1981b. History of endemic Hawaiian birds. Part 1. Population histories—species accounts, forest birds: *Vestiaria coccinea, Drepanis funerea, Drepanis pacifica.* Avian History Report 11A–11B. Cooperative National Park Resources Studies Unit, University of Hawaii, Honolulu, HI.

BANKO, W. E. 1984a. History of endemic Hawaiian birds. Part 1. Population histories—species accounts, forest birds: Amakihi, Creeper, Akepa, and Poo-uli. Avian History Report 8A–8C. Cooperative National Park Resources Studies Unit, University of Hawaii, Honolulu, HI.

BANKO, W. E. 1984b. History of endemic Hawaiian birds. Part 1. Population histories—species accounts, forest birds: Akialoa, Nukupuu, and Akiapolaau. Avian History Report 9. Cooperative National Park Resources Studies Unit, University of Hawaii, Honolulu, HI.

BANKO, W. E. 1986. History of endemic Hawaiian birds. Part 1. Population histories—species accounts, forest birds: Maui Parrotbill, Ou, Palila, Greater Koa Finch, Lesser Koa Finch, and Grosbeak Finch. Avian History Report 10. Cooperative National Park Resources Studies Unit, University of Hawaii, Honolulu, HI.

BANKO, W. E., AND P. C. BANKO. 1976. Role of food depletion by foreign organisms in historical decline of Hawaiian forest birds. Pp. 29–34 in C. W. Smith (editor). Proceedings of the First Conference in Natural Sciences in Hawaii. Cooperative National Park Research Studies Unit, University of Hawaii, Honolulu, HI.

BANKS, R. C., AND R. C. LAYBOURNE. 1977. Plumage sequence and taxonomy of Laysan and Nihoa finches. Condor 79:343–348.

BARKER, R. H., JR., T. BANCHONGAKSORN, J. M. COURVAL, W. SUWONKERD, K. RIMWUNGTRAGOON, AND D. F. WIRTH. 1992. A simple method to detect *Plasmodium falciparum* directly from blood samples using the polymerase chain reaction. American Journal of Tropical Medicine and Hygiene 46:416–426.

BARRERA, W., JR. 1971. Anaehoomalu: a Hawaiian oasis; preliminary report of salvage research in South Kohala, Hawaii. Pacific Anthropological Records No. 15. Department of Anthropology, Bernice Pauahi Bishop Museum, Honolulu, HI.

BARTLE, J. A., D. HU, J.-C. STAHL, P. PYLE, T. R. SIMONS, AND D. WOODBY. 1993. Status and ecology of gadfly petrels in the temperate North Pacific. Pp. 101–111 in K. Vermeer, K. T. Briggs, K. H. Morgan, and D. Siegel-Causey (editors). The status, ecology, and conservation of marine birds of the North Pacific. Canadian Wildlife Service Special Publication, Ottawa, Ontario.

BEAN, M. 1983. The evolution of national wildlife law. Praeger, New York, NY.

BEAN, M. J., AND M. J. ROWLAND. 1997. The evolution of national wildlife law. 3rd edition. Praeger, Westport, CT.

BEARDSLEY, J. W. 1979. New immigrant insects in Hawaii: 1962–1976. Proceedings Hawaiian Entomological Society 23:35–44.

BEATY, J. J. 1966. Guam's curious critters. The Pacific Journal. December 18:4.

BÉDARD, J., AND G. GAUTHIER. 1989. Comparative energy budgets of Greater Snow Geese (*Chen caerulesceus caerulesceus*) staging in two habitats in spring. Ardea 77:1–20.

BEISSINGER, S. B. 1995. Population trends of the Marbled Murrelet projected from demographic analyses. Pp. 385–394 in C. J. Ralph, G. L. Hunt, Jr., M. G. Martin, and J. F. Piatt (editors). Ecology and conservation of the Marbled Murrelet. USDA Forest Service General Technical Report PSW-GTR-152. USDA Forest Service, Albany, CA.

BELL, A. D. 1991. Plant form. Oxford University Press, New York, NY.

BELL, B. D. 1978. The Big South Cape Islands rat irruption. Pp. 33–40 in P. R. Dingwall, I. A. E. Atkinson, and C. Hay (editors). The ecology and control of rodents in New Zealand nature reserves. New Zealand Department of Lands and Survey Information Series 4. Wellington, New Zealand.

BELLROSE, F. C. 1976. Ducks, geese, and swans of North America. Stackpole Books, Harrisburg, PA.

BELLROSE, F. C., T. C. SCOTT, A. S. HAWKINS, AND J. B. LAW. 1961. Sex ratios and age ratios in North American Ducks. Bulletin Illinois Natural History Survey 27:6.

BELOVSKY, G. E. 1987. Extinction models and mammalian persistence. Pp. 35–58 in M. E. Soulé (editor). Viable populations for conservation. Cambridge University Press, Cambridge, UK.

BENNETT, A. F., L. F. LUMSDEN, AND A. O. NICHOLLS. 1994. Tree hollows as a resource for wildlife in remnant woodlands: spatial and temporal patterns across the northern plains of Victoria, Australia. Pacific Conservation Biology 1:222–235.

BERGER, A. J. 1966. Behavior of a captive Mockingbird. Jack-Pine Warbler 44:8–13.

BERGER, A. J. 1967. The incubation period of the Hawaiian Stilt. Auk 84:130.

BERGER, A. J. 1969a. The breeding season of the Hawaii Amakihi. Occasional Papers B. P. Bishop Museum 24:1–8.

BERGER, A. J. 1969b. The nest, eggs, and young of the Elepaio. Wilson Bulletin 81:333–335.

BERGER, A. J. 1969c. Discovery of the nest of the Hawaiian Thrush. Living Bird 8:243–250.

BERGER, A. J. 1970a. The present status of the birds of Hawaii. Pacific Science 24:29–42.

BERGER, A. J. 1970b. The eggs and young of the Palila, an endangered species. Condor 72:238–240.

BERGER, A. J. 1972. Hawaiian birdlife. University Press of Hawaii, Honolulu, HI.

BERGER, A. J. 1974, 1975. History of exotic birds in Hawaii. 'Elepaio 35:60–65, 72–80.

BERGER, A. J. 1975a. The Hawaiian Honeycreepers 1778–1974. Elepaio 35:97–100, 110–118.

BERGER, A. J. 1975b. The Warbling Silverbill, a new nesting bird in Hawaii. Pacific Science 29:51–54.

BERGER, A. J. 1975c. The Mockingbird on Hawaii Island. Elepaio 35:139.

BERGER, A. J. 1975d. The Java Sparrow in Hawaii. Elepaio 36:14–16.

BERGER, A. J. 1975e. Red-whiskered and Red-vented Bulbuls on Oahu. Elepaio 36:16–19.

BERGER, A. J. 1975f. The Japanese Bush Warbler on Oahu. Elepaio 36:19–21.

BERGER, A. J. 1977a. Aloha means goodby. National Wildlife 28–35.

BERGER, A. J. 1977b. Nesting of the Yellow-fronted Canary on O'ahu. 'Elepaio 37:128.

BERGER, A. J. 1977c. Nesting of the Japanese Bush Warbler. 'Elepaio 37:148.

BERGER, A. J. 1977d. Rothschild's Starling in Wai-kīkī. 'Elepaio 37:149.

BERGER, A. J. 1977e. Nesting seasons of some introduced birds in Hawaii. 'Elepaio 38:35–38.

BERGER, A. J. 1981. Hawaiian birdlife. 2nd edition. University of Hawaii Press, Honolulu, HI.

BERLIN, K. E., T. K. PRATT, J. C. SIMON, J. R. KOWALSKY, AND J. S. HATFIELD. 2000. Plant phenology in a cloud forest on the island of Maui, Hawaii. Biotropica 32:90–99.

BERLIN, K. E., AND E. M. VANGELDER. 1999. 'Ākohekohe (Palmeria dolei). In A. Poole and F. Gill (editors). The Birds of North America, No. 400. The Academy of Natural Sciences, Philadelphia, PA, and American Ornithologists' Union, Washington, D.C.

BEVACQUA, R. F. (EDITOR). 1972. Archaeological survey of portions of Waikoloa, South Kohala District, island of Hawaii. Department of Anthropology, Report Series No. 72–4. B. P. Bishop Museum, Honolulu, HI.

BEVERLEY, S. M., AND A. C. WILSON. 1985. Ancient origin for Hawaiian Drosophilinae inferred from protein comparisons. Proceedings of the National Academy of Science 82:4753–4757.

BEZONA, N. 1996. The tropical world in our Hawaiian gardens. Hawaii Landscape, December:4–5.

BISHOP, J. G., III, AND J. A. HUNT. 1988. DNA divergence in and around the alcohol dehydrogenase locus in five closely related species of Hawaiian Drosophila. Molecular Biology and Evolution 5:415–431.

BLACK, J. M. 1995. The Nene Branta sandvicensis Recovery Initiative: research against extinction. Ibis 137:S153-S160.

BLACK, J. M., AND P. C. BANKO. 1994. Is the Hawaiian Goose (Branta sandvicensis) saved from extinction? Pp. 394–410 in P. J. Olney, G. M. Mace, and A. T. C. Feistner (editors). Creative conservation: interactive management of wild and captive animals. Chapman and Hall, London, UK.

BLACK, J. M., C. DEERENBERG, AND M. OWEN. 1991. Foraging behaviour and site selection of Barnacle Geese Branta leucopsis in a traditional and newly colonised spring staging habitat. Ardea 79:349–358.

BLACK, J. M., A. P. MARSHALL, A. GILBURN, N. SAN-TOS, H. HOSHIDE, J. MEDEIROS, J. MELLO, C. N. HODGES, AND L. KATAHIRA. 1997. Survival, movement, and breeding of released Hawaiian Geese: an assessment of the reintroduction program. Journal of Wildlife Management 61:1161–1173.

BLACK, J. M., J. PROP, J. M. HUNTER, F. WOOG, A. P. MARSHALL, AND J. M. BOWLER. 1994. Foraging behaviour and energetics of the Hawaiian Goose Branta sandvicensis. Wildfowl 45:65–109.

BLEDSOE, A. H. 1988a. A hybrid Oporornis philadelphia x Geothlypis trichas, with comments on the taxonomic interpretation and evolutionary significance of intergeneric hybridization. Wilson Bulletin 100:1–8.

BLEDSOE, A. H. 1988b. Nuclear DNA evolution and phylogeny of the New World nine-primaried Oscines. Auk 105:504–515.

BLOOMER, J. P., AND M. N. BESTER. 1992. Control of feral cats on sub-Antarctic Marion Island, Indian Ocean. Biological Conservation 60:211–219.

BLOXOM, A. J. 1925. Diary of Andrew Bloxom, naturalist of the "Blonde." S. M. Jones (editor). B. P. Bishop Museum Special Publication 10.

BOAG, P. T. 1988. The genetics of island birds. Acta XIX Congressus Internationalis Ornithologici 19: 1550–1563.

BOCK, C. E., A. CRUZ, JR., M. C. GRANT, C. S. AID, AND T. R. STRONG. 1992. Field experimental evidence for diffuse competition among southwestern riparian birds. American Naturalist 140:815–828.

BOCK, C. E., AND R. E. RICKLEFS. 1983. Range size and local abundance of some North American songbirds: a positive correlation. American Naturalist 122:295–299.

BOCK, W. J. 1960. The palatine process of the premaxilla in the Passeres. Bulletin of the Museum of Comparative Zoology 122: 361–488.

BOCK, W. J. 1970. Microevolutionary sequences as a fundamental concept in macroevolutionary models. Evolution 24:704–722.

BOCK, W. J. 1978. Tongue morphology and affinities of the Hawaiian honeycreeper Melamprosops phaeosoma. Ibis 120:467–479.

BOCK, W. J. 1979. The synthetic explanation of macroevolutionary change—a reductionist approach. Bulletin of the Carnegie Museum of Natural History 13:20–69.

BOEKELHEIDE, R. J., AND D. G. AINLEY. 1989. Age, resource availability, and breeding effort in Brandt's Cormorant. Auk 106:389–401.

BOICE, L. P. 1997. Meeting current challenges to DoD's Conservation program. Federal Facilities Environmental Journal 8:29–37. John Wiley and Sons, New York, NY.

BORKENT, A., AND W. W. WIRTH. 1997. World species of biting midges (Diptera: Ceratopogonidae). Bulletin of the American Museum of Natural History 233:1–257

BORRIELLO, F., AND K. S. KRAUTER. 1991. Reactive site polymorphism in the murine protease inhibitor gene family is delineated using a modification of the PCR reaction (PCR+1). Nucleic Acids Research 18: 5481–5487.

BOTTIUS, E., A. GUANZIROLLI, J. F. TRAPE, C. ROGIER, L. KONATE', AND P. DRUILHE. 1996. Malaria: even more chronic in nature than previously thought: evidence for subpatent parasiteaemia detectable by the polymerase chain reaction. Transactions of the Royal Society of Tropical Medicine and Hygiene 90:15–19.

BOURKE, R. M. 1982. Sweet potato in Papua, New Guinea. Pp. 45–57 *in* R. L. Villareal and T. D. Griggs (editors). Sweet potato: proceedings of the first international symposium. AVRDC Publication No. 82–172. Asian Vegetable Research and Development Center, Shanhua, Tainan, Taiwan, China.

BOWERS, N. M. 1950. Problems of resettlement on Saipan, Tinian and Rota, Mariana Islands. Ph.D. dissertation. University Michigan, Ann Arbor, MI.

BRADLEY, J. S., R. D. WOOLLER, I. J. SKIRA, AND D. L. SERVENTY. 1989. Age-dependent survival of breeding Short-tailed Shearwaters *Puffinus tenuirostris*. Journal of Animal Ecology 58:175–188.

BRANDT, C. A., J. K. PARRISH, AND C. N. HODGES. 1995. Predictive approaches to habitat quantification: Dark-rumped Petrels on Haleakala, Maui. Auk 112:571–579.

BREGULLA, H. L. 1992. Birds of Vanuatu. Anthony Nelson, Shropshire, England.

BREITWISCH, R. 1989. Mortality patterns, sex ratios, and parental investment in monogamous birds. Current Ornithology 6:1–50.

BREMER, K. 1988. The limits of amino acid sequence data in angiosperm phylogenetic reconstruction. Evolution 42:795–803.

BRENNAN, J. 1974. The Parker Ranch of Hawaii: the saga of a ranch and a dynasty. John Day, New York, NY.

BREWBAKER, J. L., AND C. T. SORENSSON. 1994. Domestication of lesser-known species of the genus *Leucaena*. Pp. 195–204 *in* R. R. B. Leakey and A. C. Newton (editors). Tropical trees: the potential for domestication and rebuilding of forest resources. Institute of Terrestrial Ecology, HMSO, London, UK.

BRICE, A. T. 1992. The essentiality of nectar and arthropods in the diet of Anna's hummingbird (*Calypte anna*). Comparative Biochemistry and Physiology 101A:151–155.

BRICE, A. T., AND C. R. GRAY. 1991. Protein requirements of Costa's hummingbird *Calypte costae*. Physiological Zoology 64:611–626.

BRIDGES, K. W., C. H. LAMOUREUX, D. MUELLER-DOMBOIS, P. Q. TOMICH, J. R. LEEPER, J. W. BEARDSLEY, W. A. STEFFAN, Y. K. PAIK, AND K. C. SUNG. 1981. Temporal variation of organism groups studied. Pp. 391–422 *in* D. Mueller-Dombois, K. W. Bridges, and H. L. Carson (editors). Island ecosystems: biological organization in selected Hawaiian communities. Hutchinson Ross Publishing Company, Stroudsburg, PA.

BRIGHAM, W. T. 1899. Hawaiian feather work. Memoirs of the B. P. Bishop Museum 1:1–81. B. P. Bishop Museum, Honolulu, HI.

BRILES, W. E. 1954. Evidence for overdominance of the *B* blood group alleles in the chicken. Genetics 39:961–962.

BRILES, W. E., AND C. P. ALLEN. 1961. The *B* blood group system of chickens. Part II. The effects of genotype on livability and egg production in seven commercial inbred lines. Genetics 46:1273–1293.

BRILES, W. E., C. P. ALLEN, AND T. W. MILLEN. 1957. The *B* blood group system. Part I. Heterozygosity in closed populations. Genetics 42:631–648.

BRILES, W. E., R. W. BRILES, W. H. MCGIBBON, AND H. A. STONE. 1980. Identification of *B* alloalleles associated with resistance to Marek's disease. Pp. 395–416 *in* P. M. Briggs (editor). Resistance and immunity to Marek's disease. CEC Pub. EUR 6470, Luxembourg.

BRILES, W. E., R. W. BRILES, R. E. TAFFS, AND H. A. STONE. 1983. Resistance to a malignant lymphoma in chickens is mapped to a subregion of the major histocompatibility (*B*) complex. Science 219:977–979.

BRILES, W. E., R. M. GOTO, C. AUFFRAY, AND M. M. MILLER. 1993. A polymorphic system related to but genetically independent of the chicken major histocompatibility complex. Immunogenetics 37:408–414.

BRILES, W. E., W. H. MCGIBBON, AND M. R. IRWIN. 1948. Studies of the time of development of cellular antigens in the chicken. Genetics 33:97.

BRILES, W. E., AND M. OLESON. 1971. Differential depletion of *B* blood group genotypes under stress of Marek's disease. Poultry Science 50:1558.

BRILES, W. E., H. A. STONE, AND R. K. COLE. 1977. Marek's disease: effects of *B* histocompatibility alloalleles in resistant and susceptible chicken lines. Science 195:193–195.

BROCK, R. E. 1994. Final report, fish communities of the Nu'upia Fishponds, Nu'upia Ponds Wildlife Management Area, Mokapu, O'ahu, Hawai'i. Appendix B *in* R. M. Towill (editor). 1995. Environmental study of Nu'upia Ponds Wildlife Management Area, Kaneohe Bay, Hawai'i. Environmental Assessment Co., Honolulu, HI.

BROCK, V. E. 1951a. Laysan Island bird census. Elepaio 12:17–18.

BROCK, V. E. 1951b. Some observations on the Laysan Duck, *Anas wyvilliana laysanensis*. Auk 68:371–372.

BROMHAM, L., A. RAMBAUT, AND P. H. HARVEY. 1996. Determinants of rate variation in mammalian DNA sequence evolution. Journal of Molecular Evolution 43:610–621.

BROOKE, M. 1990. The Manx Shearwater. T. and A. D. Poyser, Calton, UK.

BROOKE, M. DE L., AND I. R. HARTLEY. 1995. Nesting Henderson Reed-warblers (*Acrocephalus vaughani taiti*) studied by DNA fingerprinting: unrelated coalitions in a stable habitat? Auk 112:77–86.

BROWN, C. L., R. G. MCAPLINE, AND P. P. KORMANIK. 1967. Apical dominance and form in woody plants: a reappraisal. American Journal of Botany 54:153–162.

BROWN, J. H. 1984. On the relationship between abundance and distribution of species. American Naturalist 124:255–279.

BROWN, J. H., AND A. KODRIC-BROWN. 1977. Turnover rates in insular biogeography: effect of immigration on extinction. Ecology 58:445–449.

BROWN, J. H., D. W. MEHLMAN, AND G. C. STEVENS. 1995. Spatial variation in abundance. Ecology 76:2028–2043.

BROWN, W. M., M. GEORGE, JR., AND A. C. WILSON.

1979. Rapid evolution of animal mitochondrial DNA. Proceedings of the National Academy of Sciences (USA) 76:1967–1971.

BROWN, W. Y. 1976. The breeding of sooty terns and brown noddies on Manana Island, Hawaii. Condor 78:61–66.

BROWNE, R. A., D. J. ANDERSON, J. N. HOUSER, F. CRUZ, K. J. GLASGOW, C. N. HODGES, AND G. MASSEY. 1997. Genetic diversity and divergence of endangered Galápagos and Hawaiian petrel populations. Condor 99:812–815.

BROWNE, R. A., C. R. GRIFFIN, P. R. CHANG, M. HUBLEY, AND A. E. MARTIN. 1993. Genetic divergence among populations of the Hawaiian Duck, Laysan Duck, and Mallard. Auk 110:49–56.

BROWNIE, C., J. E. HINES, AND J. D. NICHOLS. 1986. Constant-parameter capture-recapture models. Biometrics 42:561–574.

BRYAN, E. H., JR. 1938. The much maligned mongoose. Paradise Pacific 50:32–34.

BRYAN, E. H., JR. 1963. Discussion. Pp. 38 in F. R. Fosberg (editor). Man's place in the island ecosystem. B. P. Bishop Museum, Honolulu, HI.

BRYAN, E. H., JR., AND J. C. GREENWAY, JR. 1944. Contribution to the ornithology of the Hawaiian Islands. Bulletin Museum Comparative Zoology 94:80–142.

BRYAN, L. W. 1947. Twenty-five years of forestry work on the Island of Hawaii. Hawaiian Planter's Record 51:1–80.

BRYAN, W. A. 1901. A key to the birds of the Hawaiian group. Memoirs of the Bishop Museum 1:258–332.

BRYAN, W. A. 1908. Some birds of Molokai. Occasional Papers B. P. Bishop Museum 4:133–176.

BRYAN, W. A. 1917. Description of Telespiza ultima from Nihoa Island. Auk 34:70–72.

BRYAN, W. A., AND A. SEALE. 1901. Notes on the birds of Kauai. Occasional Papers B. P. Bishop Museum 1:129–137.

BUCKLAND, S. T., D. R. ANDERSON, K. P. BURNHAM, AND J. L. LAAKE. 1993. Distance sampling: estimating abundance of biological populations. Chapman and Hall, New York, NY.

BUCKLEY, F. G., AND P. A. BUCKLEY. 1974. Comparative feeding ecology of wintering adult and juvenile Royal Terns (Aves: Laridae, Sterninae). Ecology 55:1053–1063.

BUMSTEAD, N., H. WAIN, N. SALMON, AND J. SILLIBOURNE. 1995. Genomic mapping of immunological genes. Pp. 95–103 in T. F. Davison, N. Bumstead, and P. Kaiser (editors). Advances in avian immunology research. Carfax Publishing Co., Oxfordshire, UK.

BURGAN, R. E. 1970. Study plan to detect growth rings in koa. USDA Forest Service Institute of Pacific Islands Forestry, Honolulu, HI.

BURNESS, G. P., AND R. D. MORRIS. 1993. Direct and indirect consequences of mink presence in a Common Tern colony. Condor 95:708–711.

BURROWS, C. 1997. High school hikers 1997 ecology camp. Malama I ka Honua (Cherish the Earth), Journal of the Hawai'i Chapter, Sierra Club, July–September 29(3).

BURTON, P. J., AND D. MUELLER-DOMBOIS. 1984. Response of Metrosideros polymorpha seedlings to experimental canopy opening. Ecology 65:779–791.

BURY, R. B., AND J. A. WHELAN. 1984. Ecology and management of the bullfrog. U.S. Fish and Wildlife Service Resource Publication 155:1–23.

BUSTAMANTE, J. 1996. Population viability analysis of captive and released Bearded Vulture populations. Conservation Biology 10:822–831.

BUTLER, D., AND D. MERTON. 1992. The Black Robin: saving the world's most endangered bird. Oxford University Press, New York, NY.

BUTTERFIELD, B. P., W. E. MESHAKA, JR., AND C. GUYER. 1997. Nonindigenous amphibians and reptiles. Pp. 123–138 in D. Simberloff, D. C. Schmitz, and T.C. Brown (editors). Strangers in paradise: impact and management of nonindigenous species in Florida. Island Press, Washington, D.C.

BYRD, G. V., AND D. S. BOYNTON. 1979. The distribution and status of Wedge-tailed shearwaters on Kauai. 'Elepaio 39:129–131.

BYRD, G. V., J. L. SINCOCK, T. C. TELFER, D. I. MORIARTY, AND B. G. BRADY. 1984. A cross-fostering experiment with Newell's race of Manx Shearwater. Journal of Wildlife Management 48:163–168.

BYRD, G. V., AND T. C. TELFER. 1980. Barn owls prey on birds in Hawaii. 'Elepaio 41:35–36.

CADE, T. J., J. H. ENDERSON, C. G. THELANDER, AND C. M. WHITE (editors). 1988. Peregrine Falcon populations: their management and recovery. The Peregrine Fund, Boise, ID.

CALDER, W. A. 1973. Microhabitat selection during nesting of hummingbirds in the Rocky Mountains. Ecology 54:127–134.

CALDER, W. A., III. 1984. Size, function, and life history. Harvard University Press, Cambridge, MA.

CALLCOTT, A.-M. A., AND H. L. COLLINS. 1996. Invasion and range expansion of imported fire ants (Hymenoptera: Formicidae) in North America from 1918–1995. Florida Entomologist 79:240–251.

CAMPBELL, E. W. 1996. The effect of brown tree snake (Boiga irregularis) predation on the island of Guam's extant lizard assemblages. Ph.D. dissertation. Ohio State University, Columbus, OH.

CAMPBELL, R. W. 1990. The birds of British Columbia. Vol. 1. Royal British Columbia Museum, Victoria, BC.

CAMPBELL, T. W. 1995. Avian hematology and cytology. 2nd edition. University of Iowa Press, Ames, IA.

CANN, R. L., AND L. J. DOUGLAS. 1999. Parasites and conservation of Hawaiian birds. Pp. 121–136 in L. F. Landweber and A. P. Dobson (editors). Genetics and the extinction of species. Princeton University Press, Princeton, NJ.

CANN, R. L., R. A. FELDMAN, L. AGULLANA, AND L. A. FREED. 1996. A PCR approach to detection of malaria in Hawaiian birds. Pp. 202–213 in T. B. Smith and R. K. Wayne (editors). Molecular genetic approaches in conservation. Oxford University Press, New York, NY.

CAREY, A. B., AND H. R. SANDERSON. 1981. Routing to accelerate tree-cavity formation. The Wildlife Society Bulletin 9:14–21.

CARLQUIST, S. 1970. Hawaii: a natural history. Natural History Press, New York, NY.

CARLQUIST, S. 1974. Island biology. Columbia University Press, New York, NY.

CAROTHERS, J. H. 1986a. Behavioral and ecological

correlates of interference competition among some Hawaiian Drepanidinae. Auk 103:564–574.

CAROTHERS, J. H. 1986b. The effect of retreat site quality on interference-related behavior among Hawaiian honeycreepers. Condor 88:421–426.

CARPENTER, F. L. 1976a. Ecology and evolution of an Andean hummingbird (*Oreotrochilus estrella*). University of California Publications in Zoology 106:1–74.

CARPENTER, F. L. 1976b. Plant-pollinator interactions in Hawaii: pollination energetics of *Metrosideros collina* (Myrtaceae). Ecology 57:1125–1144.

CARPENTER, F. L. 1978. A spectrum of nectar-eater communities. American Zoologist 18:809–819.

CARPENTER, F. L., AND R. E. MACMILLEN. 1976. Threshold model of feeding territoriality and test with a Hawaiian honeycreeper. Science 194:639–642.

CARPENTER, F. L., AND R. E. MACMILLEN. 1980. Resource limitation, foraging strategies and community structure in Hawaiian honeycreepers. Proceedings of the 17th International Ornithological Congress 17:1100–1104.

CARRINGTON, M., G. W. NELSON, M. P. MARTIN, T. KISSNER, D. VLAHOV, J. J. GOEDERT, R. KASLOW, S. BUCHBINDER, K. HOOTS, AND S. J. O'BRIEN. 1999. HLA and HIV-1: heterozygote advantage and B*35-Cw*04 disadvantage. Science 283:1748–1752.

CARSON, H. L., AND D. A. CLAGUE. 1995. Geology and biogeography of the Hawaiian Islands. Pp. 14–29 *in* W. L. Wagner and V. A. Funk (editors). Hawaiian biogeography: evolution in a hotspot archipelago. Smithsonian Institution Press, Washington, D.C.

CARSON, H. L., J. P. LOCKWOOD, AND E. M. CRADDOCK. 1990. Extinction and recolonization of local populations on a growing shield volcano. Proceedings of the National Academy of Sciences (USA) 87:7055–7057.

CASEY, T. L. C., AND J. D. JACOBI. 1974. A new genus and species of bird from the island of Maui, Hawaii (Passeriformes: Drepanididae). Occasional Papers B. P. Bishop Museum 24:215–226.

CAUM, E. L. 1933. The exotic birds of Hawaii. Occasional Papers B. P. Bishop Museum 10:1–55.

CAVÉ, A. J. 1968. The breeding of the kestrel, *Falco tinnunculus* L., in the reclaimed area Oostelijk Flevoland. Netherlands Journal of Zoology 18:313–407.

CGAPS (COORDINATING GROUP ON ALIEN PEST SPECIES). 1996. The silent invasion. Info Grafik, Honolulu, HI.

CHALLIES, C. N. 1975. Feral pigs (*Sus scrofa*) on Auckland Island: status and effects on vegetation and nesting seabirds. New Zealand Journal of Zoology 2:478–490.

CHAPMAN, R. N. 1928. The quantitative analysis of environmental factors. Ecology 9:111–122.

CHARNOV, E. L., AND J. R. KREBS. 1974. On clutch-size and fitness. Ibis 116:217–219.

CHEKE, A. S. 1987. An ecological history of the Mascarene Islands, with particular reference to extinctions and introductions of land vertebrates. Pp. 5–89 *in* A. W. Diamond (editor). Studies of Mascarene Island birds. Cambridge University Press, Cambridge, UK.

CHURCHER, P. B., AND J. H. LAWTON. 1987. Predation by domestic cats in an English village. Journal of Zoology 212:439–455.

CID DEL PRADO VERA, A. R. MAGGENTI, AND C. VAN RIPER, III. 1985. New species of spiruridae (Nemata: Spirurida) from endemic Hawaiian honeycreepers (Passeriformes: Drepanididae) and from the Japanese White-eye (Zosteropinae: Spiruridae) and a new species of Acuriidae (Nemata: Spiruridae) collected on the island of Hawaii. Proceedings of the Helminthology Society of Washington 52:247–259.

CLAGUE, D. A., AND G. B. DALRYMPLE. 1987. Tectonics, geochronology and origin of the Hawaiian-Emperor volcanic chain. Pp. 1–54 *in* R. W. Decker, T. L. Wright, and P. H. Stauffer (editors). Volcanism in Hawaii. U.S. Geological Survey Professional Paper 1350. U.S. Government Printing Office, Washington, D.C.

CLAPP, R. B., E. KRIDLER, AND R. R. FLEET. 1977. The natural history of Nihoa Island, Northwestern Hawaiian Islands. Atoll Research Bulletin No. 207.

CLARE, R. A., R. L. TAYLOR, JR., W. E. BRILES, AND R. G. STROUT. 1989. Characterization of resistance and immunity to *Eimeria tenella* among major histocompatibility complex B-F/B-G recombinant hosts. Poultry Science 68:639–645.

CLARK, H. L. 1912. Notes on the Laysan Finch. Auk 29: 166–168.

CLUTTON-BROCK, T. H. 1991. The evolution of parental care. Princeton University Press, Princeton, NJ.

CODY, M. L. 1966. A general theory of clutch size. Evolution 20:174–184.

CODY, M. L. 1971. Ecological aspects of reproduction. Pp. 461–512 *in* D. S. Farner and J. R. King (editors). Avian biology. Vol. 1. Academic Press, New York, NY.

COGGER, H. G. 1992. Reptiles and amphibians of Australia. 5th edition. Comstock Publishers, Ithaca, NY.

COHEN, J. 1988. Statistical power analysis for the behavioral sciences. Lawrence Erlbaum, Hillsdale, NJ.

COLE, F. R., A. C. MEDEIROS, L. L. LOOPE, AND W. W. ZUEHLKE. 1992. Effects of the Argentine ant on arthropod fauna of Hawaiian high-elevation shrubland. Ecology 73:1313–1322.

COLLAR, N. J. 1996. Species concepts and conservation: a reply to Hazevoet. Bird Conservation International 6:197–200.

COLLAR, N. J. 1997. Taxonomy and conservation: chicken and egg. Bulletin of the British Ornithologists' Club 117:122–136.

COLLAR, N. J., M. J. CROSBY, AND A. J. STATTERSFIELD. 1994. Birds to watch 2: the world list of threatened birds. BirdLife International. Birdlife Conservation Series No. 4. Cambridge, UK.

COLLINS, B. G., J. GREY, AND S. MCNEE. 1990. Foraging and nectar use in nectarivorous bird communities. Studies in Avian Biology 13:110–121.

COLLINS, M. S. 1984. Observations on the nesting of the Hawaii 'Akepa. 'Elepaio 45:1–2.

COLLINS, M. W., W. E. BRILES, R. M. ZSIGRAY, W. R. DUNLOP, A. C. CORBETT, K. K. CLARK, J. L. MARKS, AND T. P. MCGRAIL. 1977. The *B* locus (Mhc) in the chicken: association with the fate of RSV-induced tumors. Immunogenetics 5:333–343.

COMPTON, W. 1997. Annual mud ops, Nu'upia Ponds get torn up. Hawaii Marine. February 13:A-4.

COMPUTER RESOURCE CENTER. 1993. Stata reference manual: Release 3.1. 6th edition. College Station, TX.

CONANT, P., A. C. MEDEIROS, AND L. L. LOOPE. 1997. A multi-agency containment program for miconia (*Miconia calvescens*), an invasive tree in Hawaiian rain forests. Pp. 249–254 *in* J. Luken and J. Thieret (editors). Assessment and management of invasive plants. Springer-Verlag, New York, NY.

CONANT, R., AND J. T. COLLINS. 1991. A field guide to reptiles and amphibians of eastern and central North America. Houghton Mifflin Co., Boston, MA.

CONANT, S. 1977. The breeding biology of the Oahu 'Elepaio. Wilson Bulletin 89:193–210.

CONANT, S. 1980. Recent records of the 'Ua'u (Dark-rumped Petrel) and the 'A'o (Newell's Shearwater) in Hawai'i. 'Elepaio 41:11–13.

CONANT, S. 1981. Recent observations of endangered birds in Hawaii's national parks. 'Elepaio 41:55–61.

CONANT, S. 1988a. Geographic variation in the Laysan Finch (*Telespiza cantans*). Evolutionary Ecology 2: 270–282.

CONANT, S. 1988b. Saving endangered species by translocation: are we tinkering with evolution? BioScience 38:254–257.

CONANT, S. 1995. Draft proposed rule for listing the Oahu 'Elepaio (*Chasiempis sandwichensis gayi*) as an endangered species under the U.S. Endangered Species Act of 1973 (as amended). Administrative report to the Ecological Services Office of the U.S. Fish and Wildlife Service, Honolulu, HI. Order No. 12200–5–0120, 1 February 1995.

CONANT, S., M. S. COLLINS, AND C. J. RALPH. 1981. Effects of observers using different methods upon the total population estimates of two resident island birds. Studies in Avian Biology 6:377–381.

CONANT, S., AND M. S. KJARGAARD. 1984. Annotated checklist of the birds of Haleakala National Park. Western Birds 15:99–110.

CONANT, S., H. D. PRATT, AND R. J. SHALLENBERGER. 1998. Reflections on a 1975 expedition to the lost world of the Alaka'i and other notes on the natural history, systematics, and conservation of Kaua'i birds. Wilson Bulletin 110:1–22.

COOCH, E. G., D. B. LANK, A. DZUBIN, R. F. ROCKWELL, AND F. COOKE. 1991. Body size variation in Lesser Snow Geese: environmental plasticity in gosling growth rates. Ecology 72:503–512.

COOK, J. 1785. A voyage to the Pacific Ocean. 2nd edition. Vols. 2–3. Hughs, London, UK.

COOPER, A. 1997. Studies of avian ancient DNA: from Jurassic Park to modern island extinctions. Pp. 345–373 *in* D. P. Mindell (editor). Avian molecular evolution and systematics. Academic Press, San Diego, CA.

COOPER, A., J. RHYMER, H. F. JAMES, S. L. OLSON, C. E. MCINTOSH, M. D. SORENSON, AND R. C. FLEISCHER. 1996. Ancient DNA and island endemics. Nature 381:484.

COORAY, R. G., AND D. MUELLER-DOMBOIS. 1981. Population structure of woody species. Pp. 259–268 *in* D. Mueller-Dombois, K. W. Bridges, and H. L. Carson (editors). Island ecosystems: biological organi-zation in selected Hawaiian communities. Hutchinson Ross, Stroudsburg, PA.

COPEYON, C. K., J. R. WALTERS, AND J. H. CARTER, III. 1991. Induction of Red-cockaded Woodpecker group formation by artificial cavity construction. Journal of Wildlife Management 55:549–556.

CORBETT, K. 1989. Key species in the Council of Europe area. Imperial House, Kent, UK.

CORDY, R. 1984. Archaeological monitoring, dredging of sand-clogged channel between Pa'akai Pond and Kailua Bay, Marine Corps Air Station, Kaneohe Bay. Technical Report prepared by R. Cordy, Waipahu, HI.

CORNELL LABORATORY OF ORNITHOLOGY. 1995. Hawaii's birds CD. Laboratory of Natural Sciences, Ithaca, NY.

COULTER, M. C., F. CRUZ, AND J. CRUZ. 1985. A programme to save the Dark-rumped Petrel, *Pterodroma phaeopygia,* on Floreana Island, Galapagos, Ecuador. Pp. 177–180 *in* P. J. Moors (editor). Conservation of island birds. International Council for Bird Preservation Technical Publication No. 3. Cambridge, UK.

COUNCIL ON ENVIRONMENTAL QUALITY, U.S. DEPARTMENTS OF AGRICULTURE, ARMY, COMMERCE, DEFENSE, ENERGY, HOUSING AND URBAN DEVELOPMENT, THE INTERIOR, JUSTICE, LABOR, STATE, TRANSPORTATION, ENVIRONMENTAL PROTECTION AGENCY, OFFICE OF SCIENCE AND TECHNOLOGY POLICY. 1995. Attachment in Memorandum of the Under Secretary of Defense, Environmental Security (ES/EQ-CO), Letter of January 23, 1996. Prepared by Office of the Under Secretary of Defense, ES. Pentagon, Washington, D.C.

COURT, A. 1992. Baedeker's Seychelles. Prentice Hall, New York, NY.

COWIE, R. H., N. L. EVENHUIS, AND C. C. CHRISTENSEN. 1995. Catalog of the native land and freshwater molluscs of the Hawaiian Islands. Backhuys Publishers, Leiden, the Netherlands.

COX, E. F., AND P. L. JOKIEL. 1997. Environmental study of Nuupia Ponds Wildlife Management Area, Marine Corps Base Hawaii, Kāne'ohe Bay. Final report. Prepared by Hawaii Institute of Marine Biology, Kāne'ohe, HI.

CRACRAFT, J. 1983. Species concepts and speciation analysis. Current Ornithology 1:159–187.

CRACRAFT, J. 1997. Species concepts in systematics and conservation biology—an ornithological viewpoint. Pp. 325–339 *in* M. F. Claridge, H. A. Dawah, and M. R. Wilson (editors). Species: the units of biodiversity. Chapman and Hall, London, UK.

CRAIG, R. J. 1989. Observations on the foraging ecology and social behavior of the Bridled White-eye. Condor 91:187–192.

CRAIG, R. J. 1990. Foraging behavior and microhabitat use of two species of white-eyes (Zosteropidae) on Saipan, Micronesia. Auk 107:500–505.

CRAIG, R. J. 1992. Territoriality, habitat use and ecological distinctness of an endangered Pacific island Reed-warbler. Journal of Field Ornithology 63:436–444.

CRAIG, R. J. 1996. Seasonal population surveys and natural history of a Micronesian bird community. Wilson Bulletin 108:246–267.

CRAIG, R. J., AND E. TAISACAN. 1994. Notes on the ecology and population decline of the Rota Bridled White-eye. Wilson Bulletin 106:165–169.

CRAWLEY, M. J. 1993. GLIM for ecologists. Blackwell Scientific Publications, Oxford, UK.

CREWS, T. E., K. KITAYAMA, J. H. FOWNES, R. H. RILEY, D. A. HERBERT, D. MUELLER-DOMBOIS, AND P. M. VITOUSEK. 1995. Changes in soil phosphorus fractions and ecosystem dynamics across a long chronosequence in Hawaii. Ecology 76:1407–1424.

CRONK, Q. C. B., AND J. L. FULLER. 1995. Plant invaders: the threat to natural ecosystems. Chapman and Hall, London, UK.

CROXALL, J. P. (EDITOR). 1991. Seabird status and conservation: a supplement. International Council for Bird Preservation Technical Publication No. 11. Cambridge, UK.

CROXALL, J. P., P. G. H. EVANS, AND R. W. SCHREIBER (EDITORS). 1984. Status and conservation of the world's seabirds. International Council for Bird Preservation Technical Publication No. 2. Cambridge, UK.

CROXALL, J. P., AND A. J. GASTON. 1988. Patterns of reproduction in high-latitude Northern- and Southern-hemisphere seabirds. Acta XIX Congressus Internationalis Ornithologici 19:1176–1194.

CUDDIHY, L. W., AND C. P. STONE. 1990. Alteration of native Hawaiian vegetation: effects of humans, their activities and introductions. University of Hawaii Press, Honolulu, HI.

DALRYMPLE, G. H. 1994. Non-indigenous amphibians and reptiles in Florida. Pp. 67–78 in D. C. Schmitz and T. C. Brown (editors). An assessment of invasive non-indigenous species in Florida's public lands. Tech. Rep. TSS-94-100. Florida Department of Environmental Protection, Tallahassee, FL.

DANIEL, J. C. 1983. The book of Indian reptiles. Oxford University Press, Bombay, India.

DANIELS, S. E., AND G. B. WALKER. 1996. Collaborative learning: improving public deliberation in ecosystem-based management. Environmental Impact Assessment Review 16:71–102.

DARWIN, C. 1859. On the origin of species. John Murray, London, UK.

DASZAK, A., A. A. CUNNINGHAM, AND A. D. HYATT. 2000. Emerging infectious diseases of wildlife—threats to biodiversity and human health. Science 287:443–449.

DE LA SALLE, H., D. HANAU, D. FRICKER, A. URLACHER, A. KELLY, J. SALAMERO, S. H. POWIS, L. DONATO, H. BAUSINGER, M. LAFORET, M. JERAS, D. SPEHNER, T. BIEBER, A. FALKENRODT, J. -P. CAZENAVE, J. TROWSDALE, AND M. -M. TONGIO. 1994. Homozygous human TAP peptide transporter mutation in HLA class I deficiency. Science 265:237–241.

DE SANTO, T. L., AND S. K. NELSON. 1995. Comparative reproductive ecology of the auks (family Alcidae) with emphasis on the Marbled Murrelet. Pp. 33–48 in C. J. Ralph, G. L. Hunt, Jr., M. G. Martin, and J. F. Piatt (editors). Ecology and conservation of the Marbled Murrelet. Gen. Tech. Rep. PSW-GTR-152. USDA Forest Service, Albany, CA.

DELACOUR, J., AND E. MAYR. 1945. The family Anatidae. Wilson Bulletin 57:3–55.

DEMENT'EV, G. P., AND N. A. GLADKOV. 1952. Birds of the Soviet Union. Vol. 4. Translated from Russian in 1967 by Israeli Program for Scientific Translation, Jerusalem.

DEPARTMENT OF DEFENSE. 1996. Instruction 4715.3. Environmental conservation program. Prepared by the Office of the Deputy Under Secretary of Defense Environmental Security, Pentagon, Washington, D.C.

DERKSEN, D. V., AND W. D. ELDRIDGE. 1980. Drought-displacement of Pintails to the Arctic coastal plain, Alaska. Journal of Wildlife Management 44:224–229.

DESALLE, R. 1992. The origin and possible time of divergence of the Hawaiian Drosophilidae: evidence from DNA sequences. Molecular Biology and Evolution 9:905–916.

DESALLE, R., AND J. A. HUNT. 1987. Molecular evolution in Hawaiian drosophilids. Trends in Ecological Evolution 2:212–216.

DIAMOND, J. M. 1972. Biogeographic kinetics: estimation of relaxation times for avifaunas of Southwest Pacific islands. Proceedings of the National Academy of Sciences (USA) 69:3199–3203.

DIAMOND, J. M. 1975. Assembly of species communities. Pp. 342–344 in M. L. Cody and J. M. Diamond (editors). Ecology and evolution of communities. Belknap Press, Cambridge, MA.

DIAMOND, J. M. 1977. Continental and insular speciation in Pacific land birds. Systematic Zoology 26:263–268.

DIAMOND, J. M. 1984. Historic extinctions: a rosetta stone for understanding prehistoric extinctions. Pp. 824–862 in P. S. Martin, and R. G. Klein (editors). Quaternary extinctions: a prehistoric revolution. University of Arizona Press, Tucson, AZ.

DIAMOND, J. 1991. A new species of rail from the Solomon Islands and convergent evolution of insular flightlessness. Auk 108:461–470.

DIAMOND, J. M., AND C. R. VEITCH. 1981. Extinctions and introductions in the New Zealand avifauna: cause and effect? Science 211:499–501.

DICKINSON, V. M. 1995. Red imported fire ant predation on Crested Caracara nestlings in south Texas. Wilson Bulletin 107:761–762.

DIXON, K. L. 1955. An ecological analysis of the interbreeding of crested titmice in Texas. University of California Publications in Zoology 54:125–206.

DOBKIN, D. S., A. C. RICH, J. A. PRETARE, AND W. H. PYLE. 1995. Nest-site relationships among cavity-nesting birds of riparian and snowpocket aspen woodlands in the northwestern Great Basin. Condor 97:694–707.

DOBSON, A. P., AND R. M. MAY. 1986. Patterns of invasions by pathogens and parasites. Pp. 58–76 in H. A. Mooney and J. A. Drake (editors.). Ecology of biological invasions of North America and Hawaii. Springer-Verlag, New York, NY.

DOCHERTY, D. E., R. I. R. LONG, E. L. FLICKINGER, AND L. N. LOCKE. 1991. Isolation of poxvirus from debilitating cutaneous lesions on four immature gackles (Quiscalus sp.). Avian Diseases 35:244–247.

DOCHERTY, D. E., AND R. I. ROMAINE LONG. 1986. Isolation of a poxvirus from a House Finch, Carpodacus mexicanus (Müller). Journal of Wildlife Disease 22:420–422.

DRAHOS, N. 1977. Population dynamics of Guam birds. Unpublished report. Guam Aquatic and Wildlife Resources Division, Guam.

DREES, B. M. 1994. Red imported fire ant predation on nestlings of colonial waterbirds. Southwestern Entomologist 19:355–359.

DRIGOT, D. C. 1996. Protecting Nu'upia ancient fishponds. Pp. 188–193 in W. B. Stapp, A. E. J. Wals, M. R. Moss, and J. E. Goodwin (editors). International case studies on watershed education. Kendall/Hunt Publishing Co., Dubuque, IA for Global Rivers Environmental Education Network (GREEN), Ann Arbor, MI.

DRIGOT, D. C., M. E. ELLIOTT, AND K. L. GLYN. 1991. Computer-aided mapping for facilities management and environmental compliance, a case study. Cartographic Perspectives, North American Cartographic Society, Bulletin No. 9, Spring 1991:3–14.

DRIGOT, D. C., AND D. TUGGLE. 1984. Request for determination of eligibility, National Register of Historic Places, Mokapu Peninsula Fishpond Complex Nu'upia Ponds. Prepared for Keeper of the National Register by Marine Corps Air Station, Kāne'ohe Bay, HI.

DUCKS UNLIMITED, INC. 1990. SPRIG: Population recovery strategy for the Northern Pintail. Ducks Unlimited Inc., Long Grove, IL.

DUFFY, D. C. 1993. Stalking the southern oscillation: environmental uncertainty, climate change, and North Pacific seabirds. Pp. 61–67 in K. Vermeer, K. T. Briggs, K. H. Morgran, and D. Siegel (editors). The status, ecology, and conservation of marine birds of the North Pacific. Canadian Wildlife Service, Ottawa, Ontario.

DUNCAN, R. P. 1997. The role of competition and introduction effort in the success of passeriform birds introduced to New Zealand. American Naturalist 149:903–915.

DUNNING, J. B. 1992. CRC handbook of avian body masses. CRC Press, Boca Raton, FL.

DUNNING, J. B., JR., AND J.H. BROWN. 1982. Summer rainfall and winter sparrow densities: a test of the food limitation hypothesis. Auk 99:123–129.

EBERHARD, T. 1954. Food habits of Pennsylvania house cats. Journal of Wildlife Mangement 18:284–286.

EDDINGER, C. R. 1970. A study of the breeding behavior of four species of Hawaiian honeycreeper (Drepanididae). Ph.D. dissertation. University of Hawaii, Honolulu, HI.

EDWARDS, S. V., E. K. WAKELAND, AND W. K. POTTS. 1995. Contrasting histories of avian and mammalian Mhc genes revealed by class II Beta sequences from songbirds. Proceedings of the National Academy of Sciences (USA) 92:12200–12204.

EEROLA, E., T. VEROMAA, AND P. TOIVANEN. 1987. Special features in the structural organization of the avian lymphoid system. Pp. 9–22 in A. Toivanen and P. Toivanen (editors). Avian immunology: basis and practice. Vol 1. CRC Press, Boca Raton, FL.

EFRON, B., AND R. J. TIBSHIRANI. 1993. An introduction to the bootstrap. Chapman and Hall, New York, NY.

EHRLICH, P. R, D. S. DOBKIN, AND D. WHEYE. 1992. Birds in jeopardy. Stanford University Press, Palo Alto, CA.

ELDER, W. H. 1958. Preliminary report on the Nene in Hawaii. Ninth Annual Report Wildlife Trust:112–117. Slimbridge, UK.

ELDER, W. H., AND D. H. WOODSIDE. 1958. Biology and management of the Hawaiian Goose. Transactions of North American Wildlife Conference 23:198–215.

ELLIS, W. 1917. Narrative of a tour through Owhyee: with remarks on history, traditions, manners, Hawaiian customs, and language of inhabitants of the Sandwich Islands. Hawaiian Gazette (reprint of London 1827 edition). Honolulu, HI.

ELLIS, S., C. KUEHLER, R. LACY, K. HUGHES, AND U. S. SEAL. 1992a. Hawaiian forest birds: conservation assessment and management plan. Captive Breeding Specialist Group, IUCN-The World Conservation Union/Species Survival Commission. U.S. Fish and Wildlife Service, Honolulu, HI.

ELLIS, S., C. KUEHLER, R. LACY, K. HUGHES, AND U. S. SEAL. 1992b. Alala, Akohekohe and Palila population and habitat viability assessments reports. Captive Breeding Specialist Group, IUCN-The World Conservation Union/Species Survival Commission, U.S. Forest Service, Hilo, HI.

ELY, C. A., AND R. B. CLAPP. 1973. The natural history of Laysan Island, Northwestern Hawaiian Islands. Atoll Research Bulletin No. 171.

EMARA, M. G., K. E. NESTOR, AND L. D. BACON. 1993. The turkey major histocompatibility complex: characterization by mixed lymphocyte, graft versus host splenomegaly, and skin graft rejections. Poultry Science 72:60–66.

ENGBRING, J. 1989. Fluctuations in bird populations on the island of Rota as related to an experimental program to control the Melon Fly. U.S. Fish and Wildlife Service, Honolulu, HI.

ENGBRING, J. 1992. Surveys of forest birds of the Republic of Palau. U.S. Fish and Wildlife Service, Honolulu, HI.

ENGBRING, J., F. L. RAMSEY, AND V. J. WILDMAN. 1986. Micronesian forest bird survey, 1982: Saipan, Tinian, Agiguan, and Rota. U.S. Fish and Wildlife Service, Honolulu, HI.

ENGILIS, A., JR. 1988. Surveys and inventories of waterbirds in the State of Hawaii. Job Progress Report, Hawaii Division of Forestry and Wildlife, Honolulu, HI.

ENGILIS, A., JR. 1990. Field notes on native forest birds in the Hanawi Natural Area Reserve, Maui. 'Elepaio 50:67–72.

ENGILIS, A., JR., AND T. K. PRATT. 1989. Kauai forest bird survey yields surprises and disappointments. Hawaii Wildlife Newsletter 4:1,10.

ENGILIS, A., JR., AND T. K. PRATT. 1993. Status and population trends of Hawaii's native waterbirds, 1977–1987. Wilson Bulletin 105:142–158.

ENGILIS, A., JR., T. K. PRATT, C. B. KEPLER, A. M. ECTON, AND K. M. FLUETSCH. 1996. Description of adults, eggshells, nestling, fledgling, and nest of the Poo-uli. Wilson Bulletin 108:607–619.

ERNST, C. H., R. W. BARBOUR, AND J. E. LOVICH. 1994. Turtles of the United States and Canada. Smithsonian Institution Press, Washington, D.C.

ESCALANTE, A. A., AND F. J. AYALA. 1994. Phylogeny of the malarial genus Plasmodium, derived from rRNA gene sequences. Proceedings of the National Academy of Sciences (USA) 91:11373–11377.

EVANS, G. C. 1972. The quantitative analysis of plant growth. University of California Press, Berkeley, CA.

EWALD, P. W. 1994. Evolution of infectious disease. Oxford University Press, New York, NY.

FAITH, D. P. 1992. Conservation evaluation and phylogenetic diversity. Biological Conservation 61:1–10.

FAIRTHORNE, R. A. 1969. Empirical hyperbolic distributions (Bradford-Zipf-Mandelbrot) for bibliometric descriptions and predictions. Journal Documentation 25:521–534.

FALANRUW, M. C., T. G. COLE, AND A. H. AMBACHER. 1989. Vegetation survey of Rota, Tinian, and Saipan, Commonwealth of the Northern Mariana Islands. USDA Forest Service, Resource Bulletin PSW-27.

FALLA, R. A., R. B. SIBSON, AND E. G. TURBOTT. 1983. The new guide to the birds of New Zealand. Collins, Auckland, New Zealand.

FALLS, J. B. 1981. Mapping territories with playback: an accurate census method for songbirds. Studies in Avian Biology 6:86–91.

FANCY, S. G. 1997. A new approach for analyzing bird densities from variable circular-plot counts. Pacific Science 51:107–114.

FANCY, S. G., J. D. JACOBI, T. K. PRATT, AND C. J. RALPH. 1994. Determining age and sex of 'Oma'o (Myadestes obscurus). 'Elepaio 54:25–27.

FANCY, S. G., T. K. PRATT, G. D. LINDSEY, C. K. HARADA, A. H. PARENT, JR., AND J. D. JACOBI. 1993a. Identifying sex and age of Apapane and Iiwi on Hawaii. Journal of Field Ornithology 64:262–269.

FANCY, S. G., AND C. J. RALPH. 1997. 'Apapane (Himatione sanguinea). In A. Poole and F. Gill (editors). The Birds of North America, No. 296. The Academy of Natural Sciences, Philadelphia, PA, and American Ornithologists' Union, Washington, D.C.

FANCY, S. G., AND C. J. RALPH. 1998. 'I'iwi (Vestiaria coccinea). In A. Poole and F. Gill (editors). The Birds of North America, No. 327. The Academy of Natural Sciences, Philadelphia, PA, and American Ornithologists' Union, Washington, D.C.

FANCY, S. G., T. J. SNETSINGER, AND J. D. JACOBI. 1997. Translocation of the Palila, an endangered Hawaiian honeycreeper. Pacific Conservation Biology 3:39–46.

FANCY, S. G., R. T. SUGIHARA, J. J. JEFFREY, AND J. D. JACOBI. 1993b. Site tenacity of the endangered Palila. Wilson Bulletin 105:587–596.

FEARE, C. J. 1984. Human exploitation. Pp. 691–700 in P. Croxall, P. G. H. Evans, and R. W. Schreiber (editors). Status and conservation of the world's seabirds. International Council for Bird Preservation No. 2. Cambridge, UK.

FEHLING, H. J., W. SWAT, C. LAPLACE, R. KÜHN, K. RAJEWSKY, U. MÜLLER, AND H. VON BOEHMER. 1994. MHC class I expression in mice lacking the proteasome subunit LMP-7. Science 265:1234–1237.

FELDMAN, R. A. 1994. Molecular evolution, genetic diversity and avian malaria in Hawaiian honeycreepers. Ph.D. dissertation. University of Hawaii, Honolulu, HI.

FELDMAN, R. A., L. A. FREED, AND R. L. CANN. 1995. A PCR test for avian malaria in Hawaiian birds. Molecular Ecology 4:663–673.

FELGER, I., L. TAVUL, AND H.-P. BECK. 1993. Plasmodium falciparum: a rapid technique for genotyping the merozoite surface protein 2. Experimental Parasitology 77:372–375.

FELGER, I., L. TAVUL, S. KABINTIK, V. MARSHALL, B. GENTON, M. ALPERS, AND H.-P. BECK. 1994. Plasmodium falciparum: extensive polymorphism in merozoite surface antigen 2 alleles in an area with endemic malaria in Papua New Guinea. Experimental Parasitology 79:106–116.

FELLERS, J. H., AND G. M. FELLERS. 1982. Status and distribution of ants in the Crater District of Haleakala National Park. Pacific Science 36:427–437.

FELSENSTEIN, M. 1988. Phylogenies from molecular sequences: inference and reliability. Annual Review of Genetics 22:521–565.

FESTA-BIANCHET, M. 1988. Seasonal range selection in bighorn sheep: conflicts between forage quality, forage quantity, and predator avoidance. Oecologia 75:580–586.

FILLON, V., R. ZOOROB, M. YERLE, C. AUFFRAY, AND A. VIGNAL. 1996. Mapping of the genetically independent chicken major histocompatibility complexes B@ and RFP-Y@ to the same microchromosome by two-color fluorescent in situ hybridization. Cytogenetics and Cell Genetics 75:7–9.

FISHER, H. 1972. The nutrition of birds. Pp. 431–469 in D. S. Farner, J. R. King, and K. C. Parkes (editors). Avian Biology. Vol. 2. Academic Press, New York, NY.

FISHER, H. I. 1948a. The question of avian introductions in Hawaii. Pacific Science 2:59–64.

FISHER, H. I. 1948b. Laysan Albatross nesting on Moku Manu islet, off Oahu. Pacific Science 2:66.

FISHER, H. I. 1949. Populations of birds on Midway and the man-made factors affecting them. Pacific Science 3:103–110.

FISHER, H. I. 1951. The avifauna of Niihau Island, Hawaiian Archipelago. Condor 67:31–42.

FISHER, H. I. 1965. Bird records from Midway Atoll, Pacific Ocean. Condor 67:355–357.

FISHER, H. I. 1967. Body weights in Laysan Albatrosses Diomedea immutabilis. Ibis 109:373–382.

FISHER, H. I. 1968. The "two-egg clutch" in the Laysan Albatross. Auk 85:134–136.

FISHER, H. I. 1969. Eggs and egg-laying in the Laysan Albatross, Diomedea immutabilis. Condor 71:102–112.

FISHER, H. I., AND P. H. BALDWIN. 1945. A recent trip to Midway Islands, Pacific Ocean. Elepaio 6:11–13.

FISHER, H. I., AND P. H. BALDWIN. 1946a. War and the birds of Midway Atoll. Condor 48:3–15.

FISHER, H. I., AND P. H. BALDWIN. 1946b. War and the birds of Midway. Paradise of the Pacific 58:4–9.

FISHER, H. I., AND P. H. BALDWIN. 1947. Notes on the Red-billed Leiothrix in Hawaii. Pacific Science 1:45–51.

FISHER, R. A. 1930. The genetical theory of natural selection. Oxford University Press, London, UK.

FISHER, W. K. 1903. Notes on the birds peculiar to Laysan Island, Hawaiian Group. Auk 20:384–397.

FITCH, H. S. 1985. Variation in clutch and litter size in

New World reptiles. Miscellaneous Publications, University of Kansas Museum of Natural History 76:1–76.

FLANNERY, T. 1995. Mammals of the southwest Pacific and Moluccan Islands. Cornell University Press, Ithaca, NY.

FLEISCHER, R. C. 1998. Genetics and avian conservation. Pp. 29–47 in J. M. Marzluff and R. Sallabanks (editors). Avian conservation. Island Press, Washington, D.C.

FLEISCHER, R. C., C. E. MCINTOSH, AND C. L. TARR. 1998. Evolution on a volcanic conveyor belt: using phylogeographic reconstructions and K-Ar-based ages of the Hawaiian Islands to estimate molecular evolutionary rates. Molecular Ecology 7:533–545.

FLEISCHER, R. C., S. L. OLSEN, H. F. JAMES, AND A. C. COOPER. 2000. Identification of the extinct Hawaiian eagle (Haliaeetus) by mtDNA sequence analysis. Auk 117:1051–1056.

FLEISCHER, R. C., C. L. TARR, AND T. K. PRATT. 1994. Genetic structure and mating system in the Palila, an endangered Hawaiian honeycreeper, as assessed by DNA fingerprinting. Molecular Ecology 3:383–392.

FONSECA, D. M., C. T. ATKINSON, AND R. C. FLEISCHER. 1998. Microsatellite primers for Culex pipiens quinquefasciatus, the vector of avian malaria in Hawaii. Molecular Ecology 7:1617–1619.

FORD, J. 1987. Hybrid zones in Australian birds. Emu 87:158–178.

FORSHAW, J. M. 1977. Parrots of the world. T. F. H. Publications, Inc., Neptune, NJ.

FORSMAN, E. D., E. C. MESLOW, AND H. M. WIGHT. 1984. Distribution and biology of the spotted owl in Oregon. Wildlife Monographs 87:1–64.

FOSBERG, F. R. 1960. The vegetation of Micronesia. Bulletin of American Museum Natural History 119: 1–75.

FOSBERG, F. R. 1966. Northern Marshall Islands land biota: birds. Atoll Research Bulletin 114:1–35.

FOSTER, M. S. 1974. Rain, feeding behavior, and clutch size in tropical birds. Auk 91:722–726.

FOSTER, M. S. 1975. The overlap of molting and breeding in some tropical birds. Condor 77:304–314.

FOSTER, M. S. 1978. Total frugivory in tropical passerines: a reappraisal. Tropical Ecology 19:131–154.

FOWLER, C. W. 1981. Density dependence as related to life history strategy. Ecology 62:602–610.

FRANKHAM, R. 1995. Inbreeding and extinction: a threshold effect. Conservation Biology 9:792–799.

FRANKIE, G. W., H. G. BAKER, AND P. A. OPLER. 1974. Comparative phenological studies of trees in tropical wet and dry forests in the lowlands of Costa Rica. Journal of Ecology 62:881–919.

FRANKLIN, I. R. 1980. Evolutionary change in small populations. Pp. 135–149 in M. E. Soule' and B. A. Wilcox (editors.) Conservation biology: an evolutionary-ecological perspective. Sinauer Associates, Sunderland, MA.

FRANKLIN, I. R., AND R. FRANKHAM. 1998. How large must populations be to retain evolutionary potential? Animal Conservation 1:69–73.

FRANKLIN, J. F., K. CORMACK, JR., W. DENISON, A. W. MCKEE, C. MASER, J. SEDELL, F. SWANSON, AND G. JUDAY. 1981. Ecological characteristics of old-growth Douglas-fir forests. USDA Forest Service Gen. Tech. Rep. PNW:118. U. S. Forest Service, Portland, OR.

FRANKLIN, J. F., F. HALL, W. LAUDENSLAYER, C. MASER, J. NUNAN, J. POPPINO, C. J. RALPH, AND T. SPIES. 1986. Interim definitions for old-growth Douglas-fir and mixed-conifer forests in the Pacific Northwest and California. USDA Forest Service Research Note PNW-447. USDA Forest Service, PNW Station, Portland, OR.

FRANKLIN, J., AND D. W. STEADMAN. 1991. The potential for conservation of Polynesian birds through habitat mapping and species translocation. Conservation Biology 5:506–521.

FRANKLIN, J. F., AND R. H. WARING. 1979. Distinctive features of the northwestern coniferous forest: development, structure, and function. Pp.59–86 in R. H. Waring (editor). Forests: fresh perspectives from ecosystem analysis. Proceedings of the 40th Annual Biology Colloquium, Oregon State University Press, Corvallis, OR.

FREED, L. A. 1999. Extinction and endangerment of Hawaiian honeycreepers: a comparative approach. Pp. 137–162 in L. F. Landweber and A. F. Dobson (editors). Genetics and the extinction of species. Princeton University Press, Princeton, NJ.

FREED, L. A., AND R. L. CANN. 1989. An integrated conservation strategy for Hawaiian forest birds. Bioscience 39:475–476.

FREED, L. A., S. CONANT, AND R. C. FLEISCHER. 1987a. Evolutionary ecology and radiation of Hawaiian passerine birds. Trends in Ecology and Evolution 2: 196–203.

FREED, L. A., T. M. TELECKY, W. A. TYLER, III, AND M. A. KJARGAARD. 1987b. Nest-site variability in the 'Ākepa and other cavity-nesting forest birds on the island of Hawaii. 'Elepaio 47:79–81.

FREELAND, J. R., AND P. T. BOAG. 1999. Phylogenetics of Darwin's finches: Paraphyly in the tree-finches, and two divergent lineages in the Warbler Finch. Auk 116:577–588.

FRENCH, N. R. 1959. Distribution and migration of the Black Rosy Finch. Condor 61:18–29.

FRITTS, T. H. 1993. The common wolf snake, Lycodon aulicus capucinus, a recent colonist of Christmas Island in the Indian Ocean. Wildlife Research 20:261–266.

FRITTS, T. H., M. J. MCCOID, AND R. L. HADDOCK. 1990. Risks to infants on Guam from the bites of the Brown Tree Snake (Boiga irregularis). American Journal of Tropical Medicine and Hygiene 42:607–611.

FRITTS, T. H., N. J. SCOTT, JR., AND J. A. SAVIDGE. 1987. Activity of the arboreal Brown Tree Snake (Boiga irregularis) on Guam as determined from electrical outages. Snake 19:51–58.

FUKUDA, T., T. GOTO, S. KITAOKA, AND H. TAKAMATSU. 1979. Experimental transmission of fowl pox by Culicoides arakawae. National Institute Animal Health Quarterly 19:104–105.

FULLER, R. W. 1953. Studies in the life history and ecology of the American Pintail (Anas acuta tzitzihoa Vieillot) in Utah. M.S. thesis. Utah State Agricultural College, Logan, UT.

FURNESS, R. W. 1987. The skuas. T. and A. D. Poyser, Calton, UK.

FURNESS, R. W. 1988. Predation on ground-nesting seabirds by island populations of red deer *Cervus elaphus* and sheep *Ovis*. Journal of Zoology 216:565–573.

FURNESS, R. W., AND P. MONAGHAN. 1987. Seabird ecology. Blackie and Son, Ltd. London, UK.

GADALLAH, F. L., AND R. L. JEFFERIES. 1995. Comparison of the nutrient contents of the principal forage plants utilized by Lesser Snow Geese on summer breeding grounds. Journal of Applied Ecology 32:263–275.

GADOW, H. 1899. Remarks on the structure of certain Hawaiian birds, with reference to their systematic position *and* Further remarks on the relationships of the Drepanididae. Pp. 219–249 *in* Wilson and Evans (1890–99) q. v.

GAILLARD, J.-M., D. PONTIER, D. ALLAINÉ, J. D. LEBRETON, J. TROUVILLIEZ, AND J. CLOBERT. 1989. An analysis of demographic tactics in birds and mammals. Oikos 56:59–76.

GALLAGHER, M. D. 1958–1959. Bulletin of the Natural History Society of Christmas Island (annual summaries 1958–59). Vol. 2–9.

GARDNER, D. E. 1997. *Botryosphaeria mamane* sp. Nov. associated with witches'-brooms on the endemic forest tree *Sophora chysophylla* in Hawaii. Mycologia 89:298–303.

GARDNER, L. L. 1925. The adaptive modifications and the taxonomic value of the tongue in birds. Proceedings of the United States National Museum 67:1–49.

GARNHAM, P. C. C. 1966. Malaria parasites and other haemosporina. Blackwell Scientific, Oxford, UK.

GARRETT, L. E., AND F. H. HARAMOTO. 1967. A catalog of Hawaii Acarina. Proceedings of the Hawaii Entomology Society 19:381–414.

GARRISON, J. 1999. Hawaii's forest birds: an inventory of research conducted 1992–1998. Secretariat for Conservation Biology, University of Hawai'i (http:\\www2.hawaii.edu/scb/).

GARWOOD, N. C., D. P. JANOS, AND N. BROKAW. 1979. Earthquake-caused landslides: a major disturbance to tropical forests. Science 205:997–999.

GASS, C. L., AND R. D. MONTGOMERIE. 1981. Hummingbird foraging behavior: decision-making and energy regulation. Pp. 159–199 *in* A. C. Kamil and T. D. Sargent (editors). Foraging ecology: ecological, ethological, and psychological approaches. Garland STPM Press, New York, NY.

GHOSH, S., AND F. S. COLLINS. 1996. The geneticist's approach to complex disease. Annual Review of Medicine 47:333–353.

GIAMBELLUCA, T. W., M. A. NULLET, AND T. A. SCHROEDER. 1986. Rainfall atlas of Hawaii. Vol. 76. Hawaii Department of Land and Natural Resources, Honolulu, HI.

GIBBONS, J., AND F. CLUNIE. 1986. Sea level changes and Pacific prehistory. Journal of Pacific History 21:58–82.

GIFFIN, J. G. 1976. Ecology of the feral sheep on Mauna Kea. Final report. Pittman-Robertson Project No. W-15-5, Study IX, 1972–1975. Hawaii State Department of Land and Natural Resources, Division of Fish and Game, Honolulu, HI.

GIFFIN, J. G. 1978. Ecology of the feral pig on the island of Hawaii. Final Report. Pittman-Robertson Project W-15-3, Study II, 1968–1972. Hawaii State Department of Land and Natural Resources, Division of Fish and Game, Honolulu, HI.

GIFFIN, J. G. 1982. Ecology of the mouflon sheep on Mauna Kea. Final report. Pittman-Robertson Project No. W-17-R, Study R-III, 1975–1979. Hawaii State Department of Land and Natural Resources, Division of Forestry, Honolulu, HI.

GIFFIN, J. G. 1993. New species of fossil birds found at Pu'u Wa'awa'a. 'Elepaio 53:1–3.

GILBERT, S. C., M. PLEBANSKI, S. GUPTA, J. MORRIS, M. COX, M. AIDOO, D. KWIATKOWSKI, B. M. GREENWOOD, H. C. WHITTLE, AND A. V. S. HILL. 1998. Association of malaria parasite population structure, HLA, and immunological antagonism. Science 279:1173–1177.

GILLESPIE, R. G., AND N. REIMER. 1993. The effect of alien predatory ants (Hymenoptera: Formicidae) on Hawaiian endemic spiders (Araneae: Tetragnathidae). Pacific Science 47:21–33.

GILPIN, M. E., AND M. E. SOULÉ. 1986. Minimum viable populations: processes of species extinctions. Pp. 19–34 *in* M. E. Soulé (editor). Conservation biology: the science of scarcity and diversity. Sinauer Associates, Sunderland, MA.

GIVNISH, T. J., K. J. SYTSMA, J. F. SMITH, AND W. J. HAHN. 1995. Molecular evolution, adaptive radiation, and geographic speciation in *Cyanea* (Campanulaceae, Lobelioideae). Pp. 288–337 *in* W. L. Wagner and V. A. Funk (editors). Hawaiian biogeography: evolution in a hotspot archipelago. Smithsonian Institution Press, Washington, D.C.

GLICK, B., T. S. CHANG, AND R. G. JAAP. 1956. The bursa of Fabricius and antibody production on the domestic fowl. Poultry Science 35:224.

GLYNN, P. W. 1988. El Niño-Southern Oscillation 1982–1983: nearshore population, community, and ecosystem responses. Annual Review of Ecology and Systematics 19:309–345.

GOFF, M. L. 1980. Mites (Thelicerata: Acari) parasitic on birds in Hawaii Volcanoes National Park. Technical Report 29. University of Hawaii Cooperative Studies Unit, University of Hawaii, Honolulu, HI.

GOFF, M. L., AND C. VAN RIPER, III. 1980. Distribution of mosquitoes (Diptera: Culicidae) on the east flank of Mauna Loa Volcano, Hawaii. Pacific Insects 22:178–188.

GOOD, M. F., D. POMBO, I. A. QUAKYI, E. M. RILEY, R. A. HOUGHTEN, A. MENON, D. W. ALLING, J. A. BERZOFSKY, AND L. H. MILLER. 1988. Human T-cell recognition of the circumsporozoite protein of *Plasmodium falciparum*: immunodominant T-cell domains map to the polymorphic regions of the molecule. Proceedings of the National Academy of Sciences (USA) 85:1199–1203.

GOODWIN, D. 1983. Pigeons and doves of the world. Cornell University Press, Ithaca, NY.

GÖTMARK, F. 1992. The effects of investigator disturbance on nesting birds. Current Ornithology 9:63–104.

GRANT, B. R., AND P. R. GRANT. 1989. Evolutionary

dynamics of a natural population. University of Chicago Press, Chicago, IL.

GRANT, P. R. 1986. Ecology and evolution of Darwin's finches. Princeton University Press, Princeton, NJ.

GRANT, P. R. 1994. Population variation and hybridization: comparison of finches from two archipelagos. Evolutionary Ecology 8:598–617.

GRANT, P. R., AND P. T. BOAG. 1980. Rainfall on the Galápagos and the demography of Darwin's finches. Auk 97:227–244.

GRANT, P. R., AND B. R. GRANT. 1992. Demography and the genetically effective sizes of two populations of Darwin's finches. Ecology 73:766–784.

GRAY, E. M., P. C. BANKO, S. J. DOUGILL, D. GOLTZ, L. JOHNSON, MEGAN E. LAUT, J. D. SEMONES, AND M. R. WILEY. 1999. 1998 Palila population census: Breeding and nonbreeding censuses of the 1998 Palila population on Mauna Kea, Hawai'i. 'Elepaio 59: 33–39.

GREEN, R. E. 1997. The influence of numbers released on the outcome of attempts to introduce exotic bird species to New Zealand. Journal of Animal Ecology 66:25–35.

GREENBERG, R., P. J. CORDERO, S. DROEGE, AND R. C. FLEISCHER. 1998. Morphological adaptation with no mitochondrial DNA differentiation in the Coastal Plain Swamp Sparrow. Auk 115:706–712.

GREENE, H. W. 1989. Ecological, evolutionary, and conservation implications of feeding biology in Old World cat snakes, genus Boiga (Colubridae). Proceedings of the California Academy of Sciences 46: 193–207.

GREENSLADE, P. J. M. 1965. Promecotheca opacicollis Gestro (Coleoptera: Chrysomelidae) on the island of Tikopia. Pacific Insects 7:661–664.

GREENWAY, J. C., JR. 1968. Family Drepanididae. Pp. 93–103 in Paynter, R. A., Editor, Check-list of Birds of the World Vol. 14. Museum Comp. Zoology, Cambridge, Ma.

GREENWOOD, A. G., AND W. F. BLAKEMORE. 1973. Pox infection in falcons. Veterinary Record 93:468–470.

GREENWOOD, J. J. D. 1997. Introduction: the diversity of taxonomies. Bulletin of the British Ornithologists' Club 117:85–96.

GREENWOOD, P. J., AND P. H. HARVEY. 1982. The natal and breeding dispersal of birds. Annual Review of Ecology and Systematics 13:1–21.

GRIFFIN, C. R., R. J. SHALLENBERGER, AND S. I. FEFER. 1989. Hawaii's endangered waterbirds: a resource management challenge. Pp. 1165–1175 in R. R. Sharitz and J. W. Gibbons (editors). Proceedings Freshwater Wetlands and Wildlife Symposium, Savannah River Ecology Lab, Aiken, GA.

GRIFFIN, C. R., P. W. C. PATON, AND T. S. BASKETT. 1998. Breeding ecology and behavior of the Hawaiian Hawk. Condor 100:654–662.

GRIFFITH, B., J. M. SCOTT, J. W. CARPENTER, AND C. REED. 1989. Translocation as a species conservation tool: status and strategy. Science 245:477–480.

GRINNELL, J. 1911. The Linnet of the Hawaiian Islands: a problem in speciation. University of California Publications in Zoology 7:179–195.

GRUE, C. E. 1985. Pesticides and the decline of Guam's native birds. Nature 316:301.

GRUMBINE, R. E. 1997. Reflections on "What is eco-system management?" Conservation Biology 11: 41–47.

GUEST, S. J. 1973. A reproductive biology and natural history of the Japanese White-eye (Zosterops japonicus japonica) in urban Oahu. Tech. Rept. 29. University of Hawaii Islands Ecosystems, Honolulu, HI.

GUINTHER, E. 1983. Hydrological patterns and water quality of the Nu'upia Ponds, Marine Corps Air Station, Kāne'ohe Bay, Island of O'ahu, Hawai'i. Prepared by AECOS, Inc., Kailua, HI.

GUINTHER, E. 1985. Biological surveys in the Nu'upia Ponds Wildlife Management Area in association with the November 1984 opening of the Paakai/Kailua Bay Channel. Prepared by AECOS, Inc., Kailua, HI.

GUSTAFSSON, L. 1988. Inter- and intraspecific competition for nest holes in a population of the collared flycatcher Ficedula albicollis. Ibis 130:11–16.

GUSTAFSSON, L., D. NORDLING, M. S. ANDERSSON, B. C. SHELDON, AND A. QVARNSTRÖM. 1994. Infectious diseases, reproductive effort and the cost of reproduction in birds. Philosophical Transactions of the Royal Society of London, Series B 346:323–331.

GUYNN, D. C., JR., R. L. DOWNING, AND G. R. ASKEW. 1985. Estimating the probability of non-detection of low density population. Cryptozoology 4:55–60.

HAIG, S. M., AND J. C. AVISE. 1996. Avian conservation genetics. Chapter 6 in J. C. Avise and J. L. Hamrick (editors). Conservation genetics: case histories from nature. Chapman and Hall, New York, NY.

HAIG, S. M., J. D. BALLOU, AND S. R. DERRICKSON. 1990. Management options for preserving genetic diversity: reintroduction of Guam Rails to the wild. Conservation Biology 4:290–300.

HAINSWORTH, F. R. 1977. Foraging efficiency and parental care in Colibri coruscans. Condor 79:69–75.

HALSE, S. A. 1978. Feeding habits of six species of honeyeater in south-western Australia. Emu 78:145–148.

HAMILTON, L. S., J. O. JUVIK, AND F. N. SCATENA (EDITORS). 1995. Ecological Studies. Vol. 110. Tropical montane cloud forests. Springer-Verlag, New York, NY.

HANDY, E. S. C., AND E. G. HANDY. 1972. Native planters in old Hawai'i: their life, lore, and environment. B. P. Bishop Museum Bulletin No. 233. Bishop Museum Press, Honolulu, HI.

HANSEN, M. P., J. N. VAN ZANDT, AND G. R. L. LAW. 1967. Differences in susceptibility to Marek's disease in chickens carrying two different blood group alleles. Poultry Science 46:1268.

HARDY, D. E. 1960. Insects of Hawaii. Vol. 10. Diptera: Nematocera-Brachycera. University of Hawaii Press, Honolulu, HI.

HARPER, J. L. 1977. Population biology of plants. Academic Press, San Diego, CA.

HARRIS, M. P. 1970. The biology of an endangered species, the Dark-rumped Petrel (Pterodroma phaeopygia), in the Galápagos Islands. Condor 72: 76–84.

HARRISON, C. S. 1990. Seabirds of Hawaii: natural history and conservation. Cornell University Press, Ithaca, NY.

HARTL, D. L., AND A. G. CLARK. 1989. Principles of

population genetics. Sinauer Associates, Inc., Sunderland, MA.

HASEGAWA, M. 1984. Status and conservation of seabirds in Japan, with special attention to the Short-tailed Albatross. Pp. 487–500 in J. P. Croxall, P. G. H. Evans, and R. W. Schreiber (editors). Status and conservation of the bird's seabirds. International Council for Bird Preservation Technical Publication No. 2. Cambridge, UK.

HASEGAWA, M., H. KISHINO, AND T. YANO. 1985. Dating of the human-ape splitting by a molecular clock of mitochondrial DNA. Journal of Molecular Evolution 22:160–174.

HATFIELD, J. S., W. R. GOULD, IV, B. A. HOOVER, M. R. FULLER, AND E. L. LINDQUIST. 1996. Detecting trends in raptor counts: power and type I error rates of various statistical tests. Wildlife Society Bulletin 24:505–515.

HAWAII AUDUBON SOCIETY. 1989. Hawaii's birds. 4th edition. Honolulu, HI.

HAWAII STATE DEPARTMENT OF LAND AND NATURAL RESOURCES, U.S. FISH AND WILDLIFE SERVICE, AND THE NATURE CONSERVANCY OF HAWAII. 1992. Hawaii's extinction crisis: a call to action. Report circulated by Hawaii State Department of Land and Natural Resources, U.S. Fish and Wildlife Service, and The Nature Conservancy of Hawaii.

HAZEVOET, C. J. 1995. The birds of the Cape Verde Islands. BOU Check-list No. 13.

HAZEVOET, C. J. 1996. Conservation and species lists: taxonomic neglect promotes the extinction of endemic birds, as exemplified by taxa from eastern Atlantic islands. Bird Conservation International 6: 181–196.

HAZLETT, R. W. 1993. Geological field guide, Kilauea Volcano. Hawaii Natural History Association, Hawaii National Park, HI.

HEDRICK, P. W., W. KLITZ, W. P. ROBINSON, M. K. KUHNER, AND G. THOMSON. 1991. Population genetics of HLA. Pp. 248–271 in R. K. Selander, A. G. Clark, and T. S. Whittam (editors). Evolution at the molecular level. Sinauer Associates Inc., Sunderland, MA.

HEITMEYER, M. E., D. P. CONNELLY, AND R. L. PEDERSON. 1989. The Central, Imperial, and Coachella valleys of California. Pp. 475–505 in L. M. Smith, R. L. Pederson, and R. M. Kaminski (editors). Habitat management for migrating and wintering waterfowl in North America. Texas Tech University Press, Lubbock, TX.

HENNY, C. J. 1973. Drought displaced movement of North American Pintails into Siberia. Journal of Wildlife Management 37:23–29.

HENRY, J., M.-T. RIBOUCHON, D. DEPETRIS, M.-G. MATTEÏ, C. OFFER, R. TAZI-AHNINI, AND P. PONTAROTTI. 1997. Cloning, structural analysis, and mapping of the B30 and B7 multigenic families to the major histocompatibility complex (MHC) and other chromosomal regions. Immunogenetics 46:383–395.

HENSHAW, H. W. 1902a. Birds of the Hawaiian Islands, being a complete list of the birds of the Hawaiian possessions with notes on their habits. Thos. G. Thrum, Honolulu, HI.

HENSHAW, H. W. 1902b. The Elepaio of Hawaii. Auk 19:221–232.

HERBERT, D. A., J. H. FOWNES, AND P. M. VITOUSEK.

1999. Hurricane damage to a Hawaiian forest nutrient suppy rate affects resistance and resilience. Ecology 80:908–920.

HERRMANN, C. M., AND T. J. SNETSINGER. 1997. Pox-like lesions on endangered Puaiohi (Myadestes palmeri) and occurrence of mosquito (Culex quinquefasciatus) populations near Koaie Stream. 'Elepaio 57:73–75.

HESS, S. C., P. C. BANKO, G. J. BRENNER, AND J. D, JACOBI. 1999. Factors related to the recovery of subalpine woodland on Mauna Kea, Hawaii. Biotropica 31:212–219.

HESTBECK, J. B. 1995. Response of Northern Pintail breeding populations to drought, 1961–92. Journal of Wildlife Management 59:9–15.

HESTBECK, J. B. 1996. Northern Pintails: have the paradigms changed? Pp. 45–49 in J. T. Ratti (editor). 7th International Wildlife Symposium. Ducks Unlimited, Memphis, TN.

HILL, A. V. S. 1996. Genetic susceptibility to malaria and other infectious diseases: from MHC to the whole genome. Symposia of the British Society of Parasitology 33:S75–S84.

HILL, A. V. S., C. E. M. ALLSOPP, D. KWIATKOWSKI, N. M. ANSTEY, P. TWUMASI, P. A. ROWE, S. BENNETT, D. BREWSTER, A. J. MCMICHAEL, AND B. M. GREENWOOD. 1991. Common West African HLA antigens are associated with protection from severe malaria. Nature 352:595–600.

HILL, A. V. S., AND D. J. WEATHERALL. 1998. Host genetic factors in resistance to malaria. Pp. 445–455 in I. W. Sherman (editor). Malaria: parasite biology, pathogenesis, and protection. ASM Press, Washington, D.C.

HILL, A. V. S., S. N. R. YATES, C. E. M. ALLSOPP, S. GUPTA, S. C. GILBERT, A. LALVANI, M. AIDOO, M. DAVENPORT, AND M. PLEBANSKI. 1994. Human leucocyte antigens and natural selection by malaria. Philosophical Transactions of the Royal Society of London, Series B. 346:379–385.

HILL, M. O. 1979. TWINSPAN—A FORTRAN program for arranging multivariate data in an ordered two-way table by classification of the individuals and attributes. Cornell University, Ithaca, NY.

HILLIS, D. M., B. K. MABLE, AND C. MORITZ. 1996. Applications of molecular systematics: the state of the field and a look to the future. Pp. 515–543 in D. M. Hillis, C. Moritz, and B. K. Mable (editors). Molecular systematics. 2nd edition. Sinauer Associates, Sunderland, MA.

HINDWOOD, K. A. 1940. The birds of Lord Howe Island. Emu 40:1–86.

HINES, J. E., AND J. R. SAUER. 1989. Program CONTRAST—a general program for the analysis of several survival or recovery rate estimates. Patuxent Wildlife Research Center, USFWS Research Publication No. 24.

HIRAI, L. T. 1975a. The Hawaiian House Finch. 'Elepaio 36:1–5.

HIRAI, L. T. 1975b. The nesting biology of the House Finch in Honolulu, Hawaii. Western Birds 6:33–44.

HIRAI, L. T. 1978. Native birds of Lanai, Hawaii. Western Birds 9:71–77.

HOBBS, R. J., AND S. E. HUMPHRIES. 1995. An integrated approach to the ecology and management of plant invasions. Conservation Biology 9:761–770.

HODGES, C. S. N. 1994. Effects of management on the survival and breeding success of the endangered Hawaiian Dark-rumped Petrel (*Pterodroma phaeopygia sandwichensis*). M.S. thesis. University of Washington, Seattle, WA.

HÖLLDOBLER, B., AND E. O WILSON. 1994. Journey to the ants. Harvard University Press, Cambridge, MA.

HOLMES, R. T. 1990. Ecological and evolutionary impacts of bird predation on forest insects: an overview. Studies in Avian Biology 13:6–13.

HOLT, A. 1996. An alliance of biodiversity, health, agriculture, and business interests for improved alien species management in Hawaii. Pp. 155–160 in O. T. Sandlund, P. J. Schei, and A. Viken (editors). 1996. Proceedings of the Norway/UN Conference on Alien Species. Directorate for Nature Management and Norwegian Institute for Nature Research, Trondheim, Norway.

HOLT, R. A., AND B. FOX. 1985. Protection status of the native Hawaiian biota. Pp. 127–141 in C. P. Stone and J. M. Scott (editors). 1985. Hawai'i's terrestrial ecosystems: preservation and management. Cooperative National Park Resources Studies Unit, University of Hawaii, Honolulu, HI.

HOOPER, L. M. 1995. The biology of the Southern Fire ant, *Solenopsis xyloni* (McCook) and its predation of the California Least Tern, *Sterna antillarum brownii* (Mearns). M.S. thesis. University of California Riverside, CA.

HOWARTH, F. G. 1985a. Impacts of alien land arthropods and mollusks on native plants and animals in Hawai'i. Pp. 149–179 in C. P. Stone and J. M. Scott (editors). Hawai'i's terrestrial ecosystems: preservation and management. Cooperative National Park Resources Studies Unit, University of Hawaii, Honolulu, HI.

HOWARTH, F. G. 1985b. Biosystematics of the *Culicoides* of Laos (Diptera: Ceratopogonidae). Pacific Insects 27:1–96.

HOWARTH, F. G., AND W. P. MULL. 1992. Hawaiian Insects and their kin. University of Hawaii Press, Honolulu, HI.

HOWARTH, F. G., AND G. W. RAMSAY. 1991. The conservation of island insects and their habitats. Pp. 71–107 in N. M. Collins and J. A. Thomas (editors). The conservation of insects and their habitats. Academic Press, New York, NY.

HOWARTH, F. G., S. H. SOHMER, AND W. D. DUCKWORTH. 1988. Hawaiian natural history and conservation efforts: what's left is worth saving. BioScience 38:232–237.

HOWE, R. W., G. J. DAVIS, AND V. MOSCA. 1991. The demographic significance of 'sink' populations. Biological Conservation 57:239–255.

HOWELL, T. R. 1952. Natural history and differentiation in the Yellow-bellied Sapsucker. Condor 54:237–282.

HUBBARD, J. P. 1977. The biological and taxonomic status of the Mexican Duck. Bulletin New Mexico Department Game and Fish. No. 16. New Mexico Department Game and Fish, Albuquerque, NM.

HUBER, L. N. 1966. Alaka'i Swamp, Kauai, March 1965. Elepaio 26:71.

HUDDLESTON, E. W., AND S. S. FLUKER. 1968. Distribution of ant species in Hawaii. Proceedings of the Hawaiian Entomological Society 20:45–69.

HUDSON, P. J. 1985. Population parameters for the Atlantic alcidae. Pp. 233–261 in D. N. Nettleship and T. R. Birkhead (editors). The Atlantic alcidae. Academic Press, New York, NY.

HUDSON, P. J. 1986. The effect of a parasitic nematode on the breeding production of Red Grouse. Journal of Animal Ecology 55:85–92.

HUFF, C. G. 1969. Exoerythrocytic stages of avian and reptilian malarial parasites. Experimental Parasitology 24:383–421.

HUGHES, A. L., AND M. NEI. 1988. Pattern of nucleotide substitution at major histocompatibility complex class I loci reveals overdominant selection. Nature 335:167–170.

HUGHES, A. L., AND M. NEI. 1992. Maintenance of MHC polymorphism. Nature 355:402–403.

HUGHES, F., P. M. VITOUSEK, AND T. TUNISON. 1991. Alien grass invasion and fire in the seasonal submontane zone of Hawai'i. Ecology 72:743–746.

HUGHES, M. K., AND A. L. HUGHES. 1995. Natural selection on *Plasmodium* surface proteins. Molecular and Biochemical Parasitology 71:99–113.

HULIER, E., P. PETOUR, G. SNOUNOU, M. P. NIVEZ, F. MILTGEN, D. MAZIER, AND L. RENIA. 1996. A method for the quantitative assessment of malaria parasite development in organs of the mammalian host. Molecular and Biochemical Parasitology 77:127–135.

HUMAR, A., C. OHRT, M. A. HARRINGTON, D. PILLAI, AND K. C. KAIN. 1997. Parasight® F test compared with the polymerase chain reaction and microscopy for the diagnosis of *Plasmodium falciparum* malaria in travellers. American Journal of Tropical Medicine and Hygiene 56:44–48.

HUNT, J. A., AND H. L. CARSON. 1983. Evolutionary relationships of four species of Hawaiian Drosophila as measured by DNA reassociation. Genetics 104:353–364.

HUTCHINS, M., AND W. G. CONWAY. 1995. Beyond Noah's Ark: the evolving role of modern zoos and aquariums in field conservation. International Zoo Yearbook 34:117–130.

HUTCHINS, M., K. WILLIS, AND R. J. WIESE. 1995. Authors' response. Zoo Biology 14:67–80.

HUTTER, K., H. BLATTER, AND A. OHMURA. 1990. Climate changes, ice sheet dynamics, and sea level variations. Geographic Institute of Zurich. Vol. 37.

INGLIS, I. R. 1977. The breeding behaviour of the Pink-footed Goose: behavioural correlates of nesting success. Animal Behaviour 25:747–764.

INNES, J. G., B. WARBURTON, D. WILLIAMS, H. SPEED, AND P. BRADFIELD. 1995. Large-scale poisoning of ship rats (*Rattus rattus*) in indigenous forests of the North Island, New Zealand. New Zealand Journal of Ecology 19:5–17.

IRWIN, D. M., T. D. KOCHER, AND A. C. WILSON. 1991. Evolution of the cytochrome B gene of mammals. Journal of Molecular Evolution 32:128–144.

JACOBI, J. D. 1978. Vegetation map of the Kau Forest Reserve and adjacent lands of Hawaii. US Forest Service Research Bulletin PSW-16. Honolulu, HI.

JACOBI, J. D. 1989. Vegetation maps of the upland plant communities on the islands of Hawai'i, Maui, Moloka'i, and Lana'i. Technical Report 68. Cooperative National Parks Studies Unit, University of Hawaii, Honolulu, HI.

JACOBI, J. D. 1993. Distribution and dynamics of *Metrosideros* dieback on the island of Hawaii: implications for management programs. Pp. 236–242 *in* O. Huettl and D. Mueller-Dombois (editors). Forest decline in the Atlantic and Pacific region. Springer-Verlag, Berlin, Germany.

JACOBI, J. D., AND C. T. ATKINSON. 1995. Hawaii's endemic birds. Pp. 376–381 *in* E. T. LaRoe, G. S. Farris, C. E. Puckett, P. D. Doran, and M. J. Mac (editors). Our living resources: a report to the nation on the distribution, abundance, and health of U.S. plants, animals, and ecosystems. U.S. Department of the Interior, National Biological Service, Washington, D.C.

JACOBI, J. D., S. G. FANCY, J. G. GIFFIN, AND J. M. SCOTT. 1996. Long-term population variability in the Palila, an endangered Hawaiian honeycreeper. Pacific Science 50:363–370.

JACOBI, J. D., G. GERRISH, D. MUELLER-DOMBOIS, AND L. WHITEAKER. 1988. Stand-level dieback and *Metrosideros* regeneration in the montane rain forest of Hawaii. Geojournal 17:193–200.

JACOBI, J. D., M. H. REYNOLDS, B. M. NIELSEN, J. K. DWYER, AND A. VIGGIANO. 1994. Surveys on the distribution and abundance of forest birds in the vicinity of proposed geothermal project subzones in the District of Puna, Hawaii. USFWS Report. Hawaii Geothermal Project Environmental Impact Statement, U.S. Department of Energy, Oak Ridge, TN.

JACOBI, J. D., AND J. M. SCOTT. 1985. An assessment of the current status of native upland habitats and associated endangered species on the Island of Hawai'i. Pp. 3–22 *in* C. P. Stone and J. M. Scott (editors). Hawai'i's terrestrial ecosystems: preservation and management. Cooperative National Parks Research Studies Unit, University of Hawaii Press, Honolulu, HI.

JAMES, F. C. 1991. Signs of trouble in the largest remaining population of Red-cockaded Woodpeckers. Auk 108:419–423.

JAMES, F. C. 1997. Nonindigenous birds. Pp. 139–156 *in* D. Simberloff, D. C. Schmitz, and T. C. Brown (editors). Strangers in paradise: impact and management of nonindigenous species in Florida. Island Press, Washington, D.C.

JAMES, F. C., AND H. H. SHUGART. 1970. A quantitative method of habitat description. Audubon Field Notes 24:727–736.

JAMES, H. F. 1987. A late Pleistocene avifauna from the island of Oahu, Hawaiian Islands. Documents des Laboratoires de Geologie de la Faculte des Sciences de Lyon 99:221–230.

JAMES, H. F. 1991. The contribution of fossils to knowledge of Hawaiian birds. Acta XX Congressus Internationalis Ornithologici 1:420–424.

JAMES, H. F. 1998. Historical perspectives on the evolution and ecology of Hawaiian birds. Part I. Phylogeny of the Hawaiian finches (Fringillidae: Drepanidini). Part II. Paleoecology of terrestrial communities. Ph.D. dissertation. Oxford University, Oxford, UK.

JAMES, H. F., AND S. L. OLSON. 1991. Descriptions of thirty-two new species of birds from the Hawaiian Islands. Part II. Passeriformes. Ornithological Monographs 46:1–88.

JAMES, H. F., T. W. STAFFORD JR., D. W. STEADMAN, S. L. OLSON, P. S. MARTIN, A. J. T. JULL, AND P. C. MCCOY. 1987. Radiocarbon dates on bones of extinct birds from Hawaii. Proceedings of the National Academy of Sciences (USA) 84:2350–2354.

JAMNBACK, H. 1965. The *Culicoides* of New York State (Diptera: Ceratopogonidae). New York State Museum Bulletin No. 399. Albany, NY.

JANACEK, L. L., R. L. HONEYCUTT, R. M. ADKINS, AND S. K. DAVIS. 1996. Mitochondrial gene sequences and molecular systematics of the Artiodactyl subfamily Bovidae. Molecular Phylogenetics and Evolution 6:107–119.

JANZEN, D. H., W. HALLWACHS, J. JIMENEZ, AND R. GÁMEZ. 1993. The role of the parataxonomists, inventory managers, and taxonomists in Costa Rica's National Biodiversity Inventory. Pp. 223–254 *in* W. V. Reid, S. A. Laird, C. A. Meyer, R. Gámez, A. Sittenfeld, D. H. Janzen, M. A. Hollin, and C. Juma (editors). Biodiversity prospecting: using genetic resources for sustainable development. World Resources Institute, Washington, D.C.

JARVI, S. I., AND W. E. BRILES. 1992. Identification of the major histocompatibility complex in the Ring-necked Pheasant, *Phasianus colchicus*. Animal Genetics 23:211–220.

JARVI, S. I., G. F. GEE, M. M. MILLER, AND W. E. BRILES. 1995. A complex alloantigen system in Florida sandhill cranes, *Grus canadensis pratensis*: evidence for the major histocompatibility (*B*) system. Journal of Heredity 86:348–353.

JARVI, S. I., R. M. GOTO, W. E. BRILES, AND M. M. MILLER. 1996. Characterization of Mhc genes in a multigenerational family of Ring-necked Pheasants. Immunogenetics 43:125–135.

JARVI, S. I., R. M. GOTO, G. F. GEE, W. E. BRILES, AND M. M. MILLER. 1999. Identification, inheritance, and linkage of B-G-like and Mhc class I genes in cranes. Journal of Heredity 90:152–159.

JEFFREY, J. J., S. G. FANCY, G. D. LINDSEY, P. C. BANKO, T. K. PRATT, AND J. D. JACOBI. 1993. Sex and age identification of Palila. Journal of Field Ornithology 64:490–499.

JEHL, J. R., AND K. C. PARKES. 1982. The status of the avifauna of the Revillagigedo Islands, Mexico. Wilson Bulletin 94:1–19.

JENKINS, C. D., S. A. TEMPLE, C. VAN RIPER, III, AND W. R. HANSEN. 1989. Disease-related aspects of conserving the endangered Hawaiian Crow. International Council for Bird Preservation Technical Publication 10:77–87.

JENKINS, J. M. 1983. The native forest birds of Guam. Ornithological Monographs 31:1–61.

JENKINS, P. 1996. Free trade and exotic species introductions. Pp. 145–147 *in* O. T. Sandlund, P. J. Schei, and A. Viken (editors). 1996. Proceedings of the Norway/UN Conference on Alien Species. Directorate for Nature Management and Norwegian Institute for Nature Research, Trondheim, Norway.

JOHNSGARD, P. A. 1961. Evolutionary relationships among the North American Mallards. Auk 78:3–43.

JOHNSGARD, P. A. 1967. Sympatry changes and hybridization incidence in Mallards and Black Ducks. American Midland Naturalist 77:51–63.

JOHNSGARD, P. A. 1978. Ducks, geese and swans of the world. University of Nebraska Press, Lincoln, NE.

JOHNSON, D. H. 1979. Estimating nest success: the Mayfield method and an alternative. Auk 96:651–661.

JOHNSON, D. H. 1995. Point counts of birds: What are we estimating? Pp. 117–123 in C. J. Ralph, J. Sauer, and S. Droege (editors). Monitoring bird populations by point counts. General Technical Report PSW-GTR-149. USDA Forest Service, Albany, CA.

JOHNSON, D. H., AND A. B. SARGEANT. 1977. Impact of red fox predation on the sex ratio of prairie Mallards. Wildlife Report 6. U.S. Fish and Wildlife Service, Washington, D.C.

JOHNSON, K. P., AND M. D. SORENSON. 1998. Comparing molecular evolution in two mitochondrial protein coding genes (Cytochrome b and ND2) in the dabbling ducks (Tribe: Anatini). Molecular Phylogenetics and Evolution 10:82–94.

JOHNSON, N. K., J. A. MARTEN, AND C. J. RALPH. 1989. Genetic evidence for the origin and relationships of Hawaiian honeycreepers (Aves: Fringillidae). Condor 91:379–396.

JOHNSON, O. W., AND P. M. JOHNSON. 1993. Counts of Pacific Golden-plovers (Pluvialis fulva) wintering on O'ahu golf courses, 1992. 'Elepaio 53:39–43.

JOHNSON, R. R., B. T. BROWN, L. T. HAIGHT, AND J. M. SIMPSON. 1981. Playback recordings as a special avian censusing technique. Studies in Avian Biology 6: 68–75.

JOHNSON, T. C., C. A. SCHOLZ, M. R. TALBOT, K. KELTS, R. D. RICKETTS, G. NGOBI, K. BEUNING, I. SSEMMANDA, AND J. W. MCGILL. 1996. Late Pleistocene desiccation of Lake Victoria and rapid evolution of cichlid fishes. Science 273:1091–1093.

JOHNSTON, J. P., W. J. PEACH, R. D. GREGORY, AND S. A. WHITE. 1997. Survival rates of tropical and temperate passerines: a Trinidadian perspective. American Naturalist 150:771–789.

JOHNSTON, R. F., AND R. K. SELANDER. 1964. House Sparrows: rapid evolution of races in North America. Science 144:548–550.

JOHNSTONE, G. W. 1985. Threats to birds on subantarctic islands. Pp. 101–121 in P. J. Moors (editor). Conservation of island birds. International Council for Bird Preservation Technical Publication No. 3. Cambridge, UK.

JUDD, C. S. 1936. Hawaii's forests winning their battle with wild animals. Honolulu Star Bulletin March 21 3rd section. Pp. 1, 7.

JUVIK, J. O., AND A. P. AUSTRING. 1979. The Hawaiian avifauna: biogeographic theory in evolutionary time. Journal of Biogeography 6:205–224.

JUVIK, J. O., AND S. P. JUVIK. 1984. Mauna Kea and the myth of multiple use: endangered species and mountain management in Hawaii. Mountain Research and Development 4:191–202.

JUVIK, J. O., AND D. NULLET. 1993. Relationships between rainfall, cloud-water interception, and canopy throughfall in a Hawaiian montane forest. Pp. 102–113 in L. S. Hamilton, J. O. Juvik, and F. N. Scatena (editors). Tropical montane cloud forests. East-West Center, Honolulu, HI.

JUVIK, J. O., D. NULLET, P. BANKO, AND K. HUGHES. 1993. Forest climatology near the tree line in Hawaii. Agricultural and Forest Meteorology 66:159–172.

KAHIOLO, G. W. 1863. Ka Nupepa kuokoa. H.M. Whitney 1861–1891, Honolulu, Hawaii

KAIN, K. C., A. E. BROWN, L. MIRABELLI, AND H. K. WEBSTER. 1993. Detection of Plasmodium vivax by polymerase chain reaction in a field study. Journal of Infectious Diseases 168:1323–1326.

KAISER, H. 1992. The trade-mediated introduction of Eleutherodactylus martinicensis (Anura: Leptodactylidae) on St. Barthélémy, French Antilles, and its implications for Lesser Antillean biogeography. Journal of Herpetology 26:264–273.

KAKESAKO, G. K. 1997. Hawaiians, Marines win with construction of walls. Honolulu Star-Bulletin, February 21:A-6.

KAMI, H. T. 1964. Foods of the mongoose on the Hamakua Coast. Zoonoses Research 3:165–170.

KANEOHE BAY TASK FORCE. 1997. Kaneohe Bay Regional Council evaluation, a report to the Nineteenth Legislature of the State of Hawaii regular session of 1988. Office of Planning, State of Hawaii, Honolulu, HI.

KARL, B. J., AND H. A. BEST. 1982. Feral cats on Stewart Island, their foods and their effects on kakapo. New Zealand Journal of Zoology 9:287–294.

KARR, J. R., J. D. NICHOLS, M. K. KLIMKIEWICZ, AND J. D. BRAWN. 1990. Survival rates of birds of tropical and temperate forests: will the dogma survive? American Naturalist 136:277–291.

KARR, J. R., AND R. R. ROTH. 1971. Vegetation structure and avian diversity in several New World areas. American Naturalist 105:423–435.

KARSTAD, L. 1971a. Arboviruses. Pp. 17–21 in J. W. Davis, R. C. Anderson, L. Karstad, and D. O. Trainer (editors). Infections and parasitic diseases of wild birds. Iowa State University Press, Ames, IA.

KARSTAD, L. 1971b. Pox. Pp. 34–41 in J. W. Davis, R. C. Anderson, L. Karstad, and D. O. Trainer (editors). Infections and parasitic diseases of wild birds. Iowa State University Press, Ames, IA.

KATAHIRA, L. K., P. FINNEGAN, AND C. P. STONE. 1993. Eradicating pigs in montane mesic habitat at Hawaii Volcanoes National Park. Wildlife Society Bulletin 21:269–274.

KAUAHIKAUA, J., S. MARGRITER, J. LOCKWOOD, AND F. TRUSDELL. 1995. Applications of GIS to the estimation of lava flow hazards on Mauna Loa Volcano, Hawaii. Pp. 315–325 in J. M. Rhodes and J. P. Lockwood (editors). Mauna Loa revealed: structure, composition, history, and hazards. Geophysical Monograph 92. American Geophysical Union, Washington, D.C.

KAUFMAN, J., S. MILNE, T. W. F. GÖBEL, B. A. WALKER, J. P. JACOB, C. AUFFRAY, R. ZOOROB, AND S. BECK. 1999. The chicken B locus is a minimal essential major histocompatability complex. Nature 401:923–925.

KAUFMAN, J., AND H. J. WALLNEY. 1996. Chicken MHC molecules, disease resistance and the evolutionary origin of birds. Current Topics in Microbiology and Immunology 212:129–141.

KEAR, J., AND A. J. BERGER. 1980. The Hawaiian Goose: an experiment in conservation. Buteo Books, Vermillion, SD.

KEEPER OF THE NATIONAL REGISTER. 1984. Determination of eligibility notification, Mōkapu Peninsula Fishpond Complex (Nuʻupia Ponds). Prepared by Keeper of the National Register, National Park Service, August 8, 1984.

KEMP, R. L., AND W. T. SPRINGER. 1978. Histomoniasis. Pp. 832–840 in M. S. Hofstad, B. W. Calnek, C. F. Helmboldt, W. M. Reid, and H. W. Yoder, Jr. (editors). Diseases of Poultry. Iowa State University Press. Ames, IA.

KENNEDY, E. D. 1991. Predicting clutch size of the House Wren with the Murray-Nolan equation. Auk 108:728–731.

KENT, J. A., AND K. PREISTER. 1997. Social ecology: a new pathway to ecosystem restoration. Pp. 28–48 in J. E. Williams, C. A. Wood, and M. P. Dombeck (editors). Watershed restoration: principles and practices. American Fisheries Society, Bethesda, MD.

KEPLER, C. B. 1967. Polynesian rat predation on nesting Laysan Albatross and other Pacific seabirds. Auk 84: 426–430.

KEPLER, C. B. 1985. Current and future roles of agencies, conservation groups, legislature, and the public in preserving and managing Hawaiian ecosystems: a summary. Pp. 483–492 in C. P. Stone and J. M. Scott (editors). Hawaiʻi's terrestrial ecosystems: preservation and management. Cooperative National Parks Research Studies Unit, University of Hawaii, Honolulu, HI.

KEPLER, C. B., AND A. K. KEPLER. 1983. A first record of nest and chicks of the Small Kauai Thrush. Condor 85:497–499.

KEPLER, C. B., T. K. PRATT, A. M. ECTON, A. ENGILIS, JR., AND K. M. FLUETSCH. 1996. Nesting behavior of the Poo-uli. Wilson Bulletin 108:620–638.

KEPLER, C. B., AND J. M. SCOTT. 1981. Reducing count variability by training observers. Studies in Avian Biology 6:366–371.

KETTLE, D. S. 1965. Biting ceratopogonids as vectors of human and animal diseases. Acta Tropica 22:356–362.

KHOO, A., T. FURUTA, N. R. ABDULLAH, N. A. BAH, S. KOJIMA, AND W. J. WAH. 1996. Nested polymerase chain reaction for detection of Plasmodium falciparum infection in Malaysia. Transactions of the Royal Society of Tropical Medicine and Hygiene 90:40–41.

KIKKAWA, J. 1977. Ecological paradoxes. Australian Journal of Ecology 2:121–136.

KIMURA, M. 1980. A simple method for estimating evolutionary rates of base substitution through comparative studies of nucleotide sequences. Journal of Molecular Evolution 16:111–120.

KING, W. B. 1984. Incidental mortality of seabirds in gillnets in the North Pacific. Pp. 709–716 in J. P. Croxall, P. G. H. Evans, and R. W. Schreiber (editors). Status and conservation of the world's seabirds. International Council for Bird Preservation Technical Publication No. 2. Cambridge, UK.

KING, W. B. 1985. Island birds: will the future repeat the past? Pp. 3–15 in P. J. Moors (editor). Conservation of island birds. International Council for Bird Preservation Technical Publication No. 3. Cambridge, UK.

KING, W. B., AND P. J. GOULD. 1967. The status of Newell's race of the Manx Shearwater. Living Bird 6:163–186.

KIRCH, J. F. 1913. The indigenous trees of the Hawaiian Islands. Published Privately, Honolulu, HI.

KIRCH, P. V. 1974. The chronology of early Hawaiian settlement. Archaelogy and Physical Anthropology in Oceania 9:110–119.

KIRCH, P. V. 1979. Marine exploitation in prehistoric Hawaii: archaeological investigations at Kalahuipuaʻa, Hawaii Island. Pacific Anthropological Records No. 29. Department of Anthropology, B. P. Bishop Museum, Honolulu, HI.

KIRCH, P. V. 1982a. The impact of the prehistoric Polynesians on the Hawaiian ecosystem. Pacific Science 36:1–14.

KIRCH, P. V. 1982b. Advances in Polynesain prehistory: three decades in review. Advance in World Archaelogy 1:51–97.

KIRCH, P. V. 1985. Feathered gods and fishhooks: an introduction to Hawaiian archaeology and prehistory. University of Hawaii Press, Honolulu, HI.

KIRCH, P. V., AND T. L. HUNT. 1997. Historical ecology in the Pacific Islands: prehistoric environmental and landscape change. Yale University Press, New Haven, CT.

KIRCH, P. V., AND M. KELLY (EDITORS). 1975. Prehistory and ecology in a windward Hawaiian valley: Halawa Valley, Molokai. Pacific Anthropological Records 24. Department of Anthropology, B. P. Bishop Museum, Honolulu, HI.

KIRCH, P. V., D. W. STEADMAN, V. L. BUTLER, J. HATHER, AND M. I. WEISLER. 1995. Pre-history and human ecology in Eastern Polynesia: excavations at Tangatatau Rockshelter, Mangaia, Cook Islands. Archeological Oceania 30:47–65.

KIRMSE, P. 1967. Host specificity and long persistence of pox infection in the flicker (Colaptes auratus). Journal of Wildlife Diseases 3:14–20.

KITAOKA, S. 1978. Serological diagnosis of chicken leucocytozoonosis. Japanese Agricultural Research Quarterly 12:157–162.

KITAOKA, S., AND T. MORII. 1963. Observations on the breeding habitats of some biting midges and seasonal population dynamics in the life cycle of Culicoides arakawae in Tokyo and its vicinity. National Institute of Animal Health Quarterly 3:198–208.

KITAYAMA, K., AND D. MUELLER-DOMBOIS. 1992. Vegetation of the wet windward slope of Haleakala, Maui, Hawaii. Pacific Science 46:197–220.

KLEIN, J. 1986. Natural history of the major histocompatibility complex. John Wiley and Sons, New York, NY.

KLEIN, J., AND C. OʻHUIGIN. 1994. MHC polymorphism and parasites. Philosophical Transactions of the Royal Society of London, Series B 346:351–358.

KLICKA, J., AND R. M. ZINK. 1997. The importance of

recent ice ages in speciation: a failed paradigm. Science 277:1666–1669.

KLOMP, H. 1970. The determination of clutch-size in birds: a review. Ardea 58:1–124.

KLOMP, H. 1980. Fluctuations and stability in Great Tit populations. Ardea 68:205–224.

KOCHER, T. D, W. K. THOMAS, A. MEYER, S, V. EDWARDS, S. PÄÄBO, F. X. VILLABLANCA, AND A. C. WILSON. 1989. Dynamics of mitochondrial DNA evolution in animals: amplification and sequencing with conserved primers. Proceedings of the National Academy of Sciences (USA) 86:6196–6200.

KÖHLER, S., C. F. DELWICHE, P. W. DENNY, L. G. TILNEY, P. WEBSTER, R. J. M. WILSON, J. D. PALMER, AND D. S. ROOS. 1997. A plastid of probable green algal origin in apicomplexan parasites. Science 275: 1485–1489.

KOMDEUR, J. 1992. Importance of habitat saturation and territory quality for evolution of cooperative breeding in the Seychelles Warbler. Nature 358:493–495.

KOMDEUR, J. 1994a. Conserving the Seychelles Warbler Acrocephalus sechellensis by translocation from Cousin Island to the islands of Aride and Cousine. Biological Conservation 67:143–152.

KOMDEUR, J. 1994b. Experimental evidence for helping and hindering by previous offspring in the cooperative breeding Seychelles Warbler (Acrocephalus sechellensis). Behavioural Ecology and Sociobiology 34:175–186.

KOMDEUR, J. 1996. Seasonal timing of reproduction in a tropical bird, the Seychelles Warbler: a field experiment using translocation. Journal of Biological Rhythms 11:333–346.

KOMDEUR, J. 1997. Interisland transfers and population dynamics of Seychelles Warblers Acrocephalus sechellensis. Bird Conservation International 7:69–80.

KOMDEUR, J., I. D. BULLOCK, AND M. R. W. RANDS. 1991. Conserving the Seychelles Warbler Acrocephalus sechellensis by translocation: a transfer from Cousin Island to Aride Island. Bird Conservation International 1:177–185.

KOMDEUR, J., S. DAAN, J. TINBERGEN, AND C. MATEMAN. 1997. Extreme adaptive modification in sex ratio of the Seychelles Warbler's eggs. Nature 385: 522–525.

KOMDEUR, J., A. HUFFSTADT, W. PRAST, G. CASTLE, R. MILETO, AND J. WATTEL. 1995. Transfer experiments of Seychelles Warblers to new islands: changes in dispersal and helping behaviour. Animal Behaviour 49:695–708.

KOZLOWSKI, T. T., AND S. G. PALLARDY. 1997a. Physiology of woody plants. 2nd edition. Academic Press, San Diego, CA.

KOZLOWSKI, T. T., AND S. G. PALLARDY. 1997b. Growth control in woody plants. Academic Press, San Diego, CA.

KRAJEWSKI, C. 1994. Phylogenetic measures of biodiversity: a comparison and critique. Biological Conservation 69:33–39.

KRAJEWSKI, C., AND D. G. KING. 1996. Molecular divergence and phylogeny: rates and patterns of cytochrome b evolution in cranes. Molecular Biology Evolution 13:21–30.

KRAMER, R. J. 1971. Hawaiian land mammals. Charles E. Tuttle Company Inc., Rutland, VT.

KRAUS, F., E.W. CAMPBELL, A. ALLISON, AND T. PRATT. 1999. Eleutherodactylus frog introductions to Hawaii. Herpetology Review 30:21–25.

KROLL, J. C., K. A. ARNOLD, AND R. F. GOTIE. 1973. An observation of predation by native fire ants on nestling Barn Swallows. Wilson Bulletin 85:478–479.

KUEHLER, C. M., AND J. GOOD. 1990. Artificial incubation of bird eggs at the Zoological Society of San Diego. International Zoo Yearbook 29:118–136.

KUEHLER, C. M., P. HARRITY, A. LIEBERMAN, AND M. KUHN. 1995. Reintroduction of hand-reared Alala Corvus hawaiiensis in Hawaii. Oryx 29:261–266.

KUEHLER, C. M., M. KUHN, J. E. KUHN, A. LIEBERMAN, N. HARVEY, AND B. RIDEOUT. 1996. Artificial incubation hand-rearing, behavior, and release of Common 'Amakihi (Hemignathus virens virens): surrogate research for restoration of endangered Hawaiian forest birds. Zoo Biology 15:541–553.

KUEHLER, C. M., M. KUHN, B. MCILRAITH, AND G. CAMPBELL. 1994. Artificial incubation and handrearing of 'Alalā (Corvus hawaiiensis) eggs removed from the wild. Zoo Biology 13:257–266.

KUEHLER, C. M., A. LIEBERMAN, B. MCILRAITH, W. EVERETT, T. A. SCOTT, M. L. MORRISON, AND C. WINCHELL. 1993. Artificial incubation and hand-rearing of Loggerhead Shrikes. Wildlife Society Bulletin 21: 165–171.

KUEHLER, C. M., A. LIEBERMAN, A. VARNEY, P. UNITT, R. M. SULPICE, J. AZUA, AND B. TEHEVINI. 1997. Translocation of Ultramarine Lories (Vini ultramarina) in the Marquesas Islands: Ua Huka to Fatu Hiva. Bird Conservation International 7:69–79.

KUEHLER, C. M., AND P. WITMAN. 1988. Artificial incubation of California Condor (Gymnogyps californianus) eggs removed from the wild. Zoo Biology 7:123–132.

KUMAR, S., K. TAMURA, AND M. NEI. 1993. MEGA: molecular evolutionary genetics analysis. Version 1.02. Pennsylvania State University, University Park, PA.

KURODA, N. 1961. The over-sea crossings of land birds in the western Pacific. Yamashina Institute for Ornithology and Zoology 3:47–53.

LA RIVERS, I. 1948. Some Hawaiian ecological notes. Wasmann Collector 7:85–110.

LAAKE, J. L., S. T. BUCKLAND, D. R. ANDERSON, AND K. P. BURNHAM. 1994. DISTANCE user's guide. Version 2.1. Colorado Cooperative Fish and Wildlife Research Unit, Colorado State University, Fort Collins, CO.

LACK, D. 1947. The significance of clutch-size. Parts I and II. Ibis 89:302–352.

LACK, D. 1948. The significance of clutch-size. Part III. Ibis 90:25–45.

LACK, D. 1954. The natural regulation of animal numbers. Clarendon Press, Oxford, UK.

LACK, D. 1966. Population studies of birds. Oxford University Press, London, UK.

LACK, D. 1968. Ecological adaptations for breeding in birds. Methuen, London, UK.

LACY, R. C. 1993. Vortex: a computer simulation model for population viability analysis. Wildlife Research 20:45–65.

LACY, R. C., K. A. HUGHES, AND P. S. MILLER. 1995. VORTEX: A stochastic simulation of the extinction process. Version 7 User's Manual. IUCN/SSC Conservation Breeding Specialist Group, Apple Valley, MN.

LAIRD, M., AND C. VAN RIPER, III. 1981. Questionable reports of *Plasmodium* from birds in Hawaii, with the recognition of *P. relictum* ssp. *capistranoae* (Russell, 1932) as the avian malarial parasite there. Pp. 159–165 *in* E. V. Canning (editor). Parasitological Topics, Special Publication No. 1. Society of Protozoologists.

LAMMERS, T. G., AND C. E. FREEMAN. 1986. Ornithophily among the Hawaiian Lobeliodeae (Campanulacae): evidence from floral nectar sugar compositions. American Journal of Botany 73:1613–1619.

LAMONT, S. J., C. BOLIN, AND N. CHEVILLE. 1987. Genetic resistance to fowl cholera is linked to the major histocompatibility complex. Immunogenetics 25:284–289.

LANDE, R. 1988. Genetics and demography in biological conservation. Science 241:1455–1460.

LANDE, R. 1995. Mutation and conservation. Conservation Biology 9:782–791.

LANDE, R., AND G. F. BARROWCLOUGH. 1987. Effective population size, genetic variation, and their use in population management. Pp. 87–123 *in* M. E. Soulé (editor). Viable populations for conservation. Cambridge University Press, New York, NY.

LAYNE, J. N. 1997. Nonindigenous mammals. Pp. 157–186 *in* D. Simberloff, D. C. Schmitz, and T. C. Brown (editors). Strangers in paradise: impact and management of nonindigenous species in Florida. Island Press, Washington, D.C.

LEISHMAN, N. J. 1986. Fulvous Whistling-ducks breeding in Hawaii: a new indigene or another exotic? 'Elepaio 46:75–76.

LEPSON, J. K. 1997. 'Anianiau (*Hemignathus parvus*). *In* A. Poole and F. Gill (editors). The Birds of North America, No. 312. The Academy of Natural Sciences, Philadelphia, PA, and American Ornithologists' Union, Washington, D.C.

LEPSON, J. K., AND L. A. FREED. 1995. Variation in male plumage and behavior of the Hawaii Akepa. Auk 112:402–414.

LEPSON, J. K., AND L. A. FREED. 1997. 'Ākepa (*Loxops coccineus*). *In* A. Poole and F. Gill (editors). The Birds of North America, No. 294. The Academy of Natural Sciences, Philadelphia, PA, and American Ornithologists' Union, Washington, D.C.

LEPSON, J. K., AND S. M. JOHNSTON. 2000. Greater 'Akialoa (*Hemignathus ellisianus*) and Lesser 'Akialoa (*Hemignathus obscurus*). *In* A. Poole and F. Gill (editors). The Birds of North America, No. 512. The Academy of Natural Sciences, Philadelphia, PA, and American Ornithologists' Union, Washington, D.C.

LEPSON, J. K., AND H. D. PRATT. 1997. 'Akeke'e (*Loxops caeruleirostris*). *In* A. Poole and F. Gill (editors). The Birds of North America, No. 295. The Academy of Natural Sciences, Philadelphia, PA, and American Ornithologists' Union, Washington, D.C.

LESLIE, M., G. K. MEFFE, J. L. HARDESTY, AND D. L. ADAMS. 1996. Conserving biodiversity on military lands: a handbook for natural resource managers. The Nature Conservancy, Arlington, VA.

LESLIE, P. H. 1945. On the use of certain matrices in population mathematics. Biometrika 33:183–212.

LEVER, C. 1987. Naturalized birds of the world. Longman Science and Technology, Essex, England.

LEVINE, N. D. 1980. Nematode parasites of domestic animals and man. Burgess Publishing Company, Minneapolis, MN.

LEVINE, N. D. 1988. Blood parasites: the malaria and related parasites. Pp. 11–34 *in* N. D. Levine (editor). The protozoan phylum apicomplexa. Vol. 2. CRC Press, Boca Raton, FL.

LEVITON, A. E. 1965. Contributions to a review of Philippine snakes, VIII. The snakes of the genus *Lycodon* H. Boie. Philippine Journal of Science 94:117–140.

LEWIN, V. 1971. Exotic game birds of the Puu Waawaa Ranch, Hawaii. Journal of Wildlife Management 35:141–155.

LEWIN, V., AND J. C. HOLMES. 1971. Helminths from the exotic game birds of the Puuwaawaa Ranch, Hawaii. Pacific Science 25:372–381.

LEWIN, V., AND G. LEWIN. 1984. The Kalij Pheasant, a newly established game bird on the island of Hawaii. Wilson Bulletin 96:634–646.

LEWIN, V., AND J. L. MAHRT. 1983. Parasites of Kalij Pheasants (*Lophura leucomelana*) on the island of Hawaii. Pacific Science 37:81–83.

LIEBERMAN, A., C. KUEHLER, A. VARNEY, P. UNITT, R. M. SULPICE, J. AZUA, AND B. TEHEVINI. 1997. A note on the 1997 survey of the translocated Ultramarine Lory (*Vini ultramarina*) population on Fatu Hiva, Marquesas Islands, French Polynesia. Bird Conservation International 7:291–292.

LIGON, J. D., AND P. B. STACEY. 1996. Land use, lag times and the detection of demographic change: the case of the Acorn Woodpecker. Conservation Biology 10:840–846.

LINDENMAYER, D. B., M. A. BURGMAN, H. R. AKÇAKAYA, R. C. LACY, AND H. P. POSSINGHAM. 1995. A review of the generic computer programs ALEX, RAMAS/Space and VORTEX for modelling the viability of wildlife metapopulations. Ecological Modeling 82:161–174.

LINDENMAYER, D. B., R. B. CUNNINGHAM, C. F. DONNELLY, M. T. TANTON, AND H. A. NIX. 1993. The abundance and development of cavities in *Eucalyptus* trees: a case study in the montane forests of Victoria, southeastern Australia. Forest Ecology and Management 60: 77–104.

LINDENMAYER, D. B., R. B. CUNNINGHAM, H. A. NIX, M. T. TANTON, AND A. P. SMITH. 1991a. Predicting the abundance of hollow-bearing trees in montane forest of southeastern Australia. Australian Journal of Ecology 16:91–98.

LINDENMAYER, D. B., R. B. CUNNINGHAM, M. T. TANTON, A. P. SMITH, AND H. A. NIX. 1991b. Characteristics of hollow-bearing trees occupied by arboreal marsupials in the montane ash forests of the Central Highlands of Victoria, south-east Australia. Forest Ecology and Management 40:289–308.

LINDSEY, G. D., S. G. FANCY, M. H. REYNOLDS, T. K. PRATT, K. A. WILSON, P. C. BANKO, AND J. D. JACOBI.

1995a. Population structure and survival of Palila. Condor 97:528–535.

LINDSEY, G. D., K. A. WILSON, AND C. HERRMANN. 1995b. Color change in Hughes's celluloid leg bands. Journal Field Ornithology 66:289–295.

LINDSEY, G. D., S. M. MOSHER, S. G. FANCY, AND T. D. SMUCKER. 1999. Population structure and movements of introduced rats in an Hawaiian rain forest. Pacific Conservation Biology 5:94–102.

LINDSEY, G. D., T. K. PRATT, M. H. REYNOLDS, AND J. D. JACOBI. 1997. Response of six species of Hawaiian forest birds to a 1991–1992 El Nino drought. Wilson Bulletin 109:339–343.

LINDSEY, G. D., E. A. VANDERWERF, H. BAKER, AND P. E. BAKER. 1998. Hawai'i (*Hemignathus virens*), Kaua'i (*Hemignathus kauaiensis*), O'ahu (*Hemignathus chloris*), and Greater 'Amakihi (*Hemignathus sagittirostris*). *In* A. Poole and F. Gill (editors). The Birds of North America, No. 360. The Academy of Natural Sciences, Philadelpia, PA, and American Ornithologists' Union, Washington, D.C.

LINLEY, J. R., AND J. B. DAVIES. 1971. Sandflies and tourism in Florida and the Bahamas and Caribbean area. Journal of Economic Entomology 64:264–278.

LITVINENKO, N. M. 1993. Effects of disturbance by people and introduced predators on seabirds in the northwest Pacific. Pp. 227–231 *in* K. T Vermeer, K. T. Briggs, K. H. Morgan, and D. Siegele-Cavsey (editors). The status, ecology, and conservation of marine birds of the north Pacific. Canadian Wildlife Service, Ottawa, Ontario.

LIVEZEY, B. C. 1991. A phylogenetic analysis and classification of recent dabbling ducks (tribe Anatini) based on comparative morphology. Auk 108:471–507.

LIVEZEY, B. C. 1993. Comparative morphometrics of *Anas* ducks, with particular reference to the Hawaiian Duck *Anas wyvilliana*, Laysan Duck *A. laysanensis*, and Eaton's Pintail *A. eatoni*. Wildfowl 44:75–100.

LIVEZEY, B. C. 1996. A phylogenetic analysis of geese and swans (Anseriformes: Anserinae), including selected fossil species. Systematic Biology 45:415–450.

LOCKLEY, T. C. 1995. Effect of imported fire ant predation on a population of the least tern—an endangered species. Southwestern Entomologist 20:517–519.

LOCKRIDGE, P. A., AND R. H. SMITH. 1984. Tsunamis in the Pacific Basin, 1900–1983. National Geophysical Data Center, Boulder, CO.

LOEW, S., AND R. C. FLEISCHER. 1996. Multilocus DNA fingerprinting. Pp. 456–461 *in* J. D. Ferraris and S. R. Palumbi (editors). Molecular zoology: advances, strategies and protocols. Wiley-Liss, New York, NY.

LOISELLE, B. A., AND J. G. BLAKE. 1991. Temporal variation in birds and fruits along an elevational gradient in Costa Rica. Ecology 72:180–193.

LONG, J. L. 1981. Introduced birds of the world. A. H. and A. W. Reed, Sydney, Australia.

LONGENECKER, B. M., AND T. R. MOSSMAN. 1981. Nomenclature for chicken MHC (*B*) antigens defined by monoclonal antibodies. Immunogenetics 13:25–28.

LONGENECKER, B. M., F. PAZDERKA, J. S. GAVORA, J.

L. SPENCER, AND R. F. RUTH. 1976. Lymphoma induced by Herpesvirus: resistance associated with a major histocompatibility gene. Immunogenetics 3:401–407.

LONGENECKER, B. M., F. PAZDERKA, G. R. LAW, AND R. F. RUTH. 1972. Genetic control of graft-versus-host competence. Transplantation 14:424–431.

LOOPE, L. L. 1997. The Hawaiian islands as a laboratory for addressing alien species problems. Pp. 259–260 *in* G. Meffe and R. Carroll (editors). Principles of conservation biology. 2nd edition. Sinauer Associates, Inc. Sunderland, MA.

LOOPE, L. L, O. HAMANN, AND C. P. STONE. 1988. Comparative conservation biology of oceanic archipelagoes: Hawaii and the Galápagos. BioScience 38:272–282.

LOOPE, L. L., AND A. C. MEDEIROS. 1994. Impacts of biological invasions on the management and recovery of rare plants in Haleakala National Park, Maui, Hawaiian Islands. Pp. 143–158 *in* M. Bowles and C. J. Whelan (editors). Restoration of endangered species. Cambridge University Press, Cambridge, UK.

LOOPE, L. L., A. C. MEDEIROS, W. MINYARD, S. JESSEL, AND W. EVANSON. 1992. Strategies to prevent establishment of feral rabbits on Maui, Hawaii. Pacific Science 46:402–403.

LOOPE, L. L., AND D. MUELLER-DOMBOIS. 1989. Characteristics of invaded islands. Pp. 257–280 *in* J.A. Drake, H. Aimoney, F. di Castri, R. H. Anoves, F. J. Kruger, M. Rejmanek, and M. Williamson (editors). Biological invasions: a global perspective. John Wiley and Sons, Chichester, UK.

LOOPE, L. L., AND C. P. STONE. 1996. Strategies to reduce erosion of biodiversity by exotic terrestrial species. Pp. 261–279 *in* R. C. Szaro and D. W. Johnston (editors). Biodiversity in managed landscapes: theory and practice. Oxford University Press, New York, NY.

LOVERIDGE, A. 1945. Reptiles of the Pacific world. MacMillan Publishing Co., New York, NY.

LOYE, J., AND S. CARROLL. 1995. Birds, bugs and blood: avian parasitism and conservation. Trends in Ecology and Evolution 10:232–235.

LWANGA, S. K., AND S. LEMESHOW. 1991. Sample size determination in health studies. World Health Organization, Geneva, Switzerland.

LYNCH, M. 1988. Estimation of relatedness by DNA fingerprinting. Molecular Biology and Evolution 5:584–589.

LYNCH, M. 1996. A quantitative-genetic perspective on conservation issues. Pp. 471–489 *in* J. C. Avise and J. L. Hamrick (editors). Conservation genetics: case histories from nature. Chapman and Hall, New York, NY.

LYNCH, M., AND R. LANDE. 1998. The critical effective size for a genetically secure population. Animal Conservation 1:70–72.

LYON, H. L. 1918. The forests of Hawaii. Hawaii Planters Record 20:276–281.

LYONS, S. W. 1979. Summer weather on Haleakala, Maui. University of Hawaii, Department of Meteorology, UHMET 79–09.

MABEN, A. F. 1982. The feeding ecology of the Black

Drongo *Dicrurus macrocercus* on Guam. M.S. thesis. California State University, Long Beach, CA.

MACARTHUR, R. H. 1972. Geographical ecology: patterns in the distribution of species. Harper and Row, New York, NY.

MACARTHUR, R. H., AND E. O. WILSON. 1967a. The theory of island biogeography. Princeton University Press, Princeton, NJ.

MACARTHUR, R. H., AND E. O. WILSON. 1967b. An equilibrium theory of insular zoogeography. Evolution 17:373–387.

MACCAUGHEY, V. 1919. The Hawaiian Elepaio. Auk 36:22–35.

MACDONALD, I. A. W., L. L. LOOPE, M. B. USHER, AND O. HAMANN. 1989. Wildlife conservation and the invasion of nature reserves by introduced species: a global perspective. Pp. 215–255 *in* J.A. Drake, H. Aimoney, F. di Castri, R. H. Anoves, F. J. Kruger, M. Rejmanek, and M. Williamson (editors). Biological invasions: a global perspective. John Wiley and Sons, Chichester, UK.

MACE, G. M., AND R. LANDE. 1991. Assessing extinction threats: towards a reevaluation of IUCN threatened species categories. Conservation Biology 5: 148–157.

MACKOWSKI, C. M. 1984. The ontogeny of hollows in Blackbutt, *Eucalyptus pilularis,* and its relevance to the management of forests for possums, gliders, and timber. Pp. 517–525 *in* A. P. Smith and I. D. Hume (editors). Possums and gliders. Surrey Beatty and Sons, Sydney, Australia.

MACMILLEN, R. E., AND F. L. CARPENTER. 1980. Evening roosting flights of the honeycreepers *Himatione sanguinea* and *Vestiaria coccinea* on Hawaii. Auk 97:28–37.

MADDISON, W. P., AND D. R. MADDISON. 1992. MacClade, Release Version 3.01. Sinauer Associates, Sunderland, MA.

MALE, T. D., AND T. J. SNETSINGER. 1998. Has the Redbilled Leiothrix disappeared from Kaua'i? 'Elepaio 58:39–43.

MALO, D., AND E. SKAMENE. 1994. Genetic control of host resistance to infection. Trends in Genetics 10: 365–371.

MALY, K., R. R. RECHTMAN, AND P. H. ROSENDAHL. 1997. Guidance for the preparation of a community caretaker/partnership plan for cultural resources stewardship at Marine Corps Base Hawaii. Final report. Prepared by Paul H. Rosendahl, Ph.D., Inc. (PHRI), Hilo, HI.

MALY, K., AND P. H. ROSENDAHL. 1995. Mokapu Peninsula oral history study, Pu'u Hawaii Loa family housing project site, Marine Corps Base Hawaii, Lands of He'eia and Kane'ohe, Island of Oa'hu. Final report. Prepared by Paul H. Rosendahl, Ph.D., Inc. (PHRI), Hilo, HI.

MANLY, B. F. J. 1992. The design and analysis of research studies. Cambridge University Press, New York, NY.

MARCHANT, S. 1960. The breeding of some S.W. Ecuadorian birds. Ibis 102:349–382; 584–599.

MARCSTRÖM, V., R. E. KENWARD, AND E. ENGREN. 1988. The impact of predation on boreal tetraonids during vole cycles: an experimental study. Journal of Animal Ecology 57:859–872.

MARKIN, G. P. 1970. Food distribution within laboratory colonies of the Argentine ant, *Iridomyrmex humilis* (Mayr). Insectes Sociaux 17:127–158.

MARSHALL, H. D., AND A. J. BAKER. 1997. Structural conservation and variation in the mitochondrial control region of fringilline finches (*Fringilla* spp.) and the greenfinch (*Carduelis chloris*). Molecular Biology and Evolution 14:173–84.

MARTIN, A. P., AND S. R. PALUMBI. 1993. Body size, metabolic rate, generation time, and the molecular clock. Proceedings of the National Academy of Sciences (USA) 90:4087–4091.

MARTIN, C. M. 1994. Recovering endangered species and restoring ecosystems: conservation planning for the twenty-first century in the United States. Ibis 137:S198-S203.

MARTIN, P. W., AND P. BATESON. 1986. Measuring behaviour. An introductory guide. Cambridge University Press, Cambridge, UK.

MARTIN, P. W., AND M. T. MYRES. 1969. Observations on the distribution and migration of some seabirds off the outer coasts of British Columbia and Washington State, 1946–1949. Syesis 2:241–256.

MARTIN, T. E. 1987. Food as a limit on breeding birds: a life-history perspective. Annual Review of Ecology and Systematics 18:453–487.

MARTIN, T. E. 1988. Habitat and area effects on forest bird assemblages: is nest predation an influence? Ecology 69:74–84.

MARTIN, T. E. 1992a. Breeding productivity considerations: what are the appropriate habitat features for management? Pp. 455–473 *in* J. M. Hagen, III, and D. W. Johnston (editors). Ecology and conservation of Neotropical migrant landbirds. Smithsonian Institution Press, Washington, D.C.

MARTIN, T. E. 1992b. Interaction of nest predation and food limitation in reproductive strategies. Current Ornithology 9:163–197.

MARTIN, T. E. 1993. Nest predation among vegetation layers and habitat types: revising the dogmas. American Naturalist 141:897–913.

MARTIN, T. E. 1995. Avian life history evolution in relation to nest sites, nest predation, and food. Ecological Monographs 65:101–127.

MARTIN, T. E., AND G. R. GUEPEL. 1993. Nest-monitoring plots: methods for locating nests and monitoring success. Journal Field Ornithology 64:507–519.

MASCIE-TAYLOR, C. G. N. 1993. The biological anthropology of disease. Pp. 1–72 *in* C. G. N. Mascie-Taylor (editor). The anthropology of disease. Oxford University Press, New York, NY.

MATTHECK, C. 1991. Trees: the mechanical design. Springer-Verlag, New York, NY.

MAYFIELD, H. F. 1975. Suggestions for calculating nest success. Wilson Bulletin 87:456–466.

MAYR, E. 1927. Die Schneefinken (Gattungen *Montifringilla* und *Leucosticte*). Journ Fur Ornithologic 75: 596–619.

MAYR, E. 1942a. Systematics and the origin of species. Columbia University Press, New York, NY.

MAYR, E. 1942b. [Review of] Speciation in the avian genus *Junco,* by A. H. Miller. Ecology 23:378–379.

MAYR, E. 1943. The zoogeographic position of the Hawaiian Islands. Condor 45:45–48.

MAYR, E. 1945. Birds of the southwest Pacific. The Macmillan Co., New York, NY.

MAYR, E. 1953. On the origin of bird migration in the Pacific. Pp 387–393 in Proceedings of the Seventh Pacific Science Congress. Vol. 4. Whitcomb and Tombs, Auckland, New Zealand.

MAYR, E. 1963. Animal species and evolution. Belknap Press, Cambridge, MA.

MAYR, E. 1969. Principles of systematic zoology. McGraw-Hill Book Co., New York, NY.

MAYR, E. 1992. A local flora and the biological species concept. American Journal of Botany 79:222–238.

MAYR, E., AND L. L. SHORT. 1970. Species taxa of North American birds. Publications of the Nuttall Ornithological Club, No. 9. Cambridge, MA.

MAZOUREK, J. C., AND P. N. GRAY. 1994. The Florida Duck or the Mallard. Florida Wildlife 48:29–31.

MCCOID, M. J. 1995. Non-native reptiles and amphibians. Pp. 433–437 in E. T. LaRoe, G. S. Farris, C. E. Puckett, P. D. Doran, and M. J. Mac (editors). Our living resources: a report to the nation on the distribution, abundance, and health of U.S. plants, animals, and ecosystems. U.S. Department of the Interior, National Biological Service, Washington, D.C.

MCCOY, M. 1980. Reptiles of the Solomon Islands. Wau Ecology Institute, Wau, Papua New Guinea.

MCCUTCHAN, T. F. 1986. The ribosomal genes of Plasmodium. International Review of Cytology 99:295–309.

MCCUTCHAN, T. F., J. C. KISSINGER, M. G. TOURAY, M. J. ROGERS, J. LI, M. SULLIVAN, E. M. BRAGA, A. U. KRETTLI, AND L. H. MILLER. 1996. Comparison of circumsporozoite proteins from avian and mammalian malarias: biological and phylogenetic implications. Proceedings of the National Academy of Sciences (USA) 93:11889–11894.

MCCUTCHAN, T. F., J. LI, G. A. MCCONKEY, M. J. ROGERS, AND A. P. WATERS. 1995. The cytoplasmic ribosomal RNAs of Plasmodium ssp. Parasitology Today 11:134–138.

MCDOWELL, D. 1997. Managing ecosystems for successful development. World Conservation Vol. 28, No. 3. International Union for Conservation of Nature and Natural Resources, Gland, Switzerland.

MCDOWELL, S. B. 1974. A catalogue of the snakes of New Guinea and the Solomons, with special reference to those in the B. P. Bishop Museum. Part I. Scolecophidia. Journal of Herpetology 8:1–57.

MCGUIRE, W., A. V. S. HILL, C. E. M. ALLSOPP, B. M. GREENWOOD, AND D. KWIATKOWSKI. 1994. Variation in the TNF-α a promoter region associated with susceptibility to cerebral malaria. Nature 371:508–511.

MCINTOSH, J., AND I. CARLSON. 1996. Archaeological monitoring during mangrove removal at Nu'upia Ponds Wildlife Management Area, Marine Corps Base Hawaii, Island of O'ahu, Hawai'i Kāne'ohe Bay, Ko'olau Poko District. Final Report TMK 4-4-08. Prepared by BioSystems Analysis, Inc., Kailua, HI.

MCKEOWN, S. 1996. A field guide to reptiles and amphibians in the Hawaiian Islands. Diamond Head Publishers, Los Osos, CA.

MEDEIROS, A. C., L. L. LOOPE, P. CONANT, AND S. MCELVANEY. 1997. Status, ecology, and management of the invasive plant, Miconia calvescens DC (Melastomataceae) in the Hawaiian Islands. Occasional Papers B. P. Bishop Museum 48:23–36.

MEDEIROS, J. S. 1950–1959. Annual waterfowl count. Job Completion Reports 1950–1959. Territory of Hawaii Fish and Game, Honolulu, HI.

MEDEIROS, J. S. 1958. Present status of migratory waterfowl in Hawaii. Journal of Wildlife Management 22:109–117.

MEDWAY, D. G. 1981. The contribution of Cook's third voyage to the ornithology of the Hawaiian Islands. Pacific Science 35:105–175.

MEFFE, G. K., AND C. R. CARROLL. 1994. Principles of conservation biology. Sinauer Associates, Inc., Sunderland, MA.

MERTON, D. V. 1975. The saddleback: its status and conservation. Pp. 61–74 in R. D. Martin (editor). Breeding endangered species in captivity. Academic Press, New York, NY.

MEYER, J.-Y. 1996. Status of Miconia calvescens (Melastomataceae), a dominant invasive tree in the Society Islands (French Polynesia). Pacific Science 50:66–76.

MEYER, J.-Y., AND J. FLORENCE. 1997. Tahiti's native flora endangered by the invasion of Miconia calvescens DC (Melastomataceae). Journal of Biogeography 23:775–781.

MEYER, J.-Y., AND J.-P. MALET. 1997. Management of the alien invasive tree Miconia calvescens DC (Melastomataceae) in the islands of Raiatea and Tahaa (Society Islands, French Polynesia): 1992–1996. Technical Report 111. Cooperative National Park Resources Studies Unit, University of Hawaii at Manoa, Honolulu, HI.

MEYER DE SCHAUENSEE, R. 1984. The birds of China. Smithsonian Press, Washington, D.C.

MICROWIZARD. 1995. Bird song master 2.2 (Hawaii). Columbus, OH.

MIGOYA, R., AND G. A. BALDASSARRE. 1995. Winter survival of female northern pintails in Sinaloa, Mexico. Journal of Wildlife Management 59:16–22.

MILBERG, P., AND T. TYRBERG. 1993. Naive birds and noble savages—a review of man-caused prehistoric extinctions of island birds. Ecography 6:229–250.

MILLER, A. H. 1937. Structural modifications in the Hawaiian Goose (Nesochen sandvicensis), a study in adaptive evolution. University of California Publications in Zoology 42(1):1–79.

MILLER, M. M., R. GOTO, A. BERNOT, R. ZOOROB, C. AUFFRAY, N. BUMSTEAD, AND W. E. BRILES. 1994a. Two Mhc class I and two Mhc class II genes map to the chicken Rfp-Y system outside of the B complex. Proceedings of the National Academy of Sciences (USA) 91:4397–4401.

MILLER, M. M., R. GOTO, S. YOUNG, J. LIU, AND J. HARDY. 1990. Antigens similar to major histocompatibility complex B-G are expressed in the intestinal epithelium in the chicken. Immunogenetics 32:45–50.

MILLER, M. M., R. GOTO, R. ZOOROB, C. AUFFRAY, AND W. E. BRILES. 1994b. Regions of homology shared by Rfp-Y and major histocompatibility B complex genes. Immunogenetics 39:71–73.

MILLER, M. R. 1985. Time budgets of Northern Pintail

wintering in the Sacramento Valley, California. Wildfowl 36:53–64.

MILLER, S. E., AND L. G. ELDREDGE. 1996. Numbers of Hawaiian species: supplement 1. Occasional Papers B. P. Bishop Museum 45:8–17.

MILLS, L. S., S. G. HAYES, C. BALDWIN, M. J. WISDOM, J. CITTA, D. J. MATTSON, AND K. MURPHY. 1996. Factors leading to different viability predictions for a grizzly bear data set. Conservation Biology 10: 863–873.

MONIZ, J. J. 1997. The role of seabirds in Hawaiian subsistence: implication for interpreting avian extinction and extirpation in Polynesia. Asian Perspectives 36:27–50.

MONROE, B. L., JR, AND C. G. SIBLEY. 1993. A world checklist of birds. Yale University Press, New Haven, CT.

MONTGOMERIE, R. D., AND C. A. REDSELL. 1980. A nesting hummingbird feeding solely on arthropods. Condor 82:463–464.

MOORE, W. S., AND V. R. DEFILIPPIS. 1997. The window of taxonomic resolution for phylogenies based on mitochondrial cytochrome b. Pp. 83–119 in D. P. Mindell (editor). Avian molecular evolution and systematics. Academic Press, San Diego, CA.

MOORE, W. S., S. M. SMITH, AND T. PRYCHITKO. In press. Nuclear gene introns versus mitochondrial genes as molecular clocks. Proceedings of the 22nd International Ornithological Congress.

MOORS, P. J., AND I. A. E. ATKINSON. 1984. Predation on seabirds by introduced animals, and factors affecting its severity. Pp. 668–690 in J. P. Croxall, P. G. H. Evans, and R. W. Schreiber (editors). Status and conservation of the world's seabirds. International Council for Bird Preservation Technical Publication No. 2. Cambridge, UK.

MORIN, M. P. 1992a. The breeding biology of an endangered Hawaiian honeycreeper, the Laysan Finch. Condor 94:646–667.

MORIN, M. P. 1992b. Laysan Finch nest characteristics, nest spacing and reproductive success in two vegetation types. Condor 94:344–357.

MORIN, M. P. 1996. Response of a remnant population of endangered waterbirds to avian botulism. Transactions of the Western Section of the Wildlife Society 32:23–33.

MORIN, M. P., AND S. CONANT. 1994. Variables influencing population estimates of an endangered passerine. Biological Conservation 67:73–84.

MORIN, M. P., AND S. CONANT. 1998. Laysan Island ecosystem restoration plan. U.S. Fish and Wildlife Service report. Hamilton Library, University of Hawaii, Honolulu, HI.

MORIN, M. P., S. CONANT, AND P. CONANT. 1997. Laysan and Nihoa Millerbird (Acrocephalus familiaris). In A. Poole and F. Gill (editors). The Birds of North America, No. 302. The Academy of Natural Sciences, Philadelphia, PA, and American Ornithologists' Union, Washington, D.C.

MORTON, E. S. 1973. On the evolutionary advantages and disadvantages of fruit eating in tropical birds. American Naturalist 107:8–22.

MOUGIN, J. L., C. JOUANIN, AND F. ROUX. 1987. Structure et dynamique de la population de Puffins Cendre Calonectris diomedea borealis de L'ile Selva-

gem Grande. L'Oiseau et Revue Ornithologie 57: 201–225.

MOULTON, D. W., AND A. P. MARSHALL. 1996. Laysan Duck (Anas laysanensis). In A. Poole and F. Gill (editors). The Birds of North America, No. 242. The Academy of Natural Sciences, Philadelphia, PA, and American Ornithologists' Union, Washington, D.C.

MOULTON, D. W., AND M. W. WELLER. 1984. Biology and conservation of the Laysan Duck (Anas laysanensis). Condor 86:105–117.

MOULTON, M. P. 1985. Morphological similarity and coexistence of congeners: an experimental test with introduced Hawaiian birds. Oikos 44:301–305.

MOULTON, M. P. 1993. The all-or-none pattern in introduced Hawaiian passeriforms: the role of competition sustained. American Naturalist 141:105–119.

MOULTON, M. P., AND J. L. LOCKWOOD. 1992. Morphological dispersion of introduced Hawaiian finches: evidence for competition and a Narcissus effect. Evolutionary Ecology 6:45–55.

MOULTON, M. P., AND S. L. PIMM. 1983. The introduced Hawaiian avifauna: biogeographic evidence for competition. American Naturalist 121:669–690.

MOULTON, M. P., AND S. L. PIMM. 1986a. The extent of competition in shaping an introduced avifauna. Pp. 80–97 in J. Diamond and T. J. Case (editors). Community ecology. Harper and Row, New York, NY.

MOULTON, M. P., AND S. L. PIMM. 1986b. Species introductions to Hawaii. Pp. 231–249 in H. A. Mooney and J. A. Drake (editors). Ecology of biological invasions of North America and Hawaii. Springer-Verlag, New York, NY.

MOULTON, M. P., AND S. L. PIMM. 1987. Morphological assortment in introduced Hawaiian passerines. Evolutionary Ecology 1:113–124.

MOULTON, M. P., S. L. PIMM, AND M. W. KRISSINGER. 1990. Nutmeg Mannikin (Lonchura punctulata): a comparison of abundances in O'ahu vs. Maui sugarcane fields: evidence for competitive exclusion? 'Elepaio 50:83–85.

MOULTON, M. P., AND J. G. SANDERSON. 1997. Predicting the fates of passeriform introductions on oceanic islands. Conservation Biology 11:552–558.

MOUNTAINSPRING, S. 1987. Ecology, behavior, and conservation of the Maui Parrotbill. Condor 89:24–39.

MOUNTAINSPRING, S., T. L. C. CASEY, C. B. KEPLER, AND J. M. SCOTT. 1990. Ecology, behavior, and conservation of the Poo-uli (Melamprosops phaeosoma). Wilson Bulletin 102:109–122.

MOUNTAINSPRING, S., J. G. GIFFIN, C. B. KEPLER, R. T. SUGIHARA, J. E. WILLIAMS, AND T. W. SUTTERFIELD. 1987. Regeneration of the subalpine woodland on Mauna Kea, Hawaii. U.S. Fish and Wildlife Service, Hawaii Volcanoes National Park, HI.

MOUNTAINSPRING, S., AND J. M. SCOTT. 1985. Interspecific competition among Hawaiian forest birds. Ecological Monographs 55:219–239.

MUELLER-DOMBOIS, D. 1980. The 'ohi'a dieback phenomenon in the Hawaiian rain forest. Pp. 153–161 in J. Cairns, Jr. (editor). The recovery process in damaged ecosystems. Ann Arbor Science Publications, Ann Arbor, MI.

MUELLER-DOMBOIS, D. 1981. Fires in tropical ecosystems. Pp. 137–176 in H. A. Mooney, T. M. Bonnicksen, N. L. Christensen, J. E. Lotan, and W. A. Reiners (editors). Fire regimes and ecosystem properties. USDA, Forest Service Gen. Tech. Rep. WO-26, Washington, D.C.

MUELLER-DOMBOIS, D. 1987. Forest dynamics in Hawaii. Trends in Ecology and Evolution 2:216–220.

MUELLER-DOMBOIS, D., K. W. BRIDGES, AND H. L. CARSON (EDITORS). 1981a. Island ecosystems: biological organization in selected Hawaiian communities. Hutchinson Ross Publishing Company, Stroudsburg, PA.

MUELLER-DOMBOIS, D., R. G. COORAY, J. E. MAKA, G. SPATZ, W. C. GAGNÉ, F. G. HOWARTH, J. L. GRESSITT, G. A. SAMUELSON, S. CONANT, AND P. Q. TOMICH. 1981b. Structural variation of organism groups studies in the Kīlauea Forest. Pp. 231–317 in D. Mueller-Dombois, K. W. Bridges, and H. L. Carson (editors). Island ecosystems: biological organization in selected Hawaiian communities. Hutchinson Ross Publishing Company, Stroudsburg, PA.

MUELLER-DOMBOIS, D., AND H. ELLENBERG. 1974. Aims and methods of vegetation ecology. John Wiley and Sons, Inc., New York, NY.

MUNRO, G. C. 1944. Birds of Hawaii. Tongg Publishing Company, Honolulu, HI.

MUNRO, G. C. 1955. Hawaii's birds in their homes: how to save them from extinction, Part VII. Elepaio 16:28–30.

MUNRO, G. C. 1960. Birds of Hawaii. Revised Edition. Charles E. Tuttle Co. Inc., Rutland, VT, and Tokyo, Japan.

MURRAY, B. G., Jr. 1971. The ecological consequences of interspecific territorial behavior in birds. Ecology 52:414–423.

MURRAY, B. G., JR. 1979. Population dynamics: alternative models. Academic Press, New York, NY.

MURRAY, B. G. 1981. The origins of adaptive interspecific territorialism. Biological Review 56:1–22.

MURRAY, B. G., JR. 1982. On the meaning of density dependence. Oecologia 53:370–373.

MURRAY, B. G., JR. 1985. Evolution of clutch size in tropical species of birds. Pp. 505–519 in P. A. Buckley, M. S. Foster, E. S. Morton, R. S. Ridgely, and F. G. Buckley (editors). Neotropical ornithology. American Ornithologists' Union, Washington, D.C.

MURRAY, B. G., JR. 1986. The structure of theory, and the role of competition in community dynamics. Oikos 46:145–158.

MURRAY, B. G., JR. 1991a. Sir Isaac Newton and the evolution of clutch size in birds: a defense of the hypothetico-deductive method in ecology and evolutionary biology. Pp. 143–180 in J. L. Casti and A. Karlquist (editors). Beyond belief: randomness, prediction, and explanation in science. CRC Press, Boca Raton, FL.

MURRAY, B. G., JR. 1991b. Measuring annual reproductive success, with comments on the evolution of reproductive behavior. Auk 108:942–952.

MURRAY, B. G., JR. 1992a. The evolution of clutch size: a reply to Wootton, Young, and Winkler. Evolution 46:1581–1584.

MURRAY, B. G., JR. 1992b. The evolutionary significance of lifetime reproductive success. Auk 109: 167–172.

MURRAY, B. G., JR. 1994a. Effect of selection for successful reproduction on hatching synchrony and asynchrony. Auk 111:806–813.

MURRAY, B. G., JR. 1994b. On density dependence. Oikos 69:520–523.

MURRAY, B. G., JR. 1997a. Population dynamics of evolutionary change: demographic parameters as indicators of fitness. Theoretical Population Biology 51:180–184.

MURRAY, B. G., JR. 1997b. On calculating birth and death rates. Oikos 78:384–387.

MURRAY, B. G., JR. 1999. Predicting the occurrence of synchronous and asynchronous hatching in birds. Pp. 624–637 in N. J. Adams and R. H. Slotow (editors). Proceedings of the 22nd International Ornithological Congress. Durban, South Africa. BirdLife South Africa, Johannesburg, South Africa. (Published on CD)

MURRAY, B. G., JR., J. W. FITZPATRICK, AND G. E. WOOLFENDEN. 1989. The evolution of clutch size. II. A test of the Murray-Nolan equation. Evolution 43: 1706–1711.

MURRAY, B. G., JR., AND V. NOLAN, JR. 1989. The evolution of clutch size. I. An equation for predicting clutch size. Evolution 43:1699–1705.

MURRAY, T. E., J. A. BARTLE, S. R. KALISH, AND P. R. TAYLOR. 1993. Incidental capture of seabirds by Japanese southern bluefin tuna longline vessels in New Zealand waters, 1988–1992. Bird Conservation International 3:181–210.

MUSSER, G. G., AND M. D. CARLETON. 1993. Family Muridae. Pp. 501–755 in D. E. Wilson and D. M. Reeder (editors). Mammal species of the world. 2nd edition. Smithsonian Institution Press, Washington, D.C.

MYERS, J. P. 1988. Dowitcher DNA. American Birds 42:1207–1209.

MYLES, D. 1985. The great waves. McGraw-Hill, New York, NY.

NAG. 1993. The GLIM system: generalised linear interactive modeling. B. Francis, M. Green, C. Payne (editors). Clarendon Press, Oxford, UK.

NAGEL, R. L., AND E. F. ROTH, JR. 1989. Malaria and red cell genetic defects. Blood 74:1213–1221.

NAGY, E., A. D. MAEDA-MACHANG'U, P. J. KRELL, AND J. B. DERBYSHIRE. 1990. Vaccination of 1-day-old chick with fowlpox virus by the aerosol, drinking water, or cutaneous routes. Avian Diseases 34:677–682.

NATIONAL PARK SERVICE. 1989. Wildland fire management and environmental assessment, HAVO. An amendment to the natural resources management plan. Unpublished report. Resources Management Division, Hawaii Volcanoes National Park, HI.

NATIONAL RESEARCH COUNCIL. 1992. The scientific bases for the preservation of the Hawaiian Crow. National Academy Press, Washington, D.C.

NEI, M. 1987. Molecular evolutionary genetics. Columbia University Press, New York, NY.

NEI, M., AND J. C. MILLER. 1990. A simple method for estimating average number of nucleotide substitutions within and between populations from restriction data. Genetics 125:873–879.

NELSON, J. T., AND F. G. FANCY. 1999. A test of the variable circular-plot method where exact density of a bird population was known. Pacific Conservation Biology 5:139–143.

NETTLESHIP, D. N., J. BURGER, AND M. GOCHFELD (EDITORS). 1994. Seabirds on islands: threats, case studies and action plans. Series No. 1. Birdlife Conservation. Cambridge, UK.

NEWELL, W. 1908. Notes on the habits of the Argentine ant or "New Orleans" ant, *Iridomyrmex humilis* Mayr. Journal of Economic Entomology 1:21–34.

NEWTON, I. 1973. Finches. Taplinger Publishing Co., New York.

NEWTON, I. 1991. Population limitation in birds of prey: a comparative approach. Pp. 3–21 *in* C. M. Perrins, J.-D. Lebreton, and G. J. M. Hirons (editors). Bird population studies. Oxford University Press, Oxford, UK.

NICE, M. M. 1957. Nesting success in altricial birds. Auk 74:305–321.

NICHOLSON, A. J. 1933. The balance of animal populations. Journal of Animal Ecology 2:132–178.

NILSSON, G. 1981. The bird business, a study of the commercial cage bird trade. Animal Welfare Institute, Washington, D.C.

NISHIDA, G. M. (EDITOR). 1994. Hawaiian terrestrial arthropod checklist. 2nd edition. B. P. Bishop Museum Technical Report 4, Honolulu, HI.

NOLAN, V., JR. 1978. The ecology and behavior of the Prairie Warbler *Dendroica discolor*. Ornithological Monographs 26:1–595.

NORRIS, K., M. ANWAR, AND A. F. READ. 1994. Reproductive effort influences the prevalence of haematozoan parasites in great tits. Journal of Animal Ecology 63:601–610.

NTOUMI, F., H. CONTAMIN, C. ROGIER, S. BONNEFOY, J.-F. TRAPE, AND O. MERCEREAU-PUIJALON. 1995. Age-dependent carriage of multiple *Plasmodium falciparum* merozoite surface antigen−2 alleles in asymtomatic malaria infections. American Journal of Tropical Medicine and Hygiene 52:81–88.

NUNN, G. B., J. COOPER, P. JOUVENTIN, C. J. R. ROBERTSON, AND G. G. ROBERTSON. 1996. Evolutionary relationships among extant albatrosses (Procellariiformes: Diomedeidae) established from complete cytochrome-b gene sequences. Auk 113:784–801.

NUNN, G. B., AND S. E. STANLEY. 1998. Body size effects and rates of cytochrome b evolution in tube-nosed seabirds. Molecular Biology and Evolution 15:1360–1371.

NUNN, P. 1990. Recent environmental changes on Pacific Islands. Geographical Journal 156:125–140.

NUR, N. 1993. Establishing demographic parameters of the Marbled Murrelet. Final report to U.S. Fish and Wildlife Service, Marbled Murrelet Recovery Team, Point Reyes Bird Observatory, Stinson Beach, CA.

NUSSBAUM, R. A. 1980. The Brahminy blind snake (*Ramphotyphlops braminus*) in the Seychelles Archipelago: distribution, variation, and further evidence for parthenogenesis. Herpetologica 36:215–221.

O'BRIEN, S. J., AND E. MAYR. 1991. Bureaucratic mischief: recognizing endangered species and subspecies. Science 251:1187–1188.

OCHMAN, H., AND A. C. WILSON. 1987. Evolution in bacteria: evidence for a universal substitution rate in cellular genomes. Journal of Molecular Evolution 26:74–86.

O'CONNOR, R. J. 1984. The growth and development of birds. John Wiley and Sons, New York, NY.

OHTA, T. 1976. Role of slightly deleterious mutations in molecular evolution and polymorphisms. Theoretical Population Biology 10:254–275.

OKAMOTO, B. 1975. Parasites of the Pacific Golden Plover and their use as biological markers. 'Elepaio 36:53–54.

OLIVER, C. D., AND B. C. LARSON. 1996. Forest stand dynamics. John Wiley and Sons, New York, NY.

OLIVER, D. L. 1961. The Pacific Islands. Doubleday and Co. Inc., Garden City, NY.

OLSEN, D. E., AND R. E. DOLPHIN. 1978. Avian pox. Veterinary Medicine/Small Animal Clinician 73: 1295–1297.

OLSON, S. L. 1989. Two overlooked holotypes of the Hawaiian flycatcher *Chasiempis* described by Leonhard Stejneger (Aves: Myiagrinae). Proceedings of the Biological Society of Washington 102:555–558.

OLSON, S. L. 1996. The contribution of the voyage of the H. M. S. *Blonde* (1825) to Hawaiian ornithology. Archives of Natural History 23:1–42.

OLSON, S. L., AND H. F. JAMES. 1982a. Fossil birds from the Hawaiian Islands: evidence for wholesale extinction by man before western contact. Science 217:633–635.

OLSON, S. L., AND H. F. JAMES. 1982b. Prodromus of the fossil avifauna of the Hawaiian Islands. Smithsonian Contributions to Zoology No. 365. Washington, D.C.

OLSON, S. L., AND H. F. JAMES. 1984. The role of Polynesians in the extinction of the avifauna of the Hawaiian Islands. Pp. 768–780 *in* P. S. Martin and R. G. Klein (editors), Quaternary extinctions: a prehistoric revolution. University of Arizona Press, Tucson, Arizona.

OLSON, S. L., AND H. F. JAMES. 1988. Nomenclature of the Kauai Amakihi and Kauai Akialoa (Drepanidini). 'Elepaio 48:13–14.

OLSON, S. L., AND H. F. JAMES. 1991. Descriptions of thirty-two new species of birds from the Hawaiian Islands: Part I. Non-passeriformes. Ornithological Monographs 45:1–88.

OLSON, S. L., AND H. F. JAMES. 1994a. A chronology of ornithological exploration in the Hawaiian Islands, from Cook to Perkins. Studies in Avian Biology 15:91–102.

OLSON, S. L., AND H. F. JAMES. 1994b. A specimen of Nuku pu'u (Aves: Drepanidini: *Hemignathus lucidus*) from the Island of Hawai'i. Pacific Science 48: 331–338.

OLSON, S. L., AND H. F. JAMES. 1995. Nomenclature of the Hawaiian 'akialoas and nukupu'us (Aves: Drepanidini). Proceedings of the Biological Society of Washington 108:373–387.

OLSON, S. L., AND A. WETMORE. 1976. Preliminary diagnoses of extraordinary new genera of birds from Pleistocene deposits in the Hawaiian Islands. Proceedings of Biological Society of Washington 89: 247–258.

OLSON, S. L., AND A. C. ZIEGLER. 1995. Remains of land birds from Lisianski Island, with observations on the terrestrial avifauna of the Northwestern Hawaiian Islands. Pacific Science 49:111–125.

OPPLIGER, A., P. CHRISTE, AND H. RICHNER. 1996. Clutch size and malaria resistance. Nature 381:565.

ORING, L. W. 1964. Behavior and ecology of certain ducks during the post breeding period. Journal of Wildlife Management 28:223–233.

ORNITHOLOGICAL SOCIETY OF JAPAN. 1974. Check-list of Japanese Birds. Gakken, Tokyo.

ORÓS, J., F. RODRÍGUEZ, J. L. RODRÍGUEZ, C. BRACO, AND A. FERNÁNDEZ. 1997. Debilitating cutaneous poxvirus infection in a Hodgson's Grandala (Grandala coelicolor). Avian Diseases 41:481–483.

O'SHEA, M. 1996. A guide to the snakes of Papua New Guinea. Independent Publishing, Port Moresby, Papua New Guinea.

OTA, H. 1998. Introduced amphibians and reptiles of the Ryukyu Archipelago, Japan. Pp. 439–452 in G. H. Rodda, Y. Sawai, D. Chiszar, and H. Tanaka (editors). Problem snake management: habu and the brown tree snake. Cornell University Press, Ithaca, NY.

OTA, Y., K. R. BERRYMAN, A. G. HULL, T. MIYAUCHI, AND N. ISO. 1988. Age and height distribution of Holocene transgressive deposits in eastern North Island, New Zealand. Paleogeography, Paleoclimatology, Paleoecology 68:135–151.

OTO, M., S. MIYAKE, AND Y. YUASA. 1993. Optimization of nonradioisotopic single strand conformation polymorphism analysis with a conventional minislab gel electrophoresis apparatus. Analytical Biochemistry 213:19–22.

OUSTALET, M. E. 1895. Les mammiferes et les oiseaux des Isles Mariannes. Nouvelles Archives du Museum D'Histoire Naturelle de Paris, Series 3, 7:141–228.

OWEN, M. 1971. The selection of feeding site by White-fronted Geese in winter. Journal of Applied Ecology 8:905–917.

OWEN, M. 1977. The role of wildfowl refuges on agricultural land in lessening the conflict between farmers and geese in Britain. Biological Conservation 11:209–222.

OWEN, M. 1981. Abdominal profile—a condition index for wild geese in the field. Journal of Wildlife Management 45:227–230.

OWEN, M., AND J. M. BLACK. 1991. Geese and their future fortune. Ibis 133:S28-S35.

PAINE, R. T., J. T. WOOTTON, AND P. D. BOERSMA. 1990. Direct and indirect effects of Peregrine Falcon predation on seabird abundance. Auk 107:1–9.

PALMER, R. S. (EDITOR). 1962. Handbook of North American birds. Vol. 1. Yale University Press, New Haven, CT.

PALMER, R. S. (EDITOR). 1976. Handbook of North American birds. Waterfowl. Vol. 2, Part 1. Yale University Press, New Haven, CT.

PARKER, J. W. 1977. Mortality of nestling Mississippi Kites by ants. Wilson Bulletin 89:176.

PARKES, K. C. 1958. Specific relations in the genus Elanus. Condor 60:139–140.

PARSONS, T. J., S. L. OLSON, AND M. J. BRAUN. 1993. Unidirectional spread of secondary sexual plumage traits across an avian hybrid zone. Science 260:1643–1646.

PAXINOS, E. A. 1998. A molecular perspective on the evolution of a Hawaiian waterfowl radiation. Ph.D. dissertation. Brown University, Providence, RI.

PAXINOS, E. A., C. MCINTOSH, K. RALLS, AND R. FLEISCHER. 1997. A non-invasive method for distinguishing among canid species: amplification and enzyme restriction of DNA from dung. Molecular Ecology 6:483–486.

PAYNE, R. B. 1969. Overlap of breeding and molting schedules in a collection of African birds. Condor 71:140–145.

PAZDERKA, F., B. M. LONGENECKER, G. R. S. LAW, AND R. F. RUTH. 1975. The major histocompatibility complex of the chicken. Immunogenetics 2:101–130.

PEALE, T. R. 1848. United States exploring expedition, 1838–1842. Mammalia and Ornithology. Vol. 8. C. Sherman, Philadelphia, PA.

PEARSON, G. L., D. A. PASS, AND E. C. BEGGS. 1975. Fatal pox infection in a Rough-legged Hawk. Journal of Wildlife Diseases 11:224–228.

PEASE, C. M., AND J. A. GRZYBOWSKI. 1995. Assessing the consequences of brood parasitism and nest predation on seasonal fecundity in passerine birds. Auk 112:343–363.

PEKELO, N., JR. 1963. Nature notes from Molokai. 'Elepaio 24:17–18.

PÉREZ-RIVERA, R. A. 1991. Change in diet and foraging behavior of the Antillean Euphonia in Puerto Rico after Hurricane Hugo. Journal of Field Ornithology 62:474–478.

PERKINS, R. C. L. 1893. Notes on collecting in Kona, Hawaii. Ibis 1893:101–114.

PERKINS, R. C. L. 1901. An introduction to the study of the Drepanididae, a family of birds peculiar to the Hawaiian Islands. Ibis 1901:562–585.

PERKINS, R. C. L. 1903. Vertebrata. Pp. 365–466 in D. Sharp (editor). Fauna Hawaiiensis. Vol. 1, part IV. The University Press, Cambridge, UK.

PERKINS, S. L., AND J. M. MARTIN. 1999. Conserved polymerase chain reaction primers fail in diagnosis of parasitic infections. Journal of Parasitology 85:982–984.

PERKINS, S. L., S. M. OSGOOD, AND J. J. SCHALL. 1998. Use of PCR for detection of subpatent infections of lizard malaria: implications for epizootiology. Molecular Ecology 7:1587–1590.

PERRINS, C. M. 1979. British tits. New Naturalist Series. Collins, London, UK.

PERRINS, C. M., AND T. A. GEER. 1980. The effect of Sparrowhawks on tit populations. Ardea 68:133–142.

PIERONI, P., C. D. MILLS, C. OHRT, M. A. HARRINGTON, AND K. C. KAIN. 1998. Comparison of ParaSight™ F-test and the ICT Malaria PF™ test with the polymerase chain reaction for the diagnosis of Plasmodium falciparum malaria in travellers. Transactions of the Royal Society of Tropical Medicine and Hygiene 92:166–169.

PIMM, S. L. 1987. The snake that ate Guam. Trends in Ecology and Evolution 2:293–295.

PIMM, S. L. 1991. The balance of nature? Ecological issues in the conservation of species and communities. University of Chicago Press, Chicago, IL.

PIMM, S. L., H. L. JONES, AND J. DIAMOND. 1988. On the risk of extinction. American Naturalist 132:757–785.

PIMM, S. L., M. P. MOULTON, AND L. J. JUSTICE. 1994. Bird extinctions in the central Pacific. Philosophical Transaction of the Royal Society of London, Series B 344:27–33.

PIMM, S. L., AND J. W. PIMM. 1982. Resource use, competition, and resource availability in Hawaiian honeycreepers. Ecology 63:1468–1480.

PIOTROWSKA, M., AND T. WESOŁOWSKI. 1989. The breeding ecology and behaviour of Phylloscopus collybita in primeval and managed stands of Bialowieza Forest (Poland). Acta Ornithologica 25:25–76.

PIRAZZOLI, P. A. 1991. World atlas of Holocene sealevel changes. Elsevier Oceanography, Series 58. Elsevier, Amsterdam, the Netherlands.

PIRAZZOLI, P. A., AND L. F. MONTAGGIONI. 1988. Holocene sea-level changes in French Polynesia. Paleogeography, Paleoclimatology, Paleoecology 68:153–175.

PLACHY, J., J. R. PINK, AND K. HALA. 1992. Biology of the chicken MHC (B complex). Critical Reviews in Immunology 12:47–79.

PLETSCHET, S. M., AND J. F. KELLY. 1990. Breeding biology and nesting success of Palila. Condor 92:1012–1021.

PODOLSKY, R., D. G. AINLEY, G. SPENCER, L. DEFOREST, AND N. NUR. 1998. Mortality of Newell's Shearwaters caused by collisions with urban structures on Kauai. Colonial Waterbirds 21:20–34.

PODOLSKY, R., AND S. W. KRESS. 1992. Attraction of the endangered Dark-rumped Petrel to recorded vocalizations in the Galápagos Islands. Condor 94:448–453.

POLIS, G. A., W. B. ANDERSON, AND R. D. HOLT. 1997. Towards an integration of landscape and foodweb ecology: the dynamics of spatially subsidized food webs. Annual Review of Ecological Systematics 29:289–316.

POLIS, G. A., AND S. D. HURD. 1996. Linking marine and terrestrial food webs: allochthonous input from the ocean supports high secondary productivity on small island and coastal land communities. American Naturalist 147:396–423.

POLLARD, J. H. 1971. On distance estimators of density in randomly distributed forests. Biometrics 27:991–1002.

POLLOCK, K. H., J. D. NICHOLS, C. BROWNIE, AND J. E. HINES. 1990. Statistical inference for capture-recapture experiments. Wildlife Monographs 107:1–97.

PORTER, J. M., AND S. G. SEALY. 1982. Dynamics of seabird multispecies feeding flocks: age-related feeding behaviour. Behaviour 81:91–109.

PORTER, J. R. 1973. The growth and phenology of Metrosideros in Hawaii. Tech. Rep. 27. US/International Biological Program Island Ecosystems IRP, Department of Botany, University of Hawaii, Honolulu, HI.

POTTS, G. R., AND N. J. AEBISCHER. 1991. Modelling the population dynamics of the Grey Partridge: conservation and management. Pp. 373–390 in C. M. Perrins, J.-D. Lebreton, and G. J. M. Hirons (editors). Bird population studies. Oxford University Press, Oxford, UK.

POULIN, B., G. LEFEBVRE, AND R. MCNEIL. 1992. Tropical avian phenology in relation to abundance and exploitation of food resources. Ecology 73:2295–2309.

PRATT, H. D. 1979. A systematic analysis of the endemic avifauna of the Hawaiian Islands. Ph.D. dissertation. Louisiana State University, Baton Rouge, LA.

PRATT, H. D. 1980. Intra-island variation in the 'Elepaio on the island of Hawaii. Condor 82:449–458.

PRATT, H. D. 1982. Relationships and speciation of the Hawaiian thrushes. Living Bird 19:73–90.

PRATT, H. D. 1987. Occurrence of the North American Coot (Fulica americana americana) in the Hawaiian Islands, with comments on the taxonomy of the Hawaiian Coot. 'Elepaio 47:25–28.

PRATT, H. D. 1989. Species limits in akepas (Drepanidinae: Loxops). Condor 91:933–940.

PRATT, H. D. 1990. Bird the world's islands now. Birding 22:10–15.

PRATT, H. D. 1992a. Is the Poo-uli a Hawaiian honeycreeper (Drepanidinae)? Condor 94:172–180.

PRATT, H. D. 1992b. Systematics of the Hawaiian "creepers" Oreomystis and Paroreomyza. Condor 94:836–846.

PRATT, H. D. 1993. Enjoying birds in Hawaii: a bird-finding guide to the fiftieth state. 2nd edition. Mutual Publishing, Honolulu, HI.

PRATT, H. D. 1994. Avifaunal change in the Hawaiian Islands 1893–1993. Studies in Avian Biology 15:103–118.

PRATT, H. D. 1996a. Voices of Hawaii's birds: an audio companion to Hawaii's birds. Hawaii Audubon Society, Honolulu, HI, and Library of Natural Sounds, Cornell Laboratory of Ornithology, Ithaca, NY.

PRATT, H. D. 1996b. Voices of Hawaii's birds, HAS's newest publication. 'Elepaio 56:33–36.

PRATT, H. D. In press. The Hawaiian honeycreepers. Oxford University Press, Oxford, UK.

PRATT, H. D., P. L. BRUNER, AND D. G. BERRETT. 1987. A field guide to the birds of Hawaii and the tropical Pacific. Princeton University Press, Princeton, NJ.

PRATT, T. K., P. C. BANKO, S. G. FANCY, G. D. LINDSEY, AND J. D. JACOBI. 1997a. Status and management of the Palila, an endangered Hawaiian honeycreeper, 1987–1996. Pacific Conservation Biology 3:330–340.

PRATT, T. K., S. G. FANCY, C. K. HARADA, G. D. LINDSEY, AND J. D. JACOBI. 1994. Identifying sex and age of Akiapolaau. Wilson Bulletin 106: 421–430.

PRATT, T. K., B. GAGNÉ, AND T. CASEY. 1993. Po'ouli again seen at Hanaw'i. Hawaii's Forests and Wildlife 8:1, 9.

PRATT, T. K., C. B. KEPLER, AND T. L. C. CASEY. 1997b. Po'ouli (Melamprosops phaeosoma). In A. Poole and F. Gill (editors). The Birds of North America, No. 272. The Academy of Natural Sciences, Philadelphia, PA, and American Ornithologists' Union, Washington, D.C.

PRIMACK, R. G. 1993. Essentials of conservation biology. Sinauer, Sunderland, Massachusetts.

PROP, J., AND C. DEERENBERG. 1991. Spring staging in Brent Geese Branta bernicla: feeding constraints and the impact of diet on the accumulation of body reserves. Oecologia 87:19–28.

PROP, J., AND T. VULNIK. 1992. Digestion by Barnacle Geese in the annual cycle: the interplay between retention time and food quality. Functional Ecology 6: 80–189.

PUKUI, M. K., AND S. H. ELBERT. 1986. Hawaiian dictionary. Revised and enlarged edition. University of Hawaii Press, Honolulu, HI.

PUKUI, M. K., S. H. ELBERT, AND E. T. MOOKINI. 1976. Place names of Hawaii. Revised and expanded edition. University of Hawaii Press, Honolulu, HI.

PULLIAM, H. R. 1975. Diet optimization with nutrient constraints. American Naturalist 109:765–768.

PULLIAM, H. R. 1988. Sources, sinks, and population regulation. American Naturalist 132:652–661.

PYKE, G. H. 1980. The foraging behaviour of Australian honeyeaters: a review and some comparisons with hummingbirds. Australian Journal of Ecology 5:343–369.

PYLE, P., S. N. G. HOWELL, R. P. YUNICK, AND D. F. DeSANTE. 1987. Identification guide to North American passerines. Slate Creek Press, Bolinas, CA.

PYLE, R. L. 1983. Hawaiian Islands region. American Birds 37:914–916.

PYLE, R. L. 1985a. Hawaiian Islands region. American Birds 37:351–353.

PYLE, R. L. 1985b. Hawaiian Islands region. American Birds 37:964–965.

PYLE, R. L. 1987a. Hawaiian Islands region. American Birds 41:148–150.

PYLE, R. L. 1987b. Hawaiian Islands region. American Birds 41:491–493.

PYLE, R. L. 1988. Hawaiian Islands region. American Birds 42:491–493.

PYLE, R. L. 1989. Hawaiian Islands region. American Birds 43:369–371.

PYLE, R. L. 1990. Native breeding birds of Hawaii. 'Elepaio 50:99–100.

PYLE, R. L. 1992. Check-list of the birds of Hawaii—1992. 'Elepaio 52:53–62.

PYLE, R. L. 1993. Hawaiian Islands region. American Birds 47:302–304.

PYLE, R. L. 1994. Hawaiian Islands region. Audubon Field Notes 48:990–992.

PYLE, R. L. 1997. Checklist of the birds of Hawaii—1997. 'Elepaio 57:129–138.

PYLE, R. L. 2000. SIGHTINGS database. Occurrence and status of birds in Hawaii projects. B. P. Bishop Museum, Honolulu, HI.

QUINN, T. W. 1992. The genetic legacy of mother goose: phylogeographic patterns of Lesser Snow Goose Chen caerulescens caerulescens maternal lineages. Molecular Ecology 1:105–117.

QUINN, T. W., G. F. SHIELDS, AND A. C. WILSON. 1991. Affinities of the Hawaiian Goose based on two types of mitochondrial DNA data. Auk 108:585–593.

QUINN, T. W., AND B. N. WHITE. 1987a. Analysis of DNA sequence variation. Pp. 163–198 in F. Cooke and P. A. Buckley (editors). Avian genetics: a population and ecological approach. Academic Press, London, UK.

QUINN, T. W., AND B. N. WHITE. 1987b. Identifications of restriction-fragment-length-polymorphisms in genomic DNA of the lesser snow goose (Anser caerulescens caerulescens). Molecular Biology and Evolution 4:126–143.

QUISENBERRY, W. B., AND G. D. WALLACE. 1959. Ar-

thropod–borne virus and encephalitis potentials in Hawaii. Hawaii Medical Journal 19:29–31.

RADUNZEL, L. A., D. M. MUSCHITZ, V. M. BAULDRY, AND P. ARCESE. 1997. A long-term study of the breeding success of Eastern Bluebirds by year and cavity type. Journal of Field Ornithology 68:7–18.

RAFFAELE, H. A. 1977. Comments on the extinction of Loxigilla portoricensis grandis in St. Kitts, Lesser Antilles. Condor 79:389–390.

RAIKOW, R. J. 1976. Pelvic appendage myology of the Hawaiian honeycreepers (Drepanididae). Auk 93: 774–792.

RAIKOW, R. J. 1977. The origin and evolution of the Hawaiian honeycreepers (Drepanididae). Living Bird 15:95–117.

RAIKOW, R. J. 1978. Appendicular myology and relationships of the New World nine-primaried oscines (Aves: Passeriformes). Bulletin of Carnegie Museum of Natural History No. 7.

RAIKOW, R. J. 1985. Problems in avian classification. Current Ornithology 2:187–212.

RAIKOW, R. J. 1986. Reshaping the avian 'tree of life.' Point Reyes Bird Observatory Newsletter 74:8–13.

RAIKOW, R. J., A. H. BLEDSOE, B. A. MYERS, AND C. J. WELSH. 1990. Individual variation in avian muscles and its significance for the reconstruction of phylogeny. Systematic Zoology 39:362–370.

RAIKOW, R. J., S. R. BORECKY, AND S. L. BERMAN. 1979. The evolutionary re-establishment of a lost ancestral muscle in the bowerbird assemblage. Condor 81:203–206.

RALLS, K., J. D. BALLOU, AND A. TEMPLETON. 1988. Estimates of lethal equivalents and the cost of inbreeding in mammals. Conservation Biology 2:185–193.

RALPH, C. J., AND S. G. FANCY. 1994a. Demography and movements of the endangered Akepa and Hawaii Creeper. Wilson Bulletin 106:615–628.

RALPH, C. J., AND S. G. FANCY. 1994b. Timing of breeding and molting in six species of Hawaiian honeycreepers. Condor 96:151–161.

RALPH, C. J., AND S. G. FANCY. 1994c. Demography and movements of the Omao (Myadestes obscurus). Condor 96:503–511.

RALPH, C. J., AND S. G. FANCY. 1995. Demography and movements of Apapane and Iiwi in Hawaii. Condor 97:729–742.

RALPH, C. J., AND S. G. FANCY. 1996. Aspects of the life history and foraging ecology of the endangered Akiapolauu. Condor 98:312–321.

RALPH, C. J., S. G. FANCY, AND T. D. MALE. 1998. Demography of an introduced Red-billed Leiothrix population in Hawaii. Condor 100:468–473

RALPH, C. J., G. R. GEUPEL, P. PYLE, T. E. MARTIN, AND D. F. DeSANTE. 1993. Handbook of field methods for monitoring landbirds. Gen. Tech. Rep. PSW-GTR-144. USDA Forest Service Pacific Southwest Research Station, Albany, CA.

RALPH, C. J., G. L. HUNT, M. G. RAPHAEL, AND J. F. PIATT (EDITORS). 1995a. Ecology and conservation of the Marbled Murrelet. USDA Forest Service General Technical Report PSW-GTR-152. Berkeley, CA.

RALPH, C. J., AND B. D. MAXWELL. 1984. Relative effects of human and feral hog disturbance on a wet forest in Hawaii. Biological Conservation 30:291–303.

RALPH, C. J., J. R. SAUER, AND S. DROEGE (EDITORS). 1995b. Monitoring bird populations by point counts. General Technical Report PSW-GTR-149. USDA Forest Service Pacific Southwest Research Station, Albany, CA.

RALPH, C. J., AND J. M. SCOTT (EDITORS). 1981. Estimating numbers of terrestrial birds. Studies in Avian Biology Number 6. Cooper Ornithological Society, Allen Press, Inc., Lawrence, KS.

RALPH, C. J., AND C. VAN RIPER, III. 1985. Historical and current factors affecting Hawaiian native birds. Bird Conservation 2:7–42.

RAMSEY, F. L., AND J. M. SCOTT. 1981. Analysis of bird survey data using a modification of Emlen's method. Studies in Avian Biology 6:483–487.

RAMSEY, F. L., V. WILDMAN, AND J. ENGBRING. 1987. Covariate adjustments to effective area in variable-area wildlife surveys. Biometrics 43:1–11.

RAND, D. M. 1994. Thermal habit, metabolic rate and the evolution of mitochondrial DNA. Trends in Ecology and Evolution 9:125–131.

RANDI, E. 1996. A mitochondrial cytochrome b phylogeny of the Alectoris partidges. Molecular Phylogenetics and Evolution 7:214–227.

RAPPOLE, J. H., AND A. R. TIPTON. 1991. New harness design for attachment of radio transmitters to small passerines. Journal Field Ornithology 62:335–337.

RAUZON, M. J. 1991. Save our shearwaters! Living Bird Quarterly 10(2):28–32.

RAUZON, M. J. 1992. Final fish and wildlife management plan for Marine Corps Air Station, Kaneohe Bay, O'ahu, Hawaii. Vols. 1, 2. Prepared by Marine Endeavors, Berkeley, CA.

RAUZON, M. J., L. MCNEIL, AND L. T. TANINO. 1997. Biological investigations at Nu'upia Ponds Wildlife Management Area, Kaneohe Bay, Marine Corps Base Hawaii. Final report. Prepared by Scientific Consultant Services/Cultural Resource Management Services (SCS/CRMS), Inc., Honolulu, HI.

RAUZON, M. J., AND L. TANINO. 1995. Endangered Hawaiian Stilt survey and assessment for improved management options, Marine Corps Base Hawaii (MCBH), Kaneohe Bay. Final report. Prepared by Marine Endeavors, Oakland, CA.

RAVE, E. H., R. C. FLEISCHER, F. DUVALL, AND J. M. BLACK. 1994. Genetic analyses through DNA fingerprinting of captive populations of Hawaiian Geese. Conservation Biology 8:744–751.

RAYNER, J. M. V. 1988. Form and function in avian flight. Current Ornithology 5:1–66.

RECHER, H. F., AND J. A. RECHER. 1969. Comparative foraging efficiency of adult and immature Little Blue Herons (Florida caerulea). Animal Behaviour 17:320–322.

REED, J. R., J. L. SINCOCK, AND J. P. HAILMAN. 1985. Light attraction in endangered procellariiform birds: reduction by shielding upward radiation. Auk 102:377–383.

REED, J. M. 1996. Using statistical probability to increase confidence of inferring species extinction. Conservation Biology 10:1283–1285.

REEDER, J. C., AND G. V. BROWN. 1996. Antigenic variation and immune evasion in Plasmodium falcipa-

rum malaria. Immunology and Cell Biology 74:546–554.

REICHARD, S. H., AND C. W. HAMILTON. 1997. Predicting invasions of woody plants introduced into North America. Conservation Biology 11:193–203.

REICHEL, J. D., AND P. O. GLASS. 1989. Micronesian Starling predation on seabird eggs. Emu 90:135–136

REICHENOW, A. 1899. Aufzeichnungen. Ornithologische Monatsberichte 7:41.

REICHENOW, A. 1901. Eine auffallende Vogelzugstrasse vom nordwestlichen nordamerika nach Polynesien. Ornithologische Monatsberichte 2:17–18.

REIMER, N. J. 1994. Distribution and impact of alien ants in vulnerable Hawaiian ecosystems. Pp. 11–22 in D. F. Williams (editor). Exotic ants: biology, impact, and control of introduced species. Westview Press, Boulder, CO.

REITER, P. 1987. A revised version of the CDC gravid mosquito trap. Journal of the American Mosquito Control Association 3:325–327.

REYNOLDS, M. H., B. A. COOPER, AND R. H. DAY. 1997a. Radar study of seabirds and bats on windward Hawai'i. Pacific Science 51:97–106.

REYNOLDS, M. H., AND G. L. RITCHOTTE. 1997. Evidence of Newell's Shearwater breeding in Puna District, Hawaii. Journal of Field Ornithology 68:26–32.

REYNOLDS, M. H., AND T. J. SNETSINGER. 1994. Critically endangered bird species located on East Maui. Hawaii's Forests and Wildlife 9:1–3.

REYNOLDS, M. H., T. J. SNETSINGER, AND C. M. HERRMANN. 1997b. Kauai's endangered solitaires: update on population status and distribution 1996. Transactions of the Western Section of the Wildlife Society 33:49–55.

REYNOLDS, R. T., J. M. SCOTT, AND R. A. NUSSBAUM. 1980. A variable circular-plot method for estimating bird numbers. Condor 82:309–313.

RHYMER, J. M., AND D. S. SIMBERLOFF. 1996. Extinction by hybridization and introgression. Annual Review of Ecology and Systematics 27:83–109.

RHYMER, J. M., M. J. WILLIAMS, AND M. J. BRAUN. 1994. Mitochondrial analysis of gene flow between New Zealand Mallards (Anas platyrhynchos) and Grey Ducks (A. superciliosa). Auk 111:970–978.

RIBIC, C. A., D. G. AINLEY, AND L. B. SPEAR. 1992. Effects of El Niño and La Niña on seabird assemblages in the Equatorial Pacific. Marine Ecology Progress Series 80:109–124.

RICE, J., R. D. OHMART, AND B. W. ANDERSON. 1983. Habitat selection attributes of an avian community: a discriminant analysis investigation. Ecological Monographs 53:263–290.

RICHARDS, L. P., AND P. H. BALDWIN. 1953. Recent records of some Hawaiian honeycreepers. Condor 55:221–222.

RICHARDS, L. P., AND W. J. BOCK. 1973. Functional anatomy and adaptive evolution of the feeding apparatus in the Hawaiian honeycreeper genus Loxops (Drepanididae). Ornithological Monographs 15.

RICHARDSON, F. 1949. Status of native land birds on Molokai. Pacific Science 3:226–230.

RICHARDSON, F. 1954. Report on the two native passerines of Nihoa, Hawaii. Condor 56:224.

RICHARDSON, F. 1957. The breeding cycles of Hawaiian sea birds. B. P. Bishop Museum Bulletin No. 218. Bishop Museum Press, Honolulu, HI.

RICHARDSON, F. 1963. Birds of Lehua Island off Niihau, Hawaii. Elepaio 23:43–45.

RICHARDSON, F., AND J. BOWLES. 1964. A survey of the birds of Kauai, Hawaii. B. P. Bishop Museum Bulletin No. 227. Bishop Museum Press, Honolulu, HI.

RICHARDSON, F., AND D. H. WOODSIDE. 1954. Rediscovery of the nesting of the Dark-rumped Petrel in the Hawaiian Islands. Condor 56:323–327.

RICHNER, H., P. CHRISTE, AND A. OPPLIGER. 1995. Paternal investment affects prevalence of malaria. Proceedings of the National Academy of Sciences (USA) 92:1192–1194.

RICKLEFS, R. E. 1968. Patterns of growth in birds. Ibis 110:419–451.

RICKLEFS, R. E. 1969. The nesting cycle of songbirds in tropical and temperate regions. Living Bird 8: 165–175.

RICKLEFS, R. E. 1973. Fecundity, mortality and avian demography. Pp. 366–435 in D. S. Farner (editor). Breeding biology of birds. National Academy of Sciences, Washington, D.C.

RICKLEFS, R. E. 1974. Energetics of reproduction in birds. Pp. 152–202 in R. E. Paynter, Jr. (editor). Avian energetics. Publications of the Nuttall Ornithological Club, No. 15. Cambridge, MA.

RICKLEFS, R. E. 1975. Patterns of growth in birds. III. Growth and development of the Cactus Wren. Condor 77:35–45.

RICKLEFS, R. E. 1992. Embryonic development period and the prevalence of avian blood parasites. Proceedings of the National Academy of Sciences (USA) 89:4722–4725.

RICKLEFS, R. E., AND D. SCHLUTER. 1993. Species diversity in ecological communities: historical and geographical perspectives. University of Chicago Press, Chicago, IL.

RIDLEHUBER, K. T. 1982. Fire ant predation on wood duck ducklings and piped eggs. Southwestern Naturalist 27:222.

RIENECKER, W. C. 1987. Migration and distribution of pintails banded in California. California Fish and Game 73:139–155.

RIENECKER, W. C. 1988. Additional notes on migration and distribution of pintails banded in California. California Fish and Game 74:61–63.

RILEY, E. M. 1996. The role of MHC- and non-MHC-associated genes in determining the human immune response to malaria antigens. Parasitology 112:S39-S51.

RIPLEY, S. D. 1960. Laysan Teal in captivity. Wilson Bulletin 72:244–247.

RIPLEY, S. D. 1962. Brief comments on the thrushes. Postilla (Yale Peabody Museum Natural History) 63: 1–5.

RIPLEY, S. D. 1977. Rails of the world. Davide. R. Goodine, Boston, MA.

ROBERTSON, H. A., J. R. HAY, E. K. SAUL, AND G. V. MCCORMACK. 1994. Recovery of the Kakerori: an endangered forest bird of the Cook Islands. Conservation Biology 8:1078–1086.

ROCK, J. F. 1913. The indigenous trees of the Hawaiian Islands. Privately published, Honolulu, HI.

ROCK, J. F. 1974. The indigenous trees of the Hawaiian Islands. Reprinted edition. Charles E. Tuttle Co., Rutland, VT, and Tokyo, Japan.

RODDA, G. H., AND T. H. FRITTS. 1992. The impact of the introduction of the colubrid snake Boiga irregularis on Guam's lizards. Journal of Herpetology 26:166–174.

RODDA, G. H., T. H. FRITTS, AND D. CHISZAR. 1997. The disappearance of Guam's wildlife. Bioscience 47:565–574.

RODDA, G. H., T. H. FRITTS, AND P. J. CONRY. 1992. Origin and population growth of the Brown Tree Snake, Boiga irregularis, on Guam. Pacific Science 46:46–57.

RODDA, G. H., T. H. FRITTS, M. J. MCCOID, AND E. W. CAMPBELL, III. 1998. An overview of the biology of the brown tree snake, Boiga irregularis, a costly introduced pest on Pacific Islands. Pp. 44–80 in G. H. Rodda, Y. Sawai, D. Chiszar, and H. Tanaka (editors). Problem snake management: habu and the brown tree snake. Cornell University Press, Ithaca, NY.

RODRIGUEZ-ESTRELLA, R., G. ARNAUD, S. A. CARDENAS, AND A. RODRIGUEZ. 1991. Predation by feral cats on birds at Isla Soccoro, Mexico. Western Birds 22: 141–142.

ROGERS, M. J., G. A. MCCONKEY, J. LI, AND T. F. MCCUTCHAN. 1995. The ribosomal DNA loci in Plasmodium falciparum accumulate mutations independently. Journal of Molecular Biology 254: 881–891.

ROHWER, F. C., AND M. G. ANDERSON. 1988. Female-biased philopatry, monogamy, and the timing of pair formation in waterfowl. Current Ornithology 5:187–221.

ROOD, J. P. 1986. Ecology and social evolution in mongooses. Pp. 131–152 in D. I. Rubenstein and R. Wrangham (editors). Ecological aspects of social evolution—birds and mammals. Princeton University Press, Princeton, NJ.

ROSE, R. G., S. CONANT, AND E. P. KJELLGREN. 1993. Hawaiian standing kāhilí in the Bishop Museum: an ethnological and biological analysis. Journal of the Polynesian Society 102:27–304.

ROSEN, P. C., AND C. R. SCHWALBE. 1995. Bullfrogs: introduced predators in Southwestern wetlands. Pp. 452–454 in E. T. LaRoe, G. S. Farris, C. E. Puckett, P. D. Doran, and M. J. Mac (editors). Our living resources: a report to the nation on the distribution, abundance, and health of U.S. plants, animals, and ecosystems. U.S. Department of the Interior, National Biological Service, Washington, D.C.

ROTHSCHILD, W. 1892. Descriptions of seven new species of birds from the Sandwich Islands. Annual Magazine of Natural History 60:108–112.

ROTHSCHILD, W. 1893–1900. The avifauna of Laysan and the neighboring islands. 3 vol. R. H. Porter, London, UK.

ROUSE, I. 1986. Migrations in prehistory. Yale University Press, New Haven, CT.

ROWLEY, I., AND E. RUSSELL. 1991. Demography of passerines in the temperate southern hemisphere. Pp. 22–44 in C. M. Perrins, J.-D. Lebreton, and G. J. M. Hirons (editors). Bird population studies: relevance to conservation and management. Oxford University Press, New York, NY.

RUDDY, D. A., G. S. KRONMAL, V. K. LEE, G. A. MINTIER, L. QUINTANA, R. DOMINGO, JR., N. C. MYER, A. IRRINKI, E. E. MCCLELLAND, A. FULLAN, F. A. MAPA, T. MOORE, W. THOMAS, D. B. LOEB, C. HARMON, Z. TSUCHIHASHI, R. K. WOLFF, R. C. SCHATZMAN, AND J. N. FEDER. 1997. A 1.1-Mb transcript map of the hereditary hemochromatosis locus. Genome Research 7:441–456.

RUSSO, C.-A. M., N. TAKEZAKI, AND M. NEI. 1995. Molecular phylogeny and divergence times of Drosophilid species. Molecular Biology and Evolution 12:391–404.

RYAN, P. G. 1991. The impact of the commercial lobster fishery on seabirds at the Tristan da Cunha Islands, South Atlantic Ocean. Biological Conservation 57:339–350.

RYAN, P. G., AND B. P. WATKINS. 1989. The influences of physical factors and orthogenic products on plant and arthropod abundance at an inland Nunatak group in Antarctica. Polar Biology 10:151–160.

SABO, S. R. 1980. Niche and habitat relations in subalpine bird communities of the White Mountains of New Hampshire. Ecological Monographs 50:241–259.

SABO, S. R. 1982. The rediscovery of Bishop's 'O'o on Maui. 'Elepaio 42:69–70.

SAITOU, N., AND M. NEI. 1987. The neighbor-joining method: a new method for reconstructing phylogenetic trees. Molecular Biology and Evolution 4:406–425.

SAKAI, H. F., AND J. R. CARPENTER. 1990. The variety and nutritional value of foods consumed by Hawaiian Crow nestlings, an endangered species. Condor 92:220–228.

SAKAI, H. F., AND T. C. JOHANOS. 1983. The nest, egg, young, and aspects of the life history of the endangered Hawaii Creeper. Western Birds 14:73–84.

SAKAI, H. F., AND C. J. RALPH. 1980a. Nest construction of the Hawaiian Creeper near Volcano, Hawaii. 'Elepaio 40:117–119.

SAKAI, H. F., AND C. J. RALPH. 1980b. An observation of 'Akiapola'au nest construction. 'Elepaio 41:4–5.

SAKAI, H. F., C. J. RALPH, AND C. D. JENKINS. 1986. Foraging ecology of the Hawaiian Crow, an endangered generalist. Condor 88:211–219.

SALOMONSEN, F. 1968. The moult migration. Wildfowl 19:5–24.

SALOMONSEN, J., D. DUNON, K. SKJØDT, D. THORPE, O. VAINIO, AND J. KAUFMAN. 1991. Chicken major histocompatibility complex-encoded B-G antigens are found on many cell types that are important for the immune system. Proceedings of the National Academy of Sciences (USA) 88:1359–1363.

SAS INSTITUTE, INC. 1985. SAS user's guide. Version 5. SAS Institute, Inc., Cary, NC.

SAS INSTITUTE, INC. 1987. SAS/STAT guide for personal computers. Version 6. SAS Institute, Inc., Cary, NC.

SASTRAPRADJA, D. S. 1965. A study of the variation in wood anatomy of Hawaiian Metrosideros (Myrtaceae). Ph.D. dissertation. University of Hawaii, Honolulu, HI.

SATCHELL, M. 1997. Parks in peril. U.S. News and World Report, July 21, 1997, pp. 23–28.

SATO, K., H. ABPLANALP, D. NAPOLITANO, AND J. REID. 1992. Effects of heterozygosity of major histocompatibility complex haplotypes on performance of leghorn hens sharing a common inbred background. Poultry Science 71:18–26.

SATTA, Y., C. O'HUIGIN, N. TAKAHATA, AND J. KLEIN. 1995. Intensity of overdominant selection at the major histocompatibility complex loci. Pp. 179–186 in M. Nei and N. Takahata (editors). Current topics on molecular evolution. Pennsylvania State University/Graduate School for Advanced Studies, Hayama, Japan.

SAUER, J. R., AND B. K. WILLIAMS. 1989. Generalized procedures for testing hypotheses about survival or recovery rates. Journal of Wildlife Management 53:137–142.

SAUNDERS, A. 1994. Translocations in New Zealand: an overview. Pp. 43–46 in M. Serna (editor). Reintroduction biology of Australian and New Zealand fauna. Surrey Beatty and Sons, Sydney, Australia.

SAUNDERS, D. A., G. T. SMITH, AND I. ROWLEY. 1982. The availability and dimensions of tree hollows that provide nest sites for cockatoos (Psittaciformes) in Western Australia. Australian Wildlife Research 9:541–556.

SAVAGE, H. M., C. J. MITCHELL, M. ROPPUL, L. T. CASTRO, R. L. KEPPLE, AND S. P. FLOOD. 1993. Mosquito faunal survey of Saipan, Mariana Islands (Diptera: Culicidae): taxonomy and larval ecology. Mosquito Systematics 25:17–24.

SAVIDGE, J. A. 1986. The role of disease and predation in the decline of Guam's avifauna. Ph.D. dissertation. University Illinois, Champaign, IL.

SAVIDGE, J. A. 1987a. Extinction of an island forest avifauna by an introduced snake. Ecology 68:660–668.

SAVIDGE, J. A. 1987b. The ecological and economic impacts of an introduced snake on Guam and its threat to other Pacific islands. Pacific Life and Environmental Studies 3:29–34.

SAVIDGE, J. A. 1988. Food habits of Boiga irregularis, an introduced predator on Guam. Journal of Herpetology 22:275–282.

SAVIDGE, J. A., L. SILEO, AND L. M. SIEGFRIED. 1992. Was disease involved in the decimation of Guam's avifauna? Journal Wildlife Diseases 28:206–214.

SCHAUINSLAND, H. H. 1899. Three months on a coral island (Laysan). (Translated from the German by M. D. F. Udvardy). Atoll Research Bulletin 432 [1996].

SCHILZ, A. J. 1996. Cultural resources management plan, Marine Corps Base Hawaii, Kaneohe Bay, Island of O'ahu, Hawaii. Final report. Prepared by Ogden Environmental and Energy Services Co., Inc., Honolulu, Hawai'i.

SCHLANGER, S. O., AND G. W. GILLETT. 1976. A geological perspective of the upland biota of Laysan Atoll (Hawaiian Islands). Biological Journal of the Linnean Society 8:205–216.

SCHMIDT, K. P., AND R. F. INGER. 1957. Living reptiles of the world. Doubleday and Co., Garden City, NY.

SCHMITT, R. C. 1971. New estimates of the precensused population of Hawaii. Journal of Polynesian Society 80:237–243.

SCHNEE, P. 1901. Eine auffallende Vogelzugstrasse vom nordwestlichen Nordamerika nach Polynesien. Ornithologische Monatsberichte 9:131–132.

SCHREIBER, R. W., AND E. A SCHREIBER. 1984. Central Pacific seabirds and the El Niño Southern Oscillation: 1982 to 1983 perspectives. Science 225:713–716.

SCHROEDER, T. 1993. Climate controls. Pp. 12–36 in M. Sanderson (editor). Prevailing trade winds: climate and weather in Hawaii. University of Hawaii Press, Honolulu, HI.

SCHUETT, G. W., P. J. FERNANDEZ, W. F. GERGITS, N. J. CASNA, D. CHISZAR, H. M. SMITH, J. B. MITTON, S. P. MACKESSY, R. A. ODUM, AND M. J. DEMLONG. 1997. Production of offspring in the absence of males: evidence for facultative parthenogenesis in bisexual snakes. Herpetological Natural History 5:1–10.

SCHULTZ, F. T., AND W. E. BRILES. 1953. The adaptive value of blood group genes in chickens. Genetics 38:34–50.

SCHWARTZ, A., AND R. W. HENDERSON. 1991. Amphibians and reptiles of the West Indies: descriptions, distributions, and natural history. University of Florida Press, Gainesville, FL.

SCHWARTZ, C. W., AND E. R. SCHWARTZ. 1949. A reconnaissance of the game birds in Hawaii. Board of Commissioners of Agriculture and Forestry, Hilo, HI.

SCOTT, J. M., AND P. W. BANKO. 2000. Hawaiian goose (Branta sandvicensis). Pp. 142–146 in R. P. Reading and B. Miller (editors). Endangered animals: a reference guide to conflicting issues. Greenwood Press, Westport, CT.

SCOTT, J. M., S. CONANT, AND H. D. PRATT. 1979. Field identification of the Hawaiian Creeper on the island of Hawaii. Western Birds 10:71–80.

SCOTT, J. M., AND C. B. KEPLER. 1985. Distribution and abundance of Hawaiian native birds: A status report. Bird Conservation 2:43–70. University of Wisconsin Press, Madison, WI.

SCOTT, J. M., C. B. KEPLER, C. VAN RIPER, III, AND S. I. FEFER. 1988. Conservation of Hawaii's vanishing avifauna. Bioscience 38:238–253.

SCOTT, J. M., C. B. KEPLER, C. VAN RIPER, III, C. STONE, AND S. I. FEFER. 1989. Reply to: Integrated conservation strategy for Hawaiian forest birds. Bioscience 39:476–479.

SCOTT, J. M., S. MOUNTAINSPRING, F. L. RAMSEY, AND C. B. KEPLER. 1986. Forest bird communities of the Hawaiian Islands: their dynamics, ecology, and conservation. Studies in Avian Biology No. 9:1–431.

SCOTT, J. M., S. MOUNTAINSPRING, C. VAN RIPER, III, C. B. KEPLER, J. D. JACOBI, T. A. BURR, AND J. G. GIFFIN. 1984. Annual variation in the distribution, abundance, and habitat response of the Palila (Loxioides bailleui). Auk 101:647–664.

SCOTT, J. M., J. L. SINCOCK, AND A. J. BERGER. 1980. Records of nests, eggs, nestlings, and cavity nesting of endemic passerine birds in Hawaii. 'Elepaio 40:163–168.

SCOTT, J. M., D. H. WOODSIDE, AND T. L. C. CASEY. 1977. Observations of birds in the Molokai Forest Reserve, July 1975. 'Elepaio 38:25–27.

SCOTT, M. E. 1988. The impact of infection and disease on animal populations: implications for conservation biology. Conservation Biology 2:40–56.

SCOTT, P. 1962. A project for a Nene park in Hawaii. Elepaio 22:80–81.

SCOWCROFT, P. G. 1983. Tree cover changes in māmane (Sophora chrysophylla) forests grazed by sheep and cattle. Pacific Science 37:109–119.

SCOWCROFT, P. G. 1992. Role of decaying logs and other organic seedbeds in natural regeneration of Hawaiian forest species on abandoned montane pasture. USDA Forest Service General Technical Report PSW-129:67–73. U.S. Forest Service, Berkeley, CA.

SCOWCROFT, P. G., AND J. G. GIFFIN. 1983. Feral herbivores suppress mamane and other browse species on Mauna Kea, Hawaii. Journal of Range Management 36:638–645.

SCOWCROFT, P. G., AND R. HOBDY. 1987. Recovery of montane koa parkland vegetation from feral goats. Biotropica 19:208–215.

SCOWCROFT, P. G., AND H. F. SAKAI. 1983. Impact of feral herbivores on mamane forests of Mauna Kea, Hawaii: bark stripping and diameter class structure. Journal of Range Management 36:495–498.

SCOWCROFT, P. G., AND H. F. SAKAI. 1984. Stripping of Acacia koa bark by rats in Hawaii and Maui. Pacific Science 38:80–86.

SEARCY, W. A. 1978. Foraging success in three age classes of Glaucous-winged Gulls. Auk 95:586–588.

SEDINGER, J. S. 1997. Adaptations to and consequences of an herbivorous diet in grouse and waterfowl. Condor 99:314–326.

SEDINGER, J. S., AND P. L. FLINT. 1991. Growth rate is negatively correlated with hatch date in black brant. Ecology 72:496–502.

SEDINGER, J. S., AND D. G. RAVELING. 1984. Dietary selectivity in relation to availability and quality of food for goslings of Cackling Geese. Auk 101:295–306.

SEDINGER, J. S., AND D. G. RAVELING. 1986. Timing of nesting by Canada Geese in relation to the phenology and availability of their food plants. Journal of Animal Ecology 55:1083–1102.

SEIGEL, R. A., AND N.B. FORD. 1987. Reproductive ecology. Pp. 210–252 in R. A. Seigel, J. T. Collins, and S. S. Novak (editors). Snakes: ecology and evolutionary biology. McGraw-Hill Publishing Co., New York, NY.

SERNA, M. (EDITOR). 1995. Reintroduction biology of Australia and New Zealand fauna. Surrey Beatty and Sons, Sydney, Australia.

SETO, N. 1994. Effects of rat predation on Bonin Petrel (Pterodroma hypoleuca) reproductive success on Midway Atoll. 'Elepaio 54:50–51.

SETO, N. W. H. 1995. Effects of rat (Rattus rattus) predation on Bonin Petrel (Pterodroma hypoleuca) reproductive success. Pacific Seabirds 22:43.

SETO, N. W. H., AND S. CONANT. 1996. The effects of rat (Rattus rattus) predation on reproductive success of the Bonin Petrel (Pterodroma hypoleuca) on Midway Atoll. Colonial Waterbirds 19:171–185.

SHAFFER, M. L. 1981. Minimum population sizes for species conservation. BioScience 31:131–134.

SHALLENBERGER, R. J., AND H. D. PRATT. 1978. Recent observations and field identification of the Oahu

Creeper (*Loxops maculata maculata*). 'Elepaio 38: 135–140.

SHALLENBERGER, R. J., AND G. K. VAUGHN. 1978. Avifaunal survey in the central Ko'olau Range, Oahu. Ahuimanu Productions, Honolulu, HI.

SHANNON, L. J., AND R. J. M. CRAWFORD. 1999. Management of the African Penguin *Spheniscus demersus*—insights from modeling. Marine Ornithology 27:119–128.

SHAW, S. L. 1981. A history of tropical cyclones in the central North Pacific and the Hawaiian Islands: 1832–1979. National Weather Service, NOAA, U.S. Department of Commerce, Washington, D.C.

SHIELDS, G. F., AND A. C. WILSON. 1987. Calibration of mitochondrial DNA evolution in geese. Journal of Molecular Evolution 24:212–217.

SHIGO, A. L. 1984. Compartmentalization: a conceptual framework for understanding how trees grow and defend themselves. Annual Review of Phytopathology 22:189–214.

SHIGO, A. L. 1991. Modern arboriculture. Shigo and Trees, Associates, Durham, NH.

SHIINA, T., A. ANDO, T. IMANISHI, H. KAWATA, K. HANZAWA, T. GOJOBORI, H. INOKO, AND S. WATANABE. 1995. Isolation and characterization of cDNA clones for Japanese Quail (*Coturnix japonica*) major histocompatibility complex (Mhc *Coja*) class I molecules. Immunogenetics 42:213–216.

SHINE, R. 1991. Strangers in a strange land: ecology of Australian colubrid snakes. Copeia 1991:120–131.

SHINE, R., AND R. A. SEIGEL. 1996. A neglected life-history trait: clutch-size variance in snakes. Journal of Zoology (London) 239:209–223.

SHOEMAKER, D. D., AND K. G. ROSS. 1996. Effects of social organization on gene flow in the fire ant *Solenopsis invicta*. Nature 383:613–616.

SHORT, L. L., JR. 1965. Hybridization in the flickers (*Colaptes*) of North America. Bulletin of the American Museum of Natural History 129:307–408.

SIBLEY, C. G. 1997. The species problem. Birding 29:215–219.

SIBLEY, C. G., AND J. E. AHLQUIST. 1982. The relationships of the Hawaiian honeycreepers (Drepanidini) as indicated by DNA-DNA hybridization. Auk 99:130–140.

SIBLEY, C. G., AND B. L. MONROE, JR. 1990. Distribution and taxonomy of birds of the world. Yale University Press, New Haven, CT.

SIBLEY, C. G., AND B. L. MONROE, JR. 1993. A supplement to distribution and taxonomy of birds of the world. Yale University Press, New Haven, CT.

SIBLEY, C. G., AND L. L. SHORT, JR. 1964. Hybridization in the orioles of the Great Plains. Auk 76:443–463.

SIBLEY, C. G., AND D. A. WEST. 1959. Hybridization in the Rufous-sided Towhees of the Great Plains. Auk 76:326–338.

SIDLE, G. R., A. J. PEARCE, AND C. L. O'LOUGHLIN. 1985. Hillslope stability and land use. American Geophysical Union, Washington, D.C.

SIKES, P. J., AND K. A. ARNOLD. 1986. Red imported fire ant (*Solenopsis invicta*) predation on Cliff Swallow (*Hirundo pyrrhonota*) nestlings in east-central Texas. Southwestern Naturalist 31:105–106.

SIMBERLOFF, D., AND W. BOECKLEN. 1991. Patterns of extinction in the introduced Hawaiian avifauna: a reexamination of the role of competition. American Naturalist 138:300–327.

SIMON, C. 1987. Hawaiian evolutionary biology: an introduction. Trends in Ecology and Evolution 2:175–178.

SIMON, J. C., P. E. BAKER, AND H. BAKER. 1997. Maui Parrotbill (*Pseudonestor xanthophrys*). *In* A. Poole and F. Gill (editors). The Birds of North America, No. 311. The Academy of Natural Sciences, Philadelpia, PA, and American Ornithologists' Union, Washington, D.C.

SIMON, J. C., T. K. PRATT, K. E. BERLIN, AND J. R. KOWALSKY. 1998. Age and sex identification of Akohekohe. Journal of Field Ornithology 69:654–660.

SIMONS, T. R. 1983. Biology and conservation of the endangered Hawaiian Dark-rumped Petrel (*Pterodroma phaeopygia sandwichensis*). CPSU/UW 83–2. National Park Service, Cooperative Parks Study Unit, College of Forest Resources, University of Washington, Seattle, WA.

SIMONS, T. R. 1984. A population model of the endangered Hawaiian Dark-rumped Petrel. Journal of Wildlife Management 48:1065–1076.

SIMONS, T. R. 1985. Biology and behavior of the endangered Hawaiian Dark-rumped Petrel. Condor 87:229–245.

SIMONS, T. R., AND C. N. HODGES. 1998. Dark-rumped Petrel (*Pterodroma phaeopygia*). *In* A. Poole and F. Gill (editors). The Birds of North America, No. 345. The Academy of Natural Sciences, Philadelphia, PA, and American Ornithologists' Union, Washington, D.C.

SINCOCK, J. L., R. E. DAEHLER, T. TELFER, AND D. H. WOODSIDE. 1984. Kauai forest bird recovery plan. U.S. Fish and Wildlife Service, Portland, OR.

SINCOCK, J. L., AND J. M. SCOTT. 1980. Cavity nesting of the Akepa on the island of Hawaii. Wilson Bulletin 92:261–263.

SINCOCK, J. L., AND G. E. SWEDBERG. 1969. Rediscovery of the nesting grounds of Newell's Manx Shearwater (*Puffinus puffinus newelli*), with initial observations. Condor 71:69–71.

SKOLMAN, R. G. 1979. Plantings of the first reserves of Hawaii, 1910–1960. Institute of Pacific Islands Forestry, Pacific Southwest Forest and Range Experiment Station. U.S. Forest Service Honolulu, HI.

SKUTCH, A. F. 1949. Do tropical birds rear as many young as they can nourish? Ibis 91:430–455.

SKUTCH, A. F. 1950. The nesting season of Central American birds in relation to climate and food supply. Ibis 92:185–222.

SKUTCH, A. F. 1985. Clutch size, nesting success, and predation on nests of Neotropcial birds; reviewed. Ornithological Monographs 36:575–594.

SMITH, C. W. 1985. Impacts of alien plants on Hawai'i's native biota. Pp. 180–250 *in* C. P. Stone and J. M. Scott (editors). Hawai'i's terrestrial ecosystems: preservation and management. Cooperative National Park Resources Studies Unit, University of Hawaii, Honolulu, HI.

SMITH, C. W. 1989. Nonnative plants. Pp. 60–68 *in* C. P. Stone and D. B. Stone (editors). Conservation biology in Hawaii. Cooperative National Park Resources Studies Unit, University of Hawaii, Honolulu, HI.

SMITH, C. W., AND J. T. TUNISON. 1992. Fire and alien plants in Hawaii: research and management implications for native ecosystems. Pp. 394–408 in C. P. Stone, C. W. Smith, and J. T. Tunison (editors). Alien plant invasions in native ecosystems of Hawaii: management and research. Cooperative National Park Resources Studies Unit, University of Hawaii, Honolulu, HI.

SMITH, H. E., AND S. J. GUEST. 1974. A survey of internal parasites of birds on the western slopes of Diamond Head, Oahu Hawaii 1972–1973. US/IBP Island Ecosystems IRP Technical Report Number 37.

SMITH, J. D. 1952. The Hawaiian Goose (Nene) restoration program. Journal of Wildlife Management 16:1–9.

SMITH, J. N. M. 1988. Determinants of lifetime reproductive success in the song sparrow. Pp. 154–172 in T. H. Clutton-Brock (editor). Reproductive success: studies of individual variation in contrasting breeding systems. University of Chicago Press, Chicago, IL.

SMITH, J. N. M., P. ARCESE, AND W. M. HOCHACHKA. 1991. Social behavior and population regulation in insular bird populations: implications for conservation. Pp. 148–167 in C. M. Perrins, J. D. Lebreton, and G. J. M. Hirons (editors). Bird population studies. Oxford University Press, Oxford, UK.

SMITH, T. B., AND S. G. FANCY. 1998. Challenges and approaches for conserving Hawaii's endangered forest birds. Pp. 306–316 in P. L. Fiedler and P. M. Kareiva (editors). Conservation biology: for the coming decade. 2nd edition. Chapman and Hall, New York, NY.

SNETSINGER, T. J., S. G. FANCY, J. C. SIMON, AND J. D. JACOBI. 1994. Diets of owls and feral cats in Hawaii. 'Elepaio 54: 47–50.

SNETSINGER, T. J., M. H. REYNOLDS, AND C. M. HERRMANN. 1998. 'Ō'ū (Psittirostra psittacea) and Lāna'i Hookbill (Dysmorodrepanis munroi). In A. Poole and F. Gill (editors). The Birds of North America, No. 335–336. The Academy of Natural Sciences, Philadelphia, PA, and American Ornithologists' Union, Washington, D.C.

SNETSINGER, T. J., K. M. WAKELEE, AND S. G. FANCY. 1999. Puaiohi (Myadestes palmeri). In A. Poole and F. Gill (editors). The Birds of North America, No. 461. The Academy of Natural Sciences, Philadelphia, PA, and American Ornithologists' Union, Washington, D.C.

SNOUNOU, G., S. VIRIYAKOSOL, X. P. ZHU, W. JARRA, L. PINHEIRO, V. E. DO ROSARIO, S. THAITHONG, AND K. N. BROWN. 1993. High sensitivity of detection of human malaria parasites by the use of nested polymerase chain reaction. Molecular and Biochemical Parasitology 61:315–320.

SNOW, D. W. 1997. Should the biological be superseded by the phylogenetic species concept? Bulletin of the British Ornithologists' Club 117:110–121.

SNYDER, N. F. R., S. R. DERRICKSON, S. R. BEISSINGER, J. W. WILEY, T. B. SMITH, W. D. TOONE, AND B. MILLER. 1996. Limitations of captive breeding in en-

dangered species recovery. Conservation Biology 10:338–348.

SOKAL, R. R., AND F. J. ROHLF. 1981. Biometry. 2nd edition. W. H. Freeman and Company, San Francisco, CA.

SORENSON, M. D., A. COOPER, E. E. PAXINOS, T. W. QUINN, H. F. JAMES, S. L. OLSON, AND R. C. FLEISCHER. 1999. Relationships of the extinct moa-nalos, flightless Hawaiian waterfowl, based on ancient DNA. Proceedings of the Royal Society of London, Series B, 266 (Nov.): 2187–2193.

SORENSON, M. D., AND R. C. FLEISCHER. 1996. Multiple independent transpositions of mitochondrial DNA control region sequences to the nucleus. Proceedings of the National Academy of Sciences (USA) 93: 15239–15243.

SOULÉ, M. E. 1980. Thresholds for survival: maintaining fitness and evolutionary potential. Pp. 151–169 in M. E. Soulé and B. A. Wilcox (editors). Conservation biology: an evolutionary-ecological perspective. Sinauer Associates, Sunderland, MA.

SOULÉ, M. E. (EDITOR). 1987. Viable populations for conservation. Cambridge University Press, London, UK.

SOUTHERN, E. M. 1975. Detection of specific sequences among DNA fragments separated by gel electrophoresis. Journal of Molecular Biology 98:503–517.

SPATZ, G., AND D. MUELLER-DOMBOIS. 1981. Age structure of Acacia koa. Pp. 268–275 in D. Mueller-Dombois, K. W. Bridges, and H. L. Carson (editors). Island ecosystems: biological organization in selected Hawaiian communities. Hutchinson Ross, Stroudsburg, PA.

SPEAR, L. B., D. G. AINLEY, N. NUR, AND S. N. G. HOWELL. 1995. Population size and factors affecting at-sea distributions of four endangered Procellariids in the tropical Pacific. Condor 97:613–638.

SPEAR, L. B., T. M. PENNIMAN, J. F. PENNIMAN, H. R. CARTER, AND D. G. AINLEY. 1987. Survivorship and mortality factors in a population of Western Gulls. Studies in Avian Biology 10:44–56.

SPIETH, H. T. 1966. Hawaiian honeycreeper, Vestiaria coccinea (Forster), feeding on lobeliad flowers, Clermontia arborescens (Mann) Hillebrand American Naturalist 100:470–473.

SPRIGGS, M. 1997. Landscape catastrophe and landscape enhancement: are either or both true in the Pacific? Pp. 80–104 in P. V. Kirch and T. L. Hunt (editors). Historical ecology in the Pacific Islands. Yale University Press, New Haven, CT.

STAFFORD, P. J. 1986. Pythons and boas. T. F. H. Publishing Co., Neptune City, NJ.

STANLEY, H. F., M. KADWELL, AND J. C. WHEELER. 1994. Molecular evolution of the family Camelidae: a mitochondrial DNA study. Proceedings of the Royal Society of London, Series B 256:1–6.

STANNARD, D. 1989. Before the horror: the population of Hawaii on the eve of Western contact. University of Hawaii Press, Honolulu HI.

STAPP, P., G. A. POLIS, AND F. SÁNCHEZ PIÑERO. 1999. Stable isotopes reveal strong marine and El Niño effects on island food webs. Nature 401:467–469.

STATE OF HAWAII. 1987. The Newell's Shearwater light attraction problem: a guide for architects, planners, and resort managers. Department of Land and Natural Resources, Division of Forestry and Wildlife, Lihue, HI.

STATTERSFIELD, A. J., M. J. CROSBY, A. J. LONG, AND D. C. WEGE. 1998. Endemic bird areas of the world: priorities for biodiversity conservation. BirdLife International. BirdLife Conservation Series No. 7. Cambridge, UK.

STEADMAN, D. W. 1991. Extinct and extirpated birds from Aitutaki and Atiu, Southern Cook Islands. Pacific Science 45:325–347.

STEADMAN, D. W. 1992. Extinct and extirpated birds from Rota, Mariana Islands. Micronesica 25:71–84.

STEADMAN, D. W. 1993. A chronstratigraphic analysis of landbird extinction on Tahuata, Marquesas Islands. Journal of Archeological Society 23:81–94.

STEADMAN, D. W. 1995. Prehistoric extinctions of Pacific island birds: biodiversity meets zooarchaeology. Science 267:1123–1131.

STEADMAN, D. W. 1997a. Human-caused extinction of birds. Pp. 139–161 in M. L. Reaka-Kudla, D. E. Wilson, and E. O. Wilson (editors). Biodiversity II. Joseph Henry Press, Washington, D.C.

STEADMAN, D. W. 1997b. Extinctions of Polynesian birds: reciprocal impacts of birds and people. Pp. 51–79 in P. V. Kirch and T. L. Hunt (editors). Historical ecology of the Pacific islands. Yale University Press, New Haven, CT.

STEADMAN, D. W., E. C. GREINER, AND C. S WOOD. 1990. Absence of blood parasites in indigenous and introduced birds from the Cook Islands, South Pacific. Conservation Biology 4:398–404.

STEARNS, H. T. 1966. Geology of the state of Hawaii. Pacific Books, Palo Alto, CA.

STEINITZ, C. (EDITOR). 1996. Biodiversity and landscape planning: alternative futures for the region of Camp Pendleton, California. Prepared by Harvard University, USDA Forest Service, U.S. Environmental Protection Agency, and The Nature Conservancy, Cambridge, MA, Logan, UT, Corvallis, OR, and Temecula, CA.

STEJNEGER, L. 1887. Birds of Kauai Island, Hawaiian Archipelago, collected by Mr. Valdemar Knudsen, with descriptions of new species. Proceedings of the United States National Museum 10:75–102.

STEJNEGER, L. 1889. Notes on a third collection of birds made in Kauai, Hawaiian Islands, by Valdemar Knudsen. Proceedings of the United States National Museum 12:377–386.

STEVENS, L. 1996. Avian biochemistry and molecular biology. Cambridge University Press, New York, NY.

STILES, F. G. 1975. Ecology, flowering phenology, and hummingbird pollination of some Costa Rican Heliconia species. Ecology 56:285–301.

STILES, F. G. 1978. Temporal organization of flowering among the hummingbird foodplants of a tropical wet forest. Biotropica 10:194–210.

STILES, F. G. 1980. The annual cycle in a tropical wet forest hummingbird community. Ibis 122:322–343.

STILES, F. G. 1985. Seasonal patterns and coevolution in the hummingbird-flower community of a Costa Rican subtropical forest. Ornithological Monographs 36:757–787.

STILES, F. G. 1988. Altitudinal movements of birds on the Caribbean slope of Costa Rica: implications for conservation. Pp. 243–258 in F. Almeda and C. M. Pringle (editors). Tropical rainforests: diversity and conservation. California Academy of Sciences, San Francisco, CA.

STILES, F. G. 1995. Behavioral, ecological and morphological correlates of foraging for arthropods by the hummingbirds of a tropical wet forest. Condor 97:853–878.

STINSON, D. W., G. J. WILES, AND J. D. REICHEL. 1997. Migrant land birds and water birds in the Mariana Islands. Pacific Science 51:314–327.

STODDARD, D. R., AND R. P. D. WALSH. 1992. Environmental variability and environmental extremes as factors in the island ecosystem. Atoll Research Bulletin 356:1–71.

STODDARD, H. L. 1931. The Bobwhite Quail, its habits, preservation and increase. Charles Scribner's Sons, New York, NY.

STONE, C. P. 1985. Alien animals in Hawai'i's native ecosystems: towards controlling the adverse effects of introduced vertebrates. Pp. 251–297 in C. P. Stone and J. M. Scott (editors). Hawaii's terrestrial ecosystems: preservation and management. Cooperative National Park Resources Studies Unit, University of Hawaii, Honolulu, HI.

STONE, C. P. 1989. Non-native land vertebrates. Pp. 88–95 in C. P. Stone and D. B. Stone (editors). Conservation biology in Hawaii. Cooperative National Park Resources Studies Unit, University of Hawaii, Honolulu, HI.

STONE, C. P., M. DUSEK, AND M. AEDER. 1995. Use of an anticoagulant to control mongooses in Nene breeding habitat. 'Elepaio 54:73–78.

STONE, C. P., AND L. L. LOOPE. 1987. Reducing negative effects of introduced animals on native biotas in Hawaii: what is being done, what needs doing, and the role of national parks. Environmental Conservation 14:245–258.

STONE, C. P., AND J. M. SCOTT (EDITORS). 1985a. Hawai'i's terrestrial ecosystems: preservation and management. Cooperative National Park Resources Studies Unit, University of Hawaii, Honolulu, HI.

STONE, C. P., AND J. M. SCOTT. 1985b. Hawai'i's native ecosystems: importance, conflicts, and suggestions for the future. Pp. 495–534 in C. P. Stone and J. M. Scott (editors). Hawai'i's terrestrial ecosystems: preservation and management. Cooperative National Park Resources Studies Unit, University of Hawaii Press, Honolulu, HI.

STONE, C. P., C. W. SMITH, AND J. T. TUNISON (EDITORS). 1992. Alien plant invasions in native ecosystems of Hawaii: management and research. Cooperative National Park Resources Studies Unit, University of Hawaii, Honolulu, HI.

STONE, C. P., AND D. B. STONE (EDITORS). 1989. Conservation biology in Hawaii. Cooperative National Park Resources Studies Unit, University of Hawaii, Honolulu, HI.

STONE, C. P., R. L. WALKER, J. M. SCOTT, AND P. C. BANKO. 1983. Hawaiian goose research and management—where do we go from here? 'Elepaio 44: 11–15.

STRAHM, W. 1996. Invasive species in Mauritius: examining the past and charting the future. Pp. 167–175 in O. T. Sandlund, P. J. Schei, and A. Viken (editors). 1996. Proceedings of the Norway/UN Conference on Alien Species. Directorate for Nature Management and Norwegian Institute for Nature Research, Trondheim, Norway.

STURMAN, W. A. 1968. Description and analysis of breeding habits of the chickadees, *Parus atricapillus* and *P. rufescens*. Ecology 49:418–431.

SUH, W.-K., M. F. COHEN-DOYLE, K. FRUH, K. WANG, P. A. PETERSON, AND D. B. WILLIAMS. 1994. Interaction of MHC class I molecules with the transporter associated with antigen processing. Science 264: 1322–1326.

SULLIVAN, K. A., AND J. J. ROPER. 1996. Impacts of predation on passerine post-fledging success. Transactions of the North American Wildlife and Natural Resource Conference 61:77–85.

SUMMERS, R. W., AND J. STANSFIELD. 1991. Changes in the quantity and quality of grassland due to winter grazing by Brent Geese (*Branta bernicla*). Agriculture, Ecosystems and Environment 36:51–57.

SUSHKIN, P. P. 1929. On the systematic position of the Drepanidae. Verhandl. VI InterNational Ornith. Kongr. Kopenhagen., pp. 379–381.

SWEDBERG, G. E. 1967. The Koloa. Division of Fish and Game, Department of Land and Natural Resources, Honolulu, HI.

SWOFFORD, D. L. 1993. PAUP: Phylogenetic analysis using parsimony. Version 3.1.1. Illinois Natural History Survey, Champaign, IL.

SWOFFORD, D. L. 1996. PAUP*: Phylogenetic analysis using parsimony*, Versions 4.0d52–60. Illinois Natural History Survey, Champaign IL.

SYKES, P. W., A. K. KEPLER, C. B. KEPLER, AND J. M. SCOTT. 2000. Kaua'i 'Ō'ō, O'ahu 'Ō'ō, Bishop 'Ō'ō, Hawai'i 'Ō'ō, and Kioea. *In* A. Poole and F. Gill (editors). The Birds of North America, No. 535. The Academy of Natural Sciences, Philadelphia, PA, and American Ornithologists' Union, Washington, D.C.

TARR, C. L. 1995. Primers for amplification and determination of mitochondrial control-region sequences in oscine passerines. Molecular Ecology 4: 527–529.

TARR, C. L., S. CONANT, AND R. C. FLEISCHER. 1998. Founder events and variation at microsatellite loci in an insular passerine bird, the Laysan Finch (*Telespiza cantans*). Molecular Ecology 7:719–731.

TARR, C. L., AND R. C. FLEISCHER. 1993. Mitochondrial-DNA variation and evolutionary relationships in the amakihi complex. Auk 110:825–831.

TARR, C. L., AND R. C. FLEISCHER. 1995. Evolutionary relationships of the Hawaiian honeycreepers (Aves, Drepanidinae). Pp. 147–159 *in* W. L. Wagner and V. A. Funk (editors). Hawaiian biogeography: evolution on a hotspot archipelago. Smithsonian Institution Press, Washington, D.C.

TAYLOR, D., AND L. KATAHIRA. 1988. Radio telemetry as an aid in eradicating remnant feral goats. Wildlife Soceity Bulletin 16:297–299.

TAYLOR, R. H. 1985. Status, habits and conservation of *Cyanoramphus* parakeets in the New Zealand region. Pp. 195–211 *in* P. J. Moors (editor). Conservation of island birds. International Council for Bird Preservation Technical Publication, No. 3. Cambridge, UK.

TEAR, T. H., J. M. SCOTT, P. H. HAYWARD, AND B.

GRIFFITH. 1993. Status and prospects for success of the Endangered Species Act: a look at recovery plans. Science 262:976–977.

TELEWSKI, F. W. 1995. Wind-induced physiological and developmental responses in trees. Pp. 237–263 *in* M. P. Coutts and J. Grace (editors). Wind and trees. Cambridge University Press, Cambridge, UK.

TELFER, T. C. 1986. Newell's Shearwater nesting colony establishment study on the island of Kauai. Final report. Statewide Pittman-Robertson Program, Department of Lands and Natural Resources, State of Hawaii, Honolulu, HI.

TELFER, T. C. 1995. Survey of the Nene population on Kauai. Pittman-Robertson Report W-18-R-20, Job R-I-G. Hawaii Department of Land and Natural Resources, Division of Forestry and Wildlife, Honolulu, HI.

TELFER, T. C. 1996. Nene surveys, Kauai County. Pittman-Robertson Report W-35-NGS, Project 1, Job 3. Hawaii Department of Land and Natural Resources, Division of Forestry and Wildlife, Honolulu, HI.

TELFER, T. C., J. L. SINCOCK, G. V. BYRD, AND J. R. REED. 1987. Attraction of Hawaiian seabirds to lights: conservation efforts and effects of moon phase. Wildlife Society Bulletin 15:406–413.

TEMPLE, S. A. 1985. Why endemic island birds are so vulnerable to extinction. Bird Conservation 2:3–6. University of Wisconsin Press, Madison, WI.

TEMPLE, S. A. 1986. The problem of avian extinctions. Current Ornithology 3:453–485.

TEMPLE, S. A., AND J. R. CARY. 1988. Modeling dynamics of habitat-interior bird populations in fragmented landscapes. Conservation Biology 2:340–347.

TEMPLETON, T. J., AND D. C. KASLOW. 1997. Cloning and cross-species comparison of the thrombospondin-related anonymous protein (TRAP) gene from *Plasmodium knowlesi*, *Plasmodium vivax* and *Plasmodium gallinaceum*. Molecular and Biochemical Parasitology 84:13–24.

TERBORGH, J. 1995. Wildlife in managed tropical forests: a Neotropical perspective. Pp. 331–342 *in* A. E. Lugo and C. Lowe (editors). Tropical forests: management and ecology. Springer-Verlag, New York, NY.

TERBORGH, J., AND B. WINTER. 1980. Some causes of extinction. Pp. 119–133 *in* M. E. Soulé and B. A. Wilcox (editors). Conservation biology: an evolutionary-ecological perspective. Sinauer Associates, Sunderland, MA.

THOMAS, D. G. 1980. Foraging of honeyeaters in an area of Tasmanian sclerophyll forest. Emu 80:55–58.

THOMAS, R. H., AND J. A. HUNT. 1991. The molecular evolution of the alcohol dehydrogenase locus and the phylogeny of the Hawaiian *Drosophila*. Molecular Biology and Evolution 8:687–702.

THOMPSON, J. N. 1996. Evolutionary ecology and the conservation of biodiversity. Trends in Ecology and Evolution 11:300–303.

THOMPSON, K. R. 1987. The ecology of the Manx Shearwater *Puffinus puffinus* on Rhum, West Scotland. Ph.D. dissertation. University of Scotland, Aberdeen, Scotland.

THROP, J. L. 1970. The Laysan Finch bill in the Honolulu Zoo: *Psittirostra cantans cantans.* Elepaio 31:31–34.

THURSTON, H. 1998. When it became a new species, a tiny songbird was thrust into the limelight. National Wildlife 36:18–19.

THURSZ, M. R., D. KWIATKOWSKI, C. E. ALLSOPP, B. M. GREENWOOD, H. C. THOMAS, AND A. V. HILL. 1995. Association between an MHC class II allele and clearance of hepatitis B virus in the Gambia. New England Journal of Medicine 332:1065.

THURSZ, M. R., H. C. THOMAS, B. M. GREENWOOD, AND A. V. S. HILL. 1997. Heterozygote advantage for HLA class II type in Hepatitis B virus infection. Nature Genetics 17:11–12.

THYAGARAJU, A. S. 1934. The King Crow (*Dicrurus macrocercus* P.). Journal of the Bombay Natural History Society 37:727–728.

TODD, I. A. 1992. WILDTRAK. Non-parametric home range analysis for Macintosh computers. Department of Zoology, Oxford University, Oxford, UK.

TOMICH, P. Q. 1969. Mammals in Hawaii. Bishop Museum Press, Honolulu, HI.

TOMICH, P. Q. 1971. Notes on foods and feeding behavior of raptorial birds in Hawaii. Elepaio 31:111–114.

TOMICH, P. Q. 1981a. Rodents. Pp. 105–110 *in* D. Mueller-Dombois, K. Bridges, and H. L. Carson (editors). Island ecosystems. U.S. International Biological Program Synthesis Series 15. Hutchinson Ross, Stroudsburg, PA.

TOMICH, P. Q. 1981b. Community structure of introduced rodents and carnivores. Pp. 301–309 in D. Mueller-Dombois, K. Bridges, and H. L. Carson (editors). Island ecosystems: biological organization in selected Hawaiian communities. U.S. International Biological Program Synthesis Series 15. Hutchinson Ross, Stroudsburg, PA.

TOMICH, P. Q. 1986. Mammals in Hawaii. 2nd edition. B. P. Bishop Museum Special Publication 76. Bishop Museum Press, Honolulu, HI.

TOMKINS, R. J. 1985. Breeding success and mortality of Dark-rumped Petrels in the Galapagos, and control of their predators. Pp. 159–175 *in* P. J. Moors (editor). Conservation of island birds. International Council for Bird Preservation Technical Publication No. 3. Cambridge, UK.

TOMKINS, R. J., AND B. J. MILNE. 1991. Differences among Dark-rumped Petrel (*Pterodroma phaeopygia*) populations within the Galapagos Archipelago. Notornis 38:1–35.

TOMONARI-TUGGLE, M. J. 1996. Bird catchers and bullock hunters in the upland Mauna Kea forest: a cultural resource overview of Hakalau Forest National Wildlife Refuge, Island of Hawaii. International Archeological Research Institute, Inc., Honolulu, HI.

TOWNS, D. R., D. SIMBERLOFF, AND I. A. E. ATKINSON. 1997. Restoration of New Zealand islands: redressing the effects of introduced species. Pacific Conservation Biology 3:99–124.

TREWICK, S. A. 1997. Flightlessness and phylogeny amongst endemic rails (Aves: Rallidae) of the New Zealand region. Philosophical Transactions of the Royal Society of London B Biological Sciences 352: 429–446.

TRIPATHY, D. N. 1993. Avipox viruses. Pp. 5–15 *in* J.

B. McFerran and M. S. McNulty (editors). Virus infections of birds. Elsevier, New York, NY.

TROWSDALE, J., J. RAGOUSSIS, AND R. D. CAMPELL. 1991. Map of the human major histocompatibility complex. Immunology Today, December 1991, centerfold.

TRYON, B. W. 1984. Additional instances of multiple egg-clutch production in snakes. Transactions of the Kansas Academy of Sciences 87:98–104.

TRYON, B. W., AND J. B. MURPHY. 1982. Miscellaneous notes on the reproductive biology of reptiles. 5. Thirteen varieties of the genus *Lampropeltis,* species *mexicana, triangulum* and *zonata.* Transactions of the Kansas Academy of Sciences 85:96–119.

TULLY, J. 1997. Pesky mangroves closing in on the bay. Kailua Sun Press, August 1–7:23.

TURNER, I. M., AND R. T. CORLETT. 1996. The conservation value of small, isolated fragments of lowland tropical rain forest. Trends in Ecology and Evolution 11:330–333.

UDVARDY, M. D. F. 1969. Dynamic zoogeography. Van Nostrand-Reinhold, New York, NY.

U.S. CONGRESS, OFFICE OF TECHNOLOGY ASSESSMENT. 1993. Harmful non-indigenous species in the United States. OTA-F-565. U.S. Government Printing Office, Washington, D.C.

U.S. DEPARTMENT OF AGRICULTURE. 1989. Results of Rota, CNMI pilot test to eradicate the melon fly by the male annihilation technique. U.S. Department of Agriculture, Agricultural Research Service, Tropical Fruit and Vegetable Research Lab, Honolulu, HI.

U.S. DEPARTMENT OF COMMERCE. 1993. Climatological data-Hawaii and Pacific. Vol. 89. NOAA. Asheville, NC.

U.S. FISH AND WILDLIFE SERVICE. 1982a. Recovery plan: Newell's Shearwater and Dark-rumped Petrel. U.S. Fish and Wildlife Service, Portland, OR.

U.S. FISH AND WILDLIFE SERVICE. 1982b. Hawaii forest bird recovery plan. U.S. Fish and Wildlife Service, Portland, OR.

U.S. FISH AND WILDLIFE SERVICE. 1982c. Alala recovery plan. U.S. Fish and Wildlife Service, Portland, OR.

U.S. FISH AND WILDLIFE SERVICE. 1982d. Recovery plan for the Laysan Duck. U.S. Fish and Wildlife Service, Portland, OR.

U.S. FISH AND WILDLIFE SERVICE. 1983a. Kauai forest birds recovery plan. U.S. Fish and Wildlife Service, Portland, OR.

U.S. FISH AND WILDLIFE SERVICE. 1983b. Hawaiian Dark-rumped Petrel and Newell's Manx Shearwater Recovery Plan. U.S. Fish and Wildlife Service, Portland, OR.

U.S. FISH AND WILDLIFE SERVICE. 1983c. Recovery plan for the Nene. U.S. Fish and Wildlife Service, Portland, OR.

U.S. FISH AND WILDLIFE SERVICE. 1984a. Northwestern Hawaiian Islands passerine recovery plan. U.S. Fish and Wildlife Service, Portland, OR.

U.S. FISH AND WILDLIFE SERVICE. 1984b. Hawaii Hawk recovery plan. U.S. Fish and Wildlife Service, Portland, OR.

U.S. FISH AND WILDLIFE SERVICE. 1984c. Maui-Molokai forest birds recovery plan. U.S. Fish and Wildlife Service, Portland, OR.

U.S. FISH AND WILDLIFE SERVICE. 1985. Hawaiian waterbirds recovery plan. U.S. Fish and Wildlife Service, Portland, OR.

U.S. FISH AND WILDLIFE SERVICE. 1986. Recovery plan for the Palila. U. S. Fish and Wildlife Service, Portland, OR.

U.S. FISH AND WILDLIFE SERVICE. 1987. Field guide to wildlife diseases. Vol. 1. General field procedures and diseases of migratory birds (M. Friend, editor). Resource Publication 167. U.S. Department of the Interior, Fish and Wildlife Service, Washington, D.C.

U.S. FISH AND WILDLIFE SERVICE. 1989. Endangered species in the wake of Hurricane Hugo. Endangered Species Technical Bulletin Nos. 9–10:3, 6–7.

U.S. FISH AND WILDLIFE SERVICE. 1996a. Endangered and threatened wildlife and plants. Tech. Rep. 50 CFR 17.11–17.12. U.S. Fish and Wildlife Service, Washington, D.C.

U.S. FISH AND WILDLIFE SERVICE. 1996b. Trends in duck breeding populations, 1955–1996. Migratory Bird Management. Office Administrative Report. Laurel, MD.

U.S. FISH AND WILDLIFE SERVICE. 1996c. Report to Congress on the recovery program for threatened and endangered species: 1996. U.S. Department of Interior, U.S. Fish and Wildlife Service, Washington, D.C.

U.S. FISH AND WILDLIFE SERVICE. 1998. Endangered and threatened wildlife and plants. Technical Report 63 FR 13150. Washington, D.C.

VAIMAN, D., L. SCHIBLER, F. BOURGEOIS, A. OUSTRY, Y. AMIGUES, AND E. P. CRIBIU. 1996. A genetic linkage map of the male goat genome. Genetics 144: 279–305.

VALLE, C. A., AND M. C. COULTER. 1987. Present status of the flightless cormorant, Galapagos Penguin and Greater Flamingo populations in the Galapagos Islands, Ecuador, after the 1982–83 El Niño. Condor 89:276–281.

VAN AARDE, R. J. 1978. Reproduction and density of the feral house cats (Felis catus) at Marion Island. Carnivore Genetics Newsletter 3:288–316.

VAN BALEN, J. H. 1980. Population fluctuations of the Great Tit and feeding conditions in winter. Ardea 68: 143–164.

VAN BALEN, J. H., C. J. H. BOOY, J. A. VAN FRANEKER, AND E. R. OSIECK. 1982. Studies on hole-nesting birds in natural nest sites. 1. Availability and occupation of natural nest sites. Ardea 70:1–24.

VAN REUSENBURG, P. J. J., AND M. N. BESTER. 1988. The effects of cats Felis catus predation on three breeding Procellariidae species on Marion Island. South African Journal of Zoology 23:301–305.

VAN RIPER, C., III. 1978. The breeding ecology of the Amakihi (Loxops virens) and Palila (Psittirostra baileui) on Mauna Kea, Hawaii. Ph.D. dissertation. University of Hawaii, Honolulu, HI.

VAN RIPER, C., III. 1980a. Observations on the breeding of the Palila (Psittirostra baileui) of Hawaii. Ibis 122:462–475.

VAN RIPER, C., III. 1980b. The phenology of the dryland forest of Mauna Kea, Hawaii, and the impact of recent environmental perturbations. Biotropica 12:282–291.

VAN RIPER, C., III. 1982. Censuses and breeding observations of the birds on Kohala Mountain, Hawaii. Wilson Bulletin 94:463–476.

VAN RIPER, C., III. 1984. The influence of nectar resources on nesting success and movement patterns of the common Amakihi (Hemignathus virens). Auk 101:38–46.

VAN RIPER, C., III. 1987. Breeding ecology of the Hawaii Common Amakihi. Condor 89:85–102.

VAN RIPER, C., III. 1991. The impact of introduced vectors and avian malaria on insular passeriform bird populations in Hawaii. Bulletin of the Society for Vector Ecology 16:59–83.

VAN RIPER, C., III. 1995. Ecology and breeding biology of the Hawaii Elepaio (Chasiempis sandwichensis bryani). Condor 97:512–527.

VAN RIPER, C., III, AND L. T. HIRAI. 1994. Coloration frequencies of male House Finches in Hawaii. Western Birds 25:163–165.

VAN RIPER, C., III, M. D. KERN, AND M. K. SOGGE. 1993. Changing nest placement of Hawaiian Common Amakihi during the breeding cycle. Wilson Bulletin 105:436–447.

VAN RIPER, C., III, AND J. M. SCOTT. 1979. Observations on distribution, diet, and breeding of the Hawaiian thrush. Condor 81:65–71.

VAN RIPER, C., III, J. M. SCOTT, AND D. M. WOODSIDE. 1978. Distribution and abundance patterns of the Palila on Mauna Kea, Hawaii. Auk 95:518–527.

VAN RIPER, C., III, S. G. VAN RIPER, M. L. GOFF, AND M. LAIRD. 1982. The impact of malaria on birds in Hawaii Volcanoes National Park. Technical Report 47. Cooperative National Park Studies Unit, University of Hawaii, Honolulu, HI.

VAN RIPER, C., III, S. G. VAN RIPER, M. L. GOFF, AND M. LAIRD. 1986. The epizootiology and ecological significance of malaria in Hawaiian land birds. Ecological Monographs 56:327–344.

VAN RIPER, C., III, S. G. VAN RIPER, AND W. R. HANSEN. In press. The epizootiology and ecological significance of avian pox in Hawaii. Auk.

VAN RIPER, S. G. 2000. Japanese White-eye (Zosterops japonicus). In A. Poole and F. Gill (editors). The Birds of North America, No. 487. The Academy of Natural Sciences, Philadephia, PA, and American Ornithologists' Union, Washington, D.C.

VAN RIPER, S. G., AND C. VAN RIPER, III. 1982. A field guide to the mammals in Hawaii. The Oriental Publishing Company, Honolulu, HI.

VAN RIPER, S. G., AND C. VAN RIPER, III. 1985. A summary of known parasites and diseases recorded from the avifauna of the Hawaiian Islands. Pp. 298–371 in C. P. Stone and J. M. Scott (editors). Hawai'i's terrestrial ecosystems: preservation and management. Cooperative National Park Studies Unit, University of Hawaii, Honolulu, HI.

VANCOUVER, G. 1798. A voyage of discovery to the North Pacific, and round the world. Vols. I–III. Robinson, London, UK.

VANDERWERF, E. A. 1993. Scales of habitat selection by foraging 'Elepaio in undisturbed and human-altered forests in Hawaii. Condor 95:980–989.

VANDERWERF, E. A. 1994. Intraspecific variation in Elepaio foraging behavior in Hawaiian forests of different structure. Auk 111:917–932.

VANDERWERF, E. A. 1997. O'ahu 'Amakihi nest in Manoa Valley. 'Elepaio 57:125–126.

VANDERWERF, E. A. 1998a. 'Elepaio (*Chasiempis sandwichensis*). *In* A. Poole and F. Gill (editors). The Birds of North America, No. 344. The Academy of Natural Sciences, Philadelphia, PA, and American Ornithologists' Union, Washington, D.C.

VANDERWERF, E. A. 1998b. Breeding biology and territoriality of the Hawaii Creeper. Condor 100:541–545.

VANDERWERF, E. A., A. COWELL, AND J. L. ROHRER. 1997. Distribution, abundance, and conservation of O'ahu 'Elepaio in the southern leeward Ko'olau Range. 'Elepaio 57:99–105.

VANDERWERF, E. A., AND J. L. ROHRER. 1996. Discovery of an 'I'iwi population in the Ko'olau Mountains of O'ahu. 'Elepaio 56:25–28.

VANGELDER, E. M. 1996. The breeding biology of the Akohekohe (*Palmeria dolei*), an endangered Hawaiian honeycreeper. M.S. thesis. San Francisco State University, San Francisco, CA.

VEITCH, C. R. 1985. Methods of eradicating feral cats from offshore islands in New Zealand. Pp. 125–141 *in* P. J. Moors (editor). International Council for Bird Preservation Technical Publication No. 3. Cambridge, UK.

VELTMAN, C. J., S. NEE, AND M. J. CRAWLEY. 1996. Correlates of introduction success in exotic New Zealand birds. American Naturalist 147:542–557.

VENABLES, W. N., AND B. D. RIPLEY. 1994. Modern applied statistics with S-Plus. Springer-Verlag, New York, NY.

VERMEER, K., AND L. RANKIN. 1984. Influence of habitat destruction and disturbance on nesting seabirds. Pp. 723–736 *in* J. P. Croxall, P. G. H. Evans, and R. W. Schreiber (editors). Status and conservation of the world's seabirds. International Council for Bird Preservation Technical Publication No. 2. Cambridge, UK.

VERNON, C. J. 1959. *Dicrurus adsimilis* killing and eating *Serinus mozambicus*. Bokmarkierie 11:3.

VINCEK, V., D. KLEIN, R. T. GRASER, F. FIGUEROA, C. O'HUIGIN, AND J. KLEIN. 1995. Molecular cloning of major histocompatibility complex class II B gene cDNA from the Bengalese Finch *Lonchura striata*. Immunogenetics 42:262–267.

VITOUSEK, P. M. 1992. Effects of alien plants on native ecosystems. Pp. 29–41 *in* C. P. Stone, C. W. Smith, and J. T. Tunison (editors). Alien plant invasions in native ecosystems of Hawai'i: management and research. Cooperative National Park Resources Studies Unit, University of Hawaii, Honolulu, HI.

VITOUSEK, P. M., C. M. D'ANTONIO, L. L. LOOPE, M. REJMANEK, AND R. WESTBROOKS. 1997. Introduced species: a significant component of human-caused global change. New Zealand Journal of Ecology 21:1–16.

VITOUSEK, P. M., L. L. LOOPE, AND C. P. STONE. 1987. Introduced species in Hawaii: biological effects and opportunities for ecological research. Trends in Ecology and Evolution 2:224–227.

VITOUSEK, P. M., D. R. TURNER, AND K. KITAYAMA. 1995. Foliar nutrients during long-term soil development in Hawaiian montane rain forest. Ecology 76:712–720.

VITOUSEK, P. M., AND L. R. WALKER. 1989. Biological invasion by *Myrica faya* in Hawai'i: plant demography, nitrogen fixation, ecosystem effects. Ecological Monographs 59:247–265.

VON HAARTMAN, L. 1956. Territory in the Pied Flycatcher, *Muscicapa hypoleuca*. Ibis 98:460–475.

VON HAARTMAN, L. 1971. Population dynamics. Pp. 391–459 *in* D. S. Farner and J. R. King (editors). Avian biology. Vol. 1. Academic Press, New York, NY.

VOS, P., R. HOGERS, M. BLEEKER, M. REIJANS, T. VAN DE LEE, M. HORNES, A. FRIJTERS, J. POT, J. PELEMAN, M. KUIPER, AND M. ZABEAU. 1995. AFLP: a new technique for DNA fingerprinting. Nucleic Acid Research 23:4407–4414.

WAGNER, H. O. 1946. Food and feeding habits of Mexican hummingbirds. Wilson Bulletin 58:69–93.

WAGNER, R. 1970. Neue Aspekte zur Stickstoffanalytik in der Wasserchemie. Vom Wasser 37:263–318.

WAGNER, W. L., AND V. A. FUNK (EDITORS). 1995. Hawaiian biogeography: evolution on a hot spot archipelago. Smithsonian Institution Press, Washington, D.C.

WAGNER, W. L., D. R. HERBST, AND S. H. SOHMER. 1990a. Manual of the flowering plants of Hawai'i. Vol. 1. University of Hawaii Press and Bishop Museum Press, Honolulu, HI.

WAGNER, W. L., D. R. HERBST, AND S. H. SOHMER. 1990b. Manual of the flowering plants of Hawai'i. Vol. 2. University of Hawaii Press and Bishop Museum Press, Honolulu, HI.

WAKELEE, K. M. 1996. Life history of the Omao (*Myadestes obscurus*). M.S. thesis. University Hawaii, Honolulu, HI.

WAKELIN, D. 1996. Immunity to parasites. 2nd edition. Cambridge University Press, Cambridge, UK.

WALKER, G. P. L. 1990. Geology and volcanology of the Hawaiian Islands. Pacific Science 44:315–347.

WALKER, R. L. 1966. Hawaii exotic game bird report. Vol. 13. Annual Report of the Western States Exotic Game Bird Committee, Honolulu, HI.

WALKER, R. L. 1967. A brief history of exotic game bird and mammal introductions into Hawaii with a look to the future. State of Hawaii, Department of Land and Natural Resources, Honolulu, HI.

WALLACE, G. D. 1973. The role of the cat in the natural history of *Toxoplasma gondii*. American Journal of Tropical Medicine and Hygiene 22:313–322.

WALLACE, G. D., D. AUAI, A. ODA, R. E. KISSLING, AND W. B. QUISENBERRY. 1964. Arthropod-borne virus survey on the island of Hawaii. Hawaii Medical Journal 23–364–386.

WALSBERG, G. E. 1983. Avian ecological energetics. Pp. 161–220 *in* D. Farner, J. King, and K. Parkes (editors). Avian biology. Vol. 7. Academic Press, New York, NY.

WARHAM, J. 1990. The petrels: their ecology and breeding systems. Academic Press, London, UK.

WARING, G. H., L. L. LOOPE, AND A. C. MEDEIROS. 1993. Study on use of alien versus native plants by nectarivorous forest birds on Maui, Hawaii. Auk 110:917–920.

WARNER, R. E. 1960. A forest dies on Mauna Kea. Pacific Discovery 13:6–14.

WARNER, R. E. 1963. Recent history and ecology of the Laysan Duck. Condor 65:3–23.

WARNER, R. E. 1967. Scientific report of the Kipahulu valley expedition. The Nature Conservancy, Honolulu, HI.

WARNER, R. E. 1968. The role of introduced diseases in the extinction of the endemic Hawaiian avifauna. Condor 70:101–120.

WARSHAUER, F. R., J. D. JACOBI, A. M. LaROSA, J. M. SCOTT, AND C. W. SMITH. 1983. The distribution, impact and potential management of the introduced vine Passiflora mollissima (Passifloraceae) in Hawaii. Technical Report 48. Cooperative National Park Research Studies Unit, University of Hawaii, Honolulu, HI.

WATERS, A. P., AND T. F. McCUTCHAN. 1989. Rapid, sensitive diagnosis of malaria based on ribosomal RNA. The Lancet 8651:1343–1346.

WAUER, R. N. 1990a. Lure of the Caribbean: Part 1. The Greater and Lesser Antilles. Birding 22:42–45.

WAUER, R. N. 1990b. Lure of the Caribbean: Part 2. West Indies endemics. Birding 22:186–189.

WAUER, R. H., AND J. M. WUNDERLE JR. 1992. The effect of hurricane Hugo on bird populations of St. Croix, U.S. Virgin Islands. Wilson Bulletin 104:656–673.

WAY, M. J., AND K. C. KHOO. 1992. Role of ants in pest management. Annual Review of Entomology 37:479–503.

WEATHERALL, D. J. 1996. Host genetics and infectious disease. Symposia of the British Society of Parasitology 33:S23-S29.

WEATHERHEAD, P. J., AND M. R. L. FORBES. 1994. Natal philopatry in passerine birds: genetic or ecological influences? Behavioral Ecology 5:426–433.

WEISS, J. B. 1995. DNA probes and PCR for diagnosis of parasitic infections. Clinical Microbiology Reviews 8:113–130.

WEISS, K. M. 1993. Genetic variation and human disease. Cambridge University Press, New York, NY.

WELLER, M. W. 1980. The island waterfowl. Iowa State University Press, Ames, IA.

WESOŁOWSKI, T. 1983. The breeding ecology and behaviour of wrens Troglodytes troglodytes under primaeval and secondary conditions. Ibis 125:499–515.

WESOŁOWSKI, T. 1989. Nest-sites of hole-nesters in a primeval temperate forest (Bialowieza National Park, Poland). Acta Ornithologica 25:321–351.

WEST, D. A. 1962. Hybridization in grosbeaks (Pheucticus) of the Great Plains. Auk 79:399–424.

WESTBROOKS, R., AND R. E. EPLEE. 1996. Strategies for preventing the world movement of invasive plants. Pp. 148–154 in O. T. Sandlund, P. J. Schei, and A. Viken (editors). 1996. Proceedings of the Norway/UN Conference on Alien Species. Directorate for Nature Management and Norwegian Institute for Nature Research, Trondheim, Norway.

WESTER, L. 1981. Introduction and spread of mangroves in the Hawaiian Islands. Association of Pacific Coast Geographers Yearbook 43:125–137.

WETMORE, A. 1924. A warbler from Nihoa. Condor 26:177–178.

WETMORE, A. 1925. Bird life among lava rock and coral sand. National Geographic Magazine 48:76–108.

WETMORE, A. 1943. An extinct goose from the island of Hawaii. Condor 45:146–148.

WHITE, G. C., AND R. A. GARROTT. 1990. Analysis of wildlife radio-tracking data. Academic Press, New York, NY.

WHITEAKER, L. D. AND D. E. GARDNER. 1985. The distribution of Myrica faya in the state of Hawaii. University Hawaii Cooperative National Park Resources Study Unit. Technical Report 55. Botany Department, University of Hawaii, Honolulu, HI.

WHITEAKER, L. D., AND D. GARDNER. 1992. Firetree (Myrica faya) distribution in Hawaii. Pp. 225–240 in C. P. Stone, C. W. Smith and J. T. Tunison (editors). Alien plant invasions in native ecosystems of Hawaii: management and research. Cooperative National Park Resources Studies Unit, University of Hawaii, Honolulu, HI.

WICHMAN, F. B. 1985. Lau-Haka. Pp. 190–124 in F. F. Winchman (editor). Kauai Tales. Bamboo Ridge Press, Honolulu, HI.

WICK, H. L. 1970. Lignin staining: a limited success in identifying koa growth rings. USDA Forest Service Research Note PSW-205. Pacific Southwest Forest and Range Experiment Station, Berkeley, CA.

WIGLEY, T. M. L., AND S. C. B. RAPER. 1993. Future changes in global mean temperature and sea level. Pp. 111–133 in R. A. Warrick, E. M. Barrow, and T. M. L. Wigley (editors). Climate and sea level change: observations, projections, and implications. Cambridge University Press, Cambridge, UK.

WILCOX, B. A. 1998. Strategic integrated resources management planning for Marine Corps Base Hawaii, Kāneʻohe Bay. Prepared by Institute for Sustainable Development, San Francisco, CA, and Kailua, HI.

WILCOX, B. A., T. DENHAM, G. AHLBORN, K. DUIN, AND R. PALMER. 1997. Integrated resources management plan for the Nuʻupia Ponds Management Zone, Marine Corps Base Hawaii (MCBH), Island of Oʻahu, State of Hawaiʻi. Final report. Prepared by Garcia and Associates, Honolulu, HI.

WILCOX, B. A., E. B. GUINTHER, K. N. DUIN, AND H. MAYBAUM. 1998. Mokapu: manual for watershed health and water quality. Final report. Prepared by Institute for Sustainable Development and AECOS, INC., Kailua, HI.

WILES, G. J. 1987a. Current research and future management of Marianas fruit bats (Chiroptera: Pteropodidae) on Guam. Australian Mammalogy 10:93–95.

WILES, G. J. 1987b. The status of fruit bats on Guam. Pacific Science 41:148–157.

WILLE, C. 1991. Paul Butler: parrot man of the Caribbean. American Birds 45:26–35.

WILLIAMS, G. C. 1966. Natural selection, the costs of reproduction, and a refinement of Lack's principle. American Naturalist 100:687–690.

WILLIAMS, R. N. 1987. Alien birds on Oahu: 1944–1985. ʻElepaio 47:87–92.

WILSON, A. C., H. OCHMAN, AND E. M. PRAGER. 1987. Molecular time scale for evolution. Trends in Genetics 3:241–247.

WILSON, D. E., AND D. M. REEDER. 1993. Mammal species of the world. 2nd edition. Smithsonian Institution Press, Washington, D.C.

WILSON, E. O. 1996. Hawaii: a world without social insects. Occasional Papers B. P. Bishop Museum 45: 3–7. Bishop Museum Press, Honolulu, HI.

WILSON, S. B. 1890. Descriptions of some new species of Sandwich-Island birds. Proceedings of the Zoology Society London 1889:445–447.

WILSON, S. B. 1891. Descriptions of two new species of Sandwich-Island birds. Annals and Magazine Natural History, Series 6, 7:460.

WILSON, S. B., AND A. H. EVANS. 1890–1899. Aves Hawaiienses: the birds of the Sandwich Islands. R. H. Porter, London, UK.

WILSON, U. W. 1991. Responses of three seabird species to El Niño events and other warm episodes on the Washington Coast, 1979–1990. Condor 93:853–858.

WIRTH, W. W. 1965. Ceratopogonidae. Pp. 121–142 in A. Stone, C. W. Sabrosky, W. W. Wirth, R. H. Toote, and J. R. Coulson (editors). A catalog of the Diptera of America north of Mexico, Agriculture Handbook 276. U.S. Department of Agriculture, Washington, D.C.

WIRTH, W. W., AND A. A. HUBERT. 1989. The Culicoides of Southeast Asia (Diptera: Ceratopogonidae). Memoirs of the American Entomological Institute No. 44. Ann Arbor, MI.

WITH, K. A. 1994. The hazards of nesting near shrubs for a grassland bird, the McCown's Longspur. Condor 96:1009–1019.

WITTZELL, H., T. VON SCHANTZ, R. ZOOROB, AND C. AUFFRAY. 1994. Molecular characterization of three Mhc class II B haplotypes in the Ring-necked Pheasant. Immunogenetics 39:395–403.

WITTZELL, H., T. VON SCHANTZ, R. ZOOROB, AND C. AUFFRAY. 1995. Rfp-Y-like sequences assort independently of pheasant Mhc genes. Immunogenetics 42:68–71.

WOLF, C. M., B. GRIFFITH, C. REED, AND S. A. TEMPLE. 1996. Avian and mammalian translocations: update and reanalysis of 1987 survey data. Conservation Biology 10:1142–1154.

WOLF, L. L. 1978. Aggressive social organization in nectarivorous birds. American Zoologist 18:765–778.

WOLF, L. L., F. G. STILES, AND F. R. HAINSWORTH. 1976. Ecological organization of a tropical, highland hummingbird community. Journal of Animal Ecology 45:349–379.

WOLFE, E. W., W. S. WISE, AND G. B. DALRYMPLE. 1997. The geology and petrology of Mauna Kea volcano, Hawaii-a study of postshield volcanism. U.S. Geological Survey Professional Paper 1557. Reston, VA.

WOODWARD, P. W. 1972. The natural history of Kure Atoll, Northwestern Hawaiian Islands. Atoll Research Bulletin 164:1–138.

WOODWORTH, B. L. 1997. Brood parasitism, nest predation, and season-long reproductive success of a tropical island endemic. Condor 99:605–621.

WOODWORTH, B. L. 1999. Modeling population dynamics of a songbird exposed to parasitism and predation and evaluating management options. Conservation Biology 13:67–76.

WOODWORTH, B. L., J. FAABORG, AND W. J. ARENDT.
1998. Breeding and natal dispersal in the Puerto Rican Vireo. Journal of Field Ornithology 69:1–7.

WOOLFENDEN, G. E., AND J. W. FITZPATRICK. 1984. The Florida Scrub Jay: demography of a cooperative-breeding bird. Princeton University Press, Princeton, NJ.

WOOLLER, R. D., J. S. BRADLEY, I. J. SKIRA, AND D. L. SERVENTY. 1989. Short-tailed Shearwater. Pp. 405–417 in I. Newton (editor). Lifetime reproduction in birds. Academic Press, London, UK.

WOOTTON, J. T., B. E. YOUNG, AND D. W. WINKLER. 1991. Ecological versus evolutionary hypotheses: demographic stasis and the Murray-Nolan clutch size equation. Evolution 45:1947–1950.

WORLD CONSERVATION UNION (WCU). 1982. The IUCN Amphibia-reptilia red book: Part I. Gland, Switzerland.

WORK, T. M., J. G. MASSEY, B. RIDEOUT, D. LEDIG, O. C. H. KWOK, AND J. P. DUBEY. 2000. Toxoplasmosis in Hawaiian Crows. Journal of Wildlife Diseases 36: 205–212.

WORK, T. M., D. BALL, M. WOLCOTT. 1999. Erysipelas in a free-ranging Hawaiian Crow (Corvus hawaiiensis). Avian Diseases 43:338–341.

WUNDERLE, J. M., JR., D. J. LODGE, AND R. B. WAIDE. 1992. Short-term effects of Hurricane Gilbert on terrestrial bird populations on Jamaica. Auk 109:148–166.

WUNZ, G. A. 1992. Wild turkeys outside their historic range. Pp. 361–384 in J. G. Dickson (editor). The wild turkey: biology and management. Stackpole Books, Harrisburg, PA.

WYLLIE, R. C. 1850. "Address." Transactions of the Royal Hawaiian Agricultural Society 1:36–49.

YAFFEE, S. L., A. F. PHILLIPS, I. C. FRENTZ, P. W. HARDY, S. M. MALEKI, AND B. E. THORPE. 1996. Ecosystem management in the United States, an assessment of current experience. Island Press, Washington, D.C.

YDENBERG, R. C., AND H. H. TH. PRINS. 1981. Spring grazing and the manipulation of food quality by Barnacle Geese. Journal of Applied Ecology 18:443–453.

YEE, R. S. N., AND W. C. GAGNE. 1992. Activities and needs of the horticulture industry in relation to alien plant problems in Hawai'i. Pp. 712–725 in C. P. Stone, C. W. Smith, and J. T. Tunison (editors). Alien plant invasions in native ecosystems of Hawaii: management and research. University of Hawaii Cooperative National Park Resources Studies Unit, Honolulu, HI.

YEN, D. E. 1974. The sweet potato and Oceania: an essay in ethnobotany. B. P. Bishop Museum Bulletin No. 236. Bishop Museum Press, Honolulu, HI.

YEN, D. E., P. V. KIRCH, P. H. ROSENDAHL AND T. RILEY. 1972. Prehistoric agriculture in the upper valley of Makaha, Oahu. Pp. 59–94 in E. Ladd and D. E. Yen (editors). Interim Report 3, Department of Anthropology, B. P. Bishop Museum, Honolulu, HI.

YOCUM, C. F. 1964. Waterfowl wintering in the Marshall Islands, Southwest Pacific Ocean. Auk 81:441–442.

YOCUM, C. F. 1967. Ecology of feral goats in Haleakala National Park, Hawaii. American Midland Naturalist 77:418–451.

YONEKURA, N., T. ISHII, Y. SAITO, Y. MAEDA, Y. MAT-
SUSHIMA, E. MATSUMOTO, AND H. KAYANNE. 1988.
Holocene fringe reefs and sea-level change in Man-
gaia Island, Southern Cook Islands. Paleogeography,
Paleoclimatology, Paleoecology 68:177–188.

YORINKS, N. 1994. Effects of malaria on the daily activity budget of experimentally-infected Hawaiian
forest birds. M.S. thesis. University of Wisconsin,
Madison, WI.

YORINKS, N., AND C.T. ATKINSON. 2000. Effects of malaria (*Plasmodium relictum*) on activity budgets of
experimentally infected juvenile Apapane (*Himatione sanguinea*). Auk 117:731–738.

YOUNG, A. M. 1971. Foraging for insects by a tropical
hummingbird. Condor 73:36–45.

YOUNG, B. E. 1994. The effects of food, nest predation
and weather on the timing of breeding in tropical
House Wrens. Condor 96:341–353.

YOUNG, H. G., AND J. M. RHYMER. 1998. Meller's

Duck: a threatened species receives recognition at
last. Biodiversity and Conservation 7:1313–1323.

ZAR, J. H. 1984. Biostatistical analysis. Prentice Hall,
NJ.

ZENNER DE POLANIA, I., AND O. M. WILCHES. 1992.
Impact ecologico de la hormiga loca, *Paratrechina
fulva* (Mayr), en el Municipo de Cimitarra (Santan-
der). Revista Colombiana de Entomologia 18:14–22.

ZINK, R. M. 1997. Species concepts. Bulletin of the
British Ornithologists' Club 117:97–109.

ZINK, R. M., AND M. C. MCKITRICK. 1995. The debate
over species concepts and its implications for ornithology. Auk 112:701–719.

ZUSI, R. L. 1978. The interorbital septum in cardueline
finches. Bulletin of the British Ornithologists' Club
98: 5–10.

ZUSI, R. L. 1989. A modified jaw muscle in the Maui
Parrotbill (*Pseudonestor*: Drepanididae). Condor 91:
716–720.